OUTL

OF THE

RELIGION AND PHILOSOPHY

OF

SWEDENBORG.

BY

THEOPHILUS PARSONS, LL.D.

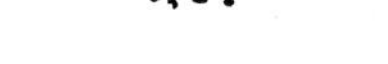

JAMES SPEIRS,

36 BLOOMSBURY STREET, LONDON.

1876.

NOTE.

This book is a reprint of an American work. The author, now nearly eighty years of age, was, for many years, Professor of Law in the University at Cambridge, in the United States; and has published many Treatises on legal subjects, which are well known to the profession in this country. He has also published books illustrative of the truths of the New-Church; as, "Deus Homo," "The Infinite and the Finite," "Essays," &c., &c. This work, lately published in America, is republished here in the belief that it is well adapted to satisfy the growing desire to know something of the system of Emanuel Swedenborg.

JAMES SPEIRS.

[illegible] Bloomsbury Street.

CONTENTS.

OUTLINES OF THE PHILOSOPHY OF THE NEW CHURCH.

CHAPTER I.

INTRODUCTORY.

A CHURCH may be defined as the collective body of those who agree together in faith and in worship.

There have been, and there are, many churches; differing from each other in their systems of faith and modes of worship.

All churches, so far as their religious tenets or doctrines have any truth, are founded upon revelation. The reason of this is, that religious doctrines relate necessarily to God and a life after death; and the human mind is incapable of forming the first or simplest idea, or having any thought whatever concerning these topics by the exercise of the senses, or of sensuous thought concerning what the senses discover. By this phrase I mean thinking, by the exercise of any or all the intellectual faculties, only on what the senses teach; drawing inferential instruction from the direct instruction which the senses give; and thus continually enlarging the knowledge which a right use of the senses enables us to acquire, but with no reference to any thing higher. It is certain that, without the senses, we could not know any thing or think any thing about the material world, or the life we pass upon this world. It is equally certain, although not so obvious, that without revelation, or information received from the other world, we could not know any thing or think any thing about that world, or an infinite Creator of that world and this.

If men did not think about what the senses acquaint them with, they would be but little better for their senses. They would not gain so much from them as the lower animals do, for these have a kind and measure of sensuous thought. Men have a far greater power of sensuous thought, that they may profit far more by their senses. This power is, indeed, far larger and higher than the analogous power which the lower animals have; for, with them, this power exists at once in the highest development it can reach, as soon as the animals are old enough to make use of it; and with but little difference among animals of the same species, or among successive generations. It stops where it begins. No animal grows much more knowing by experience, nor can the individual or the race transmit what they have learned to their successors so as to permit an accumulation or a growth of knowledge. Recently, the doctrine of "Evolution" has come into great prominence. It may be that sufficient reasons will be found for holding this process of evolution, under some form or modification, as one of the laws or methods of Divine Providence in creation. But if an animal of a new kind, a new species, may thus have come into existence from or through the agency of a lower, — a better from a worse, a higher from a lower, — it will still be true and certain that no animal below man, however he may have been formed, has the power of consciously and intentionally helping the future to know more than the past.

In all these particulars, the power of sensuous thought in men differs from that in the lower animals. In men, this power is nearly nothing in the beginning of life, but grows afterwards, or may grow, to the end of life. All that a man learns, he may teach. All that a generation acquires, it may transmit to a succeeding generation. This is done imperfectly, because of the imperfect exercise of this power of sensuous thought. Nevertheless, there is constantly much teaching of the knowledge acquired by the exercise of this power, and a large accumulation of this knowledge and a great advancement in it, from generation to generation.

There is no limit to the possible progress of this

power, if rightly exercised, either in the amount of knowledge it may acquire, or in the utilization of this knowledge for the benefit of individual and social life. It seeks to learn all it can of the forces and laws of external nature, to use these forces to make life on earth easier and more delightful, and to overcome the hinderance and obstruction with which these forces resist the designs and efforts of mankind. All this it might do, if rightfully exercised, with a continual progress, which would have neither interruption nor termination.

But it can do only this. However properly, sagaciously, or energetically exercised, it can do no more than this. It belongs to this world, to this life; and whatever it may add to the knowledge of this world or the improvement of this life, it cannot take a single step beyond or above this life. Whatever may be the enlargement, or, if we prefer to call it so, the elevation of sensuous thought in its use or its effect, it does not in this way change or make any approach to a change of its essential nature. It may embrace all the kingdoms of Nature, and penetrate the material heavens. But it continues to be sensuous thought, and only that, as entirely as it was in its beginning, or in its earliest and lowest activities. A man may master all the truths of natural science, or utilize them all to the advantage of external human life, and still employ sensuous thought as exclusively as the savage who hammers one stone with another, and so makes his hatchet.

The human mind possesses higher powers; or, if we think proper to express it differently, we may say that it is able to use all its powers in another and a higher way. The difference between these two classes of powers, or between these two ways of using all intellectual faculty, is like the difference between the two lives we lead.

We begin life in this world, as men living upon earth. We have senses exquisitely adapted to earth, and to all the information which earth can give; and intellectual faculties which, using the senses as means, may make this life one of continually greater enjoyment. But, after we have ceased to live on earth, we shall live another life in another world, and this other life will never cease. As we have faculties perfectly adapted, if rightly used, to make this life one of enjoyment, and our senses are given us as the means of attaining this end, so we have faculties as perfectly adapted to make the other life one of happiness; and revelation from or through that world provides for us the means of attaining this end by the rightful use of these faculties.

THE NECESSITY OF REVELATION.

Revelation is not an abnormal thing, coming in to supply a sudden or exceptional necessity; it is a perfectly regular part of the method of Divine Providence. It is as essential and indispensable to any knowledge or thought about spiritual life or the other world, as the senses are indispensable to any knowledge or thought about this life or this world; and it is as perfectly possible for revelation from the other world to teach us about that life and that world, as it is for the senses to teach us about this world. Then it is the business of spiritual thought — we use this phrase in contrast with sensuous thought — to make a rightful use of the instruction which revelation gives.

Revelation discloses to us the fact of another life. It is, as the derivation of the word implies, an unveiling: by it, the veil which hides that world from us is partially lifted. It tells us that there is One who made that world and this; and it tells us also somewhat about Him and His nature and method of action, His laws and His purposes. And an application of our intellectual faculties, in an appropriate way, to the truths which revelation teaches may give us an ever-growing enlargement of knowledge regarding them, and may lead us to an ever-growing happiness.

Whether we call the faculty of spiritual thought a distinct and higher faculty, or say that it is only a higher use and employment of the same faculties which give the power of sensuous thought, it is still true that spiritual thought when rightly employed about God, the soul, and other matters of religion, works, to a large extent, in like manner with sensuous thought, when that is rightly employed about its proper topics. If religion rests in some degree upon intuition or perception that certain propositions are true, so does science just as much; for the very foundation-truths of all science — axioms, or postulates — are, on the one hand, perfectly indispensable to science, and, on the other, assumed to be true in the absence of all proof; because by the constitution of human nature we cannot help believing that they are true. Religion, building upon its own foundation, which is revelation, uses logic, inference, analogy, and deduction in arguing from a general truth to its particulars, and induction in arguing from particular truths to the general truth which includes them; and religion reasons, in all these and similar ways, as freely as science.

If there are similarities, there are also essential and vital differences between spiritual and sensuous thought. One of these — that the basis of sensuous thought is sense, and the basis of spiritual thought revelation — has already been spoken of. There is another of almost equal importance.

Through all the work of sensuous thought, the intellect alone is called upon to act, and is alone permitted to act. They who would think safely are careful to exclude from their thought all influence of feeling and affection; and that this must be guarded against is one of the rules for sound and just scientific inquiry. But for the higher mode of thought the rule is otherwise. Here feeling, affection, and moral tendency come in; not to warp or obscure intellectual action or perception, but to animate and encourage and illustrate them. The results reached do not depend upon the intellect only, but upon this and upon the affections and the character also. Hence the fact to which the whole history of religion bears testimony, — that a system of religious truth is seldom received or rejected only because of the weight of argument or of evidence for or against it, but as it suits or opposes the character and tendencies, the affectional and moral wants, of those to whom it is offered. The intellect may be misled in these inquiries, and its conclusions falsified by the affections and the character. A mistaken enthusiasm may teach untruths, and cling to them. On the other hand, a coldness towards truths of this higher order, or fixed habits of thought adverse to them, or a rejoicing confidence in the strength of one's own powers and the truths they have won, with a sense of humiliation at the necessity of assistance from greater strength, — all these and similar moral difficulties have in all ages led, and will always lead, minds of great strength and culture to reject all aid from revelation, and deny all its truths. Hence always and now, some of those who are universally acknowledged as leaders of scientific thought have been, and are, unbelievers of all that merely sensuous thought is unable to grasp.

The cause of this important difference between sensuous thought which appeals only to the intellect, and super-sensuous thought which appeals also to the moral and affectional nature, may be considered more fully hereafter. Now, we say only that life in this world is but a life of preparation for another. This must be a preparation of the character, for it is that which determines the quality of life, everywhere, in this world or in the other. It is obvious that the moral character would be harmed by a compulsory intellectual reception of spiritual truth, followed by that disregard and rejection of it in life, which must spring from an antagonism to it on the part of the affections and moral tendencies. Better, it must be, that one should reject this truth intellectually, than that he should receive it intellectually by the compulsion of proof, and then harden himself against it; and so destroy or lessen the possibility that he may at some future time open his mind to the truth, and his heart to its influence.

The whole course of increase of knowledge by means of sensuous thought has been, first, to some conclusion; then to the discovery that this conclusion was erroneous, in whole or in part, and the substitution of another, — and this other, regarded as certain when it was adopted, was in its turn swept away, or greatly modified by the next wave of knowledge, and its successor took its place. Perhaps no one of what were the theories or the certainties of science two thousand, or even one thousand, years ago are held now. The cycles and epicycles of ancient astronomy have been supplanted by the circles and ellipses and other conic curves of modern astronomy. In chemistry the change is even more marked. It would seem to be impossible that the truths and principles now relied upon should ever be abandoned; but it is in the highest degree probable that the theories explanatory of them, or connected with them, will be most importantly modified. Perhaps we may believe that natural science has ascertained certain physical facts, in many branches of knowledge, which can never be disproved, because they are facts. But the inferences to be drawn from them, the laws which regulate them, and the theories which explain them, will all be subjected to changes as great as those which have attended the progress of science hitherto.

Something at least analogous to this is true in respect to the results of higher or spiritual thought, — using this phrase in distinction from sensuous thought, and meaning by it thought concerning those things about which the senses can know nothing and can teach nothing.

SUCCESSIVE REVELATIONS.

Religious truth has passed through successive phases. In the words of the apostle, "God at sundry times and in divers manners spoke in times past to the Fathers." The existence of a God, and of another life, are two great truths which all revelation from the beginning has declared, and all religion has accepted. But, with different races and in different ages, these truths have borne very different aspects, and have led to very different conclusions of faith and practice.

There are two reasons for this: one of which is, that the law of unending life must be the law of unending growth; for growth is of the essence of life. The moment when improvement comes to an end, must be a moment when that which is most valuable in life has come to an end. Goethe said that the thought of unending life sometimes oppressed him, because there must be in it a period when farther progress was impossible, and there would be nothing left but unending stagnation; but he was comforted on this point when he looked up to the stars. He might have found the same consolation in looking through the microscope; for in these days, if the telescope has disclosed the indefinite in the great and distant, the microscope has disclosed it in the little and the near. But if Goethe had known where and how to look for it, he might have found, not consolation only, but hope and joy in the prospect of a constantly growing enlargement of power, and of happiness in the exercise of power for usefulness.

There is another reason for this perpetual progress, which applies only to spiritual thought and its results. For this thought, revelation supplies the foundation and the means. And revelation has always been progressive, and always limited in its disclosures. If revelation comes from God and His heaven, and comes to tell us of Him and heaven, and how to go to heaven, why has it not been always full and clear in its instruction; telling us at once, and if need be keeping us constantly and accurately informed, of all that is knowable about Him and the other life? Surely, such knowledge is of as much more value to us as immortals than any knowledge about earth, as eternity is more than time. Surely, He could if He would give to all the nature He creates and governs, — to the leaves, the stars, the winds, — a voice to speak of Him. Why has he not done this? The answer to this question I can give much better hereafter, when I treat of human freedom, its necessities, its laws, and its effect. Now I only note the fact, that there has never been a revelation so complete as to leave nothing more to be known; so distinct that it could not be misunderstood; and so well attested that it could not be denied and rejected. And there never will be such a revelation.

It has been already said, that, to all reception and comprehension of spiritual truth, there were moral and affectional requisites as well as intellectual. Only to improve and elevate the whole nature of man, and chiefly his moral and affectional nature, is revelation given; and this improvement and elevation cannot be effectually made unless man does his part, in the freedom which is given him that he may do this. It is an easy conclusion that revelation must always, in its instruments and its method, its quantity and its character, be perfectly adapted by perfect wisdom to the needs and possibilities of those to whom it is given. Hence the fact, already referred to, but only to be understood where the nature and the purpose of all revelation are understood,—that there never has been, is not, and never will be, a revelation such in its disclosures and in its evidence, that it cannot be utterly rejected by those whom, for whatever reason, rejection suits better than acceptance.

Revelations have been usually attested by miracles. That given to the children of Israel was attended by miracles of the most striking and almost appalling character. That upon which the Christian religion was founded, rested on testimony of a different kind. In the first place, our Lord's life and character bore witness to the truth of His words. Besides this, however, they were abundantly proved by miracles; or, as the word so translated should be translated, signs.* And these were all of them works of cure, of healing, or of gift; always works of obvious mercy, and never works of terror.

THE LATEST REVELATION.

Now another revelation is given. As the Christian revelation explained and carried forward the work of the Israelitish revelation, so this new revelation explains and completes the work of the Christian revelation. As the Christian revelation advanced so far beyond the Israelitish revelation as to rest upon its own miracles of mercy instead of the terrors and trumpet-tones of Sinai, so this new revelation advances one step farther, and appeals only to reason and faith. For this is the second Christian revelation.

---

* The word "miracle," in the received English version, occurs almost exclusively in the Gospel of John. But the word so translated there occurs frequently in the other Gospels, and is there always translated "sign," as it is in some places in John. Why the word miracle was thus used in the translation of the last Gospel, and in that alone, I have never been able to learn.

This revelation was made through a man, whose life and character were most peculiar. He was the son of a Bishop, who was eminent in station and excellent in character. He was educated thoroughly in all the learning of his time; was for many years practically and busily at work as a mining engineer, holding high office in the Board which had charge of the mines of Sweden, and during this period publishing many works about the business he was engaged in, and other more general scientific subjects; and by these works winning a high reputation, and an acknowledged position among scientific men. All this continued until he had reached the age of fifty years. Then a change began, which completed itself in a few years. During his whole subsequent life, he utterly renounced the study of natural science and all worldly occupation, and devoted himself with all his former energy to spiritual science.

This he declared to be his mission, and in doing this he called himself the servant of the Lord.

Is this credible? What is the evidence of the truth of so strange a statement?

If a new revelation was to be made through him, if it was to be made by his statement of spiritual truths, they should be not merely new, but so entirely distinct from all that was ever before known, so well adapted to send the mind forward on a new path and from a new beginning, so able to supply new motives and incentives to a new moral and affectional as well as intellectual progress, and new instruction to guide this progress, as to justify and authorize this large claim.

This is precisely what his disclosures seem to give, to those who have studied them most carefully and most thoroughly. Nor do we know, or have we ever heard, of any person who studied them with care and thoroughness, and came to a different conclusion. Those who have made themselves — so far as such study could do this — competent to judge of them, believe that they answer questions as old as human thought, which have always been shrouded in darkness; that they give a rational and intelligible explanation of the nature of God and of His providence in reference to His whole creation and to every part of it, and bring into new light the laws of existence and life, and the duties, destinies, and hopes of mankind; and that they do one absolutely new thing, in destroying the separation, if not antagonism, between faith and reason, religion and science, — basing the whole world of spiritual truth upon the world of natural truth, and opening to the grasp and to the work of reason all truth equally.

There is, however, one difficulty. He declares that his spiritual senses were open through many years, and a part of his writings is occupied with describing what he saw and heard in the spiritual world. Such a statement and such descriptions must affect different classes of minds very differently. To the imaginative, who are lovers of the marvellous and not accustomed to weigh evidence, or, indeed, to ask for it, such statements come pleasantly, and are in themselves a reason for accepting all the revelations made through him.

Not so is it with thoughtful and inquiring minds, who begin with the assumption of an extreme antecedent improbability, and require evidence of sufficient weight to overthrow it; and while they admit that these claims and revelations should be judged of by evidence suited to them in kind and character, they demand that it should be conclusive. And some find this. They find it, first in the coherence, completeness, and clearness of these statements and revelations, which commend themselves to belief by their aspect of rationality and truthfulness. They find it next, by the novelty of the principles involved, and of the system of thought and faith builded upon them. Such inquirers see an all-embracing system of truth laid before them, logical in its order and consistency, solving problems which have engaged in all ages the strongest minds and never before found a solution. They say this system would have been discovered before, if merely human thought could have found it; and a large part of it, that relating to the life after death, while perfectly satisfying the demands of reason, could not, by its own nature, have been placed within the grasp of reason, excepting by revelation.

Very often have I heard a remark substantially like this: "There are many beautiful and valuable things in the writings of Swedenborg, but how can I, as a rational man, believe his assertion that he lived consciously in the spiritual world, and that God was giving to mankind a new revelation by him, without proof and adequate proof?—and there is no proof whatever." True, there is nothing which this person could regard as proof. During the many years of Swedenborg's uninterrupted intercourse with the spiritual world, there would be, perhaps there must be, instances of knowledge possessed by him, which were not to be explained except by the truth of his statement concerning himself. There were quite a number of such instances. But he utterly disclaimed and rejected any use of them as proofs of his veracity. Not only so, but it is a point in his doctrines, repeatedly stated, that all such proof of this new revelation would be not only useless but mischievous.

It is of the very essence of this revelation that it is given to man's reason; and to his reason acting in freedom. Any thing whatever which compelled or constrained his reason would be out of place in this revelation, and would tend to fetter or impair that freedom to which this revelation is given. Its doctrines must rest in every mind upon proof; but the only proof they require or permit is the proof of a rational perception of their truth, — a proof perfectly convincing, and perfectly incommunicable. There is an ancient proverb, — said to be Arabian, — "The eyes of the heart sometimes see farther than the eyes of the head." And the apostle said, "With the heart, man believeth unto righteousness."

It may be added, that the difficulty in believing the relations of Swedenborg, concerning things seen and heard in the spiritual world, does not lie in *what* he says of that world, but in the fact that he says any thing whatever, distinctly and definitely, concerning it. The belief in another life, or that men and women after death continue to live as men and women in forms and in a world suited to them, has become very feeble among thinking persons throughout Christendom. Many profess this belief, sometimes urgently; and they do so to confirm their belief and persuade themselves that they do believe. But this belief is at best a hope, more or less confident, but perfectly undefined, and not a subject of distinct conception. To such, any description whatever of that world and its inhabitants, presenting them as living persons, actively employed, must come with a shock. This fading out of belief in actual life after death constituted one of the necessities for this new revelation; and it constitutes one of the principal difficulties in its reception.

If it be a revelation, it must necessarily make its way into acceptance and belief very slowly. This point I shall consider presently. Now I will only say, that it came because it was necessary. It was necessary, because the intellectual and affectional character of the age was so far from the truth, and so far antagonistic to spiritual truth, that progress or improvement was impossible, and the loss or corruption of what was known, probable, if a new revelation were not given. And that condition of the human mind and character which made it necessary, resists it when it comes.

There are intellectual men of high powers and great cultivation, who sometimes reason about the soul and its origin and destiny. But they bring to the investigation of spiritual truth faculties and habits of thought trained and fixed into fitness for a very different kind of work, and unfitness for this. The acceptance of the mere elements and rudiments of all spiritual truth is almost impossible to them, for revelation itself, or the fact that there has been or can be any revelation, is not, perhaps cannot be, admitted by them. They would look with contempt upon those who try to work out from revelations of spiritual truth the sciences of geology or chemistry or physics; and they make the very same mistake in trying to work out spiritual truth from the senses or modes of thought proper to the consideration of what the senses teach. They do not know that, but for the indirect and diffused influence of revelation on the minds of all who live where there is any religion, they could not even think about, and therefore not even deny, God, and a soul, and another life. The inquiry into protoplasm and the reflex action of the nervous centres may be able, successful, and yield valuable results; but the chain of observation and ratiocination which led to these results will not go on, and reach up to God and the Infinite. For that purpose, reason must take a new departure; it must begin differently, and proceed differently. If any such person should read what I have written, what can he think but that I ask him to renounce logic and reason, and trust to sentiment; to abandon the realms of knowledge for those where feeling only is acknowledged as authority, and enthusiasm is the lawful sovereign? And yet I do not mean this, and I desire it just as little as he would.

Perhaps the state of mind induced in the present day, by a successful devotion to the study of natural science, may be illustrated by the fact that some among the most eminent of living scientists find it easier to believe that the wonderful order of the universe, with all the marvellous results of its laws and forces in the world — not of matter only, but of mind — are caused by the reflex action of nervous centres, or some inherent power of matter to form protoplasm, and then of protoplasm to vivify itself, or by the mutual action of atoms, than by the simple truth, almost universally believed by all races in all ages, that they are caused by a Divine Creator.

Professor Tyndall, in his address recently delivered at Belfast, says: —

"Over and above his understanding, there are many other things appertaining to man, whose prescriptive rights are quite as strong as that of the understanding itself. . . . There are such things interwoven into the nature of man as the feeling of awe, reverence, wonder, . . . the love of the beautiful, physical and moral, in Nature, poetry, and art. There is also that deep-set feeling which, since the earliest dawn of history, and probably for ages prior to the dawn of history, incorporated itself into the religions of the world. You who have escaped from these regions into the high-and-dry light of the understanding, may deride them; but, in so doing, you deride accidents of form merely, and fail to touch the immovable basis of religious sentiment in the emotional nature of man. To yield this sentiment reasonable satisfaction, is the problem of problems at the present hour."

Through the address, both before and after the passages above quoted, he throws out some hints as to the method by which he would solve this "problem of problems." The noticeable thing is, that he everywhere assumes that the understanding can have nothing to do with this work. The passage begins, "Over and above his understanding, are many other things," &c., "whose rights are as strong as that of the understanding itself." He opposes "the high-and-dry light of the understanding" to the "religious sentiment in the emotional nature of man." And the problem of the day is, to yield reasonable satisfaction to "this sentiment." All that the understanding has to do is to take care that this satisfaction is no more than reasonable. He concludes the paragraph from which we have quoted, thus: "It will be wise to recognize them [the religions of the world] as the forms of a force, mischievous, if permitted to intrude on the regions of *knowledge* over which it holds no command, but capable of being guided by liberal thought to noble issues in the region of *emotion*, which is its proper sphere. It is in vain to oppose this force with a view to its extirpation. What we should oppose, to the death if necessary, is every attempt to found, upon this elemental bias of man's nature, a system which should exercise despotic sway over his intellect."

What can be plainer or more certain than that Mr. Tyndall confines religion entirely to feeling or emotion, denying to it any hold upon the understanding, and permitting it to exist only on condition that it abstain from any reference to the understanding. It is not less than marvellous that he should suppose this religious sentiment could consider any "satisfaction" as "reasonable" or sufficient, which wholly excluded it from all connection with the understanding, and which permitted no man to hold his religious belief as a distinct and positive intellectual belief.

And yet he is perfectly right on his own ground. If the understanding were only that which he has known and cultivated as such; if its faculties were only those which he has used, and could be used only in the way in which he has used them, and had no materials to work with but those which the senses supply, and which he has worked upon and with so successfully,—then he is entirely right. Between the understanding and religion, the separation must be absolute. But, then, what can he mean when he says that the problem of the day is to satisfy the religious sentiment *reasonably?*

Elsewhere in this address, he says: "The whole process of evolution is the manifestation of a Power absolutely inscrutable to the intellect of man. As little in our day as in the days of Job, can man, by searching, find this Power out. Considered fundamentally, it is by the operation of an insoluble mystery that life is evolved," &c. An insoluble mystery! And yet the problem of this day is to solve this mystery; for what else can give "reasonable satisfaction" to the belief that it exists, and should be the object of reverence, faith and worship, obedience and love?—and surely, all these, in some way or measure, are included in all the forms of religious sentiment and emotion.

How happens it never to have occurred to Mr. Tyndall, and thinkers like him, that this Power, which, as a part of its work, has implanted in human nature this religious sentiment, may have given to it some means of intellectual satisfaction? "Certainly," they may answer, "it might have done so, but it has not. We have looked through the realms of Nature, even to their depths, and we are sure that they supply no such means." I would reply, It may be that Nature has not supplied, and could not supply, such means; or, in other words, this Power could not or would not, certainly has not, by or through Nature, provided such means. But can there be no other way? If they answer, We can see no other way, I say, Does this prove that there is no other way? May not your want of insight be your own fault? Is it not at least possible that this Power, because it would not through Nature alone give the needed information, has found another way of giving it? And if you reject at once, and without inquiry, whatever purports to be information given in this other way, may you not be rejecting truth that would offer a perfect reconciliation between religion and the understanding; giving to religion the full support of all that knowledge which you value so highly, and casting upon the dark places, even of that knowledge, a new and guiding light?

We believe that he is perfectly right in saying that, to yield this religious sentiment reasonable satisfaction, is the "problem of problems" at the present hour. And we believe, also, that the system of thought and belief introduced by Swedenborg will lead to the solution of this "problem of problems."

It is not unbelief alone which resists and prevents the acceptance of this last revelation. Still greater and wider is the effect of a firm and undoubting belief in the doctrines made familiar by education, and sanctioned in many minds by the conviction that it would be dangerous and sinful to change or renounce them. In some minds, of great power and careful culture, the doctrines of the sect they belong to are confirmed by long-continued study, by earnest efforts to maintain them and expose the errors of doctrines which oppose theirs, and by the fixed and indurated habit of loving their doctrines as their own, as a part of themselves, and thus protecting them by the invincible strength of self-love and pride of opinion.

Another cause of the slow and narrow reception of this new system of truth lies in the fact that it shares that characteristic of imperfection, which, it has been already said, is common to all revelations. This new revelation is indeed imperfect in many respects. It is given to man's reason, and to reason in its freedom; and, that this freedom may be more perfect, it is not given by inspiration. No intelligent receiver of the truths taught by Swedenborg regards him as inspired, or considers his writings as superseding or equal to the Bible. His very unusual faculties were cultivated by the most varied and thorough education possible to him, that he might be thus prepared to receive intelligently truths taught him in a most unusual way, and to profit to the utmost by this instruction. This was all. His words were not God's words, but his own; full, as we believe, of truth and wisdom, but limited in their scope, and liable to error. A most important doctrine taught by him is that of the spiritual sense of Scripture, as resting upon the correspondence of natural things with spiritual things. But he confines his interpretation to three books of the Bible, and the texts from other parts incidentally referred to. Thus he gives the principles and elements of this correspondence with much illustration, but leaves the application of them to the works and Word of God, to those who receive them. His other works are doctrinal or philosophical. But, while they contain a wisdom which opens to a receptive mind a vista that looks far into the depths of being, and truths that flash on eyes not closed to them like new sunlight, they have none of the charms of rhetoric; and are sometimes repellent to the new student, by the repetitions with which he seeks to enforce the truths he most valued, and by other characteristics, which, altogether, make his books any thing but easy reading.

If this new revelation is thus imperfect in what we may call its foundation, it is far, very far, more imperfect in its reception by those who sit at the feet of Swedenborg as learners, and would gladly impart what they know to others. We have neither his ability, nor his learning, nor his long and complete devotion to this use; and, most assuredly, we have nothing of the peculiar sources of information which were opened to him. Moreover, the causes above alluded to, as impeding the reception of this revelation in the world, act within our own minds to make this reception poor and limited. They who know these doctrines best, know best how little they know, and how imperfectly they understand what they know. They cannot study the religion which he teaches, without seeing at every step that it underlies a profound philosophy. They cannot study his philosophy without learning a lesson that continually repeats itself, — the lesson that all true philosophy rests upon religion, not only in general, but in every particular; and that a true religion finds a support and confirmation in all true philosophy. These two are in his works, distinct, and yet united; and it must depend upon the bent of his mind who studies them, whether he would call the system of truth, which these works contain, a religious philosophy or a philosophical religion.

In Swedenborg's mind and purpose, religion far outweighed philosophy, so far as they were distinct from each other. Hence it is that he teaches philosophy only as that is connected with religion. But that connection is so close and constant, that, in teaching and illustrating religious doctrines, he teaches much of philosophy. Nevertheless, one who studied all of his works to learn his philosophy would find that they gave only the Outlines of the Philosophy of the New-Church. In giving this name to my little book, I have not the slightest thought of reproducing all of Swedenborg's philosophy. I am so far from being able to do this, that an attempt to do it would be very foolish. Minds, different from those which have as yet accepted his doctrines, must engage in the study and presentation of them, and perhaps a different condition of human thought must prevail, before even the elements of this philosophy in its length and breadth can be given with clearness and accuracy.

If it be asked, then, what it is I propose to do, my answer is, Very little. I would gladly, however, if I could, offer to welcoming minds some, at least, of the foundation-truths of this new system of a philosophy that is wholly religious, and of a religion that is wholly philosophical.

We live in days in which science is declaring its divorce from religion; and some of the strongest and most influential of the minds now active are engaged in proving that men may still have a religion and retain their common sense, only on condition that they not only submit their belief to the legitimate criticism of science, but that they believe only what is permitted them to believe by the knowledge given them by the senses, added to that derived from consciousness, and, as a whole, treated in the same way which has been wonderfully successful in natural science; but with an utter rejection of all preternatural instruction or guidance. All other means of knowledge but those which are useful in the acquirement of natural knowledge, and all other methods or activities of thought, are renounced and rejected as irrational and impossible.

This work these men are doing in various ways; seldom with repulsive arrogance, or contemptuous and offensive denial. Far oftener, their gentleness and tolerance extend and strengthen their influence. This influence is as yet limited, in its full effect, to the few who are engaged in such studies; and is met, and in some degree neutralized, by the earnest, not to say passionate, defence of their assaulted citadels, by religionists of various names. So it is neutralized to some extent; but not very greatly, for the weapons of these defenders of religion, however energetically and skilfully used, are inadequate to the exigencies of this hard battle, because they are taken from an armory that was suited to other times. The most which they who use them try to do, is, to hold their own ground, without attempting to carry the war into the enemy's own territory, and make natural science itself a firm support, an earnest and trustworthy friend, of religion. Be the causes what they may, it is certain that doubting, denying, naturalistic views are now gaining ground, and threaten soon to permeate society.

It is to avert this danger and arrest the decay of religious belief, as well as to lay the foundations of a faith that will endure every test, and last through the ages, that this new revelation is given Its work of reanimating and refounding religion, of clearing away the ruins which cumber the old and immovable foundations of religion, and building upon them a new structure that will endure every test, and resist every assault, and abide the test of time, must be gradual and slow, and hardly perceptible in its early stages; for it can be wrought only through reason, and reason working in freedom, — and human reason is in these days greatly cumbered and darkened. But it is impossible for those who have studied and learned the truths taught by Swedenborg, to doubt that this work will be done; to them, the result is inevitable.

Already, a city is "descending from God out of heaven," which "the glory of God will lighten," — "and the nations of them which are saved will walk in the light of it, and the kings of the earth bring their glory and honor into it." There is a science of correspondence of natural things with spiritual things, which reveals the spiritual meaning of the Word and the works of God, and of which I shall say more presently, and am perfectly aware that even a reference to this science must seem to many minds simply irrational. The interpretation which this science gives us of this prophecy, when stated in the most general terms, is this: Now, from God, by the agency of His angels, a new system of truth and doctrine is being given to men, as a city for their minds; where, although entering each through his own among the many gates, men may dwell together in the peace of certainty, and in possession of truth irradiated with light from the knowledge that and how God is, and is the source and centre of all being; and nations will be saved from ignorance and sin by walking in this light; and the kings of the spirit, or the certain and sovereign truths of genuine knowledge of every kind, will bring their glory and honor into it, by acknowledging that it is the teacher and the mother of all wisdom.

CHAPTER II.

GOD.

There is a God. He is One. He is Infinite. He is the Cause of all that exists.

He is Infinite Love, Infinite Wisdom, and Infinite Power. He creates the universe from Himself. If we imagine Him causing something to be where nothing was, He is there by His Will, His Thought, His Action; or in and by His Love, His Wisdom, and His Power, — and they are Himself. We cannot, however, suppose something to be where nothing was; for He is everywhere, and creates, by efflux from Himself, whatever exists.

He is Infinite Love. It is of the essence of love to desire to give of its own to others; to give itself. This desire in God is infinite; and it is the moving cause of creation. It is a desire to give himself in all possible ways and all possible degrees. Therefore, He creates the universe. He creates it by efflux from Himself; and He creates it such that it may continue to be, in the highest possible degree, receptive of influx from Himself.

He creates the material world. The lowest form of this is the mineral world; above that is the vegetable world; above that is the animal world; and above that is man. All the worlds below man refer to him, and are for his use. We can see that they supply his needs, and minister to his life and enjoyment; and we may discern this in a degree which should excite in us gratitude and wonder. But they are adjusted to all our needs, natural and spiritual, in a way of which any knowledge that we acquire will never be complete, and to which any conception that we can form, although it be always growing, will never be adequate.

The reception of Him, in all of creation below man, cannot go far. In man, however feeble its beginning, it can increase indefinitely and for ever; for man is immortal. He begins to live here, because this home for the beginning of life is so constructed and so adapted to him, that he may here prepare himself for happiness hereafter. That happiness must consist in the fuller reception of Divine love and wisdom. They constitute God; and that man may receive these and appropriate them to himself, he is made in the image and likeness of God.

Anthropomorphism is, in these days, often used as a term of reproach. It means, literally, the ascribing of man's form to God; it means, actually, as used, the likening of God to man. This is an error, and a great one, just so far as it degrades God to a similitude with man, and brings the infinite down to the finite. This error has been permitted, because, even in its grosser forms, — as in those ancient religions in which the gods of popular belief were not only men, but, in much of their conduct, bad men, — even in these forms it gave a definite idea and a positive belief of the existence of God to minds which were incapable of higher views. This was good, because, for a man to be wholly destitute of a belief in God is the worst calamity that can befall him. But anthropomorphism is a truth, and not an error, just so far as it preserves the whole infinitude of God; and, asserting His absolute perfection, makes that the standard of human excellence, and founds the highest hopes of humanity upon the possible approach to divinity. There can be no religion in faith or in life, without some idea of God; and man could have no idea of God, and would have nothing upon which, or by means of which, he could form such an idea, if he were totally and perfectly different from God. If he were so different that he must exclude from his idea of God all ideas derived from himself, he would have no ideas to take their place. It is declared in Genesis, that God made man in His own image and likeness. This new philosophy neither rejects this truth, nor explains it away. It accepts it as a truth, and rests upon it its whole belief in God. And it explains this truth in such wise as to give to it new force and new distinctness, together with a clearer view of the infinite and absolute perfection of the Divine nature.

Neander, the great historian of the Christian church, finds in early Christian writers, and uses himself, the word "anthropomorphism." Of it he says: "So far as it denotes a diseased process of thought, it consists in ascribing to the Absolute Spirit the limitations and defects which cleave to the human. . . . It is based on an undeniable and inherent necessity; since man, being created in the image of God, and being a spirit in affinity with the Father of spirits, feels constraint and a warrant for framing his idea of God after this analogy. . . . It is possible to err, as well as to be right, according as the analogy is wrongly or rightly observed." In another place he says: "From the contemplation of God's self-manifestation in the creation, we are constrained to form our conception of the Divine attributes in accordance with the analogy of our own minds." We are, indeed, *constrained* to do this, by the nature He has given. And have we any right to say that He has constrained us to a falsehood?

They who make a rightful use of the resemblance

of man to God find in man love; and they carry this to the highest imaginable degree, and vest it in One who is capable of loving. They find in man wisdom, and, carrying this to its highest potency, vest it in One who can be wise. So they do with all the powers and essential attributes of manhood which they see to be good, excepting those which imply limitation and imperfection. But who or what is this One, who is thus good and wise and strong, but without limitation? They cannot imagine Him,—if, by imagination, we mean the presentment of a thing to thought, in shape. They cannot conceive of Him,—if, by conception, we mean the forming of an idea which has definite limits. But they can *believe*,—led by the tendency of a healthy human nature, and guided by a sound and intelligent logic,—they can believe that there is such a One, that there must be such a One; and, so far as above stated, He must possess the essential attributes of human nature, and so far He is a Divine Man.

A far more perfect solution of this problem is given by Christianity; and that solution is made more complete by the truths which are now given to the New-Church. But of this, I can better speak in another connection, when I treat of our Lord and Saviour, Jesus Christ,—who is Immanuel, or God with us, and God for us.

God is Man; perfect and infinite man in form: in form, but not in shape, for shape is but the expression and outward manifestation of form. It is by means of shape that form becomes apprehensible by sense and thought; and thought may then rise above shape, and think of form as it is in itself. For form we may define sufficiently, and perhaps as well as words will permit, by saying that it is the inmost nature or essential being of a thing. God is above the limitation of shape, by which all lower things are accommodated to the perceptions of his creatures. So He is above the limitations of space and time; for he is in all space without space, and in all time without time. But God is Man; and man is man, only because God's life is given to him to be his own.

God is Love and Wisdom; and man is made in the image and likeness of God, that he may receive of the Divine love and wisdom more fully. He has a will, into which the Divine love may flow, and become in him all he has of affection or feeling. He has an understanding, into which the Divine wisdom may flow, and become in him all he has of thought or perception. The infinite love of God is ever moving Him to exert, through His infinite wisdom, His infinite power. Man has strength given him, that the moving force of his will and his affections, inciting and acting through his thoughts, may cause him to be useful, and happy in being useful. This is so in man, because it is so in God, who is the one perfect Man, and the Source and Cause of all manhood; and the infinite blessedness of God, which He is ever desirous to impart in whatever measure it may be received, springs from the exercise of His power, under the direction of His wisdom, and moved by His love. The law is universal, that, without usefulness, there can be no happiness.

In the very lowest condition of human life. and in the feeblest beginnings of human strength, there is this Divine love which has become man's love, acting through his thoughts, which are but the Divine wisdom accommodated to man's capacities, and appropriated by him; and thus he is living, moving, and acting to do the least and humblest things which a living man can do. But, from this lowest beginning, a never-ending ascent is possible.

God gives to man to be his own, to be himself; not to be a partial or imperfect God, but to be himself, — a man. Because God is perfect Man, and man lives by receiving the Divine life from God, man is man. The life flowing into him is infinitely human in its source and essence, and continues to be human in him, and constitutes him man. Because this life is given him to be his own, to cause him to be himself, he is not a mere channel through which Divine life flows, nor merely an instrument which

Divine power uses. Infinite love could not be satisfied with creating so low a creature as this. It could be satisfied with nothing less than a creature capable of receiving Divine life, and appropriating this life as his own, so that he may live as from himself, and be himself; and this with an ever-growing reception and fulness of life and happiness.

Freedom is an element of the Divine life, and, like all its elements, is infinite; and this element is not severed from this life in its inflow into man. Like all the elements of this life, it is feeble and imperfect to the last degree in its incipient and early reception, but capable of perpetual growth and development. Hence and such is human freedom, with all its possible evil, and all its immeasurable good. If its evil were not possible, neither would its good be possible, for it would not be freedom; and without freedom man could not be himself, and could not fulfil the end of his creation, by living a life ever-growing in happiness by his own efforts, and ever-rising in the character of that happiness.

The doctrine that, while man's life is wholly derived from God, it is given him to be his own, — and that it is his own, and he is himself, — must often be referred to in all attempts to present the philosophy of the New-Church, for it lies near its centre, and comes forth into every part of it. The fact that

God is infinite Love, and therefore desires to give Himself fully, accounts for this further fact, that He gives to man, who is perfectly dependent upon Him, a life which is as if independent. Nor is this a mere illusion, nor is the freedom which results from it an illusion. It is through this independence in dependence, and this freedom which is given, that God endeavors to build all men into forms most capable of happiness. But He can do this only through this freedom; and therefore only through man's consent and coöperation, and only in the degree in which man consents and coöperates. It is to man himself that God commits his character, and, therefore, his destiny. And we shall begin to comprehend the wants and the failures of humanity, and the mingling and alternation of good and evil in every thing of this life, when we throw upon the clouds and darkness which now enwrap Divine Providence the light of the truths, — that we are here only in the beginning of being; that we are here only that this beginning may be rightly directed; and that we see, in this mingling of good and evil, only the conflict between the influences which would lift us up, and our refusal and opposition, or our unpreparedness to give our consent and coöperation, in our freedom.

Among mankind, there is now a strong and very general sense of independence of God, broken only by a feeling that, in some way, He is still our Master. This is permitted, because human progress begins from this idea of an absolute selfhood. But the first steps of a true progress are taken, when we come to some knowledge of the truth that all life, and all that constitutes life, — every affection and every thought and every faculty, — are constantly, instantly, and incessantly given us from God; but given to be our own, and to become what we choose to make them.

In the beginning of life, and without instruction, a man is wholly unable to have any thought that he lives from God, or otherwise than from himself. As his mind matures, if he receives instruction, he learns that there is a God, his Creator; and that he lives from Him. At first, this truth will be very obscure to him; he will see it imperfectly, and understand very little about it. As he advances in spiritual knowledge, this truth will grow clearer to him, and he will understand more about it and its consequences. This process may go on for ever. The wisest among the wise, the happiest among the happy, in that kingdom where all are happy, are those who see most clearly and know most certainly, that their whole life is His life given to them; given instantly and incessantly, so that they neither have nor can have any thought, affection, or feeling which is not derived from His influent life. And, with the growing certainty of this knowledge, there is also a growing certainty that this life is given them as their own, and that they are free, because freedom is given them as an element of this life.

The sunlight, falling upon all the individuals which make up the vegetable world, is determined in its effect and manifestation by the inmost and essential form of each; and, being so determined, causes each one to be that which it is, — beautiful and fragrant, or the reverse; fruitful or poisonous. Precisely so it is with man. It is his inmost and essential form or character which determines what the influent Divine life shall become in him, and therefore what he shall be. The sunlight and the dew, absorbed by night-shade, form and ripen poison. The heat and light from the Sun of heaven, or the Divine love and wisdom, received by the sinful man into his will and understanding, — who is sinful because he does not use the power given him to resist the proclivities of his nature, — come forth as sinfulness.

It is an universal law that this inmost form of each existing thing determines what it is, although all exist by the reception of one life. To man alone something more is given; something which belongs to him as man, and constitutes him man: it is the power over his own inmost form, or over his character. A vegetable has a kind of life, but cannot change its place; an animal has more life, for he can change his place; a man has yet more life, for he can change his character, — that is, himself; and therefore his character, and with it his destiny, are in his own hands.

If man, the creature, were utterly unlike his Creator, he would be utterly unable to have any knowledge or thought concerning his Creator; just as animals are unable. But man is in the image and likeness of God; and he is made so, that it may be possible for him to have some knowledge of God, and form some idea of Him. As he becomes better and wiser, he becomes more godlike; and as his godlikeness (or godliness) grows, so does his knowledge of God, and his wisdom concerning God. The best and most that we attain to here is but little more than nothing compared with what is possible. The wisdom of the wisest in the other life differs from our best wisdom, far more than this differs from the thought of the infant.

God is Love; pure, perfect, infinite love. Love is His motive power; it is from Him the motive power of the universe, — all the force, and all the forces of the universe, are always, and in all their action, derived from love, and are forms of love; of His love given to the universe of His creation to be its motive power. We call this force by a variety of names, because we see it under a variety of aspects.

But under all this variety of names and activities, doing the work of creation and of sustaining all that is created, force in some form is never ceasing, always active, and seen everywhere; and science is rapidly approaching the conclusion that all forces are but varying aspects of one force. As yet this is held, and that imperfectly, only in regard to material things; because science has not yet learned to look up from material things. The time will come, however, when, after science has increased its knowledge of material forces, and clearly seen their unity, it will look higher; and, becoming itself one with spiritual science, will see that all spiritual forces are one, and that they and natural forces are also, in their origin and in their inmost nature, one. What can this One be but the Divine love, which is the spring and cause of all causation?

Tell this truth now, and so tell it, if that were possible, that science would accept it, and there would be this danger: existing science would then seek to make it all material; to prove that mind was only more ethereal matter, and that "the brain secretes thought as the liver secretes bile," to use words already uttered by an eminent materialist. Already the conviction that all material forces are one has led some minds to the effort of bringing intellectual and moral forces within the same unity; and very ingenious are the arguments by which it is attempted to make mind and will only a form, or at best a product, of matter. These arguments will not be permitted to prevail. The conclusion to which they point is too absolute a falsehood; and a falsehood at once degrading to science and destructive of all true philosophy.

Love is one, and Force is one; for it is but love brought forth into an infinite variety of uses, by an infinite variety of instruments. Everywhere the universal law prevails; and this love, which has become force, is determined in its aspect and in its action by the work it has to do, and by the instruments which are adapted to this work, and by which that work is done.

All the forces of the universe in all their action are but forms of love: the tornado, the earthquake, the devastating fire, "the terror by night, the arrow that flieth by day, the pestilence that walketh in darkness, the destruction that wasteth at noon-day," and the lighter or heavier blows which fall upon us every day, and bring their gifts of pain and disappointment,—all, all of these are but forms of love. But it is an infinite love which is one with infinite wisdom; and clouds never rest upon the infinite perception that it is best for the highest and most enduring interests of man, that his spiritual freedom should not be impaired. In other words, that he should not be compelled to yield to, but led to coöperate with, the Divine goodness.

Therefore are sin, and the suffering which is its child, permitted. Therefore "are clouds and darkness round about Him." But with it all, and through it all, His love reigns and works. We are enveloped by it in the air we breathe. It shines upon us in His sunlight, and falls upon us in the soft rain and the dew, and comes to us in food and shelter; and more, infinitely more, than all this, it is ever doing all that omnipotence can do, to lead us always, in our own freedom, to look to Him with love and trust; to put away from us the hindrances that gather between Him and us; to use His gifts aright, and so convert even calamity into the blessing it was given to be.

CHAPTER III.

CREATION.

God cannot but create. Because He has and He is Infinite Love; and the desire to give what one has and is, is of the essence of love: this desire He has infinitely. Therefore He cannot but create those whom He may love, and to whom He may give from Himself; and for that purpose He creates the universe. But is the created universe eternal?— or was there a time when He who is eternal, and must desire to create, did not create? This question is irrational, because it carries the idea and the measure of time where time does not belong. We can never answer this question, nor can we ask it intelligently; for the reason that, while we live on earth, it is impossible for us to liberate our mind entirely from the influence of time, even if we are able to know and to acknowledge that time is only a thing of thought, indispensable for the necessities of this life, and adjusted to its uses.

He creates from Himself. He cannot create from nothing; for that which is created from nothing must consist of nothing, and be nothing. Therefore He creates from Himself, or by an efflux of Himself from Himself. Time belongs to us, not to Him. He creates always and incessantly. Whatever is exists by a perpetual and ever present efflux from Him. The work of creation is always now. He has methods of working, derivable from and conformed to the essential order of His own being. So far as we can discern these methods, we may call them laws. But there is no mistake which more forcibly resists all comprehension of the Divine work, than that which supposes it was once done for all time; done in the past for the present and the future; done, and dismissed from Divine action. The truth that all existence is continuously caused, in the whole and in each part, in every thing, and in all that any thing is or does, — is a central and essential element in a just and rational comprehension of the Divine work.

God is All in All. But is not this Pantheism? In all ages religious believers have looked upon Pantheism with horror. They have regarded it, and for good reasons, as the very opposite, the very antagonist, of all religion, as the most plausible and seducing enemy of religion, because it appeals to and attempts to satisfy that deep-seated and inextinguishable desire of the human heart for God, by declaring its belief in the divinity of creation, and giving to the universe the name of God. But the assertion that the universe is God, and the only God, is a most positive and emphatic denial of God. What the implanted religiousness of human nature demands is a personal God; is One to whom prayer may be directed; on whom confidence and trust may be reposed; for whom love and gratitude may be cherished, and to whom the sacrifice of obedience may be offered. Any other God than this is a God only of words, and unmeaning words; a God only of theory and not of faith or affection; a God of what may call itself philosophy, but in no possible sense a God of religion. It was of a very different God from the God of this Pantheism, that the Christian apostles four times declare Him to be All in All; and it is in a different sense from that of Pantheism that I have made use of the same phrase.

God creates the universe from Himself; but He creates it other than Himself. He creates it for His creatures, and He gives it to them. He makes it to be theirs. It is still His; but it is theirs also. He must have beings other than Himself to be objects of His love; therefore He creates them to be *themselves.*

I here again touch upon one of the points where the infinite mystery of Being comes before every mind which endeavors to investigate this mystery in the hope of learning whatever may be knowable concerning it: and that is the reconciliation of existing evil with Divine love. The little that we can learn, is so little in comparison with the stupendous whole, so nearly nothing, that it may well be regarded as nothing.

The truth to be kept in constant recollection as the basis of all consideration of this subject is, that God creates from Love. If there be a Creator, then there must be some motive power to induce creation. We may think that this motive must be far above our possible perception, and infinitely beyond our comprehension. But need we say this? Not if we believe that man is to live hereafter, and that his happiness during the whole of his unending life must be connected in some way with his relations to his Creator; for then we should admit it as probable that he would be gifted with some power of knowing the existence and apprehending the nature of his Creator; and that this power, however feeble in its beginning, would even then enable him to discern the fundamental truths on which an ever-growing structure of knowledge might rest. A part, at least, of this fundamental truth would tell him why God created him. He could learn this only from revelation; but he would be capable of so learning it, and revelation would be given him that he might know it. Hence he is taught by revelation that God is Love. Very dimly do we see this truth, but only so far as we see it do we know any thing about God; and only when we recognize this truth as truth, and keep it constantly before us so that we may walk in its light, can we hope to make any progress in our understanding of the Divine nature and work.

God creates every thing from Love; and man stands at the head of creation. How can we reconcile the oppressive imperfection and diversified unhappiness of man and his condition with the truth that an all-wise and all-powerful Being created him only from love? We cannot unless we believe that man is immortal, that he is capable of an ever-growing happiness; and that the imperfections and miseries we witness, and are conscious of, spring from causes which are the indispensable means of making this happiness more certain, more constant, more perfect. Then all that seems to be antagonistic to love may be reconciled with it, and made to wear the aspect and do the work of love.

Before attempting to show how this is, let us look for a moment at so much of the universe as is not man. The first statement to be made is, that all that is not man is for the sake of man. If we believe that God creates the universe to satisfy the desire of an infinite love, and that man satisfies this desire because he, and he only, is immortal and capable of an ever-growing and never-ending happiness, then what is not capable of this, or what is not man, can meet the demand of an infinite love only by assisting and promoting man's eternal happiness; and to this end it must be adjusted.

Let it not be supposed that because all things are for man, no other thing has any value of its own. So it might be if things were created by man, the finite; but because they are created by God, the Infinite, it is not so. Each has its own value and is itself, as if it existed for itself only and not for man. All living things have their own life, and their own happiness; and this happiness is first His, and given to them by Him, and then returns to Him, and becomes again His happiness; for He is happy because they are.

And how is it with the dead things of the universe? They also make their return to Him. He is infinitely *useful.* This word may seem a strange one to apply to God; but it is so applied, because He loves infinitely to be useful, — that is, to do good. Because this is an essential and inseparable element of His nature, it passes into all the creation which He makes of Himself and from Himself. The grain of sand, the drop of water, the rock, the ocean, the planet, the sun, — each of them has its special use, and in all these uses He rejoices.

And the beauty of the world, — vast and varied beyond all conception, escaping human observation and appreciation except in the minutest degree, — is it nothing to Him? "He that made the eye, shall He not see?" The power of perceiving and enjoying the beautiful is a part of man's nature (a power as yet most imperfectly developed), because it is a part of God's own nature; and, like every thing else which belongs to Him, is in Him perfect.

But if all this be so, why is there so much unhappiness in the world; so much that obstructs and hinders all use; so much that is not beautiful, and is its opposite; so much that is not good and is evil?

Again, let us remember that God is Love; that it is of the essence of love to give itself; that because His love is infinite, His desire to give Himself must be infinite; and that this infinite desire must prompt Him to give Himself unreservedly. It is precisely this which He does. He gives to the universe to be itself; He gives to every thing of the universe to be itself. He gives to man to be himself; He gives to him the power, or rather the necessity, to own his being, his life, his self-hood. And while God is All in All, there is no other Pantheism. In this way God makes the universe to be other than Him, even while it and every part of it depends upon His being for its being, perfectly, absolutely, and at every instant. It is other than Him because it is itself. It is itself because, while He gives being to it from Himself, He also gives to it to own the being that

He gives: to own it as its own. And in this truth we have a key to the mysteries of Providence.

To all that exist He gives being from Himself. If this were human giving, life given from Him would be severed from Him; but it is Divine giving; and the life which flows from Him to man, and is given to man that he may be himself, remains perfectly the life of God. His love is one with His wisdom; and both are constantly exercised to guide and lead and induce man to use aright the power and freedom which are given him that he may be himself. But they are always so exercised as to leave in his own hands, unimpaired, the power to form his own character, and thereby determine his own destiny.

Man, in the exercise of this power, sometimes abuses it. If he could not abuse it, he could not use it in freedom. He can abuse it, and he does abuse it. If we would form some conception of what would be the effect if man constantly used this power aright, we have but to think of what the opposite effect must be, when man abuses it. The effect of using this power aright is good, all good. Evil is the opposite of good; and the effect of abusing this power is evil, all evil,—for there is no evil which is not the exact opposite of some good, and is not caused by the wrongful use of a power, the rightful use of which would have produced that good.

As soon as men began to think, there must have been an effort to account for the evil existing within and around them. The abuse of freedom suggested itself long ago, and has been presented in many forms; in none of which has it been wholly satisfactory. Men could hardly help thinking that there was some evil power at work to produce evil. This belief was most definitely systematized in the latter part of the third century of Christianity under the name of Manicheanism. It spread from the far east into Christendom and prevailed widely. The central doctrine was that there had existed from eternity two principles, — one good, the other evil; God and Hyle, light and darkness; absolutely opposed to each other; everywhere meeting and always in conflict. This system was developed into a great number of doctrines, variously modified; the only thing common to them all being this eternal conflict of two opposite principles. The name has disappeared long ago. Perhaps the profession of such belief is not now to be met with. But the belief itself, in some degree or measure, is held very widely and almost universally. For is it not held of necessity by those who do not believe that all evil originated in some way from good? This would seem obvious. Good exists, and evil exists; and evil must exist from good, or else it exists from itself and by perpetual self-propagation. There are, undoubtedly, those who say, and with greater or less sincerity of faith believe, that a God of goodness finds the evil in the universe, and uses it as His instrument of discipline or punishment; and some I suppose think that He causes it to exist that He may so use it.

It would seem certain that we must hold Manicheanism or the belief in two antagonist principles, in some form, — either as God and His antagonist, or the two in God himself, as love and something which, whether we call it justice or by some other name, is not love; or else, that we must believe that evil is man's work, and that the power of man to do evil was given to him by Divine love, and therefore for his best good. Very many have been the efforts to establish this last theory. The difficulty is, that of the many elements of this belief every one is held feebly and imperfectly. These elements are, that there is a personal, creating, and governing God; that He is essential goodness, and only that; that whatever man has he receives from God as the gift of goodness; and that among these gifts is freedom, — given because, with all its necessary liability to abuse, it must be given as the essential foundation of all that is best in character and happiest in condition: and nothing less than the best can satisfy the infinite desire of God to give happiness.

When all these truths are clearly seen and firmly held, then, and perhaps then only, can it be clearly seen that all evil necessarily arises from the abuse of human freedom. Then, too, we shall be prepared to follow out this truth into its consequences.

It is because the destiny of man is placed in his own hands that evil comes, — moral evil and spiritual evil; evil in thought, affection, and life. And it is one of the evidences, as it is one of the effects, of the adaptation *to* man of that universe which is *for* man, that all the evil there is in man's nature or life is imaged forth in the conflicts, imperfections, and disorder in the world beneath, above, and about him. There is indeed a conflict ever going on within man and without him, between two principles, — one of which is good and the other evil. But the good one is from our Father in Heaven, and the evil is born of our abuse of the gifts of our Father. Ignorant as we are, and with our ignorance intensified and indurated by our conceit of wisdom and intellectual ability, no wonder that the relations of God with man are shrouded, not in mystery only, but in midnight darkness. No wonder that we detect in our thoughts the secret influence of the falsity which tells us that man and the universe were imperfectly constructed through a failure either of love or of power, and then left to themselves. No wonder we find it so hard to believe that perfect love, guided by perfect wisdom, is the universal motive power; and that while the power of the Omnipotent is never exerted to destroy or paralyze the freedom of the human race; while perfect love can never withdraw that gift of freedom which perfect wisdom sees to be the indispensable condition of the highest happiness,— this same love and wisdom are constantly watchful to do, through human freedom, all that can be done to prevent, or, if that can not be, to lessen, the abuse of this gift; to remedy the mischiefs which spring from it, and, as far as is possible, to use these very mischiefs as instruments of good. Immeasurable time rolls on. Patiently and slowly the work of God goes forward; and the whole universe, with all its inhabitants and every individual in this innumerable multitude, are ever advancing as fast and as far as the law of love which governs them all permits: the law that no one can advance in wisdom and in goodness, except so far as he coöperates with the Divine influence in his own freedom.

CHAPTER IV.

THIS WORLD.

We live here in material bodies and in a material world. But what is a material world? Surely we all know that. It is the world which we see and feel everywhere, and of which our bodies are made. Such is the answer which the senses give; and if it be not true and certain, what can be certain? And is not the philosophical question which has puzzled thinkers since the beginning of thought — What is matter? — a striking instance of the power and tendency of philosophy to bewilder thought, and darken with its subtleties what would never raise a doubt if quietly left to consciousness and common sense? Not so. It is a wholesome thirst of knowledge which prompts a thinking mind to ask, What is this world we live in? And the question cannot be asked, and any consideration given to the answer, without our finding that the answer is not easy.

Innumerable are the ways in which this question has been answered; but they all may be classed under two heads — Realism and Idealism. Realism holds that the world outside of us is really what it seems to be: that tree, that mountain, that cloud, are just what you see that they are, and just where you see them. But Idealism replies by easy proof of the deceitfulness of sense, and goes on to inquire into the *cause* and foundation of sensuous impressions or perceptions. It shows us that, when we look at that tree, all we see and all that the mind contemplates is a minute picture painted on the retina (or the expansion of the nerve of sight at the back of the eye); or rather, it takes a step farther, and says that all the mind can contemplate is the idea formed in the mind from that picture on the retina. For, say the Idealists, we have not and cannot have the least evidence that any thing but the idea exists, and matter is only a product or a form of thought; thus precisely reversing the materialistic theory that thought is but a product or form of matter.

Such is a very general statement of Realism and Idealism. But the modifications of each of them that have been at different times suggested, are innumerable; the main question — What is matter? — being no more and no better answered by any of these theories than it was when first asked. Supposing this question to be now before us, I think the principles of New-Church philosophy would answer it somewhat in this way.

God causes or creates the universe from Himself,

and by an efflux from Himself. This efflux is pure substance. We cannot form the slightest idea of it as it is in itself; for all that we can possibly know of it is what it appears to the mind as the mind contemplates it through the senses. It is perfectly adapted to our needs, and exquisitely adjusted to our senses, as our senses are to our mind. And the result is that this substance, becoming matter, acts on the mind through the senses, and presents all the forms and phenomena of the universe. This effect is produced in this way. The new-born babe sees the things around him; but he has no idea of distance. The moon is as near to him as the lamp on the table. He moves his limbs, and soon he moves himself. The other senses come in. He reaches toward some object, and acquires the ideas of motion, of distance, and place. He touches objects, and gets the ideas of shape and solidity. All this goes on; and, with every day, objects become more distinct to him, and stand before him, each in its place. We do all this in infancy and early childhood, from the first beginnings of sensation and thought, in the years over which oblivion rests. So we come unconsciously to those conclusions concerning external objects, which the experience of every day confirms, and which it never occurs to us to doubt. We do this, because our senses are so adjusted to our minds on the one hand as to excite these ideas in the mind; and are so adjusted to pure substance on the other hand, that through our senses that substance excites those ideas. And, in this way, we have an external world with all its indefinite variety of objects.

This view reconciles realism with idealism. It is realistic, for it asserts that there is an actual entity, a pure substance, underlying and supporting all the forms of matter. It is idealistic, for it asserts that all these forms, with all their interacting forces, are to us what they are, by reason of the adjustment of this substance to our senses, and of our senses to our minds.

It is realistic, inasmuch as it holds that there is a positive and most real *something* which is not us; and that this something exists not *in* Nature, but *as* Nature, or as the natural basis upon which rest all our conceptions of natural things. It is idealistic, inasmuch as it asserts that this substance has form and force and manifestation because, by its relation to the senses and their relation to the mind, this substance presents itself in all natural forms and forces.

In this world we begin to live. When we have ceased to live here, we at once begin to live in another world. There also we find this same substance, and there also it is adjusted to our needs. We are then in spiritual bodies with spiritual organs of sense, and with a spiritual world to live in; all formed of spiritual substance which exists, as material substance exists here, from a Divine source, and there as here is an adaptation of our senses to pure substance on the one hand, and to our minds on the other. That life will never end. It is therefore of immeasurably greater importance than this life, if we consider them separately. But they should not be considered separately. This life is a preparation for that life; and that life is the result and consummation of this life.

If this life is a preparation for that life, two questions suggest themselves. One is, What is this preparation for? The other is, How is this preparation made?

We can learn what this preparation is for, or what is the end to be attained by it, only by deducing it from the Divine purpose in creating us. This purpose is to satisfy the desire of a Being of infinite and perfect goodness, to create those whom He might love, and to whom He might impart as far as possible, and in an ever-growing measure, His own goodness and His own happiness.

Then another question occurs, and may present itself often while we are considering these topics, Why does not He create beings in whom this end is attained at once, and perfectly? He creates the birds, and gives to each one peculiar faculties tending to its preservation in life and its enjoyment of life. He creates the horse, the lion, with other faculties which have the same tendency. He creates man with still other and higher faculties which, however, tend still in the same direction. Why does He not create beings who are at once invested with the faculties and qualities which would insure the end which we are told He infinitely desires? Why has He not endowed man with these faculties and qualities? Is it a want of power which prevents it, or a want of will?

The answer is, He does not do this because this is not the best thing He can do for His creatures. Far as we are from an ability to fathom the infinite and solve the mystery of being, it should not be difficult for us to see that a created being gifted with power to be himself, and hold his life as his own; enabled and assisted to work out his own happiness by his voluntary coöperation with God; beginning at the lowest point and thence ascending, step by step, finding, as he rises, this ascent opening before him, and leading upwards forever and forever, with a constantly increasing ability to work with his Father in doing good, and enjoying the happiness of goodness, — it should not be difficult to see that we have here a picture of the happiest possible of created beings. If we think this, then we must also think that this is the being which Perfect Love would create.

The earth we live on, the air we breathe, the insect, the bird, the mammal, — all alike and equally exist and live by efflux of being or of life from Him. But we are sure that this one life is received in different ways on these different planes of being. We are sure that the higher animals receive life in another way from the lower animals; and they all receive life in another way from that in which it constitutes the being of dead matter. We may use words derived from sense to express this, and say that the higher animals receive a higher life, or receive it more largely than the lower. The point I would impress is, that there are degrees in the life received, and in the kind of reception. For then we may see that there are degrees in the gifts of Divine goodness, and that the whole of the Divine purpose in the preparation of mankind in this life for another, may be summed up as the desire and purpose of enabling man, by this preparation, to receive Divine life in the greatest possible degree, and in the best possible way.

Then we come to the question, How is this preparation effected? The first and most general answer is, Through man's voluntary coöperation in all the work, because the best result is attainable in this way. The more specific answer is, By man's resisting, suppressing, and putting away from himself the qualities and proclivities which obstruct or impair or pervert the reception of Divine life. All men receive life, and all their life, from God; for otherwise they would not live at all, for man does not live from himself. But man, and man alone, can pervert this influent Divine life, because he alone has freedom and the power of self-determination. And he receives life without perversion, and in the manner in which God desires that he should receive it, when, and as far as, love continues to be love in his will, and wisdom continues to be wisdom in his understanding. Divine love received by man must indeed continue to be in him love of some kind for ever; for otherwise he would have no motive power, no life. But only when it is the love of others does it continue to be the love it was in its Divine source. So the Divine wisdom must remain in him, or he would have no power of thought. But if the love is itself perverted into self-love, it perverts that wisdom into falsity.

It follows of necessity, that the qualities and tendencies which man must resist and put away are those which are most opposed to love and wisdom, and would therefore resist their entrance into himself, or enfeeble them, or pervert them into their opposites. The opposite of love is self-love, and its child is the love of the world for the sake of self; or, in fewer words, selfishness and worldliness. These things then are what we must resist and put away, if we would become capable of receiving Divine life without perversion, and with it, true happiness.

As all revelation is given to man to aid him in preparing for another life, it is especially aimed against the evil things which prevent or mar this preparation. All the commandments have this aim; and all are summed up in the two commandments, to love God with all the heart, and to love the neighbor as one's self. Revelation cannot go beyond this, except to explain these commands, and show why they were given, and how they may be obeyed, and what is the effect of obedience to them. And this the new revelation places in clear light.

It tells us that our life is Divine life, given us to be our own; that infinite love prompts this gift, because it is the foundation of all existence and of all happiness; that love of others is the essence of this life; and therefore the measure of our happiness must be our reception and appropriation of love,—or our happiness must be measured in kind and in degree by the kind and measure of our loving. The best and highest possible love must be our love for Him who is best and highest, and our infinite benefactor. We are therefore commanded to love the Lord our God with all the heart and soul, because, if we do so, His life, which is His love, becomes our own life without perversion; and, in the degree in which it is so, we are happy.

We must also love our brother as ourself. Our Father has given His children to each other as objects of love, that so all may learn to love, and all may be happy. In the immaturity of beginning life, we can only love each other. We are as yet incapable of knowing God or of loving Him; but we may love each other. Because the love of the neighbor is "like unto" the love of God, it trains and educates us for that consummating love. As our eyes are opened to see Him in His works and word, and in the love and wisdom manifested in them, our hearts are opened to love Him; and if we have learned to love our brethren, it is just that love which opens our hearts to this higher love. Henceforward, these two loves grow forever; not independent, but indissolubly connected; not separated but united: one as the centre, the other as the circumference. If we have learned to love our brethren aright, we love them because they and we are children of one Father, and co-partakers of His life and His love. The more we love Him in the light of this truth, the more we shall love them. The more we love them, the more we shall love Him who, as a crowning work of His infinite mercy, has given them to us that we may love them.

It is because He is Love, that He is the source of love; for all love is but His love flowing forth from Him. He creates the inanimate world for the animate world. He creates the animal world; they cannot look up to Him and return His love to Him; but He nevertheless created them in love, and cares for them in love. He creates man, and man may look up to Him; and from man, the Divine love which has become man's love, may return to Him who gave it. Then is the circle completed; and God is infinitely happy, because the end of creation is accomplished, and He has children to whom He can impart of His own happiness.

For this end all things are provided and governed, and to this end all things tend. Therefore it is that He has given us laws, obedience to which is the direct and certain way of overcoming and putting away the evil tendencies and lusts which oppose themselves to our unselfish love of the neighbor and of Him. There is no religion which has not these laws, and which does not give instruction that will save men from their sins. Hence we may now believe that all on earth, be their place and name what they may, if they are faithful to the best instruction they receive, may learn to love their brethren and their Father; and so prepare for that heaven where that love — always one with wisdom — reigns, and fills all with the light and life they are prepared to receive.

Wherever we are, whether in this world or in the other, it is the desire, the infinite desire, of our Father to give to us all the happiness He can give. But while we live here, He can not forget the end, the purpose, for which he makes us to live here; and that is, to prepare for living hereafter. In every particular of every life, a constant reference to our eternal interests governs the Divine Providence. Those interests are never subordinated to our temporal interests. These last are not forgotten or disregarded; for as much of happiness of every kind is given to us by Him while we are here as is compatible with His primal and constant regard for the things of eternity. All the events and circumstances of life are so shaped and so governed, that we may have the utmost possible aid in preparing for an eternal life. All success and all enjoyment are given us, which would not lessen or interfere with the formation of a character susceptible of true and eternal happiness. When the one great end and purpose for which we live here requires that disappointment, suffering, or calamity should befall us, they come; but they are measured precisely by our needs, and are productive of good, if we make that result possible. We die, and then enter upon our new life. And as happiness can be given to us here, only so far as it is compatible with our preparation for that life, so in that life no happiness is or can be given but that which that preparation has made it possible for us to receive, and therefore possible for Him to give.

There are those who begin life on earth, and end it before this preparation could possibly be made. They die in an hour or a day, or in infancy or childhood, or in youth, before the power of self-determination is fully developed. Or they live many years in a condition of imbecility. What is their destiny? A happy one, — always a happy one. They have not harmed themselves by the abuse of their human freedom of choice between good and evil, because they never fully possessed this freedom. They have not been able to close their hearts against good influences by the voluntary choice of evil rather than good. If they died young, they grow to maturity in the other life. If they were imbecile in this life because the material brain or nervous system was an imperfect instrument of the mind, death has cast this impediment away, and their spiritual body becomes the instrument which their material body was not. They are happy, because the impediments to happiness have never grown with them into strength, and been confirmed into dominant principles of character and life. What germs or possibilities of good are in them by inheritance become like living seeds planted in a kindly soil, where the sun of heaven shines on them, and the dews of heaven fall on them. As they grow in heaven, instruction is given them, and they welcome it. They are shielded from the assaults of those whose influence could, to them, be only harmful. They receive all the happiness of which their spiritual natures are susceptible; they know whence it comes, and who it is that protects and preserves them. They receive it in innocence, and respond to it with grateful joy.

CHAPTER V.

THE OTHER WORLD.

ALL men die; and all, when they die, live again. Death in this world is birth into another world. The first question this fact suggests is, What is this other world, — of what does it consist?

The answer is similar to that already given to the question, Of what does this present world consist? Pure substance, flowing from God, becomes matter in this world; because our senses are so adjusted to it on the one hand, and to our minds on the other, that all the phenomena of an external world exist for us. When at death we are born into another world, we have left matter behind us, but not substance. That same pure substance, flowing forth from its Divine source, is there in the other world as it was here, and of it are formed our bodies and their organs. We have senses, and these so adjusted to this substance on the one hand, and to our minds on the other, that this substance becomes for us there also an external world, as it did here.

But is that world the same as this world? It is

not the same. It is a spiritual world, and the world we live in first is a material world. In some respects it is like this world, while in others it is altogether different. Both worlds are precisely suited to our needs; this world is suited to our needs while we live in it, and that world is suited to our needs when we are there. The similarities between the two worlds come from the fact that we are the same persons there that we were while here. There is no change in our identity; none in our essential nature.

The differences between that world and this come from the fact, that the purpose for which we live in this world is altogether different from that for which we live in the other. We live in this world to prepare for the other. We live here to change our characters, our wills, our very natures; to remove from ourselves those qualities and tendencies which would hinder our happiness in the other. The Divine purpose in creating us is, that we may live forever in an unending condition of happiness. The Divine purpose in causing us to begin life in this world is to provide us with the means of removing from ourselves the hindrances to happiness. This we can only do by resisting them; by a conflict with them. Let the plain truths which belong to this matter not be forgotten. One is, that God cannot remove our tendency to selfishness and sin for us. Another is, that, while we must do this ourselves, we can not do it without His help. The third is, that His help we are sure to receive; and, by our acceptance of it, and our co-operation with Him, this work can be done, and is done.

Life in this world is a life of conflict. In a part of this conflict, we are conscious of it; and voluntarily contend against evil, and on the side of good. Another part of this conflict is waged within us, and for us, and through us, by that Divine power which is fighting our battle. We may feel it only as a season of doubt and darkness, of suffering and distress. But here, too, we have much to do in determining the issue of this conflict; and if it ends in the victory of the right over the wrong, we are strengthened for every farther conflict. The value of that which is done within us and for us, without our consciousness and coöperation, consists in its preparing us to coöperate in freedom and with consciousness in the efforts of Divine Providence to reform us. We undergo temptations; we are softened by suffering; calamity comes to weaken our selfishness and worldliness, or some strong excitement awakes or invigorates our good resolves and purposes. Then there comes a time for us to determine whether all these things are good for us or not. That time comes when calmness and quiet return, and we come into our ordinary state of feeling and of life, and our power of self-determination is restored. Then are they — our feeling and our life — better than they were? Are the lessons which were taught us in those states remembered? Are the resolutions we formed carried into effect? This is the test; for if they are, we have *in character* advanced a step forward in the way of life. If they are not, we have fallen backward. It is one battle, one conflict, from the beginning to the end. And that this battle may be fought by us and for us, matter is here vested, so to speak, in fixed, indurated, unyielding forms, by which it is capable of resisting us, and reacting against us. Moments, or it may be hours, of peace occur when we rest from the conflict, and a foretaste of the peace we may enjoy hereafter is given us. But soon the battle begins again; and, during the whole of earthly life, every man is more or less compelled to do or to be what he would not do or be, and more or less fettered and constrained by his surroundings.

This is the universal doom; because to all men is given the capacity and opportunity of preparing for another life; and this work can only be done in, by, and through effort and conflict. Therefore, this resisting and reacting world is given us wherein we may do this work. This work of establishing a permanent character is done by all who live: they can not help doing it; but they may do it as they choose. They cannot help becoming here that which they will continue to be hereafter. But they may become whatever they choose to become. Then they die; that is, they enter into another life, — another way of living. And what is the world in which they then live?

If we live in this world to prepare for that world, it would seem reasonable to believe that the two worlds cannot be altogether different. We serve here an apprenticeship to the art of living happily. Assuredly, the way in which we are to live when our apprenticeship is over cannot be so totally unlike our life here, that the habits we here form of loving and of living cease at once at death, and are impossible in that condition of being to which we are introduced by death. Of what value or what efficacy could such a preparation be? How could it be a preparation?

But if on this ground we assume a measure of similarity between these two lives, there are reasons which compel us to believe that there are also important differences. We have left the material body behind us. We live here, to prepare by effort and by conflict for the other life; and a hard, unyielding material world is given us for that purpose. We live there, not to prepare for that world, but to manifest and develop the preparation we have made in this life; and the world we there live in is not the hard, unyielding material world we live in here. We have gone away from the world in which the substance of being is vested in resisting and indurated forms. That resistance and reaction against us were needed while the conflict of preparation was going on. But the conflict is over; and, instead of it, we have now its result. The same Divine substance is where we are after death, which gave us bodies and an external world before death; it gives us now spiritual bodies, and an external world formed of spiritual substance. This substance, as spiritual substance, is as exquisitely adjusted to our senses, and through them to our minds, as it was as matter. It is as perfectly adapted to our needs now as it was before, and becomes for us an external world as it did before. But we no longer need the assistance or the encumbrance of indurated and reacting matter, and we are delivered from it. But how can this be, if we have spiritual bodies composed of organs of sense? If, in those bodies, we live in an external world composed of spiritual substance, which is adapted to our spiritual bodies and their organs as perfectly as the material external world was adapted to our material bodies and their organs, how can that spiritual substance be more yielding or less refractory than material substance is here?

An answer can be given only by some consideration of Space and Time. The strongest intellects have been exhausted in the effort to say precisely what these are. I do not propose to present the metaphysical views which have been held, nor to add another to them; but shall confine myself to those things which are certain. In the first place, they are not entities; they are not things which have a distinct and positive existence by themselves. How far they are products of thought, or in what words their relation to thought may best be expressed, has been the subject of never-ending discussion. I say, only, that they are laws or effects of thought; they are these, whatever else they may be. They are laws or effects of thought; or, if we like it better, we may say, necessities of thought. We cannot think of external things without them. We cannot think of any external object without thinking of it as existing in time and in space. Not only are space and time laws or necessities of thought, but they are as much laws or necessities of action as of thought; for we can perform no action whatever except in time and in space. Moreover, they fix impassable limits to action, and exercise an absolute control over it, and thought and will are powerless before them. I think of the next room, and wish I were there; but only, by using so much of time and passing over so much of space, can I be there. If I think of England, and wish to be there, it can be only by using much more time and passing over much more space. If a bright star attracts me and I wish I were there, time and space are too much for me; and, if there were no other hindrances, would make it impossible. They exercise this control, not in motion only, but in all action. I wish to build a house, and I form a distinct idea of what I desire it to be; but I must appropriate a portion of space, and use up in suitable efforts a portion of time, before my house can be built. And this is as true of every action; for I can not move my finger except in the requisite space and time. I may diminish these very much, but escape from them I can not.

The reason of this is, that space and time are in this world vested in that unyielding, resisting, and reacting matter which is needed for the purposes for which we live in this world, and are thus made permanent and independent of men. But when we die, these purposes no longer exist. We are no longer preparing to live, but are living in the way our preparation has fitted us for; because we need there, just as we do here, instruments by which we may take cognizance of others, and they take cognizance of us; and also need things to use, and organs and faculties by which we make use of them; we have there bodies and organs of sense and thought, and an external world of inexhaustible variety. Because we have all these, and they are so far like what we have known here that our experience will not be lost upon us, we need space and time that we may recognize ourselves and others, and make use of the things about us; or, in one word, live. But we no longer need *such* space and time as we had in this world: we no longer need their restraint and compulsion, and these pass away; but we do need as much as before their assistance, and that we have. We may express the difference in few words, thus: In this world, space and time control thought and will; in that world, thought and will control space and time.

For example: Things there have shape and place; they are near together or far apart; we move through space to approach another or go from him when we wish to do so; and we see things moving, slowly or rapidly, through space. To that extent, we have the assistance or instrumentality of space and time; but they no longer obstruct us. We move through spiritual space and time by thought and will, as we will, without painful effort. If they whom we desire to see and to be with at any moment are far off, the thought and the desire bring us together. Thought and desire produce presence in this world, but they do this subject to the impediment of space and time; and, in some cases, this impediment can not be overcome. Thought and desire produce presence in the other world; and space and time have no power to hinder it.

Externals are created through *internals*, or the objects of sense through and by thought and affection. All the various things about us, which together compose the world in which we live, were created through and by the things within human minds, —or the thoughts in their understanding, and the affections in their will. This law is in full force now, and in this world, but is almost wholly concealed from us. In the other world, it is not only in full force, but always cognizable. There we are minds, or thoughts and affections; they compose us, and constitute our personality and our identity; but not they alone. If we try to think of disembodied mind; of thinking while there is nothing that thinks, of loving while there is nothing that loves, of acting while there is nothing that acts,—we soon find that we are trying to think of that which can be only nothingness. There we are, in essence, minds; and so we are here. There we are, in existence, as much as we are here, minds in bodies, exquisitely organized, and surrounded with a world exquisitely adapted to us. Here, it is through minds that bodies are formed in adaptation to them, and the world around us is formed in adaptation to us. But we know it not. There, too, our bodies and our external world are created through our minds, and in adaptation to them. And there we know that it is so.

Here and hereafter, the external world is created through or by the instrumentality of the internal world. But here, the external world of each person is not formed through or by his thoughts or affections. Here, men of all kinds mingle; for the purposes of this life require that it should be so. An external world which corresponded to one man would not suit his neighbor. The external world of mankind is therefore the common resultant of the thought and affection of mankind through an indefinite period; and is vested in enduring matter, which gives it a measure of permanence. There, the law of affinity brings those together who are interiorly like each other; and the external world about each society corresponds to all who are within it. Because it is not vested in hard and enduring matter, it changes as they change. It is as permanent as their states are; and, therefore, in its general features, may be more permanent than any thing on earth, while in its details it may be changeful, because it is always the mirror of those whom it corresponds to and represents.

So long as we live in this world, we live here for a definite purpose, and we live only for that purpose; and, therefore, when that purpose is accomplished, as far as it will be here, we die and go elsewhere. So long as we live here for that purpose, we live in surroundings adapted thereto, and think and feel accordingly. It must be very difficult therefore for us, while we live here, to form an exactly defined idea of a life and a world so different from this, as that life and world must be. And yet, if it be one which we enter upon at death, and we are there the same persons which we are here, that life can hardly be so different from this, that it must be impossible to form any idea of it. The two essentials which are not to be lost sight of in our efforts to form this idea are, first, that we are the same persons there as here, and need and have an external world suited to our needs and capacities. The second is, that there we are free from that oppressive control of matter, and time, and space, which would not be useful to us there. Through us are formed our surroundings, and they are such as we; that is, as our thoughts and affections make them. They are our inner selves projected into *outness*, so to speak; and thus they constitute an external world, which cannot but be exactly adapted to our wants, our capacities, and our use, and a mirror in which we see ourselves.

Let us sum up what has been said of this world

and of the other, of the likeness between them and the difference between them. We have, as St. Paul says, a spiritual body. We have that body now. It is within the material body, and fills it, and gives life to it; for the material body without the spiritual body is only dead matter. The spiritual eyes look through the material eyes, the spiritual ears hear through the material ears, the spiritual fingers feel through the material fingers. In other words, the soul while in the material body makes that body live, and through it perceives the things of this material world. We die. Our material eyes, ears, and fingers remain for a time just what they were. But they neither see, nor hear, nor feel. Why? Because the spiritual body is withdrawn from them; and this is all that death means. Our spiritual body rises,—that is, we, in our spiritual body, rise from the material body. Then we are in a spiritual body, which is like our material body in limbs, members, organs, and senses. If our spiritual body had not had all these, those of our material body would not have lived; for they would have been only dead matter, which they become as soon as the spiritual body leaves them.

If we rise in a spiritual body, which is like our material body, we need an external world to live in and to make use of, just as much as we needed it here. And we have it just as much. Why should we not? This natural world is formed primarily of pure substance; and the mind, acting through the senses, perceives it as this world, and as all things in it. That same substance is there also. And there the mind, acting through the senses, perceives the spiritual world as it perceives this world while here. To our mind and our spiritual senses, the spiritual world is the same thing that the material world is to our mind and our senses when we are clothed with a material body. In some respects it is the same thing. But it differs in other most important respects. This life is a life of preparation through conflict; therefore, the things of this world are vested in untractable, indurated, and resisting forms. It would not be well for us to command them absolutely by our will; for the very purpose for which we live here is not to indulge, but to resist, our will, and change it by conflict. And during this life, the things around us are just such as may help us to fight the battle of life. Mind and will have some power over them, but that power is imperfect and obstructed; and when we wish to have our own way, this world often answers No. The other life is not a life of preparation. That work is over; and the life there is one of result and consummation. Therefore, we do not need this resistance of unyielding matter, and we do not have it. Spiritual substance is no longer clothed in untractable, indurated, and resisting forms, but is spiritual substance only. All the things of that world are the ready instruments of mind and will; and mind and will have there a supreme control of their external world.

CHAPTER VI.

THE WORLD OF SPIRITS.

We always have a spiritual body. While we live in this world, this spiritual body is clothed with a material body. It fills this material body and animates it. The material body lives only because the spiritual body fills and animates every part of it. At death, the spiritual body is withdrawn from the material body. The material body, by reason of age, disease, or injury, becomes so ill adapted to the spiritual body, that the spiritual body can no longer fill and animate and act through the material body. Then it leaves the material body, and lives out of it. This is death. The spiritual body is not created by or at death. It is only separated from the material body by death. It does not then begin to live, for it always lived within the material body, and gave life to this body; but it then begins to live as only a spiritual and substantial body, and not within a material body.

While we live within a material body, or upon earth, we live, as has been repeatedly said, for the purpose of preparing for a life out of the material body. This preparation is made by determining our will, our character, our ruling love. What that love is, we are. What that love is at death, we remain. But with very few persons is this ruling love fully developed and freed from all disguise and all admixture, so long as they live on earth. With all, or nearly all, habits are formed, motives felt, and affections indulged, which, in a greater or less degree, conflict with and modify their ruling love, and perhaps conceal it even from themselves. In this condition we pass into the spiritual world and begin to live there. But this is not the condition in which we are to live forever. That must be a condition in which the ruling love is freed from all conflicting or qualifying influences. Our external must be at one with our internal. That is to say, our life in action, our manifested character, must be the same with our inmost life or love. If we live in this world to prepare for the other world by determining here what our character shall be there, so, in the first stage of our existence there, we prepare for living in that character in a complete, unimpeded, and manifested manner.

This result is attained through various means, and in a shorter or a longer time. These means are adapted to the end they are to produce by Him who knows perfectly what we are within, and how we may best become without that which we are within. They may take the form of instruction, or of discipline; and, if need be, of painful discipline; and they are continued until their end is accomplished and the final result reached. When that end is accomplished, the result is that the man stands forth the embodiment and personification of his ruling love, which governs every feeling, every thought, every word, and every act. Precisely what he is, he seems to be; and he is known to be that, and only that, by himself and by others. Disguise is no longer possible, and is not desired or attempted. There is no longer any conflict of motives, or uncertainty of purpose, or wavering in act. The man is wholly himself; and that which he is, he is for eternity.

A principal means by which this end is accomplished consists in bringing the will and the understanding, the affections and the thoughts, the belief and the love, into unity. This is never completely the case in this world. In most men, the knowledge and the belief are above the love and the life; in some they are below. In all men there is more or less of contradiction between that which they desire, and perhaps do, and that which they know to be right, and perhaps inwardly love. St. Paul says, "What I would, that I do not; but what I hate, that I do." There are those who are always aware how much their affections and desires fall short of what the truth they know requires of them; and they are earnest in their efforts to bring them into harmony, and lament the inherited tendencies or other evil influences which obstruct their efforts. None in this world complete this work, because none subdue and suppress perfectly all tendencies to wrong. But in the other life, if the ruling love is good, by various means which infinite wisdom supplies, it works itself clear of whatever conflicts with it. And then there comes, to those who are good, peace — the peace of God, which passes all understanding that is possible in this life.

The state or condition in which these changes are going forward, and which cause not an alteration of the essential character, but a development and manifestation of it, Swedenborg calls "The world of Spirits;" giving it this name, I suppose, because those who are in that state have left the natural body, and are therefore spirits, but are not yet angels, nor have they yet gone down to be with those who have chosen not to be angels.

To some readers the thought may occur, Why carry forward into the other world the struggles and limitations, and slow and wearying progress of this? If at death the question, what we are, is settled, He who reigns there might surely assign us our place without waiting for the result of this tedious process. We may answer: He reigns in this world as in that; and yet we know that life here is a series, and, it may be, a long and painful series, of efforts, and alternate success and disappointment; and progress is, at best, gradual and slow and interrupted. That is the way of God in all of His working that we know; and it is but reasonable to infer some analogy between the known and the unknown, or between life in this world and the life of the same persons in the next world.

We might think this, even if we could see no reason why this should be so, either here or there. But we may see a reason for it, — not *the* reason; not the whole council of God, but *a* reason. For we may find it in the truth that God does all of His work through living, rational, moral, and free agents, which can be done in that way. The greatest blessing He can confer on them is that of doing His work, or working with Him. The best evidence of His infinite goodness is in the fact that He has given to His creatures this power of working with Him. All of His creatures, even to the components of the inanimate world, are His instruments, and are always doing His work. To man alone is given the power of doing this consciously and rationally, and in his freedom, or by his voluntary choice. God has given to man the ownhood of himself. This is equally true while he is living in this world and preparing for the other; and while he is in the world of spirits, removing from his character all that disguises it or conflicts with its ruling principles; and also when this work too is done, and he takes the place he has made himself fit for.

Through all this course he cannot take one step, except by the strength given him. Through it all he is guided, led, and helped in every possible way that does not take from him his freedom, or his power to make of himself, and to be himself, what he would.

In the beginning of life it is impossible for us to have any other thought than that we live from ourselves, with divers hindrances to our will, which we contend against as we can. Afterwards, we get glimpses of the truth that we live from God, and under His government; and must obey Him if we would be happy. So it is in the life of every man; and so it has been in the life of mankind. We have reached a point in human progress, in which we can at least begin to see, if we will, that we live from Him, and constantly from Him, in the highest and most absolute sense; that we depend upon Him for life, and all that constitutes life, perfectly and constantly; and that, while He is ever doing all that infinite love can prompt and infinite wisdom discern, which will help us to make our destiny a happy one, that destiny and that happiness are placed in our own hands.

They are now taught this great truth, who are willing to learn it. Only they can learn it; and they must learn it for themselves, and in their own freedom: they must see it through their own mental eyes. Very imperfectly can any see it now. Very dimly, and only in a most general way, and as a mere possibility, can some see it; and in the vision of others it will be distorted. Slowly the day may come, which this dawning light promises. But it will come surely, and as soon as shall be permitted by that law of our being, which enables these gifts of Divine Mercy to reach us only as fast and as fully as we can be brought into a condition to receive them willingly, and with all our hearts. But still there is for us the hope, that if this willingness be established within us as of our life, we may, after death has cast this body and its defilements aside, have our darkness enlightened, our weakness strengthened, and the stains of this world cleansed away; and all that is within us of true life, even if it be no more than a living germ, developed into the fulness of its stature, whatever that may be.

CHAPTER VII.

DEGREES.

One of the novel doctrines of this new philosophy is that of "Degrees." It continually presents itself in the consideration of this philosophy, and it may be well to offer now a brief sketch of it.

Degrees are of two kinds. One of them is that by which a thing grows larger or smaller, and becomes more or less, without change in its nature. Thus, that which is warm may grow warmer, or less warm; that which is bright, more or less bright; that which is sweet, more or less sweet, — and so on indefinitely. Such degrees as these Swedenborg sometimes called continuous degrees, for they run into one another by a certain continuity. The thing which changes in this way makes no change in its nature or essential character; it remains always on the same plane of being, or on the same level; as for example when it changes, by increase or diminution, from larger to smaller, from finer to grosser, or from rarer to denser, — as when the air so changes but always remains air. And as through all these changes the thing remains on the same plane of being, these degrees are also, and perhaps better, called degrees of Breadth.

There are, however, degrees of another kind; not continuous, but discrete,—by which word we mean distinctly separate. A thing changing by these degrees becomes another thing; it is higher or lower than it was before in the scale of being; and these discrete degrees are therefore called degrees of Height. The most general example I can give of them is end, cause, and effect. The end is that for which all that follows is. It moves or puts in action the cause, which then produces the effect that is sought. In that effect the cause is operative, and the end is satisfied. Of these three degrees the end is highest, the cause intermediate, and the effect lowest; or, we may say, the end is first, the cause intermediate, and the effect last. These three degrees belong necessarily to every thing which exists; for whatever exists, exists for some *purpose* which would not be accomplished if it did not exist; and it exists because for this end it is *caused* to exist; and it is itself the *effect* of the end operating through the cause. By the "end" thus used is meant much the same—but not precisely the same—as the "final cause" of the old philosophies; while what I call simply the cause is there called the "proximate" or "efficient cause;" but I prefer, and use, Swedenborg's phraseology of end, cause, and effect.

Another illustration of this same triad may be seen in affection, thought, and act. There can be no act, unless there be first some affection or feeling in the form of wish or desire for the act. This affection prompts the thought, and through the thought it causes the act. It is obvious that a man would not and could not do anything, if perfectly devoid of all affection or desire; for these are the motive force that sets in action all motion, and without them there could be no action. But it is equally certain that this desire or wish acts only through the thought which it excites. Although a man had a desire, however strong, if he had no capacity for thought, he would not be conscious of any desire, or know that he had such a desire; and still less would he know how to carry this desire into effect. But the desire sets him thinking; he becomes conscious of his desire, and devises the way of gratifying it; and then he does gratify it in the appropriate act.

These three discrete degrees exist in every act; but there are also all manner of continuous degrees in each of them, or in the strength of the affection or desire, in the adequacy of the cause, and in the completeness of the act. This man desires earnestly to have a house; and the desire prompts multitudinous thoughts about it, as to how he shall hire the house that comes nearest to his wishes; or, if he builds, he reflects, and confers with experts, until he has decided what plan within his means will best suit his wish, and then he thinks out and provides the ways of building his house, and at last builds it. That man or that boy desires to know how to read; he thinks of the means by which he may learn to read; and then, by long-continued use of these means, he acquires some measure of this learning, and reads, and completes his knowledge, more or less, by practice. This girl wishes to play upon a piano; uses the means which she thinks best adapted to enable her to do this, and, after more or less practice, plays, better or worse.

In all these instances it is obvious that there is a specific desire or affection; that this prompts the thoughts specifically adapted to the desire, and, by means of them, carries the desire into effect. But presently, the man learns to read so well that he is perfectly unconscious of the wish to read each word, or of the thought that reads it, or of the motions of his fingers by which he turns the pages. The girl practises diligently for years, and at last she will play a piece of familiar music, conversing with those who sit by her side, unconscious of the wish or the thought which causes her fingers to strike the keys; and she is equally unconscious that she strikes them, and does not know that she hears the sounds she makes, unless some mistake or discord calls her attention to them; then the desire, the thought, the effect, all come again into consciousness, and she corrects the mistake. Perhaps the most universal instance of the same kind is in walking. At first, this is learned by the process of desiring and thinking out, and then taking, each step. At last we walk without any thought of the steps we take, unless something calls our attention to them. I have read that the late Dr. Chalmers usually counted his steps as he walked; and this habit became so fixed, that he did it without effort, and without its interfering with any conversation he might be carrying on, and perhaps without consciousness unless his attention was called to it.

It has become rather a fashion in modern philosophy to deny that there is desire, or thought, or intention, in these cases where habit has made the desire, the thought, and the act so easy as to be unnoticed. The effects are sometimes said to be produced by "reflex action," a phrase recently invented; or the motions have become automatic (that is to say, they do themselves), through habit. But this is a mistake. These motions are just as voluntary; that is, they are, each of them, as much the result of a specific desire, thought, and purpose, as those earlier motions of the same kind, which required a strong desire and an earnest effort in the beginning, but of which the strength and the earnestness have gradually lessened as they became unnecessary.

An important truth in relation to these three degrees is, that as the two higher terminate in the last and lowest, all are in that: all close or ultimate in that. The end is there attained; the means are there operative and effectual, and thus the end and the means ultimate in the effect.

It has been said that this trinity, or tri-unity, of end, cause, and effect, is universal. It is so, because it is supremely in God, the author of all existence. In Him it is Love, Wisdom, and Power; all infinite because His; and all imaged forth in the love, thought, and action of man, because he is created in the likeness of God. His love is an infinite desire for such ends as are proper to perfect love. His infinite wisdom is one with His love, and directs His infinite power in producing its appropriate effects. The effect is creation; and in this His love and His wisdom are ultimated.

Firsts, intermediates, and lasts (or ultimates) are in whatever exists. The universal end of creation is to be found in God. In Him is the divine desire or purpose for which all created things exist. They are all created by Him to be His instruments, and are all used by Him as His instruments, whereby His purpose is carried into effect. But this trinity exists also, as has already been said, in each one of the things which exists. Every grain of sand exists for the sake of some use it performs or subserves. It is so created that it may perform that use. It does perform it, and in the use, which is the last or ultimate degree, the higher degrees are ultimated. Nothing whatever could exist unless the end, cause, and effect were in it; and the end and the cause are ultimated in the effect.

That which is the effect or ultimate in one series may be the instrument or mediate in another series; indeed, it always is so in one sense. Man may accomplish a purpose in producing an effect, and stop there, making no use whatever of the effect. But it is never so in Divine causation. There, every effect produced becomes at once an instrument by which a further effect is produced. One series of these degrees may be found in the Divine purpose, as the first; the spiritual world through which and by means of which the material world is created, as the intermediate; and the material world itself, as the effect in which the higher degrees of this series are ultimated. But then the Divine purpose or end at once uses this material world, and every thing in it, as the instrument for effecting a further purpose, and, when this is effected, it becomes the instrument for an effect beyond it: and this with no exception and no cessation.

While this series is in all things, it manifests itself differently in different things. It has always a tendency to manifest itself, or come into expression and form; and this is especially the case in all organisms. Thus there is in the human body that series which is universal: the end or purpose for which it is, the construction or mechanism which is the instrument by which this end is reached; and lastly, the operation of this mechanism by which this end is carried out into effect.

— But, beside this, there is in the very shape of the human body an expression of this series. The head is at the summit, and originates all movement or action. The heart and lungs, and the other viscera, are the instruments by which the vital force from the brain disseminates life and strength and activity through the frame and causes all action. Then the limbs, which are the ultimates of the series, do the work which carries into effect the purpose for which the body or the man exists.

The hands and the feet are the ultimates of the human body. They may help us to understand a law laid down by Swedenborg as widely prevailing, and often referred to by him,—the law that power resides in the ultimates. In the hands and feet, as the ultimates of the human body, the power of doing the work for which the body exists, resides. The brain is as far from them as possible; they cannot impel the blood like the heart, nor purify it like the lungs; nor can they see, or hear, or smell, or taste. But all that the other organs do ends in enabling them to do their work. Cut off the hands and feet, and however well all that remains may do its duty, the man is physically powerless. But let them do their duty, and the other organs of the body no longer work in vain, for the feet and hands are the ultimates of all the rest, and carry into effect the end and aim for which all the rest work and live.

Mr. Tyndall, in the address to which we have already referred, says: "I discern in that matter, which we in our ignorance, and notwithstanding our profound reverence for its creation, have hitherto covered with opprobrium, the promise and the potency of every form and quality of life." This is regarded by everybody as a declaration of materialism. It would seem, indeed, that he himself regards it as materialism of some sort; for he goes on to say: "The 'materialism' here enunciated may be different from what you suppose, and, therefore, I crave your gracious patience to the end." Nevertheless, these words have been considered not only as a declaration of materialism, but as a bold statement of a view held by leading scientists of the day; and not hitherto avowed, either from timidity, or from an opinion that the public mind has not heretofore been prepared to look upon this view, when presented without disguise or veil. And it has been attacked in all quarters, or by religious writers of every name; and, in fact, by all but those who welcome it, because it is a declaration of materialism. In all this there seems to me a mistake. I consider Mr. Tyndall's statement in some measure true; an imperfect, one-sided, incomplete statement of the truth. What it needs for its completeness is the farther truth that all the promise and potency in matter are derived from above matter, and are carried forth into action and effect by the inflow of that which is higher than matter.

The series of end, cause, and effect have already been presented in many forms, and the lowest and last term of the series has been called its ultimate; and it has also been stated as another law of this trinity, that its power (force, energy, *vis*) resides in the ultimates. Of the series, God, the spiritual world, and the material world, — or God, spirit, and matter, — the material world or matter is the ultimate. This series includes all that is. In God's desire, design, or purpose, is the end; or that for which all things are, and which originates all existence. He creates the spiritual world, and by and through this as the causal instrument employed He creates the material world; and here the purpose of

God is carried into effect. This purpose is the creation of a universe of beings to whom he may impart His own life, His love, and His wisdom, and give it to them as their own; while they, receiving life from Him, and knowing that He is their constant Creator and Father, using their own strength in the acknowledgement that it is their own only because He gives it them to be their own, may, under His guidance, and with His aid, enable Him to form in them a heavenly character; so that they, entering into heaven, and there growing for ever in this character and in the happiness belonging to it, satisfy the Divine purpose. This character is formed by resisting, overcoming, and putting away from the natural character whatever therein would tend to mar or pervert the life (the love and wisdom) received from its source; and so permit that life to be, when it is theirs, a life of love and wisdom that will always, in its own freedom, reject all evil and falsity. This is heavenly life. In kind and in degree it is infinitely diversified, all its varieties agreeing only in this,—that they love and choose good rather than evil.

But the work of forming this heavenly character begins on earth. Here, the free choice and the free act of every man determine his character and, therefore, his destiny. Earth, and all its laws, forces, and activities are exactly adapted to promote this end; and all these laws and forces have come down to earth from God through the spiritual world, that they might carry this end into effect. It is carried into effect just so far as men use the freedom and the strength given them aright, and so build up a heavenly character. For this end is, that God may have a universe of beings to whom He may impart His own life, and with His life His happiness, in the greatest measure in which a created being can receive it.

It might be thought the Divine purpose was not carried into effect on earth, where evil mingles so abundantly with good, but only in heaven. It is not so. No one is heavenly in heaven, who did not begin to be heavenly on earth. For if one begins on earth to love good rather than evil, truth rather than falsity, the love of God rather than the love of self, the love of others rather than the love of the world for the sake of self, — he begins to be heavenly. Immeasurably small may be this little germ of a true life, and but little more than nothing the taste of heavenly happiness. But if he has begun to love God and his neighbor, and to hate selfishness and worldliness, and to desire deliverance from them, he has begun to be heavenly, and already has had some slight foretaste of the happiness of heaven; although the new thing is to him as the manna in the desert, and he asks, as the Israelites did, "What is it?"

Heavy the burdens which still oppress him, full of pain and weariness the conflicts he may pass through before his warfare is accomplished. But he has begun to be heavenly. In him the Divine purpose for which he came into being is accomplished. All that follows is a question of degree. Of the accomplishment of this Divine purpose there can be only a beginning, a constant and perpetual beginning, which will never have an end. In the other life the burdens may fall off, the conflicts cease, the happiness be secure and great; but it will be ever-growing, for, if it were not so, it would not satisfy the infinite love of God. And after the ages of eternity have passed by, and the wisdom and the happiness are wholly beyond our present power of conception, still it will be only a beginning.

Ages ago asceticism prevailed. In eastern countries it was formulated into the doctrine that the universe had been formed and was governed by two beings or principles — one good and one evil; the good being represented by the soul, and the evil by the body. When this doctrine was suppressed, or where it was not held, the body was still regarded by many as an incarnation of evil. All indulgence of it was wrong, and all mortification of it a virtue. Much of this has survived to our own times, and causes a modified and undefined belief in many minds that sensuous pleasure is at best a weakness; and that, while a moderate enjoyment of it may be permitted, a contempt and rejection of it is better and safer for the soul.

Asceticism, even in its extreme, may be good for those who are unable to indulge at all in sensuous pleasure without running into excess, impurity, and sin. And now and always it may be well that sensuous tendencies, when very strong, should be checked by a belief that all sensuous enjoyment should be looked upon with disfavor, if these tendencies cannot otherwise be resisted. But, in itself considered, asceticism of every kind and degree is a mistake. The body and the senses, with their capacity of enjoyment, are given us to be enjoyed; and the virtues of temperance and purity give to their enjoyment endurance and a more exquisite relish. Wherever the more general elements of religion are believed, — as that there is a God whose commands are to be obeyed, — the rightful enjoyment of the senses may become itself religious, strengthening the recognition of the goodness of God, and the disposition to use in His service the added strength which well-adjusted recreation gives.

I have spoken of asceticism because this falsity is closely akin to, and may help to illustrate, another which prevails widely in these days, and is as much a mistake as asceticism. I refer to that falsity which fears or undervalues natural science, and regards it as hostile to religious truth. This is an extreme, a total, mistake. When we say that natural truth cannot contradict spiritual truth, we only utter a truism which, in some form or other, is often expressed. It is but an application of this more general proposition that falsity, either natural or spiritual, must contradict truth of the other kind. That which is thought to be truth of either kind may not be true, for mistake in either direction is very easy. Thus, that which is called spiritual or religious truth may contradict natural science, because it is spiritual falsity and not spiritual truth; and so what seem to be truths of natural science may be only its mistakes, and then they must contradict whatever is actual spiritual truth.

Is there indeed any truth so certain that it has the right to sit in judgment on all propositions that claim to be true? There can be none such, but the primary truths of religion. But these are precisely what many natural scientists deny to be certain truths; and they are so far right, as that however certain a man may rationally be of the primary religious truths, he cannot have the right to be certain that either his apprehension or his expression of these truths is beyond the possibility of mistake. Neither system of truth can practically be made the criterion for truths of the other kind, for those who are devoted to truths of that other kind must necessarily hold that it is *their* truths which have the right of final determination concerning all truths. Nevertheless, this criterion is one which men constantly, perhaps inevitably, apply. It is just this which makes so many religionists dread and hate what are called discoveries of science; and so many scientists deny and despise what are called essentials of religious truth; and so many habitually regard the rapid and inevitable growth of science as leading necessarily to the enfeeblement, if not the destruction, of religion. The fault or error is sometimes on one side, and sometimes on the other, and often divided between them.

Tyndall and Huxley and Darwin, and other leading scientists, regard as certain some at least of the results of their scientific investigation, and, because they are certain, deny the religious dogmas which are incompatible with these results; and some of their followers, although they themselves do not, reject all religion because it seems to include or imply these dogmas.

In some cases, there is an entire blindness to all spiritual truths. Where this is, religion would have been denied at any rate; for while such persons think they reject religious truth because scientific truth opposes it, they would have been as sure to reject it if presented to their minds in any way.

They reject it simply because they are unwilling and therefore unable to accept it.

In other cases, natural truth has perhaps been discovered by means, and in a way, appropriate to it. If such persons acquire the habit of believing that whatever is true is discoverable or cognizable in the same way, or by the same process, and in the same temper of mind, and that whatever cannot be so discovered cannot be true, they must necessarily reject religious truth; for that is to be seen and known only by a process and in a temper appropriate to it. For this, reason must be consulted and obeyed; but it must be a reason that is not too proud to listen to revelation, and not so proud of its own strength or its own work, that it believes itself sufficient alone and of itself to lead to all good results.

Perhaps, however, the most common cause for the rejection of religious truth by scientists and philosophers is still another. They are educated as Christians in some form or other of what is called Christian Faith; or, if not so educated, they see these various forms all around them. In none of them do they see doctrines which they can reconcile with their reason or their knowledge. The indirect influence of revelation upon them induces them perhaps still to retain the belief of a God of some sort, and of future existence of some sort; and they hold these in a dim and uncertain way as a hope or a possibility, and give what seem to them scientific or philosophic reasons for the belief or opinion they hold, utterly discarding revelation, not knowing that without the indirect effect of revelation no thought of the kind could have found its way to their minds.

Or perhaps, like Sir David Brewster, they adhere to the religion in which they were educated; holding it during active life rather loosely, not neglecting its observances, but not submitting it to investigation; and, when old age arrives and death draws near, clinging to it more closely.

Faraday — the great and good Faraday — could hold no opinion loosely or indefinitely; he could not but be religious, he could not but be scientific. But that he might hold both his religion and his science, he separated them perfectly. He placed himself very positively on the ground that they were not only distinct in their nature, but that they had no relation whatever which connected them together; and, perhaps, — if I draw a just inference from what I read in accounts of him that I have seen, — holding that both would be harmed and neither helped by any effort to bring them into harmony. Accordingly, as a scientific man, he held on his triumphant course; and, as a religious man, he left all his scientific knowledge and aspiration and thought behind, and adhered closely and earnestly to the peculiar views in which he had been brought up.

A better way than this is coming; I know not how soon or how slowly: but coming it certainly is. In the mean time, let our great scientists go on, and perform the work they are doing with so much energy and success. They are, above all, scientific men and philosophers; they must have knowledge and philosophy; they see much in the religions about them which could not be made to harmonize with their knowledge or their philosophy, and they are not led to go back to the records of revelation, and hold in their simplicity the truths they find. It is a pity when they go out of their way to sneer at religion, — which the most eminent among them do not, — for this hurts them and others. But let them go on in their course of inquiry. Let them learn all that they can about the material world, its laws, its forces, and its phenomena. This is a progress which will never end; and, when it is best for mankind. a new science will lay hold of their results. A science which is no less scientific because it is essentially and profoundly religious. A science which will have for its corner-stone the principle that there is not, and never was, and never can be, a truth of natural science which has not its correlative spiritual truth. A science which holds that the Infinite clothes itself in the finite; and which rejoices in all new light cast upon natural truth, because it may surely be reflected back upon spiritual truth. Then will Science and Religion no longer be hostile or alienated; for each will regard the other as a friend and assistant, and both will offer their fruits to Him who made them both, and gives to them both all the life they have.

CHAPTER VIII.

OWNHOOD.

SWEDENBORG frequently uses the Latin word *proprium* as a substantive. What he means by it cannot be adequately and precisely expressed by any English word. The adjective *proprius* comes very near to the English word "own." It appears in many English words; as property, propriety, appropriate, and the like. In all of these we may see the idea of own-ness: thus, a man's property is what he owns. The word is also used to signify some quality which belongs to a thing and is its own, and without which it would be another thing: thus, it is the property of flame to heat and burn, and of ice to cool; a man behaves properly, or with propriety, when his conduct accords with all the circumstances which belong to him and are his own; and he appropriates any thing when he adds it to his property (*ad* and *proprio*). In translating Swedenborg's works, in which this word *proprium* frequently occurs, some have used "self-hood;" others have used or proposed "own-ness," "owndom," or "ownhood." But it is found, on trial, that neither of these words exactly represents *proprium*, or suggests the ideas which it is intended to express by that word. Hence it has been practically concluded not to translate it at all, but to use the Latin word *proprium* as if it were an English word, leaving readers who do not know Latin to infer its meaning from the use of it; while they who do know Latin must remember that there is no word in any language which expresses more emphatically what we mean in English by the word "own." I agree that, in the translation of Swedenborg, it is best to use the word *proprium;* but, in such a work as this, I prefer to use generally the word "ownhood," explaining it as well as I can. Without using either this word or the word *proprium*, I have already referred to this doctrine, especially in Chapter II.; and must often refer to it, for it is implied in all the doctrines of the New-Church.

If it is not easy to translate the word *proprium*, it is equally difficult to exhibit the doctrine of *proprium* intelligibly. But so far as I am able to do this, it will be seen that it is novel and important, leading to consequences of great value.

Because all being is from one source, — God, who causes all things to be by an effluence from Himself, — we may hope to find the origin of this universal ownhood in God Himself, and in the nature of His working. He gives being, and all the elements of being. He gives from love; from perfect love; and He gives wholly and unreservedly. He wishes that whatsoever is should be itself; but dependent upon Him, or connected with Him, so far as it must be by the continual gift of being to it, and the continual effort on his part that its being should be complete and perfect. Because every thing exists by a constant creative effluence from Him, and could not exist otherwise, it would be a part of Him, or continuous with Him, or Him in an imperfect way, if He did not give to it to be itself, or to be its own. The whole created universe as a whole, has this ownhood of itself. In the material universe, we discern some effects of this. Modern science has come to the conclusion that there is only so much matter in the world, its quantity being constant; and all the apparent deaths or births of matter being only changes in the form and appearance of matter, — no matter ever ceasing to be, or ever now beginning to be.

More recently, and yet not so certainly, science has concluded that there is but one force in the material universe; and that constant in quantity, but ever and indefinitely varying in action and appearance. The heat we feel or cause by our own efforts disappears; but this is only because it is changed into or becomes light or magnetism or motion, or some other of the forms of force. So it is with every other of these forces. If either of them comes into manifestation, it is at the expense of some other; and when it ceases to act and appear as one force, it is because it has changed into or given birth to another. Indeed, science, in all its progress, seems to be advancing to the conclusion that the material universe is complete in itself, needing only the forces we see active in it to produce all its phenomena, and its whole succession of created beings and their circumstances. Hence it is that scientists, whose extent of knowledge gives them the widest view, see in matter "the promise and the potency" of all life. Their mistake, as we have already intimated, is that they do not see that matter has all this promise and potency, because God creates the material universe to be its own, itself; and is constantly creating, preserving, and animating it,—constantly giving this promise and potency. He continually gives it being; He continually imparts to it all force; He acts within the action of all its forces and all their effects, using them all as His instruments. And the reason of this is that the world of matter may be its own, itself,—and *as if* independent of Him,—while it is in fact instantly and constantly dependent upon Him for being, and for all its force, energy, or activity.

If we ascend to the animal world, we find the

same law or fact of ownhood, not more real, but more manifest. Every animal has some power over himself. He has will. Natural science finds it very difficult to say whether certain of the protozoa (or first forms of life) are vegetable or animal; insomuch that some scientists hold them to be neither the one nor the other, but something between, which may be developed into either. All, however, or nearly all, agree that the test is, Has the thing inquired about a will? — for if it can be seen to have a will, a choice, a power of self-determination, of any kind or any measure, it is an animal. There are sensitive plants in which motions may be produced by a touch; others in which moisture produces motion strangely like walking. Still others of which the appropriate organs close upon a fly or a morsel of flesh, and hold it firmly until all its juices are absorbed for the nourishment of the plant. Still it is only a plant, because all this is done unconsciously and involuntarily, and therefore do not entitle it to be regarded as an animal. So, too, the power which a grape vine and some other plants (perhaps all in some degree) have of sending out a root to seek distant water or rich food, or down the face of a rock to find earth, does not make the plant an animal. For an animal is a living organism which has a will; and this means that it has some power over itself, some choice whether to accept or to reject; to do this or that, or to leave it undone; and exercises this power of choice consciously and intentionally. There is, indeed, among the indefinitely numerous theories advanced in these days, one which holds that animals are only automata, or machines, with no more of consciousness or will than trees have; but this theory meets with little favor, and very limited, if indeed any, reception.

Animals have been created successively; the lower or simpler in organization first, and then, step by step, the higher or more complex. Geology tells as much as this, perhaps, with certainty. But this new science, much less than a century old, is still in its infancy; although its discoveries are so numerous and interesting, and its conclusions so important, that it seems to have reached at once a kind of maturity. But its discoveries are as yet imperfect, and few of its most important conclusions are certain. If any one is so, it is that animals have been created through countless ages in successive gradation, and that at last man was created, an animal who crowned the series. Whether evolution played any part in this successive creation, I do not care to inquire; for, as I have already intimated, if it did it was but one of the methods or means by which God created. This succession stopped with man, and we have no evidence and no reason to believe that any new animal has been created since man existed.

Man is an animal; but he is also something more and higher than an animal. As an animal he has all the ownhood which an animal has. But an animal is only a natural being, and man, as an animal, is natural; but he is also a spiritual being. He is not spiritual because he possesses all the faculties which animals possess; for some animals possess each of these faculties in greater measure than man. If he possessed all, and in a greater measure than all animals taken together, this would be a superiority only in a *continuous* degree; it would be a superiority of measure and not of kind, and only such superiority as lifts the higher animals above the lower. He is superior to all other animals by a *discrete* degree. In addition to all that they have, he has that of which they have not a particle: he has a spiritual nature; and it lifts him above all other animals by a difference not of measure but of kind, and it makes him altogether other than them. By this spiritual nature, he stands in definite relations to the spiritual world; for in this spiritual nature he lives in the spiritual world even while he lives in this natural world.

He does not know this. So long as he lives in this world, his material body covers and clothes his spiritual body; and lives only because the spiritual body fills it and animates every part of it. The material body answers two purposes, or rather it causes two entirely different effects. In the first place, as has been already said, it gives to the spiritual body an instrument by which it can recognize and make use of the material world. The material eye does not see; but the spiritual eye, or the eye of the spiritual body, through the material eye, sees the material world. When a man dies, his material eye remains for a time just what it was. It does not see, and never did see, and now the spiritual eye cannot see through it because it has gone away; for death is only the departure of the spiritual body from the material body, which then becomes dead, because all that gave it life has passed away from it. As it is with the eye, precisely so it is with the other senses and organs of sense.

The material body thus performs one of its functions in being an instrument through which the spiritual body may make use of a material world. But it accomplishes another purpose, or performs another function; and this is to serve as a veil or barrier or obstruction between the spiritual body and the spiritual world. So long as the spiritual body is clothed upon by the material body, its senses are (while we are in a normal condition) closed against all the objects in the spiritual world. How these two effects are in fact one, or if not one are closely connected, may perhaps be illustrated by a comparison. A man looks up at the sky in a cloudless night.

He sees a multitude of stars filling the whole concave. He points a good telescope at a dark space in the sky, and at once he sees a multitude of other stars, of which he could not see one before. But while the eye is fixed to the telescope, he cannot see that multitude of stars which he saw before. The instrument which enables him to see what he could not see without it, disables him from seeing what he could see without it. The material body is as the telescope. The comparison is rude, but it may at least help one to understand that, while a man lives on earth, the spiritual senses are (or the man whose senses they are, is) enabled, by the clothing of material organs, to hear, see, feel, and handle material things; while, because of these material organs, he cannot see, hear, feel, or handle the spiritual things in the midst of which he is living.

Death liberates the spiritual body from the material body; they go asunder. The material body loses all life and all sense; the spiritual body loses all recognition or perception of the material world, and gains at once full recognition and perception of the spiritual world. The man who has now no material body or organs ceases to live in this world, and begins to live consciously in that spiritual world in which he has always lived without knowing it.

If we regard God as infinite, and as the cause and source of all being, it must needs be impossible that we should have the slightest idea of Him as He is in Himself, and prior to all action or manifestation. But it is not impossible that we should discern something of His action and His manifestation of Himself. It is certain that He has given to us the power of thinking that we discern this, and of drawing some inferences in respect to His nature and His methods of action. We have also what purport to be revelations from Him, helping us in this discernment and in these inferences. If, moreover, we believe that He has made us to be immortal, we must believe that through this immortality there must be progress in knowledge and wisdom and life, or else stagnation through eternity. If we believe that there will be progress in knowledge and wisdom, this must be in knowledge of Him, and in wisdom concerning Him. For if He be the cause and source of all being, it is plain that the wiser we are concerning Him and His action, the wiser we shall be as to all things, because all things are but the products of His action. Then if we believe in immortality after death, we cannot rationally avoid the belief that we begin our immortality here, and may begin here to prepare for the life which will be more fully developed hereafter.

From all this it would seem to follow that, while the finite intellect cannot either here or there form an idea of the infinite as it is in itself, it may begin here to form an idea of Him in His action and manifestation; which idea, however imperfect in its beginning, will be enlarged and developed indefinitely. To say that our knowledge of Him may hereafter become, in comparison with our knowledge of Him while here, far more than the full-grown oak is in comparison with the acorn, is to suggest but a slight similitude. But when we remember the probable relation of this life to the next, and the probable purpose of our life here, we may believe that a knowledge of Him which is possible here may be as an acorn, a living seed, in which there exists potentially, and in its beginning, the germ of that which will come hereafter.

If any thing is certain concerning the Divine action, it is that it is gradual,—each step in advance of that behind, and each leading to a step still farther in advance. We may be disposed to see in this both the proof and the effect of the law that progress is, on the whole, eternal. However we may account for it, and however we may sometimes doubt it, because this progress advances in waves which go forward and then fall back, and in the retreating moment it seems as if progress itself were stayed,—yet, if we look over a series of sufficient extent, we cannot but be sure that the movement is, on the whole, forward. We may form two conclusions. One is, that, when we look at the past history and the present condition of human thought, we may be sure that the best idea we can form, or the sum of the knowledge we can acquire, concerning the relations of God with man must be imperfect to the last degree, and so slight as to be only more than nothing. The other conclusion is, that this knowledge may be accurate as far as it goes, and, however small in comparison with what the far future may bring forth, it may be of vast magnitude and importance in comparison with the nothingness of ignorance. It may, though small as the grain of mustard seed, have within it the capacity of perpetual growth and of indefinite multiplication by the propagation of truth from truth. This progress may be slow. We may begin from nothing; and in its early stages be only more than nothing. But progress must be constant and continual, and never end; and in all this progress man must have a share, *as of his own work*.

The conclusion from all that has been said, is, that man was created what he is, to the end that he may advance in wisdom, goodness, and happiness for ever, by his own efforts. But it is impossible to believe this without some idea of, some belief in, ownhood. For it all implies that whatever lives and advances by voluntary efforts must make these efforts as his own, and they must be most truly his own.

This doctrine of a man's ownhood of his life and being meets Pantheism; and it is the only doctrine which reconciles the truth that God is all in all, with the other truth that He is other than and distinct from the universe. True it certainly is, that God is all in all; and so far as this constitutes or implies Pantheism, that also is true. But it is not true that the All of creation is the All of God. He exists in His creation, and He exists also in Himself — in His Divine ownhood, from which proceeds creation. To this creation He gives also all the ownhood it can receive. He gives it to be itself, and therefore other than Him: as entirely other than Him as if He were not its constant and continual creator. By virtue of its ownhood, of its own being, — while it exists only from Him, and He is in it, and constitutes all of it, — He is other than it, and it is other than Him.

I have already referred to Pantheism, or the theory that the universe is God, and that God is the universe; and have said that what makes it a fatal falsity is its denial of, and its antagonism to, the idea of a personal God. The one thing which gives to Pantheism its attractiveness is its satisfying, or at least appeasing, the desire for a God, which, after revelation has once given the thought of God, is never wholly lost from the human mind and heart, — while it relieves the understanding from the effort to comprehend an Infinite person

This effort the simple-minded do not make. From the earliest ages to the present day, the great body of religious persons believed simply in a Divine man. They did not, and do not, trouble themselves to define this idea. They hold it unconsciously. If they were told that they believed only in a Divine man, they would deem it an accusation which they would reject, perhaps indignantly. "No," they would say, "we believe in a God." They do so; but all the while their God is a Divine man. He is a man, in the first place, that they may be able to think of him at all; and then they make him Divine in just such a way, and to such an extent, as they can. The old mythologies, and the religions of many heathen nations at this day, attest this. Pious Catholics cling to the worship of the Virgin Mary and of the saints, because in them they have persons to believe in, and think of, and worship.

When Pantheism relieves the understanding from the effort to comprehend an Infinite person, it does this at the cost of all that is of the essence of religion. There can be no reverence of, no obedience to, no love for, any thing which is not a person. Fetichism, which worships stocks and stones, and idolatry, may seem to worship that which is not a person; but it is worship only so far as the imagination invests the thing with the attributes of personality, or supposes it to represent a Divine person. A Pantheist believes all this a weakness from which he has escaped. He mistakes: it is a modicum of strength which he has lost. If he has succeeded in silencing or paralyzing the demand for a God whom he can love and worship, he has put away nearly all which lifts him above animal life. If he recognizes this need, and has a theory by which he worships some abstraction — as Comte and others have done or tried to do — he commits a folly which is a mere emptiness in his own mind, and which thinking people see to be an empty folly, and of which the only value is the proof it offers that man must have a God, or something which he can call a God.

How then are thinkers to deal with the problem of an Infinite person? They must resort to that anthropomorphism of which we have already spoken, and which is at once reasonable and inevitable; and is wise, so far as it lifts man up to God, and avoids degrading God to man.

An important effect of the doctrine of ownhood of human life is the perfect answer that it gives to the doctrine of final absorption into Deity. This last falsity has always prevailed very widely. Among eastern nations, and especially in Buddhism, although not in that faith alone, it was systematized and avowed. There has been, and still is, much question whether even there this absorption was carried to the extent of an entire annihilation of individuality. It is, however, certain that in the minds of its earlier and most authoritative teachers it approached very near to, if it did not reach, this extreme; while it is also certain that it stops far short of this in the views held now by the great body of Buddhists. In Christianity it has never taken the form of a positive doctrine; but it lingers, concealed perhaps and latent, in many of the most religious and reflective minds, and not unfrequently exhibits itself in poetry and speculative writing. For example, in Wordsworth's beautiful lines, if he does not mean he at least suggests this thought, where he speaks of life and death, and compares human lives to

> Streams whose murmur fills this hollow vale;
> Whether their course be turbulent or smooth,
> Their waters clear or sullied, all are lost
> Within the bosom of yon crystal lake,
> And end their journey in the same repose.

It is easy to see how thoughtful persons end, if not in this belief, at least in a strong tendency in that direction. They see that there must be a God; that He must be in some sense alone, and All in All; and that all being flows forth from Him, and through its ascending steps culminates in man. Then, what more rational hope for the next step, than that this life, going forth from God, returns to Him in the final consummation of its progress?

To all this the doctrine of ownhood has an answer. God's love, because it is infinite, cannot but give to man the infinite and endless blessing of ownhood of his life. By this is made possible that gift of reciprocation, which, if it were only understood, would vivify every human heart with the wondering gratitude that swells the heart of Heaven. If man could receive only, he could return nothing. He would have nothing of his own to give back to God, who gives him every thing. But because all that is given him is given to him as his own, he can give this back. The life which comes from God to man is none the less God's life when it is in man. When man gives back this life to God, it is none the less man's life. He does give this life back to God when the love God gives to man returns to God as man's love for Him. Man returns God's wisdom to Him, when he receives the truths God gives to him, and uses the rationality also given, to learn from those truths how to ascribe to Him all the thought and understanding he possesses, and all the wisdom that came forth from God to fill his mind with light, and all that constitutes his life and being; and thus gives to God the glory due unto Him. And this is what is meant by reciprocation. God gives to man life and love and wisdom, and man gives it all back to God, as his own free gift of that which is his own.

God always works through His instruments. He does all of His work that can be so done, by and through His free and rational instruments; for thus He blesses them. And when we think of what man may grow into, and may now be in the higher stages of his being, what limits shall we set to this possibility? God does this, because His own infinite happiness springs from the indulgence of His love and the exercise of His wisdom in His own infinite working, and in His giving of happiness; and He desires to impart as much of the same happiness to those whom He has created that He may bless them, as it is possible for them to receive, and therefore for Him to give. He does not work through them as merely passive channels, for then His end would not be attained. He creates them to be active and reacting instruments; to be men, who, in their own freedom, and in their own strength, which is given to them to be their own, do His work as their own work. In this they work with Him. Absorption into Deity is not possible, nor is a merely passive reception; but reaction and reciprocation are possible; and, thanks to His infinite goodness, conjunction with Him is therefore possible! Yes, conjunction of man, the finite creature, with God, the infinite Creator!

In the prevailing alienation from God, in our habitual looking to Him as infinitely removed from us, and as inaccessible to definite thought, and indeed to be thought of, if at all, only as a vast and hidden power, — it must be difficult to apprehend a truth which tells us that He is very near, and always seeking to come nearer. But in the light of this truth we may look upon Him as ever acting in His work of creation and preservation, and upon ourselves as working with Him: actually working with the Infinite. Far forward into an indefinite future must we extend our look, if we would see ourselves in any great measure permitting Him to accomplish the purpose for which He creates us, and has ever in view in all His dealings with us. For that purpose is that we should be, and know ourselves to be, His children; to whom He commits a share of His Divine work, that we may have a share in His Divine happiness.

But perhaps the most valuable fruit of this doctrine of the ownhood of human life is the solution of the problem presented by the mingling of order and disorder, of good and of evil, in all things that we know; in a word, that old problem, — the origin of evil, — to which we have more than once alluded, and of which we would again speak in connection with this doctrine of ownhood. Old as this problem is, and attacked by the strongest thinkers in all ages, there have been devised only three solutions: One is, that there is a power of evil in the universe, equal or nearly equal to God, and always contending with Him. Another — which is akin to the first, and, as sometimes presented, appears to be almost the same — is, that the love and power of God are limited and imperfect. The third finds the origin of evil in the freedom of man and the abuse of that freedom. It is the last which the New-Church adopts, and to which, in its doctrine of the ownhood of human life, it gives a new explanation.

This doctrine explains both how and why we have freedom, because that springs necessarily from a true ownhood of one's life. Without freedom, we should be only a machine operated by a force which we could not resist. Nor should we have even the thought or desire of resisting it, or the knowledge that it was a force controlling us; for without freedom, we could not have any idea of freedom, nor know what freedom is. Without freedom, we could not act as of ourselves, for we should be only instruments used by another, and all our acts would be the acts of him who made use of us. Because we have freedom, and this freedom is the gift of God, we stand in a relation to Him of perfect dependence, and yet are as entirely ourselves as if we were perfectly independent.

This doctrine explains what freedom is. It is the power of choosing for ourselves what we shall do, and what we shall be. There is natural freedom, and there is spiritual freedom. Natural freedom relates to this world, and to external life and conduct. Spiritual freedom relates to the spirit and the things of the spirit; to our true character; to our spiritual life in this world and in the other. Our natural freedom is much and often impaired and controlled, because we have natural freedom for the sake of our spiritual freedom; and our natural freedom is always impaired and controlled as and so far as the interests of our spiritual freedom require, but never any farther. It is impaired, suspended, and controlled in such wise as will best lead us, if we can be led, to make a good use of our spiritual freedom. That is not lessened or controlled except in the rare cases in which it is permitted that evil influences should gain possession of us; and in those cases our manhood and selfhood are suspended.

It is true that there is a sense in which it may be said that our spiritual freedom is otherwise, for a time, suspended. Divine Providence has permitted calamity or fear to oppress us, or other modes of discipline to wake us for a time to a knowledge of ourselves. We see our wrong-doings and our sins; we form earnest resolutions to abstain from them altogether. This is an excellent thing. It is just that for which these visitations are permitted. But we are not in a state of entire spiritual freedom, when, under such influences, we form such resolutions. They do not yet, therefore, as we have already said, enter into our character. For that we must wait until the storm has gone by, and we have returned into our normal condition. Then our freedom becomes again entire; and in that freedom we choose whether the repentance and reform which we had resolved upon shall be infixed into our character by our conduct. That we might form such purposes, those controlling influences were permitted; that these purposes may be carried into effect, those controlling influences have been taken away, and our freedom restored to us. For certain it is, that only what we choose in freedom, and do because we have so chosen it, becomes a part of our character and of ourselves for ever. If these resolutions of reform are sincere and earnest, they are rooted into the character, and will bear their fruits in the other life, if Divine Providence abridges this life, and so prevents them from manifesting their effects here. But in any given case, whether these purposes be so sincere and earnest, can be known only to Him who searches the heart.

There could not be manhood, and all the possibilities of a manhood growing through eternity, without ownhood of ourselves. And this implies and causes necessarily self, as the basis of character. Man, because he is free, asks of himself what he shall do and what he should be. He asks this of himself; for, if there were any one who could answer this question and decide it for him, he would not be free. He must ask this question of himself, and his answer must satisfy himself, or he cannot be happy; for he would be in a state of bondage, and that is incompatible with true happiness. He must look to himself and regard himself, or he cannot be what a man should be.

Self-love is an inevitable necessity. It belongs to man as man, and cannot be escaped from. The severest ascetic, who rejoices in the belief that he had put self-love away, has only clothed it with a disguise which cheats himself as well as others. But while it is inevitable that self-love should be positive and active in every man, it is not inevitable, and it is very far from necessary, that it should be sovereign within him. Whether it shall be so or not is precisely the question which determines his character and his destiny. As soon as he begins to live and to be conscious of life, he begins to seek indulgence for himself and for his love of himself. But he is not left long before some love of others is suggested to him and infused into him. From that moment, the contest begins between the love of self and the love of others; and it never ends until it is determined which of these two is sovereign over the other. Neither of the two can be wholly extirpated. The question is, both being there, Which shall exist and act for the sake of the other? All the aid that Infinite love and wisdom and power can give to man, to help him to give the victory to the right over the wrong, is surely and ever given to him. But there stands his ownhood of himself. Nothing can be given to him which he does not accept. In the beginning, and at the foundation of his character by birth and nature, the love of self stands first; it remains supreme, dominating the character and determining the destiny, unless the man accepts the aid that is given him, and, by the rightful use of means and powers given to this end, subjects this essence and origin of all evil — self-love — to that love of others, which is the essence and origin of all good. The question then is, Which is for the sake of the other? If self-love be supreme, the man loves himself for the sake of himself, and loves his neighbors for the sake of himself, or only as instruments for his purposes, and as contributors in some way or other to his pleasure and enjoyment. In this way, or on this ground, he may love them ardently, and persuade himself, and perhaps others, that love for others is supreme within him; but all the while it is only a servant, and perhaps a slave. But if his love for others becomes indeed supreme, then he loves himself for the sake of others. He seeks for the means of strength, that he may use it for others. He enjoys — perhaps no one more — all that sustains life and gives to it innocent pleasure;

but the foundation of all his enjoyment is that it supports and freshens and invigorates him for usefulness, and, in usefulness, happiness.

From such a love of others, as from its root, grows the love of God. For, by the unselfish love for others, man is prepared to receive this love into his heart. It is sent to him from God, as the last, best, gift, which will lead him to the love of God, and will help to accomplish the purpose of God, in making him capable of conjunction with Him and of receiving from Him the happiness which it is the happiness of God to give.

Self-love is not selfishness unless it be supreme,—making self the centre to which all things are referred. It is not selfishness when it seeks to be the servant of that love of others which uses it as its instrument. May we not here, also, look to God, the exemplar of man, his child, for instruction? We cannot err in seeing in Him a self which loves to give itself away and desires that all it gives should return to it in prayer and worship and love, only because this enables it to give itself more fully and more entirely. That He may give Himself entirely to His children, He gives to them an ownhood of their lives. Through this ownhood and the freedom which belongs to it, they may, with His unfailing help, build themselves more and more into His image and likeness, and therefore more and more into the capability of receiving His life as their own.

For all this, freedom is perfectly indispensable. Without it, man would not be man. When Huxley said, a few years ago, that he saw no good in freedom with its responsibilities, and he should be glad to be wound up periodically, like a clock, thereafter to go on as he was made to go, — this was a thoughtless remark; for no man could see more clearly that, if his wish were gratified, he would be a clock, and not a man. Freedom is indeed essential to manhood and to all idea of manhood. When disease or any cause takes it wholly from a man, he is separated from his fellows, and cared for as one who can no longer be with them. We say such a person is no longer himself, and this phrase tells the whole truth; without rational freedom and the power of self-determination, a man is not himself.

But freedom, to be real and true, must be capable of abuse. It is the power of choosing between good and evil; and no man can *choose* good unless he can *choose* evil. The choice of evil brings sin, with all its train of consequences. The world, outside of man, — and this includes his body, for the spirit is the man, — is perfectly adjusted to his spiritual needs, and is therefore in correspondence with his spiritual condition. Hence the disorder and disturbance in this external world are the effect and the symbol of the disorder in the internal world, or in the spiritual condition of mankind.

In saying that freedom, if real, must be liable to abuse, we touch again upon the great difficulty in accounting for the existence of evil. It is impossible not to believe that we are free. No sane man can doubt this any more than he can doubt his life. Freedom is as certain as life, for it is a part of life. Nor is it difficult to appreciate the good of freedom, or its indispensableness to the highest human worth or happiness. But the question remains, Why could we not have been so constructed that we might have freedom and all its beneficial results, without this liability to abuse? If we believe in heaven, do we not believe that man is free there, and yet sinless and happy?

The answer is, that only by the rightful use of a freedom liable to abuse, could we build up such a character that hereafter, when this character was fully developed, we might be free, and yet sheltered from the danger of sin.

The truth of this answer is not obvious. We shall come nearer to seeing it, as we see more clearly the worth and the essentials of a true manhood. The great difficulty in believing that a God of love, of wisdom, and of power, all infinite, should have made us and the world which is our home so full of that which we justly call evil, may be lessened by remembering how little of His work we see, and how very little of that little we understand. Many thousand years ago, men roved upon this earth in the lowest condition possible for human beings. We have, through gradual advances, reached a position which, as we look back from it upon the far-retreating past, seems to us a commanding position; which justifies us in making our reason the measure of all things, and in believing what we cannot understand to be unintelligible or non-existent. "When man has looked about him as far as he can, he concludes there is no more to be seen; when he is at the end of his line, he is at the bottom of the ocean; when he has shot his best, he is sure that no one ever did or ever can shoot better or beyond it; his own reason he holds to be the certain measure of truth, and his own knowledge, of what is possible." *

This is utter foolishness; but it is a universal foolishness from which none escape entirely. Nor can we escape it, except by a thankful reception of such truths as are within our reach, and a patient and humble hope that what we now see dimly we may grow into the ability of seeing clearly. We see here and now but a small part of the beginning of a work that is to have no end. Surely,

* Sir William Temple.

we cannot be mistaken in holding as certain that whatever evil exists, exists by God's permission; that it is permitted by Him only for the sake of good; and that His omnipotence is constantly engaged in evolving good out of all evil. But how? This may indeed be a secret of the Infinite; and the wisest may grow for ever wiser as they discern more and more of that wisdom, which they can never contemplate or comprehend in its wholeness. Little is the light now given us, because, as we now are, more would be unfit for us and harmful; but that little may guide us to the conclusion that He cannot have created any of His children for a doom which would be worse than non-existence,—for such a doom could never be the gift of perfect love.

The presence in this world of so much that is not good has always seemed, and now to many minds seems, to justify a doubt as to the existence of God; or, if He exists, then as to His goodness or wisdom or power. True it is, that we cannot believe in Him and in His infinite attributes, unless we believe that in some way He is able to deduce good from all evil. That we are unable to see clearly and always how He does this, is no argument against this belief, except with those who think that the finite can fathom the counsels of the Infinite, and who forget that we are but at the beginning of being, and that our best wisdom is but as mere foolishness in the sight of perfect wisdom. One reason why we are permitted to begin our being in a world like this is suggested by the fact that this is but the beginning. It may well be that the highest good may, in the end, or in an eternity which will not end, require eternal progress, and that this progress should begin from the bottom — from the last and lowest state in which human beings may live. And this thought helps to explain the fact which science has abundantly proved, that, prior to any civilization, men lived on earth for myriads of years in a condition removed only one step, and that not a long one, from the condition of the beasts around them.

Another view of this subject we may derive from the consideration, that what is true of individuals must be in some measure true of the whole which, taken together, they compose. And who that has made any progress in spiritual improvement can doubt that the seeming calamities which have befallen him, and have often disappointed his dearest wishes, have been the means by which he has gone forward, step by step? Even so, we may say, humbly and reverently, it may have been with our sins. We have been permitted to fall, that we might know, as otherwise we could not and would not know, what depths of iniquity were hidden in our hearts. Happy is he who is able to discern and to resist the first thoughts and emotions of evil, when they first disclose themselves to the mind! But only One, the Sinless, could do this always and perfectly. We must strive for this; and, when we fail, we may still hope that a penitence as profound as the sin calls for, may wipe the sin away, and out of its own sorrow beget such a hatred of that sin as shall make us ever thereafter safe against its influence. Happy then are we, if that repentance shall convert our love of sin into hatred of it; happy are we, if we are so changed by yielding to influences from above, that we shall hereafter be sure to hate that which otherwise we might have always loved!

For a more general view of this question we must again advert to our ownhood of ourselves. Because it has been given us, and as the end for which it is given us, we may build up our own character, — always under the leading of Providence, always with the constant help, without which we cannot take a single step; but with this leading and this constant help, we may build up our character even from the beginning. This Divine leading may take us through paths which are painful, and seem to be devious. But one of the great purposes for which the dark mysteries of life are permitted to close in upon us, may well be to strengthen our casting away of the self we know to be so stained, and our acceptance of the will of God; and to invigorate our faith in a wisdom that cannot err, and our trust in a goodness that cannot fail. And when we remember what Heaven is, and that the happiness of all who are there consists in a clear perception of Him and of His working, and in perfect love for and perfect trust in Him who gives them all their happiness, and in entire surrender of self to Him, — what price can we think too large to pay for whatever shall advance us on the way to this consummation!

CHAPTER IX.

CORRESPONDENCE.

THE basis of the philosophy which we are taught by Swedenborg, is, that all things exist from God, and that He creates them by an effluence from Himself. The whole universe is not at an equal distance from God, but some things are nearer to and other things farther from Him. Thus, spirit is nearer to Him than matter; and, in the world of spirit and in the world of matter, there are different degrees of nearness to Him or of distance. This nearness or distance is not of place, but of state or condition, and is strictly a difference of degree; and of these degrees some are continuous degrees, or degrees of breadth on the same plane, and some are discrete degrees, or degrees of height.

One of the laws in conformity to which God creates is, that He creates through, or by means of, these discrete degrees, — higher things being instruments by means of which He creates lower things; each several higher thing being an instrument by means of which each several lower thing is created. Thus, all spirit is higher than matter; and it is through spirit that matter is made to assume form. Take for example the body: if life leaves the impregnated ovum in the mother, it dies, and there is the end of it. If it lives, the life that is in it is a spiritual life; and it gathers, first from the mother, and afterwards from suitable objects brought within its reach, the materials out of which it forms the body. We know that the body grows from the first living germ to the full maturity of the adult man. So does the spirit grow from the first germ of spiritual life to its adult condition. And as the spirit grows, the material body, which is to be its clothing for a while, is formed by or through the spirit. For it is always the spirit which is formative or causative, and the material which is formed or is the effect.

What is thus true of the spirit and the body is true of the whole spiritual world, — which world includes our own spirit and all that belongs to it, — and of the whole material world. It is through that spiritual world as a whole, that the material world as a whole is created. This is true not only in the past but in the present, and continually; not only generally, but specifically: all substances and forces, and all the forms of substance, and all the activities of force, having their causes in the spiritual world. Each one of all these things is first spiritual, and then, by the creative energy passing down through it, becomes material. And this is true also of all the changes in all things, whether substance or force. These changes are continual, for it may now be considered as ascertained that all things are in perpetual motion or action, external and internal; and all this motion or action is first spiritual, and then material.

Let us return again to the example first selected, of the soul and the body. As the soul forms the body, or through the soul the body is formed, so the soul forms the body to be its representative and instrument. It can be its instrument, because it is its representative; that is, because it is so exactly adapted to it that the soul animates every part, and finds in the body clothing for all of itself; and is able to make use of every part of the body to do the act or perform the function which each portion of the soul asks of that part of the body which clothes it. In one word, the material body corresponds to the soul.

We know very well what resemblance is; and almost — not perhaps quite as well — what analogy is. But correspondence is neither resemblance nor analogy. It bears a certain likeness to them, and yet is different from them. In certain instances of correspondence, there is between the things that correspond much resemblance; in others much analogy, and in yet others neither resemblance nor analogy. Correspondence is a different relation between things; and it is difficult to present this new idea intelligibly. The word is old; but it is now used in a new sense to express a relation, not hitherto known, between spiritual things and natural things. Perhaps this new meaning of the word can only be learned gradually, as we understand in special instances the relation which it seeks to express. It might suffice as a provisional definition of correspondence, to say that it is the relation between a higher and causative thing, and the lower thing which is caused by or through the higher, and which represents the higher.

Perhaps this relation of correspondence may be illustrated by the relation between the human countenance and the affections and thoughts. Whatever they are, that becomes. Between what is felt and thought, and the expression of the face, there is no resemblance or analogy; but there is correspondence. Let a man feel some strong affection, or have a new and interesting thought, and a change takes place at once in the muscles of the face and in the brightness or sadness of the eye, which is perfectly inexplicable on mechanical grounds, but is the effect of *internals* operating upon *externals*. It is a correspondence; and this correspondence is perfect, if hypocrisy does not interfere, and if habitual repression and concealment have not impaired the response of the face to the mind and heart.

It has been said that the material world, as a whole, corresponds with the spiritual world. But there is also in each of these worlds a correspondence. For all the persons in the spiritual world think and feel, and all their thoughts and affections, taken together, constitute their internal spiritual world; but they have an outside world to live in just as men have here, and all the things thereof, taken together, constitute their external spiritual world. Their external spiritual world is formed through or by their internal spiritual world, not generally, but specifically; that is, all the several things, whether substances or forces of their external world, are formed through or by the several things — each by each — of their thoughts or affections.

So it is also, but with a difference, in this material world. Men, while they live here, have a material world, and a home and all things of it, including all animals below men, for their instruments. They have also thoughts and affections, which are of their spirits; and the things which are material are formed through and by the things of their spirits.

All things below, which are created by or through things above, correspond to them. Hence, the general correspondence between this lower world and the spiritual world, and also the correspondence between thoughts and affections, and external things, which is true of that world and of this world; specifically true of that world, where the attraction of affinity classifies all perfectly, bringing together those of like kind, and permitting the external world about them to represent, specifically, their internal world or their thoughts and affections. Here men of all kinds are mingled for the uses of this world, and the external world corresponds only generally to the world of human thought and affection; being, as it were, its common resultant.

It is indeed by means of this correspondence that creation is effected. The creative energy, flowing into one degree of existence, flows through it and creates the degree below by this law of correspondence; which may be regarded as not only a law and a fact, but also as a force, animated, like all forces, by the only primal and original force. This relation exists from the summit to the bottom, everywhere, through the whole range of existence. It is by means of it that all created things are connected together into one whole, and that this whole creation is connected with its Creator. Every thing which is caused corresponds to the higher causative thing through which it is caused; and this caused thing may become in its turn a causative thing or instrument through which a lower thing is caused, which again corresponds to its cause. And, finally, the whole creation corresponds to, expresses, and represents its Creator. Thus, correspondence is universal and all-pervading.

I have used the words cause, causative, and causation in a somewhat unusual sense. There are two kinds or modes of causation; a higher and a lower. One of these operates only between different planes or discrete degrees of being, as between spirit and matter; this is the higher. The other operates between things on the same plane of being; this is the lower. When we strike a billiard ball with another and cause it to move, when we apply flame to gunpowder and cause it to explode, when a sculptor brings out a statue from a block of marble, — these are instances of causation of the lower kind. But this is the only kind which is recognized among men. If ever they think of a spiritual cause producing a new creation, they think of it only as they would think of making some new form by the proper use of suitable instruments and substances. The idea of causation in its higher sense has not existed among men, and therefore no word has been required or used to express it. "Cause" is the only word I have, and I must use it in both senses. But I shall not be understood when I use it, if it is not remembered that I am speaking of causation as that is operative between different planes of being; of causation by corrospondence. Of course I cannot be understood by those who are unable to believe that there are different planes of being.

Some of these correspondences have always been seen, and they show themselves in all languages. A man is said to be warm or cold in his feelings or affections: burning with passion, or frozen in indifference. His thoughts are said to be luminous and bright, or dark and cloudy. Language is indeed founded upon correspondence; for leading philologists agree, that words which have a moral meaning are generally formed from those which have primarily a physical meaning; and some of our words still retain both meanings, as rule, right, and the like. Poetry discovers a multitude of correspondences; some nearer, some more remote. Indeed, the very highest poetry has always done its best and greatest work in making the splendor, the sublimity, and the beauty of the external world significant, and giving them a voice. Upon the walls of the world that is our home are hung pictures of the life within; they are veiled to our eyes, and poetry takes the veil away. When these things are thought about, and there is an attempt to analyze and account for them, they are said to be the products of imagination. This is true, but it is not true in the sense in which it is commonly said; for in their utter ignorance of the true function of the imagination, men mean by this phrase only that these things have no real existence, no actual truth. There can be no greater error. It is as much the function of imagination to supply reason with inexhaustible materials for its proper work, as it is for reason to instruct and guide imagination, that it may not wander into the paths of fantasy.

Already is it seen by some of the most eminent thinkers of the day, that imagination has always worked with reason in the progress of the profoundest sciences. Astronomy, and all the branches of physics, owe to its assistance their greatest advances; and distinguished mathematicians have said that even mathematics, the stern rebuker of fantasy, would never have reached its present fruitfulness and power had it not profited by the aid of imagination.

It is difficult to speak of what must be the effects of this doctrine, now that there is no knowledge and no recognition of it even among advanced scientists. And it cannot but seem fanciful, and offensively so, to those who habitually confine their thoughts to material things; or, if they investigate mind, so utterly invert the truth as to regard mind as the product of matter; or, if they avoid this falsity, regard mind as not only perfectly distinct from matter, but as having no definite relation to it. While mind and matter are thus regarded as perfectly separated from each other, without relation or connection, neither can be understood. Nor is there any relation or connection discoverable between them, except that of correspondence. When this is distinctly seen, the whole material world will have its significance and its voice. The realms of Nature will speak to man, for whom they are created, and their utterance will reveal truths concerning things above them. The sciences of mind and matter, no longer independent, and still less hostile, will work together while each does its own work. Many a mystery in the world of mind will be solved by light rising up to it from new discoveries in the fields of matter. Many a mystery in the world of matter will be illuminated by light falling down upon it from the world of mind.

It will be seen that all there is in the spirit of man refers itself to what is either of the will, or of the understanding, — to feelings and affections, or to thoughts; to the activities of affection or to those of thought. So it will be seen that all there is in the world of matter refers itself in its correspondence and significance to one or the other of these two great departments, — will and intellect, — which together constitute spiritual life. Innumerable and indefinitely diversified are the particulars which compose the worlds of mind and of matter. And the correspondence between the worlds is not general only, but specific; running through all these particulars and connecting them together. It is not more true that every thing which exists was caused, or had a cause, than it is that every thing which is caused corresponds to its cause. Hence it is that this world is so perfectly adjusted to our needs. We live here only to prepare for another life; and it is the perfect correspondence between those two worlds which makes the lower world perfectly adapted to be a world of preparation for the higher. The things of Nature will be made to give their moral lesson, and will be seen to have their spiritual import. A little of this is sometimes attempted, and successfully, even now, and especially by the highest poetry; but this is very little, very near to nothingness, in comparison with what may be, and therefore will be known in coming ages, when the human mind is opened to the light.

But a few correspondences have been referred to. It would be easy to go on indefinitely, and apply the same principles to other things. Indeed, it is difficult to refrain from the attempt to do so. But to those who refuse to rise above sensuous thought, and whose whole habit and condition of mind tend to resist the idea that the universe, including mind and matter, is an organic one, all its infinitely varied parts being linked together in indissoluble unity, what I have already said must needs seem to be an idle tale, a dream of unbridled fantasy; and nothing could be added that would change its aspect. To those who have learned or are willing to learn this central truth, it is possible that it might receive some illustration from farther instances of this correspondence. It seems, however, that the few which the scope of this work permits me to attempt can be given to better purpose, if at all, when I treat of the word of God. For then I shall endeavor to show that the sanctity and power and instructiveness of the word rest, in great measure, upon correspondence. By its means, inspiration from on high was able to bring that word which, in the heavens, is the inexhaustible source of the wisdom of the wisest there, down even to the dwellers upon earth, with all its transcendent truth; but covered with a veil which the science of correspondence makes, or hereafter will make, transparent.

CHAPTER X.

THE HUMAN FORM.

Form is not the same thing as shape. Every thing has a form, and only some things have shape. The correlative to form is essence. Whatever exists has both. Sensuous philosophers — Locke for example — deny and, as they think, disprove essence; and to sensuous thought there is neither form nor essence. But every thing which exists has that which makes it to be just what it is: and that is its essence. In despite of philosophy, common sense expressing itself in common language asserts an essence; for it says of this or that quality or attribute, that it is essential to this or that thing: and all that is essential to its being is of its essence. If its essence determines *what* a thing is, it is almost a definition of form to say it is that which determines *how* a thing is. Bacon, in his seventeenth aphorism, says. "Eadem res est forma calidi vel forma luminis, et lex calidi aut lex luminis;" — "The same thing is the form of heat or the form of light, and the law of heat or the law of light." As the essence of every thing determines *what* it is, and the form of it determines *how* it is, or what it shall do or act or cause, — so the form of any thing is its law.

Swedenborg uses in relation to this matter two Latin words which it has been found impossible to translate adequately; and, for the most part, they are left untranslated in our English translations of his works: these words are "*esse*" (literally, to be) and "*existere*" (literally, to exist). *Existere* is derived from two other Latin words, and means "to stand forth;" and it may help us to approach the meaning of this distinction, if we understand that the *esse* of any thing is that which it is in itself, while its *existere* is that which it is as it "stands forth," and makes itself manifest and active in its functions. This use of these two Latin words is not peculiar to Swedenborg. Spinoza makes frequent use of them in just the same sense; and I think I have met it in other writers who use scholastic Latin, but I am not sure that I remember accurately. In this work, I use "essence" and "form" as very nearly, though not quite, the equivalents of *esse* and *existere*.

In this sense, it is obvious that every thing must have an essence and a form; for, if it had no essence, it would not have that which makes it to be what it is, or to be at all, and could not have any form. And, if it had an essence and not a form, it would have no existence; for it would not have that by which it could exist and act, or stand forth in manifested and active being. But it is not so with shape; for this some things have, and other things have not. The air we breathe, the ethers from which come light, electricity, and magnetism, have no shape, but they have form. Our affections and thoughts, which are most real things, are without shape, but they have form. Shape is only an external of form, which is moulded by the form, and expresses the form to the senses of sight and touch. Where shape exists, the form is clothed by it, and in it puts on dimensions, and is cognizable by the senses and by sensuous thought. The shape does in some sort reveal and manifest the form, as the form manifests the essence. The form is not apprehensible by sensuous thought, but only by rational thought. And, in these days, rational thought for the most part submits itself to sensuous thought, and consents to call those of its intuitions or conclusions which sensuous thought cannot accept, unrealities.

Sometimes the body is called the form of the soul, and this phrase may indicate a truth. But the soul has its essence and its form, as the body has its essence and its form. The man, the human being, has his essence and his form. He is first spiritual, and then material. He is first that which makes him to be a man, and then this human essence ultimates itself in a human body, which clothes the human essence, and responds to its true form, and to some extent reveals it. In the other world, this body is formed of spiritual substance; it is so here also, for the man has a body formed of spiritual substance, — a spiritual body; and, while he lives here, he has also a body formed of material substance, deriving its life from the spiritual body which, for a time, it clothes. In both worlds, the body is an adequate instrument of the soul, and presents it forth to view. Remembering, then, that the body is itself only the shape, and not the form, of the man, but that it is adjusted to the form and reveals this form, — let us now see what lessons we may draw from the human form, as thus expressed and revealed.

In the first place, let us notice the probable perfection of this form; by which I mean that there can be no better form. If we believe what the Bible says, — that man was made in the image and likeness of God, — we shall look upon the human form as the express image of the Divine form, which must needs be perfection itself. Neither art nor science can improve upon the human form. All that can be done to represent the beautiful is to represent it as perfectly as possible; and physiology is full of acknowledgment of the wonderful adaptation of the whole and all its parts to the performance of their functions: and, as the knowledge of anatomy advances, this is seen more clearly. It may well be called the type of form; because all organisms, vegetable or animal, aspire towards the human form. In the least and lowest of them there is something which, to say the least, reminds one of some portion or some function of the human form. Science is now busy and successful in seeking through the whole organic world for organs, members, or limbs which appear to represent organs, members, or limbs of the human body; and to be indeed the same, excepting so far as they are changed by other needs and other circumstances.

In the next place, let us notice the indefinite diversity among the innumerable parts which compose this whole. No two are altogether alike. While this would be readily admitted as to all the organs or limbs, it may be thought that the minute cells and fibrils are alike in substance, shape, and function. But every cell and every fibril fills its own place, and performs precisely the function which that place requires. However similar, it is as certain that no two can perform precisely the same function in the same way, as it is that they cannot occupy the same place.

Then let us notice the law which prevails through all this immeasurable diversity of shape and place and function: it is that each part works for others, and not for itself. All the parts which compose this wonderful whole are connected together by a perfect symmetry, and the meaning and the effect of this symmetry is, that each one is so formed and so placed that it does its own especial work; and the work of each one is so adjusted to every other, that the whole work of the human body is the common resultant of the work of each part. While each one works for all, all work for each. Nor is it strictly true that no part works for itself. Each part does work for itself just so far as to profit by the work of others for it, to the extent of securing to itself the nourishment and strength necessary for its health, and for its healthy performance of the work it has to do in the organic whole. When this is perfectly true of all parts of the body, there is perfect health. Disease comes when any organ fails in its duty, and especially whenever any organ works for itself primarily, and takes more than it needs of vitality or substance. Then other organs suffer for want of that which the offending organ unduly appropriates, and the offending organ suffers for its selfishness by engorgement or inflammation. The symmetry of action is impaired or destroyed, — and that symmetry is health, and the want of it disease.

If we believe that the human form is an image of the Divine form, and therefore the most perfect of forms, we may well believe that the creative energy is always in effort to bring all things into or towards this form, but leaving all things as far away from it as their several functions may require. An important application of this principle is to human society. But we can understand that better, if we look at it in its perfection in heaven. That I will endeavor to do in my chapter on heaven. Here I will only say that the whole heaven stands before the Lord in a human form — not shape, but form; that it is composed of larger societies, and these of lesser, and these again of still less; that every society is in a true form, — that is, in the human form; that these societies differ from each other, as men differ from each other while all are men; and that the various members of a complete society correspond in character, function, and use, to the different organs of that human body which clothes and expresses the human form. This is carried to the minutest detail, and determines the order of heaven, and makes that orderly. And, as heaven grows in its completeness, its harmony becomes fuller and richer; and the whole heaven, and all the several societies — larger and smaller — approach more nearly to perfection.

There are frequent expressions which show that the idea of the human form as the type of all form has found its way to human consciousness. Thus, we speak of this man as the head of a society, and of others as its members; we say this one supplies it with brains, and that those are the strong hands that do its work. This reference goes down to the most familiar things; and thus we speak of the arms, legs, feet, face, back, and the like, of things in common use. The answer which would now be made to all this is, These are but casual analogies which the imaginative faculty, always on the lookout for materials, has laid hold of and embodied in common language.

This may be partially true, but it is very far from the whole truth. When social organization shall have advanced far beyond its present condition, and rational imagination shall have grown more acute and wiser, it will see in society many more of what it now calls analogies. Ages, perhaps ages of ages, must elapse before human society can advance so far as to recognize its own best principles of organization. Earth will always be earth, not heaven, and disorder will mingle with its order; because it will always be the state and condition in which we may prepare for heaven by conflict and by effort, and by choosing between the elements and influences of good or of evil. But even now we may learn the lessons this truth yields, and hereafter they may grow larger, and be more clearly seen, and come to us with greater power.

The first and greatest of these lessons is one which the whole universe and the whole course of

Divine Providence are constantly giving to all who are willing to receive it. This is that usefulness — working for others, and doing good to others — is the one law of health and happiness; while selfishness, in affection and in life, is the one centre from which radiate all disorder and all suffering. The Divine mercy surrounds almost every man with circumstances which compel him to be useful. The greediest self-seeker, who cares only for himself in all he does, is often in his most selfish exertions eminently useful. This has no direct effect upon his character. That he is useful to others does not render him less selfish. But it is a good thing to have the habit of usefulness. If the efforts of Providence to lead him from the love of self to the love of others are ever in any degree successful, he will not be under the additional necessity of learning to be useful. In point of fact, the highest charity for most men, or the best form of usefulness for them, lies in the complete discharge of their daily duties; for the mercy of God always so adjusts these to their spiritual needs, that the best way in any hour for men to advance spiritually is simply to do the duty of that hour.

The difference between the good man and the bad man lies in the difference in the motives which govern their acts, more than it does in the acts themselves. Of course, some acts are good and others bad; and there are persons who habitually practise those acts which all call bad, and others whose actions seem to be always good. But these are exceptions. The majority of mankind lead lives of not so much difference in appearance, while there is actually between them all the difference between good and evil, — between heaven and hell. He through whose discharge of duty there runs the desire and purpose of doing his duty and being useful to others, is good; and this goodness may be infinitely diversified in kind and in measure among men who are good. While he whose constant and dominant purpose is to serve himself and his own selfish desires, and who, when he is useful to others, is so only for the sake of himself, is not good, however he may be regarded by his fellowmen, who can judge only from appearances.

Charity, or love for others, and selfishness, are the two great opposites, between which all human life is included. If we would understand why this is so, we must go back to the original and fundamental truth that God creates man by effluence from Himself, and makes him, as far as may be, like unto Himself. His very essence is love for others. It is love which causes Him continually to create and to sustain the universe, spiritual and material; which causes Him to be infinitely useful, and to find His infinite happiness in His infinite usefulness. And it is the same love which leads Him to do all that His infinite power can do, to excite in his children a love of doing good, — a love of usefulness, that by this He may make them happy. The opposite of this love is selfishness. Between these opposites every man must *choose*, that his love of others, if he chooses that, may be his own. Between these opposites every man does choose; and this choice determines his destiny, because it determines his character.

God is One; but He is not "without form and void." He is One and Infinite; but He is an Infinite composed of infinites. One way in which He reveals Himself to us is in our own human form; and the parts and members of His Divine form, each perfectly distinct, but perfectly responsive to every other, and each in perfect sympathy with all, — all these members and activities, combining together into a perfect unity, compose or constitute God: and the correspondent to the whole and to each part is the human form. Every human being is taught and trained in this life, so far as he will permit, to take his proper place and do his proper work in that form. For it is the form of heaven, and heaven grows eternally by accessions from the earth; and the members added to it, as they rise from this world to the other, are not mere additions to a chaotic mass, only enlarging its size or the number of its components, — but each takes his own appropriate place, precisely as every part of added food, assimilated to a healthy human body and incorporated therein, takes its appropriate place. There every one is known, and his whole character and function are defined and manifested by his place in the human form of heaven. This angel is in the head, that one in the heart, and that one in the lungs; this one in the hand, and that one in the foot; this one in the eye, and that one in the ear, — and so of every part, and of every minutest part of a part. Symmetry, sympathy, and health belong to the whole; and the health and happiness of the whole belong to each.

Pride and humiliation are equally impossible where order is perfect, and it perfectly discriminates between all who are there. The highest cannot forget, and have no desire to forget, their entire dependence upon all the rest. The lowest feel and know that they are essential to the rest, and that this is seen and acknowledged by them. For each one knows that he fills a place which would not be filled or not so well filled, and does a work which would not be done or not so well done, if he were not there. All know this of all; and all help each to do his work, and the work of each is for all.

This is the perfection of human society. In its perfection it will never be found, except in the heavens. For, as already intimated, always will the earths be training schools, in which influences from above and from beneath, with the order and the disorder they bring with them, will mingle; that, through them all, man, in his ownhood of his life and in his freedom, may coöperate with God Himself in preparing to take the place which he is fit for among the happy. But, while this perfection of human society will never be reached upon the earth, it may always be approached. And it will be approached in the degree in which mutual love and the love of usefulness prevail over selfishness in all its forms, and give force and vitality to the acknowledgment of the universal brotherhood of man,—the child of our Father in the heavens.

Already has the study of the human form, and a comparison of it with other forms, suggested at least a thought of its central position among them all. Far more than this is to come; for truth is eternal, and has eternity for its development. Hereafter the study of the human form will be found to be central among human studies, as the form itself is central among forms. Unbounded treasures will repay this study; and in some future day, it will be found that an increase of knowledge of the human body (because the body is the effect, the instrument, and the expression of the human form) will enlarge the knowledge of the soul, and of the laws of all true life.

CHAPTER XI.

HEAVEN.

All men live after this life is ended; and in the next life live as they will to live, far more than they can in this life. It has already been repeatedly said that we live here to prepare for life there; and because this preparation can be made only by conflict and self-compulsion, and we are often led to this or aided in it by external compulsion, our life here is more or less a life of coercion, and all our surroundings are controlled for us, and are made to be what we need, which is only in small part what we desire. After death, the preparation we have made is developed in the world of spirits, our ruling love freed by the suppression of opposing and inconsistent tendencies, and our whole character brought into such harmony as is possible.

One effect of this is that intellectual and affectional affinity have full play. Here all live together, — the good and the evil mingled, — with but little of separation possible; because, by this mingling, we can best help each other in this life of preparation.

Not so is it there. For there the law of affinity brings the good together, and separates them from those who are not good. Where the good are is Heaven. But the attraction of affinity does far more than separate the good from the evil: it arranges them into societies, so that those who are of like kind live together. These societies in Heaven are innumerable: greater and greatest, — the larger composed of lesser, and the lesser of least; and each society has its own peculiarities and its own work, differing from every other in its character, function, and use, as every individual in every society differs from every other.

The law which pervades the whole is the law of the human form, — form, I repeat, not shape. This form I have treated of in the preceding chapter. I will repeat that it is man's form because it is God's form; and it comes to man with the life of God, which is given him to be his own, and which makes man to be man because God is Man. This Divine form is perfect; and Heaven is for ever growing into the likeness and image of this form. Hence there is an ever-growing order and harmony among all the parts of Heaven; that is, among all the societies of Heaven, and all the individuals who compose those societies. There is also order, and this an ever-growing order, in the arrangement of Heaven. The societies are lesser and greater, and all are arranged into three, — which are three heavens, and which, taken together, constitute Heaven.

THE THREE HEAVENS.

In our chapter on Degrees, and that on the Human Form, we have indicated the two principles which may help us to understand the arrangement of Heaven into three heavens. A distinction into three discrete degrees is universal, existing in God Himself, and from Him pervading all things. In Him it is love, wisdom, and power, or action. It divides Heaven into three heavens. In the highest of these, which Swedenborg calls the Heavenly heaven, love to the Lord is the ruling and all-pervading principle. In the middle heaven, called by Swedenborg the Spiritual heaven, wisdom, truth, a living faith which recognizes charity or love of the neighbor as the law of life, prevails. The lower heaven, called the natural heaven, is characterized by obedience. If we look at these heavens in the light of their correspondence with the human form, we may say that the highest heaven corresponds with the head, the middle heaven with the chest and trunk, the lowest heaven with the limbs. Nor is this correspondence general only. As each of these three great divisions of the human form is composed of larger parts, and these of lesser, and these again of still lesser, until the series closes in innumerable individual cells or molecules, so in each heaven are larger and smaller and still smaller societies. In the human form, not only are the larger members and the components of these specifically different, but it is as impossible for any two of the smallest cells or minute parts of the body to exercise precisely the same function, or stand in precisely the same relation to the rest, as it would be for them to occupy the same place at the same time. Nor is there any thing accidental or arbitrary in all this infinite variety. Every member of the body, great or small, and every minutest portion of every member, has precisely that special work to do which best enables it to promote the health, strength, and usefulness of the whole body, drawing from this general health its own well-being. All are in harmony, — each one being that and doing that which all the rest require.

Precisely so is it in Heaven. There, too, this exact distinction between all the members and component parts, this perfect harmony between them, this coöperation of all in the universal good, is the constant law of life. This is effected in a healthy and vigorous human body, because it exists in Heaven; and because Heaven is in a human form, and the human body in its true form corresponds with Heaven. Nor is this correspondence general only, for it is precise and specific. Whatever be the use or function of any part of the human body, larger or less, some part of Heaven performs a corresponding use or function, and finds therein its health and happiness. Not the whole human body only, but every member in its whole structure down to its minutest component parts, and the action of all and each, has its antitype and cause in heaven. So through the whole universe the life of God goes forth, creating all, sustaining all, pervading all; and impressing upon all, as far as that is possible, the order which exists in absolute and infinite perfection in Himself.

THE TWO KINGDOMS OF HEAVEN.

We may notice still another point in the correspondence between Heaven and man, or another fact resulting from the human form of Heaven. Every member of the human race has will and understanding; and these are distinct and yet united. In every man one or the other prevails, for they are never precisely equal. In this man, the will controls, and his affectionate and loving nature are always prominent. That man seems to be a man of intellect only; he may be as brilliant as ice, but he is as cold. All his affections seem to ask leave of his understanding to be, and to exhibit themselves. These extremes are perhaps rarely met with. But they only carry to excess a difference which is universal. Men with a perfect balance between these two elements of our being are not met with. Some come very near it, but all stand on the one side or the other, at a greater or less distance from the middle point; and are either somewhat more intellectual than affectional, or the reverse. So it is with the heavens: with each heaven, and every society in heaven, and every individual there. The highest heaven, in its relation to all below it, is a heaven of love; but it has its affectional and its intellectual side. The spiritual or middle heaven is a heaven where wisdom rules, and the love of the neighbor, founded on the truths which wisdom teaches, is the law of life; but this heaven also has its affectional and its intellectual side. The natural or lowest heaven, which is the heaven of obedience, consists of those who obey from affection, and those who obey from a sincere and intelligent recognition of the truth. This distinction, which runs through the heavens, is expressed by Swedenborg in the statement that all Heaven is divided into two kingdoms.

As the distinction into three heavens is represented in the human body, so is the distinction into two kingdoms. We have a heart, representing in its action and influence the affectional side; and lungs, representing the intellectual side. The brain is divided into two hemispheres,—one on the right side, and the other on the left. The limbs, the ears, the eyes, are on the one side and on the other. The liver has its two lobes; the kidneys are twofold; and single organs generally have, like the brain, two halves, although these are not always so apparently distinct from each other as in the case of the brain. The distinction corresponding to that of the three heavens is, if we may so express it, horizontal; while that representing the two kingdoms may be said to be vertical.

Every one who dies, and in the world of spirits has passed through such discipline and development that his ruling love dominates and forms his character without resistance or impediment, if he be good, takes his place in Heaven. This place is determined by his character. That places him not only in the heaven to which he belongs, but in that society, and in the place in that society, for which he has become fitted. He is in the closest affinity with all who are there, and they with him; and there he finds his eternal home.

THE EMPLOYMENTS OF HEAVEN.

God is infinitely active. His infinite action creates, sustains, and governs the universe of spirit and of matter. His life flows into angels and becomes their life; and His activity is in the life which is derived from Him. It follows necessarily that every angel is active and useful. In the language of Swedenborg, heaven is a kingdom of uses. Every one there gratifies the tendency and the demand of his own life in performing the use which he can best perform. These uses grow and rise as he grows and rises in Godlikeness. Every angel finds in the consciousness of this constant growth one of the elements of his happiness. But no angel becomes radically other than that he was prepared to be when he left this world. He does not change his heaven, for that depends upon the essential qualities of his character; and they are permanent and unchangeable. He finds his happiness in the performance of his use, and in the consciousness of the unending growth and elevation in his performance of it. I need not say that it must be impossible for us to form an adequate idea of the employments of the angels, for it is obvious and certain. But there are some facts and some principles which may lead our thoughts in that direction.

Many good things are done in this world. The greatest amount of human effort is of that kind. How many men are busy through life in providing food, how many in furnishing shelter or clothing, for others!—and how many in the vast variety of uses which subserve the comfort and enjoyment of life! These are all good works, and we are constrained to do them by the mercy of our Father; for so His will is done on earth, though not as it is done in heaven, for there it is done without constraint. But of this, we who adopt the doctrines of the New-Church are sure: the motives and the thoughts which induce us to do these things are all from the spiritual world, and, so far as they are good, from heaven. All the good works on earth have their prototypes in heaven; and whatsoever good things men do in an earthly way, angels are doing—not in the same, but in a heavenly way. What this way is we do not know now, for the reason that we know so little of the correspondence which connects all things of this world with all things of the other.

We may go still further. We may remember that whatsoever God can do through living and conscious instruments, He does through them; for so He blesses them. It is His sun and His rain which, coming down upon the fields He has spread out, raise and ripen all our food; but He gives to men to be His instruments in this, and thus they acquire the habit, and if they are capable of it enjoy the happiness, of usefulness. From this lowest instance of this universal law, our thoughts may go upwards indefinitely. Science now permits us to look at the material heavens, and catch a glimpse of the way in which they are builded. With the best instruments, we can but look upon an edge of the universe or a small spot within it; but we can see innumerable stars, all of which are probably suns, and may have habitable earths around them. We see nebulæ of every description: in some, we may look upon the spiral forms which indicate that they are growing into worlds of suns and earths; in others, we may see this growth so far advanced that a central sun is there already; and in others, only amorphous masses of light-mist, over which countless æons have yet to pass. And perhaps we may believe that each created sun and planet in its turn, when its work is finished, is gradually resolved into its primal atoms, which mingle with those that fill the universe; at some distant cycle again to coalesce into masses, and build up new worlds, — thus repeating, on a larger scale, the circle of death and life which we see everywhere on our own earth. We may go on in this path of what, if it be as yet only hypothesis, is at least reasonable hypothesis, until the imagination is weary and faint.

Now let us remember that all this is God's work, and that all of His work which He can He puts into the hands of His living instruments; and then what employment is there for angels in their various ranks, and in their various degrees of advancement, of wisdom, and of power! And, as in this world, beside all the external uses which are done here, there are those who find full employment for their best ability in the world of thought and truth, so in the heavens, above all the work of building and sustaining the universe as His instruments, there may be those who find their usefulness and happiness in ever learning truths which are ever ascending towards His own infinite wisdom. And they learn that they may teach, for they know how much more blessed it is to give than to receive. And from them, even the highest of them, this wisdom comes down in far descent, through all the ordered ranks of intelligences, and so modified and accommodated in this descent, that at last it reaches us, and pours into our understanding all the truth we are capable of receiving in this beginning of being.

ANGELS.

It is common for those who believe any thing about angels to regard them as a race of created beings who are altogether other than men, and far higher than men. This belief is confirmed by the text which says, "Thou hast made him a little lower than the angels." But Swedenborg declares that all angels began life as human beings, upon this or some other earth, however brief the stay of some of them upon earth. A line of thought which leads to this conclusion is suggested by the principle, that the best thing which perfect and almighty Love could do for its creatures was to create them such that, by working as of themselves in voluntary co-operation with their Father, and by the exercise of strength which He gives them as their own, they might rise, step by step, from a far-off beginning, to a condition in which it would be possible for Him to impart to them a large measure of His own life and happiness; and that this measure might increase with their constant and unending elevation towards Himself. He makes men to be themselves; that in the exercise of their own power, which is their own because He gives it to them, they might become capable, not of absorption into His infinitude, but of a conjunction with Him which may grow nearer and closer, for ever and for ever. The infinite happiness of God springs from His infinite activity in good. By their conjunction with Him, men may become at once His ministers and servants, and co-workers with Him in the whole work of creation, preservation, and government of the universe. And this, men who have become angels are. What more could angels be?

Whatever we may imagine angels to be, whatever capacity of acting as His ministers we may suppose them to have, whatever measure of love or wisdom, or of happiness resulting therefrom, we may suppose them to possess, — it is simply impossible for the most vivid and soaring imagination to surpass or to approach that point upon which human beings must stand, who, having profited by the means He gave them, through the revolving cycles which time cannot measure, have gone ever upwards in their approach to the Infinite. Higher beings than these could not be created, and could not exist. Whatever might be our belief in the desire of God to bring into being creatures whom He might bless with the utmost happiness, we may still believe that He would form for this purpose such creatures as He has formed men, with all their boundless hopes and possibilities; because to them, in the condition within their reach, might be given the highest happiness a being less than infinite could enjoy.

The idea of a race of beings higher than men has perhaps grown out of the thought that Infinite love and power could not be contented with beings so imperfect, so feeble, so far from happiness as men are, — as we see them. But when we are taught that what we see of human life is but its beginning, and think as well as we may of what will attend the full development of those powers which we here dimly discern in their germ condition, we are sure that even Infinite love and power would be satisfied with what men might become, and, in their homes in Heaven, do become.

CHAPTER XII.

THE WORD.

Here, as elsewhere in the consideration of topics of religious philosophy, we must begin with God, and with His purpose in creating and providing for mankind. This purpose was that beings might exist whom He could make happy; and therefore He made them such in capacity and character that He might for ever help them to be happy and to grow in happiness. The animals He had made He could make happy, but their happiness is not capable of eternal increase; while man's is so. Here is one of the radical distinctions between men and animals. And because of this, there exists another of these radical distinctions,—language: men have the faculty of speech, and animals have not.

God is constantly in the effort to carry into effect His own infinite purpose. The whole nature of man, and all that contributes to the constitution of that nature, is so made as to be an instrument which God can use to carry His purpose into effect. Language is one of these instruments, and a most important one. Words are the simplest things in the world: to utter them is as easy a matter as breathing; and, indeed, they are only breath made vocal. And yet words are among the most mysterious things in the world. The origin of language is wholly unknown; and no one of the many theories about it seems to be acceptable to many beside him who announces it. But the true nature of language and its influence and effect are almost as much unknown as its origin. We do know, however, much of what it is and does for man, for this is apparent at the first glance.

Words serve for means of intercourse, because they enable men to communicate to each other their thoughts and feelings, and to impress these upon each other and make them common to speaker and hearers, — and thus unite men in a common thought or feeling. Then words serve for the preservation of thoughts and feelings. They preserve them by tradition, if they are delivered for safe-keeping only to memory and transmission by repetition. Of late there have been quite interesting conclusions as to the method, and the extent and accuracy, with which a wide and complex system of doctrines could be continuously preserved by such transmission, — as in the case of the earliest Hindu beliefs. These conclusions have been drawn from distinct intimations in ancient records of the systematic and well-devised means which were successfully employed to make this transmission accurate.

Then came a farther improvement, — that of writing, — which is almost as marvellous as the origin of language. This gave to all the uses of words new power and efficacy; and when, a few centuries ago, a farther improvement in the use of words — that of printing — took place, they gained still farther power and efficacy.

If we believe that the use of words or mutual language is peculiarly human, and indispensable to human improvement; that the power of speech is given to man by God; that it is adapted to his whole nature and needs, as the means by which truth may be given him that will help him to build up in himself a heavenly character; if we believe that all human life flows into man from God, and therefore whatever is in man, humanly, must be in God, divinely, — well may it be asked, Why should not God speak to man? Why should He not make use of this instrument of language to give to man knowledge which he could not otherwise possess? The answer to this question is, He has spoken to man, and He does speak to him. He does in fact make use of man's power of hearing, of reading, and of understanding language, to communicate to men truths which could not otherwise be given to them.

God speaks to man through men into whom He

breathes His spirit. He makes use of their minds, their thoughts, their affections, their mouths, their language, to say to His children what He would. It is true that every thought and every affection which any man has comes to him from God. But the common and normal way is for these thoughts and affections to be modified and qualified by the mediums through which they flow, into affinity and adaptedness to the man's state; in order that, when they reach man, they may be given to man to be his own: and they thereby become man's, and not God's. It is sometimes said of men of great genius, — as Homer, Shakspeare, Milton, — that they were inspired. But this use of the word confounds things essentially different. Whatever comes normally to any individual is always modified into conformity with his peculiar and individual state and faculty, but always so that, when he receives it, it becomes his own. Not so is it with the subjects of inspiration. Their ownhood of themselves is for the time suspended. They are filled with the spirit of God. They utter or write what is thus given to them. This may be somewhat modified in the form it takes by the mental character, or by the habits of thought and feeling of the person employed for this use, as instruments modify the work that is done by them; but not so as to make the words their own words, for they are, and they remain, God's words.

How it was in the earliest condition of mankind we know not. There was probably a long period during which such words were only spoken, and were delivered over to memory and transmission by tradition. But at length more could be done. Our Bible, which we call emphatically the Word of God, was given to mankind, and in the languages best suited to this use. It was not given all at once. Words, perhaps preserved only by tradition from an earlier age, made a part of it. In following ages, a succession of persons employed for this use, who differed much from each other, and whose personal peculiarities are to some extent impressed upon their work, added the books of the Old Testament. At a later period, the Gospels and the Book of Revelation were added,—finally completing this Word of God.

Emanuel Swedenborg was not one of those so employed to write the words of God. He was not inspired. We repeat what we said before. He was selected for the use he performed, as a man of remarkable intellect, which was as fully cultivated and prepared by study and work as was possible; and he was then taught spiritual truth in a way in which it had never been taught to any man. He was assisted in every possible way to understand it; and as he understood it, and only so, he communicates it to others in his writings. The idea that these writings were intended to supersede in any way or measure the Word of God, or to add to it or supplement it, would have shocked him; for the purpose of his whole work was to enforce and illustrate that Word.

What must be the difference between the Word of God and the words of men? No one can answer this question fully; but some things we may say about it. For if we believe that all life proceeds from Him, that it flows forth, forming many successive spheres of being, using each higher one as the medium through which it forms the nearest lower, and finally ultimating itself in the lowest, we may believe that this is the law of the truth flowing forth from Him, and ultimating itself in the words which are given to man. This truth is the same truth in each of these degrees or spheres, — the highest and the lowest; but in each of them it has the form which is suited to that degree of being. All these degrees or forms of truth are ultimated in and are contained in the last and lowest, — the written Word. If this were a man's word, the truth would have flowed down to it through all these planes of being; but when it reached man and became his thought, it would have become his own, and would have been no longer God's truth, but what the state and character of the man made it to be. But the Word of God, although expressed by the use of human instruments, was never given to them as their own; for their ownhood of life was suspended, that they might become these instruments.

In the Word, all these higher forms of truth, or all these truths, are in the lowest or literal form. This is made possible by the law of correspondence, which connects all these degrees of being together, and all with Him from whom they flow forth as from their primal cause. By force of this law, every lower degree responds to the higher which was its causative medium, and is that higher in a lower form. By force of this law, every truth in the Word upon a lower plane responds to a truth upon a higher plane, and is that truth expressed in a lower form. All these truths are there, and we may arrange them into two classes: one, the lowest, literal sense; the other, the higher or spiritual sense.

These truths are there. But are they there *for man?* Yes, by force of this same law of correspondence; for a knowledge of this correspondence explains and applies this law, and, by the interpretation of the lowest sense, unveils the meaning of a higher sense. Each lower sense veils the higher from those who live on the lower plane of being to which that lower sense is adapted, and whose minds are not lifted above that lower plane. The knowledge of correspondences lifts the mind upwards and makes the lowest sense transparent. This knowledge may be systematized; and this systematized knowledge is the science of correspondence.

This science is now given to man; not in its fulness and entirety, for that would be beyond its possible reception, and therefore it would be given in vain. We live in the beginning of a new era. Divine Providence has waited for the need and the possibility of even this beginning. The thick darkness which has gathered through the long succession of ages of ignorance and falsity still hangs upon us all. If, through these ages, seeds of truth and light have been sown and germinated and grown, and have at last made it possible for new and greater light to be thrown upon the darkness, this great gift must still be given under the universal law of adaptation to those to whom it is given, and therefore to us only in an inchoate and incomplete manner. This science was taught to Swedenborg, and is given to mankind by him. He has given us the fact of correspondence and its general laws and principles. He has given us, by an application of these principles, the spiritual sense of Genesis, Exodus, and the Apocalypse; and, in illustration and enforcement of the meaning of these books, he has given the spiritual meaning of many passages in other books of Scripture.

The universal correspondence between all the planes of being has made it possible to include all truths within the form and expression of literal truth. The science of correspondence teaches the higher truths which lie within the lower. In doing this, it will show that whatever thing exists in Nature had a spiritual cause, and from that a spiritual meaning. All the order and beauty and magnificence of Nature, which, even in their mystery, have lifted up some happy hearts to their Creator, — all will be made vocal; and their songs of praise — perfect in harmony, and ever-growing in melody — will sound, even to men's hearts, the wisdom and power, and, more than all, the goodness of Him who is the All-Father. Then will the prophecy be fulfilled; for "He will destroy in this mountain the face of the covering cast over all people, and the veil that is spread over all nations."

Is this a work to be done at once or soon? The science of astronomy, from the far-distant ages when the watchers of the stars on the plains of Chaldea first observed them, has been growing to this day; when, however perfect some may think it, other and wise men regard it as only in its beginning. This new science is as much more radiant than the other as the stars of the spirit are brighter than the stars of the sky, as much higher as the laws of heaven are higher than the laws of material worlds; and who will count the ages which must elapse before it can attain what may be regarded as a full development?

Man is not born into the faculty of speech or of reading and writing, but with the capacity of acquiring these faculties; and they can be acquired only step by step, and by continuous effort. So must it be with learning to read the spiritual sense of Scripture and the meaning of the book of Nature. These things also must be learned only step by step, and by continuous effort. He who enters upon the investigation of the science of correspondence, and gives it up because of the difficulties he meets with at the beginning of his study, acts like the petulant child, who, discouraged by the efforts required, casts his book away, insisting that it cannot be read, or that it is not worth reading. Speech was given to man, probably, soon after he began to be; then, after a long period, came written language, and, after another period, the invention of printing. Now, a new faculty is placed within his reach; for the fact of correspondence of all that is without with all that is within is made known to him; and with this fact the principles are given which will enable him to acquire some knowledge of the science that discovers and explains these correspondences. It would be impossible to forecast the whole effect of this consummating gift; it is the close of an ascending series: the close, because it deals with infinites and universals, and can never be exhausted; and nothing more can be given but added means of acquiring, comprehending, and applying this science. We may regard it as a reasonable conclusion, that so much as the arts of writing and printing have done towards elevating and advancing men beyond the point they could have reached had these gifts been withheld, so much will the science of correspondence — in the far-distant ages, when its work shall reach a high development — do towards elevating and advancing men beyond the point which they could have reached had this science never been given.

As yet we have nothing like an elementary or educational work adapted to beginners in the study of this science. Swedenborg assumes it as existing, and applies it as he has occasion to the passages of Scripture he explains. He does little more than this, and nothing more has been done; but he lays down with great clearness the principles of the science, and from these will be evolved in coming time all that will be necessary or useful to those who would learn this science.

THE BIBLE.

Of the Bible which we have, a few of the earliest chapters were taken from an earlier Word, which differed from the present, inasmuch as it contained only truths of correspondence; that is, only a spiritual meaning, and not literal truth. Under the form of an historical account of the creation of the natural world, and the fall of man, and finally the almost total extinction of men, — they describe the beginning, the decay, and termination of a spiritual creation; or of the establishment and decline of the earliest church among men. These chapters were placed as an introduction to the Word which we have, in part because, by their apparent description of the creation and early history of the world, they serve as a fitting introduction to the historical Word. They are placed there far more because in their spiritual meaning they set forth truths of infinite moment, eternal duration, and universal application, concerning the birth, growth, and perils of spiritual goodness in every man and every age and every church.

After the long period during which primeval man lived "*sicut feræ*," or in a way of life but little higher than that of animals, "The spirit of God moved upon the face of the waters." Spiritual light dawned upon the heaving waste of his merely natural life, and the first Church was established. Swedenborg says it was established in Mesopotamia and the countries adjacent for a considerable distance; when or how many ages ago we know not. He calls this the "Most Ancient Church." It was very peculiar, responding to the needs of the infancy of mankind. In its beginning, it was pure and holy; and it subsequently fell away, and became wholly corrupted, through the abuse of that freedom which is given to man for his highest good. This abuse caused an evil influence to come forth from elements of human nature which are inseparable from it, — the ownhood of life, and power of self-determination, — because without them man would be incapable of "working out his salvation," and building himself into the largest receptibility of the gift of happiness. He was told not to eat of the "tree of the knowledge of good and evil." To eat, is to appropriate to ourselves; we make what we eat our own and a part of ourselves. He was permitted to discern most distinctly the difference between good and evil; and all good influences told him and taught him, that this knowledge was given him from God for his guidance; and all evil influences told him and taught him, that this knowledge was his own, not by gift from his Creator, but in its origin, — that it was self-acquired, and belonged to him by virtue of the power and intelligence which were self-derived and self-possessed. These evil influences told him to cast away all grateful acknowledgment of God as the giver of all knowledge and of all truth, to eat of this tree, and be to himself "as God, knowing good and evil" from himself. To these influences he yielded. He denied and deserted his

God, and strove to avoid the thought of Him, or to hide from His presence; he became as God to himself, and worshipped himself. So he fell from his high estate. So the Church fell from its early innocence; not by the disobedience of one man, nor by one act, but by a long-descending course of failure in temptation, until there grew up a state of mind in which man gave the victory within himself to evil influences over good ones, — to evil over good. And this is symbolized in the account of what we call the Fall of Man.

When the spirit of God moves upon the face of the waters in any mind, and there is in it the first germination of good, there is some foretaste of peace. But soon the tempter comes. He moves us to look upon our goodness as our own work. A conflict begins between this influence, this temptation, and all within us which recognizes our own impurity, and our inability to cope with it without strength from on high, and which inspires humble gratitude to the Divine mercy which has given us this strength. Every feeling of this kind is insidiously attacked by our sensuous nature; for this tells us that we have conquered by our own strength, and the very goodness we are conscious of becomes an evil thing, for it is corrupted into food for self-pride and self-love, and builds up a barrier against all recognition, obedience, worship, or love of Him to whom these are due. If this enemy of our souls prevails, we fall. Well is this sensuous nature symbolized by the serpent, which cannot leave the ground; and, if it conquers in this strife and holds its victory, will creep upon its belly and feed on dust for evermore. And in these days how it clings to the ground, looking upon sense and sensuous thought as the only teacher of truth, and finding all its nourishment in the dust of the earth! Happily we are told, that while it will continue to bruise the heel, or that part of human nature which comes in contact with all that belongs to earth, "the seed of the woman" shall eventually bruise its head.

This first fall of man, which includes all subsequent decline, is followed by the successive decay of this Church, which is treated of in the following chapters.

The next prominent fact narrated symbolizes the next essential element of spiritual death. Because of the long-continued indulgence and confirmation of the evil thing, we are now born with the inheritance of a proclivity to self-pride and self-love. We can resist and overcome it, only by learning the truth which exposes its true nature and tells us how to suppress it, and then by obeying this truth. In this work, the understanding must take the lead, and gradually reform and purify the will, which will then be filled with true life — the life of love. Faith must take the lead, and open the way for charity. Faith is the first born, and is represented by Cain, while charity is represented by Abel. Faith, truth, must take the lead; but only in the beginning, and until charity comes into full life, — for all the worth of faith consists in its leading to charity. But in human nature there lies deeply hidden the propensity to exalt faith over charity, belief over life, the understanding over the will. Faith seeks to rule alone, to claim all sovereignty, to be the master while charity is the servant; and at length charity is wholly thrown aside as valueless, while to faith alone is attributed the whole work of salvation. Then the end is reached, and Cain kills Abel.

It is commonly thought, by those who think about the matter at all, that "faith alone" is to be found only in the theological doctrines which rest upon it as their basis. This is indeed a very great mistake. They are but a consummation of that which in less intensity is very common. "Faith alone" shows itself everywhere to those who know how to recognize its presence in its influence and effects. Wheresoever there is a preference of belief over life and act, a disposition to think that character and destiny are determined by belief rather than by the affections which govern the life (a disposition which easily passes into the substitution of profession for belief); wherever there is any tendency to consider profession and a name as having some virtue in themselves, whether it be slight or strong enough to make us prominent and violent in defence of the doctrines which we think are saving us without the trouble of goodness; wherever there is a willingness to consider mere belief and loud assertion of truth as the equivalent of loving it and living it; wheresoever the intellect is placed above the heart, and culture, knowledge, and mere belief have a value assigned to them which is disconnected from life and character,—there is faith alone. And are not its traces everywhere?

This most ancient Church continued to decline through a period which was probably a very long one. The stages of this decline were marked, each having its own peculiarities; and they constituted what may be regarded as derivative or subordinate churches of the most ancient Church. They are designated by the series of antediluvian patriarchs, none of whom were persons. The peculiarities of each were described in the events which befell each, and intimated in their names. At length the consummation came. Falsities had overwhelmed the Church like a deluge. They were so extreme and intense that they suffocated even natural life, and this was nearly extinguished in that Church. A few only survived, who were represented by Noah, and with them there began a new Church, differing altogether from that which preceded it. This Ancient Church, — for so this Church, beginning with Noah, is called by Swedenborg, — continued for many ages, which were represented by "the generations of Noah," and described symbolically by the events and the persons named, until at length it passed away, and was succeeded by the Hebraic Church, which takes its name from Eber, or Heber. This Church also continued through many spiritual changes and generations, and with Abraham, or his immediate ancestry, the history becomes literally true.* Abraham was an actual living man; and

* Within the last half-century, the peculiar learning necessary for a critical examination of the Scriptures has greatly increased, and it has been used by many writers, some of great ability, to prove that the books of the Bible were written by other authors than those whose names they bear, and not in the forms which they now have, nor at the times supposed. It does not fall within the scope of this work to consider these speculations, nor would it be necessary, for these writers do most conclusively refute each other. Of their speculations, which are numerous and utterly discordant, Dean Milman said well, that the authors do not attempt "to make bricks without straw, but to make them wholly of straw, and offer them as solid materials." Among those opposed to them, some adhere to the literal truth of every word of Scripture, in the belief that a failure in any part of this truth would impeach, if not destroy, the authority of the Scriptures. I do not share this belief nor this fear. The difficulties in holding to the literal truth of the whole Scripture are very great. I do not possess the learning which would enable me to judge of them critically; but of one thing I am entirely confident, and that is, that the books which compose what I consider the inspired Scriptures, were written at such times and by such persons, as to admit of the inspiration which makes them the Word of God.

I have said that the assailants of the literal truth of the Bible hold with his grandson Jacob, or Israel, the Israelitish Church began,—although it was not fully established until a later day, when the Israelites were led forth from Egypt.

---

discordant theories, and conclusively refute each other. This they do in most particulars. But there are some general propositions in which they mainly agree; arguments in their favor derived from recent investigations have great force, and they are accepted by most of the defenders of the Bible who do not hold to its exact literal truth. These are,—that the first chapters of Genesis were derived from earlier traditions or scriptures, and are without exact literal truth; that the names of the Patriarchs, which, like all other Hebrew names, are significant, probably served to indicate different races or tribes; that those early chapters, so far as they are histori-cal, refer to a part only of mankind, and to a limited region of the earth; and that there are passages of Scripture which, whether or not interpolated, will not bear a literal construction. Now it is, to say the least, remarkable that Swedenborg, more than a hundred years ago, without the especial learning such investigations require, and before the critical apparatus necessary for them existed, came, in his own way, to conclusions, not in exact, but still in singular, accordance with these. For he holds, as I have already stated, that Genesis, as far as Eber (or rather Heber, from whom came the name of the Hebrews), was taken from an earlier Word, which was so writ-ten as to express spiritual truths under the form of a constructed history; that the names of the Patriarchs indicate (not successive tribes or races, but) successive churches, or systems and modes of faith and worship; that the history in these chapters, so far as it is history, relates to a part only of mankind, and to a limited region of the earth (Mesopotamia and the countries adjacent, to a considerable distance); and that in the books which are actually historical are passages in which the spiritual truths to be expressed by correspond-ence required some departure from literal natural truth, and hence these passages do not describe an actual occurrence, but have a differ-ent meaning. This last statement applies, I suppose, not only to the ages of the Patriarchs, but to the numbers in the historical books which seem to present insuperable difficulties.

Recently, there have been earnest efforts to reconcile the established facts of science with the early chapters of Genesis; nor have they been wholly unsuccessful. By supposing a day to mean, not a natural day, but a distinct period of great length, regarding Adam as the parent of a special race, confining the deluge to a limited tract of country, and other similar accommodations, the creation of earth, of animals, and of man as narrated in Genesis, is made to coincide, though very loosely, with the conclusions of geology and other paleontological sciences. So, too, recent discoveries and theories in philology and ethnology have led some persons,—not wholly without reason,—to see in history the Hamites, Shemites, and Japhethites fulfilling the statements and prophecies concerning them. And yet we say that the first eleven chapters of Genesis, as far as the immediate ancestry of Abraham, are without literal truth.

An explanation of this we can give only by referring to the doctrine of correspondences. In those chapters of Genesis we have a spiritual history of mankind, and of the earlier churches. This spiritual history is adequately expressed in what purports to be an external history of mankind, by reason of the correspondence between spiritual things and natural things. These natural things were narrated without reference to actual occurrences, but in just such a form as would suffice to represent and signify the spiritual history. But the correspondence between internal and causative facts, and external facts or effects, causes this external history to have some literal truth, or some accordance with actual facts, though only of the most general kind. Times are mentioned as the ages of the patriarchs with so much exactness, that a chronology has been constructed, and, until of late, generally received. But by these patriarchs were signified not men but churches; and as times, like all other natural things, have their correspondence, and through their correspondence their significance, these times, while without literal truth as the lives of men, have their spiritual significance in reference to the churches which bear the names of the patriarchs. If natural science is, or shall be, able to construct a chronology of those primeval times, nothing in the Scripture narrative will, in our view, give to it either support or contradiction.

With Abraham a new order of things begins, and there is a great change in the letter of the Word. It becomes literally historical, although the literal sense continues to be, in the whole and in every part, correspondent to spiritual truth, and significant of that truth.

The Israelitish Church was a most peculiar Church. In fact it never was a true Church, but only a representative Church, or rather the representative of a true Church. The Israelitish nation were selected not because they were among the best of men, but because they were very far from this. They were so entirely natural or sensual in thought, character, and disposition, that they could be led along through a series of events such that the narration of them would be made perfectly correspondent and significative, with less harm or peril to themselves than might have been caused to any other race.

To explain this, I must say something of profanation; and the doctrines which relate to this grievous and destructive evil are among the new truths which are now given to men. If truth is offered to a man, he may be perfectly insensible to it; wholly unable to understand it, or to receive it. It will then do him neither good nor harm, for it will not enter into him and make a part of him. It may be asked how can truth do any man harm? If truth be understood, received, and acknowledged, it at once carries with it the duty of obedience, of preservation and cultivation, and of a life in accordance with it. Where truth has been received because the evidence of it or its own inherent light are for the time irresistible, and afterwards, when opposing elements of character come into full force, is rejected and denied and cast out of the life,— there the truth has been the means of great harm:

falsehood is confirmed, and the possibility of a future recovery is diminished. This is the sin of profanation. It is frequently referred to in the Bible, but generally under the veil of symbols. It is represented in the law of Moses by leprosy, that most distressing disease which it is so difficult to cure. In the Gospels, it is referred to as the unpardonable sin. If a man has listened to the truth as the gift of God, and suffered it to amend his heart and life, and afterwards, deluded by the uprising of self-confidence and the pride of self-intelligence, believed that it was all his own work, ascribing it to his self-intelligence and self-excellence, regarding his former belief that it was wrought only by the strength that God gave, as an illusion and a folly, — wofully is that man's state changed for the worse. The devil that left him has returned with seven more to find his former home swept and garnished for his reception and his permanent abode.

Not in Scripture only, but in life and in all Providence, we may see the Divine effort to guard men from this great danger. We may thus understand those texts which say that the Lord hath blinded their eyes and hardened their hearts, lest they should see and understand, "and I should heal them." Better is it that they should not be healed, if their temporary health would bring with it more fatal disease.

The Word of God as a whole is addressed to all possible conditions of human beings. Therefore, in its higher and highest senses it speaks to those in the higher and highest of these conditions; and in its lowest and literal sense to those in the lowest of them. It was addressed to the Jews, primarily, in this literal sense; and was in exact adaptation to them, that it might be in exact adaptation to all in all ages, who stand where they stood. There is scarcely a reference in it to another life. All the motives to obedience, whether of promise or of threat, of reward or of punishment, are drawn from this life. In the same sense, it is and always will be addressed to all who, like the Jews, are only natural, and therefore incapable of being moved by any thing more spiritual. To them, as to the Jews, God is a hard and jealous master. So He awakens in them that "fear of the Lord" which is said in the Psalm to be "the beginning of wisdom." Even in this literal sense, there are passages unequalled in sublimity by any human composition, because in them the spiritual shines through the natural; and the good of all ages have found in them instruction, consolation, hope, and joy. But these passages were to the Jews, generally, a dead letter; and if the whole Word had been, in its literal sense, higher than it was, it would have been to them, and to all like them, dead, or worse than dead. It was in mercy that their eyes were blinded and their hearts hardened by their naturalness; and so it is to-day with all in whom this naturalness and worldliness prevail. They are taught only what will lift them up, — one step, and then another, and another, if they will; until at length they rise out of the darkness of mere naturalism, and stronger and purer light from God out of heaven can reach them without exposing them to the fearful danger of profanation.

This same principle has governed the action of Divine Providence throughout the history of mankind, and in all His dealings with races, nations, and churches, and with every individual. First, stands the law that only through man's free and voluntary coöperation will God give to man His greatest gifts, for only so can they be given in the fullest measure; and therefore from the humblest and lowest condition must mankind and every man of his kind work himself upwards by the strength given him to that end. And with this law comes another: the gifts of truth are always so measured, so qualified, or so withheld, that, while they are ever enough to teach the willing mind and lead the willing heart, they are forced upon no reluctant acceptance, but may be rejected by all who are not willing to receive them. And most of all is Providential care exerted, that spiritual truth shall not become accessible and attractive to those who, when their ruling loves again become triumphant, would be sure to reject or pervert it. Therefore is this great sin of profanation rare. But wholly prevented it cannot be; for whatsoever is given to man is given to his freedom, and he may abuse it even to the extent of profanation if he will, — and he sometimes does.

It may indeed be asked by some, If this new gift of truth on which the New-Church is founded, be of such transcendent worth as I have supposed, why has not He who has given it for the good of mankind provided for its wider and more rapid growth? Why has He deposited it in such feeble hands, and not called some of the princes of knowledge to impart to it the prestige of their greatness, and set it forth with all the charm of eloquence, and all the glory which genius could cast upon it? The answer is, Because it is better for mankind that it should obey the universal law of adaptation. It is better that the progress of this truth should be slow, and its reception so narrow as to be almost unseen, rather than it should be so presented to unprepared multitudes as that some, however excellent in the ways which the truths they possess have shown them, would be unable to receive this new truth, and harm themselves by its rejection; and others would receive it only to expose it to perversion and profanation. This truth is permitted to find its way to the hearts and minds of the few who have received it, not because they are better or worse than others, but because they could be helped by it more than by any other truth.

THE ISRAELITISH CHURCH.

Under the guidance of this principle of adaptation, the Israelites were chosen as a race among whom could be established a perfect representative of a Church; but under the protecting veil of a symbolic representation. This was effected by positive revelations, variously but stringently enforced, which, in the tabernacle and temple worship, and in a law and ritual which penetrated into social, family, and daily life, expressed in symbolic language precisely the requirements and the characteristics of a true spiritual Church. These literal expressions signify by correspondence, answering spiritual truths and laws. Then the race was carried through a history which, told for the most part with literal accuracy, expressed in its literal language what in its spiritual correspondence was a spiritual history,— as true of one race as of another, of one time as of another, and of one man as of another. Not that all which is spiritually told there befalls all races and all men, but that nothing can befall any race or any men which does not find its lesson there. It would be impossible, without going too far beyond the scope and character of this little work, to give these lessons in any detail. That the history of the Israelites has some spiritual meaning has always been seen by all who looked upon the Scriptures as holy. For example, the journey from Egypt to Canaan, the sanctity of the temple and of Mount Zion, are matters frequently referred to in the sermons and religious writings of most Christian sects. In the early ages of Christianity, the spiritual sense of Scripture was generally acknowledged; and some — Origen, for example — labored earnestly to discover and exhibit this sense. But the time had not come when the laws and principles of correspondence could be given; and by them alone can this spiritual sense be made accurate, continuous, and coherent.

For a long succession of ages, the Bible has been protected against the assaults of a purely natural criticism by the reverence which hung about it an impenetrable armor. That time has gone by. Now, reverence for any thing is feeble, and seems to be growing feebler every day. The Bible which, to some persons, is still a most interesting topic of investigation on religious grounds, is to others an interesting topic of inquiry on the most external and purely natural grounds. Learned and able men devote themselves to the work of disproving its inspiration, and exposing what such criticism as theirs holds to be its errors. Its defenders are feeble, however earnest; and it is impossible to deny that the Bible has fallen in men's minds far below its former high estate. The ground taken by modern criticism is, that the Bible must be investigated and criticised, and accepted or rejected as this criticism determines, precisely like any other book, — which would be true if the Bible were like other books; and is just as untrue as that is. It may be that this conclusion has not been generally reached; and certainly it is not by all religious men. But equally certain it is that the Bible seems to be falling under the blows of its adversaries, and needs a new and stronger defence, if any portion of its ancient sanctity is to be restored to it. These late assaults upon it, and this decay of an unreasoning reverence, have been permitted, because means are now given for awakening a reverence for it far deeper than has ever been felt, and of founding this reverence on grounds which the strictest rationality will maintain.

The assaults upon the Bible have been almost wholly on the following grounds: First, that there is not and cannot be any such thing as inspiration, or as an inspired book. Then, the uncertainty as to the authorship and dates of the several books, and of the canon of Scripture. Then, the apparent contradiction by passages of Scripture of the most certain principles of morality, and its imputation to the Deity of wrath, cruelty, and vengeance. Then, its inconsistencies. And then, the demonstrable inaccuracy of some of its statements. To all these objections an answer can be given, and against them there is now an adequate defence.

As to the first and most general objection, — that there is no such thing as inspiration or an inspired book, — this is an objection which cannot but prevail with all those who do not believe in spirit as a real existence, distinct from matter; that is, with all those whose thoughts are only sensuous thoughts, and whose reason is only a sensuous reason, whether that reason be coarse, rude, and wholly uncultivated, or carried forward to the highest point of external culture and refinement. And to this objection the answer is given by the truths now made known concerning the relation of God to man, and of spirit to matter. As these are understood, inspiration will be understood, and an inspired book be seen to be a communication from God to man, and to the highest reason of man.

As to the uncertainty of the authorship and dates of the several books, so far as we think of it at all, we recognize in it a provision which lessens the tendency to regard the books as merely human books, which would certainly be stronger if the individual writers were well known. The canon of Scripture has greatly fluctuated as to both Testaments. There is but one standard which can be depended upon. No book contains the Word of God, unless it contains from beginning to end, and in all its parts, a continuous spiritual sense founded on the correspondence between spirit and matter. We should not venture, on our own knowledge of this correspondence, to apply this test rigorously. On this point we accept the statement of Swedenborg, who, on this ground, excludes from the commonly accepted canon of Protestant Scripture, Ruth, Chronicles, Ezra, Nehemiah, Esther, Job, Proverbs, Ecclesiastes, and the Song of Solomon; and, from the New Testament, the Acts, and all the Epistles.

Of the opposition of some parts of the Bible to a pure morality, and of the imputation to God of the qualities of a bad man, the explanation is to be found in the nature and purpose of the Word, and the method in which that purpose is accomplished. God has spoken that Word to men to lift them up. It addresses them in the very lowest moral and spiritual condition in which they can exist. It speaks to them in a way they can understand, and addresses to them motives by which they can be influenced. For this purpose, God is represented very differently in different places, because He is presented to all as that which their God would be. It is said in Psalm xviii., "With the merciful thou wilt show thyself merciful; with an upright man thou wilt show thyself upright; with the pure thou wilt show thyself pure; and with the froward thou wilt show thyself froward." Let a man's disposition be what it may, it will be sure to give color and form to the conception he will have of God from reading the Bible. If he be down in the depths of sinfulness, and his heart and mind are closed against all but the lowest motives, the terror of an angry and avenging God may restrain and help him. If he accepts the help, and is restrained from his evil ways, and gradually grows better, at whatever point of elevation he may reach, he will find, even in the literal sense of the Word, assurances of a gracious Father, of perfect mercy, and unfailing love.

As to the objection to the Bible, founded on the immorality of some of its chief persons, and the savage cruelty of the chosen people, — we reply that this people were chosen that they might exhibit, in their extirpation of the corrupted heathen who then possessed Palestine, the processes, often painful and distressing, by which correspondent corruptions may be extirpated from the heart which they have taken possession of. The inhabitants of Canaan at that time were descendants from the ancient and Hebraic churches, and had reached that fulness of depravity that it was well for them that they should pass away. The Israelites were in their own nature hard and savage, and were permitted to obey the dictates of their nature, wholly unconscious of what they were representing. Vice and sin of every kind grew by indulgence among all ranks of them, until at length they completed their own work, and brought destruction on the nation. Thus they represented in their whole career, the establishment, the growth, the decay, and the death of a church among men; and not this only, but of the church — or the good and the truth — in every man who afterwards pursues a downward path. These paths are as many and as various as the men who take them; but all are included in this representation.

Perhaps it may be well to show what different construction the spiritual meaning gives to the natural meaning. Let us, in the difficulty of choosing, take almost without choice, as an example, the closing verses of Psalm cxxxvii., in which it is said, "O daughter of Babylon who is to be destroyed, . . . happy he that taketh and dasheth thy little ones against the stones." I have more than once heard this cited as giving great difficulty to those who would see in the Psalms only songs of praise and prayer to a God of love. In the literal sense, these words are full of the most savage cruelty; in the spiritual sense, they describe a blessedness which the best man may well pray for every day of his life. As the whole world of matter corresponds to the whole world of spirit, so, as has been said, all that is material must correspond either to what belongs to the understanding or to the will; for these two compose and constitute the whole of the spirit, each half being indefinitely diversified. Rocks and stones are perfectly devoid of life, and are among the things which correspond to and represent the things of the understanding; and more especially those truths which are positive, abiding, and fundamental. Thus our Lord speaks of the house that is founded upon a rock, that the floods and the winds assail it in vain; for so it is with the house of faith, — the intellectual structure in which a man makes his home, and which spiritual floods and winds beat upon in vain, if it be founded upon a clear perception and firm belief of the foundation truths upon which all genuine faith must rest. So He said to Peter, "Upon this rock will I build my church," referring to the truth Peter had just declared, — "Thou art the Christ, the Son of the living God;" for against a church, whether of many or of one, built on this foundation, the gates of hell cannot prevail. Stones are more special truths, of like kind, each of which forbids and rebukes the sin opposed to it; and the power to dash the little ones of the enemies of our souls against the stones is a power from our Heavenly Father to dash the earliest emotions of evil, — the newly-born children of sin, — even in their infancy, against the truths which expose and defeat them, and take their life away.

All good may be perverted into evil, and all truth into falsity; and there is no evil which is not a perverted good, and no falsity which is not a perverted truth. Hence, most things mentioned in the Scriptures have a twofold significance; in one place representing what is good or true, and in another what is evil or false. Thus stones are often used to represent falsities; as, when our Lord said, "I and my Father are one," the Jews, representing the natural man or mind, "took up stones to stone him." And in the parable in Matthew xiii., and Mark iv., the "stony places" and "stony ground" represent a mind so overstrewn with falsities, that truths sown there could not take abiding root.

That modern criticism has established the opposition between some of the facts stated in the Bible and those which the progress of science has demonstrated, cannot be denied; and some Biblical statements, especially where numbers are concerned, are impossible. To objections of this kind, the answer is that God has not spoken to man to reveal to him either natural science or the history of the race, or of a nation. His purpose was altogether other than this. This has been often said before; but now, and not until now, we can understand the true nature and purpose of the Bible, and the way in which it accomplishes its purpose. God gives to man, as inherent in his nature, powers entirely adequate in their normal and natural exercise to the gradual acquirement of all knowledge of a natural kind, or needed for this life. God speaks to him in a way that is higher than his nature, to give him truth which he could not otherwise possess; spiritual truth, religious truth, — of which not one particle could come to him any more than it comes to animals, if it did not come to him in a supra-natural way. This spiritual sense or meaning of the Bible is the primary thing. It is preserved at all events and perfectly. By means of the correspondence between spirit and matter, it could be expressed in natural forms which are for the most part literally true, and in this natural form it could come to natural men, and reach their understandings and their hearts. But where this expression was impossible, because no natural forms which were literally true were capable of containing this spiritual sense, there natural forms which were not literally true were of necessity employed. For this spiritual truth is the gift of God to men in every possible condition, even to the highest which created beings can attain, and therefore it is perfect. Our eyes are opened to see it only partially and imperfectly. In coming ages, as the race rises into higher needs and higher capacities, more and yet more of this truth will be seen, and seen with greater distinctness. The limit is all of it in the seer and none of it in the truth, for infinite truth is condensed and embodied in this literal truth.

Of the Gospels I shall have more to say when I speak of the acts and words of our Lord. The Acts and the Epistles, it has been already stated, are excluded from the canon of the New Testament, because they were not inspired in the sense already given to the word inspiration. They are excellent and valuable writings, containing much religious truth of great importance, and have been useful not only for the truth they contain, but for their protection of the inspired books, by drawing away from them the assaults of a sceptical and hostile criticism, or of a false and pernicious interpretation, which have, in large measure, exhausted themselves upon the Epistles.

The prophetical writings are not everywhere prophecies of the future. In some passages they regard the present; and describe, in words of fearful denunciation, the corruptions prevailing all around the prophet. In others, they threaten calamity and destruction as the doom of transgressors. But in many others they describe, as in a far future, the coming of the Messiah, the establishment of His kingdom, the restoration of Israel, and a reign of peace that is to know no end. This prophecy has always been referred by Christians to the coming of the Lord. This is well. But in an interior sense it refers to His second coming. So understood, the prophets bear testimony, not only in general but in their details, to the establishment of the New-Church; and to its growth, its character, and its influence, as a whole, and in every mind to which it can find entrance.

The Psalms are quite distinct from any other parts of Scripture. In their literal sense, they are songs of praise and prayer. In their spiritual sense they set forth the spiritual history of our Lord: His temptations, His conflicts, His sufferings, and His victories. Because there is no way to heaven but to take up our cross and follow Him, and this not merely in a general way but most specifically, the Psalms in their spiritual sense are applicable to every man who is seeking to walk in the path which our Saviour trod; and at every step they give him, and always have given him, guidance, strength, and consolation.

Of the book of Job we have already said that it has not a constant and continuous spiritual sense, and therefore is not properly a part of Holy Scripture; nor does Swedenborg say much of it, although he sometimes quotes from it. He tells us that some knowledge of correspondences existed among very ancient races, who had very little of natural science;

and that the book of Job was composed when much of that knowledge remained with the posterity of those races. It may be regarded as a long parable. Under the guise of a good and very wealthy man, who is bereft of every thing, and long and sorely tempted but never overcome, and in the end restored to greater wealth and prosperity,—it narrates the spiritual history of a good man, who is conscious and proud of his goodness, and suddenly awakes to a sense of the taint which lies upon that goodness, and, by long and painful temptation, is brought to a knowledge of his utter wretchedness without God; and when at length, accepting and taking to his heart the truth that all human goodness is the gift of God only, he gives to Him the glory, he is restored to more than his former peace and happiness.

Of the Apocalypse we must say more. Very many have been the efforts to explain this book as a prophecy of external history, by applying its statements to various historical events. These efforts have been utterly vain and useless, for the plain reason that this book refers solely and exclusively to the spiritual history of the Christian Church. After describing the falsities and errors which beset it even in its beginning, it goes on to describe its gradual decay and decline, until its corruption was consummated. It then relates the judgment which took place in the spiritual world, establishing new heavens, under whose influence a new earth would be created by the descent to earth from heaven of a new church, which is called the New Jerusalem. A great number of details concerning all these topics are specifically set forth. All of these are wholly unintelligible, unless a knowledge of the correspondences in accordance with which the book is composed casts its light upon them. Then they are full of information; not speculative, and not merely general; but intensely practical, and infinitely greater in interest and importance to the well-being of mankind than any prophecy concerning political or external history could be.

There are undoubtedly some passages in the Word to which, if they are regarded only in the literal sense, it is difficult to attach any meaning; and many, especially in the historical narratives, to which it is impossible to attach any religious meaning, if they are so regarded. But these were necessary to the continuity and completeness of the spiritual sense. There is also much — indeed, nearly all the ritualistic portion of the Old Testament — which has no longer obligatory force or application in the literal sense. But all these portions — as will be seen when their correspondences are known — contain in their spiritual sense instruction of inestimable value. And there are other passages, in which the spiritual sense shines forth with its own light, imparting a sublimity to which none can be dead but those who are wholly blinded by sense or sin. Swedenborg compares these passages to the face which is not clothed, and in which the character shines forth unveiled.

Let it not be supposed for a moment that the belief in the spiritual sense of the Bible has the slightest tendency to depreciate the literal sense. On the contrary, a firm belief that it is the basis, the continent, and the expression of a heavenly and an infinite sense gives to it new force and sanctity. The commandments therein set forth are the words of God to man, given to guide him to happiness and to heaven. In their literal sense, they are addressed to him in his lowest and most external condition. But this is a condition which no man can ever pass through in such wise that it no longer belongs to him. Among the heresies which have darkened the Christian Church, have been some which permitted men to believe that they could rise to so lofty a spiritual state that the natural or external became utterly unimportant, and that it was then safe for them to disregard the commandments of the Word, and to indulge their lusts. What truth can more effectually rebuke this terrible falsity than that which teaches us that internal goodness (if it were possible) without a corresponding life, would be a soul without a body, an essence without a form, — a mere impossibility!

Gladly would I close this most imperfect view of the Bible with fitting words; but I have none such. How can the words of man speak adequately of the Word of God? For the Bible is that, in no poetical way, and by no figure of speech, but with a reality which surpasses all other reality. Not to men only upon earth is it spoken; but when they leave this lowest life and ascend to heaven, even to the Heaven of heavens, they find it there also, — the Word of God to men: ascending in its meaning as they ascend, and ever in its inmost infinitely above them, and ever bringing down from His infinitude and His blessedness light and life to His children.

CHAPTER XIII.

THE LORD.

They who can form any conception of the incarnation of God the Father, in Jesus Christ, whether they believe it or not, may see that it must be, if true, the central fact of Divine Providence, — for which every thing that preceded it prepared, and from which every thing which follows it proceeds. They may see, too, that any comprehension of this fact must be, if not founded upon, assisted by some general understanding of the laws and order and purposes of Divine Providence, and of a personal immortality or a spiritual existence after life in this world has terminated.

Nothing of all this can be clearly understood without some knowledge of the doctrine of ownhood, or of *proprium*, as I have elsewhere called it. This has already been referred to, and must be repeatedly referred to; for I deem it fundamental to all truth that relates to Divine Providence. Of this doctrine I will endeavor again to make such a statement as seems necessary in connection with the subject of this chapter.

God loves infinitely; He *is* Love. It is the essence of love to desire to give whatever it has or is — to give itself — to an object which must be other than itself, or outside of itself.

To satisfy this desire God created and creates whatever exists; and so created and creates every thing, that it shall be other than Himself or outside of Himself.

And yet He cannot but create every thing from Himself. His infinite and perfect love would move him to do this: nor could He otherwise create, for whatever is created only of nothingness would consist only of nothingness; nor can we believe this, or indeed think it. We can think He caused thoughts or affections which belonged to His being to be embodied and existent outside of Himself, and that thus an external universe came into being. This, however, is an inadequate expression of the fact. So must any of our words be. Nor can we ever comprehend fully and adequately the method of creation. But something we may know and comprehend about it; and all of this knowledge may grow in quantity and in clearness for ever. Now, all that I venture to say is, that God creates the universe from Himself and of Himself.

But love requires an object out of itself, or other than itself. If God continually creates the universe from Himself and of Himself, how can it satisfy His infinite desire for an object of His love, which object must be other than Himself? It is precisely this question which this doctrine of *proprium* answers.

He gives to the universe He creates to be itself. He gives to it ownhood of itself, or *proprium*, that it may be itself and not God; and so may be other than Him, while created of and from Him, and an object of His love. He does not cause it to be other than Himself by creating it apart, and infusing into it a certain measure of life or energy or force, and impressing upon it certain laws in accordance wherewith this force shall continue to operate, and then letting it alone to go on of itself. With Him there is no time. He gives us the idea of time to satisfy a necessity of our finite nature; and it is difficult for us to think even of Him and His work without time. But we are capable of seeing clearly that with Him there is no time, and that His work of creation is a constant and ever-present work. And as He creates by perpetual creation, He always imparts to His creation to be itself; and so other than Him, even while its being and all that constitutes its being are incessantly derived from Him.

The universe consists of dead matter and of living creatures. All of it and all things in it are the objects of His care. But only living creatures can receive from Him happiness; and all that is not living is for the sake of what is living, and is instrumental in enabling Him to give them happiness. But what is happiness? This word expresses a feeling which cannot be defined. We may use other words, more or less synonymous, but they do not define it. It needs no definition. All men know what it is, for it is that which all men know that they desire. In form it is infinitely diversified, and so it is in measure. But all forms and all measures of it are, like life, — which is equally diversified in form and measure, — derived from one source, one infinite happiness, which is the happiness of God. Of this, which is His own happiness, He imparts to all His creatures in the form and measure in which they are capable of receiving it. Only where there is life is there happiness; and in created life, only in its highest form, — only in human life, — is there a consciousness of happiness.

Only to men does He give this consciousness of happiness; but He also gives to men much more than this. He gives to them selfhood, *proprium*, — ownership of themselves and of their life in a far higher sense than that in which He gives this to any other of His creatures. And *therefore* He gives to them the power of determining for themselves the kind and the measure of the happiness which they will make themselves capable of receiving from Him.

In Him, in life in its origin and in itself, happiness is an element of life, and is one with life. The gift of *proprium*, and of the free will or power of self-determination which flows from it, is given to man not only because Infinite Love must have objects out of itself, and could not otherwise have such objects, but because, by means of this gift, the highest possible measure of happiness may be given to those of His creatures who possess this freedom of the will; that is, to human beings. For that greatest happiness is the happiness of working with Him by choice and as of themselves, to build themselves up into the possibility of a likeness with Him, which admits of conjunction with Him; and of the perpetual and eternal growth of this likeness and this conjunction, which is at every step the result of God's working and man's free coöperation with God.

As man cannot have one particle of goodness or truth unless God gives them to him, so He cannot give them to man unless man accepts them. And man may accept the gifts of God, and utterly pervert them. He may receive from God that which should be truth in his understanding and good in his affection, and, by the abuse of his power of self-determination, he may make it falsity and evil.

It has been already said that man has no consciousness that he lives from God, or that his thoughts and affections are other than self-derived; and he begins life with no other consciousness than that his life is his own. Soon the difference between right and wrong becomes known to him. Then, if he chooses good rather than evil, he believes not only that the power of choice which he exerts is his own, which is true, but that this power belongs to and is derived from his own nature, which is false. This is, however, a falsehood which then may do no harm; for it is necessary that he should so begin his human consciousness that his selfhood, or free-will, or *proprium*, may be complete and unimpaired. But so long as he so believes, his choosing good in act has less power to make him good in spirit; for it tends to nourish self-love, self-pride, and self-contentment, — all of which are the opposites of good. There is but one real good, and that is godlikeness; for only that tends to make him capable of conjunction with God. Hence, from near the beginning of his consciousness, influences around him and within him endeavor to open his mind gradually to the truth, and to lead his will to the good which belongs to that truth. The idea of God is soon presented to him. Then other religious truths; those which, as the Commandments, tell him to avoid doing those things which would darken his thoughts and corrupt his affections. These truths are taught him in various ways, and with progressive increase and elevation in their character, if he profits by them, always being adapted by perfect wisdom to his capacities, that he may make use of them; and always rising and growing as his capacities grow by his reception of these truths in his understanding and his will, and his incorporating them into his life. By these means, and at every step forwards, his *proprium* or selfhood is vivified with a true life, and regenerated. Whensoever he rejects or abuses the means of this improvement thus given him, his *proprium* or selfhood remains what it originally was, and that is only self-love, which, when unchecked and uncontrolled, is the source and origin of all evil; and therefore his *proprium* remains only self-love, or only and altogether evil, and all that he thinks or feels or does from it is evil and only evil. Therefore also truth is never given him such in form or in measure that he cannot receive it, or, if he receives, must reject or pervert it; but always only such that he may receive it if he will, and may profit by it if he will.

The same law or principle of order, by which Divine Providence is governed in reference to individual men, governs this Providence also as to all men or the race. From the beginning, God came down to men always in forms and in measures perfectly suited to their capacities and needs. At first, by revelations and influences of which we know but little, and only as we gather that from the first chapters of Genesis, when their spiritual meaning is disclosed by the science of correspondence. Then followed successive revelations, and churches built upon them. To the Jewish Church was given a written Word. It was given, not to this church only, but to mankind; and will endure as long as mankind. It is adapted, even in its literal sense, to all men in all ages. To those who are only natural, it speaks in tones of command, — prohibiting sin and threatening disobedience with the consuming wrath of an Omnipotent God. To those capable of receiving into the understanding, heart, and life, higher truths, they are given even in the literal sense; and such men have always found them there. These truths are all expressed under natural forms; but these natural forms clothed spiritual forms, by virtue of that correspondence between spiritual things and natural things, which causes all natural things to exist as the effects of their spiritual causes.

At length, more could be done for mankind. He who had heretofore given them of His truth and His influence through all these instrumentalities, came down Himself; came to man in a human body and in a human nature; was born and grew and lived as a man among men, — Immanuel, God with us, — through the years of one generation.

There is no life but His life. Whenever conception takes place in a mother's womb, it is because life from Him, through the child's father, and therefore modified and limited by that father, came down and vivified the seed in the mother. But to the virgin Mary life came directly from Him who is Life; for He Himself, without any instrumental medium, vivified the seed in Mary's womb, and Jesus Christ was conceived and born of a virgin.

In assuming a human body and a human nature, He assumed a human *proprium;* that *proprium*, ownhood, or selfhood, which has been repeatedly spoken of. For what purpose and with what effect He assumed this *proprium*, I will endeavor to state.

It may well seem an idle thing, or worse than idle, to attempt to fathom the designs of the Omniscient and Almighty. But, thanks to His infinite mercy, it is not impossible for us to see with some clearness some part of His infinite purpose. We venture, therefore, to say that the incarnation of our Lord may be considered under five heads: —

1. The redemption of mankind.

2. The bringing of the spiritual world into order.

3. The making of the assumed humanity Divine.

4. The providing thereby of a new medium for saving influence.

5. The giving to mankind for evermore a definite object of intelligent faith, of worship, and of love.

THE REDEMPTION OF MANKIND.

Any presentation of the working of Divine Providence which supposes that He works according to a certain plan and method, and makes use of means and instruments, and advances slowly, step by step, —is open to the objection that it forgets His Omniscience and Omnipotence, and likens Him to man in a way that degrades Him. It will be said that He who knows every thing needs not to grope His way through experiments and by circuitous paths; and that He who can do what He will needs not to employ instruments or methods, nor to approach gradually the end that He would reach. All this is for man to do. He who has all knowledge and all power has but to will, and it is; as when God said "Be light," and "light was."

This objection has great weight with many minds; more perhaps than they are aware of. The obvious and immediate answer, that in point of fact growth and movement by steps, and by instruments, is the way and method of divine action, in all we see and know of it, does not satisfy them. The fact is undisputable. The whole universe, and all its parts and operations, proves and illustrates this fact or law. And not only does the dead universe prove it, but the universe of mind as well. Every thing that lives acts by its instrument, and if by no other instrument then by its body, which is its instrument. Nothing marks the elevation of man above all lower animals, more than the variety and multiplicity of the instruments which he uses. And gradual progress is another universal fact, for the law of life is growth, and when that ceases decay begins, and death approaches. Not more certain is it, that the babe grows through childhood and youth into manhood, than that the mind grows also, and in every hour of its growth, or every step of its progress, makes use of means and instruments that it may grow. Nor, is this more true of the individual than of the race. Age follows age; there is much alternation, — apparent advance being followed by apparent retreat; and advance in some places is accompanied by retreat in others. Events occur which promote advance, and then those which cause retreat; and not unfrequently those circumstances which seemed to promise advance or threaten retreat are utterly falsified by the actual result. But through it all, and as the common resultant of it all, the race does grow, and does go forward.

Either, then, there is no God, — or He has left this world to take care of itself, — or else this method of action, by successive steps, by the use of diversified instrumentalities, and in ways suited to varying conditions and needs, is the universal law of Divine action. If it be so, any method of promoting the salvation of mankind, which has not this character, would stand in exact opposition to all that we know, and all we might expect from what we know of Divine Providence.

This answer, however, to the objection above stated would tend rather to silence than to satisfy it. There is a better answer. Because this is the method of Divine action, to man can be given the blessing of using the instruments which God provides, and of unending advancement in goodness and in the happiness of working with God.

Before going farther, let me advert to a mistake on which rests much of the unwillingness to consider the Almighty as working step by step, and upon a definite plan or method. This mistake is, that there are no limits to the power of God; whereas there is a sense in which, or an aspect under which, this power is limited; for it is self-limited by the Divine love and wisdom. God *can* do nothing which He does not desire because it is the best thing for his creatures. He *can* do nothing which He does not see to be the best way of promoting that result. The Divine omnipotence is the willing and obedient servant of the Divine love and wisdom. Herein we see one of the instances of the likeness of man to God. For what can be more obvious, than that we grow in Godlikeness, or godliness, in the measure in which the strength we have is the willing and obedient servant of whatever love and wisdom there may be in us?

Let us again refer to the fact, that while God creates the universe constantly and incessantly, and always from Himself, He so creates it that it shall always be itself, or other than Him; and should always and in all things, small or great, act as of itself.

The first and perpetual effect is, that man, for whom the universe is, and to whom it is always accommodated, adjusted, and adapted by correspondence, — man must always do his part of the work in all that God does for him, wherein man can work. Innumerable, yea, infinite, are the things which God does for him, wherein he does and can do nothing; as in all that belongs to his infancy and immaturity, and in various circumstances of his life and condition. All these things, however, have but one end; and that is, to lead and help him, by all the aid which Omnipotence can yield, freely to accept the blessing offered him, and in the exercise of his own free will, and by the strength given him to that end, do what there is for him to do, that this blessing may be his. It can be his only, on the condition that he thus coöperates with God. He could not so coöperate, unless his free agency or free self-determination in spiritual things were perfectly preserved; and therefore it is preserved. And thus, while he is perfectly and instantly dependent upon God, he is always himself. In the measure in which we understand this truth or law, we shall find it easier to understand the mystery of life. And let us endeavor to cast the light of this truth upon the redemption of man by the incarnation of God in Jesus Christ.

Life flows into man in two ways: immediately and mediately. That which flows into him from God immediately, forms the basis of his life. It flows into the inmost of his being, and does not reach his consciousness. That which flows into him mediately, comes to him through angels and spirits. They who are most like him are nearest to him by the law of affinity. The life which flows through them is modified by them, and is thereby suited to him because they are like him, and are brought into connection with him by this resemblance; not by a blind law, for this influent life is always controlled by our Father, and made to be the best for him which it can be. This life forms and constitutes the whole of his conscious life. He would have no consciousness of being, no feeling, no thought, no action, and no character, but for this mediate life. It must be suited to him, that it may become his; and it is suited to him by those through whom it flows to him, because they are like to him. They are many. They are good so far as he has any thing of good in him to bring the good near to him; they are evil so far as he has evil in his character to bring evil spirits near to him. And in this way every thing in him which lives is vivified.

But not every thing within him is thus vivified. Far, very far more of that which is in him is never brought forth into his consciousness. They must have little experience or knowledge of themselves, who do not know what it is to find some trait or tendency which was wholly unexpected brought into consciousness and activity. "Is thy servant a dog, that he should do this thing?" has been the indignant exclamation of many who afterwards found themselves doing just that thing. There is no one of us who would not be amazed and shocked, could he see all the proclivities to evil which are in him by a long inheritance. But it is here that the goodness and wisdom of Providence come in especially. These proclivities do us no harm, and are not really a part of us or of our living self, while they remain latent and suppressed. And our Father so controls the influent life by which we live, that no evil tendency shall be called forth, which it is beyond our power to resist and overcome. But why, we may ask, does not His mercy, by a similar control, prevent any tendency to evil from acquiring vitality within us? Nor is there any answer to this question, excepting so far as we understand and remember that Providence places our character in our own hands, and we are gifted with the power of preparing for eternal happiness, by building up, as of ourselves, a character receptive thereof. Nor can we do this in any other way than by resisting and putting away from us, as of ourselves, an evil tendency, and then the love of the opposite good flows in, and is appropriated — or added to our *proprium* — and becomes a part of ourselves. Unless we do something of this, we do not take one step in the path of happiness; and the more of this we do, the farther we advance in this path.

That we may do this, our free-will is perfectly preserved. The influences by which we live are so balanced and equilibrated that we stand between them, living from them, and yet free: free to turn to the right or to the wrong; free to accept and appropriate and make our own the good or the evil that are within our reach; free "to choose this day whom we will serve," — and every day of our lives we make that choice.

Good spirits have no desire to disturb this equilibrium, or coerce us in any way. They know that upon the rightful exercise of our free-will depends our happiness. Evil spirits seek nothing more than to fetter this free-will, and coerce us into evil; for that will bring us into servitude to them. And now we come to the great fact which made the incarnation of our Lord necessary.

All conscious life comes to men through those in the spiritual world. Evil men become evil spirits, and the life which flows through them is evil. This evil life is equilibrated in the manner already stated. But the amount and strength of evil had gradually so increased in the spiritual world that this equilibrium had become difficult; and, if the same increase of evil had gone on, would have become impossible. Then would the free-will of mankind have perished, and with it all the hope of eternal happiness. Mankind were made captive by the enemies of their souls, and were passing under a bondage from which there would be no escape. From this captivity, from this bondage, our Lord came to redeem them. And in coming as He did come, He only pursued to its end the path He had ever followed in enabling and assisting men to work out their salvation.

Heretofore, from the beginning, truth had been given to men to help them in their combat with evil. It always came from the Divine wisdom; it always was that wisdom accommodated to man. A word is the expression of a thought. The Divine Word is the form and expression of the Divine wisdom. Always it was the Word of God which taught men how to escape from the hell within themselves, — the hell of self-love. It had come in many forms; it had come in many revelations; it had come as a written Word. But now, in man's greatest need, it came itself to men.

Let it not for a moment be supposed that the Divine wisdom came alone, or separated from the Divine love. With God, this is impossible. In man, as we all know, truth and goodness, the understanding and the will, are separated, and sometimes far apart. For we all know what it is to love that which the understanding rebukes, and have no love for that which it approves and enjoins. The will and the understanding, which are vessels for and instruments of love and wisdom, are separated and opposed when the will seeks and enjoys that which the understanding condemns.

In God, love and wisdom exist together in a perfect unity. They are separated in man during his life on earth, but that life is given him to bring them again into unity. This is done when the understanding succeeds in bringing the will, first into acknowledgment, then into obedience, and then into love for that which the understanding knows to be good. They are brought into unity also when an evil will subdues the understanding into agreement with itself, and, by its seductions, causes the understanding to see as good and to call good the evil things — the worldliness and selfishness —

which the unregenerated will loves. Blessed is he whom truth has taught the way of goodness, and who has followed that way until his will and understanding have become one in the knowledge and the love of good.

In God, love and wisdom are perfectly and absolutely one. The wisdom is always the guide, the expression, and the instrument of the love, and the love always the only motive force of the wisdom. Always, in the earliest, the later, and the latest action and manifestation of the Word, or of the wisdom of God, His love was in His wisdom as its source and life. For the Word was always with God, and was always God, and without it was nothing made (or done) which was made. In the Word made flesh, the Infinite and Divine love, and the Infinite and Divine wisdom, were together as one; and as one became flesh by assuming a human nature from the virgin Mary.

If it be asked how we can hope that a finite mind can be lifted to a conception or to an intellectual belief of an infinite, and therefore inexpressible and inconceivable, fact, — the answer is, that here also God has revealed Himself, not in His Word only, but in His work; and even in ourselves has so placed His image, that we gain from it some knowledge even of Him. Whatsoever thing a man has ever done, he did because some desire or affection moved him to do it, and caused a thought of how to do it; and when it was done, the affection and the thought met together in the act. Were there no affection, there would be no motive power; were there no thought, the motive power could not act; and only in the act could both come forth and be. From this faint image of the Infinite, we may look up, not wholly without light, even to the Infinite itself, — although the image is as far from its prototype as earth is from heaven; but earth reflects the forms of heaven.

Thus the Word made flesh was God with us, — Immanuel. He was a man, conceived within a human mother, and born of a human mother. But within that assumed humanity there was God Himself.

The Word was made flesh by the impregnation of a virgin. We have already said, that, whenever a human child begins to live, life through its father impregnates the ovum in its mother; and the child grows, and is born. But, in the case of our Lord, life came to the mother directly, and not through any human father.

When a man is regenerated, it is by resisting and overcoming the proclivities to evil, which belong to his inherited nature. Precisely so it was with our Lord; but with this difference. No evil spirits are permitted to have access to any man, and waken any of his inherited proclivities to evil, excepting those which he may, if he will, resist and srbdue. Precisely so was it with our Lord; but with this difference. In any man, the life which is his came to him through a human father, and was modified by this transmission; his power of resisting and subduing his evils is thereby modified and limited, and the evils which present themselves to his consciousness are those only which this limited power is adequate to subdue. But the life within our Lord was infinite, possessing all power; therefore all the evil tendencies in the nature inherited from the mother came forth into consciousness and conscious effort, because the life within was strong enough to resist them all, and overcome them all: and it did resist, subdue, and extirpate all of them.

With every man, the evil tendencies which awaken within him, and tempt him to sin in thought, affection, or act, are animated by evil spirits in whom those very evils have become their life. If he resists in these temptations, if he overcomes in these conflicts, he overcomes these evil spirits, and lessens and at length destroys their power to do him harm.

Precisely so was it with our Lord; but with this difference. The evil spirits by whom He was tempted, and whom He overcame, were the whole company of evil spirits; for all the powers of hell were permitted to rise up against Him; in His mother, Mary, were by long inheritance germs of all possible evil, and the work which our Lord came to do, He could therefore do completely. All of these evil spirits He conquered, and conquered perfectly; and all of them He reduced into such order, that never thereafter should they exert an overpowering influence upon man, or any influence beyond what might subserve his best interests in bringing to his knowledge and within his reach the sinful tendencies which he might overcome, — and thus giving him the means and opportunity of removing from himself those hindrances which opposed the good influences that seek to give him the life of heaven.

Thus our Lord became our Redeemer. Thus He redeemed us from slavery to sin, and bondage to evil and unhappiness.

It is common to consider redemption and salvation as the same thing. It is not so. Redemption makes salvation possible. It supplies the means, and gives the opportunity of securing salvation; it gives salvation to all who will make use of those means, and profit by that opportunity. Redemption is an accomplished fact, and is universal. Salvation comes to all who are willing to profit by their redemption, and accept the offer of salvation. Redemption means the deliverance from all those influences which would have made our salvation impossible. Salvation means an escape from sin by our acceptance of, and coöperation with, the Divine effort to save us.

Again it may be asked, Why has an Omniscient and Omnipotent Being taken this indirect and circuitous method of accomplishing His purpose, instead of reaching this result at once by the exercise of His Sovereign will? And, again, we refer to this gift of man to himself, to this *proprium* or ownhood of life, without which man would not be man, for he would lose all that distinguishes and characterizes his nature. It may help us to believe that this work of redemption was done in the manner we have attempted to describe, if we remember that man alone can sin. To him alone among the creatures of God is this fearful power given. For man alone can choose between good and evil, and his choice of evil makes sin. Man alone can resist sin and put it away. For he alone can choose between good and evil, and his choice of good resists sin and puts it away. Human nature alone can be defiled with sin; and only in and by human nature can this defilement be cleansed away.

So has our Lord created us; so has He created human nature. He has made it to be itself, its own. He has given it power to do its own work; and that it might do this fully, that its choice of good might be its own and entirely its own, He has so formed it, that only by and through human nature can the work of resisting evil and choosing good be done. Therefore, our Lord Himself assumed this human nature, that in it, by it, and through it, He might contend against and overcome and put away all evil; which work, even He could not do in any other way. There have been those who, oppressed by the magnitude of this fact, have held that it was all unreal, not a fact, but only an appearance. They were terribly mistaken. It was the greatest reality in heaven or in earth. He, the Infinite and Eternal, was born of a woman, and lay in the manger in Bethlehem, — a babe, — a human babe. From this humble infancy He grew into childhood, youth, and manhood. And in His human nature, from the power it derived from the Almightiness within, He resisted all the tendencies to evil of this nature, and contended with and overcame the evil spirits who animated these evils and brought them into His consciousness, and strove to bring them into will and act.

He conquered them; and by this victory He wrought the redemption of mankind.

THE BRINGING OF THE SPIRITUAL WORLD INTO ORDER.

It will be recollected as a part of this statement, that all our conscious life comes to us through those in the spiritual world, who are brought near to us by affinity or resemblance; that we neither think nor love nor do evil, except from the influence of those who, finding in us the germ of the evil which has reached its maturity in them, animate that germ with their own life; that, at the time of the coming of our Lord, our enemies had become so numerous and strong, that it had become difficult, and would have become impossible, so to balance their evil influences with good influences as to leave our spiritual freedom unimpaired. By our Lord's victories over these evil spirits, our redemption was wrought; and, that it might be complete, all the powers of darkness and of death were permitted to assail Him, and all were conquered.

These conflicts or temptations, and the sufferings attendant upon them, grew even to the end. They were like those which men suffer from like causes, with the exception repeatedly made before, that they were boundless and unlimited; they were *all*, of which no man can know more than a part. We cannot conceive of them adequately; but, that we may not be wholly ignorant, we have the story of Gethsemane. In this we have a picture of the sharpest agony that man ever endured; for where else was it ever seen that a human mind could be tortured, until the sweat fell from the brow in drops of blood?

It is commonly supposed that His suffering in Gethsemane arose from His anticipation of what was awaiting Him in Calvary. But this supposition does Him fearful injustice. How many of his followers went rejoicingly to a similar but more protracted and painful death! No. The suffering in that garden was from conflicts at that moment going on within Him. When, in His intolerable distress, perfect patience for a moment gave way, and He said, "Let this cup pass from me," — it was the cup He was at that moment drinking. He drank it all. They crucified Him, and He died *on* the cross; but he did not die *from* the cross. Capital punishment by crucifixion was well known and often practised in those days, nor is it now wholly unknown in the East. Different writers, ancient and modern, tell us about it. The nails did not pierce a vital organ, and a crucified person who was not interfered with usually lived from three to seven days. Our Lord hung on the cross six hours, and then gave up the ghost. The two who were crucified with Him were alive when the soldiers came, and were put to death. What then did our Lord die of? He died because the intensity of His spiritual suffering laid at last upon his physical frame a heavier burden than it could bear. He died of intolerable agony.

It may be that there are few in these days who can form any conception of this kind of suffering.

It has not been so always. There have been those who have felt and have manifested from similar conflicts, an extremity of distress which shattered the mind and convulsed the body. Here, as so often elsewhere, we have but to enlarge indefinitely a thing of human experience to reach a higher experience. That our redemption might be accomplished, all the powers of evil were permitted to assail Him. They were conquered; but more than that was necessary, that our redemption might be permanent and perpetual. It was necessary that these evil spirits from whom all evil influences come, should be so disposed of, so arranged, and so circumstanced, that never, or very seldom and only for a time, should there be an irruption from the abode of the false and the evil, of force enough to break down man's will.

When we speak of the people of the spiritual world as undergoing some process of disposition and arrangement which should have a material and permanent effect upon their condition and their power, we encounter the difficulty arising from the prevailing dimness and feebleness of the belief that there are any such people, or, as a matter of fact, any other world but this. A mind in such a state can scarcely believe that words have any meaning which describe that world as most real, and as having inhabitants who are men and women still, and subject to various changes of condition, some slow and gradual, some rapid and sudden, much as it is in this world. Yet even this must be believed, if we would understand at all the effect of our Lord's life and death on earth, in establishing new order in the spiritual world.

THE MAKING OF THE ASSUMED HUMANITY DIVINE.

The conflict and agony endured by our Lord was a conflict between the immeasurable evil of the assumed humanity and the perfect good within. It belonged to and was felt in that human nature. Again, we must refer to our own experience as men, to help us to form some conception of this. Every one who has resisted any evil thought or wish in himself, must know that something within him, something higher than his lower nature, opposed and resisted the tendencies of this lower nature. He must know that he himself consisted, if we may so speak, of two natures, — one lower and more external than the other, to which all the influences of sense and self and worldliness had access, and the other higher and more internal, in which better thoughts and better feelings prevailed. He must know, if much conflict between what is worse and what is better has taught him the lesson, that these two are so distinct that he may look upon himself as in some sense two men, — a natural man and a spiritual man. And not only his own experience, but his observation of all around him, teaches him that what the whole man becomes depends upon the issue of this conflict: natural, if the lower nature prevails and suppresses or silences the higher nature, which would rebuke and reform the lower; spiritual, if this higher nature prevails in the conflict, and succeeds in subduing the impulses of the lower, and these grow weaker and less urgent until their power disappears, and they are suppressed.

Carry this conception upwards, as far as our limited faculties permit, and it will help us to understand the effect of our Lord's temptations and victories. It will help us, too, to understand how He spake and acted differently in these two states. At times, when that which was only natural was urgent and prominent, He spake as a suffering man, and of the Father as distinct and afar from Him; when the conflict had ended in victory, He spake of the Father as one with Him. At one time appearing to the disciples as distraught with the agony of Gethsemane, and at another as glorified with the glory of the Father, as on the mount of transfiguration. These conflicts and victories were constant, and covered the whole ground. He cleansed His assumed human nature perfectly from defilement, from every thing belonging to it which opposed the divine within. It was full of all evil, and all this evil He expelled; and as the evil passed away, the opposite good, divine good, took its place. He brought this lower nature into perfect harmony, into oneness, with the divine within. The human nature became glorified; without ceasing to be human, it became a divine nature. He was at once perfect Man and perfect God.

THEREBY WAS PROVIDED A NEW MEDIUM FOR SAVING INFLUENCE.

In this divine-human nature, God has a new and nearer access to us in our human nature. He always works by instruments or means, and we can see, dimly if not clearly, that, excepting by instruments or media of some kind, the Infinite could not reach and act upon the finite. Many are the instruments he has used and is using, — as many as the things He has created and creates; but by His incarnation and His unition of His assumed humanity with His essential divinity, He has a new instrument perfectly adjusted to our human needs; for while it is divine with the essential Divinity, it is human in the Divine external. The nature which He assumed is our nature, and the proclivities to evil, which in that nature He resisted and subdued, are our proclivities to evil. If we would resist our own proclivities to evil, we must follow His example, and resist them as he resisted them. There is no other way. And, while we acknowledge His omniscience and perfect love, we may think that in every step of the way, — in every effort, every pain, every trial, in the dark hours of temptation, in the darker hours when despair is drawing near, — He is with us in His divine-human experience, and with His divine-human sympathy. All that, too, He has known; for His trials and His sufferings include all trial, and all suffering.

In all our conflicts with the enemies of our souls, it is He who fights for us and in us, even as He fought against those same enemies when He stood on earth. By His victory over them He reduced them to order, so that they could never more assail us with a strength He could not enable us to resist, as of ourselves and in our own freedom. More He did not do. He did not take from us the necessity of doing our part, because He loved us too well to take from us the blessing that comes, when we do our part. It is only His strength that fights the battle, but He gives this strength to us to be our own, if we are willing to accept it, and make use of it; for we, too, must fight that battle, as of ourselves. We are fighting for life; we must conquer or die: and in all the days or years we pass in this world this battle is going on, although we know it not. This is the battle between right and wrong, between truth and falsehood, between good and evil. The power to choose comes only from Him; but He gives us this power, and our choice is our own. Over us His infinite goodness is watching, exactly adapting all the circumstances of life to our spiritual needs, bringing to us every day in the form of that day's duty the means by which we may advance along the path He trod. He helps us always with a power which cannot fail, and leads us always with a wisdom which cannot mistake, but which we are often utterly incapable of comprehending. And He leaves it always to us, to choose whether we will reject His mercies, or accept them in the only way in which we can accept them; and that is, by doing the duty of each day, in the strength He gives us, and with the acknowledgment that it is His strength, given to us, by which we do it.

Mankind has reached a point in human progress, at which it is given us to know, if we will, that we live from God, constantly and in the highest and most absolute sense; that we depend upon Him for life, and for all the thought and feeling and power which constitute life, instantly, incessantly, and perfectly; that He is ever doing all that infinite love can prompt, and all that perfect wisdom can discern, to make our destiny a happy one. But that, nevertheless, He has placed our destiny in our own hands.

Perhaps ages must elapse before the human mind

can be so far cleansed from its obstructions and defilements, that this central truth of man's ownhood of his life, which perfectly reconciles the omnipotence of God and our perfect dependence upon Him, with our perfect freedom; which reconciles His omniscience and almightiness with the necessity and efficacy of our Lord's life and death on earth, — before this truth can be seen with entire fulness and clearness. But so far as it is seen, it stands in the mind as indeed a central truth. From it radiates light into all the departments of thought which concern themselves with the relations of God with man, or with the laws of being in this life or in the other. Resting upon it we may have doctrines on all these subjects, which illuminate the sorrow, the danger, and the mystery of life. Unspeakable the hope and consolation, the trust and peace they offer when pain and peril press upon us most heavily. They solve hard questions of duty, and fall as sunshine upon the pathway that leads to heaven and to God.

THE GIVING TO MANKIND FOR EVERMORE A DEFINITE OBJECT OF INTELLIGENT FAITH, OF WORSHIP, AND OF LOVE.

Throughout this work I have assumed the immortality of man, and the existence of God. The system of Swedenborg would have much to say, if these fundamental truths were disputed. But they are topics by themselves, and I have thought it best not to enter upon any direct investigation of them in this sketch. One reason is, that I suppose them to be generally and almost universally believed in some form or other, and have therefore confined myself to some attempts to rectify and improve this belief. But they who hold it in any form whatever would probably admit that a correct knowledge of God, and just views of His nature and action, if it were possible to attain to them, would have a vast importance, not only in this life, but during the whole of that immortality. The religious philosophy I am attempting to exhibit goes still farther. It asserts that the whole condition of every man through eternity is governed and determined by his relation, or the relation of his thoughts and affections, to God. We are told by our Lord, that the first and greatest commandment is to love God. This, like every commandment in the Word, is not merely a positive requirement, but it is a revelation. It discloses to us the truth, that our love to God measures our capacity of happiness; that the entire absence of this love implies the entire absence of that capacity; and that the quality of that love determines the quality of our happiness. Hence, from the very beginning, it has been the constant endeavor of Divine Providence to give to men this knowledge and this love, so far as it was possible for men to receive them in freedom, and give them a cordial welcome.

All the earlier revelations, however they began, ended in idolatry. This was permitted, because even this was always better than no recognition and no worship of a being or beings above men. And while in many instances this idolatry ran to extremes which were awful in their wickedness, we have also much reason to believe that through them a light shone upon many minds, which suggested, sometimes to the intellect, perhaps oftener to the heart, a belief in and a love for a Supreme, Almighty Father.

Through many fluctuations, far more than history takes note of, there was on the whole a gain or enlargement of the human capacity for truth and goodness, even from the first existence of mankind, when they lived only as animals live. These fluctuations were inevitable. Every revelation of truth became dim, and every church founded upon these revelations ran through its course of morning, noon, and night. For every revelation, like every spiritual gift of God, was given to and submitted to man's freedom. We may liken the whole course of Divine Providence to the advancing and retreating waves of a rising tide; or, better, to the tide that rises and falls back, but is ever slowly but surely gaining on the shore, on which it seems to break ineffectually. So the influence of truth and of good has been slowly but surely gaining upon the indurated self-love, the natural *proprium* of mankind. And, as they gained, new and larger gifts, making still greater gains possible, could be and therefore were given to mankind.

A step of vast importance was taken, when a written word was given. But a further step of infinitely greater moment was taken, when our Lord came upon earth. And then the Gospels were written, containing His words and acts. Then the Apocalypse was written, containing little literal truth, but in its spiritual meaning disclosing the spiritual history of Christianity, — thus completing the Word of God. Nothing more remained but that second coming of the Lord, His coming in the Spirit, which was distinctly intimated in the Gospels, and of which the Apocalypse of St. John is, in its spiritual sense, a perfectly definite prophecy.

Our Lord was a man; certainly He was a man. But there was that in His words and works which distinctly indicated that He was a divine person; and when one of His disciples called Him, "My Lord and my God," He accepted this address. During the first centuries, He was worshipped as divine by all; for those most earnest to find in the early centuries a denial of His divinity have wholly failed. He was regarded as a manifestation of the Father, as Himself divine; and was not unfrequently called or spoken of as God. At first, there was little effort to determine His relation to the Father, beyond the accepted phrase, "Son of God." But at length, some three centuries after His death, these inquiries took definite shape; and then the controversy between Arius and Athanasius arose. At the Council of Nice, in the year 325, it was determined in favor of Athanasius; and what was called the heresy of Arius was condemned. The essence of that heresy was, that Jesus Christ was a created person, whom God the Father called into being; and Arians and Semi-Arians gave unto Him, in various forms, all the glory and exaltation that were compatible with His distinctness from and subordination to the Father. This heresy, subdued with much difficulty, retained sufficient power in the church to be very troublesome for some ages, and has never been eradicated.

The Nicene Council decided that the Father, the Son, and the Holy Ghost were of the *same* essence; the Arians contending that they were of *like* essence. The dominant or orthodox party contended that while they were One, they were also Three. But three what? It is impossible that this question must not have greatly exercised the minds of thinking men. Among the most noticeable things in church history is the indistinctness, the delay, not to say the reluctance, with which the church answered this question. I must be very brief in noticing this answer, and perhaps cannot do better than to refer for illustration to the three creeds, — the Apostles', the Nicean, and the Athanasian.

Of the first the origin is unknown; but it is certainly of extreme antiquity, and settled down into its present form in less than two centuries after our Lord's birth. It is not so much a creed of opinions or beliefs, as an assertion of facts; but of such facts as they who framed it supposed all Christians should and would admit. Very possibly it was soon after its general adoption used as a test-creed, as setting forth what it was on the one hand necessary, and on the other hand sufficient, for a Christian to believe in order to entitle him to that name. As to the point under consideration, it says nothing about our Lord except by stating the facts narrated in the Gospels, and nothing concerning His nature or His relation to the Father beyond calling Him "His only begotten Son."

Then came the Nicean creed; agreed upon at that council only after long, and earnest, and furious debate, and, perhaps, the coercive authority of the Emperor. In this creed, description and epithets are used without stint to mark with reprobation the heresy of Arius. It calls our Lord, "God of God, Light of Light, very God of very God, begotten, not made, being of one substance with the Father." But they do not go further and say what the Father, the Son, and the Holy Spirit are in respect to each other. And then came the Athanasian creed; formed, probably, a century or two after Athanasius, and called by his name, because it was intended and believed to express his views. However, when ever, or by whomsoever composed, it gradually worked its way into general acceptance; and for more than a thousand years, and until recently, has been the authoritative symbol or creed of Catholic, Greek, and Protestant, and indeed of Christendom, with the exception of those who have strayed wholly away from the old paths. This creed is as definite as words can make it, and labors after words to make it perfectly definite. The sum of the whole matter is, that there are three Persons and one God; "for there is one person of the Father, another of the Son, and another of the Holy Ghost; but the Godhead of the Father, of the Son, and of the Holy Ghost is all one; the glory equal, the majesty coeternal."

I do not pause to consider the Greek "hypostatis," or "prosopon," or the etymological and original meaning of Person. That which is certain about the matter is, that Christendom, as a general thing, settled down into the worship of three persons who formed one God. They were understood to be distinct individualities, so distinct as to have different characteristics and functions, and enter into arrangements with each other founded upon these characteristics and the different work they did. This is made certain by the vicarious atonement, or the scheme of salvation which was founded upon and indissolubly connected with this distinctness of persons. For this scheme or system was, that the First person of the Trinity accepted the self-sacrifice of the Second person as atoning for the sin of the sinner, and satisfying the requirement of the First person's justice; whereby the Third person became able to do for the sinner the work of regeneration and salvation. It would seem difficult, not to say impossible, to hold this system in substance and reality, and not to look upon these three persons as separate from each other, as much as three men are; and any dimness or uncertainty about this distinct separation must make the belief of this scheme of salvation proportionally dim and indistinct; and if this distinct separation were wholly lost, then all belief in this scheme must be wholly lost from thought, whatever words might continue to be used. A few words concerning the history of this doctrine may illustrate our meaning.

We have a right to say of Augustine, Bishop of

Hippo, that he was a great and good man, if any evidence can authorize us to attach these words to any person. And yet, to him more than to any other, the Christian Church owes its system of election, predestination, and salvation by faith alone. Of course it is always said by those who hold this system, that its foundations are to be found in the epistles of Paul. There, undoubtedly, Augustine did find these foundations; but it was his great logical power which built upon them the fabric that has lasted to our own time.

His early life was, perhaps, dissolute. But the instruction of his admirable mother, Monica, who was a most devout Christian, at length bore fruit. While still a young man he determined to change his life. At first he sought help and guidance in philosophy; but he soon saw or felt its insufficiency, and, turning to religion, he became a Manichean. To that doctrine of two sovereigns of the world, one good and the other evil, he was impelled by the profound conviction of his own sinfulness. After a few years he renounced it, and became an orthodox Christian. Still the conviction of his sinful nature haunted him, and the business of his intellectual life was to account for this. He thought the accepted doctrines of the church, especially as expounded by St. Paul, enabled him to do so; for he understood from them that Adam by his disobedience,—by doing his own will instead of the will of God, which is at once the root and the sum and substance of all evil, — fixed upon his own nature the stain of rebellion, and imparted that nature to his children, whereby they are irresistibly inclined to evil; that is, to the love of self rather than the love of God. By this taint all men became sinful, and all merit from the perfect justice of God the punishment of damnation. They could be saved only by the self-sacrifice of the only-begotten Son of God, who thereby atoned for their sins; and the benefit of this atonement fell on those who had been elected as its recipients, and predestined to salvation. At first, and for some years, he held only to conditional predestination; that is, to predestination founded upon foreknowledge. The Omniscient could not but foreknow who would accept the grace offered to all, and them He would predestinate to salvation. But in his later years he abandoned all condition, and maintained the doctrine of absolute predestination, with no reference to the individual man. In those days this doctrine was, and ever since has been, opposed by those who saw in it the great danger of telling men that conduct could have no influence upon destiny; and in Augustine's day this opposition was the more urgent, because his doctrine had impelled some to avowed Antinomianism (or the worthlessness of obedience to law), and to the misconduct which would flow therefrom. Nevertheless, his great influence established this as the doctrine of the church. In succeeding ages, this doctrine came sometimes into controversy, and sometimes faded out of notice. Later, in the centuries immediately preceding Luther, it yielded practically to a view of the efficacy of works, which was carried to an extreme.

Then came Luther. Partly from constitutional tendency, more from his needing it as a weapon against the papacy, he took up Augustine's whole system, dwelling especially upon salvation by faith alone. I have read a quotation from one of his sermons, in which he says that good works can have nothing to do in causing regeneration, because before regeneration our works cannot be good, and after regeneration they cannot cause what has been already effected. He and his disciples — the kind and gentle Melancthon especially — preached and pressed this doctrine unreservedly; and, as one of its almost inevitable consequences, Antinomianism, or disregard of the law, broke forth with fury, and did vast mischief.

It is, however, to Calvin more than to any or all others, that the prevalence of the doctrine of salvation by faith alone among Protestants is due. He rested this doctrine upon the atonement by vicarious punishment, and that upon the doctrine of three persons in one God. With his powerful logic he bound together with such consistency and coherence these elements of his system, that it has resisted all assault until recently. Now, while it has caused some to be unbelievers in any religion, and has led more to construct a religion which did not require the divinity of Jesus Christ, it has exhibited its inherent weakness more clearly by its universal decay. There are still a few who from time to time preach or publish some assertion of old Orthodoxy in its hardest form, as if to show that it was not quite dead yet. Nor is it; for to many it is all the religion they have, and any obscurity or weakening of the system in their minds, or of its foundation (the tripersonality of the Godhead), is an obscurity and a weakening of their religion.

The strongest minds, — profoundly impressed with the necessity of upholding the doctrine of an atonement by vicarious suffering, on the one hand, and of maintaining the unity of God on the other, — have expended all their strength in the endeavor to reconcile a trinity of persons with a unity of person. But in vain, because reason is incapable of the thought. Some have said it is not a truth for reason, because we cannot understand it; but that it is a truth for faith, because we can believe it. But this is a mere misuse of the word "belief." If a scholar whom we trusted read to us some Arabic words of which we knew not the meaning, and told us they expressed a truth, we might learn the sounds and repeat them as a formula, and insist that they were true. But this would be a belief of the man who told us, and in no sense a belief of the wholly unknown ideas which the words express. So, if our religious teachers assure us that God is one person, but is also three persons, we may say it is so; but we attach no meaning to the words, nor is there any meaning in our faith; for the human mind is wholly unable to attach a meaning to such words.

Those who hold this doctrine as an article of faith may be divided into three classes: First, those who hold it only in words, and do not think about it at all. Then, those who profess the doctrine, but forget the tripersonality, and believe in one God. Then, those who, clinging to the tripersonality, believe in three Gods. It would seem to be impossible to believe actually in three persons and one God, because this is unthinkable. The old maxim, "Credo quia impossibile est," — "I believe because it is impossible," — was used to mark the distinction between a religious faith and a merely rational faith. Now none would avow it, and all would agree that it was ludicrously absurd. And yet it would express accurately the condition of that mind which really believed that there were three persons, each one of whom was God, and that, nevertheless, there was but one God.

It is to this condition of the Christian mind, that the New-Church comes to give for evermore a definite object of religious Faith, of Worship, and of Love. This object is our Lord and Saviour Jesus Christ; in whose person is a Trinity analogous to that in every man. For in every man there is Love or affection, which is the motive power of every act; Thought, which is produced from love or affection, and is the instrument by means of which the affection or desire acts; and Action, or operation, wrought by the love through the thought. And in these we have, by as close an analogy as can exist between the infinite and the finite, what is meant by Jehovah the Father, His only-begotten Son, and the Holy Spirit. When we address a man, and ask of him a favor, we do not address his affections alone, nor his thoughts alone, nor his action alone; but we address the whole man. Precisely so should we address in thought, in faith, in prayer, and in love, our Lord and Saviour Jesus Christ. He is Jehovah in His divine humanity. He is the Holy Spirit in His divine providence. He is our Lord and our God. Will, understanding, and action are as distinct in God as they are in man, and are distinct in man because they are distinct in God; and they are no more three persons in God than they are three persons in man.

Without recognizing the likeness between God and man, as has been repeatedly said, it will be impossible to have any idea whatever of God. From very early in the history of thought on this subject, — at least in the early Hindu and Greek religious philosophies, — there were those who urgently and eloquently maintained the doctrine of one God, the All-father, the Infinite, Absolute, and Impersonal; towards whom or which, in their view, all the many and diversified forms of popular religion pointed. Of late years this doctrine seems to be revived; for there are those who think they are giving clearness and accuracy to their religious ideas by going back, not to the early name, but to this early doctrine. That God should be a person they hold to be an absurdity, and almost a contradiction in terms. He must be infinite, and therefore without limitation or definition; and therefore without personality. But it should be obvious, for it is certain, and by some of the strongest thinkers who hold this view it is admitted, that of such a Being it is necessarily impossible to form any idea or conception. Such an idea of God may be held in words, but not in mind; it may be said, but it can not be thought; for if this infinitude makes personality impossible, it necessarily makes all idea or conception impossible. The whole effect upon the mind of such a view must be negative. It leads to the denial of every form of doctrine which implies personality, but it substitutes nothing in its place. With some it may lead to the deification of Nature, or to some form of Pantheism; but these, whatever words may be used, are but ways of denying that there is any God. For the human mind is such, that, to extinguish all idea of a God possessing the incidents of personality, is to exclude all idea of God. A religious sense, which is satisfied with such a God, must be satisfied with a God whom it can not love, nor worship, nor think of definitely. Far more might be said of the inexpressible mistake of attempting to believe in an impersonal God. But it would all end in this,—that an impersonal God is a word only, and not a thought.

It is to guard against this peril, and lift men out of this utter darkness, that in all ages Divine Providence has permitted them to find personal objects of worship in the many forms of heathenism; for even these might train the good among them into the possibility of receiving more and higher truth in their subsequent state of being. The Jews were taught that there was but one God, and that he was a spirit. But they always regarded Him as a personal Being of unlimited power, who had chosen their race as the object of His especial favor.

Our Lord came; and He disclosed His divinity sufficiently to lead to faith in Him, and to love and worship of Him. And in all subsequent ages, through all the clouds which have gathered about His revelation of Himself, and all distortions of the truth, He has lifted towards Himself the thoughts and the hearts of all who have not chosen to grovel upon the earth.

He has come again. He has come in the spirit, and has given to mankind the revelation which lay within the former revelation as the soul within the body. He has come to satisfy, fully and for ever, the requirement of human nature for a Divine Man, who may be the object of love and worship without limit. He has come not merely to satisfy this requirement, but to show that it springs from the very nature of God Himself, and of man, and of the relation of man to God. We may know now, what has always been known by those who could profit by the knowledge, that it was impossible to form any idea of Him, excepting through the ideas of human nature which we derive from self-consciousness. But we may also know now, that in this way we can form an idea of Him, founded upon His true nature and the actual working of His Providence; which idea, however imperfect and inadequate, may, as far as it goes, be just, and be capable of unending increase in its development and its truth. He has come to teach us that as all things exist from Him, so all our life is from Him, and is His life given to us to be our own; that our humanity is the effect and the image of His humanity, our personality the effect and image of His personality; and that we are men because He is perfect man.

CHAPTER XIV.

CONCLUSION.

In this last chapter, I propose to touch upon some of those topics which have not yet been considered, but of which some notice seems necessary even to the sketch I am endeavoring to make.

OF MARRIAGE.

This topic, from the place it holds in the philosophy of the New-Church, might seem to merit a chapter to itself. Nothing more, however, will be attempted, than a brief statement of the peculiar views held concerning this subject.

In the faith of tho New-Church, marriage is connected with the order of the whole universe, from the bottom to the summit. In all ages, a kind of duality, answering somewhat to that of the sexes, has been recognized as everywhere existing. Modern science has proved that this distinction of sexes, and the propagation of life by their conjunction, exists throughout the vegetable kingdom as much as in the animal kingdom. Elsewhere are traces of the same principle, not so obvious or so certain, but which many writers have referred to, in many ways. All of this, whatever be its form or its manifestation, refers to the primary and essential duality between the Divine love and the Divine wisdom. This duality is perfect, and their union into oneness is perfect. They are, to translate Swedenborg's phrase, "distinctly one;" that is, distinct and yet one. In mankind, these two divine elements come down into the human will and the human understanding, which are formed for their reception. Below the spirit of man, these divine elements come forth into the human form, and cause the distinction of the sexes. Farther down and outside of man, they cause a distinction of the sexes in the animal and vegetable kingdom. Still farther down, in the world of dead matter, they cause the innumerable correspondences which make this dead world representative, in this respect, of the world of life.

In man, this correspondence is necessarily higher than in the world outside of him, for the whole of that world is lower than he is. Of the two sexes, the correspondence changes somewhat with the change in the state of the individuals. Generally, however, the intellectual prevails in man, and the affectional in woman.

In God these two elements are perfectly united,—are one. It has been already said that it is the constant effort of Providence to make the will and the understanding in man united into oneness; for then, what the understanding sees as true the will loves as good, and there is the joy of peace in the whole man. The chief instrument to this end, and the most prominent example of the influence of this effort, is a marriage between two who may become one, by the union of the will and the understanding. The husband representing the understanding, and the wife representing the will, they two become one, when they are perfectly adapted to each other, and bound together by mutual love; they are a one formed of two whom God has joined together. Then the husband draws for every thought warmth and vitality from the wife, and every affection of her heart draws truth, enlightenment, and guidance from the wisdom of the husband.

The distinction between the sexes is not bodily only; it is primarily spiritual, and exists in the body only by derivation from the spirit. It is complete in the body; for no smallest part in a masculine body is precisely the same with the answering part in the feminine body. The distinction is also perfect in the spirit. Nothing in the soul, or in the thought, or affection, or motive, or action, of the one is precisely the same with any thing in the other. Therefore this distinction survives the death of the body. It is as perfect in the spiritual world as it was in the natural world. The two who have made each other happy, and who have helped each other while here to advance hand in hand along the way of life, were, while bound by the ties of a natural marriage, united in a spiritual marriage even in this world; and this marriage, so far from being weakened by the death of the body, rises as they rise, and is for ever the means of their ascent, and grows in strength and in happiness with every step of their ascent.

And they, too, who have not known on earth the happiness of such a marriage, because the wisdom of their Father saw that it was not well for them to find it here, if they choose good rather than evil, and by that choice become angels, will be sure to find it in heaven, and to find in it a large part of all that heaven can give them.

Hence, in the view of the New-Church, marriage stands invested, not with an importance merely, but with a sanctity, that it can not know elsewhere. The best influences of heaven have formed it, and bless it; and through it descend to earth and find a home in human hearts.

Hence, too, all that is hostile to, or inconsistent with, the holiness and purity of marriage, — all unchastity, infidelity, impurity, and lust, in thought, or word, or act, — are seen in the new light now dawning, to come direct from hell, and to be the surest means of dragging down their victims to the dark abodes from which they spring.

Only when the true nature of the marriage relation and its origin in the Divine nature itself are understood, can we form a just conception of the truth, that whatever is hostile to this relation pollutes the source of all good, and threatens the destruction of all happiness. The Scriptures bear testimony to this truth in the very peculiar phraseology often recurring in the prophetical writings, which is quite unintelligible without the aid of this truth. For in the most terrible denunciations of the prophets, the charge of adultery and fornication is constantly brought upon churches and races, and so applied that a literal understanding of it is impossible; as in Jeremiah iii., 8, 9, it is said, that "backsliding Israel" and "her treacherous sister Judah" "committed adultery with stocks and stones." And in Isaiah xxiii., 18, it is said that, "Tyre shall commit fornication with all the kingdoms of the world upon the face of the earth." In all the many texts of this kind, these sins are used to express the direst perversion and corruption of all that is good, and the falsification of all that is true; and thus the consummation of all evil.

OF THOUGHT.

What is Thought? And here, as so often elsewhere, I must go back to the central truth, that all our life is derived from God,—is His life given to us to be our own. His being consists of that which when received by our will — which is formed for its reception — constitutes love and affection of every kind; and of that which when received by our understanding — which is formed for its reception — constitutes thought, or rather the capacity of thought; for thought exists only when the understanding becomes active. The activity of the understanding is thought. For our understanding is formed first, to receive life from the Divine wisdom; and then, by its own action, to manifest this life in all the forms and varieties of thought. Our thoughts are not the thoughts of God in us; for they are our own thoughts, caused by the action of our own minds, by virtue of the life which is given to us to be our own.

Animals think; but men have far higher and wider capacities of thought. There have been endless discussions of the question, What constitutes the difference between human thought and animal thought? Some, who have looked only or mainly at the enormous difference between them, have come to the conclusion that animals are little or nothing more than self-acting machines, without thought or even sensation. Others, who have looked only or mainly at the great similitude between animal and human thought, have concluded that they are much the same in kind, differing only in degree.

Our first answer to the question,—What constitutes the difference between men and animals?—is this. We have heretofore spoken of the internal man and the external man, or of man's internal nature and his external nature. Animals have no internal nature. The human external is like the animal external in kind, though larger and fuller in measure. But a man is essentially more than an animal, because he has also an internal nature. Animals are not immortal. Their life begins and ends on earth; and their whole nature is adapted to life on earth. Man is immortal, and lives here to prepare for a life which begins when this life ends. Besides an external, which with him as with animals is adapted to life on earth, he has also an internal; whence he has the power while living here, to take thought for an eternal morrow, and to prepare for living hereafter. A man who makes no use of his internal, but suffers it to grow torpid and wholly inactive, leads a life which is only an animal life, however far above it he may seem to be, from the larger capacities of his external nature.

Intellectually considered, the difference between

men and animals is this: Animals have not, and men have, the power of *thinking about their thoughts;* and all the differences between them are derivable from this difference; and this again is derived from the primary difference, that animals have only an external nature, while men have both an external and an internal. Men and animals think, first, in their external minds. Animals stop there because they have no other mind. But men have another and a higher mind, and from that look down upon, recognize, and think about, the thoughts in that lower mind.

Thought is certainly possible without words; for the youngest infants think, and animals think: but neither of them can speak. At first, all thought is caused by sensation. The thoughts of an infant, thus caused, are very few. Soon, however, he begins to think about his thoughts; or, in other words, his thoughts become the subjects of thought. Then it is possible to use words, and the child slowly learns to speak. An animal never speaks. A dog can see that a cherry is red, and that blood or raw flesh are red, as well as man can, and can recognize the things as well as man can; but he can not think of the thought, and therefore he can not think of *redness,* aside from any one or more red things; and he has no word which would apply to all red things, because he has no such thought. To use the terms of logic, he can think in the concrete but not in the abstract; and words which are abstract, or which represent abstract thoughts, form so large and so important a portion of language, that without them there could be no language. Such words are not derived directly from sensation, but from thought about the thoughts which sensation excites. Men, as we have said, can think from sensation, and can then rise to a higher plane of thought and look down upon the thoughts derived directly from sensation. Animals have not this higher plane of thought. Because animals have no such thoughts they have no words. They make sounds which are often very significant, and communicate information to their fellows or to men. These sounds may be said to be their words, and to constitute their language. And it is much what our language would be if it lost all its abstract words, and contained none but those expressive of some one specific object. Human language can signify specific objects, but it is only by the use of words which limit and specialize these objects. *Generic* words are thus made *specific* words. I can think and speak of *pens;* but if I would speak of a pen on my table, or the pen in my hand, I must use apposite words, or perhaps use apposite gestures, — as when I say *this* pen, and show it, or point to it.

Animals can have no abstract words, because they have no abstract thoughts; and they have no abstract thoughts, because they do not need them; and they do not need them, because they are not immortal. Men owe to language (which they could not have without abstract thought) civilization, with all that it implies or includes, and all science, with the immense addition which it makes to human enjoyment. These things belong to this life; and it may be said that men would lose a vast deal, even were this life all, if they were without language. But it should be remembered that this life, with all that is in it, is intended to promote the preparation of mankind for another life, by the development and elevation of both the intellect and the affections. It is left to human freedom to determine whether and in what degree this effect shall be produced; but such is the purpose of every thing which is comprehended within or produced by civilization. And it is for this purpose that civilization, and language as the means of civilization, are given.

But language can do far more to effect this purpose of preparation for eternity. It is the instrument of thought; and thought can not only use it to express itself, but, by means of language, can advance gradually and slowly to an elevation it could not otherwise have reached: and this ascending pathway will know no end. A profound thought which is clothed in words gains definiteness and ultimation. It stands distinctly before the mind, and becomes the step from which a higher ascent can be made. And words may rise as thoughts rise; and, in that future life where much that fetters them here will pass away, both words and thoughts will reach an elevation far transcending our present capacity of conception.

In this upward progress of thought, three stages may be recognized, answering to the three degrees which play so important a part in the system of Swedenborg. To these three stages we give the names of knowledge, intelligence, and wisdom. We must begin with knowing; for, if we know nothing, there is nothing for us to understand. We may, however, know much, very much, and understand little or nothing of what we know. We take an entirely distinct step forward when we begin to know, not only the thing, but its place in Nature or in thought, its relations with those other things which touch it upon all sides, the end for which it is, the cause which produces it, and the effects which it produces. Then we have ascended from knowledge to intelligence. We may know very much, and understand much about what we know, and yet have little or no wisdom. For here also we take another distinct step forward, when we inquire into and ascertain the relation of a thing or a truth to life and character, and apply it in accordance with what we learn. It is for the sake of wisdom that we possess the faculties of knowing, and of understanding what we know; and only in the measure in which we acquire wisdom are these faculties put to their proper use.

Either knowledge, intelligence, or wisdom may exist in any degree, small or great. Where the knowledge is large there may be little of intelligence or wisdom; where it is small there may still be much of these. And of these two either may be small while the other is large, or the converse. We often meet knowing men of active intellects, who are far from wise, and men of little knowledge or active thought, who are wise with what they know. Always one law holds good. Knowledge and intelligence are for the sake of wisdom; if they do not end in this, they may as well not be, and will cease to be at death. Only when, only as far as, knowledge and intelligence have ripened into wisdom, and their fruits are rooted in the life and character, and so belong to the ownhood of the man, do they rise with him from the grave of the dead body, and abide with him for evermore. These fruits may be small; but, if they belong to the life, they will be as living seeds, possessing the power of indefinite multiplication and unending duration in that increase.

OF INSTINCT.

The instinct of animals is another topic of frequent discussion. By some means animals know, from the beginning of life, what they must do to preserve life and make it comfortable, and how they must do it. Neither instruction nor imitation have much to do with it, if any thing. Birds might perhaps profit by the example of their parents, and there are some indications of animals teaching their young. But, after the utmost is made of instances of this kind, it is still certain that instinct teaches to all animals much, and to some animals all that they know, without any other instruction; as in the case of those insects which never knew their parents, and cannot know their children. There is something of instinct also with human beings, as when new-born babes take their mother's milk at once, as perfectly the first time as ever. What then is instinct?

To answer this question, we must again go back to the primal truth, that all life is God's life, imparted to those who live by receiving it. But to this we must now add another truth, or law. It is, that, while life is one, it is determined in its action, manifestation, aspect, and effect, by the form of the recipient. My readers must remember what I have repeatedly said, that I do not mean by form, shape, but the inmost nature of the thing; that which gives to the *form* of a thing, according to Bacon, almost the same meaning as the *law* of the thing: for its form is the law which determines what it is. The doctrine above stated is not a new one. It is indeed much the same with the old maxim, "Quicquid recipitur, recipitur ad modum recipientis," — "whatever is received, is received after the manner of the receiver," — provided we add to the maxim that the "*modus*," or manner, is determined by the form, or inmost nature, of the receiver; and that this form is itself determined by and adjusted to the use or function of the receiver in the universe.

Every thing has its form, and could not exist without it. It is created in this form, through parents if it be an organized and living thing, to the end that it may so live by the life it receives as to carry into effect the end for which it exists. Therefore it has by creation the form by means of which it will manifest the life it receives in the way which that end requires.

The variety in these forms, and in the way in which they accomplish the ends for which they are, is simply infinite. No two leaves in a forest, no two grains of sand upon a seashore, are absolutely alike. But all things are arranged in classes, which man can often discern, in each of which all the individuals resemble each other, while no two are precisely alike. These classes gradually rise, from beings so small that they are only indicated but not shown by our best instruments, to the larger beings which are yet so small that only these instruments can discern them; and from these up through all the range of animal life, and at last to man himself, who, while also an animal, is not merely the highest of animals, but above all animals. Through this infinite variety, the one law prevails which makes each one, while it lives by receiving the same Divine life which gives life to all, at the same time itself, and by its form determined in its action and function.

The bud on every tree wraps the living germ that is to break forth next spring in the tenderest, softest leaflets, imbricated around that central germ with a skill human art cannot imitate, and covers the whole with a thick and leathery coat, cemented together so as to resist the winter storm and cold, and protect the tender life within while it needs protection. An insect lays its eggs in an exact order upon the twigs of the tree that its offspring when hatched can eat, and covers them too with a protective and sufficient cement. The bird that builds in the tree builds its nest carefully in the appropriate season, lays its eggs, sedulously covers and warms them with her own heat during the appointed period, and, when her young break forth, rejoices to find food for them and to protect them to the utmost of her power, even, if need be, at the peril of her own life. The human mother delights in caring for her new-born, and, as it lies in its cradle, covers it when too much cold threatens, with one and another blanket, as the tree protected its germ by the leaflets it folded around it. So much for the affections; and the same law holds good as to the intellect. For thousands of years, the honey-bee has constructed its marvellous cells, all upon the same model. A few generations ago, a human mind was able to discover its mathematical accuracy, and to demonstrate that it solved practically a most difficult problem,—how to construct cells which should afford the utmost storage room and have the utmost strength which were possible, by the use of a certain quantity of building material.

And now, What is instinct? It is action by a recipient of life, promotive of the ends for which that recipient exists, but without its conscious, intelligent, and voluntary coöperation. When the tree so shapes the bud as to protect the germ at its centre, it is wholly unconscious of what it is doing. The insect lays, arranges, and seals up its eggs on the tree, without the slightest thought of why it does this, but probably finds pleasure in what it does; for its desire and determination to do it are intense and regardless of obstacles. The bird has perhaps something more of consciousness as to the why and the wherefore of its acts; and certainly, when its young become the objects of its care, finds great enjoyment in that care. The human mother knows what she does, and why she does it, and is happy in doing it; and sometimes makes great mistakes, and sometimes fails utterly in that which, because she possesses rational power, has become her duty, but is subjected to that rational power.

Here is the dividing line. Animals are so constituted that the very form of their being causes the life received to manifest itself in all the knowledges and all the acts which are necessary for them. To man more is given, for he has the power of voluntarily carrying into effect the purposes for which he lives; and, that he may exercise this power, they cannot be and will not be carried into effect without his coöperation. The bee knew at the beginning how to make his cell perfectly, or rather did make his cell perfectly, by the influence of the mind within him of which he had no consciousness, and over which he had no control. But innumerable ages rolled along before man, from the ability to count his fingers, — and this he had to learn, — rose up through the series of gradually-acquired knowledges, into the ability to comprehend the mathematical character of the cell.

The animal is not wholly without reason, and the man not wholly without instinct. And yet it is certain that reason characterizes man, and instinct animals. The mother who tenderly cares for her child may do this only from instinct, and only as instinct prompts; and so far she is only an animal. But she may rise far higher than this; for she may look upon her child as an immortal being, given to her by God, entrusted to her care, and bringing with it a boundless responsibility so to deal with it as to promote its eternal welfare. And she may, through all the years that she is spared to it, use all her rational faculties to discern and pursue the path that leads to this end. Nothing of all this can the animal mother even think of. The human mother can if she will, and can neglect this duty if she will; but only so far as she does it, is she a woman, a human mother. The universal law which is founded upon the inmost nature of man, and man alone, and governs his whole being and destiny, comes in here as everywhere. For man only is capable of a voluntary coöperation with his Father; he only is capable of a voluntary reception of the gifts which his Father is ever seeking to bestow; and he only is capable of a voluntary refusal of this coöperation or this reception. But only by them can man become so far His child as to know the full blessedness of that relation.

THE SLOW GROWTH OF THE NEW-CHURCH.

It is more than a century since the foundation of this church was laid, by the publication of the theological writings of Emanuel Swedenborg. For more than half of that time, individuals and societies have been active in translating them, and in publishing them widely. There have been many preachers of these doctrines, and not a few writers of books and periodicals. The sale of Swedenborg's writings, and of books intended to present the doctrines of the church, has been constant and large. How happens it, under these circumstances, that the growth of this church has been and is so slow, if its doctrines are all that we who hold them suppose them to be?

There are many answers to this question. One among them is, that its growth has been greater than is apparent. It is not a sect. Its faith does not consist of a few specific tenets, easily stated and easily received. It is a new way of thinking about God and man, this life and another, and every topic connected with these. And this new way of thinking has made and is making what may well be called great progress. It may be discerned everywhere, in the science, literature, philosophy, and theology of the times; not prevalent in any of them, but existing, and cognizable by all who are able to appreciate these new truths with their bearings and results. If we hold that the spiritual world is the world of causes, and this world the world of effects, then we must hold that the New-Church will be an effect of influences which come, as the New Jerusalem is said by John to come, "from God out of heaven."

These influences are constantly at work to promote the establishment of this New-Church upon earth. Not suddenly, not violently, for the Lord is infinitely patient; but slowly, step by step, and only in such wise as is compatible with that spiritual freedom of mankind which is never violated.

Let it not be supposed that by the New-Church is meant the organized societies calling themselves by that name. In one sense, that is their name. Swedenborg says there are three essentials of this Church: a belief in the Divinity of the Lord, and in the sanctity of the Scriptures, and a life of charity, which is a life governed by a love of the neighbor. Where these are, there is the Church. Whoever holds these essentials in faith and life is a member of the New-Church, whatever may be his theological name or place. Only in the degree in which he so holds these essentials is any one a member of that church. Those who, holding or desiring to hold these essentials in faith and life, unite and organize that they may be assisted and may assist each other in so holding them, constitute the visible or professed New-Church. But very false would they be to its doctrines, if they supposed themselves to be exclusively members of that Church, or if they founded their membership upon their profession or external organization. For there is no other true foundation for this membership than every man's own internal reception of the essentials of the church, and his leading the life which its truths require.

It would demand a volume to indicate all those effects the new influences now constructing new heavens and a new earth have already produced, that we who can see but a very small part of the whole are able to discern. But we may mention as one of these effects, that Calvinism — old, hard, uncompromising — has almost disappeared. Where should we read in any new book, where should we hear in any sermon, of the damnation of infants, absolute election and predestination; or an atonement which presented God as vindictive and merciless, condemning a large part of His children, before their birth, to eternal misery, and hating with infinite and eternal wrath, not only sin but sinners, whom He had foreordained to be sinners? The Orthodox community has generally gone so far from such doctrines, that many may deny that they ever were preached, and charge me with error and injustice. I would advise persons who do so, to read the "spider sermon," so called, of Jonathan Edwards, lately republished. In all ages there have been those who turned their minds away from such pictures, and, even while assenting in words, greatly modified these views in their thoughts and feelings. But that such views were widely preached, and, indeed, passionately urged, is a matter of history.

One other instance of the diffused and indirect influence of the New-Church is the change which has taken place in the thought and feeling concerning death. Mr. Ralph Waldo Emerson, in an essay on Immortality, contained in a volume lately published, — in which he gives in his own inimitable manner what we may regard as his latest views on many interesting subjects, — says: "Swedenborg had a vast genius, and announced many things true and admirable, though always clothed in somewhat sad and Stygian colors. These truths, passing out of his system into general circulation, are now met with every day, qualifying the views and creeds of all churches, and of men of no church. And I think we are all aware of a revolution in opinion. Sixty years ago, the books read, the sermons and prayers heard, the habits of thought of religious persons, — were all directed on death. All were under the shadow of Calvinism, and of the Roman Catholic purgatory; and death was dreadful. The emphasis of all the good books given to young people was on death. We were all taught that we were born to die; and over that, all the terrors that theology could gather from savage nations were added to increase the gloom. A great change has occurred: death is seen as a natural event, and is met with firmness." Mr. Emerson is a good judge of this, and he is an impartial judge; for he is very far indeed from accepting the system of Swedenborg. The fact is undoubtedly as he states it. The indirect influence of the New-Church has produced just that effect; but it is as yet most imperfect and incomplete. What will it be, and what changes in thought and feeling will it cause, when the darkness and dread which have in all ages rested upon the grave, pass away? — when the inexpressible folly of bewailing the dead, with the feeling that they have ceased to live, or "are sleeping in the grave," is effectually exposed, not by faith only, but by a close and exact reason, which, while receiving warmth from faith, gives to it light? — when the shuddering horror which now shrouds the dead body, gives way to the certainty that death is but *a step forward in life?*

It may be said, and indeed often is said, that all this fading out or modification of ancient error is due to "the spirit of the age." This is true, — exactly true; for the spirit of the age is the spirit of the New-Church, doing its work wherever it can.

If it can do but a little here, it does that little; if it can do more there, it does more: everywhere doing all it can, always in subordination to the principle that no more can be done for man than he is willing to accept.

Another answer to the question — Whence the slow growth of the church? — may be this: Christians may now be divided into those who care for religion, and those who do not. They who do care for religion constantly nourish their religious faith, value it, and make some effort to live in accordance with it. They are therefore confirmed in that faith, and, if not wholly satisfied with it, they are at least convinced that there is no better, and that it would be a great mistake, if not a sin, to wander away from it. The stronger their faith, and the more they value it, the greater would be their dislike of a heresy which claimed, as they must think, to supersede it, and the more unwilling they must be even to inquire into it. While they who feel no interest in religion, and whose observance of it is merely formal, — a thing of habit, but not of meaning, — would feel no interest whatever in this new form of religion. It is nothing to them, and threatens only to disturb the routine of their thought and life. If they are led by mere curiosity to look into it at all, it is unintelligible to them, or it presents difficulties they do not care enough about the matter to encounter; and they pass it by with indifference or contempt.

This would be a sufficient answer, if the division above made were exhaustive; that is, if there were none in the Christian Church but those who were wedded to the faith that they held and satisfied with it, and those who held no faith and had no desire to hold any. But there is a third class; perhaps not inconsiderable now, and continually increasing. This class consists of those who have much religious sentiment, and some, perhaps much, desire to learn religious truth that they may have the support and comfort of distinct and firm religious belief; but who have no such belief and indeed no faith, because the forms or systems of faith in which they have been educated or which are within their reach are entirely unsatisfactory, and seem to them irrational or unsupported by competent evidence. The question then takes this form: Why do not these persons come to the New-Church and find there all they want? The answer I would now make to this question rests upon a principle which only of late has been clearly seen and appreciated. The best recent writers upon the philosophy of history have solved some of the most difficult problems which it presents, by the recognition of the law, that the peculiar and distinctive characteristics of an age cannot fail to exert an almost irresistible influence upon all its phenomena and all the individuals then living and acting.

One of the statements of Swedenborg is to the effect, that every substance puts forth from itself what may be called a sphere of itself, which contains or consists of its essential qualities. By this sphere, every thing exerts an influence upon its surroundings. In living organisms it is more active than in dead matter; in the animal world more active than in the vegetable world; and in men more active than in animals, for the sphere of men includes all their character. What is sometimes called — for want of a better word — the magnetic power of certain persons, by which, as orators, preachers, statesmen, generals, or in society, they exert an influence upon other men that seems, in some cases at least, inexplicable, may be accounted for by the spheres which flow from them. This power is sometimes said to be the power which a strong will exerts over a weaker. It is certainly stronger in him whose will is stronger, and is more energetic when the man himself is strongly excited and his will intensified.

The sphere of an age is the combined sphere of all who compose that age. Its power is very great, and can hardly be withstood by persons of ordinary power of resistance; and still less by those in whom this power is feeble, or who make no effort.

What then is the prevailing sphere of this age? Let us compare it with that of other ages.

So far as the records of human thought instruct us, we must believe that there never has been a period in which *naturalism* prevailed to the same extent as in the present. By this word, I mean a looking to and thinking about and caring for and recognition of things of this world rather than of the other; nature rather than spirit; secular interests of all kinds rather than those of religion. We may go back to ages so remote that we know little of them, but their monuments remain and tell us what a vast proportion of the labor of different races was expended in the service of religion; and we may infer what a hold it had upon the thought and care of rulers and peoples. Coming down through the ages, we shall find evidence of a similar condition of human interest. In the centuries of Christianity we find the strongest men — and very strong were some of them, especially in what we call "the dark ages" — devoting their most earnest thought to religion. The magnificent cathedrals of the middle ages tell the same story. We say nothing as to the value or worthlessness of the speculations about which so much profound thought was employed, or of the truth or falsity of the religions which were so highly valued; but only that, in all those days a strong and general interest was felt in the religious questions of the time, and a very large proportion of the best and most strenuous intellectual effort was given to them.

Coming to our own age, what do we see? Let the railroad, the steam-engine, the telegraph, answer. We see a more earnest and successful devotion of human effort to science and arts in their application to this life than was ever before known. It may safely be said, that within the last hundred years there have been more inventions promotive of human activity and effort in the direction of the enjoyments of this life, and a greater utilization of all the forces of Nature to that end, than all the previous centuries taken together have contributed. Natural science has flourished and is flourishing as it never did, drawing into its service the best intellects; and their investigations and discoveries are presented in popular form in leading periodicals as the most acceptable and interesting reading they can offer to the public. In a word, never was there known a period approaching this in the earnest devotion of thought to every thing which is of the earth, earthly, and in the decay and feebleness of interest in that which concerns the spirit of man and his eternal life. Of course all the forms of religion remain, although so large a portion of the people attend to them not at all, or only with indifference. Of course there are still those who professionally, or from their personal taste, write and publish on religious topics. But looking at the matter as a whole, who that has any real belief in another and an eternal world, and therefore regards this life as only introductory and preparatory, can fail to see that the set and tendency of human thought and care in these days is strongly and decidedly away from whatever belongs to man as an immortal, and towards this world and all that belongs to it; or away from spiritualism and towards naturalism?

I have used a word which suggests to me one answer that may be made. Is not the Spiritualism (so called, but I like better to call it spiritism) now so popular, a proof that I am wrong as to the prevalence and power of naturalism? On the contrary, I find in it cogent evidence that I am right. Of this spiritism, whatever else may be said of it, this much I think is certain (and my opinion is grounded upon much study of its phenomena, and much acquaintance with its literature. I do not speak of persons. Undoubtedly the many believers in spiritism are of all kinds; and some of them are good, and perhaps find aliment for their goodness in what they believe. But from what I have seen and heard and read, I write of the system and its fundamental doctrines; for these it seems to have), — spiritism does nothing more than extend this life beyond the grave. If its theories, or its dreams, are realized, the other life is but a continuation of this. So far is it from opposing naturalism, that it gives to the merest, lowest, and grossest naturalism an element of perpetuity; and this is its highest idea of immortality. So far from spiritism being an opponent of naturalism, I believe that its popularity and rapid spread spring from its naturalism, and from its supplying food for the hunger of mankind for some knowledge of what is to follow death, without making any demand for an elevation of either the will or the understanding above the common thoughts, cares, or interests of this world. I believe spiritism to be the consummation of naturalism. It brings the thought of heaven itself down to earth, — not to lift the earthly up, but to be itself submerged in the very dregs of earthliness.

Naturalism at this day dominates the thought of Christendom as it never did before. The metaphysical philosophy of the day is characterized by a prevailing — not a universal — tendency to limit its inquiry into the nature and functions of mind to this life, not seldom with an express or distinctly implied denial of any other.

So, as to the philosophy of history, whether general or confined to some special subject, as that of civilization. Writers who are most successful do not seem to have a thought of Providential action or purpose. Buckle went farther; his naturalism was aggressive. He knew that something other than naturalism had vast power in other ages, and has some power in this; and the main purpose of his book was to extinguish its embers. These writers consider and analyze the course of events with utter ignorance or positive denial of Providential action or purpose. If it be true that there is a God, and that He is the Supreme Governor of the world, what sort of work must such writers make in their explanation of events and consequences? Just such work as they would make if they undertook to explain the mechanism and action of a clock, in utter ignorance or denial that there was any weight or pendulum. And yet their labor may not be wholly lost. They may supply to those who believe that there is a weight and pendulum, or a motive force and a governing wisdom, the means of tracing their influence through the intricate machinery, and of discerning more distinctly the purpose of the whole, and the way in which this purpose is accomplished.

We repeat, that naturalism at this day dominates the thought of Christendom as it never did before. And yet it may be that in this way and for this reason this age may be eminently preparatory for the new era of the New-Church. It is a fundamental principle of the new truths which will prevail in this new era, that Nature and spirit, when viewed aright, are not distinct from each other in the way in which they have been thought to be. They are distinct — perfectly distinct — from each other; but Nature is the effect, the clothing, and the mirror of spirit: spirit is the cause, the inmost essence, and the soul of Nature. In the present generation, the most active and energetic thought is devoted to an investigation of Nature and of all its laws, forces, and phenomena. It has made a wonderful progress in this direction; and never did it seem to be advancing more rapidly than at this moment. But in all this, natural science is but laying up a vast store of materials which spiritual science is hereafter to make use of.

It is now a very common question, What is the use of all this knowledge, and what is the value of the truth which is sought with so much labor? One answer is, that truth, merely as truth and for its own sake, is a noble object of human pursuit; and much eloquence has been expended in proving this. Another answer is, that truths of the most abstract kind are found serviceable to the practical good of mankind. Mathematics, so profound that few men on earth are equal to its demands, is now applied to all natural science, and especially to astronomy; and astronomy directly assists the whole navigation of the civilized world. Chemistry, in some hands, is penetrating into all the physical secrets of Nature, and by other hands its discoveries as soon as made are utilized for practical art. And so it is with all the branches of natural science.

But a far better answer remains to be made to the question, What is the worth of natural science? The New-Church will bring back to the knowledge of mankind what, if it has known, it has forgotten, — that this life and this world are but preparatory for another, and that their value in this respect is as much more than their value in themselves, as eternity is more than time. Then, when the light of spiritual science is cast upon natural science, it will be seen that what is true of the whole of Nature is true of all the science which teaches us about Nature. Building upon the relation of Nature to spirit as that of an effect to its cause, and upon the correspondence between all things of Nature and the things of spirit, it will begin a work which will last through the ages: the work of showing that all natural science is but the clothing, the outer form, the mirror of spiritual science. Then it will be found that the age which busied itself successfully in gathering the stores of natural science was gathering a treasury of knowledge for spiritual science to lift up far above Nature. Then will it be seen that this naturalistic age was doing a work which was not only useful but indispensable for the work of that coming age.

And even the prevailing worldliness of this age

may possibly become instrumental for the growth of its opposite, — charity. Swedenborg is continually speaking about charity. It holds with him the same high place which Paul gives it when he says, "Though I speak with the tongues of men and of angels, and understand all mysteries, and have all faith, and bestow all my goods on the poor, and give my body to be burned, — all profiteth me *nothing*, if I have not charity." But what is charity? Swedenborg gives this definition: "Charity itself is to act justly and faithfully in the office, business, and work in which one is, and with whomsoever he has any intercourse." He does not object to or undervalue that which in the present opinion of the world is alone thought to be charity, — the caring for the poor (a mistake which Paul's express declaration might have prevented); for this, he says, should always be done, but with prudence. Whatever is done outside of one's regular employment may be a beneficent act; but it does not deserve the higher name of charity, for that belongs to the full and faithful discharge of all the duties of our office, place, function, or employment. And, whenever this charity prevails, there will be little need of that almsgiving which is now called charity. Swedenborg says of a true charity, "And so the common good is provided for as well as that of each individual." And how universally would the good of each individual be provided for, if all men performed all the duties of their employment justly and faithfully! Charity may be described as love in action. And a true charity is the love of the neighbor, and of all as our neighbors; recognizing the place and mode of work which belongs to us as that assigned to us by our Lord's perfect wisdom, because it is the best way in which we can exercise and manifest our love. And it is not the least among the novelties of Swedenborg's system, that he puts what is now called charity in its proper place, lifting up the word to its just meaning, and the thing itself to its high position. What will the earth be when the unremitted industry and active energy in all the uses of life which characterize this age are unabated, but the fever of greed is quelled, and selfishness is no longer dominant, order is unbroken, and usefulness universal, and the happiness of usefulness fills the human heart with the happiness it was made to enjoy?

I have asked what earth would be then. There is but one answer, — it would be heaven. For, by the influence of such truth and the infusion of such life, earth would be lifted up to heaven.

Countless ages of ages have rolled away since this earth was made ready to be the home of human life. Gradually and very slowly mankind have reached their present condition. It may be that as many ages must come forth from the womb of the future and join the long procession of the past, before such a hope can be, even in a moderate degree, fulfilled. But it is certain that for that happiness man was made; and to it, led by his Father's hand, he will approach while earth exists. How far away such a result may be; how slowly and with what alternations we may approach it; how long it will be before the fetters of naturalism and worldliness will be broken, or at least loosened, so far as to permit some decided relaxation of their influence, — we know not. What we do know is, that, while their influence remains dominant as it is now, the reception of this latest and consummating revelation must be slow, narrow, imperfect, and fragmentary; because New-Church doctrine and influence, and naturalism and worldliness, are exact antagonists. The New-Church strikes a deadly blow at naturalism, and must needs be resisted by all the influences of naturalism. Where one is strong, the other must be weak. Where one holds possession, the other cannot enter. None who live in this age can wholly escape the influence of the age; and that influence tends powerfully to close the mind against spiritual truth, and to bar the heart against the entrance of spiritual life.

Hinweise zur Benutzung

VELDEN AM WÖRTHERSEE – Kärnten – 730 09 – 8 55
Wintersport: 440 m
Wien 321 – Klagenfurt 26 – Villach 18 – St. Veit an
Villacher Str. 19, ✉ 9220, ✆ (04274) 21 03, info@v
Veranstaltungen
24.6.-15.08.: Wörtherseefestspiele
08.09-10.09.: Weinfest
Wörther See★ – Maria Wörth★ (Ost: 10 km) –
(West: 13 km) – Villach★ (West: 15 km) – Reifn
Bären
Europaplatz. 1 ✉ 9220 – ✆ (0474) 2 66 00
–baren-hotel@aon.at – Fax (07431) 266001
12 Zim – 59/76 € 90/122 € – Rest (ge
und Montag)– Menü 25 € – Karte 13/28 €
• Ein tadellos geführtes kleines Hotel in ein
und besonders im Anbau ganz modernen

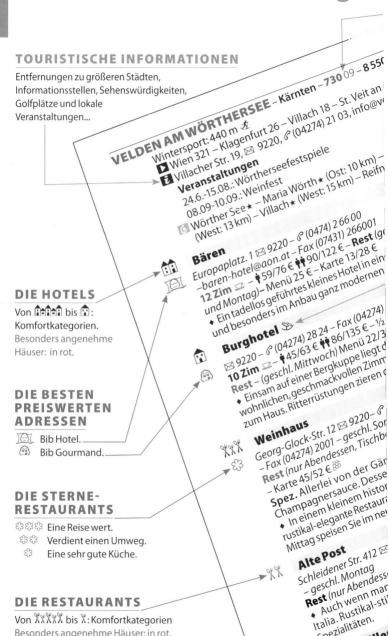

TOURISTISCHE INFORMATIONEN

Entfernungen zu größeren Städten, Informationsstellen, Sehenswürdigkeiten, Golfplätze und lokale Veranstaltungen...

DIE HOTELS

Von 🏨🏨🏨🏨 bis 🏨: Komfortkategorien. Besonders angenehme Häuser: in rot.

Burghotel
✉ 9220 – ✆ (04274) 28 24 – Fax (04274)
10 Zim – 45/63 € 86/135 € – ½
Rest – (geschl. Mittwoch) Menü 22/3
• Einsam auf einer Bergkuppe liegt d
wohnlichen, geschmackvollen Zimm
zum Haus. Ritterrüstungen zieren d

DIE BESTEN PREISWERTEN ADRESSEN

Bib Hotel.

Bib Gourmand.

Weinhaus
Georg-Glock-Str. 12 ✉ 9220– ✆
– Fax (04274) 2001 – geschl. Son
Rest (nur Abendessen, Tischbe
– Karte 45/52 €
Spez. Allerlei von der Gär
Champagnersauce. Desse
• In einem kleinem histor
rustikal-elegante Restaura
Mittag speisen Sie im neu

DIE STERNE-RESTAURANTS

✿✿✿ Eine Reise wert.

✿✿ Verdient einen Umweg.

✿ Eine sehr gute Küche.

Alte Post
Schleidener Str. 412 ✉
– geschl. Montag
Rest (nur Abendess
• Auch wenn man
Italia. Rustikal-sti
Spezialitäten.

DIE RESTAURANTS

Von XXXXX bis X: Komfortkategorien Besonders angenehme Häuser: in rot.

Windmülle
Feldhäuser Str.
(04274)

MICHELIN-KARTE

Angabe der Michelin-Karte, auf der der Ort zu finden ist.

LAGE DER STADT

Markierung des Ortes auf der Regionalkarte am Ende des Buchs (Nr. der Karte und Koordinaten).

LAGE DES HAUSES

Markierung auf dem Stadtplan (Planquadrat und Koordinate).

RUHIGE HOTELS

ruhiges Hotel.

sehr ruhiges Hotel.

BESCHREIBUNG DES HAUSES

Atmosphäre, Stil, Charakter und Spezialitäten.

EINRICHTUNG UND SERVICE

PREISE

öhe 450 m 3 **B2**

n 43

t

Gail (Flügelaltar★★)

amidenkogel★ (Ost: 18 km)

AU **z**

ug. 3 Wochen Samstagmittag

hngebiet mit freundlichem Service

nr wohnlich gestalteten Zimmern.

öllen-und Modeltal Zim

BF **n**

geschl. Jan.-März

arte 18/26 €

g von 1938, die das kleine Hotel mit seinen

erherbergt. Auch ein kleines Museum gehört

tikale Restaurant. Kreative Regionalküche.

CY **a**

4) 20 00 – weinhaus@langwies.at

-Montag

ng erforderlich) Menü 30/65 €

pfleber. Steinbutt unter der Pinienkruste mit

er «Weinhaus».

n Stadthause führt Familie Kreus dieses gemütliche

t angenehmer Atmosphäre und klassischer Küche. Am

chen Bistro oder auf der Terrasse vor dem Haus.

BU **g**

) – ☎ (04274) 51 00 – *alterpost@utanet.at*

schbestellung ratsam)– Menü 55/70 € – Karte 36/40 €

on außen nicht vermutet: Hier erwartet Sie ein Stück Bella

s Ambiente, herzliche Atmosphäre und natürlich typische

Zim

CS **e**

57439– ☎ (04274) 20 09 – info@windmuller.at

– geschl. Sonntag-Montag

58/65 €– **Rest** – Menü 22 € – Karte 12/23 €

nsreiche Ambiente des Gewölberestaurants, den geschul-

saisonal beeinflusste Küche.

DS **e**

ller.at

rustikal

Grundsätze

„Dieses Werk hat zugleich mit dem Jahrhundert das Licht der Welt erblickt, und es wird ihm ein ebenso langes Leben beschieden sein."

Das Vorwort der ersten Ausgabe des MICHELIN-Führers von 1900 wurde im Laufe der Jahre berühmt und hat sich inzwischen durch den Erfolg dieses Ratgebers bestätigt. Der MICHELIN-Führer wird heute auf der ganzen Welt gelesen. Den Erfolg verdankt er seiner konstanten Qualität, die einzig den Lesern verpflichtet ist und auf festen Grundsätzen beruht.

Die Grundsätze des MICHELIN-Führers:

Anonymer Besuch: Die Inspektoren testen regelmäßig und anonym die Restaurants und Hotels, um deren Leistungsniveau zu beurteilen. Sie bezahlen alle in Anspruch genommenen Leistungen und geben sich nur zu erkennen, um ergänzende Auskünfte zu den Häusern zu erhalten. Für die Reiseplanung der Inspektoren sind die Briefe der Leser im Übrigen eine wertvolle Hilfe.

Unabhängigkeit: Die Auswahl der Häuser erfolgt völlig unabhängig und ist einzig am Nutzen für den Leser orientiert. Die Entscheidungen werden von den Inspektoren und dem Chefredakteur gemeinsam getroffen. Über die höchsten Auszeichnungen wird sogar auf europäischer Ebene entschieden. Die Empfehlung der Häuser im Michelin-Führer ist völlig kostenlos.

Objektivität der Auswahl: Der MICHELIN-Führer bietet eine Auswahl der besten Hotels und Restaurants in allen Komfort- und Preiskategorien. Diese Auswahl erfolgt unter strikter Anwendung eines an objektiven Maßstäben ausgerichteten Bewertungssystems durch alle Inspektoren.

Einheitlichkeit der Auswahl: Die Klassifizierungskriterien sind für alle vom Michelin-Führer abgedeckten Länder identisch.

Jährliche Aktualisierung: Jedes Jahr werden alle praktischen Hinweise, Klassifizierungen und Auszeichnungen überprüft und aktualisiert, um ein Höchstmaß an Zuverlässigkeit zu gewährleisten.

... und sein einziges Ziel – dem Leser bestmöglich behilflich zu sein, damit jede Reise und jeder Restaurantbesuch zu einem Vergnügen werden, entsprechend der Aufgabe, die sich Michelin gesetzt hat: die Mobilität in den Vordergrund zu stellen.

Lieber Leser

Lieber Leser,

Wir freuen uns, Ihnen die 4. Ausgabe des MICHELIN-Führers Österreich vorstellen zu dürfen. Diese Auswahl der besten Hotels und Restaurants in allen Preiskategorien wird von einem Team von Inspektoren mit Ausbildung in der Hotellerie erstellt. Sie bereisen das ganze Jahr hindurch das Land. Ihre Aufgabe ist es, die Qualität und Leistung der bereits empfohlenen und der neu hinzukommenden Hotels und Restaurants kritisch zu prüfen.

In unserer Auswahl weisen wir jedes Jahr auf die besten Restaurants hin, die wir mit ✪ bis ✪✪✪ kennzeichnen. Die Sterne zeichnen die Häuser mit der besten Küche aus, wobei unterschiedliche Küchenstilrichtungen vertreten sind. Als Kriterien dienen die Qualität der Produkte, die fachgerechte Zubereitung, der Geschmack der Gerichte, die Kreativität und das Preis-Leistungs-Verhältnis, sowie die Beständigkeit der Küchenleistung. Darüber hinaus werden zahlreiche Restaurants für die Weiterentwicklung ihrer Küche hervorgehoben. Um die neu hinzugekommenen Häuser des Jahrgangs 2008 mit einem, zwei oder drei Sternen zu präsentieren, haben wir diese mit einem„**N**" gekennzeichnet .

Außerdem möchten wir die *"Hoffnungsträger"* für die nächsthöheren Kategorien hervorheben. Diese Häuser sind in der Sterne-Liste und auf unseren seiten in Rot aufgeführt. Sie sind die besten ihrer Kategorie und könnten in Zukunft aufsteigen, wenn sich die Qualität ihrer Leistungen dauerhaft und auf die gesamte Karte bezogen bestätigt hat. Mit dieser besonderen Kennzeichnung möchten wir Ihnen die Restaurants aufzeigen, die in unseren Augen die Hoffnung für die Gastronomie von morgen sind.

Ihre Meinung interessiert uns! Bitte teilen Sie uns diese mit, insbesondere hinsichtlich dieser *"Hoffnungsträger"*. Ihre Mitarbeit ist für die Planung unserer Besuche und für die ständige Verbesserung des MICHELIN-Führers von großer Bedeutung.

Wir danken Ihnen für Ihre Treue und wünschen Ihnen angenehme Reisen mit dem MICHELIN-Führer 2008.

Den MICHELIN-Führer finden Sie auch im Internet unter
www.ViaMichelin.com
oder schreiben Sie uns eine E-mail:
der.michelinfuehrer-austria@de.michelin.com

Kategorien & Auszeichnungen

KOMFORTKATEGORIEN

Der MICHELIN-Führer bietet in seiner Auswahl die besten Adressen jeder Komfort- und Preiskategorie. Die ausgewählten Häuser sind nach dem gebotenen Komfort geordnet; die Reihenfolge innerhalb jeder Kategorie drückt eine weitere Rangordnung aus.

		Großer Luxus und Tradition
		Großer Komfort
		Sehr komfortabel
		Mit gutem Komfort
		Mit Standard-Komfort
garni		Hotel ohne Restaurant
mit Zim		Restaurant vermietet auch Zimmer

AUSZEICHNUNGEN

Um Ihnen behilflich zu sein, die bestmögliche Wahl zu treffen, haben einige besonders bemerkenswerte Adressen dieses Jahr eine Auszeichnung erhalten. Die Sterne bzw. „Bib Gourmand" sind durch das entsprechende Symbol bzw. und Rest gekennzeichnet. Unsere „Hoffnungsträger" für die nächst höhere Küchenauszeichnung finden Sie auf der Sterne-Liste. Außerdem ist der Name dieser Häuser im Buch in rot gedruckt.

DIE BESTEN RESTAURANTS

Die Häuser, die eine überdurchschnittlich gute Küche bieten, wobei alle Stilrichtungen vertreten sind, wurden mit einem Stern ausgezeichnet. Die Kriterien sind: die Qualität der Produkte, die Kreativität, die fachgerechte Zubereitung und der Geschmack sowie das Preis-Leistungs-Verhältnis und die immer gleich bleibende Qualität.

Eine der besten Küchen: eine Reise wert
Man isst hier immer sehr gut, öfters auch exzellent.

Eine hervorragende Küche: verdient einen Umweg

Ein sehr gutes Restaurant in seiner Kategorie

DIE BESTEN PREISWERTEN HÄUSER

Bib Gourmand
Häuser, die eine gute Küche bis 30 € bieten (Preis für eine dreigängige Mahlzeit ohne Getränke). In den meisten Fällen handelt es sich um eine regional geprägte Küche.

Bib Hotel
Häuser, die eine Mehrzahl ihrer komfortablen Zimmer bis 90 € anbieten (Preis für 2 Personen inkl. Frühstück).

DIE ANGENEHMSTEN ADRESSEN

Die rote Kennzeichnung weist auf besonders angenehme Häuser hin. Dies kann sich auf den besonderen Charakter des Gebäudes, die nicht alltägliche Einrichtung, die Lage, den Empfang oder den gebotenen Service beziehen.

bis **Angenehme Hotels**

bis **Angenehme Restaurants**

BESONDERE ANGABEN

Neben den Auszeichnungen, die den Häusern verliehen werden, legen die Michelin-Inspektoren auch Wert auf andere Kriterien, die bei der Wahl einer Adresse oft von Bedeutung sind.

LAGE

Wenn Sie eine ruhige Adresse oder ein Haus mit einer schönen Aussicht suchen, achten Sie auf diese Symbole:

Ruhiges Hotel

Sehr ruhiges Hotel

Interessante Sicht

Donau **Besonders schöne Aussicht**

WEINKARTE

Wenn Sie ein Restaurant mit einer besonders interessanten Weinauswahl suchen, achten Sie auf dieses Symbol:

Weinkarte mit besonders attraktivem Angebot
Aber vergleichen Sie bitte nicht die Weinkarte, die Ihnen vom Sommelier eines großen Hauses präsentiert wird, mit der Auswahl eines Gasthauses, dessen Besitzer die Weine der Region mit Sorgfalt zusammenstellt.

Einrichtung & Service

30 Zim	Anzahl der Zimmer
	Fahrstuhl
A/C	Klimaanlage (im ganzen Haus bzw. in den Zimmern oder im Restaurant)
	Nichtraucherzimmer vorhanden bzw. separater Restaurantraum für Nichtraucher reserviert
	Internetzugang mit W-LAN in den Zimmern möglich
	Für Körperbehinderte leicht zugängliches Haus
	Spezielle Angebote für Kinder
	Terrasse mit Speisenservice
Spa	Wellnessbereich
	Freibad oder Hallenbad
	Badeabteilung, Thermalkur
	Sauna, Fitnessraum
	Tennisplatz oder –halle
18	Golfplatz und Lochzahl
	Garten, Liegewiese - Park
	Strandbad
	Bootssteg
	Konferenzraum (übliche Tagungstechnik vorhanden)
	Veranstaltungsraum (bei Restaurants)
	Hotelgarage (wird gewöhnlich berechnet)
P	Parkplatz reserviert für Gäste
	Hunde sind unerwünscht (im ganzen Haus bzw. in den Zimmern oder im Restaurant)
U	Nächstgelegene U-Bahnstation (in Wien)

Preise

Die in diesem Führer genannten Preise wurden uns im Sommer 2007 angegeben. Bedienung und MwSt. sind enthalten. Es sind Inklusivpreise, die sich nur noch durch die evtl. zu zahlende Kurtaxe erhöhen können. Sie können sich mit den Preisen von Waren und Dienstleistungen ändern.
Der erste Preis ist der Mindestpreis in der Nebensaison, der zweite Preis der Höchstpreis in der Hauptsaison. Die Häuser haben sich verpflichtet, die von den Hoteliers selbst angegebenen Preise den Kunden zu berechnen.
Anlässlich größerer Veranstaltungen, Messen und Ausstellungen werden von den Hotels in manchen Städten und deren Umgebung erhöhte Preise verlangt.
Erkundigen Sie sich bei den Hoteliers nach eventuellen Sonderbedingungen.

RESERVIERUNG UND ANZAHLUNG

Einige Hoteliers verlangen zur Bestätigung der Reservierung eine Anzahlung oder die Nennung der Kreditkartennummer. Dies ist als Garantie sowohl für den Hotelier als auch für den Gast anzusehen. Bitten Sie den Hotelier, dass er Ihnen in seinem Bestätigungsschreiben alle seine Bedingungen mitteilt.

KREDITKARTEN

AE ⓓ MC VISA	Akzeptierte Kreditkarten: American Express – Diners Club – Mastercard (Eurocard) - Visa

ZIMMER

Zim – 🚹60/75 €	Mindest- und Höchstpreis für ein Einzelzimmer/
🚹🚹70/120 €	Mindest- und Höchstpreis für ein Doppelzimmer
Zim ☕ –	Zimmerpreis inkl. Frühstück
☕ 10 €	Preis des Frühstücks
Suiten	Preise auf Anfrage
☼ – ❄	Preise im Sommer – Preise im Winter

HALBPENSION

½ P 10 €	Aufschlag zum Zimmerpreis für Halbpension pro Person und Tag
(inkl. ½ P)	Zimmerpreis inkl. Halbpension

RESTAURANT

Menü 20/42 €	**Menüpreise:** mindestens 20 €, höchstens 42 €
Karte 30/41 €	**Der erste Preis** entspricht einer einfachen Mahlzeit mit Suppe, Hauptgericht, Dessert. Der zweite Preis entspricht einer reichlicheren Mahlzeit (mit Spezialität) aus Vorspeise, Hauptgang und Dessert (Getränke nicht inbegriffen).

Städte

ALLGEMEINES

✉ *1010*	Postleitzahl
L	Landeshauptstadt
730 *R 20*	Nummer der Michelin-Karte mit Koordinaten
24 000 Ew	Einwohnerzahl
Höhe 175 m	Höhe
Heilbad *Kneippkurort* *Heilklimatischer Kurort-Luftkurort* *Erholungsort* *Wintersport*	Art des Ortes
1 000 m	Maximal- Höhe des Wintersportgeländes
2	Anzahl der Kabinenbahnen
4	Anzahl der Schlepp- oder Sessellifts
	Langlaufloipen
AX A	Markierung auf dem Stadtplan
	Rundblick, Aussichtspunkt
18	Golfplatz mit Lochzahl
	Flughafen
	Ladestelle für Autoreisezüge – Nähere Auskünfte bei allen Fahrkartenausgaben
	Autofähre, Personenfähre
	Informationsstelle

SEHENSWÜRDIGKEITEN

BEWERTUNG

★★★	Eine Reise wert
★★	Verdient einen Umweg
★	Sehenswert

LAGE

	In der Stadt
	In der Umgebung der Stadt
6 km	Entfernung in Kilometern

Stadtpläne

Hotels
Restaurants

SEHENSWÜRDIGKEITEN

Sehenswertes Gebäude
Sehenswerte Kirche

STRASSEN

Autobahn, Schnellstraße
Nummern der Anschluss-Stellen:
Autobahnein – und/oder–ausfahrt
Hauptverkehrsstraße
Einbahnstraße – Gesperrte Straße,
mit Verkehrsbeschränkungen
Fußgängerzone – Straßenbahn
Karlstr. P P Einkaufsstraße – Parkplatz – Parkhaus, Tiefgarage
Park-and-Ride-Plätze
Tor – Passage – Tunnel
Bahnhof und Bahnlinie
Standseilbahn – Seilschwebebahn
F Bewegliche Brücke – Autofähre

SONSTIGE ZEICHEN

Informationsstelle
Moschee – Synagoge
Turm – Ruine – Windmühle – Wasserturm
Garten, Park, Wäldchen – Friedhof – Bildstock
Stadion – Golfplatz – Pferderennbahn – Eisbahn
Freibad – Hallenbad
Aussicht – Rundblick
Denkmal – Brunnen – Fabrik – Leuchtturm
Jachthafen – Autobusbahnhof
Flughafen – U-Bahnstation, S-Bahnhof
Schiffsverbindungen: Autofähre – Personenfähre
Hauptpostamt (postlagernde Sendungen) und Telefon
Krankenhaus – Markthalle
Öffentliches Gebäude, durch einen Buchstaben gekennzeichnet:
L R – Sitz der Landesregierung – Rathaus
J – Gerichtsgebäude
M T U – Museum – Theater – Universität, Hochschule
POL. – Polizei (in größeren Städten Polizeipräsidium)

Mode d'emploi

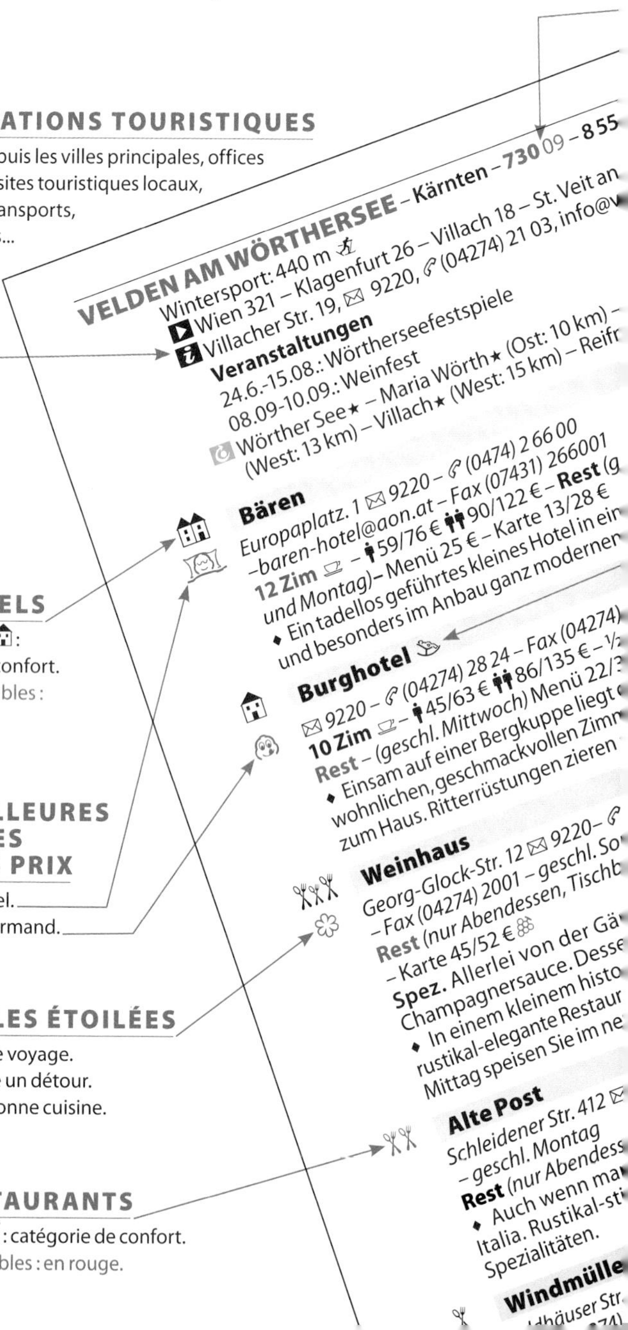

INFORMATIONS TOURISTIQUES

Distances depuis les villes principales, offices de tourisme, sites touristiques locaux, moyens de transports, golfs et loisirs...

LES HÔTELS

De 🏠🏠🏠🏠🏠 à 🏠 : catégorie de confort.
Les plus agréables : en rouge.

LES MEILLEURES ADRESSES À PETITS PRIX

Bib Hôtel.
Bib Gourmand.

LES TABLES ÉTOILÉES

✿✿✿ Vaut le voyage.
✿✿ Mérite un détour.
✿ Très bonne cuisine.

LES RESTAURANTS

De XXXXX à X : catégorie de confort.
Les plus agréables : en rouge.

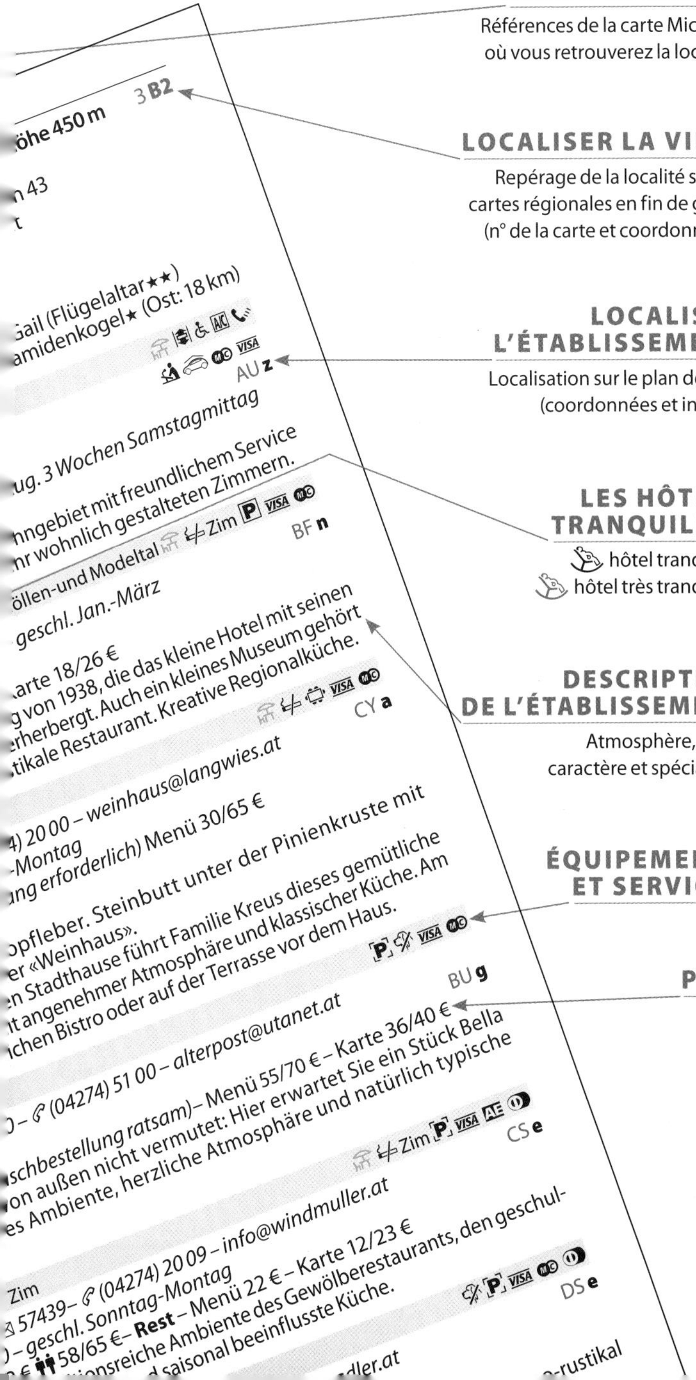

CARTE MICHELIN

Références de la carte Michelin où vous retrouverez la localité.

LOCALISER LA VILLE

Repérage de la localité sur les cartes régionales en fin de guide (n° de la carte et coordonnées).

LOCALISER L'ÉTABLISSEMENT

Localisation sur le plan de ville (coordonnées et indice).

LES HÔTELS TRANQUILLES

hôtel tranquille.
hôtel très tranquille.

DESCRIPTION DE L'ÉTABLISSEMENT

Atmosphère, style, caractère et spécialités.

ÉQUIPEMENTS ET SERVICES

PRIX

Engagements

« Ce guide est né avec le siècle
et il durera autant que lui. »

Cet avant-propos de la première édition du Guide MICHELIN 1900 est devenu célèbre au fil des années et s'est révélé prémonitoire. Si le Guide est aujourd'hui autant lu à travers le monde, c'est notamment grâce à la constance de son engagement vis-à-vis de ses lecteurs.
Nous voulons ici le réaffirmer.

Les engagements du Guide MICHELIN :

La visite anonyme : les inspecteurs testent de façon anonyme et régulière les tables et les chambres afin d'apprécier le niveau des prestations offertes à tout client. Ils paient leurs additions et peuvent se présenter pour obtenir des renseignements supplémentaires sur les établissements. Le courrier des lecteurs nous fournit par ailleurs une information précieuse pour orienter nos visites.

L'indépendance : la sélection des établissements s'effectue en toute indépendance, dans le seul intérêt du lecteur. Les décisions sont discutées collégialement par les inspecteurs et le rédacteur en chef. Les plus hautes distinctions sont décidées à un niveau européen. L'inscription des établissements dans le guide est totalement gratuite.

La sélection : le Guide offre une sélection des meilleurs hôtels et restaurants dans toutes les catégories de confort et de prix. Celle-ci résulte de l'application rigoureuse d'une même méthode par tous les inspecteurs.

La mise à jour annuelle : chaque année toutes les informations pratiques, les classements et les distinctions sont revus et mis à jour afin d'offrir l'information la plus fiable.

L'homogénéité de la sélection : les critères de classification sont identiques pour tous les pays couverts par le Guide Michelin.

… et un seul objectif : tout mettre en œuvre pour aider le lecteur à faire de chaque sortie un moment de plaisir, conformément à la mission que s'est donnée Michelin : contribuer à une meilleure mobilité.

Édito

Cher lecteur,

Nous avons le plaisir de vous proposer notre 4e édition du Guide MICHELIN Österreich. Cette sélection des meilleurs hôtels et restaurants dans chaque catégorie de prix est effectuée par une équipe d'inspecteurs professionnels, de formation hôtelière. Tous les ans, ils sillonnent le pays pour visiter de nouveaux établissements et vérifier le niveau des prestations de ceux déjà cités dans le Guide.

Au sein de la sélection, nous reconnaissons également chaque année les meilleures tables en leur décernant de ✿ à ✿✿✿. Les étoiles distinguent les établissements qui proposent la meilleure qualité de cuisine, dans tous les styles, en tenant compte des choix de produits, de la créativité, de la maîtrise des cuissons et des saveurs, du rapport qualité/prix ainsi que de la régularité.

Cette année encore, de nombreuses tables ont été remarquées pour l'évolution de leur cuisine. Un « **N** » accompagne les nouveaux promus de ce millésime 2008, annonçant leur arrivée parmi les établissements ayant une, deux ou trois étoiles.

De plus, nous souhaitons indiquer les établissements « *espoirs* » pour la catégorie supérieure. Ces établissements, mentionnés en rouge dans notre liste et dans nos pages, sont les meilleurs de leur catégorie. Ils pourront accéder à la distinction supérieure dès lors que la régularité de leurs prestations, dans le temps et sur l'ensemble de la carte, aura progressé. Par cette mention spéciale, nous entendons vous faire connaître les tables qui constituent à nos yeux, les espoirs de la gastronomie de demain.

Votre avis nous intéresse, en particulier sur ces « *espoirs* » ; n'hésitez pas à nous écrire. Votre participation est importante pour orienter nos visites et améliorer sans cesse votre Guide. Merci encore de votre fidélité. Nous vous souhaitons de bons voyages avec le Guide MICHELIN 2008.

Consultez le Guide MICHELIN sur
www.ViaMichelin.com
et écrivez-nous à :
der.michelinfuehrer-austria@de.michelin.com

Classement & Distinctions

LES CATÉGORIES DE CONFORT

Le Guide MICHELIN retient dans sa sélection les meilleures adresses dans chaque catégorie de confort et de prix. Les établissements sélectionnés sont classés selon leur confort et cités par ordre de préférence dans chaque catégorie.

🏨🏨🏨🏨🏨	XXXXX	Grand luxe et tradition
🏨🏨🏨🏨	XXXX	Grand confort
🏨🏨🏨	XXX	Très confortable
🏨🏨	XX	De bon confort
🏨	X	Assez confortable
garni		L'hôtel n'a pas de restaurant
mit Zim		Le restaurant possède des chambres

LES DISTINCTIONS

Pour vous aider à faire le meilleur choix, certaines adresses particulièrement remarquables ont reçu une distinction : étoiles ou Bib Gourmand. Elles sont repérables dans la marge par ✿ ou ☺ et dans le texte par **Rest**.

LES ÉTOILES : LES MEILLEURES TABLES

Les étoiles distinguent les établissements, tous les styles de cuisine confondus, qui proposent la meilleure qualité de cuisine. Les critères retenus sont : le choix des produits, la créativité, la maîtrise des cuissons et des saveurs, le rapport qualité/prix ainsi que la régularité.

✿✿✿ **Cuisine remarquable, cette table vaut le voyage**
On y mange toujours très bien, parfois merveilleusement.

✿✿ **Cuisine excellente, cette table mérite un détour**

✿ **Une très bonne cuisine dans sa catégorie**

LES BIBS : LES MEILLEURES ADRESSES À PETIT PRIX

☺ **Bib Gourmand**
Établissement proposant une cuisine de qualité, souvent de type régional, jusqu'à 30 € (Prix d'un repas hors boisson).

Bib Hôtel
Établissement offrant une prestation de qualité avec une majorité de chambres jusqu'à 90 €. Prix pour 2 personnes, petit-déjeuner inclus.

LES ADRESSES LES PLUS AGRÉABLES

Le rouge signale les établissements particulièrement agréables. Cela peut tenir au caractère de l'édifice, à l'originalité du décor, au site, à l'accueil ou aux services proposés.

🏠 à 🏠🏠🏠🏠🏠 **Hôtels agréables**

✕ à ✕✕✕✕✕ **Restaurants agréables**

LES MENTIONS PARTICULIÈRES

En dehors des distinctions décernées aux établissements, les inspecteurs Michelin apprécient d'autres critères souvent importants dans le choix d'un établissement.

SITUATION

Vous cherchez un établissement tranquille ou offrant une vue attractive ? Suivez les symboles suivants :

Hôtel tranquille

Hôtel très tranquille

Vue intéressante

Donau **Vue exceptionnelle**

CARTE DES VINS

Vous cherchez un restaurant dont la carte des vins offre un choix particulièrement intéressant ? Suivez le symbole suivant :

Carte des vins particulièrement attractive
Toutefois, ne comparez pas la carte présentée par le sommelier d'un grand restaurant avec celle d'une auberge dont le patron se passionne pour les vins de sa région.

Équipement & Services

30 Zim	Nombre de chambres
	Ascenseur
A/C	Air conditionné (dans tout ou partie de l'établissement)
	Établissement disposant de chambres ou d'une salle réservées aux non-fumeurs
	Connexion Internet « Wireless Lan » dans la chambre
	Établissement en partie accessible aux personnes à mobilité réduite
	Équipements d'accueil pour les enfants
	Repas servi au jardin ou en terrasse
Spa	Wellness-Center : bel espace de bien-être et de relaxation
	Piscine : de plein air ou couverte
	Cure thermale, hydrothérapie
	Sauna - salle de remise en forme
	Court de tennis
18	Golf et nombre de trous
	Jardin de repos - Parc
	Plage aménagée
	Ponton d'amarrage
	Salle de conférence
	Salon privé (dans les restaurants)
	Garage dans l'hôtel (généralement payant)
P	Parking réservé à la clientèle
	Accès interdit aux chiens (dans tout ou partie de l'établissement)
U	Station de métro la plus proche (à Vienne)

Prix

Les prix indiqués dans ce guide ont été établis à l'été 2007. Ils sont susceptibles de modifications, notamment en cas de variation des prix des biens et des services. Ils s'entendent taxes et service compris.

Le premier prix est le prix minimum en basse saison, le deuxième prix le prix maximum en haute saison. Les hôteliers et restaurateurs se sont engagés, sous leur propre responsabilité, à appliquer ces prix aux clients.

À l'occasion de certaines manifestations : congrès, foires, salons, festivals, événements sportifs ..., les prix demandés par les hôteliers peuvent être sensiblement majorés.

ARRHES

Pour la confirmation de la réservation certains hôteliers demandent le numéro de carte de crédit ou un versement d'arrhes. Il s'agit d'un dépôt-garantie qui engage l'hôtelier comme le client. Bien demander à l'hôtelier de vous fournir dans sa lettre d'accord toutes les précisions utiles sur la réservation et les conditions de séjour.

CARTES DE PAIEMENT

	Cartes de paiement acceptées :
AE ① MC VISA	American Express – Diners Club –Mastercard (Eurocard) – Visa.

CHAMBRES

25 Zim	Nombre de chambres
Zim – 🚹60/75 €	Prix des chambres mini/maxi pour 1 et
🚹🚹70/120 €	2 personne(s)
Zim ☕ –	Petit-déjeuner compris
☕ 10 €	Petit-déjeuner en sus
Suiten	Suites : se renseigner auprès de l'hôtelier
☼	Prix pour l'été
❄	Prix pour l'hiver

DEMI-PENSION

½ P 10 €	Prix du supplément pour la demi-pension par personne/jour.
(inkl. ½ P)	Prix de la chambre, demi-pension inclus

RESTAURANT

Menü 20/42 €	**Menu à prix fixe :** minimum 20 €, maximum 42 €
Karte 30/41 €	**Repas à la carte** hors boisson. Le premier prix correspond à un repas simple comprenant une soupe, un plat du jour et un dessert. Le 2e prix concerne un repas plus complet comprenant une entrée, un plat (avec spécialité), et un dessert.

Villes

GÉNÉRALITÉS

✉ *1010*	Numéro de code postal
L	Capitale de Province
730 *R 20*	Numéro de la carte Michelin et carroyage
24 000 Ew	Population résidente
Höhe 175 m	Altitude de la localité
Heilbad	Station thermale
Kneippkurort	Station de cures Kneipp
Heilklimatischer	Station climatique
Kurort-Luftkurort	Station climatique
Erholungsort	Station de villégiature
Wintersport	Sports d'hiver
1 000 m	Altitude maximale atteinte par les remontées mécaniques
2	Nombre de téléphériques ou télécabines
4	Nombre de remonte-pentes et télésièges
	Ski de fond
AX A	Lettres repérant un emplacement sur le plan
	Panorama, point de vue
18	Golf et nombre de trous
	Aéroport
	Localité desservie par train-auto
	Transports maritimes : passagers et voitures – passagers seulement
i	Information touristique

INFORMATIONS TOURISTIQUES

INTÉRÊT TOURISTIQUE

★★★	Vaut le voyage
★★	Mérite un détour
★	Intéressant

SITUATION DU SITE

	Dans la ville
	Aux environs de la ville
6 km	Distance en kilomètres

Plans

Hôtels
Restaurants

CURIOSITÉS

Bâtiment intéressant
Édifice religieux intéressant

VOIRIE

Autoroute, double chaussée de type autoroutier
Numéro d'échangeur
Grande voie de circulation
Sens unique – Rue réglementée ou impraticable
Zone à circulation réglementée – Rue piétonne – Tramway
Karlstr. Rue commerçante
Parking – Parking couvert
Parking Relais
Porte – Passage sous voûte – Tunnel
Gare et voie ferrée
Funiculaire – Téléphérique, télécabine
Pont mobile – Bac pour autos

SIGNES DIVERS

Information touristique
Mosquée – Synagogue
Tour – Ruines – Moulin à vent – Château d'eau
Jardin, parc, bois – Cimetière – Calvaire
Stade – Golf – Hippodrome – Patinoire
Piscine de plein air – couverte
Vue – Panorama
Monument – Fontaine – Usine – Phare
Port de plaisance – Gare routière
Aéroport – Station de métro
Transport par bateau :
passagers et voitures, passagers seulement
Bureau principal de poste
Hôpital – Marché couvert
Bâtiment public repéré par une lettre
L R Conseil provincial – Hôtel de ville
J Palais de justice
M T U Musée – Théâtre - Université
POL. Police (Commissariat central)

How to use this guide

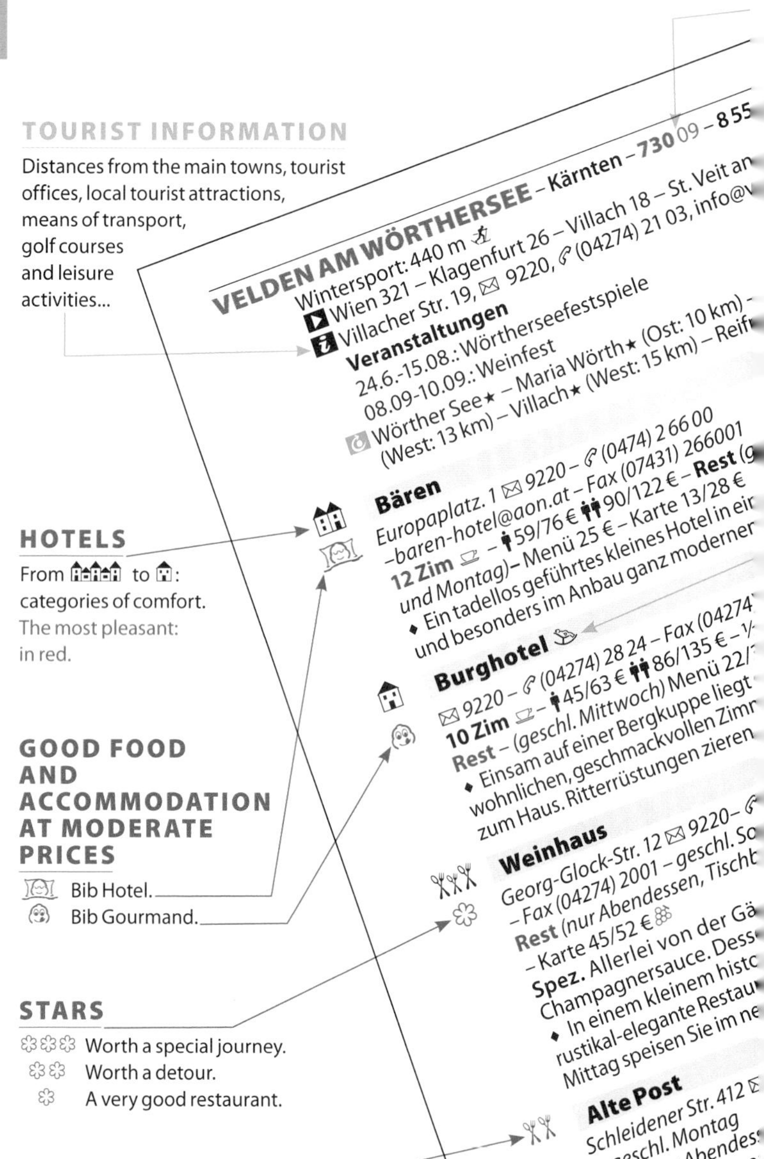

TOURIST INFORMATION

Distances from the main towns, tourist offices, local tourist attractions, means of transport, golf courses and leisure activities...

HOTELS

From 🏠🏠🏠🏠🏠 to 🏠: categories of comfort.
The most pleasant: in red.

GOOD FOOD AND ACCOMMODATION AT MODERATE PRICES

Bib Hotel.
Bib Gourmand.

STARS

✿✿✿ Worth a special journey.
✿✿ Worth a detour.
✿ A very good restaurant.

RESTAURANTS

From XXXXX to X: categories of comfort
The most pleasant: in red.

MICHELIN MAPPING

References for the Michelin map which covers the area.

LOCATING THE TOWN

Locate the town on the map at the end of the guide (map number and coordinates).

LOCATING THE ESTABLISHMENT

Located on the town plan (coordinates and letters giving the location).

QUIET HOTELS

quiet hotel.
very quiet hotel.

DESCRIPTION OF THE ESTABLISHMENT

Atmosphere, style, character and specialities.

FACILITIES AND SERVICES

PRICES

Commitments

"This volume was created at the turn of the century and will last at least as long".

This foreword to the very first edition of the MICHELIN Guide, written in 1900, has become famous over the years and the Guide has lived up to the prediction. It is read across the world and the key to its popularity is the consistency of its commitment to its readers, which is based on the following promises.

The MICHELIN Guide's commitments:

Anonymous inspections: our inspectors make regular and anonymous visits to hotels and restaurants to gauge the quality of products and services offered to an ordinary customer. They settle their own bill and may then introduce themselves and ask for more information about the establishment. Our readers' comments are also a valuable source of information, which we can then follow up with another visit of our own.

Independence: Our choice of establishments is a completely independent one, made for the benefit of our readers alone. The decisions to be taken are discussed around the table by the inspectors and the editor. The most important awards are decided at a European level. Inclusion in the Guide is completely free of charge.

Selection and choice: The Guide offers a selection of the best hotels and restaurants in every category of comfort and price. This is only possible because all the inspectors rigorously apply the same methods.

Annual updates: All the practical information, the classifications and awards are revised and updated every single year to give the most reliable information possible.

Consistency: The criteria for the classifications are the same in every country covered by the MICHELIN Guide.

... and our aim: to do everything possible to make travel, holidays and eating out a pleasure, as part of Michelin's ongoing commitment to improving travel and mobility.

Dear reader,

We are delighted to introduce the 4th edition of The MICHELIN Guide Österreich

This selection of the best hotels and restaurants in every price category is chosen by a team of full-time inspectors with a professional background in the industry. They cover every corner of the country, visiting new establishments and testing the quality and consistency of the hotels and restaurants already listed in the Guide.

Every year we pick out the best restaurants by awarding them from ✿ to ✿✿✿. Stars are awarded for cuisine of the highest standards and reflect the quality of the ingredients, the skill in their preparation, the combination of flavours, the levels of creativity and value for money, and the ability to combine all these qualities not just once, but time and time again.

Additionnally, we highlight those restaurants which, over the last year, have raised the quality of their cooking to a new level. Whether they have gained a first star, risen from one to two stars, or moved from two to three, these newly promoted restaurants are marked with an '**N**' next to their entry to signal their new status in 2008.

We have also picked out a selection of *"Rising Stars"*. These establishments, listed in red, are the best in their present category. They have the potential to rise further, and already have an element of superior quality; as soon as they produce this quality consistently, and in all aspects of their cuisine, they will be hot tips for a higher award. We've highlighted these promising restaurants so you can try them for yourselves; we think they offer a foretaste of the gastronomy of the future.

We're very interested to hear what you think of our selection, particularly the *"Rising Stars"*, so please continue to send us your comments. Your opinions and suggestions help to shape your Guide, and help us to keep improving it, year after year. Thank you for your support. We hope you enjoy travelling with the MICHELIN Guide 2008.

Consult the MICHELIN Guide at
www.ViaMichelin.com
and write to us at:
der.michelinfuehrer-austria@de.michelin.com

Classification & awards

CATEGORIES OF COMFORT

The MICHELIN Guide selection lists the best hotels and restaurants in each category of comfort and price. The establishments we choose are classified according to their levels of comfort and, within each category, are listed in order of preference.

🏨🏨🏨🏨🏨	XXXXX	Luxury in the traditional style
🏨🏨🏨🏨	XXXX	Top class comfort
🏨🏨🏨	XXX	Very comfortable
🏨🏨	XX	Comfortable
🏨	X	Quite comfortable
garni		This hotel has no restaurant
mit Zim		This restaurant also offers accommodation

THE AWARDS

To help you make the best choice, some exceptional establishments have been given an award in this year's Guide. They are marked ✿ or ☺ and Rest.

THE BEST CUISINE

Michelin stars are awarded to establishments serving cuisine, of whatever style, which is of the highest quality. The cuisine is judged on the quality of ingredients, the skill in their preparation, the combination of flavours, the levels of creativity, the value for money and the consistency of culinary standards.

✿✿✿ **Exceptional cuisine, worth a special journey**
One always eats extremely well here, sometimes superbly.

✿✿ **Excellent cooking, worth a detour**

✿ **A very good restaurant in its category**

GOOD FOOD AND ACCOMMODATION AT MODERATE PRICES

☺ **Bib Gourmand**
Establishment offering good quality cuisine, often with a regional flavour, up to € 30 (Price of a three course meal, not including drinks).

☺ **Bib Hotel**
Establishment offering good levels of comfort and service, with most rooms priced up to € 90. Price of a room for 2 people, including breakfast.

PLEASANT HOTELS AND RESTAURANTS

Symbols shown in red indicate particularly pleasant or restful establishments: the character of the building, its décor, the setting, the welcome and services offered may all contribute to this special appeal.

🏠 to 🏠🏠🏠🏠🏠	**Pleasant hotels**
✗ to ✗✗✗✗✗	**Pleasant restaurants**

OTHER SPECIAL FEATURES

As well as the categories and awards given to the establishment, Michelin inspectors also make special note of other criteria which can be important when choosing an establishment.

LOCATION

If you are looking for a particularly restful establishment, or one with a special view, look out for the following symbols:

🐴	**Quiet hotel**
🐴	**Very quiet hotel**
⋞	**Interesting view**
⋞ Donau	**Exceptional view**

WINE LIST

If you are looking for an establishment with a particularly interesting wine list, look out for the following symbol:

🍇	**Particularly interesting wine list** This symbol might cover the list presented by a sommelier in a luxury restaurant or that of a simple inn where the owner has a passion for wine. The two lists will offer something exceptional but very different, so beware of comparing them by each other's standards.

Facilities & services

30 Zim	Number of rooms
	Lift (elevator)
A/C	Air conditioning (in all or part of the establishment)
	Non smoking rooms or restaurant available
	Wireless Lan in bedrooms
	Establishment at least partly accessible to those of restricted mobility
	Special facilities for children
	Meals served in garden or on terrace
Spa	Spa : an extensive facility for relaxation and well-being
	Swimming pool: outdoor or indoor
	Hydrotherapy
	Sauna – Exercise room
	Tennis court
18	Golf course and number of holes
	Garden - Park
	Beach with bathing facilities
	Landing stage
	Equipped conference room
	Private dining rooms (in restaurants)
	Hotel garage (additional charge in most cases)
P	Car park for customers only
	Dogs are excluded from all or part of the establishment
U	Nearest metro station (in Vienna)

Prices

Prices quoted in this Guide were supplied in summer 2007. They are subject to alteration if goods and service costs are revised. The rates include tax and service charge.

The first price is the minimum rate in low season, the second price the maximum rate in high season. By supplying the information, hotels and restaurants have undertaken to maintain these rates for our readers.

In some towns, when commercial, cultural or sporting events are taking place the hotel rates are likely to be considerably higher.

RESERVATION AND DEPOSITS

Some hotels will ask you to confirm your reservation by giving your credit card number or require a deposit which confirms the commitment of both the customer and the hotelier. Ask the hotelier to provide you with all of the terms and conditions applicable to your reservation in their written confirmation.

CREDIT CARDS

	Credit cards accepted by the establishment:
AE ⓓ MC VISA	American Express – Diners Club – MasterCard (Eurocard) – Visa

ROOMS

25 Zim	Number of rooms
Zim – 👤 60/75 €	Lowest price/highest price for a single and
👥 70/120 €	a double or twin room
Zim ☕ –	Breakfast included
☕ 10 €	Breakfast supplement
Suiten	Suites: check with the hotelier for prices
☼	Summer prices
❄	Winter prices

HALF BOARD

½ P 10 €	This supplement per person per day should be added to the cost of the room in order to obtain the half board price.
(inkl. ½ P)	Price of the room including half board

RESTAURANT

Menü 20/42 €	**Set meals:** Lowest € 20 and highest € 42
Karte 30/41 €	**A la carte meals:**
	The first figure is for a plain meal and includes soup, main dish of the day with vegetables and dessert. The second figure is for a fuller meal and includes hors d'œuvre, main course and dessert (excluding drinks).

Towns

GENERAL INFORMATION

✉ *1010*	Postal code
L	Capital of the province
730 *R 20*	Michelin map number
24 000 Ew	Population
Höhe 175 m	Altitude (in metres)
Heilbad	Spa
Kneippkurort	Health resort (Kneipp)
Heilklimatischer	Health resort
Kurort-Luftkurort	Health resort
Erholungsort	Holiday resort
Wintersport	Winter sports
1 000 m	Altitude (in metres) of highest point reached by lifts
2	Number of cable cars
4	Number of ski and chair lifts
	Cross-country skiing
AX A	Letters giving the location of a place on the town plan
	Panoramic view, view
18	Golf course and number of holes
	Airport
	Shipping line (passengers & cars)
	Passenger transport only
i	Tourist Information Centre

SIGHTS

STAR RATING

★★★	Highly recommended
★★	Recommended
★	Interesting

LOCATION

	Sights in town
	In the surrounding area
6 km	Distance in kilometres.

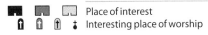

- Hotels
- Restaurants

SIGHTS

Place of interest
Interesting place of worship

ROADS

Motorway, Dual carriageway
Motorway, Dual carriageway with motorway characteristics
Number of junction
Major thoroughfare
One-way street – Unsuitable for traffic, street subject to restrictions
Area subject to restrictions
Pedestrian street – Tramway
Karlstr. Shopping street – Low headroom – Car park
Park and Ride
Gateway – Street passing under arch – Tunnel
Low headroom (16'6" max.) on major through routes
Station and railway
Funicular – Cable-car
Lever bridge – Car ferry

VARIOUS SIGNS

Tourist Information Centre
Mosque – Synagogue
Tower – Ruins – Windmill – Water Tower
Garden, park, wood – Cemetery – Cross
Stadium – Golf course – Racecourse – Skating rink
Outdoor or indoor swimming pool
View – Panorama
Monument – Fountain – Factory – Lighthouse
Pleasure boat harbour – Coach station
Airport – Underground station
Ferry services: passengers and cars, passengers only
Main post office
Hospital – Covered market
Public buildings located by letter:
L R - Provincial Government office – Town Hall
J - Law Courts
M T U - Museum – Theatre – University-College
POL. - Police (in large towns police headquarters)

Come leggere la guida

INFORMAZIONI TURISTICHE

Distanza dalle città di riferimento, uffici turismo, siti turistici locali, mezzi di trasporto, golfs e tempo libero...

GLI ALBERGHI

Da 🏨🏨🏨🏨🏨 a 🏨: categorie di confort.
I più ameni: in rosso.

I MIGLIORI ESERCIZI A PREZZI CONTENUTI

- Bib Hotel.
- Bib Gourmand.

LE TAVOLE STELLATE

- ✿✿✿ Vale il viaggio.
- ✿✿ Merita una deviazione.
- ✿ Ottima cucina.

I RISTORANTI

Da XXXXX a X: categorie di confort
I più ameni: in rosso.

CARTE MICHELIN

Riferimento alla carta Michelin in cui figura la località.

LOCALIZZARE LA CITTÀ

Posizione della località sulla carta regionale alla fine della guida (n° della carta e coordinate).

LOCALIZZARE L'ESERCIZIO

Localizzazione sulla pianta di città (coordinate ed indice).

GLI ALBERGHI TRANQUILLI

Albergo tranquillo.
Albergo molto tranquillo.

DESCRIZIONE DELL'ESERCIZIO

Atmosfera, stile, carattere e spécialità.

INSTALLAZIONI E SERVIZI

PREZZI

Principi

« Quest'opera nasce col secolo e durerà quanto esso. »

La prefazione della prima Edizione della Guida MICHELIN 1900, divenuta famosa nel corso degli anni, si è rivelata profetica. Se la Guida viene oggi consultata in tutto il mondo è grazie al suo costante impegno nei confronti dei lettori.

Desideriamo qui ribadirlo.

I principi della Guida MICHELIN:

La visita anonima: per poter apprezzare il livello delle prestazioni offerte ad ogni cliente, gli ispettori verificano regolarmente ristoranti ed alberghi mantenendo l'anonimato. Questi pagano il conto e possono presentarsi per ottenere ulteriori informazioni sugli esercizi. La posta dei lettori fornisce peraltro preziosi suggerimenti che permettono di orientare le nostre visite.

L'indipendenza: la selezione degli esercizi viene effettuata in totale indipendenza, nel solo interesse del lettore. Gli ispettori e il caporedattore discutono collegialmente le scelte. Le massime decisioni vengono prese a livello europeo. La segnalazione degli esercizi all'interno della Guida è interamente gratuita.

La selezione: la Guida offre una selezione dei migliori alberghi e ristoranti per ogni categoria di confort e di prezzo. Tale selezione è il frutto di uno stesso metodo, applicato con rigorosità da tutti gli ispettori.

L'aggiornamento annuale: ogni anno viene riveduto e aggiornato l'insieme dei consigli pratici, delle classifiche e della simbologia al fine di garantire le informazioni più attendibili.

L'omogeneità della selezione: i criteri di valutazione sono gli stessi per tutti i paesi presi in considerazione dalla Guida MICHELIN.

... e un unico obiettivo: prodigarsi per aiutare il lettore a fare di ogni spostamento e di ogni uscita un momento di piacere, conformemente alla missione che la Michelin si è prefissata: contribuire ad una miglior mobilità.

Editoriale

Caro lettore,

Abbiamo il piacere di presentarvi la nostra 4a edizione della Guida MICHELIN Austria.

Questa selezione, che comprende i migliori alberghi e ristoranti per ogni categoria di prezzo, viene effettuata da un'équipe di ispettori professionisti del settore. Ogni anno, percorrono l'intero paese per visitare nuovi esercizi e verificare il livello delle prestazioni di quelli già inseriti nella Guida.

All'interno della selezione, vengono inoltre assegnate ogni anno da ✿ a ✿✿✿ alle migliori tavole. Le stelle contraddistinguono gli esercizi che propongono la miglior cucina, in tutti gli stili, tenendo conto della scelta dei prodotti, della creatività, dell'abilità nel raggiungimento della giusta cottura e nell'abbinamento dei sapori, del rapporto qualità/prezzo,ma anche della continuità.

Anche quest'anno, numerose tavole sono state notate per l'evoluzione della loro cucina. Una « **N** » accanto ad ogni esercizio prescelto dell'annata 2008, ne indica l'inserimento fra gli esercizi con una, due o tre stelle.

Desideriamo inoltre segnalare le « *promesse* » per la categoria superiore. Questi esercizi, evidenziati in rosso nella nostra lista e nelle nostre pagine, sono i migliori della loro categoria e potranno accedere alla categoria superiore non appena le loro prestazioni avranno raggiunto un livello costante nel tempo, e nelle proposte della carta. Con questa segnalazione speciale, è nostra intenzione farvi conoscere le tavole che costituiscono, dal nostro punto di vista, le principali promesse della gastronomia di domani.

Il vostro parere ci interessa, specialmente riguardo a queste « *promesse* ». Non esitate quindi a scriverci, la vostra partecipazione è importante per orientare le nostre visite e migliorare costantemente la vostra Guida. Grazie ancora per la vostra fedeltà e vi auguriamo buon viaggio con la Guida MICHELIN 2008.

Consultate la Guida MICHELIN su
www.ViaMichelin.com
e scriveteci a :
der.michelinfuehrer-austria@de.michelin.com

Categorie & simboli distintivi

LE CATEGORIE DI CONFORT

Nella selezione della Guida MICHELIN vengono segnalati i migliori indirizzi per ogni categoria di confort e di prezzo.Gli esercizi selezionati sono classificati in base al confort che offrono e vengono citati in ordine di preferenza per ogni categoria.

		Gran lusso e tradizione
		Gran confort
		Molto confortevole
		Di buon confort
		Abbastanza confortevole
garni		L'albergo non ha ristorante
mit Zim		Il ristorante dispone di camere

I SIMBOLI DISTINTIVI

Per aiutarvi ad effettuare la scelta migliore, segnaliamo gli esercizi che si distinguono in modo particolare. Questi ristoranti sono evidenziati nel testo con o e Rest.

LE MIGLIORI TAVOLE

Le stelle distinguono gli esercizi che propongono la miglior qualità in campo gastronomico, indipendentemente dagli stili di cucina. I criteri presi in considerazione sono : la scelta dei prodotti, l'abilità nel raggiungimento della giusta cottura e nell'abbinamento dei sapori, il rapporto qualità/prezzo nonché la costanza.

Una delle migliori cucine, questa tavola vale il viaggio
Vi si mangia sempre molto bene, a volte meravigliosamente.

Cucina eccellente, questa tavola merita una deviazione

Un'ottima cucina nella sua categoria

I MIGLIORI ESERCIZI A PREZZI CONTENUTI

Bib Gourmand
Esercizio che offre una cucina di qualità, spesso a carattere tipicamente regionale, fino a 30 €, prezzo di un pasto, bevanda esclusa.

Bib Hotel
Esercizio che offre un soggiorno di qualità fino a 90 € per la maggior parte delle camere. Prezzi per 2 persone, prima colazione compresa.

GLI ESERCIZI AMENI

Il rosso indica gli esercizi patricolarmente ameni. Questo per le caratteristiche dell'edificio, le decorazioni non comuni, la sua posizione ed il servizio offerto.

🏠	a 🏠🏠🏠🏠🏠	**Alberghi ameni**
X	a XXXXX	**Ristoranti ameni**

LE SEGNALAZIONI PARTICOLARI

Oltre alle distinzioni conferite agli esercizi, gli ispettori Michelin apprezzano altri criteri spesso importanti nella scelta di un esercizio.

POSIZIONE

Cercate un esercizio tranquillo o che offre una vista piacevole? Seguite i simboli seguenti :

🐎	**Albergo tranquillo**
🐎	**Albergo molto tranquillo**
⋞	**Vista interessante**
⋞ Donau	**Vista eccezionale**

CARTA DEI VINI

Cercate un ristorante la cui carta dei vini offra una scelta particolarmente interessante? Seguite il simbolo seguente:

🍇	**Carta dei vini particolarmente interessante**

Attenzione a non confrontare la carta presentata da un sommelier in un grande ristorante con quella di una trattoria dove il proprietario ha una grande passione per i vini della regione.

Installazioni e servizi

30 Zim	Numero di camere
	Ascensore
	Aria condizionata (in tutto o in parte dell'esercizio)
	Esercizio con camere riservate in parte ai non fumatori Una sala del ristorante è riservata ai non fumatori
	Connessione Internet "Wireless Lan" in camera
	Esercizio accessibile in parte alle persone con difficoltà motorie
	Attrezzatura per accoglienza e ricreazione dei bambini
	Pasti serviti in giardino o in terrazza
	Spa / Wellness center: centro attrezzato per il benessere ed il relax
	Piscina: all'aperto, coperta
	Cura termale, Idroterapia
	Sauna - Palestra
	Campo di tennis
	Golf e numero di buche
	Giardino - Parco
	Spiaggia attrezzata
	Pontile d'ormeggio
	Sale per conferenze
	Saloni particolari
	Garage nell'albergo (generalmente a pagamento)
	Parcheggio riservato alla clientela
	Accesso vietato ai cani (in tutto o in parte dell'esercizio)
U	Stazione della metropolitana più vicina (a Vienna)

I prezzi

I prezzi che indichiamo in questa guida sono stati stabiliti nell'estate 2007; potranno subire delle variazioni in relazione ai cambiamenti dei prezzi di beni e servizi. Essi s'intendono comprensivi di tasse e servizio.

Il primo prezzo è il prezzo minimo in bassa stagione, il secondo prezzo il prezzo massimo in alta stagione. Gli albergatori e i ristoratori si sono impegnati, sotto la propria responsabilità, a praticare questi prezzi ai clienti.

In occasione di alcune manifestazioni (congressi, fiere, saloni, festival, eventi sportivi...) i prezzi richiesti dagli albergatori potrebbero subire un sensibile aumento.

LA CAPARRA

Alcuni albergatori chiedono il versamento di una caparra. Si tratta di un deposito-garanzia che impegna sia l'albergatore che il cliente. Chiedete all'albergatore di fornirvi nella sua lettera di conferma ogni dettaglio sulla prenotazione e sulle condizioni di soggiorno.

CARTE DI CREDITO

	Carte di credito accettate :
AE ⓓ ⓜⓒ VISA	American Express – Diners Club –Mastercard (Eurocard) – Visa.

CAMERE

25 Zim	Numero di camere
Zim – 🚹60/75 €	Presso minimo/massimo per camera singola
🚹🚹70/120 €	e doppia
Zim ☕ –	Prima colazione compresa
☕ 10 €	Supplemento per la prima colazione
Suiten	Suite: informarsi presso l'albergatore
☼	Prezzi estivi
❄	Prezzi invernali

MEZZA PENSIONE

½ P 10 €	Questo supplemento per persona al giorno va aggiunto al prezzo della camera per ottenere quello della mezza pensione.
(inkl. ½ P)	Prezzo della camera mezza pensione inclusa.

RISTORANTE

Menü 20/42 €	**Menu a prezzo fisso:** minimo 20 €, massimo 42 €
Karte 30/41 €	**Pasto alla carta** bevanda esclusa. Il primo prezzo corrisponde ad un pasto semplice comprendente: zuppa, piatto del giorno e dessert. Il secondo prezzo corrisponde ad un pasto più completo (con specialità) comprendente: antipasto, secondo e, dessert.

Le città

GENERALITÀ

✉ *1010*	Codice di avviamento postale
L	Capoluogo di Provincia
730 *R 20*	Numero della carta Michelin e coordinate riferite alla quadrettatura
24 000 Ew	Popolazione residente
Höhe 175 m	Altitudine
Heilbad	Stazione termale
Kneippkurort	Stazione di cure Kneipp
Heilklimatischer	Stazione climatica
Kurort-Luftkurort	Stazione climatica
Erholungsort	Stazione di villeggiatura
Wintersport	Sport invernali
1 000 m	Altitudine massima raggiungibile con gli impianti di risalita
2	Numero di funivie o cabinovie
4	Numero di sciovie e seggiovie
	Sci di fondo
	Panorama, vista
18	Golf e numero di buche
	Aeroporto
	Località con servizio auto su treno
	Trasporti marittimi: passeggeri ed autovetture
	Solo passegeri
	Ufficio informazioni turistiche

INFORMAZIONI TURISTICHE

INTERESSE TURISTICO

★★★	Vale il viaggio
★★	Merita una deviazione
★	Interessante

UBICAZIONE

	Nella città
	Nei dintorni della città
6 km	Distanza chilometrica

Le piante

- Alberghi
- Ristoranti

CURIOSITÀ

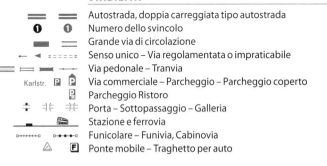

Edificio interessante
Costruzione religiosa interessante

VIABILITÀ

Autostrada, doppia carreggiata tipo autostrada
Numero dello svincolo
Grande via di circolazione
Senso unico – Via regolamentata o impraticabile
Via pedonale – Tranvia
Karlstr. P P Via commerciale – Parcheggio – Parcheggio coperto
Parcheggio Ristoro
Porta – Sottopassaggio – Galleria
Stazione e ferrovia
Funicolare – Funivia, Cabinovia
F Ponte mobile – Traghetto per auto

SIMBOLI VARI

Ufficio informazioni turistiche
Moschea – Sinagoga
Torre – Ruderi – Mulino a vento – Torre dell'acquedotto
Giardino, parco, bosco – Cimitero – Calvario
Stadio – Golf – Ippodromo - Pattinaggio
Piscina: all'aperto, coperta
Vista – Panorama
Monumento – Fontana – Fabbrica - Faro
Porto turistico – Stazione di Autobus
Aeroporto – Stazione della Metropolitana
Trasporto con traghetto:
passeggeri ed autovetture, solo passeggeri
Ufficio postale centrale
Ospedale – Mercato coperto
Edificio pubblico indicato con lettera:
L R Sede del Governo della Provincia –Municipio
J Palazzo di Giustizia
M T U Museo – Teatro - Università
POL. Polizia (Questura, nelle grandi città)

Auszeichnungen 2008

Distinctions 2008

Awards 2008

Le distinzioni 2008

Die Sterne 2008

Filzmoos	✻✻	Ort mit mindestens einem 2-Sterne-Restaurant
Linz	✻	Ort mit mindestens einem 1-Stern-Restaurant

Feuersbrunn
Krems an der Donau
Mautern
Wien
Linz
Mayerling
Baden
Weiden am See
Grieskirchen
Schützen am Gebirge
Vorchdorf
Irdning
Filzmoos
Mauterndorf
Bad Sankt Leonhard im Lavanttal
Straden
Leutschach
Tainach
Klagenfurt
Velden am Wörthersee
Nassfeld

Die Sterne-Restaurants

Les tables étoilées

Starred establishments

Gli esercizi con stelle

✿✿ 2008

Alland/Mayerling	*Restaurant Hanner*	
Filzmoos	*Hubertus*	
Hermagor / Naßfeld	*Arnold Pucher*	N
Mautern	*Landhaus Bacher*	
Schützen am Gebirge	*Taubenkobel*	
Wien	*Steirereck*	N
Zell am See	*Mayer's*	

✿ 2008

In rot *die Hoffnungsträger 2008 für* ✿✿
➜ **En rouge** *les espoirs 2008 pour* ✿✿
➜ **In red** *the 2008 Rising Stars for* ✿✿
➜ **In rosso** *le promesse 2008 per* ✿✿

Baden bei Wien	*Primavera*	
Bergheim	*Zur Plainlinde*	
Fügenberg im Zillertal / Hochfügen	*Alexander*	
Golling	*Döllerer*	
Grafenwörth / Feuersbrunn	*Toni M.*	N
Grieskirchen	*Waldschänke*	
Hallwang	*Pfefferschiff*	
Hof bei Salzburg	*Imperial*	N
Innsbruck	*Wirtshaus Schöneck*	
Irdning	*Villa Falkenhof*	
Ischgl	*Paznaunerstube*	
Kirchberg in Tirol	*Rosengarten*	
Kitzbühel	*Neuwirt*	
Kitzbühel	*Tennerhof*	
Klagenfurt	*Dolce Vita*	
Kötschach-Mauthen	*Sissy Sonnleitner-Landhaus Kellerwand*	
Krems an der Donau	*Mörwald Kloster UND*	
Lauterach	*Guth*	
Lech am Arlberg	*Brunnenhof*	
Lech am Arlberg	*Griggeler Stuba*	
Lech am Arlberg	*Post Stuben*	
Lech am Arlberg / Zürs	*KochArt*	
Leutschach	*Kreuzwirt am Pössnitzberg*	N
Linz	*Verdi*	
Lochau	*Mangold*	
Mauterndorf	*Mesnerhaus*	
Salzburg	*Brandstätter*	
Salzburg	*Esszimmer*	
Salzburg	*Ikarus*	
Salzburg	*Magazin*	
Salzburg	*Riedenburg*	
Sankt Leonhard im Lavanttal, Bad	*Trippolt Zum Bären*	
Schruns	*Edel-Weiß*	
Söll	*Schindlhaus*	
Straden	*Saziani*	
Tainach	*Sicher*	
Tannheim	*Hohenfels das Landhotel - Tannheimer Stube*	
Velden am Wörthersee	*Schlossstern*	N
Vorchdorf	*Tanglberg*	
Weiden am See	*Zur Blauen Gans*	
Werfen	*Karl und Rudolf Obauer*	
Wien	*Mraz und Sohn*	
Wien	*Restaurant Coburg*	
Wien	*RIeGi*	
Wien	*Walter Bauer*	

N *Neu* ➜ *Nouveau* ➜ *New* ➜ *Nuovo*

Die Hoffnungsträger 2008 für ✿

Les espoirs 2008 pour ✿

The 2008 Rising Stars for ✿

Le Promesse 2008 per ✿

Eisenstadt	*Bodega La Ina*	**Steyr**	*Tabor Turm*
Innsbruck	*Pavillon*	**Velden am Wörthersee**	*Caramé*
Lech am Arlberg / Zürs	*Thurnhers Alpenhof*		

N *Neu* → *Nouveau* → *New* → *Nuovo*

Bib Gourmand 2008

● Orte mit mindestens einem Bib Gourmand-Haus

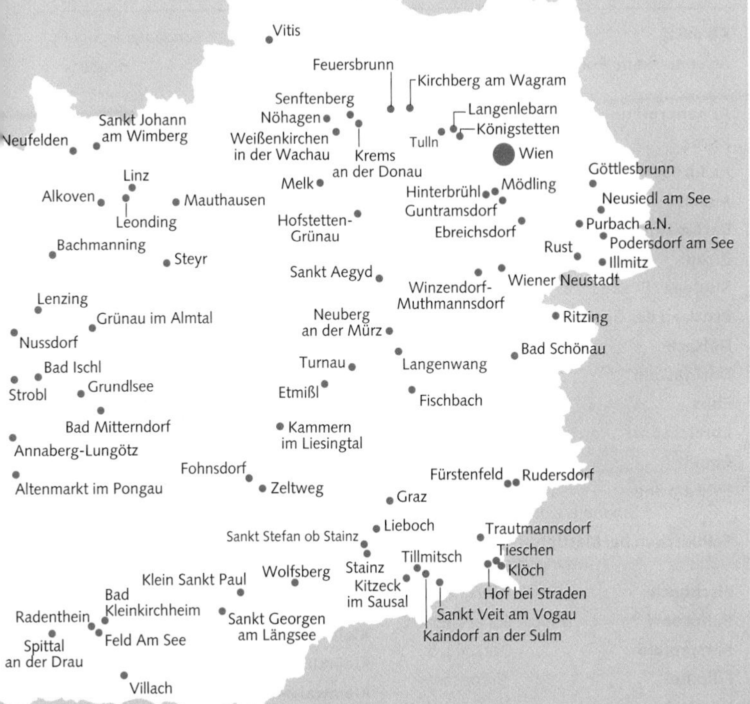

Bib Gourmand

Sorgfältig zubereitete, preiswerte Mahlzeiten
Repas soignés à prix modérés
Good food at moderate prices
Pasti accurati a prezzi contenuti

Alkoven	*Gasthof Schrot*	
Altenmarkt im Pongau	*Lebzelter - Moser*	
Annaberg-Lungötz	*Winterstellgut*	
Anras	*Pfleger*	
Au im Bregenzerwald	*Krone*	N
Axams	*Bürgerstuben*	
Bachmanning	*Weinwirt*	
Bizau	*Schwanen*	
Bludenz / Braz	*Gasthof Rössle*	
Bruck an der Glocknerstraße	*Taxhof*	
Dölsach	*Tiroler Hof*	
Dorfgastein	*Unterbergerwirt*	
Ebbs	*Unterwirt*	
Ebreichsdorf	*Rosenbauchs - Wirtshaus*	
Etmißl	*Gasthof Hubinger*	
Feld am See	*Landhotel Lindenhof - Vinum*	
Feldkirchen bei Mattighofen	*Maria vom guten Rat*	
Fischbach	*Gasthof Forsthaus*	
Fohnsdorf	*Schloss Gabelhofen*	N
Fürstenfeld	*Das Leitgeb*	
Fulpmes	*Gröbenhof*	
Göttlesbrunn	*bittermann*	N
Goldegg	*Zum Bierführer*	
Golling	*Wirtshaus - Döllerer*	
Grafenwörth / Feuersbrunn	*Mörwald-Villa Katharina - Zur Traube*	
Graz	*Iohan*	
Graz	*Kehlberghof*	
Graz	*Santa Clara*	
Grünau im Almtal	*Almtalhof*	
Grundlsee	*Post am See*	
Guntramsdorf	*Landhotel Jagdhof*	
Gurten	*Bauböck*	
Hinterbrühl	*Hexensitz*	N
Hittisau	*Gasthof Krone*	
Hofgastein, Bad	*Bertahof*	
Hofstetten-Grünau	*Landgasthof 3erlei*	
Hohenems	*Gasthaus Adler*	
Illmitz	*Presshaus*	
Innervillgraten	*Der Gannerhof*	
Ischl, Bad	*Goldenes Schiff*	
Jochberg	*Gasthaus Bärnbichl*	
Kaindorf an der Sulm	*Winzerhaus Kogelberg*	
Kammern im Liesingtal	*Spary*	
Kaprun	*Jagawirt*	N
Kauns	*Gasthof Falkeis*	
Kirchberg am Wagram	*Gut Oberstockstall*	
Kitzbühel	*Schwedenkapelle*	N
Kitzeck im Sausal	*Kirchenwirt*	
Kitzeck im Sausal	*Weinhof Kappel*	
Klein Sankt Paul	*Zum Dorfschmied*	
Kleinkirchheim, Bad	*Drage*	
Kleinwalsertal / Riezlern	*Almhof Rupp*	
Kleinwalsertal / Riezlern	*Alpenhof Jäger*	
Kleinwalsertal / Riezlern	*Scharnagl's Alpenhof*	
Klöch	*Schöne Aussichten*	
Königstetten	*Zum weißen Adler*	
Köstendorf	*Fritzenwallner*	
Krems an der Donau	*Jell*	
Krems an der Donau	*Zum Kaiser von Österreich*	

N *Neu* → *Nouveau* → *New* → *Nuovo*

Langenlebarn *Floh*
Langenlebarn *Zum Roten Wolf*
Langenwang *Krainer* N
Lans *Wilder Mann*
Lenzing *Wengermühle*
Lieboch *Kohnhauser*
Linz *Verdi Einkehr*
Linz / Leonding *Bergdiele*
Matrei am Brenner *Gasthof Lamm*
Mauthausen *Weindlhof*
Melk an der Donau *Stadt Melk - Légere*
Mitterndorf, Bad *Grimming-Wurz'n*
Mödling *Florians*
Mondsee *Seegasthof Lackner*
Nauders *Alpengasthof Norbertshöhe* N
Neuberg an der Mürz *Gasthof Holzer*
Neufelden *Mühltalhof*
Neumarkt am Wallersee *Gasthaus Kienberg* N
Neusiedl am See *Am Nyikospark*
Nussdorf am Attersee *1er Beisl im Lex'nhof*
Oberndorf in Tirol *Penzinghof*
Podersdorf am See *Zur Dankbarkeit*
Purbach am Neusiedlersee *Gut Purbach* N
Radenthein *Metzgerwirt*
Ritzing *Horvath*
Röthis *Torggel*
Rudersdorf *Zum alten Weinstock*
Rust am See *Wirtshaus im Hofgassl*
Salzburg *Gasthof Auerhahn*
Salzburg *Gasthof Schloss Aigen*
Salzburg *Pomodoro*
Salzburg *Zum Eigenherr* N
Sankt Aegyd *Zum Blumentritt*
Sankt Georgen am Längsee *Gasthof Liegl*
Sankt Jakob in Defereggen *Jesacherhof - Jakobistube*
Sankt Johann am Wimberg *Keplingerwirt*
Sankt Stefan ob Stainz *Landgasthof Gerngroß*
Sankt Veit am Vogau *Thaller*
Sankt Veit im Pongau *Sonnhof*
Schönau, Bad *Triad*
Schruns *Montafoner Stube - Löwen* N
Schwarzenberg *Gasthof Adler*
Schwendau im Zillertal *Sieghard*
Senftenberg *Weinhaus Nigl*
Spittal an der Drau *Kleinsasserhof*
Stainz *Engelweingarten*
Steyr *Rahofer*
Straden / Hof bei Straden *Stöcklwirt*
Strassen *Strasserwirt*
Strobl *Strobler Hof*
Stumm im Zillertal *Landgasthof Linde*
Sulz *Altes Gericht*
Telfs / Mösern *Habhof*
Tieschen *Königsberghof*
Tillmitsch *Schmankerlstub'n Temmer*
Trautmannsdorf *Steira Wirt*
Tulln *Sodoma*
Turnau *Wirtshaus Steirereck*
Uderns *Der Metzgerwirt*
Vigaun, Bad *Kellerbauer* N
Villach *Kaufmann und Kaufmann*
Villach *Urbani-Weinstuben* N
Vitis *Zum Topf*
Volders *Rossstall-Taverne*
Wattens *Zum Schwan*
Weinzierl am Walde / Nöhagen *Gasthaus Schwarz*
Weißenkirchen in der Wachau *Florianihof*
Weißenkirchen in der Wachau *Holzapfels Prandtauerhof*
Weißenkirchen in der Wachau *Jamek*
Wien *Artner*
Wien *Fadinger*
Wien *Mezzo*
Wien *Tempel*
Wien *Vestibül*
Wien *Vikerl's Lokal* N
Wiener Neustadt *Gastwirtschaft Brod*
Winzendorf-Muthmannsdorf *Schmutzer*
Wolfsberg *Alter Schacht*
Zell am See *Landhotel Erlhof*
Zell am See *Zum Hirschen*
Zeltweg *Schlosstaverne*

N *Neu* → *Nouveau* → *New* → *Nuovo*

Bib Hotel

Hier übernachten Sie gut und preiswert
Bonnes nuits à petits prix
Good accomodation at moderate prices
Buona sístemazione a prezzo contenuto

Abtenau	*Gutjahr*
Achenkirch	*Panorama*
Aigen-Schlägl	*Bärnsteinhof*
Altenmarkt im Pongau	*Alpenland*
Altenmarkt im Pongau	*Landhaus Kristall*
Anif	*Pension Schiessling*
Berwang	*Rotlechhof*
Bizau	*Schwanen*
Blumau, Bad	*Landhaus Florian*
Deutschlandsberg	*Pension Pölzl*
Dornbirn	*Dreiländerblick*
Eben am Achensee / Pertisau	*Gasthof Golfvilla*
Eben am Achensee / Pertisau	*Sonnenhof*
Erl	*Beim Dresch*
Feldkirch	*Gasthof Schäfle*
Finkenberg im Zillertal	*Dornauhof* N
Fiss	*Am Sonnberg*
Fulpmes	*Gröbenhof*
Fuschl am See	*Landgasthaus Hochlackenhof* N
Gamlitz	*Weingut Söll*
Gamlitz	*Weinlandhof*
Göstling an der Ybbs	*Gasthof Fahrnberger*
Gols	*Birkenhof*
Graz	*Der Marienhof*
Greifenburg	*Erbhof Kohlmayr*
Grödig	*Gasthof Schorn*
Großgmain	*Gasthof Steinerwirt* N
Hartberg	*Zum Alten Gerichtshof*
Heiligenkreuz	*Gasthof Gerlinde Gibiser*
Illmitz	*Johannes-Zeche*
Ischgl	*Valülla*
Jennersdorf	*Oasis*
Kirchberg am Wagram	*Alter Winzerkeller*
Kirchberg am Wechsel	*Landgasthof Fally*
Kleinwalsertal / Mittelberg	*Ingeborg*
Krumbach	*Gasthof Adler*
Krumpendorf	*Krumpendorferhof*
Kuchl	*Wagnermigl*
Leibnitz	*Weinland*
Leibnitz	*Zur alten Post*
Lermoos	*Klockerhof*
Leutschach	*Weingut Tauss*
Lienz	*Haidenhof*
Lingenau	*Gasthof zum Löwen*
Lölling	*Landgasthof Neugebauer* N
Loipersdorf	*Loipen Hof*
Maria Alm	*Edelweiss*
Mariapfarr	*Häuserl im Wald*
Mariapfarr	*Zum Granitzl*
Marz	*Müllner*
Mauterndorf	*Binggl* N
Minihof-Liebau	*Landhofmühle*
Mondsee	*Gasthof Drachenwand*
Moosburg	*Gasthof Bärnwirt*
Nauders	*Via Claudia*
Neustift im Stubaital	*Schönherr-Haus*
Neustift im Stubaital	*Sportpension Elisabeth*
Oberndorf in Tirol	*Gartenhotel Rosenhof*
Pfunds	*Pension Schöne Aussicht*
Pöllauberg	*Berggasthof König*

N *Neu* → *Nouveau* → *New* → *Nuovo*

Saalbach-Hinterglemm	*Schachner*	
Salzburg	*Blobergerhof*	
Salzburg	*Zur Post*	
Sankt Florian bei Linz	*Zur Kanne*	
Sankt Gilgen	*Schernthaner*	N
Sankt Johann in Tirol	*Gruber*	
Sankt Stefan ob Stainz	*Wirtshaus Jagawirt*	
Schattwald	*Alpengasthof Zur Post*	
Seefeld	*Alpengruss*	
Seefeld	*Christina*	N
Seefeld	*Lindauer*	
Seefeld	*St. Georg*	
Spitz an der Donau	*Weinberghof*	
Stans	*Brandstetterhof*	
Steeg	*Stern*	
Tulwitz	*Gasthof Knoll Pröllhofer*	
Turnau	*Seeberghof*	N
Vigaun, Bad	*Gasthof Langwies*	
Waltersdorf, Bad	*Safenhof*	N
Weißenkirchen in der Wachau	*Donauwirt*	
Wildschönau	*Landhaus Marchfeld*	
Wilhelmsburg	*Landgasthof Reinberger*	

N *Neu* → *Nouveau* → *New* → *Nuovo*

Angenehme Hotels

Hébergement agréable

Pleasant Lodging

Allogio ameno

Ischgl *Trofana Royal*
Velden am Wörthersee *Schloss Velden*
Wien *Imperial*
Wien *Palais Coburg*

Achenkirch *Posthotel*
Finkenberg im Zillertal *Sport- und Wellnesshotel Stock*
Going am Wilden Kaiser *Bio-Hotel Stanglwirt*
Hof bei Salzburg *Schloss Fuschl*
Kitzbühel *Tennerhof*
Lech am Arlberg *Almhof Schneider*
Lech am Arlberg / Zürs *Zürserhof*
Leogang *Der Krallerhof*
Maria Wörth / Sekirn *aenea*
Mieming *Alpenresort Schwarz*
Mondsee *Seehof*
Salzburg *Sacher*
Sankt Anton / Sankt Christoph *Arlberg Hospiz*
Serfaus *Schalber*
Wien *Bristol*
Wien *Sacher*
Zell am See *Salzburgerhof*

Alland / Mayerling *Hanner*
Alpbach *Böglerhof*
Dürnstein *Schloss Dürnstein*
Eben am Achensee / Maurach *Alpenrose*
Ellmau *Kaiserhof*
Feldkirchen an der Donau *Schloss Mühldorf*
Gastein, Bad *Grüner Baum*
Grän-Haldensee *Wellness-Hotel Engel*
Graz *Schlossberg Hotel*
Innsbruck *Schlosshotel*
Irdning *Schloss Pichlarn*
Lech am Arlberg *Burg Vital Hotel*
Lech am Arlberg *Gasthof Post*
Lech am Arlberg / Zürs *Thurnhers Alpenhof*
Salzburg *Goldener Hirsch*
Salzburg *Schloss Mönchstein*
Sankt Anton *Raffl's St. Antoner Hof*
Sebersdorf *Schloss Obermayerhofen*
Sölden / Hochgurgl *Top Hotel Hochgurgl*
Thiersee *Juffing Residenz*
Turracher Höhe *Hochschober*
Wien *Do und Co Hotel Vienna*

Afiesl *Romantik Resort Bergergut*
Bregenz *Deuring-Schlössle*
Brixen im Thale *Residenz Hubertus*
Filzmoos *Hubertus*
Fischbach *Dorfhotel Fasching*
Gargellen *Alpenhotel Heimspitze*
Gaschurn *Pfeifer*
Gerlos *Schönruh*
Gmunden *Schlosshotel Freisitz Roith*
Graz *Zum Dom*
Grünau im Almtal *Almtalhof*
Heiligenblut *Haus Senger - Chalet*
Innervillgraten *Der Gannerhof*
Innsbruck *Schwarzer Adler*
Jennersdorf *Landhaus Römerstein*
Längenfeld *Naturhotel Waldklause*
Lech am Arlberg *Angela*
Lech am Arlberg *Kristiania*
Millstatt am See *Bio-Hotel Alpenrose*
Mitterndorf, Bad *Landhaus Schloss Grubegg*
Nesselwängle *Sunneschlössli*
Pörtschach *Seehotel Porcia*
Rust am See *Bürgerhaus*
Salzburg *Rosenvilla*
Salzburg *Villa Pace*
Sankt Anton *Himmlhof*
Sankt Wolfgang im Salzkammergut *Landhaus zu Appesbach*
Schönegg *Guglwald*
Semmering *Panoramahotel Wagner*
Serfaus *3 Sonnen*
Straden *Castell Puccini*
Tannheim *Hohenfels das Landhotel*
Velden am Wörthersee *Seeschlössl*
Weißenkirchen in der Wachau *Donauhof*
Weißensee / Neusach *Ronacherfels*
Weißensee / Techendorf *Die Forelle*
Wien *Hollmann Beletage*
Wien *Kaiserhof*
Wien *Rathaus*
Zell am See *Schloss Prielau*

Hofkirchen im Mühlkreis *Landhotel Falkner*
Kleinwalsertal / Hirschegg *Sonnenberg*
Klöch *Schöne Aussichten*
Lech am Arlberg *Alpenrose*
Lech am Arlberg *Alpina*
Mariapfarr *Häuserl im Wald*
Oberalm *Schloss Haunsperg*
Sankt Leonhard im Pitztal *Gasthof Kirchenwirt*
Seefeld *Alpengruss*
Velden am Wörthersee *Gästehaus Gudrun*

Angenehme Restaurants

Restaurants agréables

Particularly pleasant restaurants

Ristoranti ameni

Salzburg	*Ikarus*
Velden am Wörthersee	*Schlossstern*
Wien	*Steirereck*

Alland / Mayerling	*Restaurant Hanner*
Ellmau	*Schloss-Stube im Kaiserhof*
Hallwang	*Pfefferschiff*
Hermagor / Naßfeld	*Arnold Pucher*
Ischgl	*Paznaunerstube*
Kirchberg in Tirol	*Rosengarten*
Lech am Arlberg	*Brunnenhof*
Mautern	*Landhaus Bacher*
Schruns	*Edel-Weiß*
Schützen am Gebirge	*Taubenkobel*
Straden	*Saziani*
Weißenkirchen in der Wachau	*Holzapfels Prandtauerhof*
Werfen	*Karl und Rudolf Obauer*
Zell am See	*Mayer's*

Annaberg-Lungötz	*Winterstellgut*
Bergheim	*Zur Plainlinde*
Brixlegg	*Sigwart's Tiroler Weinstuben*
Gamlitz	*Jaglhof*
Gargellen	*Montafoner Stöbli*
Innsbruck	*Pavillon*
Kirchberg am Wagram	*Gut Oberstockstall*
Kötschach-Mauthen	*Sissy Sonnleitner-Landhaus Kellerwand*
Lech am Arlberg	*Griggeler Stuba*
Lech am Arlberg	*Post Stuben*
Salzburg	*Esszimmer*
Sankt Anton	*Museum*
Sankt Anton / Sankt Christoph	*Hospiz Alm*
Senftenberg	*Weinhaus Nigl*
Spittal an der Drau	*Mettnitzer*
Tschagguns	*Montafoner Stube*
Velden am Wörthersee	*Caramé*
Weiden am See	*Zur Blauen Gans*
Weißenkirchen in der Wachau	*Florianihof*
Wien	*Zum Schwarzen Kameel*
Wien	*Zum weißen Rauchfangkehrer*
Zell am See	*Landhotel Erlhof*

Bruck an der Glocknerstraße	*Taxhof*
Gamlitz	*Erikas*
Innsbruck	*Lichtblick*
Innsbruck	*Wirtshaus Schöneck*
Lech am Arlberg	*Klösterle*
Rust am See	*Rusterhof*
Sankt Anton	*Schindler*
Schönau, Bad	*Triad*
Turnau	*Wirtshaus Steirereck*

Gut zu wissen

Pour en savoir plus

Further information

Per sapere di piú

Wellness-Hotels

Bel espace de bien-être et de relaxation

Extensive facility for relaxation and well-being

Centro attrezzato per il benessere ed il relax

Achenkirch	*Landhotel Reiterhof*
Achenkirch	*Posthotel*
Afiesl	*Romantik Resort Bergergut*
Aigen-Schlägl	*Almesberger*
Alpbach	*Böglerhof*
Aussee, Bad	*Falkensteiner Hotel Wasnerin*
Baden bei Wien	*Grand Hotel Sauerhof*
Bartholomäberg	*Fernblick*
Bergheim	*Gasthof Gmachl*
Berwang	*Kaiserhof*
Berwang	*Singer Sporthotel und Spa*
Bezau	*Gams*
Bezau	*Post*
Bleiberg, Bad	*Bleibergerhof*
Bludenz	*Val Blu Resort*
Brand	*Sporthotel Beck*
Brand	*Walliserhof*
Bürserberg	*Berghotel Schillerkopf*
Burgauberg-Neudauberg	*Das Gogers Golf und Spa*
Damüls	*Damülser Hof*
Dellach im Gailtal	*Biohotel Daberer*
Dienten am Hochkönig	*Die Übergossene Alm*
Dienten am Hochkönig	*Mitterwirt*
Dornbirn	*Rickatschwende*
Eben am Achensee / Maurach	*Alpenrose*
Eben am Achensee / Maurach	*Vier Jahreszeiten*

Eben am Achensee / Pertisau	*Caroline*
Eben am Achensee / Pertisau	*Der Wiesenhof*
Eben am Achensee / Pertisau	*Fürstenhaus*
Eben am Achensee / Pertisau	*Post*
Ehrwald	*Sporthotel Alpenhof*
Elbigenalp	*Alpenrose*
Ellmau	*Kaiserhof*
Erpfendorf in Tirol	*Vital-Hotel Berghof*
Eugendorf	*Landhotel Gschirnwirt*
Faistenau	*Alte Post*
Finkenberg im Zillertal	*Sport- und Wellnesshotel Stock*
Fiss	*Alpenresort Schlosshotel Fiss*
Flachau	*Felsenhof*
Flachau	*Lacknerhof*
Fontanella	*Faschina*
Fügen	*Crystal*
Fügen	*Held*
Fügen	*Schiestl*
Fuschl am See	*Ebner's Waldhof am See*
Gars am Kamp	*Dungl Bio-Vital Hotel*
Gastein, Bad	*Europäischer Hof*
Gastein, Bad	*Grüner Baum*
Gerlos	*Alpenhof*
Gerlos	*Gaspingerhof*
Gleichenberg, Bad	*Schlössl-Hotel-Kindl*
Gnadenwald	*Alpenhotel Speckbacher Hof*
Going am Wilden Kaiser	*Bio-Hotel Stanglwirt*
Grän-Haldensee	*Liebes Rot-Flüh*
Grän-Haldensee	*Sonnenhof*
Grän-Haldensee	*Tyrol*
Grän-Haldensee	*Wellness-Hotel Engel*
Großarl	*Edelweiss*
Häring, Bad	*Panorama Royal*
Hall, Bad	*Tassilo Hotel*

Hermagor	*Falkensteiner Hotel Carinzia*
Hermagor / Naßfeld	*Sonnenalpe*
Hermagor / Naßfeld	*Wulfenia*
Hof bei Salzburg	*ArabellaSheraton Hotel Jagdhof*
Hof bei Salzburg	*Schloss Fuschl*
Hofgastein, Bad	*Astoria*
Hofgastein, Bad	*Grand Park Hotel*
Hofgastein, Bad	*Palace*
Hofgastein, Bad	*Thermenhotel Sendlhof*
Innsbruck	*Sporthotel Igls*
Irdning	*Schloss Pichlarn*
Ischgl	*Brigitte*
Ischgl	*Madlein*
Ischgl	*Post*
Ischgl	*Trofana Royal*
Jennersdorf	*Landhaus Römerstein*
Jerzens	*Jerzner Hof*
Kals	*Taurerwirt*
Kirchberg in Tirol	*Elisabeth*
Kitzbühel	*A-ROSA*
Kitzbühel	*Erika*
Kitzbühel	*Schwarzer Adler*
Kitzbühel	*Sport-Wellnesshotel Bichlhof*
Kitzbühel	*Weisses Rössl*
Kitzeck im Sausal	*Weinhof Kappel*
Kleinkirchheim, Bad	*Die Post*
Kleinkirchheim, Bad	*Felsenhof*
Kleinkirchheim, Bad	*Pulverer-Thermenwelt*
Kleinkirchheim, Bad	*Thermenhotel Ronacher*
Kleinwalsertal / Hirschegg	*Birkenhöhe*
Kleinwalsertal / Hirschegg	*Naturhotel Chesa Valisa*
Kleinwalsertal / Hirschegg	*Walserhof*
Kleinwalsertal / Mittelberg	*Leitner*
Kleinwalsertal / Mittelberg	*IFA-Hotel Alpenhof Wildental*

Kleinwalsertal / Riezlern	*Almhof Rupp*
Kössen	*Alpina*
Kössen	*Peternhof*
Krems an der Donau	*Steigenberger Avance Hotel Krems*
Kukmirn	*Brennerei und Wellnesshotel Lagler*
Laa an der Thaya	*Therme Laa Hotel und Spa*
Längenfeld	*Aqua Dome - Tirol Therme*
Langenlois	*LOISIUM*
Lavant	*Dolomitengolf*
Lech am Arlberg	*Almhof Schneider*
Lech am Arlberg	*Arlberg*
Lech am Arlberg	*Burg Hotel*
Lech am Arlberg	*Burg Vital Hotel*
Lech am Arlberg	*Goldener Berg*
Lech am Arlberg	*Gotthard*
Lech am Arlberg	*Krone*
Lech am Arlberg	*Sonnenburg*
Lech am Arlberg / Zürs	*Zürserhof*
Leogang	*Der Krallerhof*
Lermoos	*Alpenrose*
Lermoos	*Post und Postschlößl*
Lesachtal	*Almwellness-Hotel Tuffbad*
Leutasch	*Quellenhof*
Leutasch	*Sporthotel Xander*
Loipersdorf	*Thermenhotel Stoiser*
Mieming	*Alpenresort Schwarz*
Millstatt am See	*Alexanderhof*
Mittersill	*Kinderhotel Felben*
Mörbisch	*Das Schmidt*
Nauders	*Alpin-Spa-Hotel Naudererhof*
Nesselwängle	*Laternd'l Hof*
Neuhofen an der Ybbs	*Kothmühle*
Neukirchen am Großvenediger	*Gassner*
Neusiedl am See	*Helga Dolezal Beauty-Vital-Residenz*

Neustift im Stubaital	*Jagdhof*
Neustift im Stubaital	*Sporthotel Neustift*
Obertauern	*Steiner*
Pamhagen	*Vila Vita Hotel Pannonia*
Pettneu am Arlberg	*Gridlon*
Pichl an der Enns	*Pichlmayrgut*
Pill	*Bio-Aktiv-Hotel Grafenast*
Pörtschach	*Parkhotel*
Pörtschach	*Schloss Seefels*
Pörtschach	*Werzer's Hotel Resort*
Puch bei Hallein	*Kurhotel Vollererhof*
Radenthein	*Seefischer am See*
Radkersburg, Bad	*Hotel im Park*
Radstadt	*Gut Weissenhof*
Radstadt	*Zum Jungen Römer*
Rauris	*Rauriserhof*
Reith im Alpbachtal	*Pirchner Hof*
Reuthe	*Gesundhotel Bad Reuthe*
Ried im Oberinntal	*Linde*
Ried im Zillertal	*Magdalena*
Rohrmoos	*Schwaigerhof*
Saalbach-Hinterglemm	*Feriengut Ellmauhof*
Saalbach-Hinterglemm	*Kendler*
Saalbach-Hinterglemm	*Sport- und Vitalhotel Ellmau*
Saalbach-Hinterglemm	*Theresia Gartenhotel*
Saalfelden	*Gut Brandlhof*
Saalfelden	*Schörhof*
Sankt Anton	*Alte Post*
Sankt Anton	*Schwarzer Adler*
Sankt Anton / Sankt Christoph	*Alpenhotel St. Christoph*
Sankt Anton / Sankt Christoph	*Arlberg Hospiz*
Sankt Anton / Sankt Christoph	*Maiensee*
Sankt Anton im Montafon	*Adler*
Sankt Georgen am Längsee	*Moorquell*

Sankt Georgen im Attergau	*Winzer*
Sankt Jakob in Defereggen	*Jesacherhof*
Sankt Johann im Pongau	*Berghof*
Sankt Johann im Pongau	*Dorfhotel Tannenhof*
Sankt Johann im Pongau	*Oberforsthof*
Sankt Johann im Pongau	*Zinnkrügl*
Sankt Kanzian	*Wellnesshotel Mori*
Sankt Leonhard im Lavanttal, Bad	*Moselebauer*
Sankt Leonhard im Pitztal	*Sport- und Vitalhotel Seppl*
Sankt Leonhard im Pitztal	*Vier Jahreszeiten*
Sankt Leonhard im Pitztal	*Wildspitze*
Sankt Michael im Lungau	*Eggerwirt*
Sankt Michael im Lungau / Katschberg	*Falkensteiner Hotel Cristallo*
Sankt Veit in Defereggen	*Gourmethotel Defereggental*
Sankt Wolfgang im Salzkammergut	*Im Weissen Rössl*
Schallerbach, Bad	*Paradiso*
Scheffau am Wilden Kaiser	*Kaiser in Tirol*
Schönegg	*Guglwald*
Schruns	*Alpenhotel Bitschnau*
Schruns	*Alpenrose*
Schruns	*Löwen*
Schruns	*Vitalquelle Gauenstein*
Seeboden	*Koller's Hotel am See*
Seefeld	*Astoria Relax und Spa-Hotel*
Seefeld	*Das Hotel Eden*
Seefeld	*Dorint Vital Royal Spa*
Seefeld	*Gartenhotel Tümmlerhof*
Seefeld	*Klosterbräu*
Seefeld	*Lärchenhof*
Seefeld	*Sonnenresidenz Alpenpark*
Seefeld	*Wellnesshotel Schönruh*
Seefeld / Reith	*Alpenkönig Tirol*
Serfaus	*Cervosa*

Serfaus	*Schalber*	
Silbertal im Montafon	*Bergkristall*	
Sillian	*Dolomiten Residenz Sporthotel Sillian*	
Sölden	*Castello Falkner*	
Sölden	*Central*	
Sölden / Hochgurgl	*Top Hotel Hochgurgl*	
Sölden / Obergurgl	*Alpina*	
Sölden / Obergurgl	*Bergwelt*	
Sölden / Obergurgl	*Hochfirst*	
Stans	*Schwarzbrunn*	
Stegersbach	*Balance Resort*	
Stegersbach	*Larimar*	
Tannheim	*Jungbrunn*	
Tannheim	*Schwarzer Adler - Sonnenheim*	
Tannheim	*Sägerhof*	
Tatzmannsdorf, Bad	*AVITA*	
Tatzmannsdorf, Bad	*Kur- und Thermenhotel*	
Tatzmannsdorf, Bad	*Reiter's Avance Hotel*	
Tatzmannsdorf, Bad	*Reiter's Supreme Hotel*	
Tatzmannsdorf, Bad	*Simon - Das Vitalhotel*	
Telfs	*Interalpen-Hotel Tyrol*	
Telfs / Mösern	*Inntalerhof*	
Thiersee	*Sonnhof*	
Turracher Höhe	*Hochschober*	
Turracher Höhe	*Seehotel Jägerwirt*	
Tux / Hintertux	*Neuhintertux*	
Tux / Vorderlanersbach	*Tuxerhof*	
Unken	*Familien Erlebnis Hotel Post*	
Velden am Wörthersee	*Schloss Velden*	
Velden am Wörthersee	*Seehotel Europa*	
Villach / Egg am Faakersee	*Karnerhof*	
Villach / Warmbad	*Warmbaderhof*	
Wagrain	*Sporthotel*	
Walchsee	*Schick*	

Walchsee	*Seehof-Seeresidenz*
Waltersdorf, Bad	*Der Steirerhof*
Waltersdorf, Bad	*Thermenhof Paierl*
Warth	*Lechtaler-Hof*
Westendorf	*Vital Landhotel Schermer*
Wildschönau	*Wastlhof*
Windischgarsten	*Dilly's Wellness-Hotel*
Zell am See	*Badhaus*
Zell am See	*Landgasthof Stadt Wien*
Zell am See	*Mavida*
Zell am See	*Salzburgerhof*
Zell am See	*Sporthotel Alpenblick*
Zell am See	*Tirolerhof*
Zell am Ziller	*Theresa SPA-Wellness Hotel*

Weinbau in Österreich

Österreich hat eine Weinanbaufläche von knapp 50 000 Hektar und ist in Weinbauregionen und -gebiete unterteilt. Die Herkunft aus einem der Weinbaugebiete wird bei Qualitätsweinen stets angegeben. Rebsorten und Qualtitätsstufen: S. 69

Le vignoble en Autriche

Le vignoble autrichien s'étend sur une surface de 50 000 hectares subdivisée en régions et zones de viticulture. L'origine des zones de viticulture est indiquée pour chaque vin de qualité. Les cépages et niveaux de qualité : p. 71

Austrian wines

Austria has almost 50 000 ha of vineyards and is divided into wine regions and wine appellations or Gebiete. A superior quality wine, or Qualitätswein, always includes the region of production on the label. Grape varieties and quality grades: p. 73

I vigneti in Austria

La superficie vinicola austriaca è di 50 000 ettari ed è suddivisa in regioni e zone di viticoltura. L'origine di queste ultime è indicata in ogni vino di qualità. I vitigni e livelli di qualità: p. 75

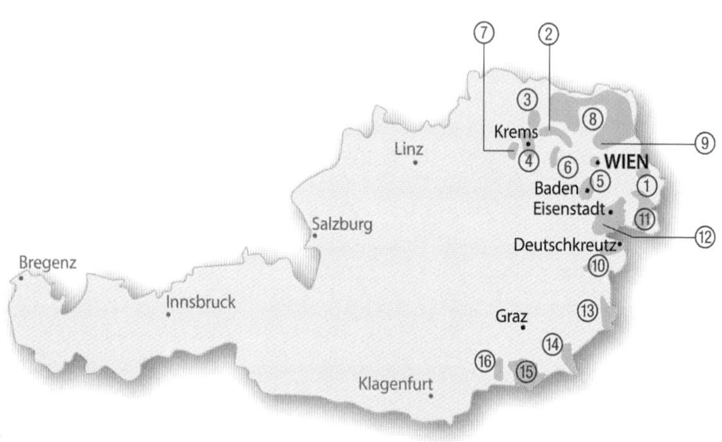

① Carnuntum
② Donauland
③ Kamptal
④ Kremstal
⑤ Thermenregion
⑥ Traisental
⑦ Wachau
⑧ Weinviertel
⑨ Wien
⑩ Mittelburgenland
⑪ Neusiedler See
⑫ Neusiedler See-Hügelland
⑬ Südburgenland
⑭ Südosteiermark
⑮ Südsteiermark
⑯ Weststeiermark

Rebsorten

DIE WICHTIGSTEN WEISSWEINSORTEN

Chardonnay: wird vor allem in der Steiermark angebaut und heißt dort Morillon. Hier liefert er meist frische und blumige Weine.

Grüner Veltliner: Klassisch kommt die österreichische Nationalrebe aus Niederösterreich und Wien. Die jungen Veltliner sind pfeffrig und spritzig; gereifte Veltliner sehr extraktreich.

Müller-Thurgau (Rivaner): Die ehemals weitverbreitete Traube ist eine Kreuzung aus Riesling und Gutedel und erzeugt milde, säurearme Weine.

Riesling: Er wächst vor allem in der Wachau, im Kamptal und im Donauland. Typisch sind sein Duft nach Aprikosen und Zitrusfrüchten sowie die rassige Säure.

Sauvignon blanc: wird vor allem in der Steiermark angebaut. Dort ergibt er einen eleganten Wein mit exotischen Aromen und feiner Säure.

Weißer Burgunder (Pinot blanc, Klevner): ist vorwiegend im Burgenland und in Niederösterreich angesiedelt. Aus dieser Traube entstehen harmonische, dezente Weine mit feiner Säure.

Welschriesling: Mit seinem frisch-fruchtigen Aroma wird er zumeist jung als Alltagswein getrunken. Am Neusiedler See erzeugt man aber auch hochwertige edelsüße Botrytisweine.

DIE WICHTIGSTEN ROTWEINSORTEN

Blauburgunder (Pinot Noir): wächst vor allem in Niederösterreich und im Burgenland. Sie ergibt feine, vollmundige Rotweine mit sehr gutem Alterungspotenzial.

Blauer Wildbacher: beliebte Traube in der Steiermark, wird fast ausschließlich als Rosé ausgebaut, zum sogenannten Schilcher. Der Schilcher ist kernig, mit kräftiger Säure; er wird am besten im Jahr nach der Lese getrunken.

Blaufränkisch (Lemberger, Kekfrankos): ist die typische Traube des Burgenlands, aus der fruchtige, gerbstoffhaltige Rotweine entstehen.

Portugieser: die ertragsreiche Rebsorte wird fast ausschließlich in Niederösterreich angebaut. Der Portugieser ist ein milder und fruchtiger Rotwein, der jung getrunken wird.

Zweigelt (Rotburger): Kreuzung aus St. Laurent und Blaufränkisch, aus der sowohl fruchtige und leichte Weine entstehen, als auch kraftvolle, lagerfähige Gewächse mit eleganter Weichselfrucht.

St. Laurent: Kennzeichnend für diesen Wein ist die kräftige, dunkelrote Farbe und das samtige Kirschbukett. Gutes Alterungspotential.
Eine ständig zunehmende Tendenz bei den hochwertigen Rotweinen ist der Ausbau von Weinen aus gemischtem Traubengut als Cuvée.

QUALITÄTSSTUFEN

Nach dem Weingesetz wird zwischen Tafelwein, Landwein und Qualitätswein unterschieden. Zur höchsten Stufe, den Qualitätsweinen, gehören auch die Kabinett- und Prädikatsweine, für die zusätzliche Anforderungen in Bezug auf Mostgewicht und Verarbeitung gelten.

Besonderheiten sind der Strohwein aus Trauben, die mindestens drei Monate auf Stroh getrocknet wurden, und der Ausbruch, der ähnlich dem ungarischen Aszú aus überreifem, eingetrocknetem Traubengut hergestellt wird, dem frisch gekelterter Most zugesetzt werden kann (hauptsächlich im Burgenland).

In der Wachau hat die Vereinigung "Vinea Wachau" für trocken ausgebaute Weine spezielle Kategorien geschaffen:

Steinfeder - leichte, fruchtige Weine mit höchstens 10,7° Alk.

Federspiel - elegante Weine, maximal 12,5° Alk.

Smaragd - kraftvolle, ausgereifte Weine; Bezeichnung für die besten Spätlesen

Zusätzlich zur Einteilung der Weine in Qualitätsstufen gibt es im österreichischen Weingesetz auch den noch neuen Begriff DAC (Districtus Austria Controllatus). Als DAC-Weine dürfen nur "gebietstypische" Qualitätsweine vermarktet werden.

Les cépages

PRINCIPAUX CÉPAGES BLANCS

Chardonnay : cultivé principalement en Styrie où on le nomme Morillon. C'est un vin frais et bouqueté.

Grüner Veltliner : cépage autrichien classique provenant de la Basse-Autriche et de Vienne. Les jeunes Veltliner sont piquants et vifs, les vieux Veltliner sont très aromatiques.

Müller-Thurgau (Rivaner) : ce cépage, autrefois très répandu, est un croisement entre Riesling et Gutedel ; il produit un vin fruité et peu acide.

Riesling : pousse avant tout dans la région de la Wachau, au Kamptal et dans la vallée du Danube. Ses arômes d'abricots et d'agrumes sont typiques. Vin nerveux.

Sauvignon blanc : cultivé en Styrie. Vin élégant avec des saveurs epicées et une acidité subtile.

Weißer Burgunder (Pinot blanc, Klevner) : est surtout planté au Burgenland et en Basse-Autriche. Vin harmonieux et équilibré.

Welschriesling : avec sa saveur fraîche et fruitée, il est généralement consommé jeune comme vin de table. Par contre au Neusiedler See, on produit des vins moëlleux de haute qualité (grains à pourriture noble).

PRINCIPAUX CÉPAGES ROUGES

Blauburgunder (Pinot Noir) : pousse avant tout en Basse-Autriche et au Burgenland. Vin rouge fin et velouté avec un bon potentiel de vieillissement.

Blauer Wildbacher : cépage courant en Styrie, presque uniquement vinifié comme rosé sous la dénomination Schilcher. Vin piquant et charnu. Il est bu dans l'année qui suit les vendanges.

Blaufränkisch (Lemberger, Kekfrankos) : Raisin typique du Burgenland, vin fruité et tanique.

Portugieser : cépage presque exclusivement cultivé en Basse-Autriche. Vin rouge doux et fruité, à boire jeune.

Zweigelt (Rotburger) : Croisement entre St. Laurent et Blaufränkisch, dont naissent non seulement des vins fruités et légers, mais aussi des vins vigoureux et élégants avec potentiel de garde.

St. Laurent : la caractéristique de ce vin est la couleur de sa robe, très marquée ainsi que son arôme de cerises. Bon potentiel de vieillissement.

Une tendance croissante parmi les vins rouges de grande qualité est l'assemblage de différents cépages pour une cuvée.

NIVEAUX DE QUALITÉ

La législation vinicole établit une distinction entre vins de table, vins du pays et vins de qualité. Les vins Kabinett et Prädikat font partie des vins de qualité, pour lesquels prévaut une réglementation particulière concernant la teneur en sucre et la méthode de vinification.

Dans le Burgenland on trouve des particularités comme le Strohwein, élaboré avec des raisins séchés sur la paille pendant au moins 3 mois - et l'Ausbruch, élaboré comme l'Aszú hongrois, à partir de grains à pourriture noble ajoutés à un moût traditionnel.

En Wachau, l'association « Vinea Wachau » a créé des catégories spéciales pour les vins secs :

Steinfeder : léger, fruité avec un degré alcoolique max. de 10,7°.

Federspiel : élégant, avec un degré alcoolique max de 12,5°.

Smaragd : vigoureux, mûr ; désignant les meilleurs vins de vendanges tardives.

En plus de la répartition des vins en niveaux de qualité, il existe dans la législation vinicole autrichienne une nouvelle définition, DAC (Districtus Austria Controllatus). Seuls les vins typiques du terroir peuvent être commercialisés en tant que vin DAC.

Grape varieties

THE MAIN WHITE WINES

Chardonnay: Produced mostly in Styria, where it is known as Morillon. It generally makes fresh and flowery wines.

Grüner Veltliner: Austria's national grape is traditionally grown in Lower Austria and around Vienna. A young Veltiner is lively and peppery, mature vintages gain in body and complexity.

Müller-Thurgau (Rivaner): Once far more widespread, this cross between Riesling and Gutedel produces soft wines with light acidity.

Riesling (Rheinriesling, Weisser Riesling): Most commonly found in Wachau, Kamptal and along the Danube, Riesling is easily recognised by its apricot and citrus bouquet and its vivacious acid character.

Sauvignon Blanc: Cultivated mainly in Styria, where it gives elegant wines with exotic tones and a very delicate acidic quality.

Weißer Burgunder (Pinot Blanc, Klevner): Grows best in Lower Austria and the Burgenland. This grape makes subtle and well-balanced wines with an understated acid note.

Welschriesling (Italian Riesling): Generally a fresh and fruity young wine, good for everyday drinking, although vineyards around the Neusiedler See use the noble rot, or Edelfäule, method to produce highly-prized sweet wines.

THE MAIN RED WINES

Blauburgunder (Pinot Noir): This delicate yet full-flavoured red ages very well. It is mainly grown in Lower Austria and the Burgenland.

Blauer Wildbacher: Popular in Styria, where it is used almost exclusively to make a type of rosé known as Schilcher. Robust with a sharp acid note, Schilcher is best drunk in the year after its harvest.

Blaufränkisch (Lemberger, Kekfrankos): Fruity with heavy tannins, this is the typical grape of the Burgenland.

Portugieser: this high-yield variety comes almost exclusively from Lower Austria. Portugieser is a soft and fruity wine which is best enjoyed young.

Zweigelt (Rotburger): The cross between St. Laurent and Blaufränkisch produces light and fruity wines as well as powerful vintages with elegant cherry flavour that mature well over the years.

St. Laurent: This variety is appreciated for its strong, dark-red robe and a silky nose with a hint of cherries. One to lay down.

An increasing trend away from varietal wines has led to the production of more and more quality red blends, or cuvées.

By law, Austrian wines must fall into one of three categories: Tafelwein, Landwein and the most prestigious Qualitätswein. This highest level includes the Kabinettweine and Prädikatsweine: these additional distinctions are dictated by the way the wine is produced and aged and by the specific gravity of the grape must.

Among the wines unique to Austria are Strohwein, produced from grapes which have been dried on a bed of straw for at least three months, and Ausbruch, which is similar to Hungarian Aszú Tokay, in that it is made from overripe dried grapes to which some producers add a fresh pressing of must. Both wines are particularly popular in Burgenland.

The «Vinea Wachau» association have created three special categories for wines varieties produced from dried grapes.

They are:

Steinfeder - light and fruity with a maximum of 10,7% alcohol by volume

Federspiel - elegant wines up to 12,5%.

Smaragd - Powerful, mature wines. The best Spätlesen, or late-harvested wines, fall into this category.

In addition to the quality categories above, Austrian wine legislation - the Weingesetz - now includes the new designation DAC (Districtus Austria Controllatus). As with the French "Appellation Contrôlée", only wines deemed "typical of the region" may be sold under a DAC label.

I vitigni

PRINCIPALI VITIGNI BIANCHI

Chardonnay: è coltivato soprattutto nello Steinmark dove è denominato Morillon. E' un vino fresco e aromatico.

Gruner Veltliner: vitigno nazionale classico originario della Niederosterreich e di Vienna. I giovani Veltliner sono vivaci e frizzanti, quelli invecchiati molto aromatici.

Muller-Thurgau (Rivaner): un tempo molto diffuso, si tratta di un incrocio tra il Riesling e il Gutedel, fruttato e poco acido.

Riesling: è coltivato soprattutto nel Wachau, nel Kamptal e nel Donauland. Vino nervoso, sono tipici i suoi profumi di albicocca e agrumi.

Sauvignon: coltivato nello Steiermark, è un vino elegante con sapore esotico e finemente acido.

Burgunder bianco (Pinot bianco, Klevner): cresce soprattutto nel Burgenland e nella Niederosterreich. Armonico ed equilibrato.

Welschriesling: fresco e fruttato, è consumato soprattutto giovane come vino di tutti i giorni mentre, coltivato sul lago Neusiedler, diventa un vino morbido di alta qualità (Botrytiswein).

PRINCIPALI VITIGNI ROSSI

Blauburgunder (Pinot Nero): è coltivato soprattutto nella Niederosterrreich e nel Burgenland. Fine e vellutato, dimostra buone capacità di invecchiamento.

Blauer Wildbacher: uva diffusa nello Steinmark, è quasi esclusivamente coltivata per produrre vini rosati. Chiamato Schilcher, è un vino frizzante e carnoso che viene bevuto un anno dopo la vendemmia.

Blaufrankish (Lemberger, Kekfrankos): tipico del Burgerland, è tannico e fruttato.

Portugieser: quasi esclusivamente coltivato nella Niederosterreich, bevuto giovane è un vino dolce e fruttato.

Zweigelt (Rotburger): incrocio tra il St. Laurent e il Blaufrankisch da cui nascono non solo dei vini fruttati e leggeri ma anche vigorosi ed eleganti con possibilità di invecchiamento.

St. Laurent: caratteristica di questo vitigno è il colore acceso e il profumo di ciliegie. Buone potenzialità di invecchiamento.

Una tendenza in costante crescita è quella di produrre vini unendo diversi vitigni.

LIVELLO DI QUALITÀ

La legge sul vino stabilisce una distinzione tra vino da tavola, vino regionale e vino di qualità. I vini Kabinett e Pradikat fanno parte dei vini di qualità per i quali sono previste esigenze ulteriori relativamente a zuccheri e trattamento.

Vini particolari come lo Strohwein (prodotto con uva lasciata seccare per almeno 3 mesi sulla paglia) e l'Ausbruch (prodotto come l'Aszù ungherese dove aggiungono gli acini con muffa nobile al mosto tradizionale) si trovano soprattutto nel Burgerland.

Nel Wachau l'associazione «Vinea Wachau» ha creato delle categorie speciali per i vini secchi:

- **Steinfeder:** leggero, fruttato con tasso alcolico massimo del 10,7°.

- **Federspiel:** elegante, contenuto alcolico massimo del 12,5°.

- **Samaragd:** vigoroso e maturo, designa i migliori vini a vendemmia tardiva.

Oltre alla suddivisione dei vini di qualità, esiste nelle leggi austriache una nuova denominazione DAC (Districtus Austria Controllatus) con cui possono essere commercializzati solo i vini tipici del territorio.

Die österreichische Küche

Wenn man heute von der typisch österreichischen Küche spricht, meint man im Allgemeinen die Wiener Küche, die sich zu Beginn des 19. Jahrhunderts in Konkurrenz zur französischen Hochküche entwickelte. Sie gilt als bodenständig und sehr vielseitig. Die Wiener Küche vereinigt zahlreiche Einflüsse aus den Landesküchen des Habsburger Kaiserreichs, u.a. aus der böhmischen, ungarischen, türkischen und italienischen Küche.

Berühmt sind die unzähligen Spezialitäten aus gekochtem Rindfleisch, die variantenreichen Kaffeesorten und vor allem die traditionellen Mehlspeisen.
Hier wird zwischen kalten Mehlspeisen wie Brot, Torten, Kaffeegebäck usw. und warmen Mehlspeisen unterschieden. Sie sind aus - ursprünglich ungezuckerten - Gerichten für die Fastentage entstanden; auch heute noch gehören herzhafte Gerichte wie Aufläufe oder Nudeln dazu.

Die österreichische Gastronomie ist ebenso vielfältig wie die Küche des Landes. Gerade in ländlichen Gebieten pflegt man oft eine sehr traditionelle Küche, die regional geprägt ist. So ist z.B. im Burgenland der ungarische Einfluss besonders ausgeprägt, während auf den Speisekarten im seenreichen Kärnten viel Fisch angeboten wird. Viele Köche verbinden heute aber auch ihre österreichischen Wurzeln mit einer modernen internationalen Küche; teilweise werden sogar asiatische Einflüsse und exotische Gewürze integriert.

Sehr beliebt bei Besuchern und Einheimischen sind auch die Buschenschanken, Beisln und Heurigenlokale. In den Buschenschanken dürfen ausschließlich Erzeugnisse aus eigener Herstellung und kalte Speisen verkauft werden. Sie sind in allen österreichischen Weinbauregionen verbreitet. In den Wiener Beisln wird preiswerte Hausmannskost angeboten. Die Heurigen schließlich, in den Winzerdörfern rund um Wien, haben wie die Buschenschanken eine Sondererlaubnis zum Ausschank des eigenen jungen Weins (also des Heurigen) und bieten einfache Speisen, meist vom Buffet. Typisch für die Wiener Heurigen ist außerdem die traditionelle Schrammelmusik.

La cuisine autrichienne

A l'évocation de la cuisine traditionnelle autrichienne, on pense aussitôt à son fleuron, la cuisine viennoise, la grande rivale de la gastronomie française au 19e s. Alors capitale du vaste Empire austro-hongrois, qui englobait des pays aussi divers que la Bohème, la Hongrie, d'anciennes régions de l'Empire ottoman ou d'Italie, Vienne bénéficiait de nombreuses influences qui se reflétaient entre autres dans sa cuisine.

La réputation de la cuisine viennoise repose sur les spécialités de bœuf bouilli, la grande variété de cafés (héritage des Turcs) et les traditionnels entremets à base de farine (Mehlspeisen). Ceux-ci, froids (gâteaux, variétés de pains, petits fours) ou chauds, à l'origine non sucrés, étaient réservés à la période du Carême avant de se décliner sous forme de délicieux soufflés ou de pâtes savoureuses.

La gastronomie autrichienne puise également sa richesse dans la variété des cuisines du terroir ; rustique dans les régions agricoles, elle est à l'inverse imprégnée de « saveurs » hongroises en Burgenland et s'appuie, dans les régions des lacs, sur les préparations de poisson.
Aujourd'hui de nombreux chefs combinent ces recettes traditionnelles avec une cuisine plus actuelle et internationale et y associent des épices exotiques ou des parfums asiatiques

Mais on ne peut parler de la cuisine autrichienne sans évoquer ces petits établissements bien caractéristiques que sont les Heurigen, les Beisln, ou les Buschenschanken.

Les Heurigen, guinguettes dans les villages vinicoles autour de Vienne, appartiennent à des producteurs qu'une loi autorise à servir leur vin nouveau. Viennois et étrangers y affluent, attirés par la dégustation accompagnée de quelques mets simples, et, surtout, par l'ambiance gaie qui règne sous la tonnelle au son du violon et de l'accordéon.
Dans les Buschenschanken de la route du Vin, la même atmosphère joviale se manifeste autour d'un verre et de préparations froides, cuisinées à la maison.

À Vienne, c'est dans les « Beisln », sorte de petits bistrots, que l'on se retrouve pour manger une cuisine familiale bon marché.

Kleines Lexikon zur österreichischen Küche
Petit lexique sur la cuisine autrichienne

Österreichisch	Deutsch	Français
Agrasel	Stachelbeere	Groseille à maquereau
Aranzini	kandierte Fruchtstücke	fruits confits
Aschanti	Erdnuss	cacahuète
Baunzerl	Milchbrötchen	petit pain au lait
Beigel	Flügel und Schlegel vom Hühnchen	aile et cuisse de poulet
Beinfleisch	Querrippe	plat de côtes
Beiried	Roastbeefentrecôte	
Beizkräutel	Thymian	thym
Bertram	Estragon	estragon
Beuschel	Lunge	mou de veau
Blunze	Blutwurst	boudin
Brimsen	Schafskäse	fromage de brebis
Buchtel	Hefegebäck	pâtisserie au levain
Busserln	Makronen	macarons
Dalken	Pfannkuchen aus Hefeteig	crêpe de pâte levée
Eierschwammerl	Pfifferling	girolle
Erdäpfel	Kartoffeln	pommes de terre
Eitrige	Wiener Wurstspezialität	spécialité de saucisse viennoise
Faschiertes Laberl	Frikadelle	boulette de viande hachée
Filz	Schweinespeck	poitrine de porc fumée
Fisolen	Bohnen	haricots
Fleck	Kutteln	tripes
Fleckerln	in Quadrate geschnittener Nudelteig	pâte à nouilles
Fledermaus	Teil der Rinderhüfte	araignée de bœuf
Fogosch	Zander	sandre
Fritatten	Pfannkuchenstreifen	lamelles de crêpes
Gansljunges	Gänseklein	abattis d'oie
Gekröse	Innereien	abats
Germ	Hefe	levure
Geselchtes	Rauchfleisch	viande de porc fumée
Gickerl	Hühnchen	poulet
Goderl	Schweinskinn	gorge de porc
Golatschen	Plundergebäck	pâte feuilletée levée
Grammerl	ausgelassener Speck	lard fondu
Gröstl	Tiroler Pfannengericht	pommes de terre et viande sautées
Häuptlsalat	Kopfsalat	laitue
Herrenpilz	Steinpilz	cèpe
Hetscherln	Hagebutten	cynorrdhon
Heurige	neue Kartoffeln	pommes de terre nouvelles

Österreichisch	**Deutsch**	**Français**
Heuriger	neuer Wein	vin nouveau
Hieferscherzel	Rinderhüfte	rumsteck
Holler	Holunder	sureau
Jause	kalte Speisen	plats froids
Jungfernbraten	Schweinslende mit Kümmel	longe de porc au cumin
Kaiserfleisch	Geräucherter Schweinebauch	poitrine de porc fumée
Kaiserschmarrn	Mehlspeise mit Eiern und Rosinen	entremet aux œufs et raisins secs
Kalbsvögerl	ausgelöste Haxe	jarret désossé
Kaneel	Zimt	canelle
Kaprizen	kleine Mehlspeise	petit entremet
Karfiol	Blumenkohl	chou-fleur
Kavaliersspitz	Schulterdeckel vom Rind	partie de l'épaule du bœuf
Kipferl	Hörnchen	croissant
Kletzen	getrocknete Birnen	poires sechées
Knofel	Knoblauch	ail
Kohlsprossen	Rosenkohl	choux de Bruxelles
Krammetsbeer	Wacholderbeere	baie de genièvre
Kren	Meerettich	raifort
Kronsbeere	Preiselbeere	airelles
Kruspelspitz	ausgelöste Zwischenrippe	entrecôte
Kukuruz	Mais	maïs
Kuttelkraut	Thymian	thym
Latwerge	Fruchtmus	marmelade
Lebzelten	Lebkuchen	pain d'epices
Lembraten	Rindsniere	rognon de bœuf
Liptauer	Quark mit Gewürzen	fromage blanc et épices
Lungenbraten	Filet	filet
Mageres Meisel	vorderster Teil der Rinderschulter	paleron
Marille	Aprikose	abricot
Mehlspeis	Kuchen, Torten	pâtisserie
Melanzani	Auberginen	aubergines
Neugewürz	Piment	piment
Nockerln	Spätzle	pâtes aux œufs
Obers	Sahne	crème
Ochsenschlepp	Ochsenschwanz	queue de bœuf
Palatschinken	gefüllter Pfannkuchen	crèpe farcie
Paradeiser	Tomate	tomate
Pflanzl	Frikadelle	boulette de viande hachée
Plenten	Maisgrieß	semoule de mais
Pofesen	gebackene Semmelschnitten	entremets de Bohème
Pomeranze	Bitterorange	orange amère
Porree	Lauch	poireau

Österreichisch	Deutsch	Français
Powidltascherl	mit Pflaumenmus gefüllter Knödel	ravioles à la confiture de prune
Quargel	Sauermilchkäse	fromage caillé
Reibedatschi	Kartoffelpuffer	pommes de terre râpées rissolées
Ribisel	Johannisbeere	groseille
Ringlotten	Reineclauden	reine-claude
Risibisi	Reis mit Erbsen	riz aux petits pois
Rissole	Fleischpastete	paté de viande
Saumeise	gewürztes Schweinefleisch	crépinette de porc
Schauferl	Schulter	épaule de porc
Schill	Zander	sandre
Schmetten	Sauerrahm	crème aigre
Schöberl	gebackene Suppeneinlage	garniture de potage
Schöpsernes	Hammelfleisch	viande de mouton
Schopfbraten	Schweinehals	collier de porc
Schulterscherzel	Teil der Rinderschulter	macreuse
Schwammerl	Pilz	champignon
Stanitzel	Hörnchen	cornet
Stelze	Schweinshaxe, Eisbein	jarret de porc
Sterzkrusten	gebratene Polentaschnitten	polenta poêlée
Striezel	längliches Hefegebäck	pâtisserie en pâte levée
Surfleisch	Pökelfleisch	viande salée
Sturm	Federweißer	vin nouveau
Tafelspitz	gekochtes Rindfleisch	bœuf gros sel
Topfen	Quark	fromage blanc
Vogerlsalat	Feldsalat	mâche
Wadschinken	Teil des Rinderbeins	jarret de bœuf
Wammerl	Bauchfleisch vom Schwein	poitrine de porc
Weichsel	Sauerkirsche	griotte
Zeller	Sellerie	céleri
Zelten	Lebkuchen	pain d'épice
Zibeben, Ziberln	Rosinen	raisins secs
Ziemer	Rückenstück (beim Wild)	selle (gibier)
Zwetschgenröster	Pflaumenkompott	compote de prunes

The cuisine of Austria

To the wider world, Austria's culinary reputation rests largely on the Viennese tradition, which came to rival the high gastronomic culture of France in the early 19C. The capital's cuisine drew inspiration from all corners of the vast Hapsburg Empire, including Bohemia, Hungary, northern Italy and the former Ottoman provinces, to create a style which was diverse yet still strongly rooted in local tastes and character.

Its most famous specialities are the numerous recipes for beef, a remarkable variety of coffees - one of the more positive legacies of the Turkish wars - and countless dishes based on flour or meal (Mehl). These hot and cold Mehlspeisen were originally unsweetened Lenten foods, but developed into a delicious range of cakes and breads as well as hearty bakes and savoury noodle dishes.

Austrian gastronomy also reflects the variations in its regional dishes. The influence of neighbouring Hungary comes through strongly in recipes from the Burgenland, while the lake district of Carinthia prides itself on its freshwater fish. More and more of today's chefs are experimenting with a blend of traditional recipes, Asian flavours and exotic spices to create a new style of Austrian fusion cooking; this innovative version of national cuisine coexists happily alongside three enduringly popular and inimitably Austrian institutions: the Heurige, the Beisl and the Buschenschanken.

Shortly after the harvest, visitors and locals alike flock to the wine villages around Vienna, where wine producers traditionally nail a pine branch above their doorways to show that they have been granted a special license to open their little bar-parlour or garden and sell the year's young wine - the Heuriger - and a buffet of simple dishes. A Heurige is also the place to hear genuine Austrian, folk-inspired Schrammelmusik, played on the accordion, violin and guitar. Buschenschanken, found throughout the Austrian wine regions, also serve home- made wine and cold dishes, while the traditional Viennese Beisl, something between a bistro and a pub, offers "little bites" of good value home cooking.

La cucina austriaca

La cucina tradizionale austriaca è spesso associata al suo esempio più celebre, la gastronomia viennese, grande rivale della cucina francese nel XIX secolo. Vienna, allora capitale del vasto impero austro-ungarico che comprendeva paesi tanto diversi quanto la Boemia, l'Ungheria, regioni del vecchio impero ottomano o dell'Italia, beneficiava di diverse influenze che si riflettevano, tra l'altro, sulla sua cucina.

La fama della cucina viennese si fonda sul manzo bollito, la grande varietà di caffè (eredità turca) e i tradizionali dolci a base di farina (Mehlspeisen). Questi, sia freddi (torte, diversi tipi di pane, pasticceria) che caldi, in origine non zuccherati, erano serviti all'epoca di Careme prima di differenziarsi nelle forme di deliziosi soufflé o saporite paste.

La gastronomia austriaca affonda le radici della sua ricchezza anche nella varietà della cucina del territorio; rustica nelle regioni agricole, è viceversa impregnata di sapori ungarici nel Burgenland per abbracciare infine preparazioni a base di pesce nelle regioni dei laghi.
Oggi molti cuochi uniscono le ricette tradizionali ad una cucina più moderna e internazionale unendovi delle spezie esotiche o profumi asiatici.

Ma non si può parlare di cucina austriaca senza evocare le Heurigen, i Beisln e le Buschenschanken, piccole e caratteristiche strutture.
Le Heurigen, trattorie di campagna in villaggi vinicoli nei dintorni di Vienna, appartengono a dei produttori autorizzati dalla legge a servire i loro vini novelli. Sono frequentate da viennesi e stranieri attirati da degustazioni accompagnate da piatti semplici e, soprattutto, da un ambiente allegro sotto pergolati al suono di violini e fisarmoniche.

Nelle Buschenschanken, lungo la strada del vino, si ritrova la stessa atmosfera gioviale intorno ad un bicchiere e piatti freddi preparati in casa.

A Vienna infine ci si ritrova nei Beisln, sorta di piccoli bistrot per gustare una cucina familiare a buon mercato.

A short glossary of Austrian cuisine
Piccolo glossario della cucina austriaca

Österreichisch	**English**	**Italiano**
Agrasel	Groosberry	uva spina
Aranzini	candied fruits	frutta candita
Aschanti	peanut	arachide
Baunzerl	roll made with milk and sugar	pane al latte
Beigel	wing & leg of young chicken	ala e coscia di pollo
Beinfleisch	rib of beef	entrecôte
Beiried	roast beef	entrecôte
Beizkräutel	thyme	timo
Bertram	tarragon	estragone
Beuschel	calf's lung hash	polmone di vitello
Blunze	blood sausage	sanguinaccio
Brimsen	ewe's milk cheese	formaggio di pecora
Buchtel	Danish pastry	pasticceria lievitata
Busserln	macaroon	amaretti
Dalken	yeast dough pancake	crepe di pasta lievitata
Eierschwammerl	chanterelle	cantarello
Erdäpfel	potato	patate
Eitrige	Viennese speciality sausage	insaccati viennesi
Faschiertes Laberl	rissole	polpette di carne tritata
Filz	smoked belly of pork	petto di maiale affumicato
Fisolen	beans	fagioli
Fleck	tripe	trippa
Fleckerln	noodle squares	tagliatelle
Fledermaus	cut of beef haunch	taglio di manzo
Fogosch	zander	lucioperca
Fritatten	pancake strips	millefoglie di crepe
Gansljunges	goose giblets & wings	frattaglie
Gekröse	offal	frattaglie
Germ	yeast	lievito
Geselchtes	smoked meat	carne di maiale affumicata
Gickerl	chicken	pollo
Goderl	neck of pork	guancia di maiale
Golatschen	pastries	pasta sfoglia
Grammerl	melted pork fat	lardo battuto
Gröstl	meat & potato hash	patate e carne saltati
Häuptlsalat	lettuce	lattuga
Herrenpilz	cep	porcini
Hetscherln	rose hip	rosa canina
Heurige	new potatoes	patate novelle
Heuriger	new wine	vino novello

Österreichisch	English	Italiano
Hieferscherzel	haunch of beef	girello di manzo
Holler	elderberry	sambuco
Jause	cold food	piatti freddi
Jungfernbraten	loin of pork with kümmel	lombo di maiale affumicato
Kaiserfleisch	smoked belly of pork	petto di maiale affumicato
Kaiserschmarrn	sugared raisin pancake	dolce alle uova e uva passa
Kalbsvögerl	calf's knuckle off the bone	stinco disossato
Kaneel	cinammon	cannella
Kaprizen	small flummery	piccolo dolce
Karfiol	cauliflower	cavolfiore
Kavaliersspitz	beef shoulder fillet	taglio di spalla di manzo
Kipferl	croissant	croissant
Kletzen	dried pears	pere essiccate
Knofel	garlic	aglio
Kohlsprossen	Brussels sprouts	cavoli di Bruxelles
Krammetsbeer	juniper berry	ginepro
Kren	horseradish	rafano
Kronsbeere	cranberry	mirtilli
Kruspelspitz	sirloin steak	entrecôte
Kukuruz	maize	mais
Kuttelkraut	thyme	timo
Latwerge	jam	marmellata
Lebzelten	gingerbread	pane speziato
Lembraten	beef kidneys	rognone di manzo
Liptauer	spiced fromage blanc	formaggio bianco e spezie
Lungenbraten	fillet	filetto
Mageres Meisel	chuck steak	paletta
Marille	apricot	albicocca
Mehlspeis	cakes & tarts	pasticceria
Melanzani	aubergines	melanzane
Neugewürz	pimento	peperoncino
Nockerln	spaetzle	gnocchetti
Obers	cream	panna
Ochsenschlepp	oxtail	coda di manzo
Palatschinken	stuffed pancake	crepe farcita
Paradeiser	tomato	pomodoro
Pflanzl	rissole	polpetta di carne tritata
Plenten	semolina/polenta	semola di mais
Pofesen	small filled cakes	dolce della Boemia
Pomeranze	bitter orange	arancia amara
Porree	leek	porro
Powidltascherl	dumplings filled with plum compote	ravioli con marmellata di prugne
Quargel	curd	formaggio cagliato

Österreichisch	English	Italiano
Reibedatschi	grated potato dumplings	patate pelate e saltate
Ribisel	redcurrant	uva spina
Ringlotten	greengage	susine regina claudia
Risibisi	rice with peas	risibisi
Rissole	meat pasty or pie	paté di carne
Saumeise	smoked spiced pork	salsiccia schiacciata
Schauferl	shoulder of pork	spalla di maiale
Schill	zander	lucioperca
Schmetten	sour cream	panna acidulata
Schöberl	small baked soup dumplings	pastina in brodo
Schöpsernes	mutton	montone
Schopfbraten	neck of pork	guanciale di maiale
Schulterscherzel	shoulder of beef	spalla di manzo
Schwammerl	mushroom	funghi
Stamperl	small stemless schnapps glass	bicchierino d'acquavite
Stanitzel	croissant	cornetto
Stelze	knuckle of pork	stinco di maiale
Sterzkrusten	pan-fried polenta	polenta spadellata
Striezel	sweet plaited loaf	pasticceria di pasta lievitata
Surfleisch	salted meat	carne salata
Sturm	new wine	vino novello
Tafelspitz	haunch of beef	manzo stufato
Topfen	fromage blanc	formaggio bianco
Vogerlsalat	mache	dolcetta
Wadschinken	knuckle of beef	stinco di manzo
Wammerl	belly of pork	petto di maiale
Weichsel	sour cherry	visciola
Zeller	celery	sedano
Zelten	gingerbread	pane speziato
Zibeben, Ziberln	raisin	uvetta passa
Ziemer	saddle (game)	sella (di selvaggina)
Zwetschgenröster	plum compote	marmellata di prugne

Unterwegs mit dem Auto

ALLGEMEINE BESTIMMUNGEN

In Österreich besteht allgemeine Gurtpflicht. Die maximal zulässige Alkoholgrenze liegt bei 0,5 Promille. Telefonieren am Steuer ist ausschließlich mit einer Freisprechanlage erlaubt. Es gilt eine ganzährige Lichtpflicht, auch tagsüber.

GESCHWINDIGKEITSREGELUNGEN

Höchstgeschwindigkeiten für PKW:
Autobahn: 130 km/h (mit Anhänger 100 km/h)
Landstraße: 100 km/h
Stadtgebiet: 50 km/h

GEBÜHREN

Auf den österreichischen Autobahnen und Schnellstraßen besteht Vignettenpflicht. Die Vignetten sind an den grenznahen Autabahnraststätten und beim ÖAMTC erhältlich.

AUTOMOBILCLUBS

ÖAMTC, Schubertring 1, ✉ 1010 Wien, ✆ (01) 71 19 90, www.oeamtc.at, Pannenhilfe ✆ 120

ARBÖ, Mariahilfer Str. 180, ✉ 1150 Wien, ✆ (01) 89 12 17, www.arboe.or.at, Pannenhilfe ✆ 123

URLAUBSINFORMATION ÖSTERREICH

Margaretenstr. 1, ✉ 1040 Wien, ✆ (01) 58 86 63 29, Fax (01) 5 88 66 41, urlaub@austria.info

L'aide au voyage

RÉGLEMENTATION GÉNÉRALE

Le port de la ceinture de sécurité en Autriche est obligatoire. Le taux maximum d'alcoolémie autorisé est de 0,5g .
Durant la conduite, l'usage du téléphone portable n'est autorisé qu'avec une installation mains libres. L'usage des feux de route tout au long de l'année même durant la journée est obligatoire.

LIMITES DE VITESSE

Vitesses maximales autorisées pour les voitures :
Autoroute : 130 km/h (avec remorque 100 km/h)
Route départementale : 100 km/h
Agglomération : 50 km/h

TAXES ET PÉAGES

Sur les autoroutes et certaines routes nationales, les vignettes sont obligatoires . Elles sont en vente dans les stations-services proche des frontières, auprès des automobiles-clubs et dans les bureaux de tabac.

AUTOMOBILES-CLUBS

ÖAMTC, Schubertring 1, F 1010 Wien, ✆ (01) 71 19 90, www.oeamtc.at, service dépannage ✆ 120
ARBÖ, Mariahilfer Str. 180, F 1150 Wien, ✆ (01) 89 12 17, www.arboe.or.at, service dépannage ✆ 123

MAISON DE L'AUTRICHE

Margaretenstr. 1, ✉ 1040 Wien, ✆ (01) 58 86 63 29, Fax (01) 5 88 66 21, urlaub@austria.info

Driving in Austria

GENERAL REGULATIONS

The wearing of seatbelts is compulsory for drivers and all passengers.
The alcohol limit for drivers is 0.5g/100ml.
Mobile telephones may only be used with a hands-free kit. The use of headlights is compulsory during the day, all year round.

SPEED LIMITS

Maximum speeds for cars:
Motorway : 130 km/h: 80mph (100 km/h with a trailer)
All other roads : 100 km/h-62mph
Built-up areas : 50 km/h-31mph

MOTORWAY TOLLS

Drivers on motorways and certain main roads must display a valid toll disc or "Vignette". Vignettes are available at motorway service stations near the border and through the ÖAMTC (see below).

AUTOMOBILE CLUBS

ÖAMTC, Schubertring 1, ✉ 1010 Wien, ✆ (01) 71 19 90, www.oeamtc.at, Breakdown assistance ✆ 120

ARBÖ, Mariahilfer Str. 180, ✉ 1150 Wien, ✆ (01) 89 12 17, www.arboe.or.at, Breakdown assistance ✆ 123

AUSTRIAN NATIONAL TOURIST OFFICE

Margaretenstr. 1, ✉ 1040 Wien, ✆ (01) 58 86 63 29, Fax (01) 5 88 66 42, urlaub@austria.info

Consigli per il viaggio

REGOLE GENERALI

In Austria è obbligatorio indossare le cinture di sicurezza.
Il tasso alcolico massimo consentito è di 0,5g.
L'uso del cellulare durante la guida è consentito solo con auricolare.
Obbligo di fari accesi di giorno.

LIMITI DI VELOCITÀ

Velocità massima consentita per le vetture:
-autostrada: 130km/h (100km/h con rimorchio)
-strade provinciali: 100km/h
-centri abitati 50km/h

TASSE E PEDAGGI

Il bollo di circolazione ("vignette") è obbligatorio sulle autostrade e su alcune strade nazionali. E' in vendita nelle stazioni di servizio nei pressi delle frontiere, nei club automobilistici e nelle tabaccherie.

CLUB AUTOMOBILISTICI

(assistenza)
ÖAMTC, Schubertring 1, ✉ 1010 Wien, ✆ (01) 71 19 90, www.oeamtc.at, servizio d'emergenza ✆ 120
ARBÖ, Mariahilfer Str. 180, ✉ 1150 Wien, ✆ (01) 89 12 17, www.arboe.or.at, servizio d'emergenza ✆ 123

AUSTRIA TURISMO

Margaretenstr. 1, ✉ 1040 Wien, ✆ (01) 58 86 63 29, Fax (01) 5 88 66 21, urlaub@austria.info

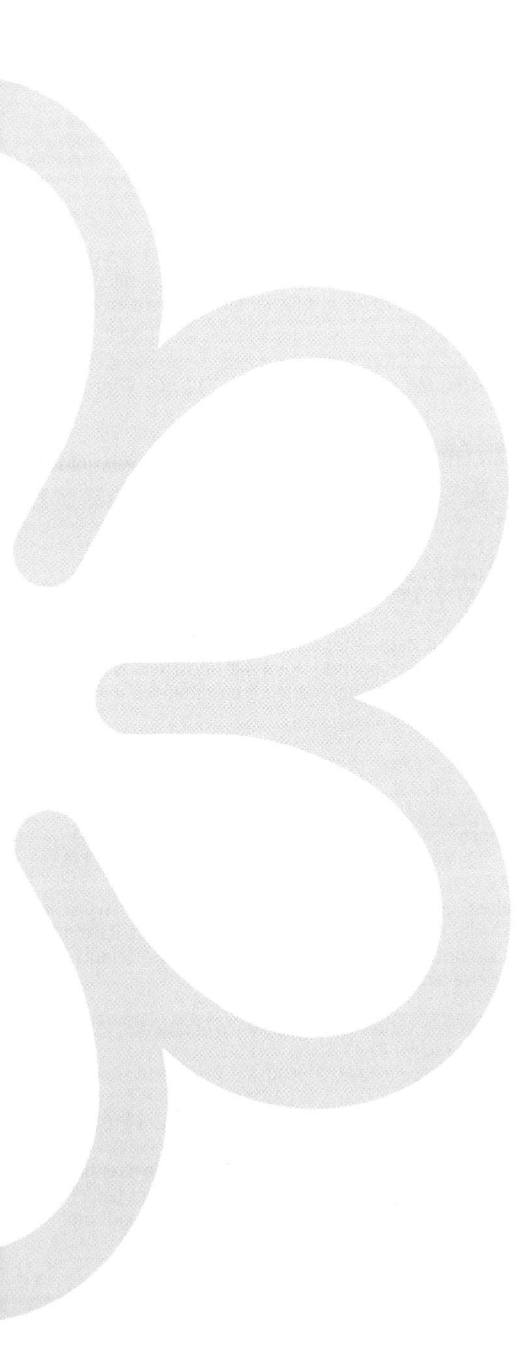

Städte
von A bis Z

Villes
de A à Z

Towns
from A to Z

Città
da A a Z

ABSAM – Tirol – 730 G7 – 6 370 Ew – Höhe 632 m – Wintersport:

7 **D5**

Wien 440 – Innsbruck 13 – Hall in Tirol 3 – Schwaz 23

Dörferstr. 37, 6067, (05223) 5 31 90, absam@regionhall.at

Landgasthof Bogner

Walburga-Schindl-Str. 21 6067

– (05223) 5 79 87 – info@hotel-bogner.at – Fax (05223) 579877

34 Zim – 70/175 € 110/188 € – ½ P 15 €

Rest – Karte 20/36 €

◆ Der Tiroler Erbhof ist zu einem komfortablen Hotel geworden, das über mit hellem Naturholz eingerichtete Zimmer verfügt – alle mit sehr gutem Platzangebot. Teils neuzeitlich, teils ländlich präsentiert sich das gepflegte Restaurant.

ABTENAU – Salzburg – 730 M6 – 5 680 Ew – Höhe 712 m – Wintersport: 1 260 m 1 6

8 **G4**

Wien 308 – Salzburg 48 – Bischofshofen 44 – Bad Aussee 52

Markt 165, 5441, (06243) 40 40 54, ferien@lammertal.info

Gutjahr

Rest,

Markt 187 5441 – (06243) 24 34 – hotel@gutjahr.at

– Fax (06243) 243433

geschl. 1. – 27. April und 27. Oktober – 30. November

58 Zim (inkl. ½ P.) – 63/69 € 102/137 € 67/75 € 111/149 € – 4 Suiten

Rest – (nur Abendessen für Hausgäste)

◆ Dieses in einer Seitenstraße liegende Hotel mit hübschen, wohnlichen Zimmern mit Balkon hat zudem einen netten Freizeitbereich mit Kosmetik- und Massageangebot.

Gasthof Post

Zim,

Markt 39 5441 – (06243) 2 20 90 – office@hotel-post-abtenau.at

– Fax (06243) 3353

geschl. April, November

56 Zim (inkl. ½ P.) – 63/75 € 102/124 € 66/80 € 108/136 €

Rest – Karte 16/27 €

◆ Der 400 Jahre alte Gasthof der Familie Windhofer im regionstypischen Stil, verfügt über helle, nett eingerichtete Zimmer, teils mit Balkon. Im Restaurant finden sie unterteilte Stuben mit reichlicher Holzeinrichtung und bürgerlicher Speisekarte.

Goldener Stern

Zim,

Markt 29 5441 – (06243) 22 40

– hotel@goldenerstern.at – Fax (06243) 224040

geschl. April, November

33 Zim (inkl. ½ P.) – 60/64 € 98/110 € 62/71 € 102/122 €

Rest – Karte 19/33 €

◆ Seit 1592 in Familienbesitz befindet sich der rustikale Gasthof am Markt. Besonders hübsch sind die Zimmer im Anbau und der helle Frühstücksraum. Zum Restaurantbereich gehört eine sehr gute Konditorei.

Gute und preiswerte Häuser kennzeichnet das MICHELIN-Männchen, der „Bib": der rote „Bib Gourmand" für die Küche, der blaue „Bib Hotel" bei den Zimmern.

ACHENKIRCH – Tirol – 730 H6 – 2 070 Ew – Höhe 930 m – Wintersport: 1 800 m 10 7 D5

Wien 437 – Innsbruck 56 – Schwaz 29 – München 84

Rathaus 387, 6215, (05246) 53 00, achenkirch@achensee.info

Alpengolf, (05246) 66 04

Achensee★★ Süd: 4 km – Sylvenstein-Stausee★ Nord-West: 14 km

Posthotel

(geheizt)

Nr. 382 6215 – (05246) 65 22 – posthotel@posthotel.at – Fax (05246) 6522468

150 Zim (inkl. ½ P.) – 179/226 € 288/372 € – 27 Suiten

Rest *Gaststube* – (Tischbestellung erforderlich) Menü 44/78 € (abends) – Karte 29/47 €

♦ Ein großer, luxuriöser Wellnessbereich, der sich auf 6000 qm erstreckt, erwartet Sie in diesem schönen Alpenhotel. Elegante Zimmer und ein reichhaltiges Freizeitangebot ebenso. Ein ländlich-gemütliches A-la-carte-Restaurant ist die Gaststube.

Landhotel Reiterhof

Zim, Rest,

Nr. 380 6215 – (05246) 66 00 – info@reiterhof.com – Fax (05246) 66007

42 Zim (inkl. ½ P.) – 95/120 € 160/204 € 100/130 € 180/216 €

Rest – (nur für Hausgäste)

♦ Das Hotel mit eigener Landwirtschaft hält wohnliche und meist geräumige, mit Naturmaterialien eingerichtete Zimmer bereit. Idyllisch ist die Gartenanlage mit Badeteich.

Panorama

Zim,

Nr. 130a 6215 – (05246) 63 81 – info@pensionpanorama.at – Fax (05246) 638149

geschl. 1. – 26. April, 27. Okt. – 29. Nov.

15 Zim – 36/40 € 58/70 € 39/47 € 64/88 € – ½ P 9/12 €

Rest – (nur Abendessen für Hausgäste)

♦ Die gepflegten Zimmer dieses Hotels wurden unterschiedlich, mal in Kirsche, mal mit hellem Holz eingerichtet. Panoramasuite mit eigener Dachterrasse. Sonnenterrasse.

AFIESL – Oberösterreich – 730 O3 – 430 Ew – Höhe 820 m 2 H2

Wien 230 – Linz 52 – Wels 72 – Rohrbach 13

4170, (07216) 44 51, office@romantik.at

Romantik Resort Bergergut

(geheizt)

Afiesl 7 4170 – (07216) 44 51 – bergergut@romantik.at – Fax (07216) 445131

35 Zim (inkl. ½ P.) – 220/260 €

Rest – (nur für Hausgäste)

♦ Ganz besonders auf Paare zielt das Angebot des Romantikhotels mit seinen aufwändig gestalteten Themensuiten und Wellnessangebot (z.B. Paarmassagen) ab. In intimer Atmosphäre speist man in dem eleganten Restaurant.

AFLENZ KURORT – Steiermark – 730 R6 – 1 040 Ew – Höhe 770 m – Wintersport: 1 810 m ⛷8 ⛷ 10 **J4**

▶ Wien 159 – Graz 77 – Leoben 41

Post Karlon Zim, VISA

Mariazeller Str. 10 ✉ 8623 – ✆ (03861) 2 20 30 – hotel.post.karlon@aon.at – Fax (03861) 22034
geschl. Ende Nov. 2 Wochen
36 Zim – ♦53/65 € ♦♦74/94 € – ½ P 12 € – 6 Suiten
Rest – *(geschl. März – April Dienstag und Okt. Dienstag)* Karte 14/27 €

◆ In dem erweiterten Gasthof a. d. 16. Jh. erwarten Sie solide, unterschiedlich möblierte Zimmer – einige im Landhausstil sowie auch einige Romantikzimmer mit Holzfußboden. Mit viel Holz rustikal bis bürgerlich gestaltete Gasträume.

Wie entscheidet man sich zwischen zwei gleichwertigen Adressen?
In jeder Kategorie sind die Häuser nochmals geordnet,
die besten Adressen stehen an erster Stelle.

AICH – Steiermark – 730 N6 – 820 Ew – Höhe 740 m – Wintersport: 2 015 m 2 13 9 **H4**

▶ Wien 279 – Graz 157 – Salzburg 99 – Bischofshofen 59

Zum Grafen Wirt mit Zim VISA

Aich 1 ✉ 8966 – ✆ (03686) 43 07 – info@grafenwirt.at – Fax (03686) 430720
geschl. Ende April 2 Wochen, Nov. und Montag
12 Zim – ☼ ♦36/40 € ♦♦72/80 € ❄ ♦86/90 € ♦♦86/90 € – ½ P 15 €
Rest – Menü 13/18 € – Karte 16/30 €

◆ Der im Ortszentrum gelegene Gasthof beherbergt ein ländlich gestaltetes Restaurant, in dem man eine überwiegend bürgerlich ausgerichtete Küche bietet. Im Gästehaus Zur Gräfin befinden sich moderne Appartements.

AIGEN-SCHLÄGL – Oberösterreich – 730 N3 – 1 930 Ew – Höhe 596 m – Wintersport: 1 337 m 8 2 **H2**

▶ Wien 234 – Linz 56 – Passau 52 – Freistadt 60
ℹ Hauptstr. 2, ✉ 4160, ✆ (07281) 2 00 65, info@boehmerwald.at
Böhmerwald- Ulrichsberg, Seitelschlag 50 ✆ (07288) 82 00
Stift Schlägl★ (Stiftskirche★, Bildergalerie★)
Moldaublick★ (Nord: 17 km)

Almesberger (geheizt) Zim, VISA

Marktplatz 4 ✉ 4160 – ✆ (07281) 87 13 – hotel@almesberger.at – Fax (07281) 871376
80 Zim (inkl. ½ P.) – ♦91/168 € ♦♦160/222 € – 4 Suiten
Rest – Karte 15/32 €

◆ Die Ferienanlage direkt am Markt besteht aus drei Häusern. Die wohnlich-funktionell eingerichteten Zimmer, schöne Suiten und der 5000 qm große Wellnessbereich überzeugen. Restaurantstuben mit regionalem und teils auch einfachem mexikanischem Angebot.

Bärnsteinhof

Marktplatz 12 ✉ 4160 – ✆ (07281) 62 45 – info@baernsteinhof.at – Fax (07281) 624513

geschl. Nov. 2 Wochen

12 Zim – 42/46 € 84/92 € – ½ P 13 €

Rest – *(geschl. Mittwoch)* Karte 16/27 €

♦ Individuelle, mit schönen Möbeln wohnlich eingerichtete Gästezimmer mit neuzeitlichen Bädern machen dieses kleine Hotel aus. Gemütliche, ländliche Gaststube.

ALKOVEN – Oberösterreich – 730 O4 – 5 200 Ew – Höhe 268 m 2 H3

Wien 200 – Linz 18 – Wels 22 – Steyr 61

Gasthof Schrot mit Zim

Alte Hauptstr. 38 ✉ 4072 – ✆ (07274) 7 14 00 – essen@gasthofschrot.at – Fax (07274) 71400

geschl. 5. – 17. März und Montag - Dienstag

3 Zim – 28 € 50 €

Rest – Menü 29 € – Karte 19/42 €

♦ Das Gasthaus in der Ortsmitte ist ein sympathischer Familienbetrieb mit rustikalem Ambiente und regionaler Küche. Sehr schön sitzt man auch im Innenhof.

ALLAND – Niederösterreich – 730 U4 – 2 410 Ew – Höhe 333 m 3 K3

Wien 32 – St. Pölten 46 – Baden 17 – Wiener Neustadt 45

Stift Heiligenkreuz★ Ost: 4 km

In Mayerling Süd-Ost: 2 km über die B 210 Richtung Baden:

Hanner Zim,

Heinz Hanner Platz 1 ✉ 2534 – ✆ (02258) 23 78 – hanner@hanner.cc – Fax (02258) 237841

20 Zim – 102/146 € 165/212 €

Rest *Hanner* – separat erwähnt

Rest *Hanner leger* – Karte 20/35 €

♦ Bereits in der Eingangshalle fällt das moderne, puristische Design des Hotels auf. Dieser Stil zieht sich durch das gesamte Haus, bis in die interessanten Zimmer. Ein Bistro für Kleinigkeiten und Jausen ist das Hanner leger.

Restaurant Hanner

Heinz Hanner Platz 1 ✉ 2534 – ✆ (02258) 23 78 – hanner@hanner.cc – Fax (02258) 237841

Rest – Menü 99/138 € – Karte 70/95 €

Spez. Scharfe Entenzungen und Königskrabbe. Filet, Sugo und geschmorter Bauch vom Wienerwald-Schwein mit Waldmeisterkaviar. 7 x Geschmack von Schokolade.

♦ Mit der hellen und angenehm schlichten Einrichtung hat man den richtigen Rahmen für die schmackhafte kreative Küche des Restaurants geschaffen. Schöne Sicht in den Garten.

Unsere „Hoffnungsträger" sind die Restaurants, deren Küche wir für die nächste Ausgabe besonders sorgfältig auf eine höhere Auszeichnung hin überprüfen. Der Name dieser Restaurants ist in „rot" gedruckt und zusätzlich auf der Sterne-Liste am Anfang des Buches zu finden.

ALPBACH – Tirol – 730 H6 – 2 490 Ew – Höhe 1 000 m – Wintersport: 2 100 m 3 18 7 E5

Wien 412 – Innsbruck 53 – Kufstein 40 – Schwaz 24

Alpbach 175, 6236, (05336) 2 00 94, alpbach@alpbachtal.at

Böglerhof
Rest, Rest,

Nr. 166 6236 – (05336) 52 27 – info@boeglerhof.at – Fax (05336) 5227402

geschl. 4. Nov. – 15. Dez.

74 Zim (inkl. ½ P.) – 79/146 € 142/208 € 94/175 € 156/266 € – 17 Suiten

Rest – Karte 26/38 €

◆ In angenehmem Naturholz wurden die Zimmer des Hofguts aus dem 14. Jh. eingerichtet, ausgestattet mit modernen Bädern. Ein schöner Freizeit- und Beautybereich gehört zum Hotel. Noch aus der Bauzeit des Anwesens stammen die gemütlichen Restaurantstuben.

Post
(geheizt) Rest,

Alpbach 184 6236 – (05336) 52 03 – info@hotel-post.cc – Fax (05336) 5685

geschl. Ostern – Mitte Mai, Anfang Nov. – Mitte Dez.

23 Zim – 54/67 € 90/130 € 63/76 € 108/154 € – ½ P 8 €

Rest – Karte 15/32 €

◆ Der ehemalige Gasthof aus dem 16. Jh. beherbergt heute solide, in regionstypischem Stil eingerichtete Zimmer und Suiten – zum Teil auch mit Balkon. Das Restaurant: eine ganz mit Holz vertäfelte Stube mit Kachelofen und Dielenboden.

ALTAUSSEE – Steiermark – 730 N6 – 1 890 Ew – Höhe 719 m – Wintersport: 1 800 m 9 – Luftkurort 9 H4

Wien 286 – Graz 164 – Salzburg 81 – Gmunden 60

Kurhaus, Fischerndorf 61, 8992, (03622) 7 16 43, info.altaussee@ausseerland.at

Veranstaltungen

22.05. – 25.05.: Narzissenfes

14.08.: Berge in Flammen

Altausseer See★

Loser Panoramastraße★ (Nord: 12 km)

Seevilla
Rest, Rest,

Fischerndorf 60 8992 – (03622) 7 13 02 – hotel@seevilla.at – Fax (03622) 713028

53 Zim (inkl. ½ P.) – 118/165 € 214/290 € – 3 Suiten

Rest – Menü 21/38 € – Karte 22/51 €

◆ Das sehr schön am See gelegene Hotel verfügt über wohnliche, teilweise seeseitige Gästezimmer sowie einen hübschen modernen Saunabereich. Auch Kosmetik wird angeboten.

Am See

Fischerndorf 2 8992 – (03622) 7 13 61 – office@hotelamsee.at – Fax (03622) 7136113

geschl. 5. November – 15. Dezember

19 Zim – 80/100 € 140/170 € 60/80 € 100/130 € – 3 Suiten

Rest – *(geschl. Dienstag)* Karte 18/33 €

◆ Seit 1326 ist der Gasthof im Familienbesitz – einige antike Einrichtungsstücke bewahren den historischen Charme des Hauses. Die Zimmer bieten teils Blick auf See und Berge. Restaurant in rustikalem Stil.

ALTENFELDEN - Oberösterreich - 730 N3 - 2 240 Ew - Höhe 598 m

2 **H2**

Wien 213 - Linz 35 - Wels 50 - Freistadt 65

Veldenstr. 3, 4121, (07282) 55 55, gemeindeamt@altenfelden.at

Kleebauer

Rest,

Mairhof 4 4121 - (07282) 55 88 - info@kleebauer.at - Fax (07282) 599232

23 Zim (inkl. ½ P.) - 100/145 € 200/290 € - 4 Suiten

Rest - (nur Abendessen für Hausgäste)

♦ Der denkmalgeschützte ca. 700 Jahre alte Gutshof gefällt mit seiner ruhigen Lage und wohnlichen Zimmern in rustikalem Stil. Eigene Pferde sowie Unterbringung von Gastpferden.

ALTENMARKT IM PONGAU - Salzburg - 730 M6 - 3 490 Ew - Höhe 850 m - Wintersport: 2 188 m 3 20

9 **G5**

Wien 311 - Salzburg 69 - Bischofshofen 29 - Zell am See 63

Sportplatzstr. 486, 5541, (06452) 56 11, info@altenmarkt-zauchensee.at

Das Urbisgut

Rest,

Urbisweg 22 5541 - (06452) 7 22 70 - info@urbisgut.com - Fax (06452) 72278

geschl. 12. April - 1. Mai, 18. Oktober - 29. November

42 Zim (inkl. ½ P.) - 55/75 € 118/128 € 78/98 € 148/178 € - 4 Suiten

Rest - (nur Abendessen für Hausgäste)

♦ Aus einem alten Bauernhof wurde ein Hotel mit großzügigem Rahmen. Die Zimmer sind überwiegend mit hellem, rustikalem Mobiliar ausgestattet. Kosmetik und Massage im Haus.

Lebzelter

Zim,

Marktplatz 79 5541 - (06452) 69 11 - office@lebzelter.com - Fax (06452) 7823

geschl. 5. April - 1. Mai,12. Oktober - 1. November

30 Zim - 50/75 € 100/126 € 60/90 € 120/186 € - 3 Suiten

Rest *Moser* - Karte 23/37 €

♦ Alpenländischer Gasthof im Zentrum bei der Kirche. Wohnliche Atmosphäre in den Zimmern mit hellem Naturholz, hübschen Stoffen und Bildern sowie zeitgemäßen Bädern. Im Moser: schön gedeckte Tische, Gewölbedecke und rustikale Eleganz; dazu eine Zirbelstube.

Kesselgrub

(geheizt) Rest,

Lackengasse 86 5541 - (06452) 52 32 - info@kesselgrub.at - Fax (06452) 523244

50 Zim (inkl. ½ P.) - 58/78 € 110/170 € 70/100 € 120/240 € - 3 Suiten

Rest - Menü 12 € (mittags) - Karte 16/38 €

Rest *s'Kessei* - *(geschl. im Sommer Sonntag, nur Abendessen)* Karte 19/43 €

♦ Das Salzburger Wirtshaus bietet wohnliche, teils etwas neuzeitlicher möblierte Zimmer. Garten mit Kinderspielplatz und Naturschwimmteich. Im Sommer auf Wunsch all inclusive. Restaurant in ländlichem Stil. S'Kessei: rustikal mit Bar und Weinprobierstube.

Scheffer's (mit Gästehaus)
Zauchenseestr. 184 ✉ 5541 – ✆ (06452) 55 06 – office@scheffers-hotel.at – Fax (06452) 7421
geschl. 7. April – 5. Mai
31 Zim (inkl. ½ P.) – ☼ 65/76 € 108/138 € ❄ 81/114 € 140/206 €
Rest – *(nur Abendessen)* Menü 17/22 €
◆ Sehr individuell eingerichtete Zimmer bietet dieses engagiert geführte Hotel. Moderne Technik in einem kuppelförmig angelegten Veranstaltungsbereich. Massage-Angebote.

Alpenland garni
Zauchenseestr. 278 ✉ 5541 – ✆ (06452) 55 66 – info@alpenland.cc – Fax (06452) 556614
geschl. Nov.
22 Zim – ☼ 53/58 € 86/96 € ❄ 64/81 € 108/142 €
◆ Das freundlich und familiär geführte Hotel beherbergt hinter seiner Balkonfassade eine geschmackvoll gestaltete Lobby und wohnliche Zimmer mit Parkettfußboden.

Landhaus Kristall garni
Palfen 9 ✉ 5541 – ✆ (06452) 73 54 – kristall@sbg.at – Fax (06452) 735438
geschl. Mai, Okt. – Nov.
17 Zim – ☼ 34/40 € 52/64 € ❄ 45/56 € 74/96 €
◆ Durchgängig im regionstypischen Landhausstil präsentiert sich das freundlich geführte Haus mit schönem Garten. Neben komfortablen Zimmern bietet man auch Familienappartements.

Gasthof Markterwirt mit Zim
Marktplatz 4 ✉ 5541 – ✆ (06452) 54 20 – info@markterwirt.at – Fax (06452) 542031
geschl.15. – 30.April, Nov.
29 Zim (inkl. ½ P.) – ☼ 46/59 € 91/111 € ❄ 52/76 € 109/161 €
Rest – Karte 16/34 €
◆ Charmanter Gasthof a. d. 11. Jh. mit verschiedenen Bereichen: gemütliches Café, "Alte Kuch'l" mit Gewölbe und Kamin, Gaststube mit rötlicher Kieferntäfelung und Terrasse. Übernachtungsgäste können zwischen zwei Zimmerkategorien wählen: Standard und Komfort.

Zum Steirerwirt
Zauchenseestr. 44 ✉ 5541 – ✆ (0664) 1 31 83 89 – info@steirerwirt.at – Fax (06452) 4826
geschl. Juni, Nov. und Montag, im Sommer Montag – Dienstag
Rest – *(wochentags nur Abendessen)* (Tischbestellung ratsam) Karte 19/31 €
◆ Freundlicher Service und regionale Küche erwarten Sie in dem an einen Campingplatz angeschlossenen Restaurant. Netter Zierrat trägt zum gemütlich-rustikalen Ambiente bei.

In Altenmarkt-Zauchensee **Süd-Ost: 11 km – Höhe 1 352 m**

Salzburger Hof
Palfen 185 ✉ 5541 – ✆ (06452) 40 15 – info@salzburgerhof.net
– Fax (06452) 401556
geschl. Mai, Oktober – November
44 Zim (inkl. ½ P.) – ☼ 54/94 € 98/164 € ❄ 88/170 €
158/294 € – 14 Suiten
Rest – (nur Abendessen für Hausgäste) Karte 22/41 €
♦ Nahe der Lifte gelegenes komfortables Hotel mit schönem Relax- und Fitnessbereich im obersten Stock. Besonders wohnlich: Penthouse Junior Suite unterm Dach mit toller Sicht.

Alpenhof
Zim,
Palfen 119 ✉ 5541 – ✆ (06452) 4 01 40
– info@alpenhof.net – Fax (06452) 401481
geschl. 20. April – 1. Juni
49 Zim (inkl. ½ P.) – ☼ 57/117 € 114/194 € ❄ 99/166 €
158/278 € – 29 Suiten
Rest – *(im Winter nur Abendessen)* Karte 17/40 €
♦ Das Hotel liegt unweit der Skilifte und bietet sehr unterschiedlich geschnittene Gästezimmer sowie einen hübschen, mediterran gestalteten Saunabereich. Der A-la-carte-Gast speist in getäfelten Stuben. Sonnenterrasse.

ALTHOFEN – **Kärnten** – 730 P8 – **4 740 Ew – Höhe 700 m** 10 **I5**

Wien 266 – Klagenfurt 35 – St. Veit an der Glan 16 – Wolfsberg 42

Bachler
Silberegger Str. 1 ✉ 9330 – ✆ (04262) 38 35 – restaurant@bachler.co.at
– Fax (04262) 38354
geschl. Karwoche, Mitte – Ende August und Sonntagabend
Rest – Menü 36/49 € – Karte 25/43 €
♦ Mit Engagement leitet Familie Bachler das "Kärntner Kulturwirtshaus", in dem man regionale Küche bietet. Gäste nehmen im Wirtshaus oder im etwas eleganteren Restaurant Platz.

AMLACH – **Tirol** – siehe Lienz

AMSTETTEN – **Niederösterreich** – 730 Q4 – **22 600 Ew – Höhe 276 m** 2 **I3**

Wien 121 – St. Pölten 64 – Linz 59 – Steyr 44
Hauptplatz 29, ✉ 3300, ✆ (07472) 60 14 54, tourismus@amstetten.at
Swarco Amstetten-Ferschnitz, Gut Edla 18 ✆ (07473) 82 93
Schloss Greinburg (Innenhof★) Nord: 19 km – Strudengau★ Nord: 23 km – Burg Clam★ Nord-West: 26 km

Exel
Zim,
Alte Zeile 14 ✉ 3300 – ✆ (07472) 2 58 88 – office@hotelexel.com
– Fax (07472) 2588825
50 Zim – 88 € 135 € – ½ P 16 €
Rest – Karte 19/33 €
♦ Ein modernes und ganz auf den Geschäftsreisenden ausgerichtetes Hotel nahe der Fußgängerzone mit gut ausgestatteten, funktionellen Zimmern unterschiedlicher Größe. Parkettfußboden und neuzeitliches Mobiliar bestimmen den Stil des Restaurants.

Wien 308 – Salzburg 9 – Bad Reichenhall 20 – Hallein 12
Gemeindeamt, Anifer Str. 10, ✉ 5081, ✆ (06246) 7 23 65, tourist@info-anif.co.at
Schoss Hellbrunn★ (Nord: 2 km)

Friesacher

Hellbrunner Str. 17 ✉ 5081
– ✆ (06246) 89 77 – first@hotelfriesacher.com
– Fax (06246) 897749
90 Zim – 80/110 € 135/180 €
Rest – Menü 16/21 € – Karte 29/44 €
◆ In zeitlos elegantem Landhausstil gehalten sind die Zimmer des Familienbetriebes mit 150 Jahren Tradition. Besonders hübsch: die Zimmer im Gartenhaus und der Badebereich. Das Restaurant ist unterteilt in mehrere rustikale Stuben mit regionaler Küche.

Hubertushof

Alpenstr. 110 (Neu Anif, nahe der Autobahnausfahrt Salzburg Süd) ✉ 5081 – ✆ (06246) 89 70 – hotel@hubertushof-anif.at
– Fax (06246) 76036
85 Zim – 77/102 € 117/159 € – ½ P 17 €
Rest – *(geschl. Februar 2 Wochen, Juli 3 Wochen)* Karte 20/40 €
◆ Ein gewachsener regionstypischer Gasthof in verkehrsgünstiger Lage. Die meisten Zimmer sind im eleganten Landhausstil eingerichtet und verfügen über einen Balkon. Gepflegtes Restaurant mit regionaler Küche.

Schlosswirt zu Anif (mit Gästehaus)

Salzachtal Bundesstr. 7 ✉ 5081
– ✆ (06246) 7 21 75 – info@schlosswirt-anif.com
– Fax (06246) 721758
28 Zim – 70/86 € 130/158 €
Rest – *(geschl. Sonntag, außer Festspielzeit)* Menü 62 €
– Karte 35/58 €
◆ Neben dem Wasserschloss Anif liegt eines der ältesten Gasthäuser Salzburgs (1350 erbaut); angeboten werden wohnliche Zimmer im Biedermeierstil sowie Seminarräume. In gepflegter Atmosphäre isst man hier regionale Küche und wird freundlich bedient.

Pension Schiessling garni

Hellbrunnerstr. 14 ✉ 5081 – ✆ (06246) 7 24 85
– Fax (06246) 724854
7 Zim – 40/45 € 65/70 €
◆ Mitten im Ort liegt dieser kleine Familienbetrieb. Die wohnlich gestalteten Gästezimmer – fast alle mit Balkon – bieten teils eine schöne Sicht auf die Berge.

Unsere „Hoffnungsträger" sind die Restaurants, deren Küche wir für die nächste Ausgabe besonders sorgfältig auf eine höhere Auszeichnung hin überprüfen. Der Name dieser Restaurants ist in „rot" gedruckt und zusätzlich auf der Sterne-Liste am Anfang des Buches zu finden.

ANNABERG-LUNGÖTZ – Salzburg – 730 M6 – 2 300 Ew – Höhe 777 m – Wintersport: 1620 m 2 31 9 G4

Wien 337 – Salzburg 58 – Hallein 44 – Bischofshofen 30

Winterstellgut mit Zim – Lammertal und Berge, Rest, VISA AE
Braunötzhof 4 (Nord-Ost: 2,5 km ab Annaberg) ✉ 5524 Annaberg – ✆ (06463) 60 07 80 – willkommen@winterstellgut.at – Fax (06463) 6007810 – geschl. nach Ostern – April, Nov.
4 Zim – 200/280 € 200/280 € – 3 Suiten
Rest – *(geschl. Montag – Dienstag)* (Tischbestellung ratsam) Menü 39 € – Karte 20/41 €
◆ In malerischer Lage findet man das Gasthaus mit behaglichen Stuben und schöner Aussicht. Schmackhafte regionale Küche wird hier durchgehend angeboten. Geschmackvolle, ländlich-elegante Suiten und ein großer Naturbadeteich gehören zum Haus.

ANRAS – Tirol – 730 J8 – 1 340 Ew – Höhe 1 261 m 8 F6

Wien 426 – Innsbruck 157 – Matrei in Osttirol 49 – Lienz 22

Pfleger Rest, VISA
Dorf 15 ✉ 9912 – ✆ (04846) 62 44 – info@hotel-pfleger.at – Fax (04846) 624420 geschl. 31. März – 1. Mai, 26. Okt. – 20. Dez.
34 Zim (inkl. ½ P.) – 62/70 € 102/120 € 65/83 € 110/140 €
Rest – *(geschl. Mittwoch)* Karte 23/38 €
◆ Das im alpenländischen Stil erbaute Hotel beherbergt mit hellem Holzmobiliar wohnlich eingerichtete Gästezimmer, alle mit Balkon. Auch Familienzimmer. Neuzeitlich-ländliches Ambiente im Restaurant. Internationales Angebot mit einigen Wirtshausgerichten.

ANSFELDEN – Oberösterreich – 730 O4 – 14 790 Ew – Höhe 289 m 2 H3

Wien 172 – Linz 12 – Wels 25 – Steyr 38
18 GC Stärk Linz – Ansfelden, Im Golfwinkel 11 ✆ (07229) 7 85 78

In Ansfelden-Kremsdorf Süd-West: 2 km, nahe der BAB-Ausfahrt Traun:

Stockinger Zim, VISA AE
Ritzlhofstr. 65 ✉ 4052 – ✆ (07229) 88 32 10 – hotel@stocki.at – Fax (07229) 8832172
100 Zim – 49 € 80 € – ½ P 11 € – 6 Suiten
Rest – Karte 13/35 €
◆ Ein zum Hotel gewachsener familiengeführter Gasthof in verkehrsgünstiger Lage. Besonders komfortabel sind die schönen Zimmer im neueren Anbau. Ländlich-rustikale Gaststube mit Kachelofen.

ANTHERING – Salzburg – 730 L5 – 3 110 Ew – Höhe 422 m 8 F4

Wien 299 – Salzburg 9 – Burghausen 47 – Hallein 34

Ammerhauser Zim, VISA AE
Dorfstr. 1 ✉ 5102 – ✆ (06223) 22 04 – info@ammerhauser.at – Fax (06223) 220462
49 Zim – 70/78 € 120/135 € – ½ P 25 €
Rest – Karte 24/35 €
◆ Der gewachsene Gasthof in Familienbesitz wurde zeitgemäß aus- und umgebaut und bietet nun wohnliche, ländlich-elegante Zimmer. Moderne Tagungsräume. Regionale Küche wird in behaglichem Ambiente angeboten. Schöner Wintergarten zur Terrasse.

In Anthering-Acharting Nord-West: 4 km über B 156a Richtung Oberndorf:

Im Wald – Hammerschmiede Zim,
Acharting 22 ✉ 5102
– ✆ (06223) 25 03 – info@hammerschmiede.at
– Fax (06223) 250377
20 Zim – 65/85 € 110/140 € – ½ P 19 € – 4 Suiten
Rest – (nur für Hausgäste) Karte 21/28 €
◆ Die ehemalige Hammerschmiede aus dem Jahre 1850 wurde von der Chefin sorgfältig restauriert und ist nun ein charmantes Hotel. Lage mitten im Wald und hauseigene Pfauen.

ARZL IM PITZTAL – **Tirol** – 730 E7 – **2 790 Ew** – **Höhe 880 m** – **Wintersport: 1 850 m** 6 **C5**

Wien 502 – Innsbruck 58 – Imst 6 – Garmisch-Partenkirchen 62
Arzl 210, ✉ 6471, ✆ (05414) 8 69 99, info@pitztal.com

Arzlerhof
Osterstein 31 (Nord: 1 km) ✉ 6471 – ✆ (05412) 69 00
– hotel@arzlerhof.at – Fax (05412) 6900100
geschl. 30. März – 10. Mai, 26. Okt. – 1.Dez.
70 Zim (inkl. ½ P.) – 62/69 € 104/118 € 68/88 € 116/156 €
Rest – (nur Abendessen für Hausgäste)
◆ Ein Teil der Zimmer dieses familiengeführten Hauses ist ganz modern und freundlich gestaltet, auch Allergikerzimmer mit Holzfußboden. Heller, neuzeitlicher Freizeitbereich.

ASCHAU IM ZILLERTAL – **Tirol** – 730 H7 – **1 540 Ew** – **Höhe 580 m** – **Wintersport:** 7 **E5**

Wien 429 – Innsbruck 56 – Kitzbühel 79 – Schwaz 28
Aschau 215, ✉ 6274, ✆ (05282) 29 23, tvb-aschau@zillertal-mitte.at

Apparthotel Aschauerhof Rest,
Höhenstr. 17 ✉ 6274 – ✆ (05282) 29 25
– info@apparthotel-aschauerhof.at – Fax (05282) 292529
geschl. 5. April – 1. Mai, 26. Okt. – 15. Dez.
36 Suiten (inkl. ½ P.) – 42/68 € 64/102 € 70/102 € 106/184 €
Rest – Menü 27 € – Karte 17/28 €
◆ Ein familienfreundliches All-Suite-Alpenhotel mit Gästezimmern im Landhausstil mit Kachelofen – einige mit zwei Schlafzimmern. Gutes Freizeit- und Kinderbetreuungsangebot. Angenehme Atmosphäre herrscht in den mit hellem Holz vertäfelten Gaststuben.

Bestecke und Sterne sollten nicht verwechselt werden!
Die Bestecke stehen für eine Komfortkategorie, die Sterne zeichnen Häuser mit besonders guter Küche aus - in jeder dieser Kategorien.

ATTERSEE – Oberösterreich – 730 M5 – 1 500 Ew – Höhe 469 m – Wintersport: 660 m 1 1 G3

Wien 246 – Linz 86 – Salzburg 52 – Wels 55

Nussdorfer Str. 15, 4864, (07666) 77 19, info@attersee.at

Seegasthof Oberndorfer

Attersee, Zim,

Hauptstr. 18 4864
– (07666) 7 86 40 – hotelobernderfer@attersee.at – Fax (07666) 786491
geschl. Feb.

23 Zim – 108/136 € 130/224 € 96/132 € 122/229 €

Rest – Karte 17/30 €

♦ Seit 1898 befindet sich das Haus im Besitz der Familie Oberndorfer. Immer wieder erweitert und modernisiert, bietet es neuzeitlich-funktionelle Zimmer, meist mit Seeblick. Sehr schön ist der Gastgarten mit Kastanienbäumen direkt am See.

AU IM BREGENZERWALD – Vorarlberg – 730 B7 – 1 650 Ew – Höhe 800 m – Wintersport: 2 060 m 2 6 5 A5

Wien 593 – Bregenz 43 – Dornbirn 33 – Sankt Anton 51

Argenau 376, 6883, (05515) 22 88, info@au-schoppernau.at

Adler

Zim,

Lisse 90 6883 – (05515) 22 64 – hotel@adler-au.at
– Fax (05515) 22644
geschl. 31. März – 30. April, 10. Nov. – 20. Dez.

31 Zim – 60/72 € 104/128 € 68/82 € 120/152 €
– ½ P 12 €

Rest – *(geschl. Dienstag)* Karte 27/34 €

♦ Etwas oberhalb des Zentrums liegt dieses neuzeitliche Hotel. Wohnlich und modern sind die großzügigen, hochwertig ausgestatteten Zimmer. Angenehmer Saunabereich. Restaurantstuben in gemütlich-ländlichem Stil. Licht und leicht elegant: der Wintergartenanbau.

Krone

Zim,

Jaghausen 4 (B 200) 6883 – (05515) 2 20 10 – office@krone-au.at
– Fax (05515) 2201201
geschl. 30. März – 15. Mai, 15. Okt. – 20. Dez.

67 Zim (inkl. ½ P.) – 74/90 € 138/184 € 83/103 € 156/210 €

Rest – *(geschl. Sonntagabend – Montag)* (Tischbestellung ratsam) Karte 26/49 €

♦ Das gewachsene Hotel am Ortsrand bietet zum Teil sehr modern und in geraden Linien gehaltene Zimmer – einige mit schönem Blick. Naturbadeteich. Im Restaurant serviert man eine schmackhafte Regionalküche, für die überwiegend heimische Produkte verwendet werden.

Alpenrose

Rest,

Rehmen 91 (Süd-Ost: 1,5 km, über B 200 Richtung Schoppernau, dann links ab) 6883 – (05515) 22 47 – hotel@alpenrose-au.at
– Fax (05515) 22477
geschl. 6. April – 29. Mai, 26. Okt. – 13. Dez.

30 Zim (inkl. ½ P.) – 76/84 € 136/152 € 87/100 € 158/184 €

Rest – Karte 17/37 €

♦ Von der Fassade bis in die gepflegten Gästezimmer zeigt sich das etwas außerhalb gelegene familiengeführte Alpenhotel im regionstypischen Stil. Freundliches, ländlich-modern gestaltetes Restaurant.

Rössle Rest,

Argenau 96 ✉ 6883 – ✆ (05515) 22 16 – hotel@roessle-au.at – Fax (05515) 22166
geschl. 30. März – 30. April, 22. Okt. – 20. Dez.
32 Zim – ☼ 48/58 € 80/100 € ❄ 56/68 € 96/120 € – ½ P 12 €
Rest – (nur Abendessen für Hausgäste)
◆ Hinter einer hübschen Schindelfassade erwarten Sie solide, rustikal möblierte Zimmer. Gemütlich: eine 300 Jahre alte Stube mit niedriger Decke und ganz in Holz.

Gasthof Post Zim,

Argenau 100 ✉ 6883 – ✆ (05515) 41 03 – info@motorradhotel.at – Fax (05515) 41034
geschl. 21. Okt. – 15. Dez., 6. April – 26. Mai
21 Zim (inkl. ½ P.) – ☼ 47/60 € 94/120 € ❄ 52/77 € 104/150 € – 9 Suiten
Rest – Karte 15/29 €
◆ Gut unterhaltene und solide möblierte Gästezimmer stehen in diesem mit Schindeln verkleideten Alpenhotel bereit. Tourenvorschläge für Motorradfans. Ländlich gestaltetes Restaurant.

AURACH BEI KITZBÜHEL – Tirol – siehe Kitzbühel

AUSSEE, BAD – Steiermark – 730 N6 – 5 090 Ew – Höhe 650 m – Wintersport: 1 800 m 9 – Kurort

9 **H4**

Wien 282 – Graz 160 – Salzburg 82 – Bad Ischl 28
Bahnhofstr. 132 (Eingang Pratergasse), ✉ 8990, ✆ (03622) 5 23 23, info.badaussee@ausseerland.at
Ausseerland, Sommersbergseestr. 19 ✆ (03622) 5 41 85
Veranstaltungen 22.05. – 25.05.: Narzissenfest
Ausseer Kammerhofmuseum (Kaiserzimmer★)
Grundlsee★ (Ost: 5 km) – Altausseer See★ (Nord: 5 km)

Falkensteiner Hotel Wasnerin < Dachstein, Loser und Trisselwand, (Solebad, geheizt) Rest,

Sommersbergseestr. 19 ✉ 8990 – ✆ (03622) 5 21 08 – wasnerin@falkensteiner.com – Fax (03622) 52108400
90 Zim (inkl. ½ P.) – ☼ 105/130 € 180/230 € ❄ 105/155 € 180/250 € – 9 Suiten
Rest – (nur für Hausgäste)
◆ In diesem Hotel erwarten Sie mit hellem Holz modern und wohnlich eingerichtete Zimmer mit Balkon sowie ein Freizeitbereich, der auf "Medical Wellness" setzt.

Erzherzog Johann (freier Zugang zur Therme) Rest,

Kurhausplatz 62 ✉ 8990 – ✆ (03622) 5 25 07 – info@erzherzogjohann.at – Fax (03622) 52507680
geschl. 15. – 30. Nov.
62 Zim (inkl. ½ P.) – 98/128 € 166/224 €
Rest – Karte 26/40 €
◆ Das im Zentrum gelegene Stadthaus beherbergt zeitgemäße, nach Süden hin angelegte Gästezimmer im Landhausstil. Schön ist der helle, moderne Saunabereich mit Kosmetikangebot. Restaurantstuben mit rustikal-elegantem Ambiente.

AXAMS – Tirol – 730 F7 – **5 300 Ew** – **Höhe 878 m** – **Wintersport: 2 340 m**
1 9 6 **D5**

Wien 450 – Innsbruck 12 – Seefeld in Tirol 20

Sylvester-Jordan-Str. 12, Gemeindeamt, 6094, (05234) 6 81 78, axams@innsbruck.info

XX **Bürgerstuben**

Georg-Bucher-Str. 7 6094 – (05234) 6 83 57 – info@buergerstuben.at – Fax (05234) 67702

geschl. 19. – 31. Mai, 4. – 16. Nov. und Montag

Rest – *(nur Abendessen)* (Tischbestellung ratsam) Menü 30/49 € – Karte 23/39 €

♦ Schon seit über 20 Jahren betreiben die Inhaber dieses gemütliche Restaurant. In den mit Bildern dekorierten Stuben wird sorgfältig zubereitete internationale Küche serviert.

XX **Sonnpark**

Gerichtsäcker 1 6094 – (05234) 6 62 20

geschl. März 2 Wochen, Okt. – Nov. 2 Wochen und Montag

Rest – *(Dienstag – Freitag nur Abendessen)* Karte 19/33 €

♦ Gut eingedeckte Tische und farblich abgestimmte Stoffe unterstreichen das klassische Ambiente in den Räumen dieses familiengeführten Restaurants.

BACHMANNING – Oberösterreich – 730 N4 – **640 Ew** – **Höhe 435 m**
2 **H3**

Wien 217 – Linz 57 – Salzburg 91 – Wels 22

XX **Weinwirt**

Grünbachstr. 20 4672 – (07735) 71 31 – office@weinwirt.at – Fax (07735) 20171

geschl. Mitte – Ende Juli und Montag – Dienstag

Rest – Karte 21/36 €

♦ Viele Stammgäste schätzen diesen soliden und gut geführten Familienbetrieb, der Ihnen in gepflegter Atmosphäre eine sorgfältig zubereitete regionale Küche bietet.

BAD...

siehe Eigenname des Ortes (z. B. Bad Aussee siehe Aussee, Bad).
voir au nom propre de la localité (ex.: Bad Aussee voir Aussee, Bad).
see under second part of town name (e.g. for Bad Aussee see under Aussee, Bad).vedere nome proprio della località (es.: Bad Aussee vedere Aussee, Bad).

BADEN BEI WIEN – Niederösterreich – 730 U4 – **24 510 Ew** – **Höhe 220 m**
4 **L3**

Wien 27 – St. Pölten 63 – Wiener Neustadt 29 – Mödling 12

(Leopoldsbad), Brusattiplatz 3, 2500, (02252) 22 60 06 00, info@baden.at

Enzesfeld, (02256) 8 12 72

Kurpark★ – Bäderarchitektur★ – Doblhoffpark (Rosarium★) X

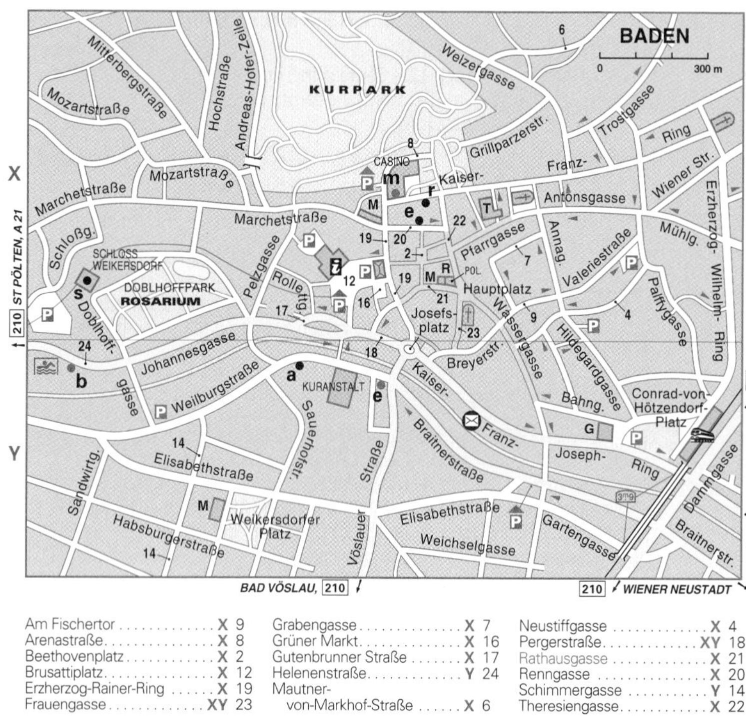

Am Fischertor	X 9		Grabengasse	X 7		Neustiffgasse	X 4
Arenastraße	X 8		Grüner Markt	X 16		Pergerstraße	XY 18
Beethovenplatz	X 2		Gutenbrunner Straße	X 17		Rathausgasse	X 21
Brusattiplatz	X 12		Helenenstraße	Y 24		Renngasse	X 20
Erzherzog-Rainer-Ring	X 19		Mautner-von-Markhof-Straße	X 6		Schimmergasse	Y 14
Frauengasse	XY 23					Theresiengasse	X 22

Grand Hotel Sauerhof

Weilburgstr. 11 ✉ 2500
– ✆ (02252) 4 12 51 – reservation@sauerhof.at
– Fax (02252) 48047 Y **a**

88 Zim – 112/137 € 187/212 € – ½ P 27 € – 3 Suiten
Rest *Rauhenstein* – ✆ (02252) 41 25 16 – Menü 22/39 €
– Karte 33/45 €

◆ In einem 3000 qm großen Park liegt dieses Biedermeier-Palais a. d. J. 1820, dessen Ursprung bis ins 14. Jh. zurückgeht. Stilvolle Zimmer. Geschulter Service und klassische Küche im elegant-rustikalen Restaurant Rauhenstein. Mittags einfachere Karte.

Schloss Weikersdorf (mit Gästehaus)

Zim, Rest, P VISA AE

Schlossgasse 9 ✉ 2500 – ✆ (02252) 48 30 10
– weikersdorf@hotelschlossweikersdorf.at
– Fax (02252) 48301150 X **s**

100 Zim – 140/160 € 175/198 € – ½ P 25 € – 15 Suiten
Rest – Karte 21/38 €

◆ Das im Rosenpark gelegene Schloss a. d. 13. Jh. beherbergt funktionell ausgestattete, in modernem Stil gehaltene Zimmer und Suiten. Kosmetikangebot. Hohe Decken, Stuckverzierungen und sehr gut eingedeckte Tische prägen das Restaurant. Terrasse zum Rosarium.

Herzoghof garni
Kaiser-Franz-Ring 5 ✉ 2500 – ✆ (02252) 4 43 86
– reservierung@hinteregger-hotels.com – Fax (02252) 80578 X **r**
34 Zim – 120 € 170 € – 4 Suiten
◆ 1258 erstmals urkundlich erwähnt, bietet das gepflegte klassische Stadthotel heute modern eingerichtete Zimmer, teils mit Balkon und Blick auf den Kurpark.

Sacher Baden Zim, Rest,
Helenenstr. 55 (über Y) ✉ 2500 – ✆ (02252) 4 84 00
– office@sacher-baden.at – Fax (02252) 42979
44 Zim – 79/86 € 114/140 €
Rest – Karte 17/25 €
◆ In den zwei modernen Anbauten dieses 1881 gegründeten Hotels erwarten den Gast mit italienischen Stilmöbeln solide und elegant gestaltete Zimmer. Gepflegtes Restaurant mit gediegener Einrichtung.

Admiral am Kurpark garni
Renngasse 8 ✉ 2500 – ✆ (02252) 8 67 99
– reservierung@hotel-admiral.at – Fax (02252) 867998 X **e**
22 Zim – 115 € 174 € – 5 Suiten
◆ Ein freundlich geführtes Hotel in der Nähe von Kurpark und Kasino. Man verfügt über wohnliche Zimmer und Suiten sowie ein großzügiges Penthouse. Internet-Corner in der Lobby.

Primavera (Franz Pigel)
Weilburgstr. 3 ✉ 2500 – ✆ (02252) 8 55 51 – Fax (02252) 85551
geschl. 15. Juli – 17. Aug. und Sonntag – Montag Y **e**
Rest – (Tischbestellung ratsam) Menü 59/69 € – Karte 35/58 €
Spez. Parfait von der Stopfgansleber. Pot au feu von Edelfischen mit Noilly Prat und Safran. Lammrücken "Primavera" (2 Pers.).
◆ In dem eleganten kleinen Restaurant in der Stadt kann man eine sehr klassische, auf das Produkt bezogene Küche genießen. Der Chef macht den Service teilweise selbst.

Do & Co Casino
Kaiser-Franz-Ring 1 ✉ 2500 – ✆ (02252) 4 35 02 – baden@doco.com
– Fax (02252) 43502430 X **m**
Rest – Karte 28/47 €
◆ In das größte Kasino Europas hat man mehrere Bars, ein modernes Bistro und ein klassisch-gediegenes Restaurant integriert. Mit schönem Terrassenbereich.

BAIRISCH KÖLLDORF – Steiermark – 730 T8 – 980 Ew – Höhe 390 m

Wien 189 – Graz 70 – Leibnitz 50 – Feldbach 18 11 **L5**

Landhaus Legenstein (geheizt) (Thermal) Rest,
Bairisch Kölldorf 14
✉ 8344 – ✆ (03159) 22 20 – info@legenstein.at – Fax (03159) 22204
44 Zim (inkl. ½ P.) – 68/81 € 122/132 €
Rest – Menü 14/18 € – Karte 14/27 €
◆ In dem familiengeführten Hotel erwartet Sie ein neuzeitliches Ambiente. Ein Teil der Gästezimmer ist für Allergiker reserviert. Schöner Freizeitbereich mit Innenhofgarten. Hell und freundlich wirkt das Restaurant.

BARTHOLOMÄBERG – Vorarlberg – 730 B7 – 2 240 Ew – Höhe 1 087 m – Wintersport: 1 250 m 1 5 A6

Wien 586 – Bregenz 64 – Bludenz 12 – Feldkirch 32
Pfarrkirche (barocke Innenausstattung★, Friedhof ★)

Fernblick
Bergpanorama, Rest,
Panoramastr. 32 6780
– *(05556) 73 11 50 – fernblick@ferienhotel.at – Fax (05556) 7311565*
69 Zim (inkl. ½ P.) – 87/136 € 172/272 € 87/159 €
172/284 € – 10 Suiten – **Rest** – (nur für Hausgäste)
◆ Ein durch und durch wohnlich gestaltetes Hotel mit großzügigem Rahmen. Besonders geschmackvoll sind die neueren, z. T. als Maisonetten angelegten Zimmer. Schöne freie Sicht. Restaurant mit elegantem Landhausambiente und Aussichtsterrasse.

BERGHAUSEN – Steiermark – 730 S8 – 600 Ew – Höhe 400 m 11 K6

Wien 237 – Graz 52 – Maribor 23 – Leibnitz 14

Weingut Firmenich-Steinberghof
(Buschenschank)
Wielitsch 62 (Süd-West: 4 km, Richtung Südsteirische Weinstr, nach 3,5 km rechts ab) 8461 – (03453) 24 35 – Fax (03453) 4417
geschl. 17. Dez. – 22. Feb. und Dienstag – Mittwoch
Rest – Karte ca. 16 €
◆ Behaglich-rustikales Lokal nahe der slowenischen Grenze mit typischem, auch über Jausen hinausgehendem Speisenangebot. Schöne Aussicht über die steirischen Weinberge.

BERGHEIM – Salzburg – 730 L5 – 4 840 Ew – Höhe 420 m 8 F4

Wien 294 – Salzburg 4 – Bad Reichenhall 22
Moosfeldstr. 2, 5101, (0662) 45 45 05,
info@bergheim-tourismus.at

Gasthof Gmachl
(geheizt)
Dorfstr. 35 5101
– *(0662) 45 21 24 – info@gmachl.at – Fax (0662) 45212468*
geschl. Anfang – Mitte Juli
70 Zim – 127/164 € 214/246 € 91/111 € 164/196 €
– ½ P 26 € – 6 Suiten – **Rest** – Karte 26/37 €
◆ Der Gasthof in der Ortsmitte empfängt Sie mit einem großzügigen, eleganten Hallenbereich mit Galerie, offenem Kamin und einer Bar. Schöner Park mit Freizeiteinrichtungen. Von der Terrasse unter Bäumen genießt man die regionale Küche und eine wundervolle Sicht.

In Bergheim-Lengfelden Nord-Ost: 2 km Richtung Obertrum:

Gasthof Bräuwirt
Zim,
Lengfelden 21 5101 – (0662) 45 21 63 – gasthof@braeuwirt.at – Fax (0662) 45216353
geschl. 2. – 13. Jan., Juni, 22. – 28. Dez.
39 Zim – 55/90 € 80/140 € – ½ P 20 €
Rest – *(geschl. Samstag, Sonntagabend, außer Messen)* Karte 13/31 €
◆ Die Gästezimmer des bereits seit über 350 Jahre bestehenden Gasthofs sind elegant-ländlich eingerichtet und zeitgemäß ausgestattet. Zum Restaurant gehört ein schöner Gastgarten.

In Bergheim-Maria Plain Süd-Ost: 1 km:

Maria Plain

Plainbergweg 41 ✉ 5101 – ✆ (0662) 4 50 70 10 – info@mariaplain.com – Fax (0662) 45070119
geschl. Juli 1 Woche
25 Zim – 55/75 € 99/134 € – ½ P 19 € – 5 Suiten
Rest – *(geschl. Ende Jan. – Anfang März und Mittwoch – Donnerstag außer Festspielzeit)* Karte 23/26 €
◆ Unmittelbar bei der berühmten Basilika Maria Plain liegt der aus dem 17. Jh. stammende Gasthof, dessen Zimmer mit Stilmöbeln eingerichtet wurden. In den unterschiedlichen Stüberln und im Gastgarten serviert man bürgerliche Küche.

Zur Plainlinde (Gerhard Brugger)

Plainbergweg 30 ✉ 5101 – ✆ (0662) 45 85 57 – restaurant@plainlinde.at – Fax (0662) 458270
geschl. Anfang Jan. 2 Wochen, Anfang Sept. 1 Woche und Montag – Dienstag, außer Festspielzeit
Rest – (Tischbestellung ratsam) Menü 22 € (mittags)/62 € – Karte 43/60 €
Spez. Gambastortellini mit Tomaten und Pistou. Blutwurst mit Taube und Steinpilzen. Rehrücken im Salzteig mit Kumquats und Sellerie.
◆ Das freundlich geführte Restaurant mit geschmackvoller und dezenter Einrichtung bietet kreative Regionalküche und hat eine schöne Auswahl an österreichischen Weinen.

Sie suchen ein besonderes Hotel für einen sehr angenehmen Aufenthalt?
Reservieren Sie in einem roten Haus: … .

BERWANG – Tirol – 730 E6 – 640 Ew – Höhe 1 350 m – Wintersport: 1 740 m 14

6 C5

Wien 507 – Innsbruck 82 – Reutte 16 – Garmisch-Partenkirchen 38
Berwang 82, ✉ 6622, ✆ (05673) 20 00 04 00, info@berwang.at

Singer Sporthotel & Spa

(geheizt) Rest,

Berwang 52 ✉ 6622 – ✆ (05674) 81 81 – office@hotelsinger.at – Fax (05674) 818183
geschl. 5. – 9. April, 2. Nov. – 13. Dez.
57 Zim (inkl. ½ P.) – 100/185 € 200/270 € 120/275 € 240/410 € – 5 Suiten
Rest – *(im Winter nur Abendessen)* Menü 56/65 € – Karte 32/52 €
Rest *Singerstub'n* – *(geschl. 1. April – 18. Dez. und Montagabend, Mittwochabend, Freitagabend, Sonntagabend)* Karte 18/35 €
◆ Wohnlich-traditionelles Ambiente erwartet Sie in diesem Alpenhotel. Direkt gegenüber (unterirdisch verbunden): der sehr schöne, großzügige Spabereich mit Kosmetikangebot. Klassisch-alpenländischer Speisesaal mit Holzdecke. Rustikal: die Singerstub'n.

Kaiserhof Rest, P
Berwang 78 ✉ 6622 – ☎ (05674) 82 85 VISA AE
– hotel@kaiserhof.at – Fax (05674) 828695
100 Zim (inkl. ½ P.) – ☼ 90/112 € 170/199 € ❄ 112/133 €
224/266 € – 6 Suiten
Rest – Karte 27/34 €
◆ Recht ruhig etwas oberhalb des Ortes gelegenes Alpenhotel mit gutem Wellnessangebot. Einige der Zimmer bieten eine schöne Aussicht. Skilift und Loipen ganz in der Nähe. Restaurant mit regionaler und internationaler Küche. Im Sommer nette Terrasse.

Rotlechhof P

Rinnen 26 (Süd-West: 2 km) ✉ 6622 – ☎ (05674) 82 70
– info@rotlechhof.at – Fax (05674) 8421
geschl. Ende März – 1.Mai, Mitte Okt. – 20. Dez.
30 Zim – ☼ 39 € 65 € ❄ 46/68 € 74/118 € – ½ P 10 €
Rest – Karte 13/44 €
◆ Der Landgasthof überzeugt mit seiner Lage in Liftnähe und gut unterhaltenen, mit hellen Holzmöbeln ausgestatteten Zimmern – zum Großteil mit separatem Wohnteil. Gepflegte Atmosphäre im unterteilten Restaurant. Sehr nette Sonnenterrasse mit schöner Aussicht.

Almrausch Zim, Rest, P
Rinnen 36 (Süd-West: 2 km) ✉ 6622 – ☎ (05674) 81 67
– besler@hotel-almrausch.com – Fax (05674) 8356
geschl. Ende März – Mitte Mai, Mitte Okt. – Mitte Dez.
20 Zim (inkl. ½ P.) – ☼ 35/55 € 66/106 € ❄ 45/105 € 90/200 €
Rest – (nur Abendessen für Hausgäste)
◆ Das familiengeführte Ferienhotel mit seinen sehr gepflegten Zimmern liegt etwas außerhalb von Berwang in einem hübschen kleinen Dorf. Liftanlagen unweit des Hauses.

Rot steht für unsere besonderen Empfehlungen!

BEZAU – **Vorarlberg** – 730 B6 – **1 880 Ew** – **Höhe 650 m** – **Wintersport: 1 650 m** 2 5 **A5**

Wien 607 – Bregenz 31 – Dornbirn 21 – Lindau 41
Platz 39, ✉ 6870, ☎ (05514) 22 95, Fax (05514) 3129, bezau.tourismus@aon.at

Post Zim, P
Brugg 35 ✉ 6870 – ☎ (05514) 22 07 VISA AE
– office@hotelpostbezau.com – Fax (05514) 220722
geschl. Dez. 2 Wochen
52 Zim (inkl. ½ P.) – ☼ 132/172 € 232/316 € ❄ 126/182 €
222/348 €
Rest – *(geschl. Ende Mai 2 Wochen, Juli 1 Woche, Anfang Dez. 2 Wochen und Sonntagabend, Montag – Samstag nur Abendessen)* Menü 48/60 € – Karte 39/51 €
◆ Sowohl moderner als auch traditioneller Stil findet sich in diesem gewachsenen Hotel. Geradlinig und ganz in Weiß ist der Spabereich gehalten, mit eigener Naturkosmetiklinie. Teils klassisch, teils neuzeitlich gestaltetes Restaurant.

Gams ⋖ (geheizt) Zim, P VISA MC

Platz 44 ✉ 6870 – ✆ (05514) 22 20 – info@hotel-gams.at
– Fax (05514) 222024
52 Zim – 146/280 € – ½ P 12 €
Rest *Gourmetstube* – *(geschl. Montag – Dienstag, nur Abendessen)* (Tischbestellung ratsam) Menü 51/58 € – Karte 37/44 €
Rest *Das Wirtshaus* – *(geschl. Montag – Dienstag, nur Mittagessen)* Karte 24/33 €

♦ Ein interessanter Kontrast zu dem 1648 als Gasthof erbauten Haus ist das Blütenschloss mit ganz modernen Kuschel-Juniorsuiten und geschmackvollem Wellnessbereich auf 1000 qm. Schöne historische Gourmetstube mit gemütlichem Ambiente und kreativer Küche.

Gasthaus Engel mit Zim P VISA MC

Platz 29 ✉ 6870 – ✆ (05514) 22 03 – office@gasthaus-engel.de
– Fax (05514) 28935
geschl. 23. Juni – 6. Juli, 6. -19. Okt.
6 Zim – 55 € 90 €
Rest – *(geschl. Donnerstag, nur Abendessen)* Karte 19/35 €

♦ Das Gasthaus aus dem 18. Jh. beherbergt schöne rustikale Bregenzer Stuben, die mit Holztäfelung, Kachelofen, alten Tischen und Ölgemälden gemütlich eingerichtet sind. Zum Übernachten stehen einige gepflegte Gästezimmer bereit.

BILDSTEIN – Vorarlberg – 730 B6 – 740 Ew – Höhe 650 m 5 A5

Wien 633 – Bregenz 17 – Dornbirn 9
Dorf 83, ✉ 6858, ✆ (05572) 5 83 84, gemeinde.bildstein@cnv.at

Traube mit Zim ⋖ Rheintal und Bergpanorama, Zim, VISA MC AE

Dorf 85 ✉ 6858 – ✆ (05572) 58 36 90
– office@hotel-traube.at – Fax (05572) 583693
geschl. Jan. – Feb.
8 Zim – 78/90 € 128/150 € – ½ P 25 €
Rest – (Tischbestellung ratsam) Menü 26/41 € – Karte 30/48 €

♦ Neben der Kirche liegt das erweiterte Gasthaus mit blauen Holzschindeln und roten Fensterläden – ein klassisch-rustikales Restaurant mit schöner Aussicht. Elegante Zimmer.

BIRKFELD – Steiermark – 730 T6 – 1 710 Ew – Höhe 623 m – Wintersport: 11 K4

Wien 148 – Graz 50 – Bruck a.d. Mur 62 – Wiener Neustadt 99
Stift Vorau★ (Nord-Ost: 20 km)

Forellengasthaus Kulmer P VISA MC

Haslau 63 (Nord-West: 4,5 km, Richtung Gasen) ✉ 8190
– ✆ (03174) 44 63 – franz.kulmer@kulmer-fisch.at – Fax (03174) 4378
geschl. Nov. und Montag – Dienstag
Rest – Karte 14/27 €

♦ Ein Gasthaus a. d. J. 1722 mit rustikalen Stuben und wechselnder Bilderausstellung. Die kleine bürgerliche Karte wird ergänzt durch meist mündlich empfohlene Forellengerichte.

BISCHOFSHOFEN – Salzburg – 730 L6 – 10 090 Ew – Höhe 550 m – Wintersport: 1 000 m 1 — 8 G5

Wien 346 – Salzburg 50 – Villach 147 – Zell am See 51

Salzburger Str. 1, 5500, (06462) 24 71, info@bischofshofen.com

Lage★

Salzachtal★ – Liechtensteinklamm★ (Süd: 9 km) – Erlebnisburg Hohenwerfen★ (Nord-West: 9 km) – Höhlen Eisriesenwelt★★ (Nord-West: 12 km)

Ortners

Alte Bundesstr. 4 5500 – (06462) 3 29 78 – Fax (06462) 32978
geschl. Mitte Juli 2 Wochen und Sonntag – Montag
Rest – Menü 19/35 € – Karte 22/28 €

◆ Ein Mix aus Restaurant und Bar ist diese Adresse in der Innenstadt. Dunkles Holz, Backsteinwände und Erdtöne bestimmen das Ambiente. Terrasse zur verkehrsberuhigten Straße.

BIZAU – Vorarlberg – 730 B6 – 960 Ew – Höhe 681 m – Wintersport: 1 700 m — 5 A5

Wien 609 – Bregenz 34 – Dornbirn 24 – Lech am Arlberg 47

Schwanen

VISA

Krichdorf 77 6874 – (05514) 21 33 – schwanen.moosbrugger@vol.at – Fax (05514) 213329
geschl. 10. Nov. – 22. Dez.
20 Zim – 43/50 € 74/96 € – ½ P 18 €
Rest – *(geschl. Mittwoch)* Menü 25/36 € – Karte 25/39 €

◆ Der familiär geführte kleine Gasthof am Dorfplatz verfügt über wohnliche, freundliche Zimmer mit Holzfußboden, einige mit Balkon. Die schmackhaften Speisen basieren zum Teil auf der Küche Hildegard von Bingens.

BLEIBERG, BAD – Kärnten – 730 N9 – 2 760 Ew – Höhe 920 m – Wintersport: 1 200 m — 9 H6

Wien 341 – Klagenfurt 52 – Villach 16 – Spittal an der Drau 44

Bleibergerhof

(geheizt)

P VISA AE

Drei Lärchen 150 9530 – (04244) 22 05 – office@bleibergerhof.at – Fax (04244) 220570
108 Zim (inkl. ½ P.) – 115/125 € 198/250 € – 7 Suiten
Rest – *(nur Abendessen)* Menü 49/70 € – Karte 31/52 €

◆ Ein angenehmer, zeitgemäßer Spabereich und helle, schöne Gästezimmer in warmen Tönen machen dieses Hotel aus. Hübsch ist auch der Garten mit Badeteich. Das Restaurant teilt sich in moderne und regional-rustikale Räume.

Gartenpension Lindenbauer

P VISA

Bleiberg – Nötsch 131 9530 – (04244) 22 49 – pension@lindenbauer.co.at – Fax (04244) 25911
geschl. 7. Jan. – 1. Feb., 3. Nov. – 20. Dez.
11 Zim – 35/45 € 70/90 € – ½ P 12 €
Rest – (nur Abendessen für Hausgäste)

◆ Die familiäre kleine Pension ist ein tipptopp gepflegtes Haus mit hellen, freundlichen Zimmern und schön angelegtem Garten mit Liegestühlen und Sonnenterrasse.

BLUDENZ - Vorarlberg - 730 B7 - 13 710 Ew - Höhe 588 m 5 A6

Wien 580 - Bregenz 53 - Feldkirch 21 - Sankt Anton 46

Rathaus, Werdenbergerstr. 42, 6700, (05552) 6 21 70, tourismus@bludenz.at

Bludenz - Braz, Oberradin 60 (05552) 33 50 30

Arlberggebiet★★

Schlosshotel Dörflinger Zim,

Schlossplatz 5 6700 - (05552) 6 30 16
- info@schlosshotel.cc - Fax (05552) 630168

42 Zim - 69/85 € 110/120 € - ½ P 18 €

Rest - Karte 18/31 €

◆ Schön ist die erhöhte Lage des Hotels mit Blick über die Stadt, im Haus erwartet Sie eine wohnlich-gediegene Atmosphäre. Mountainbikes und Fahrräder für Hotelgäste gratis. Klassisch-rustikales Restaurant und überdachte, beheizte Terrasse mit toller Aussicht.

Val Blu Resort (geheizt) Zim,

Haldenweg 2a 6700
- (05552) 6 31 06 - valblu@bludenz.at - Fax (05552) 631064

56 Zim - 55/93 € 90/110 €

Rest - *(nur Abendessen)* Karte ca. 17 €

◆ Ein Hotel mit moderner, lichter Architektur und farbenfrohem, sachlich-klarem Design. Der Spabereich ist großzügig und vielseitig. Direkt nebenan: das Freibad von Bludenz.

In Braz Ost: 8 km, Richtung Innsbruck:

Gasthof Traube Rest,

Klostertalerstr. 12 6751 - (05552) 2 81 03 - office@traubebraz.at
- Fax (05552) 2810340
geschl. Nov.

36 Zim - 62/82 € 110/136 € 65/94 € 116/160 €
- ½ P 26 €

Rest - Menü 17/57 € - Karte 23/46 €

◆ Dieser Landgasthof liegt günstig im 5-Täler-Stern und wird seit mehreren Generationen von der Familie geleitet. Die gemütlichen Zimmer verfügen teils über einen Balkon. Jagdtrophäen und ein Kachelofen schmücken das ländliche, holzvertäfelte Restaurant.

Gasthof Rössle mit Zim Zim,

Arlbergstr. 67 6751 - (05552) 28 10 50 - office@roesslebraz.at
- Fax (05552) 281056
geschl. 23. Juni - 23. Juli., 17. - 24. Dez. und Montag

10 Zim - 45/50 € 80/90 € 50/55 € 90/100 €
- ½ P 23 €

Rest - (Tischbestellung ratsam) Menü 25/40 € - Karte 20/42 €

◆ Neben der Kirche liegt der gut geführte Gasthof von 1776. In 2 holzvertäfelten Stuben im 1. Stock serviert man schmackhafte regionale und internationale Küche. Nette Terrasse. Zum Übernachten stehen funktionelle Zimmer zur Verfügung.

BLUMAU, BAD - Steiermark - 730 U7 - 1 530 Ew - Höhe 280 m - Heilbad 11 L5

Wien 144 - Graz 62 - Fürstenfeld 10

Hauptstr. 113, 8283, (03383) 23 77, info@tvbadblumau.at

Thermenoase garni

Hauptstr. 6 ✉ 8283 – ✆ (03383) 26 60 – perl@thermenoase.at
– Fax (03383) 266042
17 Zim – 35/41 € 58/70 €
◆ Ein kleines Hotel mit familiärer Atmosphäre sowie funktionell und wohnlich eingerichteten Zimmern, die alle einen eigenen Namen tragen. Schöner großer Garten mit Pool.

Landhaus Florian garni

Hauptstr. 12 ✉ 8283 – ✆ (03383) 20 94 – office@landhaus-florian.com
– Fax (03383) 20944
11 Zim – 32 € 54 €
◆ In diesem netten kleinen Landhotel erwarten Sie Zimmer, die mit hellem Naturholz wohnlich gestaltet sind, sowie ein gemütlicher Frühstücksraum. Feng-Shui-Garten mit Badeteich.

Bad Blumauerhof

Zim,

Bad Blumau 29 ✉ 8283 – ✆ (03383) 51 15 – office@badblumauerhof.at
– Fax (03383) 511550
20 Zim – 37 € 64 € – ½ P 15 €
Rest – Karte 12/30 €
◆ Vor allem die schöne ruhige Lage am Waldrand spricht für dieses Haus. Die solide möblierten Zimmer verteilen sich auf eine kleine Pension und einen Hotelanbau. Restaurant in ländlichem Stil.

BODENSDORF – Kärnten – 730 N8 – 3 590 Ew – Höhe 505 m 9 H6

Wien 315 – Klagenfurt 34 – Villach 14 – Spittal an der Drau 47
10.-Oktober-Str. 1, ✉ 9551, ✆ (04243) 83 83 23, steindorf.tourist@ktn.gde.at
Ossiacher See★
Gerlitzen★★ (Nord-West: 12 km)

Seerose

Ossiacher See, Rest,

Fischerweg 7 ✉ 9551 – ✆ (04243) 25 14 – hotel@seerose.info
– Fax (04243) 251433
geschl. 12. Okt. – 17. April
40 Zim – 53/80 € 110/178 €
Rest – (nur für Hausgäste)
◆ Schön ist die Lage dieses Ferienhotels direkt am See. Eine große Wiese und ein hauseigener Badestrand stehen den Gästen zur Verfügung. Alle Zimmer mit Balkon und Seesicht.

In Bodensdorf-Sankt Urban Süd-West: 1 km über B 94 Richtung Villach:

Falkensteiner Hotel Urbani

(geheizt) Rest,

St. Urbanweg 16
✉ 9551 – ✆ (04243) 22 86 – urbani@falkensteiner.com
– Fax (04243) 228661
geschl. 1. – 30. Nov.
51 Zim (inkl. ½ P.) – 51/98 € 118/216 € 53/98 €
110/172 €
Rest – *(nur für Hausgäste)*
◆ Die Lage direkt am Ossiacher See, wohnliche (Familien-) Zimmer sowie viele Freizeitangebote für die ganze Familie (Falky-Land für Kinder) machen dieses Hotel aus.

In Bodensdorf-Steindorf Nord-Ost: 2 km über B 94 Richtung Feldkirchen:

Seehotel Hoffmann (mit Gästehaus) Ossiacher See, Zim, Rest, VISA
Stiegl (B 94)
✉ 9552 – ✆ (04243) 87 04 – seehotel.hoffmann@aon.at
– Fax (04243) 8704100
geschl. Okt. – April
33 Zim (inkl. ½ P.) – 55/85 € 100/168 €
Rest – Karte 21/31 €
♦ Ein netter Familienbetrieb mit schönem Garten- und Strandbereich. Die Gästezimmer sind teilweise als Appartements angelegt, modern sind die Zimmer im Gästehaus. Kleiner, leicht eleganter Speisesaal und schöne überdachte Terrasse mit Seesicht.

Ossiacher See Ossiacher See, Rest, VISA
Seeblickweg 17 ✉ 9552 – ✆ (04243) 24 84
– info@hotel-ossiacher-see.at – Fax (04243) 248450
geschl. 1. Nov. – 22. Dez.
28 Zim (inkl. ½ P.) – 42/65 € 80/130 €
Rest – (nur Abendessen für Hausgäste)
♦ Wunderschön oberhalb des Ortes liegt diese tadellos gepflegte, familiär geführte Pension – mit Seeblick. Es stehen zeitgemäß und solide eingerichtete Zimmer zur Verfügung. Zum Restaurant gehören ein Wintergartenvorbau und eine Terrasse mit Sicht auf den See.

BRAMBERG AM WILDKOGEL – **Salzburg** – 730 J7 – **3 900 Ew** – **Höhe 820 m** – **Wintersport: 2100 m** 1 10 7 **E5**

Wien 410 – Salzburg 118 – Kitzbühel 43 – Zell am See 40
Stoitznergasse 3, ✉ 5733, ✆ (06566) 72 51, info@bramberg.at

Grundlhof Rest, VISA
Habach 16 (Süd: 1,5 km) ✉ 5733 – ✆ (06566) 73 85 – info@grundlhof.at
– Fax (06566) 738533
geschl. 15.April – 15. Mai, 25. Okt. – 10. Dez.
30 Zim (inkl. ½ P.) – 48/62 € 88/108 €
Rest – Karte 16/30 €
♦ Der im hiesigen Stil erbaute Gasthof unter familiärer Leitung verfügt über solide und neuzeitlich möblierte Zimmer und eigene Landwirtschaft. In hellem Holz gehaltene Gasträume.

Weyerhof mit Zim VISA
Weyer 9 (West: 2,5 km) ✉ 5733 – ✆ (06566) 72 38 – info@weyerhof.at
– Fax (06566) 723811
geschl. April und Nov.
6 Zim – 35/45 € 60/90 € – ½ P 14 €
Rest – Karte 16/35 €
♦ In dem Wirtshaus aus dem 17. Jh. hat man ein gemütliches Restaurant eingerichtet, teils als holzgetäfelte Stube, teils unter einer hübschen Gewölbedecke. Ländliche Zimmer.

BRAND – **Vorarlberg** – 730 B7 – **710 Ew** – **Höhe 1 050 m** – **Wintersport: 2 000 m** 2 12 5 **A6**

Wien 589 – Bregenz 60 – Feldkirch 29 – Bludenz 11
Mühledörfle 40, ✉ 6708, ✆ (05559) 5 55, brand@brand.vol.at
Brand, ✆ (05559) 4 50
Brandnertal★★ (Süd: 5 km)

Sporthotel Beck (Badeteich) Rest, VISA
Mühledörfle 91 ✉ 6708
– ✆ (05559) 3 06 – info@sporthotel-beck.at – Fax (05559) 30670
geschl. 24. März - Mitte Mai, Ende Okt. – Mitte Dez.
50 Zim (inkl. ½ P.) – 95/103 € 162/174 € 107/166 € 185/272 €
Rest – (nur für Hausgäste)
◆ Ganz auf Familien ist das aus einem landwirtschaftlichen Betrieb entstandene Hotel ausgelegt: Kinderprogramm, Reiten und Biotop-Badesee. U. a. recht geräumige Appartements.

Scesaplana Rest, VISA
Mühledörfle 158 ✉ 6708 – ✆ (05559) 2 21 – scesaplana@s-hotels.com
– Fax (05559) 445
geschl. 20. Okt. – 13. Dez.
61 Zim (inkl. ½ P.) – 75/102 € 136/192 € 82/166 € 130/310 €
Rest – Karte 33/37 €
◆ In dem neuzeitlich gestalteten Hotel erwarten Sie ein großzügiger öffentlicher Bereich sowie unterschiedlich geschnittene, wohnliche Gästezimmer. Kunstobjekte zieren das Haus. Das nette kleine Bauernstüberl dient als A-la-carte-Restaurant.

Walliserhof VISA
Gufer 42 ✉ 6708 – ✆ (05559) 2 41 – office@walliserhof.at
– Fax (05559) 24162
geschl. 30. Nov. – 20. Dez.
52 Zim (inkl. ½ P.) – 90/111 € 144/270 € 120/165 € 192/390 € – 4 Suiten
Rest – Karte 24/41 €
◆ Ein engagiert geführtes Haus mit klarem, modernem Ambiente. Fast alle Zimmer sind im Designerstil gehalten: Edelweiß-, Romantik- und Almrauschzimmer. Komfortabler Spabereich. Neuzeitlich gestaltetes Restaurant.

Valschena VISA
Studa 58 ✉ 6708 – ✆ (05559) 3 31 – hotel.valschena@cable.vol.at
– Fax (05559) 331113
geschl. 30. März – 26. Mai, 9. Okt. – 18. Dez.
16 Zim (inkl. ½ P.) – 66/71 € 122/132 € 76/96 € 152/192 €
Rest – (nur für Hausgäste)
◆ Das von der Inhaberfamilie geleitete kleine Hotel im regionstypischen Stil verfügt über solide möblierte Gästezimmer und einen rustikal eingerichteten Frühstücksraum.

Brandner Hof VISA
Studa 57 ✉ 6708 – ✆ (05559) 2 60 – restaurant.brandnerhof@aon.at
– Fax (05559) 2604
geschl. 31. März – Ende Mai, 13. Okt. – 15. Dez.
Rest – Menü 42 € – Karte 25/43 €
◆ In dem zum Hotel Valschena gehörenden Restaurant erwartet Sie ein sehr gepflegtes Ambiente mit ländlicher Note. Geboten wird internationale, teils auch regionale Küche.

BRAZ – Vorarlberg – siehe Bludenz

BREGENZ – Vorarlberg – 730 B6 – **26 760 Ew** – **Höhe 396 m** – **Wintersport: 1 064 m** 2 5 **A5**

Wien 627 – Dornbirn 13 – Feldkirch 36 – Lindau 10

Rathausstr. 35a, 6900, (05574) 4 95 90, tourismus@bregenz.at

Veranstaltungen

23.07. – 23.08.: Festspiele

Seeufer (★vom Hafendamm) – Vorarlberger Landesmuseum★ – Martinsturm ★ BY

Pfänder★★ (auch mit)

Deuring-Schlössle Rest,

Ehre-Guta-Platz 4 6900 – (05574) 4 78 00 – rezeption@deuring-schloessle.at – Fax (05574) 4780080

geschl. Feb. BZ **a**

15 Zim – 95/180 € 176/210 €

Rest – *(geschl. Sonntag, nur Abendessen, außer Festspielzeit)* (Tischbestellung ratsam) Menü 58/76 € – Karte 35/68 €

◆ Einen schönen Rahmen verspricht das hübsche Schlösschen auf einem Felsen über der Stadt. Die geschmackvolle Einrichtung mit vielen Antiquitäten zeichnet das kleine Hotel aus. Stilvoll: das Restaurant mit klassischer Küche. Terrasse mit Blick auf die Stadt.

Weisses Kreuz

Römerstr. 5 6900 – (05574) 4 98 80 – hotelweisseskreuz@kinz.at – Fax (05574) 498867 BY **w**

44 Zim – 109/166 € 126/226 € – ½ P 17 €

Rest *Stadtgasthaus* – *(geschl. Sonntag, außer Festspielzeit)* Menü 25/59 € – Karte 22/48 €

◆ Das alte Stadthaus im Zentrum ist ein engagiert geführtes Hotel, seit über 20 Jahren in Familienhand. Technisch gut ausgestattete Zimmer in modernem Design stehen bereit. In dem stilvoll dekorierten Restaurant Stadtgasthaus bietet man regionale Küche.

Schwärzler Rest,

Landstr. 9 (über AZ) 6900 – (05574) 49 90 – schwaerzler@s-hotels.com – Fax (05574) 47575

83 Zim – 92/130 € 128/180 € – ½ P 28 €

Rest – Menü 25/36 € – Karte 26/44 €

◆ Ein gut geführtes Hotel am Stadtrand, das Ihnen leicht elegante, meist mit hellen Möbeln eingerichtete Zimmer und sehr komfortable Juniorsuiten bietet. Verschiedene Restauranträume in ländlichem Stil.

Germania Zim,

Am Steinenbach 9 6900 – (05574) 42 76 60 – office@hotel-germania.at – Fax (05574) 427664

20. Dez. – 7. Jan. BY **a**

38 Zim – 89/110 € 125/169 € – ½ P 35 €

Rest – *(geschl. Sonntag und Feiertag, außer Festspielzeit, nur Abendessen)* Menü 24/28 € – Karte 24/37 €

◆ Der kleine Gasthof mit einem großen modernen Anbau verfügt über funktionell ausgestattete Zimmer und eine neuzeitliche Hotelhalle mit Internet-Corner. Das Restaurant: recht schlicht und angenehm hell gestaltet, teils leicht rustikal.

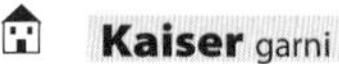

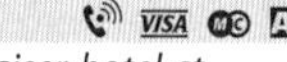

Kaiser garni

Kaiserstr. 2 ✉ 6900 – ✆ (05574) 5 29 80 – office@kaiser-hotel.at – Fax (05574) 52982 BY **k**

8 Zim ☕ – 🚹70/90 € 🚹🚹114/132 €

◆ Mitten im Zentrum steht das kleine Altstadthaus aus dem 15. Jh. Die Zimmer wirken klassisch-elegant und verfügen über Bäder mit Whirlwanne.

BREGENZ

Amtstorstr.	BZ	2
Am Steinenbach	BY	14
Anton-Schneider-Str.	BY	3
Bahnhofstr.	AY	
Kaiserstr.	BY	5
Kirchstr.	BYZ	6
Kornmarktstr.	BY	8
Leutbühel	BY	9
Maurachgasse	BY	1
Mehrerauer Str.	AY	1
Rathausstr.	BY	1
Thalbachgasse	BZ	1

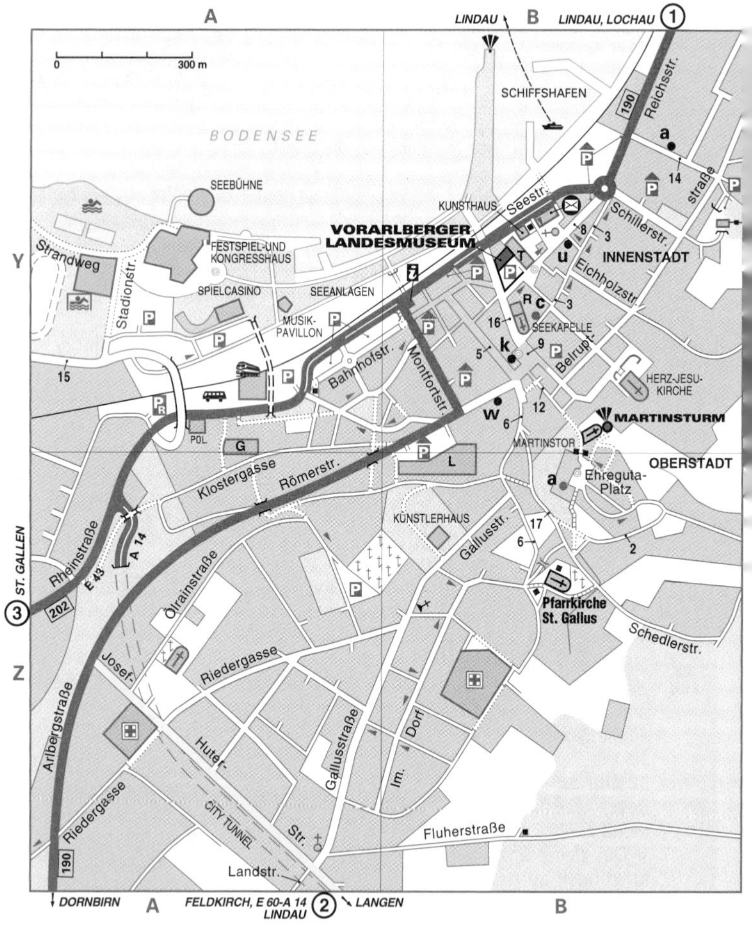

Neubeck
Anton-Schneider-Str. 5 ✉ 6900 – ✆ (05574) 4 36 09
– restaurant@neubeck.at – Fax (05574) 43710
geschl. Sonntag - Montag, Feiertage BY **c**
Rest – Menü 24/49 € (abends) – Karte 24/46 €
◆ In der Innenstadt befindet sich dieses modern-elegant gehaltene Restaurant. Sehr nett sitzt man auch in dem zum Garten hin gelegenen kleinen Wintergarten.

BREITENWANG – Tirol – 730 E6 – 1 580 Ew – Höhe 854 m 6 C5

Wien 500 – Innsbruck 90 – Reutte 2 – Garmisch-Partenkirchen 46

Moserhof Rest,
Planseestr. 44 ✉ 6600 – ✆ (05672) 6 20 20 – info@hotel-moserhof.at
– Fax (05672) 6202040
33 Zim – 50/60 € 80/100 € – ½ P 9 € – **Rest** – Karte 15/28 €
◆ Das familiengeführte Landhotel verfügt über funktionelle, mit soliden Naturholzmöbeln eingerichtete Gästezimmer – fast alle mit Balkon – sowie eine hauseigene kleine Kapelle. Gepflegt dekoriertes Restaurant mit freundlichem Service und netter Terrasse.

BRIXEN IM THALE – Tirol – 730 I6 – 2 580 Ew – Höhe 800 m – Wintersport: 1 829 m 6 84 7 E5

Wien 376 – Innsbruck 78 – Wörgl 20 – Kitzbühel 12
Dorfstr. 93, ✉ 6364, ✆ (05334) 84 33, info@kitzbuehel-alpen.at

Residenz Hubertus Zim,
Ahornweg 4 ✉ 6364 – ✆ (05334) 81 87
– info@hubertus-brixen.at – Fax (05334) 8187333
geschl. Mitte April – Ende Mai, Mitte Okt. – Mitte Dez.
23 Zim – 47/63 € 62/82 € 87/114 € 96/146 €
Rest – (nur für Hausgäste)
◆ Sehr schön sind die wohnlichen Zimmer sowie der Sauna-, Kosmetik- und Massagebereich dieses familiär geleiteten Hauses. Im Garten befindet sich ein kleiner Badeteich. Ganz rustikal ist die Tiroler Zirbenholzstube für Nichtraucher.

Loipenstub'n
Feuringweg 36 ✉ 6364 – ✆ (05334) 83 81 – info@hotelloipenstubn.at
– Fax (05334) 838118 – geschl. Oktober – November
24 Zim (inkl. ½ P.) – 42/52 € 64/84 € 58/68 € 126/136 €
Rest – *(geschl. im Sommer Dienstag)* Karte 19/33 €
◆ Das in einem Wohngebiet gelegene Ferienhotel verfügt über hübsche, rustikal-gemütliche Gästezimmer mit komfortablen Bädern und einen freundlichen kleinen Saunabereich. In den regionstypischen Restaurantstuben bietet man bürgerliche Küche.

Reitlwirt Rest,
Dorfstr. 31 (B 170) ✉ 6364 – ✆ (05334) 81 19 – info@hotelreitlwirt.at
– Fax (05334) 81194
geschl. 1. April – 9. Mai, 5. Okt. – 15. Dez.
29 Zim – 38 € 70/76 € 59/75 € 112/144 € – ½ P 10 €
Rest – *(nur Abendessen)* Karte 16/32 €
◆ Aus dem Jahre 1556 stammt das familiär geleitete Haus. Es erwarten Sie solide, mit hellem Holzmobiliar ausgestattete Zimmer und ein ansprechend gestalteter Saunabereich. Restaurantstuben mit behaglicher Atmosphäre.

XX **Thalhof**

Schwimmbadweg 8 ✉ 6364 – ✆ (05334) 84 68
– kulinarium@thalhof.at
Fax (05334) 2829
– geschl. 16. Juni – 9. Juli, 27. Okt. – 5. Dez. und Dienstag
Rest – *(Montag und Mittwoch - Freitag nur Abendessen)*
Karte 25/40 €

◆ Dieser nette Familienbetrieb ist ein im alpenländischen Stil gehaltenes Restaurant mit Nichtraucherstübchen. Der Chef kocht, die Chefin leitet freundlich den Service.

Wir bemühen uns bei unseren Preisangaben um größtmögliche Genauigkeit. Aber alles ändert sich! Lassen Sie sich daher bei Ihrer Reservierung den derzeit gültigen Preis mitteilen.

BRIXLEGG – Tirol – 730 H6 – 2 780 Ew – Höhe 534 m – Wintersport: 7 E5

Wien 404 – Innsbruck 45 – Schwaz 16 – Wörgl 17
Römerstr. 1, ✉ 6230, ✆ (05337) 6 25 81, info@alpbachtal.at

XX **Sigwart's Tiroler Weinstuben**

Marktstr. 40 ✉ 6230 – ✆ (05337) 6 33 90
– tiroler-weinstuben@aon.at
– Fax (05337) 6339015
– geschl. 3. – 31. Juli. und Montag – Mittwoch
Rest – Menü 39/57 € – Karte 39/57 €

◆ Ein Gasthof von 1774 beherbergt die ländlich-rustikalen Stuben, in denen man gute regionale Küche mit internationalem Einfluss serviert. Hübsche Terrasse im Hof.

BRUCK AN DER GLOCKNERSTRASSE – Salzburg – 730 K7 – 4 430 Ew – Höhe 758 m – Wintersport: 2 8 F5

Wien 376 – Salzburg 92 – Zell am See 6 – Saalfelden 21

X **Taxhof** mit Zim ← Tal und Glocknermassiv,

Hundsdorf 15 (Nord: 3,5 km) ✉ 5671
– ✆ (06545) 62 61 – taxhof@sbg.at
– Fax (06545) 62616
– geschl. 31. März – 29. April, 5. – 29. Nov. und Montag, im Winter Montag – Dienstag
7 Zim (inkl. ½ P.) – †68/86 € ††116/180 €
Rest – *(nur Abendessen)* Menü 28 € – Karte 19/31 €

◆ Über 300 Jahre in Familienbesitz ist der in 1020 m Höhe gelegene Hof, zu dem noch eigene Landwirtschaft gehört. In historischem Ambiente isst man regional. Gemütliche Gästezimmer mit stimmigen Bauernmöbeln. Hübsch: die kleine Maisonette im alten Holzstadl.

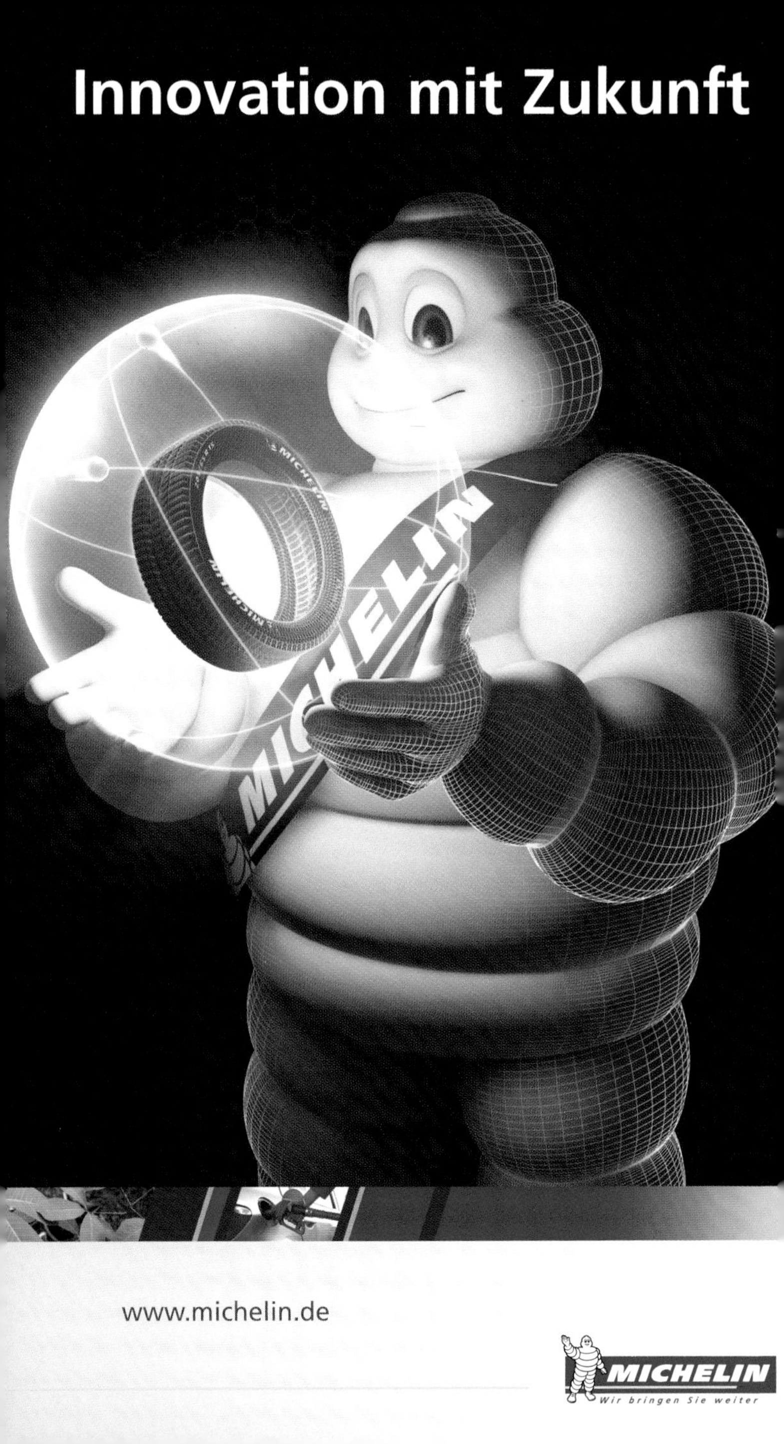

Zacherl-Bräu mit Zim
Glocknerstr. 14 ✉ 5671 – ✆ (06545) 72 42 – gasthof@zacherlbraeu.at – Fax (06545) 7242
geschl. Mitte Mai 2 Wochen, Mitte Okt. 2 Wochen
7 Zim – 40/44 € 64/72 € – ½ P 19 €
Rest – *(geschl. außer Saison Montag)* Karte 17/36 €
♦ Kachelofen, Zirbenholztäfelung und Kreuzgewölbe verleihen dem Gasthaus aus dem 16. Jh. ein gemütliches Ambiente. Im Sommer serviert man auf der lauschigen Gartenterrasse.

BRUCK AN DER MUR – Steiermark – 730 R6 – 13 440 Ew – Höhe 491 m 10 J4

Wien 148 – Graz 54 – Wiener Neustadt 99 – Leoben 16
Koloman-Wallisch-Platz 1, ✉ 8600, ✆ (03862) 89 01 21, stadtmarketing@bruckmur.at
St. Lorenzen, Gassing 22 ✆ (03864) 3 96 10
Oberaich, Am Golfplatz 1 ✆ (03862) 5 57 11
Eiserner Brunnen★★ – Kornmesserhaus★ – Pfarrkirche (Sakristeitür★) – St.-Ruprechts-Kirche (Weltgerichtsfresko★)
Leoben (Stadtpfarrkirche St. Xaver★) Süd-West: 13 km

Landskron Rest, Zim,
Am Schiffertor 3 ✉ 8600 VISA AE
– ✆ (03862) 58 45 80 – info@hotel-landskron.at – Fax (03862) 584586
44 Zim – 75/90 € 90/110 €
Rest – Karte 17/31 €
♦ Durch die historische Stadtmauer betreten Sie den direkt angeschlossenen geräumigen und lichten Hallenbereich dieses komfortablen Hotels. Die Zimmer sind modern ausgestattet. Neuzeitlich-elegantes Restaurant im 2. Stock und Terrasse mit Blick auf die Mur.

BUCH – Tirol – 730 H6 – 2 430 Ew – Höhe 560 m 7 D5

Wien 413 – Innsbruck 35 – Garmisch-Partenkirchen 89 – Schwaz 6
St. Margarethen 107, ✉ 6200, ✆ (05244) 6 58 94, tvb.buch.tirol@aon.at

Gasthof Esterhammer Rest,
Rotholz 362 (Nord-Ost: 3 km Richtung Wörgl) VISA AE
✉ 6200 – ✆ (05244) 6 22 12 – hotel@esterhammer.com – Fax (05244) 622126
geschl. Nov. 3 Wochen
18 Zim – 43/46 € 68/80 € – ½ P 14 €
Rest – Karte 12/29 €
♦ Die Zimmer des historischen, im Jahre 1481 erstmals erwähnten Gasthofs sind im Landhausstil oder mit bemalten Bauernmöbeln ausgestattet. In Holz gehaltene Gaststuben a. d. 18. und 19. Jh. mit regionaler Küche. Terrasse unter Kastanienbäumen mit schöner Sicht.

BÜRSERBERG – Vorarlberg – 730 B7 – 550 Ew – Höhe 900 m – Wintersport: 1 850 m 13 5 A6

Wien 583 – Bregenz 55 – Feldkirch 24 – Bludenz 6

Berghotel Schillerkopf ← Bludenz und Vorarlberg,
Tschengla 1 ✉ 6707 Zim,
– ✆ (05552) 6 31 04 – info@schillerkopf.at – Fax (05552) 67487
geschl. April - Mai
35 Zim (inkl. ½ P.) – ☼ 69/79 € 126/146 € ❄ 83/98 € 142/210 € – 10 Suiten
Rest – (Tischbestellung ratsam) Karte 16/30 €
◆ Bereits seit Generationen ist dieses Haus im Familienbesitz. Herrlich: die Lage mitten im Skigebiet sowie der große Garten. Zimmer im neuzeitlichen oder im ländlichen Stil. Rustikale Restaurantstube.

BURGAUBERG-NEUDAUBERG – Burgenland – 730 U7 – 1 320 Ew – Höhe 350 m 11 L4

Wien 145 – Eisenstadt 110 – Fürstenfeld 16 – Oberwart 21
GC Golfschaukel, Neudauberg 18 ✆ (03326) 5 50 00

Im Stadtteil Neudauberg Nord: 3 km, ab Burgauberg:

Das Gogers Golf und Spa
Neudauberg 240 ✉ 8292 Rest,
– ✆ (03326) 5 52 22 – office@dasgogers.at – Fax (03326) 5522215
geschl. 10. – 27. Dez., 6. Jan. – 8. Feb.
40 Zim – 99/119 € 139/165 € – ½ P 29 €
Rest – *(nur Abendessen)* Karte 26/36 €
◆ Ein nicht alltägliches Hotel, das in seiner beeindruckenden Bauweise buchstäblich eins ist mit der grünen Hügellandschaft der Golfschaukel Lafnitz. Geradlinig das Design.

DAMÜLS – Vorarlberg – 730 B7 – 330 Ew – Höhe 1 431 m – Wintersport: 2 010 m 11 5 A5

Wien 606 – Bregenz 52 – Feldkirch 36 – Bludenz 26
Kirchdorf 138, ✉ 6884, ✆ (05510) 6 20, info@damuels.at

Damülser Hof ← Bergpanorama,
Furkastr. 147 ✉ 6884 – ✆ (05510) 2 10
– hotel@damuelserhof.at – Fax (05510) 543
geschl. Mai, November
52 Zim (inkl. ½ P.) – ☼ 70/90 € 140/180 € ❄ 90/120 € 180/220 €
Rest – Karte 20/36 €
◆ Solide und funktionelle Zimmer, fast alle mit Balkon, sowie ein nett gestalteter Freizeitbereich mit modern ausgestattetem Fitnessraum bietet dieses Hotel oberhalb des Ortes. Mit hellem Holz in rustikalem Stil eingerichtetes Restaurant.

Alpenblume ← Zim,
Uga 78 ✉ 6884 – ✆ (05510) 2 65 – hotel-alpenblume@lanner.at
– Fax (05510) 2656
geschl. 7. April – Mitte Mai, November
26 Zim (inkl. ½ P.) – ☼ 48/56 € 90/112 € ❄ 68/76 € 124/144 €
Rest – Karte 16/35 €
◆ Das Hotel liegt etwas unterhalb des Ortes bei der Uga-Sesselbahn. Eine geräumige Halle mit Kamin sowie solide, hell möblierte Zimmer, auch Familienzimmer, erwarten Sie. Zur Halle hin offenes Restaurant in rustikalem Stil.

S'Ländle Bergpanorama, Zim,
Uga 53 ✉ 6884 – ✆ (05510) 6 10
– office@laendlehotel.at – Fax (05510) 61016
geschl. 6. April – 15. Juni, 5. Okt. – 5. Dez.
11 Zim (inkl. ½ P.) – ☼ 60/63 € 90/96 € ❄ 78/90 € 130/186 €
Rest – *(nur Abendessen)* (im Sommer nur für Hausgäste) Karte 17/39 €
◆ Ruhig liegt das familiengeführte kleine Hotel im Skigebiet. Die Zimmer verfügen z. T. über einen Balkon mit schöner Sicht. Für jeden Gast steht hier eine Garage bereit. Ländliches Restaurant mit netter Terrasse.

DELLACH – Kärnten – siehe Maria Wörth

DELLACH IM GAILTAL – Kärnten – 730 L9 – 1 380 Ew – Höhe 672 m
8 **G6**

Wien 398 – Klagenfurt 103 – Villach 68 – Lienz 39

Biohotel Daberer Berge, Rest,
St. Daniel 32 (West: 1 km) ✉ 9635
– ✆ (04718) 5 90 – info@biohotel-daberer.at – Fax (04718) 590310
geschl. 9. Nov. – 20. Dez.
43 Zim (inkl. ½ P.) – 71/99 € 152/204 € – 6 Suiten
Rest – (nur Abendessen für Hausgäste)
◆ Das ruhig gelegene Alpenhotel mit den wohnlichen Zimmern wurde nach baubiologischen Richtlinien gestaltet. Natur, Gesundheit und Wellness stehen im Mittelpunkt. Helle, freundliche Restauranträume mit schöner Sicht auf die Umgebung.

DEUTSCHKREUTZ – Burgenland – 730 V6 – 3 230 Ew – Höhe 192 m
4 **M3**

Wien 77 – Eisenstadt 33 – Wiener Neustadt 55 – Sopron 10
Hauptstr. 54, ✉ 7301, ✆ (02613) 2 02 00, tourismus@deutschkreutz.at

Weingasthof – Hotel Schreiner (geheizt)
Girmerstr. 45 ✉ 7301 – ✆ (02613) 8 03 22
– info@hotel-schreiner.at – Fax (02613) 803224
geschl. Feb.
35 Zim – 35/45 € 64/76 €
Rest – *(geschl. Montag)* Karte 18/25 €
◆ In einer ruhigen Nebenstraße in einem Wohngebiet liegt der zum Hotel erweiterte familiengeführte Gasthof mit schönem Garten. Besonders hübsch sind einige neuere Zimmer. In bürgerlichem Stil gehaltenes Restaurant.

DEUTSCHLANDSBERG – Steiermark – 730 R8 – 7 990 Ew – Höhe 368 m
10 **K5**

Wien 228 – Graz 42 – Maribor 67 – Leibnitz 36
Hauptplatz 34, ✉ 8530, ✆ (03462) 75 20, tourismus@schilcherheimat.at
18 Schloss Frauenthal, Ulrichsberg 7 ✆ (03462) 57 17
Steirische Weinstraße★ – Kitzeck★ (Süd-Ost: 25 km)

Pension Pölzl garni

Narzissenweg 6 ✉ 8530 – ☎ (03462) 2 07 35 – info@pension-poelzl.at – Fax (03462) 2073535
geschl. 22. Dez. – 10. Jan.
10 Zim – 39 € 70 €
◆ Etwas zurückversetzt von der Straße liegt das neuzeitliche kleine Hotel mit leicht mediterran wirkendem Eingangsbereich und geräumigen, hell möblierten Gästezimmern.

Burghotel Deutschlandsberg

Burgplatz 1 ✉ 8530
– ☎ (03462) 5 65 60 – info@burghotel-dl.at – Fax (03462) 565622
geschl. Januar – Februar
21 Zim – 57/72 € 94/144 € – ½ P 21 € – 6 Suiten
Rest – *(geschl. Sonntagabend - Montag)* Menü 20/40 € – Karte 25/36 €
◆ Mit Möbeln verschiedener Epochen eingerichtet, fügen sich die Zimmer und Suiten des Hotels harmonisch in den historischen Rahmen der Burg a. d. 11. Jh. ein. Netter Garten. Schöne Aussicht auf Deutschlandsberg von der Terrasse und z. T. vom Restaurant aus.

Kaminstub'n

Kreßbach 100 (Süd: 2 km über B 76, dann rechts ab Richtung Trahütten)
✉ 8530 Hollenegg – ☎ (03462) 47 37 – kaminstubn@aon.at
– Fax (03462) 370112
geschl. Sonntagabend – Montag
Rest – Karte 16/32 €
◆ Aus mehreren steirischen Bauernhäusern a. d. 19. Jh. ist dieser Gasthof entstanden. Altes Holz und Steinboden, Kamin und Zierrat schaffen ein rustikales Umfeld. Netter Garten.

DIENTEN AM HOCHKÖNIG – Salzburg – 730 L6 – 800 Ew – Höhe 1 071 m – Wintersport: 1 826 m 1 17 8 G5

Wien 366 – Salzburg 70 – Bischofshofen 20 – Saalfelden 19
Dorf 44, ✉ 5652, ☎ (06461) 2 63, info@dienten.co.at

Die Übergossene Alm (geheizt) Rest,

Sonnberg 54
(Ost: 2 km) ✉ 5652 – ☎ (06461) 23 00 – welcome@uebergossenealm.at
– Fax (06461) 23062
geschl. Ende März – Anfang Juni, Mitte November – Mitte Dezember
83 Zim (inkl. ½ P.) – 115 € 200/250 € 148/180 € 262/346 €
Rest – (nur für Hausgäste)
◆ Gediegen-ländlich ist das Ambiente in diesem gewachsenen Ferienhotel etwas außerhalb des Ortes. Sehr schöner Wellnessbereich mit 7 Saunen und Badebiotop.

Mitterwirt (geheizt) Rest,

Dorf 23 ✉ 5652 – ☎ (06461) 2 04 – hochkoenig@hotel-mitterwirt.at
– Fax (06461) 204200
geschl. April – 7. Juni
48 Zim (inkl. ½ P.) – 72/82 € 156/172 € 92/128 € 184/276 €
Rest – (nur Abendessen für Hausgäste)
◆ In der Ortsmitte liegt das regionstypische Hotel unter Leitung der Inhaberfamilie. Man verfügt über wohnlich mit hellem Holz möblierte Gästezimmer.

Salzburger Hof (geheizt) Rest,
Dorf 6 ✉ 5652 – ✆ (06461) 21 70 – hotel@salzburger-hof.at – Fax (06461) 21731
geschl. Mitte April – Ende Mai, Anfang Okt. – Mitte Dez.
28 Zim (inkl. ½ P.) – ☼ 47/68 € 94/136 € ❄ 78/105 € 140/188 €
Rest – Karte 14/37 €
♦ Die Zimmer dieses gepflegten Hotels sind teils mit rustikaler Eiche, teils mit hellem Naturholz eingerichtet und haben einen eigenen Balkon – mit Eisstockbahn hinter dem Haus. Das Essen wird in ländlich-rustikalen Restaurantstuben serviert.

DÖLSACH – Tirol – 730 K8 – 2 190 Ew – Höhe 780 m – Wintersport:

8 **F6**

Wien 399 – Innsbruck 193 – Lienz 7 – Spittal an der Drau 65

Tiroler Hof mit Zim Zim,
✉ 9991 – ✆ (04852) 6 41 11 – tirolerhof—doelsach@hotmail.com – Fax (04852) 64141
geschl. 7. – 22. Jan
6 Zim – 40/45 € 80/85 €
Rest – *(geschl. Montag)* Menü 26/36 € – Karte 25/45 €
♦ In diesem familiär geleiteten Gasthaus in der Ortsmitte bietet man Ihnen in freundlichem, recht neuzeitlichem Ambiente regionale und internationale Speisen.

DONNERSKIRCHEN – Burgenland – 730 V5 – Höhe 193 m – 1 650 Ew

4 **L3**

Wien 69 – Eisenstadt 15

Check In Rest,
Am Seeblick 6 (Süd: 1,5 km über B 50) ✉ 7082 – ✆ (02683) 3 01 10 – office@checkin-hotel.at – Fax (02683) 30116
geschl. 21. Dez. – 31. Jan.
45 Zim – 44/47 € 70/78 € – ½ P 12 €
Rest – Karte 13/20 €
♦ Funktionell und modern ist dieses Hotel etwas außerhalb des Ortes eingerichtet. Ruhiger sind die nach hinten gelegenen Gästezimmer.

DORFGASTEIN – Salzburg – 730 L7 – 1 650 Ew – Höhe 840 m – Wintersport: 2 033 m 5 13

8 **G5**

Wien 376 – Salzburg 80 – Bischofshofen 32 – Zell am See 34
Nr.16, ✉ 5632, ✆ (06432) 3 39 34 60, info@dorfgastein.com

Dorfhotel Kirchenwirt Zim,
Dorfgastein 8 ✉ 5632 – ✆ (06433) 72 51 – info@kirchenwirt-gastein.at – Fax (06433) 739137
geschl. 6. April – 10. Mai
28 Zim (inkl. ½ P.) – ☼ 64 € 108/114 € ❄ 73/83 € 140/152 €
Rest – *(im Winter Montag – Freitag nur Abendessen)* Karte 20/45 €
♦ Im Zentrum neben der kleinen Kirche gelegenes Alpenhotel mit Balkonfassade. Wohnliche Zimmer und Appartements sowie ein schöner Relaxbereich mit fachkundiger Betreuung. Restaurant mit rustikalem Ambiente.

In Dorfgastein-Unterberg Nord-West: 2,5 km:

XX **Unterbergerwirt** mit Zim — Zim, P

Unterberg 7 ✉ 5632 – ✆ (06433) 70 77 – info@unterbergerwirt.com – Fax (06433) 707777
geschl. 7. April – 9. Mai, 13. Okt. – 5. Dez. und Dienstag
7 Zim – 55/60 € 92/102 € – ½ P 17 €
Rest – (abends Tischbestellung ratsam) Menü 34 € – Karte 23/34 €
◆ Produkte vom eigenen Bauernhof und Rindfleisch aus eigener Zucht sind die Grundlagen für die vorwiegend regionale Küche des Hausherrn. Hübsches Dekor im ländlichen Restaurant.

Außerhalb Nord-Ost: 2,5 km Richtung Schischaukel:

Hauserbauer — Bergpanorama, Zim, P

Maierhofen 25 ✉ 5632 Dorfgastein VISA
– ✆ (06433) 73 39 – info@hauserbauer.com – Fax (06433) 733933
geschl. April, Nov.
25 Zim (inkl. ½ P.) – 61/64 € 110/148 € 78/89 € 144/192 €
Rest – *(geschl. Montag)* Karte 17/33 €
◆ In 1080 m Höhe liegt das teilweise mit Holzschindeln verkleidete regionstypische Gasthaus. Den Freizeitbereich hat man mit Naturmaterialien im alpenländischen Stil gestaltet. Geschmackvolle ländliche Restauranträume und hübsche Panoramaterrasse vor dem Haus.

Der Stern ✿ zeichnet Restaurants mit exzellenter Küche aus.
Er wird an Häuser vergeben, für die man gerne einen Umweg in Kauf nimmt!

DORNBIRN – **Vorarlberg** – 730 B6 – **42 310 Ew** – **Höhe 437 m** – **Wintersport: 1 458 m** 1 11 — 5 **A5**

Wien 688 – Bregenz 13 – Feldkirch 26 – Lindau 22
Kulturhaus, Rathausplatz 1, ✉ 6850, ✆ (05572) 2 21 88, tourismus@dornbirn.at

Veranstaltungen
03.04. – 06.04.: Fühjahrsmesse
31.07. – 03.08.: art bodensee
16.10. – 18.10.: GEWINN-Messe

Bregenzerwald★★ – Rappenlochschlucht★

Four Points by Sheraton — Zim, Rest, P VISA AE

Messestr. 1 (über B204 Z, an der Messe)
✉ 6854 – ✆ (05572) 3 88 80 – info@4p-sheraton-dornbirn.at
– Fax (05572) 388830
106 Zim – 120/168 € 150/198 €
Rest – Karte 31/57 €
◆ In den oberen Etagen des Panoramahauses ist das Hotel mit modern-komfortablem Ambiente und tollem Rundumblick auf die Region untergebracht. Schöner Spabereich gegen Gebühr. Zum Restaurant im elften Stock gehört eine um das Haus herum angelegte Balkonterrasse.

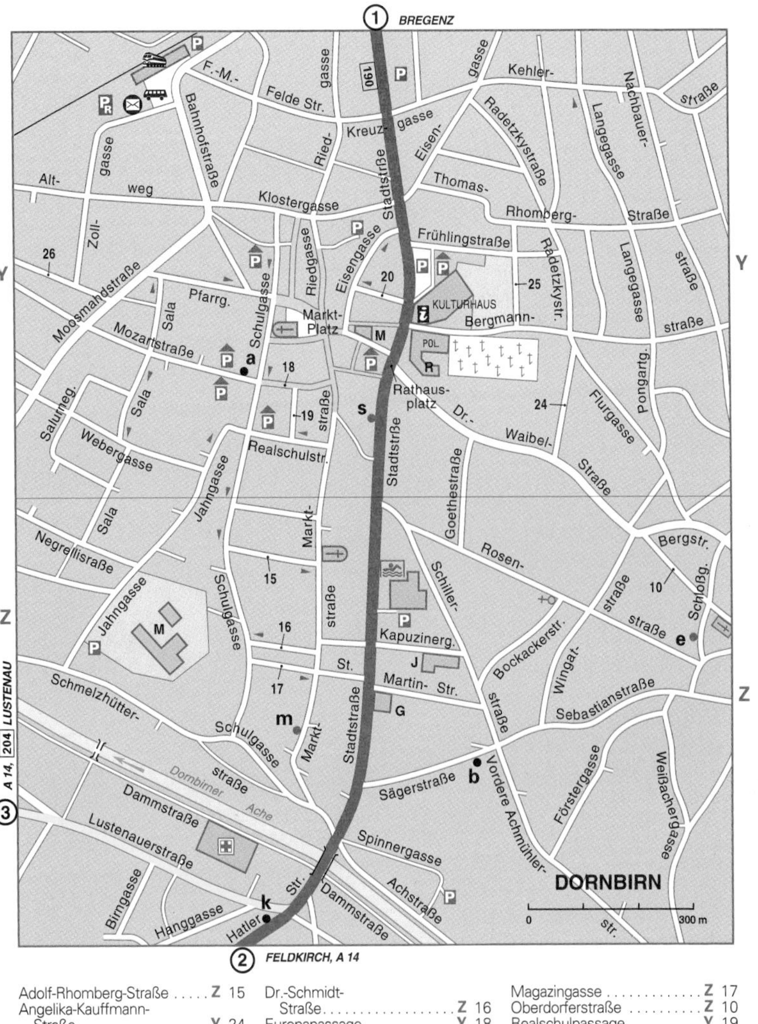

Adolf-Rhomberg-Straße	Z 15	Dr.-Schmidt-Straße	Z 16	Magazingasse	Z 17
Angelika-Kauffmann-Straße	Y 24	Europapassage	Y 18	Oberdorferstraße	Z 10
Apfelgasse	Y 26	Klaudiastraße	Y 25	Realschulpassage	Y 19
				Viehmarktstrasse	Y 20

Martinspark Zim, Zim,

Mozartstr. 2 ✉ *6850 – ☎ (05572) 37 60*

– rezeption@martinspark.at – Fax (05572) 3760376 Y **a**

98 Zim – 102/152 € 132/182 € – 10 Suiten

Rest – *(geschl. Sonn- und Feiertage)* Karte 23/38 €

◆ Moderne Gestaltung, klare Linien und zeitgenössische Kunst prägen den Stil des Hauses, das als erstes Designhotel Austrias bekannt wurde. Zimmer in verschiedenen Kategorien. Im Restaurant: Palmen, helles Holz und eine luftige Atmosphäre.

Krone Zim,

Hatlerstr. 2 ✉ 6850 – ✆ (05572) 2 27 20 – info@kronehotel.at
– Fax (05572) 2272073
geschl. 23. – 26. Dez. Z **k**
91 Zim – 47/118 € 77/159 € – ½ P 20 €
Rest – Karte 14/46 €

◆ Ein moderner Empfangsbereich sowie funktionelle Zimmer verschiedener Kategorien erwarten Sie in dem verkehrsgünstig gelegenen Hotel. Drei unterschiedlich, aber immer rustikal ausgestattete Restauranträume.

Sonne garni

Sägerstr. 8 ✉ 6850 – ✆ (05572) 2 22 12 – sonne@vol.at
– Fax (05572) 222126 Z **b**
23 Zim – 54/70 € 84/100 €

◆ Das Haus liegt in der Nähe der Dornbirner Ache. Die Zimmer sind unterschiedlich groß und mit hellem Holz ausgestattet, die meisten haben einen Balkon. Moderner Frühstücksraum.

M

Lustenauer Str. 64 (über B 204 Z) ✉ 6850 – ✆ (05572) 21 03 96
– info@m-dornbirn.at – Fax (05572) 21039619
geschl. 16. Juli – 31. Juli und Sonntag
Rest – Menü 55 € – Karte 33/53 €

◆ In einem verglasten Bürohaus befindet sich dieses puristisch designte Restaurant mit Bar. Im Sommer sitzt man sehr nett im überdachten Innenhof, dem Palmengarten.

Zum Verwalter mit Zim Rest,

Schlossgasse 1 ✉ 6850 – ✆ (05572) 2 33 79 – hotel@zumverwalter.at
– Fax (05572) 233796
geschl Anfang – Mitte Jan., Anfang – Mitte Aug. Z **e**
8 Zim – 59 € 96 €
Rest – *(geschl. Sonntag – Montag)* Menü 39 € (mittags) – Karte 28/43 €

◆ Ein modernerer Bistrobereich und gemütliche rustikale Stuben bilden das Restaurant. Hübsche historische Holzdecke in einem der Räume. Mediterran beeinflusste regionale Küche.

Faerber's

Färbergasse 15 (über B 190 Y, im Betriebsgebiet Färbergasse) ✉ 6850
– ✆ (05572) 39 84 00 – lorenzin@restaurant-faerbers.at
– Fax (05572) 398139
geschl. 24. Dez. – 6. Jan., Samstagmittag, Sonn- und Feiertage
Rest – Karte 26/54 €

◆ Moderner Stil und eine wechselnde Bilderausstellung bestimmen hier das Ambiente. Terrasse mit altem Baumbestand vor dem Haus. Mittags preiswerte kleine Karte.

Sinohaus

Marktstr. 23 ✉ 6850 – ✆ (05572) 2 03 90 – Fax (05572) 20390
geschl. Juni und Mittwoch Y **s**
Rest – Menü 48 € – Karte 22/40 €

◆ Lampen aus Japanpapier, Bambusrollos, Palmen und Rattanstühle erzeugen im eleganten Restaurant eine dem Küchenstil entsprechende asiatische Atmosphäre. Sehr gute Weinauswahl !

Gasthaus Gemsle

Marktstr. 62 ✉ 6850 – ✆ (05572) 20 09 18 – gemsle@gemsle.at – Fax (05572) 203919
geschl. 28. Jan – 10. Feb., 28. Juli – 17. Aug. und Juni – Aug. Samstag – Sonntag sowie Sept. – April Dienstag Z m
Rest – Karte 18/32 €
♦ Der Gasthof von 1822 befindet sich seit mehreren Generationen in Familienbesitz. Traditionelle Gaststuben mit Kachelofen, Holzvertäfelung, hübschem Dekor und regionaler Küche.

Gasthaus Schiffle

Mühlebacherstr. 25 (über Halter Str. Z und Mittelfeldstraße) ✉ 6850 – ✆ (05572) 3 30 23 – schiffle@gmx.at – Fax (05572) 330234
geschl. Sonntagabend – Montag
Rest – Karte 16/42 €
♦ Ein altes gepflegtes Holzhaus ist die Heimat dieses rustikalen Restaurants. Auch im Inneren bestimmt Holz das Bild: Wandvertäfelungen und blanke Tische mit Blumendekorationen.

Auf dem Bödele **Nord-Ost: 8,5 km:**

Rickatschwende

< Rheintal und Bodensee,
Rickatschwende 1
✉ 6850 Dornbirn – ✆ (05572) 2 53 50 – office@rickatschwende.com – Fax (05572) 2535070
geschl. 17. – 31. Dez.
47 Zim – †100/128 € ††150/194 € – 4 Suiten
Rest *Schwende Stüble* – ✆ (05572) 25 35 04 08 *(geschl. Sonntagabend – Montag)* Menü 36/64 € – Karte 33/51 €
♦ Sehr schön liegt das Hotel oberhalb der Stadt. Die neuzeitlichen, wohnlichen Zimmer bieten Blick zum Rheintal oder zum Wald – alle mit Balkon. Medizinische Abteilung. Schwende Stüble im modernen Stil.

Berghof Fetz

< Bregenzerwald,
Bödele 574 ✉ 6850 Dornbirn – ✆ (05572) 7 74 00 – info@berghoffetz.at – Fax (05572) 774007
geschl. April 2 Wochen, Nov. 2 Wochen
10 Zim – †55/101 € ††116/140 € – ½ P 20 €
Rest – *(geschl. Montag außer Saison)* Karte 20/36 €
♦ Hotel mit interessanter Holzarchitektur. Alle Zimmer mit Balkon und Blick auf den Bregenzer Wald. Sauna und Ruheraum mit großer Glasfront zum Berg. Gediegenes Restaurant mit rustikalem Ambiente. Schöne Panoramaterrasse.

Dreiländerblick

< Dornbirn und Schweizer Berge,
Oberfallenberg 14 ✉ 6850 Dornbirn Zim, Zim,
– ✆ (05572) 2 11 28 – gasthof.dreilaenderblick@.aon.at – Fax (0662) 234669432
geschl. Jan. 2 Wochen, Ende Okt. – Mitte Nov.
9 Zim – †54/58 € ††88/96 €
Rest – *(geschl. Donnerstag)* Karte 18/32 €
♦ Gasthof in schöner Lage oberhalb von Dornbirn mit herrlicher Sicht auf die Schweizer Alpen. Im Zimmerbereich rustikal mit variierenden Einrichtungen. Restaurant mit großer Fensterfront und Kachelofen.

Auf dem Karren Süd-Ost: 2 km, mit erreichbar – Höhe 971 m

Panoramarestaurant Karren Dornbirn und Rheintal,
Gütlestr. 6 ✉ 6850 Dornbirn
– (05572) 5 47 11 – panorama@karren.at
– Fax (05572) 547114
geschl. 3. März – 4. April, 3. – 14. Nov.
Rest – Menü 33 € – Karte 20/42 €
◆ Nach fünf Minuten Fahrt mit der Seilbahn erreicht man das Ausflugslokal auf der Bergspitze. Der ältere Teil ist rustikal, im säulengetragenen Glasanbau geht es moderner zu.

DROBOLLACH AM FAAKER SEE – Kärnten – siehe Villach

Dieser Führer lebt von Ihren Anregungen, die uns stets willkommen sind.
Egal ob Sie uns eine besonders angenehme Überraschung
oder eine Enttäuschung mitteilen wollen – schreiben Sie uns!

DÜRNSTEIN – Niederösterreich – 730 S3 – 940 Ew – Höhe 209 m 3 J2

Wien 84 – St. Pölten 30 – Krems a. d. Donau 8 – Melk 33
Dürnstein 132, ✉ 3601, (02711) 2 00, info.duernstein@aon.at
Pfarrkirche (Kirchturm★)
Wachau★★★ Straße zwischen Melk und Krems

Schloss Dürnstein Donautal, Zim, Rest,
Dürnstein 2
✉ 3610 – (02711) 2 12 – hotel@schloss.at
– Fax (02711) 21230
geschl. 3. Nov. – 20. März
47 Zim – 153/218 € 195/365 € – ½ P 30 €
Rest – Menü 31/70 € – Karte 28/56 €
◆ Herrlich liegt das Barockschloss von 1630, das mit seinen individuellen, mit Antiquitäten versehenen Zimmern und schönem Innenhof mit Freibad besticht. Von Säulen wird das elegante Restaurantgewölbe getragen. Reizvolle Terrasse mit Blick auf die Donau.

Richard Löwenherz (geheizt)
Dürnstein 8 ✉ 3601 – (02711) 2 22 – loewenherz@duernstein.at
– Fax (02711) 22218
geschl. Nov. – März
39 Zim – 96/136 € 166/191 € – ½ P 30 €
Rest – Menü 29/34 € – Karte 28/43 €
◆ Das Hotel befindet sich in den Wirtschaftsgebäuden des einstigen Klosters und beherbergt meist mit Stilmobiliar eingerichtete Zimmer, fast alle mit Blick auf die Donau. Rustikal-gemütliche Restauranträume mit Gewölbedecke und schöner Terrasse zur Donau hin.

Gartenhotel

Dürnstein 122 ✉ 3601 – ✆ (02711) 2 06 – info@pfeffel.at – Fax (02711) 2068

geschl. 15. Nov. – 15. März

45 Zim – 61/75 € 84/132 € – ½ P 22 €

Rest – *(nur Abendessen)* Karte 20/29 €

◆ Aus drei Häusern bestehendes familiengeführtes Hotel. Recht komfortabel sind die mit Stilmöbeln eingerichteten Zimmer im Haupthaus, etwas schlichter die in den Nebengebäuden. Teil des Restaurants ist ein Wintergarten.

Sänger Blondel

Dürnstein 64 ✉ 3601 – ✆ (02711) 2 53 – saengerblondel@aon.at – Fax (02711) 2537

geschl. 16. November – 14. März

15 Zim – 65 € 94/110 € – ½ P 21 €

Rest – *(geschl. Sonntagabend – Dienstag)* Karte 20/33 €

◆ Das kleine Hotel – ein Gasthhof a. d. 17. Jh. – befindet sich in der Ortsmitte und verfügt über praktische und solide in altdeutschem Stil möblierte Gästezimmer. Hübsche Restaurantterrasse mit Aussicht auf den bekannten Dürnsteiner Kirchturm.

Loibnerhof

Unterloiben 7 (Ost: 2 km) ✉ 3601 – ✆ (02732) 8 28 90 – Fax (02732) 828903

geschl. 1. – 28. Januar und Montag – Dienstag

Rest – Menü 37 € – Karte 21/40 €

◆ Ein ländlich-rustikales Restaurant auf beiden Seiten der Straße: freundlich gestaltete Stuben und ein romantischer, z. T. als Veranda angelegter Gastgarten unter Obstbäumen.

Wie entscheidet man sich zwischen zwei gleichwertigen Adressen?
In jeder Kategorie sind die Häuser nochmals geordnet,
die besten Adressen stehen an erster Stelle.

EBBS – Tirol – 730 I6 – 4 890 Ew – Höhe 600 m – Wintersport: 1 100 m

7 E4

Wien 376 – Innsbruck 80 – Kufstein 9 – Kitzbühel 42

Unterer Stadtplatz 8, ✉ 6330, ✆ (05372) 6 22 07, info@kufstein.com

Postwirt

Zim, Zim,

Wildbichler Str. 25 ✉ 6341 – ✆ (05373) 4 22 24 – tirol@hotelpostwirt.at – Fax (05373) 42924

geschl. 29. März – April

50 Zim – 57/60 € 104/108 € – ½ P 10 €

Rest – *(geschl. Mittwoch)* Karte 17/25 €

◆ Der alpenländische Stil dieses zentral gelegenen Hotels begleitet Sie von der Fassade bis in die wohnlich gestalteten Gästezimmer. Ländlich dekorierte Gaststuben mit freundlichem Service.

Oberwirt Zim, P

Wildbichler Str. 36 ✉ 6341 – ✆ (05373) 4 22 46 – info@oberwirt-ebbs.at – Fax (05373) 42256
geschl. 15. Nov. – 15. Dez.
47 Zim – 48 € 78 € – ½ P 12 €
Rest – *(geschl. Donnerstag)* Karte 15/27 €

◆ Der neben der Kirche gelegene Tiroler Gasthof aus dem 15. Jahrhundert beherbergt recht unterschiedliche Zimmer, die teils mit solidem Naturholz wohnlich möbliert sind. Restaurantstuben mit rustikalem Ambiente und nettem Barbereich.

Kaiserhotel Ebbs Rest, P VISA

Haflingerweg 6 ✉ 6341 – ✆ (05373) 4 24 24 – ebbs@kaiserhotel.at – Fax (05373) 42283
geschl. Anfang Nov. – 20. Dezember
47 Zim (inkl. ½ P.) – 52/68 € 88/120 €
Rest – (nur Abendessen für Hausgäste)

◆ Recht ruhig liegt das Ferienhotel mit der regionstypischen Balkonfassade am Ortsrand. Man bietet solide Zimmer und einige Appartements, z. T. als Maisonetten angelegt.

Unterwirt mit Zim Zim, P VISA

Wildbichlerstr. 38 ✉ 6341 – ✆ (05373) 4 22 88 – info@gourmethotel-unterwirt.at – Fax (05373) 42253
geschl. April 2 Wochen, 10. Nov. – 13. Dez.
25 Zim – 40/60 € 76/96 € – ½ P 13 €
Rest – *(geschl. Dienstag – Mittwochmittag)* Menü 45/58 € – Karte 27/45 €

◆ Der im 15. Jh. erstmals urkundlich erwähnte Gasthof beherbergt zwei hübsch dekorierte, in warmen Farben gehaltene Restaurantstuben. Schöner Gartenbereich mit Terrasse.

In Ebbs-Oberndorf **Süd: 1,5 km über B 175:**

Sattlerwirt Zim, P VISA

Oberndorf 89 ✉ 6341 – ✆ (05373) 4 22 03 – info@sattlerwirt.at – Fax (05373) 422037
geschl. Ende Okt. – Ende Nov.
33 Zim – 41/45 € 68/73 € – ½ P 11 €
Rest – *(geschl. Montag)* Karte 16/40 €

◆ Seit über 100 Jahren befindet sich der Gasthof mit der bemalten Fassade im Besitz der Familie. Die Zimmer sind unterschiedlich möbliert und zeitgemäß ausgestattet. In rustikalem Stil gehaltene Restaurantstuben.

Wir bemühen uns bei unseren Preisangaben um größtmögliche Genauigkeit. Aber alles ändert sich! Lassen Sie sich daher bei Ihrer Reservierung den derzeit gültigen Preis mitteilen.

EBEN AM ACHENSEE – Tirol – 730 H6 – 6 610 Ew – Höhe 980 m 7 D5

Wien 415 – Innsbruck 37 – Schwaz 11 – Kufstein 44
GC Achensee, Pertisau ✆ (05243) 53 77

Huber & Hochland
Rest, Rest,

Eben 28 ✉ 6212 – ✆ (05243) 53 11 – ferien@hotelhuber.at – Fax (05243) 6210
geschl. 30. März – 8. Mai, 19. Okt. – 19. Dez.
50 Zim (inkl. ½ P.) – 56/63 € 96/122 €
Rest – (nur Abendessen für Hausgäste)
◆ Zwei unterirdisch verbundene Häuser bilden diesen Familienbetrieb mit sehr gepflegten und sauberen Gästezimmern, die mit unterschiedlichen Holzmöbeln eingerichtet sind.

In Maurach Nord-West: 1,5 km – Wintersport: 1 900 m 1 5

Maurach Hnr. 82, ✉ 6212, ✆ (05243) 53 55, maurach@achensee.info

Alpenrose
(geheizt) Rest, Rest,

Nr. 68 ✉ 6212 – ✆ (05243) 5 29 30
– info@alpenrose.at – Fax (05243) 5466
geschl. Nov. 2 Wochen
92 Zim (inkl. ½ P.) – 136/175 € 272/350 € 125/174 € 250/438 € – 10 Suiten
Rest – (nur für Hausgäste)
◆ Das schmucke Ferienhotel bietet neben den attraktiven und geschmackvollen Landhauszimmern einen reizvollen Freizeit- und Wellnessbereich. Mit Kinderclub für die kleinen Gäste.

Vier Jahreszeiten
Rest, VISA AE

Maurach 127a ✉ 6212
– ✆ (05243) 53 75 – hotel@4jahreszeiten.at – Fax (05243) 591245
geschl. April – Juni, 16. Nov. – 15. Dez.
76 Zim (inkl. ½ P.) – 77/100 € 124/164 € 79/118 € 124/196 €
Rest *Michl Stub'n* – *(geschl. Mittwoch, Montag – Samstag nur Abendessen)*
Menü 34/62 € – Karte 27/49 €
◆ Die Zimmer in diesem gewachsenen regionstypischen Hotel sind recht unterschiedlich in Einrichtung und Größe, von rustikal bis modern. Gediegen: Michl Stub'n mit klassischem Angebot.

Sonnalp

Maurach 127e ✉ 6212 – ✆ (05243) 54 40 – hotel@sonnalp.net
– Fax (05243) 544030
geschl. Ende März – Ende April, Anfang Nov. – Mitte Dez.
32 Zim (inkl. ½ P.) – 95/182 € 162/214 € 98/228 € 168/264 €
Rest – (nur Abendessen für Hausgäste)
◆ Im Zentrum, nicht sehr weit vom See liegt dieses Hotel mit seinen wohnlich-funktionellen Zimmern und einem sehr gepflegten Freizeitbereich mit Kosmetik und Bäderabteilung.

Naturhotel Alpenblick
(geheizt) Rest,

Maurach 207 ✉ 6212 – ✆ (05243) 53 15
– info@naturhotel-alpenblick.at – Fax (05243) 531515
geschl. Nov. – Mitte Dez.
30 Zim (inkl. ½ P.) – 45/56 € 82/130 €
Rest – (nur Abendessen für Hausgäste)
◆ Ein familiengeführtes Haus mit schöner Liegewiese am Waldrand und wohnlichen, teilweise besonders hübsch im Landhausstil eingerichteten Gästezimmern.

In Pertisau Nord-West: 6 km – Wintersport: 1 510 m 1 4

Pertisau Nr. 53d, 6213, (05243) 43 07, pertisau@achensee.info

Fürstenhaus

See und Berge, (geheizt) Rest,

Pertisau Nr. 63

6213 – (05243) 5 44 20 – fuerstenhaus@travelcharme.com
– Fax (05243) 5442555

geschl. 16. Nov. – 19. Dez.

119 Zim (inkl. ½ P.) – 140/242 € 224/414 € – 9 Suiten

Rest – (nur für Hausgäste)

◆ Das historische Haus a. d. 15. Jh., das einst Kaiser Maximilian als Jagdschloss diente, ist heute ein modernes Hotel mit großzügigen Zimmern und ansprechendem Wellnessbereich.

Der Wiesenhof

(geheizt)

Nr. 9 6213 – (05243) 52 46
– info@wiesenhof.at – Fax (05243) 524648

geschl. 4. Nov. – 18 Dez.

71 Zim (inkl. ½ P.) – 98/120 € 196/248 €

Rest – (nur für Hausgäste)

◆ Aus einem alten Bauernhof entstand dieser schöne, von Wiesen umgebene Alpengasthof. Zimmer in verschiedenen Kategorien, schöner Wellnessbereich und viele Freizeitangebote.

Post

Rest,

Seepromenade 82 6213 – (05243) 52 07 – hotel@postamsee.at
– Fax (05243) 521180

geschl. Ende März – April, Anfang Nov. – Mitte Dez.

70 Zim (inkl. ½ P.) – 86/106 € 168/222 €

Rest – Karte 18/46 €

◆ Direkt an der Seepromenade findet man diesen Alpengasthof mit gelber Fassade. Größtenteils Zimmer im Landhausstil. Wohnliche Halle und gepflegter Wellnessbereich. Restaurant im alpenländischen Stil.

Kristall

(geheizt)

Pertisau Nr. 51 6213 – (05243) 54 90 – info@kristall-pertisau.at
– Fax (05243) 549019

50 Zim (inkl. ½ P.) – 73/144 € 106/180 € 73/154 € 106/192 €

Rest – Karte 17/42 €

◆ Wohnlich und funktionell sind die mit hellem Ahornmobiliar modern eingerichteten Gästezimmer in diesem Hotel in der Ortsmitte. Auch einige Familienzimmer sind vorhanden. Ländliche Atmosphäre im Restaurant mit Wintergarten und sonniger Terrasse.

Christina

Pertisau Nr. 61 6213 – (05243) 53 61 – info@hotel-christina.at
– Fax (05243) 53618

geschl. 17. März – 26. April, 20. Okt. – 20. Dez.

19 Zim (inkl. ½ P.) – 84/139 € 114/162 € 100/194 € 136/216 €

Rest – Karte 17/37 €

◆ Das familiengeführte Hotel liegt in Seenähe und bietet hübsche, freundlich gestaltete Zimmer, die z. T. über einen Balkon verfügen. Das pavillonartige Restaurant sorgt für ein lichtes Ambiente.

Caroline Rest,
Achensee 10 ✉ 6213 – ✆ (05243) 53 94 – info@caroline.at
– Fax (05243) 539450 – geschl. April, Nov. – Mitte Dez.
27 Zim (inkl. ½ P.) – 75/80 € 140/160 €
Rest – (nur Abendessen für Hausgäste)
◆ Nette, gewachsene Pension mit freundlicher Atmosphäre. In den Zimmern teils bemalte Bauernmöbel, teils helles Naturholz. Direkter Zugang zum Wellnessbereich des Wiesenhofs.

Gasthof Golfvilla Rest,
Pertisau 15 b ✉ 6213 – ✆ (05243) 58 23 – info@golfvilla.at
– Fax (05243) 58765 – geschl. 6. – 26. April, 26. Okt. – 17. Dez.
13 Zim (inkl. ½ P.) – 39/60 € 66/118 €
Rest – *(geschl. im Sommer Dienstagmittag)* Karte 14/25 €
◆ Ein netter, recht ruhig gelegener Gasthof aus den 50er Jahren. Die Zimmer sind sehr gepflegt, haben ein gutes Platzangebot und sind teils allergikergeeignet. Restaurant im Landhausstil mit freundlichem Service.

Sonnenhof Rest,
Pertisau Nr. 26b ✉ 6213 – ✆ (05243) 54 54 – info@hotelsonnenhof.at
Fax (05243) 545454 – geschl. Ende März – Anfang Mai, Mitte Okt. – Mitte Dez.
23 Zim – 35/50 € 62/88 €
Rest – (nur Abendessen für Hausgäste)
◆ Sie finden dieses regionstypische kleine Hotel in der Ortsmitte. Hier überzeugt neben den wohnlich gestalteten Zimmern eine engagierte Führung.

EBREICHSDORF – Niederösterreich – 730 V5 – 8 790 Ew – Höhe 211 m 4 L3

Wien 31 – St. Pölten 88 – Eisenstadt 23 – Wiener Neustadt 25
Schloss Ebreichsdorf, Schlossallee 1 ✆ (02254) 7 38 88

Rosenbauchs
Rechte Bahnzeile 9 ✉ 2483 – ✆ (02254) 7 23 38 – rosenbauchs@aon.at
– Fax (02254) 72338
Rest – *(geschl. Montag – Dienstag)* Karte 28/54 €
Rest *Wirtshaus* – *(geschl. Montag – Dienstag)* Karte 17/24 €
◆ Das Gasthaus befindet sich bereits seit 1921 in den Händen der Familie. In modernen Räumen serviert man internationale, kreative Küche. Zum Haus gehört eine Vinothek. Das gasthauseigene Wirthaus hat regionale Gerichte auf seiner Speisekarte.

EFERDING – Oberösterreich – 730 O4 – 3 400 Ew – Höhe 271 m 2 H3

Wien 201 – Linz 27 – Wels 24 – Steyr 55
Stadtplatz 31, ✉ 4070, ✆ (07272) 5 55 51 60, tourismusverband@eferding.ooe.gv.at

Seminarhotel Brummeier Zim,
Stadtplatz 35 ✉ 4070 – ✆ (07272) 24 62 – seminar@brummeier.at
– Fax (07272) 2462220 – geschl. 23. Dez. – 7. Jan., 21. Juli – 3. Aug.
25 Zim – 49 € 86 € – ½ P 16 €
Rest – *(geschl. Samstagabend–Sonntag)* Menü 24/43 € (abends) – Karte 17/36 €
◆ Direkt im Zentrum liegt der ehemalige Gasthof, den man zu einem Seminarhotel mit solide möblierten, zeitgemäßen Zimmern erweitert hat. Mit dunklem Holz, angenehmen Farben und Bildern nett gestaltetes Restaurant.

EGG AM FAAKER SEE – Kärnten – siehe Villach

EHENBICHL – Tirol – 730 E6 – 700 Ew – Höhe 862 m 6 C5

Wien 523 – Innsbruck 96 – Reutte 3 – Imst 51

Maximilian Rest, P VISA

Reuttener Str. 1 ✉ 6600 – ✆ (05672) 6 25 85 – info@hotelmaximilian.at – Fax (05672) 6258554 – geschl. 15. März – 28. April, Ende Okt. – 20. Dez.
34 Zim – 50/65 € 99/130 €
Rest – *(geschl. Dienstagmittag – Mittwochmittag)* Karte 15/28 €
◆ Ein familiengeführter Gasthof mit recht unterschiedlich eingerichteten Zimmern, die im oberen Stock über kleine Wintergärten verfügen. In ländlichem Stil gehaltenes Restaurant.

In Ehenbichl-Rieden Süd-West: 6 km:

Gasthof Kreuz P VISA AE

Rieden 4 ✉ 6671 – ✆ (05678) 52 02 – kreuz.rieden@aon.at – Fax (05678) 520275
geschl. 8. – 30. Jan., 25. Nov. – 9. Dez. und Montag – Dienstag
Rest – Menü 42 € (abends) – Karte 17/34 €
◆ Bei dieser Adresse handelt es sich um einen netten Gasthof unter freundlicher Führung mit ländlich-gepflegtem, gemütlichem Ambiente und regionaler Küche. Schöne Terrasse.

EHRENHAUSEN – Steiermark – 730 S8 – 1 090 Ew – Höhe 267 m 11 K6

Wien 237 – Graz 52 – Leibnitz 10 – Feldbach 51

Georgi Schlössl P VISA

Georgigasse 68 ✉ 8461 – ✆ (03453) 2 57 77 – office@georgi-schloessl.at – Fax (03453) 257777 – geschl. 18. – 26. Feb., Juli 1 Woche
Rest – *(geschl. Montag – Dienstag und Sonntagabend)* Menü 32/48 € – Karte 25/45 €
◆ Das Restaurant mit schöner geschnitzter Holzdecke und Kamin ist in einem hübschen Schlösschen untergebracht. Durch eine Glasscheibe ist die Küche einsehbar. Regionale Karte.

EHRWALD – Tirol – 730 E6 – 2 560 Ew – Höhe 1 000 m – Wintersport: 3 000 m 2 12 6 C5

Wien 494 – Innsbruck 73 – Garmisch-Partenkirchen 25 – Reutte 25
Kirchplatz 1, ✉ 6632, ✆ (05673) 20 00 02 08, ehrwald@zugspitzarena.com
Zugspitze★★★ (Nord-Ost: 5 km)

Sporthotel Alpenhof ← Alpen und Umgebung, (geheizt) Rest, P VISA

Alpenhofstr. 13 ✉ 6632 – ✆ (05673) 23 45 – hotel@alpenhof-ehrwald.at – Fax (05673) 234552
geschl. 30. März – 30. April, 2. Nov. – 17. Dez.
45 Zim (inkl. ½ P.) – 100/125 € 190/290 € 115/160 € 220/330 € – 8 Suiten
Rest – *(geschl. Montag)* Karte 22/36 €
◆ Großzügige Zimmer und Appartements sowie ein gepflegter Wellness-, Beauty- und Freizeitbereich sprechen für dieses gewachsene Alpenhotel. Rustikale kleine Stuben ergänzen das stilvoll dekorierte Restaurant.

Spielmann (geheizt) Rest, VISA

Wettersteinstr. 24 ✉ 6632 – ✆ (05673) 2 22 50
– info@hotel-spielmann.com – Fax (05673) 22255
geschl. 3. März – 25. Juni, 11. Okt. – 20. Dez.
38 Zim (inkl. ½ P.) – 85/100 € 147/224 € 90/122 €
161/279 € – 5 Suiten
Rest – *(geschl. 30. März – 25. Mai, 7. Okt. – 22. Dez. und Montag,)* Karte 19/44 €

♦ Dieses Haus im Tiroler Stil ist eine ehemalige Pension a. d. 19. Jh. Individuelle Zimmer in neun verschiedenen Kategorien – einige sehr großzügig. Skilift direkt vor der Tür. Zum Restaurant gehört eine Terrasse mit schöner Sicht auf die Berge.

Sporthotel Schönruh Rest, VISA

Florentin Wehner-Weg 32 ✉ 6632 – ✆ (05673) 2 32 20
– info@hotel-schoenruh.com – Fax (05673) 232230
geschl. 30. März - 4. Mai, 19. Okt. – 20. Dez.
45 Zim (inkl. ½ P.) – 74/101 € 114/172 € 87/130 €
141/227 €
Rest – Karte 19/44 €

♦ Das zentral und dennoch relativ ruhig gelegene Haus verfügt über unterschiedlich eingerichtete Zimmer sowie für Familien geeignete Appartements. Netter Freizeitbereich. Zum Restaurant gehört eine Terrasse mit herrlicher Sicht auf die Sonnenspitze.

Alpen Residence Rest, VISA

Florentin-Wehner-Weg 37 ✉ 6632
– ✆ (05673) 2 25 50 – hotel@alpenresidence.at – Fax (05673) 225555
geschl. 30. April – 1. Juli
42 Zim (inkl. ½ P.) – 83/107 € 120/144 € 107/150 €
170/250 €
Rest – (nur Abendessen für Hausgäste)

♦ Recht geräumige, technisch gut ausgestattete Zimmer sowie ein neuzeitlicher Freizeitbereich stehen in diesem relativ ruhig gelegenen Hotel zur Verfügung.

Alpin Zim, Rest, VISA

Hauptstr. 29 ✉ 6632 – ✆ (05673) 22 79 – alpin@tirol.com
– Fax (05673) 227929
geschl. April – Mai, 3. Nov. – 20. Dez.
15 Zim (inkl. ½ P.) – 42/50 € 84/103 € 64/91 € 143/205 €
– 3 Suiten
Rest – (nur Abendessen für Hausgäste, im Sommer garni)

♦ Freundlich kümmert man sich in diesem kleinen Hotel um die Gäste. Die Zimmer sind mit hellem Naturholz wohnlich gestaltet, teils mit Kachelofen.

Stern Rest, VISA

Innsbrucker Str. 8 ✉ 6632 – ✆ (05673) 2 28 70 – hotelstern@netway.at
– Fax (05673) 2287222
geschl. 26. März – 10. Mai, 11. Okt. – 19. Dez.
36 Zim (inkl. ½ P.) – 60/78 € 102/124 € 70/113 €
120/190 €
Rest – (nur für Hausgäste)

♦ Mitten im Ort liegt dieses familiengeführte Hotel mit seinen sehr gepflegten Gästezimmern – die Zimmer nach hinten bieten eine schöne Sicht auf Lermoos und die Berge. In ländlichem Stil gehaltene Gaststube.

EICHENBERG - Vorarlberg - 730 B6 - 390 Ew - Höhe 795 m 5 A5

Wien 617 – Bregenz 11 – Dornbirn 23 – Lindau 10

Dorf 53, Gemeindeamt, ✉ 6911, ☎ (05574) 4 24 29, eichenberg.tourismus@cnv.at

Schönblick

< Bodensee, Lindau und Alpen,

Dorf 6 ✉ 6911

– ☎ (05574) 4 59 65 – hotel.schoenblick@schoenblick.at

– Fax (05574) 459657

geschl. 7. Jan. – 15. Feb., 10. Nov. – 16. Dez.

23 Zim – ♦70/89 € ♦♦120/136 € – ½ P 23 €

Rest – *(geschl. Montag – Dienstagmittag)* Menü 36 € – Karte 26/45 €

◆ Der Name des Hauses verspricht eine freie Sicht auf den Bodensee. Hell und neuzeitlich sind die Zimmer eingerichtet. Netter Saunabereich. Kosmetik- und Massageangebote. Die große Fensterfront im Restaurant ermöglicht einen schönen Ausblick. Aussichtsterrasse.

EISENSTADT L - Burgenland - 730 V5 - 11 340 Ew - Höhe 182 m 4 L3

Wien 49 – Wiener Neustadt 29 – Baden 36 – Sopron 20

Rathaus, Hauptstr. 35, ✉ 7000, ☎ (02682) 6 73 90, tourism@eisenstadt.at

Neusiedler See Donnerskirchen, Am Golfplatz 1 ☎ (02683) 81 71

Veranstaltungen

04.09. – 14.09.: Internationale Haydntage

Schloss Esterházy★ (Leopoldinentempel★) – Österreichisches Jüdisches Museum★ **M¹** – Burgenländisches Landesmuseum (römische Mosaike★) **M²** – Kalvarienberg und Bergkirche★ (Kreuzweg★) A

Rust★ Süd-Ost: 15 km – Mörbisch am See★ Süd-Ost: 20 km

Ohr

Zim,

Ruster Str. 51 ✉ 7000 – ☎ (02682) 6 24 60 – info@hotelohr.at

– Fax (02682) 624609

geschl. Feb. B **n**

39 Zim – ♦68/88 € ♦♦98/118 €

Rest – *(geschl. Okt. – April Sonntagabend – Montag)* Karte 21/38 €

◆ Ein gepflegtes, seit vielen Jahren familiengeführtes Haus unweit des Zentrums, das man um einen Anbau mit ganz modern eingerichteten Zimmern erweitert hat. Restaurant mit rustikalem Charakter, teils komplett in Zirbenholz gehalten.

Bodega La Ina

Hauptstr. 48 ✉ 7000 – ☎ (02682) 6 23 05 – info@laina.at

– Fax (02382) 62305

geschl. 7. – 22. Feb. und Sonntag – Montag, Feiertage B **b**

Rest – Menü 44/65 € – Karte 35/47 €

◆ In der Fußgängerzone liegt das geschmackvoll gestaltete Restaurant mit südländischem Touch. Die kreative Küche serviert man auch auf der schön eingedeckten Innenhofterrasse.

Esterházy

Esterházyplatz 5 ✉ 7000 – ☎ (02682) 6 28 19 – office@imesterhazy.at

– Fax (02682) 628194 A **c**

Rest – Menü 25/45 € – Karte 24/37 €

◆ Der ehemalige Pferdestall des Schlosses Esterházy beherbergt heute dieses Restaurant in modernem Stil. Eine hohe weiße Gewölbedecke schafft eine angenehm luftige Atmosphäre.

EISENSTADT

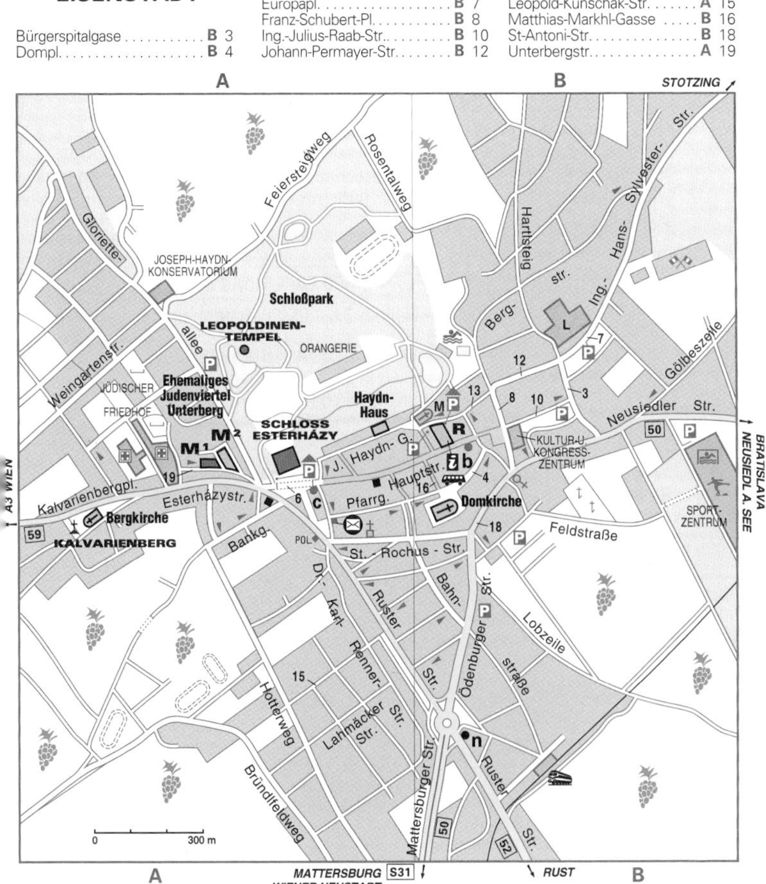

ELBIGENALP – **Tirol** – 730 D7 – **840 Ew** – **Höhe 1 040 m** – **Wintersport: 1 200 m** 5 **B5**

Wien 538 – Innsbruck 94 – Reutte 34
Elbigenalp 52, ✉ 6652, ✆ (05634) 53 15, lechtal@tirol.com

Alpenrose
Untergiblen 21 ✉ 6652 – ✆ (05634) 66 51 – info@alpenrose.net – Fax (05634) 665287 VISA
100 Zim (inkl. ½ P.) – †92/135 € ††174/248 €
Rest – Karte 18/32 €
◆ Hier beeindruckt vor allem das Wellness-Schlössl mit großzügiger Saunalandschaft, modernem Fitnessstudio und Garten mit Badeteich. Individuelle Zimmer im alpenländischen Stil. Großer Speisesaal und gemütliche rustikale Stuben.

Stern (mit Gästehaus) Zim, Rest,
Dorf 7 ✉ 6652 – ✆ (05634) 62 02
– info@hotel-stern.at – Fax (05634) 62029
geschl. 10. – 30. April, 25. Okt. – 3. Dez.
40 Zim – 55/69 € 93/121 € – ½ P 12 €
Rest – *(geschl. Dienstag)* Karte 21/34 €
◆ In einer ruhigen Seitenstraße befindet sich dieser gepflegte Landgasthof mit soliden Zimmern. Im Gästehaus stehen auch einige Appartements zur Verfügung. Eine bürgerlich-regionale Küche wird in den Restaurantstuben serviert.

ELIXHAUSEN – Salzburg – 730 L5 – 2 690 Ew – Höhe 600 m 8 F4

Wien 296 – Salzburg 9 – Hallein 31 – Bad Reichenhall 24

Gmachl (geheizt) Zim,
Dorfstr. 14 ✉ 5161
– ✆ (0662) 4 80 21 20 – romantikhotel@gmachl.com
– Fax (0662) 48021272
geschl. 22. – 26. Dez.
57 Zim – 85/127 € 135/220 € – 7 Suiten
Rest – Menü 35/59 € – Karte 29/47 €
◆ Der gewachsener Gasthof anno 1334, der ehemals eine Benediktinertaverne war, ist im Landhausstil eingerichtet und verfügt über heimelige und charmante Zimmer. In den gemütlichen Restaurantstuben mit schöner Ausstattug bietet man regionale Küche an.

ELLMAU – Tirol – 730 I6 – 2 530 Ew – Höhe 820 m – Wintersport: 1 550 m

10 104 7 E5

Wien 366 – Innsbruck 80 – Wörgl 22 – Kitzbühel 17
✉ 6352, ✆ (05358) 23 01, info@ellmau.at
27 Wilder Kaiser, Dorf 2 ✆ (05358) 42 82
9 Kaisergolf Ellmau, Steinerner Tisch 17 ✆ (05358) 23 79
Kaisergebirge★★

Kaiserhof Wilder Kaiser,
Harmstätt 8 (Süd-West: 2,5 km) ✉ 6352
– ✆ (05358) 20 22 – info@kaiserhof-ellmau.at – Fax (05358) 2022600
geschl. 30. März – 10. Mai, 2. Nov. – 18. Dez.
31 Zim (inkl. ½ P.) – 112/162 € 212/276 € 142/260 € 248/428 € – 6 Suiten
Rest *Schloss-Stube im Kaiserhof* – separat erwähnt
◆ Neben der Skipiste liegt das familiengeführte Hotel, in dem der Gast aufmerksam umsorgt wird. In ruhiger Umgebung und in wohnlichen Zimmern können Sie sich erholen.

Hochfilzer (mit Gästehaus) Rest,
Dorf 33 ✉ 6352 – ✆ (05358) 25 01 – info@hotel-hochfilzer.com
– Fax (05358) 3152
geschl. Ende März – Mitte Mai , Ende Okt. – Mitte Dez.
90 Zim (inkl. ½ P.) – 51/93 € 102/150 € 74/138 € 148/258 €
Rest – Karte 18/30 €
◆ Ein ehemaliger Gasthof in einem 600 Jahre alten Gebäude hat sich zu diesem zeitgemäßen Hotel mit großem Freizeitbereich entwickelt. Einige Zimmer sind besonders komfortabel. Gemütliches A-la-carte-Stüberl.

Alte Post Zim,

Dorf 24 6352 – (05358) 22 25 – info@hotelaltepost.com – Fax (05358) 3292
geschl. April, Nov.
32 Zim – 52/61 € 86/98 € 85/99 € 152/180 € – ½ P 10 €
Rest – Karte 17/32 €
◆ Traditionsreicher Alpengasthof im Ortszentrum mit zum Teil holzverkleideter Balkonfassade und einer Einrichtung im regionstypischen Stil. Rustikales Ambiente mit Kachelofen und freundlichem Service im Restaurant.

Schloss-Stube im Kaiserhof – Hotel Kaiserhof

Harmstätt 8 (Süd-West: 2,5 km) 6352 – (05358) 20 22 – info@kaiserhof-ellmau.at – Fax (05358) 2022600
geschl. 30. März – 10. Mai, 25. Okt. – 18. Dez.
Rest – *(geschl. Sonntag – Dienstag, nur Abendessen)* Menü 42/89 €
◆ Sowohl auf der Panoramaterrasse wie auch in der kleinen, eleganten Schloss-Stube genießen Sie die klassische Küche und das freundliche Personal.

EMMERSDORF – Niederösterreich – 730 S4 – 1 710 Ew – Höhe 227 m

3 **J2**

Wien 87 – St. Pölten 26 – Krems 36 – Melk 5

Zum Schwarzen Bären

Marktplatz 7 3644 – (02752) 7 12 49 – hotel@hotelpritz.at – Fax (02752) 7124944
geschl. Feb.
50 Zim – 60/81 € 90/132 € – ½ P 15 €
Rest – Menü 21/46 € – Karte 19/38 €
◆ Seit 1908 befindet sich dieser Landgasthof im Besitz der Familie. Es erwarten Sie mit Naturholz solide möblierte, wohnliche Zimmer. Das Restaurant: teils ländliche Stube, teils als Wintergarten angelegt.

Donauhof Zim,

An der Donau 40 (B 3) 3644 – (02752) 7 17 77 – hotel@donauhof.com – Fax (02752) 7177744
geschl. 1. – 6. Jan.
32 Zim – 48/73 € 96/126 € – ½ P 15 €
Rest – *(geschl. Nov. – März Sonntagabend)* Karte 14/34 €
◆ Ein solides Landhotel unter familiärer Leitung, das über wohnliche, mit hellen Naturholzmöbeln eingerichtete Gästezimmer verfügt. Gemütliche kleine Gaststube, ganz in Holz gehalten.

Landhotel Wachau Zim,

Luberegg 20 (West: 2 km) 3644 – (02752) 7 25 72 – info@landhotel-wachau.at – Fax (02752) 7257288
geschl. Nov.
34 Zim – 60/76 € 110/126 € 50/69 € 90/106 € – ½ P 15 €
Rest – *(geschl. Sonntagabend – Montag, außer Saison)* Karte 12/29 €
◆ Hell möblierte und funktionell ausgestattete Gästezimmer bietet Ihnen dieser Familienbetrieb, das Schwesterhotel des Donauhofs. Das Restaurant ist in nette Stuben und einen Pavillon unterteilt.

Hafer Kast'n
(Heuriger)

Luberegg 18 (West: 2 km) ✉ 3644 – ✆ (02752) 7 17 77 60
– heuriger@donauhof.com – Fax (02752) 7177744
geschl. 1. Nov. – 5. April
Rest – *(ab 16 Uhr geöffnet)* Karte 13/18 €
◆ In einem ehemals zum Schloss gehörenden Gebäude hat man dieses gemütliche und urige, über zwei Etagen angelegte Heurigen-Lokal eingerichtet. Netter Gartenbereich.

ENNS – Oberösterreich – 730 P4 – 10 620 Ew – Höhe 281 m 2 I3

Wien 157 – Linz 24 – Wels 40 – Steyr 22
Hauptplatz 1, ✉ 4470, ✆ (07223) 8 27 77, info.enns@oberoesterreich.at
Stadtturm (≤★) – Basilika St. Laurenz★

Lauriacum

Wiener Str. 5 ✉ 4470 – ✆ (07223) 8 23 15 – hotel@lauriacum.at
– Fax (07223) 8233229
31 Zim – 64/84 € 98/117 € – 3 Suiten
Rest – *(geschl. Samstag – Sonntag, nur Abendessen)* Karte 13/35 €
◆ Ein familiengeführtes Hotel im Stadtzentrum, das wegen seiner funktionell ausgestatteten, teils großzügigen Zimmer vor allem von Geschäftsreisenden gerne besucht wird. Gediegenes A-la-carte-Restaurant.

Römer garni

Mauthausnerstr. 39 ✉ 4470 – ✆ (07223) 8 49 00
– pension@zumroemer.at – Fax (07223) 849003
21 Zim – 39/45 € 60/64 €
◆ Etwas außerhalb des Zentrums gelegenes Hotel mit sachlich-modern eingerichteten Zimmern und einem freundlichen Frühstücksraum mit kleiner Terrasse.

ERL – Tirol – 730 I5 – 1 420 Ew – Höhe 470 m – Wintersport: 7 E4

Wien 380 – Innsbruck 85 – München 85 – Kufstein 15

Blaue Quelle mit Zim

Mühlgraben 52 (Süd: 1 km) ✉ 6343 – ✆ (05373) 81 28
– info@blauequelle.at – Fax (05373) 81284
geschl. 1. – 31. Jan.
12 Zim – 35/40 € 56/70 € – ½ P 15 €
Rest – *(geschl. Montag – Dienstag)* Karte 15/38 €
◆ Der gut geführte, über 350 Jahre alte Tiroler Gasthof bietet gemütliche Stuben, teils mit Zirbenholztäfelung, teils mit gewölbeartigen Decken und Bögen.

Beim Dresch mit Zim

Oberweidau 2 ✉ 6343 – ✆ (05373) 81 29 – anker@dresch.at
– Fax (05373) 81293
geschl. Anfang Nov. 2 Wochen
11 Zim – 35/45 € 70/100 € – ½ P 15 €
Rest – *(geschl. Mittwoch – Donnerstagmittag)* Karte 18/35 €
◆ Das Landgasthaus am Ortsanfang beherbergt eine rustikale Gaststube und ein gepflegtes, ländlich wirkendes Restaurant mit Kachelofen. Einige der Gästezimmer sind nach Feng-Shui-Richtlinien gestaltet.

ERNSTHOFEN – Niederösterreich – 730 P4 – 2 110 Ew – Höhe 267 m 2 I3

Wien 165 – St. Pölten 108 – Linz 33 – Steyr 15

Fischerwirt mit Zim Zim,
Mühlrading 11 4432 – (07435) 84 66 – info@fischerwirt.cc – Fax (07435) 846615
geschl. Anfang Jan. 2 Wochen, Ende Juli 2 Wochen und Dienstag – Mittwoch
4 Zim – 28 € 56 €
Rest – Karte 16/29 €
◆ Stammgäste schätzen das ländlich-schlicht gehaltene, etwas außerhalb an der Enns gelegene Lokal mit freundlichem Service. Hell und neuzeitlich möblierte Zimmer.

Gute Küche zu günstigem Preis? Folgen Sie dem „Bib Gourmand"

ERPFENDORF IN TIROL – Tirol – 730 J6 – 3 500 Ew – Höhe 630 m – Wintersport: 1 831 m 2 7 F4

Wien 359 – Innsbruck 99 – Kitzbühel 18 – Kufstein 37

Vital-Hotel Berghof (mit Gästehaus) (geheizt) Zim,
Dorf 24 6383 – (05352) 82 21 – hotel@berghof-tirol.at – Fax (05352) 8460
geschl. 28. März – 1. Juli, 31. Okt. – 10. Dez.
70 Zim (inkl. ½ P.) – 66/105 € 112/152 € 68/126 € 120/218 €
Rest – Karte 16/38 €
◆ Das gewachsene Haus ist ein solider Familienbetrieb mit alpenländisch-wohnlichen Zimmern und schönem Wellnessbereich. Großer Garten mit Minigolf und Eisstockschießen (Winter). A-la-carte-Restaurant mit bürgerlicher Küche. Gemütliche Bar.

ESCHENAU – Niederösterreich – 730 S4 – 1 170 Ew – Höhe 404 m 3 K3

Wien 82 – St. Pölten 20 – Amstetten 79 – Krems 56

In Eschenau-Rotheau Nord-Ost: 3 km:

Gasthof Pils Zim,
Rotheau 6 3153 – (02762) 6 86 13 – service@gasthof-pils.at – Fax (02762) 686137
20 Zim – 33 € 56 € – ½ P 14 €
Rest – *(geschl. Donnerstag – Freitag, Sonn- und Feiertage abends)* Karte 13/27 €
◆ Seit 100 Jahren wird das Haus mit der gelben Fassade als Gasthof genutzt. Im Hotelbereich stehen zeitgemäß eingerichtete Zimmer zur Verfügung. Freundlich gestaltetes Restaurant in ländlichem Stil.

ETMISSL – Steiermark – 730 R6 – 540 Ew – Höhe 720 m – Wintersport: 930 1 – Erholungsort 10 J4

Wien 160 – Graz 78 – Bruck a.d. Mur 23 – Leoben 42

Etmißlerhof (mit Gästehaus) (geheizt)
Etmißl 43 ✉ 8622
– ✆ (03861) 84 44 – info@etmisslerhof.at – Fax (03861) 844440
30 Zim (inkl. ½ P.) – 🚹45/61 € 🚹🚹80/118 €
Rest – *(geschl. Mittwoch)* Karte 12/23 €
◆ Über wohnlich eingerichtete Zimmer und Appartements verfügt dieses aus Stamm- und Gästehaus bestehende familienfreundliche Hotel mit Angebot für Kinder. Bürgerlicher Restaurantbereich.

XX **Gasthof Hubinger** mit Zim
Etmißl 25 ✉ 8622 – ✆ (03861) 81 14 – office@hubinger.com
– Fax (03861) 811423
geschl. Nov. 2 Wochen
8 Zim – 🚹38/40 € 🚹🚹76 €
Rest – *(geschl. Sonntagabend – Montag)* Menü 10 € – Karte 12/35 €
◆ A. d. J. 1494 stammt der Gasthof der Familie Wöls. Gemütlich-ländlich sind die Räume gestaltet, teils mit Gewölbe, teils mit Kachelofen. Regionale Küche. Nette Zimmer.

Gute Küche zu günstigem Preis? Folgen Sie dem „Bib Gourmand".
– Das freundliche MICHELIN-Männchen heißt „Bib"
und steht für ein besonders gutes Preis-Leistungs-Verhältnis!

EUGENDORF – **Salzburg** – 730 L5 – **6 120 Ew** – **Höhe 558 m** – **Wintersport: 700 m** 1 8 **G4**

Wien 286 – Salzburg 14 – Burghausen 64 – Vöcklabruck 50
Salzburger Str. 7, ✉ 5301, ✆ (06225) 84 24, info@eugendorf.com
Salzburg-Eugendorf, Golfplatz 1, ✆ (06225) 7 00 00

Landhotel Gschirnwirt Rest,
Alte Wiener Str. 49 (Nord-Ost: 1,5 km
an der B 1) ✉ 5301 – ✆ (06225) 82 29 – schinagl@gschirn.at
– Fax (06225) 822939
40 Zim – 🚹61/86 € 🚹🚹103/212 € – ½ P 19 €
Rest – *(geschl. 13. – 27. Nov. und Montag sowie Freitagmittag)*
Menü 27/35 € – Karte 18/32 €
◆ Dieses gewachsene Landhotel hält für Sie mit Naturholz eingerichtete, wohnliche Zimmer bereit. Ebenso wie einen netten Wellnessbereich und moderne Tagungsräume. Ländliches Restaurant mit Nischen im rustikalen Stil und bürgerlicher Küche.

Landgasthof Holznerwirt
Dorfstr. 4 ✉ 5301 – ✆ (06225) 82 05
– hotel@holznerwirt.at – Fax (06225) 820519
geschl. 4. – 14. Jan., 20. – 25. Dez.
58 Zim – 🚹63/83 € 🚹🚹114/166 € – ½ P 17 €
Rest – *(geschl. Sonntagabend - Montag)* Karte 15/31 €
◆ Der im Zentrum des Ortes liegende Alpengasthof a. d. 14. Jh. verfügt über komfortable, unterschiedlich eingerichte Zimmer mit Holzfußboden. Historischer Gewölbekeller mit guter Schnapsauswahl, Jägerstübl und netter Gastgarten.

Landhotel Drei Eichen
Kirchbergstr. 1 (Nord-Ost: 4 km an der B 1) VISA MC AE
✉ *5301 – ✆ (06225) 85 21 – landhotel.drei.eichen@sbg.at*
– Fax (06225) 85215
28 Zim – 58/65 € 90/130 € – ½ P 18 €
Rest – *(geschl. Mittwoch – Donnerstagmittag)* Karte 15/43 €
◆ Besonders auf Geschäftsreisende ausgerichtet ist dieses Hotel im Landhausstil mit moderner Tagungstechnik, großzügigen Zimmern mit Balkon, Seminargarten und Saunabereich. In den Gaststuben mit ländlichem Dekor herrscht eine gemütliche Atmosphäre.

Gasthof Neuwirt Zim, P VISA MC
Dorf 16 ✉ 5301 – ✆ (06225) 82 07 – neuwirt@sbg.at – Fax (06225) 82075
geschl. Karwoche, 23. – 26. Dez.
15 Zim – 45/50 € 70/75 € – ½ P 17 €
Rest – *(geschl. Freitag – Samstag)* Karte 13/29 €
◆ Einen kleinen, ländlichen Gasthof mit tadellos gepflegten Zimmern finden die Besucher hier. Ruhiger, schattiger Garten und Kinderspielplatz. Regionstypische Gaststuben mit Herrgottswinkel.

Gasthof zur Strass bei Bruno mit Zim VISA MC AE
Salzburgerstr. 25 ✉ 5301 – ✆ (06225) 82 18 – reservierung@beibruno.at
– Fax (06225) 8526
geschl. Anfang Sept. 1 Woche
9 Zim – 56 € 90 €
Rest – *(geschl. Sept. – Juni Sonn- und Feiertage)* Menü 35/50 € – Karte 27/56 €
◆ In dem gemütlichen Gasthof am Rande des Ortes mit nettem Gastgarten serviert man regionale und internationale Küche. Es werden Kochkurse angeboten.

EURATSFELD – Niederösterreich – 730 Q4 – 2 320 Ew – Höhe 305 m 3 J3

Wien 122 – St. Pölten 65 – Linz 67

Gafringwirt P VISA MC
Mittergafring 4 (Süd-Ost: 2,5 km) ✉ 3324 – ✆ (07474) 2 68
– info@gafringwirt.at – Fax (07474) 26828
geschl. 28. Jan. – 10. Feb., 10. – 20. Nov.
18 Zim – 36/48 € 64/76 € – ½ P 12 €
Rest – *(geschl. Dienstag, Sonntagabend)* Karte 15/28 €
◆ Ein sympathischer kleiner Landgasthof unter familiärer Leitung. Die Zimmer sind teils recht groß und alle mit hellen Naturholzmöbeln eingerichtet. Solide ländliche Gaststuben.

FAAK AM SEE – Kärnten – siehe Finkenstein

FAISTENAU – Salzburg – 730 L5 – 2 850 Ew – Höhe 786 m – Wintersport: 1 000 m 3 8 G4

Wien 289 – Salzburg 22 – Bad Ischl 41 – Hallein 18
Am Lindenplatz 1, ✉ 5324, ✆ (06228) 23 14, faistenau@fuschlseeregion.com

Alte Post

Lindenplatz 5 ✉ 5324 – ✆ (06228) 2 20 50 – info@altepost-faistenau.at – Fax (06228) 220528
geschl. 5. – 25. April.
43 Zim (inkl. ½ P.) – ☼ 55/70 € 110/138 € ❄ 61/79 € 120/170 €
Rest – *(geschl. Donnerstagmittag)* Karte 23/34 €
◆ Neben einem schönen Wellnessbereich und zahlreichen Freizeitangeboten bietet dieses familiär geleitete Gasthaus zeitgemäße und teilweise große Zimmer an. Der Stil des Restaurants wird bestimmt durch die rustikale Einrichtung und die bürgerliche Küche.

FEICHTEN – Tirol – siehe Kaunertal

FELD AM SEE – Kärnten – 730 N8 – 1 190 Ew – Höhe 746 m 9 H6

Wien 323 – Klagenfurt 57 – Villach 24 – Spittal an der Drau 26

Landhotel Lindenhof

Dorfstr. 8 ✉ 9544 – ✆ (04246) 22 74 – urlaub@landhotel-lindenhof.at – Fax (04246) 227450
geschl. 30. März – 1. Mai, 25. Okt. – 25. Dez.
26 Zim (inkl. ½ P.) – 50/70 € 100/150 €
Rest *Vinum* – *(geschl. 6. Jan. – 3. Mai, 1. Okt. – 25. Dez. und Montag)* Karte 19/39 €
◆ Zu dem wohnlichen Hotel im Landhausstil gehören ein eigenes Strandbad am Brennsee, ein Bade- und Saunabereich sowie Massage- und Kosmetikangebote. Das Restaurant Vinum besteht aus zwei gemütlichen Stuben, in denen man gute regionale Küche serviert.

FELDBACH – Steiermark – 730 T8 – 4 680 Ew – Höhe 282 m 11 L5

Wien 173 – Graz 53 – Fürstenfeld 28 – Leibnitz 44
Hauptplatz 1, ✉ 8330, ✆ (03152) 3 07 90, tourismusverband@feldbach.at
Riegersburg★ (Nord-Ost: 10 km)

Csejtei (mit Gästehaus)

Ungarstr. 12 ✉ 8330 – ✆ (03152) 22 05 – Fax (03152) 22054
27 Zim – 50/65 € 100/110 €
Rest – *(geschl. Sonntag)* Karte 16/24 €
◆ In der Ortsmitte steht dieser familiengeführte Gasthof mit gelber Fassade. Besonders schön sind die eleganten Zimmer in einem kleinen Gästehaus. Im Bistro-Stil gehaltenes Restaurant mit Terrasse unter Kastanienbäumen.

Gute und preiswerte Häuser kennzeichnet das MICHELIN-Männchen, der „Bib": der rote „Bib Gourmand" für die Küche, der blaue „Bib Hotel" bei den Zimmern.

FELDKIRCH – Vorarlberg – 730 A7 – 28 610 Ew – Höhe 458 m 5 A6

Wien 600 – Bregenz 36 – Vaduz 15 – Bludenz 21

Palais Lichtenstein, Schlossergasse 8, ✉ 6800, ✆ (05522) 73 46 70, tourismus@feldkirch.at

Altstadt★ – Domkirche St.Nikolaus (Beweinung Christi★)

Holiday Inn

Zim, Rest

Leonhardsplatz 2 ✉ 6800 – ✆ (05522) 7 46 00
– reservation@holiday-inn-feldkirch.com – Fax (05522) 78646 **a**

92 Zim – 85/99 € 116/130 €, ☕ 14 €

Rest – Karte 20/28 €

◆ Das neuzeitliche Hotel unterhalb der Burg bietet funktionelle Zimmer mit hellem Holzmobiliar und einen gepflegten Freizeitbereich. Helles Restaurant mit großer Fensterfront.

Bären garni

Bahnhofstr. 1 ✉ 6800 – ✆ (05522) 3 55 00 – office@hotel-baeren.at
– Fax (05522) 72577
geschl. Ende Okt. – Anfang Nov. 2 Wochen **b**

47 Zim ☕ – 53/78 € 78/126 €

◆ Ein zentral gelegenes Patrizierhaus aus dem 14. Jh. mit roter Putzfassade beherbergt dieses Hotel mit klassischer Halle und Zimmern in zwei Kategorien.

Alpenrose

Zim

Rosengasse 6 ✉ 6800 – ✆ (05522) 72 17 50
– hotel.alpenrose@cable.vol.at – Fax (05522) 721755 **c**

27 Zim ☕ – 71/76 € 122 €

Rest – *(geschl. Samstagmittag, Sonntag)* Karte 19/40 €

◆ Das in der Altstadt gelegene Bürgerhaus a. d. 16. Jh. bietet stilvoll mit Nussbaummöbeln und gut abgestimmtem Dekor ausgestattete Zimmer. Restaurant in klassischer, eleganter Aufmachung.

FELDKIRCH

Ardetzenbergtunnel 2
Bahnhofstr. 3
Burggasse 4
Dompl. 5
Fidelisstr. 7
Ganahlstr. 8
Herrengasse 9
Johannitergasse 10
Kreuzgasse 12
Leonhardsplatz 13
Montfortgasse 15
Neustadt 16
Rosengasse 24
Schillerstr. 17
Schloßgraben 19
Schloßsteig 20
Schmiedgasse 22
Vorstadt 23
Wichnergasse 26
Zeughausgasse 30

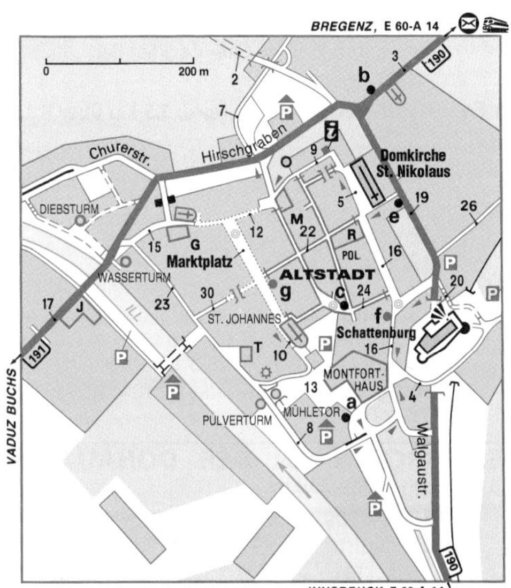

Montfort das Hotel

Galuragasse 7 (über B 190 Richtung Bregenz) ✉ 6800 – ✆ (05522) 7 21 89 – office@montfort-dashotel.at – Fax (05522) 7479911

53 Zim – 75/85 € 125/195 €

Rest – Karte 21/35 €

◆ Ein gewachsenes Stadthotel mit modernem Ambiente. Zeitgemäßes, helles Mobiliar, warme Farben und zeitgenössische Bilder machen die Zimmer wohnlich. Unterteilter Restaurantbereich mit Bar.

Post garni

Schlossgraben 5 ✉ 6800 – ✆ (05522) 7 28 20 – hotel.post@utanet.at – Fax (05522) 728206

geschl. 20. Dez. – 10. Jan. **e**

14 Zim – 65/69 € 90/98 €

◆ Gut geführtes, gepflegtes Hotel in einem älteren Stadthaus im Zentrum mit solide ausgestatteten Zimmern. Zum Haus gehört ein Café.

Dogana

Neustadt 20 ✉ 6800 – ✆ (05522) 75 12 63 – dogana@dogana.com – Fax (05522) 751265

geschl. Sonntag – Montag, Feiertage **f**

Rest – Menü 30/48 € – Karte 18/37 €

◆ Das Dogana besteht aus einer Bar, einem Café im Bistrostil und einem modern-eleganten Restaurant im 1. Stock. Bilder, farbige Wände und zeitgemäße Musik prägen die Atmosphäre.

Rauch

Marktgasse 12 ✉ 6800 – ✆ (05522) 7 63 55 – info@rauch.sonderbar.at – Fax (05572) 36673 **g**

Rest – *(geschl. Dienstag)* (Tischbestellung ratsam) Menü 49/73 € – Karte 32/51 €

◆ In dem modernen Restaurant mit markantem Kreuzgewölbe bietet man saisonale Gerichte – am Mittag ist die Küche einfacher und die Stimmung etwas legerer. Café/Cocktail-Bar.

In Feldkirch-Altenstadt **Nord: 3,5 km über B 190, Richtung Götzis:**

Gasthof Schäfle (mit Gästehaus)

Naflastr. 3 ✉ 6804 – ✆ (05522) 7 22 03 – office@schaefle.cc – Fax (05522) 7220317

geschl. 22. Dez. – 20. Jan.

30 Zim – 56/60 € 86/95 €

Rest – *(geschl. Samstag – Sonntag)* Karte 24/43 €

◆ Ein netter, familiär geführter Landgasthof, der neuzeitlich eingerichtete Zimmer und Appartements bietet. Mit Gästehaus in einer Nebenstraße des Ortsteils. In den gemütlichen Gaststuben serviert man u. a. selbst gebackenes Brot und Wein vom eigenen Weinberg.

FELDKIRCHEN AN DER DONAU – Oberösterreich – 730 O3 – 5 070 Ew – Höhe 268 m 2 **H2**

Wien 200 – Linz 22 – Wels 35 – Passau 62

Hauptstr. 1, ✉ 4101, ✆ (07233) 71 90, tv.feldkirchen.donau@direkt.at

Donau, Golfplatzstr. 12 ✆ (07233) 76 76

Schloss Mühldorf (mit Gästehaus)

Mühldorf 1 (Süd-Ost: 2 km) Zim, VISA AE
4101 – (07233) 72 41 – schloss@muehldorf.co.at
– Fax (07233) 72414
35 Zim – 105/158 € 180/220 € 85/138 € 140/180 €
– ½ P 25 €
Rest – *(wochentags nur Abendessen)* Karte 24/39 €
Rest *Mühldorferie* – *(geschl. Sonntag – Mittwoch , nur Abendessen)* *(Tischbestellung ratsam)* Menü 44/54 € – Karte 27/36 €

◆ Ansprechend wurde in der alten Schlossanlage das historische Gemäuer mit modernem Komfort kombiniert. Freuen Sie sich auf den Rosengarten, den Schwimmteich und den Reitstall. Schönes Restaurant mit Kreuzgewölbe. Mühldorferie: kleines Gourmet-Restaurant.

Luxuriös oder eher schlicht?
Die Symbole und kennzeichnen den Komfort.

FELDKIRCHEN BEI MATTIGHOFEN – Oberösterreich – 730 L4 – 1 830 Ew – Höhe 571 m

1 **F3**

Wien 289 – Linz 125 – Salzburg 38 – Traunreut 51

Maria vom guten Rat VISA

Gstaig 1 (Ost: 2 km in Richtung Mattighofen) 5143 – (07748) 5 01 95
– info@gstaig.at – Fax (07748) 5019595
geschl. 14. Jan. – 5. Feb., 19. – 27. Nov. und Montag – Dienstag
Rest – Menü 27/34 € – Karte 14/37 €

◆ Das komplett sanierte Dorfgasthaus beherbergt im 1. Stock ein ländlich-modern gestaltetes Restaurant, im EG eine nette Stube. Regionale Küche. Sehr schöner Garten mit Salettl.

FELDKIRCHEN IN KÄRNTEN – Kärnten – 730 O8 – 14 030 Ew – Höhe 550 m – Wintersport: 1 350m 8

9 **I6**

Wien 303 – Klagenfurt 23 – Pörtschach 16 – Villach 25

Amthofgasse 3, 9560, (04276) 21 76, tourismus@feldkirchen.at

Nudelbacher (geheizt) Rest,

Bösenlacken 6 (Süd: 2,5 km) 9560 VISA AE
– (04276) 32 75 – hotel@nudelbacher.at – Fax (04276) 327566
geschl. 20. März – 26. April, 1. Nov. – 27. Dez.
27 Zim (inkl. ½ P.) – 52/69 € 92/130 €
Rest – (nur Abendessen für Hausgäste)

◆ Aus einer Frühstückspension entwickelte sich dieses nette Ferienhotel mit wohnlicher Atmosphäre. Am Haus: ein sehr hübscher Garten mit großem Pool und Spielplatz.

FERLACH – Kärnten – 730 O9 – 7 610 Ew – Höhe 466 m – Wintersport: 1 200 m 3

9 **I6**

Wien 335 – Klagenfurt 16 – Villach 45 – St. Veit an der Glan 37

In Ferlach-Ressnig Nord: 1 km:

Plasch – Auf der Huabn (mit Gästehaus)
Ressnig 17 ✉ 9170 – Zim, P VISA MC AE
– *✆ (04227) 23 70 – info@gasthof-plasch.at – Fax (04227) 237050*
23 Zim – 30/38 € 58/70 € – ½ P 11 €
Rest – Karte 14/32 €
♦ Der nahegelegene Badesee und ein Spielpark direkt am Haus machen diese ländliche Urlaubsadresse mit zeitgemäßen Zimmern für Familien mit Kindern interessant. Radlerservice. Rustikales Restaurant mit Produkten aus eigener Schlachtung und Landwirtschaft.

Außerhalb Nord-Ost: 2,5 km, über B 85 Richtung Sankt Margareten im Rosental:

Antonitsch Glainach P
Glainach/Glinje 12 ✉ 9170 – ✆ (04227) 22 26
– antonitsch.glainach@aon.at – Fax (04227) 4236
geschl. Nov. – 22. März und Montag
Rest – Karte 13/29 €
♦ Ein 350 Jahre altes Gasthaus mit gemütlichen Alt-Kärntner Stuben und hübschem Kastaniengarten. Man pflegt eine traditionelle regionale Küche mit Kärntner Spezialitäten.

FEUERSBRUNN – Niederösterreich – siehe Grafenwörth

FILZMOOS – Salzburg – 730 M6 – 1 360 Ew – Höhe 1 057 m – Wintersport: 1 645 m 1 7 9 G4

Wien 309 – Salzburg 75 – Bischofshofen 35 – Bad Ischl 78
Nr. 50, ✉ 5532, ✆ (06453) 82 35, info@filzmoos.at
Lage★
Gerzkopf★★ – Salzkammergut★★★ – Roßbrand★★

Hubertus (Johanna Maier) (geheizt) P
✿✿ *Am Dorfplatz 1 ✉ 5532* VISA MC AE
– ✆ (06453) 82 04 – info@hotelhubertus.at – Fax (06453) 82046
geschl. April, Nov.
15 Zim – ☼ 150/190 € 210/280 € ❄ 170/210 € 240/310 €
Rest – *(geschl. Montag – Dienstag, Mittwoch – Freitag nur Abendessen)* (Tischbestellung ratsam) Menü 98/135 €
Spez. Variation vom Saibling. Kalb und Reh in zwei Gängen serviert. Johannas Topfenteller.
♦ Mit viel Engagement führt die Familie Maier ihr Hotel, dessen wohnliche und hübsche Landhauszimmer den Gast überzeugen. Freibad und Liegewiese in unmittelbarer Nähe. Ländlich-elegant sind die Hubertus- und die Jägerstube mit klassischer saisonaler Kost.

Dachstein Zim, P
Filzmoos 31 ✉ 5532 – ✆ (06453) 8 21 80 – info@hotel-dachstein.at
– Fax (06453) 821845 – geschl. 5. April – 1. Mai, 25. Okt. – 20. Dez.
34 Zim (inkl. ½ P.) – ☼ 61/72 € 121/154 € ❄ 79/109 € 130/222 €
Rest – Karte 17/32 €
♦ Zeitgemäße, komfortable Zimmer mit einem Touch Landhausstil bietet das engagiert geführte Alpenhotel seinen Gästen. Im UG gepflegter Freizeitbereich mit zahlreichen Angeboten. Stilvoll-ländliches Ambiente im Restaurant.

Filzmooserhof (geheizt) Rest,
Neuberg 85 ✉ 5532 – ✆ (06453) 82 32 – hotel@filzmooserhof.at – Fax (06453) 823266
geschl. 1. – 30. April, 1. Nov. – 22. Dez.
35 Zim (inkl. ½ P.) – ☼ 65/80 € 118/166 € ❄ 83/104 € 164/222 € – 4 Suiten
Rest – (Tischbestellung ratsam) Karte 22/33 €
♦ Besonders auf Familien ist dieses Hotel ausgelegt: Freizeitaktivitäten für Groß und Klein, einige Familienzimmer sowie All-inclusive-Angebot für Kinder. Bürgerlich-rustikales Restaurant mit Sonnenterrasse.

Alpenkrone Rest,
Filzmoos 133 ✉ 5532 – ✆ (06453) 8 28 00 – alpenkrone.filzmoos@aon.at – Fax (06453) 828048
geschl. 1. April – 9. Mai, 6. Okt. – 19. Dez.
65 Zim (inkl. ½ P.) – ☼ 51/61 € 88/108 € ❄ 55/110 € 96/204 €
Rest – Karte 16/38 €
♦ Ruhig liegt das Hotel oberhalb des Ortes. Ein Teil der Zimmer mit Berg-/Talblick. Mit Südamerika-Souvenirs dekorierter Freizeitbereich mit Massage und Bädern. Von der Terrasse des Restaurants genießt man eine schöne Aussicht. Bürgerliches Speisenangebot.

In Filzmoos-Neuberg **Nord-West: 6 km Richtung Eben im Pongau:**

Neubergerhof Zim, Rest,
Neuberg 84 ✉ 5532 – ✆ (06453) 83 81 – urlaub@hotel-neubergerhof.at – Fax (06453) 838163
geschl. 5. April – 9. Mai, 21. Okt. – 20. Dez.
30 Zim (inkl. ½ P.) – ☼ 55/65 € 100/120 € ❄ 61/82 € 108/150 €
Rest – Karte 16/31 €
♦ Das im regionstypischen Stil erbaute Familienhotel verfügt über wohnlich eingerichtete Zimmer und Freizeitangebote wie Indoor-Kletterwand, Bogenschießen und Reiten für Kinder. Alpenländisch gestaltetes Restaurant mit schöner Aussicht und Terrasse zum Tal hin.

FINKENBERG IM ZILLERTAL – Tirol – 730 H7 – 1 530 Ew – Höhe 840 m – Wintersport: 2 095 m 1 8 7 E5

Wien 443 – Innsbruck 70 – Schwaz 41 – Kufstein 71
✉ 6292, ✆ (05285) 6 26 73, info@finkenberg.at
Wanderung zum Rastkogel★★ (mit zum Penken)

Sport- & Wellnesshotel Stock Berge und Mayrhofen, (geheizt) Rest,
Dorf 142 ✉ 6292 – ✆ (05285) 67 75 – sporthotel@stock.at – Fax (05285) 6775421
geschl. 6. – 25. April
96 Zim (inkl. ½ P.) – ☼ 145/183 € 250/330 € ❄ 157/270 € 290/380 € – 44 Suiten
Rest – (nur Abendessen für Hausgäste)
♦ Ein elegantes Alpenhotel, das mit einem Wellnessbereich auf 4000 qm beeindruckt. Die individuellen Zimmer sind liebevoll und warm gestaltet. Gutes All-inclusive-Angebot. Schön sind die geschmackvoll dekorierten Restaurantstuben. Begehbarer Weinkeller.

Olympia-Relax-Hotel-Leonhard-Stock

(geheizt) Rest,

Dorf 151 ✉ 6292 – ✆ (05285) 6 26 88 – info@olympiahotel.at
– Fax (05285) 6268833
geschl. 4. – 12. Nov.
22 Zim (inkl. ½ P.) – ☼ 48/66 € 96/144 € ❄ 45/98 € 90/226 €
Rest – (nur für Hausgäste)
♦ In dem im Zentrum gelegenen Hotel erwarten Sie solide im regionstypischen Stil eingerichtete Gästezimmer sowie ein netter rustikaler Frühstücksraum.

Dornauhof

Dornau 308 ✉ 6292 – ✆ (05285) 6 26 96 – info@dornauhof.at
– Fax (05285) 626967
geschl. 13. April – 10. Mai, 31. Okt. – 1. Dez.
31 Zim (inkl. ½ P.) – ☼ 43/55 € 74/96 € ❄ 66/89 € 118/164 €
Rest – (nur Abendessen für Hausgäste)
♦ Recht ruhig in einer Nebenstraße liegt dieses freundlich und familiär geleitete Hotel im alpenländischen Stil. Direkt am Haus führt der Donauradweg vorbei. Restaurant mit rustikalem Ambiente.

Landgasthof Persal

Finkenberg und Berge, Zim, Rest,

Persal 261 ✉ 6292
– ✆ (05285) 6 21 14 – info@persal.at – Fax (05285) 63355
geschl. 1. April – 30. Juli
26 Zim (inkl. ½ P.) – ☼ 40/50 € 80/100 € ❄ 51/77 €
100/140 €
Rest – Karte 16/35 €
♦ Ein großer, familiengeführter Alpengasthof am Ortsende mit Balkonfassade, funktionell ausgestatteten Zimmern und gepflegtem Saunabereich. Rustikale Gaststuben mit regionaler Küche. Man verwendet u. a. Produkte aus eigener Landwirtschaft.

FINKENSTEIN AM FAAKER SEE – Kärnten – 730 N9 – 8 200 Ew – Höhe 554 m

9 **H6**

Wien 343 – Klagenfurt 48 – Villach 8 – Spittal a. d. Drau 48
Dietrichsteinerstr. 2 (Faak), ✉ 9583, ✆ (04254) 21 10, faakersee@ktn.gde.at

Veranstaltungen

04.09. – 06.09.: European Bike Week – Harley Davidson

In Faak am See Nord-Ost: 4 km:

Inselhotel

See, Zim, Rest,

Inselweg 10 ✉ 9583
– ✆ (04254) 21 45 – info@inselhotel.at – Fax (04254) 213677
geschl. 17. Sept. – 23. Mai
32 Zim (inkl. ½ P.) – 73/104 € 142/260 €
Rest – Karte 23/28 €
♦ Per Bootstaxi erreicht man das Hotel auf der kleinen Insel im Faaker See. Schön: das alte Badehaus mit Sauna und Kosmetik sowie das Strandbad mit Beachvolleyball und Tennis. Saalartiges Restaurant und Terrasse mit toller Aussicht.

FISCHAMEND – Niederösterreich – 730 V4 – 4 420 Ew – Höhe 150 m

4 **L2**

Wien 23 – St. Pölten 98 – Baden 47 – Bratislava 45

Petronell-Carnuntum (Archäologischer Park★) Ost: 20 km – Rohrau (Harrach'sche Gemäldegalerie★★) Süd-Ost: 25 km

Merzendorfer

Hainburgerstr. 1 ✉ 2401 – ✆ (02232) 7 63 14 – merzendorfer@utanet.at – Fax (02232) 763144

geschl. über Ostern 1 Woche, Ende Dez. 2 Wochen und Sonntag – Montag

Rest – Karte 24/43 €

◆ Ein gepflegtes familiengeführtes Restaurant - optisch in zwei Räume unterteilt - mit solider bürgerlicher Einrichtung und freundlichem Service. Überwiegend Fischgerichte.

FISCHBACH – Steiermark – 730 S6 – 1 620 Ew – Höhe 1 050 m – Wintersport: 1 200 m 3 – Luftkurort

11 **K4**

Wien 142 – Graz 61 – Bruck a.d. Mur 38 – Wiener Neustadt 94

Dorfhotel Fasching

Rest, Rest, VISA

Fischbach 3c ✉ 8654 – ✆ (03170) 2 62 – dorfhotel.fasching@aon.at – Fax (03170) 26280

geschl. 22. Nov. – 13. Dez.

40 Zim (inkl. ½ P.) – 59/72 € 104/142 € – 5 Suiten

Rest – Karte 26/32 €

◆ Das familiär geführte Hotel in schöner, ruhiger Lage überzeugt mit wohnlichen, in modernem Stil eingerichteten Zimmern und freundlichen Mitarbeitern. Das Restaurant teilt sich in gemütliche Stuben und einen wintergartenartigen Bereich.

Gasthof Forsthaus

VISA AE

Fischbach 2 ✉ 8654 – ✆ (03170) 2 01 – office.forsthaus@utanet.at – Fax (03170) 20114

geschl. Mittwoch, Sonntagabend

Rest – Karte 21/37 €

◆ Das 400 Jahre alte Haus ist ein solider, von der Inhaberfamilie geleiteter Gasthof mit bürgerlich-rustikal eingerichteten Stuben.

FISS – Tirol – 730 D7 – 860 Ew – Höhe 1 436 m – Wintersport: 2 700 m 10 31

6 **C6**

Wien 533 – Innsbruck 90 – Landeck 21 – Serfaus 4

Unteregasse 2, ✉ 6533, ✆ (05476) 64 41, info@serfaus-fiss-ladis.at

Alpenresort Schlosshotel Fiss

(geheizt) Rest, Rest, VISA

Laurschweg 28 ✉ 6533 – ✆ (05476) 63 97 – info@schlosshotel-fiss.com – Fax (05476) 639757

geschl. 13. April – 21. Juni

103 Zim (inkl. ½ P.) – ☼ 140/160 € 230/390 € ❄ 160/225 € 260/390 € – 24 Suiten

Rest – (nur für Hausgäste)

◆ Dieses Alpenhotel ist komfortabel und elegant von der Lobby bis zum Wellnessbereich. Für Kinder: das "Kids-Schlössl". Ein Aufzug bringt Sie vom Skiraum direkt auf die Piste.

Lasinga Rest,

Laurschweg 2 ✉ 6533 – ✆ (05476) 68 86 – info@lasinga.at – Fax (05476) 6886150
geschl. Mitte April – Anfang Dez.
30 Zim (inkl. ½ P.) – 🚹89/133 € 🚹🚹148/284 € – 6 Suiten
Rest – (nur für Hausgäste)

◆ Ein familiär geleitetes Haus im Zentrum mit gemütlicher Lobby und geräumigen, wohnlichen Gästezimmern. Der Freizeitbereich ist ansprechend im modernen Stil gehalten.

Chesa Monte Rest,

Platzergasse 4 ✉ 6533 – ✆ (05476) 64 06 – office@chesa-monte.at – Fax (05476) 64067
geschl. Mitte April – Mitte Juni, Mitte Okt. – Anfang Dez.
26 Zim (inkl. ½ P.) – ☼ 🚹71/78 € 🚹🚹128/156 € ❄ 🚹98/145 € 🚹🚹196/320 €
Rest – *(geschl. Mitte April - Mitte Dez. und Dienstag, nur Abendessen)* Karte 25/40 €

◆ In dem Ferienhotel im Zentrum erwarten Sie eine schöne Halle mit Bar und Kamin sowie solide Zimmer. Appartements befinden sich im 50 m entfernten Gästehaus.

St. Laurentius Rest,

Leiteweg 26 ✉ 6533 – ✆ (05476) 67 14 – info@laurentius.at – Fax (05476) 671467
geschl. 8. April – 9. Juni, 22. Okt. – 7. Dez.
63 Zim (inkl. ½ P.) – ☼ 🚹84/98 € 🚹🚹126/184 € ❄ 🚹106/157 € 🚹🚹152/310 €
Rest – (nur Abendessen für Hausgäste)

◆ Hier ist man ganz auf Familien mit Kindern aller Altersklassen ausgerichtet: Familienzimmer, "Kids STAR-Club" und Kinder-Buffet. Highlight: das Schwimmbad mit 40-m-Rutsche.

Am Sonnberg garni

Kaiweg 1 ✉ 6533 – ✆ (05476) 2 01 39 – info@amsonnberg.at – Fax (05476) 2013910
geschl. 7. April – 12. Juni, 15. Okt. – 6. Dez.
15 Zim – ☼ 🚹35/43 € 🚹🚹46/62 € ❄ 🚹57/72 € 🚹🚹90/120 €

◆ Dieses nette kleine Hotel wird freundlich von der Inhaberfamilie geführt und verfügt über alpenländisch eingerichtete Zimmer mit Balkon oder Terrasse. 2 Appartements.

Hubertushof Rest,

Via Claudia Augusta 39 ✉ 6533 – ✆ (05476) 67 27 – info@hubertushof-fiss.at – Fax (05476) 672733
geschl. 15. Okt. – 7. Dez.
20 Zim – ☼ 🚹30 € 🚹🚹52/56 € ❄ 🚹40/59 € 🚹🚹72/118 € – ½ P 14/23 €
Rest – (nur Abendessen für Hausgäste)

◆ Die zentrale Lage und solide, rustikal möblierte Zimmer sprechen für den gut geführten Alpengasthof. Alle Zimmer verfügen über einen Balkon oder eine kleine Terrasse.

Gebhard mit Zim

Via Claudia Augusta 36 ✉ 6533 – ✆ (05476) 66 17
– info@hotel-gebhard.at – Fax (05476) 661784
geschl. 15. April – 15. Mai, 24. Okt. – 5. Dez.
7 Zim (inkl. ½ P.) – ☼ 65 € 118 € ❄ 120 € 240 €
Rest – *(geschl. Mitte Mai – Mitte Okt. Dienstag)* Karte 21/35 €
◆ Dieses Restaurant teilt sich in einen angenehm hell und zeitlos gehaltenen Raum sowie eine gemütlich-rustikale Stube. Serviert werden bürgerliche Speisen. Gepflegte Gästezimmer und ein kleiner Saunabereich.

FLACHAU – **Salzburg** – 730 M6 – **2 630 Ew** – **Höhe 925 m** – **Wintersport: 1 980 m** 9 44 9 **G5**

Wien 317 – Salzburg 74 – Bischofshofen 34 – Bad Ischl 78
Dorfstr. 172, ✉ 5542, ✆ (06457) 22 14, info@flachau.com

Lacknerhof

(geheizt) Rest, VISA AE

Unterberggasse 172
✉ 5542 – ✆ (06457) 2 37 90 – info@lacknerhof.at
– Fax (06457) 237946
geschl. 1. April – 15. Mai, 15. Nov. – 10. Dez.
71 Zim (inkl. ½ P.) – ☼ 92/104 € 154/178 € ❄ 114/184 € 180/342 € – 5 Suiten
Rest – Karte 20/33 €
◆ Hier erwarten Sie wohnliche Zimmer im Landhausstil (im Anbau etwas größer) sowie ein schöner Saunabereich. Pub und Disko befinden sich im kleinen Burgschlössl. All inclusive. Eine nette Stube dient als A-la-carte-Restaurant.

Tirolerhof

Zim, Rest, VISA

Hofgasse 214 ✉ 5542 – ✆ (06457) 2 77 90
– info@hotel-tirolerhof.com – Fax (06457) 27797
geschl. 13. April – 10. Mai, 18. Okt. – 7. Dez.
50 Zim (inkl. ½ P.) – ☼ 62/68 € 120/130 € ❄ 78/105 € 156/204 € – 4 Suiten
Rest – Karte 17/32 €
◆ Ein schöner, alpenländisch gestalteter unterirdischer Gang verbindet die 3 Hotelgebäude. Im Bioholzhaus Bründlhof befindet sich neben einigen Zimmern ein hübsches Hallenbad. Eine Holzdecke trägt zum gemütlichen Ambiente im Restaurant bei.

Reslwirt (mit Gästehaus)

Zim, Rest, VISA

Dorfstr. 10 ✉ 5542 – ✆ (06457) 22 16
– hotel@reslwirt.at – Fax (06457) 202127
geschl. 14. April – 9. Mai, 2. Nov. – 1. Dez.
56 Zim (inkl. ½ P.) – ☼ 77/87 € 134 € ❄ 110/124 € 210/244 €
Rest – Karte 15/30 €
◆ Das a. d. J. 1774 stammende Gasthaus wurde größtenteils neu aufgebaut und bietet mit Vollholzmöbeln wohnlich ausgestattete Zimmer. 2 Allergikerzimmer. Netter Saunabereich. Rustikale Gaststube mit teilweise alter Holztäfelung.

Waidmannsheil

Wastlgasse 195 ✉ 5542 – ✆ (06457) 23 68 – info@hotel-waidmannsheil.at – Fax (06457) 23686
geschl. 7. April – 24. Juni, 28. Sept. – 5. Dez.
42 Zim (inkl. ½ P.) – ☼ 74/76 € 118/122 € ❄ 103/117 € 156/184 €
Rest – (nur für Hausgäste)

◆ Das familiengeführte regionstypische Haus beherbergt hell möblierte Zimmer – besonders geräumig sind die beiden Suiten – und ein lichtes Hallenbad. Kosmetik und Massage.

Montanara Rest,

Unterberggasse 167 ✉ 5542 – ✆ (06457) 24 03 – flachau@montanara.com – Fax (06457) 24038
geschl. 7. April – 1. Juni, Okt. – Nov.
28 Zim (inkl. ½ P.) – ☼ 77 € 104/150 € ❄ 105/135 € 160/268 €
Rest – (nur für Hausgäste)

◆ Das neben einer Seilbahn gelegene Hotel wird freundlich von der Inhaberfamilie geleitet und verfügt über im alpenländischen Stil gehaltene Gästezimmer. Ein freundlicher Wintergarten ergänzt das Restaurant. Alle Weine auf der Karte werden auch offen ausgeschenkt.

Bergdiamant garni

Unterberggasse 349 ✉ 5542 – ✆ (06457) 3 35 46 – hotel@bergdiamant.at – Fax (06457) 3354614
25 Zim – ☼ 44/50 € 58/72 € ❄ 61/69 € 98/108 €

◆ Ein freundlich geführtes Hotel mit Gästezimmern in neuzeitlichem alpenländischem Stil und einem hellen Frühstücksraum mit Terrasse.

In Flachau-Flachauwinkl Süd: 6 km über Flachauwinklstraße:

Gasthof Wieseneck

Flachauwinklstr. 218 ✉ 5542 – ✆ (06457) 22 76 – info@wieseneck.at – Fax (06457) 2879
geschl. April – Mai, Okt. – Nov.
35 Zim (inkl. ½ P.) – ☼ 47/51 € 74/82 € ❄ 73/88 € 130/160 €
Rest – Karte 16/34 €

◆ Direkt an der Talstation der Kabinenbahn liegt dieses sehr gepflegte familiengeführte Haus mit seinen wohnlich ausgestatteten Gästezimmern. Ländlich gestaltetes Restaurant mit rustikaler Stube.

In Flachau-Reitdorf Nord: 2 km:

Felsenhof

Kreuzmoosstr. 88 ✉ 5542 – ✆ (06457) 22 51 – hotel@felsenhof.com – Fax (06457) 213462
geschl. 6. April – 31. Mai
61 Zim (inkl. ½ P.) – ☼ 54/72 € 108/130 € ❄ 82/99 € 164/198 €
Rest – (nur Abendessen für Hausgäste)

◆ Vor allem auf Familien ist das Hotel in ruhiger Ortsrandlage ausgerichtet. Die zeitgemäßen Zimmer sind teilweise Familienzimmer, Studios und Appartements.

FLATSCHACH - Steiermark - 730 Q7 - 180 Ew - Höhe 680 m 10 J5

Wien 196 - Graz 74 - Leoben 36 - Klagenfurt 47

Forellenhof Gursch

Flatschach 6 ✉ 8720 Knittelfeld - ✆ (03577) 2 20 10
- forellenhof.gursch@a1.net - Fax (03577) 22009
geschl. Montag - Mittwoch
Rest - Karte 13/30 €

◆ Ein Haus in der Ortsmitte beherbergt dieses bürgerliche Restaurant mit rustikal-schlichtem Ambiente und nettem, kompetentem Service durch den Chef.

Der Stern ✿ zeichnet Restaurants mit exzellenter Küche aus.
Er wird an Häuser vergeben, für die man gerne einen Umweg in Kauf nimmt!

FLATTACH IM MÖLLTAL - Kärnten - 730 L8 - 1 380 Ew - Höhe 820 m - Wintersport: 3 120 m 2 9 8 G6

Wien 371 - Klagenfurt 114 - Villach 79 - Lienz 40

Flattacher Hof

Flattach 13 ✉ 9831 - ✆ (04785) 81 00 - info@flattacherhof.at
- Fax (04785) 810040
40 Zim (inkl. ½ P.) - ☼ 80/93 € 136/156 € ❄ 90/130 €
150/200 € - 10 Suiten
Rest - (nur für Hausgäste)

◆ In dem freundlich geführten, gewachsenen Gasthof stehen recht großzügige, als Suiten, Juniorsuiten und Appartements angelegte Zimmer zur Verfügung. Schöner Freizeitbereich.

FOHNSDORF - Steiermark - 730 Q7 - 8 530 Ew - Höhe 800 m 10 I5

Wien 203 - Graz 81 - Knittelfeld 14 - Leoben 42

In Fohnsdorf-Hetzendorf Süd: 3,5 km Richtung Pöls und Judenburg:

Schloss Gabelhofen Rest, Rest,

Schlossgasse 54 ✉ 8753 - ✆ (03573) 5 55 50
- hotel-schloss@gabelhofen.at - Fax (03573) 55556
57 Zim - 89/145 € 158/198 € - ½ P 24 €
Rest - *(geschl. Sonntag)* Menü 38/59 € - Karte 27/41 €

◆ Der Charme des historischen Schlosses sowie wechselnde Kunstausstellungen machen dieses Hotel interessant. Einige Zimmer in den Türmen der Wehrmauer. Kommunikationszentrum. Alte Burgräume mit schönem Kreuzgewölbe beherbergen das Restaurant.

FONTANELLA - Vorarlberg - 730 B7 - 480 Ew - Höhe 1 200 m - Wintersport: 2 000 m 4 5 A5

Wien 600 - Bregenz 61 - Feldkirch 30 - Bludenz 20
Kirchberg 25, ✉ 6733, ✆ (05554) 51 50, info@walsertal.at

In Fontanella-Faschina Nord: 4 km – Höhe 1 492 m

Faschina ← Bergpanorama, (geheizt) Rest,
Faschina 55 ✉ 6733
– ✆ (05510) 2 24 – hotel@faschina.at – Fax (05510) 22426
geschl. 15. April – 15. Juni, 10. Okt. – 15. Dez.
40 Zim (inkl. ½ P.) – 68/78 € 136/144 € 88/100 € 168/188 €
Rest – Karte 13/37 €
◆ Die Lage an der Skipiste, solide möblierte, funktionelle Gästezimmer und ein mit viel Holz gemütlich gestalteter Saunabereich sprechen für dieses Alpenhotel. Rustikal gestaltetes Restaurant – der Speisesaal mit schöner Sicht.

FRANKING – Oberösterreich – 730 K4 – 850 Ew – Höhe 457 m 1 F3

Wien 306 – Linz 146 – Salzburg 36 – Burghausen 19
Nr. 26, ✉ 5131, ✆ (06277) 81 19, info.franking@netway.at

In Franking-Dorfibm Nord-Ost: 2,5 km

Landhotel Moorhof Zim, Rest,
Dorfibm 2 ✉ 5131 – ✆ (06277) 81 88
– moorhof@landhotels.at – Fax (06277) 818875
geschl. 15. – 28. Dez.
30 Zim – 56/68 € 90/110 € – ½ P 14 €
Rest – *(geschl. Sonntagabend – Montagmittag)* Karte 17/44 €
◆ Ruhig liegt der Familienbetrieb mit seinen zeitgemäßen, hell möblierten Zimmern in einem kleinen Ortsteil. Freizeitbereich mit Bierbad und Heubett sowie Panorama-Hallenbad.

FRASTANZ – Vorarlberg – 730 A7 – 6 220 Ew – Höhe 510 m 5 A6

Wien 627 – Bregenz 39 – Feldkirch 31 – Dornbirn 5

Gasthof Maria Grün mit Zim ← Zim, Zim,
Mariagrünerstr. 30 ✉ 6820 – ✆ (05522) 73 56 90
– office@mariagruen.at – Fax (05522) 735694
geschl. 28. Juli – 10. Aug., 22. Dez. – 14. Jan.
14 Zim – 50/55 € 80/86 €
Rest – *(geschl. Freitag – Samstag)* Karte 26/39 €
◆ Ruhig liegt das persönlich geführte Haus oberhalb des Dorfes – ein Restaurant in modernem, klarem Stil mit guter regionaler Küche. Reizvolle Terrasse im Sommer. Nett sind die neuzeitlich eingerichteten Gästezimmer.

FRAUENTAL – Steiermark – 730 R8 – 3 000 Ew – Höhe 324 m 10 K5

Wien 223 – Graz 37 – Maribor 66 – Leibnitz 35

Sorgerhof Zim,
Grazerstr. 260 ✉ 8523 – ✆ (03462) 32 79 – buero@sorgerhof.at
– Fax (03462) 5137
geschl. 23. Dez. – 7. Jan.
28 Zim – 41/47 € 72/79 € – ½ P 12 €
Rest – *(geschl. Sonn- und Feiertage abends)* Karte 19/30 €
◆ Der im Ortskern gelegene, vom Inhaber geführte Gasthof mit der gelben Fassade verfügt über behaglich und funktionell eingerichtete Zimmer, teils mit Balkon. Restaurant mit ländlichem Charakter.

FREISTADT – Oberösterreich – 730 P3 – 7 360 Ew – Höhe 560 m – Wintersport: 1 2 I2

Wien 198 – Linz 39 – Passau 116 – Zwettl 61

Hauptplatz 14, 4240, (07942) 7 57 00, kernland@oberoesterreich.at

St. Oswald-Freistadt, Am Golfplatz 1 (07945) 79 38

SternGartl Oberneukirchen, Schauerschlag 4 (07212) 2 13 33

Hauptplatz★ – Befestigungsanlagen★★ – Stadtpfarrkirche (Altarbild des Barockaltars★)

Mühlviertel★

Gasthof Deim – Zum Goldenen Hirschen

Böhmergasse 8 4240
– (07942) 72 25 80 – goldener.hirsch@hotels-freistadt.at
– Fax (07942) 7225840
geschl. 14. Jan – 28. Feb.

32 Zim – 45/55 € 75/88 € – ½ P 10 €

Rest – *(geschl. Nov. – März Sonntagabend)* Karte 13/28 €

◆ Gut unterhaltene, mit unterschiedlichen Naturholzmöbeln wohnlich eingerichtete Zimmer stehen in diesem Gasthof aus dem 13. Jh. zur Verfügung. Historische Gaststuben, teils mit schwerer Holzdecke, teils mit Kreuzgewölbe.

FROHNLEITEN – Steiermark – 730 R7 – 6 600 Ew – Höhe 438 m 10 J4

Wien 169 – Graz 28 – Leoben 39 – Bruck a. d. Mur 25

Murhof, Adriach 53 (03126) 30 10

Schloss Feistritz, Schlosspark (03126) 30 00 43

Peggau (Lurgrotte★) Süd: 8 km

Frohnleitnerhof

Hauptplatz 14a 8130 – (03126) 41 50 – info@frohnleitnerhof.at
– Fax (03126) 4150555

29 Zim – 59 € 96 € – ½ P 11 €

Rest – Karte 16/34 €

◆ Ein im Zentrum oberhalb der Mur gelegenes Hotel mit neuzeitlich ausgestatteten Gästezimmern – einige mit Blick auf den Fluss. Modern-elegantes Restaurant mit großer Fensterfront sowie rustikale Stube mit Braukesseln.

FÜGEN IM ZILLERTAL – Tirol – 730 H6 – 3 410 Ew – Höhe 550 m – Wintersport: 2 400 m 3 16 7 E5

Wien 418 – Innsbruck 46 – Schwaz 17 – Kufstein 47

Hauptstr. 1, 6263, (05288) 6 22 62, tvb.fuegen@aon.at

Schiestl

Zim, Rest,

Hochfügener Str. 29 6263 – (05288) 62 32 60
– info@hotel-schiestl.com – Fax (05288) 64118

93 Zim (inkl. ½ P.) – 75/78 € 132/138 € 84/94 € 150/170 €

Rest – Karte 15/33 €

◆ Die gewachsene Hotelanlage ist eine familienfreundliche Urlaubsadresse mit modernem Kinder- und Familienschwimmbad. Einige der Zimmer sind besonders komfortabel und geräumig. Das gemütliche Restaurant mit Zirbenstube bietet internationale und regionale Küche.

Held Zim,

Kapfing 95 (Süd: 1 km) ✉ 6263 – ✆ (05288) 6 23 86
– reservierung@held.at – Fax (05288) 623867
geschl. 14. April – 1. Mai, 1. Nov. – Ende Dez.
71 Zim (inkl. ½ P.) – ☼ 🚹101/109 € 🚹🚹142/176 € ❄ 🚹106/150 € 🚹🚹162/228 €
Rest – (nur Abendessen für Hausgäste)

♦ Eine große, gepflegte Gartenanlage mit Schwimmteich und Spielplatz gehört zu dem gewachsenen Alpenhotel mit Landhaus. Verschiedene Zimmervarianten. Moderner Freizeitbereich.

Haidachhof Zim, Rest,

Hochfügener Str. 280 ✉ 6263 – ✆ (05288) 6 23 80
– hotel@haidachhof.com – Fax (05288) 6338866
geschl. Mitte April – Mitte Mai, Mitte Okt. – Mitte Dez.
32 Zim (inkl. ½ P.) – ☼ 🚹91 € 🚹🚹126 € ❄ 🚹105/135 € 🚹🚹148/180 € – 7 Suiten
Rest – (nur für Hausgäste)

♦ Der mit Engagement geleitete Familienbetrieb bietet u. a. sehr schöne und wohnliche Landhaussuiten mit Panorama-Badewanne und Blick auf die Zillertaler Berge.

Crystal Rest, Rest,

Hochfügener Str. 305 ✉ 6263
– ✆ (05288) 6 24 25 – info@crystal-vital.at – Fax (05288) 62426
geschl. 12. April – 10. Mai, 31. Okt. – 10. Dez.
88 Zim (inkl. ½ P.) – ☼ 🚹83/131 € 🚹🚹144/240 € ❄ 🚹64/144 € 🚹🚹126/266 €
Rest – (nur für Hausgäste)

♦ Die Zimmer des familiengeführten Alpenhotels sind unterschiedlich in Zuschnitt und Einrichtung. Großzügiger Freizeitbereich mit Wellnessangeboten.

Bruno Rest,

Haidach 373 ✉ 6263 – ✆ (05288) 6 24 60 – info@hotelbruno.at
– Fax (05288) 63035
geschl. April, Nov.
50 Zim (inkl. ½ P.) – ☼ 🚹55/63 € 🚹🚹94/114 € ❄ 🚹57/99 € 🚹🚹114/184 €
Rest – (nur Abendessen für Hausgäste)

♦ Das recht ruhig oberhalb des Ortes gelegene Alpenhotel bietet sehr unterschiedlich geschnittene und möblierte Gästezimmer – auch Familienzimmer sind vorhanden.

Elisabeth Rest, Rest,

Hochfügener Str. 393 ✉ 6263 – ✆ (05288) 6 29 72
– info@elisabeth-fuegen.at – Fax (05288) 62972311
geschl. 10. April - 9. Mai, 25. Okt. – 12. Dez.
35 Zim (inkl. ½ P.) – ☼ 🚹53/60 € 🚹🚹86/100 € ❄ 🚹69/96 € 🚹🚹118/172 €
Rest – (nur Abendessen für Hausgäste)

♦ Das familiengeführte Ferienhotel nahe der Seilbahn verfügt über z. T. recht großzügige Gästezimmer. Zum Haus gehört eine Kinderskischule mit Lift.

Landhaus Zillertal
Pankrazbergstr. 420 ✉ 6263 – ✆ (05288) 6 21 50
– info@landhaus-zillertal.at – Fax (05288) 6215050
geschl. Nov.
30 Zim – ☼ 55 € 94 € ❄ 63/67 € 110/118 €
Rest – (nur Abendessen für Hausgäste)
◆ Zeitgemäße, mit hellem Naturholz eingerichtete Gästezimmer – einige auch für Familien geeignet – sowie ein netter Garten sprechen für dieses Haus.

Landgasthof Thomas
Pankrazbergstr. 529 ✉ 6263 – ✆ (05288) 6 37 40 – Fax (05288) 637405
geschl. April 2 Wochen, Nov. 2 Wochen und im Sommer Montag – Dienstag
Rest – Karte 16/34 €
◆ Familiär geführter gemütlicher Gasthof mit 2 ländlich-rustikalen, hübsch dekorierten Stuben. Man kocht bürgerlich mit regionalen Produkten – im Winter etwas einfachere Küche.

Sie suchen ein besonderes Hotel für einen sehr angenehmen Aufenthalt?
Reservieren Sie in einem roten Haus: ... .

FÜGENBERG IM ZILLERTAL – Tirol – 730 H6 – 1 170 Ew – Höhe 650 m
7 **E5**

Wien 121 – Innsbruck 48 – Schwaz 20 – Kufstein 49

In Hochfügen Süd-West: 15 km über Fügen – Höhe 1 500 m

Lamark
Zim,
Hochfügen 5 ✉ 6263 – ✆ (05280) 2 25 – info@lamark.at
– Fax (05280) 227
geschl. Mai – Nov.
51 Zim (inkl. ½ P.) – 120/145 € 200/270 €
Rest *Alexander* – separat erwähnt
Rest – (abends Tischbestellung ratsam) Karte 18/44 €
◆ Sehr freundlich kümmert man sich in dem engagiert geführten Haus um den Gast. Schön ist die Lage ganz in der Nähe der Skilifte. Man bietet u. a. großzügige Familienzimmer. Hübsches Restaurant mit Barbereich, am Abend teilweise mit Live-Pianomusik.

Almhof
Rest,
Hochfügen 10 ✉ 6263 – ✆ (05280) 2 11
– hotel—almhof@hochfuegen.com – Fax (05280) 2218
geschl. Mitte April – Mitte Juni, Ende Sept. – Anfang Dez.
22 Zim (inkl. ½ P.) – ☼ 54 € 94 € ❄ 87/115 € 154/210 €
Rest – Karte 16/32 €
◆ In dem schönen, teilweise holzverkleideten Gasthof mit bemaltem Erker stehen im regionstypischen Landhausstil eingerichtete Zimmer und Appartements zur Verfügung. Gepflegte, ländliche Gaststube und nette Weinstube.

XXX **Alexander** (Alexander Fankhauser) – Hotel Lamark 
Hochfügen 5 ✉ 6263 – ✆ (05280) 2 25 – info@lamark.at
– Fax (05280) 227
geschl. Mai – Nov. und Montag – Dienstag
Rest – *(nur Abendessen)* Menü 85 €
Spez. Hausgemachte Blutwurst und Flusskrebserl mit Kartoffelsoufflé. Knusprig gebratenes Bachforellenfilet mit Schweinsbackerl und Sauerkraut. Cannelloni vom Zillertaler Frischkäse mit sautiertem Kalbsbries und Alba-Trüffel (Saison).
◆ Eine alpenländisch-elegante Atmosphäre herrscht in diesem holzvertäfelten Restaurant mit angenehm aufmerksamem Service. Geboten wird kreative Küche auf klassischer Basis.

FÜRSTENFELD – Steiermark – 730 U7 – 5 990 Ew – Höhe 267 m 11 L5

Wien 158 – Graz 60 – Maribor 117 – Leibnitz 90
Haupstr. 2a, ✉ 8280, ✆ (03382) 55 47 00, infoffld@twin.at

X **Das Leitgeb** 
Ledergasse 13 ✉ 8280 – ✆ (03382) 5 30 39 – leitgeb@dasleitgeb.at
– Fax (03382) 54074
geschl. 7. – 21. Jan., Mittwoch und Sonntagabend
Rest – Menü 34/48 € – Karte 24/38 €
◆ Ein gepflegter Gasthof mit bürgerlich-rustikaler Einrichtung, in dem man Ihnen traditionelle Küche und ein Genießermenü serviert.

Rot steht für unsere besonderen Empfehlungen!

FULPMES – Tirol – 730 G7 – 3 900 Ew – Höhe 937 m – Wintersport: 2 260 m 1 7 6 D5

Wien 460 – Innsbruck 18 – Schwaz 43 – Neustift 6
Bahnstr. 17, ✉ 6166, ✆ (0) 5 01 88 12 00, info@stubai.at
Stubaital★★

Sporthotel Brugger 
Am Bichl 1 ✉ 6166 – ✆ (05225) 6 28 70
– info@sporthotel-brugger.at – Fax (05225) 628707
50 Zim (inkl. ½ P.) – 50/82 € 86/140 €
Rest – (nur für Hausgäste)
◆ Die ruhige Lage im Ort sowie mit hellem Holz wohnlich gestaltete Zimmer sprechen für das Haus mit der alpenländischen Balkonfassade. Familienzimmer.

Hubertus garni 
Medrazerstr. 10 ✉ 6166 – ✆ (05225) 6 22 94 – hotel@hubertus-fulpmes.at
– Fax (05225) 62741
geschl. 23. April – 17. Mai, 14. Okt. – 13. Dez.
23 Zim – 30/40 € 60/80 € 38/52 € 76/92 €
◆ Das Hotel befindet sich in einer Villa von 1911, die durch Anbauten erweitert wurde. Es erwarten Sie Zimmer von unterschiedlicher Größe mit zeitlos-gediegener Einrichtung.

Habicht Fulpmes und Bergpanorama, (geheizt)
Tschaffinis 2 6166 Zim, Rest, VISA
– (05225) 6 23 17 – k.hupfauf@tirol.com – Fax (05225) 62062
25 Zim (inkl. ½ P.) – 49/54 € 98/108 € 54/77 € 108/162 €
Rest – (nur für Hausgäste)
◆ Helles Schleiflackmobililar findet sich in den Zimmern dieses Hauses. Eine kleine Halle mit offenem Kamin lädt zum Verweilen ein. Mit eigener Skischule.

Gröbenhof mit Zim Bergpanorama, Zim,
Gröben 1 (Süd-West: 2 km, über Herrengasse und Gröbenweg) 6166 – (05225) 6 24 42 – groebenhof@tirol.com – Fax (05225) 6244214 VISA AE
geschl. 10. – 30. April, 10. – 30. Nov. und Mittwoch
8 Zim – 31/37 € 61/73 €
Rest – (Tischbestellung ratsam) Karte 16/36 €
◆ Oberhalb des Ortes liegt das Haus mit den freundlich-rustikalen Stuben. Die Sonnenterrasse bietet einen tollen Blick auf die Berge. Regionale Küche aus heimischen Produkten. Fast alle der wohnlichen Zimmer bieten eine schöne Aussicht.

In Fulpmes-Medraz **Süd-West: 1,5 km:**

Atzinger Rest,
Sonnegg 22 6166 – (05225) 6 31 35 VISA
– hotel@atzinger.at – Fax (05225) 63580134
geschl. 6. April – 31. Mai, 19. Okt. – 20. Dez.
32 Zim (inkl. ½ P.) – 67/80 € 114/140 € 79/110 € 138/200 € – 3 Suiten
Rest – (nur Abendessen für Hausgäste)
◆ Das persönlich geführte Alpenhotel bietet einen schönen Blick auf das gesamte Stubaital. Wohnliches Ambiente im ganzen Haus. Viele Kinderbetreuungsangebote.

Auenhof Rest, VISA
Auenweg 14 6166 – (05225) 6 27 63 – hotel@auenhof.at
– Fax (05225) 6225250
geschl. 1. April – 14. Juni, 18. Okt. – 21. Dez.
25 Zim (inkl. ½ P.) – 60/64 € 104/128 € 70/86 € 140/192 €
Rest – (nur Abendessen für Hausgäste)
◆ Ein rustikal-eleganter Freizeitbereich auf 2 Etagen, Spielplatz und Spielzimmer mit Kletterwand sowie ein schöner Garten zählen zu den Vorzügen des Hotels.

Medrazerhof VISA
Deniflestr. 7 6166 – (05225) 6 37 74 – medrazerhof@aon.at
– Fax (05225) 63450
geschl. Juni
36 Zim (inkl. ½ P.) – 49/56 € 80/92 € 57/82 € 94/144 €
Rest – *(nur Abendessen)* Karte 19/28 €
◆ Der familiengeführte, regionstypische Gasthof hält solide ausgestattete Gästezimmer – z. T. mit Balkon – bereit. Netter, heller Freizeitbereich im UG. Restaurant im alpenländisch-rustikalen Stil.

FUSCHL AM SEE - Salzburg - 730 L5 - 1 340 Ew - Höhe 669 m 8 G4

Wien 291 – Salzburg 25 – St. Gilgen 7 – Bad Ischl 30
Dorfplatz 1, 5330, (06226) 82 50, fuschl@fuschlseeregion.com

Ebner's Waldhof am See

Seestr. 30 Rest, VISA
5330 – (06226) 82 64 – info@ebners-waldhof.at
– Fax (06226) 8644
geschl. 30. März – 26. April, 2. Nov. – 13. Dez.
120 Zim (inkl. ½ P.) – 104/178 € 184/304 € – 20 Suiten
Rest *Gütlstuben* – *(geschl. Sonntagabend – Montag)* (Tischbestellung ratsam) Menü 31/65 € – Karte 24/47 €

◆ In idyllischer Umgebung und schön am See liegt das großzügige Ferienhotel mit Wellnessangebot auf fünf Etagen. Wohnliche Zimmer und teils aufwändig gestaltete Suiten. Elegant und regionstypisch: die Gütlstuben mit ebensolchem Angebot.

Sonnleitn Gartenhotel

Rest,
Seestr. 4 5330 – (06226) 84 05 VISA
– info@gartenhotel-sonnleitn.at – Fax (06226) 84058
geschl. 30. März – 26. April, 2. – 29. Nov.
22 Zim (inkl. ½ P.) – 88/110 € 130/190 €
Rest – (nur Abendessen für Hausgäste)

◆ Äußerst freundlich von der Familie geführt wird das alpenländische, wohnliche Hotel. Mit rustikalem Freizeitbereich, Naturschwimmteich und 150 m entferntem Badestrand.

Seerose

Zim, VISA AE
Dorfstr. 20 5330 – (06226) 82 16 – office@hotel-seerose.at
– Fax (06226) 821644
geschl. April 2 Wochen, Nov.
31 Zim – 62/79 € 104/192 € – ½ P 16 €
Rest – *(geschl. Montag, Dez. – April Montag – Dienstag)* Karte 24/37 €

◆ Sehr schön liegt das familiengeführte Haus direkt am See. Den Gast erwarten freundlich eingerichtete, wohnliche Zimmer. Vom Hallenbad aus blickt man auf den See.

Lindenhof garni

VISA
Oberdorfstr. 20 5330 – (06226) 82 63 – pension.lindenhof@gmx.at
– Fax (06226) 826322
geschl. Okt. – April
15 Zim – 27/35 € 50/64 €

◆ Nette, familiäre Pension mit funktionellen Zimmern, die teils über einen Balkon verfügen. Gutes Preis-Leistungs-Verhältniss !

Brunnwirt

VISA AE
Wolfgangseestr. 11 5330 – (06226) 82 36 – office@brunnwirt.at
– Fax (06226) 823613
geschl. 1. – 15. Sept., 23. Dez. – 7. Jan. und Sonntag – Montag
Rest – (Tischbestellung erforderlich) (nur Abendessen) Menü 49 € – Karte 31/44 €

◆ Außerhalb gelegener Landgasthof mit rustikalen Gaststuben. Das regionale Angebot ist international beeinflusst. Bezaubernde Terrasse zum See hin.

Im Ellmautal **Süd-Ost: 4 km über Ellmaustraße Richtung Mozartblick:**

Landgasthaus Hochlackenhof

Ellmaustr. 80 (geheizt) Zim, Zim,
5330 Fuschl am See – (06226) 83 30 – info@hochlackenhof.at
– Fax (06226) 83306
geschl. Mitte Jan. – Ende April, Mitte Okt. – Anfang Dez.
16 Zim – 44/53 € 69/83 €
Rest – *(geschl. Dienstag)* Karte 18/32 €

♦ Traditioneller, freundlich-familiär geführter Gasthof in ruhiger Lage. Man wohnt in rustikalen Zimmern und kann Liegewiese und Freibad nutzen. Spielplatz für die Kinder. Ländliches Ambiente in den Gaststuben.

GALLIZIEN – Kärnten – 730 P9 – 1 830 Ew – Höhe 460 m 10 I6

Wien 310 – Klagenfurt 23 – Villach 63 – Völkermarkt 18

Albert's Schlemmerstube

Gallizien 32 9132 – (04221) 21 84 – Fax (04221) 2184
geschl. Montag – Dienstag, Juni – Okt. Montag
Rest – Karte 13/33 €

♦ Ein Landgasthof mit leicht unterteilten Restauranträumen und bürgerlicher Einrichtung. Freundlicher Service durch die Chefin und bürgerliches Speisenangebot.

GALTÜR – Tirol – 730 C8 – 780 Ew – Höhe 1 600 m – Wintersport: 2 297 m 1 10 – Lufkurort 5 B6

Wien 555 – Innsbruck 112 – Landeck 40 – Ischgl 10
Gemeindehaus Nr. 39, 6563, (05443) 85 21, info@galtuer.com

Veranstaltungen
31.08.: Silvretta-Ferwall-Marsch/Marathon
27.09.: Almkäseolympiade

Silvretta-Hochalpenstraße★★ – Bielerhöhe (Silvretta-Stausee★, Aufstieg zum Hohen Rad★★★) Süd-West: 9 km

Rössle

Am Dorfplatz 47 6563 – (05443) 8 23 20 – info@roessle.com
– Fax (05443) 84605
geschl. Mitte April – Anfang Juni, Okt. – Anfang Dez.
34 Zim (inkl. ½ P.) – 71/83 € 130/147 € 96/182 € 166/340 € – 5 Suiten
Rest – Karte 22/39 €

♦ Ein traditionsreicher Familienbetrieb im Zentrum mit behaglicher Lobby und soliden Zimmern in rustikalem Stil. Besonders wohnlich: die geräumigen Suiten und Juniorsuiten. Teil des Restaurants ist eine 400 Jahre alte komplett holzgetäfelte Stube mit Ofen.

Luggi

Zim,
Galtür 23e 6563 – (05443) 83 86 – luggi@galtuer.at
– Fax (05443) 83864
geschl. Mai, Okt. – Nov.
25 Zim (inkl. ½ P.) – 39/46 € 74/92 € 75/90 € 150/179 €
Rest – (nur Abendessen für Hausgäste, im Sommer Garni)

♦ Am Zentrumsrand liegt das familiengeführte Alpenhotel mit seinen neuzeitlich-wohnlich eingerichteten Zimmern. Originell: die in Pyramiden-Form gebaute Bar neben dem Haus.

Gampeler Hof Zim,
Galtür 66a ✉ 6563 – ✆ (05443) 83 07 – gampelerhof@galtuer.at
– Fax (05443) 830720
geschl. 2. – 26. Mai
18 Zim (inkl. ½ P.) – ☼ 40 € 66/75 € ❄ 54/75 € 88/130 €
Rest – (nur Abendessen für Hausgäste)
♦ Eine gepflegte Fassade und ein neuzeitlich-ländlicher Eingangsbereich empfangen Sie in dem Hotel im Zentrum. Mit soliden dunklen Holzmöbeln ausgestattete Zimmer.

Marangun Rest,
Galtür 39b ✉ 6563 – ✆ (05443) 82 77 – marangun@galtuer.at
– Fax (05443) 82777
geschl. Mai, Nov.
16 Zim (inkl. ½ P.) – ☼ 56 € 84/92 € ❄ 72/84 € 130/168 €
Rest – (nur Abendessen für Hausgäste)
♦ Ein familiengeführtes kleines Hotel am Zentrumsrand, in dem wohnliche, z. T. neuzeitlich möblierte Gästezimmer zur Verfügung stehen.

In Galtür-Wirl West: 2 km:

Wirlerhof Zim, VISA
Wirl 8a ✉ 6563 – ✆ (05443) 82 31
– wirlerhof@huber-hotels.at – Fax (05443) 823159
geschl. 13. April – 24. Mai, 11. Okt. – 7. Dez.
79 Zim (inkl. ½ P.) – ☼ 70/79 € 124/144 € ❄ 105/166 € 184/304 € – 8 Suiten
Rest *Stuba* – Karte 26/43 €
♦ Nahe dem Skilift befindet sich das Haus der Familie Huber. Ein Teil der Zimmer ist besonders hübsch in neuzeitlich-rustikalem Stil eingerichtet. Halle mit Bar und Kamin. Behaglich ist das Ambiente in dem ganz in Holz gehaltenen Restaurant.

Almhof Paznauntal und Bergpanorama, Rest, Zim, VISA
Wirl 4 ✉ 6563
– ✆ (05443) 82 53 – almhof@huber-hotels.at – Fax (05443) 844371
geschl. 13. April – Mai, 11. Okt. – 7. Dez.
80 Zim (inkl. ½ P.) – ☼ 58/60 € 104/110 € ❄ 99/152 € 182/288 €
Rest *Zirbenstube* – *(geschl. 13. April – 7. Dez.)* Karte 21/49 €
♦ Schön liegt das Alpenhotel etwas oberhalb des kleinen Ortes. Die ländlich eingerichteten Gästezimmer verfügen meist über einen Balkon. Hübsch: die holzvertäfelte Zirbenstube mit Ofen. Terrasse direkt an der Piste.

Gasthof Alpkogel Rest, VISA
Silvrettastr. 8b ✉ 6563 – ✆ (05443) 82 81 – alpkogel@tirol.com
– Fax (05443) 8518
geschl. Mai – Juni, Okt. – Nov.
19 Zim (inkl. ½ P.) – ☼ 22/29 € 50/54 € ❄ 67/78 € 122/144 €
Rest – *(geschl. Mai – Nov., im Sommer Garni)* Karte 14/24 €
♦ Familiäre Atmosphäre und bürgerlich-rustikaler Charakter machen diesen kleinen Gasthof unweit der Liftanlagen aus. Gepflegte, dunkel möblierte Zimmer. Regionstypisch gestaltetes Restaurant.

Wien 236 - Graz 51 - Maribor 28 - Leibnitz 13

Marktplatz 41, ✉ 8462, ✆ (03453) 39 22, gamlitz.tourismus @aon.at

Sattlerhof (mit Landhaus) Zim, P
Sernau 2a (Süd-West: 2 km, Richtung Leutschach über B 69, Ortsende links ab Richtung Steinbach)
✉ 8462 – ✆ (03453) 4 45 40 – restaurant@sattlerhof.at
– Fax (03453) 445444
geschl. Mitte Dez. – Mitte März
15 Zim – 100/128 € 124/166 €
Rest – *(geschl. Sonntag – Montag, nur Abendessen)* Menü 44/63 € – Karte 39/46 €
Rest *Wirtshaus* – *(geschl. Montag – Dienstag, nur Mittagessen)* Karte 19/23 €
◆ Haupthaus und Landhaus dieses an ein abseits gelegenes Weingut angeschlossenen kleinen Hotels beherbergen freundliche Zimmer in warmen Tönen. Das Restaurant: teils im Landhausstil, teils als Wintergarten mit versenkbaren Fenstern. Wirtshaus mit offener Küche.

Weinlandhof
Untere Hauptstr. 15 ✉ 8462 – ✆ (03453) 25 84
– weinlandhof-wratschko@aon.at
– Fax (03453) 271510
58 Zim – 53/70 € 88/104 € – ½ P 14 €
Rest – *(geschl. Ende Nov. – Mitte März)* Karte 15/28 €
◆ Neuzeitliche, wohnliche Zimmer, teils zum Garten hin gelegen, ein hell gestalteter Freizeitbereich sowie ein umfangreiches Frühstücksbuffet erwarten Sie in diesem Hotel. Elegant-rustikal wirkender Restaurantbereich.

Am Marktplatz
Marktplatz 9 ✉ 8462 – ✆ (03453) 26 47 – office@wratschko.at
– Fax (03453) 26474
14 Zim – 57/70 € 84/110 € – ½ P 12 €
Rest – *(geschl. Dez. – Juni Mittwoch)* Karte 14/29 €
◆ In dem von der Familie geleiteten Landgasthof stehen dem Besucher funktionelle Zimmer, teils auch mit Balkon, zur Verfügung. Zum Haus gehört ein Weingut. Restaurant in bürgerlich-rustikalem Stil.

Weingut Söll garni Weinberge, P
Steinbach 63a (Süd-West: 3,5 km, Richtung Leutschach über B 69, am Ortsende links ab Richtung Sernau) ✉ 8462
– ✆ (03454) 66 67 – familie@weingut-soell.at
– Fax (03454) 666777
geschl. Mitte Dez. – Ende März
5 Zim – 47/57 € 74/94 €
◆ In dem kleinen Gästehaus dieses traumhaft gelegenen Weinguts hat man moderne, wohnliche Zimmer eingerichtet, teils mit Terrasse oder großen Dachfenstern. Gute Weine.

Jaglhof mit Zim — Steirisches Weinland, Rest, P
Sernau 25 (Süd-West: 4 km, Richtung Leutschach über B 69, am Ortsende links ab) ✉ *8462 –* ✆ *(03454) 66 75 – jaglhof@anderlage.at – Fax (03454) 667512*
geschl. Jan. – Feb.
7 Zim – 130 € 160 €
Rest – *(geschl. Dienstag – Mittwoch, Sonntagabend, Sept. – Okt. nur Sonntagabend)* Menü 54/69 € – Karte 30/50 €
◆ Traumhaft ist die Lage des Hauses in den Weinbergen, phantastisch die Aussicht. Zu dem Restaurant im eleganten Landhausstil gehört eine Vinothek mit Weinen aus der Region. Wohnliche Gästezimmer mit Balkon.

Buschenschänken – (nur kalte Speisen – Jausen):

Erikas mit Zim — Weinberge, P
Kranach 3 (West: 3 km, über B 69 Richtung Leutschach, nach 2 km rechts ab) ✉ *8462 –* ✆ *(03453) 55 65 – erikas.buschenschank@1044.net – Fax (03453) 5565*
gesch. Mitte Dez. – Mitte Feb.
5 Zim – 38/50 € 60/84 €
Rest – *(geschl. Montag – Mittwoch)* (Tischbestellung ratsam) Karte ca. 14 €
◆ Das einstige Weinpresshaus a. d. 19. Jh. beherbergt heute die urig-gemütlichen Stuben des Buschenschanks. Typisches Jausenangebot. Schöne Terrasse mit Sicht. Mit Balkonen versehene, wohnliche Gästezimmer.

Bacchuskeller Weingut Lambauer mit Zim — P
Eckberg 37 (Süd: 4 km, Richtung Sulztal an der Weinstraße) ✉ *8462 –* ✆ *(03453) 25 70 – eva.lambauer@bacchuskeller.at – Fax (03453) 257070*
geschl. Dez. – Feb.
13 Zim – 62 € 100 €
Rest – *(geschl. Montag)* Karte ca. 14 €
◆ Weingut unter familiärer Leitung mit gemütlichem Buschenschank: Dielenboden und Antiquitäten prägen das Ambiente für den Genuss von Wein und Jausen. Wohnliche, helle Zimmer.

Brolli-Arkadenhof — Weinberge, P
Eckberg 43 (Süd: 4,5 km, Richtung Sulztal an der Weinstraße) ✉ *8462 –* ✆ *(03453) 23 41 – weingut@brolli.at – Fax (03453) 23414*
geschl. Mitte Nov. – Mitte März und Montag
Rest – Karte ca. 12 €
◆ In der rustikalen, mit modernen Bildern dekorierten Buschenschänke bietet man neben den eigenen Weinen auch kalte Gerichte. Sehr schön: der Gastgarten mit altem Baumbestand.

Weingut Hack-Gebell mit Zim — Weinberge, Zim, P
Eckberg 100 (Süd: 6 km, Richtung Sulztal an der Weinstr.) ✉ *8462 –* ✆ *(03454) 3 03 – office@weingut-hack.at – Fax (03454) 303*
geschl. Dez. – Feb.
10 Zim – 30/45 € 44/84 €
Rest – *(Dienstag – Sonntag ab 13 Uhr und Montag ab 18 Uhr geöffnet)* Karte ca. 12 €
◆ Sympathischer Buschenschank mit sehr gemütlichem, urigem Ambiente und typischem Jausenangebot. Besonders komfortabel sind die Zimmer im Haupthaus. Auch Familienzimmer gibt es.

GARGELLEN – Vorarlberg – 730 B8 – 2 270 Ew – Höhe 1 423 m – Wintersport: 2 300 m 1 7 – Höhenluftkurort 5 **A6**

Wien 667 – Bregenz 79 – Feldkirch 48 – Schruns 16
Haus Valisera Nr. 28a, 6787, (05557) 63 03, info@gargellen.at

Alpenhotel Heimspitze (mit Gästehaus)
Haus 53 6787 – (05557) 63 19
– hotel@heimspitze.com – Fax (05557) 631920
geschl. Ende April – Ende Juni, Anfang Okt. – Anfang Dez.
23 Zim (inkl. ½ P.) – 74/85 € 136/204 € 91/106 €
172/250 € – 4 Suiten
Rest ***Montafoner Stöbli*** – separat erwähnt
♦ Eine heimelige Atmosphäre herrscht in diesem engagiert und aufmerksam geführten Haus. Zentral und doch recht ruhig ist die Lage. Im Gästehaus befinden sich moderne Suiten.

Alpenrose
Zim, Rest, VISA
Haus 74 6787 – (05557) 63 14 – office@alpenrose-gargellen.at
– Fax (05557) 63146
gescl. 14. April – 19. Juni, 13. Okt. – 19. Dez.
18 Zim (inkl. ½ P.) – 73/77 € 126/134 € 96/113 €
168/202 €
Rest – (nur Abendessen für Hausgäste)
♦ Schön ist die Lage dieses Hauses auf einer Anhöhe oberhalb des Ortes. Die wohnlichen Zimmer bieten teilweise Aussicht auf Gargellen und die Berge. Das Restaurant teilt sich in sehr nette kleine Stuben.

Landhaus Mateera
Rest, VISA
Haus Nr. 78 6787 – (05557) 6 38 70 – info@mateera.at
– Fax (05557) 63875
geschl. 15. April – 20. Juni, 30. Sept. – 1. Dez.
20 Zim (inkl. ½ P.) – 59/67 € 102/116 € 83/101 €
152/186 €
Rest – (nur Abendessen für Hausgäste)
♦ Ein alpenländisches kleines Hotel mit behaglichen Zimmern in ländlichem Stil. Im Sommer stehen eigene Pferde zum Reiten zur Verfügung.

Montafoner Stöbli – Alpenhotel Heimspitze
VISA
Haus 53 6787 – (05557) 63 19
– hotel@heimspitze.com – Fax (05557) 631920
geschl. Ende April – Ende Juni, Anfang Okt. – Anfang Dez. und Montag
Rest – *(ab 14 Uhr geöffnet)* (Tischbestellung erforderlich) Menü 32/39 €
– Karte 29/50 €
♦ Ein Schmuckstück ist diese über 200 Jahre alte Montafoner Stube mit schöner Holztäfelung, Kachelofen und Zierrat. Der Service ist kompetent, die Küche klassisch und regional.

GARS AM KAMP – Niederösterreich – 730 T3 – 3 540 Ew – Höhe 256 m 3 **K2**

Wien 82 – St. Pölten 54 – Krems 31 – Altenburg 10
Hauptplatz 83, 3571, (02985) 26 80, info@gars.at
Schloss Rosenburg★ (Nord: 5 km) – Stift Altenburg★★ (Nord-West: 10 km) – Schloss Greillenstein★ (Nord-West: 16 km)

Dungl Bio-Vital Hotel
Zim,

Hauptplatz 58 ✉ 3571
– ✆ (02985) 2 66 60 – bio-vitalhotel@willidungl.info
– Fax (02985) 2666745
102 Zim – 105/110 € 159/163 € – ½ P 22 €
7 Suiten
Rest – Karte 22/34 €
◆ Zu diesem komfortablen Hotel gehört ein großzügiger Freizeit- und Therapiebereich. Die wohnlichen Zimmer bieten teils Balkon und Burgblick. Sehr geschmackvoll: die Suiten. Gepflegte Gaststube in bürgerlichem Stil.

Dungl Aktiv – Vital Hotel garni

Kremser Str. 656 ✉ 3571
– ✆ (02985) 2 66 68 00 – aktiv-vitalhotel@willidungl.info
– Fax (02985) 2666805
49 Zim – 79/91 € 132/146 €
◆ Neuzeitlich und funktionell sind die mit Vollholzmöblen eingerichteten Zimmer und Juniorsuiten dieses nahe dem Kurpark gelegenen Hotels.

GASCHURN – Vorarlberg – 730 C8 – 1 660 Ew – Höhe 1 000 m – Wintersport: 2 300 m 4 24 5 B6

Wien 580 – Bregenz 79 – Sankt Anton 68 – Feldkirch 48

Haus des Gastes, Dorfstr. 2, ✉ 6793, ✆ (05558) 8 20 10, info@gaschurn-partenen.com

Versettla-Kabinenbahn★

Sporthotel Silvretta Nova
Rest,

Dorfstr. 11b ✉ 6793
– ✆ (05558) 88 88 – sporthotel@silvrettanova.at
– Fax (05558) 8267
geschl. 7. April – 22. Mai, 13. Okt. – 5. Dez.
61 Zim (inkl. ½ P.) – 85/112 € 141/173 € 111/226 € 194/346 € – 6 Suiten
Rest *Fässle* – *(im Winter Dienstag)* Menü 29/40 € – Karte 23/35 €
◆ In der Hotelhalle wie auch in den Gästezimmern erwartet Sie ein gediegen-elegantes Ambiente. Großer, ansprechender Freizeitbereich mit Natursteinkuppel. Blickfang in dem gemütlich-rustikalen Restaurant Fässle ist das markante Weinfass. Internationale Küche.

Pfeifer
(beheizt) Rest,

Haus 186c ✉ 6793 – ✆ (05558) 86 20 – ydomig@domig.vol.at
– Fax (05558) 8808
geschl. Mitte April – Mitte Juni
21 Zim (inkl. ½ P.) – 80/86 € 123/141 € 146/197 € 224/317 € – 8 Suiten
Rest – (nur Abendessen für Hausgäste)
◆ Sehr gemütlich ist die Atmosphäre in diesem Haus, angenehm die Betreuung durch Familie Domig. Mit Geschmack hat man den Hallenbereich und die individuellen Zimmer gestaltet. Im Restaurant bietet man eine hochwertige Halbpension.

Posthotel Rössle (geheizt) VISA

Dorfstr. 4 ✉ 6793 – ✆ (05558) 8 33 30
– info@posthotel-roessle.at – Fax (05558) 833350
geschl. 30. März - Mai, 15. Okt. – 15. Dez.
59 Zim (inkl. ½ P.) – 65/90 € 114/184 € 106/288 € 180/350 € – 10 Suiten
Rest – (nur Abendessen) Karte 19/33 €
◆ Ein geschichtsträchtiges Haus, in dem schon Hemingway zu Gast war. Stammhaus und Anbau dieses traditionsreichen Familienbetriebs unterscheiden sich etwas in der Einrichtung. Rustikales Restaurant und kleine alpenländische Stube.

Verwall Rest, VISA

Haus 129 (B 188) ✉ 6793 – ✆ (05558) 82 06 – info@verwall.com
– Fax (05558) 820670
geschl. 6. April – 10. Mai, 28. Sept. – 15. Dez.
46 Zim (inkl. ½ P.) – 73/78 € 118/142 € 101/150 € 170/272 € – 3 Suiten
Rest – (nur Abendessen für Hausgäste)
◆ Das gewachsene Ferienhotel am Ortseingang verfügt über neuzeitliche, individuell möblierte Gästezimmer. Im Freizeitbereich bietet man auch Kosmetik.

Lucas Rest, VISA

Haus 19 ✉ 6793 – ✆ (05558) 82 36 – info@hotel-lucas.at
– Fax (05558) 82365
geschl. 7. April – 15. Juni, 5. Okt. – 15. Dez.
27 Zim (inkl. ½ P.) – 97/125 € 116/160 € 160/215 € 222/296 €
Rest – *(nur Abendessen)* (Tischbestellung ratsam) Menü 40/80 €
◆ Wohnlich ist das Ambiente in dem von der Inhaberfamilie geleiteten Hotel im Ortszentrum. Ein Teil der Gästezimmer ist in ganz modernem Stil gehalten. Nett ist das neuzeitliche kleine A-la-carte-Restaurant.

Tschanun Zim,

Innere Gosta 16 B ✉ 6793 – ✆ (05558) 86 62
– aparthotel.tschanun@aon.at – Fax (05558) 86624
geschl. Ende April – Anfang Juni, Mitte Okt. – Mitte Dez.
17 Zim – 45/60 € 82/120 € 75/94 € 136/216 € – ½ P 18/35 €
Rest – (nur Abendessen für Hausgäste)
◆ Oberhalb des Ortes liegt dieses Hotel im alpenländischen Stil. Alle Zimmer mit Balkon und kleiner Sitzgelegenheit. Terrasse mit schönem Panoramablick.

Versettla Gaschurn und Bergpanorama, VISA

Haus 112a (West 2 km, ab der Versettla-Bahnstation) ✉ 6793 – ✆ (05558) 82 33 – versettla@aon.at
– Fax (05558) 82338
geschl. Mitte April – Anfang Juni, Mitte Okt. – Mitte Dez.
12 Zim (inkl. ½ P.) – 46/53 € 92/106 € 84/92 € 168/184 €
Rest – *(geschl. im Sommer Dienstag)* Karte 20/36 €
◆ Hier beginnt der Skispaß gleich vor der Tür: oberhalb des Ortes gelegenes kleines Hotel mit gepflegten Zimmern und Appartements. Auch im Sommer viele Freizeitaktivitäten.

GASPOLTSHOFEN – Oberösterreich – 730 N4 – 3 600 Ew – Höhe 455 m

Wien 218 – Linz 58 – Salzburg 92 – Wels 26 2 **H3**

Gasthof Klinger mit Zim

Jeding 1 4673 – (07735) 69 13 – gasthof.klinger@fnet.cc – Fax (07735) 7193 – geschl. Montagabend – Dienstag

4 Zim – 38/42 € 65/69 €

Rest – Karte 17/27 €

◆ Zu diesem soliden historischen Gasthof a. d. 16. Jh. gehören ein schöner Gastgarten unter zwei Kastanienbäumen und eine nette Weinlaube mit Kamin.

GASTEIN, BAD – Salzburg – 730 L7 – 5 840 Ew – Höhe 1 000 m – Wintersport: 2 686 m 7 20 8 **G5**

Wien 392 – Salzburg 96 – Spittal an der Drau 44 – Lienz 58

Kaiser Franz Josef-Str. 27, 5640, (06432) 3 39 35 60, info@badgastein.at

Gastein, Golfstr. 6 (06434) 27 75

Lage★ – Unterer Wasserfall der Gasteiner Ache★ – Kaiser-Wilhelm-Promenade★ (★)

Stubnerkogel★★ mit – Kreuzkogel★★★ mit (Süd: 6 km) – Zitterauer Tisch und Bockhartsee★★★ (Tageswanderung ab Stubnerkogel)

Europäischer Hof

(Thermal) Rest,

Miesbichlstr. 20 (Nord-Ost: 5 km über B 167 in Kötschachdorf) 5640 – (06434) 2 52 60 – reservierung@europaeischerhof.at – Fax (06434) 2526262

111 Zim – 88/104 € 154/194 € 120/220 € 172/294 € – ½ P 24 €

Rest – Karte 22/43 €

◆ Nur wenige Schritte vom Golfplatz entfernt liegt das komfortable Hotel mit großzügiger Halle sowie wohnlichen Zimmern und kleinen Suiten. Greenfee-Ermäßigung. Kosmetik. Gediegen-rustikales Restaurant. Gasteiner Klause am Wochenende und für Veranstaltungen.

Wildbad

Gasteinertal, Rest,

Karl-Heinrich-Waggerlstr. 20 5640 – (06434) 37 61 – info@hotel-wildbad.com – Fax (06434) 376170 geschl. 19. April – Mitte Mai, 30. Sept. – Mitte Dez.

37 Zim (inkl. ½ P.) – 63/85 € 126/170 € 78/128 € 156/256 €

Rest – (nur Abendessen für Hausgäste)

◆ Das zentral am Hang gelegene Hotel unter Leitung der Familie bietet klassisch eingerichtete Zimmer mit Balkon, eine schöne Saunalandschaft sowie ein gutes Frühstücksbuffet.

Cordial Sanotel (mit Gästehaus)

Conrad-Strochner Str. 2 5640 – (06434) 2 50 10 – chbadgastein@cordial.at – Fax (06434) 250177 geschl. 20. April – 6. Juni, 2. Nov. – 5. Dez.

73 Zim – 60/90 € 90/224 € 63/105 € 96/180 € – ½ P 22 € – 28 Suiten

Rest – *(nur Abendessen)* Karte 25/41 €

◆ Dieses Hotel bietet von einem Teil seiner Zimmer sowie vom Ruhebereich aus eine schöne Sicht auf den nahe gelegenen Gasteiner Wasserfall. Einige der Suiten mit Küchenzeile. Helles Restaurant mit großer Fensterfront zum Wasserfall.

Lutter & Wegner mit Zim — Zim,
Kaiser-Franz-Josef-Str. 16 ✉ 5640 – ✆ (06434) 51 01
– info@villasolitude.com – Fax (06434) 51012
geschl. Nov
9 Zim (inkl. ½ P.) – 75/125 € 150/250 €
Rest – Karte 27/41 €
◆ Ein gemütliches Restaurant mit hübschem Gewölbe in der Villa Solitude von 1838 – erste österreichische Dependance des Berliner Weinhauses. Terrassen mit Blick auf Bad Gastein. In den Gästezimmern vermitteln alte Holztäfelungen und Böden historischen Charme.

Im Kötschachtal Nord-Ost: 4,5 km:

Grüner Baum (mit Gästehäusern) (geheizt)
(Thermal) Zim,
Kötschachtal 25 ✉ 5640 – ✆ (06434) 2 51 60 – urlaub@hoteldorf.com
– Fax (06434) 251625
geschl. 30. März – 1. Mai, 2. – 5. Nov.
80 Zim (inkl. ½ P.) – 107/148 € 214/296 € 112/183 €
224/366 € – 7 Suiten
Rest – Karte 23/41 €
◆ Malerisch am Nationalpark Hohe Tauern liegt das Hoteldorf, das den Gast mit originellen und hübschen Zimmern und vielen Freizeitmöglichkeiten erwartet. Abends ergänzt die mit Originalstichen dekorierte Ridinger Stube den A-la-carte-Wintergarten.

GATSCHACH – Kärnten – siehe Weissensee

GERLOS – Tirol – 730 I7 – 820 Ew – Höhe 1 300 m – Wintersport: 2 300 m
3 45 7 **E5**

Wien 448 – Innsbruck 75 – Schwaz 47 – Zell am Ziller 16
Gerlos 141, ✉ 6281, ✆ (05284) 5 24 40, info@gerlos.at

Gaspingerhof (geheizt)
Gerlos 153 ✉ 6281 Zim, Rest,
– ✆ (05284) 5 21 60 – info@gaspingerhof.at – Fax (05284) 533549
geschl. 14. April – 21. Juni, 20. Okt. – 15. Dez.
79 Zim (inkl. ½ P.) – 79/96 € 158/178 € 102/156 €
204/300 €
Rest – Karte 14/36 €
◆ Das Alpenhotel im Tiroler Stil mit teils holzverkleideter Fassade verfügt über meist recht geräumige Zimmer sowie einen großzügigen Wellnessbereich. Ländlich-rustikales Restaurant mit regionaler und internationaler Küche.

Schönruh
Gerlos 285 ✉ 6281 – ✆ (05284) 53 68 – info@schoenruh.com
– Fax (05284) 55377
geschl. 6. April – 15. Juni, 20. Okt. – 6. Dez.
22 Zim (inkl. ½ P.) – 65/85 € 150/170 € 90/135 €
180/260 € – 3 Suiten
Rest – (nur für Hausgäste)
◆ In der freundlichen, familiären Atmosphäre des Hotels mit hübschen Zimmern fühlt man sich als Gast wohl. Entspannen kann man auch im Freizeitbereich. Hausgästen bietet man aufwändige Halbpension-Menüs.

Alpenhof Rest, VISA AE
Gerlos 125 ✉ 6281 – ✆ (05284) 53 74
– hotel@alpenhof-gerlos.at – Fax (05284) 537455
geschl. 10. April – 20. Juni, 30. Okt. – 10. Dez.
70 Zim (inkl. ½ P.) – ☼ 54/60 € 101/115 € ❄ 83/120 € 150/200 € – 8 Suiten
Rest – (nur Abendessen für Hausgäste)
◆ Das familiengeführte Alpenhotel liegt am Ortseingang und bietet solide und funktionell ausgestattete Gästezimmer, die im Anbau etwas großzügiger ausfallen.

Sportalm Rest, VISA AE
Gerlos 169 ✉ 6281 – ✆ (05284) 52 42 – info@sportalm-gerlos.at
– Fax (05284) 5555
geschl. 20. April – 15. Mai, Nov.
23 Zim (inkl. ½ P.) – ☼ 38/45 € 76/90 € ❄ 70/95 € 140/190 €
Rest – Karte 17/41 €
◆ Die Zimmer dieses Hotels im Zentrum sind rustikal-elegant möbliert und technisch modern ausgestattet. Schön: die großen Balkone/Terrassen sowie der Saunabereich auf dem Dach. Rustikales Restaurant mit Wintergarten und bürgerlichem Angebot.

Edelweiss Zim, Rest, VISA
Gerlos 135 ✉ 6281 – ✆ (05284) 52 08 – hotelgerlos@aon.at
– Fax (05284) 5509
geschl. 15. April – 15. Juni, 15. Sept. – 5. Dez.
52 Zim – ☼ 55 € 72 € ❄ 70/110 € 110/148 € – ½ P 38 €
Rest – *(nur Abendessen)* Menü 45 € – Karte 23/38 €
◆ Teils im Landhausstil, teils ganz modern sind die Zimmer in diesem Alpenhotel gestaltet – auch allergikerfreundliche Zimmer sind vorhanden. Kleine Bar im Brasserie-Stil.

Innertalerhof Rest,
Innertal 320 ✉ 6281 – ✆ (05284) 52 97 – innertalerhof@.utanet.at
– Fax (05284) 529730
geschl. 25. März – 2. April, Anfang Okt. – Anfang Dez.
33 Zim (inkl. ½ P.) – ☼ 50/63 € 70/96 € ❄ 75/95 € 152/184 €
Rest – Karte 17/38 €
◆ Ruhig liegt das familiengeführte Haus am Ortsrand. Die Zimmer sind mit hellen massiven Holzmöbeln wohnlich eingerichtet, meist mit Ahorn-Parkettböden. Rustikales Restaurant mit bürgerlicher Karte – für Wanderer: kleines Angebot am Mittag. Nette Sonnenterrasse.

Vitalhotel Glockenstuhl Rest,
Oberhof 250 ✉ 6281 – ✆ (05284) 52 17
– gerlos@glockenstuhl.at – Fax (05284) 544226
geschl. April – 28. Juni, 4. Okt. – Mitte Dez.
27 Zim (inkl. ½ P.) – ☼ 60/69 € 108/133 € ❄ 75/109 € 136/232 €
Rest – Karte 17/34 €
◆ Aus einem Bauernhof von 1680 ist ein zeitgemäßes, familiär geleitetes Hotel entstanden. Die Zimmer sind mit hellem Naturholz wohnlich gestaltet. Netter Freizeitbereich. Ländlich-rustikales Restaurant, ein Teil mit historischer Holzdecke.

Kristall Rest,

Gerlos 124 6281 – (05284) 52 48 – info@hotel-kristall.com – Fax (05284) 524850

geschl. 5. April – 30. Mai, 4. Okt. – 15. Dez.

18 Zim (inkl. ½ P.) – 59/64 € 98/108 € 65/116 € 110/212 €

Rest – (nur Abendessen für Hausgäste)

♦ Leicht elegant und komfortabel sind die Gästezimmer dieses kleinen Hotels möbliert. Zu den Annehmlichkeiten zählt auch ein recht großzügiger Freizeitbereich.

Alpenland garni

Gerlos 145 6281 – (05284) 52 80 – alpenland.gerlos@aon.at – Fax (05284) 52807

geschl. 6. April – 10. Mai, 20. Okt. – 2. Dez.

20 Zim – 32/34 € 60/70 € 46/58 € 90/120 €

♦ Das Haus liegt in der Ortsmitte, im Erdgeschoss einige Geschäfte. Komfortable Zimmer und Appartements, einer der Frühstücksräume mit aufwändig gearbeiteter Holzdecke.

Gasthof Riederhof

Gerlos 101 6281 – (05284) 52 89 – riederhof@tirol.com – Fax (05284) 54645

geschl. 7. April – 5. Juli, 30. Sept. – 18. Dez.

20 Zim (inkl. ½ P.) – 41/44 € 72/82 € 60/68 € 114/132 €

Rest – Karte 15/32 €

♦ Am Ortseingang liegt der kleine, familiär geführte Gasthof mit Balkonfassade. Die Zimmer sind funktionell ausgestattet, hell oder dunkel möbliert – auch einige Familienzimmer. Gaststuben im regionstypischen Stil.

GLEICHENBERG, BAD – Steiermark – 730 T8 – 2 170 Ew – Höhe 300 m – Heilbad

11 **L5**

Wien 186 – Graz 67 – Maribor 54 – Fürstenfeld 38

Brunnenstr. 11, 8344, (03159) 22 03, info@bad-gleichenberg.at

Bad Gleichenberg, Am Hoffeld 3 (03159) 37 17

Bad Radkersburg★ (Süd-Ost: 24 km)

Schlössl-Hotel-Kindl (Thermal) Rest, Rest,

Nr. 44 8344 – (03159) 23 32 – info@schloessl-hotel.at – Fax (03159) 233222

geschl. 16. Dez. – 6. Jan.

34 Zim (inkl. ½ P.) – 70/81 € 116/138 €

Rest – Karte 16/29 €

♦ Hinter einer hübschen Fassade in kräftigem Gelb verbergen sich mit italienischen Stilmöbeln eingerichtete Zimmer und ein netter Wellnessbereich mit gepflegter Außenanlage.

Stenitzer Rest, VISA
Schulstr. 51 ✉ 8344 – ✆ (03159) 22 50 – hotel.stenitzer@aon.at – Fax (03159) 225060
30 Zim – 70/76 € 120/132 € – ½ P 10 € – 4 Suiten
Rest – Karte 17/30 €
◆ Durch eine beeindruckende Atriumhalle – früher der Innenhof dieses ehemaligen herrschaftlichen Guts – gelangen Sie in teils neuzeitlich, teils leicht elegant möblierte Zimmer. Restaurant mit angeschlossenem Café.

GLEINSTÄTTEN – Steiermark – 730 S8 – 1 500 Ew – Höhe 285 m 10 K5

Wien 245 – Graz 60 – Leibnitz 17 – Deutschlandsberg 18

Zur Hube
Sausal 51 (Nord-West: 3km, Richtung Pistorf) ✉ 8443 – ✆ (03457) 32 71 – restaurant@zurhube.at – Fax (03457) 3271
geschl. Sonntagabend – Mittwoch
Rest – (Tischbestellung erforderlich) Menü 29 € – Karte 26/38 €
◆ Ein 300 Jahre altes, idyllisch in den Weinbergen gelegenes Bauernhaus, das weitgehend seinen Originalzustand bewahrt hat, beheimatet dieses Restaurant mit regionaler Küche.

GLEISDORF – Steiermark – 730 T7 – 5 230 Ew – Höhe 343 m 11 K5

Wien 178 – Graz 29 – Weiz 16 – Fürstenfeld 32

Sonnenwirt A/C VISA
Franz-Josef-Str. 7 ✉ 8200 – ✆ (03112) 3 64 00 – info@sonnenwirt.at – Fax (03112) 36401
geschl. Sonntag – Montag
Rest – Menü 45 € – Karte 18/38 €
◆ Aus guten Produkten bereitet man in diesem modern und farbenfroh gestalteten Restaurant hinter den Mauern des einstigen Klosters eine kreative Küche zu. Kompetenter Service.

GLOGGNITZ – Niederösterreich – 730 T5 – 6 160 Ew – Höhe 442 m 3 K3

Wien 83 – St. Pölten 119 – Wiener Neustadt 34 – Mürzzuschlag 28

In Gloggnitz-Kranichberg Süd-Ost: 8 km – Höhe 640 m

Burghotel Kranichberg
Kranichberg 1 Zim, Rest, P VISA AE
✉ 2640 – ✆ (02662) 82 42 – hotel@kranichberg.at – Fax (02662) 8386
geschl. 22. Dez. – 6. Jan.
52 Zim – 70/82 € 116/142 € – ½ P 17 €
Rest – *(geschl. Sonntagabend)* Karte 18/33 €
◆ In die aus dem Mittelalter stammende Burg hat man ein Seminarhotel mit hell möblierten, funktionellen Zimmern integriert. Besonders geräumig sind die Ritterzimmer mit Gewölbe. Klassisch-rustikal gehaltenes Speisezimmer mit offenem Kamin.

Sie suchen ein besonderes Hotel für einen sehr angenehmen Aufenthalt?
Reservieren Sie in einem roten Haus: ... .

GMÜND - Niederösterreich - 730 Q2 - 5 870 Ew - Höhe 507 m 2 I1

Wien 140 - St. Pölten 98 - Freistadt 56 - Zwettl 27
Weitra, Hausschachen 313 (02856) 20 58
Sgraffitohäuser★ - Blockheide★★
Burg Heidenreichstein★ (Nord-Ost: 19 km)

Goldener Stern

Rest, Zim,

Stadtplatz 15 3950 - (02852) 54 54 50 - hotel@goldener-stern.eu - Fax (02852) 54548

VISA

40 Zim - 79 € 110 € - ½ P 16 €

Rest - Menü 29/59 € - Karte 19/38 €

♦ Mit soliden Eichenholzmöbeln wohnlich eingerichtete Zimmer mit guter Technik sowie funktionelle Tagungsmöglichkeiten bietet das Hotel im Zentrum. Kleiner, netter Saunabereich. Gast-, Zunft- und Kaminstube sind die Restauranträume: von einfach bis etwas edler.

GMUNDEN - Oberösterreich - 730 N5 - 13 190 Ew - Höhe 425 m - Wintersport: 1 000 m 1 2 - Luftkurort 2 H3

Wien 229 - Linz 68 - Salzburg 79 - Bad Ischl 33
Toscanaplatz 1, 4810, (07612) 7 44 51, info@traunsee.at
Traunsee-Kirchham, Kampesberg 38 (07619) 25 76
Esplanade★ - Schloss Ort★ - Kammerhofmuseum★
Gmundnerberg★ (Süd-West: 9 km) - Almtal★ (Ost: 16 km)

Schlosshotel Freisitz Roith

Traunsee, Zim,

Traunsteinstr. 87

VISA AE

4810 - (07612) 6 49 05 - info@freisitzroith.at - Fax (07612) 6490517

geschl. 14. Jan. - 30. April, Nov. - Dez.

23 Zim - 80/93 € 190/230 €

Rest - Menü 38/58 € - Karte 30/50 €

♦ Angenehm ist die ruhige, erhöhte Lage dieses a. d. 16. Jh. stammenden kleinen Schlosses, sehr schön ist die Aussicht. Wohnliche Zimmer und ein gepflegter Garten erwarten Sie. Modernes Wintergartenrestaurant mit Blick auf den Traunsee und klassischer Küche.

Hois'n Wirt

Traunsee und Berge, Zim,

Traunsteinstr. 277 4810 - (07612) 7 73 33 - reception@hoisnwirt.at - Fax (07612) 7733395

VISA AE

geschl. 1. Nov. - 28. Feb.

20 Zim - 58/75 € 96/116 € - ½ P 15 €

Rest - Karte 13/31 €

♦ Der gewachsene Landgasthof ist ein familiengeführtes kleines Hotel direkt am See. Die Zimmer verfügen alle über einen Balkon und bieten eine schöne Aussicht. Zum Restaurant gehört eine nette Terrasse mit alten Kastanien.

Gasthof Grünberg am See

Traunsteinstr. 109 4810 - (07612) 7 77 00 - gruenberg@vpn.at - Fax (07612) 7770033

VISA AE

38 Zim - 58/78 € 106/146 € - ½ P 18 €

Rest - Karte 17/31 €

♦ Zeitgemäß und praktisch ausgestattete Zimmer, teils mit Seeblick, und ein eigener Strand mit Bootsverleih zählen zu den Annehmlichkeiten dieses Familienbetriebs. Bürgerliches Restaurant mit regionaler Karte und Terrasse mit Seeblick.

XX **Orther Stub'n** 

Orth 1 (Seeschloss Orth) ✉ 4810 – ✆ (07612) 6 24 99 – info@schlossorth.com – Fax (07612) 63724

Rest – Menü 29/58 € – Karte 28/44 €

◆ Malerisch liegt das Schloss Orth im Traunsee – durch einen Holzsteg mit dem Festland verbunden. Hier finden Sie eine hübsche gemütliche Stube mit netter Innenhofterrasse.

GNADENWALD – **Tirol** – 730 G7 – **610 Ew** – **Höhe 920 m** – **Wintersport:** 1 – **Luftkurort** 7 **D5**

Wien 433 – Innsbruck 16 – Schwaz 14 – Hall in Tirol 6

Alpenhotel Speckbacher Hof 

St. Martin 2 ✉ 6060 – ✆ (05223) 5 25 11 – info@speckbacherhof.at – Fax (05223) 5251155

55 Zim – 58/95 € 96/186 € – ½ P 25 €

Rest – Karte 18/46 €

◆ Der in einem kleinen Weiler gelegene Gasthof beherbergt in einem modernen Anbau großzügige, wohnlich-elegante Zimmer. Man bietet auch Kosmetik und Massage. Die Restaurantstuben sind mit viel Holz gemütlich-rustikal gestaltet. Großer Gastgarten.

Gute Küche zu günstigem Preis? Folgen Sie dem „Bib Gourmand"

GNESAU – **Kärnten** – 730 N8 – **1 250 Ew** – **Höhe 963 m** – **Wintersport: 1 150 m** 1 9 **H6**

Wien 317 – Klagenfurt 35 – Villach 37 – Spittal an der Drau 46

X **Seebacher**

Gurk 23 (Ost: 3 km) ✉ 9563 – ✆ (04278) 2 57 – gasthof.seebacher@aon.at – Fax (04278) 2574

geschl. 18. Juni – 11. Juli und Mittwoch – Donnerstagmittag

Rest – Menü 25 € – Karte 15/35 €

◆ Seit über 50 Jahren wird dieser nette Betrieb der Familie Seebacher als Gasthof geführt. Zwei rustikal-gemütliche Restauranträume – einer mit Kachelofen – empfangen die Gäste.

GÖSING – **Niederösterreich** – **siehe Puchenstuben**

GÖSTLING AN DER YBBS – **Niederösterreich** – 730 Q5 – **2 190 Ew** – **Höhe 532 m** – **Wintersport: 1 878 m** 9 3 **J3**

Wien 158 – St. Pölten 101 – Mariazell 46

Markt 1, ✉ 3345, ✆ (07484) 50 20 19, info@goestling-hochkar.at

Mandl-Scheiblechner

Stixenlehen 48 ✉ 3345 – ✆ (07484) 22 44 – info@rafting-mandl.at – Fax (07484) 2938

geschl. November

22 Zim – 48/53 € 76/86 € 53/58 € 86/98 € – ½ P 12 €

Rest – *(geschl. Dienstagabend – Mittwoch)* Karte 14/28 €

◆ Das Hotel bietet meist mit hellem Naturholz möblierte, zeitgemäß ausgestattete Gästezimmer, einige sind recht großzügig angelegt. Man organisiert Rafting-Touren. Gaststuben in ländlichem Stil.

In Göstling-Lassing Süd-West: 8 km über B 25 Richtung Hochkar:

Gasthof Fahrnberger (mit Gästehaus)
Lassing 19 ✉ 3345 – ☎ (07484) 7 23 40
– office@gasthof-fahrnberger.at – Fax (07484) 723450
geschl. April, Nov.
12 Zim (inkl. ½ P.) – †52/64 € ††103/128 €
Rest – *(geschl. Mai – Juni Dienstag – Mittwoch und Sept. – Okt. Dienstag – Mittwoch, Dez. – März nur Abendessen)* Karte 14/31 €
♦ Das gut geführte kleine Hotel ist ein älterer Gasthof mit Anbau und Gästehaus und verfügt über recht individuelle Zimmer, teils hell möbliert, z. T. auch mit Holzfußboden. Mit viel Holz rustikal gestaltetes Restaurant.

GÖTTLESBRUNN – Niederösterreich – 730 W4 – 1 320 Ew – Höhe 171 m

▶ Wien 42 – St Pölten 115 4 **M2**

bittermann
Abt-Bruno-Heinrich-Platz 1 ✉ 2464 – ☎ (02162) 8 11 55
– info@bittermann-vinarium.at – Fax (02162) 8115566
Rest – Menü 38 € – Karte 19/37 €
♦ Geschmackvoll, modern und hell sind sowohl die Vinothek im ersten Stock wie auch das eigentliche Lokal, beides befindet sich in einer ehemaligen Volksschule. Regionale Küche.

GÖTZIS – Vorarlberg – 730 A7 – 10 100 Ew – Höhe 450 m 5 A5

▶ Wien 675 – Bregenz 23 – Dornbirn 12 – Feldkirch 14

24 7 Hotel garni
Montfortstr. 6 ✉ 6840 – ☎ (05523) 6 92 47 – office@hotel247.at
– Fax (05523) 692477 – geschl. 23. Dez. – 7. Jan.
39 Zim – †71 € ††110 €
♦ 24 Stunden lang und das 7 mal in der Woche kümmert man sich in diesem modernen, in klarem Design gehaltenen Hotel um die Gäste. Freizeitbereich mit Sauna und Dampfbad.

Dorfpark Rest,
Im Buch 1 ✉ 6840 – ☎ (05523) 5 52 50 – office@hotel-dorfpark.at
– Fax (05523) 55250410
38 Zim – †61/66 € ††90/96 €
Rest – *(geschl. 1. Juli – 26. Aug. Sonntag)* Karte 16/22 €
♦ Modernes Hotel im Zentrum in einer Anlage mit Einkaufsmarkt und Wohnungen. Man bietet zeitgemäße Gästezimmer mit wohnlichem Ambiente. Indische und internationale Küche im Restaurant Ingwer.

Cantinetta Leonetti 
Hauptstr. 23 ✉ 6840 – ☎ (05523) 6 22 54 – Fax (05523) 62254
geschl. Samstagmittag, Sonntag
Rest – Karte 17/35 €
♦ Italienische Küche in einem mit rötlichen Schindeln verkleideten alpenländischen Gasthaus. Innen: Kachelofen und z. T. Holztäfelung. Hinter dem Haus eine hübsche Terrasse.

kult-t Am Bach
Am Bach 10 ✉ 6840 – ☎ (05523) 5 48 60 – info@kul-t.at
– Fax (05523) 54830
geschl. 26. Juli – 17. Aug. sowie Sonn- und Feiertage

Rest – Karte 17/37 €

◆ In das Kulturhaus hat man dieses Restaurant integriert. Moderne Architektur, eine große Fensterfront und legerer Service bestimmen die Atmosphäre. Mittags günstiges Tagesmenü.

GOING AM WILDEN KAISER – Tirol – 730 J6 – 1 730 Ew – Höhe 800 m – Wintersport: 1 500 m 1 25 7 E5

Wien 364 – Innsbruck 82 – Kitzbühel 14 – Kufstein 21

Dorfstr. 10, 6353, (05358) 24 38, going@wilderkaiser.info

Bio-Hotel Stanglwirt

Wilder Kaiser, (geheizt) Rest, P VISA AE

Kaiserweg 1
(Ost: 1 km über die B 178) 6353 – (05358) 20 00
– info@stanglwirt.com – Fax (05358) 200031

151 Zim (inkl. ½ P.) – 134/175 € 236/416 € – 18 Suiten

Rest *Gasthof Stanglwirt* – separat erwähnt

◆ Luxuriöses Alpenhotel mit wohnlich-charmanter Atmosphäre und vielfältigem Angebot wie Felsensauna, Kinderbauernhof und Lipizzanergestüt. Zimmer nach Norden mit toller Sicht.

Cordial (mit Gästehaus)

Rest, P VISA AE

Marchstr. 63 6353 – (05358) 21 25
– chgoing@cordial.co.at – Fax (05358) 212548
geschl. 3. Nov. – 6. Dez.

48 Zim – 71/133 € 85/145 € 71/157 € 85/169 € – ½ P 22 €

Rest – *(nur Abendessen)* Karte 21/28 €

◆ Das solide geführte Hotel liegt etwas außerhalb des Zentrums, direkt an einer Skipiste. Die Gästezimmer verfügen größtenteils über Balkone.

Lanzenhof

P

Dorfstr. 16 6353 – (05358) 35 34 – info@lanzenhof.at
– Fax (05358) 3592 – geschl. April, Nov.

16 Zim (inkl. ½ P.) – 45/50 € 80/94 € 55/60 € 100/110 €

Rest – *(geschl. Sonntag)* Karte 19/39 €

◆ Mitten im Ort finden Sie diese freundlich-familiäre Adresse, die über gepflegte, mit Naturholz möblierte Gästezimmer verfügt – einige bieten zwei separate Schlafräume. Urige Restaurantstuben und netter Weinkeller für Degustationen.

Gasthof Stanglwirt – BioHotel Stanglwirt

P VISA AE

Kaiserweg 1 (Ost:1 km) 6353
– (05358) 20 00 – info@stanglwirt.com – Fax (05358) 200031

Rest – Karte 25/46 €

◆ Gemütlich sind die Stuben in dem Gasthof a. d. 17. Jh. Sehr hübsch: das Alm-Restaurant und die Kuhstall-Stube mit Blick in den Stall. Internationale und regionale Küche.

GOISERN, BAD – Oberösterreich – 730 M6 – 7 610 Ew – Höhe 504 m – Wintersport: 1 004 m 1 – Luftkurort 9 G4

Wien 274 – Linz 113 – Salzburg 63 – Bad Ischl 10

Kirchengasse 4, 4822, (06135) 83 29, goisern@inneres-salzkammergut.at

Veranstaltungen

11.01. – 13.01.: Schneespektakel

Gasthof Goiserer Mühle

Kurparkstr. 9 ✉ 4822 – ✆ (06135) 82 06 – goiserermuehle@eunet.at – Fax (06135) 820666

34 Zim – 55/75 € 110/150 € – ½ P 18 €

Rest – *(geschl. Dienstag)* Karte 21/38 €

♦ Ein ländlich-wohnliches Ambiente prägt den traditionellen Gasthof mit den vielen Dachgauben. Modern: die Gästezimmer im Anbau. Fahrradverleih im Haus. Besonders hübsch: die nostalgisch anmutende Gaststube und die Terrasse. Regional ausgelegte Karte.

In Bad Goisern-Sankt Agatha Süd-Ost: 2,5 km über B 145 Richtung Bad Aussee:

Landhotel Agathawirt (geheizt) Zim, Zim,

St. Agatha 10 (B 145) ✉ 4822 – ✆ (06135) 83 41 – office@agathawirt.at – Fax (06135) 7557

geschl. 7. – 30. April, 3. Nov. – 24. Dez.

29 Zim – 44/69 € 70/104 € – ½ P 12 €

Rest – Karte 16/27 €

♦ Das hübsche, unter Denkmalschutz stehende Stammhaus des Gasthofs wurde 1517 erbaut. Alle Zimmer befinden sich im neueren Teil und bieten zeitgemäßen Komfort. Eine der Gaststuben liegt im historischen Gebäude. Terrasse mit altem Kastanienbaum.

GOLDEGG – Salzburg – 730 L7 – 2 220 Ew – Höhe 850 m – Wintersport: 1 250 m 4 8 G5

Wien 364 – Salzburg 68 – Zell am See 36 – Bad Gastein 33

Hofmark 18, ✉ 5622, ✆ (06415) 81 31, tourismus@goldeggamsee.at

Goldegg, Maierhof 5 ✆ (06415) 88 15

Der Seehof Rest,

Hofmark 8 ✉ 5622 – ✆ (06415) 8 13 70 – seehof@salzburg.co.at – Fax (06415) 8276

geschl. 25. März – 25. April, 26. Okt. – 5. Dez.

28 Zim – 78/138 € 146/206 € – ½ P 38 €

Rest – *(geschl. Mittwochmittag außer Juni – Sept.)* Menü 46/49 € – Karte 30/40 €

♦ Hier erwarten Sie hell und schlicht-modern eingerichtete Zimmer mit Parkett und teils Blick auf den See – einige mit durch Glas abgetrennten Bädern. Neuzeitliches Restaurant mit Holzfußboden und umlaufender roter Polsterbank. Holzvertäfelte Nichtraucherstube.

Zur Post Zim, Rest,

Hofmark 9 ✉ 5622 – ✆ (06415) 8 10 30 – hotel@hotelpost-goldegg.at – Fax (06415) 8104

geschl. Mitte März – Anfang Mai, Mitte Okt. – 20. Dez.

37 Zim (inkl. ½ P.) – 65/86 € 130/178 € 65/102 € 130/204 €

Rest – *(geschl. Mittwochmittag)* Karte 20/30 €

♦ Das seit über 40 Jahren von der Inhaberfamilie geführte Hotel mit regionstypischer Fassade bietet in ländlichem Stil gehaltene Zimmer. Im Winter beginnen am Haus die Loipen. Unterteiltes Restaurant mit rustikalem Ambiente.

Zum Bierführer mit Zim — Zim,

Hofmark 19 ✉ 5622 – ✆ (06415) 81 02 – info@bierfuehrer.sbg.at – Fax (06415) 810222

25 Zim – 48/58 € 96/116 € – ½ P 20 €

Rest – *(geschl. 10. – 30. Jan. und Montag – Dienstagmittag)* Karte 19/43 €

♦ Die gemütlichen Restauranträume sind rustikal ausgestattet und mit alten Fotos, Bildern und ländlichem Zierrat dekoriert. Neuzeitliche Zimmer im Gästehaus hinter dem Gasthof.

GOLLING – Salzburg – 730 L6 – 3 910 Ew – Höhe 476 m – Wintersport: 1 010m 2

8 G4

Wien 325 – Salzburg 29 – Bischofshofen 25 – Bad Ischl 63

Markt 51, ✉ 5440, ✆ (06244) 43 56, office@golling.info

Kirche St. Nikolaus (Lage★) – Gollinger Wasserfall★★

Salzbachtal★ – Höhlen Eisriesenwelt★★ (Süd: 10 km) – Erlebnisburg Hohenwerfen★ (Süd: 15 km)

Döllerer — Zim,

Am Marktplatz 56 ✉ 5440 – ✆ (06244) 4 22 00 – office@doellerer.at – Fax (06244) 691242

geschl. 7. – 21. Jan., Anfang Juli 2 Wochen

12 Zim – 80/120 € 110/160 €

Rest Wirtshaus – separat erwähnt

Rest – *(geschl. Sonntag – Montag, außer Aug.)* Menü 69/105 €

Spez. Gravensteiner Apfel mit Blunz'n gefüllt und gegrillte Langoustinen. Knuspriger Schweinebauch mit Alba-Trüffel (Nov.). Dukatenbuchteln mit Rumeis und Nougatfondue.

♦ Ein aus dem 14. Jh. stammendes Gasthaus im Ortszentrum gegenüber der alten Burg beherbergt geschmackvoll und elegant eingerichtete Zimmer. Im Gourmetrestaurant erwarten Sie internationale Küche mit regionalen Einflüssen und netter, kompetenter Service.

Wirtshaus – Hotel Döllerer

Am Marktplatz 56 ✉ 5440 – ✆ (06244) 4 22 00 – office@doellerer.at – Fax (06244) 691242

geschl. 7. – 21. Jan., Anfang Juli 2 Wochen

Rest – *(geschl. Sonntag – Montag, außer Aug.)* Menü 25 € – Karte 24/36 €

♦ Ein schöner Ort zum geselligen Zusammensein ist das ländliche Wirtshaus mit historischem Steingewölbe, in dem man regionale Küche serviert.

GOLS – Burgenland – 730 W5 – 3 520 Ew – Höhe 130 m

4 M3

Wien 60 – Eisenstadt 39 – Wiener Neustadt 67 – Bratislava 46

Birkenhof

Birkenplatz 1 ✉ 7122 – ✆ (02173) 2 34 60 – info@birkenhofgols.at – Fax (02173) 234633

geschl. 10. – 25. Feb., 22. Dez. – 10. Jan.

30 Zim – 59/81 € 88/118 € – ½ P 16 €

Rest – *(geschl. 12. Jan. – 10. Feb. Sonntagabend – Montag, 26. Feb. – 14. Juli und 15. Sept. – 22. Dez. Montag,)* 55 € – Karte 21/39 €

♦ Am Neusiedlersee befindet sich der hübsche Landgasthof mit eigenem Weingut, dessen Zimmer im zeitlosen, freundlichen Landhausstil gehalten sind. Verschiedene, individuell eingerichtete Restauranträume in ländlichem Stil. Schöner Gartenbereich.

Preisinger garni
Untere Quergasse 27 ✉ 7122 – ✆ (02173) 23 89
– gaestehaus@preisinger.at – Fax (02173) 238922
geschl. Jan. – März
7 Zim – 46 € 92 €
♦ Neuzeitliche, behaglich gestaltete Zimmer, ein sehr gepflegter Frühstücksraum und ein netter Innenhof zählen zu den Vorzügen dieser kleinen familiengeführten Pension.

GOSAU – Oberösterreich – 730 M6 – 1 950 Ew – Höhe 760 m – Wintersport: 1 800 m 2 35

9 **G4**

Wien 291 – Linz 130 – Salzburg 62 – Bad Ischl 27
Gosau 547, ✉ 4824, ✆ (06136) 82 95, gosau@inneres-salzkammergut.at
Vorderer Gosausee★★★ (Süd: 7 km)

Landhaus Koller (mit Gästehaus) (geheizt) Zim, Rest,
Gosau 353 ✉ 4824
– ✆ (06136) 8 84 10 – office@hotel-koller.com – Fax (06136) 884150
geschl. April, Nov.
22 Zim (inkl. ½ P.) – 82/128 € 164/212 € 109/139 € 218/234 €
Rest – (nur Abendessen für Hausgäste)
♦ Die 1850 erbaute Jagdvilla mit Blick auf den Gosaukamm bietet Ihnen wohnlich-rustikale Zimmer, meist mit Balkon, sowie einen netten Garten mit Pool. Appartements im Gästehaus.

Gasthof Kirchenwirt
Gosau 2 ✉ 4824 – ✆ (06136) 81 96 – gasthof.kirchenwirt@aon.at
– Fax (06136) 819615
24 Zim – 26/28 € 52/56 € 33/35 € 66/70 € – ½ P 9 €
Rest – Karte 13/24 €
♦ Auf eine über 400-jährige Geschichte kann dieser Gasthof zurückblicken. Man bietet einfache, aber gepflegte Zimmer und eine persönliche Atmosphäre. Gemütliche, rustikale Gaststuben und eine hübsche Terrasse mit schöner Aussicht.

GRÄN-HALDENSEE – Tirol – 730 D6 – 600 Ew – Höhe 1 134 m – Wintersport: 1 883 m 1 3

5 **B5**

Wien 525 – Innsbruck 112 – Kempten 44 – Reutte 22
Dorfstr. 1 (Grän) ✉ 6673, ✆ (05675) 62 85, info@tannheimertal.com

Liebes Rot-Flüh (geheizt) Rest,
Seestr. 26 (Haldensee) ✉ 6673
– ✆ (05675) 64 31 – traumhotel@rotflueh.com – Fax (05675) 643146
101 Zim (inkl. ½ P.) – 135/188 € 248/346 € – 23 Suiten
Rest *La Cascata Nobile* – separat erwähnt
Rest *Via Mala* – ✆ (05675) 64 31 95 *(nur Abendessen)* Karte 22/44 €
Rest *Loch Ness* – ✆ (05675) 64 31 88 *(nur Abendessen)* Karte 30/51 €
♦ Ein luxuriöses Ferienhotel unweit des Sees mit sehr individuell eingerichteten Zimmern und Suiten, schönem Garten, großem Wellnessbereich und freundlichem Service. Das Restaurant Via Mala im UG wurde authentisch einem Bergdorf nachempfunden.

Wellness-Hotel Engel

Dorfstr. 35 (Grän) ✉ 6673 Rest,
– ☎ (05675) 64 23 – post@engel-tirol.com – Fax (05675) 6702
70 Zim (inkl. ½ P.) – ☼ 100/170 € 188/260 € ❄ 109/187 €
188/294 € – 15 Suiten
Rest – *(geschl. Dienstag)* Karte 23/46 €
◆ Freundliches, geschultes Personal kümmert sich in dem Hotel mit sehr wohnlichen Zimmern und einem hochwertig ausgestatteten, vielfältigen Wellnessbereich um Sie. Das rustikal-elegante Restaurant bietet regionale und internationale Küche.

Sonnenhof

Füssener Jöchle Str. 5 (Grän) ✉ 6673 – ☎ (05675) 63 75
– post@sonnenhof-tirol.com – Fax (05675) 63755
geschl. Mitte April – Mitte Mai, Anfang Nov. – Mitte Dez.
46 Zim (inkl. ½ P.) – ☼ 92/122 € 134/174 € ❄ 108/139 €
166/244 € – 3 Suiten
Rest – Karte 21/31 €
◆ Direkt am Skilift gelegenes Hotel mit einer schmucken Tiroler Balkonfassade. Die Zimmer sind überwiegend großzügig geschnittenen und wohnlich eingerichtet. Gediegene Restauranträume und nette Aussichtsterrasse.

Tyrol

(geheizt) Zim, Zim,
Seestr. 24 (Haldensee) ✉ 6673 – ☎ (05675) 62 45
– info@tyrol-haldensee.com – Fax (05675) 6073
geschl. 11. Nov. – 10. Dez.
57 Zim (inkl. ½ P.) – ☼ 65/95 € 125/210 € ❄ 75/105 €
140/230 € – 7 Suiten
Rest – Karte 18/34 €
◆ Ein gut geführtes Urlaubshotel mit wohnlichen, teilweise in neuzeitlichem Stil möblierten Zimmern und einem ansprechenden Freizeitangebot mit Kosmetik und Massage. Zur Halle hin offenes A-la-carte-Restaurant.

Lumberger Hof

Zim,
Am Lumberg 1 (Grän) ✉ 6673 – ☎ (05675) 63 92
– hotel@lumbergerhof.at – Fax (05675) 613146
geschl. 1. – 28. April, 6. Nov. – 15. Dez.
43 Zim (inkl. ½ P.) – 77/122 € 144/214 €
Rest – Karte 22/38 €
◆ Dieses familiengeführte Alpenhotel am Ortsrand beherbergt in warmen Farbtönen angenehm wohnlich gestaltete, z. T. besonders großzügige Zimmer. Kosmetik und Massage im Angebot. Ländlich-gediegenes Restaurant mit freundlichem Service.

Apparthotel Told

Zim, Rest,
Engetalstr. 1 (Grän) ✉ 6673 – ☎ (05675) 62 94 – told@magnet.at
– Fax (05675) 619122
geschl. 30. März – 30. April, 26. Okt. – 19. Dez.
32 Zim (inkl. ½ P.) – ☼ 64/71 € 114/128 € ❄ 74/81 €
134/160 €
Rest – *(geschl. Dienstag)* Karte 19/32 €
◆ Das im Tiroler Stil gebaute Haus bietet u. a. einige als Appartement angelegte Zimmer mit Küchenzeile. Fahrräder werden kostenlos zur Verfügung gestellt. Rustikales Restaurant mit regional-bürgerlicher Küche und schöner Terrasse.

La Cascata Nobile - Hotel Liebes Rot-Flüh
Seestr. 26 (Haldensee) ✉ 6673
– ☎ (05675) 64 31 68 – traumhotel@rotflueh.com – Fax (05675) 643146
Rest – *(geschl. Dienstag – Mittwoch, nur Abendessen)* Menü 76/97 € – Karte 45/64 €
◆ In gediegen-eleganter Atmosphäre speist man hier klassische, teils regional beeinflusste Küche und wird vom freundlichen Servicepersonal zuvorkommend bedient.

GRAFENWÖRTH – Niederösterreich – 730 T3 – 2 620 Ew – Höhe 216 m 3 K2

Wien 64 – St. Pölten 36 – Krems 15 – Stockerau 36

In Feuersbrunn Nord: 4 km:

Mörwald – Villa Katharina
Kleine Zeile 10 ✉ 3483 – ☎ (02738) 22 98
– reception@moerwald.at – Fax (02738) 229860
10 Zim – †81/96 € ††108/128 € – ½ P 39 €
Rest Toni M. – separat erwähnt
Rest *Zur Traube* – Menü 29 € (mittags)/69 € – Karte 26/45 €
Rest *Bistro m.wirts.haus* – ☎ (02738) 22 98 41 – Karte 13/21 €
◆ Angeschlossen an das Stammhaus der Familie Mörwald ist dieses moderne kleine Hotel mit seinen geschmackvollen, nach Rebsorten benannten Gästezimmern. Restaurant Zur Traube mit verschiedenen schönen Stuben und drei Terrassen. Regionale und klassische Karte.

Toni M. – Hotel Mörwald – Villa Katharina
Kleine Zeile 15 ✉ 3483 – ☎ (0676) 84 22 98 81
– toni@moerwald.at – Fax (02738) 229860
geschl. Jan. – Feb., Mitte Juli – Aug. und Samstag – Sonntag
Rest – *(nur Abendessen)* (Tischbestellung erforderlich) Menü 75/125 €
Spez. Tranche vom hausgebeizten Seesaibling mit gedämpftem Weinkraut und Honig. Würfel vom Zander mit Thymian gebraten und roten Rüben. Heimische Walnüsse in Souffléform mit Pistazieneis.
◆ Im Stil der 70er Jahre wurde das Restaurant elegant und hübsch eingerichtet. Ein Küchenstudio, eine eigene Vinothek und klassische Küche erwarten hier den Gast.

GRAMBACH – Steiermark – 730 S7 – 1 330 Ew – Höhe 350 m 11 K5

Wien 192 – Graz 8 – Leibnitz 42

Landhaus Hammerl
Weiherweg 1 ✉ 8071 – ☎ (0316) 40 14 41
– restaurant@landhaus-hammerl.at – Fax (0316) 401441
geschl. Sonntagabend – Montag
Rest – Menü 35/42 € – Karte 21/40 €
◆ Das von der Inhaberfamilie geleitete Restaurant am Orstrand bietet internationale und regionale Speisen, die man auch im hübschen, teilweise überdachten Gastgarten serviert.

Office National de Tourisme Autrichien

GRAZ

L **Bundesland:** Steiermark
Michelin-Karte: **730** S7
Wien 201 – Salzburg 257 – Klagenfurt 140 – Maribor 72

Einwohnerzahl: 226 250 Ew
Höhe: 365 m

10 K5

Die Hauptstadt der Steiermark erschließt sich dem Gast nicht gleich auf den ersten Blick. Denn gerade die zahlreichen für die Stadt charakteristischen Innenhöfe verleihen ihr das vielgerühmte südländische Flair. Weitläufige Parkanlagen hatten ihr einst den Titel Gartenstadt eingebracht und die Ernennung zur Kulturhauptstadt Europas 2003 brachte neue Akzente ins Stadtbild: die Murinsel und die hypermoderne Architektur des Kunsthauses "A Friendly Alien" sind unübersehbar. Im Sommer verwandeln sich ganze Straßenzüge in einen großen Gastgarten, wo man unter freiem Himmel steirische Spezialitäten bei einem Glas heimischen Weins genießen kann. Und ist man erst mal auf den Geschmack gekommen, ist es gut zu wissen, dass Graz auch einen hervorragender Ausgangspunkt zur Erkundung der Steirischen Weinstraßen darstellt.

PRAKTISCHE HINWEISE

Tourist-Information

Herrengasse 16 (im Landhaus) DZ, 8010, (0316) 8 07 50, info@graztourismus.at

Flughafen

Feldkirchen/Graz (Süd: 8 km über B 67 AX), (0316) 2 90 20

Messen

Messecenter Graz, Messeplatz 1, 8010, (0316) 8 08 80

17.01. – 20.01.: Häuslbauer

25.01. – 27.01.: Ferien – Vital

01.05. – 04.05.: Lebensart

07.09. – 10.09.: Gastronomia

27.09. – 05.10.: Herbstmesse

Veranstaltungen

26.01.: Grazer Opernredoute

01.04. – 06.04.: Diagonale (Festival des österreichischen Films)

27.06. – 27.07.: Styriarte

01.07. – 31.08.: Jazzsommer

26.07. – 02.08.: La Strada

02.10. – 26.10.: Steirischer Herbst

Golfplätze

27 Grazer Golf Club, Graz-Thal, Windhof 137 ✆ (0316) 57 28 67

9 Golfzentrum Andritz, Andritzer Reichsstr. 157 ✆ (0316) 69 58 00

9 Golf-Club Liebenau, Neu Oedt 14 ✆ (03182) 35 55

18 Gut Freiberg, Gleisdorf, Ludersdorf 32 ✆ (03112) 6 27 00

SEHENSWÜRDIGKEITEN

ALTSTADT

Hauptplatz★ – Mittelalterliches Viertel★ CZ – Landhaus★★ CDZ – Palais Attems (Fassaden★★) **D** CY – Treppenturm★★ **B** DY – Zeughaus★★★ – Stadtpfarrkirche zum Hl. Blut (Glockenzentrum★) – Mausoleum★★ – Domkirche★ (Reliquienschreine★★★) DZ

PARKANLAGEN UND ANDERE SEHENSWÜRDIGKEITEN

Schlossberg★ (Herbersteingarten: ⩽★★) – Mariahilf-Kirche★ – Murinsel★ CY – Alte Galerie des Steiermärkischen Landesmuseums Joanneum (Mittelalterliche Kunst★) **M**[3] – Kunsthaus Graz★★ CZ – Leechkirche (Westportal★, Glasmalereien★) – Stadtpark★ DY

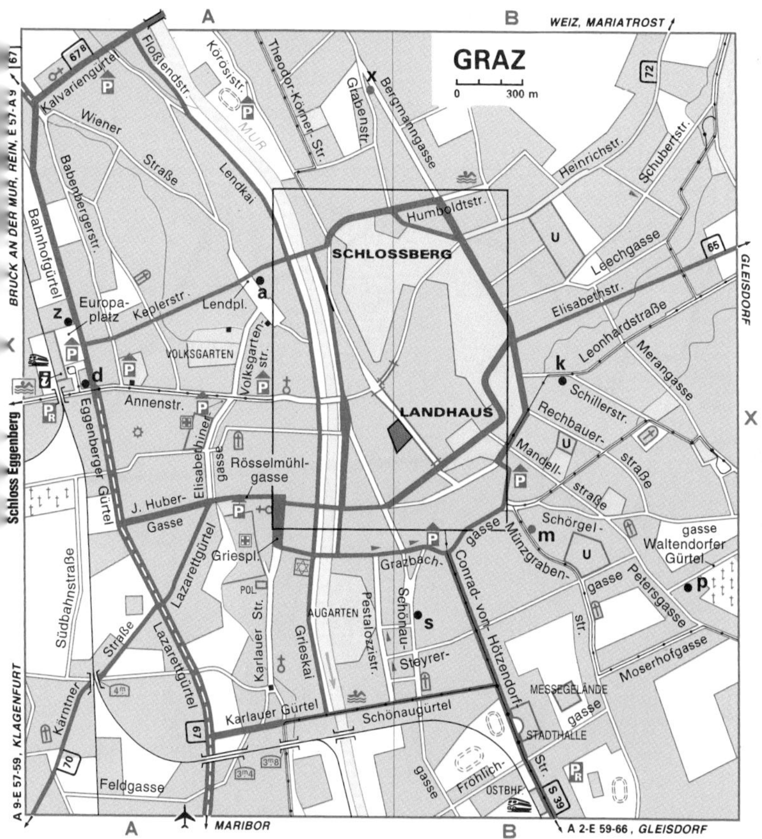

Grand Hotel Wiesler Zim, VISA AE

Grieskai 4 ✉ *8020 – ✆ (0316) 7 06 60 – direktion@hotelwiesler.com – Fax (0316) 706676* CZ **f**

96 Zim ☕ – 🚹185/205 € 🚹🚹245/265 € – 4 Suiten

Rest – *(geschl. Sonntag)* Menü 39/48 € – Karte 26/46 €

◆ Im Zentrum liegt das Jugendstilhotel, dessen Zimmer und elegante Suiten alle über eine hohe Decke verfügen. Schön frühstücken kann man im Grand Café mit Jugenstilmosaiken. Kräftige Farben, Philippe-Starck-Design und ein helles, nettes Ambiente im Restaurant.

Schlossberg Hotel garni VISA AE

Kaiser-Franz-Josef-Kai 30 ✉ *8010 – ✆ (0316) 8 07 00 – office@schlossberg-hotel.at – Fax (0316) 807070*

geschl. Weihnachten – Silvester CY **h**

54 Zim – 🚹145/185 € 🚹🚹190/235 €, ☕ 17 € – 4 Suiten

◆ Die Gästezimmer des Bürgerhauses a. d. 16. Jh. hat man mit feinen Antiquitäten ergänzt. Bilder und Skulpturen finden Sie überall im Haus, auch im hübschen Frühstücksraum.

GRAZ

Abraham-a-Santa-Clara-Gasse . . . . . DZ 2
Altstadtpassage . . . . DZ 3
Färbergasse . . . . DZ 5
Färberpl. . . . . DZ 6
Franziskanergasse . . . . CZ 8
Franziskanerpl. . . . . CZ 9
Freiheitspl. . . . . DY 10
Girardigasse . . . . DZ 35
Glockenspielpl. . . . . DZ 12
Griespl. . . . . CZ 13
Hauptbrücke . . . . CZ 16
Keplerbrücke. . . . . CY 19
Luthergasse . . . . DZ 20
Mehlpl. . . . . DZ 22
Neue-Welt-Gasse . . . . CZ 23
Paradeisgasse. . . . . CZ 26
Radetzkybrücke . . . . CZ 27
Schloßbergpl. . . . . CY 29
Stempfergasse. . . . . DZ 30
Tegetthoffbrücke . . . . CZ 32

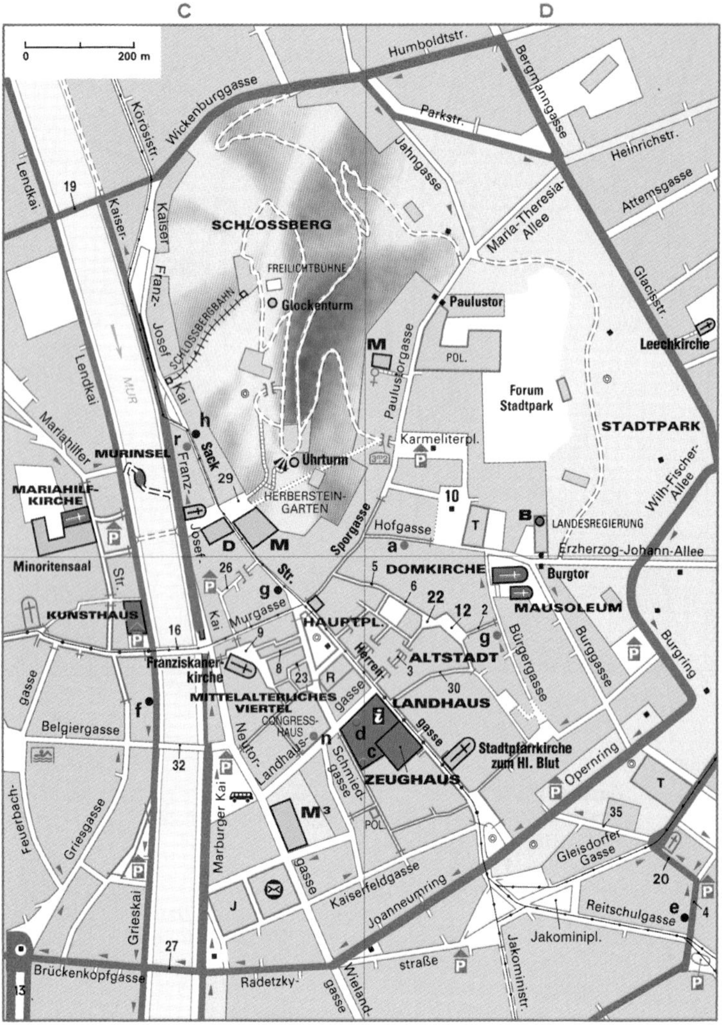

Wir bemühen uns bei unseren Preisangaben um größtmögliche Genauigkeit. Aber alles ändert sich! Lassen Sie sich daher bei Ihrer Reservierung den derzeit gültigen Preis mitteilen.

augartenhotel Zim, Rest,

Schönaugasse 53 ✉ *8010* VISA AE

– ✆ *(0316) 2 08 00 – office@augartenhotel.at – Fax (0316) 2080080* BX **s**

56 Zim – 115/155 € 140/180 €, 13 €

Rest *Magnolia* – ✆ (0316) 82 38 35 *(geschl. Aug. 2 Wochen und Samstag – Sonntag)* Menü 40/60 € – Karte 36/42 €

◆ Modernes, farbenfrohes Design prägt die Innenarchitektur dieses Hotels mit der verspiegelten Glasfassade. Gemälde und Skulpturen schmücken Zimmer und Konferenzräume. Im hinteren Trakt befindet sich das kleine Restaurant Magnolia mit offener Küche.

Erzherzog Johann Zim, VISA AE

Sackstr. 3 ✉ *8010 – ✆ (0316) 81 16 16 – office@erzherzog-johann.com – Fax (0316) 811515* CZ **g**

59 Zim – 109/172 € 160/240 €

Rest – *(geschl. 4. – 26. Aug. und Montag – Dienstag)* Menü 38/50 € – Karte 27/37 €

◆ Stilvoll ist das Ambiente in diesem ehemaligen Barockpalais am Hauptplatz. Hohe, stuckverzierte Decken und schöne Stilmöbel bestimmen das Interieur. Restaurant im überdachten und begrünten Innenhof.

Parkhotel Graz Zim, Rest, P

Leonhardtstr. 8 (am Meranpark) VISA AE

✉ *8010 – ✆ (0316) 3 63 00 – romantik@parkhotel-graz.at – Fax (0316) 363050* BX **k**

70 Zim – 95/145 € 165/230 €

Rest – Menü 20 € (abends) – Karte 23/35 €

◆ Die gastronomische Tradition dieses Hauses reicht zurück bis ins 16. Jh. Heute erwarten Sie hier ein stilvoller Hallenbereich und zeitgemäße, behagliche Zimmer. Gediegenes Restaurant mit Wintergarten. Schön: der Biedermeier-Gastgarten.

Zum Dom garni VISA AE

Bürgergasse 14 ✉ *8010 – ✆ (0316) 82 48 00 – domhotel@domhotel.co.at – Fax (0316) 8248008* DZ **b**

29 Zim – 80/120 € 150/165 € – 7 Suiten

◆ Das einstige Rokokopalais ist heute ein Hotel, das nichts von seinem Charme eingebüßt hat. Individuelle, aufwändig gestaltete Zimmer schaffen eine edle Atmosphäre.

Gollner garni P VISA AE

Schlögelgasse 14 ✉ *8010 – ✆ (0316) 82 25 21 – hotel.gollner@chello.at – Fax (0316) 8225217* DZ **e**

54 Zim – 105/130 € 150/240 € – 4 Suiten

◆ Ein klassisches Stadthotel, gediegen und individuell eingerichtet. Besonders empfehlenswert sind die Zimmer zum rückwärtig gelegenen, liebevoll gepflegten Garten.

Mercure Graz City garni P

Lendplatz 36 ✉ *8020 – ✆ (0316) 75 14 05* VISA AE

– h5742@accor.com – Fax (0316) 751405555 X **a**

96 Zim – 75/105 € 85/123 €, 11 €

◆ Nicht weit vom neuen Grazer Wahrzeichen, dem futuristischen Kunsthaus, und der Murinsel wohnen Sie in zeitgemäßen, geräumigen Zimmern. Die Altstadt ist zu Fuß erreichbar.

Mercure Graz Messe
Zim, Rest,

Waltendorfer Gürtel 8 ✉ *8010 – ✆ (0316) 82 63 00 – h2212@accor.com – Fax (0316) 826300630* BX **p**

101 Zim – ♦99 € ♦♦137 €

Rest – Karte 18/24 €

♦ Ein modernes Hotel, das mit seinen funktionellen Zimmern hauptsächlich auf die Bedürfnisse von Geschäftsreisenden und Tagungsteilnehmern eingestellt ist. Zur Halle hin offenes, schlicht gestaltetes Restaurant.

daniel garni

Europaplatz 1 ✉ *8020 – ✆ (0316) 71 10 80 – hello@hoteldaniel.com – Fax (0316) 711085* AX **d**

102 Zim – ♦59/79 € ♦♦79/99 €, ☕ 9 €

♦ Direkt im Zentrum befindet sich dieses Hotel mit modern eingerichteten Zimmern. Nett ist der Frühstücksraum mit Wasserbecken und Wasserfall. Hoteleigene Roller zum Verleih.

Ibis garni

Europaplatz 12 ✉ *8020 – ✆ (0316) 7 78 – h1917-re@accor.com – Fax (0316) 778303* AX **z**

108 Zim – ♦62 € ♦♦79 €, ☕ 10 €

♦ Die Lage am Bahnhof und die funktionelle Einrichtung machen das moderne Hotel besonders für Geschäftsreisende interessant. Vom Frühstücksraum blicken Sie auf den Europaplatz.

Iohan

Landhausgasse 1 ✉ *8010 – ✆ (0316) 82 13 12 – restaurant@iohan.at – Fax (0316) 82131212*

geschl. Sonntag – Montag und Feiertage CZ **d**

Rest – *(nur Abendessen)* Menü 36 € – Karte 25/47 €

♦ Ein wunderbares Kreuzgewölbe, getragen von schweren Steinsäulen, gibt dem großen, minimalistisch gestylten Raum ein ganz spezielles Flair. Schöner Renaissance-Innenhofgarten.

Landhaus Keller

Schmiedgasse 9 ✉ *8010 – ✆ (0316) 83 02 76 – mahlzeit@landhaus-keller.at – Fax (0316) 8302766*

geschl. 1. – 6. Januar und Sonntag CDZ **c**

Rest – (Tischbestellung ratsam) Karte 20/45 €

♦ Eines der ältesten und größten Wirtshäuser in Graz – 1596 als Schenke eröffnet. Das Restaurant besteht aus mehreren rustikalen Stuben, teils mit schönen Gewölbedecken.

Casino Restaurant

Landhausgasse 10 ✉ *8010 – ✆ (0316) 8 21 38 00 – office@revita.at – Fax (0316) 82138010* CZ **n**

Rest – *(nur Abendessen)* Menü 36 € – Karte 23/38 €

♦ Im Casino Restaurant sitzen Sie mitten im Geschehen! Wer nicht spielen möchte, genießt in klassischem Ambiente an gut eingedeckten Tischen die spannende Atmosphäre.

Mayers

Sackstr. 29/III ✉ *8010 – ✆ (0316) 81 33 91 – restaurant@mayers.cc – Fax (0316) 814191*

geschl. 1. – 7. Jan. und Samstag – Sonntag CY **r**

Rest – *(nur Abendessen)* Karte 26/40 €
♦ Im dritten Stock eines modernen Geschäftshauses mit auffallender Glasfassade finden Sie dieses ansprechende, im Bistrostil gestaltete Restaurant mit schöner Aussicht.

Hofkeller

Hofgasse 8 ✉ 8010 – ✆ (0316) 83 24 39 – office@hofkeller.at
geschl. Sonn- und Feiertage DY **a**
Rest – Karte 26/36 €
♦ Südländische Farbgestaltung und eine hübsche Gewölbedecke machen den Reiz des kleinen Restaurants aus. Das Angebot ist überwiegend mediterran ausgelegt.

Corti

Münzgrabenstr. 17 ✉ 8010 – ✆ (0316) 81 70 80 – info@ristorantecorti.at – Fax (0316) 817080
geschl. 24. – 28. Dez. und Sonntag BX **m**
Rest – Menü 60 € – Karte 22/43 €
♦ Alle, die italienische Regionalküche und nostalgisches Ambiente lieben, werden sich hier – im ältesten italienischen Restaurant der Stadt – zweifelsohne wohlfühlen.

Santa Clara

Bürgergasse 6 (Innenhof) ✉ 8010 – ✆ (0316) 81 18 22 – Fax (0316) 811400
geschl. Feb. 2 Wochen, Sonn- und Feiertage DZ **g**
Rest – *(nur Abendessen)* Karte 21/38 €
♦ Etwas versteckt liegt das Restaurant in einem Innenhof in der Altstadt. Unter einem schönen Kreuzgewölbe empfiehlt man Ihnen mündlich die mediterranen Speisen. Gastgarten.

In Graz-Andritz **Nord: 3 km über Bergmannstraße und Grabenstraße AX:**

Sporthotel Players

Weinzöttlstr. 6 ✉ 8045 – ✆ (0316) 67 29 26 – office@sporthotel-players.at – Fax (0316) 67292643
geschl. 22. – 25. März, 10. – 13. Mai, 24. – 27. Dez.
34 Zim – 62/64 € 97/104 €
Rest – *(Montag – Freitag nur Abendessen)* Karte 12/24 €
♦ Zum Freizeitangebot dieses Hotels zählt ein komplett ausgestattetes Fitnesscenter auf 600 qm – für Hotelgäste gratis. Sie wohnen in sehr gepflegten, zeitgemäßen Zimmern. Kleines Restaurant mit offener Küche und Pizza-Ofen.

In Graz-Eggenberg **West: 5 km über Annenstraße AX:**

Bokan Exclusiv garni

Mainersbergstr. 1 ✉ 8051 – ✆ (0316) 57 14 34 – office@bokan-exclusive.at – Fax (0316) 57143475
69 Zim – 77 € 128 € – 4 Suiten
♦ Hinter einer auffälligen modernen Fassade finden Geschäftsreisende und Tagungsgäste ein ebenso modernes Interieur vor, das mit Funktionalität überzeugt.

In Graz-Geidorf

Vital Hotel Teuschler garni

Mariatroster Str. 12 (über Heinrichstr. BX) ✉ *8043 – (0316) 32 14 48 – hotel@teuschler.at – Fax (0316) 3214484*
geschl. 15. Dez. – 6. Jan.
25 Zim – 59/79 € 98/138 €

◆ Ein neuzeitliches Hotel, dessen Zimmer mit hellem, funktionellem Mobiliar ausgestattet sind und alle über W-Lan verfügen. Frühstücksbuffet mit Vitalecke.

Das Wirtshaus Greiner mit Zim

Grabenstr. 64 ✉ *8010 – (0316) 68 50 90 – das@wirtshaus-greiner.at – Fax (0316) 6850904* AX x
8 Zim – 48 € 78/82 €
Rest – *(geschl. Ende Juli – Mitte August 3 Wochen, Ende Dez. – Anfang Jan. 2 Wochen und Samstag – Sonntag)* Menü 19/35 € (abends) – Karte 15/32 €

◆ Mit viel Holz hat man das von der Inhaberfamilie geführte Haus aus dem 16. Jahrhundert rustikal und gemütlich eingerichtet. Nette, recht individuelle Gästezimmer.

In Graz-Mariatrost **Nord-Ost: 4 km über Heinrichstraße BX:**

Stoiser's Hotel Garni garni

Mariatroster Str. 174 ✉ *8044 – (0316) 39 20 55 – graz@stoiser.com – Fax (0316) 39205555*
geschl. 21. – 28. Dez.
53 Zim – 64/71 € 108/122 €

◆ Geeignet für Geschäftsreisende und Tagungsgäste: solide, neuzeitliche und technisch gut ausgestattete Zimmer – teils ruhiger nach hinten gelegen – sowie moderne Seminarräume.

Pfeifer Kirchenwirt Zim,

Kirchplatz 9 ✉ *8044 – (0316) 3 91 11 20 – office@kirchenwirtgraz.com – Fax (0316) 39111249*
31 Zim – 85/115 € 110/140 €
Rest – *(geschl. Sonntagabend)* Karte 15/40 €

◆ Aus einem alten Gasthof ist dieses zeitgemäße Hotel an der imposanten Wallfahrtskirche entstanden. Einige der funktionellen Zimmer sind besonders geschmackvoll und gediegen. Bürgerlich-ländliche Restaurantstuben. Hübscher Gastgarten unter Kastanienbäumen.

Häuserl im Wald (mit Gästehäusern) Zim,

Roseggerweg 105 ✉ *8044 – (0316) 39 11 65 – legenstein@aon.at – Fax (0316) 392277*
22 Zim – 44/55 € 78/95 €
Rest – *(geschl. Montag)* Karte 13/32 €

◆ Ruhig liegt dieses Hotel am Rand des Leechwalds. Zimmer im Landhausstil verteilen sich auf das Haupthaus, eine Villa und ein ca. 10 Min. entferntes Bauernhaus. Mehrere unterschiedlich gestaltete Räume und eine große Terrasse bilden den Restaurantbereich.

In Graz-Strassgang Süd-West: 6 km über Kärntner Straße AX:

Paradies Rest, P VISA AE
Strassganger Str. 380b ✉ 8054 – ☎ (0316) 28 21 56 – info@hotelparadies.at – Fax (0316) 2821566
85 Zim – 75/91 € 110/140 € – 4 Suiten
Rest – Karte 16/34 €
♦ An eine Tennishalle hat man das moderne Tagungshotel angebaut. Hier erwarten Sie funktionelle, solide möblierte Zimmer mit gutem Platzangebot sowie ein großer Freizeitbereich. Hell und freundlich wirkt das Restaurant.

XX **Kehlberghof** ← Graz, P VISA AE
Kehlbergstr. 83 ✉ 8054 – ☎ (0316) 28 41 25 – restaurant@kehlberghof.at – Fax (0316) 286825
geschl. Karwoche, 12. Aug. – 3. Sept., über Weihnachten 2 Wochen und Sonntag – Montag
Rest – (Tischbestellung ratsam) Karte 18/40 €
♦ Regionale Produkte sind die Grundlage dieser schmackhaften Küche – ein angenehm helles und freundliches Ambiente umgibt den Gast. Schöner Blick auf die Stadt. Nette Terrasse.

In Graz-Waltendorf Ost: 3 km über Schillerstraße BX:

Der Marienhof garni P VISA
Waltendorfer Hauptstr. 81 ✉ 8010 – ☎ (0316) 42 98 42 – hotel@dermarienhof.at – Fax (0316) 42984214
geschl. 19. Dez. – 6. Jan.
20 Zim – 57 € 90 €
♦ Hinter einer frischen gelben Fassade stehen neuzeitliche und allergikerfreundliche Zimmer mit hellem Holzmobiliar, Parkett und guter Technik bereit – teils mit Blick auf Graz.

In Graz-Webling Süd: 3 km über Lazarettgürtel AX:

Kern Buam garni P VISA AE
Kärntner Str. 245 ✉ 8054 – ☎ (0316) 29 14 30 – hotel@kernbuam.at – Fax (0316) 291430555
44 Zim – 58/69 € 94/108 €
♦ Eine funktionelle Ausstattung und die verkehrsgünstige Lage machen dieses Hotel vor allem für Geschäftsleute interessant.

Unsere „Hoffnungsträger" sind die Restaurants, deren Küche wir für die nächste Ausgabe besonders sorgfältig auf eine höhere Auszeichnung hin überprüfen. Der Name dieser Restaurants ist in „rot" gedruckt und zusätzlich auf der Sterne-Liste am Anfang des Buches zu finden.

GREIFENBURG – Kärnten – 730 L8 – 1 920 Ew – Höhe 620 m 8 G6

Wien 367 – Klagenfurt 110 – Lienz 38 – Spittal an der Drau 33

Erbhof Kohlmayr garni

Tirolerstr. 12 ✉ 9761 – ✆ (04712) 3 36 – Fax (04712) 33620
geschl. Feb. – März, Nov.
10 Zim – 42/50 € 64/80 €

◆ Um 1600 wurde der Gasthof mit den soliden, wohnlichen Zimmern erstmals erwähnt. Man bietet seinen Gästen freien Eintritt zum Greifenburger Badesee. Eigene Hochalm in 2200 m.

GRIES IM SELLRAIN – Tirol – 730 F7 – 570 Ew – Höhe 1 238 m 6 C5

Wien 506 – Innsbruck 25 – Imst 64 – Schwaz 54

Sporthotel Antonie (geheizt) Rest,

Nr. 16 ✉ 6182 – ✆ (05236) 2 03
– info@hotel-antonie.at – Fax (05236) 20349
geschl. 6. April – 20. Mai, 5. Okt. – 30. Nov.
42 Zim (inkl. ½ P.) – 57/63 € 95/108 € 67/88 € 119/161 €
Rest – Karte 19/33 €

◆ Der gewachsene Gasthof in der Dorfmitte verfügt über solide, mit hellem Holz eingerichtete Zimmer sowie einen recht großzügigen Saunabereich. Café mit hausgemachtem Kuchen.

GRIESKIRCHEN – Oberösterreich – 730 N4 – 4 810 Ew – Höhe 340 m

Wien 211 – Linz 51 – Wels 24 – Passau 61 2 H3

Gasthof Zweimüller-Zum Weissen Kreuz Zim,

Stadtplatz 4 ✉ 4710
– ✆ (07248) 6 22 26 – zweimueller@vitalwelt.at – Fax (07248) 6222631
geschl. 1. – 19. August
18 Zim – 65 € 98 €
Rest – *(geschl. Samstag, Sonntagabend)* Karte 14/33 €

◆ In der Ortsmitte finden Sie diesen Gasthof a. d. J. 1604. Durch Flure mit auffallenden Kreuzgewölbe-Decken gelangen Sie in wohnliche, farblich angenehm gestaltete Zimmer. Rustikale Gaststuben mit überdachter Terrasse. Serviert werden regionale Speisen.

Castelvecchio

Bahnhofstr. 7 ✉ 4710 – ✆ (07248) 6 43 80 – pizza.pasta@aon.at
– Fax (07248) 61426
geschl. Aug. 2 Wochen und Montag – Dienstag
Rest – *(Mittwoch – Samstag nur Abendessen)* Menü 33/48 € – Karte 33/43 €

◆ Ziegelsteinwände, ein altes Gewölbe und nettes Dekor unterstreichen den gemütlichen Charakter dieses Restaurants und sorgen für leicht toskanisches Flair. Italienische Karte.

Waldschänke (Elisabeth Grabmer)

Kickendorf 15 (Nord: 2 km, Richtung Pollham) ✉ 4710
– ✆ (07248) 6 23 08 – waldschaenke@utanet.at – Fax (07248) 66644
geschl. 1. – 9. Jan., 28. Juli – 13. Aug. und Sonntagabend – Dienstag
Rest – *(Mittwoch – Freitag nur Abendessen)* (Tischbestellung ratsam)
Menü 42/56 € – Karte 30/46 €

Spez. Marinierter Kalbsstafelspitz mit milder Krensauce und Gemüsesalat. Pochiertes grünes Ei mit Saiblingskaviar und Blattspinat. Tournedos vom Bio-Stier mit Petersilienkruste.

◆ Klassische, aus regionalen Produkten zubereitete Küche, sehr gute Weinberatung und geschultes Personal erwarten Sie in dem engagiert geführten, netten Landgasthof.

GRÖBMING – Steiermark – 730 N6 – 2 500 Ew – Höhe 776 m – Wintersport: 2 048 m 3 – Heilklimatischer Kurort 9 **H4**

Wien 271 – Graz 149 – Liezen 32 – Bad Ischl 72

Kirchplatz 15, 8962, (03685) 22 13 10, info@groebmingerland.at

Schloss Thannegg

Schloss 1, (Moosheim) (Süd: 2 km) 8962 – (03685) 23 21 00 – info@schloss-thannegg.at – Fax (03685) 232106

geschl. 31. März – 4. Mai, 19. Okt. – 21. Dez.

18 Zim – 59/79 € 102/145 € 79/92 € 142/167 € – 5 Suiten

Rest – *(geschl. Montagmittag, Dienstag – Mittwochmittag)* Karte 17/33 €

◆ Das Schloss a. d. J. 1150 beherbergt dieses engagiert geführte, charmante kleine Hotel mit meist rustikal möblierten Zimmern. Turmsuite über zwei Etagen. Im Restaurant: viel Holz, ein alter Herd und historischer Zierrat. Bürgerlich-regionale Küche.

Häuserl im Wald

Mitterberg 71, (Mitterberg) (Ost: 3 km) 8962 – (03685) 2 22 80 – hotel@haeuserlimwald.at – Fax (03685) 2228055

geschl. 10. – 25. Dez.

35 Zim (inkl. ½ P.) – 49/54 € 84/98 € 57/63 € 104/140 €

Rest – Karte 16/33 €

◆ Etwas außerhalb liegt dieses regionstypische, familiengeführte Hotel mit eigener kleiner Landwirtschaft. Die Zimmer sind mit hellem Naturholz wohnlich eingerichtet. Rustikal gestalteter Restaurantbereich.

Landhaus St. Georg

Rest,

Kulmweg 555 8962 – (03685) 2 27 40 – office@st-georg.at – Fax (03685) 2274060

geschl. April, November

21 Zim (inkl. ½ P.) – 61/99 € 96/198 € 77/115 € 126/230 € – 7 Suiten

Rest – *(geschl. Donnerstag)* Karte 17/30 €

◆ Die schöne ruhige Lage und wohnliche Gästezimmer im Landhausstil – teilweise mit gemütlichem Kachelofen – machen dieses Hotel aus. Restaurantstuben mit behaglichem gediegenem Ambiente.

Amadeus

Rest,

Stoderstr. 878 8962 – (03685) 2 38 39 – office@landhaus-amadeus.at – Fax (03685) 238394

geschl. 15. Okt. – 22.Dez.

12 Zim (inkl. ½ P.) – 65/75 € 114/134 € 75/85 € 134/152 €

Rest – (nur Abendessen für Hausgäste)

◆ Das kleine Hotel am Ortsrand verfügt über wohnlich-rustikale Gästezimmer im Landhausstil, die meist als Appartements angelegt sind.

Reisslerhof

Rest,

Zirting 24, (Mitterberg) (Ost: 2 km) 8962 – (03685) 2 23 64 – info@reisslerhof.at – Fax (03685) 2236410

geschl. Nov.

35 Zim (inkl. ½ P.) – ☼ 45/47 € 78/102 € ❄ 53/60 € 84/122 €
Rest – (nur Abendessen für Hausgäste)
♦ Die Zimmer in diesem familiengeführten Haus sind zeitgemäß und funktionell eingerichtet - die nach hinten gelegenen bieten eine schöne Aussicht.

GRÖDIG – **Salzburg** – 730 L5 – **6 640 Ew** – **Höhe 446 m** – **Wintersport: 1 805 m** 1 — 8 **F4**

Wien 309 – Salzburg 10 – Hallein 9 – Berchtesgaden 16
Gartenauerstr. 8 (Gartenau), ✉ 5083, (06246) 7 35 70, info@groedig.net

In Grödig-Eichet Nord-West: 2 km Richtung Salzburg:

Gasthof Pflegerbrücke — Biergarten Zim, P VISA MC
Pflegerstr. 53 ✉ 5082 – (0662) 82 17 25 – office@pflegerbruecke.at – Fax (0662) 82172515
geschl. Feb.
22 Zim – 44/48 € 74/78 €
Rest – *(geschl. Mittwoch – Donnerstag)* Karte 14/31 €
♦ Der familiengeführte Landgasthof mit freundlich-gelber Fassade verfügt über neuzeitliche Zimmer und einen Spielplatz für Kinder. Bürgerlich essen kann man in der ländlichen Gaststube mit großem Biergarten.

In Grödig-Gartenau Süd-Ost: 1 km Richtung Hallein:

Untersberg (mit Gästehaus) — Zim, P VISA MC AE
Dr. Friedrich Ödlweg 1 ✉ 5083 – (06246) 7 25 75 – hoteluntersberg@salzburg.co.at – Fax (06246) 725755
53 Zim – 61/81 € 100/132 € – ½ P 15 €
Rest – Karte 16/33 €
♦ Das Hotel im ländlich-rustikalen Stil nahe Salzburg bietet komfortable, wohnliche Gästezimmer und für Seminare geeignete Räume an. Kleiner Speisesaal und rustikale Gaststube mit internationalem Angebot.

In Grödig-Sankt Leonhard Süd-Ost: 1,5 km Richtung Hallein:

Gasthof Schorn — P VISA MC AE
Sankt Leonhard Str. 1 ✉ 5083 – (06246) 7 23 34 – info@gasthofschorn.at – Fax (06246) 7233440
20 Zim – 46/52 € 74/84 € – ½ P 14 €
Rest – *(geschl. Montag)* Karte 15/28 €
♦ Hinter Wandmalereien an der Fassade verbirgt sich ein freundlicher Familienbetrieb mit modernen, in warmen Tönen gestalteten, behaglichen Zimmern. In rustikale Stuben unterteiltes Restaurant mit regionalem Angebot.

GROSSARL – **Salzburg** – 730 L7 – **3 640 Ew** – **Höhe 920 m** – **Wintersport: 2 033 m** 4 17 — 8 **G5**

Wien 345 – Salzburg 73 – Bischofshofen 25 – St. Johann im Pongau 15
Markt 1, ✉ 5611, (06414) 2 81, info@grossarl.co.at

Tauernhof

Unterberg 85 ✉ 5611 – ✆ (06414) 26 40 – info@tauernhof.com – Fax (06414) 26455

100 Zim (inkl. ½ P.) – ☼ 🚹69/74 € 🚹🚹111/129 € ❄ 🚹73/125 € 🚹🚹119/234 €

Rest – Karte 16/34 €

◆ In dem Ferienhotel mit regionstypischer Balkonfassade erwarten den Gast wohnlich-ländlich gestaltete Zimmer sowie ein schöner Bade- und Saunabereich und Kosmetik. A-la-carte-Stube in rustikalem Stil.

Edelweiss

Zim, Rest,

Unterberg 83 ✉ 5611 – ✆ (06414) 30 00 – info@edelweiss-grossarl.at – Fax (06414) 30066

geschl. 13. – 27. April

100 Zim (inkl. ½ P.) – ☼ 🚹114/130 € 🚹🚹176/210 € ❄ 🚹114/191 € 🚹🚹176/294 €

Rest – Karte 16/40 €

◆ Ein über mehrere Etagen angelegter Wellnessbereich mit Beauty-Abteilung zählt neben den alpenländisch eingerichteten Zimmern zu den Vorzügen dieses gut geführten Hotels. Verschiedene Stuben und eine Pizzeria bilden das Restaurant.

Waldhof

(geheizt) Zim,

Markt 272 ✉ 5611 – ✆ (06414) 88 66 – info@hotel-waldhof.com – Fax (06414) 886688

geschl. 4. Nov. – 1. Dez., 5. April – 1. Mai

43 Zim (inkl. ½ P.) – ☼ 🚹74/106 € 🚹🚹134/172 € ❄ 🚹89/156 € 🚹🚹164/253 €

Rest – Karte 15/25 €

◆ Vor allem auf Familien ist dieses Ferienhotel eingestellt. Neben einem umfangreichen Kinderprogramm bietet man auch einen natürlichen Badesee und ein Erlebnis-Hallenbad. Neuzeitlich gestaltetes Restaurant in warmen Farben sowie ein separates Pub.

Neuwirt

Rest,

Markt 6 ✉ 5611 – ✆ (06414) 2 51 – info@hotel-neuwirt.com – Fax (06414) 2514

geschl. Mai, Nov.

22 Zim (inkl. ½ P.) – ☼ 🚹64/74 € 🚹🚹98/118 € ❄ 🚹85/103 € 🚹🚹136/176 €

Rest – (nur Abendessen) Karte 16/28 €

◆ Mit hübschen Stoffen dekorierte Gästezimmer im Landhausstil sowie eine persönliche Führung sprechen für dieses im Ortskern gelegene kleine Hotel. Eine der beiden Restaurantstuben ist die besonders gemütliche holzgetäfelte Zirbenstube für Nichtraucher.

Hubertushof

Rest,

Markt 158 ✉ 5611 – ✆ (06414) 2 27 – info@hotel-hubertus.cc – Fax (06414) 2274

geschl. 14. April – 1. Mai, 26. Okt. – 28. Nov.

32 Zim (inkl. ½ P.) – ☼ 🚹58/76 € 🚹🚹99/111 € ❄ 🚹73/115 € 🚹🚹130/167 €

Rest – (nur Abendessen für Hausgäste)

◆ In dem familiengeführten Hotel in einer Nebenstraße erwarten Sie mit Zirbenholzmöbeln regionstypisch eingerichtete Zimmer sowie ein hübsch gestalteter Saunabereich.

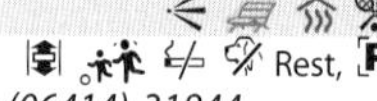

Familien-Erlebnis-Hotel Moar-Gut
Bach 19 (Süd: 3 km) ✉ 5611 Rest,
– ✆ (06414) 3 18 – info@hotel-moargut.com – Fax (06414) 31844
geschl. 2. Nov. – 15. Dez.
21 Zim (inkl. ½ P.) – 170/190 € 180/240 €
Rest – (nur Abendessen für Hausgäste)
◆ Nettes ländliches Ambiente erwartet Sie in dem ganz auf Familien eingestellten Hotel mit Bauernhof. Zimmer mit Küchenzeile und hübscher Saunabereich im alpenländischen Stil.

Kristall Zim, Rest,
Unterberg 158 ✉ 5611 – ✆ (06414) 87 67 – info@kristall.eu
– Fax (06414) 876755
geschl. 13. April – 20. Mai, 30. Okt. – 10. Dez.
25 Zim (inkl. ½ P.) – 40/60 € 80/104 € 50/90 € 100/180 €
Rest – (nur Abendessen für Hausgäste)
◆ Das im alpenländischen Stil gebaute Hotel liegt unweit des Skilifts und gefällt mit seinen freundlichen, neuzeitlich-wohnlichen Gästezimmern. Hübscher Saunabereich.

Wir bemühen uns bei unseren Preisangaben um größtmögliche Genauigkeit. Aber alles ändert sich! Lassen Sie sich daher bei Ihrer Reservierung den derzeit gültigen Preis mitteilen.

GROSS-ENZERSDORF – Niederösterreich – 730 V4 – 8 130 Ew – Höhe 156 m 4 L2

Wien 18 – St. Pölten 92 – Baden 42 – Bratislava 53

Am Sachsengang Zim,
Schloßhofer Str. 60 ✉ 2301 VISA
– ✆ (02249) 29 01 – hotel@sachsengang.at – Fax (02249) 2905
106 Zim – 80/110 € 135/150 € – ½ P 23 €
Rest *Taverne am Sachsengang* – Karte 22/50 €
◆ In diesem gewachsenen familiengeführten Hotel am Ortsrand wohnen Sie in funktionell ausgestatteten, im Laura-Ashley-Stil gehaltenen Zimmern. In einem separaten Gebäude ist die Taverne am Sachsengang untergebracht – ländliches Ambiente mit elegantem Touch.

GROSSGMAIN – Salzburg – 730 K5 – 2 420 Ew – Höhe 520 m 8 F4

Wien 307 – Salzburg 15 – Berchtesgaden 18 – Bad Reichenhall 6
Salzburger Str. 250, ✉ 5084, ✆ (06247) 82 78, info@tourist-grossgmain.co.at

In Großgmain-Hinterreit Nord-Ost: 2 km Richtung Salzburg:

Gasthof Steinerwirt

Salzburger Str. 25 ✉ 5084 – ✆ (06247) 73 11
– info@gasthof-steinerwirt.at – Fax (06247) 73115
22 Zim – 45/49 € 70/80 € – ½ P 12 €
Rest – *(geschl. Donnerstag)* Karte 18/32 €
◆ Ein sehr gepflegter Gasthof mit modernen, geräumigen und hellen Zimmern, die fast alle über einen Balkon verfügen. Man betreibt eine eigene Landwirtschaft und Hausmetzgerei. Gemütliches Restaurant im regionstypischen Stil mit bürgerlicher Kost.

Im Naturpark Untersberg

Latschenwirt

Buchhöhenstr. 122 (Nord-Ost: 5,5 km, Richtung Salzburg, nach 4 km rechts ab) ✉ 5084 – ✆ (06247) 73 51 – info@latschenwirt.at – Fax (06247) 73511

geschl. 18. – 23. Feb. und Dienstag – Mittwoch

Rest – (Tischbestellung ratsam) Menü 31/36 € (abends) – Karte 22/38 €

◆ Die gemütliche alpenländische Bauernstube bietet klassisches und regionales Essen. Besonders schön für Wanderer ist der Gastgarten zum Einkehren.

GROSSKIRCHHEIM – Kärnten – 730 K8 – 1 610 Ew – Höhe 1 095 m – Wintersport: 1 401 m

8 **F6**

Wien 407 – Klagenfurt 151 – Spittal an der Drau 73 – Lienz 28

Schloßwirt Zim,

Döllach 100 ✉ 9843 – ✆ (04825) 4 11 – info@schlosswirt.net – Fax (04825) 411165

geschl. 14. Okt. – 20. Dez.

22 Zim (inkl. ½ P.) – 58/80 € 110/150 €

Rest – Menü 19 € (abends) – Karte 25/30 €

◆ Individuell und wohnlich-verspielt hat man die Zimmer in diesem 60 Jahre alten Gasthof eingerichtet. Alpines Reiten mit Haflingern ist möglich. Schön: die Römersauna. Nett sitzt man in den ländlichen Gaststuben mit freundlichem Service.

GRÜNAU IM ALMTAL – Oberösterreich – 730 N5 – 2 120 Ew – Höhe 528 m – Wintersport: 1 600 m 2 10

2 **H3**

Wien 228 – Linz 68 – Wels 48 – Gmunden 23

Im Dorf 17, ✉ 4645, ✆ (07616) 82 68, gruenau@almtal.at

Cumberland Wildpark★

Almsee★ (Süd: 12 km)

Almtalhof Rest,

Almeggstr. 1 ✉ 4645 – ✆ (07616) 60 04 – almtalhof@almtal.at – Fax (07616) 600466

geschl. 17. März – 28. April, 15. Okt. – 15. Dez.

23 Zim – 70/94 € 136/196 € – ½ P 23 €

Rest – Menü 43 € – Karte 21/36 €

◆ In dem von der Familie geführten Hotel herrscht eine gemütliche Atmosphäre, erzeugt durch den rustikalen Stil und das nette Dekor. Internationale und regionale Speisen gibt es in den holzverkleideten Restaurantstuben.

Waldpension Göschlseben Zim, Rest,

Göschlseben 5 ✉ 4645 – ✆ (07616) 82 80 – goeschlseben@almtal.at – Fax (07616) 828048

geschl. Mitte Okt. – Mitte Dez.

16 Zim – 40/60 € 76/120 € – ½ P 23 €

Rest – (nur Abendessen für Hausgäste)

◆ Eine ruhig gelegene kleine Urlaubsadresse unter familiärer Leitung, die über solide und zeitgemäß eingerichtete Gästezimmer verfügt.

GRUNDLSEE – Steiermark – 730 N6 – 1 290 Ew – Höhe 710 m – Wintersport: 850 m 2 9 H4

Wien 288 – Graz 166 – Salzburg 87 – Bad Ischl 34

Mosern 25, 8993, (03622) 86 66, info.grundlsee@ausseerland.at

Veranstaltungen

22.05. – 25.05.: Narzissenfest

Seehotel
Grundlsee und Bergpanorama, Zim,

Mosern 22 8993
– (03622) 8 60 44 – office@seehotelgrundlsee.at – Fax (03622) 860444
geschl. April 2 Wochen, Nov. 2 Wochen

17 Zim – 88/204 € 130/214 € – ½ P 15 €

Rest *Max's* – (nur Abendessen) Karte 20/40 €

◆ Eine schöne und individuelle kleine Adresse ist dieses mit viel Holz hell und modern gestaltete Hotel direkt am See. Zimmer mit Seeblick erwarten hier den Gast. Restaurant Max's mit internationaler Küche.

Post am See
Grundlsee und Bergpanorama,

Bräuhof 94 8993 – (03622) 2 01 04 – postamsee@utanet.at
– Fax (03622) 20104
geschl. 25. März – 23. April, Nov. und Montag – Dienstag, im Aug. nur Montag

Rest – Menü 19 € (mittags)/37 € – Karte 24/37 €

◆ Ein von der Inhaberfamilie geführtes Restaurant mit gediegenem Ambiente. Sehr schön sitzt man auf der Terrasse zum See. Aufmerksamer Service.

GUMPOLDSKIRCHEN – Niederösterreich – 730 U4 – 3 240 Ew – Höhe 260 m 4 L3

Wien 22 – St. Pölten 68 – Wiener Neustadt 31 – Mödling 5

Schrannenplatz 5, 2352, (02252) 6 35 36, tourismus@gumpoldskirchen.at

Richardhof, Hagenau am Richardhof 248 (02236) 89 23 05

Turmhof garni

Josef Schöffel Str. 9 2352 – (02252) 6 07 33 30
– office@hotel-turmhof.at – Fax (02252) 6073336
geschl. 21. Dez. – 7. Jan.

21 Zim – 75 € 110 €

◆ Ruhig liegt das freundlich und engagiert geführte Hotel am Ortsrand unterhalb der Weinberge. Man bietet moderne, in klaren Linien gehaltene Zimmer.

Krug Altes Zechhaus mit Zim
(Heuriger)

Kirchenplatz 1 2352 – (02252) 6 22 47 – office@krug.at
– Fax (02252) 622474

10 Zim – 45 € 70 €

Rest – *(Montag – Freitag nur Abendessen)* Menü 17 € (Buffet)

◆ Im Jahre 1549 wurde das Weinhaus erstmals erwähnt. Der Gotische Dachboden und der Zechhauskeller mit urigem Gewölbe bieten rustikales Ambiente und regionale Küche.

Luxuriös oder eher schlicht?
Die Symbole und kennzeichnen den Komfort.

GUNDERSHEIM – Kärnten – siehe Kirchbach

GUNTERSDORF – Niederösterreich – 730 U3 – 1 130 Ew – Höhe 247 m
3 **K1**

Wien 65 – St. Pölten 92 – Stockerau 36

Gasthaus an der Kreuzung
Oberort 110 ✉ 2042 – ✆ (02951) 22 29 – Fax (02951) 22294
geschl. 21. Juli – 7. Aug. und Mittwoch – Donnerstag
Rest – Menü 22 € – Karte 11/22 €
♦ In der Ortsmitte gelegener Gasthof mit freundlicher gelber Fassade, ländlichem und gepflegtem Ambiente und aufmerksamem Service. Terrasse im Innenhof.

GUNTRAMSDORF – Niederösterreich – 730 U4 – 8 430 Ew – Höhe 193 m
4 **L3**

Wien 19 – St. Pölten 70 – Baden 9 – Mödling 5

Refugium Zim, Zim,
Kirchengasse 4 ✉ 2353 – ✆ (02236) 50 66 50 – office@hotel-refugium.at
– Fax (02236) 50665050
geschl. 22. Dez. – 2. Jan.
16 Zim – 78 € 125 € – ½ P 21 €
Rest – (nur Abendessen) Karte 21/47 €
♦ Engagiert führt Familie Swoboda das kleine Hotel im Zentrum. Die freundlichen, wohnlichen Zimmer sind mit Parkettfußboden und guter Technik ausgestattet. In einem Wintergarten befindet sich das Restaurant.

Landhotel Jagdhof
Hauptstr. 41 ✉ 2353 – ✆ (02236) 5 22 25 – info@jagdhof.cc
– Fax (02236) 5222540
geschl. 24. – 26. Dez.
34 Zim – 75 € 110/125 € – ½ P 25 €
Rest – *(geschl. Sonntag)* Karte 27/45 €
♦ Der ehemalige Zehenthof bietet heute wohnliche Gästezimmer – einige mit Laura-Ashley-Dekor, der größte Teil befindet sich im Hotelanbau, in neuzeitlichem Stil eingerichtet. Klassisches Restaurant mit Wintergarten.

GURTEN – Oberösterreich – 730 M4 – 1 230 Ew – Höhe 400 m
1 **G3**

Wien 248 – Linz 88 – Braunau 28 – Ried im Innkreis 12

Bauböck
Gurten 16 ✉ 4942 – ✆ (07757) 62 02 – bauboeck@utanet.at
– Fax (07757) 62024
geschl. Sonntagabend – Montag
Rest – Karte 21/45 €
♦ Seit 1541 existiert dieses Gasthaus, in dem man in einer rustikalen Stube mit schwerer Holzdecke und nettem Dekor eine solide regionale Küche bietet.

GUTTARING – Kärnten – 730 P8 – 1 570 Ew – Höhe 860 m
10 **I5**

Wien 270 – Klagenfurt 39 – St. Veit an der Glan 20 – Judenburg 66

XX **Brunnwirt-Kassl** mit Zim

Unterer Markt 2 ✉ 9334 – ✆ (04262) 81 25 – brunnwirtkassl@aon.at – Fax (04262) 812521

geschl. Jan. 2 Wochen und Mittwoch sowie Jan. – April Mittwoch – Donnerstag

15 Zim – 42/48 € 80/90 € – ½ P 18 €

Rest – Menü 18 € – Karte 18/44 €

♦ Seit sieben Generationen ist der gut geführte Gasthof in Familienbesitz. Freundlich bewirtet man Sie hier mit regionaler Küche. Hübsch: die Gartenanlage mit Obstbäumen. Gepflegte Gästezimmer.

HAAG – Niederösterreich – 730 P4 – 5 170 Ew – Höhe 345 m 2 I3

Wien 148 – St. Pölten 91 – Steyr 18 – Amstetten 27

XX **Mitter** mit Zim

Linzer Str. 11 ✉ 3350 – ✆ (07434) 4 24 26 – mitter@stadthaag.at – Fax (07434) 4242642

geschl. 19. Aug. – 3. Sept., 27. Dez. – 6. Jan. und Donnerstag

10 Zim – 35/39 € 70/80 €

Rest – Menü 28/48 € – Karte 23/40 €

Rest *Gaststube* – Menü 28 € – Karte 13/30 €

♦ Hinter einer schmucken gelb-weißen Fassade führt Familie Hawel engagiert ein gepflegtes Restaurant in bürgerlichem Stil. Schöner Garten mit Terrassenbereich. Ländlich-rustikal gestaltete Gaststube.

HÄRING, BAD – Tirol – 730 I6 – 2 270 Ew – Höhe 625 m – Wintersport: 1 594 m 1 7 E5

Wien 398 – Innsbruck 66 – Kufstein 13 – Kitzbühel 37

✉ 6323, ✆ (05372) 6 22 07, info@kufstein.com

Panorama Royal ← Wörgl und Inntal, Zim,

Schönau 110

(Süd-West: 1 km in Richtung Wörgl) ✉ 6323 – ✆ (05332) 7 71 17 – office@panorama-royal.at – Fax (05332) 7711777

43 Zim – 77/120 € 138/216 € – ½ P 20 €

Rest – Menü 39/48 € – Karte 23/42 €

♦ Das Hotel liegt auf einer kleinen Anhöhe und bietet komfortable Zimmer, die mit modernen italienischen Stilmöbeln eingerichtet sind. Das Ambiente der unterteilten Restauranträume: rustikal bis elegant.

Schermer Zim,

Dorf 158 (am Kurzentrum) ✉ 6323 – ✆ (05332) 8 73 09 – hotelschermer@aon.at – Fax (05332) 87309

geschl. 3. – 14. März, 7. – 18. Juli, 17. – 28. Nov.

20 Zim (inkl. ½ P.) – 55/62 € 110/124 €

Rest – *(geschl. Mittwoch)* Karte 14/32 €

♦ Der Gasthof liegt direkt neben dem Kurzentrum. Die Zimmer sind alle mit Naturholz möbliert und funktionell ausgestattet – einige mit separatem Wohnbereich. Ganz in Holz gehaltenes Restaurant.

HAIMING – Tirol – 730 E7 – 3 910 Ew – Höhe 700 m – Wintersport: 1 850 m 2 8 6 C5

Wien 488 – Innsbruck 44 – Imst 16 – Seefeld in Tirol 29

Siedlungsstr. 2, ✉ 6425, ✆ (05266) 8 83 07, info@haiming.at

Föhrenhof Rest, VISA
Siedlungsstr. 6 ✉ 6425 – ✆ (05266) 8 85 88 – info@foehrenhof.com – Fax (05266) 8858850
20 Zim (inkl. ½ P.) – †42/74 € ††84/148 €
Rest – Karte 20/28 €
♦ Funktionell ausgestattete, einheitlich mit hellem Naturholz möblierte Gästezimmer sprechen für das kleine Hotel in der Ortsmitte. Das Restaurant ist teils neuzeitlich gestaltet, teils ganz in rustikalem Holz gehalten.

In Haiming-Ochsengarten Süd-Ost: 12 km ab der B 171 in Richtung Kühtai – Höhe 1 560 m

Gasthof Burkert Zim, Rest, VISA
Nr. 34 ✉ 6433 – ✆ (05252) 69 47 – info@gasthof-burkert.at – Fax (05252) 69474
geschl. 30. April – 31. Mai, 18. Okt. – 8. Dez.
19 Zim (inkl. ½ P.) – ☼ †36/38 € ††62/68 € ❄ †46/51 € ††84/94 €
Rest – Karte 17/22 €
♦ Die Zimmer dieses alpenländischen Gasthofs unterscheiden sich in der Größe und sind meist mit hellen, neuzeitlich-rustikalen Möbeln ausgestattet. Ländliches Restaurant mit lichtem Wintergartenanbau.

In Haiming-Haimingerberg Süd: 4 km

Ferienschlössl Zim, VISA
Haimingerberg 42 ✉ 6425 – ✆ (05266) 8 71 78 – hotel@ferienschloessl.at – Fax (05266) 871787
geschl. April 2 Wochen
42 Zim (inkl. ½ P.) – †86/102 € ††150/182 €
Rest – Karte 19/36 €
♦ Schön ist die Sicht von dem ruhig in einem kleinen Weiler gelegenen Hotel mit Garten. Man bietet unterschiedlich eingerichtete, wohnliche Zimmer und einen netten Badebereich. Restaurant mit gepflegter ländlicher Atmosphäre.

HAINZENBERG – Tirol – 730 H7 – 680 Ew – Höhe 500 m — 7 **E5**

Wien 467 – Innsbruck 66 – Schwaz 38 – Mayrhofen 12

Dörflwirt Rest, VISA
Dörfl 398 ✉ 6280 – ✆ (05282) 31 62 – info@doerflwirt.at – Fax (05282) 4231
geschl. Mitte April – Anfang Mai, Mitte Okt. – Mitte Dez.
29 Zim (inkl. ½ P.) – ☼ †79 € ††138 € ❄ †83 € ††146 €
Rest – Karte 17/32 €
♦ Das Haus mit der teilweise holzverkleideten Balkonfassade liegt über dem Tal und verfügt über freundliche, neuzeitliche Gästezimmer. Im Sommer All-inclusive-Angebot. Restaurant mit bürgerlicher Küche.

HALL IN TIROL – Tirol – 730 G7 – 11 500 Ew – Höhe 574 m – Wintersport: 2 304 m 7 — 7 **D5**

Wien 438 – Innsbruck 11 – Seefeld in Tirol 32 – Schwaz 21
Wallpachgasse 5, ✉ 6060, ✆ (05223) 4 55 44, info@regionhall.at
Veranstaltungen
30.05. – 31.05.: Festival der kleinen historischen Städte
Obere Stadt★ (Stadtpfarrkirche★) – Damenstift (Kirchenfassade★)

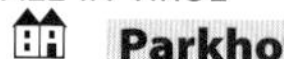

Parkhotel
Zim,

Thurnfeldgasse 1a 6060 – (05223) 5 37 69 – info@parkhotel-hall.com – Fax (05223) 54653
geschl. über Weihnachten
59 Zim – 92/100 € 146/164 € – ½ P 17 €
Rest – Karte 17/33 €
♦ Hypermodern vom puristischen Foyer bis in die überwiegend in einem Turmbau aus Glas und Stahl untergebrachten Designerzimmer mit Laptop und kostenlosem 24-h-Internetzugang. Das Restaurant: komplett verglast und schlicht im Stil.

Gartenhotel Maria Theresia
Reimmichlstr. 25 6060 – (05223) 5 63 13 – info@gartenhotel.at – Fax (05223) 5631366
27 Zim – 65/70 € 110/120 € – ½ P 20 € – 3 Suiten
Rest – Karte 18/42 €
♦ Die Zimmer dieses Familienbetriebs hat man mit warmen Tönen wohnlich und zeitgemäß gestaltet. Schön sind auch die kleine Kaminhalle und der gepflegte Garten mit Streichelzoo. Sehr angenehm sitzt man im Gastgarten des Restaurants unter Kastanien.

Goldener Engl
Rest,

Unterer Stadtplatz 5 6060 – (05223) 54 62 10 – info@goldener-engl.at – Fax (05223) 5462125
18 Zim – 90/100 € 150/180 € – ½ P 18 €
Rest – Karte 23/36 €
♦ Das 700 Jahre alte denkmalgeschützte Gebäude direkt an der Stadtmauer ist heute ein hübsches, gemütliches Hotel mit historischem Flair und wohnlichen Zimmern im Landhausstil. Sie speisen in schönen rustikalen Restaurantstuben oder im gotischen Gewölbekeller.

Heiligkreuz
Zim,

Reimmichlstr. 18 (Heiligkreuz) 6060 – (05223) 5 71 14 – info@heiligkreuz.at – Fax (05223) 571145
geschl. 26. Okt. – 26. Dez.
30 Zim – 68/89 € 106/140 € – ½ P 18 €
Rest – *(geschl. Sonntag, nur Abendessen)* Karte 17/31 €
♦ Seit dem 15. Jh. besteht diese Adresse als Gasthaus. In einigen Zimmern leuchtet nachts ein Sternenhimmel über dem Bett. Zum Haus gehört eine kleine Sternwarte. Gepflegtes Restaurant mit Buffetbereich.

HALL, BAD – Oberösterreich – 730 O4 – 4 760 Ew – Höhe 388 m 2 H3

Wien 182 – Linz 35 – Wels 28 – Steyr 18
Kurpromenade 1, 4540, (07258) 72 00, info.bad-hall@oberoesterreich.at
Herzog Tassilo, Blankenbergerstr. 30 (07258) 54 80

Tassilo Hotel

(Thermal) Rest,

Parkstr. 4 4540 – (07258) 2 61 10 – rezeption@tassilotherme.at – Fax (07258) 26115
72 Zim (inkl. ½ P.) – 79/134 € 158/238 €
Rest – Karte 16/34 €
♦ Schön liegt das Haus mit der gepflegten gelb-weißen Fassade im Kurpark. Fast schon luxuriös sind die Zimmer im Vital Club. Großer Freizeitbereich mit Beauty-Anwendungen. Neuzeitliches Restaurant mit gut eingedeckten Tischen.

Parkhotel Zur Klause Rest,
Am Sulzbach 10 ✉ 4540 – ✆ (07258) 4 90 00
– info@parkhotelzurklause.at – Fax (07258) 4900180
geschl. 10. Jan. – 5. Feb.
50 Zim – 46/60 € 86/114 €
Rest – (nur für Hausgäste)
◆ In einer Seitenstraße, am Kurpark, liegt dieser gewachsene Gasthof mit seinen neuzeitlich und funktionell ausgestatteten Zimmern mit gutem Platzangebot.

HALLEIN – Salzburg – 730 L5 – 18 400 Ew – Höhe 460 m – Wintersport: 1 322 m 3 8 G4

Wien 315 – Salzburg 19 – Bischofshofen 35 – Berchtesgaden 15
Mauttorpromenade 6, ✉ 5400, ✆ (06245) 8 53 94, office@hallein.com
Salzburg-Rif, Schlossallee 50a ✆ (06245) 7 66 81
Veranstaltungen
06.09. – 07.09.: Kunsthandwerksmarkt
Salzachtal★

In Hallein – Taxach-Rif Nord: 5,5 km über B 159 Richtung Salzburg:

Gasthof Hohlwegwirt mit Zim
Salzburgerstr. 84 (Taxach) ✉ 5400 – ✆ (06245) 82 41 50
– gasthof@hohlwegwirt.at – Fax (06245) 8241572
5 Zim – 62/96 € 80/131 € – ½ P 18 €
Rest – *(geschl. Sonntagabend – Montag, außer Festspielzeit)* Menü 31/48 € – Karte 15/44 €
◆ In den Restaurantstuben können Gäste hier Regionales oder Mediterranes von der Speisekarte wählen. Serviert wird in rustikaler gemütlicher Umgebung. Gepflegte Zimmer mit antiker Einrichtung.

HALLWANG – Salzburg – 730 L5 – 3 500 Ew – Höhe 523 m 8 G4

Wien 299 – Salzburg 12 – Bischofshofen 65 – Bad Reichenhall 26

Gasthof Kirchbichl Zim, Rest,
Dorfstr. 41 ✉ 5300 – ✆ (0662) 66 19 54
– kontakt@landgasthof-kirchbichl.at – Fax (0662) 66590055
geschl. 7. – 16. Juli
18 Zim – 52/60 € 90/120 € – ½ P 14 €
Rest – *(geschl. Montagmittag)* Karte 12/25 €
◆ Der in der Ortsmitte gelegene ländliche Gasthof wurde um ein separates Hotelgebäude mit wohnlichen und zeitgemäßen Zimmern erweitert. Bürgerliche Küche serviert man in den rustikalen Stuben des Gasthauses.

In Hallwang-Söllheim Süd-West: 3 km:

Pfefferschiff (Klaus Fleischhaker)
Söllheim 3 ✉ 5300 – ✆ (0662) 66 12 42 – restaurant@pfefferschiff.at
– Fax (0662) 661841
geschl. 22. Juni – 14. Juli und Sonntag – Montag, Festspielzeit nur Montag
Rest – *(Dienstag – Freitag nur Abendessen)* (Tischbestellung ratsam)
Menü 38 € (mittags)/75 € – Karte 45/67 €
Spez. Renkenfilet mit Trüffel. Kalbsrücken mit Risotto und Eierschwammerl. "Heiße Liebe" von der Himbeere.
◆ Das 350 Jahre alte Pfarrhaus beherbergt ein familiär geführtes Restaurant, in dessen drei Stuben sehr gute regionale Küche und Weine geboten werden. Moderne Bilderausstellung.

HARTBERG – Steiermark – 730 T7 – 6 550 Ew – Höhe 360 m – Wintersport: 795 m
11 L4

Wien 128 – Graz 62 – Bruck an der Mur 90 – Wiener Neustadt 79
Rochusplatz 3, 8230, (03332) 66 50 50 , tourismusverband@htb.at

Zum Alten Gerichtshof garni
Rest,
Herrengasse 4 8230 – (03332) 6 33 56
– info@hotel-altergerichtshof.at – Fax (03332) 633566
geschl. 22. Dez. – 7. Jan.
16 Zim – 42/50 € 72/80 €
◆ Das schön in der Altstadt am Schloss gelegene einstige Bezirksgericht ist ein hübsch eingerichtetes kleines Hotel mit historischem Flair. Stilvoll sind die Mansardenzimmer.

Berghof
Oststeirisches Hügelland,
Ring 3 (Nord-West: 1,5 km) 8230
– (03332) 6 23 05 – schreiners.berghof@aon.at – Fax (03332) 6230516
geschl. Nov. – März
13 Zim – 40/42 € 70/74 € – ½ P 9 €
Rest – *(geschl. Sonntagabend – Montag)* Karte 16/26 €
◆ Herrlich liegt das Hotel über den Weingärten des Ringkogels. Die Zimmer sind in modernem Design gehalten und teils mit Holzfußboden ausgestattet – alle mit schöner Aussicht. Helles, freundliches Restaurant in ländlichem Stil.

Sonne garni
Hauptplatz 9 8230 – (03332) 6 23 42 – rezeption@sonne-hotel.at
– Fax (03332) 6234225
13 Zim – 40 € 70 €
◆ In dem ehemaligen Gasthof mit gelber Fassade stehen neuzeitlich und funktionell ausgestattete Zimmer und Maisonetten bereit. Modernes Café in der früheren Gaststube.

Pusswald
Grazerstr. 18 8230 – (03332) 6 25 84 – info@restaurant-pusswald.at
– Fax (03332) 666224
geschl. 7. – 13. Jan., 1. – 11. Sept. und Sonntag – Montag
Rest – Karte 28/43 €
◆ Familie Pusswald bietet in ihrem modern in klaren Linien gehaltenen Restaurant regional, mediterran und leicht asiatisch beeinflusste Küche. Mit Vinothek.

HAUGSCHLAG – Niederösterreich – 730 R2 – 530 Ew – Höhe 520 m
2 I1

Wien 155 – St. Pölten 126 – Waidhofen a. d. Thaya 33 – Gmünd 30
36 Waldviertel & Resort Haugschlag, Haugschlag 160 (02865) 84 41
18 Herrensee-Litschau, Buchenstr. 1 (02865) 4 38

Golfresort Haugschlag
Haugschlag 160 3874
– (02865) 84 41 – info@golfresort.at – Fax (02865) 844122
geschl. 3. Nov. – 14. März
38 Zim – 93/113 € 138/178 € – ½ P 19 €
Rest – Karte 15/31 €
◆ Inmitten einer großzügigen Golfanlage steht das mit dem Clubhaus verbundene Hotel. Technisch sehr gut ausgestattete Zimmer in modern-elegantem Landhausstil überzeugen. Neuzeitlich gestaltetes Restaurant mit Terrasse zum Golfplatz.

HAUS IM ENNSTAL – Steiermark – 730 N6 – 2 530 Ew – Höhe 740 m – Wintersport: 2 015 m 2 9 9 H4

Wien 284 – Graz 162 – Salzburg 95 – Bischofshofen 55
Raiffeisenstr. 188, 8967, (03686) 22 34, info@haus.at
Dachstein Tauern, Oberhaus 59 (03686) 26 30

Zur Herrschaftstaverne

Rest,

Marktstr. 39 8967 – (03686) 23 92 – info@herrschaftstaverne.at – Fax (03686) 23927
geschl. Ende April 1 Woche
38 Zim (inkl. ½ P.) – 61 € 106 € 72/89 € 128/178 €
Rest – Karte 15/30 €

◆ In dem regionstypischen familiengeführten Haus im Zentrum erwarten Sie wohnlich im alpenländischen Stil eingerichtete Zimmer und ein neuzeitlicher Freizeitbereich. Hübsche holzgetäfelte Stube und gediegenrustikales Restaurant mit Wintergartenanbau.

Kirchenwirt

VISA AE

Kirchengasse 56 8967 – (03686) 22 28 – office@kirchenwirt.net – Fax (03686) 22285
geschl. 6. April – Anfang Mai, Anfang Okt. – Anfang Dez.
30 Zim (inkl. ½ P.) – 60/67 € 102/116 € 74/88 € 130/158 €
Rest – Karte 14/32 €

◆ Der familiär geleitete Gasthof steht in der Ortsmitte und verfügt über funktionell ausgestattete Zimmer mit gutem Platzangebot sowie einen modernen kleinen Saunabereich. In nette Stuben unterteiltes Restaurant.

Gute und preiswerte Häuser kennzeichnet das MICHELIN-Männchen, der „Bib": der rote „Bib Gourmand" für die Küche, der blaue „Bib Hotel" bei den Zimmern.

HEILIGENBLUT – Kärnten – 730 K7 – 1 190 Ew – Höhe 1 300 m – Wintersport: 2 912 m 4 10 8 F5

Wien 420 – Klagenfurt 161 – Lienz 38 – Zell am See 51
Hof 4, 9844, (04824) 20 01 21, office@heiligenblut.at
Kirche★
Oberes Mölltal★ – Schareck★★ mit (Nord: 8 km) – Franz-Josephs-Höhe★★★ (Nord: 16 km)

Haus Senger – Chalet

Berge, Zim, Rest, VISA AE

Großglocknerstr. 23 9844 – (04824) 22 15 – office@romantic.at – Fax (04824) 22159
geschl. Ende März – Mitte Juni, Mitte Okt. – Mitte Dez.
15 Zim (inkl. ½ P.) – 84/102 € 126/158 € 62/110 € 144/180 € – 6 Suiten
Rest – Karte 18/33 €

◆ Das familiengeführte Hotel ist ein über 300 Jahre altes Bauernhaus, das seinen netten rustikalen Charakter bewahrt hat. Wohnliche Zimmer und sehr großzügige Suiten. Gemütliche Gaststuben mit regionaler Küche.

Glocknerhof Rest,
Hof 6 ✉ 9844 – ✆ (04824) 22 44
– glocknerhof@pichlers.at – Fax (04824) 2244166
geschl. Mitte April – Ende Mai, Okt. – Nov.
52 Zim (inkl. ½ P.) – 72/99 € 126/180 € 88/123 € 158/220 €
Rest – Karte 19/31 €
♦ In dem Alpenhotel erwarten Sie eine gemütliche Halle, ein gepflegter Freizeitbereich und unterschiedlich geschnittene, solide Zimmer. Besonders hübsch: die Tauerngold-Zimmer. Zum Restaurant gehört eine Terrasse mit schöner Aussicht.

Lärchenhof Berge, Rest,
Hof 70 ✉ 9844 – ✆ (04824) 22 62 – info@ski-heiligenblut.at
– Fax (04824) 226245
geschl. 15. April – 20. Juni, 30. Sept. – 20. Dez.
26 Zim (inkl. ½ P.) – 62/98 € 124/144 € 85/101 € 150/220 €
Rest – *(Weihnachten – Ostern nur Abendessen)* Karte 14/25 €
♦ Schön ist die ruhige Lage dieses Hotels oberhalb des Ortes. Die Zimmer sind meist recht geräumig – mehr Komfort bieten die Erker-Panorama-Suiten. Panorama-Restaurant und gemütliche Bauernstube.

Kärntnerhof Rest, Rest,
Winkl 3 ✉ 9844 – ✆ (04824) 2 00 40
– info@hotel-kaerntnerhof.com – Fax (04824) 200489
geschl. 12. April – 7. Juni, 25. Okt. – 23. Dez.
40 Zim (inkl. ½ P.) – 66/70 € 124/152 € 86/92 € 150/206 €
Rest – (nur Abendessen für Hausgäste)
♦ Das gewachsene familiengeführte Hotel in zentrumsnaher Lage verfügt über wohnliche, unterschiedlich geschnittene Zimmer und Appartements sowie einen netten Freizeitbereich.

Bei schönem Wetter isst man gern im Freien!
Wählen Sie ein Restaurant mit Terrasse:

HEILIGENBRUNN – Burgenland – 730 V7 – 990 Ew – Höhe 226 m

11 **L5**

Wien 173 – Eisenstadt 151 – Fürstenfeld 40 – Güssing 14
Heiligenbrunn 33, ✉ 7522, ✆ (03324) 72 81, post@heiligenbrunn.bgld.gv.at

Krutzler Zim,
Heiligenbrunn 16 ✉ 7522 – ✆ (03324) 72 40 – post@hotel-krutzler.at
– Fax (03324) 7255
geschl. 9. – 17. Feb.
34 Zim – 67 € 108 € – ½ P 12 €
Rest – Karte 16/30 €
♦ Der Gasthof ist ein charmanter Familienbetrieb. Gepflegte, helle Zimmer findet man im ruhigen Hinterhaus. Des Weiteren besteht die Möglichkeit, Fahrräder zu leihen. In Stuben unterteiltes Restaurant mit ländlichem Ambiente.

HEILIGENKREUZ - Burgenland - 730 U8 - 1 250 Ew - Höhe 230 m

Wien 175 - Eisenstadt 153 - Graz 78 - Fürstenfeld 18 11 L5

Gasthof Gerlinde Gibiser (mit Gästehäusern) Zim,
Obere Hauptstr. 10 7561 - (03325) 42 16 - g.gibiser@aon.at - Fax (3325) 424644
15 Zim - 51 € 70/110 €
Rest - *(geschl. Montag)* Karte 17/40 €
◆ Der kleine Gasthof besticht durch seinen rustikal-ländlichen Charme. Strohdachbungalows ("Kellerstöckl") mit Kachelofen sorgen für gemütliche Stimmung. Hübsches rustikales, teils leicht elegant wirkendes Restaurant.

HEITERWANG - Tirol - 730 E6 - 560 Ew - Höhe 1 000 m - Wintersport: 1 233 m 2 6 C5

Wien 508 - Innsbruck 83 - Reutte 8 - Garmisch-Partenkirchen 39
Oberdorf 4, 6611, (05673) 20 00 07 00, r.pahle@zugspitzarena.com

Landhotel Heiterwangerhof
Ennet der Ach 4 6611 - (05674) 51 04 - heiterwangerhof@aon.at - Fax (05674) 5652
geschl. 30. März - 30. April, 14. Okt. - 19. Dez.
13 Zim - 36/49 € 72/98 € - ½ P 16 €
Rest - *(nur Abendessen)* Karte 17/19 €
◆ Das kleine Landhotel mit regionstypischer Balkonfassade bietet mit hellen Naturholzmöbeln solide eingerichtete Zimmer, meist mit Küchenzeile und unterteiltem Wohn-/Schlafraum. Bürgerliche Gaststube mit separater Bar.

HERMAGOR - Kärnten - 730 M9 - 7 240 Ew - Höhe 612 m - Wintersport: 2 020 m 5 25 9 G6

Wien 374 - Klagenfurt 79 - Spittal an der Drau 46 - Villach 43
Gösseringlände 7, 9620, (04282) 20 43, info@hermagor.at

Bürgerbräu Zim,
Gasserplatz 1 9620 - (04282) 2 50 85 - office@buergerbrau.at - Fax (04282) 2508514
geschl. über Weihnachten
15 Zim - 52/55 € 86/92 € - ½ P 12 €
Rest - *(geschl. Sonntag, außer Saison)* Karte 14/22 €
◆ Das im Zentrum gelegene Hotel verfügt über neuzeitlich und funktionell eingerichtete Zimmer und wird auch von Geschäftsleuten geschätzt. Rustikales Restaurant.

Panoramahotel Hauserhof Gailtal und Alpenlandschaft, Rest,
Kreuth 1 (Nord-West: 2,5 km Richtung Guggenberg) 9620 - (04282) 22 86 - info@panoramahotel.at - Fax (04282) 228640
geschl. April, Nov.
30 Zim (inkl. ½ P.) - 65/75 € 108/128 € 63/80 € 106/138 €
Rest - (nur Abendessen für Hausgäste)
◆ Wunderschön ist die ruhige Lage oberhalb des Ortes. Das Ferienhotel bietet zeitgemäße Zimmer, einen Garten mit gepflegter Liegewiese und eine Terrasse mit Panoramablick.

Lerchenhof Zim,
Untermöschach 8 (Nord-West: 1 km Richtung Weißensee)
9620 – (04282) 21 00 – info@lerchenhof.at
– Fax (04282) 21009
geschl. 7. – 30. April, 20. Okt. – 29. Nov.
20 Zim – 46/53 € 80/90 € 48/60 € 84/102 €
– ½ P 16 €
Rest – *(geschl. Montag außer Saison)* Karte 20/29 €
◆ Der schöne ehemalige Gutshof ist ein familiär geführtes Hotel mit individuellen, wohnlichen Zimmern und kleinem Saunabereich mit Ruhezone. In der Küche der ländlich-rustikalen Gaststuben verwendet man Produkte aus der eigenen Landwirtschaft. Hübsche Terrasse.

In Hermagor-Presseggen Ost: 5 km über B 111 Richtung Villach:

Alpen-Adria-Hotel (geheizt) Zim,
Presseggersee 2 9620 – (04282) 26 66
– info@alpenadriahotel.at – Fax (04282) 266666
geschl. 28. Okt. – 8. Dez.
50 Zim (inkl. ½ P.) – 71/90 € 102/150 €
Rest – (nur für Hausgäste)
◆ In diesem gewachsenen Ferienhotel erwarten Sie solide Gästezimmer, eine nette Gartenanlage mit Pool und Liegewiese sowie diverse Freizeitangebote, auch für Kinder. Modern gestaltetes Restaurant mit Weinlounge.

In Hermagor-Tröpolach West: 9 km über B 111 Richtung Kötschach-Mauthen:

Falkensteiner Hotel Carinzia (geheizt) Rest, Zim,
Tröpolach 156 9631 – (04285) 7 20 00 – carinzia@falkensteiner.com
– Fax (04285) 720005
160 Zim (inkl. ½ P.) – 89/209 € 178/418 €
7 Suiten
Rest – (nur Abendessen für Hausgäste)
◆ Ein klarer moderner Stil kennzeichnet Architektur und Einrichtung dieses direkt an der Seilbahn-Talstation gelegenen Hotels. Beeindruckend: Acquapura Spa auf 2400 qm.

In Nassfeld Süd-West: 20 km über Tröpolach – Höhe 1 550 m

Wulfenia Bergpanorama, (geheizt)
Nassfeld 7 9620 – (04285) 81 11
– info@wulfenia.at – Fax (04285) 8124
geschl. Mai – Nov.
65 Zim (inkl. ½ P.) – 121/270 € 248/374 €
6 Suiten
Rest *Arnold Pucher* – separat erwähnt
◆ Die Lage direkt an der Skipiste, wohnlich-komfortable Zimmer (auch viele Familienzimmer) sowie ein schöner Wellnessbereich und Kinderbetreuung sprechen für dieses Haus.

Sonnenalpe ← Gartnerkofel und Hohe-Tauern,
Nassfeld 9 (geheizt)
✉ 9620 – ✆ (04285) 82 11 – info@sonnenalpe.at – Fax (04285) 8128
geschl. 7. April – 30. Nov.
59 Zim (inkl. ½ P.) – 125/180 € 260/360 € – 6 Suiten
Rest – (nur für Hausgäste)
◆ Ein engagiert geführtes Haus, das über moderne, mit heimischem Holz möblierte Zimmer verfügt. Sie nutzen den Freizeitbereich des durch einen Gang verbundenen Hotels Wulfenia.

Alpenhof Plattner ← Berglandschaft,
Nassfeld 99 ✉ 9620 Zim, Rest, VISA
– ✆ (04285) 82 85 – reception@plattner.at – Fax (04285) 828587
geschl. 7. April – 31. Mai, 13. Okt. – 5. Dez.
18 Zim (inkl. ½ P.) – 60/67 € 120/134 € 70/115 € 140/230 €
Rest – Karte 18/34 €
◆ Das Alpenhotel liegt auf einer Alm, die nur im Sommer per Auto erreichbar ist. Solide Zimmer mit Balkon und heller Naturholzeinrichtung. Im Winter meist Wochenpauschale. Regionstypisches Restaurant und Terrasse mit beeindruckender Aussicht.

Arnold Pucher – Hotel Wulfenia VISA
Nassfeld 7 ✉ 9620 – ✆ (04285) 81 11 – restaurant@arnold-pucher.at
– Fax (04285) 8124
geschl. Mai – Nov. und Montag – Dienstag
Rest – *(nur Abendessen)* (Tischbestellung ratsam) Menü 90/110 € – Karte ca. 68 €
Spez. Rotbarbe im "Plastiksackerl" mit zweierlei Paprika. Mandarinen Bouillabaisse von heimischen Fischen. Lammrücken im Grissinimantel mit Bohnen.
◆ Charmant umsorgt Frau Pucher den Gast hier mit den kreativen Menüs ihres Mannes. Zu den einzelnen Gängen werden verschiedene erstklassige Olivenöle zur Degustation gereicht.

HINTERBRÜHL – Niederösterreich – 730 U4 – 4 020 Ew – Höhe 252 m

Wien 20 – St. Pölten 61 – Wiener Neustadt 41 – Baden 16 4 **L2**
Seegrotte★
Wienerwald★

Höldrichsmühle Zim, VISA AE
Gaadnerstr. 34 ✉ 2371 – ✆ (02236) 26 27 40 – hoeld@eunet.at
– Fax (02236) 48729
44 Zim – 69/78 € 99/119 € – ½ P 19 €
Rest – Karte 17/30 €
◆ Die ehemalige Mühle a. d. 18. Jh. wurde zu einem Seminar- und Businesshotel umgebaut. Eine Bilderausstellung des Künstlers H. Danko ziert das Haus. In Stuben unterteiltes Restaurant mit Gewölbedecke.

Beethoven Rest, VISA AE
Beethovengasse 8 ✉ 2371 – ✆ (02236) 2 62 52 – info@beethoven-hotel.at
– Fax (02236) 277017
25 Zim – 64/74 € 84/98 €
Rest – *(geschl. 23. Dez. – 2. Jan. und Freitagabend – Sonntag)* Karte 16/24 €
◆ Das nach dem gegenüberliegenden Park benannte familiengeführte Hotel verfügt über funktionelle, zeitgemäß mit Kirschholzmobiliar eingerichtete Gästezimmer. Ein netter Gastgarten vor dem Haus ergänzt das Café-Restaurant Fidelio.

Hexensitz VISA

Johannesstr. 35 ✉ 2371 – ☎ (02236) 2 29 37 – restaurant@hexensitz.at – Fax (02236) 893184
geschl. Sonntagabend – Dienstagmittag
Rest – 35 € – Karte 24/40 €

◆ Warme Farben, Holzfußboden und eine elegante Note bestimmen das Ambiente dieses über zwei Ebenen angelegten Restaurants. Sehr schön: der Gastgarten unter Kastanienbäumen.

HINTERSTODER – Oberösterreich – 730 O5 – 1 010 Ew – Höhe 600 m – Wintersport: 1860 m 1 9 — 9 H4

Wien 217 – Linz 85 – Steyr 55 – Liezen 38
Hinterstoder 38, ✉ 4573, ☎ (07564) 52 63, hinterstoder@pyhrn-priel.net

Vital-Hotel Stoderhof Rest, VISA

Hinterstoder 10 ✉ 4573 – ☎ (07564) 52 66 – stohof@aon.at – Fax (07564) 5401
geschl. Mitte April – Mitte Mai, Nov.
28 Zim (inkl. ½ P.) – ☼ 74 € 138 € ❄ 83/98 € 154/170 €
Rest – (nur Abendessen für Hausgäste)

◆ Das in der Ortsmitte gelegene Hotel bietet Ihnen mit hellem Naturholzmobiliar wohnlich gestaltete Zimmer und einen Gesundheitsbereich auf der Grundlage chinesischer Medizin.

HINTERTUX – Tirol – siehe Tux

HIPPACH IM ZILLERTAL – Tirol – 730 H7 – 1 400 Ew – Höhe 650 m – Wintersport: 1 830 m 1 13 — 7 E5

Wien 436 – Innsbruck 63 – Schwaz 34 – Mayrhofen 5

Zenzerwirt Zim,

Dorf 14 ✉ 6283 – ☎ (05282) 36 02 – hotel@zenzerwirt.at – Fax (05282) 3350
geschl. 6. April – 10. Mai, 19. Okt. – 20. Dez.
50 Zim (inkl. ½ P.) – ☼ 59/60 € 98/118 € ❄ 72/95 € 126/190 €
Rest – Karte 18/31 €

◆ Mehr als die Hälfte der Zimmer des netten Alpengasthofs ist großzügig geschnitten, hell und wohnlich. Der Rest ist kleiner, rustikal ausgestattet, aber sehr gepflegt. Kachelöfen und Zierrat sorgen in den Gaststuben für eine gemütliche Atmosphäre.

HIRSCHEGG – Vorarlberg – siehe Kleinwalsertal

HITTISAU – Vorarlberg – 730 B6 – 1 810 Ew – Höhe 792 m – Wintersport: 1 600 m 6 — 5 A5

Wien 712 – Bregenz 25 – Dornbirn 22 – Kempten 55
Gemeindehaus, Platz 370, ✉ 6952, ☎ (05513) 62 09 50, tourismus@hittisau.at

Das Schiff Rest,
Heideggen 311 ✉ 6952 – ✆ (05513) 62 20 – info@schiff-hittisau.com – Fax (05513) 622019
geschl. 1. – 14. April, 17. Nov. – 15. Dez.
28 Zim – 70 € 120 € – ½ P 28 €
Rest – *(geschl. Sonntagabend – Montag)* Menü 39/60 € – Karte 30/50 €
♦ Der mit Holzschindeln verkleidete Alpengasthof von 1840 wurde um einen Hotelanbau erweitert. Dort findet man modern und geschmackvoll eingerichtete Zimmer. Hübsche rustikale Gaststuben mit schmackhaften Gerichten der regionalen und klassischen Küche.

Landhotel Hirschen Rest,
Platz 187 ✉ 6952 – ✆ (05513) 23 20 – info@landhotel-hirschen.at – Fax (05513) 232077
geschl. Juli 2 Wochen, Mitte Nov. – Mitte Dez.
18 Zim – 48 € 96 € – ½ P 16 €
Rest – *(geschl. Dienstag – Mittwochmittag)* Karte 18/32 €
♦ Traditioneller, holzschindelverkleideter Gasthof im Zentrum mit soliden, wohnlichen Zimmern. Im Haus bietet man auch energetische Therapien. Alpe mit Schaukäserei. Kachelöfen, Deckenbilder und Zierrat schmücken die Gaststuben.

Gasthof Krone
Am Platz 185 ✉ 6952 – ✆ (05513) 62 01 – gasthof@krone-hittisau.at – Fax (05513) 620116
geschl. 31. März – 24. April, 3. Nov. – 14. Dez.
28 Zim – 58/62 € 98/104 €
Rest – *(geschl. Mittwoch – Donnerstag)* Karte 25/41 €
♦ Das stattliche Bregenzerwälderhaus hält für seine Gäste solide und gepflegte Zimmer bereit, denen hübsche Stoffe ein wohnliches Ambiente geben. Moderne Tagungsmöglichkeiten. Gemütliche, rustikale Gaststube mit alter Holztäfelung.

Pension Bals Zim, Rest,
Bühl 31 ✉ 6952 – ✆ (05513) 2 61 20 – pension@bals.at – Fax (05513) 261226
geschl. Ende März – Anfang Mai, Ende Okt. – 26. Dez.
13 Zim (inkl. ½ P.) – 52 € 90/104 €
Rest – (nur Abendessen für Hausgäste)
♦ Alpenländischer Gasthof am Ortseingang mit gepflegten Zimmern und freundlicher Atmosphäre. Schönes Saunahaus, in dem ein Panoramafenster den Blick auf die Berge freigibt.

HOCHBURG-ACH – Oberösterreich – 730 K4 – 2 980 Ew – Höhe 462 m 1 F3

Wien 300 – Linz 140 – Salzburg 46 – Braunau 23

Burgblick garni
Ach 31 (im Ortsteil Ach) ✉ 5122 – ✆ (07727) 40 04 – info@altstadthotels.net – Fax (07727) 40043666
43 Zim – 79/86 € 108/115 €
♦ Direkt an der Salzach gelegenes Hotel mit modern und wohnlich eingerichteten Gästezimmern. Schön: die Aussicht auf die Burg von Burghausen.

HOCHFÜGEN - Tirol - siehe Fügenberg im Zillertal

HOCHGURGL - Tirol - siehe Sölden

HÖCHST - Vorarlberg - 730 A6 - 7 100 Ew - Höhe 400 m 5 A5

Wien 696 - Bregenz 10 - Lindau 19 - Dornbirn 13

 **Gasthof Die Linde** 

Kirchplatz 16 ✉ 6973 - ✆ (05578) 75 37 80 - office@die-linde.at - Fax (05578) 753786

30 Zim - 75/85 € 190 € - ½ P 14 €

Rest - Karte 24/46 €

◆ Das familiär geleitete Haus befindet sich im Ortszentrum bei der Kirche und verfügt über wohnliche, freundliche, mit naturbelassenem Holz eingerichtete Gästezimmer. Mit Jagdtrophäen und Kachelofen dekorierte Gaststuben.

HÖFEN - Tirol - 730 E6 - 1 260 Ew - Höhe 864 m 6 C5

Wien 507 - Innsbruck 94 - Reutte 5 - Garmisch-Partenkirchen 44

 **Landgasthof Lilie** 

Alte Bundesstr. 19 ✉ 6600 - ✆ (05672) 6 32 11 - urlaub@gasthof-lilie.at - Fax (05672) 62051

geschl. 1. - 4. Mai, 11. - 30. Nov.

28 Zim - 39/48 € 74/88 € - ½ P 12 €

Rest - *(geschl. Dienstag)* Karte 17/29 €

◆ Der gestandene Gasthof ist ein solider Familienbetrieb, der gepflegte, mit unterschiedlichem Holzmobiliar ausgestattete Zimmer bietet. Die gemütliche Zirbenstube ergänzt das gediegene Restaurant.

Frühstück inklusive? Die Tasse steht gleich hinter der Zimmeranzahl.

HOF BEI SALZBURG - Salzburg - 730 L5 - 3 410 Ew - Höhe 730 m - Wintersport: 900 m 2 8 G4

Wien 282 - Salzburg 16 - Bad Ischl 38 - Hallein 24

Salzburg-Schloss Fuschl, Schlossstr. 19 ✆ (06229) 23 90

Schloss Fuschl 

Schloss-Str. 19 Zim, Rest,

✉ 5322 - ✆ (06229) 2 25 30 - schloss.fuschl@arabellastarwood.com - Fax (06229) 22531531

110 Zim - 310/522 € 360/572 € - 26 Suiten

Rest Imperial - separat erwähnt

Rest *Schloss Restaurant* - Karte 45/68 €

◆ Dieses attraktive Hotel, ansässig in einem Jagdschloss von 1450 direkt am See, bietet luxuriöse und elegante Suiten sowie nicht minder schöne Zimmer und sehr guten Service. Im Schloss Restaurant: regional-internationale Küche und bezaubernder Seeblick.

ArabellaSheraton Hotel Jagdhof Biergarten
Schloss-str. 1 Zim, VISA AE
✉ 5322 – ✆ (06229) 2 37 20 – *jagdhof.fuschl@arabellastarwood.com*
– Fax (06229) 23722531
143 Zim – 170/305 € 200/335 € – ½ P 26 € – 13 Suiten
Rest – Karte 26/44 €
Rest *Osteria* – *(geschl. Montag – Dienstag im Winter, im Winter nur Abendessen)* Karte 26/33 €
◆ Oberhalb des Sees liegt die aus einem Gasthof und zwei Gebäuden im Landhausstil bestehende Anlage, die mit Großzügigkeit und Stil überzeugt. Schöner Wellnessbereich. Rustikale Restaurantstuben mit netter Terrasse. Osteria: Italienische Küche.

Imperial – Hotel Schloss Fuschl Zim,
Schloss-Str. 19 ✉ *5322* – ✆ *(06229) 2 25 30* VISA AE
– schloss.fuschl@arabellastarwood.com – Fax (06229) 22531531
geschl. Anfang Dez. 2 Wochen und Sonntag – Montag
Rest – *(nur Abendessen)* Menü 110/140 € – Karte 65/80 €
Spez. Langoustine mit Mango und Sauerkrautsauce. Filet vom Bio-Milchkalb mit Schinken-Tramezzini und Tomatenconfit. Erdbeeren in Zitronengrasgelee mit Basilikummousse.
◆ Elegantes Restaurant mit geschmackvoller Einrichtung in Silber und Schwarz, in dem der Gast klassisch-internationale Küche genießt.

HOF BEI STRADEN – Steiermark – siehe Straden

HOFGASTEIN, BAD – Salzburg – 730 L7 – 6 730 Ew – Höhe 860 m – Wintersport: 2 300 m 7 16 – Kurort 8 G5

Wien 384 – Salzburg 87 – St. Johann im Pongau 32 – Zell am See 41
Tauernplatz 1, ✉ 5630, ✆ (06432) 3 39 32 60, info@badhofgastein.com
Schossalm★ (mit)

Grand Park Hotel (Thermal)
Kurgartenstr. 26 Rest, VISA AE
✉ *5630* – ✆ *(06432) 6 35 60* – *office@grandparkhotel.at*
– Fax (06432) 8454
geschl. 2. Nov. – 5. Dez.
89 Zim (inkl. ½ P.) – 107/155 € 204/354 € 121/233 € 234/494 € – 4 Suiten
Rest – Karte 34/50 €
◆ Stilvoll und elegant ist das Ambiente in diesem Hotel mit großzügigem und geschmackvollem "Grand Park Spa" auf 2000 qm. Alle Zimmerkategorien bieten einen Balkon.

Thermenhotel Sendlhof (Thermal)
Pyrkerstr. 34 ✉ *5630* Rest,
– ✆ *(06432) 3 83 80 – info@sendlhof.co.at – Fax (06432) 383860*
geschl. 6. April – 3. Mai, 2. Nov. – 15. Dez.
60 Zim (inkl. ½ P.) – 76/101 € 142/222 € 86/111 € 182/252 €
Rest – (nur Abendessen für Hausgäste)
◆ Das familiär geleitete gewachsene Hotel verfügt über wohnlich-elegante Gästezimmer sowie eine schöne Badelandschaft und einen großen Garten zum Entspannen.

Bismarck (mit Gästehaus) (Thermal) Rest, VISA
Alpenstr. 6 ✉ 5630
– ✆ (06432) 6 68 10 – info@hotel-bismarck.com – Fax (06432) 66816
geschl. 12. Nov. – 13. Dez.
75 Zim (inkl. ½ P.) – ☼ 81/91 € 136/176 € ❄ 85/124 € 166/276 € – 12 Suiten
Rest – (nur für Hausgäste)
♦ Alpine Eleganz erwartet den Gast im Fürstenhaus dieses aus mehreren Trakten bestehenden Hotels, im Schlössl befinden sich moderne und großzügige Appartements/Suiten. In fünf Stuben unterteilter Speisesaal.

Palace (Thermal) Spa Rest, Rest, P VISA AE
Alexander Moser Allee 13
✉ 5630 – ✆ (06432) 6 71 50 – info@kurhotelpalace.at
– Fax (06432) 671567
198 Zim (inkl. ½ P.) – 83/110 € 166/182 €
Rest – (nur für Hausgäste)
♦ Dieses Hotel am Ortsrand – umgeben von einem schönen, 30 000 qm großen Hotelpark – verfügt über unterschiedlich ausgestattete Gästezimmer und ein vielfältiges Freizeitangebot.

Astoria Spa Zim, Rest, P
Salzburger Str. 24 ✉ 5630 – ✆ (06432) 6 27 70
– info@kur-sporthotel-astoria.com – Fax (06432) 627777
geschl. Nov.
74 Zim (inkl. ½ P.) – ☼ 68/156 € 110/166 € ❄ 91/186 € 128/264 €
Rest – (Abendessen nur für Hausgäste) Karte 20/30 €
♦ In dem Hotel mit der Balkonfassade finden Sie neben komfortablen Zimmern auch Spa-Angebote. Die Senior-Chefin selbst bietet Chi Gong an. Klassisches Restaurant.

Österreichischer Hof (Thermal) Rest, P VISA
Kurgartenstr. 9 ✉ 5630
– ✆ (06432) 6 21 60 – info@oehof.at – Fax (06432) 621651
geschl. 25. April – 15. Mai, 9. Nov. – 20. Dez.
68 Zim (inkl. ½ P.) – ☼ 85/95 € 164/184 € ❄ 103/134 € 192/260 € – 6 Suiten
Rest – (nur für Hausgäste)
♦ Hell und praktisch eingerichtete Zimmer sowie kostenloser Zugang zur Therme erwarten Sie hier. Das Hotel organisiert auch geführte Wanderungen.

Arkadenhof Zim, Rest, P VISA
Tauernstr. 53 ✉ 5630 – ✆ (06432) 82 44
– arkadenhof@colombohotel.com – Fax (06432) 824444
geschl. 5. Nov. – 20. Dez.
36 Zim – ☼ 59/75 € 98/128 € ❄ 59/82 € 98/136 € – ½ P 14 €
Rest – *(nur Abendessen)* Karte 21/33 €
♦ Das am Ortsrand gelegene Urlaubshotel bietet z. T. für mehrere Personen geeignete Zimmer mit alpenländischem Mobiliar, kleiner Küchenzeile und überwiegend mit Balkon.

Rauscher und Paracelsus (geheizt) Rest, Rest, P VISA

Kurpromenade 20 ✉ 5630
– ☎ (06432) 6 41 20 – info@hotel-rauscher.com – Fax (06432) 641218
geschl. Anfang April – Mitte Mai, Ende Okt. – Mitte Dez.
55 Zim (inkl. ½ P.) – ☼ 52/58 € 100/116 € ❄ 65/78 € 120/156 €
Rest – (nur Abendessen für Hausgäste)
◆ Nahe dem Kurpark liegt das aus zwei miteinander verbundenen Häusern bestehende Hotel. Die meisten der zeitgemäßen Zimmer befinden sich im Hotel Rauscher. In verschiedene Stuben unterteiltes Restaurant.

Zum Toni Zim, Rest, P VISA

Eisenstein 1 ✉ 5630 – ☎ (06432) 66 29 – hotelzumtoni@aon.at
– Fax (06432) 662933
16 Zim (inkl. ½ P.) – ☼ 37/39 € 76/86 € ❄ 44/58 € 88/128 €
Rest – Karte 17/34 €
◆ In dem familiengeführten Hotel stehen solide, mit Naturholz regionstypisch eingerichtete Gästezimmer mit neuzeitlichen Bädern zur Verfügung. Restaurantstuben mit nettem Terrassenbereich im Sommer. Im Winter bietet man auch Fondue.

In Bad Hofgastein-Hundsdorf **Süd: 1,5 km Richtung Bad Gastein und Anger:**

Zum Stern Rest, Rest, P

Weitmoserstr. 33 ✉ 5630 – ☎ (06432) 84 50 VISA AE
– info@zumstern.com – Fax (06434) 845085
geschl. 20. April – 10. Mai
40 Zim (inkl. ½ P.) – ☼ 92/100 € 148/222 € ❄ 93/164 € 158/298 €
Rest – Karte 20/31 €
◆ Eine alpenländische Hotelanlage mit komfortablen Zimmern, einige auch für Familien. Besonders schön: die Landhauszimmer mit Kachelofen. Heller, freundlicher Hallenbadbereich. Stilvoll-rustikales Ambiente und gut eingedeckte Tische im Restaurant.

Weitmoser Schlössl P VISA

Schlossgasse 14 ✉ 5630 – ☎ (06432) 66 01 – weitmoser@netway.at
– Fax (06432) 66015
geschl. 25. März - 10. Mai, 30. Sept. – 20. Dez. und Montag
Rest – (abends Tischbestellung ratsam) Karte 21/39 €
◆ In dem Schloss a. d. J. 1554 serviert man internationale und regionale Küche – hier werden Produkte aus der eigenen Landwirtschaft verarbeitet. Wintergarten-Café im 1. Stock.

Außerhalb **Süd: 4 km Richtung Bad Gastein:**

Bertahof P VISA

Vorderschneeberg 15 ✉ 5630 Bad Hofgastein – ☎ (06432) 76 08
– landgasthof@bertahof.at – Fax (06432) 76084
geschl. Nov. und Mittwoch
Rest – (Tischbestellung ratsam) Karte 21/37 €
◆ Ein historischer Alpengasthof mit schmackhaftem internationalem und regionalem Angebot, für das man frische, vorwiegend regionale Zutaten verwendet.

HOFKIRCHEN IM MÜHLKREIS – Oberösterreich – 730 N3 – 1 440 Ew – Höhe 600 m
2 **H2**

Wien 228 – Linz 50 – Wels 58 – Passau 41
Markt 8, ✉ 4142, ✆ (07285) 70 11, gemeindeamt@hofkirchen.at
Pfarrkirchen i. Mühlviertel, ✆ (07285) 64 20

In Hofkirchen-Marsbach Süd-Ost: 4 km Richtung Niederkappl, dann rechts:

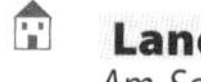

Landhotel Falkner ← Donautal, Zim, Rest, VISA

Am Schloss Marsbach 2 ✉ 4142
– ✆ (07285) 2 23 – falkner@resi.at – Fax (07285) 22320
geschl. 6. Jan. – 16. März, 26. Okt. – 21. Dez.

12 Zim (inkl. ½ P.) – ☼ 104/134 € 174/214 € ❄ 111/141 € 200/240 €

Rest – (nur Abendessen für Hausgäste)

◆ Das ehemalige Jagdhaus a. d. 16. Jh. ist ein schönes kleines Hotel, das bereits in der 5. Generation von Familie Falkner geleitet wird. Beeindruckend: die Panoramalage.

HOFSTETTEN-GRÜNAU – Niederösterreich – 730 S4 – 2 570 Ew – Höhe 320 m
3 **J3**

Wien 80 – St. Pölten 18 – Amstetten 77 – Krems 54

Landgasthof 3erlei mit Zim Zim, VISA AE

Kammerhoferstr. 1 (an der B 39, Nord-Ost: 1,5 km) ✉ 3202
– ✆ (02723) 82 51 – office@3erlei.at – Fax (02723) 825133
geschl. 2.- 6. Jan. und Sonn- und Feiertage abends

20 Zim – 40 € 70 € – ½ P 15 €

Rest – Menü 35 € – Karte 17/38 €

◆ In drei gemütlich-ländlichen Restaurantstuben – Fichtenstüberl, Kaminstüberl und Landhausstüberl – serviert man seinen Gästen regionale Speisen.

Luxuriös oder eher schlicht?
Die Symbole und kennzeichnen den Komfort.

HOHENEMS – Vorarlberg – 730 B6 – 13 900 Ew – Höhe 432 m
5 **A5**

Wien 635 – Bregenz 19 – Feldkirch 19 – Dornbirn 7
Schweizer Str. 10, ✉ 6845, ✆ (05576) 4 27 80, tourismus@hohenems.at

Schiffle Zim, VISA AE

Radetzkystr. 38 (B 190) ✉ 6845 – ✆ (05576) 7 24 32
– office@hotel-schiffle.at – Fax (05576) 7243288
geschl. 2. – 13. Jan.

40 Zim – 56/69 € 88/125 € – ½ P 17 €

Rest – *(geschl. 2. – 20. Jan. und Sonntagabend – Montag, Dienstag – Samstag nur Abendessen)* Karte 22/39 €

◆ Bereits in der 3. Generation wird das Haus von der Wirtsfamilie geführt. Die Zimmer verteilen sich auf Stamm- und Gästehaus und bieten zeitgemäßen Komfort. Hübsch gedeckte Tische und nette Dekorationen im Restaurant.

Lorenz garni

Bahnhofstr. 17 ✉ 6845 – ✆ (05576) 7 23 32 – cafe-lorenz@aon.at – Fax (05576) 723325

geschl. 28. Juli – 20. Aug.

21 Zim – 43/50 € 80/98 €

◆ Die Zimmer dieses im Zentrum gelegenen Hotels sind mit dunklen oder neuzeitlichen hellen Holzmöbeln ausgestattet. Mit im Haus: eine eigene Bäckerei/Konditorei mit Café.

Gasthaus Adler

Kaiser-Franz-Josef-Str. 104 (L 190) ✉ 6845 – ✆ (05576) 7 22 92 – martin-adler@gmx.at

geschl. 13. – 30. Mai, 7. – 31. Okt. und Dienstag

Rest – Menü 30/42 € – Karte 17/37 €

◆ Das familiengeführte Gasthaus ist ein bürgerlich-rustikal gehaltenes Restaurant, in dem man eine gute, teils regional ausgelegte Küche bietet. Toller Weinkeller.

HOHENTAUERN – Steiermark – 730 P6 – 540 Ew – Höhe 1 274 m – Wintersport: 1 800 m 5 9 I4

Wien 227 – Graz 105 – Leoben 67 – Liezen 34

Gemeindeamt, Hohentauern 8, ✉ 8785, ✆ (03618) 3 35, info@hohentauern.at

Gasthof Passhöhe ← Niedere Tauern, Zim,

Hohentauern 110, (B 114) ✉ 8785 – ✆ (03618) 2 19 – haas@passhoehe.at – Fax (03618) 2194

geschl. 7. – 30. April, 4. – 30. Nov.

14 Zim – 34/38 € 68/76 € – ½ P 15 €

Rest – *(geschl. außer Saison Mittwoch)* Karte 13/23 €

◆ Ein an der Passstraße gelegener kleiner Gasthof unter Leitung der Inhaberfamilie mit solide und zeitlos möblierten Zimmern. Rustikales Restaurant.

HOLLERSBACH – Salzburg – 730 J7 – 1 160 Ew – Höhe 806 m – Wintersport: 1 000 m 2 7 F5

Wien 423 – Salzburg 126 – Kitzbühel 35 – Zell am See 33

Nr.13, ✉ 5731, ✆ (06562) 81 05, hollersbach@sbg.at

Kaltenhauser Zim,

Hollersbach 17 ✉ 5731 – ✆ (06562) 8 11 70 – info@kaltenhauser.com – Fax (06562) 811750

geschl. 7. April – 9. Mai, 27. Okt. – 5. Dez.

33 Zim (inkl. ½ P.) – 52/61 € 94/108 € 64/94 € 118/174 €

Rest – Karte 15/34 €

◆ Aus dem 14. Jh. stammt der gestandene Gasthof in der Ortsmitte mit rustikal gehaltenen, teils holzgetäfelten Zimmern und gemütlichem Aufenthaltsbereich. Feng-Shui-Garten. Behagliche, z. T. mit Zirbelholz eingerichtete Gaststuben.

HOLZGAU – Tirol – 730 D7 – 470 Ew – Höhe 1 103 m – Wintersport: 5 B5

Wien 547 – Innsbruck 103 – Reutte 43 – Lech 25
Holzgau 45, 6654, (056331) 53 56, oberlechtal@tirol.com

Ober-Lechtalerhof
Rest,

Holzgau 40 6654 – (05633) 56 88 – oberlechtalerhof@tirol.com – Fax (05633) 568841
geschl. 20. April – 10. Mai, 25. Okt. – 15. Dez.
18 Zim (inkl. ½ P.) – 58/77 € 118/152 €
Rest – (nur für Hausgäste)

♦ Hinter seiner z. T. bemalten Fassade beherbergt das von Familie Blaas geführte Haus meist als Appartement angelegte Zimmer mit kleiner Kochzeile, einige auch mit Kinderzimmer.

Gasthof Bären

Holzgau 56 6654 – (05633) 52 17 – baeren@holzgau.net – Fax (05633) 5359
geschl. 6. – 30. April, 12. Okt. – 19. Dez.
25 Zim (inkl. ½ P.) – 45/51 € 72/84 € 47/68 € 76/118 €
Rest – Karte 15/31 €

♦ Der von der Inhaberfamilie geleitete Gasthof liegt zentral unterhalb der Kirche und bietet solide, regionstypisch eingerichtete Gästezimmer. Ländlich dekoriertes Restaurant mit bürgerlicher Küche.

Berg Heil
Rest,

Leehtal 114 6654 – (05633) 52 15 – info@bergheil.com – Fax (05633) 521575
20 Zim (inkl. ½ P.) – 38/41 € 80/96 € 43/49 € 90/114 €
Rest – Karte 16/24 €

♦ Dieser nette Familienbetrieb am Ortseingang bietet sehr gepflegte Zimmer, die mit hellem Holzmobiliar angenehm zeitgemäß eingerichtet sind. Restaurant in neuzeitlichem Stil.

HOPFGARTEN – Tirol – 730 I6 – 5 270 Ew – Höhe 620 m – Wintersport: 1 825 m 12 84 7 E5

Wien 383 – Innsbruck 69 – Kitzbühel 21 – Wörgl 10
Brixentalerstr. 41, 6361, (05335) 23 22, hopfgarten@hohe-salve.com

s'Platzl

Brixentaler Str. 3 6361 – (05335) 23 33 – Fax (05335) 3501
geschl. August 2 Wochen und Sonntag – Montag
Rest – *(nur Abendessen)* Karte 29/44 €

♦ Ein kleines modern gestaltetes, in Pastellfarben gehaltenes Restaurant mit Bar, in dem man Ihnen eine wechselnde international ausgelegte Tageskarte reicht.

IGLS – Tirol – siehe Innsbruck

ILLMITZ – Burgenland – 730 W5 – 2 600 Ew – Höhe 117 m 4 M3

Wien 77 – Eisenstadt 56 – Wiener Neustadt 85 – Sopron 50

Obere Hauptstr. 2, 7142, (02175) 23 83, illmitz@illmitz.co.at

Nationalpark (geheizt)

Apetlonerstr. 56 7142 – (02175) 36 00 – salzl@hotel-nationalpark.com – Fax (02175) 36004
VISA

geschl. 20. Dez. – 6. Jan.

42 Zim – 82/91 € 120/142 € – ½ P 16 €

Rest – Karte 19/30 €

◆ Großzügige, technisch gut ausgestattete Zimmer und ein gepflegter Freizeitbereich charakterisieren dieses für Seminare geeignete Hotel. Unterteilter Restaurantbereich in neuzeitlichem Stil.

Johannes-Zeche (mit Gästehaus Tauber)

VISA

Florianigasse 10 7142 – (02175) 23 35 – tauber-johannes-zeche@burgenland.org – Fax (02175) 23355

geschl. Feb.

30 Zim – 37/42 € 60/80 € – ½ P 10 €

Rest – *(geschl. Mitte Nov. – Mitte März Montag – Donnerstag)* Karte 14/29 €

◆ Neben gemütlichen, zeitgemäßen Zimmern im 200 m entfernten Gästehaus bietet dieses Hotel noch eine Halle mit integrierter Vinothek. Heurigenähnlich ist das nett dekorierte, gemütliche Restaurant.

Presshaus

VISA AE

Apetloner Str. 13 7142 – (02175) 27 30 – presshaus@bnet.at – Fax (02175) 26025

geschl. Feb. 3 Wochen und Montag – Dienstag außer Juli – Aug.

Rest – Karte 27/41 €

◆ In rustikalem Ambiente mit reichlich Holzdekor kann man hier schmackhafte regionale Küche zu sich nehmen, welche von freundlichem Personal serviert wird.

IMST – Tirol – 730 E7 – 8 690 Ew – Höhe 830 m – Wintersport: 2 100 m 3 6 C5

Wien 503 – Innsbruck 59 – Landeck 20 – Sankt Anton 46

Johannesplatz 4, 6460, (05412) 69 10, info@imst.at

Rosengartenschlucht★ – Stams: Stift Stams★★ (Nord-Ost: 26 km)

Post

Zim, VISA

Eduard-Wallnöfer-Platz 3 6460 – (05412) 6 65 54 – info@romantikhotel-post.com – Fax (05412) 6651955

geschl. April, Nov. – 22. Dez.

26 Zim – 58/68 € 90/110 € – ½ P 25 €

6 Suiten

Rest – Karte 24/46 €

◆ 1450 erstmals urkundlich erwähntes Hotel im früheren Schloss Sprengenstein. Die Zimmer: mit italienischen Stilmöbeln klassisch-elegant eingerichtet, z. T. mit Holzfußboden. Mit viel altem Holz geschmackvoll gestaltetes Restaurant. Hübsche Veranda zum Park.

In Imst-Weinberg **Süd-West: 2 km über B 171 Richtung Landeck, dann rechts:**

Landhotel Hohe Warte
Rottweilerstr. 2 ✉ 6460 – ☎ (05412) 6 64 14 – info@hohewarte.at – Fax (05412) 664144
geschl. 5. April – 3. Mai, 18. Okt. – 20. Dez.
10 Zim – 36/44 € 64/77 € – ½ P 11 €
Rest – *(geschl. Montag, Dienstag – Freitag nur Abendessen)* Karte 17/30 €
◆ Recht ruhig liegt das kleine Hotel in einem Ortsteil. Die Zimmer sind rustikal eingerichtet, sauber und gepflegt. In einem separaten Haus befinden sich 4 Suiten. Restaurant mit ländlichem Charakter – einer der Räume mit Wandmalerei.

INNERVILLGRATEN – Tirol – 730 J8 – 990 Ew – Höhe 1 400 m – Wintersport: 1 4

7 **F6**

Wien 442 – Innsbruck 224 – Lienz 38
Gasse 78, ✉ 9932, ☎ (04843) 51 94, innervillgraten@hochpustertal.com

Der Gannerhof
Innervillgraten 93 ✉ 9932 – ☎ (04843) 52 40 – gannerhof@aon.at – Fax (04843) 5506
geschl. 24. März – 2. April, 1. Nov. – 15. Dez. und Montag – Dienstag
22 Zim (inkl. ½ P.) – 96/102 € 162/250 € – 6 Suiten
Rest – Karte 29/47 €
◆ Das schöne Bauernhaus mit ursprünglichem Charme ist ein engagiert geleitetes Hotel nahe der italienischen Grenze. Sehr hübsch: Ganner-Schupfer-Biohaus aus heimischem Vollholz. Mit Produkten aus eigenem Anbau wird regionale Küche zubereitet.

Hautemaniere Noël/SCOPE

INNSBRUCK

L **Bundesland:** Tirol
Michelin-Karte: **730** G7
Wien 484 – München 170 – Salzburg 190 – Bozen 120

Einwohnerzahl: 113 400 Ew
Höhe: 580 m

7 D5

Innsbrucks Panorama gleicht einem Gesamtkunstwerk. Hervorragende Zeugnisse der Baukunst aus der großen Vergangenheit verschmelzen mit der prächtigen Kulisse der zum Karwendelgebirge gehörenden Nordkette: traumhaft schön! Mit dem Goldenen Dachl und seinem Grabmal in der Hofkirche hinterließ Kaiser Maximilian I. hier bedeutende Zeugnisse der Renaissance, die bis heute nichts von ihrer Faszination verloren haben. Die Stadt steht jedoch auch für den manchmal herben, aber dennoch immer herzlichen Charme Tirols, dem eine bodenständige und auch sehr deftige Küche entspricht. Und Innsbruck war schon zweimal, 1964 und 1976, Austragungsort der Olympischen Winterspiele – zweifelsohne ein Beweis für die hervorragenden Wintersportmöglichkeiten in und um die Stadt.

PRAKTISCHE HINWEISE

Tourist-Information

Burggraben 3 CZ, ✉ 6021, ☎ (0512) 5 98 50, office@innsbruck.info

Autoreisezug

Amraser Straße

Flughafen

Innsbruck (West: 4,5 km), ☎ (0512) 22 52 50

Messen

Innsbrucker Messe, Falkstr. 2, ✉ 6020, ☎ (0512) 5 38 30

26.01. – 27.01.: Reisetrend u. Wellness & Gesundheit

07.02. – 11.02.: ART

29.02. – 02.03.: Die Weinmesse

13.03. – 16.03.: Tiroler Frühjahrsmesse

14.09. – 17.09.: fafga

04.10. – 12.12.: Herbstmesse

Veranstaltungen

03.01. – 04.01.: Vierschanzentournee – Bergiselspringen

17.01. – 22.01.: SPECIAL OLYMICS

01.03. – 23.03.: Osterfestival Tirol

12.04. – 19.04.: Eishockey WM

22.06. – 15.07.: Tanzsommer

08.07. – 24.08.: Festwochen der Alten Musik

24.11. – 06.01.: Christkindlmarkt

Fußball-Europameisterschaft

10.06., 14.06., 18.06.: Vorrundenspiele

Golfplätze

18 Innsbruck-Igls, Rinn, Oberdorf 11 ✆ (05223) 7 81 77

9 Innsbruck-Igls, Lans, Sperberegg ✆ (0512) 37 71 65

SEHENSWÜRDIGKEITEN

ALTSTADT

Maria-Theresien-Straße★ (≤★★) – Goldenes Dachl★ – Helblinghaus★ – Dom zu St. Jakob (Grabmal★) – Hofburg★ (Riesensaal★★) – Hofkirche (Grabmal Kaiser Maximilians I★★). – Silberne Kapelle★★ – Tiroler Volkskunstmuseum★★ CZ – Tiroler Landesmuseum "Ferdinandeum" **M²** DZ – Stadtbild★★

WEITERE SEHENSWÜRDIGKEITEN

Hungerburg★, Hefelekar★★ mit 🚡 – Basilika von Wilten★ AY – Schloss Ambras★ (Rüstkammern★, Porträtgalerie★, Spanischer Saal★) BY

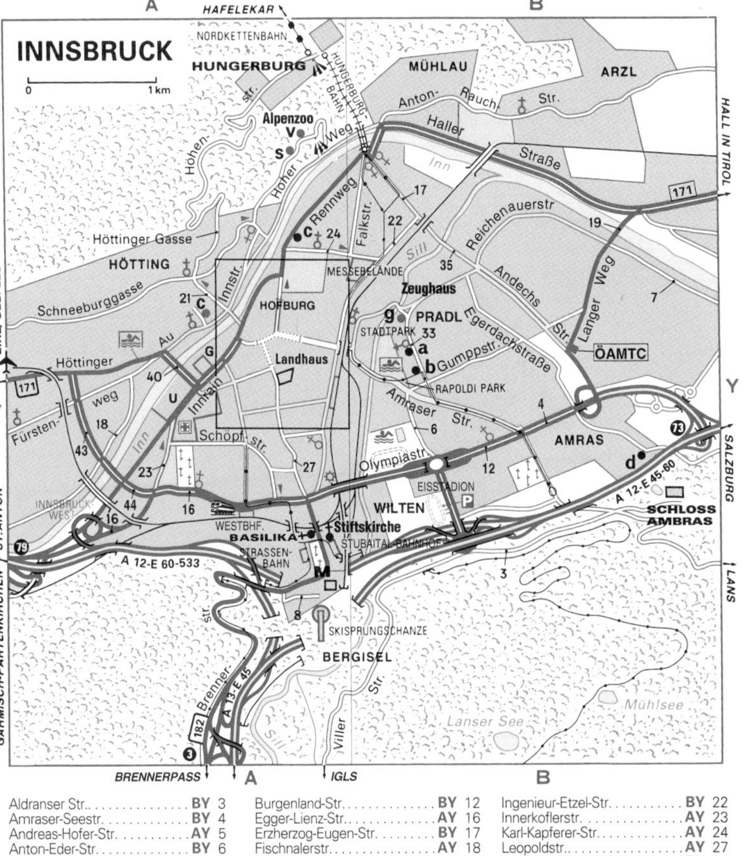

Straße		Nr.
Aldranser Str.	BY	3
Amraser-Seestr.	BY	4
Andreas-Hofer-Str.	AY	5
Anton-Eder-Str.	BY	6
Archenweg	BY	7
Bachlechnerstr.	AY	43
Bergiselweg	AY	8
Burgenland-Str.	BY	12
Egger-Lienz-Str.	AY	16
Erzherzog-Eugen-Str.	BY	17
Fischnalerstr.	AY	18
Grenobler Brücke	BY	19
Höttinger Gasse	AY	21
Holzhammerstr.	AY	44
Ingenieur-Etzel-Str.	BY	22
Innerkoflerstr.	AY	23
Karl-Kapferer-Str.	AY	24
Leopoldstr.	AY	27
Pradlerstr.	BY	33
Prinz-Eugen-Str.	BY	35
Universitäts-Brücke	AY	40

Grand Hotel Europa

Südtiroler Platz 2 ✉ 6020 – ✆ (0512) 59 31 – hotel@europatyrol.com – Fax (0512) 587800 DZ **a**

122 Zim – ☼ 130/150 € 176/202 € ❄ 154/180 € 212/246 €, 20 € – 4 Suiten

Rest *Europa-Stüberl* – separat erwähnt

◆ Gediegene Atmosphäre bestimmt das aus dem Jahre 1869 stammende Hotel in zentraler Lage gegenüber dem Bahnhof. Prächtig ist der denkmalgeschützte Barocksaal.

Hilton

Salurner Str. 15 ✉ 6010 – ✆ (0512) 5 93 50 – info.innsbruck@hilton.com – Fax (0512) 5935220 CDZ **b**

176 Zim – 109/169 € 144/204 €, 22 € – 4 Suiten

Rest *Guggeryllis* – Karte 27/39 €

◆ Die Lage direkt im Zentrum, moderne Zimmer mit sehr funktionell ausgestattetem Arbeitsplatz sowie eine schöne Aussicht zeichnen das Hotel aus. Kasino im Haus. Ein Hofnarr a. d. 16. Jh. gab dem klassisch gestalteten, reich dekorierten Guggeryllis den Namen.

INNSBRUCK

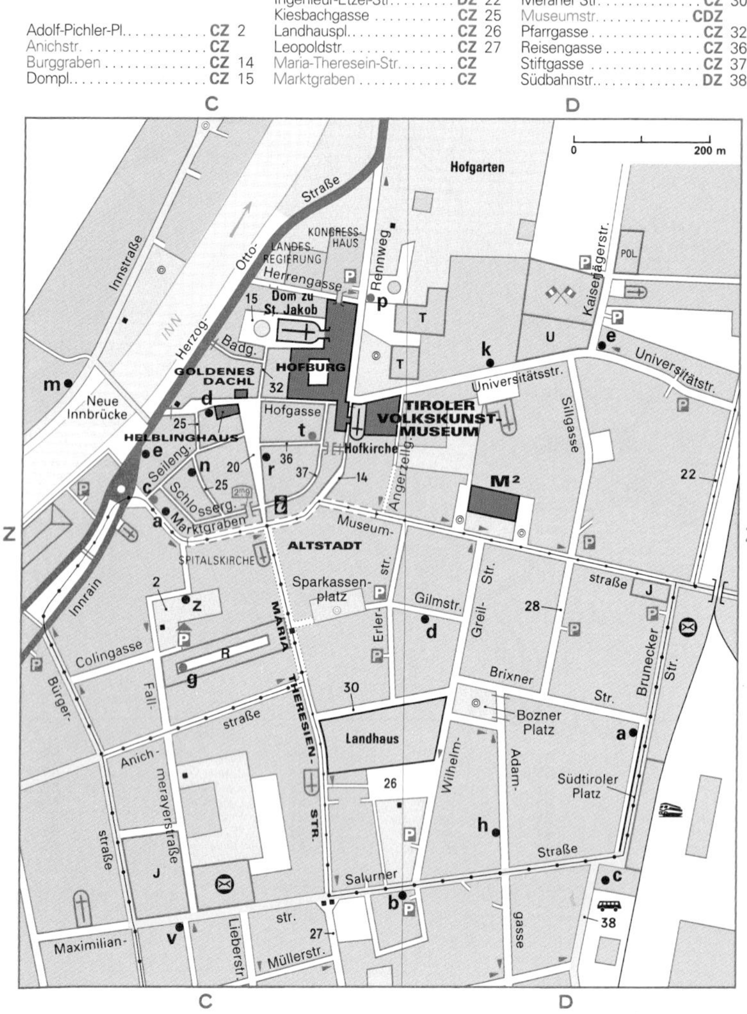

The Penz garni
Adolf-Pichler-Platz 3 ✉ 6020 – ✆ (0512) 5 75 65 70
– office@thepenz.com
– Fax (0512) 5756579 CZ **z**

94 Zim ☕ – 👤140/210 € 👥180/260 €

◆ Das Hotel mit der verglasten Fassade liegt nahe der Altstadt und schließt an eine Geschäftspassage an. Geradliniges modernes Design überall. Bar mit Dachterrasse im 5. OG.

Schwarzer Adler
Kaiserjägerstr. 2 ✉ 6020 – ✆ (0512) 58 71 09 – info@deradler.com – Fax (0512) 561697 DZ **e**
39 Zim – 105/165 € 149/220 € – 4 Suiten
Rest – Menü 30/49 € – Karte 21/37 €
◆ Geschmackvoll und sehr individuell hat man die Zimmer in diesem engagiert geführten Haus eingerichtet. Besonders aufwändig gestaltet sind die Suiten und Versace-Maisonetten. Gemütlich: die hübschen Restaurantstuben. Toll ist die Sicht von der Dachterrasse.

Congress
Zim, Rest,
Rennweg 12a ✉ 6020 – ✆ (0512) 21 15 – congress@austria-trend.at – Fax (0512) 2115500 AY **c**
106 Zim – 149/164 € 190/209 €
Rest – Karte 22/39 €
◆ Am Innufer, nahe der Messe gelegenes Haus mit modernen Gästezimmern. Die Innenstadt mit dem Goldenen Dachl ist zu Fuß gut erreichbar.

Neue Post
Zim,
Maximilianstr. 15 ✉ 6020 – ✆ (0512) 5 94 76 – innsbruck@hotel-neue-post.at – Fax (0512) 581818 CZ **v**
52 Zim – 99/135 € 123/190 €
Rest – *(geschl. Samstagmittag, Sonn- und Feiertage)* Karte 26/45 €
◆ 1902 wurde das Gebäude im späthistorisierenden Stil errichtet und mauserte sich vom Beisl zum sehr gut geführten klassischen Stadthotel mit teilweise eleganten Zimmern. Stilvolles Restaurant mit Wintergarten.

Grauer Bär
Zim,
Universitätsstr. 7 ✉ 6020 – ✆ (0512) 5 92 40 – grauer-baer@innsbruck-hotels.at – Fax (0512) 574535 DZ **k**
196 Zim – 109/145 € 149/185 € – 4 Suiten
Rest – Menü 23 € – Karte 23/37 €
◆ In dem nur 200 m vom historischen Zentrum entfernten Hotel erwarten den Gast eine große Halle mit schöner Bar sowie technisch gut ausgestattete, teils ganz moderne Zimmer.

Innsbruck
Zim,
Innrain 3 ✉ 6020 – ✆ (0512) 59 86 80 – office@hotelinnsbruck.com – Fax (0512) 572280 CZ **e**
112 Zim – 115/189 € 155/229 €
Rest – (nur Abendessen für Hausgäste)
◆ Das auf den Fundamenten der ehemaligen Stadtmauer erbaute Hotel verfügt über zeitgemäße und wohnliche Zimmer mit gutem Platzangebot.

Sporthotel Penz
Rest,
Fürstenweg 183 (über AY) ✉ 6020 – ✆ (0512) 2 25 14 – office@sporthotel-penz.at – Fax (0512) 22514124
77 Zim – 88/128 € 130/155 €
Rest – *(geschl. Sonntag)* (nur für Hausgäste)
◆ Unweit eines Sportzentrums in Flughafennähe gelegenes Hotel mit funktionellen Zimmern. Freundlich und modern: der Saunabereich auf dem Dach mit Blick auf Stadt und Berge. Angenehm hell gestaltetes Restaurant.

Central Zim, Rest,

Gilmstr. 5 6020 – (0512) 59 20 – office@central.co.at
– Fax (0512) 580310 DZ **d**
85 Zim – 99/123 € 115/161 €
Rest – Karte 18/26 €
◆ Ganz in der Nähe der Altstadt gelegenes Hotel mit unterschiedlich gestalteten, teils recht großzügigen Zimmern – auch Mehrbettzimmer für Familien. Im Restaurant: Wiener Kaffeehaustradition seit 1875. Lüster, Säulen und Stuckverzierung prägen das Ambiente.

Sailer Zim, Zim,

Adamgasse 8 6020 – (0512) 53 63 – hotel@sailer-innsbruck.at
– Fax (0512) 53637 DZ **h**
90 Zim – 75/145 € 120/240 €
Rest – Karte 17/44 €
◆ Aus einem über 100 Jahre alten Gasthof ist dieses gepflegte Stadthotel entstanden. Besonders wohnlich: die Zimmer in der 5. und 6. Etage. Das Restaurant: mehrere gemütliche kleine Stuben, z. T. ganz mit Holz vertäfelt.

Goldener Adler

Herzog-Friedrich-Str. 6 6020 – (0512) 57 11 11
– office@goldeneradler.com – Fax (0512) 584409 CZ **d**
35 Zim – 90/100 € 129/190 € – ½ P 15 €
Rest – Karte 17/43 €
◆ Diese traditionsreiche Adresse in der Fußgängerzone existiert bereits seit über 600 Jahren als Gasthaus und beherbergt solide, unterschiedlich eingerichtete Zimmer. Das Restaurant teilt sich in verschiedene Stuben, teilweise mit historischer Ausstattung.

Maximilian garni

Marktgraben 7 6020 – (0512) 5 99 67 – hotel.maximilian@eunet.at
– Fax (0512) 577450 CZ **a**
46 Zim – 80/130 € 110/170 €
◆ Am Rand der Altstadt liegt das familiengeführte Hotel mit soliden Zimmern. Modern sind der schöne Hallenbereich und der in klaren Linien gehaltene Frühstücksraum.

Weisses Rössl

Kiebachgasse 8 6020 – (0512) 58 30 57 – weisses@roessl.at
– Fax (0512) 5830575
geschl. April 2 Wochen, Nov. 2 Wochen CZ **n**
13 Zim – 75/85 € 115/140 €
Rest – *(geschl. Sonn- und Feiertage)* Karte 15/34 €
◆ Der a. d. J. 1410 stammende Gasthof in der Innsbrucker Fußgängerzone ist ein familiär geführtes kleines Haus mit zeitgemäß und wohnlich ausgestatteten Zimmern. Getäfelte Wände und Holzbalken an der Decke geben den Gaststuben rustikales Flair.

Weisses Kreuz garni

Herzog-Friedrich-Str. 31 6020 – (0512) 59 47 90
– hotel@weisseskreuz.at – Fax (0512) 5947990 CZ **r**
40 Zim – 59/95 € 93/118 €
◆ In der Altstadt befindet sich das nette traditionsreiche Haus von 1465, in dem schon Mozart zu Gast war. Es stehen unterschiedlich eingerichtete Zimmer zur Verfügung.

Ibis garni
Sterzingerstr. 1 ✉ 6020 – ✆ (0512) 5 70 30 00 – h5174@accor.com – Fax (0512) 570300555 DZ **c**
75 Zim – †61 € ††76 €, ☕ 9 €
◆ Die zentrale Lage neben dem Bahnhof sowie neuzeitliche Gästezimmer in sachlich-funktionellem Stil sprechen für dieses Hotel.

Europa-Stüberl – Grand Hotel Europa
Südtiroler Platz 2 ✉ 6020 – ✆ (0512) 59 31 – hotel@europatyrol.com – Fax (0512) 587800 DZ **a**
Rest – Menü 38/48 € – Karte 29/60 €
◆ Hübsche Holztäfelungen verleihen den Restaurantstuben ihr gemütliches Ambiente. Der Service ist aufmerksam und freundlich, die Küche überwiegend international.

Pavillon
Rennweg 4 (1. Etage, am Landestheaterplatz) ✉ 6020 – ✆ (0512) 25 70 00 – office@der-pavillon.at – Fax (0512) 908288
geschl. April 2 Wochen, September 2 Wochen und Sonntag – Montag CZ **p**
Rest – *(nur Abendessen)* (Tischbestellung ratsam) Menü 42/79 € – Karte 39/68 €
◆ Das moderne Restaurant in geradlinigem Stil befindet sich in einem Glasbau mitten im Zentrum. Geboten wird ambitionierte kreative Küche. Café im EG.

Villa Blanka ≤ Innsbruck und Bergpanorama,
Weiherburggasse 8 ✉ 6020 – ✆ (0512) 27 60 70 – marketing@villablanka.com – Fax (0512) 29241370
geschl. 18. – 29. Feb. AY **v**
Rest – Karte 22/46 €
◆ An die Hotelfachschule angegliedertes Restaurant mit moderner, fast puristischer Einrichtung und schönem Blick über Innsbruck. Regionale Karte mit internationalem Einfluss.

Wirtshaus Schöneck (Alfred Miller)
Weiherburggasse 6 ✉ 6020 – ✆ (0512) 27 27 28 – info@wirtshaus-schoeneck.com – Fax (0512) 272729
geschl. Ende Feb. – Anfang März., Ende Aug. – Anfang Sept. und Sonntag – Dienstagmittag AY **s**
Rest – (Tischbestellung erforderlich) Menü 19 € (mittags)/76 € (abends) – Karte 43/53 €
Spez. Jakobsmuschel und Garnelen mit Safranmelange. In Lagrein geschmortes Kalbswangerl mit getrüffeltem Erdäpfelpüree. Kalbskutteln mit Riesling, Thymian und Kümmel.
◆ Das Wirtshaus a. d. 19. Jh. besticht durch gemütliche Atmosphäre – altes Holz und Zierrat prägen die Stuben. Am Abend: klassisches Angebot, mittags einfachere regionale Karte.

Lichtblick ≤ Innsbruck,
Maria-Theresienstr. 18 (7. Etage, Rathauspassage) ✉ 6020 – ✆ (0512) 56 65 50 – office@restaurant-lichtblick.at
geschl. Samstagabend – Sonntag CZ **g**
Rest – (Tischbestellung ratsam) Menü 32/42 € – Karte 21/44 €
◆ Eine phantastische Sicht über die Stadt bietet das moderne Restaurant mit gehobener kreativer Küche. Einfachere und preiswertere Mittagskarte. 360°-Bar in klarem Design.

Dengg
Riesengasse 13 ✉ 6020 – ☎ (0512) 58 23 47 – dengg@chello.at – Fax (0512) 5823477
geschl. Samstagmittag, Sonn- und Feiertage CZ **t**
Rest – Menü 42/57 € – Karte 29/42 €
◆ Ein Altstadthaus in einer kleinen Gasse beherbergt drei Restaurantstuben, Bar und Café. In trendigem Ambiente bietet man Fusion-Küche.

Thai Li
Marktgraben 3 ✉ 6020 – ☎ (0512) 56 28 13 – service@thai-li-ba.at – Fax (0512) 5678885
geschl. Sonntagmittag, Montag CZ **c**
Rest – (Tischbestellung ratsam) Karte 19/30 €
◆ Ein gut besuchtes, schlicht gehaltenes Restaurant am Rande der Altstadt. In der offenen Küche bereitet man thailändische Spezialitäten.

In Innsbruck-Amras

Bierwirt Zim,
Bichlweg 2 ✉ 6020 – ☎ (0512) 34 21 43 – hotel@bierwirt.com – Fax (0512) 3421435 BY **d**
66 Zim – 80/90 € 120/130 €
Rest – Karte 17/26 €
◆ Ein stattlicher alpenländischer Gasthof mit langer Tradition. Die Zimmer sind mit hellem Naturholz wohnlich eingerichtet, im Gästehaus fallen sie etwas großzügiger aus. Verschiedene Restaurantstuben in regionalem Stil.

In Innsbruck-Igls **Süd: 6 km über Viller Straße** AY – **Höhe 900 m**

Schlosshotel Berge, Rest,
Viller Steig 2 ✉ 6080 – ☎ (0512) 37 72 17 – hotel@schlosshotel-igls.com – Fax (0512) 377217198
geschl. April, Mitte Okt. – Mitte Dez.
18 Zim – ☼ 160/225 € 300 € ❄ 160/300 € 300/400 € – ½ P 30 € – 6 Suiten
Rest – Karte 31/48 €
◆ In herrlicher Lage oberhalb von Innsbruck befindet sich das schlossähnliche Hotel. Elegant sind die individuellen Zimmer und die kleine Halle. Frühstück im Blauen Salon. Restaurant mit klassischem Ambiente.

Sporthotel Igls
Hilber Str. 17 ✉ 6080 – ☎ (0512) 37 72 41 – hotel@sporthotel-igls.com – Fax (0512) 378679
geschl. Nov.
74 Zim – ☼ 85/109 € 150/230 € ❄ 93/194 € 170/368 € – ½ P 18 € – 4 Suiten
Rest – Karte 24/43 €
◆ In dem typisch alpenländischen Hotel erwarten Sie Zimmer im wohnlich-eleganten Landhausstil und ein großzügiger Freizeitbereich. Ein offener Kamin macht die Halle gemütlich. Klassisch gehaltenes Restaurant.

In Innsbruck-Mariahilf

Mondschein garni
Mariahilfstr. 6 ✉ 6020 – ✆ (0512) 2 27 84 – office@mondschein.at – Fax (0512) 2278490 CZ **m**
34 Zim – 75/105 € 105/160 €
◆ In der ältesten, denkmalgeschützten Häuserzeile der Stadt steht das Hotel direkt am Inn. Neben wohnlichen Zimmern hat man eine schöne Bar mit Kreuzgewölbe und offenem Kamin.

Trattoria da Peppino
Kirschentalgasse 6 ✉ 6020 – ✆ (0512) 27 56 99 – Fax (0512) 275699
geschl. Sonntag – Montag AY **c**
Rest – *(nur Abendessen)* Karte 25/40 €
◆ Ein Restaurant im Trattoria-Stil, das einen sehr freundlichen Service sowie italienische Küche mit einer guten Auswahl an frischem Fisch bietet.

In Innsbruck-Pradl

Leipziger Hof Zim,
Defreggerstr. 13 ✉ 6020 – ✆ (0512) 34 35 25 – info@leipzigerhof.at – Fax (0512) 394357 BY **b**
55 Zim – 90/150 € 130/220 €
Rest – *(geschl. Sonn- und Feiertage)* Karte 20/36 €
◆ Das Hotel der Familie Perger liegt direkt gegenüber dem Stadtpark. Man verfügt über neuzeitliche Gästezimmer – hübsch: die Zimmer mit Erker. Gemütliches Restaurant im Tiroler Stil, mit Nischen und einem Kachelofen.

Alpinpark
Pradlerstr. 28 ✉ 6020 – ✆ (0512) 34 86 00 – alpinpark@innsbruck-hotels.at – Fax (0512) 364172 BY **a**
87 Zim – 70/95 € 110/166 € – ½ P 10 €
Rest – Karte 17/32 €
◆ In dem Hotel am Rande der Innenstadt stehen funktionell eingerichtete Zimmer zur Verfügung. Im Winter zählt ein Gratis-Skibus zum Angebot. Netter Saunabereich. Restaurant und bäuerlich dekorierte Stube.

Jabinger – Hotel Altpradl
Pradlerstr. 8 ✉ 6020 – ✆ (0512) 34 16 34 – office@jabinger.at – Fax (0512) 341634
geschl. Dienstag BY **g**
Rest – Menü 54 € – Karte 29/44 €
◆ In den ländlich-rustikal gehaltenen Restaurantstuben bietet man regionale und internationale Küche sowie eine gute Auswahl an österreichischen Weinen.

Bestecke und Sterne sollten nicht verwechselt werden!
Die Bestecke stehen für eine Komfortkategorie, die Sterne zeichnen Häuser mit besonders guter Küche aus - in jeder dieser Kategorien.

IRDNING – Steiermark – 730 O6 – 2 640 Ew – Höhe 645 m – Wintersport: 750 m 1 9 H4

Wien 257 – Graz 135 – Liezen 18 – Bad Ischl 58

Irdning 220, 8952, (03682) 2 32 43, info@urlaubsland.at

Schloss Pichlarn, Gatschen 28 (03682) 22 84 15 40

Schloss Pichlarn Grimming und Ennstal, (geheizt) Rest, Rest, Rest,

Zur Linde 1 (Ost: 1,5 km, Richtung Aigen, dann rechts ab) 8952 – (03682) 2 44 40 – reservierung@pichlarn.at – Fax (03682) 228416

120 Zim (inkl. ½ P.) – 130/170 € 260/366 € – 11 Suiten

Rest – (abends Tischbestellung ratsam) Menü 59 € – Karte 34/49 €

◆ Das über 900 Jahre alte Schloss ist heute eine 100 ha große Hotelanlage mit elegantem Rahmen. Zum Freizeitangebot zählen u. a. Ayurveda-Behandlungen und Reiten. Klassische Küche im hübschen, gemütlich-alpenländischen Schloss-Stüberl.

Villa Falkenhof (Dietmar Dorner) mit Zim Rest,

Falkenburg 23 (Süd: 1 km)

8952 – (03682) 2 24 45 – office@falkenhof.at – Fax (03682) 224455

14 Zim – 75/110 € 110/180 €, 15 €

Rest – (Tischbestellung ratsam) Menü 48 € (mittags)/105 € – Karte ca. 65 €

Spez. Sashimi von Thunfisch, Lachs und Hummer. Rindsfilet "Café de Paris". Schokodôme.

◆ Die Jagdvilla am Waldrand beherbergt dieses Restaurant, in dem man die kreative Küche Dietmar Dorners genießen kann, serviert von kompetentem Personal.

ISCHGL – Tirol – 730 C7 – 1 490 Ew – Höhe 1 400 m – Wintersport: 2 872 m 5 36 5 B6

Wien 611 – Innsbruck 102 – Bludenz 63 – Imst 48

Nr. 320, 6561, (05444) 5 22 60, info@ischgl.com

Silvretta-Hochalpenstraße★★

Trofana Royal

Nr. 334 6561 – (05444) 6 00 – office@trofana.at – Fax (05444) 60090

geschl. Anfang Mai – Ende Juni, Mitte Okt. – Ende Nov.

82 Zim (inkl. ½ P.) – 140/160 € 220/300 € 220/320 € 390/620 € – 12 Suiten

Rest *Paznaunerstube* – separat erwähnt

◆ Beispielhaft kümmert sich das Serviceteam in diesem luxuriösen Haus um den Gast. Ebenso angenehm: die großzügigen und hochwertigen Zimmer sowie das umfassende Wellnessangebot.

Madlein

Nr. 144 6561 – (05444) 52 26 – info@madlein.com – Fax (05444) 5226202

geschl. 4. Mai – 7. Juni, 14. Sept. – 28. Nov.

70 Zim (inkl. ½ P.) – 100/225 € 150/300 € 188/488 € 280/650 € – 3 Suiten

Rest – Karte 19/45 €

◆ Puristisches Design begleitet Sie von der Lobby über den Spabereich bis in den Zen-Garten. Auch ein Teil der Zimmer ist in diesem klaren, modernen Stil gehalten.

Post Rest, Rest, VISA

Nr. 7 6561 – (05444) 52 32 – hotel@post-ischgl.at – Fax (05444) 561733

geschl. 5. Mai – 20. Juni, 22. Sept. – 27. Nov.

85 Zim (inkl. ½ P.) – 80 € 140 € 106/178 € 194/338 € – 22 Suiten

Rest – (nur für Hausgäste)

♦ Gewachsenes Alpenhotel im Zentrum mit geräumiger Halle, komfortablen Zimmern (auch Familienzimmer) und schönem großzügigen Wellness- und Beautybereich. Luxus-Kristall-Suite.

Seiblishof Rest, P VISA AE

Nr. 111 6561 – (05444) 54 25 – info@seiblishof.com – Fax (05444) 542566

geschl. 1. Mai – 22. Juni, 20. Sept. – 29. Nov.

60 Zim (inkl. ½ P.) – 80/92 € 170/198 € 121/181 € 264/384 €

Rest – (nur Abendessen für Hausgäste)

♦ Das am Ortsrand gelegene Hotel verfügt über einen komfortablen Vitalbereich und ist mit Kinderbetreuung und einigen "Family-Zimmern" ganz auf Familien eingestellt.

Tirol Rest, P VISA

Nr. 79 6561 – (05444) 52 16 – hotel@tirol-ischgl.at – Fax (05444) 52166

geschl. 2. Mai – 24. Juni, 16. Sept. – 29. Nov.

53 Zim (inkl. ½ P.) – 63/65 € 110/114 € 96/135 € 158/251 €

Rest – Karte 21/33 €

♦ Im Zentrum befindet sich das Hotel mit rundem, turmähnlichem Anbau. Die Zimmer sind großzügig geschnitten und mit einem behaglichen Wohnbereich ausgestattet. Rund angelegtes Restaurant mit rustikalem Ambiente.

Brigitte Zim, Rest, P VISA

Nr. 236 6561 – (05444) 56 46 – info@hotel-brigitte.com – Fax (05444) 564666

geschl. Anfang Mai – Ende Nov.

63 Zim (inkl. ½ P.) – 129/202 € 218/383 € – 10 Suiten

Rest – (nur Abendessen für Hausgäste)

♦ Eine großzügige Lobby mit Kamin und Bar empfängt Sie in dem gut geführten Hotel mit wohnlichen Zimmern und schönem Freizeitbereich mit Kosmetik und Massage.

Schlosshotel Romantica VISA AE

Nr. 276 6561 – (05444) 56 33 – info@romantica.at – Fax (05444) 5634666

geschl. 5. Mai – 27. Nov.

60 Zim – 145/165 € 156/290 € – ½ P 38 €

Rest *Schloss-Alm* – Menü 48/77 € – Karte 40/56 €

♦ Ein Hotel mit alpenländischem Ambiente mitten im Zentrum. Eine schöne Terrasse bietet Sonne bis in die Abendstunden. Hübscher Freizeitbereich. Die Gastronomie Schloss-Alm umfasst gehobenen Après-Ski, Restaurant und Disko.

Goldener Adler

Nr. 6 ✉ 6561 – ✆ (05444) 52 17 – hotel@goldener-adler.at
– Fax (05444) 5571
geschl. 4. Mai – 14. Juni, 7. Sept. – 30. Nov.
35 Zim (inkl. ½ P.) – ☼ †63/68 € ††116/122 € ❄ †103/153 €
††154/238 €
Rest – (nur Abendessen für Hausgäste)

♦ In dem über 370 Jahre alten Gasthof hat man Tradition und Moderne gelungen kombiniert. Die Zimmer sind geschmackvoll und individuell eingerichtet.

The Hotel

Nr. 352 ✉ 6561 – ✆ (05444) 2 01 50 – welcome@thehotel.at
– Fax (05444) 2015050
geschl. Anfang Mai – Ende Nov.
20 Zim (inkl. ½ P.) – †78/121 € ††124/234 €
Rest – (nur Abendessen für Hausgäste)

♦ Das in neuzeitlichem Stil gebaute kleine Hotel beherbergt freundlich und funktionell eingerichtete Gästezimmer mit individueller Note.

Sonne

Nr. 23 ✉ 6561 – ✆ (05444) 53 02 – office@sonne-ischgl.at
– Fax (05444) 547322
geschl. Anfang Mai – Ende Juni, Ende Sept. – Ende Nov.
54 Zim (inkl. ½ P.) – ☼ †59/69 € ††98/118 € ❄ †94/170 €
††164/314 € – 3 Suiten
Rest – *(geschl. Anfang Mai – Anfang Juli, Mitte Sept. – Ende Nov.)*
Karte 18/52 €

♦ Wohnliches regionstypisches Ambiente und persönliche Gästebetreuung machen das am Rand des Zentrums gelegene Alpenhotel aus. Rustikales Restaurant mit freundlichem Service.

Christine garni

Nr. 9 ✉ 6561 – ✆ (05444) 53 46 – info@hotel-christine.at
– Fax (05444) 534646
geschl. Anfang Mai – Ende Nov.
35 Zim ☕ – †90/132 € ††130/224 €

♦ Gediegenes Ambiente begleitet Sie vom Empfangsbereich bis in die zeitgemäß und solide ausgestatteten Gästezimmer dieses Hauses.

Alpenresidenz Trisanna garni

Nr. 65 ✉ 6561 – ✆ (05444) 52 27
– hotel@trisanna.at – Fax (05444) 52276
geschl. Mai – Nov.
30 Zim ☕ – †58/99 € ††114/190 €

♦ In dem engagiert geführten Hotel erwarten den Gast wohnliche, teilweise mit kleinem Kachelofen ausgestattete Zimmer sowie ein ansprechend gestalteter Freizeitbereich.

Almhof garni

Nr. 353 ✉ 6561 – ✆ (05444) 2 01 99 – info@almhof-ischgl.at
– Fax (05444) 201995
geschl. 4. Mai – Juni, Sept. – Nov.

21 Zim – ☼ 🕴34/36 € 🕴🕴64/68 € ❄ 🕴58/98 € 🕴🕴116/196 €
◆ Das Hotel liegt bei der Talstation der Silvrettabahn. Die Zimmer sind wohnlich mit Naturholzmöbeln eingerichtet, manche mit Whirlwanne und Kachelofen. Gepflegter Saunabereich.

Fliana — VISA MC

Nr. 280 ✉ 6561 – ☎ (05444) 55 43 – hotel@fliana.at – Fax (05444) 55435
geschl. 1. Mai – 20. Juni, 1. Okt. – 1. Dez.
30 Zim (inkl. ½ P.) – ☼ 🕴70/90 € 🕴🕴140/180 € ❄ 🕴70/110 € 🕴🕴140/220 €
Rest – (nur Abendessen für Hausgäste, im Winter garni)
◆ Ein sympathisches Haus im alpenländischen Stil mit zeitgemäßer Ausstattung und freundlicher Atmosphäre. Man bietet auch Familienzimmer mit separatem Kinderschlafraum.

Ischgl — Rest, P VISA MC

Nr. 197 ✉ 6561 – ☎ (05444) 53 51 – info@hotelischgl.at
– Fax (05444) 53515
geschl. 4. Mai – 28. Juli
28 Zim (inkl. ½ P.) – ☼ 🕴58/93 € 🕴🕴116/186 € ❄ 🕴126/177 € 🕴🕴170/238 € – 3 Suiten
Rest – (nur Abendessen für Hausgäste)
◆ Das hübsche Hotel am Ortseingang bietet wohnliche Zimmer im alpenländischen Stil mit guter technischer Ausstattung. Nett ist auch der Saunabereich.

Yscla — Rest, VISA MC

Nr. 125 ✉ 6561 – ☎ (05444) 52 75 – info@yscla.at – Fax (05444) 52754
geschl. 4. Mai – 5. Aug., 14. Sept. – 28. Nov.
31 Zim (inkl. ½ P.) – ☼ 🕴65/75 € 🕴🕴110/160 € ❄ 🕴110/165 € 🕴🕴170/320 €
Rest *Stüva* – separat erwähnt
◆ Yscla bedeutet "Au am Wasser" und ist der rätoromanische Namen Ischgls. Ein engagiert geführtes Hotel mit komfortablen Zimmern, Après-Ski und mehreren Restaurants.

Olympia — P VISA MC

Nr. 62a ✉ 6561 – ☎ (05444) 54 32 – hotel@olympia-ischgl.at
– Fax (05444) 5432100
geschl. 2. Mai – 28. Juni, 30. Aug. – 28. Nov.
42 Zim (inkl. ½ P.) – ☼ 🕴61 € 🕴🕴108/116 € ❄ 🕴91/131 € 🕴🕴152/247 €
Rest – (nur Abendessen für Hausgäste)
◆ In dem gewachsenen familiär geführten Alpenhotel stehen hell möblierte, solide Gästezimmer von unterschiedlicher Größe zur Verfügung.

Sylvia — Rest, P VISA MC AE

Nr. 297 ✉ 6561 – ☎ (05444) 56 90 – hotel-sylvia@ischgl.at
– Fax (05444) 56917
geschl. Mai – Ende Nov.
18 Zim (inkl. ½ P.) – 🕴110/190 € 🕴🕴140/260 €
Rest – (nur Abendessen für Hausgäste)
◆ Das mit Holzschindeln verkleidete Hotel liegt bei der Pardatschgrat-Bahn. Man bietet zeitgemäß ausgestattete Zimmer und eine nett gestaltete Hotelhalle.

Sporthotel Piz Buin Zim, Rest,

Nr. 64 ✉ 6561 – ✆ (05444) 53 00
– piz-buin@ischgl.at – Fax (05444) 5673
geschl. Anfang Mai – Ende Juni, Mitte Sept. – Anfang Dez.
31 Zim (inkl. ½ P.) – 69/77 € 137/153 € 87/151 € 187/293 €
Rest – (nur Abendessen für Hausgäste)

◆ Wohnliches Ambiente im ganzen Haus: gemütliche Halle mit offenem Kamin, mit hellem Holz vertäfelte, rustikale Gaststube und unterschiedlich eingerichtete Zimmer.

Piz Tasna Rest,

Nr. 174 ✉ 6561 – ✆ (05444) 52 77 – hotel@piztasna.at
– Fax (05444) 527755
geschl. Mai – Juni, Okt. – Nov.
33 Zim (inkl. ½ P.) – 54/62 € 108/124 € 80/125 € 160/250 €
Rest – (nur Abendessen für Hausgäste)

◆ Das Alpenhotel mit bemalter Fassade liegt recht ruhig abseits des Zentrums. Solide Zimmer und ein sehr netter Freizeitbereich mit diversen Angeboten.

Albona Rest, Rest,

Nr. 282 ✉ 6561 – ✆ (05444) 55 00 – office@albona-ischgl.at
– Fax (05444) 56727
geschl. Anfang Mai – Ende Nov.
34 Zim (inkl. ½ P.) – 118/200 € 198/308 €
Rest – (nur Abendessen für Hausgäste)

◆ Ein familiengeführtes Hotel am Rand des Zentrums mit zeitgemäßen, soliden Gästezimmern und einem netten, gepflegten Saunabereich.

Palin garni

Nr. 234 ✉ 6561 – ✆ (05444) 54 45 – hotel@palin.at – Fax (05444) 54456
geschl. 4. Mai - 28. Nov.
20 Zim – 45/85 € 90/170 €

◆ Ruhig liegt das Hotel etwas oberhalb des Zentrums. Es erwarten Sie eine gemütliche Halle, zeitgemäße Zimmer und ein Saunabereich.

Valülla garni

Nr.19 ✉ 6561 – ✆ (05444) 52 54 – info@valuella.at – Fax (05444) 52544
geschl. Anfang Mai – Ende Juni, Ende Sept. – Ende Nov.
21 Zim – 25/40 € 50/76 € 51/85 € 96/156 €

◆ Das Haus befindet sich in recht ruhiger Lage etwas außerhalb des Zentrums, die Seilbahn ist nicht weit entfernt. Die Zimmer sind geräumig und technisch gut ausgestattet.

Ida garni

Nr. 355 ✉ 6561 – ✆ (05444) 5 00 05 – hotel@ida-ischgl.at
– Fax (05444) 500055
geschl. 4. Mai – 28. Nov.
18 Zim – 60/77 € 100/144 €

◆ Das im regionstypischen Stil erbaute Hotel ist ein kleiner Familienbetrieb mit Zimmern in hellem Naturholz – alle mit Balkon, einige auch mit Küchenzeile.

Arnika Zim, Rest,

Nr. 36 ✉ 6561 – ✆ (05444) 52 44 – info@hotelarnika.at
– Fax (05444) 524414
geschl. 5. Mai – Ende Juni
19 Zim (inkl. ½ P.) – ☼ 49 € 92/106 € ❄ 79/126 € 132/272 €
Rest – *(geschl. Ende Juni – Mitte Okt. Dienstag) (im Winter nur Abendessen für Hausgäste)* Karte 19/33 €
♦ Die familiengeführte Ferienpension in einer Nebenstraße im Zentrum verfügt über solide Gästezimmer und einen hübschen holzvertäfelten Frühstücksraum. Freundliches Restaurant mit Terrasse.

Caroline garni

Nr. 45 ✉ 6561 – ✆ (05444) 52 89 – hotel-caroline@ischgl.at
– Fax (05444) 528911
geschl. Anfang Mai – Ende Nov.
20 Zim – 52/88 € 94/166 €
♦ Ein relativ ruhig gelegenes Haus mit solide möblierten, teilweise recht geräumigen Zimmern und einem ansprechend gestalteten Freizeitbereich.

Germania Zim,

Nr. 221 ✉ 6561 – ✆ (05444) 52 30 – germania@ischgl.at
– Fax (05444) 52303
geschl. Mai – Juni, Okt. – Nov.
20 Zim – ☼ 40 € 70/80 € ❄ 130 € 140/180 € – ½ P 20 €
Rest – *(nur Abendessen)* Karte 18/43 €
♦ Etwas abseits des Trubels und dennoch zentrumsnah liegt dieses Hotel mit seinen soliden Gästezimmern und kleinem, aber sehr gepflegtem Saunabereich. Neuzeitliches Restaurant.

Paznaunerstube – Hotel Trofana Royal

Nr. 334 ✉ 6561 – ✆ (05444) 6 00 – office@trofana.at – Fax (05444) 60090
geschl. Anfang Mai – Ende Juni, Mitte Okt. – Ende Nov. und im Sommer Dienstag
Rest – (Tischbestellung erforderlich) Menü 52/99 € – Karte 36/71 €
Spez. Das Beste von der Gänseleber. Paznauner Schaf'l in der Senfsaatkruste. Süße Versuchung von Bitterschokolade, Bauerntopfen und Trüffel in vier Gängen serviert.
♦ Ein schönes Restaurant mit elegantem alpenländischem Ambiente. Der Service ist aufmerksam und kompetent, die ideenreiche Karte bietet harmonisch zubereitete Speisen.

Stüva – Hotel Yscla

Nr. 125 ✉ 6561 – ✆ (05444) 52 75 – info@yscla.at – Fax (05444) 52754
geschl. 4. Mai – 5. Aug., 14. Sept. – 28. Nov.
Rest – *(nur Abendessen)* Menü 42/58 € – Karte 27/48 €
♦ Eine rustikale Atmosphäre herrscht in den zwei kleinen Restaurantstuben. Freundlich serviert man seinen Gästen internationale Speisen.

Café Loba Bauernküche

Nr. 286 ✉ 6561 – ✆ (05444) 52 89 – hotel-caroline@ischgl.at
– Fax (05444) 528911
geschl. Mai – Ende Nov.
Rest – *(nur Abendessen)* (Tischbestellung ratsam) Karte 21/37 €
♦ Dieses im Tiroler Stil gebaute Haus beherbergt eine urig-gemütliche, ganz mit Altholz verkleidete Stube, in der man regionale Küche bietet. Zittermusikabende.

In Ischgl-Mathon Süd-West: 4 km Richtung Galtür:

Alp Larain

Rest,

Hauptstr. 62a ✉ 6562 – ✆ (05444) 51 76 – info@alp-larain.com
– Fax (05444) 51778
geschl. Anfang Mai – Anfang Dez.
27 Zim (inkl. ½ P.) – 92/108 € 142/200 €
Rest – (nur Abendessen für Hausgäste)
◆ Ein Alpenhotel mit gemütlicher Halle und Gästezimmern im regionalen Landhausstil – alle verfügen über einen Wohnbereich und einen Balkon.

Belavita

Zim,

Nr. 74 ✉ 6562 – ✆ (05444) 54 84 – hotel@belavita.at
– Fax (05444) 54846
geschl. Mai – Juni, Sept. – Nov.
23 Zim (inkl. ½ P.) – 45/50 € 70/90 € 70/100 € 116/186 €
Rest – (nur Abendessen für Hausgäste)
◆ Eine netter Halle mit Kachelofen empfängt Sie in diesem Hotel. Die Zimmer sind im alpenländischen Landhausstil eingerichtet. Im UG befindet sich ein gepflegter Saunabereich.

Residenz Glöckner

Zim,

Mathon 75 ✉ 6562 – ✆ (05444) 51 67 – gloeckner@aon.at
– Fax (05444) 516710
geschl. Mai, Okt. – Nov.
15 Zim – 82 € 138/148 €
Rest – Karte 20/33 €
◆ Solide Zimmer in rustikalem Stil, z. T. mit Dachschräge, sowie ein gemütlicher kleiner Barbereich stehen in dem regionstypischen Hotel in zentraler Lage zur Verfügung.

Wirtshaus Walserstube

Mathon 12 ✉ 6562 – ✆ (05444) 59 31 – ischgl@restaurant-walserstube.at
– Fax (05444) 20013
geschl. Anfang Mai – Anfang Juni, Anfang Okt. – Mitte Nov., im Sommer Dienstag
Rest – (Tischbestellung ratsam) Karte 20/27 €
◆ Das Paznauner Gasthaus a. d. 16. Jh. beherbergt heute ganz in Holz gehaltene, mit hübschem Dekor liebevoll eingerichtete Stuben sowie ein kleines Bauernmuseum im 1. Stock.

ISCHL, BAD – Oberösterreich – 730 M5 – 14 090 Ew – Höhe 468 m – Wintersport: 1 450 m 1 2 9 G4

Wien 265 – Linz 104 – Salzburg 53 – Gmunden 33
Kurdirektion, Bahnhofstr. 6, ✉ 4820, ✆ (06132) 2 77 57, office@badischl.at
Salzkammergut, Wirling 36 ✆ (06132) 2 63 40

Veranstaltungen
23.03.: Osterfestspiele
21.05. – 25.05.: Shake the lake
12.07. – 31.08.: Operettenfestspiele

Kaiservilla★ A
Salzkammergut★★★ – Ebensee (Traunsee★, Zeitgeschichte-Museum Ebensee★) Nord-Ost: 17 km

BAD ISCHL

Johannes-Brücke .... B 5
Kaiser-Franz-Josef-Str. .... B 7
Kaltenbachstr. .... A 9
Kurhausstr. .... A 12
Leitenbergerstr. .... A 13
Maxquellgasse .... B 15
Pfarrgasse .... B 16
Steinfeldstr. .... B 18
Traunkai .... A 20
Voglhuberstraße .... B 2

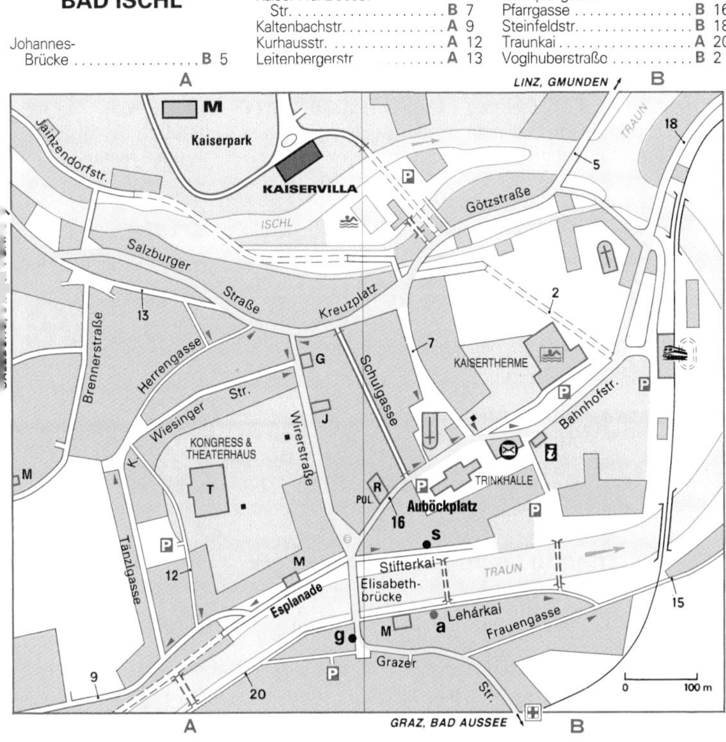

Goldener Ochs Zim,

Grazer Str. 4 ✉ 4820 – ✆ (06132) 2 35 29 – info@goldenerochs.at – Fax (06132) 2352950 A **g**

48 Zim – 43/64 € 78/110 € – ½ P 14 €

Rest – Karte 13/33 €

◆ An der Traun liegt der um einen hübschen Hotelanbau erweiterte traditionsreiche Gasthof. Zimmer mit elegantem Touch, zum Garten hin mit Holzbalkonen. Restaurant teils mit Gewölbe und Kachelofen, teils klassisch-rustikal. Schön: der großzügige Wintergarten.

Goldenes Schiff Zim, Zim,

Adalbert-Stifter-Kai 3 ✉ 4820 – ✆ (06132) 2 42 41 – office@goldenes-schiff.at – Fax (06132) 2424158 B **s**

55 Zim – 78/88 € 108/152 € – ½ P 22 €

Rest – *(geschl. März 2 Wochen, Nov. 2 Wochen und Montag)* Menü 36/59 € – Karte 16/36 €

◆ Das moderne Hotel im Zentrum bietet helle, wohnliche Zimmer in unterschiedlichen Größen, teilweise mit schönem Blick auf die Traun, die Lehárvilla und die Berge. Freundlich gestaltetes Restaurant und Terrasse am Fluss.

Villa Schratt mit Zim Rest, VISA AE
Steinbruch 43 (über Salzburger Straße A) ✉ 4820 – ☎ (06132) 2 76 47 – hanke@villaschratt.at – Fax (06132) 276474
4 Zim – 56/100 € 80/144 €
Rest – *(geschl. Dienstag – Mittwoch)* Menü 38/69 € – Karte 43/56 €
◆ Gemütlich sitzt man in den beiden hübschen Gaststuben der historischen alpenländischen Villa. Geboten werden zwei saisonale Menüs.

Weinhaus Attwenger VISA
Leharkai 12 ✉ 4820 – ☎ (06132) 2 33 27 – weinhausattwenger@aon.at – Fax (06132) 23327
geschl. Montag, Nov. – April Montag – Dienstag B **a**
Rest – Menü 26/30 € – Karte 17/41 €
◆ Die Bürgerstube mit Jagdtrophäen, die Heurigenstube mit dunkler Holztäfelung und die Attwengerstube mit hübschem Gewölbe bilden dieses Gasthaus mit historischem Charme.

JENNERSDORF – Burgenland – 730 U8 – 4 240 Ew – Höhe 241 m 11 L5

Wien 173 – Eisenstadt 151 – Graz 75 – Fürstenfeld 15
Eisenstädter Str. 11, ✉ 8380, ☎ (03329) 4 86 83, jennersdorf@suedburgenland.co.at

Nahe der Therme Loipersdorf Nord-Ost: 7 km:

Landhaus Römerstein
Therme 18 ✉ 8282 Loipersdorf – ☎ (03329) 4 67 77 – hotel@roemerstein.at – Fax (03329) 46290
geschl. Mitte Dez. – Mitte März
15 Zim – 80/100 € 140/180 € – ½ P 10 €
Rest – (nur Abendessen für Hausgäste)
◆ Schön über der Therme gelegenes Hotel, das mit Engagement von der Familie geführt wird. Hübsche Einrichtung mit vielen Details und ein ansprechender Wellnessbereich.

Maria Theresien Hof garni Rest, VISA AE
Therme 111 ✉ 8380 Jennersdorf – ☎ (03329) 4 54 98 – maria@theresienhof.net – Fax (03329) 4566611
geschl. 15. – 27. Dez.
30 Zim – 40/45 € 72/76 €
◆ In dem etwas abseits der Straße gelegenen Hotel erwarten Sie mit hellem Naturholz möblierte Gästezimmer und ein gutes Frühstücksbuffet.

Oasis garni
Oberhenndorf 27 ✉ 8380 Jennersdorf – ☎ (03329) 4 57 21 – info@pension-oasis.at – Fax (03329) 4572133
16 Zim – 36 € 72 €
◆ Das neuzeitliche kleine Hotel beherbergt hinter seiner gelben Fassade mit Kiefernmobiliar eingerichtete Zimmer mit gutem Platzangebot. Reichhaltiges Frühstück.

JERZENS – Tirol – 730 E7 – 910 Ew – Höhe 1 104 m – Wintersport: 2 450 m 1 7 6 C6

Wien 513 – Innsbruck 70 – Imst 17 – Landeck 34
Dorf 220, ✉ 6474, ☎ (05414) 8 69 99, info@pitztal.com

Jerzner Hof Pitztal und Bergwelt, Rest, VISA
Hochzeigerstr. 170
6474 – (05414) 85 10 – info@jerznerhof.at – Fax (05414) 851012
geschl. Mai
48 Zim (inkl. ½ P.) – 82/100 € 164/200 € 90/130 €
180/260 € – 4 Suiten
Rest – (nur Abendessen für Hausgäste)
◆ Alpenhotel oberhalb des Ortes mit wohnlichen Zimmern, fast alle mit Balkon. Teil des Freizeitbereichs ist ein recht großer, moderner Fitnessraum.

In Jerzens-Liss **Ost: 3,5 km Richtung Hoch Zeiger – Höhe 1 450 m**

Alpen Royal Bergpanorama, Rest, VISA
Liss 300 6474 – (05414) 8 60 86
– info@alpen-royal.at – Fax (05414) 8608640
geschl. Anfang April – Mitte Juni, Mitte Okt. – Anfang Dez.
28 Zim (inkl. ½ P.) – 54/58 € 108/116 € 72/102 €
144/204 €
Rest – (nur Abendessen für Hausgäste)
◆ Ganz in der Nähe der Talstation liegt das familiengeführte Hotel, das mit hellen und freundlichen, neuzeitlich gestalteten Zimmern überzeugt.

JOCHBERG – **Tirol** – 730 J6 – **1 540 Ew** – **Höhe 924 m** – **Wintersport: 2 000 m** 16 7 **F5**

Wien 375 – Innsbruck 105 – Kitzbühel 10 – Wörgl 40
Dorf 22, 6373, (05356) 7 77 42, info.jochberg@kitzbuehel.com

Jochbergerhof VISA
Martensgasse 6 6373 – (05355) 52 24 – office@jochbergerhof.at
– Fax (05355) 522455
geschl. 5. April – 4. Mai, 26. Okt. – 14. Dez.
30 Zim – 63 € 116 € 84/87 € 160/172 € – ½ P 18 €
Rest – Karte 22/43 €
◆ Das von der Inhaberfamilie geführte Ferienhotel liegt in einer Seitenstraße im Ortskern und bietet solide eingerichtete Zimmer, zwei davon mit Himmelbett und eigener Sauna. Gaststube mit bürgerlich-ländlichem Ambiente.

Gasthaus Bärnbichl Jochberg und Berglandschaft,
Bärenbichlweg 35 6373 – (05355) 53 47 – Fax (05355) 5347
geschl. nach Ostern – Mitte Mai, Nov. und Dienstag
Rest – (abends Tischbestellung ratsam) Karte 19/31 €
◆ Familiäre Atmosphäre und schmackhafte traditionelle Tiroler Wirtshausküche machen den heimeligen Berggasthof aus. Sehr nett sitzt man auf der Sonnenterrasse mit Aussicht.

JUNGHOLZ IN TIROL – **Tirol** – 730 D6 – **320 Ew** – **Höhe 1 058 m** – **Wintersport: 1 500 m** 6 – **Luftkurort** 5 **B5**

Wien 532 – Innsbruck 129 – Kempten (Allgäu) 31 – Füssen 32
Tannheim, Oberhöfen 110, 6675, (05675) 6 22 00, info@tannheimertal.com

Alpenhof Rest,

Am Sonnenhang 23 ✉ 6691 – ✆ (05676) 8 11 40
– info@landhotel-alpenhof.com – Fax (05676) 820150
geschl. 31. März – 27. April, 3. Nov. – 13. Dez.
27 Zim – 48/67 € 77/99 € 58/81 € 93/119 €
– ½ P 13 €
Rest – Karte 19/39 €
◆ Ein in regionstypischem Stil gehaltenes Haus unter Leitung der Familie. Wanderwege und Loipen finden Sie direkt vor der Tür. In gemütlich-rustikalen Stuben bewirtet man Sie mit heimischen Speisen.

JUNS – Tirol – siehe Tux

KAINDORF AN DER SULM – Steiermark – 730 S8 – 2 420 Ew – Höhe 276 m

11 **K5**

Wien 223 – Graz 38 – Maribor 34 – Leibnitz 3

Staribacher

Grottenhof 5 (Nord-West: 1,5 km, über B 74 Richtung Eibiswald, dann rechts ab) ✉ 8430 – ✆ (03452) 8 25 50 – hotel@staribacher.at
– Fax (03452) 825509
geschl. 23. – 25. Dez.
31 Zim – 69 € 104/120 € – ½ P 19 € – 4 Suiten
Rest – Menü 32 € – Karte 19/40 €
◆ Im Hotel erwarten Sie in neuzeitlichem Stil eingerichtete und technisch funktionell ausgestattete Zimmer in angenehmen Farben, einige mit Terrasse oder Balkon. Das Restaurant ist in mehrere freundliche, z. T. leicht rustikale Räume unterteilt.

Auf dem Kogelberg Nord-West: 4 km über B 74 Richtung Eibiswalde:

Winzerhaus Kogelberg Sulmtal,

Kogelberg 10 ✉ 8430 Kaindorf an der Sulm – ✆ (03452) 8 34 51
– Fax (03452) 83451
geschl. 22. Dez. – Jan., Aug. 1 Woche
Rest – *(geschl. Sonntag – Dienstag)* (Tischbestellung ratsam) Karte 15/35 €
◆ Gemütlich sitzt man in den rustikalen, mit viel altem Zierrat dekorierten Restaurantstuben dieses a. d. 17. Jh. stammenden Winzerhauses.

KALS – Tirol – 730 J8 – 1 340 Ew – Höhe 1 325 m – Wintersport: 2 305 m 6

8 **F6**

Wien 443 – Innsbruck 178 – Lienz 33 – Matrei in Osttirol 21
Ködnitz 17, ✉ 9981, ✆ (04876) 88 00, kals@tirol.com

Taurerwirt (geheizt) Zim,

Burg 12 (Nord: 3 km) ✉ 9981
– ✆ (04876) 82 26 – info@taurerwirt.at – Fax (04876) 822611
geschl. 5. April – 11. Mai, 11. Okt. – 20. Dez.
35 Zim (inkl. ½ P.) – 86/106 € 142/198 € 95/115 €
160/200 €
Rest – Karte 17/45 €
◆ Die ruhige Lage am Ende des Tales, Zimmer in neuzeitlich-ländlichem Stil und ein schöner Beautybereich mit diversen Anwendungen sprechen für dieses Haus. Rustikales Restaurant mit Wintergarten.

KAMMERN IM LIESINGTAL - Steiermark - 730 Q6 - 1 660 Ew - Höhe 670 m 10 J4

Wien 182 - Graz 60 - Leoben 22 - Knittelfeld 33
GC Reiting-Gai, Golfplatzweg 1 (03847) 50 08

In Kammern-Liesing Ost: 3 km über B 113, dann rechts ab Richtung Mötschendorf:

Spary
Liesing 21 8773 - (03844) 86 77 - gasthaus.spary@gmx.at - Fax (03844) 8677
geschl. Mittwoch
Rest - (Tischbestellung ratsam) Karte 17/34 €
◆ Ein nettes ländliches Dekor und der alpenländische Charakter schaffen in dem in Stuben unterteilten Restaurant ein behagliches Ambiente.

KANZELHÖHE - Kärnten - siehe Treffen am Ossiachersee

KAPFENBERG - Steiermark - 730 R6 - 22 240 Ew - Höhe 501 m 10 J4

Wien 144 - Graz 62 - Wiener Neustadt 95 - Leoben 26
Grazer Str. 8, 8605, (03862) 2 46 76, info@kapfenberg.at

Böhlerstern Zim,
Friedrich-Böhler-Str. 13 8605 - (03862) 20 63 75 - reception@boehlerstern.at - Fax (03862) 206165
geschl. 24. Dez. - 6. Jan.
47 Zim - 71/84 € 112/116 €
Rest - *(geschl. Sonn- und Feiertage)* Karte 17/33 €
◆ 1919 wurde das schmucke Haus als Gästehaus für Geschäftspartner der Böhler Metallwerke gebaut. Heute stehen hier technisch gut ausgestattete Zimmer in modernem Stil bereit. Bürgerlich-rustikale Restauranträume, teils mit Zirbenholz vertäfelt.

Sporthotel Grabner Zim,
Johann-Brandl-Gasse 25, (Stadion) 8605 - (03862) 2 17 70 - sporthotel-kapfenberg@tsk.at - Fax (03862) 217703
38 Zim - 63/73 € 95/130 €
Rest - Karte 15/33 €
◆ Das beim Sportzentrum gelegene Hotel verfügt über hell eingerichtete, neuzeitlich-funktionelle Zimmer und eine mit viel Holz gemütlich-alpenländisch gestaltete Romantik-Suite.

Schicker
Grazer Str. 9 8605 - (03862) 2 26 12 - office@schicker-kapfenberg.at - Fax (03862) 223144
geschl. Juni - Aug. Sonntag
Rest - Karte 15/31 €
◆ Die Stube, der Florentiner und das elegante kleine Schwarze bilden dieses Restaurant an der Mürz. In ganz modernem Design: Mocca Café-Bar. Mit Schanigarten.

Sie suchen ein besonderes Hotel für einen sehr angenehmen Aufenthalt? Reservieren Sie in einem roten Haus: ... .

KAPFENSTEIN – Steiermark – 730 T8 – 1 700 Ew – Höhe 300 m 11 L5

Wien 178 – Graz 70 – Maribor 59 – Fürstenfeld 24

Schloss Kapfenstein
Region und Weinberge, Zim, VISA AE

Kapfenstein 1 ✉ 8353
– ✆ (03157) 30 03 00 – hotel@schloss-kapfenstein.at
– Fax (03157) 3003030
geschl. 21. Dez. – 6. März

15 Zim – 91/113 € 132/176 € – ½ P 30 €

Rest – Menü 26 € (mittags)/38 € – Karte 26/41 €

◆ Das Schloss a. d. J. 1065 beherbergt hübsche, recht individuell eingerichtete Gästezimmer, z. T. mit Antiquitäten. Schöner Saal mit altem Kachelofen und Holzfußboden. Überwiegend rustikal gestaltetes Restaurant. Einen Blick über die Region bietet die Terrasse.

KAPPL – Tirol – 730 D7 – 2 590 Ew – Höhe 1 258 m – Wintersport: 2 690 m 1 7 5 B6

Wien 537 – Innsbruck 93 – Landeck 21 – Sankt Anton 37

Dorf 112, ✉ 6555, ✆ (05445) 62 43, kappl@kappl-see.com

Dorfstadl
VISA AE

Dorf 452 ✉ 6555 – ✆ (05445) 62 55 – dorfstadl@hoteldorfstadl.at
– Fax (05445) 6753
geschl. 1. Mai – 28. Juni, 20. Sept. – 28. Nov.

26 Zim (inkl. ½ P.) – 70 € 140 € 86/174 € 150/214 €

Rest – (im Sommer nur für Hausgäste) Karte 15/35 €

◆ Ein netter Empfangsbereich mit kleinem Kamin sowie recht geräumige, wohnliche Gästezimmer erwarten Sie in diesem Familienbetrieb im Ortskern nahe der Diasbahn.

In Kappl-Bach Süd: 1,5 km:

Edelweiß-Schlössl
Paznauntal und Bergpanorama, Zim, VISA

Bach 47 ✉ 6555 – ✆ (05445) 62 66
– edelweiss@waibl.at – Fax (05445) 62666
geschl. Mai, Okt. – Nov.

19 Zim (inkl. ½ P.) – 46/51 € 82/132 € 74/92 € 118/168 €

Rest – (nur für Hausgäste)

◆ Das familiengeführte kleine Ferienhotel befindet sich oberhalb des Ortsteils und bietet eine tolle Aussicht sowie mit schönen Holzmöbeln ausgestattete Gästezimmer.

In Kappl-Sinsnerau Süd-West: 3,5 km über B 188 Richtung Ischgl:

Höllroah

Sinsnerau 438 ✉ 6555 – ✆ (05445) 65 54 – info@hoellroah.at
– Fax (05445) 65544
geschl. Juli, Sept. – Dez.

28 Zim (inkl. ½ P.) – 43/66 € 72/88 € 56/85 € 102/126 €

Rest – Karte 16/31 €

◆ In dem von der Inhaberfamilie geleiteten Hotel an der Straße nach Ischgl stehen neuzeitlich-rustikal eingerichtete Zimmer und ein netter Saunabereich zur Verfügung. Restaurant in ländlichem Stil mit Wintergartenanbau.

In Kappl-Untermühl Nord: 2 km über B 188 Richtung Landeck:

Sunshine Zim,
Untermühl 612 ✉ 6555 – ✆ (05445) 66 00 – sunshine@kappl.at
– Fax (05445) 660066
geschl. Mitte Juni – Mitte Juli, 27. Okt. – 8. Nov.
21 Zim (inkl. ½ P.) – ☼ 65/75 € 98/124 € ❄ 85/105 € 134/190 €
Rest – *(geschl. Montag – Dienstag, Mittwoch – Samstag nur Abendessen)* (Tischbestellung ratsam) Menü 31/55 € – Karte 27/37 €
◆ Ein sehr gepflegter Familienbetrieb in einem Ortsteil oberhalb von Kappl. Das zu den Wanderhotels gehörende Haus bietet neben zeitgemäßen Zimmern auch geführte Touren. Freundlich gestaltetes Restaurant.

KAPRUN – Salzburg – 730 K7 – 2 910 Ew – Höhe 760 m – Wintersport: 3 029 m 6 22 8 F5

Wien 396 – Salzburg 100 – Kitzbühel 51 – Zell am See 9
Salzburger Platz 601, ✉ 5710, ✆ (06547) 80 80, welcome@europasportregion.info
Kaprunertal★★ – Kitzsteinhorn★★★ (mit) Süd-West: 9 km

Steigenberger (geheizt) Zim, Rest,
Schlossstr. 751 ✉ 5710
– ✆ (06547) 76 47 – kaprun@steigenberger.at – Fax (06547) 7680
125 Zim – ☼ 83/104 € 136/168 € ❄ 108/133 € 186/226 € – ½ P 28 €
Rest – Karte 29/50 €
◆ Durch eine großzügige Halle betreten Sie dieses im Zentrum gelegene komfortable Hotel. Die Zimmer sind mit hellem Naturholzmobiliar funktionell ausgestattet. Mit dunklem Holz rustikal gestaltete Gaststube.

Rudolfshof Vitality (mit Rudolfshof)
Lechnerdorfgasse 606 ✉ 5710
– ✆ (06547) 71 83 – vitality@rudolfshof.com – Fax (06547) 71838
57 Zim (inkl. ½ P.) – ☼ 73/95 € 116/160 € ❄ 119/195 € 178/350 €
Rest – *(im Sommer nur Abendessen)* Karte 19/39 €
◆ Angenehm ruhig liegt der gewachsene Familienbetrieb oberhalb des Ortes. Die Zimmer gefallen mit einem wohnlichen, leicht eleganten Ambiente – im Rudolfshof etwas einfacher.

Barbarahof
Nikolaus-Gassner-Str. 692 ✉ 5710 – ✆ (06547) 7 24 80
– info@hotel-barbarahof.at – Fax (06547) 72486
geschl. Juni
40 Zim (inkl. ½ P.) – ☼ 72/91 € 120/146 € ❄ 101/149 € 166/262 € – 7 Suiten
Rest – (nur Abendessen für Hausgäste)
◆ Wohnliche Zimmer mit Balkon und Blick auf das Bergpanorama sowie ein hübscher Freizeitbereich bietet das familiengeführte Haus. Besonders schön: die Zimmer im Neubau.

Active by Leitner's garni (mit Gästehaus)
Sportplatzstr. 755 ✉ 5710
– ☎ (06547) 87 82 – info@active-kaprun.at – Fax (06547) 878259
geschl. 26. Mai – 6. Juli, 7. Sept. – 19. Okt.
21 Zim – ☼ 🚹59/69 € 🚹🚹88/108 € ❄ 🚹77/90 € 🚹🚹124/150 €
– 5 Suiten
◆ Modernes Design begleitet Sie vom Empfang bis in die in klaren Linien gehaltenen Zimmer. Im Gästehaus: Suiten im neuzeitlichen Landhausstil.

Vötter's Sportkristall Rest,
Schlossstr. 621 ✉ 5710 – ☎ (06547) 7 13 40
– hotel@sport-kristall.at – Fax (06547) 713450
geschl. 15. Mai – 15. Juni, 15. Sept. – 20. Okt.
50 Zim (inkl. ½ P.) – ☼ 🚹74/87 € 🚹🚹124/154 € ❄ 🚹84/147 €
🚹🚹142/264 € – 11 Suiten
Rest – *(nur Abendessen)* Karte 18/38 €
◆ Das familiengeführte Hotel verfügt über wohnliche, teils etwas rustikalere Zimmer sowie schöne Suiten in warmen Farben. Dachterrasse. Sehenswert: hauseigenes Oldtimer-Museum. Hell und freundlich gestaltetes Restaurant.

Orgler
Schlossstr. 22 ✉ 5710 – ☎ (06547) 82 05 – kaprun@hotel-orgler.at
– Fax (06547) 7567
geschl. 25. Mai – 8. Juni, 28. Sept. – 10. Okt.
36 Zim (inkl. ½ P.) – ☼ 🚹79/122 € 🚹🚹150/180 € ❄ 🚹96/162 €
🚹🚹188/274 €
Rest – *(geschl. Mai sowie Okt. Mittwoch)* Karte 24/41 €
◆ Das von der Inhaberfamilie geleitete Hotel befindet sich mitten im Zentrum und hält für seine Gäste solide möblierte und wohnliche Zimmer bereit. Das Restaurant ist eine Zirbenstube aus den 30er Jahren.

Antonius (geheizt)
Schlossstr. 744 ✉ 5710 – ☎ (06547) 76 70
– info@hotel-antonius.at – Fax (06547) 76706
geschl. 15. Sept. – 25. Okt.
50 Zim (inkl. ½ P.) – ☼ 🚹🚹112/136 € ❄ 🚹🚹144/250 € – 46 Suiten
Rest – Karte 21/28 €
◆ Etwas abseits vom Zentrum liegt dieses familiär geführte Haus. Die Zimmer sind zeitgemäß eingerichtet, meist mit getrenntem Wohn- und Schlafbereich. Helles Holz gibt dem neuzeitlichen Restaurant einen ländlichen Touch.

Zur Burg Rest,
Burglindgasse 481 ✉ 5710 – ☎ (06547) 83 06 – office@hotel-zur-burg.at
– Fax (06547) 830660
35 Zim (inkl. ½ P.) – ☼ 🚹82/104 € 🚹🚹127/163 € ❄ 🚹84/142 €
🚹🚹124/240 €
Rest – (nur Abendessen für Hausgäste)
◆ Etwas außerhalb des Zentrums, unterhalb der Burgruine liegt das familiengeführte Hotel mit wohnlichen, meist in rustikaler Eiche gehaltenen Zimmern. Zeitweise "all inclusive".

Kapruner Hof

Rest, P VISA MC

Schulstr. 559 ✉ 5710 – ✆ (06547) 72 34 – hotel@kaprunerhof.at – Fax (06547) 8581
geschl. 4. April – 22. Mai
28 Zim (inkl. ½ P.) – ☼ 85/93 € 140/182 € ❄ 105/140 € 180/300 €
Rest – Karte 17/37 €
♦ Recht ruhig liegt dieses Haus in einer Sackgasse. Die Zimmer sind teils in dunkler Eiche, teils mit neuzeitlicheren Holzmöblen funktionell ausgestattet. Mit viel Holz eingerichtete kleine Gaststube.

Gasthof Mitteregger

P VISA MC

Schlossstr. 13 ✉ 5710 – ✆ (06547) 82 07 – hotel@mitteregger.at – Fax (06547) 820763
geschl. Mai
39 Zim (inkl. ½ P.) – ☼ 52/73 € 90/116 € ❄ 69/116 € 124/206 €
Rest – Karte 15/34 €
♦ Mitten im Zentrum liegt dieser gestandene familiengeführte Gasthof aus dem 15. Jh., der über wohnlich-rustikale Zimmer verfügt. In mehrere Stuben unterteiltes Restaurant mit bürgerlich-ländlichem Charakter.

Wüstlau-Kitzalm

Zim, P VISA MC

Kesselfallstr. 647 (Süd-West: 4,5 km) ✉ 5710 – ✆ (06547) 84 61 – hotel@wuestlau.at – Fax (06547) 846162
geschl. 13. – 27. Sept.
21 Zim (inkl. ½ P.) – ☼ 53/61 € 106/122 € ❄ 64/97 € 128/194 €
Rest – *(geschl. Mittwoch, nur Abendessen)* Karte 16/32 €
♦ Ein solider Landgasthof unter familiärer Leitung, dessen Zimmer mit hellen Holzmöblen praktisch und zeitgemäß eingerichtet sind. Urig wirkt das A-la-carte-Restaurant Kitzalm. Sehr nett: der Naturgastgarten.

Dorfstadl

P VISA MC AE

Kellnerfeldstr. 691 ✉ 5710 – ✆ (06547) 72 80 – appartment@dorfstadl-kaprun.at – Fax (06547) 72804
geschl. 10. Mai – 10. Juli, außer Saison Montag
Rest – *(nur Abendessen)* Karte 24/37 €
♦ In einem alten, am Zentrumsrand wieder aufgebauten Bauernhaus hat man dieses urgemütliche Restaurant eingerichtet. Bäuerliches Dekor ziert das ganze Haus.

Jagawirt

P

Kesselfallstr. 404 (Süd-West: 2,5 km) ✉ 5710 – ✆ (06547) 87 37 – info@jagawirt-kaprun.at – Fax (06547) 70567
geschl. Sonntagabend – Montag
Rest – *(wochentags ab 15.00 Uhr geöffnet)* (Tischbestellung ratsam) Karte 27/44 €
♦ Rustikales Ambiente mit modernem Touch in einem alten Jagdhaus. Hier oder auf der Terrasse mit Blick auf das Kitzsteinhorn wird regionale und internationale Küche serviert.

Bei schönem Wetter isst man gern im Freien!
Wählen Sie ein Restaurant mit Terrasse:

KARTITSCH – Tirol – 730 J8 – 900 Ew – Höhe 1 356 m – Wintersport: 1 820 m 2 8 F6

Wien 436 – Innsbruck 218 – Lienz 32 – Bruneck 51
Gemeindehaus 80, 9941, (04848) 63 01, info@kartitsch.com

Panorama Hotel Cis
Wiese 39 9941 – (04848) 53 33 – info@hotelcis.at – Fax (04848) 533333
17 Zim (inkl. ½ P.) – 44/66 € 88/94 € 43/73 € 86/104 €
Rest – *(geschl. Sonntagabend)* Karte 15/31 €
♦ Sehr gepflegt ist dieses familiengeführte kleine Hotel am Ortseingang, das über mit soliden Eichenmöbeln und Sitzgruppe ausgestattete Zimmer verfügt. Ein Wintergartenanbau ergänzt das Restaurant.

KASTEN BEI BÖHEIMKIRCHEN – Niederösterreich – 730 T4 – 1 240 Ew – Höhe 271 m 3 K2

Wien 55 – St. Pölten 18 – Baden 55

XXX **Pedro's Landhaus** mit Zim
Dörfl 19 (Süd-Ost: 1 km) 3072 – (02744) 73 87 – office@pedros-landhaus.at – Fax (02744) 7389
geschl. 10. Juli – 8. Aug. und Sonntag
15 Zim – 65/80 € 120 €
Rest – Karte 32/48 €
♦ Schön liegt das ehemalige Palais a. d. J. 1850 in einem 4 ha großen Park. Klassisches Ambiente, gut eingedeckte Tische und aufwändiger Service machen das Restaurant aus.

KATSCHBERG – Salzburg – siehe Sankt Michael im Lungau

KATSDORF – Oberösterreich – 730 P4 – 2 740 Ew – Höhe 303 m 2 I2

Wien 175 – Linz 24 – Steyr 42 – Freistadt 29

Mader Zim,
Baderberg 7 4223 – (07235) 88 58 50 – office@hotel-mader.at – Fax (07235) 88585112
27 Zim – 61/65 € 90/98 €
Rest – Karte 15/33 €
♦ Zeitgemäße, einheitlich mit weiß eingefärbtem Holzmobiliar eingerichtete Gästezimmer bietet Ihnen dieses Seminarhotel am Ortsrand. Neuzeitlich gestaltetes Restaurant.

KAUNERTAL – Tirol – 730 E7 – 600 Ew – Höhe 1 273 m – Wintersport: 3 160 m 1 14 6 C6

Wien 538 – Innsbruck 94 – Landeck 25 – Sankt Anton 53
Feichten 134, 6524, (05475) 29 20, info@kaunertal.com

In Feichten

Weisseespitze
Platz 30 ✉ 6524 – ✆ (05475) 3 16 – info@weisseespitze.com – Fax (05475) 31665
75 Zim (inkl. ½ P.) – ☼ †76/92 € ††130/162 € ❄ †76/104 € ††130/186 € – 4 Suiten
Rest – Karte 18/34 €
♦ Ein Teil dieses Hotels ist mit besonders komfortablen, großzügigen Zimmern und einem geräumigen Saunabereich rollstuhlgerecht angelegt. Zum Haus gehört auch ein Campingplatz. Restaurant mit neuzeitlich-rustikalem Ambiente.

Bödele
Rest,
Feichten 172 ✉ 6524 – ✆ (05475) 2 53 – boedele@aon.at – Fax (05475) 25357
27 Zim (inkl. ½ P.) – ☼ †42/50 € ††78/94 € ❄ †48/69 € ††90/132 €
Rest – (nur Abendessen für Hausgäste)
♦ Das familiengeführte Hotel im alpenländischen Stil befindet sich am Ortsrand und bietet solide eingerichtete Zimmer sowie einige Familienappartements. Bar mit Wintergarten.

Rot = angenehm. Richten Sie sich nach den Symbolen und in Rot.

KAUNS – Tirol – 730 E7 – 450 Ew – Höhe 1 050 m 6 C6

▶ Wien 528 – Innsbruck 84 – Landeck 15 – Sankt Anton 44

Gasthof Falkeis mit Zim
Kauns 47 ✉ 6522 – ✆ (05472) 62 25 – info@gasthof-falkeis.at – Fax (05472) 6142
geschl. 16. – 30. Juni, 20. Nov. – 10. Dez.
7 Zim – †31/36 € ††54/80 € – ½ P 10 €
Rest – *(geschl. Montag)* (Tischbestellung ratsam) Karte 17/35 €
♦ Neuzeitlich und leicht rustikal ist das Ambiente in diesem familiär geführten Gasthof. Serviert wird eine frische regionale Küche. Wohnliche, zeitgemäße Zimmer.

KEUTSCHACH AM SEE – Kärnten – 730 O9 – 2 350 Ew – Höhe 490 m 9 I6

▶ Wien 315 – Klagenfurt 12 – Villach 31 – St. Veit an der Glan 37
ℹ Keutschach 1, ✉ 9074, ✆ (04273) 2 45 00, keutschach@ktn.gde.at

Seehotel Hafnersee (mit Gästehaus)
Zim,
Plescherken 5 (West: 3 km, Richtung Schiefling) ✉ 9074 – ✆ (04273) 23 75 – info@hafnersee.at – Fax (04273) 237516
73 Zim – †75/77 € ††126/132 € – ½ P 15 €
Rest – Karte 16/33 €
♦ Das auf einem 40 ha großen Grundstück gelegene Hotel überzeugt mit freundlichen, modern und funktionell eingerichteten Zimmern und dem Badesee im Naturschutzgebiet.

In Keutschach-Höhe Nord-West: 4 km Richtung Schiefling und Pyramidenkogel:

Der Höhenwirt Karawankengruppe, Zim,
Höhe 4 (Am Pyramidenkogel) ✉ 9074
– ✆ (04273) 23 28 – office@hoehenwirt.at – Fax (04273) 232866
geschl. Ende Okt. – Ostern
20 Zim (inkl. ½ P.) – 55/60 € 95/110 €
Rest – *(geschl. Ostern – Anfang Mai Montag – Mittwoch, Oktober Dienstag)* Karte 17/28 €
◆ Ein gut geführtes, abgelegenes Hotel in ländlich-idyllischer Umgebung mit recht großzügigen Zimmern. Sammlerstücke aus einstigen Herrenhäusern und Villen zieren das Haus. Im Restaurant serviert man Produkte aus der eigenen Landwirtschaft nebenan.

KIRCHBACH – **Kärnten** – 730 L9 – **2 890 Ew** – **Höhe 642 m** 9 **G6**

Wien 389 – Klagenfurt 94 – Villach 59 – Spittal a.d. Drau 62

In Gundersheim West: 5 km über B 111 Richtung Kötschach-Mauthen:

Landhof Lenzhofer Rest,
Landhof 1 ✉ 9634 – ✆ (04718) 33 70
– info@landhof-lenzhofer.at – Fax (04718) 3374
geschl. nach Ostern 3 Wochen, Nov. – Mitte Dez.
16 Zim (inkl. ½ P.) – 83/96 € 154/176 € 88/119 € 158/218 €
Rest – *(geschl. außer Saison Mittwoch, nur Abendessen)* (Tischbestellung ratsam) Karte 27/39 €
◆ Abseits der Straße liegt dieses gut geführte und tipptopp gepflegte kleine Hotel mit seinen wohnlichen Landhauszimmern. Netter Garten mit Teich. Freundlich gestaltete Restauranträume.

KIRCHBERG – **Tirol** – 730 I6 – **4 960 Ew** – **Höhe 860 m** – **Wintersport: 1 995 m 7 45** 7 **E5**

Wien 371 – Innsbruck 83 – Wörgl 25 – Kitzbühel 7
Hauptstr. 8, ✉ 6365, ✆ (05357) 20 00, info@kitzbuehel-alpen.com

Elisabeth (geheizt) Rest, Rest,
Aschauer Str. 75 ✉ 6365
– ✆ (05357) 22 77 – office@hotel-elisabeth-tirol.at – Fax (05357) 3701
100 Zim (inkl. ½ P.) – 75/110 € 130/200 € 103/177 € 186/334 € – **Rest** – Karte 17/33 €
◆ Ein Urlaubshotel mit wohnlich-ländlichem Ambiente, schönem Spabereich auf drei Etagen sowie Naturbadeteich. Besonders komfortabel sind die Juniorsuiten mit schöner Aussicht. Das Restaurant teilt sich in verschiedene gediegen-rustikale Räume.

Tyroler Hof Rest,
Möselgasse 11 ✉ 6365 – ✆ (05357) 26 66
– info@tyrolerhof.at – Fax (05357) 266565
geschl. 6. April – 22. Mai, 5. Okt. – 20. Dez.
26 Zim (inkl. ½ P.) – 60/69 € 106/130 € 87/112 € 150/230 € – 3 Suiten – **Rest** – (nur Abendessen für Hausgäste)
◆ Das familiengeführte Haus verfügt über recht unterschiedliche Zimmer von alpenländisch bis klassisch-elegant, viele nach Süden gelegen. Man bietet auch Kosmetik und Massage.

Bräuwirt
Neugasse 9 ✉ *6365 – ✆ (05357) 22 29 – info@hotel-braeuwirt.at – Fax (05357) 3879*
33 Zim (inkl. ½ P.) – ☼ 60/70 € 100/120 € ❄ 90/120 € 160/220 €
Rest – Karte 19/38 €
◆ Aus einem alten Gasthof ist dieses behindertenfreundliche Hotel mit modernen, geräumigen Zimmern entstanden, die Südzimmer bieten eine schöne Sicht. Eigene Alm mit Sennerei. Gemütliche Restaurantstuben.

Rosengarten (Simon Taxacher) – Hotel Taxacherhof
Aschauer Str. 46 ✉ *6365 – ✆ (05357) 25 27 – info@geniesserrestaurant.at – Fax (05357) 4201*
geschl. 3. Juni – 10. Juli, Mitte Okt. – Anfang Dez. und Mittwoch
Rest – *(nur Abendessen)* (Tischbestellung erforderlich) Menü 55/93 € – Karte 54/80 €
Spez. Marinierte Gänsestopfleber mit Zartbitterschokolade und Banyulsgelee. Suprême vom Steinbutt mit feiner Trüffelinfusion und Sellerie. Le Noir de Bigorre in Salbei-Milch gegart mit Knusper-Kümmel.
◆ In dem modern-eleganten Restaurant unter der Leitung des ambitionierten Küchenchefs Simon Taxacher bietet man kreative Speisen auf klassischer Basis.

Seefeldstub'n
Stöcklfeld 33 ✉ *6365 – ✆ (05357) 21 58 – office@seefeldstubn.at – Fax (05357) 215821*
geschl. April, 19. Okt. – 7. Dez.
Rest – Karte 20/41 €
◆ Ein familiär geleitetes Restaurant direkt an der Loipe mit bürgerlichem Speisenangebot. Kachelofen und ländliches Dekor unterstreichen das rustikale Ambiente.

In Kirchberg-Klausen **Ost: 1 km Richtung Kitzbühel:**

Sportalm
Rest,
Brandseitweg 26 ✉ *6365 – ✆ (05357) 27 78 – info@hotel-sportalm.at – Fax (05357) 334730*
geschl. 31. März – 30. April
27 Zim (inkl. ½ P.) – ☼ 50/60 € 122/132 € ❄ 105/186 € 140/252 € – 7 Suiten
Rest – (nur Abendessen für Hausgäste)
◆ Solide eingerichtete Gästezimmer mit gutem Platzangebot sowie ein neuzeitlicher Saunabereich sprechen für dieses familiengeführte regionstypische Ferienhotel.

Alpenhof
Zim,
Brandseitweg 18 ✉ *6365 – ✆ (05357) 23 89 – haus.alpenhof@gbh.oegb.or.at – Fax (05357) 238933*
geschl. 5. April – 9. Mai, 4. Okt. – 5. Dez.
54 Zim (inkl. ½ P.) – 61/83 € 110/162 €
Rest – Karte 16/31 €
◆ Schön liegt das Hotel im Grünen unweit der Gondelbahn. Zum Haus gehören ein großzügiger Freizeitbereich mit Sonnenterrasse und eine gepflegte Außenanlage mit Teich. Restaurant in bürgerlichem Stil.

KIRCHBERG AM WAGRAM – Niederösterreich – 730 T3 – 3 350 Ew – Höhe 240 m
3 **K2**

Wien 60 – St. Pölten 47 – Krems 27 – Stockerau 32

Alter Winzerkeller garni

Rossplatz 1 ✉ 3470 – ✆ (0664) 5 95 86 07 – office@alterwinzerkeller.at – Fax (02279) 502119
geschl. Mitte Dez. – Ende Feb.
6 Zim – 55 € 88 €

◆ Das ehemalige Presshaus a. d. 19. Jh. verfügt heute über großzügige Gästezimmer mit Parkettfußboden. Eine Original-Weinpresse ziert den Hallenbereich. Schöner Weinkeller.

Gut Oberstockstall

Oberstockstall 1 (Nord: 1 km) ✉ 3470 – ✆ (02279) 23 35 – restaurant@gutoberstockstall.at – Fax (02279) 23356
geschl. Mitte Dez. – Ende Feb. und Sonntagabend – Mittwochmittag
Rest – Menü 60/78 € – Karte 24/46 €

◆ Seit über 200 Jahren in Familienbesitz ist der aus dem 14. Jh. stammende Gutshof mit nettem Wintergarten und schönem Terrassenbereich im Innenhof. Kreative Regionalküche.

KIRCHBERG AM WECHSEL – Niederösterreich – 730 T6 – 2 350 Ew – Höhe 578 m – Wintersport: 1 500 m 2
11 **L4**

Wien 93 – Sankt Pölten 102 – Mürzzuschlag 42 – Wiener Neustadt 40
Markt 63, ✉ 2880, ✆ (02641) 24 60, tourismus@kirchberg-am-wechsel.at

Landgasthof Fally

Ödenkirchen 28 (Nord: 8 km, Richtung Rams, nach 4 km am Ramssattel rechts ab) ✉ 2880 – ✆ (02629) 72 05 – mail@landgasthof-fally.at – Fax (02629) 720550
geschl. Mitte Jan. – Mitte Feb.
11 Zim – 32/37 € 60/70 € – ½ P 9 €
Rest – *(geschl. Dienstagabend – Mittwoch)* Karte 16/22 €

◆ Einsam und ruhig liegt das von Familie Fally geführte kleine Haus am Waldrand. Die Zimmer sind freundlich und wohnlich im Landhausstil eingerichtet. Netter ländlicher Restaurantbereich.

KITZBÜHEL – Tirol – 730 J6 – 8 580 Ew – Höhe 800 m – Wintersport: 2 000 m 9 55
7 **E5**

Wien 445 – Innsbruck 96 – Kufstein 35 – Bad Reichenhall 58
Hinterstadt 18 AZ, ✉ 6370, ✆ (05356) 77 70, info@kitzbuehel.com
18 Kitzbühel-Schwarzsee-Reith, Golfweg Schwarzsee 35 ✆ (05356) 7 77 70
18 Eichenheim, Kitzbühel-Aurach ✆ (05356) 6 66 15
9 Kitzbühel, Schloss Kaps ✆ (05356) 6 30 07
9 Rasmushof, Ried Ecking 15 ✆ (05356) 6 52 52

Veranstaltungen

18.01. – 20.01.: Hahnenkamm-Rennen
23.06. – 28.06.: Golf Festival

Kitzbüheler Horn★★ (mit) – Ehrenbachhütte (Hahnenkamm-Massiv)★ (mit) – Schwarzkogel★★ (mit und Spazierweg)

KITZBÜHEL

Bichlstr. . . . . **BZ** 2
Gänsbachgasse . . . . **BY** 4
Hinterstadt . . . . **BZ** 6
Klostergasse . . . . **AZ** 8
Malinggasse . . . . **BZ** 10
Schulgasse . . . . **BZ** 12
Steinergasse . . . . **AY** 14
Vorderstadt . . . . **BZ** 16
Wagnerstrasse . . . . **BZ** 18

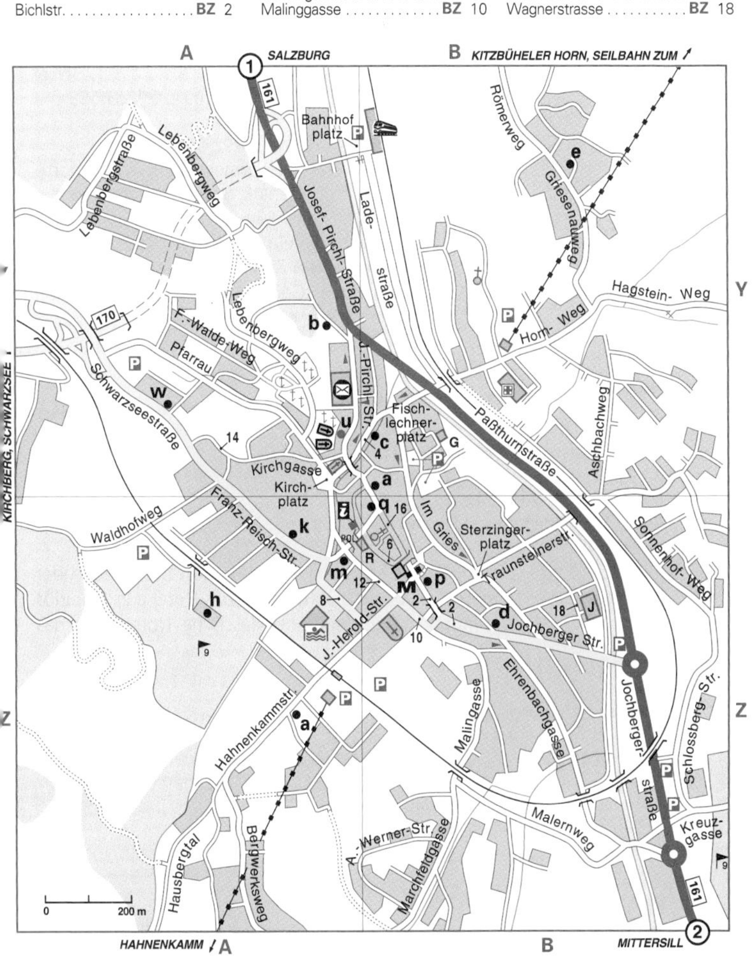

A-ROSA ← Kitzbühel, Hahnenkamm und Streif, (geheizt)
Rest, VISA AE

Ried Kaps 7 (über Kreuzgasse BZ) ✉ 6370 – ✆ (05356) 65 66 00
– *info.kitzbuehel@a-rosa.de* – Fax (05356) 65660819

150 Zim (inkl. ½ P.) – ☼ 189/269 € 149/458 € ❄ 229/339 €
189/598 € – 46 Suiten

Rest Golfhaus – separat erwähnt

Rest *KAPS* – ✆ (05356) 65 66 07 32 *(nur Abendessen)* (Tischbestellung ratsam) Menü 64/89 €

◆ Schön liegt die einem Schloss nachempfundene Hotelanlage am Golfplatz. Das geschmackvolle SPA-ROSA erstreckt sich über 3000 qm und lässt keine Wünsche offen. Moderne Zimmer. Restaurant KAPS im Tiroler Stil.

Tennerhof (mit Residenz Römerhof) Streif und Alpenpanorama, (geheizt) Rest, VISA AE
Griesenauweg 26 ✉ 6370 – (05356) 6 31 81 – office@tennerhof.com – Fax (05356) 6318170
geschl. 8. Okt. – 14. Dez., 31. März – 21. Mai BY **e**
40 Zim – ☼ 138/150 € 220/328 € ❄ 168/269 € 263/558 € – ½ P 43 € – 9 Suiten
Rest – *(geschl. Dienstag, nur Abendessen)* Menü 54/92 €
Spez. Steinbutt mit confierter Entenkeule und Parmesanfond. Geschmorte Kalbsbackerl mit Jakobsmuschel und Ochsenmark. Sauerrahmsoufflé mit Rhabarber.
◆ Das einstige Hofgut von 1679 ist heute ein engagiert geführtes Hotel, das mit hochwertigen, äußerst wohnlichen Zimmern besticht. Im Römerhof bietet man Familienappartements. Gediegen-rustikales Restaurant mit kompetentem Service und klassischer Küche.

Weisses Rössl Rest, VISA AE
Bichlstr. 5 ✉ 6370 – (05356) 7 19 00 – hotel@roesslkitz.at – Fax (05356) 7190099
geschl. Mitte April – Mitte Mai, Nov. – Anfang Dez. BZ **p**
68 Zim (inkl. ½ P.) – ☼ 130/185 € 250/410 € ❄ 180/345 € 265/815 € – 13 Suiten
Rest – *(nur Abendessen)* (Tischbestellung ratsam) Menü 65/90 € – Karte 35/58 €
◆ Die zentrale Lage sowie das elegante Ambiente von der Lobby über die Zimmer bis hin zum Wellnessbereich machen das Hotel aus. Luxuriös sind vor allem die Zimmer im Anbau. Eine klassische Note prägt das Restaurant.

Sport-Wellnesshotel Bichlhof Bergwelt, (geheizt) Rest, VISA
Bichlnweg 153 (über Jochberger Str. BZ, dann links ab Richtung Bichlalm) ✉ 6370 – (05356) 6 40 22 – office@bichlhof.at – Fax (05356) 63634
geschl. nach Ostern – Mitte Mai, Ende Okt. – Mitte Dez.
52 Zim – ☼ 95/125 € 150/240 € ❄ 145/185 € 240/300 € – ½ P 20 € – 9 Suiten
Rest – Karte 28/39 €
◆ Ruhig liegt das engagiert geführte Haus etwas außerhalb des Ortes. Die Zimmer sind wohnlich und individuell gestaltet, der Freizeitbereich bietet einen tollen Panoramablick. Ein Wintergartenvorbau ergänzt das gemütlich-ländliche Restaurant.

Schwarzer Adler VISA AE
Floriangasse 15 ✉ 6370 – (05356) 69 11 – hotel@adlerkitz.at – Fax (05356) 73939
geschl. Ende April – Mitte Mai, Nov. – Mitte Dez. BZ **d**
71 Zim (inkl. ½ P.) – ☼ 158/210 € 240/330 € ❄ 173/270 € 270/620 € – 5 Suiten
Rest *Neuwirt* – separat erwähnt
◆ Das Haus verfügt über einen imponierenden Wellnessbereich – großzügig über mehrere Ebenen angelegt und ganz modern gestaltet. Sommer-Spa mit Dachpool. Suiten mit Sauna.

Zur Tenne

Rest,

Vorderstadt 8 ✉ 6370 – ✆ (05356) 6 44 44
– info@hotelzurtenne.com – Fax (05356) 6480356 BZ **q**

51 Zim – ☼ 92/143 € 148/242 € ❄ 92/306 € 148/381 € – ½ P 34/42 € – 6 Suiten

Rest – Karte 27/57 €

♦ Mitten im Zentrum liegt das im Tiroler Stil gehaltene Urlaubshotel. Besonders schön sind die Suiten mit offenem Kamin. Nett: der kleine Saunabereich. Hübsches alpenländisch gestaltetes Restaurant.

Golf-Hotel Rasmushof

Rest,

Ried Ecking 15 ✉ 6370
– ✆ (05356) 6 52 52 – office@rasmushof.at – Fax (05356) 6525249 AZ **h**

49 Zim – ☼ 150/180 € 205/260 € ❄ 230/350 € 260/415 € – ½ P 26/31 € – 15 Suiten

Rest – Karte 20/55 €

♦ Schön ist die Lage des Hauses am eigenen Golfplatz und an der Streif-Abfahrt. Einige der großen, geschmackvollen Zimmer sind besonders hübsch mit viel Altholz ausgestattet. Urig-rustikal ist die Atmosphäre in den Restaurantstuben.

Tiefenbrunner

Vorderstadt 3 ✉ 6370 – ✆ (05356) 6 66 80 – hotel.tiefenbrunner@kitz.net
– Fax (05356) 6668080
geschl. Mitte April – Mitte Mai, Mitte Okt. – Mitte Dez. BY **a**

76 Zim – ☼ 66/104 € 116/148 € ❄ 108/204 € 200/308 € – ½ P 20/25 €

Rest – *(geschl. Ende April 2 Wochen, Ende Nov. 2 Wochen)* Karte 18/37 €

♦ Seit 1810 ist dieses Haus im Familienbesitz. Zum Freizeitbereich zählen Kosmetik, Massage und ein schönes Panoramahallenbad. Luxus-Juniorsuiten mit Sauna oder Infrarotkabine. Gediegen-rustikal ist das Ambiente im Restaurant.

Kaiserhof

Zim, Rest,

Hahnenkammstr. 5 ✉ 6370 – ✆ (05356) 7 55 03
– kitz@hotel-kaiserhof.at – Fax (05356) 7550355
geschl. 30. März - 9. Mai, 19. Okt. – 6. Dez. AZ **a**

51 Zim (inkl. ½ P.) – ☼ 95/140 € 150/230 € ❄ 147/275 € 220/410 € – 4 Suiten

Rest – *(nur Abendessen)* (Tischbestellung ratsam) Menü 28/55 €

♦ An der Talstation der Hahnenkammbahn liegt dieses hübsche, ganz im modernen Landhausstil gehaltene Hotel. Die geräumigen Zimmer sind hochwertig und sehr wohnlich eingerichtet. Kleines Abendrestaurant mit klassischer und regionaler Küche.

Erika

(geheizt) Rest,

Josef-Pirchl-Str. 21 ✉ 6370 – ✆ (05356) 6 48 85 – office@erika-kitz.at
– Fax (05356) 6488513
geschl. Ende März – Mitte Mai AY **b**

48 Zim (inkl. ½ P.) – ☼ 83/120 € 166/200 € ❄ 120/180 € 240/320 € – 22 Suiten

Rest – (nur Abendessen für Hausgäste)

♦ In dem schmucken Haus von 1897 erwarten Sie eine Wintergarten-Lobby, stilvolle Zimmer und ein schöner Wellnessbereich mit Kosmetik, Naturbadeteich und Hallenbad mit Rutsche.

Kitzhof Rest, VISA AE

Schwarzseestr. 8 ✉ 6370 – ✆ (05356) 63 21 10 – info@hotel-kitzhof.com – Fax (05356) 6321115 AY **w**

166 Zim (inkl. ½ P.) – ☼ 182/266 € 260/380 € ❄ 210/350 € 300/500 €

Rest – (nur für Hausgäste)

♦ In diesem Haus hat man gelungen moderne und regionstypisch rustikale Elemente kombiniert. Einige der nach hinten gelegenen Zimmer bieten einen schönen Blick aufs Kitzhorn.

Sporthotel Reisch Rest, P

Franz-Reisch-Str. 3 ✉ 6370 VISA AE

– ✆ (05356) 63 36 60 – sporthotel-reisch@kitz.net – Fax (05356) 63291

geschl. 10. April – 15. Mai, 10. Okt. – 30. Nov. AZ **m**

43 Zim – ☼ 80/120 € 140/180 € ❄ 120/195 € 198/360 € – ½ P 25 €

Rest – Karte 25/48 €

♦ Das Ferienhotel befindet sich im Zentrum und bietet seinen Gästen wohnlich-rustikale Zimmer sowie diverse Kosmetik- und Massageangebote. Das Restaurant teilt sich in verschiedene gemütlich-ländliche Stuben. Zur Straße hin liegt die überdachte Terrasse.

Hahnenhof P

Hausstattfeld 18 (über Marchfeldgasse B) ✉ 6370 – ✆ (05356) 6 25 82 – info@hahnenhof.at – Fax (05356) 71613

20 Zim (inkl. ½ P.) – ☼ 35/70 € 70/140 € ❄ 80/195 € 160/390 €

Rest – *(nur Abendessen)* (im Sommer Garni) Karte 32/45 €

♦ Das in einer Wohngegend am Ortsrand gelegene 300 Jahre alte ehemalige Bauernhaus beherbergt heute ein kleines Hotel mit wohnlich im Landhausstil eingerichteten Zimmern. Rustikales, nett dekoriertes Restaurant.

Villa Licht garni P VISA AE

Franz-Reisch-Str. 8 ✉ 6370 – ✆ (05356) 6 22 93 – hotel-licht@tirol.com – Fax (05356) 6229333

geschl. April – Mai, Okt. – Nov. AZ **k**

18 Zim – ☼ 65/70 € 120/140 € ❄ 90/145 € 160/240 €

♦ Mit Liebe zum Detail hat man das über 100 Jahre alte familiengeführte Haus gestaltet. Einige der hübschen Gästezimmer sind als Suiten angelegt und besonders komfortabel.

Ehrenbachhöhe < Kitzbüheler Alpen und Wilder Kaiser, Rest,

Hahnenkamm 22 (über Kirchberger Str. B 170 AY, nur mit , Fleckalmbahn ab Klausen) ✉ 6370 – ✆ (05356) 6 21 51 – info@ehrenbachhoehe.at – Fax (05356) 6215199

geschl. Mai – Juni, Mitte Sept. – Anfang Dez.

47 Zim (inkl. ½ P.) – ☼ 75 € 120 € ❄ 110/125 € 170/200 €

Rest – (im Sommer nur für Hausgäste) Karte 18/35 €

♦ Die etwas mühsame Anreise mit Fleckalmbahn und kleinem Fußmarsch ist angesichts der schönen Zimmer und der einsamen Berglage schnell vergessen. Auch einfachere Zimmer. Bürgerliches Restaurant mit herrlicher Aussicht.

Gasthof Eggerwirt

Gänsbachgasse 12 ✉ 6370 – ✆ (05356) 6 24 55 – info@eggerwirt-kitzbuehel.at – Fax (05356) 6243722 – geschl. April, Nov. BY **c**

19 Zim – ☼ 52/63 € 88/104 € ❄ 74/106 € 118/162 € – ½ P 16/22 € – **Rest** – Karte 15/40 €

♦ In dem über 300 Jahre alten regionstypischen Gasthof erwarten Sie solide Zimmer, die teilweise besonders freundlich im neuzeitlich-alpenländischen Stil eingerichtet sind. Schön sitzt man in dem an das Restaurant angeschlossenen Wintergarten.

Neuwirt – Hotel Schwarzer Adler

Florianigasse 15 ✉ 6370 – ✆ (05356) 69 11 – hotel@adlerkitz.at – Fax (05356) 73939

geschl. Ende April – Mitte Mai, Nov. – Mitte Dez. BZ **d**

Rest – *(nur Abendessen)* Menü 68/84 € – Karte 35/59 €

Spez. Lauwarme Gazpacho mit Hummer und Kräuterbrotsalat. Milchkalbsfilet mit Olivenöl und Langostinos. Mohnschupfnudeln und Powidltascherl mit weißem Mohneis.

♦ In den beiden gemütlichen Restaurantstuben serviert man regional beeinflusste kreative Küche – kompetent empfiehlt man Ihnen den passenden Wein.

Schwedenkapelle

Klausenbach 67 (über Kirchberger Str. B 170 AY, und Gundhabing) ✉ 6370 – ✆ (05356) 6 58 70 – Fax (05356) 658704

geschl. Mitte April – Ende Mai, Okt. – Mitte Dez. und Montag, im Sommer Montag – Dienstagmittag

Rest – *(im Winter nur Abendessen)* Menü 31/45 € – Karte 23/48 €

♦ Das ehemaligen Bauernhaus, ursprünglich als Kapelle erbaut, beherbergt heute ein rustikales Restaurant mit regionalem Speisenangebot.

Lois Stern

Josef Pirchl-Str. 3 ✉ 6370 – ✆ (05356) 7 48 82

geschl. 4. – 28. Nov. und Sonntag – Montag AY **u**

Rest – *(nur Abendessen)* Menü 45/75 € – Karte 35/53 €

♦ Im Zentrum befindet sich dieses modern gestaltete Restaurant. Während die Chefin freundlich den Service leitet, bereitet der Chef in der offenen Küche euro-asiatische Speisen.

Wirtshaus Zum Rehkitz

Am Rehbühel 30 (über Jochberger Str. BZ, dann links ab Richtung Bichlalm) ✉ 6370 – ✆ (05356) 6 61 22 – Fax (05356) 661224

geschl. April 1 Woche, 9. Juni – 4. Juli, 10. Nov. – 5. Dez., außer Saison Mittwoch – **Rest** – Karte 27/44 €

♦ Eine gemütliche Atmosphäre herrscht in den drei charmanten, ganz in Holz gehaltenen Stuben dieses sorgsam sanierten historischen Bauernhauses. Hübsche Terrasse vor dem Haus.

Golfhaus – Hotel A-ROSA

Hahnenkamm und Streif,

Ried Kaps 7 (über Kreuzgasse BZ) ✉ 6370 – ✆ (05356) 65 66 08 35 – info.kitzbuehel@a-rosa.de – Fax (05356) 65660819

Rest – (Tischbestellung ratsam) Karte 24/38 €

♦ Im Golf-Clubhaus des Hotel A-ROSA befindet sich dieses nette modern-rustikale Restaurant mit regionaler Küche – mittags kleine Karte. Herrlich ist der Blick von der Terrasse.

In Kitzbühel-Oberaigen Süd-Ost: 4,5 km über Jochberger Straße BZ und B 161:

Rosi's Sonnbergstub'n Kitzbüheler Bergwelt,
Oberaigenweg 101 ✉ 6370
– ✆ (05356) 6 46 52 – mail@sonnbergstuben.at – Fax (05356) 6465210
geschl. Nov.
15 Zim – 62/72 € 94/100 € 69/86 € 116/150 €
Rest – Karte 21/40 €
◆ Traumhaft liegt dieses Haus in 1200 m Höhe. Sehr freundlich kümmert man sich in dem kleinen Berghotel mit den wohnlichen, individuell geschnittenen Zimmern um seine Gäste. Behagliche alpenländische Gaststuben mit wunderschöner Sonnen-Panoramaterrasse.

In Aurach bei Kitzbühel Süd-Ost: 5 km über Jochberger Straße BZ:

Gigglingstube
Gigglingweg 17 ✉ 6370 – ✆ (05356) 6 48 88 – Fax (05356) 73205
geschl. Mitte April – Ende Juni, Mitte Nov. – Mitte Dez. und Montag
Rest – *(nur Abendessen)* (Tischbestellung ratsam) Karte 31/47 €
◆ Eine nette, gemütlich-rustikale Atmosphäre herrscht in diesem familiär geleiteten Restaurant. Geboten wird klassische Küche mit regionalem Einfluss.

In Reith bei Kitzbühel Nord-West: 3,5 km über Schwarzseestraße AY Richtung Wörgl:

Biohotel Florian (mit Gästehaus) Rest,
Bichlach 41 ✉ 6370 – ✆ (05356) 6 52 42
– info@biohotel-florian.at – Fax (05356) 652424
geschl. 16. Nov. – 20. Dez.
31 Zim (inkl. ½ P.) – 88/98 € 152/176 € 91/106 €
158/200 €
Rest – (nur Abendessen für Hausgäste)
◆ Engagiert führt Familie Pointner dieses ruhig gelegene Hotel mit eigener Bio-Landwirtschaft und Yoga-Seminarhaus. Solide Gästezimmer mit Vollholzmöbeln und Holzfußboden.

Zum Tischlerwirt VISA AE
Kitzbühlerstr. 46 ✉ 6370 – ✆ (05356) 6 54 16 – info@tischlerwirt.at
– Fax (05356) 654164
geschl. 26. Mai – 27. Juni, 9. Nov. – 5. Dez. und Dienstag
Rest – *(Montag – Donnerstag nur Abendessen)* Menü 35/43 € –
Karte 30/50 €
◆ Ein 150 Jahre altes Gasthaus beherbergt dieses nette Restaurant mit rustikalem Charakter. Der Chef Reinhard Brandner bereitet eine regional beeinflusste klassische Küche.

KITZECK IM SAUSAL – Steiermark – 730 S8 – 1 200 Ew – Höhe 564 m

11 **K5**

Wien 236 – Graz 51 – Maribor 47 – Leibnitz 16
Steirische Weinstraße★

Weinhof Kappel ⩤ (geheizt)
Steinriegel 25 ✉ 8442 – ✆ (03456) 23 47
– office@weinhof-kappel.at – Fax (03456) 234730
geschl. 7. Jan. – 14. März
21 Zim – 82/105 € 164/210 € – ½ P 17 €
Rest – *(geschl. Mittwoch – Donnerstag)* (Tischbestellung ratsam)
Menü 30/48 € – Karte 22/38 €
♦ Die wohnlichen Zimmer dieses Hauses sind z. T. mit naturbelassenen Holzmöbeln und Holzboden eingerichtet und bieten eine schöne Sicht. Meerwasser-Außenpool mit Panoramablick. Eine Bilderausstellung ziert das in bürgerlich-rustikalem Stil gehaltene Restaurant.

Steirerland ⩤ Steirisches Umland und Weinberge, Zim,
Höch 10 ✉ 8442 – ✆ (03456) 23 28
– office@steirerland.co.at – Fax (03456) 232828
geschl. Jan. – Feb.
12 Zim – 50/70 € 100/120 € – ½ P 15 €
Rest – *(geschl. Sonntagabend – Montag)* Menü 29/45 € – Karte 16/36 €
♦ Das gut geführte kleine Hotel liegt auf dem höchsten Weinberg Österreichs. Wohnliche Zimmer mit schöner Aussicht – besonders hübsch: die in Vollholz gehaltenen Winzerzimmer. Bürgerliches Restaurant mit Fensterfront.

Kirchenwirt
Steinriegel 52 ✉ 8442 – ✆ (03456) 22 25 – kirchenwirt.kitzeck@aon.at
– Fax (03456) 22254
geschl. Feb. – 11. März, Ende Juni 1 Woche und Sonntag – Dienstag
Rest – (Tischbestellung ratsam) Menü 32/41 € – Karte 21/33 €
♦ Ein familiengeführtes Gasthaus mit rustikalem, leicht elegantem Ambiente. Sehr schön: die Terrasse mit Blick auf die Weinberge. Selbst gebrannte Schnäpse und eigene Weine.

Weingut Warga-Hack mit Zim Buschenschank Zim,
Gauitsch 20 ✉ 8442 – ✆ (03456) 2 28 20
– warga-hack@warga-hack.at – Fax (03456) 228220
geschl. 6. – 22. Juli
8 Zim – 46/68 € 56/78 €
Rest – *(geschl. Jan. – Mitte März Montag – Donnerstag, Mitte März – Ende August Sonntag – Montag, Sept. – Dez. Montag , ab 14.00 Uhr geöffnet)*
Karte ca. 12 €
♦ Hinter der gelben Fassade verbirgt sich ein gemütlicher Buschenschank mit Kamin und Holztäfelung – ein nettes Umfeld zur Verkostung von Wein und Jausen. Wohnliche Gästezimmer in ländlichem Stil.

Weingut Schwarz mit Zim Buschenschank Zim,
Greith 35 ✉ 8442 – ✆ (03456) 30 64 Zim,
– weingut-schwarz@aon.at – Fax (03456) 27452
geschl. Ende Nov. – Ende März
5 Zim – 39/40 € 56/78 €
Rest – *(geschl. Sonntag – Dienstag, geöffnet ab 14 Uhr)* Karte ca. 12 €
♦ Neben einem Weingut findet man hier in einem separaten Gebäude auch einen rustikal-gemütlichen Buschenschank, in dem Jausen zum Wein gereicht werden. Hübsche Gästezimmer.

Weingut Lambauer mit Zim Buschenschank

Greith 19 ✉ 8442 Zim, VISA

– *(03456) 22 35 – info@weingut-lambauer.at – Fax (03456) 27497*
geschl. Nov. – März
5 Zim – 35 € 64 €
Rest – *(geschl. Sonntag – Montag , geöffnet Dienstag – Donnerstag ab 16 Uhr, Freitag – Samstag ab 14 Uhr)* Karte ca. 12 €

◆ Auf einer Anhöhe liegt das familiengeführte Weingut. Im mediterran gestalteten Buschenschank werden Jausen serviert. Hübsche Terrasse mit schönem Ausblick in die Weinberge. Funktionelle Gästezimmer mit Balkon. Nette Liegewiese hinter dem Haus.

KLAGENFURT L – **Kärnten** – 730 OP9 – **90 150 Ew** – **Höhe 444 m** – **Wintersport: 528 m** 3 9 **I6**

Wien 299 – Salzburg 221 – Graz 133 – Villach 39

Neuer Platz (Rathaus), ✉ 9010, (0463) 5 37 22 23, tourismus@klagenfurt.at

Klagenfurt-Seltenheim, (0463) 4 02 23

Veranstaltungen

18.01. – 20.01.: Agrarmesse Alpen-Adria
08.02. – 10.02.: Der Häuslbauer
10.04. – 13.04.: Freizeit u. Auto & Bike
13.07.: Kärnten Ironman Austria
13.09. – 21.09.: Herbstmesse
31.10. – 02.11.: Pferdemesse Alpen-Adria
21.11. – 23.11.: Gesund Leben u. Kärntner Brauchtumsmesse

Fußball-Europameisterschaft

08.06., 12.06., 16.06.: Vorrundenspiele

Altstadt★★ – Neuer Platz (Lindwurmbrunnen★) – Alter Platz★ – Landhaus (Renaissance-Innenhof★, Großer Wappensaal★) – Bergbaumuseum★ Y – Dom★ – Landesmuseum★ **M**[1] – Diözesanmuseum★ **M**[2] Z

Wörther See★ – Viktring (Stift: Deckenfresken★) Süd: 7 km – Schloss Hollenburg (Innenhof★) Süd: 10 km

Das Salzamt Palais Hotel Landhaushof A/C

Landhaushof 3 ✉ 9020 Zim, VISA AE

– *(0463) 59 09 59 – office@landhaushof.at – Fax (0463) 59095909* Y **a**
27 Zim – 135/165 € 200/230 €
Rest – Menü 21/36 € (abends) – Karte 13/36 €

◆ Das aufwändig restaurierte ehemalige Renaissancepalais – einst als Salzamt genutzt – beherbergt heute sehr moderne und geschmackvolle Zimmer, einige mit freigelegten Fresken. Speisen werden im eleganten Arkadenhof oder im rustikalen Salzamt serviert.

Palais Porcia garni A/C VISA AE

Neuer Platz 13, (3. Etage) ✉ 9020 – (0463) 51 15 90
– *hotel@palais-porcia.at – Fax (0463) 51159030* Y **e**
35 Zim – 84/182 € 113/197 €

◆ Der einstige Fürstensitz beeindruckt mit einem nicht alltäglichen, stilvollen Ambiente. Die Zimmer sind elegant und sehr individuell eingerichtet – von Barock bis Biedermeier.

Arcotel Moser Verdino garni VISA AE

Domgasse 2 ✉ 9020 – (0463) 5 78 78 – moserverdino@arcotel.at
– *Fax (0463) 516765* Y **b**

KLAGENFURT

Straße	Planquadrat	Nr.
August-Jaksch Str.	Z	2
Benediktinerpl.	Z	3
Domgasse	YZ	11
Feldkirchner Str.	Y	4
Feldm.-Conrad-Pl.	Y	5
Heiligengeistpl.	Y	6
Herbertstraße	Y	19
Herrengasse	Y	7
Heuplatz	Y	16
Karfreitstraße	YZ	14
Kramergasse	Y	9
Landhaushof	Y	8
Pernhartgasse	Y	10
Purtscherstr.	Y	12
St.-Veiter Str.	Y	13
Sterneckstraße	Y	20
Theaterpl.	Y	15
Wienergasse	Y	17
Wiesbadener Str.	Y	18

71 Zim – 🚹74/162 € 🚹🚹108/240 €, ☕ 12 €

◆ Das Jugendstilhaus von 1858 befindet sich in der Altstadt und verfügt über neuzeitlich und funktionell eingerichtete Zimmer und großzügige Juniorsuiten sowie ein nettes Café.

Der Sandwirth

Pernhartgasse 9 ✉ *9020* – ✆ *(0463) 5 62 09 – hotel@sandwirth.at – Fax (0463) 514322* Y **s**

VISA MC AE D

68 Zim ☕ – 🚹95/114 € 🚹🚹149/174 €

Rest – *(geschl. Sonntagabend)* Menü 28 € – Karte 24/36 €

◆ Eine Halle in modernem Stil sowie neuzeitlich-funktionell ausgestattete Zimmer erwarten Sie in diesem gut geführten Businesshotel. Café-Bar und Cigar Lounge.

Goldener Brunnen garni

Karfreitstr. 14, (1. Etage) ✉ 9020 – ✆ (0463) 5 73 80 – hotel@goldener-brunnen.at – Fax (0463) 516520

geschl. 19. – 29. Dez. Z **r**

26 Zim – 79/98 € 110/130 €

◆ Im Zentrum, gegenüber dem Dom liegt das ehemalige Kloster – heute ein Hotel mit komfortablen und funktionellen Gästezimmern in zeitlosem Stil.

Atrigon garni

Kinoplatz 6 ✉ 9020 – ✆ (0463) 35 19 50 – info@atrigon.at – Fax (0463) 3519520 Z **t**

39 Zim – 86 € 120 €

◆ In dem neuzeitlichen Etagenhotel nur wenige Schritte vom Bahnhof erwarten Sie funktionell eingerichtete Zimmer mit gutem Platzangebot und ein ansprechendes Frühstücksbuffet.

Carinthia Stadthotel garni

8. Mai-Str. 41, (3. Etage) ✉ 9020 – ✆ (0463) 51 16 45 – carinthia@chello.at – Fax (0463) 51167210

geschl. 21. Dez. – 7. Jan. Y **n**

28 Zim – 72/99 € 110/150 €

◆ Ein typisches Stadthotel nahe der Altstadt von Klagenfurt. Die Gästezimmer sind meist mit hellem Naturholz wohnlich eingerichtet.

Dermuth

Kohldorfer Str. 52 (über Sterneckstr. Y) ✉ 9020 – ✆ (0463) 2 12 47 – dermuth@klagenfurt.net – Fax (0463) 2124717

geschl. 22. Dez. – 13. Jan.

54 Zim – 77/108 € 128/146 €

Rest – Karte 21/36 €

◆ Das traditionelle Gasthaus mit rustikalem Charakter wurde um einen Hotelbau mit gediegenen, meist mit Parkettfußboden ausgestatteten Zimmern ergänzt, einige mit Balkon. Das Restaurant teilt sich in mehrere gemütliche Stuben und einen neuzeitlicheren Pavillon.

Plattenwirt garni (mit Gästehaus)

Friedelstrand 2 (über Villacher Straße YZ) ✉ 9020 – ✆ (0463) 2 11 73 – hotel@plattenwirt.at – Fax (0463) 2117325

37 Zim – 80/100 € 100/160 €

◆ Das Hotel nahe dem Wörthersee ist ein ehemaliger Gasthof mit Gästehaus. Ein Teil der Zimmer ist besonders modern gestaltet und großzügig geschnitten. Heller Frühstücksraum.

Geyer garni

Priesterhausgasse 5 ✉ 9020 – ✆ (0463) 5 78 86 – info@hotelgeyer.com – Fax (0463) 5788620

geschl. über Weihnachten Y **g**

25 Zim – 68/78 € 92/105 €

◆ Ein durch die Inhaberin solide geführtes Hotel im Zentrum, das über mit hellem Holzmobiliar zeitgemäß eingerichtete Gästezimmer verfügt.

Aragia Zim, Zim, VISA AE

Völkermarkter Str. 100, (B 70) (über Y) ✉ 9020 – ✆ (0463) 3 12 22 – hotel@aragia.at – Fax (0463) 3122213

geschl. 18. – 28. Dez.

40 Zim – 58/68 € 88/102 € – **Rest** – *(geschl. im Winter Samstag-Sonntag, nur Abendessen)* Menü 11 € – Karte 13/31 €

◆ Vor allem Geschäftsreisende schätzen die funktionell ausgestatteten Gästezimmer dieses am Stadtrand gelegenen familiengeführten Hotels. Eine nach hinten gelegene Terrasse ergänzt das Restaurant.

Dolce Vita (Stephan Vadnjal) VISA AE

Heuplatz 2 ✉ 9020 – ✆ (0463) 5 54 99 – restaurant.dolcevita@aon.at – Fax (0463) 554994

geschl. Ende Aug. – Anfang Sept. und Samstag – Sonntag, Feiertage Y **m**

Rest – (Tischbestellung ratsam) Menü 58/80 € – Karte ca. 32 € (mittags)

Spez. Roh marinierte Scampetti in Kräuterduft. Panna Cotta von weißem Spargel mit Jakobsmuscheln (Saison). Wolfsbarsch in der Salzkruste.

◆ Guten Service mit mündlichen Empfehlungen am Tisch und mediterrane Küche bietet Ihnen diese Adresse. Großes Degustationsmenü am Abend. Mittags: günstigere A-la-carte-Auswahl.

Oscar VISA AE

St. Veiter Ring 43 ✉ 9020 – ✆ (0463) 50 01 77 – haas@gut-essen-trinken.at – Fax (0463) 507517

geschl. Sonn- und Feiertage Y **f**

Rest – Menü 35 € (abends) – Karte 27/44 €

◆ Eine moderne Einrichtung und die gepflegte Atmosphäre machen dieses zentral gelegene Restaurant mit italienischer Küche aus. Vor dem Haus: die nette Terrasse.

Gasthaus im Landhaushof VISA AE

Landhaushof 1 ✉ 9020 – ✆ (0463) 50 23 63 – haas@gut-essen-trinken.at – Fax (0463) 507517 Y **c**

Rest – Menü 25 € (abends) – Karte 16/34 €

◆ Im Seitenflügel des Kärntner Landhauses wird Ihnen unter einem schönen Kreuzgewölbe regionale Küche serviert. Nett sitzt man auch auf der Terrasse.

ANDO VISA AE

Lakeside B06, (Lakeside Science & Technology Park) (West: 4 km, über Villacher Straße YZ in Richtung Maria Wörth) ✉ 9020 – ✆ (0463) 89 01 90 – restaurant@ando.at – Fax (0463) 89019015

geschl. 2. – 7. Jan. und Samstag – Sonntag

Rest – Menü 39 € – Karte 24/34 €

◆ Mit klarem modernem Design besticht das Restaurant auf dem Gelände des Lakeside-Technologieparks. Die Küche verbindet Kärntne Speisen mit asiatischen Elementen.

Der Franzos VISA

Villacher Str. 11, (B 83) ✉ 9020 – ✆ (0664) 4 66 55 00 – derfranzos@aon.at – Fax (0463) 501535

geschl. Anfang Jan. 1 Woche, Ende Aug. – Mitte Sept. 3 Wochen sowie Samstag, Sonn- und Feiertage YZ **a**

Rest – *(nur Abendessen)* Menü 28/42 € – Karte 27/37 €

◆ Das kleine Lokal am Rande des Zentrums gehört zu den ältesten Gasthäusern der Stadt. Französische Bistroküche im urig-gemütlichen Ambiente. Kleiner weinberankter Gastgarten.

In Klagenfurt-Sankt Georgen am Sandhof Nord-Ost: 5 km über St. Veiter Straße Y :

Schloss St. Georgen garni
Sandhofweg 8 ✉ 9020
– ✆ (0463) 46 84 90 – hotel@schloss-st-georgen.at – Fax (0463) 4684970
geschl. 20. Dez. – 1. Feb.
16 Zim – 80/120 € 120/160 €
◆ Schön liegt das im Jahre 1216 erstmals erwähnte ehemalige Schloss in einem 1,7 ha großen Park. Sehr individuell und wohnlich-elegant hat man die Gästezimmer gestaltet.

In Klagenfurt-Viktring Süd-West: 6 km über Villacher Straße YZ:

Weidenhof
Süduferstr. 66 (Nord-West: 1,5 km, Richtung Maria Wörth) ✉ 9073
– ✆ (0463) 28 15 40 – hotel@weidenhof.at
– Fax (0463) 2815408
geschl. über Weihnachten
34 Zim – 58/62 € 95/100 € – ½ P 14 €
Rest – *(geschl. Montag)* Karte 17/30 €
◆ Eine solide familiengeführte Adresse, die mit ihren funktionellen und zeitgemäßen Zimmer vor allem von Geschäftsreisenden gerne genutzt wird. Gemütliches, in verschiedene Stuben unterteiltes Restaurant.

KLAUS – Vorarlberg – 730 A7 – 2 800 Ew – Höhe 490 m   5 A5

Wien 673 – Bregenz 26 – Feldkirch 13 – Dornbirn 15

Sternen   Rest,
Im Tobel 14 ✉ 6833 – ✆ (05523) 6 24 43 – info@sternen.at
– Fax (05523) 624436
geschl. Nov.
31 Zim – 49/54 € 76/86 € – ½ P 12 €
Rest – *(geschl. Sonntag – Montag, nur Abendessen)* Karte 13/27 €
◆ Zimmer mit hellem Mobiliar und meist mit Balkon – nach Süden hin mit schöner Aussicht – sowie eine nette Gartenanlage zählen zu den Annehmlichkeiten dieses Familienbetriebs. Unterteiltes Restaurant von bürgerlich bis rustikal mit netter Terrasse.

KLEIN SANKT PAUL – Kärnten – 730 P8 – 2 200 Ew – Höhe 635 m   10 I6

Wien 279 – Klagenfurt 38 – Wolfsberg 58

Zum Dorfschmied mit Zim
Marktstr. 16 ✉ 9373 – ✆ (04264) 22 80 – zumdorfschmied@aon.at
– Fax (04273) 22804
18 Zim – 38 € 65 €
Rest – *(geschl. Sonn- und Feiertage abends, Montag)* (Tischbestellung ratsam) Karte 22/45 €
◆ Der Familienbetrieb im Ortskern ist ein freundliches Restaurant in ländlichem Stil. Produkte aus der eigenen Bio-Landwirtschaft prägen das Angebot. Kleine Schnapsbrennerei.

KLEINARL – Salzburg – 730 L7 – 750 Ew – Höhe 1 014 m – Wintersport: 1 980 m 8 9 G5

Wien 331 – Salzburg 73 – St. Johann im Pongau 15

Dorf 28, 5603, (06418) 2 06, welcome@kleinarl.info

Guggenberger
(geheizt) Zim,

Dorf 45 5603 – (06418) 2 22 – info@hotel-guggenberger.at – Fax (06418) 22240

geschl. Mitte April – Ende Mai, Mitte Okt. – Anfang Dez.

43 Zim (inkl. ½ P.) – 66/73 € 122/132 € 74/105 € 134/196 €

Rest – Karte 16/29 €

♦ Ein Teil der soliden Gästezimmer dieses Alpenhotels sind besonders großzügig und neuzeitlich-rustikal möbliert – einige auch mit allergikerfreundlichem Parkettfußboden. Sie speisen in ländlichem Ambiente an gut eingedeckten Tischen. Im Sommer nette Terrasse.

Zirbenhof
Zim, VISA

Viehofstr. 14 5603 – (06418) 2 21 – info@zirbenhof.at – Fax (06418) 22125

geschl. 12. April – 28. Juni, 6. Sept. – 5. Dez.

18 Zim (inkl. ½ P.) – 48/60 € 96/120 € 60/155 € 120/190 €

Rest – Karte 18/30 €

♦ Die Lage direkt an der Liftanlage sowie wohnliche Zimmer in angenehm warmen und frischen Farben machen dieses familiengeführte kleine Hotel aus.

Landhaus Lärchenhof
(geheizt) Zim,

Rupertiweg 3 5603 – (06418) 26 50 – info@laerchenhof.de – Fax (06418) 2658

geschl. 7. April – 24. Juli, 10. Sept. – 15. Dez.

12 Zim (inkl. ½ P.) – 76/99 € 116/140 € 86/112 € 138/212 €

Rest – Karte 18/29 €

♦ Eine sehr gepflegte Adresse ist dieser solide geführte Familienbetrieb mit seinen teilweise hell im Landhausstil oder auch rustikaler ausgestatteten Gästezimmern. Ländlich gestaltetes Restaurant. Eine schöne Sicht bietet die Terrasse hinter dem Haus.

Aichhorn
VISA AE

Peilsteingasse 15 5603 – (06418) 3 74 – info@restaurant-aichhorn.at – Fax (06418) 3744

geschl. Nov. 2 Wochen und außer Saison Montag

Rest – Menü 23 € (mittags)/52 € – Karte 18/44 €

♦ Regionale, z. T. klassische Küche serviert man in dem regionstypisch gestalteten Restaurant – sehr freundlich leitet die Chefin den Service. Terrasse mit schönem Tauernblick.

Bestecke und Sterne sollten nicht verwechselt werden! Die Bestecke stehen für eine Komfortkategorie, die Sterne zeichnen Häuser mit besonders guter Küche aus - in jeder dieser Kategorien.

KLEINKIRCHHEIM, BAD – Kärnten – 730 N8 – 1 870 Ew – Höhe 1 050 m – Wintersport: 2 055 m 4 22 – Kurort 9 H6

Wien 312 – Klagenfurt 50 – Villach 36 – Spittal a.d. Drau 31
Dorfstr. 30, 9546, (04240) 82 12, info@badkleinkirchheim.at
Bad Kleinkirchheim-Reichenau, Plass 19 (04275) 5 94

Thermenhotel Ronacher

(Thermal) (Thermal) Rest, VISA
Thermenstr. 3 9546 – (04240) 2 82 – thermenhotel@ronacher.com – Fax (04042) 282606
geschl. April
90 Zim (inkl. ½ P.) – 150/188 € 266/359 € 165/213 € 288/383 € – 9 Suiten
Rest – (Tischbestellung erforderlich) Menü 36 € (mittags)/70 € (abends) – Karte 25/36 €

◆ Das Hotel überzeugt mit seiner schön gestalteten Thermen- & Wohlfühlwelt auf 4000 qm – das Angebot reicht von Beauty- und Massageanwendungen bis hin zur Almhütten-Sauna. Gemütlich sind die verschiedenen Restaurantstuben.

Pulverer-Thermenwelt

(Thermal) (Thermal) VISA
Thermenstr. 4 9546 – (04240) 7 44 – hotel@pulverer.at – Fax (04240) 793
geschl. 6. April – 1. Mai, 24. Nov. – 5. Dez.
100 Zim (inkl. ½ P.) – 100/123 € 202/264 € 93/158 € 180/316 € – 6 Suiten
Rest *Loystub'n* – separat erwähnt

◆ Ein traditionelles alpenländisches Ferienhotel mit wohnlichen Gästezimmern und einem großzügigen Wellnessbereich mit vielfältigem Angebot.

Die Post

(geheizt) Zim, Rest, VISA
Dorfstr. 64 9546 – (04240) 2 12 – ronacher@diepost.com – Fax (04240) 650
geschl. April
94 Zim (inkl. ½ P.) – 96/140 € 162/292 € 108/123 € 176/316 €
Rest – (nur für Hausgäste)

◆ In dem gewachsenen Ferienhotel erwarten Sie wohnliche Gästezimmer und ein aufwändig gestalteter Wellnessbereich mit Kinderbetreuung.

Felsenhof

(geheizt) (geheizt) Rest, VISA AE
Mozartweg 6 9546 – (04240) 68 10 – office@hotelfelsenhof.at – Fax (04240) 68320
geschl. 25. März – 20. April- 25. Mai, 2. Nov. – 20. Dez.
34 Zim (inkl. ½ P.) – 90/120 € 150/186 € 100/140 € 170/246 €
Rest – (nur für Hausgäste)

◆ Freundlich wird das leicht erhöht gelegene Ferienhotel von Familie Lercher geführt. Man bietet wohnliche Zimmer und Wellness auf 800 qm. Schön ist die Sicht auf die Umgebung.

Almrausch (geheizt) Zim, Rest,
Wasserfallweg 7 ✉ 9546 – ✆ (04240) 84 84
– hotel.almrausch@aon.at – Fax (04240) 848418
geschl. 1. April – 22. Mai
33 Zim (inkl. ½ P.) – ☼ 64/80 € 124/156 € ❄ 77/94 €
124/192 € – 6 Suiten
Rest – (nur Abendessen für Hausgäste)
◆ In diesem Familienbetrieb am Ortsrand erwarten Sie hell und freundlich eingerichtete Zimmer mit gutem Platzangebot. Nett ist der Empfangsbereich mit Blick in den Weinkeller.

Eschenhof (geheizt) Rest,
Wasserfallweg 12 ✉ 9546
– ✆ (04240) 82 62 – hotel@eschenhof.at – Fax (04240) 826282
geschl. 11. April – 25. Mai, 14. Nov. – 15. Dez.
42 Zim (inkl. ½ P.) – ☼ 76/88 € 156/186 € ❄ 85/110 €
184/240 €
Rest – (nur Abendessen für Hausgäste)
◆ Am Ortsrand liegt das gewachsene Landhotel unter familiärer Leitung mit seinen hell und freundlich eingerichteten Zimmern und einem ansprechenden Frühstücksbuffet.

Sonnalm (geheizt) Rest,
Quellenweg 3 ✉ 9546 – ✆ (04240) 5 07 – office@sonnalm.at
– Fax (04240) 50715
geschl. 1. April – 7. Juni, 19. Nov. – 20. Dez.
27 Zim (inkl. ½ P.) – ☼ 67/79 € 128/162 € ❄ 80/115 €
148/238 €
Rest – (nur Abendessen für Hausgäste)
◆ Wohnliche Gästezimmer und ein netter, gepflegter Freizeitbereich machen dieses gut geführte Hotel aus. Auch eine eigene Bibliothek ist vorhanden.

Prägant (geheizt) Rest,
Kirchheimerweg 6 ✉ 9546
– ✆ (04240) 45 20 – praegant@hhbkk.at – Fax (04240) 45317
geschl. April – Mai
36 Zim (inkl. ½ P.) – ☼ 89/135 € 150/270 € ❄ 91/147 €
144/296 €
Rest – (nur Abendessen für Hausgäste)
◆ Ein kleiner Park umgibt das von der Inhaberfamilie gut geführte Urlaubshotel. Man bietet u. a. sehr schöne Themenzimmer (Mond, Erde, Venus und Sonne).

Trattlerhof Rest, Rest,
Gegendtaler Weg 1 ✉ 9546
– ✆ (04240) 81 72 – hotel@trattlerhof.at – Fax (04240) 8124
geschl. April, Nov.
47 Zim (inkl. ½ P.) – 73/99 € 128/274 €
Rest – (nur für Hausgäste)
◆ Aus einem Gasthof von 1356 ist dieses Hotel entstanden. Im Sommer stehen den Gästen Pferde zur Verfügung. Tennisplätze und Angelteich bei der nahen hauseigenen Einkehrhütte.

Loystub'n – Hotel Pulverer Thermenwelt
Thermenstr. 4 ✉ 9546 – ✆ (04240) 7 44 – hotel@pulverer.at – Fax (04240) 793
geschl. 6. April – 1. Mai, 24. Nov. – 5. Dez.
Rest – Karte 32/41 €
◆ Das Restaurant teilt sich in behaglich-rustikale kleine Stuben mit regionstypischem Charme. Freundlich und kompetent kümmert man sich um seine Gäste.

Drage
Rottensteinerweg 1 (Ost: 2,5 km über B 88, dann links ab) ✉ 9546 – ✆ (04240) 2 77 – gasthof.drage@aon.at – Fax (04240) 20408
geschl. 16. Juni – 11. Juli und Montag – Dienstag
Rest – Karte 20/40 €
◆ Gut isst man in den ländlichen Gaststuben dieses ehemaligen Bauernhauses. Geboten werden Gerichte aus der Kärntner Wirtshausküche sowie internationale Speisen.

In Bad Kleinkirchheim-St. Oswald Nord-West: 4,5 km – Höhe 1 358 m

St. Oswald Rest, Rest,
Schartenweg 5 ✉ 9546 – ✆ (04240) 59 10 – reservierung@hotel-st-oswald.at – Fax (04240) 58372
geschl. 31. März – 1. Juni, 27. Okt. – 15. Dez.
53 Zim (inkl. ½ P.) – ☼ 88/110 € 162/198 € ❄ 100/138 € 198/276 € – 14 Suiten
Rest – *(geschl. Dienstag, Sonntagabend)* Karte 26/62 €
◆ Vor allem die ruhige Lage auf einer Anhöhe und die schöne Aussicht sprechen für dieses Urlaubshotel. Die Zimmer sind zeitgemäß ausgestattet und verfügen über einen Balkon. Klassisch-gediegenes Restaurant mit sehr netter Terrasse.

KLEINWALSERTAL – Vorarlberg – 730 C6 – 4 720 Ew – Wintersport: 2 000 m 2 34

5 **B5**

Wien 583 – Bregenz 83 – Kempten 49
Tal★
Oberstdorf★★

In Riezlern – Höhe 1 100 m

Walserstr. 54, ✉ 6991, ✆ (05517) 51 14 18

Almhof Rupp Rest,
Walserstr. 83 ✉ 6991 – ✆ (05517) 50 04 – info@almhof-rupp.de – Fax (05517) 3273
geschl. 15. April – 15. Mai, 10. Nov. – 20. Dez.
32 Zim (inkl. ½ P.) – ☼ 80/110 € 140/180 € ❄ 105/140 € 180/250 €
Rest – *(geschl. Montag)* (Tischbestellung erforderlich) Menü 20/58 € – Karte 24/41 €
◆ Eine ländlich-gediegene Atmosphäre erwartet den Gast in diesem ruhig gelegenen alpenländischen Haus mit behaglichen Zimmern und einem großzügigen Wellnessbereich. In der netten Walserstube serviert man sorgfältig zubereitete Speisen.

Riezler Hof

Walserstr. 57 ✉ 87567 – ✆ (05517) 5 37 70 – info@riezlerhof.at – Fax (05517) 537750
geschl. Mitte April – Mitte Mai, Mitte Okt. – Mitte Dez.
28 Zim – ☼ †66/76 € ††132/152 € ❄ †66/108 € ††132/216 €
Rest – *(geschl. Montag)* Karte 19/32 €
♦ Das Hotel im Ortszentrum verfügt über neuzeitlich eingerichtete Gästezimmer mit solider Technik – besonders ruhig sind die Zimmer nach hinten. Heller Holzboden und holzgetäfelte Wände machen das Restaurant gemütlich.

Alpenhof Jäger

Unterwestegg 17 ✉ 6991 – ✆ (05517) 52 34 – alpenhof.jaeger@aon.at – Fax (05517) 523450
geschl. 6. – 27. April, 22. Juni – 12. Juli, 23. Nov. – 20. Dez.
12 Zim (inkl. ½ P.) – ☼ †52/59 € ††98/118 € ❄ †68/79 € ††124/170 €
Rest – *(geschl. Dienstag – Mittwoch, nur Abendessen)* Menü 26/47 € – Karte 22/44 €
♦ Herzstück des kleinen Hotels ist ein liebevoll restauriertes Walserhaus von 1690. Hier sowie in einem Anbau im regionstypischen Stil befinden sich behaglich-rustikale Zimmer. Urige Gaststube im historischen Teil des Hauses mit guter, teils regionaler Küche.

Walserstuba Rest,

Eggstr. 2 ✉ 6991 – ✆ (05517) 5 34 60 – info@walserstuba.at – Fax (05517) 534613
geschl. 6. April – 1. Mai, 26. Okt. – 13. Dez.
23 Zim (inkl. ½ P.) – ☼ †59 € ††108/118 € ❄ †71/76 € ††138/152 €
Rest – *(geschl. Montag – Dienstagmittag)* Karte 32/50 €
♦ Der familiengeführte Alpengasthof mit Holzbalkonen bietet mit regionstypischen Naturholzmöbeln solide eingerichtete Zimmer. Die Gaststuben sind teils getäfelt, teils mit dunklen Holzbalken eines alten Bauernhauses ausgestattet.

Wagner Zim, Rest,

Walserstr. 1 ✉ 6991 – ✆ (05517) 52 48 – info@hotel-wagner.de – Fax (05517) 3266
geschl. Mitte April – Mitte Mai, Ende Okt. – Mitte Dez.
21 Zim (inkl. ½ P.) – ☼ †62/67 € ††100/116 € ❄ †89/155 € ††146/210 €
Rest – (nur Abendessen für Hausgäste)
♦ Direkt am Waldrand und wenige Minuten vom Ortskern entfernt liegt das gemütlich-rustikale Landgasthaus mit seinen unterschiedlich möblierten Zimmern.

Scharnagl's Alpenhof mit Zim

Zwerwaldstr. 28 ✉ 6691 – ✆ (05517) 52 76 – alpenhof@scharnagls.de – Fax (05517) 52763
geschl. 14. – 30. April, 3. Nov. – 4. Dez.
5 Zim (inkl. ½ P.) – ☼ †45/50 € ††84/98 € ❄ †62/67 € ††118/132 €
Rest – *(geschl. Mittwoch – Donnerstagmittag)* Menü 34/42 € – Karte 28/39 €
♦ Ganz in hellem Holz ist dieses engagiert geführte Restaurant gehalten. Der Patron bereitet deftige Hausmannskost und klassische Gerichte.

In Hirschegg – Höhe 1 125 m

im Walserhaus, 6992, (05517) 5 11 40, info@kleinwalsertal.com

Walserhof

Rest,

Walserstr. 11 6992 – (05517) 56 84 – walserhof@aon.at – Fax (05517) 5938

geschl. 2. Nov. – 15. Dez.

52 Zim (inkl. ½ P.) – 83/117 € 126/160 € 94/149 € 148/242 €

5 Suiten

Rest – Karte 18/39 €

◆ Das gemütlich-rustikal eingerichtete Hotel bietet neben wohnlichen Zimmern und Wellnessangeboten auch eine hübsche Gartenanlage. Alpenländisch ist das Ambiente im Restaurant.

Birkenhöhe

Kleinwalsertal,

Oberseitestr. 34 6992 – (05517) 55 87 – info@birkenhoehe.com – Fax (05517) 558712

VISA

geschl. 12. April – 31. Mai, 2. Nov. – 17. Dez.

38 Zim (inkl. ½ P.) – 80/100 € 150/200 € 90/125 € 170/206 €

3 Suiten

Rest – *(geschl. Sonntag – Montag, nur Abendessen)* (Tischbestellung ratsam) Menü 28/65 €

◆ Ein familiär geleitetes Hotel in Hanglage mit schöner Aussicht, wohnlicher und zeitgemäßer Einrichtung und einem ansprechenden Wellnessbereich mit Kosmetik und Massage. Das A-la-carte-Restaurant ist eine kleine Stube in alpenländisch-elegantem Stil.

Naturhotel Chesa Valisa (mit Gästehaus)

(geheizt) Rest, VISA

Gerbeweg 18 6992 – (05517) 5 41 40 – info@naturhotel.at – Fax (05517) 5108

geschl. 6. April – 28. Juni, 11. Nov. – 15. Dez.

45 Zim (inkl. ½ P.) – 78/88 € 136/170 € 88/125 € 156/246 €

Rest – Karte 25/37 €

◆ Mit Vollholzmöbeln und Parkett sind die Zimmer des familiengeführten Hauses im Skigebiet neuzeitlich eingerichtet. Wellness- und Bio-Arrangements sowie diverse Aktivprogramme. Regionale Küche aus Naturprodukten im ländlichen Restaurant. Schöner Weinkeller.

Gemma

Rest, VISA

Schwarzwassertalstr. 21 6992 – (05517) 5 36 00 – info@gemma.at – Fax (05517) 5360300

geschl. 6. April – 20. Mai, 2. Nov. – 12. Dez.

26 Zim (inkl. ½ P.) – 57/65 € 104/144 € 75/102 € 136/214 €

Rest – (nur Abendessen für Hausgäste)

◆ Ruhig liegt der alpenländische Gasthof mit der typischen holzverkleideten Fassade oberhalb des Ortes. Die Zimmer sind rustikal gestaltet, einige auch in neuzeitlichem Stil.

Sonnenberg Kleinwalsertal, Rest,
Am Berg 26 ✉ 6992 – ☎ (05517) 54 33
– info@kleinwalsertal-sonnenberg.de – Fax (05517) 543333
geschl. April, Ende Okt. – Mitte Dez.
16 Zim (inkl. ½ P.) – ☼ 71/94 € 148/162 € ❄ 77/114 €
160/198 €
Rest – (nur Abendessen für Hausgäste)
♦ Aus dem 16. Jh. stammt der freundliche Familienbetrieb, der mit viel altem Holz eingerichtet wurde und urigen Charme versprüht. Netter Garten mit schöner Sicht.

In Mittelberg – Höhe 1 220 m

Walserstr. 89, ✉ 6993, ☎ (05517) 51 14 19

IFA-Hotel Alpenrose
Walserstr. 46 ✉ 6993 – ☎ (05517) 3 36 40 VISA
– alpenrose@ifahotels.com – Fax (05517) 3364888
geschl. 15. – 31. Nov.
100 Zim (inkl. ½ P.) – ☼ 65/85 € 100/130 € ❄ 85/105 €
130/200 €
Rest – (nur Abendessen für Hausgäste)
♦ Moderne und wohnliche Zimmer hält dieser familienfreundliche Alpengasthof mit im Sommer blumengeschmückter Fassade bereit. Fragen Sie nach den Familienzimmern für 4 Personen.

Leitner
Walserstr. 55 ✉ 6933 – ☎ (05517) 5 78 80 – info@hotel-leitner.de
– Fax (05517) 578839
geschl. 7. April – 12. Mai, 6. Nov. – 16. Dez.
35 Zim (inkl. ½ P.) – ☼ 75/100 € 108/172 € ❄ 95/126 €
157/240 € – 13 Suiten
Rest – (nur Abendessen für Hausgäste)
♦ Gemütliche, meist als Suiten angelegte Zimmer und ein schöner Spabereich auf 1000 qm machen diesen kleinen Familienbetrieb zu einem netten Ferienhotel. Behaglich ist das teilweise mit Zirbelholz ausgestattete Restaurant, hübsch die Terrasse.

Lärchenhof
Schützabühl 2 ✉ 6993 – ☎ (05517) 65 56
– naturhotel.laerchenhof@aon.at – Fax (05517) 6500
geschl. 7. April – 9. Mai, 27. Okt. – 18. Dez.
24 Zim (inkl. ½ P.) – ☼ 55/70 € 100/116 € ❄ 56/79 € 114/140 €
Rest – *(geschl. Dienstag)* (nur Abendessen für Hausgäste)
♦ Auf 1 250 m Höhe, inmitten der schönen Bergwelt, finden Sie ein Hotel, das nach baubiologischen Grundsätzen gestaltet wurde. Zimmer teils im Landhausstil.

Ingeborg garni
Im Hag 3 ✉ 6993 – ☎ (05517) 5 75 80 – ingeborg@vlbg.at
– Fax (05517) 575859
7 Zim – ☼ 45/55 € 64/88 € ❄ 45/68 € 72/116 €
♦ Eine familiengeführte kleine Pension in ruhiger Lage, die mit sehr wohnlichen und gediegenen Zimmern (z. T. mit Küchenzeile) und einem hübschen Saunabereich gefällt.

In Mittelberg-Höfle Süd: 2 km, Zufahrt über die Straße nach Baad:

IFA-Hotel Alpenhof Wildental

Höfle 8 ✉ 6993 – ✆ (05517) 6 54 40
– wildental@ifahotels.com – Fax (05517) 65448
geschl. 8. – 29. Nov.
57 Zim (inkl. ½ P.) – ☼ 74/99 € 144/186 € ❄ 80/118 €
118/246 €
Rest – Menü 20/23 €
◆ In dem schön und sehr ruhig gelegenen Hotel erwarten Sie neuzeitliche Zimmer – teilweise mit Aussicht – sowie Wellness mit verschiedenen Massage- und Kosmetikanwendungen.

KLÖCH – Steiermark – 730 T8 – 1 330 Ew – Höhe 290 m 11 L5

Wien 194 – Graz 79 – Leibnitz 43 – Fürstenfeld 40
Gemeindeamt, Klöch 110, ✉ 8493, ✆ (03475) 50 70, info-kloech@aon.at

Schöne Aussichten

Weinberge, Zim,
Hochwarth 10 (Nord: 1,5 km) ✉ 8493
– ✆ (03475) 75 45 – schoene.aussichten@aon.at – Fax (03475) 7545
geschl. 11. Nov. – 6. April
12 Zim – 65/78 € 90/116 € – ½ P 25 €
Rest – *(geschl. Montag-Dienstag, Sonntagabend, Mittwoch – Donnerstag nur Abendessen)* (Tischbestellung ratsam) Karte 28/38 €
◆ In den Weinbergen liegt das kleine, nette und familiär geleitete Haus, dessen Zimmer im regionstypischen Stil eingerichtet wurden. Wie der Name schon sagt, hat man von der Terrasse des Restaurants eine schöne Aussicht. Regionale Küche.

Frühwirth

Buschenschank
Deutsch Haseldorf 46 (Nord: 1,5 km) ✉ 8493 – ✆ (03475) 23 38
– weingut@fruehwirth.at – Fax (03475) 23384
geschl. Dez. – Feb. und Dienstag
Rest – *(ab 15 Uhr geöffnet)* Karte ca. 12 €
◆ Zu einem Weingut gehört die rustikal-gemütliche Buschenschänke, die zum Wein natürlich auch Jausen anbietet. Terrasse mit Blick auf die Weinberge.

Gießauf-Nell

Buschenschank
Hochwarth 63 (Nord: 1,5 km) ✉ 8493 – ✆ (03475) 72 65
– giessauf-nell@aon.at – Fax (03476) 7265
geschl. 8. Dez. – 8. Feb., Juli 1 Woche, Mittwoch
Rest – *(ab 14 Uhr geöffnet)* Karte ca. 12 €
◆ In dem ländlich-behaglichen Buschenschank bewirtet Sie die Inhaberfamilie mit selbst hergestellten Produkten. Hübsch: die rustikale Terrasse mit schöner Aussicht.

KLÖSTERLE AM ARLBERG – Vorarlberg – 730 C7 – 770 Ew – Höhe 1 069 m – Wintersport: 2 300 m 1 9 5 B6

Wien 558 – Bregenz 75 – Bludenz 24 – Sankt Anton 24
Arlbergstr. 59, ✉ 6754, ✆ (05582) 7 77, tourismus@kloesterle.com

In Stuben am Arlberg **Ost: 6 km in Richtung Lech am Arlberg – Höhe 1 409 m**

Hubertushof Klostertal, Rest, Rest,
Stuben 48 ✉ 6762 – ☎ (05582) 7 71
– info@hubertushof-arlberg.at – Fax (05582) 77153
geschl. 23. April – 30. Nov.
33 Zim (inkl. ½ P.) – 97/170 € 163/302 €
Rest – Karte 23/40 €
◆ Schön liegt das Hotel oberhalb des Dorfes, reizvoll ist die Aussicht von hier. Die Zimmer sind zeitgemäß möbliert und teilweise mit Parkettboden ausgestattet. Das Restaurant: teils modern, teils traditionell-rustikal.

Post (mit Gästehaus) Rest, VISA
Im Dorf 17 ✉ 6762 – ☎ (05582) 7 61 – info@hotelpost.eu
– Fax (05582) 76136
geschl. 21. April – 14. Juni, 28. Sept. – 1. Dez.
54 Zim (inkl. ½ P.) – 53/68 € 106/166 € 80/132 € 146/284 €
Rest – Karte 25/39 €
◆ Gleich am Ortseingang steht der traditionsreiche Gasthof mit rosa Fassade und Holzfensterläden. Die Zimmer sind individuell und dennoch alle im alpenländischen Stil gehalten. Gemütlich ist die uralte A-la-carte-Stube.

Sporthotel Arlberg Zim, VISA
Arlbergstr. 50 ✉ 6762 – ☎ (05582) 5 21 – hotel@arlberg-stuben.at
– Fax (05582) 524
geschl. Nov. 3 Wochen
18 Zim – 48/55 € 76/90 € (inkl. ½ P.) 67/155 € 120/260 €
Rest – Karte 17/28 €
◆ Ein sehr gepflegter Familienbetrieb an der Passstraße. Besonders schön: die großen Deluxe-Zimmer und der moderne Saunabereich. Unterschiedliche behagliche Restaurantstuben mit netter Terrasse.

Gasthof Mondschein Zim, Rest, VISA
Hannes-Schneider-Promenade 9 ✉ 6762
– ☎ (05582) 5 11 – hotel@mondschein.com – Fax (05582) 736
geschl. 13. April – 7. Dez.
33 Zim (inkl. ½ P.) – 76/128 € 132/270 €
Rest – *(geschl. 13. April – 14. Dez. und Montag, nur Abendessen)* Karte 23/38 €
◆ Im Zentrum liegt dieser familiengeführte Alpengasthof mit Grundmauern aus dem Jahre 1739. Die Zimmer sind meist in ländlichem Stil eingerichtet. Kachelofen und blanke alte Holztische geben den Gaststuben ihren ganz rustikalen Charakter.

KLOSTERNEUBURG – Niederösterreich – 730 U4 – 24 800 Ew – Höhe 192 m – Wintersport: 4 L2

Wien 14 – St. Pölten 67 – Baden 47 – Krems 63
Niedermarkt 4, ✉ 3400, ☎ (02243) 3 20 38, tourismus@klosterneuburg.net
Stift (Stiftskirche★, Barocktrakt★, Stiftsmuseum★) – Sammlung Essl★

Schrannenhof garni

Niedermarkt 17 ✉ 3400 – ✆ (02243) 3 20 72 – info@schrannenhof.at – Fax (02243) 3207213

19 Zim – 59/85 € 94/130 €

◆ Das Bürgerhaus a. d. 15. Jh. beherbergt hübsche, in hellen Farben gehaltene und individuell geschnittene Zimmer mit Naturholzmöbeln im ländlichen Stil, z. T. mit Gewölbedecke.

KÖFLACH – Steiermark – 730 R7 – 10 680 Ew – Höhe 420 m – Wintersport: 1 700 m 2

10 **J5**

Wien 226 – Graz 40 – Knittelfeld 40 – Wolfsberg 49

An der Quelle 3, ✉ 8580, ✆ (03144) 72 77 70, office@lipizzanerheimat.com

Maria Lankowitz, Puchbacherstr. 109 ✆ (03144) 69 70

Gestüt Piber★ Nord-Ost: 3 km – Bärnbach: Pfarrkirche St. Barbara★ Ost: 8 km

Thermenhotel Nova Köflach (Thermal) Zim, Rest,

An der Quelle 1

✉ 8580 – ✆ (03144) 70 10 00 – info@novakoeflach.at – Fax (03144) 7010099

131 Zim (inkl. ½ P.) – 109/116 € 178/192 €

Rest – (nur Abendessen für Hausgäste)

◆ Ein modernes Haus, zu dessen Besonderheiten ein Thermenexpress und fernöstliche Behandlungen zählen, die teilweise von einem Shaolin-Mönch durchgeführt werden.

Außerhalb Nord-West: 9,5 km über B 77 Richtung Judenburg, in Krenhof geradeaus Richtung Graden, 0,5 km nach Krenhof links ab:

Bergwirt Bergwelt, Rest,

Graden 127 ✉ 8593 Graden – ✆ (03144) 23 80 – office@bergwirt.com – Fax (03144) 2380325

50 Zim – 69/79 € 114/134 € – ½ P 12 €

Rest – Karte 21/37 €

◆ Der Familienbetrieb befindet sich in reizvoller Lage am Berghang in 1000 m Höhe. Man verfügt über neuzeitliche, funktionelle Zimmer, nach Süden mit besonders schöner Sicht.

KÖNIGSLEITEN – Salzburg – siehe Wald im Pinzgau

KÖNIGSTETTEN – Niederösterreich – 730 U4 – 1 890 Ew – Höhe 160 m

3 **K2**

Wien 25 – St. Pölten 47 – Baden 49 – Tulln 10

Zum weißen Adler

Wiener Str. 40 ✉ 3433 – ✆ (02273) 22 46 – weisseradler@aon.at – Fax (02273) 2246

geschl. 4. – 16. Feb., Juli – Aug. 2 Wochen und Montag – Dienstag

Rest – *(Mittwoch – Donnerstag nur Abendessen)* Menü 28 € – Karte 23/40 €

◆ In Stube und Restaurant erwarten Sie gemütlich-ländliches Ambiente, freundlicher familiärer Service und schmackhafte Regionalküche. Gastgarten unter alten Kastanien.

KÖSSEN – Tirol – 730 J5 – 3 940 Ew – Höhe 591 m – Wintersport: 1 700 m

1 10 7 **E4**

Wien 363 – Innsbruck 99 – Wörgl 42 – Kitzbühel 30
Kössen, Dorf 15, 6345, (0501) 1 00, info@kaiserwinkl.com
Kaiserwinkel Kössen, Mühlau 1 (05375) 21 22
Reit im Winkl-Kössen, (0049-8640) 79 82 50

Alpina

(geheizt) VISA

Ausserkapelle 2, (B 172) 6345 – (05375) 21 46 – gruber@hotel-alpina.at – Fax (05375) 6853
geschl. 6. – 30. April, 3. Nov. – 18. Dez.
85 Zim (inkl. ½ P.) – 50/90 € 114/180 € 59/105 € 120/220 €
Rest – Karte 16/36 €

♦ Ein familiär geleitetes Alpenhotel mit wohnlichen Gästezimmern. Besonders komfortabel: der Neubau mit schönen Zimmern und großzügigem Spa. Gut ausgestatteter Fitnessbereich. Erlebnisrestaurant Alt Tyrol mit alpinem Charakter.

Waidachhof (mit Gästehaus)

Waidach 22, (B 172) 6345 – (05375) 64 15 – waidachhof@aon.at – Fax (05375) 64159
geschl. 30. März – 30. April, 28. Okt. – 18. Dez.
45 Zim (inkl. ½ P.) – 45/50 € 82/92 € 56/58 € 90/108 €
Rest – *(geschl. Mittwoch)* Karte 13/28 €

♦ Die Zimmer und geräumigen Juniorsuiten dieses regionstypischen Familienbetriebs sind mit hellem Holzmobiliar zeitgemäß eingerichtet und verfügen über Balkon oder Loggia. Restaurant in bürgerlichem Stil.

Sonnenhof

Dorf 16 6345 – (05375) 2 92 00 – Fax (05375) 2920051
geschl. 1. Nov. – 15. Dez. und Montag
Rest – Menü 15 € – Karte 19/28 €

♦ Das im Zentrum hinter der Kirche gelegene Restaurant teilt sich in gemütlichen Stuben, die mit Holztäfelung oder Backsteingewölbe hübsch gestaltet sind.

An der Straße nach Schwendt Süd-Ost: 2 km, nach 1,5 km links:

Lucknerhof

Kaisergebirge,

Lucknerstr. 20 6345 Schwendt – (05375) 63 14 – lucknerhof@hotmail.com – Fax (05375) 2747
geschl. 14. – 25. April, Juni 2 Wochen und im Sommer Dienstag
Rest – Karte 18/30 €

♦ Direkt an einer Loipe liegt der einfache Gasthof mit freundlichem Service und regionaler Küche. Die Terrasse bietet bei klarem Wetter eine schöne Sicht auf das Kaisergebirge.

Auf dem Moserberg Ost: 6 km Richtung Reit im Winkl, dann links:

Peternhof

Reit im Winkl, Kaisergebirge und Unterberg, (geheizt) Rest,

Moserbergweg 60 6345 Kössen – (05375) 62 85 – info@peternhof.com – Fax (05375) 6944
geschl. 7. – 25. April, 10. Nov. – 19. Dez.

156 Zim (inkl. ½ P.) – ☼ 86/93 € 154/188 € ❄ 88/118 € 160/242 € – 42 Suiten
Rest – Karte 18/34 €
◆ Die komfortable Hotelanlage liegt einsam auf einer Anhöhe nahe dem Wald. Besonders elegant und stilvoll sind die Suiten im Kaiserschlössl und im Romantikschlössl. Das Restaurant teilt sich in alpenländische Stuben und einen gediegenen Speisesaal.

KÖSTENDORF – Salzburg – 730 L5 – 2 460 Ew – Höhe 560 m 1 G3

Wien 273 – Salzburg 28 – Burghausen 47 – Vöcklabruck 40

XX **Fritzenwallner**
Dorfplatz 6 ✉ 5203 – ✆ (06216) 53 02 – restaurant@fritzenwallner.at – Fax (06216) 53024
geschl. Montag – Dienstag
Rest – *(Mittwoch – Samstag nur Abendessen)* (Tischbestellung ratsam)
Menü 38/50 € – Karte 18/37 €
◆ Die schmackhafte, mediterran angehauchte Küche, zubereitet aus guten Produkten, zeichnet diesen familär geleiteten Gasthof aus.

KÖTSCHACH-MAUTHEN – Kärnten – 730 L8 – 3 620 Ew – Höhe 710 m – Wintersport: 1 300 m 4 8 G6

Wien 406 – Klagenfurt 111 – Lienz 34 – Spittal a.d. Drau 65
(Rathaus in Kötschach) Nr. 390, ✉ 9640, ✆ (04715) 85 16, info@koemau.com

Veranstaltungen
27.09. – 28.09.: Käsefestival

Pfarrkirche Unsere Liebe Frau (Gewölbe★)
Lesachtal★

Im Ortsteil Mauthen

XX **Sissy Sonnleitner-Landhaus Kellerwand** mit Zim
Mauthen 24 ✉ 9640 – ✆ (04715) 2 69 – sonnl@utanet.at – Fax (04715) 26916
geschl. Mitte März – Anfang April, Ende Nov. – Mitte Dez.
11 Zim – 68/90 € 116/160 € – ½ P 29 € – 6 Suiten
Rest – *(geschl. Montag – Dienstag)* Menü 30/61 € – Karte 30/49 €
Spez. Tortellini vom Gailtaler Almkäse mit Lauch und Mandeln in Chiantisaft. Gebratene Ente mit Löwenzahnhonigsaft und Mohngnocchi. Kleine Milchdesserts.
◆ Sehr angenehm ist die Atmosphäre im Haus der Familie Sonnleitner. Geboten wird mediterran beeinflusste regionale Küche – im Sommer speist man mit Blick in den Garten. Zum Übernachten stehen wohnliche Gästezimmer im Landhausstil bereit.

KORNEUBURG – Niederösterreich – 730 V3 – 11 040 Ew – Höhe 158 m 4 L2

Wien 18 – Sankt Pölten 92 – Floridsdorf 14 – Döbling 15

XX **Tuttendörfl**
Tuttendörfl 6 (Süd: 3 km in Richtung Langenzersdorf, dann rechts) ✉ 2100 – ✆ (02262) 72 48 50 – donaurestaurant@aon.at – Fax (02262) 61535
geschl. 23. Dez. – 15. Jan. und Sonntag – Montag

Rest – Karte 18/37 €

♦ Hier genießt man den schönen Blick auf die Donau. Zur Wahl stehen Schankstube, Restaurant und Wintergarten sowie zwei sehr hübsche Terrassen, eine davon unter Kastanienbäumen.

KOTTINGBRUNN – Niederösterreich – 730 U5 – 6 590 Ew – Höhe 251 m 4 L3

Wien 39 – St. Pölten 69 – Baden 23 – Wiener Neustadt 7

Tennis & Golf Hotel Höllrigl (mit Gästehäusern)

Zim,

Hauptstr. 29

2542 – (02252) 7 76 16 – hotel@hoellrigl.at – Fax (02252) 7761660

30 Zim – 63/93 € 98/118 € – ½ P 18 €

Rest – (nur für Hausgäste)

♦ Neben neuzeitlichen Zimmern bietet das Hotel auf seinem 5 ha großen Grundstück auch einen Freizeitbereich mit Beach-Volleyball, Tennisplätzen, Golf-Übungsanlage und Badeteich.

KRAMSACH – Tirol – 730 H6 – 4 410 Ew – Höhe 520 m – Wintersport: 1 800 m 8 7 E5

Wien 469 – Innsbruck 45 – Kitzbühel 54 – Schwaz 18

Zentrum 1, 6233, (05336) 60 06 15, kramsach@alpbachtal-seenland.at

Sporthotel Sonnenuhr

(geheizt)

Rest, Zim,

Ebnat 45 (Nord: 1,5 km, Richtung Brandenberg) 6233 – (05337) 6 26 04 – info@sporthotel-sonnenuhr.at – Fax (05337) 6260444

geschl. Nov.

52 Zim (inkl. ½ P.) – 62/80 € 108/152 €

Rest – Karte 15/34 €

♦ Die Zimmer dieses gewachsenen, gut geführten Familienbetriebs sind unterschiedlich eingerichtet, teils zeitlos, teils besonders hübsch im neuzeitlichen Landhausstil. Kleines Restaurant in ländlich-elegantem Stil und angenehm heller Wintergarten.

Kramsacher Hof

Zim, Rest,

Claudiaplatz 9 6233 – (05337) 6 39 87 – info@kramsach.com – Fax (05337) 65740

geschl. 20. – 26. Dez.

50 Zim – 67 € 114 €

Rest – *(geschl. Samstagmittag, Sonntagmittag)* Karte 17/45 €

♦ Dieses familiengeführte Hotel in der Ortsmitte verfügt über funktionell ausgestattete Zimmer, größenteils in modernem Stil möbliert. Sehr nett ist der Saunabereich. Neuzeitlich-ländlich gestaltetes Restaurant mit Stubencharakter.

KREMS AN DER DONAU – Niederösterreich – 730 S3 – 23 720 Ew – Höhe 221 m 3 J2

Wien 78 – St. Pölten 28 – Melk 37 – Zwettl 50

Undstr. 6, 3500, (02732) 8 26 76, pegasus.krems@pegasus.at

Lengenfeld, Am Golfplatz 1 (02719) 87 10

Piaristenkirche★ – Weinstadtmuseum★ BZ

Stift Göttweig★ Süd: 6 km – Dürnstein★ West: 9 km – Schloss Grafenegg★ Ost: 12 km

KREMS

Am Goldberg . . . . **AY** 4
Bertschingerstr. . . . . **BY** 2
Dominikanerpl. . . . . **BZ** 5
Dreifaltigkeitspl. . . . . **BZ** 6
Gartenaugasse . . . . **BZ** 9
Gaswerkgasse . . . . **AY** 10
Heinemannstr. . . . . **BY, BZ** 12
Körnermarkt . . . . **BZ** 13
Kreuzbergstr. . . . . **AY** 14
Mosepl. . . . . **BZ** 16
Obere Landstr. . . . . **BZ** 18
Pfarrpl. . . . . **BZ** 20
Schillerstr. . . . . **BY** 30
Untere Landstr. . . . . **BZ** 26
Wachtertorgasse . . . . **BY** 28
Minoritenpl. . . . . **AZ** 15
Neutorgasse . . . . **AZ** 17
Philosophensteig . . . . **AY** 21
Rathauspl. . . . . **AZ** 2
Schürepl. . . . . **AZ** 2

STEIN

Dr-Dorrek-Str. . . . . **AY** 3

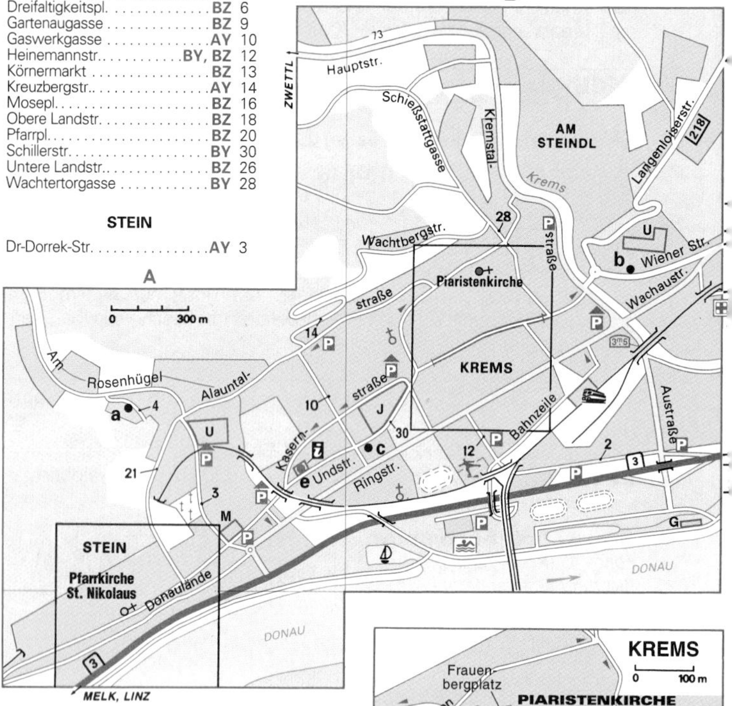

Luxuriös oder eher schlicht?
Die Symbole und kennzeichnen den Komfort.

Steigenberger Avance

Rest,

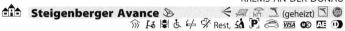

Am Goldberg 2 ✉ 3500 – ✆ (02732) 71 01 00 – krems@steigenberger.at – Fax (02732) 7101050 AY **a**

143 Zim – 111/131 € 182/202 € – 10 Suiten

Rest – Karte 27/51 €

◆ Das oberhalb der Weinberge liegende Hotel bietet neben schönen Zimmern und Suiten einen modern gestalteten Wellnesbereich an. Wintergartenlounge für Raucher. Teil des Restaurants sind die netten Wachauer Weinstuben.

Klinglhuber

Wiener Str. 2 ✉ 3500 – ✆ (02732) 8 69 60 – hotel@klinglhuber.com – Fax (02732) 8214350

geschl. 27. Dez. – 7. Jan. BY **b**

46 Zim – 67/78 € 96/104 € 56/65 € 78/90 € – ½ P 15 €

Rest – *(geschl. Sonntag)* Karte 12/28 €

◆ Den Gasthof am Kremsfluss hat man durch einen modernen Hotelbau gegenüber erweitert. Hier sind die Zimmer besonders komfortabel und neuzeitlich. Das Restaurant ist in mehrere gemütliche Gaststuben unterteilt.

Unter den Linden garni

Schillerstr. 5 ✉ 3500 – ✆ (02732) 8 21 15 – hotel@udl.at – Fax (02732) 8211520

geschl. Jan. – 17. Feb. BY **c**

39 Zim – 49/78 € 73/97 €

◆ Herzstück dieses seit fünf Generationen von der Inhaberfamilie geleiteten Hotels ist ein Altbau von 1867. Wohnlich sind die recht individuellen, freundlich gestalteten Zimmer.

Mörwald Kloster UND

Undstr. 6 ✉ 3500 – ✆ (02732) 7 04 93 – und@moerwald.at – Fax (02732) 7049360

geschl. Sonntag – Montag AY **e**

Rest – Menü 75/95 € – Karte 46/71 €

Spez. Tatar vom Limousin in gelierter Consommé mit roten Rüben. Medaillon vom St. Pierre mit Artischockenragout. Taube und Landhendl im Brotteig.

◆ Das Restaurant befindet sich in einem a. d. 17. Jh. stammendem Kloster mit rustikal-modernen Räumen. Die Küche ist kreativ französisch. Angenehm sitzt man auch im Innenhof.

Zum Kaiser von Österreich

Körnermarkt 9 ✉ 3500 – ✆ (02732) 8 60 01 – kaiser.von.oesterreich@aon.at – Fax (02732) 860014

geschl. 1. – 5. Jan., 18. Juli – 12. Aug. und Sonntag – Montag BZ **n**

Rest – Menü 24/48 € – Karte 25/44 €

◆ Im Herzen der Altstadt befindet sich das gemütliche Restaurant, das regionale und saisonale Küche anbietet, die mit Sorgfalt zubereitet wird.

Jell

Hoher Markt 8 ✉ 3500 – ✆ (02732) 8 23 45 – amon-jell@utanet.at – Fax (02732) 823454
geschl. Anfang Feb. 3 Wochen, Anfang Juli 2 Wochen und Samstagabend, Sonntagabend – Montag BZ **r**
Rest – (Tischbestellung ratsam) Karte 15/35 €
◆ Eine lebendige Atmosphäre herrscht in dem mit viel Holz und Kachelofen urig-rustikal gestalteten Restaurant in der Altstadt. Man bietet Regionalküche mit kreativen Einflüssen.

KREMSMÜNSTER – Oberösterreich – 730 O4 – 6 440 Ew – Höhe 345 m 2 H3

Wien 202 – Linz 41 – Wels 19 – Steyr 29
Rathausplatz 1, ✉ 4550, ✆ (07583) 72 12, tourismus@kremsmuenster.at
Stift Kremsmünster★ (Tassilokelch★★★)

Schlair garni (mit Gästehaus)

Franz-Hönig-Str. 16 ✉ 4550 – ✆ (07583) 52 58 – schlair@hotelschlair.at – Fax (07583) 525852
geschl. 20. Dez. – 10. Jan.
35 Zim – 53/63 € 80/88 € – ½ P 16 €
◆ Ein engagiert geführtes Hotel mit 700 Jahre altem Gästehaus in der Altstadt. Unterschiedlich gestaltete, funktionelle Zimmer von rustikal bis neuzeitlich. Eigenes Kaffeehaus.

KREUZBERG – Kärnten – siehe Weissensee

KRIMML – Salzburg – 730 I7 – 890 Ew – Höhe 1 076 m – Wintersport: 2 040 m 5 61 7 E5

Wien 432 – Salzburg 134 – Kitzbühel 55 – Zell am Ziller 54
OK 37, ✉ 5743, ✆ (06564) 7 23 90, info@krimml.at
Krimmler Wasserfälle★★★

Krimmlerfälle (geheizt)

Wasserfallstr. 42 ✉ 5743 – ✆ (06564) 72 03 – info@krimmlerfaelle.at – Fax (06564) 7473
geschl. 15. Okt. – 20. Dez., 24. März – 15. Mai
45 Zim (inkl. ½ P.) – ☼ 68/78 € 108/154 € ❄ 78/120 € 128/230 €
Rest – Karte 15/25 €
◆ Dieser gepflegte Familienbetrieb ist ein regionstypisches Haus in der Ortsmitte, das über behagliche, solide eingerichtete Zimmer und Appartements verfügt. Teil des Restaurants ist eine gemütliche, freundlich gestaltete Gaststube.

KRONSTORF – Oberösterreich – 730 P4 – 3 010 Ew – Höhe 276 m 2 I3

Wien 163 – Linz 31 – Wels 46 – Steyr 14
Metzenhof, Dörfling 2 ✆ (07225) 73 89 10

Rahofer mit Zim

Hauptstr. 56 ✉ 4484 – ✆ (07225) 83 03 – eva-rahofer@yahoo.de – Fax (07225) 830315

geschl. 1. – 7. Jan., 16. – 31. Aug. und Sonntagabend – Montag

5 Zim – 55/65 € 80/95 €

Rest – Karte 22/38 €

◆ Dieser familiengeführte Gasthof ist ein in Stuben unterteiltes Restaurant in bürgerlichem Stil, teils mit Gewölbedecke, teils mit Theke. Netter Gastgarten im Innenhof.

KRUMBACH – Vorarlberg – 730 B6 – 940 Ew – Höhe 730 m 5 A5

Wien 713 – Bregenz 26 – Dornbirn 24 – Kempten 51

Gemeindeamt, Dorf 2, ✉ 6942, ✆ (05513) 81 57, tourismus@krumbach.at

Rossbad

Rain 81 (West: 4 km Richtung Dornbirn, nach 2 km rechts)

✉ 6942 – ✆ (05513) 51 10 – info@rossbad.com – Fax (05513) 511031

geschl. 13. – 27. April, 9. Nov. – 31. Dez.

38 Zim (inkl. ½ P.) – 63/82 € 110/148 €

Rest – (nur für Hausgäste)

◆ Die schöne, einsame Lage, helle, wohnlich-rustikale Zimmer mit gutem Platzangebot und ein geräumiger Freizeitbereich machen dieses im alpenländischen Stil erbaute Hotel aus.

's Schulhus

Glatzegg 58 (West: 2 km Richtung Dornbirn) ✉ 6942 – ✆ (05513) 83 89 – schulhus@aon.at – Fax (05513) 8715

geschl. Montag – Dienstag

Rest – Karte 30/42 €

◆ Seit 1994 dient die frühere Dorfschule als Restaurant, in dem man regionale Produkte sorgfältig und schmackhaft verarbeitet. Bilder einer Behindertenwerkstatt zieren den Raum.

Gasthof Adler mit Zim

Dorf 5 ✉ 6942 – ✆ (05513) 81 56 – mail@adler-krumbach.at – Fax (05513) 815614

geschl. März

8 Zim – 42 € 72 € – ½ P 18 €

Rest – *(geschl. Mittwoch, Montag – Freitag nur Abendessen)* Menü 40 € – Karte 21/42 €

◆ Seit mehreren Generationen befindet sich der schmucke Gasthof a. d. J. 1852 in Familienbesitz. Ein neuzeitlicher, klarer Stil und der warme Holzton bestimmen das Ambiente. Hübsch sind die hellen, modernen Gästezimmer mit Naturholzböden.

KRUMPENDORF – Kärnten – 730 O9 – 2 850 Ew – Höhe 446 m 9 I6

Wien 304 – Klagenfurt 9 – Villach 35 – St. Veit an der Glan 25

Hauptstr. 145, ✉ 9201, ✆ (04229) 23 43 31, krumpendorf@ktn.gde.at

Strandhotel Habich
Walterskirchenweg 10 ✉ 9201 – ☎ (04229) 26 07 – strandhotel.habich@happynet.at – Fax (04229) 260776
geschl. Okt. – April
38 Zim (inkl. ½ P.) – 🚹49/74 € 🚹🚹112/148 € – **Rest** – (nur für Hausgäste)
◆ Schön liegt das familiengeführte Haus mit nettem Garten und eigenem Strand direkt am See. Recht unterschiedlich geschnittene Zimmer, meist in rustikaler Eiche eingerichtet.

Krumpendorferhof
Hauptstr. 164 ✉ 9201 – ☎ (04229) 23 01 – office@krumpendorferhof.at – Fax (04229) 230123 – geschl. Feb. 3 Wochen
19 Zim – 🚹46/62 € 🚹🚹76/104 € – ½ P 12 €
Rest – *(geschl. Dienstag, Juli – Aug. Dienstagmittag und Mittwochmittag)*
Karte 12/42 €
◆ Der über 600 Jahre alte Gasthof ist ein kleines, von der Familie Hammerschlag freundlich geleitetes Hotel mit wohnlichen Zimmern im Landhausstil. In einem der Restauranträume schaffen Krumpendorfer Werkzeuge Museumsatmosphäre.

Kärnten Rest,
Wieningerallee 12 A ✉ 9201 – ☎ (04229) 39 19 – office@hotelkaernten.at – Fax (04229) 391933
40 Zim – 🚹45/51 € 🚹🚹72/82 € – ½ P 12 €
Rest – (nur Abendessen für Hausgäste)
◆ Zu den Annehmlichkeiten dieses Familienbetriebs nahe dem Seebad zählen neuzeitlich mit hellen Naturholzmöbeln eingerichtete Gästezimmer und ein netter Garten.

KUCHL – Salzburg – 730 L6 – 6 440 Ew – Höhe 470 m – Wintersport:

Wien 321 – Salzburg 25 – Hallein 8 – Bischofshofen 29 8 G4
Markt Nr. 38, ✉ 5431, ☎ (06244) 62 27, info.kuchl@salzburg.co.at

Wagnermigl garni
Markt 61 ✉ 5431 – ☎ (06244) 51 39 – wagnermigl@kuchl.com – Fax (06244) 51394 – geschl. Nov. – Mitte Mai
23 Zim – 🚹40/46 € 🚹🚹68/80 €
◆ Das von der Inhaberfamilie sehr gut geführte Haus überzeugt durch freundliche Gästebetreuung und geschmackvoll gestaltete Zimmer.

KÜHTAI – Tirol – 730 F7 – 2 380 Ew – Höhe 2 020 m – Wintersport: 2 520 m 12 6 C5

Wien 481 – Innsbruck 38 – Imst 34 – Seefeld in Tirol 40
Kühtai 42, ✉ 6183, ☎ (05239) 52 22, info@schneegarantie.at

Sporthotel Bergpanorama,
Nr. 9 ✉ 6183 – ☎ (05239) 52 17 – info@sporthotel-kuethai.com – Fax (05239) 521780
geschl. Mitte April – Ende Juni, Mitte Sept. – Anfang Dez.
53 Zim (inkl. ½ P.) – ☼ 🚹59 € 🚹🚹110/116 € ❄ 🚹105/160 € 🚹🚹190/340 € – 15 Suiten – **Rest** – (nur für Hausgäste)
◆ Das Alpenhotel mit Türmchen und Balkonfassade überzeugt mit schöner Lage und neuzeitlichen, wohnlich eingerichteten, meist recht geräumigen Zimmern.

Konradin ← Rest, Rest, P
Nr. 39 6183 – (05239) 52 20 VISA MC
– hotel@konradin.at – Fax (05239) 5293
geschl. Mai – Juni, Sept. – Dez.
63 Zim (inkl. ½ P.) – 65 € 120 € 100/145 € 170/270 €
– 13 Suiten
Rest – Karte 27/49 €
♦ Das regionstypische Hotel unter familiärer Leitung verfügt über solide im ländlichen Stil möblierte Gästezimmer, überwiegend mit Balkon. Kleine Indoor-Golfanlage. Restaurant mit bürgerlich-rustikalem Ambiente.

Astoria ← Bergpanorama, Rest, P
Nr. 33 6183 – (05239) 52 15 VISA MC AE
– astoria.kuehtai@tirol.com – Fax (05239) 521580
geschl. 5. April – 14. Juni, 8. Sept. – 13. Dez.
41 Zim (inkl. ½ P.) – 64 € 120 € 95/150 € 190/300 €
Rest – (nur für Hausgäste, im Sommer garni)
♦ Ein rustikaler Hallenbereich mit Kamin und Bar empfängt Sie in dem direkt an der Skipiste gelegenen Hotel. Gepflegte, teils hell, teils dunkel eingerichtete Zimmer. Gediegenes, holzvertäfeltes Restaurant und Terrasse mit toller Aussicht.

Gute Küche zu günstigem Preis? Folgen Sie dem „Bib Gourmand".
– Das freundliche MICHELIN-Männchen heißt „Bib"
und steht für ein besonders gutes Preis-Leistungs-Verhältnis!

KUFSTEIN – Tirol – 730 I6 – 15 360 Ew – Höhe 500 m – Wintersport: 1 900 m 9 85

7 E4

Wien 385 – Innsbruck 74 – Kitzbühel 35 – Wörgl 15
Unterer Stadtplatz 8, 6330, (05372) 6 22 07, info@kufstein.com
Festung (Lage★, Kaiserturm★)
Ursprungpass-Straße★ (von Kufstein nach Bayrischzell)

Alpenrose Zim, P VISA MC AE D
Weißachstr. 47 6330 – (05372) 6 21 22 – alpenrose.telser@kufnet.at
– Fax (05372) 621227
geschl. 16. – 30. März
22 Zim – 75/90 € 119/134 €
Rest – Menü 18 € – Karte 22/42 €
♦ Ein engagiert und freundlich geführter Alpengasthof, der von ländlicher Eleganz geprägt ist. Die komfortablen Zimmer sind im Landhausstil eingerichtet. Gediegenes Restaurant mit regionstypischer Holztäfelung.

Andreas Hofer Zim, Rest,
Georg-Pirmoser-Str. 8 6330 VISA MC AE D
– (05372) 69 80 – info@andreas-hofer.com – Fax (05372) 698090
95 Zim – 55/75 € 130/160 € – ½ P 15 €
Rest – *(geschl. Sonntag)* Karte 25/33 €
♦ Direkt im Zentrum liegt das mit funktionellen, teils recht großzügigen Gästezimmern ausgestattete Hotel. Auch Familienzimmer sind vorhanden. Bürgerliches Restaurant mit Kamin.

Auracher Löchl Zim, Zim,

Römerhofgasse 2 ✉ 6330 – ✆ (05372) 6 21 38 – hotel-weinhaus@auracher-loechl.at – Fax (05372) 6213851

35 Zim ☕ – 🚹56/85 € 🚹🚹112/126 € – ½ P 18 €

Rest – Karte 15/38 €

◆ Eine Art Brücke über die Altstadtgasse verbindet das Wirtshaus von 1409 mit dem Hotel am Innufer. Die wohnlichen Zimmer im Tiroler Stil bieten teils Altstadt- oder Flussblick. Urige Restaurantstuben im historischen Gasthaus – hier entstand das Kufsteiner Lied.

Gasthof Felsenkeller

Kienbergstr. 35 ✉ 6330 – ✆ (05372) 6 27 84 – kufstein@felsenkeller.at – Fax (05372) 6278444

geschl. 2. Nov. – 12. Dez.

26 Zim ☕ – 🚹46/65 € 🚹🚹72/88 € – ½ P 15 €

Rest – *(geschl. Dienstag)* Karte 14/28 €

◆ Am Fuße des Kaisergebirges liegt dieser direkt an den Felsen gebaute Gasthof im Tiroler Stil. Sie wohnen in rustikalen Zimmern mit Balkon und Sitzecke. Ganz in Holz gehaltenes A-la-carte-Restaurant. Forellen aus eigener Zucht.

Zum Bären

Salurner Str. 36 ✉ 6330 – ✆ (05372) 6 22 29 – kufstein@hotelbaeren.at – Fax (05372) 636894

33 Zim ☕ – 🚹49/56 € 🚹🚹78/95 €

Rest – *(geschl. Sonn- und Feiertage, nur Abendessen)* Karte 18/34 €

◆ Der gewachsene alpenländische Gasthof am Ortsrand erwartet seine Gäste mit soliden, unterschiedlich eingerichteten, teils recht geräumigen Zimmern. Fahrradverleih. Teil des Restaurants ist eine gemütliche kleine Stube mit Kachelofen.

Goldener Löwe

Oberer Stadtplatz 14 ✉ 6330 – ✆ (05372) 6 21 81 – goldener.loewe@kufnet.at – Fax (05372) 621818

38 Zim ☕ – 🚹49 € 🚹🚹85 €

Rest – Karte 17/34 €

◆ Hinter der hellgelben Fassade des Gasthofs im Zentrum hält man für die Gäste saubere und gepflegte Zimmer bereit, die alle mit soliden, dunklen Möbeln ausgestattet sind. Bürgerliche Gaststube mit Holztäfelung.

KUKMIRN – Burgenland – 730 U7 – 2 040 Ew – Höhe 254 m 11 L5

Wien 153 – Eisenstadt 131 – Fürstenfeld 16 – Graz 75

Brennerei und Wellnesshotel Lagler Zim, Rest,

Kukmirn 137 ✉ 7543 – ✆ (03328) 3 20 03 – info@lagler.cc – Fax (03328) 3200340

27 Zim ☕ – 🚹64/81 € 🚹🚹104/138 € – ½ P 19 € – 4 Suiten

Rest – Karte 16/35 €

◆ Etwas außerhalb des Ortes an einem Badesee liegt das Wellnesshotel mit angeschlossener Brennerei. Gepflegt, zeitgemäß und teils mit Parkett eingerichtet sind die Zimmer. Restaurant mit nettem rustikalem Ambiente.

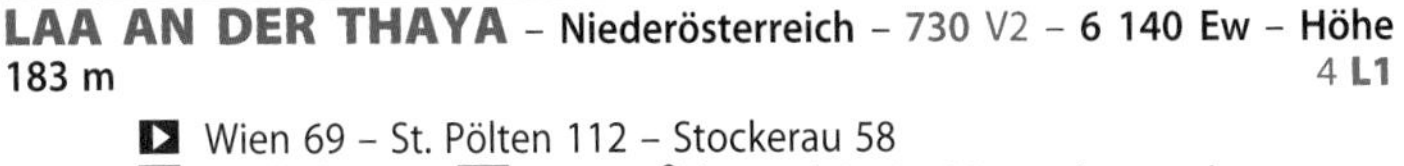

LAA AN DER THAYA – Niederösterreich – 730 V2 – 6 140 Ew – Höhe 183 m 4 L1

Wien 69 – St. Pölten 112 – Stockerau 58
Stadtplatz 43, 2136, (02522) 25 01 29, tourismus@laa.at

Therme Laa Hotel & Spa

(freier Zugang zur Therme Laa) Zim,
Thermenplatz 1 2136 – (02522) 8 47 00 – sinne@therme-laa.at – Fax (02522) 84700755
122 Zim – 137/142 € 224/234 € 147/152 € 264/274 € – ½ P 24 € – 6 Suiten
Rest – Karte 14/27 €
◆ Ein Glasgang verbindet dieses modern designte Hotel direkt mit der Therme. In den Zimmern hat man klare Linien mit kräftigen Farben und warmem Holz kombiniert. Ganz neuzeitliches, fast schon puristisch wirkendes Restaurant.

Zum Brüdertor

Raiffeisenplatz 5 2136 – (02522) 82 86 – office@bruedertor.at – Fax (02522) 8156
31 Zim – 49/51 € 92 € – ½ P 14 €
Rest – Karte 12/26 €
Rest *Pueblo de la Luna* – *(nur Abendessen)* Karte 11/38 €
◆ Mitten im Zentrum liegt das gepflegte familiengeführte Hotel mit der gelb-weißen Fassade. Die Zimmer sind einheitlich mit solidem, zeitgemäßem Mobiliar eingerichtet. Hotelrestaurant mit Café-Charakter. Im Pueblo: Gerichte von mexikanisch bis indonesisch.

Gute Küche zu günstigem Preis? Folgen Sie dem „Bib Gourmand"

LAABEN – Niederösterreich – 730 T4 – 1 160 Ew – Höhe 380 m 3 K3

Wien 46 – St. Pölten 32 – Baden 46
Wienerwald Brand-Laaben, Forsthof 211 (0664) 4 31 54 96

Laabnerhof

(geheizt) Zim,
Laaben 32 3053 – (02774) 83 55 – laabnerhof@aon.at – Fax (02774) 835540
26 Zim – 62/66 € 94/102 € – ½ P 25 €
Rest – *(geschl. Sonntagabend)* Menü 35/69 € – Karte 24/44 €
◆ Ein völlig modernisierter Gasthof unter familiärer Leitung, der über technisch gut ausgestattete und mit hellen Naturholzmöbeln und Parkett eingerichtete Zimmer verfügt. Freundliches, neuzeitliches Restaurant mit begehbarem Weinkeller.

Zur Post

Laaben 33 3053 – (02774) 83 63 – info@hotelpost-laaben.at – Fax (02774) 8363333
geschl. 9. – 18. Feb.
64 Zim – 51 € 90 € – ½ P 11 €
Rest – *(geschl. Montag)* Karte 12/28 €
◆ Besonders auf Seminare ist der gewachsene Gasthof in der Ortsmitte ausgelegt. Man bietet wohnliche, funktionelle Zimmer sowie einen hübschen Sauna- und Badebereich. Ländliche Gaststube und ein über den Bach gebauter Restaurantraum.

Zur Linde mit Zim — Rest,
Hauptplatz 28 ✉ 3053 – ☏ (02774) 83 78
– linde@landgasthof-zur-linde.at – Fax (02774) 837820
geschl. 9. Jan. – 1. Feb.
10 Zim – 42/47 € 64/74 € – ½ P 9 €
Rest – *(geschl. Mittwoch – Donnerstag)* Karte 15/35 €
◆ Der von der Familie geführte Gasthof teilt sich in eine ländliche Gaststube mit schwerer Holzdecke und einen hellen, freundlichen Raum. Hübsche Terrasse.

LADIS – Tirol – 730 D7 – 540 Ew – Höhe 1 180 m – Wintersport: 2 700 m 10 33

6 C6

Wien 531 – Innsbruck 87 – Sankt Anton 47 – Landeck 18
Haus 27, ✉ 6533, ☏ (05472) 66 01, info@serfaus-fiss-ladis.at

Sonnleit'n — Rest,
Dorfstr. 42 ✉ 6531 – ☏ (05472) 26 60 – hotel@sonnleiten.co.at
– Fax (05472) 26605
geschl. 10. Okt. – 9. Dez.
20 Zim (inkl. ½ P.) – ☼ 48/52 € 96/104 € ❄ 122/155 €
152/194 €
Rest – (nur Abendessen für Hausgäste)
◆ Neben der Liftstation liegt das familiengeführte Hotel mit wohnlich und hell im rustikalen Stil eingerichteten Zimmern und Appartements mit kleiner Küche.

Goies — Rest,
Grunesweg 2 ✉ 6531 – ☏ (05472) 6 13 30 – office@hotel-goies.at
– Fax (05472) 613333
geschl. Anfang April – Anfang Mai, Nov. – Anfang Dez.
40 Zim (inkl. ½ P.) – ☼ 85/115 € 140/200 € ❄ 100/140 €
170/240 € – 5 Suiten
Rest – (nur Abendessen für Hausgäste)
◆ Ein regionstypisches Hotel im Zentrum, zu dessen Freizeitbereich ein Panorama-Erlebnis-Hallenbad sowie Massage- und Beautyangebote zählen. Teils besonders komfortable Zimmer.

LÄNGENFELD – Tirol – 730 E7 – 4 070 Ew – Höhe 1 200 m – Wintersport: 2

6 C6

Wien 515 – Innsbruck 72 – Imst 37 – Sölden 14
Ötztaler Heimat- und Freilichtmuseum★ (West: 5 km) – Stuibenfall★★ (Nord: 11 km)

Aqua Dome – Tirol Therme — (geheizt) Rest,
Oberlängenfeld 140 ✉ 6444 – ☏ (05253) 64 00 – office@aqua-dome.at
– Fax (05253) 6400480
140 Zim (inkl. ½ P.) – ☼ 145/165 € 250/290 € ❄ 190/200 €
300/320 € – 26 Suiten
Rest – (nur für Hausgäste)
◆ Modernes Design von der Lobby bis in die schönen Zimmer. Großzügig angelegt und aufwändig gestaltet: die angegliederte Thermenlandschaft – für Hotelgäste kostenlos.

Naturhotel Waldklause  Rest,

Unterlängenfeld 190 ✉ 6444 – ✆ (05253) 54 55 – office@waldklause.at – Fax (05253) 54554

48 Zim (inkl. ½ P.) – 🚹122/140 € 🚹🚹210/274 €

Rest – (nur für Hausgäste)

♦ Das Holzhaus wurde sehr modern und ansprechend designt. Mit seinen puristischen, mit Farbakzenten versehenen Zimmern erzeugt es eine warme Atmosphäre. Kosmetik und Massage.

Rita Rest,

Oberlängenfeld 44a ✉ 6444 – ✆ (05253) 53 07 – info@hotel-rita.com – Fax (05253) 5061

42 Zim (inkl. ½ P.) – ☼ 🚹65/80 € 🚹🚹112/140 € ❄ 🚹75/99 € 🚹🚹130/184 €

Rest – Karte 22/45 €

♦ Ein hübsch gestalteter, recht vielfältiger Freizeitbereich sowie ein schöner Garten zählen zu den Annehmlichkeiten dieses regionstypischen Hauses. Geräumig: die Juniorsuiten. Neuzeitlich-ländliches Restaurant und Wintergarten für Kaffee und Kuchen.

Dieser Führer lebt von Ihren Anregungen, die uns stets willkommen sind. Egal ob Sie uns eine besonders angenehme Überraschung oder eine Enttäuschung mitteilen wollen – schreiben Sie uns!

LANDECK – Tirol – 730 D7 – 7 340 Ew – Höhe 817 m – Wintersport: 2 212 m 1 6 5 B6

Wien 518 – Innsbruck 75 – Imst 20 – Sankt Anton 29

Malserstr. 10, ✉ 6500, ✆ (05442) 6 56 00, info@tirolwest.at

Trisannabrücke★ (Nord-West: 9 km)

Schrofenstein Rest,

Malserstr. 31 ✉ 6500 – ✆ (05442) 6 23 95 – info@schrofenstein.at – Fax (05442) 6495455

geschl. 1. – 17. April, 26. Okt. – 10. Dez.

60 Zim – ☼ 🚹69/114 € 🚹🚹78/128 € ❄ 🚹62/148 € 🚹🚹98/196 € – ½ P 18/22 €

Rest – Karte 24/36 €

♦ Das 150 Jahre alte Gasthaus im Ortskern ist heute ein familiär geleitetes Hotel mit funktionell ausgestatteten, z. T. leicht eleganten Zimmern. Mehrfach unterteiltes Restaurant in ländlichem Stil.

Enzian Rest,

Adamhofgasse 6 ✉ 6500 – ✆ (05442) 6 20 66 – info@hotel-enzian.com – Fax (05442) 620666

geschl. 15. – 22. Okt.

31 Zim (inkl. ½ P.) – ☼ 🚹59/73 € 🚹🚹98/142 € ❄ 🚹50/84 € 🚹🚹86/168 €

Rest – *(geschl. Mitte Okt. – Mitte Nov.) (nur Abendessen für Hausgäste)*

♦ Motorradfahrer schätzen den Biker-Service dieses familengeführten Hotels etwas außerhalb des Zentrums. Die Zimmer sind sehr solide mit hellen Naturholzmöbeln eingerichtet.

Mozart Rest, Rest, VISA

Adamhofgasse 7 ✉ 6500 – ✆ (05442) 6 42 22 – landeck@mozarthotels.at – Fax (05442) 6422211
geschl. 15. – 30. April, 27. Okt. – 10. Dez.
23 Zim – 49/53 € 98/106 € 55/65 € 110/130 € – ½ P 12 €
Rest – (nur Abendessen für Hausgäste)
◆ Ruhig liegt dieser Familienbetrieb im Wohngebiet. Es erwarten Sie wohnlich-rustikale Zimmer mit Balkon (die nach Süden hin etwas geräumiger) und eine hübsche Bar mit Kamin.

LANERSBACH – Tirol – siehe Tux

LANGENEGG – Vorarlberg – 730 B6 – 1 030 Ew – Höhe 700 m 5 A5

Wien 591 – Bregenz 21 – Dornbirn 56 – Kempten 19
Bach 127, ✉ 6941, ✆ (05513) 41 01 14, tourismus@langenegg.at

Krone VISA

Gfäll 107 ✉ 6941 – ✆ (05513) 61 78 – info@krone-langenegg.at – Fax (05513) 617822
30 Zim – 60/80 € 114/144 € – ½ P 25 €
Rest – *(geschl. Montag – Dienstag und Sonntagabend)* Menü 65 € – Karte 28/45 €
◆ Ein familiär geführtes Haus mit wohnlichen Gästezimmern und einem modernen Saunabereich. Besonders schön und komfortabel sind die Zimmer im neueren Anbau. Gemütliches, ganz in Holz gehaltenes Restaurant.

LANGENLEBARN – Niederösterreich – 730 – 13 600 Ew – Höhe 180 m

Wien 47 – Sankt Pölten 55 3 K2

Floh VISA

Tullner Str. 1 ✉ 3425 – ✆ (02272) 6 28 09 – floh@derfloh.at – Fax (02272) 628094
geschl. 15. – 24. Sept. und Dienstag – Mittwoch
Rest – (Tischbestellung ratsam) Karte 14/39 €
◆ Bewusst hat man hier den Wirtshaus-Charakter bewahrt. Die Küche: regional, schmackhaft und schnörkellos. Beeindruckende Weinauswahl mit eigener Karte für Großflaschen.

Zum Roten Wolf VISA

Bahnstr. 58 ✉ 3425 – ✆ (02272) 6 25 67 – Fax (02272) 62567
geschl. Aug. 2 Wochen und Montag – Dienstag
Rest – Menü 42 € – Karte 29/46 €
◆ In Bahnhofsnähe befindet sich das Gasthaus mit drei kleinen Stuben im rustikal-bürgerlichen Stil. Hier wird man mit einfallsreicher Regionalküche bewirtet.

LANGENLOIS – Niederösterreich – 730 T3 – 6 880 Ew – Höhe 213 m 3 K2

Wien 74 – Sankt Pölten 44 – Krems an der Donau 11 – Tulln an der Donau 40

 **LOISIUM** (geheizt) Zim,

Loisiumallee 2 ✉ 3550
– ✆ (02734) 77 10 00 – buchen@loisium.at
– Fax (02734) 77100100
82 Zim – 120/140 € 160/190 € – ½ P 35 €
Rest *Vineyard* – ✆ (02734) 77 10 05 00 – Menü 40/55 € (abends) – Karte 30/47 €

◆ Der moderne Hotelbau inmitten der Weinberge trägt die Handschrift des US-Architekten Steven Holl. Durch und durch klares, fast puristisches Design. Hochwertiger Spabereich. Geradlinig gestaltetes Restaurant.

Heurigenhof Bründelmayer

Walterstr. 14 ✉ 3550 – ✆ (02734) 28 83 – office@heurigenhof.at
– Fax (02734) 28834
geschl. 24. Dez. – 5. Feb., 7. – 15. Juli und Montag – Dienstag
Rest – *(Mittwoch – Freitag ab 15 Uhr geöffnet)* Menü 29 € – Karte 17/29 €

◆ Ein uriges Heurigenlokal, in dem man unter einer recht niedrigen Gewölbedecke an blanken Tischen Platz nimmt – ein offener Kamin unterstreicht das gemütliche Ambiente.

LANGENWANG – Steiermark – 730 S6 – 4 060 Ew – Höhe 637 m – Wintersport: 1 256 m 4 — 10 K4

Wien 114 – Graz 87 – Leoben 51 – Wiener Neustadt 65

Krainer Rest,

Grazerstr. 12 ✉ 8665 – ✆ (03854) 20 22 – restaurant@hotel-krainer.com
– Fax (03854) 20224
15 Zim – 60 € 104 € – ½ P 15 €
Rest – *(geschl. Sonntagabend – Montag)* Menü 37/48 € – Karte 20/32 €

◆ Das im Stil eines Landhauses erbaute, familiengeführte Hotel im Ortskern bietet wohnliche, zeitlos eingerichtete Zimmer und einen modernen kleinen Saunabereich. Der Sohn der Familie Krainer bereitet schmackhafte regionale Speisen. Kuchen im neuzeitlichen Café.

LANS – Tirol – 730 G7 – 910 Ew – Höhe 900 m – Wintersport: — 7 D5

Wien 444 – Innsbruck 8 – Schwaz 27 – Seefeld in Tirol 34
9 Innsbruck-Igls, Lans ✆ (0512) 37 71 65
18 Innsbruck-Igls – Rinn, Oberdorf 11 ✆ (05223) 7 81 77

Walzl

Dorfstr. 56 ✉ 6072 – ✆ (0512) 37 03 80 – info@gasthof-walzl.at
– Fax (0512) 37038050
30 Zim – ☼ 51/63 € 80/110 € ❄ 63/75 € 100/130 € – ½ P 12/15 €
Rest – Karte 20/31 €

◆ Das von der Inhaberfamilie geleitete Haus ist ein zeitgemäßes, kinderfreundliches Hotel in einem netten Dorf nahe Innsbruck. Angenehmer Saunabereich und moderne Weinkapelle. Sie speisen in der holzgetäfelten Zirbenstube oder im ländlich-eleganten Restaurant.

Isserwirt Zim, VISA AE

Lans 9 ✉ 6072 – ✆ (0512) 3 77 26 10 – hotel@isserwirt.at – Fax (0512) 37726129
geschl. 19. Okt. – 9. Nov.
30 Zim – 55/86 € 90/150 € – ½ P 12 €
Rest – *(geschl. außer Saison Montag)* Karte 18/38 €

◆ Der bereits im 14. Jh. urkundlich erwähnte Gasthof ist seit 15 Generationen in Familienbesitz. Die Zimmer sind solide und rustikal, einige modern-komfortabel. Mit dunklem Holz und z. T. mit Kachelofen ausgestattete Gaststuben. Netter Gastgarten mit Pavillon.

Wilder Mann mit Zim Zim, VISA AE

Römerstr. 12 ✉ 6072 – ✆ (0512) 37 96 96 – info@wildermann-lans.at – Fax (0512) 379139
14 Zim – 55/87 € 140/154 €
Rest – Karte 26/46 €

◆ In den Stuben dieses beliebten Gasthofs erwarten Sie eine sehr gemütliche Atmosphäre, freundlicher Service und regionale Küche aus einheimischen Produkten. Im Gästehaus gegenüber befinden sich wohnliche Zimmer mit gutem Platzangebot.

LASSNITZHÖHE – Steiermark – 730 S7 – 2 530 Ew – Höhe 558 m – Heilklimatischer Kurort 11 K5

Wien 181 – Graz 20 – Leibnitz 50 – Fürstenfeld 45
Obere Bahnstr. 1, ✉ 8301, ✆ (03133) 22 04, lassnitzhoehe.info@aon.at

Gasthof Großschedl zum Kramerwirt Zim,

Hönigtaler Str. 20 (Nord-West: 3 km, Richtung Graz) ✉ 8301 – ✆ (03133) 25 03 – office@grosschedl.at – Fax (03133) 250315
21 Zim – 35/55 € 58/76 € – ½ P 11 €
Rest – *(geschl. Feb. 1 Woche, Juli 3 Wochen und Sonntagabend – Montag)* Karte 11/27 €

◆ Der in ländlichem Stil gehaltene Gasthof unter familiärer Leitung beherbergt meist neuzeitlich eingerichtete und teils mit Holzfußboden ausgestattete Zimmer und Appartements. Teil des Restaurants ist die gemütliche alte Bauernstube a. d. J. 1801.

An der A 2 Ausfahrt Lassnitzhöhe Süd: 2 km:

Gasthof Höchschmied (mit Gästehaus) Zim, VISA AE

Schemerlhöhe 12 ✉ 8301 Lassnitzhöhe – ✆ (03133) 22 15 – gasthof@hoechschmied.at – Fax (03133) 22154
16 Zim – 39 € 72 € – ½ P 10 €
Rest – *(geschl. Dienstag)* Karte 11/23 €

◆ Verkehrsgünstig nahe der Autobahnausfahrt liegt der um ein Gästehaus erweiterte kleine Gasthof mit seinen meist neuzeitlichen, in angenehmen Farben gestalteten Zimmern. Restaurant mit rustikalem Charakter.

Dieser Führer lebt von Ihren Anregungen, die uns stets willkommen sind. Egal ob Sie uns eine besonders angenehme Überraschung oder eine Enttäuschung mitteilen wollen – schreiben Sie uns!

LAUTERACH – Vorarlberg – 730 B6 – 8 680 Ew – Höhe 412 m 5 A5

Wien 622 – Bregenz 4 – Dornbirn 8 – Feldkirch 32

Guth (Thomas Scheucher)

Wälderstr. 10 ✉ 6923 – ✆ (05574) 7 24 70 – tisch@restaurantguth.at – Fax (05574) 724706
geschl. 24. Dez. – 6. Jan., 25. Aug. – 14. Sept. und Samstag – Sonntag, Festspielzeit Samstagabend geöffnet
Rest – (Tischbestellung ratsam) Karte 38/62 €
Spez. Kalbskutteln in Riesling mit Parmesan gratiniert. Gröstl vom Bodenseezander mit Liebstöckel und altem Balsamico. Lamm mit Gewürzkräutern und cremiger Polenta.
◆ Modernes, klares Design bestimmt das Bild in dem persönlich geführten Familienbetrieb. Serviert wird feine regionale und leicht mediterrane Küche. Schön: der Blick zum Garten.

LAVANT – Tirol – 730 K8 – 280 Ew – Höhe 675 m 8 F6

Wien 400 – Innsbruck 184 – Lienz 10 – Spittal a.d. Drau 65

Dolomitengolf

Am Golfplatz 1 (Nord: 2 km) ✉ 9900 – ✆ (04852) 6 11 22 – info@hotel-dolomitengolf.com – Fax (04852) 61122444
geschl. Ende Okt. – Mitte Dez.
80 Zim (inkl. ½ P.) – ☼ 🚹103/117 € 🚹🚹158/184 € ❄ 🚹110/160 € 🚹🚹180/250 € – 3 Suiten
Rest – Karte 24/42 €
◆ Die ruhige Lage direkt am hauseigenen Golfplatz sowie mit hübschen Stoffen und hellem Holz wohnlich gestaltete Zimmer mit neuester Technik machen dieses Hotel aus. Moderne Bilder und Holzfußboden unterstreichen das neuzeitliche Ambiente im Restaurant.

LECH AM ARLBERG – Vorarlberg – 730 C7 – 1 470 Ew – Höhe 1 450 m – Wintersport: 2 444 m 5 28 5 B6

Wien 628 – Bregenz 92 – Bludenz 41 – Landeck 48
Dorf 2 (Lech), ✉ 6764, ✆ (05583) 2 16 10, info@lech-zuers.at
Lage★
Hochtannbergstraße★ (Nord: 12 km) – Aussichtspunkte: Zuger Hochlicht★★, Rüfikopf★ (mit) – Spullersee★ und Formarinsee★ (Anfahrt mit dem Bus: Süd-West: 10 km)

Almhof Schneider

Tannberg 59 ✉ 6764 – ✆ (05583) 35 00 – info@almhof.at – Fax (05583) 350033
A/C Rest, Zim,
geschl. 14. April – Anfang Dez.
54 Zim (inkl. ½ P.) – 🚹270/840 € 🚹🚹580/980 € – 21 Suiten
Rest – *(geschl. Ende April – Mitte Dez.)* Menü 55/94 € – Karte 50/82 €
◆ Das traditionsreiche Haus steht für Exklusivität in Ausstattung und Service, gepaart mit alpenländischem Charme und der Herzlichkeit der Familie Schneider. Restaurant mit geschmackvollem Ambiente sowie klassischer und regionaler Küche – mittags kleine Karte.

Arlberg (geheizt) Zim, Rest,
Tannberg 187 ✉ 6764
– ✆ (05583) 2 13 40 – info@arlberghotel.at – Fax (05583) 213425
geschl. Ende April – Anfang Juli, Ende Sept. – Anfang Dez.
49 Zim (inkl. ½ P.) – ☼ 139/156 € 280/296 € ❄ 227/304 € 426/652 € – 7 Suiten
Rest *La Fenice* – *(geschl. Ende April – Anfang Dez. und Dienstag, nur Abendessen)* Menü 70 € – Karte 39/73 €
Rest *Arlberg Stube* – Karte 33/49 €
♦ Aufmerksam und persönlich kümmert man sich in dem familiengeführten Hotel um die Gäste. Schöne wohnlich-elegante Zimmer und moderner, hochwertiger Spabereich. La Fenice mit klassischer italienischer Küche. Regionales in der Arlberg Stube – abends auch Fondue.

Gasthof Post
Lech 11 ✉ 6764 – ✆ (05583) 2 20 60 – postlech@relaischateaux.com
– Fax (05583) 220623 – geschl. Mai – Juni, Okt. – Nov.
39 Zim – ☼ 140/180 € 240/420 € ❄ 230/330 € 410/750 € – ½ P 30 € – 6 Suiten
Rest *Post Stuben* – separat erwähnt
♦ Beispielhafter Service und die freundlich-familiäre Atmosphäre zeichnen das Hotel der Moosbruggers aus. Ein hübsches Haus mit alpenländischem Charakter. Sehr gute Halbpension.

Krone Rest,
Lech 13 ✉ 6764 – ✆ (05583) 25 51 – email@romantikhotelkrone-lech.at
– Fax (05583) 255181
geschl. 20. April – 28. Juni
57 Zim (inkl. ½ P.) – ☼ 121/131 € 188/240 € ❄ 190/300 € 310/570 € – 6 Suiten
Rest – Menü 73 € – Karte 37/66 €
♦ Hinter der dunklen Schindelfassade findet man alpenländisch-elegante Zimmer verschiedener Kategorien und einen großzügigen Wellnessbereich. Das Restaurant: eine mit viel Holz gestaltete Stube sowie ein Rundbau mit großer Fensterfront. Mittags einfachere Karte.

Auriga Zim, Rest,
Omesberg 330 ✉ 6764 – ✆ (05583) 25 11 – hotel-auriga@lech.at
– Fax (05583) 251155
geschl. 25. April – Ende Nov.
27 Zim (inkl. ½ P.) – 150/225 € 250/550 € – 8 Suiten
Rest – (nur für Hausgäste)
♦ Mit gutem Service und wohnlich gestalteten Gästezimmern überzeugt dieses von der Inhaberfamilie engagiert geleitete Hotel. Schön ist der großzügige Freizeitbereich. Man bietet eine hochwertige Halbpension und ausgesuchte Weine. Weinkeller für Degustationen.

Brunnenhof Rest,
Lech 146 ✉ 6764 – ✆ (05583) 23 49 – info@brunnenhof.com
– Fax (05583) 234959
geschl. Mai – Nov.
35 Zim (inkl. ½ P.) – 150/200 € 210/360 €
Rest *Brunnenhof* – separat erwähnt
♦ Hier erwartet Sie freundliches Personal und eine wohnliche Atmosphäre von der Halle bis in die Gästezimmer. In neuzeitlichem Stil zeigt sich der Saunabereich.

Der Berghof Omeshorn, Schafberg, Zim,
Dorf 161 6764
– (05583) 26 35 – info@derberghof.at – Fax (05583) 26355
geschl. 20. April – 21. Juni, 21. Sept. – 29. Nov.
57 Zim (inkl. ½ P.) – 80/128 € 160/256 € 136/267 €
272/534 €
Rest – Karte 39/53 €
♦ Hotel mit wohnlich-alpenländischen Gästezimmern und einem schönen Saunabereich. Besonders hochwertig sind die modern-eleganten Zimmer im neueren Teil. Lift vom Hotel ins Dorf. Gemütliches Restaurant mit Panoramaterrasse. Regionale und internationale Küche.

Kristiania Rest,
Omesberg 331 6764 – (05583) 2 56 10 – kristiania@lech.at
– Fax (05583) 3550
geschl. Mai – Nov.
29 Zim – 225/500 € 400/750 € – ½ P 35 € – 7 Suiten
Rest – Karte 50/80 €
♦ Sehr geschmackvolle, individuelle Zimmer und der zuvorkommende Service verleihen diesem Haus eine exklusive Note. Kunstgegenstände setzen interessante Akzente. Das Restaurant bietet internationale und regionale Küche sowie eine gute Weinauswahl.

Angela Lech und Bergpanorama,
Tannberg 62 6764 – (05583) 24 07
– angela.hotel@lech.at – Fax (05583) 240715
geschl. Mai – Nov.
33 Zim (inkl. ½ P.) – 145/350 € 250/470 € – 6 Suiten
Rest – (nur für Hausgäste)
♦ Herrlich liegt das Hotel oberhalb des Ortes direkt neben der Skipiste. Sehr nett und persönlich kümmert man sich hier um seine Gäste. Einige Zimmer sind besonders komfortabel.

Kristberg (mit Gästehaus) Lech und Bergpanorama, Zim,
Lech 316 6764
– (05583) 24 88 – office@hotel-kristberg.at – Fax (05583) 2800
geschl. Mai – Nov.
43 Zim (inkl. ½ P.) – 110/227 € 260/494 €
Rest – (nur für Hausgäste)
♦ Oberhalb des Ortes finden Sie das vom ehemaligen Skirennfahrer Egon Zimmermann geleitete Haus. Die schöne Sicht und wohnliche Zimmer, teils mit Balkon, machen das Hotel aus.

Monzabon Zim,
Tannberg 228 6764 – (05583) 21 04 – hotel.monzabon@lech.at
– Fax (05583) 210436
geschl. Mitte April- Anfang Dez.
30 Zim (inkl. ½ P.) – 138/246 € 232/472 € – 10 Suiten
Rest – Karte 28/48 €
♦ Ein Familienbetrieb im gediegen-rustikalen Stil eines Jagdhauses. Die Lage nahe den Bergbahnen und wohnliche, teilweise recht großzügige Zimmer sprechen für das Haus. Nett ist die Jägerstube mit Blick in die hauseigene Eishalle.

Schmelzhof (mit Gästehaus) Rest,
Omesberg 370 ✉ 6764
– ✆ (05583) 3 75 00 – hotel@schmelzhof.at – Fax (05583) 375030
geschl. Mai – Juni, Okt. – Nov.
32 Zim (inkl. ½ P.) – ☼ 78/90 € 140/210 € ❄ 135/160 € 270/390 € – 5 Suiten
Rest – *(geschl. Dienstag)* (nur für Hausgäste)
◆ Wohnliche Gästezimmer in freundlichen Farben und der familiäre Service erzeugen hier im Haus eine sympathische, frische Atmosphäre. Schön sind die Lage und die Aussicht.

Pfefferkorn's
Dorf 138 ✉ 6764 – ✆ (05583) 2 52 50 – info@pfefferkorns.net
– Fax (05583) 25258
geschl. Mai – Juni, Okt – Nov.
29 Zim – ☼ 53/70 € 90/140 € ❄ 120/190 € 220/300 € – ½ P 25 € – 22 Suiten
Rest – *(geschl. Mai – Nov.)* (Tischbestellung ratsam) Karte 33/48 €
Rest *s'Pfefferkörndl* – Karte 18/34 €
◆ Das regionstypische Hotel im Zentrum bietet dem Gast wohnlich eingerichtete Zimmer, einige davon im modern-rustikalen Alpin-Stil. Trendige Club-Lounge im UG. Hübsches, alpenländisch gehaltenes Restaurant. Leger geht's im Pfefferkörndl zu.

Aurora Zim, Rest,
Omesberg 209 ✉ 6764 – ✆ (05583) 23 54 – hotel@aurora-lech.com
– Fax (05583) 235430
geschl. Mai – Juni, Okt. – Nov.
22 Zim (inkl. ½ P.) – ☼ 70/80 € 140/184 € ❄ 108/182 € 196/384 €
Rest – *(geschl. im Sommer Sonntag, im Winter Donnerstag)* (nur Abendessen für Hausgäste)
◆ Eine nette Lobby mit Kamin und Bergblick, wohnliche Zimmer und ein ganz modern gestalteter Saunabereich machen dieses gut geführte Hotel aus.

Omesberg
Omesberg 5 ✉ 6764 – ✆ (05583) 22 12 – bucher@omesberg.lech.at
– Fax (05583) 3756
geschl. 20. April – 1. Juli, 20. Sept. – 1. Dez.
29 Zim (inkl. ½ P.) – ☼ 73/79 € 130/150 € ❄ 122/170 € 210/316 €
Rest – Karte 18/23 €
◆ Ein alpenländisches und zeitgemäßes Ambiente begleitet Sie vom Empfangsbereich bis in die komfortablen Zimmer dieses am Ortsrand gelegenen Hotels.

Gotthard Zim, Rest,
Omesberg 119 ✉ 6764 – ✆ (05583) 35 60
– hotel@gotthard.at – Fax (05583) 356052
geschl. Mitte April – Mitte Juni, Mitte Okt. – Mitte Dez.
54 Zim – ☼ 57/66 € 104/180 € ❄ 85/135 € 146/300 € – ½ P 35 €
Rest – Karte 27/42 €
◆ Wohnlich ist die Atmosphäre in diesem aus zwei Gebäuden bestehenden Hotel. Die Zimmer sind teils im gediegenen Landhausstil eingerichtet. Schöner, großzügiger Freizeitbereich. Mit viel Holz ländlich-rustikal gestaltetes Restaurant. Bäckerei, Café-Konditorei.

Filomena garni
Omesberg 211 ✉ 6764 – ✆ (05583) 22 11 – apart@filomena.at
– Fax (05583) 26038
geschl. Mai – Juni, Okt. – Nov.
20 Zim – ☼ 49 € 98 € ❄ 71/132 € 143/384 €
◆ Hinter einer Holzfassade erwarten Sie eine großzügige Hotelhalle, wohnliche Appartements mit gutem Platzangebot und kleiner Küche sowie ein schöner Freizeitbereich.

Auenhof
Rest, Rest,
Tannberg 345 ✉ 6764 – ✆ (05583) 25 41
– auenhof.lech@vol.at – Fax (05583) 25413
geschl. 14. April – 26. Juni, 8. Sept. – Nov.
26 Zim (inkl. ½ P.) – ☼ 63/69 € 130/145 € ❄ 94/165 €
190/332 € – 4 Suiten
Rest – (nur Abendessen für Hausgäste)
◆ Ein freundlich und familiär geleitetes Haus an einem kleinen Fluss am Ortsrand. Behagliche Zimmer, meist mit Balkon, und ein hübscher, recht vielfältiger Freizeitbereich.

Haldenhof
Tannberg 347 ✉ 6764 – ✆ (05583) 2 44 40 – reservation@haldenhof.at
– Fax (05583) 244421
geschl. Mai – Juni, Okt – Nov.
24 Zim (inkl. ½ P.) – ☼ 61/73 € 122/146 € ❄ 102/180 €
176/360 € – 6 Suiten
Rest – (nur Abendessen für Hausgäste)
◆ Zu diesem solide geführten Haus gehören eine behagliche Bar mit Kaminhalle und ein netter Saunabereich. Auch einige gemütliche Familienzimmer stehen zur Verfügung.

Hinterwies
Rest, Zim, Rest,
Tannberg 186 ✉ 6764 – ✆ (05583) 25 31
– hotel.hinterwies@lech.at – Fax (05583) 253151
geschl. Mai - Anfang Dez.
27 Zim (inkl. ½ P.) – 145/234 € 228/380 € – 5 Suiten
Rest – Karte 24/48 €
◆ Schön und recht ruhig liegt das Haus am Ortsrand. Man bietet unterschiedlich eingerichtete Zimmer – darunter einige ganz moderne – und einen neuzeitlichen Freizeitbereich. Hübsches, hell gestaltetes Restaurant, teilweise mit rustikalem Touch.

Theodul
Lech 332 ✉ 6764 – ✆ (05583) 23 08 – office@theodul.at
– Fax (05583) 25218
geschl. 21. April – 1. Juli, 15. Sept. – 30. Nov.
29 Zim (inkl. ½ P.) – ☼ 70/78 € 128/150 € ❄ 103/160 €
185/320 €
Rest – (nur Abendessen für Hausgäste)
◆ Der solide geführte Familienbetrieb verfügt über zeitgemäße, wohnliche Zimmer, teilweise mit Balkon. Der Freizeitbereich ist recht großzügig und sehr modern. Gutes Frühstück.

Antonius Rest,

Tannberg 289 ✉ 6764 – ✆ (05583) 24 62 – hotel@antonius.at – Fax (05583) 24622
geschl. Mai – Juni, Sept. – Ende Nov.
20 Zim (im Winter inkl. ½ P.) – ☼ 46/98 € 92/127 € ❄ 106/173 € 209/380 € – 4 Suiten
Rest – *(geschl. Dienstag)* (nur Abendessen für Hausgäste, im Sommer Garni)
◆ In dem familiär geleiteten Hotel erwarten Sie ein hübscher Hallen- und Barbereich sowie behagliche, meist hell möblierte Zimmer. Eine der Suiten: über zwei Etagen, mit Küche.

Anemone (mit Gästehaus) Rest, AE

Tannberg 431 ✉ 6764 – ✆ (05583) 3 53 90 – info@hotelanemone.com – Fax (05583) 35394
geschl. Mai – Nov.
42 Zim (inkl. ½ P.) – 118/211 € 238/393 €
Rest – (nur Abendessen für Hausgäste)
◆ Das Haus mit der z. T. holzverkleideten Balkonfassade beherbergt wohnliche Gästezimmer mit bemalten Bauernmöbeln oder hellem Naturholz. Modern: der Freizeitbereich.

Lech (mit Gästehaus)

Lech 263 ✉ 6764 – ✆ (05583) 2 28 90 – hotel.lech@lech.at – Fax (05583) 2727
31 Zim (im Winter inkl. ½ P.) – ☼ 49/69 € 98/138 € ❄ 99/149 € 198/298 €
Rest – (nur Abendessen für Hausgäste, im Sommer Garni)
◆ Eine schöne Lobby mit Kamin empfängt Sie in dem Hotel am Ortseingang. Man verfügt über wohnliche, teils rustikal gestaltete Zimmer. Saunabereich im griechisch-römischen Stil.

Alpina garni

Omesberg 6 ✉ 6764 – ✆ (05583) 23 09 – strolz@lech-alpina.at – Fax (05583) 4118
geschl. Ende April – Anfang Dez.
11 Zim – 80/110 € 150/220 €
◆ Die äußerst gemütliche Atmosphäre dieses hübschen kleinen Holzhauses begleitet Sie von der Kaminhalle über die 200 Jahre alte Frühstücksstube bis in die individuellen Zimmer.

Sursilva (mit Gästehaus)

Lech 487 ✉ 6764 – ✆ (05583) 2 97 00 – office@hotel-sursilva.at – Fax (05583) 297022
geschl. Mai – Juni, Okt. – Nov.
14 Zim (im Winter inkl. ½ P.) – ☼ 43 € 74 € ❄ 112/140 € 170/300 €
Rest – (nur für Hausgäste, im Sommer Garni)
◆ Relativ ruhig liegt das kleine Hotel etwas zurückversetzt von der Straße. Eine sehr familiär geführte Adresse mit individuellen Zimmern. Einige Appartements im Gästehaus.

Alpenrose Rest,

Oberstubenbach 237 ✉ 6764 – ✆ (05583) 22 92 – office@pensionalpenrose.com – Fax (05583) 32713
geschl. 22. April - 29. Juni

18 Zim – ☼ 42/65 € 74/120 € ❄ 80/95 € 150/198 € – ½ P 32 €
Rest – (nur Abendessen für Hausgäste)
◆ Mit Geschmack und Liebe zum Detail hat die Inhaberin ihr kleines Hotel gestaltet – antike Möbelstücke und hübsche Dekorationen verleihen den Zimmern ihre individuelle Note.

Alpenland

Anger 198 ✉ 6764 – ☎ (05583) 23 51 – alpenland@daskleinehotel.at – Fax (05583) 23515
geschl. 19. April – Juni, 28. Sept. – 1. Dez.
17 Zim (im Winter inkl. ½ P.) – ☼ 40/45 € 76/84 € ❄ 140/150 € 260/300 € – **Rest** – (nur Abendessen für Hausgäste, im Sommer Garni)
◆ Individuell hat man die Zimmer dieses von der Inhaberfamilie geführten, alpenländischen kleinen Hotels im leicht eleganten Landhausstil eingerichtet.

Fernsicht

Anger 233 ✉ 6764 – ☎ (05583) 24 32 – fernsicht@lech.at – Fax (05583) 24326
geschl. 13. April – 12. Juli, 7. Sept. – 5. Dez.
18 Zim (im Winter inkl. ½ P.) – ☼ 38/40 € 70/80 € ❄ 89/112 € 148/224 €
Rest – *(geschl. 13. Juli – 6. Sept. und Donnerstag)* (nur Abendessen für Hausgäste)
◆ Ein freundlich geleitetes Hotel mit wohnlichen Zimmern, die sich in Einrichtung und Zuschnitt unterscheiden. Zum Haus gehört auch ein hübscher Freizeitbereich.

Roggal garni

Omesberg 184 ✉ 6764 – ☎ (05583) 22 74 – roggal@lech.at – Fax (05583) 26804
geschl. Mai, Okt. – Nov.
22 Zim – ☼ 38/44 € 76/88 € ❄ 62/91 € 114/182 €
◆ Hier erwarten Sie zeitgemäße Zimmer, ein uriger Aufenthaltsraum mit Kachelofen und ein mediterran gestalteter Freizeitbereich. Gemütlich: der Frühstücksraum mit gutem Buffet.

Almrausch

Strass 42 ✉ 6764 – ☎ (05583) 29 85 – hotel@almrausch.at – Fax (05583) 298519
geschl. Mai – Nov.
12 Zim (inkl. ½ P.) – 148/250 € 148/250 €
Rest – *(geschl. Mittwoch)* (nur Abendessen für Hausgäste)
◆ Wohnlich-rustikales Ambiente, der Blick auf die Berge und die familiäre Führung machen dieses kleine Hotel oberhalb des Ortes aus. Nett ist auch der neuzeitliche Saunabereich.

Brunnenhof – Hotel Brunnenhof

Lech 146 ✉ 6764 – ☎ (05583) 23 49 – info@brunnenhof.com – Fax (05583) 234959
geschl. Mai – Nov.
Rest – *(geschl. Sonntag – Montag, nur Abendessen)* (Tischbestellung ratsam) Karte 46/69 €
Spez. Gänseleber und Wachtel. Milchkalb im Kräuterbisquit mit Ricottatortelli. Vanille Traum.
◆ Versiert und aufmerksam ist der Service in diesem Restaurant, klassisch das Speisenangebot. Holzvertäfelung und hübsches Dekor schaffen in den Stuben ein gemütliches Ambiente.

XX **Post Stuben** - Gasthof Post

Lech 11 ✉ 6764 – ✆ (05583) 2 20 60 – postlech@relaischateaux.com
– Fax (05583) 220623
geschl. Mai – Juni, Okt. – Nov.
Rest – *(nur Abendessen)* Menü 45/105 € – Karte 44/76 €
Spez. Rahmsuppe von Erbsen und Zitronenblätter mit Garnelenrolle. Seeteufelmedaillons mit Kürbispüree und Mandel-Tortellini. Wiener Tafelspitz mit Cremespinat, Apfelkren, Schnittlauchsauce und Rösterdäpfel.
◆ In den gemütlichen holzvertäfelten Restaurantstuben umsorgt Sie ein aufmerksames und geschultes Team mit klassischer Küche.

XX **Fux**

Omesberg 587 ✉ *6764* – ✆ *(05583) 29 92* – *fux@fux-mi.net*
– *Fax (05583) 29928*
geschl. Ende April – Anfang Dez.
Rest – *(nur Abendessen)* Karte 40/105 €
Rest *Steakhouse* – *(nur Abendessen)* Karte 33/79 €
◆ Schlicht-modern ist das Ambiente in diesem euro-asiatischen Restaurant, sensationell die Weinauswahl mit über 1700 verschiedenen Positionen. Mit Sushi-Buffet. Ein hoher Raum mit großen Fenstern beherbergt das Steakhouse mit Restaurantbar und Galerie.

X **Rud-Alpe** ≤ Berge und Lech,

Tannberg 185 ✉ *6764* – ✆ *(05583) 41 82 50* – *rud-alpe@skiarlberg.at*
– *Fax (05583) 4182510*
geschl. 28. April – 1. Juli, 6. Okt. – 1. Dez. und Juli – Anfang Okt. Mittwoch
Rest – Menü 39/62 € – Karte 26/48 €
◆ Oberhalb von Lech, mitten auf der Piste liegt das urige Holzhaus mit seinen gemütlich-rustikalen Stuben. Nur zu Fuß oder per Ski zu erreichen. Sehr schöne Sonnenterrasse.

In Lech-Oberlech **Nord: 3,5 km, im Winter autofrei, mit erreichbar – Höhe 1 700 m**

Burg Hotel ≤ Bergpanorama, Rest,

Oberlech 266
✉ *6764* – ✆ *(05583) 2 29 10* – *info@burghotel.at*
– *Fax (05583) 2291120*
geschl. 21. April – 18. Juli, 6. Okt. – 28. Nov.
65 Zim (inkl. ½ P.) – ☼ 112/142 € 202/212 € ❄ 167/304 € 307/476 € – 6 Suiten
Rest *Lechtaler Stube* – *(nur Abendessen)* Menü 48 € (veg.)/95 €
Rest *Panorama-Terrassenrestaurant* – *(nur Mittagessen)* Karte 28/60 €
◆ Lebendig ist die Atmosphäre in dem Ferienhotel neben der Seilbahnstation mit wohnlichen Zimmern und vielseitigem Freizeitbereich. Lechtaler Stube mit zeitgemäßer Küche auf klassischer Basis. Im Sommer ergänzt eine Almhütte das Panorama-Terrassenrestaurant.

Burg Vital Hotel ≤ Bergpanorama, Rest,

Oberlech 568
✉ *6764* – ✆ *(05583) 31 40* – *office@burgvitalhotel.at*
– *Fax (05583) 314016*
geschl. 20. April - Ende Juni, Mitte Okt. – Anfang Dez.

40 Zim (inkl. ½ P.) – ☼ 135/174 € 220/327 € ❄ 147/273 € 296/552 € – 3 Suiten
Rest *Griggeler Stuba* – separat erwähnt
Rest *Bella Vita* – *(nur Mittagessen)* Karte 22/43 €
◆ Das Hotel besticht durch seine exklusive Lage im Skigebiet, den aufmerksamen Service und das behagliche alpenländische Ambiente im ganzen Haus. Großzügiger Wellnessbereich. Ländlich-elegant ist das Restaurant Bella Vita mit hübscher Terrasse.

Sonnenburg Bergpanorama, Rest, VISA AE
Oberlech 55 ✉ 6764 – ✆ (05583) 21 47 – hotel@sonnenburg.at – Fax (05583) 214736
geschl. Mai – Nov.
74 Zim (inkl. ½ P.) – 164/219 € 268/372 €
Rest *Schüna* – Karte 31/57 €
◆ Der Familienbetrieb bietet im Stamm- und im Landhaus wohnliche, meist geräumige Zimmer. Auch eine wechselnde Bilderausstellung befindet sich im Hotel. Hochwertige Halbpension. Im Schüna: tagsüber Crêpes, am Abend auf Vorbestellung Fondue oder Raclette.

Montana Bergpanorama, A/C Rest, Rest, VISA
Oberlech 279
✉ 6764 – ✆ (05583) 24 60 – montanaoberlech@aon.at – Fax (05583) 246038
geschl. Mai – Nov.
45 Zim (inkl. ½ P.) – 130/260 € 240/490 € – 25 Suiten
Rest – Menü 45/85 € – Karte 45/60 €
◆ Ein familiengeführtes Hotel in unmittelbarer Nähe der Pisten mit wohnlich gestalteten Gästezimmern, meist mit Balkon. Etwas aufwändiger sind die Zimmer im Chalet. Restaurant in ländlichem Stil.

Bergkristall Bergpanorama, Rest, VISA
Oberlech 382 ✉ 6764 – ✆ (05583) 26 78 – bergkristall@wrann.at – Fax (05583) 267814
geschl. 15. April – 10. Dez.
33 Zim (inkl. ½ P.) – 114/189 € 250/358 € – 3 Suiten
Rest – Karte 30/54 €
◆ Das von Familie Wrann engagiert geführte Hotel verfügt über freundlich gestaltete Gästezimmer, teilweise mit Balkon, und einen netten kleinen Freizeitbereich. Rustikales Restaurant und Sonnenterrasse mit herrlicher Sicht auf die Berge.

Petersboden Zim, Rest, VISA AE
Oberlech 278 ✉ 6764 – ✆ (05583) 32 32 – hotel@petersboden.com – Fax (05583) 323238
geschl. 13. April – 29. Nov.
19 Zim (inkl. ½ P.) – 124/237 € 220/456 €
Rest – Karte 32/54 €
◆ Das mit Holz verkleidete Haus direkt neben der Skipiste ist ein solider Familienbetrieb mit wohnlichen Zimmern und mediterranem Freizeitbereich. Multi-Media-Raum. Gemütlich-rustikales Restaurant mit guter internationaler Küche – einfacheres Mittagsangebot.

Goldener Berg Bergpanorama, Rest, VISA

Oberlech 117 ✉ 6764
– ✆ (05583) 2 20 50 – info@goldenerberg.at – Fax (05583) 250513
geschl. Mai – Juni, Okt. – Nov.
41 Zim (inkl. ½ P.) – 80/102 € 164/224 € 165/385 €
280/730 € – 9 Suiten
Rest *Johannisstübli* – Menü 48/75 € – Karte 26/52 €
Rest *Alter Goldener Berg* – Karte 18/51 €
◆ Hotel oberhalb der Gondelstation mit recht unterschiedlichen Zimmern. Sehr schön in Naturstein, Glas und Holz gehalten: Alpin Spa mit toller Aussicht. Gute internationale und regionale Küche im Johannisstübli. Alter Goldener Berg mit Fondue-Auswahl am Abend.

Burgwald Bergpanorama, Zim, Rest, VISA

Oberlech 151 ✉ 6764 – ✆ (05583) 23 10
– mail@hotelburgwald.com – Fax (05583) 32166
geschl. 13. April – 29. Nov.
20 Zim (inkl. ½ P.) – 145/200 € 280/390 €
Rest – Karte 28/54 €
◆ In dem an der Skipiste gelegenen kleinen Hotel unter familiärer Leitung stehen gepflegte Gästezimmer mit wohnlichem Ambiente und meist mit Balkon zur Verfügung. Gemütliche Restaurantstuben und sehr netter Terrassenbereich.

Murmeli VISA AE

Oberlech 297 ✉ 6764 – ✆ (05583) 38 44 – hotel@murmeli.at
– Fax (05583) 24674
geschl. Mai – Ende Nov.
12 Zim (inkl. ½ P.) – 115/140 € 260/296 € – 7 Suiten
Rest – *(nur Mittagessen)* Karte 30/52 €
◆ Seine überschaubare Größe und wohnliche, mit Birnenholz möblierte Zimmer – teilweise als kleine Suiten angelegt – sprechen für dieses familiengeführte Hotel. Eine Terrasse vor dem Haus ergänzt das nett gestaltete Restaurant.

Griggeler Stuba – Burg Vital Hotel Bergpanorama, P VISA AE

Oberlech 568 ✉ 6764 – ✆ (05583) 31 40
– office@burgvitalhotel.at – Fax (05583) 314016
geschl. 20. April - Ende Juni, Mitte Okt. – Anfang Dez. und im Winter Samstag, im Sommer Dienstag
Rest – *(nur Abendessen)* (Tischbestellung ratsam) Menü 69/106 € – Karte 44/56 €
Spez. Tatar vom Tiroler Graurind mit gelierter Suppe und Feldgurken. Taube mit Kräuterbröseln und cremigen Linsen. Buttermilch-Cremeschnitte mit Rumtopf von Waldbeeren.
◆ Eine gemütliche, geschmackvoll-rustikale Stube. Die kreative Regionalküche ist saisonal geprägt, verfeinert mit einer Vielzahl an Kräutern. Weinkarte mit ca. 700 Positionen.

In Lech-Zug **Süd-West: 3 km:**

Rote Wand (mit Gästehaus) (geheizt) P VISA

Zug 5 ✉ 6764 – ✆ (05583) 3 43 50
– gasthof@rotewand.com – Fax (05583) 343540
geschl. Mai, Nov.

38 Zim (inkl. ½ P.) – 174/186 € 248/384 € 182/306 € 254/436 € – 12 Suiten
Rest – *(geschl. Sonntag)* Karte 47/59 €
♦ Das familiär geführte Hotel bietet großzügige Zimmer, die ganz modern in sachlichem, geradlinigem Stil gehalten sind, sowie Maisonetten und Appartements/Suiten. Skiservice. Nette Restaurantstuben mit internationaler Küche und einer großen Fondue-Auswahl.

Hartenfels Rest, VISA

Zug 490 6764 – (05583) 31 04 – hotel.hartenfels@netway.at – Fax (05583) 31044 – geschl. 6. April – 1. Juli, Anfang Sept. – Mitte Dez.
15 Zim (inkl. ½ P.) – 70 € 100 € 104/160 € 168/296 €
Rest – *(geschl. Mittwoch)* Karte 24/50 €
♦ Ein im regionstypischen Stil erbautes kleines Hotel mit solide und wohnlich ausgestatteten Gästezimmern und Appartements, teils mit Balkon. Unterteilter Restaurantbereich mit rustikalem Ambiente.

Gasthof Alpenblick AE

Zug 10 6764 – (05583) 27 55 – kh.zimmermann@vol.at – Fax (05583) 2766 – geschl. Mai – Mitte Dez.
Rest – Karte 26/46 €
♦ In den holzvertäfelten, im alpenländischen Stil gehaltenen Restaurantstuben serviert man regionale Küche mit internationalem Touch. Schön gelegene Terrasse mit Bergblick.

s'Achtele mit Zim VISA

Zug 525 6764 – (05583) 3 93 70 – info@staefeli.at – Fax (05583) 39377 – geschl. Mai – Juni, Okt. – Nov.
8 Zim – 45 € 84 € 90/105 € 160/170 €
Rest – *(geschl. Sonntag, nur Abendessen)* Karte 23/44 €
♦ Gemütlich ist dieses nett dekorierte, mit viel Holz ausgestattete Restaurant. Terrasse mit Blick auf Madloch-Joch und Omeshorn. Die Küche ist bürgerlich. Zum Übernachten stehen wohnliche Zimmer zur Verfügung.

Klösterle VISA AE

Zug 27 6764 – (05583) 31 90 – Fax (05583) 3190 geschl. Mitte April – Anfang Dez.
Rest – *(geschl. Montag)* (Tischbestellung erforderlich) Karte 46/70 €
♦ Eine urige Atmosphäre herrscht in dem Bauernhaus a. d. 15. Jh. Geboten werden regionale Gerichte – mittags Jausenkarte und Kuchen. Auch mit dem Orts- und Nachtbus erreichbar.

In Zürs am Arlberg Süd-Ost: 6 km – Höhe 1 720 m

Haus Nr. 76 (Zürs), 6763, (05583) 22 45, info@lech-zuers.at

Zürserhof Zim, VISA

Haus 75 6763 – (05583) 25 13 – hotel@zuerserhof.at – Fax (05583) 3165 geschl. Mitte April – Anfang Dez.
104 Zim (inkl. ½ P.) – 230/475 € 380/795 € – 16 Suiten
Rest – (Tischbestellung ratsam) Karte 45/67 €
♦ Äußerst angenehm sind der klassisch-rustikale Rahmen des Hauses und der perfekte Service. Wahrhaft luxuriös: Royal Suite mit Butler. Spa- und Freizeitangebote tun ein Übriges. Elegantes Restaurant mit Sonnenterrasse direkt an der Skipiste.

Thurnhers Alpenhof

Zim, Rest,

Haus 295 ✉ 6763
– ✆ (05583) 21 91 – mail@thurnhers-alpenhof.com
– Fax (05583) 3330
geschl. Mitte April – Anfang Dez.
39 Zim (inkl. ½ P.) – 250/490 € 380/660 € – 7 Suiten
Rest – (Tischbestellung erforderlich) Menü 65 € – Karte 37/60 €
◆ Geschmackvolles Ambiente und freundliches, geschultes Personal zeichnen das Hotel aus. Der Freizeitbereich erstreckt sich über 3 Ebenen. Dachterrasse mit Blick über Zürs. Restaurant mit klassisch inspirierter internationaler Küche – kleines Angebot am Mittag.

Edelweiss

Rest,

Haus 79 ✉ 6763 – ✆ (05583) 26 62 – hotel@edelweiss.net
– Fax (05583) 3533
geschl. Ende April – Anfang Dez.
63 Zim (inkl. ½ P.) – 132/299 € 278/558 € – 3 Suiten
Rest *Chesa* – *(geschl. Montag)* Karte 27/55 €
◆ Ganz individuell und wohnlich-elegant hat man hier die Zimmer gestaltet, aufwändig dekoriert und mit schönen Bädern ausgestattet. Originell und sehr beliebt: die Bar Zürserl. Das Chesa ist gemütlich-rustikal, mit antiken Einzelstücken und viel Zierrat.

Sporthotel Lorünser

Rest,

Haus 112 ✉ 6763 – ✆ (05583) 2 25 40
– hotel@loruenser.at – Fax (05583) 225444
geschl. Ende April – Anfang Dez.
71 Zim (inkl. ½ P.) – 168/311 € 328/546 € – 4 Suiten
Rest – Karte 35/47 €
◆ Die familiäre Atmosphäre und der behagliche alpenländisch-rustikale Stil machen dieses Hotel aus. Auf Wunsch ist auch Vollpension möglich. Restaurant mit regionstypischem Ambiente.

Albona Nova

Rest,

Haus 217 ✉ 6763 – ✆ (05583) 23 41 – office@albonanova.at
– Fax (05583) 234112
geschl. Mitte April – Mitte Dez.
34 Zim (inkl. ½ P.) – 128/308 € 228/388 €
Rest *Die Ente von Zürs* – *(geschl. Donnerstag, nur Abendessen)* (Tischbestellung ratsam) Menü 59/99 € – Karte 39/60 €
◆ Ein sehr familienfreundliches Ferienhotel, in dem Sie eine gemütliche Atmosphäre und recht unterschiedlich gestaltete Gästezimmer erwarten. In dem kleinen, klassisch-rustikalen A-la-carte-Restaurant bietet man u. a. Entenspezialitäten.

Arlberghaus

Rest,

Haus 126 ✉ 6763 – ✆ (05583) 22 58 – skihotel@arlberghaus.com
– Fax (05583) 225855
geschl. 18. April – 3. Dez.
46 Zim (inkl. ½ P.) – 120/217 € 223/424 €
Rest – Karte 26/54 €
◆ Eine solide Adresse in der Ortsmitte mit teils behaglich-rustikalen, teils hell und neuzeitlich gestalteten Gästezimmern. Im zweiten Stock befindet sich die Sonnenterrasse. Gemütlich ist das Restaurant Walserstube.

Enzian

Haus 84 ✉ 6763 – ✆ (05583) 2 24 20 – office@hotelenzian.com
– Fax (05583) 3404
geschl. Mitte April - Mitte Dez.
40 Zim (inkl. ½ P.) – †114/199 € ††228/410 € – 6 Suiten
Rest *Enzianstube* – Karte 28/48 €

♦ Neben recht unterschiedlichen Zimmern bietet dieses direkt an einem Skihang gelegene Haus eine Vielzahl an Freizeitaktivitäten, wie z. B. Indoor-Golf, Squash, Badminton. Das A-la-carte-Restaurant ist in einer Zirbenstube a. d. J. 1925 untergebracht.

Erzberg

Haus 383 ✉ 6763 – ✆ (05583) 2 64 40 – hotel.erzberg.zuers@aon.at
– Fax (05583) 264444
geschl. Mai – Nov.
26 Zim (inkl. ½ P.) – †93/170 € ††176/336 €
Rest – (nur Abendessen für Hausgäste)

♦ In dem von der Inhaberfamilie geleiteten Hotel stehen wohnlich-solide ausgestattete Gästezimmer zur Verfügung, teilweise mit Balkon.

KochArt – im Robinson Club Alpenrose

Haus 82 ✉ 6763 – ✆ (05583) 2 27 10 – alpenrosezuers@robinson.de
– Fax (05583) 227179
geschl. Anfang April – Anfang Dez. und Sonntag – Montag
Rest – *(nur Abendessen)* (Tischbestellung ratsam) Menü 48/165 € – Karte 50/84 €

Spez. Weißer Biolachs mit Fleur de sel und Risotto von schwarzem Kaiser-Reis. Schnee-Ei mit Kaviar gefüllt und kalte Hummersauce. Rehrücken in der Kastanie mit schwarzen Nüssen.

♦ In einem Nebengebäude des Robinson Clubs serviert man dem Gast auf recht lebendige und nicht ganz alltägliche Weise die kreative Küche von Otto Koch.

LECHASCHAU – Tirol – 730 E6 – 1 940 Ew – Höhe 853 m — 6 C5

Wien 522 – Innsbruck 95 – Reutte 2 – Imst 50

Gasthof Krone — Zim, Zim

Wängler Str. 6 ✉ 6600 – ✆ (05672) 6 23 54 – info@romantik-krone.at
– Fax (05672) 623546
geschl. April, 6. Okt. – 15. Nov.
27 Zim – †43/48 € ††72/84 € – ½ P 17 €
Rest – *(geschl. im Winter Mittwoch)* Karte 19/33 €

♦ Seit dem 19. Jh. wird das Haus der Familie Pohler als Gasthof geführt. Es stehen hier rustikal möblierte Zimmer sowie drei hübsche Appartements zur Verfügung. Das Sommerhaus, eine mit Holz überbaute Terrasse, ergänzt die gemütlichen Restaurantstuben.

Wir bemühen uns bei unseren Preisangaben um größtmögliche Genauigkeit. Aber alles ändert sich! Lassen Sie sich daher bei Ihrer Reservierung den derzeit gültigen Preis mitteilen.

LEIBNITZ – Steiermark – 730 S8 – 6 900 Ew – Höhe 276 m 11 K5

Wien 225 – Graz 40 – Maribor 30

Sparkassenplatz 4a, 8430, (03452) 7 68 11, office@leibnitz.info

Gut Murstätten Lebring, Neu-Oedt 14 (03182) 35 55

Ehrenhausen: Mausoleum★ (Süd: 10 km)

Zur alten Post

Zim, Zim, VISA

Grazer Gasse 7, (Zufahrt über Sparkassenplatz) 8430 – (03452) 8 23 73 – office@zur-alten-post.at – Fax (03452) 8237350

22 Zim – 52 € 80 € – ½ P 11 €

Rest – *(Nov. – Mai nur Mittagessen)* Karte 14/28 €

◆ Mit einem neuzeitlichen Hotelbau hat man den im Zentrum gelegenen Gasthof um moderne, geschmackvolle Zimmer in freundlichen Farben erweitert. Das Restaurant: teils bürgerlich-rustikal, teils als mediterran gestaltetes, lichtes Atrium.

Weinland garni

VISA AE

Konradweg 5 8430 – (03452) 8 43 10 – hotel.weinland@aon.at – Fax (03452) 8431020

8 Zim – 51/89 € 90/128 €

◆ Recht ruhig liegt das familiengeführte kleine Hotel in einer Seitenstraße. Besonders schön sind die geräumigen Zimmer im rückwärtigen Bereich. Hübscher Garten mit Pool.

LENZING – Oberösterreich – 730 M5 – 5 040 Ew – Höhe 485 m 1 G3

Wien 247 – Linz 83 – Wels 54

In Lenzing-Neuhausen

Wirt z' Neuhausen

Neuhausen 1 4860 – (07662) 27 25 – wirt-zneuhausen@utanet.at

geschl. Montag – Dienstag und über Weihnachten

Rest – *(nur Abendessen)* Karte 22/43 €

◆ Der rustikale Gasthof mit regionaler und internationaler Karte erzeugt eine freundliche Atmosphäre durch die gemütlichen Stuben und den schönen Innenhof.

In Lenzing-Oberachmann

Wengermühle

VISA AE

Oberachmannerstr. 2 4860 – (07662) 42 23 – restaurant@wengermuehle.com – Fax (07662) 4091

geschl. Sonntagabend – Dienstagmittag, Mai – Sept. nur Montag

Rest – (Tischbestellung ratsam) Menü 20/65 € – Karte 24/56 €

◆ Gelungen wurden in der ehemaligen Mühle historische Stilmerkmale erhalten und mit modernen verbunden. Die regionale Küche serviert man auch auf der Terrasse am Fluss.

LEOGANG – Salzburg – 730 K6 – 3 040 Ew – Höhe 800 m – Wintersport: 1 914 m 11 45 8 F5

Wien 363 – Salzburg 94 – Bad Reichenhall 56 – Kitzbühel 42

Löwenhof Zim, P VISA

Dorf 119 ✉ 5771 – ✆ (06583) 74 28 – loewenhof@loewe.at – Fax (06583) 74295
geschl. 8. April – 29. Mai, 7. Okt. – 30. Nov.
39 Zim (inkl. ½ P.) – ☼ †94 € ††156/166 € ❄ †136/144 € ††230/258 €
Rest – Karte 22/40 €
◆ Mit einer großen Halle im Landhausstil empfängt Sie das Hotel mitten im Zentrum. Die Zimmer sind mit hellen Naturholzmöblen und Dielenböden freundlich eingerichtet. Badeteich. Ländlich-elegantes Restaurant.

Kirchenwirt Zim, Zim, P VISA

Dorf 3 ✉ 5771 – ✆ (06583) 82 16 – hotelkirchenwirt@nextra.at – Fax (06583) 8459
geschl. 30. März – 30. April, 7. Nov. – 15. Dez.
23 Zim – ☼ †72 € ††120 € ❄ †89/120 € ††149/199 € – ½ P 10/15 €
Rest – *(geschl. Dienstag außer Saison)* Karte 19/42 €
◆ Der im Jahre 1326 erstmals erwähnte Gasthof ist ein solide geführter Familienbetrieb, in dem man mit viel altem Holz bewusst den ursprünglichen Charakter bewahrt hat. Restaurant in bürgerlich-rustikalem Stil.

In Leogang-Hütten West: 4 km Richtung Sankt Johann:

Landhotel Rupertus Zim, Rest, P VISA

Hütten 40 ✉ 5771 – ✆ (06583) 84 66 – info@rupertus.at – Fax (06583) 846655
geschl. 5. April - 9. Mai, 11. Okt. – 1. Dez.
38 Zim (inkl. ½ P.) – ☼ †62/68 € ††104/116 € ❄ †80/99 € ††130/168 €
Rest – Karte 17/34 €
◆ Das nahe der Lifte gelegene familiengeführte Haus bietet solide möblierte Gästezimmer sowie im Sommer einen eigenen Badeteich. In hellem Holz gehaltenes Restaurant.

In Leogang-Rain West: 2 km Richtung Sankt Johann:

Der Krallerhof Spa Rest, P VISA AE

Rain 6 ✉ 5771 – ✆ (06583) 82 46 – office@krallerhof.com – Fax (06583) 824685
geschl. 1. April – 1. Mai
118 Zim (inkl. ½ P.) – ☼ †139/165 € ††280/330 € ❄ †140/184 € ††280/336 € – 22 Suiten
Rest – Karte 28/44 €
◆ Das luxuriöse Alpenhotel war einst ein Bauernhof und bietet seinen anspruchsvollen Gästen Zimmer, eingerichtet in einem wohnlichen Mix aus Landhaus- und Designerstil. Leicht elegantes, vorwiegend rustikales Restaurant.

In Leogang-Rosental Nord-Ost: 1 km Richtung Saalfelden, dann links:

Gasthof Wachter P VISA

Rosental 8 ✉ 5771 – ✆ (06583) 83 04 – gasthof-wachter@aon.at – Fax (06583) 83046 – geschl. 14. April - 15. Mai, 28. Sept. - 29. Nov.
27 Zim (inkl. ½ P.) – ☼ †44/51 € ††78/88 € ❄ †59/73 € ††106/130 €
Rest – Karte 19/27 €
◆ Hinter der alpenländischen Balkonfassade beherbergt der Gasthof zeitgemäße, mit hellem Naturholz möblierte Zimmer – auch die etwas einfacheren mit Pakettfußboden und Balkon. Ländlicher Restaurantbereich mit Kachelofen und z. T. Holztäfelung.

Lindenhof
Rosental 10 ✉ 5771 – ✆ (06583) 82 80 – hotel-lindenhof@aon.at
– Fax (06583) 828095
geschl. 14. April – 12. Mai, 10. Okt. – 12. Dez.
24 Zim (inkl. ½ P.) – ☼ 44/50 € 68/90 € ❄ 61/75 € 100/140 €
Rest – (nur Abendessen für Hausgäste)
◆ Recht ruhig liegt das familiengeführte Haus in einer Nebenstraße. Die Zimmer sind mit hellem Landhausmobiliar eingerichtet und unterschiedlich in der Größe.

In Leogang-Sonnberg West: 2 km Richtung Sankt Johann:

Bachmühle mit Zim
Sonnberg 148 ✉ 5771 – ✆ (06583) 71 32 – bachmuehle@sbg.at
– Fax (06583) 7132
geschl. April, Nov.
10 Zim – ☼ 37/42 € 74/84 € ❄ 48/60 € 96/120 €
– ½ P 15 €
Rest – *(geschl. Mittwoch)* Karte 17/36 €
◆ Ganz in hellem Holz ist die Einrichtung dieses Gasthofs gehalten, passend dazu das Dekor. Die Karte ist weitgehend regional ausgelegt.

LEONDING – Oberösterreich – siehe LINZ

LERMOOS – Tirol – 730 E6 – 1 070 Ew – Höhe 1 004 m – Wintersport: 2 250 m 1 8 6 C5

Wien 495 – Innsbruck 73 – Reutte 21 – Garmisch-Partenkirchen 26
Unterdorf 15, ✆ (05673) 24 01, info@lermoos.at
Lage★★ – Maria Opferung ★★

Alpenrose (geheizt) Rest,
Danielstr. 3 ✉ 6631
– ✆ (05673) 24 24 – info@hotelalpenrose.at – Fax (05673) 242424
72 Zim (inkl. ½ P.) – ☼ 105/135 € 218/326 € ❄ 145/252 €
299/620 € – 23 Suiten
Rest – (nur für Hausgäste)
◆ Luxuriöses Familienhotel mit elegantem Landhausambiente. Der vielfältige Kinderbereich bietet u. a. Piratenschiff, Kino, Kindergarten. Hochwertiges All-inclusive-Angebot.

Post & Postschlößl (mit Gästehaus) (geheizt)
Kirchplatz 6
✉ 6631 – ✆ (05673) 2 28 10 – hotel@post-lermoos.at
– Fax (05673) 2281841
geschl. 2. Nov. – 5. Dez.
60 Zim (inkl. ½ P.) – ☼ 103/136 € 168/234 € ❄ 116/178 €
194/318 € – 21 Suiten
Rest – Karte 21/49 €
◆ Der großzügige Rahmen, Spa auf 2000 qm sowie überaus geräumige und wohnliche Zimmer zeichnen die Post heute aus. Etwas kleinere Zimmer im denkmalgeschützten Schlössl von 1560. Als A-la-carte-Restaurant dient eine gemütliche alte Stube. Terrasse mit Bergblick.

Sporthotel Zugspitze (mit Gästehaus) Zim,
Innsbruckerstr. 51 ✉ 6631
– ✆ (05673) 26 30 – h.zugspitze@tirol.com – Fax (05673) 263015
geschl. 6. April – 31. Mai, 3. Okt. – 20. Dez.
34 Zim (inkl. ½ P.) – 77/92 € 124/144 € 90/146 € 150/252 €
Rest – Karte 20/31 €
◆ In erhöhter Lage finden Sie dieses alpenländische Hotel. Besonders schön sind die Appartements im Gästehaus. Man bietet Kutschfahrten mit hauseigenen Pferden an. Eine Terrasse mit toller Sicht auf die Zugspitze ergänzt das rustikale Restaurant.

Klockerhof < Zugspitze und Sonnenspitze, Rest,
Widum 12 ✉ 6631 – ✆ (05673) 21 16 – info@klockerhof.at
– Fax (05673) 21166
geschl. April – Mai
23 Zim (inkl. ½ P.) – 38/44 € 72/84 € 60/67 € 112/128 €
Rest – (nur Abendessen für Hausgäste)
◆ Das familiengeführte Hotel liegt an einem Hang im Wohngebiet und bietet neben wohnlichen Gästezimmern einen schönen Saunabereich mit Wasserbetten und Sicht auf die Berge.

LESACHTAL – Kärnten – 730 K8 – 1 560 Ew – Höhe 1 043 m 8 F6

Wien 426 – Klagenfurt 131 – Villach 96 – Lienz 55

In Lesachtal-Sankt Lorenzen

Almwellness-Hotel Tuffbad
Tuffbad 3 (Nord-Ost: 3 km)
✉ 9654 – ✆ (04716) 6 22 – info@almwellness.com – Fax (04716) 62255
geschl. 24. März - 1. Mai, 15. Nov. – 15. Dez.
38 Zim (inkl. ½ P.) – 104/134 € 178/238 €
Rest – (nur für Hausgäste)
◆ Malerisch liegt das Hotel in einem ruhigen Seitental in 1200 m Höhe. Schöne Zimmer und Appartements im Landhausstil sowie diverse Beauty- und Wellnessangebote erwarten Sie. Nette rustikale Stuben ergänzen das freundlich gestaltete Restaurant.

LEUTASCH – Tirol – 730 F6 – 1 990 Ew – Höhe 1 130 m – Wintersport: 1 605 m 3 6 C5

Wien 474 – Innsbruck 31 – Seefeld 8 – Garmisch-Partenkirchen 31
Weidach 320, ✉ 6105, ✆ (050) 5 08 80 10, info@leutasch.com
Leutaschtal★★ – Seefelder Sattelstraßen★★

Quellenhof (geheizt) Rest,
Weidach 288 ✉ 6105
– ✆ (05214) 67 82 – info@quellenhof.at – Fax (05214) 6369
83 Zim (inkl. ½ P.) – 115/152 € 210/260 € 135/198 € 226/352 €
Rest – (nur Abendessen für Hausgäste)
◆ Ein freundlich geführtes und von Stammgästen geschätztes Hotel mit z. T. sehr geräumigen, neuzeitlichen Zimmern. Der vielfältige Spabereich bietet auch chinesische Heilkunst.

Sporthotel Xander (mit Gästehaus)
Kirchplatzl 147 ✉ 6105 Zim, P VISA
– ☎ (05214) 65 81 – xander.leutasch@tirol.com – Fax (05214) 6943
geschl. 30. März – 1. Mai, 2. Nov. – 6. Dez.
68 Zim (inkl. ½ P.) – ☼ 64/100 € 100/186 € ❄ 88/164 €
128/340 €
Rest – Karte 18/38 €
◆ Der denkmalgeschützte Gasthof ist eines der ältesten Gasthäuser im Ort. Die Zimmer sind mit soliden Holzmöbeln ausgestattet, im Gästehaus etwas schlichter. Familienzimmer. Restaurant Kirchenwirt mit bürgerlichem Angebot.

Hubertushof Rest, P VISA
Reindlau 230a ✉ 6105 – ☎ (05214) 65 61
– office@hubertushof-leutasch.at – Fax (05214) 6961
geschl. 20. März – 20. Mai, 12. Okt. – 20. Dez.
30 Zim (inkl. ½ P.) – ☼ 60/82 € 110/136 € ❄ 92/121 €
158/214 €
Rest – *(geschl. Dienstag)* Karte 15/39 €
◆ Gepflegt und gut geführt ist dieses alpenländische Hotel mit seinen rustikal möblierten, wohnlich und zugleich funktionell gestalteten Zimmern. Bürgerlich-rustikal eingerichtete Gaststube.

Bergland – Jodlerwirt Rest, P VISA
Obern 42 ✉ 6105 – ☎ (05214) 62 53 – st.draxl@jodlerwirt.at
– Fax (05214) 600426
geschl. April, Nov.
30 Zim (inkl. ½ P.) – ☼ 46/73 € 80/112 € ❄ 73/114 €
126/176 €
Rest – Karte 19/27 €
◆ In einem kleinen Weiler liegt das Hotel des in der Region bekannten "Jodlerwirts", das über behagliche Zimmer mit hellem Holzmobiliar verfügt. Unterhaltungsabend. Kosmetik.

Kristall Rest, P VISA
Weidach 300m ✉ 6105 – ☎ (05214) 63 19 – office@hotel-kristall.at
– Fax (05214) 631947
geschl. 24. März – 24. Mai, 12. Okt. – 21. Dez.
43 Zim (inkl. ½ P.) – ☼ 60/92 € 120/146 € ❄ 98/133 €
182/228 €
Rest – (nur für Hausgäste)
◆ Leicht erhöht in einer Seitenstraße gelegenes Hotel unter familiärer Leitung. Die Zimmer sind z. T. mit hellem Naturholz möbliert, einige auch als große Appartements angelegt.

Lehnerhof garni P
Lehner 199 ✉ 6105 – ☎ (05214) 62 78 – lehnerhof@tirol.com
– Fax (05214) 62785
geschl. 24. März – 21. Mai, 19. Okt. – 20. Dez.
13 Zim – ☼ 32/38 € 54/62 € ❄ 41/48 € 74/88 €
◆ Viele Stammgäste schätzen diesen recht ruhig gelegenen kleinen Familienbetrieb mit sehr gepflegten rustikalen Zimmern und drei Ferienwohnungen.

Forellenhof
Weidach 290 (am Weidachsee) ✉ 6105 – ✆ (05214) 64 55 – forellen.hof@nextra.at – Fax (05214) 6455
geschl. Anfang April – Pfingsten, Anfang Okt. – Weihnachten und Montag
Rest – Karte 17/35 €
◆ Teil dieses Restaurants sind zwei mit 150 Jahre altem Holz ausgestattete Stuben. Fisch aus dem Weidachsee bestimmt das Angebot. Im Sommer sehr beliebt: die Terrasse.

Wie entscheidet man sich zwischen zwei gleichwertigen Adressen? In jeder Kategorie sind die Häuser nochmals geordnet, die besten Adressen stehen an erster Stelle.

LEUTSCHACH – Steiermark – 730 S9 – 630 Ew – Höhe 350 m 11 K6

Wien 248 – Graz 62 – Maribor 25 – Leibnitz 24
Hauptplatz 2, ✉ 8463, ✆ (03454) 70 70 10, info@rebenland.at
Veranstaltungen
17.05.: Weinkulinarium
03.05.: Welschlauf

Tscheppe's Langgasthof Zim,
Hauptplatz 6 ✉ 8463 – ✆ (03454) 2 46 – office@tscheppes-gasthof.com – Fax (03454) 644621
26 Zim – 58/65 € 84/110 € – ½ P 13 €
Rest – *(geschl. Mai – Nov. Sonntagabend, Nov. – Mai Dienstag – Mittwoch)* Karte 15/32 €
◆ Ein erweiterter Gasthof im Zentrum des Ortes, der mit wohnlichen und funktionellen Zimmern in neuzeitlichem Stil überzeugt. Eine ständige Bilderausstellung ziert das Haus. Restaurant mit rustikalem Ambiente.

Moserhof (geheizt)
Grosswalz 80 ✉ 8463 – ✆ (03454) 66 61 – office@moserhof.at – Fax (03454) 666120 – geschl. 23. Dez. – 23. März
24 Zim – 63 € 126 € – ½ P 4/12 € – 7 Suiten
Rest – *(Ende März – Mitte Aug. Montag – Mittwoch nur Mittagessen)* Karte 18/27 €
◆ Sehr ruhig, an der malerischen Weinpanoramastraße liegt dieses familiengeführte Hotel. Alle Zimmer bieten einen sehr schönen Ausblick auf die Weinberge. Eigenes Weingut. Teils rustikales, teils elegantes Restaurant mit regionalem Speisenangebot. Terrasse.

Außerhalb – Lagehinweise siehe bei den einzelnen Häusern:

Weingut Tschermonegg (mit Gästehaus) (geheizt) Zim,
Glanz 50 (Nord-Ost: 6 km über Südsteirische Weinstraße) ✉ 8463 Glanz a.d. Weinstr. – ✆ (03454) 3 26 – weingut@tschermonegg.at – Fax (03454) 32650
geschl. 10. Dez. – 14. März
17 Zim – 46/52 € 72/84 €
Rest – *(geschl. Mittwoch)* Karte ca. 10 €
◆ Ein familiengeführtes Weingut mit neuzeitlichen, wohnlich eingerichteten Zimmern – einige größere Zimmer im Weingartenhaus. Sehr schön: Freibad mit Blick auf die Weinberge. In einem netten Buschenschank serviert man hausgemachte Jausen.

Weingut Tauss garni (geheizt) P VISA

Schloßberg 80 (Süd: 2 km Richtung Schlossberg und Großwalz)
8463 Leutschach – (03454) 67 15 – weingut-tauss@gmx.at
– Fax (03454) 70050
geschl. 16. – 30. Dez.
10 Zim – 50/56 € 76/88 €
◆ Das ruhig gelegene Weingut besticht durch seine hübschen, mit viel Holz behaglich eingerichteten Weißwein-/Rotwein-Zimmer sowie eine schöne Liegewiese mit Pool.

Kreuzwirt am Pössnitzberg P VISA

Pössnitz 168a (Süd-Ost: 5,5 km über Südsteirische Weinstraße)
8463 Leutschach – (03454) 20 56 00 – office@gasthaus-kreuzwirt.at
– Fax (03454) 205690
geschl. 8. Jan. – 21. Feb., Juli 2 Wochen und Dienstag – Donnerstagmittag, Juni – Aug. nur Dienstag – Mittwochmittag
Rest – (Tischbestellung ratsam) Menü 35 € (mittags)/89 €
– Karte 46/69 €
Spez. Gebratenes Wallerfilet mit Kalbskopf und Krenbutter. Brust vom Kapaun mit Flusskrebsen und Morcheln. Warme Marillentarte mit Lavendelblüteneis.
◆ Das Gasthaus mit der gelben Fassade beherbergt in seinem lichten Holzanbau ein freundliches, geradlinig-modern gestaltetes Restaurant mit regional inspirierter Küche.

Abels Wirtshaus am Käsehof P

Fötschach 9 (Ost: 2,5 km über Südsteirische Weinstraße)
8463 Leutschach – (03454) 63 84 – info@kaesehof-abel.com
– Fax (03454) 6384
geschl. Mittwoch – Donnerstag, außer Feiertage
Rest – Menü 21/37 € – Karte 17/29 €
◆ Unter dem schönen Gurtengewölbe des ehemaligen Schafstalls hat man ein gemütlich-rustikales Restaurant eingerichtet. Erzeugnisse der hauseigenen Käserei bereichern die Karte.

Sabathihof mit Zim P

Pössnitz 142 (Ost: 5 km über Südsteirische Weinstraße) 8463 Leutschach – (03454) 4 95 – familie@sabathihof.com – Fax (03454) 4954
geschl. Mitte Dez. – Mitte März
17 Zim – 35/53 € 53/90 € – ½ P 13 €
Rest – *(geschl. Montag – Dienstag, außer Feiertage, Sept. – Okt. Montagmittag, Dienstagmittag)* Karte 15/31 €
◆ Das schön in den Weinbergen gelegene Haus ist ein nettes Restaurant, in dem warme Töne und nettes Dekor ein behagliches Ambiente schaffen. Die meisten der Gästezimmer sind hübsche Winzerzimmer.

Repolusk P

Glanz an der Weinstraße 41 (Nord-Ost: 6,5 km über Südsteirische Weinstraße) 8463 Leutschach – (03454) 3 13 – weingut@repolusk.at
– Fax (03454) 3134
geschl. Dez. – Mitte März und Dienstag – Mittwoch
Rest – Karte ca. 12 €
◆ Sehr gemütlich hat man den Buschenschank mit angenehmen Farben gestaltet. Aus einem großen Ofen kommt das frische Brot für die Jause. Gastgarten mit Blick auf die Weinberge.

LIEBOCH – Steiermark – 730 S8 – 4 000 Ew – Höhe 333 m 10 K5

Wien 202 – Graz 15 – Bruck an der Mur 63 – Maribor 64

Kohnhauser mit Zim

Radlstr. 60 (an der A 2 Ausfahrt Lieboch) ✉ 8501 – ✆ (03136) 6 24 96 – kochkunst@kohnhauser.at – Fax (03136) 6230735

geschl. 1. – 25. Mai

14 Zim – 59 € 90 €

Rest – *(geschl. Samstag, Sonn- und Feiertage)* Menü 25/56 € – Karte 26/51 €

◆ Hell und freundlich eingerichtetes Restaurant mit mächtiger Holzdecke. Idyllisch: die Terrasse in einem hübschen Garten mit großem, schön angelegtem Teich. Solide, hell möblierte Gästezimmer.

LIENZ – Tirol – 730 K8 – 12 080 Ew – Höhe 673 m – Wintersport: 2 290 m

1 16 8 F6

Wien 405 – Innsbruck 175 – Spittal a.d. Drau 70

Europaplatz 1, ✉ 9900, ✆ (04852) 6 52 65, tvblienz@aon.at

Veranstaltungen

22.07. – 26.07.: Olala Straßentheaterfestival

09.08. – 11.08.: Altstadtfest

06.09.: Dolomitenmann

Pfarrkirche St. Andrä (Grabsteine★)

Pustertaler Höhenstraße★ bis Bannberg (Süd-West: 10 km)

Traube Zim,

Hauptplatz 14 ✉ 9900 – ✆ (04852) 6 44 44 – info@hoteltraube.at – Fax (04852) 64184

56 Zim – 88/109 € 136/178 € 79/109 € 124/178 € – ½ P 14 €

Rest *La Taverna* – ✆ (04852) 6 44 44 77 *(geschl. Montag)* Karte 18/31 €

◆ Aus dem 18. Jh. stammt das weinrote Bürgerhaus am Lienzer Hauptplatz. Man bietet Einzel-, Traube- oder klassisch-gediegene, teils antik möblierte Romantik-Zimmer. Im Untergeschoss: das in rustikalem Stil gehaltene Restaurant La Taverna.

Moarhof (geheizt) Rest,

Moarfeldweg 18 ✉ 9900 – ✆ (04852) 6 75 67 – info@hotel-moarhof.at – Fax (04852) 6756750

geschl. 6. – 21. April sowie im Nov. Freitag – Sonntag

57 Zim (inkl. ½ P.) – 54/65 € 104/126 € 51/71 € 102/138 €

Rest – *(geschl. 6. – 21. April, Nov.)* Menü 38 € – Karte 18/39 €

◆ In dem Hotel am Ortsrand erwarten Sie wohnliche Gästezimmer – die nach Süden hin gelegenen alle mit Balkon – sowie ein freundlicher Frühstücksraum in hellem Holz. Hübsch: die gemütliche rustikale A-la-carte-Stube mit internationalem Angebot.

Haidenhof Lienzer Dolomiten, Zim, Zim,

Grafendorfer Str. 12 ✉ 9900 – ✆ (04852) 6 24 40 – info@haidenhof.at – Fax (04852) 624406

geschl. Anfang April 3 Wochen, Anfang Nov. 3 Wochen

23 Zim – 44/62 € 80/124 € – ½ P 15 €

Rest – Menü 45 € – Karte 18/37 €

◆ Das einstige Schloss Grafenberg ist heute ein familiengeführtes Gasthaus mit sehr wohnlichen, neuzeitlichen Zimmern. Schön ist die Lage oberhalb der Stadt. Bürgerliches Restaurant und hübsche Stube mit alter Täfelung. Zum Tal hin angelegte Terrasse.

Goldener Fisch

Kärntner Str. 9 ✉ 9900 – ✆ (04852) 6 21 32 – info@goldener-fisch.at – Fax (04852) 6213248
geschl. 7. – 20. April, 3. – 23. Nov.
30 Zim – 45/53 € 80/92 € – ½ P 12 €
Rest – Karte 14/31 €
◆ Nahe dem Flussufer und nur wenige Schritte vom Zentrum liegt der Gasthof mit den roten Fensterläden. Es erwarten Sie helle, neuzeitlich und funktionell möblierte Zimmer. Das Restaurant teilt sich in bürgerliche Gaststuben.

In Amlach **Süd: 2,5 km über Amlacher Straße:**

Parkhotel Tristachersee

Zim,
Tristachersee 1 (Ost: 3 km) ✉ 9900 – ✆ (04852) 6 76 66 – parkhotel@tristachersee.at – Fax (04852) 67699
geschl. 25. März – 30. April, 3. Nov. – 20. Dez.
53 Zim (inkl. ½ P.) – 85/129 € 124/222 € 82/128 € 124/216 €
Rest – Karte 17/46 €
◆ Idyllisch liegt das engagiert geführte Haus am See. Wohnliche Zimmer mit Balkon und ein schöner Garten mit Fischteichen. Besonders komfortabel: See-Studios und See-Suiten. Mit viel Holz behaglich gestaltete Restaurantstuben. Wintergarten und Terrasse zum See.

Ferienhotel Laserz

Rest,
Ulrichsbichl (Ost: 1 km) ✉ 9900 – ✆ (04852) 6 24 88 – info@laserz.at – Fax (04852) 6248813
geschl. 13. Okt. – 13. Dez.
23 Zim (inkl. ½ P.) – 59/73 € 110/138 € 49/75 € 104/144 €
Rest – Karte 13/29 €
◆ Der im alpenländischen Stil erbaute Gasthof unter familiärer Leitung bietet rustikal eingerichtete Zimmer, die alle über einen Balkon verfügen. Restaurant mit ländlichem Charakter.

LIGIST – Steiermark – 730 R8 – 3 200 Ew – Höhe 392 m 10 **J5**

Wien 215 – Graz 30 – Köflach 16 – Wolfsberg 50
Ligist 22, ✉ 8563, ✆ (03143) 2 22 90, tourismus@ligist.info

Landgasthaus Krämerwirt

Ligist 35 ✉ 8563 – ✆ (03143) 30 40 – zolgar@landgasthaus-kraemerwirt.at – Fax (03143) 3040
geschl. Mitte Feb. 2 Wochen, Mitte Aug. 2 Wochen und Montag – Dienstag
Rest – Karte 15/29 €
◆ Gepflegtes, mit Holzmobiliar, hübschen Stoffen und nettem Dekor in ländlich-rustikalem Stil gehaltenes Restaurant unter familiärer Leitung.

Bestecke und Sterne sollten nicht verwechselt werden!
Die Bestecke stehen für eine Komfortkategorie, die Sterne zeichnen Häuser mit besonders guter Küche aus - in jeder dieser Kategorien.

LINGENAU - Vorarlberg - 730 B6 - 1 330 Ew - Höhe 650 m 5 A5

Wien 593 - Bregenz 21 - Dornbirn 19 - Feldkirch 47

Verkehrsamt, Hof 258, ✉ 6951, ☎ (05513) 63 21, tourismus@lingenau.at

Gasthof zum Löwen

Hof 30 ✉ 6951 – ☎ (05513) 63 60 – info@loewen-lingenau.com – Fax (05513) 63606

geschl. 15. Nov. – 15. Dez.

29 Zim – †48/52 € ††72/80 € – ½ P 12 €

Rest – *(geschl. Mittwoch)* Karte 19/31 €

◆ Ein Anbau mit hellen, in modernem Stil gehaltenen Zimmern – ausgestattet mit großen Fenstern – ergänzt den im Ortszentrum gelegenen Gasthof. Unterteilter Restaurantbereich mit rustikalem Ambiente.

Ball David/PHOTONONSTOP

LINZ

🄻 **Bundesland:** Oberösterreich
Michelin-Karte: **730** O4
▶ Wien 186 – Salzburg 138 – Graz 222 – Passau 82

Einwohnerzahl: 183 510 Ew
Höhe: 260 m

2 H2

Die Lage an der Donau begünstigte die Entwicklung von Linz zum oberösterreichischen Industriezentrum. Noch heute hat die Produktion landesweite Bedeutung, in der Innenstadt ist davon aber nichts zu spüren. Hier gruppieren sich um den gewaltigen Hauptplatz Monumente verschiedenster Epochen, die als Zeugnisse der städtischen Blüten vom Frühmittelalter bis zur Gegenwart stehen. Und der Blick ist schon in die Zukunft gerichtet: Mit dem Ars Electronica Center und dem Lentos Kunstmuseum verfügt Linz über zwei renommierte hochkarätige Museen zu Medien und moderner Kunst. Ausflugsziele locken in allen Himmelsrichtungen: Nördlich der Donau dringt man in die urwüchsige Hügellandschaft des Mühlviertels vor, im Westen entdeckt man die Stiftskirche Wilhering, ein Juwel des Rokoko, im Süden die barocken Anlagen von Schloss Hohenems und Stift St. Florian und im Osten Enns, eine der ältesten Städte Österreichs.

PRAKTISCHE HINWEISE

Tourist-Information

Hauptplatz 1 Z, ✉ 4020, ✆ (0732) 70 70 17 77, tourist.info@linz.at

Flughafen

✈ Linz (Süd-West: 16 km), ✆ (07221) 60 00

Messen

Europaplatz 1, ✉ 4020, ✆ (0732) 69 66

01.02. – 03.02.: Tourist

29.02. – 02.03.: fepo 08 – Die Messe der Unternehmerinnen

15.03. – 16.03.: Linzer Autofrühling

28.03. – 30.03.: Bleib g'sund

23.04. – 27.04.: LITERA

26.09. – 28.09.: Öko Intakt Messe

14.11. – 16.11.: Haus & Wohnen

Veranstaltungen

10.05. – 12.05.: Linz Fest

01.05. – 31.09.: Linzer Donausommer

17.07. – 19.07.: Pflasterspektakel

03.09. – 09.09.: Ars Electronica

14.09. – 04.10.: Brucknerfest

27.09. – 05.10.: Urfahraner Herbstmarkt

15.11. – 24.12.: Christkindlmarkt

Golfplätze

- 9 GC Stärk Linz Pichling, Auhirschgasse 52 ✆ (0732) 32 01 88 20
- 18 GC Stärk Linz Ansfelden, Im Golwinkel 11 ✆ (07229) 7 85 78
- 18 Linzer GC Luftenberg, Am Luftenberg 1a ✆ (07237) 38 93
- 27 Golfclub Donau-Feldkirchen, Golfplatzstr. 12 ✆ (07233) 76 76
- 18 SternGartl – Oberneukirchen, Schauerschlag 4 ✆ (07212) 2 13 33

SEHENSWÜRDIGKEITEN

Pöstlingberg★ (≤★) X – Altstadt★ (Schlossmuseum★) – Priesterseminarkirche★ – Lentos Kunstmuseum★ Z – Stiftskirche Wilhering★★★ (West: 8 km) – Mühlviertel★ (Nord: 15 km)

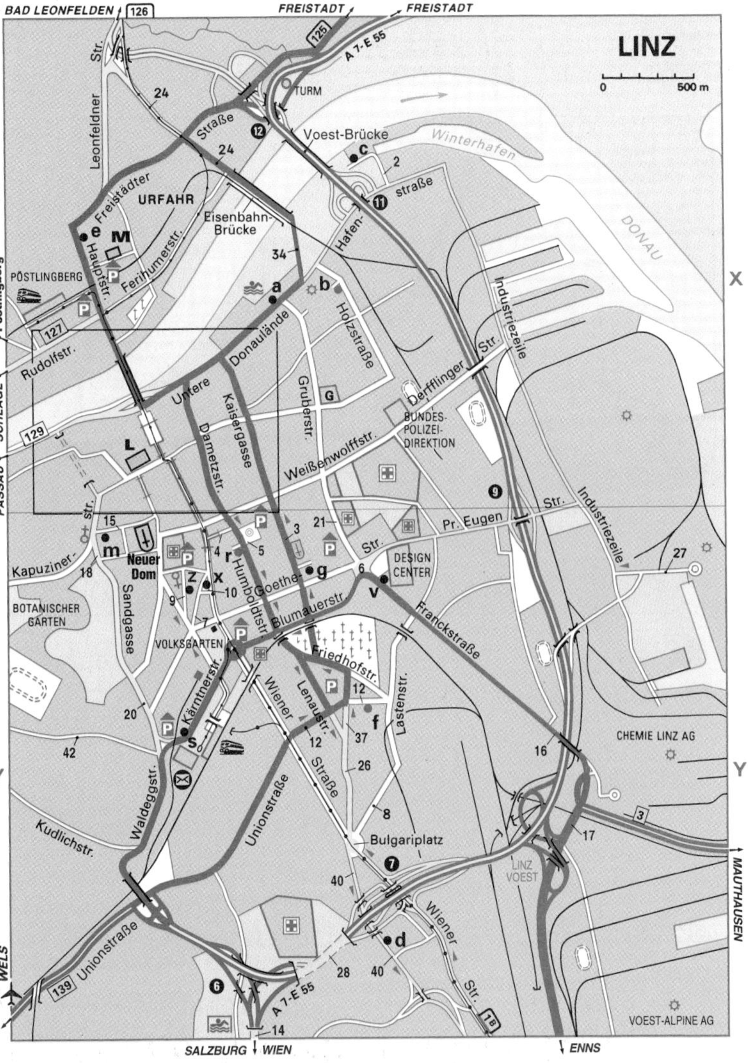

LINZ

Straße	Planquadrat	Nr.
Aigengutstr.	Y	17
Am Winterhafen	X	2
Baumbachstr.	XY	15
Dinghoferstr.	Y	3
Einhausung Niedernhart	Y	28
Europaplatz	Y	6
Gesellenhausstr.	Y	9
Gürtelstr.	Y	8
Hamerlingstr.	Y	12
Henssenplatz	Y	5
Hopfengasse	Y	18
Johann-Konrad-Vogel-Str.	Y	4
Kellergasse	Y	20
Khevenhüllerstr.	X	21
Linke-Brückenstr.	X	24
Makartstr.	Y	26
Nebingerstr.	Y	27
Rainerstr.	Y	7
Rechte Brückenstr.	X	34
Rilkestr.	Y	37
St. Peter Str.	Y	16
Schillerplatz	Y	10
Tunnel Bindermichl	Y	14
Wankmüllerhofstr.	Y	40
Ziegeleistr.	Y	42

Rot = angenehm. Richten Sie sich nach den Symbolen ✗ und ⌂ in Rot.

LINZ

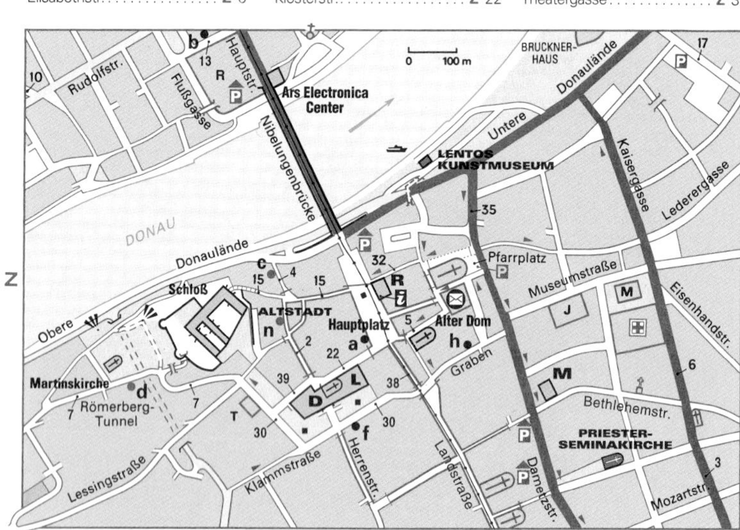

Schillerpark Zim, Rest,
Schillerplatz ✉ *4020 –* ✆ *(0732) 6 95 00* VISA MC AE D
– schillerpark@austria-trend.at – Fax (0732) 69509 Y **x**
111 Zim – 82/194 € 119/268 €
Rest *Primo Piano* – ✆ (0732) 6 95 01 17 *(geschl. Montag, Sonn- und Feiertage, nur Abendessen)* Karte 27/43 €
Rest *Tafelspitz* – ✆ (0732) 6 95 01 09 – Karte 20/29 €
◆ Hinter seiner verglasten Fassade beherbergt das unweit der Fußgängerzone gelegene Hotel eine großzügige Halle und moderne Zimmer unterschiedlicher Kategorien. Primo Piano im 1. Stock mit großer Fensterfront zum Schillerplatz. Tafelspitz in zeitlosem Stil.

Courtyard by Marriott Zim,
Europaplatz 2 ✉ *4020 –* ✆ *(0732) 6 95 90* VISA MC AE D
– cy.lnzcy.dos@courtyard.com – Fax (0732) 606090 Y **v**
236 Zim – 115/130 € 115/130 €, 16 € – 3 Suiten
Rest – Karte 21/43 €
◆ Zu den Annehmlichkeiten dieses modernen Hotels zählen hell eingerichtete Zimmer mit guter Technik, ein gepflegter Freizeitbereich sowie ein Businesscenter. Neuzeitliches Restaurant in freundlichen Farben und mit großer Fensterfront.

ARCOTEL Nike Zim, P
Untere Donaulände 9 ✉ *4020* VISA MC AE D
– ✆ *(0732) 7 62 60 – nike@arcotel.at – Fax (0732) 76262* X **a**
176 Zim – 82/170 € 82/170 €, 14 €
Rest – *(geschl. Samstagmittag)* Karte 22/52 €
◆ Hier überzeugen die Lage direkt an der Donau und ganz in der Nähe der Altstadt sowie neuzeitliche, funktionelle Zimmer. Sehr moderne Executive-Zimmer in den obersten Etagen. Elegantes Restaurant mit Terrasse.

Drei Mohren garni

Promenade 17 ✉ 4020 – ✆ (0732) 7 72 62 60 – hotel@drei-mohren.at – Fax (0732) 7726266 Z **f**

23 Zim ☕ – 🚹108 € 🚹🚹142 €

♦ Dieser über 400 Jahre alte, persönlich geführte Traditionsbetrieb bietet wohnlich-komfortable Gästezimmer und elegante Suiten. Schön ist das Foyer mit offenem Kamin.

Steigenberger Zim,

Am Winterhafen 13 ✉ 4020 – ✆ (0732) 7 89 90 – linz@steigenberger.at – Fax (0732) 789999 X **c**

168 Zim – 🚹73/120 € 🚹🚹146/290 €, ☕ 12 €

Rest – Karte 28/43 €

♦ Außen moderne Architektur, innen nostalgisches Ambiente im US-amerikanischen Club-Stil. Rattanmobiliar und Deckenventilatoren in den Zimmern runden das Bild ab. Bistroähnlicher Stil prägt das Restaurant.

Wolfinger garni

Hauptplatz 19 ✉ 4020 – ✆ (070) 7 73 29 10 – office@hotelwolfinger.at – Fax (070) 77329155 Z **a**

50 Zim ☕ – 🚹80/87 € 🚹🚹116/126 €

♦ In den ehrwürdigen Mauern des 1616 erstmals als Gasthof erwähnten Hauses finden Besucher geschmackvoll mit Stilmobiliar bestückte Zimmer – teils mit Parkett und Gewölbedecke.

Dom-Hotel garni (mit Gästehaus)

Baumbachstr. 17 ✉ 4020 – ✆ (0732) 77 84 41 – domhotel—linz@aon.at – Fax (0732) 775432 Y **m**

44 Zim ☕ – 🚹105 € 🚹🚹130 €

♦ Zentral, in Domnähe, liegt dieses zeitgemäße Hotel. Die Zimmer im 5. Stock verfügen über Balkon oder Wintergarten. Individuell: die Zimmer im ruhig gelegenen Gästehaus.

City-Hotel garni

Schillerstr. 52 ✉ 4020 – ✆ (070) 65 26 22 – cityhotel—linz@aon.at – Fax (070) 651308 Y **g**

40 Zim ☕ – 🚹105 € 🚹🚹130 €

♦ Hier erwarten Sie funktionelle, in hellen Farben und modernem Stil eingerichtete Gästezimmer und ein neuzeitlicher, angenehm lichter Frühstücksraum.

Kolping garni

Gesellenhausstr. 5 ✉ 4020 – ✆ (0732) 66 16 90 – office@hotel-kolping.at – Fax (0732) 66169055 Y **z**

52 Zim ☕ – 🚹82 € 🚹🚹106 €

♦ Im Herzen der Stadt, am Beginn der Fußgängerzone, liegt diese saubere und gepflegte Übernachtungsadresse, die über praktisch ausgestattete Zimmer verfügt.

Novotel Rest, Zim,

Wankmüllerhofstr. 37 ✉ 4020 – ✆ (070) 3 47 28 10 – h0519@accor.com – Fax (070) 349335 Y **d**

115 Zim ☕ – 🚹78/95 € 🚹🚹90/122 €

Rest – Karte 17/40 €

♦ Vor allem Tagungsgäste schätzen die freundlichen, neuzeitlich ausgestatteten Zimmer dieses Hotels sowie die stadtnahe, verkehrsgünstige Lage direkt an der Autobahn.

Mühlviertlerhof garni
Graben 24 ✉ 4020 – ✆ (0732) 77 22 68 – office@hotel-muehlviertlerhof.at – Fax (0732) 77226834 Z **h**
26 Zim – 64/78 € 94/108 €
◆ Ganz individuell eingerichtete Themenzimmer – vom Indischen Zimmer über das Burgzimmer bis zum Afrikanischen Zimmer – erwarten Sie in dem kleinen Hotel im Stadtzentrum.

Ibis
Zim,
Kärntner Str. 18 ✉ 4020 – ✆ (0732) 6 94 01 – h1722@accor.com – Fax (0732) 694019 Y **s**
146 Zim – 61 € 76 €, 9 €
Rest – Karte 15/26 €
◆ Besonders für Geschäftsreisende eignet sich diese beim Hauptbahnhof gelegene Übernachtungsadresse mit ihren praktisch und zeitgemäß ausgestatteten Zimmern.

Nöserlgut
Landwiedstr. 69 (über Unionsstraße Y, dann links ab) ✉ 4020 – ✆ (070) 68 33 26 – hotel@noeserlgut.at – Fax (070) 68332620
18 Zim – 65 € 94 €
Rest – *(geschl. Samstag, Sonn- und Feiertage)* Karte 16/24 €
◆ Dieses Haus besticht durch familiäre Atmosphäre und gut ausgestattete, wohnliche Zimmer, deren Mobiliar aus dem Holz des 500 Jahre alten Dachstuhls gefertigt wurde. Gewölbedecke, ländliches Dekor und blanke Tische geben dem Heurigenrestaurant rustikales Flair.

herberstein
Altstadt 10 ✉ 4020 – ✆ (0732) 78 61 61 – office@herberstein-linz.at – Fax (0732) 78616111
geschl. Sonntag Z **n**
Rest – *(nur Abendessen)* (Tischbestellung ratsam) Karte 30/41 €
◆ Modernes Restaurant in historischen Mauern – mit Asia Lounge, Oriental Lounge (hier speist man im Liegen) und Enoteca mit schönem Kreuzgewölbe. Hübscher begrünter Innenhof.

Der neue Vogelkäfig
Holzstr. 8 ✉ 4020 – ✆ (0732) 77 01 93 – vogelkaefig@utanet.at – Fax (0732) 7701932
geschl. Feb. 1 Woche, Aug. – Sept. 3 Wochen und Samstag – Montag X **b**
Rest – (Tischbestellung ratsam) Menü 29 € (mittags)/71 € (abends) – Karte 39/62 €
◆ Seit vielen Jahren führt Georg Essig dieses leicht rustikale, mit Bildern und Vogelkäfigen dekorierte Restaurant. Das Angebot: klassisch und regional. Nette Gartenterrasse.

La Cave
Römerstr. 21 ✉ 4020 – ✆ (070) 77 62 03 – office@la-cave.at – Fax (070) 682157
geschl. 25. Juli – 16. Aug. sowie Sonn- und Feiertage Z **d**
Rest – *(nur Abendessen)* Karte 27/43 €
◆ Verteilt auf drei Etagen eines Eckhauses befindet sich ein Restaurant, das durch dunkles Holz, gedämpfte Beleuchtung und schön gedeckte Tische romantisch und gemütlich wirkt.

XX **Nabuu**

Hamerlingstr. 42 ✉ 4020 – ☎ (0732) 60 03 16 – office@nabuu.at – Fax (0732) 6003164

geschl. Anfang Aug. 1 Woche, Sonn- und Feiertage Y **f**

Rest – Menü 7 € (mittags) – Karte 26/37 €

♦ Sehr modern, mit verglaster Front, dunklen Böden und heller Möblierung ist das zweistöckige Restaurant, das Ihnen internationale Küche mit asiatischen Einflüssen offeriert.

X **Schwarzer Anker**

Hessenplatz 14 ✉ 4020 – ☎ (0732) 77 82 46 – anker@schwarzer-anker.at – Fax (0732) 77865917

geschl. 4. – 24. Aug. und Sonntagabend – Montag Y **r**

Rest – Karte 12/30 €

♦ Das Traditionslokal am Hessenplatz lockt mit Wirtshauscharakter und bodenständiger Küche. Im Keller des Hauses finden auch Live-Konzerte in geselliger Atmosphäre statt.

X **Zum kleinen Griechen**

Hofberg 8 ✉ 4020 – ☎ (070) 78 24 67 – info@zumkleinengriechen.at – Fax (070) 944096

geschl. Sonntagabend Z **c**

Rest – Menü 58 € – Karte 30/52 €

♦ Alte Gewölbe aus dem 15. Jh. bilden den Rahmen dieses kleinen, familiär geführten Lokals, dessen Küche mediterran-levantinische Speisen bietet. Handverlesenes Zigarrenangebot!

Dieser Führer lebt von Ihren Anregungen, die uns stets willkommen sind. Egal ob Sie uns eine besonders angenehme Überraschung oder eine Enttäuschung mitteilen wollen – schreiben Sie uns!

In Linz-Urfahr

Spitz garni

Fiedlerstr. 6 ✉ 4040 – ☎ (070) 73 37 33 – office@spitzhotel.at – Fax (070) 733733833 Z **b**

73 Zim – ☼ 139/198 € 168/227 € ❄ 153/219 € 182/248 €

♦ Ein moderner Hallenbereich empfängt Sie in einem der ersten Kultur- und-Style Hotels, wie sich das Spitz bezeichnet. Die Zimmer sind je nach Stockwerk unterschiedlich gestaltet.

Goldener Adler (mit Gästehaus)

Hauptstr. 56 ✉ 4040 – ☎ (0732) 73 11 47 – office@goldeneradler.at – Fax (0732) 7311475 X **e**

43 Zim – 65 € 90 €

Rest – *(geschl. 24. Dez. – 2. Jan. und Sonntag, im Sommer Samstag – Sonntag)* Karte 16/36 €

♦ Im Haupthaus wie auch in den beiden Gästehäusern bietet man Reisenden solide möblierte Zimmer mit zeitgemäßer Ausstattung. Auch Appartements stehen zur Verfügung. Ein bürgerlich-rustikales Ambiente erwartet Sie im Restaurant und in der Schmankerl Hütt'n.

XXX **Verdi** (Erich Lukas)

Pachmayrstr. 137 (über Leonfeldner Straße X) ✉ 4040 – ✆ (070) 73 30 05 – lukas@verdi.at – Fax (070) 7330054
geschl. Sonntag – Montag, Feiertage
Rest *Verdi Einkehr* – separat erwähnt
Rest – *(nur Abendessen)* (Tischbestellung ratsam) Menü 45/62 € – Karte 31/50 €
Spez. Regionale Impressionen serviert in vier Gängen. In Barolo geschmorte Kalbsbackerl mit Karfiolcreme und Gemüse-Schnittlauchnage. Schokodôme mit Trester und Tonkabohnen-Semifreddo.
◆ Modern-elegant wurde das Restaurant mit dem aufmerksamen Service gestaltet. Die mediterrane und internationale Küche wird auch auf der Terrasse mit Blick ins Grüne serviert.

X **Verdi Einkehr**

Pachmayrstr. 137 (über Leonfeldner Str. X) ✉ 4040 – ✆ (070) 73 30 05 – lukas@verdi.at – Fax (070) 7330054
geschl. Sonntag – Montag, Feiertage
Rest – *(nur Abendessen)* (Tischbestellung ratsam) Menü 30 € – Karte 22/30 €
◆ Dies ist die etwas einfachere Alternative zum Restaurant Verdi. Die Gäste nehmen in gemütlich-ländlicher Atmosphäre Platz und lassen sich regionale Gerichte schmecken.

In Leonding-Berg **West: 3,5 km über Kapuzinerstraße Y:**

XX **Bergdiele**

Holzheimerstr. 7 ✉ 4060 – ✆ (0732) 78 10 54 – info@bergdiele.at – Fax (0732) 774357
geschl. Samstag, Sonn- und Feiertage
Rest – (Tischbestellung ratsam) Menü 35/49 € – Karte 26/45 €
◆ Das Haus mit der markanten gelben Fassade beherbergt ein helles, freundliches Restaurant im Landhausstil. Aufmerksam serviert man eine gute regionale und internationale Küche.

Gute Küche zu günstigem Preis? Folgen Sie dem „Bib Gourmand". – Das freundliche MICHELIN-Männchen heißt „Bib" und steht für ein besonders gutes Preis-Leistungs-Verhältnis!

LOCHAU – Vorarlberg – 730 B6 – 5 250 Ew – Höhe 412 m – Wintersport: 1 064 m 2

5 **A5**

Wien 613 – Bregenz 6 – Dornbirn 19 – Lindau 6
Landstr. 22, Gemeindeamt, ✉ 6911, ✆ (05574) 4 53 04, tourismus@lochau.cnv.at

Gästehaus Bernhard garni

Landstr. 16 ✉ 6911 – ✆ (05574) 4 77 56 – wb.gaestehaus@aon.at – Fax (05574) 477566
11 Zim – 41/46 € 68/78 €
◆ 10 Minuten vom See entfernt liegt dieses nette, ca. 400 Jahre alte kleine Gasthaus mit gepflegten Zimmern. Sie frühstücken in einer behaglichen holzvertäfelten alten Stube.

Mangold (Michael Schwarzenbacher)

Pfänderstr. 3 ✉ 6911 – ✆ (05574) 4 24 31 – office@restaurant-mangold.at – Fax (05574) 424319
geschl. Feb. 3 Wochen und Montag
Rest – Menü 40/67 € – Karte 35/54 €
Spez. Roh marinierte Jakobsmuscheln mit Granny Smith und Ingwereis. Kalbs T-Bone mit Spargel und Spinattortellini. Topfenschmarren mit Mango und Sauerrahmeis.

◆ In gemütlichem Ambiente serviert man freundlich und aufmerksam feine Regionalküche mit mediterranem Einfluss. Schön sitzt man auch im Innenhof oder im lichten Wintergarten.

LÖLLING – Kärnten – 730 P8 – 1 810 Ew – Höhe 900 m 10 I5

Wien 253 – Klagenfurt 48 – Graz 89 – St. Veit an der Glan 29

Landgasthof Neugebauer mit Zim

Graben 6 ✉ 9335 – ✆ (04263) 4 07 – neugebauer@loelling.at – Fax (04263) 4074
geschl. 11. – 24. Feb. und Montag
5 Zim – 38 € 76 €
Rest – Karte 16/35 €

◆ Seit über 100 Jahren leitet Familie Neugebauer ihren ländlich-rustikalen Landgasthof. Es erwarten Sie freundlicher Service und regionale Küche. Nett: der Gastgarten am Bach. Gemütlich und tipptopp gepflegt sind die Zimmer im Gästehaus.

LOFER – Salzburg – 730 K6 – 1 950 Ew – Höhe 640 m – Wintersport: 1 630 m 2 14 8 F4

Wien 332 – Salzburg 41 – Zell am See 38 – Bad Reichenhall 25
Lofer 310, ✉ 5090, ✆ (06588) 8 32 10, info@lofer.com
Stadtbild★★
Saalachtal★ (Süd-Ost: 10 km)

Dax

Rest,

Lofer 250 ✉ 5090 – ✆ (06588) 83 89 – hoteldax@lofer.net – Fax (06588) 83899
40 Zim (inkl. ½ P.) – 58/70 € 100/118 € 72/94 € 128/166 € – 6 Suiten
Rest – Karte 19/32 €

◆ Ein gewachsenes, sehr gepflegtes Alpenhotel unter familiärer Leitung, dessen Gästezimmer mit Altholz, in hellem Naturholz oder im italienischen Stil eingerichtet sind. Regionstypisch gestaltetes Restaurant. Abends zusätzlich Pizza-Pasta-Restaurant.

Salzburger Hof

Lofer 128 ✉ 5090 – ✆ (06588) 83 33 – info@hotel-salzburgerhof.at – Fax (06588) 7663
geschl. 10. April – 4. Mai, 20. Okt. – 15. Dez.
25 Zim (inkl. ½ P.) – 38/51 € 72/96 € 45/62 € 84/120 €
Rest – Karte 15/36 €

◆ Die Zimmer dieses Familienbetriebs sind mit soliden Holzmöbeln ausgestattet, gepflegt und verfügen über ein gutes Platzangebot. In Stuben unterteiltes Restaurant mit ländlichem Ambiente.

Neuwirt

Lofer 177 ✉ 5090 – ✆ (06588) 83 15 – landgasthof.neuwirt@aon.at – Fax (06588) 83154
geschl. April, Nov.
14 Zim – 43/46 € 74/78 € 45/51 € 76/88 € – ½ P 9 €
Rest – *(geschl. Montag)* Karte 17/32 €
◆ Der kleine alpenländische Gasthof befindet sich in leicht erhöhter Lage und bietet seinen Gästen zeitgemäße Zimmer mit Balkon sowie ein Biofrühstück. Restaurant in rustikalem Stil.

Rot steht für unsere besonderen Empfehlungen!

LOIPERSDORF – **Steiermark** – 730 U7 – **1 340 Ew** – **Höhe 249 m** – **Wintersport: 330 m** 11 **L5**

Wien 164 – Graz 65 – Fürstenfeld 6
Therme Loipersdorf 152, ✉ 8282, ✆ (03382) 88 33, info@loipersdorf.at
Thermengolfclub Loipersdorf-Fürstenfeld, Gillersdorf 50 ✆ (03382) 85 33

Loipen Hof garni

Loipersdorf 223 (Süd-Ost: 3 km, Richtung Jennersdorf, dann rechts ab) ✉ 8282 – ✆ (03382) 85 74 – info@loipenhof.at – Fax (03382) 857442
geschl. Juli 1 Woche, Jan. 2 Wochen
25 Zim – 44/50 € 68/80 €
◆ Das am Waldrand gelegene familiengeführte Hotel beherbergt wohnliche, hübsch eingerichtete Gästezimmer und einen behaglichen Frühstücksraum.

Im Ortsteil Therme Loipersdorf Süd-West: 3,5 km Richtung Jennersdorf:

Loipersdorf Spa & Conference

(freier Zugang zur Therme) Rest,

Loipersdorf 219 ✉ 8282 – ✆ (03382) 2 00 00 – info@loipersdorfhotel.com – Fax (03382) 2000088
244 Zim – 157/213 € 220/275 € – ½ P 25 €
Rest – Karte 19/41 €
◆ An der Therme liegt die Hotelanlage mit großzügigem Rahmen und guten Konferenzmöglichkeiten, die in allen Bereichen neuesten Gesichtspunkten entspricht. Restaurant mit schöner Terrasse und Blick.

Thermenhotel Stoiser

(geheizt) (freier Zugang zur Therme) Rest,

An der Therme 153 ✉ 8282 – ✆ (03382) 82 12 – thermenhotel@stoiser.com – Fax (03382) 821233
geschl. 15. – 24. Dez.
142 Zim (inkl. ½ P.) – 72/122 € 210/224 € – 8 Suiten
Rest – Karte 15/31 €
◆ Freundlich eingerichtete Zimmer mit funktioneller Ausstattung sowie ein gepflegter Freizeitbereich mit Gartenanlage zählen zu den Vorzügen dieses Hauses.

Thermalhotel Leitner

(freier Zugang zur Therme) Zim, VISA AE

Therme Loipersdorf 218 ✉ 8282 – ☎ (03382) 86 16
– thermal@hotel-leitner.at – Fax (03382) 861686
74 Zim (inkl. ½ P.) – 99/108 € 142/184 €
10 Suiten
Rest – (nur für Hausgäste)
◆ Durch eine helle, modern gestaltete Hotelhalle gelangen Sie in wohnliche Gästezimmer, meist mit Balkon – von einigen hat man einen Blick auf die Therme.

Thermenhotel Kowald

(freier Zugang zur Therme) Rest, VISA AE

Loipersdorf 215 ✉ 8282
– ☎ (03382) 82 82 – info@kowald.com – Fax (03382) 828228
geschl. 15. – 25. Dez.
45 Zim (inkl. ½ P.) – 85/93 € 142/172 €
Rest – *(nur Abendessen)* Karte 19/26 €
◆ Ein gut unterhaltenes Hotel unter familiärer Leitung. Parkettfußboden trägt in den zeitgemäß ausgestatteten Zimmern zu einem behaglichen Ambiente bei. Viel Holz und warme Farben lassen das Restaurant freundlich-rustikal wirken.

Riegler's

Buschenschank

Therme Loipersdorf 161 ✉ 8282 – ☎ (03382) 2 00 01
– hannes.riegler@utanet.at – Fax (03382) 8435
geschl. Jan. – 25. März, 23. Juni – 20. Juli und Sonntag – Montag
Rest – *(geöffnet ab 17 Uhr)* Karte ca. 12 €
◆ Die rustikale Einrichtung mit Kamin bestimmt das gemütlich-ländliche Flair dieses Buschenschankes. Serviert werden zum Wein Jausen aus Produkten der eigenen Landwirtschaft.

LUSTENAU – Vorarlberg – 730 A6 – 19 710 Ew – Höhe 405 m   5 A5

Wien 630 – Bregenz 11 – Dornbirn 8 – Feldkirch 29

Gasthof Krönele

VISA

Reichsstr. 12, (B 203) ✉ 6890 – ☎ (05577) 8 21 18
– gasthof@kroenele.com – Fax (05577) 8211850
74 Zim – 58/78 € 78/110 €
Rest – Karte 18/43 €
◆ Die einstige bäuerliche Gastwirtschaft von 1875 ist ein familiengeführtes Hotel mit wohnlichen, zeitgemäßen Zimmern, die sich teilweise in einem neuen Anbau befinden. In Stuben unterteiltes rustikales und nett dekoriertes Restaurant.

Frühlingsgarten

VISA

Hofsteigstr. 39 (Nord-Ost: 3 km, Richtung Bregenz über L 203, nach 2 km rechts ab) ✉ 6890 – ☎ (05577) 8 24 12
– Fax (05577) 82412
geschl. Karwoche, Mitte Aug. – Anfang Sept., Freitag – Samstagmittag
Rest – Karte 15/26 €
◆ Dieses schlichte, gepflegte Restaurant unter familiärer Leitung ist in bürgerlichem Stil gehalten und bietet eine ebenfalls bürgerliche Speisenauswahl.

LUTZMANNSBURG – Burgenland – 730 V6 – 950 Ew – Höhe 204 m 11 **M4**

Wien 96 – Eisenstadt 62 – Szombathely 37

Sonnenpark (direkter Zugang zur Therme) Zim,

Thermengelände 1 ✉ 7361
– ☎ (02615) 8 71 71 – info@sonnenpark.at – Fax (02615) 8717119
geschl. 22. – 25. Dez.
87 Zim (inkl. ½ P.) – 122/132 € 194/214 €
Rest – (nur Abendessen für Hausgäste)
◆ Ganz modern: eine Atriumhalle mit aufwändiger Stahl-/Glaskonstruktion sowie die großzügig geschnittenen und funktionell ausgestatteten Zimmer. Auch Familienzimmer.

Thermenhotel All in Red (geheizt) (direkter Zugang zur Therme) Rest,

Thermenplatz 7 ✉ 7361 – ☎ (02615) 8 13 13 – hotel@allinred.at
– Fax (02615) 81313813
geschl. Nov. 1 Woche, Dez. 1 Woche
71 Zim – 109/139 € 198/258 €
Rest – (nur für Hausgäste)
◆ Äußerst modern in Form und Farbe – von der Halle bis in die Zimmer. Überall in diesem All-inclusive-Haus setzt Rot farbige Akzente. Vier Top-Appartements mit Dachterrasse.

Thermenhof Derdak Zim,

Thermenstr. 1 ✉ 7361 – ☎ (02615) 8 77 11 – office@thermenhofderdak.at
– Fax (02615) 877114
31 Zim – 45/50 € 70/80 € – ½ P 12/15 €
Rest – Karte 19/23 €
◆ Vom Baustil bis zur Zimmereinrichtung präsentiert sich das familiengeführte Hotel ganz neuzeitlich. In nur 10 Gehminuten erreichen Sie die Sonnentherme. In freundlichen Farben ist das Restaurant gehalten – nette Terrasse im Innenhof.

Sonnenhof garni

Thermenstr. 29 ✉ 7361 – ☎ (02615) 8 12 86
– sonnenhof-lutzmannsburg@gmx.at – Fax (02615) 8128633
36 Zim – 42/48 € 64/76 €
◆ Modern und angenehm hell gestaltete Zimmer sowie die überschaubare Größe sprechen für diese sehr gepflegte Frühstückspension unter familiärer Leitung.

MADSEIT – Tirol – siehe Tux

Wir bemühen uns bei unseren Preisangaben um größtmögliche Genauigkeit. Aber alles ändert sich! Lassen Sie sich daher bei Ihrer Reservierung den derzeit gültigen Preis mitteilen.

MAISHOFEN – Salzburg – 730 K6 – 3 030 Ew – Höhe 757 m – Wintersport: 1 8 F5

Wien 366 – Salzburg 74 – Kitzbühel 61 – Saalfelden 11
Saalhofstr. 2, ✉ 5751, ✆ (06542) 6 83 18, info@maishofen.com

Landgasthof Schloss Kammer

Kammererstr. 22 ✉ 5751 – ✆ (06542) 6 82 02 – schloss.kammer@sbg.at – Fax (06542) 682024
geschl. 1. Nov. – 2. Dez.
13 Zim – 46/62 € 82/114 € 49/70 € 88/130 € – ½ P 13 €
Rest – *(geschl. Mai – Juni und Sept. – Okt. Montag)* Karte 14/31 €
◆ Das kleine Schloss im Stil eines Landgasthofs ist seit über 200 Jahren familiengeführt – mit eigener Kapelle. Individuell mit Antiquitäten und Naturholz eingerichtete Zimmer. Freundlicher Service in den drei ländlichen Stuben mit Gewölbe.

Gute Küche zu günstigem Preis? Folgen Sie dem „Bib Gourmand"

MALLNITZ – Kärnten – 730 L8 – 1 030 Ew – Höhe 1 200 m – Wintersport: 2 650 m 2 5 – Heilklimatischer Luftkurort 8 G5

Wien 373 – Klagenfurt 116 – Badgastein 6 – Spittal a.d. Drau 38
✉ 9822, ✆ (04784) 2 90, info@mallnitz.at
Ankogelbahn★★ – Obervellach (Pfarrkirche★, Triptychon★) Süd: 9 km

Alpengarten

Zim, Rest,

Rabisch 11 (Süd: 1,5 km) ✉ 9822 – ✆ (04784) 81 00 – info@alpengarten.at – Fax (04784) 810015
geschl. 14. April – 24. Mai, 6. Okt. – 16. Dez.
30 Zim (inkl. ½ P.) – 71/78 € 118/150 € 76/115 € 126/216 €
Rest – (nur für Hausgäste)
◆ Zu dem familiengeführten Ferienhotel mit soliden Gästezimmern gehört eine nette Gartenanlage mit Naturschwimmteich und Kinderspielplatz sowie ein Streichelzoo.

MARBACH AN DER DONAU – Niederösterreich – 730 R4 – 1 670 Ew – Höhe 220 m 3 J2

Wien 103 – St. Pölten 46 – Amstetten 40 – Melk 18

Wachauerhof

Wachau-Krummnußbaum 43 ✉ 3671 – ✆ (07413) 70 35 – info@wachauerhof.at – Fax (07413) 703533
geschl. Jan. – April
16 Zim – 54/58 € 82/90 € – ½ P 14 €
Rest – *(geschl. Montag – Dienstag)* Karte 13/29 €
◆ Das an der Donau gelegene familiengeführte Urlaubshotel verfügt über wohnliche, mit hellem Naturholz möblierte Gästezimmer, Fahrrad-Service und einen eigenen Bootssteg. Unterteiltes, ländlich gestaltetes Restaurant.

MARIA ALM – Salzburg – 730 K6 – 2 150 Ew – Höhe 800 m – Wintersport: 2 000 m 2 31 8 **F5**

Wien 362 – Salzburg 70 – Saalfelden 6 – Zell am See 20
Dorf 65, ✉ 5761, ✆ (06584) 78 16, infoalm@hochkoenig.at

Veranstaltungen

27.07.: Jakobi-Ranggeln am Hundstein

Edelweiss

Bachstr. 23 ✉ 5761 – ✆ (06584) 78 28 – info@hoteledelweissmariaalm.at – Fax (06584) 782896

geschl. 6. April – 3. Mai, 2. Nov. – 13. Dez.

31 Zim – ☼ 45/64 € 74/112 € ❄ 63/74 € 110/132 € – ½ P 15 €

Rest – Karte 21/35 €

◆ Relativ ruhig liegt das im regionstypischen Stil gebaute Hotel in einer Seitenstraße. Man bietet neuzeitliche Zimmer und einen großen Sauna-, Dampfbad- und Rasulbereich. Leicht rustikales Restaurant.

Der Thalerhof

Rest, P

Dorf 88 ✉ 5761 – ✆ (06584) 74 47 – thalerhof@sbg.at – Fax (06584) 744717

geschl. 1. Nov. – 15. Dez.

38 Zim (inkl. ½ P.) – ☼ 69/89 € 118/138 € ❄ 81/115 € 142/190 €

Rest – Karte 16/29 €

◆ Hinter seiner alpenländischen Balkonfassade beherbergt das tadellos geführte Hotel mit Wurzelholz eingerichtete sowie großzügigere, hell und modern gestaltete Zimmer. Restaurant mit gepflegtem ländlichem Ambiente und gemütliche Weinbar mit Backsteingewölbe.

In Maria Alm – Hinterthal Ost: 8 km:

Schafhuber

Urslaustr. 4 ✉ 5761 – ✆ (06584) 81 47 – landhotel-schafhuber@sbg.at – Fax (06584) 81477

geschl. Ende März – Mitte Mai, Mitte Okt. – Mitte Dez.

16 Zim (inkl. ½ P.) – ☼ 63/70 € 106/138 € ❄ 85/121 € 146/202 €

Rest – Karte 14/30 €

◆ In dem kleinen Hotel am Ortseingang erwarten Sie in ländlichem Stil eingerichtete Gästezimmer – besonders hübsch sind die Romantikzimmer mit Holzfußboden. In gemütlich-rustikale, nett dekorierte Stuben unterteiltes Restaurant. Die Spezialität: Strudel.

Urslauerhof

Urslaustr. 2 ✉ 5761 – ✆ (06584) 81 64 – urslauerhof@sbg.at – Fax (06584) 8208

geschl. 1. Nov. – 15. Dez.

30 Zim (inkl. ½ P.) – ☼ 60/75 € 100/130 € ❄ 86/104 € 150/182 €

Rest – Menü 20 € – Karte 15/35 €

◆ Ein neuzeitlicher alpenländischer Gasthof unter familiärer Leitung. Die Zimmer verteilen sich auf Neubau und Stammhaus und sind in Ahorn oder Esche möbliert. Neo-rustikal gestaltetes Restaurant.

MARIA ENZERSDORF AM GEBIRGE – Niederösterreich – 730 U4 – 8 210 Ew – Höhe 225 m 4 L2

Wien 22 – Sankt Pölten 70 – Baden 16 – Mödling 2

Restaurant im Schloss Hunyadi

Schlossgasse 6 ✉ 2344 – ✆ (02236) 89 39 89 – geniessen@schlosshunyadi.at – Fax (02236) 89398939
geschl. 17 – 24. März, 1. – 20. Sept. und Samstag – Sonntag
Rest – Menü 21 € (mittags)/49 € – Karte 27/34 €

◆ Das spätbarocke Schloss bietet diesem eleganten Restaurant einen stilvollen Rahmen. Herr Winter bereitet klassische Küche. Schöner Park mit altem Baumbestand.

MARIA TAFERL – Niederösterreich – 730 R4 – 880 Ew – Höhe 443 m

Wien 103 – St. Pölten 46 – Krems 52 – Amstetten 40 3 J2
Maria Taferl, Maria Taferl 43 ✆ (07413) 3 50
Lage★

Schachner (mit Gästehaus) Donautal und Alpenvorland, (geheizt) Zim,

Maria Taferl 24 ✉ 3672 – ✆ (07413) 63 55 – office@hotel-schachner.at – Fax (07413) 635583
geschl. Anfang Feb. 2 Wochen
80 Zim – 64/84 € 106/146 € – ½ P 16/35 €
Rest – *(geschl. Jan. – Feb.)* Menü 28/65 € – Karte 27/38 €

◆ Die schöne Panoramalage sowie wohnlich und funktionell, teils ganz modern eingerichtete Gästezimmer machen dieses gewachsene Hotel aus. Das Restaurant teilt sich in einen klassisch-gediegenen und einen neuzeitlicheren Bereich.

MARIA WÖRTH – Kärnten – 730 O9 – 1 260 Ew – Höhe 450 m 9 I6

Wien 314 – Klagenfurt 15 – St. Veit an der Glan 36 – Villach 28
Seepromenade 5, ✉ 9082, ✆ (04273) 22 40, mariawoerthinfo@ktn.gde.at
Dellach, Golfstr. 3 ✆ (04273) 25 15

Veranstaltungen
21.05. – 25.05.: GTI Treffen in Reifnitz

Linde Wörthersee, Rest,

Lindenplatz 3 ✉ 9082 – ✆ (04273) 22 78 – info@h-linde.at – Fax (04273) 2501 – geschl. Okt. – April
30 Zim – 110/280 € 150/280 € – ½ P 30 €
Rest *Linde* – separat erwähnt
Rest *Seebar* – Karte 22/62 €

◆ Auf einer Halbinsel, direkt am See liegt das engagiert geführte gewachsene Ferienhotel. Es erwarten Sie eine lichte, moderne Halle und gediegen-wohnliche Zimmer. Unmittelbar am Wasser: die Seebar.

Seehof

Kirchenweg 1 ✉ 9082 – ✆ (04273) 22 86 – info@seehof.cc – Fax (04273) 2286
geschl. 6. Okt. – 30. April
15 Zim – 49/69 € 90/178 € – ½ P 15 € – **Rest** – (nur für Hausgäste)

◆ Ein nettes Urlaubshotel ist die schmucke Villa a. d. 19. Jh. Zum Haus gehört eine schöne Gartenanlage mit Zugang zum See und Bootsanleger. Zimmer mit Bio-Gesundheitsbetten.

Linde – Hotel Linde — Wörthersee,
Lindenplatz 3 ✉ 9082 – ✆ (04273) 22 78 – info@h-linde.at
– Fax (04273) 2501
geschl. Okt. – April
Rest – Karte 25/51 €
◆ Restaurant mit klassisch-elegantem Ambiente und internationaler Karte. Einen sehr schönen Blick auf den See genießt man von der Terrasse. Mit Loungebereich.

In Reifnitz Süd-Ost: 1,5 km Richtung Klagenfurt:

Strandhotel Sille — Zim,
Wörthersee Süduferstr. 108 ✉ 9081
– ✆ (04273) 22 37 – reservierung@hotel-sille.com – Fax (04273) 244853
geschl. 2. Jan. – 25. März
28 Zim – 64/103 € 92/150 € – ½ P 18 € – 4 Suiten
Rest – Karte 18/33 €
◆ Das aus zwei miteinander verbundenen Häusern bestehende Hotel befindet sich im Ortszentrum, direkt am Wörthersee. Die hübschen Zimmer sind teilweise seeseitig gelegen. Das Restaurant bietet eine schöne Terrasse zum See.

In Dellach West: 4 km Richtung Velden:

Seewirt
Fischerweg 12 ✉ 9082 – ✆ (04273) 22 57 – office@hotelseewirt.at
– Fax (04273) 28052
geschl. Okt. – Anfang Mai
26 Zim (inkl. ½ P.) – 75/150 € 110/204 €
Rest – Karte 19/34 €
◆ Die Lage direkt am See – mit eigenem Bootsverleih – sowie neuzeitlich ausgestattete Zimmer und Appartements machen dieses für Familien gut geeignete Hotel aus. Eine Terrasse mit Seeblick ergänzt das Restaurant. Bürgerliche Karte mit vielen Fischgerichten.

In Sekirn Süd-Ost: 4,5 km Richtung Klagenfurt:

aenea — Wörthersee, (geheizt) Rest, Zim,
Wörthersee Süduferstr. 86 ✉ 9081 – ✆ (04273) 2 62 20 – aenea@aenea.at
– Fax (04273) 2622020
geschl. Nov. – April
15 Suiten – 300/500 € 350/550 €
Rest – Menü 58/98 € (abends) – Karte 50/79 €
◆ Das Hotel oberhalb des Sees beeindruckt mit hochwertiger Ausstattung in geschmackvollem topmodernem Design. Ein gläserner Lift bringt Sie zum Strand. Zum modern-eleganten Restaurant gehört eine Terrasse mit phantastischem Seeblick. Mittags kleine Karte.

Gute und preiswerte Häuser kennzeichnet das MICHELIN-Männchen, der „Bib": der rote „Bib Gourmand" für die Küche, der blaue „Bib Hotel" bei den Zimmern.

MARIAPFARR – Salzburg – 730 N7 – **2 220 Ew** – **Höhe 1 120 m** – **Wintersport: 2 050 m** 5 – **Heilklimatischer Kurort** 9 **H5**

Wien 295 – Salzburg 125 – Villach 100

Gemeindeamt, Pfarrstr. 7, ✉ 5571, ☎ (06473) 87 66, mariapfarr@lungautourismus.at

Häuserl im Wald

Niederrain 140 (West: 4 km, Richtung Weißpriach, dann rechts ab) ✉ 5571 – ☎ (06473) 82 88 – haus.i.wald@aon.at – Fax (06473) 82888
geschl. 30. März – 11. Mai, 13. Okt. – 7. Dez.
12 Zim – ☼ †34/37 € ††60/70 € ❄ †40/43 € ††72/110 € – ½ P 10 €
Rest – *(geschl. Montag)* Karte 14/29 €
◆ In versteckter Waldlage liegt dieses kleine Hotel mit wohnlichen Zimmern und freundlicher Betreuung. Von der hauseigenen Sauna aus gelangt man direkt in den Garten. Zum Restaurant gehört eine Stube mit schönem Blick und neuzeitlich-ländlicher Einrichtung.

Zum Granitzl

Grabendorf 52 (Nord–West: 3 km) ✉ 5571 – ☎ (06473) 82 39 – info@granitzl.at – Fax (06473) 82396
geschl. 1. April – 10. Mai, 3. Nov. – 15. Dez.
16 Zim (inkl. ½ P.) – ☼ †45/50 € ††80/98 € ❄ †50/60 € ††88/120 €
Rest – *(Montag – Donnerstag nur Abendessen)* Karte 13/27 €
◆ Ein vom Inhaber gut geführter kleiner Berggasthof oberhalb des Ortes, in dem solide mit hellem Holz eingerichtete Zimmer und eine nette Saunalandschaft zur Verfügung stehen. Teils wintergartenartig angelegtes Restaurant und Terrasse mit toller Sicht.

Thomalwirt

Pfarrstr. 15 ✉ 5571 – ☎ (06473) 82 04 – info@thomalwirt.at – Fax (06473) 820478
– geschl. 6. April – 9. Mai, 2. Nov. – 6. Dez.
30 Zim (inkl. ½ P.) – ☼ †47/55 € ††94/110 € ❄ †52/78 € ††104/156 €
Rest – Karte 15/26 €
◆ Das Hotel im verkehrsberuhigten Ortskern bietet neben solide ausgestatteten Zimmern auch einen neuzeitlichen Saunabereich und einen Ruheraum mit Aussicht. Unterteiltes Restaurant mit rustikalem Ambiente.

Panoramagasthof Steiner

Rest, VISA

Bergstr. 144 ✉ 5571 – ☎ (06473) 82 72 – albert.steiner@aon.at – Fax (06473) 82722 – geschl. Nov.
9 Zim – ☼ †33/38 € ††66/76 € ❄ †38/43 € ††76/86 €
Rest – *(geschl. Dienstag)* Karte 19/34 €
◆ Der etwas oberhalb des Ortes gelegene kleine Familienbetrieb überzeugt durch neuzeitliche, mit hellem Naturholzmobiliar und Parkettboden ausgestattete Zimmer. Gepflegtes, freundliches Restaurant in ländlichem Stil. Mit Panoramaterrasse.

Post-Örglwirt

Rest, Rest,

Pfarrstr. 18 ✉ 5571 – ☎ (06473) 82 07 – info@oerglwirt.com – Fax (06473) 820722 – geschl. 30. März – 30. Mai, 19. Okt. – 18. Dez.
24 Zim (inkl. ½ P.) – ☼ †48/52 € ††90/100 € ❄ †57/68 € ††106/130 €
Rest – *(geschl. 30. März – 14. Juni, 19. Okt. – 18. Dez. und Montag)* Karte 18/29 €
◆ Ein durch die Inhaberfamilie solide geführter Gasthof in der Ortsmitte. Die Zimmer sind gepflegt und im ländlichen Stil möbliert. Regionstypisch gestaltete Gaststuben.

MARIASTEIN – Tirol – 730 I6 – 280 Ew – Höhe 650 m 7 E5

Wien 399 – Innsbruck 68 – Kufstein 15 – Kitzbühel 44

Mariasteinerhof

Mariastein 14 ✉ 6322 – ✆ (05332) 5 67 17 – hotel@mariasteinerhof.at – Fax (05332) 567177

geschl. April, Nov.

30 Zim – ☼ 53/69 € 90/122 € ❄ 61/87 € 106/158 € – ½ P 19 €

Rest – *(geschl. Montagmittag, Dienstagmittag) (im Winter nur für Hausgäste)* Karte 16/32 €

♦ In dem familiengeführten Haus oberhalb der Kirche stehen solide, neuzeitliche Gästezimmer mit Balkon zur Verfügung. Moderner Saunabereich und Kosmetikanwendungen. Zwei Stuben und ein Wintergarten mit netter Aussicht bilden das Restaurant.

MARIAZELL – Steiermark – 730 R5 – 1 730 Ew – Höhe 864 m – Wintersport: 1 235 m 1 4 3 J3

Wien 131 – Graz 117 – St. Pölten 77 – Bruck a.d. Mur 62

Hauptplatz 13, ✉ 8630, ✆ (03882) 23 66, info@mariazeller-land.at

Basilika★★

Annaberg ★ Nord-Ost: 24 km

Goldenes Kreuz Rest,

Wiener Str. 7 ✉ 8630 – ✆ (03882) 23 09 – scherfler@mariazell.at – Fax (03882) 230966

32 Zim – 49/69 € 78/118 € – ½ P 12 €

Rest – Menü 10/15 € – Karte 15/32 €

♦ Hinter seiner stilvollen Fassade verbirgt das von Familie Scherfler geführte Hotel gediegen eingerichtete Zimmer – einige liegen rückwärtig und bieten eine schöne Aussicht. In mehrere Räume unterteiltes Restaurant mit klassisch-rustikalem Ambiente.

Brauhaus Mariazell mit Zim Zim,

Wiener Str. 5 ✉ 8630 – ✆ (03882) 2 52 30 – brauhaus@mariazell.at – Fax (03882) 25238

geschl. 14. – 24. Jan., 25. März – 24. April, 3. – 28. Nov.

2 Zim – 47/109 € 94/218 €

Rest – *(geschl. Donnerstag, Sonntagabend)* (Tischbestellung ratsam) Karte 16/28 €

♦ Gemütlich sitzt man in den alten Gewölben und Stuben des traditionsreichen Gasthofs von 1673. In der Hausbrauerei wird obergäriges Bier gebraut – Schank neben den Sudkesseln. Die zwei Gästezimmer sind das Braumeister- und das Wasserreich-Zimmer.

Gute und preiswerte Häuser kennzeichnet das MICHELIN-Männchen, der „Bib": der rote „Bib Gourmand" für die Küche, der blaue „Bib Hotel" bei den Zimmern.

MARZ - Burgenland - 730 V5 - 2 030 Ew - Höhe 365 m 4 L3

Wien 64 - Eisenstadt 20 - Wiener Neustadt 19 - Sopron 29

Müllner (mit Gästehaus)

Hauptstr. 101 ✉ 7221 - ☎ (02626) 6 39 67 - office@hotel-muellner.at - Fax (02626) 639674

geschl. 21. Dez. - 7. Jan.

54 Zim - 40/52 € 70/84 € - ½ P 12 €

Rest - *(geschl. Donnerstagmittag)* Karte 13/25 €

◆ Ein familiengeführter Gasthof in der Ortsmitte mit gepflegten, funktionell ausgestatteten Zimmern - im Gästehaus sind die Zimmer moderner mit Kirschholzmöbeln eingerichtet. Unterteiltes Restaurant in ländlichem Stil.

Frühstück inklusive? Die Tasse steht gleich hinter der Zimmeranzahl.

MATREI AM BRENNER - Tirol - 730 G7 - 1 000 Ew - Höhe 992 m - Wintersport: 7 D5

Wien 465 - Innsbruck 23 - Schwaz 48 - Seefeld 42

Brennerstr. 104, ✉ 6143, ☎ (05273) 62 78, info.matrei@wippregio.at

Parkhotel

Brennerstr. 83 (B 182) ✉ 6143 - ☎ (05273) 62 69 - mail@parkhotel-matrei.at - Fax (05273) 626966

geschl. 31. Okt. - 1. Dez.

44 Zim - 60/75 € 95/115 € - ½ P 24 €

Rest - Karte 15/41 €

◆ Solide möblierte, wohnliche Zimmer und ein Garten mit Naturbadeteich zählen zu den Annehmlichkeiten dieses gut von der Familie geführten Hauses. Mit viel hellem Holz alpenländisch gestaltetes Restaurant, teils leicht elegant, und Wintergarten-Pavillon.

Krone Zim,

Brennerstr. 54 (B 182) ✉ 6143 - ☎ (05273) 62 28 - office@krone-matrei.at - Fax (05273) 6644

geschl. 3. Nov. - 4. Dez.

50 Zim - 50/54 € 78/84 € - ½ P 14 €

Rest - *(geschl. außer Saison Mittwoch)* Karte 16/31 €

◆ Der bereits seit 1447 in Familienbesitz befindliche Gasthof mit über 1000-jähriger Tradition hat seinen historischen Rahmen bewahrt. Zimmer teils mit Balkon/Terrasse. In ländlichem Stil gehaltenes Restaurant mit Thekenbereich.

Gasthof Lamm mit Zim

Brennerstr. 36 (B 182) ✉ 6143 - ☎ (05273) 62 21 - info@gasthoflamm.at - Fax (05273) 622111

6 Zim - 50 € 80 € - ½ P 25 €

Rest - *(geschl. Montag)* Karte 16/39 €

◆ Der Gasthof a. d. 15. Jh. beherbergt ein Restaurant mit rustikal-elegantem Ambiente und eine behagliche Gaststube. Der Chef bereitet regionale Speisen. Zum Übernachten stehen solide eingerichtete Zimmer bereit.

In Mühlbachl Nord: 1 km:

 **Stolz**

Brennerstr. 30 (B 182) ✉ 6143 – ✆ (05273) 63 12 – kontakt@hotel-stolz.at – Fax (05273) 6312606

55 Zim – 55 € 88 € – ½ P 11 € – **Rest** – Karte 14/27 €

◆ Das sehr gepflegte familiengeführte Hotel am Ortseingang verfügt über solide und wohnlich eingerichtete Gästezimmer, meist mit Balkon. Gemütliche Restaurantstuben mit Kachelofen und nettem Dekor.

In Pfons Nord-Ost: 1,5 km:

Gasthof Fuchs

Pfons 16 ✉ 6143 – ✆ (05273) 62 02 – info@hotel-fuchs.at – Fax (05273) 620250

geschl. Nov.

22 Zim – 42/45 € 68/74 € – ½ P 8 €

Rest – *(nur Abendessen)* Karte 14/23 €

◆ Dieser regionstypische Gasthof mit eigener Landwirtschaft ist ein alteingesessener Familienbetrieb mit unterschiedlich möblierten, gut unterhaltenen Zimmern. Bürgerlich gestaltetes Restaurant.

MATREI IN OSTTIROL – **Tirol** – 730 J7 – **4 910 Ew** – **Höhe 1 000 m** – **Wintersport: 2 400 m** 1 7 — 8 **F6**

Wien 433 – Innsbruck 161 – Lienz 28 – Kitzbühel 66

Rauterplatz 1, ✉ 9971, ✆ (04875) 65 27, matrei@hohetauern-osttirol.at

St.Nikolaus-Kirche (Fresken★)

Europa-Panoramaweg★★ (mit) – Goldriedbahn (★★) – Spaziergang zum Kals-Matrei-Törlhaus★★ – Kalsertal★★ (Süd-Ost: 9 km)

Outside — Rest,

Virgener Str. 3 ✉ 9971 – ✆ (04875) 52 00 – office@hotel-outside.at – Fax (04875) 520052

geschl. 25. März – 8. Mai, 26. Okt. – 20. Dez.

40 Zim (inkl. ½ P) – 80/100 € 154/174 € 80/140 € 160/240 €

Rest – (nur Abendessen für Hausgäste)

◆ Ein gut geführtes Hotel nahe dem Zentrum, das Ihnen freundliche Zimmer mit mediterranem Touch bietet. Zum Freizeitbereich gehört ein Garten mit Badeteich.

MATTSEE – **Salzburg** – 730 L5 – **2 850 Ew** – **Höhe 530 m** – **Wintersport:** — 1 **F3**

Wien 282 – Salzburg 21 – Burghausen 39 – Bad Reichenhall 35

Passauerstr. 3, ✉ 5163, ✆ (06217) 60 80, info@mattsee.co.at

Schlosshotel Iglhauser — Rest,

Schlossbergweg 1 ✉ 5163 – ✆ (06217) 52 05 – schlosshotel@iglhauser.at – Fax (06217) 520533

geschl. Anfang Nov. 1 Woche

39 Zim – 79/153 € 156/189 € – ½ P 20 € – 16 Suiten

Rest – *(geschl. Sonntagabend, außer Festspielzeit)* Menü 26 € – Karte 29/45 €

◆ Schön am See liegt das a. d. 11. Jh. stammende Schloss, das Zimmer, unterschiedlich in Kategorie und Stil, für Sie bereithält sowie aufwändig gestaltete Suiten. Tagungsräume. Im historischen Restaurant und auf der netten Terrasse serviert man Regionales.

MAUERBACH BEI WIEN - Niederösterreich - 730 U4 - 3 420 Ew - Höhe 280 m 4 L2

Wien 18 - St. Pölten 50 - Baden 39 - Krems 55

Auf dem Tulbingerkogel Nord-West: 5,5 km Richtung Tulln - Höhe 495 m

Berghotel Tulbingerkogel Wienerwald und Tullnerfeld, (geheizt) P VISA AE
Tulbingerkogel 1 3001 Mauerbach - (02273) 73 91 - hotel@tulbingerkogel.at - Fax (02273) 739173
44 Zim - 72/180 € 108/196 € - ½ P 28 €
Rest - Menü 46 € - Karte 31/48 €
♦ Ein schön gelegenes Hotel mit funktionellen, teils ganz modern gestalteten Zimmern, einem neuzeitlichen Freizeitbereich und freundlichem Service. Gute Tagungsmöglichkeiten. Zum Restaurant gehört eine hübsche Terrasse. Begehbarer Weinkeller mit seltenen Weinen.

MAURACH AM ACHENSEE - Tirol - siehe Eben am Achensee

MAUTERN - Niederösterreich - 730 S3 - 3 080 Ew - Höhe 201 m 3 J2

Wien 79 - St. Pölten 24 - Krems 4 - Melk 34

Landhaus Bacher mit Zim A/C Rest, VISA
Südtiroler Platz 2 3512 - (02732) 8 29 37 - info@landhaus-bacher.at - Fax (02732) 74337
geschl. Jan. - 8. März
10 Zim - 85/105 € 125/182 €
Rest - *(geschl. Montag - Dienstag)* Menü 36 € (mittags)/99 € - Karte 59/83 €
Spez. Das gebackene Caviarei. Gebratene Langostinos auf weißer Mandelcreme und getrockneten Marillen. Himbeertörtchen mit Sauerrahm und Hollersorbet.
♦ Familie Wagner-Bacher bietet zu der hervorragenden klassischen Küche auch die passende Atmosphäre. Ein Kamin ziert das Restaurant im eleganten Landhausstil. Schöner Garten. Das kleine Gästehaus beherbergt wohnliche Zimmer, die zum Stil des Hauses passen.

MAUTERNDORF - Salzburg - 730 N7 - 1 850 Ew - Höhe 1 122 m - Wintersport: 2 360 m 1 9 9 H5

Wien 297 - Salzburg 117 - Spittal a.d. Drau 54 - Tamsweg 12
Markt 52, 5570, (06472) 79 49, info@mauterndorf.at
Burg Mauterndorf★
Schloss Moosham★ Süd: 4 km - Radstädter Tauernstraße★

Steffner-Wallner Zim, Zim, P
Markt 90 5570 - (06472) 72 14 - hotel-steffner@sbg.at - Fax (06472) 7794
geschl. Mitte April - Mitte Mai, Mitte Okt. - Ende Nov.
19 Zim (inkl. ½ P.) - 58/65 € 96/110 € 72/86 € 124/148 €
Rest - Karte 17/38 €
♦ Aus dem Jahre 1207 stammt der von der Familie geführte Gasthof im Zentrum, der über wohnliche, in rustikalem Stil eingerichtete Zimmer verfügt. Teilweise mit Holz vertäfelte Gaststube und Hausgast-Restaurant mit schöner alter Natursteinwand.

Binggl garni

Markt 91 ✉ 5570 – ✆ (06472) 72 04 – urlaub@binggl.com – Fax (06472) 720416

22 Zim – ☼ 42/55 € 70/76 € ❄ 51/56 € 88/98 €

◆ In dem Hotel erwarten Sie helle, freundliche Zimmer sowie ein alpenländisch gestalteter Saunabereich. Schön ist die Maisonette-Suite. Mit im Haus: eigene Bäckerei und Café.

Stegmühlhof garni

Markt 323 ✉ 5570 – ✆ (06472) 74 00 – info@stegmuehlhof.com – Fax (06472) 740033

geschl. 14. – 26. April, 11. Okt. – 1. Dez.

19 Zim – ☼ 42/46 € 72/88 € ❄ 54/60 € 80/116 €

◆ In dem kleinen Hotel erwarten Sie familiäre Atmosphäre und solide möblierte, gut gepflegte Gästezimmer. Ein Holzhäuschen am Fluss dient als Grillplatz.

Gasthof Weitgasser Rest,

Markt 106 ✉ 5570 – ✆ (06472) 73 66 – weitgasser@sbg.at – Fax (06472) 73666

12 Zim (inkl. ½ P.) – ☼ 38/45 € 68/100 € ❄ 50/66 € 98/148 €

Rest – Karte 25/37 €

◆ Der Gasthof a. d. J. 1651 ist ein kleiner Familienbetrieb mit geschmackvollen, wohnlichen Zimmern in ländlich-rustikalem Stil und nettem Saunabereich mit Balkon zur Taurach. Regionstypisch gestaltetes Restaurant.

Mesnerhaus

Markt 56 ✉ 5570 – ✆ (06472) 75 95 – info@mesnerhaus.at – Fax (06472) 759514

geschl. Juni 3 Wochen, Nov. 3 Wochen und Montag – Dienstag

Rest – (Tischbestellung ratsam) Menü 39/127 € – Karte 48/58 €

Rest *Maria & Josef* – Karte 22/39 €

Spez. Marinierter Saibling, Mohn-Stampf-Kartoffeln, Saiblingskaviar. Ochsenschwanz, Selleriepüree, Brennesseln. Schokoladentörtchen, Kirschtabakeis, Schokoladenwhisky.

◆ Schön harmonieren in diesem Restaurant im 1. Stock moderner Stil und der historische Rahmen des Hauses. Serviert wird kreative Küche. Maria & Josef nennt sich der gemütliche Bistrobereich mit regionalem Speisenangebot.

MAUTHAUSEN – Oberösterreich – 730 P4 – 4 850 Ew – Höhe 230 m

2 **I3**

Wien 168 – Linz 25 – Perg 12 – Steyr 38

Weindlhof mit Zim

Kirchenweg 12 ✉ 4310 – ✆ (07238) 26 41 – office@weindlhof.at – Fax (07238) 26416

geschl. Jan. 2 Wochen, 28. Juni – 10. Aug.

11 Zim – 30/40 € 55 €

Rest – *(geschl. Sonntag – Montag)* Menü 31/42 € – Karte 17/30 €

◆ Recht ruhig liegt der kleine Gutshof oberhalb des Ortes. In gemütlichen Restaurantstuben mit ländlichem Charakter bietet man regionale Küche. Sehr gepflegte, freundlich eingerichtete Gästezimmer.

MAYERLING – Niederösterreich – siehe Alland

MAYRHOFEN IM ZILLERTAL – Tirol – 730 H7 – 3 760 Ew – Höhe 680 m – Wintersport: 2 500 m 8 41 7 E5

Wien 439 – Innsbruck 66 – Kufstein 67 – Schwaz 38

(Europahaus), Dursterstr. 225, 6290, (05285) 6 45 06, info@mayrhofen.at

Zell am Ziller (Kirche★) Nord: 7 km – Zillertal★★ Nord: 7 km – Zemmtal★★ Süd-West: 8 km – Stilluppgrund★ Süd: 9 km – Tuxertal★★★ Süd-West: 11 km

Elisabeth

Zim, Rest, P VISA AE

Mayrhofen 432 6290 – (05285) 67 67 – info@elisabethhotel.com – Fax (05285) 676767

geschl. Mai, Nov.

32 Zim (inkl. ½ P.) – 110/140 € 170/250 € 140/260 € 196/570 € – 4 Suiten

Rest – *(geschl. Mai – Nov., nur Abendessen)* (Tischbestellung ratsam) Menü 39/49 €

◆ Hübsche, wohnliche Landhauszimmer und großzügige Suiten sowie ein schöner Freizeitbereich machen dieses komfortable Alpenhotel aus. Gediegen-elegant ist die Sissi Stube mit klassischer Küche auf regionaler Basis.

Gutshof zum Stillupper

(geheizt) P VISA

Tuxerstr. 826 6290 – (05285) 81 24 – info@gutshof.cc – Fax (05285) 8328

21 Zim (inkl. ½ P.) – 105/128 € 140/170 € 90/135 € 150/240 €

Rest – *(geschl. außer Saison Montag)* Karte 18/38 €

◆ Ein modernisierter und erweiterter Gutshof a. d. 17. Jh. Es erwarten Sie mit modernster Technik ausgestattete Zimmer im Landhausstil und ein Freizeitbereich mit Almsauna. In zwei holzvertäfelten Stuben serviert man u. a. Erzeugnisse der eigenen Landwirtschaft.

Sporthotel Manni

(geheizt) Zim, P VISA AE

Hauptstr. 439 6290 – (05285) 6 33 01 – sporthotel@mannis.at – Fax (05285) 6330110

geschl. Mitte April – Mitte Mai, Anfang Nov. – Mitte Dez.

52 Zim – 73/118 € 126/186 € 103/203 € 166/346 € – ½ P 25/30 €

Rest – *(geschl. Mitte April – Mitte Juni, Mitte Okt. – Mitte Dez.)* Karte 30/60 €

◆ Mitten im Zentrum gelegenes Hotel mit wohnlich und funktionell eingerichteten Zimmern. Sehr schön: das Dach-Schwimmbad mit toller Sicht. Sportgeschäft im Haus.

Zillertaler Hof

(geheizt) Rest, P VISA

Am Marienbrunnen 341 6290 – (05285) 6 22 65 – info@zillertalerhof.at – Fax (05285) 6226544

45 Zim (inkl. ½ P.) – 61/78 € 98/136 € 70/150 € 120/280 €

Rest – (nur Abendessen für Hausgäste)

◆ Das zentral gelegene Alpenhotel verfügt über Zimmer im Tiroler Stil oder im Landhausstil sowie eine nette Kamin-Lounge und einen hübschen, modernen Sauna- und Badebereich.

Edenlehen (mit Gästehaus)
Mayrhofen 676 ✉ 6290 – ✆ (05285) 6 23 00 – edenlehen@tirol.com – Fax (05285) 6230015
geschl. Nov.
40 Zim (inkl. ½ P.) – ☼ 🚹63/70 € 🚹🚹110/146 € ❄ 🚹72/78 € 🚹🚹126/166 €
Rest – Karte 19/35 €
◆ Hinter seiner regionstypischen Fassade bietet dieses familiengeführte Haus etwas außerhalb des Zentrums wohnlich gestaltete Gästezimmer mit Balkon.

Ferienhof garni
Rest,
Rauchenwald 671 ✉ 6290 – ✆ (05285) 6 26 03 – info@ferienhof.at – Fax (05285) 6260333
geschl. 1. April – 1. Juli, 6. Okt. – 25. Dez.
17 Zim ☕ – ☼ 🚹52/66 € 🚹🚹76/87 € ❄ 🚹63/119 € 🚹🚹92/159 €
◆ In einem Wohngebiet liegt der neuzeitliche Familienbetrieb, der über unterschiedlich geschnittene Zimmer mit hellem Naturholzmobiliar und funktioneller Ausstattung verfügt.

Pension Waldheim
Fischerstr. 509 ✉ 6290 – ✆ (05285) 6 22 11 – info@hotelwaldheim.at – Fax (05285) 6221130
geschl. 1. April – 11. Mai, 28. Sept. – 15. Dez.
20 Zim (inkl. ½ P.) – ☼ 🚹66/86 € 🚹🚹113/147 € ❄ 🚹76/108 € 🚹🚹132/187 €
Rest – (nur Abendessen für Hausgäste)
◆ Ruhig, aber dennoch nicht weit vom Zentrum gelegenes kleines Hotel unter familiärer Leitung. Die Zimmer sind gediegen eingerichtet und bieten einen Balkon.

Apparthotel König garni
Jakob-Moser-Weg 578 ✉ 6290 – ✆ (05285) 6 22 35 – info@apparthotel-koenig.at – Fax (05285) 620665
geschl. 15. April – 1. Juni, 10. Okt. – 10. Dez.
11 Zim – ☼ 🚹🚹74/88 € ❄ 🚹🚹86/104 €, ☕ 10 €
6 Suiten
◆ Die ruhige Lage am Ortsrand, eine familiäre Atmosphäre und wohnliche, fast elegante Zimmer und Appartements sprechen für dieses Haus.

Pramstraller
Dursterstr. 248 ✉ 6290 – ✆ (05285) 6 21 19 – info@pramstraller.at – Fax (05285) 621195
geschl. Ende März – Mitte Mai, Mitte Okt. – Mitte Dez.
23 Zim (inkl. ½ P.) – ☼ 🚹67/72 € 🚹🚹110/120 € ❄ 🚹79/92 € 🚹🚹134/160 €
4 Suiten
Rest – Karte 14/40 €
◆ Das gepflegte, familiär geleitete Hotel verfügt über mit viel Holz solide eingerichtete Gästezimmer mit Balkon – auch Familienzimmer. Nett gestaltete Vitaloase. Ein 300 Jahre altes Wasserrad ziert das alpenländisch-rustikale Restaurant. Terrasse zum Garten.

Karlsteg

Dornauberg 2 (Süd: 4 km Richtung Ginzling) ✉ 6295 – ✆ (05286) 52 50 – info@karlsteg.at – Fax (05286) 52505
15 Zim (inkl. ½ P.) – ☼ 44 € 88 € ❄ 55 € 110 €
Rest – Karte 17/33 €
◆ Im Tal, direkt an einem Bach liegt das um einen Anbau erweiterte Gasthaus a. d. J. 1890. Unterschiedlich geschnittene, zeitgemäße Zimmer und ein großer moderner Saunabereich. Gemütlich: die drei regionstypischen Restaurantstuben.

Jägerhof

Tuxerstr. 722 ✉ 6290 – ✆ (05285) 6 25 40 – hotel-jaegerhof@happynet.at – Fax (05285) 6251840
27 Zim (inkl. ½ P.) – ☼ 53/63 € 90/110 € ❄ 68/78 € 120/140 €
Rest – Karte 17/38 €
◆ Viele Stammgäste schätzen diesen familiengeführten Gasthof mit seinen praktischen, mit hellem Naturholzmobiliar ausgestatteten Zimmern. Restaurant mit rustikalem Charakter.

In Mayrhofen-Zillergrund **Nord-Ost: 4 km Richtung Brandberg, nach dem Brandbergtunnel halbrechts ab:**

Zillergrund

Zillergrund 903 ✉ 6290 – ✆ (05285) 6 23 77 – info@zillergrund.at – Fax (05285) 623776
geschl. 7. April – 15. Mai
31 Zim (inkl. ½ P.) – ☼ 55/69 € 110/138 € ❄ 69/83 € 138/166 €
Rest – (nur für Hausgäste)
◆ Ruhig liegt das gewachsene Alpenhotel in einem kleinen Tal. Die Zimmer sind unterschiedlich geschnitten und mit hellem Holzmobiliar und warmen Farben eingerichtet. Das Restaurant: teils bürgerlich-rustikal, teils im Landhausstil.

MELK AN DER DONAU – Niederösterreich – 730 S4 – 5 230 Ew – Höhe 209 m

3 **J2**

- Wien 86 – St. Pölten 29 – Amstetten 40 – Krems 37
- Babenbergerstr. 1, ✉ 3390, ✆ (02752) 52 30 74 10, touristinfo@stadt-melk.at
- Stift Melk★★★
- Wachau★★★ – Donautal★★ – Schloss Schallaburg★ (Süd: 6 km) – Burgruine Aggstein★ (Nord-Ost: 12 km)

Zur Post

Linzer Str. 1 ✉ 3390 – ✆ (02752) 5 23 45 – info@hotelpost-melk.at – Fax (02752) 5234550
geschl. 2. Jan. – 15. Feb.
28 Zim ☕ – 56/63 € 91/100 € – ½ P 15 €
Rest – *(geschl. Mitte Okt. – April Sonntagabend – Montag)* Karte 18/34 €
◆ Funktionelle, aber wohnliche Zimmer sprechen für diesen solide geführten Familienbetrieb, ein etwa 80 Jahre alter Gasthof mitten im Zentrum. Das Restaurant: die rustikale Poststube und drei hell gestaltete Räume mit Gewölbedecke.

Wachau Zim,

Am Wachberg 3 ✉ 3390 – ✆ (02752) 5 25 31 – info@hotel-wachau.at – Fax (02752) 5253113
geschl. 20. – 27. Dez.
30 Zim – ♦60/70 € ♦♦85/110 € – ½ P 18/40 €
Rest – *(geschl. Nov. – März Samstag – Sonntag, nur Abendessen)* Karte 19/36 €
♦ Wohnliche, meist mit hellem Kirschbaummobiliar eingerichtete und mit guter Technik ausgerüstete Gästezimmer erwarten Sie in diesem familiengeführten Landhaushotel am Ortsrand.

Stadt Melk – Tom's Restaurant mit Zim

Hauptplatz 1 ✉ 3390 – ✆ (02752) 5 24 75 – hotel.stadtmelk@netway.at – Fax (02752) 5247519
geschl. Jan.
13 Zim – ♦58/65 € ♦♦75/93 € – ½ P 18 €
Rest – *(geschl. Mittwoch)* Menü 48/78 €
Rest *Légere* – *(geschl. Mittwoch)* Karte 27/39 €
♦ Ein Restaurant mit persönlicher Atmosphäre, in dem man seinen Gästen nur ein Menü offeriert – dazu reicht man die passenden Weine. Das Légere befindet sich im Wintergarten, von wo aus man einen schönen Blick auf den Hauptplatz hat. Geboten wird Regionalküche.

MELLAU – Vorarlberg – 730 B6 – 1 290 Ew – Höhe 700 m – Wintersport: 1 750 m 1 6 — 5 A5

Wien 602 – Bregenz 34 – Dornbirn 24 – Feldkirch 50
Platz 292, ✉ 6881, ✆ (05518) 22 03, tourismus@mellau.at

Kanisfluh (mit Gästehaus) Rest,

Platz 60 ✉ 6881 – ✆ (05518) 22 56 – hotel@kanisfluh.com – Fax (05518) 2256500
geschl. 15. – 29. Juni, 26. Okt. – 21. Dez.
35 Zim (inkl. ½ P.) – ♦70/89 € ♦♦128/142 €
Rest – Karte 20/28 €
♦ Ein gepflegtes familiengeführtes Hotel mit wohnlichen Gästezimmern in rustikalem Stil. Eine eigene Tennisanlage befindet sich wenige Gehminuten entfernt.

MICHELBACH – Niederösterreich – 730 T4 – 930 Ew – Höhe 370 m — 3 K3

Wien 61 – St. Pölten 24 – Baden 61

Schwarzwallner mit Zim

Untergoin 6 (Süd-Ost: 1 km) ✉ 3074 – ✆ (02744) 82 41 – landgasthaus@schwarzwallner.at – Fax (02744) 8494
geschl. 11. – 28. Feb.
3 Zim – ♦32 € ♦♦58 €
Rest – *(geschl. Dienstag – Mittwoch)* Menü 24 € – Karte 14/30 €
♦ Das familiengeführte Gasthaus a. d. 18. Jh. teilt sich in ländlich-gemütliche Stuben sowie einen neuzeitlicheren Wintergarten. Ruhig gelegene Zimmer.

MICHELHAUSEN – Niederösterreich – 730 T4 – 2 530 Ew – Höhe 181 m

Wien 44 – St. Pölten 30 – Baden 61 – Krems 35 — 3 K2
2000 Tullnerfeld-Atzenbrugg, Am Golfplatz 1 ✆ (02275) 2 00 85
The Country Club Atzenbrugg, Am Golfplatz 1 ✆ (02275) 2 00 75

Hütt mit Zim

Dorfstrasse 2 (Süd-West: 2 km) ✉ 3452 – ☎ (02275) 52 54 – huett@eunet.at – Fax (02275) 52543

8 Zim – 33 € 60 € – ½ P 16 €

Rest – *(geschl. Freitag – Samstag)* Menü 36 € – Karte 23/36 €

◆ Der Landgasthof mit der gelben Fassade beherbergt 3 ländlich gehaltene, z. T. leicht elegant wirkende Restauranträume sowie einfache, aber saubere und individuelle Zimmer.

MIEMING – Tirol – 730 E7 – 2 890 Ew – Höhe 884 m – Wintersport: 1

Wien 479 – Innsbruck 35 – Seefeld in Tirol 19 – Imst 29 6 **C5**

Obermieming 175a (B 189), ✉ 6414, ☎ (05264) 52 74, info@mieming.at

Mieminger Plateau, Obermieming ☎ (05264) 53 36

Alpenresort Schwarz (geheizt) Zim, Rest,

Obermieming 141 ✉ 6414 – ☎ (05264) 5 21 20 – hotel@schwarz.at – Fax (05264) 52127

117 Zim (inkl. ½ P.) – 164/364 € 278/494 € – 22 Suiten

Rest – Karte 25/50 €

◆ Komfortable Zimmer im Tiroler Landhausstil und Wellnessangebote aller Art finden Sie in dem 32 000 qm großen, charmanten Luxusthotel mit "Natur-Erlebnis-See". All-inclusive. Aufwändig dekorierte Restaurantstuben mit regionalem Angebot.

In Wildermieming Nord-Ost: 3 km über B 189 Richtung Telfs:

Adlerhof garni

Wildermieming 9a ✉ 6414 – ☎ (05264) 51 17 – adlerhof@aon.at – Fax (05264) 511730

geschl. 27. Okt. – 16. Dez.

10 Zim – 28/38 € 42/76 €

◆ Das frei am Ortsrand stehende, familiär geführte Haus verfügt über mit hellen Holzmöbeln in ländlichem Stil eingerichtete Gästezimmer und Appartements mit kleiner Küche.

MILLSTATT AM SEE – Kärnten – 730 M8 – 3 360 Ew – Höhe 588 m

Wien 345 – Klagenfurt 74 – Spittal a.d. Drau 10 – Villach 37 9 **H6**

Marktplatz 8 (Rathaus), ✉ 9872, ☎ (04766) 2 02 20, info@millstatt.at

Millstätter See, Am Golfplatz 1 ☎ (04762) 8 25 48

Veranstaltungen

23.08.: Kaiserfest

Stift★ (romanisches Westportal★★)

Die Forelle Millstätter See, (geheizt)

Fischergasse 65 ✉ 9872 – ☎ (04766) 2 05 00 – office@hotel-forelle.at – Fax (04766) 205011

geschl. Ende Okt. – März

59 Zim (inkl. ½ P.) – 61/105 € 130/268 € – 4 Suiten

Rest – Karte 23/42 €

◆ Die Lage direkt am See, meist stilvoll-gediegen eingerichtete Zimmer verschiedener Kategorien und ein ansprechender Freizeitbereich machen dieses Hotel aus. Klassisch gestaltete Speiseräume mit Terrasse zum See.

Alexanderhof ← Millstätter See, Rest,
Alexanderhofstr. 16 ✉ 9872
– ✆ (04766) 20 20 – alexanderhof@peak.at – Fax (04766) 202070
geschl. Nov. – April
70 Zim (inkl. ½ P.) – 69/85 € 106/150 €
Rest – Karte 14/25 €
◆ Aus einem ehemaligen Bauernhof ist dieses Ferienhotel in schöner Lage oberhalb des Ortes entstanden. Die wohnlichen Gästezimmer bieten überwiegend einen tollen Seeblick. Restaurant in neuzeitlich-ländlichem Stil.

In Millstatt-Obermillstatt Nord-Ost: 2 km:

Bio-Hotel Alpenrose ← Millstätter See und Berglandschaft, (geheizt) Rest,
Obermillstatt 84
✉ 9872 – ✆ (04766) 25 00 – info@biohotel-alpenrose.at
– Fax (04766) 3425
geschl. Mitte Jan. – Feb.
27 Zim (inkl. ½ P.) – 93/109 € 186/236 €
Rest – (nur Abendessen für Hausgäste)
◆ Die Panorama-Lage und angenehme Ruhe machen dieses nach biologischen Gesichtspunkten gebaute Hotel aus. Die Zimmer sind mit Naturhölzern eingerichtet, Technik nur auf Wunsch.

MINIHOF-LIEBAU – Burgenland – 730 U8 – 1 180 Ew – Höhe 270 m

Wien 182 – Eisenstadt 160 – Graz 80 – Fürstenfeld 24 11 **L5**

Landhofmühle garni
✉ 8384 – ✆ (03329) 28 14 – landhofmuehle@aon.at
– Fax (03329) 2847
geschl. 20. Dez. – 25. Feb.
12 Zim – 40 € 72/84 €
◆ In ländlicher Umgebung findet man die ehemalige Mühle a. d. J. 1898 mit warmer Atmosphäre. Hübsche Zimmer im Landhausstil und einen gemütlichen Frühstücksraum finden Sie hier.

MISTELBACH – Niederösterreich – 730 V3 – 10 650 Ew – Höhe 218 m

Wien 51 – St. Pölten 109 – Klosterneuburg 51 – Stockerau 51 4 **L1**
Asparn an der Zaya (Freilichtmuseum★) Nord-West: 8 km

Zur Linde Zim,
Bahnstr. 49 ✉ 2130 – ✆ (02572) 24 09 – fam.polak@zur-linde.at
– Fax (02572) 240990
22 Zim – 55/61 € 86/104 € – ½ P 9 €
Rest – *(geschl. 1. – 14. Jan. und Sonntagabend – Montag)* Menü 42/55 € (abends) – Karte 21/39 €
◆ Ein modernisierter Gasthof unter familiärer Leitung, der über neuzeitlich und wohnlich mit Naturholzmöbeln im Landhausstil eingerichtete Zimmer verfügt. In mehrere Bereiche unterteiltes Restaurant, teils klassisch, teils ländlich.

MITTELBERG – Vorarlberg – siehe Kleinwalsertal

MITTERBACH – Niederösterreich – 730 R5 – 620 Ew – Höhe 800 m – Wintersport: 1 626 m 12 3 J3

Wien 125 – St. Pölten 71 – Bruck a.d. Mur 67 – Mariazell 6

Gemeindeamt, Hauptstr. 14, 3224, (03882) 42 11, tourismus@mitterbach.at

Filzwieser mit Zim
Rest,

Bundesstr. 78 3224 – (03882) 2 50 40 – filzi@mariazell.at – Fax (03882) 250431

geschl. Nov.

6 Zim – 31/36 € 62 € 33/38 € 66 € – ½ P 16 €

Rest – *(geschl. Mittwoch)* Karte 21/38 €

◆ Bereits in der dritten Generation leitet Familie Filzwieser diesen Gasthof. Die beiden Stuben sind gemütlich im regionstypischen Stil eingerichtet.

Bestecke und Sterne sollten nicht verwechselt werden!
Die Bestecke stehen für eine Komfortkategorie, die Sterne zeichnen Häuser mit besonders guter Küche aus - in jeder dieser Kategorien.

MITTERNDORF, BAD – Steiermark – 730 N6 – 3 220 Ew – Höhe 812 m – Wintersport: 1 965 m 19 – Heilbad, Luftkurort 9 H4

Wien 267 – Graz 145 – Liezen 28 – Bad Aussee 14

Nr. 59, 8983, (03623) 24 44, info.badmitterndorf@ausseerland.at

Grimmingblick
(geheizt) Rest,

Nr. 279 8983 – (03623) 24 91 – info@hotelgrimmigblick.at – Fax (03623) 249175

geschl. 5. – 25. April, 2. – 28. Nov.

64 Zim (inkl. ½ P.) – 67/68 € 137/139 €

Rest – Karte 13/26 €

◆ In diesem Hotel im Ortszentrum stehen zeitgemäß und funktionell ausgestattete Zimmer, teils mit Balkon, und ein netter Saunabereich zur Verfügung.

Kogler
Rest,

Winkel 129 8983 – (03623) 2 32 50 – info@hotelkogler.at – Fax (03623) 3107

geschl. 15. April – 15. Mai, 26. Okt. – 2. Dez.

34 Zim (inkl. ½ P.) – 40/65 € 80/130 € 60/95 € 120/190 €

Rest – *(geschl. Sonntag, nur Abendessen)* Karte 18/35 €

◆ Das familiengeführte Haus beherbergt hinter seiner gepflegten Balkonfassade wohnliche, solide Gästezimmer und einige Appartements.

Apparthotel Montana garni

Thörl 53 8983 – (03623) 2 45 30 – info@apparthotel-montana.com – Fax (03623) 245344

geschl. 7. – 26. April, Nov.

19 Zim – 41/47 € 68/88 € 54/60 € 86/102 €

◆ Ein kleines Hotel mit wohnlich eingerichteten Gästezimmern und großzügigen Appartements sowie einem freundlich gestalteten Frühstücksraum mit Terrasse.

Grimming-Wurz'n

Heilbrunn-Str. 354 ✉ 8983 – ☎ (03623) 31 32 – grimmingwurzn@aon.at – Fax (03623) 3132

geschl. April 3 Wochen, 10. Nov. – 6. Dez. und Dienstag – Mittwoch

Rest – (abends Tischbestellung ratsam) Menü 11 € (mittags)/48 € – Karte 24/43 €

◆ Eine offene Decke mit Holzbalkenkonstruktion und ein Kamin, in dem im Winter ein echtes Feuer lodert, tragen zum rustikalen Charakter dieses Restaurants bei.

In Bad Mitterndorf-Neuhofen Süd: 1 km:

Landhaus Schloss Grubegg garni

Neuhofen 23 ✉ 8983 – ☎ (03623) 2 65 45 – info@schlossgrubegg.at

10 Zim – 75/95 € 140/180 €

◆ Mit hochwertigem, geschmackvollem Interieur bewahrt das idyllisch gelegene, liebevoll restaurierte Haus von 1591 den historischen Charme. Individuelle Zimmer mit antiken Öfen.

MITTERSILL – Salzburg – 730 J7 – 5 590 Ew – Höhe 789 m – Wintersport: 1 894 m 15 7 F5

Wien 397 – Salzburg 121 – Wörgl 60 – Kitzbühel 30

Marktplatz 1, ✉ 5730, ☎ (06562) 42 92, info@mittersill-tourismus.at

Golfclub Mittersill-Stuhlfelden, Felben 133 ☎ (06562) 57 00

Stubachtal★★★ (Ost: 6 km) – Schößwendklamm ★ (Süd: 8 km) – Hintersee★ (Süd: 11 km)

Kinderhotel Felben

Felberstr. 51 ✉ 5730 – ☎ (06562) 44 07 – info@felben.at – Fax (06562) 440772

geschl. 28. – 30. April, Nov. 3 Wochen

38 Zim (inkl. ½ P.) – 98/137 € 156/240 €

Rest – (nur für Hausgäste)

◆ Etwas abseits in einem Wohngebiet liegt das auf Familienferien ausgerichtete Hotel mit behaglichen Räumen, Kinderprogramm und angeschlossenem Bauernhof.

Bräurup

Kirchgasse 9 ✉ 5730 – ☎ (06562) 62 16 – hotel@braurup.at – Fax (06562) 6216502

geschl. 7. – 26. April

55 Zim (inkl. ½ P.) – 68/76 € 104/160 €

Rest – Karte 17/41 €

◆ Der traditionsreiche Gasthof wurde mit einem Nebenhaus verbunden und bietet nun hell und zeitgemäß eingerichtete sowie rustikal gestaltete Zimmer. Sie speisen in gemütlichen holzvertäfelten Stuben a. d. 18. Jh. oder unter einer Gewölbedecke. Eigene Brauerei.

In Mittersil-Rettenbach West: 3,5 km:

Sonnberghof Rest,

Lämmerbichl 8 ✉ 5730 – ☎ (06562) 83 11 – info@sonnberghof.at – Fax (06562) 83114

geschl. 5. April – 3. Mai

24 Zim (inkl. ½ P.) – 52/69 € 94/152 € – 10 Suiten
Rest – *(nur Abendessen)* Karte 16/36 €
◆ Herrlich liegt der kleine Familienbetrieb inmitten von Bergwiesen. Die 200 qm große Vitalalm bietet verschiedene Saunen. Zum Haus gehört auch ein Schwimmbiotop. Im gemütlichen Restaurant verarbeitet man Produkte vom eigenen Bio-Bauernhof.

MÖDLING – Niederösterreich – 730 U4 – 20 410 Ew – Höhe 228 m 4 L2

Wien 17 – St. Pölten 63 – Baden 12 – Wiener Neustadt 37
Kaiserin Elisabethstr. 2, 2340, (02236) 2 67 27, tourismus@moedling.at
Achau, Biedermannsdorfer Straße (02236) 7 36 01
Leopoldsdorf, Ödenburger Straße (B16) (02235) 43 79 00

Florians

Neudorferstr. 68 2340 – (02236) 89 24 54 – essen@florians.at – Fax (02236) 89245411
geschl. Sonntag – Montag, Feiertage
Rest – (Tischbestellung ratsam) Menü 39/52 € – Karte 26/45 €
◆ Ein schönes modern-elegantes Restaurant, das eine unkomplizierte regionale und mediterrane Küche bietet. Nebenan befinden sich die kleine Genusshandlung und die Vinothek.

MÖRBISCH AM SEE – Burgenland – 730 V5 – 2 330 Ew – Höhe 115 m 4 M3

Wien 67 – Eisenstadt 19 – Wiener Neustadt 44 – Baden 53
Hauptstr. 23, 7072, (02685) 84 30, tourismus@moerbisch.com
Veranstaltungen
10.07. – 24.08.: Seefestspiele
Rust★ – Neusiedler See★★

Das Schmidt

Rest, Rest,

Raiffeisenstr. 8 7072 – (02685) 82 94 – das-schmidt@speed-tiscali.at – Fax (02685) 844834
geschl. Nov. – Ende April
29 Zim – 69/76 € 98/138 € – ½ P 12 €
Rest – Karte 15/37 €
◆ Ein gut unterhaltenes Haus unter familiärer Leitung, das über wohnliche und funktionelle, hell möblierte Zimmer verfügt. Liegewiese mit Badeteich und Schlammbad. In Stuben unterteiltes Restaurant mit bürgerlicher Einrichtung.

Sonnenhof garni

Nussau 18 7072 – (02685) 6 09 73 – sonnenhof-moerbisch@aon.at – Fax (02685) 609734
geschl. Nov. – Ende März
15 Zim – 32/40 € 56/70 €
◆ Die familiengeführte Pension bietet solide, in rustikaler Eiche eingerichtete Zimmer und einen eigenen Fahrradverleih. Im Sommer frühstücken Sie auf der netten Terrasse.

MÖSERN – Tirol – siehe Telfs

MONDSEE – Oberösterreich – 730 M5 – 3 210 Ew – Höhe 481 m – Wintersport: 8 G4

Wien 269 – Linz 109 – Salzburg 31 – Gmunden 54

Dr.-Franz-Müller-Str. 3, 5310, (06232) 22 70, info@mondsee.at

Am Mondsee, Schwarzindien 200 (06232) 3 83 50

Drachenwand- St. Lorenz, Am Golfplatz 4 (06232) 56 56

Veranstaltungen

01.08. – 03.08.: Seefest Mondsee

30.08. – 10.09.: Mondseetage

Pfarrkirche zum Hl. Michael★ – Mondsee★

Schloss Mondsee

Zim, Zim, VISA AE

Schlosshof 1a 5310

– (06232) 50 01 – office@schlossmondsee.at – Fax (06232) 500122

68 Zim – 105/135 € 160/190 € – ½ P 30 € – 4 Suiten

Rest – Karte 29/46 €

◆ Das 763 erstmals erwähnte Schloss beherbergt heute ein interessantes modernes Hotel, das mit funktionellen Zimmern/Maisonetten und historischem Rahmen überzeugt. Ein schmuckes Gewölbe ziert das Restaurant.

Leitnerbräu garni

VISA

Steinerbachstr. 6 5310 – (06232) 65 00 – hotel@leitnerbraeu.at

– Fax (06232) 650022 – geschl. 6. – 27. Jan.

30 Zim – 80/115 € 135/170 € 73/90 € 120/160 €

◆ Zentral in der Innenstadt liegt diese gepflegte Adresse. Mit italienischen Stilmöbeln hat man die Gästezimmer wohnlich eingerichtet.

Villa Drachenwand

VISA

Am Golfplatz 4 (Süd-West 2 km, am Golfplatz Drachenwand) 5310

– (06232) 44 37 – office@gastfreundlich.at – Fax (06232) 36070

geschl. Nov. – März

11 Zim – 65/75 € 115/125 € – ½ P 18 € – **Rest** – Karte 13/33 €

◆ Direkt am Golfplatz liegt dieses nette und gepflegte Haus. Für die Gäste stehen wohnliche Zimmer mit guter Technik und Schreibgelegenheiten zum Einzug bereit. Neuzeitliches Restaurant mit Wintergartenvorbau – hell und freundlich.

Seegasthof Lackner mit Zim

Mondsee und Voralpenlandschaft, VISA

Mondseestr. 1 5310

– (06232) 23 59 – office@seehotel-lackner.at – Fax (06232) 235950

geschl. Donnerstag

16 Zim – 50/75 € 86/170 € – ½ P 30 €

Rest – Menü 40/65 € – Karte 27/57 €

◆ In dem freundlich gestalteten Gasthof direkt am Mondsee serviert man regionale und internationale Speisen. Zum Haus gehören eine schöne Terrasse am See und eine Vinothek.

In Mondsee-Sankt Lorenz Süd: 2,5 km:

Gasthof Drachenwand

St. Lorenz 46 5310 – (06232) 33 56 – drachenwand@aon.at

– Fax (06232) 335610

geschl. Ende Jan. – Mitte März, Mitte Nov. – Anfang Dez.

7 Zim – 45 € 80 €

Rest – *(geschl. Montag, im Winter Montag – Dienstag)* Karte 17/28 €

◆ Ein gut geführter kleiner Gasthof im regionalen Stil. Eine angenehm familiäre Atmosphäre und wohnliche, großzügige Zimmer mit Parkettfußboden machen diese Adresse aus. Im Restaurant erwarten Sie ein bürgerlich-rustikales Ambiente und ein netter Service.

Am nördlichen Mondseeufer **Süd-Ost: 6 km:**

Seehof Rest,
Auhof 1 5311 Loibichl – (06232) 50 31
– seehof@nextra.at – Fax (06232) 503151
geschl. 14. Sept. – Mitte Mai
30 Zim – 140/285 € 156/484 € – ½ P 32 € – 13 Suiten
Rest – Karte 34/49 €
♦ Aus fünf Häusern setzt sich die Hotelanlage mit eigenem Park und Strand am See zusammen. Die Zimmer sind elegant-geräumig, das Personal ist zuvorkommend und engagiert. Gediegenes Restaurant mit hübscher überdachter Gartenterrasse. Küche auf regionaler Basis.

MOOSBURG – Kärnten – 730 09 – 4 470 Ew – Höhe 790 m 9 **I6**

Wien 305 – Klagenfurt 13 – Sankt Veit a.d. Glan 27 – Villach 31
Kirchplatz 1, 9062, (04272) 8 34 00 10, moosburg@ktn.gde.at
Austria Wörthersee, Golfstr. 2 (04272) 8 34 86

Sagmeisterei
Feldkirchner Str. 5 9062 – (04272) 8 28 98 – sagmeisterei@aon.at
– Fax (04272) 828984
geschl. Jan. und Montag – Dienstagmittag sowie Nov. – April Montag – Dienstag
Rest – Menü 52 € – Karte 28/55 €
♦ Eine gemütliche Atmosphäre herrscht in diesem mit bunt gemischten Accessoires originell dekorierten Restaurant von Robert Sagmeister. Geboten wird internationale Küche.

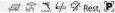

Golfrestaurant
Golfstr. 2 (West: 1,5 km, Richtung Pörtschach) 9062
– (04272) 8 33 15 – Fax (04272) 83314
geschl. Dez. – März
Rest – Karte 25/67 €
♦ Golfclub-Restaurant mit freundlichem, leicht mediterranem Ambiente und internationaler Küche – das Thema Wein bestimmt das Dekor. Schön ist der Blick auf den Golfplatz.

In Moosburg-Bärndorf **West: 3 km Richtung Pörtschach, nach dem Golfplatz rechts:**

Gasthof Bärnwirt Rest,
Bärndorf 3 9062 – (04272) 8 30 13 – gasthof@baernwirt.at
– Fax (04272) 830134
geschl. Nov.
15 Zim – 32/47 € 70/84 € – ½ P 6 €
Rest – *(geschl. Okt. – April, Mai Dienstag – Mittwoch)* Karte 15/25 €
♦ Ein gut geführter Familienbetrieb in ruhiger Lage. Die Zimmer sind mit Naturholz wohnlich eingerichtet und meist sehr geräumig. Schön: das Freibad mit Liegewiese und Aussicht. In der Gaststube serviert man bürgerliche Küche.

Gute Küche zu günstigem Preis? Folgen Sie dem „Bib Gourmand"

MÜHLBACH AM HOCHKÖNIG – Salzburg – 730 L6 – 1 630 Ew – Höhe 854 m – Wintersport: 1 826 m 1 26 8 G5

Wien 356 – Salzburg 59 – Bischofshofen 9

Mühlbach 154 a, 5505, (06467) 72 35, info@muehlbach.co.at

Veranstaltungen

30.03.: Volksmusikalische Skihüttenroas

Bergheimat Tal und Berge, Zim,
Mandlwandstr. 159 (Nord: 4 km) 5505 – (06467) 72 26 – hotel@bergheimat.com – Fax (06467) 722613
geschl. 30. März – 2. Juni, 5. Okt. – 19. Dez.
38 Zim (inkl. ½ P.) – 50/90 € 90/140 € 60/120 € 120/190 €
Rest – Karte 15/32 €

◆ Das Hotel liegt sehr ruhig oberhalb des Ortes in 1200 m Höhe. Die Zimmer sind recht unterschiedlich: von gepflegt-einfach bis hin zum großzügigen Appartement mit Whirlwanne. Gediegenes Ambiente im Restaurant – netter Terrassenbereich im Sommer.

Alpengasthof Birgkarhaus (geheizt) Zim,
Mühlbach 191 (West 7 km, auf dem Dientner Sattel) 5505 – (06467) 72 87 – office@birgkarhaus.at – Fax (06467) 72874
geschl. Mitte April – Mitte Mai, Nov. – 15. Dez.
16 Zim (inkl. ½ P.) – 64/76 € 101/119 € 76/97 € 119/152 €
Rest – *(geschl. im Sommer Sonntagabend)* Karte 19/30 €

◆ In fast 1400 m Höhe gelegener, familiär geführter kleiner Gasthof mit regionstypisch eingerichteten Zimmern und großem Garten mit beheiztem Schwimmteich. Rustikale Restaurantstuben mit Sonnenterrasse.

Alpengasthof Kopphütte Hochkönig und Niedere Tauern, Zim,
Mitterberg. 188 (Nord: 7 km) 5505 – (06467) 72 64 – office@kopphuette.at – Fax (06467) 72648
geschl. 29. März – 10. Mai, Mitte Okt. – 24. Dez.
20 Zim (inkl. ½ P.) – 46/51 € 82/92 € 57/58 € 104/106 €
Rest – Karte 15/22 €

◆ Von der Familie geleiteter Gasthof in 1307 m Höhe, unterhalb des Hochkönig. Die meisten Zimmer mit Bergblick, teils auch kleine Familienzimmer. Panoramasauna auf 2 Etagen. Restaurantstuben in ländlichem Stil.

MÜHLBACHL – Tirol – siehe Matrei am Brenner

MÜHLDORF – Niederösterreich – 730 S3 – 1 450 Ew – Höhe 400 m 3 J2

Wien 102 – St. Pölten 47 – Krems 26 – Melk 26

Burg Oberranna garni
In Oberranna 1 (Nord-West: 1,5 km) 3622 – (02713) 82 21 – reservierung@burg-oberranna.at – Fax (02713) 8366
geschl. Nov. – 25. April
12 Zim – 84 € 122/144 €

◆ Diese bis auf das 12. Jh. zurückgehende romantische Burganlage bietet mit Antiquitäten ausgestattete Zimmer und Appartements – z. T. mit Blick ins Mühltal. Romanische Kapelle.

MURAU – Steiermark – 730 O7 – 2 340 Ew – Höhe 830 m – Wintersport: 2 004 m 5 9 I5

Wien 249 – Graz 127 – St. Veit an der Glan 67 – Judenburg 45
Bundesstr. 13a, 8850, (03532) 27 20, tourismus@murau.at
Stadtpfarrkirche St. Matthäus★ – Leonardikapelle★
Sankt Lambrecht (Stiftskirche: Hochaltar★) Süd-Ost: 15 km

Lercher

Zim, VISA AE

Schwarzenbergstr. 10 8850 – (03532) 24 31 – hotel.lercher@murau.at – Fax (03532) 3694

50 Zim – 61/95 € 92/164 €

Rest Lercher's Panorama – separat erwähnt

Rest – Karte 16/33 €

♦ Das gewachsene traditionsreiche Hotel in der Altstadt bietet im Anbau wohnliche und leicht elegante Gästezimmer, im Stammhaus etwas einfachere. Bürgerliches Restaurant mit günstigem Mittagsbuffet.

Gasthof Ferner

Rest, Zim, VISA

Roseggerstr. 9 8850 – (03532) 23 18 – info@hotel-ferner.at – Fax (03532) 23185

geschl. 10. – 30. Nov.

8 Zim – 40/42 € 70/76 € – ½ P 12 €

Rest – Karte 15/33 €

♦ Aus dem Jahre 1500 stammt dieser gestandene Gasthof – seit 14 Generationen unter familiärer Leitung. Man verfügt über unterschiedlich eingerichtete, gepflegte Zimmer. Gemütlich-rustikales Restaurant, teils mit Kreuzgewölbe. Schön ist der schattige Gastgarten.

Lercher's Panorama – Hotel Lercher

Stolzalpe, VISA AE

Schwarzenbergstr. 10 8850 – (03532) 24 31 – hotel.lercher@murau.at – Fax (03532) 3694

Rest – *(geschl. April, Juli 3 Wochen, Nov. und Sonntag – Montag, nur Abendessen)* (Tischbestellung ratsam) Menü 55/90 € – Karte 39/48 €

♦ Lercher's Panorama ist ein nettes kleines Restaurant mit elegantem Touch und Sicht auf Stadt und Berge. Das Angebot ist international ausgelegt, mit regionalen Elementen.

MUTTERS – Tirol – 730 G7 – 1 940 Ew – Höhe 830 m – Wintersport: 1 801 m 1 2 7 D5

Wien 450 – Innsbruck 6 – Schwaz 32 – Seefeld 27
Kirchplatz 11, 6162, (0512) 54 84 10, mutters@innsbruck.info

Mutterehof

VISA AE

Nattererstr. 20 6162 – (0512) 54 84 91 – muttererhof@tirol.com – Fax (0512) 5484915

geschl. April, Nov.

22 Zim – 35/55 € 60/80 € 35/65 € 60/90 € – ½ P 10/18 €

Rest – (nur Abendessen für Hausgäste)

♦ Die Zimmer dieses gepflegten Hotels verfügen teilweis über einen Balkon, die nach hinten gelegenen bieten einen schönen Blick ins Tal. Rustikale, regionstypisch dekorierte Gaststuben und hübsche Terrasse mit Aussicht.

Sonnhof Rest,

Burgstall 12 6162 – (0512) 5 48 47 00 – hotel@sonnhof-mutters.at – Fax (0512) 548471
geschl. April, Nov.
28 Zim – 50/74 € 80/110 € 56/81 € 92/144 € – ½ P 10 €
Rest – Menü 21 € – Karte 18/29 €
♦ Das in Zentrumsnähe gelegene, von der Besitzerfamilie geführte Haus bietet rustikal gehaltene Gästezimmer unterschiedlicher Größe, teils mit Balkon. Bürgerliches Restaurant.

An der Alten Brennerstraße Süd-Ost: 4 km Richtung Matrei am Brenner:

Gasthof Schupfen mit Zim

Unterberg 5 (B 182) 6020 Mutters – (0512) 56 24 26 – info@schupfen.at – Fax (0512) 562426
geschl. Montag – Dienstag
6 Zim – 40/50 € 70/100 € – ½ P 15 €
Rest – Karte 20/39 €
♦ Hinter der denkmalgeschützten Fassade des durch den Freiheitskämpfer Andreas Hofer 1809 bekannt gewordenen Hauses verbergen sich heute rustikale Stuben und wohnliche Zimmer.

Luxuriös oder eher schlicht?
Die Symbole und kennzeichnen den Komfort.

NASSEREITH – Tirol – 730 E7 – 2 090 Ew – Höhe 860 m – Wintersport: 1 120 m 2 6 C5

Wien 497 – Innsbruck 53 – Garmisch-Partenkirchen 46 – Reutte 38
Fernpassstraße★ – Fernsteinsee★ (Nord: 10 km)

Schloss Fernsteinsee (mit Gästehaus und Schloss)

(Nord-West: 3,5 km Richtung Fernpass) 6465 – (05265) 52 10 – hotel@fernsteinsee.at – Fax (05265) 52174
geschl. 4. Nov. – 1. April
34 Zim (inkl. ½ P.) – 61/106 € 122/212 €
Rest – Karte 16/39 €
♦ Sie haben die Wahl zwischen gediegenen Zimmern im Hotel, Appartements in der Villa Lorea oder stilvoll-luxuriösen, mit Antiquitäten bestückten Zimmern und Suiten im Schloss. A-la-carte-Stube mit bürgerlich-rustikalem Charakter.

NASSFELD – Kärnten – siehe Hermagor

NAUDERS – Tirol – 730 D8 – 1 540 Ew – Höhe 1 394 m – Wintersport: 2 850 m 3 27 5 B6

Wien 556 – Innsbruck 113 – Sankt Anton 72 – Landeck 44
Dr.-Tschiggfrey-Str. 66, 6543, (05473) 8 72 20, nauders@reschenpass.info
Oberes Inntal★ – Finstermünzpass★ (Nord: 8 km)

Alpin-Spa-Hotel Naudererhof

Karl-Blaas-Gasse 160
Rest, VISA
✉ 6543 – ✆ (05473) 8 77 04 – info@naudererhof.at – Fax (05473) 87777
geschl. 15. April – 20. Mai, 20. Okt. – 10. Dez.
45 Zim (inkl. ½ P.) – ☼ 70/85 € 130/170 € ❄ 92/130 € 184/276 € – 8 Suiten
Rest – Karte 16/42 €
◆ Eine behagliche, geräumige Halle mit Kamin und Wintergartenanbau empfängt Sie in dem familiengeführten Hotel. Der moderne Wellnessbereich bietet eine Vielzahl an Anwendungen. Gediegenes Restaurant und gemütliche Stube.

Hochland

Rest,
Dr. Tschiggfrey-Str. 183 ✉ 6543 – ✆ (05473) 8 62 22 – hotel@hochland.at – Fax (05473) 862228
geschl. 13. April – 1. Mai, 19. Okt. – 15. Dez.
45 Zim (inkl. ½ P.) – ☼ 55/71 € 90/144 € ❄ 74/109 € 122/222 €
Rest – (nur für Hausgäste, im Winter nur Abendessen) Karte 14/34 €
◆ Die wohnlichen, unterschiedlich geschnittenen Zimmer dieses Hotels verteilen sich auf zwei miteinander verbundene Häuser. Auch Familienzimmer sind vorhanden. Restaurant in rustikal-klassischem Stil.

Central

Rest,
Unterdorfweg 196 ✉ 6543 – ✆ (05473) 87 22 10 – info@hotel-central.at – Fax (05473) 8722146
geschl. 7. April – 10. Mai, 4. Okt. – 15. Dez.
35 Zim (inkl. ½ P.) – ☼ 77/81 € 112/156 € ❄ 99/147 € 160/271 € – 10 Suiten
Rest – (nur Abendessen für Hausgäste)
◆ Eine rustikale Halle mit Kamin, die gemütliche 400 Jahre alte Stube sowie solide, teilweise neuere, modern gestaltete Zimmer sprechen für dieses regionstypische Haus.

Schwarzer Adler

Rest,
Dr. Tschiggfrey-Str. 33 ✉ 6543 – ✆ (05473) 87 25 40 – info@adlerhotel.at – Fax (05473) 87624
geschl. Mitte April – Anfang Juni, Mitte Okt. – Mitte Dez.
40 Zim (inkl. ½ P.) – ☼ 63/84 € 101/150 € ❄ 79/127 € 140/234 €
Rest – Menü 10/17 € – Karte 15/24 €
◆ Der regionstypisch-rustikale Stil begleitet Sie von der großzügigen Halle bis in die gepflegten, meist mit Balkon ausgestatteten Gästezimmer dieses Familienbetriebs.

Tia Monte

Rest, Rest, VISA
Dr.-Tschiggfrey-Str. 30 ✉ 6543 – ✆ (05473) 8 62 40 – office@hotel-tiamonte.at – Fax (05473) 862406
geschl. April – Mai
27 Zim (inkl. ½ P.) – ☼ 64/68 € 83/112 € ❄ 57/92 € 98/168 €
Rest – (nur Abendessen für Hausgäste)
◆ Das Hotel im Zentrum beherbergt hinter seiner modernen hellblau-weißen Fassade neuzeitliche, teils recht geräumige Gästezimmer, einige mit Balkon.

Alpengasthof Norbertshöhe ← Engadin, P
Martinsbrucker Str. 223 (Nord-West: 2 km Richtung St. Moritz) ✉ 6543 – ✆ (05473) 87 24 10 – norbertshoehe.hotel@tirol.com – Fax (05473) 872417
geschl. 6. April – Mitte Juni, Ende Sept. – Mitte Dez.
20 Zim (inkl. ½ P.) – ☼ †54 € ††94 € ❄ †67/79 € ††120/144 €
Rest – *(geschl. Montag)* Karte 21/40 €
♦ Schön liegt der familiengeführte Gasthof an der Straße nach St. Moritz. Die Zimmer sind wohnlich-rustikal eingerichtet und bieten fast alle Bergblick. Helles, neuzeitliches Restaurant und Terrasse mit Aussicht.

Via Claudia garni ← P
Unterdorfstr. 406 ✉ 6543 – ✆ (05473) 8 77 07 – info@viaclaudia-nauders.at – Fax (05473) 877077
geschl. Mitte April – Mitte Mai, Mitte Okt. – Mitte Dez.
13 Zim – ☼ †35/45 € ††60/80 € ❄ †50/60 € ††80/100 €
♦ Ein mit viel hellem Holz und nettem Dekor gemütlich gestalteter kleiner Familienbetrieb im alpenländischen Stil, der über wohnliche Gästezimmer verfügt.

NECKENMARKT – Burgenland – 730 V6 – 1 730 Ew – Höhe 225 m 4 L3

Wien 94 – Eisenstadt 50 – Sopron 19 – Oberpullendorf 14

Gasthof Zur Traube (mit Gästehaus) P
Herrengasse 42 ✉ 7311 – ✆ (02610) 4 22 56 – info@gasthof-zur-traube.at – Fax (02610) 423064 VISA AE
geschl. über Weihnachten
15 Zim – †34/40 € ††56/68 € – ½ P 15 €
Rest – *(geschl. Montagabend)* Menü 36 € – Karte 15/35 €
♦ Ein familiengeführter erweiterter Gasthof in der Ortsmitte. Besonders modern und recht geräumig sind die Zimmer im neuzeitlichen Gästehaus. Im Restaurant – Lärchenstüberl und Nusszimmer – bietet man klassische Küche, die durch regionale Gerichte ergänzt wird.

NESSELWÄNGLE – Tirol – 730 D6 – 470 Ew – Höhe 1 147 m – Wintersport: 1 560 m 4 5 B5

Wien 518 – Innsbruck 105 – Reutte 16 – Sonthofen 32
✉ 6672, ✆ (05675) 82 71, nesselw@netway.at

Laternd'l Hof ← Spa Rest, P
Seestr. 16, (Haller) (Nord-West: 2 km) ✉ 6672 – ✆ (05675) 82 67 – info@laterndlhof.com – Fax (05675) 8205
geschl. Ende März – Ende April, Anfang Nov. – Mitte Dez.
32 Zim (inkl. ½ P.) – †93/111 € ††172/208 €
Rest – *(geschl. Montag)* Karte 18/39 €
♦ Das Haus verfügt über Zimmer im regionstypischen Landhausstil – alle mit Balkon und Sicht auf See und Berge – sowie einen nett gestalteten Wellnessbereich mit Kosmetik. Zum Restaurant gehört eine schöne Terrasse mit Seeblick.

Via Salina ← Haldensee, Zim, P
Haller 11 ✉ 6672 – ✆ (05675) 2 01 04 – office@via-salina.at – Fax (05675) 2010444 VISA AE
geschl. 19. Nov. – 15. Dez.

28 Zim (inkl. ½ P.) – ☼ 80/95 € 130/160 € ❄ 84/120 € 138/210 € – 3 Suiten
Rest – Menü 30 € – Karte 20/38 €
◆ Die schöne Lage direkt am Haldensee sowie sehr wohnliche, großzügige Gästezimmer mit Kachelofen machen dieses Ferienhotel aus. Restaurant mit gemütlichen kleinen Stuben und Terrasse am See.

Sunneschlössli garni < Krinnenspitze und Gaichtspitze,
Haus 124 ✉ 6672
– ✆ *(05675) 83 83 – welcome@sunneschloessli.com – Fax (05675) 838365*
7 Suiten – 80/120 € 92/165 €, ☕ 12 €
◆ Geschmackvoll und mit Antiquitäten versehen sind die Zimmer und Suiten dieses Hauses mit individueller, privater Atmosphäre. Man kümmert sich mit Engagement um die Gäste.

Gasthof Köllenspitze mit Zim
Nesselwängle 7 ✉ 6672 – ✆ (05675) 82 28 – info@koellenspitze.at
– Fax (05675) 8406
geschl. 1. April – 8. Mai, 9. Juni – 4. Juli, 27. Okt. – 20. Dez. und Mittwoch
10 Zim ☕ – ☼ 34 € 58 € ❄ 35 € 60 € – ½ P 10 €
Rest – Karte 18/35 €
◆ Ein einfacher, solider Gasthof unter Leitung der Inhaberfamilie mit ländlichem Ambiente und überwiegend regional ausgerichteter Küche.

NEUBERG AN DER MÜRZ – Steiermark – 730 S6 – 1 550 Ew – Höhe 732 m – Wintersport: 10 K4

Wien 116 – Graz 105 – Bruck a.d. Mur 56 – Mürzzuschlag 12
Münster★
Semmering★ (Süd-Ost: 25 km)

Gasthof Holzer mit Zim Zim,
Hauptstr. 9 ✉ 8692 – ✆ (03857) 83 32 – gasthof@hubertholzer.com
– Fax (03857) 833224
geschl. Nov., Dienstag – Mittwoch
6 Zim ☕ – 36/50 € 58/98 € – ½ P 20 €
Rest – Karte 19/42 €
◆ Ein familiengeführter Gasthof im Ortskern mit bürgerlich-rustikalem Charakter. Man serviert regionale Gerichte zu fairen Preisen.

NEUDAUBERG – Burgenland – siehe Burgauberg-Neudauberg

NEUFELDEN – Oberösterreich – 730 O3 – 1 250 Ew – Höhe 517 m – Wintersport: 2 H2

Wien 212 – Linz 34 – Wels 49 – Passau 57
Markt 22, ✉ 4120, ✆ (07282) 62 55, gemeinde@neufelden.ooe.gv.at

Mühltalhof mit Zim
Unternberg 6 ✉ 4120 – ✆ (07282) 6 25 80 – reception@muehltalhof.at
– Fax (07282) 62583
20 Zim ☕ – 65/95 € 110/180 € – ½ P 30 €
Rest – *(geschl. Sonntagabend – Dienstag)* Karte 28/48 €
◆ In dem über 300 Jahre alten Gasthaus an der Großen Mühl serviert man in 2 Stuben eine kreative Regionalküche. Moderne Kunst ziert das Haus. Nette Terrasse zum Fluss. Recht individuell eingerichtete Zimmer.

NEUHOFEN AN DER KREMS – Oberösterreich – 730 O4 – 5 410 Ew – Höhe 303 m 2 H3

Wien 181 – Linz 21 – Wels 29 – Steyr 24

Moser

Marktplatz 9 ✉ 4501 – ✆ (07227) 42 29 – gasthofmoser@neuhofen.at – Fax (07227) 42294

Rest – Menü 35 € – Karte 22/35 €

◆ Seit 1449 wird dieses Haus als Gasthof betrieben. Eine rustikale Stube mit Kachelofen und Theke und das in Holz gehaltene Salettl mit reichlich Zierrat. Schöne Gewölbedecke.

NEUHOFEN AN DER YBBS – Niederösterreich – 730 Q4 – 2 540 Ew – Höhe 320 m – Wintersport: 1 2 I3

Wien 133 – St. Pölten 76 – Steyr 39 – Amstetten 12

Kothmühle

Zim, Rest,

Kothmühle 1 (Süd-Ost: 3,5 km)

✉ 3364 – ✆ (07475) 52 11 20 – office@kothmuehle.at – Fax (07475) 521128

95 Zim – 84/126 € 126/168 € – ½ P 19 €

Rest – Karte 18/39 €

◆ Seit 1866 ist der Gutshof a. d. 14. Jh. im Besitz der Familie Scheiblauer. Ein Seminarhotel mit individuellen, wohnlichen Zimmern, schönem Spabereich und Naturschwimmbiotop. Helle, freundliche Restauranträume mit Blick in den Garten.

NEUKIRCHEN AM GROSSVENEDIGER – Salzburg – 730 I7 – 2 620 Ew – Höhe 856 m – Wintersport: 2 150 m 1 15 7 E5

Wien 416 – Salzburg 140 – Wörgl 79 – Kitzbühel 49

Marktstr. 171, ✉ 5741, ✆ (06565) 62 56, info@neukirchen.at

Veranstaltungen

10.07. – 03.08.: Freiluftfestspiele

Gassner

Hadergasse 167 ✉ 5741 – ✆ (06565) 62 32 – info@hotel-gassner.at – Fax (06565) 6232400

geschl. 31. März - 21. Mai, 12. Okt. – 20. Dez.

50 Zim (inkl. ½ P.) – ☼ 62/75 € 123/152 € ❄ 74/90 € 132/184 € – 3 Suiten

Rest – Karte 17/34 €

◆ Viel Holz gibt dem gewachsenen Familienbetrieb oberhalb des Ortskerns sein wohnliches Ambiente. Die Zimmer sind unterschiedlich geschnitten und teils mit Holz vertäfelt. Ein rustikaler älterer Teil und ein neuzeitlicher Bereich bilden das geräumige Restaurant.

Steiger

Kreuzschiedstr. 259 ✉ 5741 – ✆ (06565) 63 59 – info@hotel-steiger.at – Fax (06565) 635955

geschl. 7. – 28. April, 5. Nov. – 1. Dez.

40 Zim (inkl. ½ P.) – ☼ 52/66 € 128/143 € ❄ 61/89 € 121/183 €

Rest – Karte 18/29 €

◆ Ein Hotel aus zwei miteinander verbundenen Gasthöfen. Mit hübschen Farben und Stoffen hat man die teils ganz hell, teils in rustikaler Eiche gehaltenen Zimmer gestaltet. Angenehm hell und neuzeitlich-ländlich eingerichtetes Restaurant.

Hubertus

Am Waldrand 278 ✉ 5741 – ✆ (06565) 64 80 – hotel-hubertus@sbg.at – Fax (06565) 64808
geschl. 15. April – 31. Mai, 10. Okt. – 15. Dez.
35 Zim (inkl. ½ P.) – ☼ 61/70 € 112/130 € ❄ 66/77 € 122/154 €
Rest – Karte 16/31 €
◆ Relativ ruhig liegt das im hiesigen Stil erbaute Hotel mit Holzbalkonen. Man verfügt über praktisch ausgestattete, wohnliche Gästezimmer und ein Kosmetikstudio. Gemütliche Gaststuben.

Abelhof Großvenediger,

Rossberg 116 ✉ 5741 – ✆ (06565) 6 23 00 – abelhof@aon.at – Fax (06565) 62305
geschl. 5. April – 1. Mai, 19. Okt. – Mitte Dez.
32 Zim (inkl. ½ P.) – ☼ 40/47 € 74/88 € ❄ 47/55 € 88/110 €
Rest – Karte 15/31 €
◆ Die sehr schöne Lage auf einer Almwiese oberhalb des Ortes spricht für diesen typischen Gasthof. Die Zimmer sind in rustikalem Stil eingerichtet. Freundliche Gaststuben mit großem Kachelofen.

Unsere „Hoffnungsträger" sind die Restaurants, deren Küche wir für die nächste Ausgabe besonders sorgfältig auf eine höhere Auszeichnung hin überprüfen. Der Name dieser Restaurants ist in „rot" gedruckt und zusätzlich auf der Sterne-Liste am Anfang des Buches zu finden.

NEUMARKT AM WALLERSEE – Salzburg – 730 L5 – 5 420 Ew – Höhe 510 m 1 G3

Wien 270 – Salzburg 24 – Burghausen 52 – Vöcklabruck 37

Winkler mit Zim

Thalham 12 (Süd-Ost: 2,5 km) ✉ 5202 – ✆ (06216) 52 70 – info@seehotel.at – Fax (06216) 527033
geschl. Sept. – Juni Dienstag
11 Zim – ☼ 80/100 € 120/160 € ❄ 60/80 € 100/140 €
Rest – Karte 23/43 €
◆ Das ruhig an der Bucht des Sees gelegene historische Landhaus bietet vorwiegend Fischgerichte aus den hauseigenen Fischbecken an. Schöne Terrasse mit Blick auf den See. Solide Zimmer mit schönem Ausblick.

Gasthaus Kienberg

Neufahrn 39 (Ost: 6 km, ab Neufahrn Richtung Kienberg) ✉ 5202 – ✆ (06216) 2 01 03 – gasthaus@kienberg.at – Fax (06216) 20103
geschl 28. Jan. – 3. März und Montag – Dienstag
Rest – Karte 20/38 €
◆ In einsamer Lage mit herrlicher Sicht befindet sich der Gasthof der Familie Huber. Zubereitet werden regionale und internationale Gerichte.

NEUNKIRCHEN – Niederösterreich – 730 U5 – 11 030 Ew – Höhe 369 m

4 **L3**

Wien 65 – St. Pölten 101 – Wiener Neustadt 17 – Baden 39

Osterbauer

Rest, Zim, P, VISA, MC, AE, D

Minoritenplatz ✉ 2620 – ✆ (02635) 6 31 55 – hotel.osterbauer@utanet.at – Fax (02635) 631555

26 Zim – 55/75 € 75/90 €

Rest – *(geschl. Sonntagabend)* Karte 14/28 €

◆ Ein familiengeführtes Hotel in zentraler Lage mit zeitgemäß ausgestatteten Gästezimmern. Im 3. Stock befindet sich eine schöne Suite mit Blick auf die Umgebung. Zum Restaurant gehört ein netter Gastgarten hinter dem Haus.

Brunnenstöckl

VISA, MC, AE, D

Hauptplatz 12, (Hauptplatzpassage) ✉ 2620 – ✆ (02635) 6 18 44 – brunnenstoeckl@aon.at – Fax (02635) 618444

geschl. Anfang Aug. 2 Wochen und Sonntag – Montag

Rest – Karte 20/34 €

◆ Im 1. Stock eines ehemaligen Bürgerhauses a. d. 17. Jh. – heute Teil der Hauptplatzpassage – befindet sich dieses ländlich gehaltene Restaurant mit freundlichem Service.

NEUSACH – Kärnten – siehe Weißensee

NEUSIEDL AM SEE – Burgenland – 730 W5 – 5 590 Ew – Höhe 131 m

4 **M3**

Wien 53 – Eisenstadt 32 – Baden 76 – Sopron 54

Hauptplatz 1, ✉ 7100, ✆ (02167) 22 29, info@neusiedlamsee.at

Neusiedler See★★

Schloss Halbturn (Fresken★) Süd-Ost: 13 km – Frauenkirchen★ Süd-Ost: 16 km

Wende

Zim, P, VISA, MC, D

Seestr. 40 ✉ 7100 – ✆ (02167) 81 11 – anfrage@hotel-wende.at – Fax (02167) 8111649

geschl. Anfang Feb. 2 Wochen, 22. – 25 Dez.

105 Zim (inkl. ½ P.) – 83/94 € 132/164 €

Rest – Karte 19/38 €

◆ Durch einen recht großen Hallenbereich mit Sitzgruppen und Friseur gelangen Sie in die zeitgemäß und funktionell ausgestatteten Gästezimmer dieses gewachsenen Hotels. Freundlich wirkendes Hotelrestaurant.

Helga Dolezal Beauty-Vital-Residenz

Seestr. 37

Zim, Rest, P, VISA, MC, AE, D

✉ 7100 – ✆ (02167) 24 39 – h.dolezal@beauty-vital-residenz.at – Fax (02167) 243926

geschl. 15. – 25. Dez.

40 Zim (inkl. ½ P.) – 95/140 € 190/320 €

Rest – (nur für Hausgäste)

◆ Das Hotel hat sich auf Wellness und Kosmetikanwendungen verschiedenster Art spezialisiert. Die Zimmer sind teils im Laura-Ashley-Stil gehalten und mit vielen Details versehen.

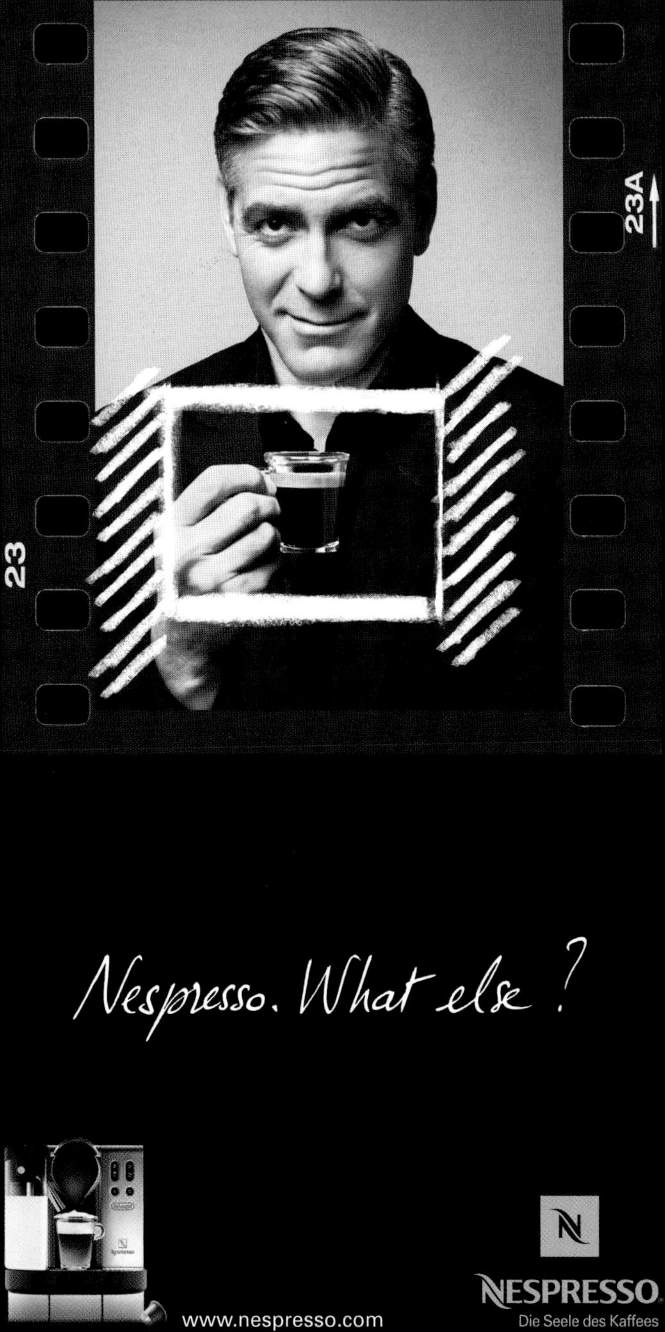

Am Nyikospark mit Zim — AC Zim, Zim, P VISA AE
Untere Hauptstr. 59 ✉ 7100 – ✆ (02167) 4 02 22
– landgasthaus@nyikospark.at – Fax (02167) 7778
geschl. Anfang Feb. 2 Wochen und Montag – Dienstag
5 Zim – 70/90 € 100 €, 10 €
Rest – Karte 16/41 €
◆ Die Gaststube aus dunklem Holz befindet sich in einem ehemaligen Offizierscasino. Unter anderem stehen ein Gastgarten und ein moderner Wintergarten zur Verfügung. Neuzeitlich designte Appartements im Gästehaus.

NEUSTIFT IM STUBAITAL – Tirol – 730 F7 – 4 330 Ew – Höhe 1 000 m – Wintersport: 3 250 m 9 35 — 6 D6

Wien 466 – Innsbruck 23 – Schwaz 48 – Seefeld 43
Stubaitalhaus, Dorf 3, ✉ 6167, ✆ (0) 5 01 88 10, info@stubai.at
Stubaital★★

Jagdhof — (geheizt) Rest, P VISA AE
Scheibe 44 ✉ 6167
– ✆ (05226) 26 66 – mail@hotel-jagdhof.at – Fax (05226) 2666503
geschl. 13. April – 31. Mai
70 Zim (inkl. ½ P.) – 145/238 € 310/396 € 161/287 € 340/474 € – 8 Suiten
Rest *Pfurtschellers Hubertus Stube* – *(nur Abendessen)* (Tischbestellung ratsam) Menü 80/107 € – Karte 49/90 €
◆ Wohnlich-alpenländisch ist das Ambiente in den teils mit antiken Möbelstücken versehen Zimmern. Eleganter und großzügiger, in warmen Tönen gehaltener Wellnessbereich. Pfurtschellers Hubertus Stube ist schön im regionstypischen Stil eingerichtet.

Sporthotel Neustift — (geheizt) P VISA
Moos 7 ✉ 6167
– ✆ (05226) 25 10 – sporthotel@neustift.at – Fax (05226) 251019
geschl. Mai
64 Zim (inkl. ½ P.) – 84/116 € 168/178 € 93/162 € 192/270 € – 6 Suiten
Rest – (nur für Hausgäste)
◆ Das Hotel an der Talstation gefällt mit einer großzügigen Lobby, komfortablen Zimmern und einem Freizeitbereich auf 3 Etagen. Suiten teils mit Parkett und Kachelofen.

Schönherr-Haus garni  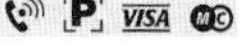
Stubaitalstr. 79 ✉ 6167 – ✆ (05226) 35 30
– schoenherrhaus@schoenherr.cc – Fax (05226) 353030
20 Zim – 41/44 € 74/81 € 60/83 € 98/144 €
7 Suiten
◆ Das familiengeführte Hotel bietet hübsche, mit kleiner Küche ausgestattete Junior Suiten und Suiten, die auch als Ferienwohnung gemietet werden können. Gutes Frühstücksbuffet.

Alpenhotel Fernau — (geheizt) Rest, P VISA
Scheibe 66 ✉ 6167
– ✆ (05226) 2 71 70 – info@hotel-fernau.at – Fax (05226) 2698116
geschl. Anfang Mai – Mitte Juni, Anfang Okt. 3 Wochen

45 Zim (inkl. ½ P.) – ☼ 59/88 € 98/146 € ❄ 66/116 € 112/202 € – 3 Suiten
Rest – (nur Abendessen für Hausgäste)
◆ Unterschiedlich geschnittene und eingerichtete Zimmer mit Balkon – vom Einzelzimmer bis zur Suite – bietet dieses familiengeführte Hotel. Schöne Aussicht von der Liegewiese.

Berghof

Moos 11 ✉ 6167 – ✆ (05226) 23 50 – info@berghof-tirol.com – Fax (05226) 235042
geschl. Mai, Ende Sept. – Ende Okt.
34 Zim (inkl. ½ P.) – ☼ 52/72 € 94/124 € ❄ 59/106 € 114/192 €
Rest – (nur Abendessen für Hausgäste)
◆ Das von der Inhaberfamilie geleitete Haus liegt bei der Bergbahn-Talstation und bietet wohnliche Zimmer im regionstypischen Stil sowie ein hübsches Saunadorf. Zur Halle mit Barbereich hin offen angelegtes Restaurant.

Der Hoferwirt

Zim,

Dorf 12 ✉ 6167 – ✆ (05226) 22 01 – der-hoferwirt@neustift.at – Fax (05226) 220122
26 Zim (inkl. ½ P.) – ☼ 49/53 € 82/98 € ❄ 58/82 € 100/152 €
Rest – *(geschl. außer Saison Dienstag)* Menü 12/20 € – Karte 17/29 €
◆ Das im Ortszentrum gelegene Haus ist seit drei Generationen in Familienbesitz. Die Zimmer sind überwiegend mit hellem Naturholz neuzeitlich und freundlich eingerichtet. Rustikale Restaurantstuben und lichter Wintergarten.

Sportpension Elisabeth garni

Oberdorf 2 ✉ 6167 – ✆ (05226) 22 32 – info@sportpension-elisabeth.at – Fax (05226) 3496
geschl. Mai
17 Zim – ☼ 42/45 € 64/70 € ❄ 51/60 € 82/100 €
◆ Zu den Annehmlichkeiten dieses persönlich geführten Hauses zählen Gästezimmer mit freundlicher und wohnlicher Einrichtung und ein gemütlicher Frühstücksraum.

Jagdhütte

Stubaitalstr. 82 ✉ 6167 – ✆ (05226) 26 68 – office@jagdhuette.at – Fax (05226) 266844
geschl. 7. April – 8. Mai, 6. – 29. Okt., im Mai, Sept. und Nov. Montag
Rest – Karte 15/39 €
◆ Dunkles Holz, ein mittig angelegter Kamin und eine offene Deckenkonstruktion geben dem Restaurant seinen rustikalen Charakter. Pub im Erdgeschoss.

Kratzerwirt mit Zim

Obergasse 15 (Richtung Gletscherbahn, nach 500 m Ortsausgang links ab) ✉ 6167 – ✆ (05226) 31 52 – info@kratzerwirt.at – Fax (05226) 315220
16 Zim – ☼ 36/48 € 36/48 € ❄ 51/61 € 51/61 €, 8 € – ½ P 11 €
Rest – Karte 15/30 €
◆ Das im alpenländischen Stil erbaute Haus oberhalb des Ortes beherbergt ein in Stuben unterteiltes Restaurant mit heller, rustikaler Einrichtung. Die Gästezimmer werden auch als Ferienwohnungen vermietet – einige für bis zu neun Personen.

In Neustift-Kampl Nord-Ost: 2,5 km Richtung Innsbruck:

Steuxner (geheizt) Rest,
Feldgasse 3 6167 – (05226) 22 42 – hotel@steuxner.at
– Fax (05226) 28317
geschl. Ende April 1 Woche, Anfang Juni 1 Woche, Anfang Okt. 2 Wochen
31 Zim (inkl. ½ P.) – 41/45 € 74/90 € 46/57 € 84/114 €
Rest – Karte 14/27 €
◆ Hinter seiner Balkonfassade beherbergt dieses familiär geführte Haus sehr gepflegte Zimmer mit Balkon und schöner Aussicht. Freibad mit Blick auf die Berge. Bürgerlich-rustikales Restaurant.

In Neustift-Milders Süd-West: 2 km Richtung Oberbergtal:

Sonne garni
Franz-Senn-Str. 164 6167 – (05226) 24 33
– office@hotel-garni-sonne.at – Fax (05226) 283335
geschl. Ende April – Mitte Juli
17 Zim – 27/36 € 50/66 € 41/52 € 76/96 €
◆ Ein familiengeführtes kleines Hotel mit freundlich und neuzeitlich gestalteten Gästezimmern, teils mit schöner Aussicht, und gemütlichem Frühstücksraum.

NIEDERNSILL – Salzburg – 730 J7 – 2 420 Ew – Höhe 768 m – Wintersport: 1 000 m 3 8 F5

Wien 384 – Salzburg 92 – Mittersill 15 – Zell am See 15

Kehlbachwirt Biergarten Zim,
Jesdorferstr. 3 5722 – (06548) 82 87 – info@kehlbachwirt.at
– Fax (06548) 82877
geschl. 14. – 30. April, 22. Sept. – 14. Dez.
30 Zim (inkl. ½ P.) – 47/57 € 81/101 € 48/65 € 84/118 €
Rest – *(geschl. außer Saison Montag – Dienstag)* Karte 16/31 €
◆ In der Ortsmitte finden Sie diesen gewachsenen Gasthof, der über gepflegte und unterschiedlich eingerichtete Zimmer in ländlichem Stil verfügt. Rustikales Ambiente im mehrfach unterteilten Restaurantbereich. Garten mit Terrasse und Biergarten.

NIKLASDORF – Steiermark – 730 R6 – 2 700 Ew – Höhe 521 m 10 J4

Wien 156 – Graz 64 – Leoben 6 – Bruck a.d. Mur 11

Brücklwirt Zim,
Leobner Str. 90 (West: 1,5 km über B 116 Richtung Leoben) 8712
– (03842) 8 17 27 – reception@bruecklwirt.co.at – Fax (03842) 817275
70 Zim – 64 € 98 €
Rest – *(geschl. Jan. 1 Woche sowie Sonn- und Feiertage abends)* Menü 13 €
– Karte 20/34 €
◆ Ein solide geführtes Hotel mit teils neuzeitlich und funktionell ausgestatteten, teils etwas älter möblierten Zimmern und einer Gartenanlage. Gemütliche, holzvertäfelte Gaststuben.

NÖHAGEN – Niederösterreich – siehe Weinzierl am Walde

NUSSDORF AM ATTERSEE – Oberösterreich – 730 M5 – 1 100 Ew – Höhe 500 m – Wintersport: 9 G4

Wien 250 – Linz 90 – Salzburg 56 – Gmunden 36

Dorfstr. 50, 4865, (07666) 80 64, info.nussdorf@attersee.at

Aichinger (geheizt) Zim,

Am Anger 1 4865 – (07666) 80 07

– office@hotel-aichinger.at – Fax (07666) 700750

geschl. 7. Jan. – 17. Feb.

23 Zim – 65/105 € 110/170 € 65/85 € 110/130 € – ½ P 25 €

Rest – *(geschl. Montag, Juli- August Montagmittag)* Menü 42 € – Karte 19/46 €

◆ Der gut geführte Familienbetrieb befindet sich nur wenige Minuten vom Strandbad entfernt und verfügt über hübsche, wohnliche Gästezimmer und einen netten Garten. In dem geschmackvollen, rustikal-eleganten Restaurant kocht man auf regionaler Basis.

Landgasthof Ragginger (mit Gästehaus) Zim, Zim,

Dorfstr. 42 4865

– (07666) 80 05 – ragginger@aon.at – Fax (07666) 800577

geschl. 1. Nov. – 25. Dez.

30 Zim – 44/60 € 88/110 €

Rest – *(geschl. Mittwoch außer Juni – August)* Karte 15/31 €

◆ Im Ortszentrum steht der familiengeführte Gasthof mit gegenüberliegendem Gästehaus und Metzgerei. Ganz in der Nähe hat man ein eigenes Strandbad am See. Rustikales Restaurant mit bürgerlicher Karte.

1er Beisl im Lex'nhof mit Zim Zim,

Am Anger 4 4865 – (07666) 8 00 00

– einserbeisl@lexenhof.at – Fax (07666) 80000

geschl. Nov. – März (Hotel)

12 Zim – 36/48 € 60/98 €

Rest – *(geschl. Feb. – März 3 Wochen, Nov. 3 Wochen, Okt. – April Dienstag – Mittwoch, Mai - Sept. Dienstag)* Menü 38/58 € – Karte 30/47 €

◆ Holztäfelung und Kachelofen schaffen in den Restaurantstuben ein gemütliches Ambiente. Serviert wird internationale und regionale Küche. Zum Übernachten stehen solide, behagliche Gästezimmer und eine Ferienwohnung bereit.

OBERALM – Salzburg – 730 L5 – 3 850 Ew – Höhe 452 m 8 G4

Wien 316 – Salzburg 14 – Bad Reichenhall 29 – Berchtesgaden 18

Schloss Haunsperg garni

Hammerstr. 51 5411 – (06245) 8 06 62

– info@schlosshaunsperg.com – Fax (06245) 85680

geschl. 15. Okt. – 15. März

8 Zim – 90/100 € 135/210 € – 5 Suiten

◆ Das pittoreske Schloss a. d. 14. Jh. ist seit über 100 Jahren in Familienbesitz und beherbergt ein Hotel mit feinen, antik eingerichteten Zimmern. Kleiner Park mit Kirche.

Landgasthof Hammerwirt

Messinghammerstr. 1 5411 – (06245) 8 36 64

– landgasthaus.hammerwirt@sbg.at – geschl. Montag

Rest – Karte 14/33 €

◆ Am Ortsrand befindet sich der ländliche Gasthof mit rustikalen Stuben und nettem Gastgarten. Die Küche ist bürgerlich-rustikal.

OBERGURGL - Tirol - siehe Sölden

OBERNDORF IN TIROL - Tirol - 730 J6 - 1 950 Ew - Höhe 700 m - Wintersport: 1 470 m 2 15 7 E5

Wien 360 - Innsbruck 90 - Kitzbühel 7 - Kufstein 29
Josef-Hager-Str. 23, 6372, (05352) 6 29 27, oberndorf@ferienregion.at

Penzinghof

Zim, VISA

Penzingweg 14, (an der Penzing-Bergbahn) 6372 - (05352) 6 29 05 - info@penzinghof.at - Fax (05352) 65466
geschl. Nov.
35 Zim (inkl. ½ P.) - 58/75 € 114/158 € 72/115 € 145/280 €
Rest - Menü 20/32 € - Karte 18/35 €
♦ Das Ferienhotel direkt an der Bergbahn ist ein engagiert geführter Familienbetrieb mit hellen, wohnlichen Zimmern und hübschem Garten mit Badeteich. Man bietet auch Kosmetik. Freundliches Restaurant mit nettem Terrassenbereich.

Lindner

VISA AE

Josef-Hager-Str. 20 6372 - (05352) 69 69 - urlaub@hotel-lindner.at - Fax (05352) 696977
geschl. April, Nov.
53 Zim (inkl. ½ P.) - 75/105 € 126/148 € 81/174 € 138/228 €
Rest - Karte 20/32 €
♦ Hinter seiner regionstypischen Balkonfassade beherbergt das familiengeführte Hotel solide und gepflegte Gästezimmer in rustikaler Eiche. Ländlich-gediegener Restaurantbereich.

Gartenhotel Rosenhof

(geheizt) Rest, VISA

Kreuzgasse 23 6372 - (05352) 6 29 28 - rosenhof@aon.at - Fax (05352) 629287
geschl. Nov.
15 Zim - 42/52 € 64/94 € 44/69 € 70/128 € - ½ P 15 €
Rest - *(geschl. Dienstag) (nur Abendessen für Hausgäste)*
♦ Ein familiär geleitetes kleines Hotel in ruhiger Lage. Die Zimmer (z. T. Appartements) liegen meist zum Tal hin, mit schöner Sicht. Hübscher Garten mit drei Holz-Ferienhäuschen.

Schmiedboden

VISA

Schmiedboden 12 (Süd - West: 1 km) 6372 - (05356) 6 46 46 - info@schmiedboden.at - Fax (05356) 646466
geschl. April - Mai, Okt. - Nov.
11 Zim - 46/56 € 62/82 € 56/69 € 88/98 € - ½ P 8 €
Rest - (nur für Hausgäste)
♦ Das schmucke Tiroler Holzhaus beherbergt ländlich-wohnlich gestaltete Zimmer, überwiegend mit Balkon. Auch Familienappartements stehen zur Verfügung.

OBERTAUERN – **Salzburg** – 730 M7 – **460 Ew** – **Höhe 1 750 m** – **Wintersport: 2 335 m** 1 25 9 **G5**

Wien 327 – Salzburg 91 – Spittal a.d. Drau 73

Obertauern 161, 5562, (06456) 72 52, info@obertauern.com

Seekarspitze★★ – Wildsee★★

Das Seekarhaus

Zim, Rest,

Nr. 35 5562 – (06456) 2 00 10 – info@seekarhaus.at – Fax (06456) 2001010

geschl. Mai – Anfang Nov.

50 Zim (inkl. ½ P.) – 116/241 € 152/384 € – 5 Suiten

Rest – Karte 25/46 €

◆ Das Hotel liegt oberhalb des Orts direkt am Skihang. Wohnlich: die ländlich-eleganten Zimmer mit gutem Platzangebot. Schönes Saunadorf und gemütlicher kleiner Kosmetikbereich. Restaurant mit alpenländischem Charme. Montagabends Fondue.

Steiner

Rest, Rest,

Nr. 103 5562 – (06456) 73 06 – info@hotel-steiner.at – Fax (06456) 747045

geschl. 22. April – 27. Nov.

80 Zim (inkl. ½ P.) – 102/150 € 184/300 €

Rest – (nur Abendessen für Hausgäste)

◆ Mit gediegen-geschmackvoll eingerichteten Gästezimmern gefällt dieses gewachsene Hotel mit seiner in unterschiedlichen freundlichen Farben gehaltenen Fassade.

Enzian

Rest, Rest,

Obertauern 116 5562 – (06456) 7 20 70 – hotel@enzian.net – Fax (06456) 720750

geschl. 14. Mai – 22. Nov.

58 Zim (inkl. ½ P.) – 110/169 € 166/338 € – 10 Suiten

Rest – Karte 22/39 €

◆ Ein familiengeführtes Haus mit moderner Lobby und z. T. als Appartement angelegten Zimmern, einige mit Wintergarten. Hallenbad und Ruhebereich bieten eine nette Sicht. Buffetrestaurant mit Zirbenstube für Nichtraucher. Raucherzone mit Glasdach und Bergblick.

Apparthotel Landhaus St. Georg garni

Rest,

Obertauern 189 5562 – (06456) 76 50 – office@st-georg.cc – Fax (06456) 765033

geschl. 21. April – 27. Nov.

40 Zim – 124/222 €

◆ Dieses Hotel verfügt über einheitlich mit Fichtenholzmobiliar eingerichtete Gästezimmer, teils mit Küchenzeile, sowie ein Kinderspielzimmer und eine Internetecke.

Apparthotel Auerhahn garni

Rest,

Nr. 197 5562 – (06456) 2 00 80 – info@auerhahn-obertauern.at – Fax (06456) 200805

10 Zim – 73 € 73/160 €

◆ In Liftnähe liegt das kinderfreundliche kleine Hotel unter familiärer Leitung. Zimmer mit gutem Platzangebot, teils mit Parkettboden. Nette Aussicht vom Ruheraum der Sauna.

Apparthotel Breitlehenalm garni

Obertauern 177 ✉ 5562 – ✆ (06456) 75 66 – info@breitlehenalm.at – Fax (06456) 76175

16 Zim – 62/78 € 88/130 €

◆ Hinter einer gelben Balkonfassade erwarten Sie tadellos gepflegte und regionstypisch gestaltete Gästezimmer, die in Größe und Zuschnitt unterschiedlich ausfallen.

Alpenland Zim, Rest, VISA

Obertauern 137 ✉ 5562 – ✆ (06456) 7 34 50 – alpenland@obertauern.net – Fax (06456) 73456

geschl. 21. April – 27. Nov.

33 Zim (inkl. ½ P.) – 85/112 € 142/224 €

Rest – (nur für Hausgäste)

◆ Das Hotel bietet wohnliche, mit Fichtenholzmöbeln ausgestattete Gästezimmer, größtenteils mit Balkon, sowie den Sauna-, Kosmetik- und Ruhebereich "Alpen-Relax-Land".

Kristall garni

Obertauern 136 ✉ 5562 – ✆ (06456) 73 23 – kristall@kindl.at – Fax (06456) 73237

geschl. Mai – Mitte Nov.

35 Zim – 54/60 € 100/118 €

◆ Oberhalb des Ortes finden Sie dieses von der Inhaberfamilie freundlich geleitete Hotel. Die wohnlichen Zimmer verfügen z. T. über einen getrennten Wohn- und Schlafraum.

Haus Barbara Rest, VISA

Obertauern 121 ✉ 5562 – ✆ (06456) 72 75 – info@hotel-barbara.at – Fax (06456) 759533

geschl. Mai, Mitte Sept. – Mitte Nov.

21 Zim (inkl. ½ P.) – ☼ 42 € 84 € ❄ 54/80 € 112/166 €

Rest – *(geschl. Juni – Mitte Sept. Samstag, Juni – Mitte Sept. nur Abendessen) (nur für Hausgäste)*

◆ Direkt neben einem Skilift gelegenes Hotel mit hell und zeitgemäß eingerichteten Zimmern – Familienzimmer verfügen über einen zweiten Schlafraum. Après-Ski-Bar mit Terrasse.

Tauernblick Rest,

Obertauern 132 ✉ 5562 – ✆ (06456) 72 76 – info@tauernblick.com – Fax (06456) 72768

20 Zim (inkl. ½ P.) – 72/88 € 122/158 €

Rest – (nur für Hausgäste)

◆ Das persönlich geführte Haus beherbergt gepflegte, mit Fichtenholzmöbeln in ländlichem Stil ausgestattete Zimmer, die sich in Größe und Zuschnitt unterscheiden.

OBERTILLIACH – Tirol – 730 J8 – 800 Ew – Höhe 1 450 m – Wintersport: 2 250 m 5 — 8 F6

Wien 440 – Innsbruck 162 – Lienz 41 – Matrei in Osttirol 68

Dorf 4, ✉ 9942, ✆ (04847) 52 55, info@obertilliach.com

Unterwöger

Dorf 26 ✉ 9942 – ✆ (04847) 52 21 – hotel.unterwoeger@tirol.com – Fax (04847) 522122

geschl. Mai 2 Wochen, Nov. 2 Wochen

28 Zim – 36/51 € 64/94 € – ½ P 12 €

Rest – Karte 16/24 €

◆ Der Gasthof a. d. J. 1750 beherbergt Zimmer in bäuerlichem Stil, meist mit altem Parkett, einige auch mit Antiquitäten. Neuzeitlicher sind die Zimmer im Anbau. Die Gaststuben sind mit rustikaler Einrichtung, Holzfußboden und Täfelung regionstypisch gestaltet.

OBERTRAUN – **Oberösterreich** – 730 N6 – **770 Ew** – **Höhe 513 m** – **Wintersport: 2 100 m** 1 4 9 **H4**

Wien 294 – Linz 130 – Salzburg 80 – Gmunden 59

Obertraun 180, ✉ 4831, ✆ (06131) 3 51, obertraun@inneres-salzkammergut.at

Krippenstein★★ – Dachstein-Rieseneishöhle★★ – Hallstatt★★ (West: 4 km)

Haus am See Rest,

Obertraun 169 ✉ 4831 – ✆ (06131) 2 67 77 – hotel-hausamsee@aon.at – Fax (06131) 26788

24 Zim – 36/43 € 74/86 € – ½ P 14 €

Rest – Karte 14/23 €

◆ Vor allem die schöne Lage am Hallstätter See macht dieses Hotel aus. Die Gästezimmer sind neuzeitlich-rustikal möbliert – einige mit netter Aussicht. Restaurant und Terrasse bieten Seeblick.

OBERTRUM AM SEE – **Salzburg** – 730 L5 – **4 210 Ew** – **Höhe 511 m** – **Wintersport:** 1 **F3**

Wien 296 – Salzburg 17 – Burghausen 40 – Bad Reichenhall 32

Gasthof Neumayr

Dorfplatz 8 ✉ 5162 – ✆ (06219) 63 02 – gasthof.neumayr@aon.at – Fax (06219) 630240

geschl. 22. Dez. – 7. Jan.

17 Zim – 45/56 € 70/86 € – ½ P 12 €

Rest – *(geschl. Dienstag, Freitagmittag)* Karte 11/30 €

◆ Zimmer in ländlichem Stil und eine nette kleine Sauna stehen in dem familiengeführten Gasthof in der Ortsmitte zur Verfügung. Zwei Restaurantstuben: eine kleine Fischerstube und die rustikale Gaststube, beide mit bürgerlicher Küche. Schöner Gastgarten.

OBSTEIG – **Tirol** – 730 E7 – **970 Ew** – **Höhe 1 000 m** – **Wintersport: 1 500 m** 3 6 **C5**

Wien 484 – Innsbruck 41 – Seefeld 25 – Imst 24

Oberstrass 218, ✉ 6416, ✆ (05264) 81 06, info@mieminger-plateau.at

Holzleiten

Holzleiten 84 (Nord-West: 3 km über B 189 Richtung Nassereith, dann rechts ab) ✉ 6416 – ☎ (05264) 82 44 – hotel@holzleiten.at – Fax (05264) 83788
geschl. April, 9. Nov. – 15. Dez.
27 Zim (inkl. ½ P.) – ☼ 71/96 € 130/156 € ❄ 79/108 € 142/184 €
Rest – *(Montag – Freitag nur Abendessen)* Karte 24/34 €
♦ Ein freundlicher Service und gepflegte, zeitlos möblierte Gästezimmer mit Balkon oder Terrasse sprechen für das in einem kleinen Weiler gelegene Hotel. Rustikal gehaltenes Restaurant.

Alpenhof garni

Oberstraß 226 ✉ 6416 – ☎ (05264) 83 05 – alpenhof@familienpension.at – Fax (05264) 83056
12 Zim – 38/46 € 60/95 €
♦ Die zentrale und doch freie Lage sowie ein gemütliches, alpenländisches Ambiente machen das kleine Hotel unter familiärer Leitung aus.

OETZ – Tirol – 730 E7 – 2 210 Ew – Höhe 820 m – Wintersport: 2 200 m 2 9 6 C5

Wien 497 – Innsbruck 58 – Imst 19 – Telfs 27
Hauptstr. 66, ✉ 6433, ☎ (05252) 66 69, info@oetz.com
Ötztal★★ – Stuibenfall★★ (Süd-Ost: 12 km) – Ötztaler Heimat- und Freilichtmuseum★ (Süd: 17 km)

Waldhof

Habichen 5 (Süd-Ost: 1 km über B 186) ✉ 6433 – ☎ (05252) 62 49 – hotel@waldhof.at – Fax (05252) 61526
geschl. 14. April – 3. Mai, 20. Okt. – 19. Dez.
40 Zim (inkl. ½ P.) – ☼ 52/60 € 100/120 € ❄ 68/99 € 136/210 €
Rest – Karte 13/34 €
♦ Die Zimmer dieses in einem kleinen Ortsteil gelegenen Hotels sind im rustikalen Stil eingerichtet – auch einige Appartements/Ferienwohnungen stehen zur Verfügung. Restaurant mit ländlichem Charakter.

Il Giardino

Hauptstr. 86 ✉ 6433 – ☎ (05252) 2 11 80 – office@ilgiardino-oetz.com – Fax (05252) 211818
geschl. 7. – 17. Jan., 2. Nov. – 10. Dez.
Rest – *(geschl. Montag, nur Abendessen)* Karte 24/44 €
♦ Das seit vielen Jahren von der Inhaberin geführte Restaurant ist teils als Wintergarten angelegt, teils als leicht rustikale Stube mit blanken Tischen und sehr gutem Gedeck.

OHLSDORF – Oberösterreich – 730 N5 – 4 530 Ew – Höhe 505 m 2 H3

Wien 227 – Linz 63 – Wels 38 – Steyr 61

Waldesruh

Kohlwehr 1 (Nord: 5 km in Richtung Steyrermühl) ✉ 4694 Ohlsdorf – ☎ (07613) 31 43 – restaurant@waldesruh.at – Fax (7613) 31434
geschl. Montag – Dienstag
Rest – Menü 45 € – Karte 18/37 €
♦ Seit 130 Jahren befindet sich der schön im Auwald gelegene Landgasthof in Familienbesitz. Man bietet eine regional-internationale Küche aus frischen Produkten.

OLLERSDORF IM BURGENLAND - Burgenland - 730 U7 - 990 Ew - Höhe 360 m 11 L4

Wien 138 – Eisenstadt 116 – Fürstenfeld 23 – Graz 94

Vitalhotel Strobl Zim, Rest, P VISA MC AE D

Hauptstr. 64 ✉ 7533 – ✆ (03326) 5 26 15 – info@vitalhotel-strobl.at – Fax (03326) 5261522

21 Zim – 52 € 90 € – ½ P 15 €

Rest – Karte 15/28 €

◆ Der zeitgemäße Stil sowie angenehme warme Farben finden sich in dem ganzen Haus wieder. Die Zimmer sind solide und gut ausgestattet. Helles, rustikales Restaurant mit Pizzaofen und bürgerlichem Angebot.

OSSIACH - Kärnten - 730 N8 - 750 Ew - Höhe 510 m 9 H6

Wien 328 – Klagenfurt 50 – Villach 15

Stiftsschmiede P VISA MC AE D

Ossiach 4 ✉ 9570 – ✆ (04243) 4 55 54 – office@stiftsschmiede.at – Fax (04243) 45553

geschl. 7. Jan. – 15. März, Okt. – Juni Sonntag – Dienstag und Sonntag

Rest – *(nur Abendessen)* Karte 24/37 €

◆ Eine Schmiede a. d. 9. Jh. beherbergt dieses rustikal-elegante Restaurant. Spezialität des Hauses sind Süßwasserfische, die an der ehemaligen Feuerstelle zubereitet werden.

PAMHAGEN - Burgenland - 730 W5 - 1 770 Ew - Höhe 121 m 4 M3

Wien 87 – Eisenstadt 66 – Sopron 39 – Bratislava 65

Bahnstr. 2c, ✉ 7152, ✆ (02174) 20 93, tourismus.pamhagen@aon.at

Vila Vita Hotel Pannonia (geheizt) Spa Rest, P VISA MC AE D

Storchengasse 1 (Nord-Ost: 6 km) ✉ 7152 – ✆ (02175) 2 18 00 – info@vilavitapannonia.at – Fax (02175) 2180444

geschl. Mitte Nov. – Mitte Dez.

160 Zim – 100 € 176 € 85/91 € 140/152 € – ½ P 24 €

Rest – Karte 16/32 €

Rest *Vita Tella* – *(geschl. Montag – Dienstag, Mittwoch – Samstag nur Abendessen)* Menü 45/59 € – Karte 32/44 €

◆ Eine großzügige Hotelanlage auf einem Grundstück von 200 ha mit Bungalow-Dorf und eigenem Badesee sowie einem vielfältigen Sportangebot. Restaurant mit internationaler Küche und hübschem Sandsteinweinkeller. Saisonale Speisen im eleganten Vita Tella.

PARTENEN - Vorarlberg - 730 C8 - 1 660 Ew - Höhe 1 050 m - Wintersport: 2 300 m 4 25 5 B6

Wien 576 – Bregenz 83 – Sankt Anton am Arlberg 72 – Bludenz 32

Haus des Gastes, Dorfplatz 8, ✉ 6794, ✆ (05558) 8 31 50, info@gaschurn-partenen.com

Golfclub Hochmontafon Silvretta, ✆ (05558) 81 00

Silvretta-Hochalpenstraße★★ – Hohes Rad★★★ (Süd-Ost: 16 km)

Tiroler Hof garni

Dorfstr. 21e ✉ 6794 – ✆ (05558) 83 18 – tirolerhof@partenen.net – Fax (05558) 83188

17 Zim – ☼ 35 € 54 € ❄ 37/40 € 66/98 €

♦ Das kleine Hotel bietet sehr gepflegte, mit hellem Holzmobiliar wohnlich eingerichtete Gästezimmer, meist mit Balkon, sowie einen neuzeitlichen Saunabereich.

PERCHTOLDSDORF – Niederösterreich – 730 U4 – 14 000 Ew – Höhe 280 m

4 **L2**

Wien 16 – St. Pölten 56 – Wiener Neustadt 41 – Baden 17

Marktplatz 10, ✉ 2380, ✆ (01) 86 68 34 00, info@markt-perchtolds-dorf.at

GC Laab – Walde, Hoffeldstrasse ✆ (02239) 43 92

Pfarrkirche zum hl. Augustinus (Marientod★)

Wienerwald★ – Stift Heiligenkreuz★ (Süd-West: 18 km)

In Vino Veritas garni

Hochstr. 78a ✉ 2380 – ✆ (01) 8 65 27 81 – office@invinoveritas.at – Fax (01) 865278140

geschl. 24. Dez. – 6. Jan.

19 Zim – 75 € 112 €

♦ In einer Seitenstraße liegt das solide geführte kleine Hotel, in dem zeitgemäße, mit hellen Naturholzmöbeln im Landhausstil eingerichtete Zimmer bereitstehen.

PERG – Oberösterreich – 730 P4 – 7 130 Ew – Höhe 250 m

2 **I3**

Wien 160 – Linz 30 – Steyr 38 – Amstetten 38

Waldhör garni

Herrenstr. 28 ✉ 4320 – ✆ (07262) 54 34 50 – hotel@hotel-waldhoer.at – Fax (07262) 5434545

geschl. 5. – 8. Dez., 22. Dez. – 2. Jan.

24 Zim – 47/79 € 85/99 €

♦ Hinter der historischen Fassade des Stadthotels verbergen sich individuell gestaltete, freundliche Zimmer und ein heller, wintergartenartiger Frühstücksraum.

PERTISAU AM ACHENSEE – Tirol – siehe Eben am Achensee

PETTNEU AM ARLBERG – Tirol – 730 D7 – 1 460 Ew – Höhe 1 228 m – Wintersport: 2 040 m 4

5 **B6**

Wien 539 – Innsbruck 96 – Landeck 24 – Sankt Anton 7

Gridlon (geheizt) Rest,

Garnen 36 ✉ 6574 – ✆ (05448) 82 08 – hotel@gridlon.com – Fax (05448) 820868

geschl. 15. März – 22. Juni, 9. Sept. – 7. Dez.

50 Zim (inkl. ½ P) – ☼ 68/108 € 132/166 € ❄ 85/149 € 132/238 €

Rest – (nur Abendessen für Hausgäste)

♦ Das von der Inhaberfamilie engagiert geleitete Haus verfügt über zeitgemäße, etwas unterschiedlich eingerichtete Zimmer, auch Familienzimmer, sowie diverse Wellnessangebote. Ein Weinkeller mit Verkostungen ergänzt das in Stuben unterteilte Restaurant.

Gasthof Traube Rest, Rest,

Schnann 34 (Ost: 3 km, in Richtung Landeck) ✉ 6574 – ✆ (05447) 56 14 – info@gasthof-traube.at – Fax (05447) 561480
geschl. 1. Mai – 20. Juni, 1. Okt. – 15. Dez.
16 Zim (inkl. ½ P.) – ☼ 47/50 € 84/100 € ❄ 65/76 € 108/148 €
Rest – *(geschl. Juni – Sept. Montag)* Karte 13/26 €

◆ Der kleine familiengeführte Gasthof an der Ortsdurchfahrt verfügt über saubere, wohnlich und praktisch ausgestattete Zimmer sowie einen kleinen Badeteich. Gepflegte Gaststube mit gemütlicher Atmosphäre.

Pettneuerhof

Steinig 207 (West: 1,5 km, Arlbergbundesstraße Ausfahrt Vadiesen) ✉ 6574 – ✆ (05448) 83 91 – pettneuerhof@aon.at – Fax (05448) 83914
geschl. Okt. – Nov., Mai
30 Zim (inkl. ½ P.) – ☼ 78 € 120/150 € ❄ 94/97 € 162/194 €
Rest – Karte 20/38 €

◆ In einem kleinen Ortsteil liegt dieser nette Landgasthof, den man um einen Anbau mit neuzeitlichem Hallenbereich und mit in hellem Naturholz möblierten Zimmern erweitert hat. Rustikales Restaurant mit dunkler Holzdecke. Im UG gibt es eine Bar im Stil einer Skihütte.

Luxuriös oder eher schlicht?
Die Symbole und kennzeichnen den Komfort.

PETZENKIRCHEN – Niederösterreich – 730 R4 – 1 300 Ew – Höhe 260 m

3 **J3**

Wien 101 – St. Pölten 44 – Amstetten 25 – Krems 55

Landgasthof Bärenwirt mit Zim Zim, VISA AE

Ybbser Str. 3 ✉ 3252 – ✆ (07416) 5 21 53 – baerenwirt@aon.at – Fax (07416) 5215310
geschl. Sonn- und Feiertage abends
20 Zim – 42/47 € 64/72 € – ½ P 15 €
Rest – Menü 28 € – Karte 13/34 €

◆ Der Gasthof in der Ortsmitte beherbergt eine schlichte Gaststube sowie ein Restaurant mit bürgerlichem Charakter und freundlichem Service. Nette Terrasse. Zum Übernachten stehen neuzeitlich möblierte Gästezimmer bereit.

PFUNDS – Tirol – 730 D8 – 2 490 Ew – Höhe 970 m – Wintersport: 2 850 m 3 25

5 **B6**

Wien 543 – Innsbruck 99 – Landeck 30 – Sankt Anton 59
Stuben 40, ✉ 6542, ✆ (05474) 52 29, info@pfunds.at

Kreuz Rest,

Stubener Str. 43 (Stuben) ✉ 6542 – ✆ (05474) 52 18 – info@hotelkreuz.at – Fax (05474) 5750
geschl. Nov. – Mitte Dez., Mitte April – Mitte Mai
30 Zim (inkl. ½ P.) – ☼ 43/48 € 84/92 € ❄ 53/62 € 92/120 €
Rest – Karte 20/36 €

◆ In dem gepflegten Familienbetrieb erwarten Sie eine helle, leicht elegante Halle mit Bar sowie funktionelle, teilweise zum netten Garten hin gelegene Gästezimmer. Gemütlich-rustikaler Restaurantbereich.

Pension Schöne Aussicht  Zim,

Gatter 354, (Dorf) ✉ 6542 – ✆ (05474) 52 38 – office@schoene.aussicht-pfunds.at – Fax (05474) 5721

35 Zim – 22/25 € 44/50 € – ½ P 10 €

Rest – (nur Abendessen für Hausgäste, Ostern – Weihnachten Garni)

◆ Die Lage am Ortsrand sowie neuzeitlich-rustikal gestaltete Zimmer sprechen für dieses Hotel mit eigener Landwirtschaft. Außerdem: vier Ferienwohnungen im Nachbarhaus.

In Pfunds-Lafairs Nord: 3,5 km über B 180 Richtung Landeck:

Lafairser Hof Zim,

Lafairs 373 (B 180) ✉ 6542 – ✆ (05474) 57 57 – info@lafairserhof.at – Fax (05474) 575740

geschl. 15. Okt. – 15. Dez., 1. April – 10. Mai

40 Zim (inkl. ½ P.) – 75/86 € 132/154 € 81/95 € 144/172 € – 7 Suiten

Rest – Karte 15/41 €

◆ Ein regionstypisches Hotel mit gemütlicher Halle, freundlichen, wohnlich eingerichteten Zimmern und einer Saunaanlage im mediterranen Stil. Klassisch gestaltetes Restaurant.

PICHL AN DER ENNS – Steiermark – 730 M6 – 900 Ew – Höhe 840 m – Wintersport: 2 000 m 1 18 9 H5

Wien 296 – Graz 174 – Salzburg 83 – Liezen 57

Gemeindeamt, Pichl 100, ✉ 8973, ✆ (06454) 73 80, info@pichl.at

Pichlmayrgut (geheizt, Solebad) Rest,

Pichl 54 (B 320) ✉ 8973 – ✆ (06454) 73 05 – info@pichlmayrgut.at – Fax (06454) 730550

123 Zim (inkl. ½ P.) – 100/115 € 160/280 € 114/148 € 212/414 € – 3 Suiten

Rest – Karte 19/41 €

◆ Aus einem 1117 erstmals erwähnten Gut ist dieses Hotel entstanden. Ähnlich einem kleinen Dorf sind die Gebäude um einen Hof angelegt. Zimmer im Landhausstil. Rustikales Restaurant mit Wintergarten und Terrasse mit schöner Sicht. Weitere Terrasse im Innenhof.

PILL – Tirol – 730 H7 – 1 050 Ew – Höhe 550 m 7 D5

Wien 423 – Innsbruck 25 – Schwaz 4 – Kufstein 52

In Pill-Hochpillberg Süd-Ost: 10 km – Höhe 1 300 m

Bio-Aktiv-Hotel Grafenast Inntal und Karwendel, (geheizt) Rest,

Pillbergstr. 205 ✉ 6130 – ✆ (05242) 6 32 09 – sehnsucht@grafenast.at – Fax (05242) 6320999

geschl. Ende Okt. – 22. Dez., 26. März – 9. Mai.

25 Zim (inkl. ½ P.) – 94/120 € 184/240 € 96/160 € 192/320 €

Rest – Karte 20/35 €

◆ Die idyllische Lage, eine natürlich-wohnliche Einrichtung, Kunst und ein Seminarraum nach asiatischem Vorbild kennzeichnen die Philosophie des 100 Jahre alten Holzhauses. Original erhaltene alte Gaststube mit urigem Charakter und Küche aus Bio-Produkten.

PINKAFELD – Burgenland – 730 U6 – 5 190 Ew – Höhe 399 m 11 L4

Wien 112 – Eisenstadt 90 – Wiener Neustadt 63 – Fürstenfeld 52

Stadthotel
Rest,

Hauptplatz 18 ✉ 7423 – ✆ (03357) 4 33 35 – stadthotel-pinkafeld@aon.at – Fax (03357) 4333535

30 Zim – 57 € 84 €

Rest – *(geschl. 28. Juli – 10. Aug. und Sonntagabend, Feiertage)* Karte 16/26 €

◆ Mit hellen modernen Naturholzmöbeln und guter Technik hat man die Zimmer dieses direkt im Zentrum gelegenen Hotels wohnlich wie auch funktionell ausgestattet. In neuzeitlichem Stil eingerichtetes Restaurant.

PINSWANG – Tirol – 730 E6 – 450 Ew – Höhe 850 m 6 C5

Wien 496 – Innsbruck 99 – Reutte 13 – Füssen 5

Gutshof zum Schluxen

Unterpinswang 24 ✉ 6600 – ✆ (05677) 89 03 – info@schluxen.com – Fax (05677) 890323

geschl. 7. Jan. – 16. Feb.

33 Zim – 35/55 € 70/88 € – ½ P 15 €

Rest – Karte 14/39 €

◆ Am Ortsende finden Sie diesen gepflegten Landgasthof. Ländlich-gediegenes Ambiente in den sauberen Gästezimmern – mit Parkettfußboden und z. T. separatem WC. Mehrfach unterteiltes Restaurant mit freundlichem Service. Schöne Aussicht von der Terrasse.

PLANK AM KAMP – Niederösterreich – 730 T3 – 1 830 Ew – Höhe 254 m 3 K2

Wien 85 – Sankt Pölten 58 – Krems an der Donau 25 – Horn 18

Schwillinsky

Kremser Str. 8 ✉ 3564 – ✆ (02985) 3 04 00 – karl@schwillinsky.com

geschl. Mitte Jan. – Ostern und Sonntag – Montag

Rest – (Tischbestellung ratsam) Karte 17/35 €

◆ Dieses auf den ersten Blick ganz schlichte, ländliche Gasthaus beherbergt ein nettes, mediterran angehauchtes kleines Restaurant mit sehr freundlichem Service.

PODERSDORF AM SEE – Burgenland – 730 W5 – 2 000 Ew – Höhe 121 m 4 M3

Wien 66 – Eisenstadt 45 – Wiener Neustadt 73 – Bratislava 52

Hauptstr. 2, ✉ 7141, ✆ (02177) 22 27, info@podersdorfamsee.at

Gasthof Seewirt (mit Gästehaus Attila)

Strandplatz 1 ✉ 7141 Zim,

– ✆ (02177) 24 15 – seewirtkarner@netway.at – Fax (02177) 241530

geschl. Ende Nov. – Ende Jan.

70 Zim – 72/97 € 102/188 € 61/76 € 84/168 € – ½ P 13 €

Rest – *(geschl. Jan. – April sowie Sept. – Nov. Montag – Dienstag)* Karte 15/27 €

◆ Nahe dem Schiffsanleger liegen der Gasthof von 1924 und das ca. 100 m entfernte Gästehaus. Einige der Zimmer sind mit Stilmobiliar eingerichtet, andere ganz modern. Das Restaurant ist teils neuzeitlich, teils ländlich gestaltet.

Pannonia (mit Gästehaus) (geheizt) Zim, P

Seezeile 20 ✉ 7141 – ✆ (02177) 22 45 – pannonia.florian@nextra.at – Fax (02177) 22454

geschl. Jan. – März

43 Zim – 47/72 € 71/122 € – ½ P 13 €

Rest – Karte 15/35 €

◆ Das Hotel in Nähe der Strandpromenade empfängt sie mit einem modernen Eingangsbereich inklusive kleiner Vinothek. Die Zimmer sind unterschiedlich eingerichtet. Regionale und bürgerliche Küche.

Die Herberge garni P

Seeweingärten III/1 ✉ 7141 – ✆ (02177) 23 46 – herberge@netway.at – Fax (02177) 23464

geschl. 12. Nov. – 15. März

24 Zim – 30/34 € 50/62 €

◆ Der am Ortsende gelegene Familienbetrieb mit privater Atmosphäre verfügt über zeitgemäß eingerichtete Gästezimmer und Appartements sowie einen gepflegten Garten.

Zur Dankbarkeit

Hauptstr. 39 ✉ 7141 – ✆ (02177) 22 23 – dankbarkeit@magnet.at – Fax (02177) 22234

geschl. 24. Dez. – 3. Jan. und Mittwoch – Donnerstag, Dez. – März Montag – Donnerstag

Rest – Karte 17/34 €

◆ Ländlicher Charakter und schmackhafte regionale Küche zeichnen das familiengeführte Gasthaus aus. An das Haus angeschlossen ist ein 100 m entfernter netter Heuriger.

PÖLLAUBERG – Steiermark – 730 T7 – 2 230 Ew – Höhe 757 m 11 K4

Wien 142 – Graz 71 – Bruck a.d. Mur 81 – Fürstenfeld 53

Maria Pöllauberg★

Pöllau★ (Süd-West: 6 km)

Retter P VISA AE

Pöllauberg 88 (Süd-Ost: 3 km) ✉ 8225 – ✆ (03335) 26 90 – hotel@retter.at – Fax (03335) 269051

geschl. Weihnachten

50 Zim – 95 € 156 € – ½ P 16 € – 10 Suiten

Rest *Muskat* – *(geschl. Sonn- und Feiertage abends)* Karte 17/42 €

◆ Ein professionell geführtes Seminarhotel in schöner Lage mit neuzeitlichen Zimmer und Suiten in hellem Holz – mit Balkon/Terrasse. Netter Garten mit Naturschwimmteich. Muskat: puristisch-modern gehaltenes Restaurant.

Berggasthof König Rest, P VISA

Pöllauberg 5 ✉ 8225 – ✆ (03335) 23 11 – office@berggasthof-koenig.at – Fax (03335) 23115

geschl. 4. – 24. Feb.

7 Zim – 51 € 82 €

Rest – *(geschl. Montag, Nov. – März Montag – Dienstag)* Karte 17/31 €

◆ Der a. d. J. 1628 stammende Weingasthof am Dorfplatz beherbergt mit hellen Naturholzmöbeln und Holzfußboden freundlich im ländlichen Stil eingerichtete Zimmer. Gemütliche Gaststube mit Kachelofen und alter Holzbalkendecke.

PÖRTSCHACH AM WÖRTHERSEE – Kärnten – 730 09 – 2 670 Ew – Höhe 446 m

9 **I6**

Wien 309 – Klagenfurt 15 – Villach 26 – St. Veit an der Glan 31

Hauptstr. 153, 9210, (04272) 23 54, info@poertschach.at

Veranstaltungen

18.05. – 24.05.: ATP Tennisturnier

Wörther See★

Velden★★ Nord-West: 10 km – Winterkirche in Maria Wörth (romanische Wandmalereien★) Süd: 22 km – Maria Gail (Flügelaltar★★) Süd-West: 24 km

Werzer's Hotel Resort

Rest, VISA AE

Werzerpromenade 8 9210 – (04272) 2 23 10 – resort@werzers.at – Fax (04272) 2251113

geschl. Nov. – März

119 Zim – 94/185 € 138/280 € – ½ P 19 €

8 Suiten

Rest *Werzer's à la Carte* – Karte 28/47 €

◆ Vor allem die schöne Lage spricht für dieses neuzeitliche Ferienhotel. Es erwarten Sie geräumige, wohnliche Zimmer – in den oberen Etagen mit Blick auf den See. Modern gestaltet: Werzer's à la Carte.

Parkhotel

Wörthersee, Rest, VISA AE

Elisabethstr. 22

9210 – (04272) 2 62 10 – office@parkhotel-poertschach.at – Fax (04272) 2621731

geschl. 20. Okt. – 20. April

200 Zim (inkl. ½ P.) – 113/169 € 182/272 €

14 Suiten

Rest *Palmenrestaurant* – *(geschl. Mitte Sep. – Mitte Mai und Montag, nur Abendessen)* Menü 32/49 € – Karte 32/50 €

◆ Die reizvolle Lage in einem 18 000 qm großen Park direkt am See, ein großzügiger Rahmen und individuell eingerichtete Gästezimmer machen dieses Hotel aus. Gediegenes Restaurant mit freundlichem, geschultem Service.

Seehotel Porcia garni

Wörthersee, VISA AE

Hauptstr. 231, (B 83) 9210 – (04272) 20 87 – office@seehotel-porcia.at – Fax (04272) 208787

13 Zim – 170/531 € 170/531 €

6 Suiten

◆ Nur durch Klingeln gelangen Sie in das klassisch-stilvolle kleine Hotel. Die Zimmer sind individuell, mit vielen Antiquitäten eingerichtet, darunter auch ein Versace-Zimmer.

Seehotel Dr. Jilly

Rest, VISA

Alfredweg 5 9210 – (04272) 22 58 – seehotel@jilly.at – Fax (04272) 22587

geschl. Nov. – März

35 Zim (inkl. ½ P.) – 75/150 € 150/260 €

Rest – Karte 14/41 €

◆ Nur wenige Schritte vom See entfernt liegt dieses Hotel. Ein Großteil der Zimmer ist recht modern und wohnlich in hellen Farben gestaltet. Die ruhige Lage verspricht Erholung.

Schloss Leonstain Rest,

Leonstainerstr. 1, (B 83) 9210 – (04272) 28 16 – info@leonstain.at – Fax (04272) 2823

geschl. Okt. – April

32 Zim – 85/165 € 170/232 € – ½ P 25 €

6 Suiten

Rest *Leon* – separat erwähnt

♦ A. d. J. 1492 stammt das ehemalige Gehöft mit kleinem Park – ein sehr schön und individuell eingerichtetes Hotel im Stil eines Schlosses, in dem schon Johannes Brahms wohnte.

Striedinger's Lust & Laune Hotel Zim,

Seeuferstr. 33 9210 – (04272) 23 34 – lust@laune.at – Fax (04272) 233440

geschl. 15. Okt. – 15. April

20 Zim (inkl. ½ P.) – 77/120 € 154/254 €

Rest – (nur Abendessen für Hausgäste)

♦ Das hübsch anzusehende Landhaus mit Holzfensterläden, Balkonen und Turm ist ein familienfreundliches Hotel mit individuellen Zimmern – nett ist die farbenfrohe Gestaltung.

Villa Riva Zum Goldenen Löwen (mit Gästehaus) Rest,

Hauptstr. 293, (B 83) 9210 – (04272) 3 21 00 – villariva@aon.at – Fax (04272) 321071

13 Zim (inkl. ½ P.) – 80/155 € 160/310 €

Rest – (nur Mittagessen für Hausgäste)

♦ Schön ist die Lage der beiden im Villenstil erbauten Häuser direkt am Wasser. Es erwarten Sie ein eleganter Rahmen und gediegen-gemütliche Zimmer mit Seeblick.

Leon – Hotel Schloss Leonstain

Leonstainerstr. 1, (B 83) 9210 – (04272) 28 16 – info@leonstain.at – Fax (04272) 2823

geschl. Okt. – April

Rest – *(nur Abendessen)* Menü 49/64 € – Karte 40/54 €

♦ Gelungen hat man in diesem Restaurant altes Gemäuer mit modern-eleganter Einrichtung kombiniert. Besonders angenehm ist die Atmosphäre im begrünten Innenhof.

In Pörtschach-Pritschitz **Ost: 4 km über B 83 in Richtung Klagenfurt:**

Villa Rainer Rest,

Werftenstr. 57 9210 – (04272) 23 00 – hotel@rainer.at – Fax (04272) 230017

geschl. Mitte Okt. – Mitte April

41 Zim (inkl. ½ P.) – 86/155 € 210/372 €

5 Suiten

Rest – (nur für Hausgäste)

♦ Malerisch ist die Lage der eleganten Villa auf einem ca. 13 000 qm großen Gartengrundstück direkt am See. Sehenswert: eine Waffensammlung sowie Bilder und Antiquitäten.

In Pörtschach-Sallach **Ost: 3 km über B 83 in Richtung Klagenfurt:**

Das Landhaus Zim, Rest,
Kogelweg 4 ✉ 9210 – ☎ (04272) 2 59 10
– info@landhaus.at – Fax (04272) 25918
10 Zim – ☼ 70/95 € 90/140 € ❄ 65/80 € 80/110 €
– ½ P 19 €
Rest – (nur Abendessen für Hausgäste)
◆ Das familiengeführte, schöne kleine Landhaus liegt verkehrsgünstig unweit der Autobahn. Ein tadellos gepflegtes Hotel mit behaglichen, zeitgemäßen Gästezimmern.

In Pörtschach-Töschling **West: 1,5 km über B 83 Richtung Villach:**

Schloss Seefels (geheizt) Rest, Rest,
Töschling 1
✉ 9210 – ☎ (04272) 2 37 70 – office@seefels.at – Fax (04272) 3704
geschl. Anfang Nov. – 7. Dez.
71 Zim (inkl. ½ P.) – ☼ 170/350 € 360/480 € ❄ 140/265 €
266/400 € – 30 Suiten
Rest *La Terrasse* – separat erwähnt
Rest *Portobello* – ☎ (04272) 2 37 76 45 *(geschl. Mitte Okt. – Mitte Mai, nur Mittagessen außer Juli – Aug.)* Karte 31/54 €
◆ Das ehemalige Privatschloss ist ein elegantes Hotel in schöner Lage am See mit großzügigen, in angenehmen mediterranen Farben gehaltenen Zimmern und Suiten. Das Portobello ist ein Seerestaurant mit Terrasse direkt am Wasser.

Werzer's Seehotel Wallerwirt Wörthersee,
Töschling 96 ✉ 9212
– ☎ (04272) 2 31 60 – wallerwirt@werzers.at – Fax (04272) 231676
geschl. Okt. – 1. Mai
50 Zim – 85/142 € 128/214 € – ½ P 17 €
Rest – (nur für Hausgäste)
◆ Die schöne Lage am See sowie funktionell gestaltete, teils recht geräumige Zimmer – überwiegend mit Seeblick – machen dieses Hotel aus. Bahnhaltestelle vor dem Haus.

Ferienhotel Wörthersee Rest,
Töschling 82 ✉ 9210
– ☎ (04272) 25 09 – info@ferienhotel-woerthersee.at – Fax (04272) 2504
71 Zim (inkl. ½ P.) – 84/120 € 138/210 €
Rest – (nur Abendessen für Hausgäste)
◆ Leicht erhöht über dem See liegt dieses in neuzeitlichem Stil gebaute Hotel mit seinen modern und funktionell eingerichteten Zimmern und Appartements.

La Terrasse – Hotel Schloss Seefels Wörthersee,
Töschling 1 ✉ 9210
– ☎ (04272) 2 37 76 13 – office@seefels.at – Fax (04272) 3704
geschl. Anfang Nov. – 7. Dez.
Rest – *(nur Abendessen)* Menü 71/91 € – Karte 49/69 €
◆ Warmes Rot, Kronleuchter und Ölgemälde sowie aufwändig eingedeckte Tische unterstreichen das klassisch-elegante Ambiente dieses Restaurants.

PÖTTSCHING – Burgenland – 730 V5 – 2 680 Ew – Höhe 218 m 4 L3

Wien 54 – Eisenstadt 19 – Baden 43 – Wiener Neustadt 12

XX **Der Reisinger**

Hauptstr. 83 ✉ 7033 – ☎ (02631) 22 12 – info@der-reisinger.at – Fax (02631) 2090

geschl. Juli – Aug. und Sonntagabend – Mittwoch

Rest – Menü 20/33 € – Karte 24/34 €

♦ Der sehr gepflegte und gut geführte Familienbetrieb mit freundlichem Service teilt sich in eine bürgerliche Stube und zwei leicht klassisch wirkende Restauranträume.

PRUTZ – Tirol – 730 D7 – 1 670 Ew – Höhe 866 m – Wintersport: 1 5

6 C6

Wien 525 – Innsbruck 82 – Sankt Anton 41 – Imst 27

Prutz 93 (B 180), ✉ 6522, ☎ (05472) 62 67, tiroler.oberland-prutz@netway.at

Ausflug zur Karlesspitze mit Wiesejaggl-Sessellift★★★ – Pillerpass-Straße nach Wenns★ (Nord: 10 km) – Kaunertal★★★ (Ost: 12 km)

Gasthof Post Zim,

Prutz 17 (B 180) ✉ 6522 – ☎ (05472) 62 17 – hotel@postprutz.at – Fax (05472) 62176

geschl. 7. April – 1. Mai, 19. Okt. – 22. Dez.

37 Zim (inkl. ½ P.) – ☼ †47/50 € ††74/80 € ❄ †56/70 € ††92/120 €

Rest – Karte 18/29 €

♦ Am Ortseingang liegt der familiengeführte Gasthof mit Hotelanbau. Hier stehen neuzeitlich wie auch funktionell eingerichtete Zimmer zur Verfügung. Rustikales Restaurant mit hoher Holzbalkendecke.

PUCH BEI HALLEIN – Salzburg – 730 L5 – 4 090 Ew – Höhe 446 m

Wien 304 – Salzburg 12 – Hallein 5 – Bad Reichenhall 31 8 G4

Gemeindeamt, Hallener Landesstr. 26, ✉ 5412, ☎ (06245) 8 41 66, tourist.puch@salzburg.at

Außerhalb Nord-Ost: 4 km Richtung Salzburg, dann rechts – Höhe 800 m

Kurhotel Vollererhof (mit Gästehaus) Salzachtal, (geheizt) Zim, Rest,

Vollererhofstr. 158 ✉ 5412 Puch bei Hallein – ☎ (06245) 89 91 – kurhotel@vollererhof.at – Fax (06245) 899166

geschl. 7. – 21. Jan.

39 Zim (inkl. ½ P.) – †113/156 € ††226/282 € – 4 Suiten

Rest – Karte 23/46 €

♦ Im gemütlichen Salzburger Stil eingerichtete Zimmer, meist mit Talblick, und ein reichhaltiges Wellnessangebot stehen den Gästen des Alpenhotels in 800 m Höhe zur Verfügung.

Im Puch-Sankt Jakob am Thurn Nord: 3 km über Elsbethen:

X **Gasthaus Schützenwirt**

Dorf 96 ✉ 5412 – ☎ (0662) 63 20 20 20 – Fax (0662) 63202024

Rest – *(Montag – Freitag nur Abendessen)* Karte 19/35 €

♦ In diesem Haus bereitet man die Speisen nur aus Bioprodukten zu, serviert werden sie in der modernen Gaststube oder auf der hübschen Terrasse hinter dem Haus.

PUCHBERG AM SCHNEEBERG – Niederösterreich – 730 T5 – 2 840 Ew – Höhe 577 m – Wintersport: 2 075 m 3 – Heilklimatischer Kurort
3 **K3**

Wien 76 – St. Pölten 97 – Wiener Neustadt 29 – Neunkirchen 18

Sticklergasse 3, ✉ 2734, ☎ (02636) 22 56, tourismusbuero@puchberg.at

Schneeberg★

Schneeberghof

Zim, Rest,

Wiener Neustädter Str. 24 ✉ 2734
– ☎ (02636) 35 00 – info@schneeberghof.at
– Fax (02636) 3233

74 Zim – 78/86 € 130/146 € – ½ P 10 €

Rest – Karte 19/28 €

◆ Aus einem Gasthaus ist dieses komfortable Seminarhotel an der Ortsdurchfahrt entstanden, das über funktionell ausgestattete Zimmer mit gutem Platzangebot verfügt.

In Puchberg-Losenheim West: 6 km:

Forellenhof

Losenheimer Str. 132 ✉ 2734 – ☎ (02636) 36 11
– info@forellenhof-puchberg.at – Fax (02636) 361142
geschl. Nov.

20 Zim (inkl. ½ P.) – 44 € 88 €

Rest – *(geschl. Montag)* Karte 16/33 €

◆ Der gewachsene familiengeführte Gasthof liegt schön in einem kleinen Dorf, mit Blick auf den Schneeberg. Zum Haus gehören eine Kinderskischule und ein eigener Skilift. Ländliche, z. T. auch ganz mit Holz ausgekleidete Gaststuben.

PUCHENSTUBEN – Niederösterreich – 730 R5 – 310 Ew – Höhe 871 m – Wintersport: 1 195 m 5
3 **J3**

Wien 109 – St. Pölten 52 – Amstetten 56 – Mariazell 32

In Gösing Süd: 10 km Richtung Mariazell, nach 7 km rechts ab:

Alpenhotel Gösing

Rest, Rest,

Gösing 4 ✉ 3221
– ☎ (02728) 2 17 – alpenhotel@goesing.at
– Fax (02728) 217116

73 Zim – 80/83 € 132/166 € – ½ P 20/28 €

Rest – Karte 16/36 €

◆ In einem großen Naturpark am Fuße des Ötschers liegt dieses Ferienhotel mit schönem, komfortablem Hallenbereich und ganz unterschiedlich gestalteten Zimmern. Gemütlich-ländliche Gaststuben. Wildspezialitäten.

Wir bemühen uns bei unseren Preisangaben um größtmögliche Genauigkeit. Aber alles ändert sich! Lassen Sie sich daher bei Ihrer Reservierung den derzeit gültigen Preis mitteilen.

PURBACH AM NEUSIEDLERSEE - Burgenland - 730 W5 - 2 570 Ew - Höhe 124 m 4 M3

Wien 63 - Eisenstadt 18 - Wiener Neustadt 47 - Sopron 40

Kloster Am Spitz mit Zim

Waldsiedlung 2 ✉ 7083 - ✆ (02683) 55 19 - weingasthof@klosteramspitz.at - Fax (02683) 551920
geschl. 7. Jan. - 6. März
18 Zim - 68/73 € 116/136 €
Rest - *(geschl. Montag - Mittwochmittag außer Feiertage)* Menü 50/55 € - Karte 22/48 €

♦ Inmitten der Weinberge liegt das ehemals zum Kloster gehörende Gebäude. Das Restaurant hat eine schöne Terasse mit Aussicht auf den See. Regionale Küche und eigene Weine. Moderne Gästezimmer.

Gut Purbach mit Zim

Hauptgasse 64 ✉ 7083 - ✆ (02683) 5 60 86 - gutpurbach@aon.at
geschl. Jan. und Dienstag - Mittwoch
4 Zim - 106 € 106 €
Rest - Menü 27/54 € - Karte 24/36 €

♦ Der aufwändig restaurierte ehemalige Vierkanthof a. d. 16. Jh. beherbergt seit 1860 ein Gasthaus. Heute bietet man hier in modernem Ambiente schmackhafte regionale Küche. Die als Appartements angelegten Gästezimmer wurden von einem Künstler gestaltet.

RAABA - Steiermark - 730 S7 - 1 930 Ew - Höhe 350 m 11 K5

Wien 194 - Graz 7 - Maribor 67

Am Mühlengrund garni

Am Mühlengrund 8 ✉ 8074 - ✆ (0316) 40 31 01 - office@hotel-auer.at - Fax (0316) 4031014
geschl. 22. Dez. - 7. Jan.
23 Zim - 75/130 € 110/190 €

♦ Modernes Hotel an einem kleinen Teich, das mit seinem funktionellen, recht puristischen Stil besonders auf Geschäftsleute ausgelegt ist. Auf Anfrage kocht man für Gruppen.

RAABS AN DER THAYA - Niederösterreich - 730 S2 - 3 120 Ew - Höhe 420 m 3 J1

Wien 112 - St. Pölten 92 - Gemünd 46 - Zwettl 49
18 Thayatal Drosendorf, Autendorf 18 ✆ (02915) 62 62 5
Stift Geras★ (Süd-Ost: 23 km)

In Raabs-Liebnitz **West: 5 km Richtung Groß-Siegharts, nach 3 km rechts ab:**

Liebnitzmühle

Liebnitz 38 ✉ 3820 - ✆ (02846) 75 01 - liebnitzmuehle@friedreich.com - Fax (02846) 750159
44 Zim - 69 € 108/116 € - ½ P 11 €
Rest - Karte 13/29 €

♦ Sehr schön liegt die ehemalige Mühle an der Thaya. Zum Freizeitbereich gehören ein lichtes, ganz verglastes Hallenbad und eine original finnische Blockhaussauna. Rustikal-gemütliche Gaststube, klassisch-gediegener Speisesaal und Reiterstüberl mit Gewölbedecke.

RADENTHEIN – Kärnten – 730 N8 – 6 620 Ew – Höhe 746 m 9 H6

Wien 319 – Klagenfurt 61 – Spittal a.d. Drau 23 – Villach 28

Metzgerwirt mit Zim Rest, VISA AE
Hautpstr. 22 ✉ 9545 – ✆ (04246) 20 52
– stadler.emanuel@metzgerwirt.co.at – Fax (04246) 3976
17 Zim – 38/45 € 70/80 € – ½ P 15 €
Rest – Menü 30 € – Karte 16/37 €
◆ Das von Familie Stadler gut geführte Haus ist aus einem ehemaligen Metzgereigasthof entstanden. Freundlich serviert man in verschiedenen Restauranträumen regionale Küche. Recht schlichte, gepflegte Gästezimmer.

In Radentheim-Döbriach Süd-West: 5 km über B 98 in Richtung Millstatt:

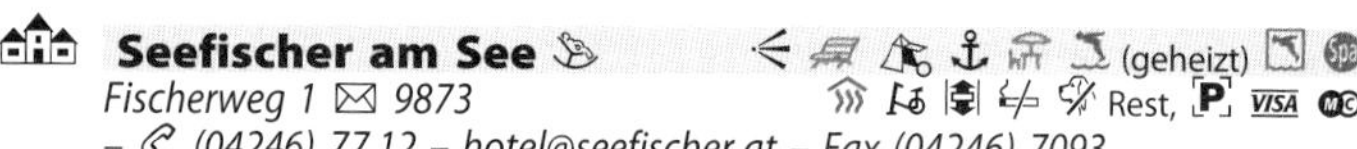

Seefischer am See (geheizt) Rest, VISA
Fischerweg 1 ✉ 9873
– ✆ (04246) 77 12 – hotel@seefischer.at – Fax (04246) 7093
geschl. 2. Nov. – 20. Dez., 25. März – 10. Mai
40 Zim (inkl. ½ P.) – 83/108 € 158/236 € 83/93 € 158/212 € – 4 Suiten
Rest – Menü 29 € – Karte 23/38 €
◆ Herrlich liegt das Ferienhotel am Millstätter See. Neben wohnlichen Zimmern, teils mit Seesicht, erwarten Sie hier Wellnessangebote auf 2000 qm und eine Liegewiese am Seeufer. Restaurant im Landhausstil mit Blick auf den Yachthafen.

Dieser Führer lebt von Ihren Anregungen, die uns stets willkommen sind. Egal ob Sie uns eine besonders angenehme Überraschung oder eine Enttäuschung mitteilen wollen – schreiben Sie uns!

RADKERSBURG, BAD – Steiermark – 730 T8 – 1 600 Ew – Höhe 209 m – Wintersport: – Heilbad 11 L5

Wien 209 – Graz 79 – Maribor 41 – Leibnitz 43
Hauptplatz 14, ✉ 8490, ✆ (03476) 25 45, info@brbg.at
Stadtbild ★

Hotel im Park (Thermal) VISA AE
Kurhausstr. 5 ✉ 8490
– ✆ (03476) 2 57 10 – res@kip.or.at – Fax (03476) 208545
96 Zim (inkl. ½ P.) – 97/115 € 194/240 € – 7 Suiten
Rest – (nur für Hausgäste)
◆ Die Lage am Kurpark, ein hübsch gestalteter Wellnessbereich sowie ein schöner Garten mit Pool und Bar sprechen für dieses elegant wirkende Haus.

Triest (Thermal) Rest, Rest, VISA
Alfred-Merlini-Allee 5 ✉ 8490
– ✆ (03476) 4 10 40 – info@hoteltriest.at – Fax (03476) 410407070
63 Zim (inkl. ½ P.) – 103 € 176 €
Rest – (nur für Hausgäste) Karte 12/17 €
◆ Ein warmer Holzton und Stoffe in angenehmen Farben schaffen in den im italienischen Stil möblierten Zimmern ein behagliches Ambiente. Lage am Kurpark, in Thermalbadnähe.

Thermalhotel Fontana (Thermal) (Thermal) Rest, Rest,
Alfred Merlini Allee 6 8490 – (03476) 4 15 50 – info@hotelfontana.at – Fax (03476) 4155050
140 Zim (inkl. ½ P.) – 88 € 156 €
Rest – (nur für Hausgäste) Karte 12/21 €
♦ Das moderne Bade- und Kurhotel ist in den Bad Radkersburger Kurpark eingebettet. Zweckmäßig sind die komplett ausgestatteten Zimmer gestaltet.

Landhaus Vier Jahreszeiten Rest,
Thermenstr. 11 8490 – (03476) 36 66 – info@4-jahreszeiten.at – Fax (03476) 36664
21 Zim – 80 € 130 € – ½ P 16 €
Rest – (nur für Hausgäste)
♦ Vom Empfangsbereich bis in die Zimmer hat man dieses Landhaus mit freundlichen Farben im Landhausstil eingerichtet. Schöne Feng-Shui-Gartenanlage mit Naturschwimmteich.

Markowitsch Buschenschank
Alt-Weindörfl 144 (Nord: 1 km Richtung Klöch, Mitte Ungarbrücke links) 8490 – (03476) 28 39 – buschenschank.markowitsch@utanet.at – Fax (03476) 2839
geschl. Juli und Mittwoch
Rest – Karte ca. 12 €
♦ In dem mit viel Holz gemütlich-rustikal gestalteten Bauernhaus bewirtet man Sie mit Wein und hausgemachten Spezialitäten. Schöner Arkadenhof.

RADSTADT – Salzburg – 730 M6 – 4 710 Ew – Höhe 856 m – Wintersport: 1 677 m 9 9 G5

Wien 309 – Salzburg 70 – Bischofshofen 30
Stadtplatz 17, 5550, (06452) 74 72, info@radstadt.com
Radstadt Tauerngolf, Römerstr. 18 (06452) 51 11

Veranstaltungen

18.05.: Amadé – Radmarathon
01.08. – 03.08.: Gardefest
06.09. – 08.09.: Kunsthandwerksmarkt

Lage★
Radstädter Tauernstraße★

Gut Weissenhof Rest,
Weissenhof 6 5550 – (06452) 70 01 – info@weissenhof.at – Fax (06452) 7006
geschl. nach Ostern – Mitte Mai, Ende Okt. – Mitte Dez.
77 Zim (inkl. ½ P.) – 107/118 € 206/226 € 109/139 € 208/268 € – 6 Suiten
Rest – (nur für Hausgäste)
♦ Die Lage direkt am Golfplatz sowie wohnlich-komfortable Zimmer in ländlichem Stil machen das großzügig angelegte Gut aus. Reitpferde und -halle. Recht aufwändige Halbpension.

Zum Jungen Römer – Zim, Rest,

Römerstr. 18 ✉ 5550
– ✆ (06452) 67 12 – hotel@roemer.at
– Fax (06452) 671250
geschl. Ende Okt. – Anfang Dez., Ende März - Anfang Mai
36 Zim (inkl. ½ P.) – ☼ 89/98 € 132/176 € ❄ 95/136 € 148/194 € – 4 Suiten
Rest – Karte 20/37 €
◆ Ideal ist die Lage dieses Alpenhotels unmittelbar am Golfplatz und nahe der Bergbahn. Wohnliche, teils neuzeitlich-hell, teils dunkler möblierte Gästezimmer. Zeitlos-gediegenes Restaurant mit Terrasse zum Golfplatz.

Taxerhof – Zim,

Taxerweg 5 ✉ 5550 – ✆ (06452) 75 42 – info@taxerhof.at
– Fax (06452) 754244
geschl. 20. April – 16. Mai
27 Zim – ☼ 47/55 € 74/96 € ❄ 42/49 € 64/84 € – ½ P 12 €
Rest – (nur Abendessen für Hausgäste, im Winter Garni)
◆ Das familiengeführte Hotel in Golfplatznähe bietet neuzeitlich eingerichtete Zimmer und viele Appartements mit Küche sowie einen netten Saunabereich.

RAMSAU AM DACHSTEIN – Steiermark – 730 M6 – 2 710 Ew – Höhe 1 100 m – Wintersport: 2 700 m 1 17 – Luftkurort 9 H4

Wien 296 – Graz 174 – Salzburg 89 – Liezen 57
Ramsau 40, ✉ 8972, ✆ (03687) 8 18 33, info@ramsau.com
Langlaufgebiet★★★ – Hunerkogel ★★★ (mit) Nord: 10 km
Verkehrsleitsystem in Farben (siehe Hinweis hinter der Hausnummer)

Lindenhof – Rest,

Ort 301, (gelb 632) ✉ 8972 – ✆ (03687) 8 15 55 – info@hotel-lindenhof.at
– Fax (03687) 815557
geschl. 5. Nov. – 6. Dez., 30. März – 30. April
15 Zim (inkl. ½ P.) – ☼ 45/65 € 106/121 € ❄ 52/84 € 132/159 € – 4 Suiten
Rest – (nur Abendessen für Hausgäste)
◆ Der schön an einem lichten Lärchenwald gelegene Familienbetrieb im regionstypischen Stil verfügt über wohnlich-alpenländische Gästezimmer.

Berghof ≤ Dachstein Massiv, Planai und Hauser Kaibling, – Rest,

Ramsau 192,
(rot 507) ✉ 8972 – ✆ (03687) 81 84 80 – office@hotel-berghof.at
– Fax (03687) 818485
geschl. 6. April – 31. Mai 5. Okt. – 8. Nov.
36 Zim (inkl. ½ P.) – ☼ 66/85 € 132/150 € ❄ 70/86 € 140/178 €
Rest – Karte 18/32 €
◆ Ein eigener Biobauernhof und ein Naturbadeteich gehören zu diesem familiär geleiteten Hotel. Die Zimmer sind alle gut gepflegt und zeitgemäß ausgestattet. Rustikal eingerichtetes Restaurant mit Wintergarten.

Landhaus Ramsau (geheizt) Zim, Rest,

Schildlehen 36 (blau 709) 8972
– (03687) 8 12 91 – landhaus.ramsau@aon.at – Fax (03687) 8124935
geschl. Nov., April – Mai
25 Zim (inkl. ½ P.) – 55/60 € 110/130 € 68/85 € 140/170 € – 5 Suiten
Rest – (nur Abendessen für Hausgäste)
◆ Dieses Hotel in regionaler Bauweise verfügt über mit hellem Holzmobiliar solide eingerichtete Gästezimmer sowie mit einem Computer ausgestattete Suiten.

Neuwirt Zim, Rest,

Obere Leiten 113, (violett 281) 8972 – (03687) 8 19 46
– info@neuwirt-ramsau.at – Fax (03687) 819467
geschl. 7. April – 20. Mai, 27. Okt. - 4. Dez.
21 Zim – 48/64 € 86/123 € 58/81 € 104/150 €
Rest – *(geschl. Dienstag, außer Saison)* Karte 15/35 €
◆ Der einstige Gasthof ist ein gewachsener Familienbetrieb mit rustikalen Zimmern im Haupthaus und großzügigen, modern-eleganten Zimmern im Anbau. Schöner Saunabereich. Mit viel Holz behaglich gestaltetes Restaurant.

RAMSAU IM ZILLERTAL – Tirol – 730 H7 – 1 420 Ew – Höhe 600 m 7 E5

Wien 436 – Innsbruck 63 – Schwaz 35 – Kitzbühel 86
Hippach und Umgebung, Ramsau 20a, 6283, (05282) 36 30, info@hippach.at

Theresia Zim,

Ramsau 78a (Süd: Richtung Mayrhofen, dann links ab) 6284
– (05282) 37 02 – info@theresia.at – Fax (05282) 4435
geschl. 7. April – 17. Mai, 20. Okt. – 28. Nov.
25 Zim (inkl. ½ P.) – 54/66 € 92/116 € 63/91 € 110/150 €
Rest – *(geschl. Dienstag)* Karte 17/38 €
◆ In einem kleinen Wohngebiet liegt der modernisierte Gasthof, dessen Zimmer einheitlich mit hellem Holzmobiliar und guter Technik neuzeitlich und funktionell ausgestattet sind. Ländlich eingerichtetes Restaurant mit gemütlicher Atmosphäre.

Eder (mit Gästehaus) Rest,

Ramsau 73a (Süd: Richtung Mayrhofen, dann links ab) 6283
– (05282) 32 86 – info@hotel-eder.com – Fax (05282) 32864
geschl. 14. Okt. – 8. Dez.
28 Zim (inkl. ½ P.) – 44/56 € 88/108 € 55/75 € 112/148 €
Rest – Karte 14/33 €
◆ Das familiengeführte Hotel am Ortsrand verfügt über meist hell eingerichtete, zeitgemäß und funktionell ausgestattete Gästezimmer. Das Restaurant teilt sich in die rustikale Zirbenstube und einen neuzeitlichen, zur Halle hin offenen Raum.

RANKWEIL – Vorarlberg – 730 A7 – 11 180 Ew – Höhe 465 m 5 A5

Wien 669 – Bregenz 33 – Dornbirn 23 – Feldkirch 9
Gemeindeamt, Am Marktplatz, 6830, (05522) 40 50, buerger-service@rankweil.at

Hoher Freschen Zim,

Kreuzlingerstr. 2 ✉ 6830 – ✆ (05522) 4 42 37 – hotel@freschen.at – Fax (05522) 44555

33 Zim – 60/88 € 91/130 € – ½ P 15 €

Rest – *(geschl. Sonn- und Feiterage, nur Abendessen)* Karte 19/36 €

♦ In Bahnhofsnähe liegt der um einem neueren Anbau erweiterte Gasthof. Die Zimmer sind überwiegend modern möbliert und mit Parkettfußboden ausgestattet. In bürgerlichem Stil gehaltenes Restaurant und nette Stube mit Holztäfelung.

Gasthof Mohren

Stiegstr. 17 ✉ 6830 – ✆ (05522) 4 42 75 – office@mohren.at – Fax (05522) 442755

22 Zim – 49/58 € 82/104 €

Rest – *(geschl. Sonntagabend – Montag)* Menü 38 € – Karte 20/42 €

♦ Aus dem Jahre 1904 stammt dieses Haus, das gut unterhaltene, solide und zeitgemäß eingerichtete Gästezimmer beherbergt, teils mit Balkon. Neuzeitliches, gemütliches Restaurant. Für Veranstaltungen: eine urige Scheune im Garten.

Gasthof Schäfle

Sigmund-Nachbaur-Str. 14 ✉ 6830 – ✆ (05522) 4 45 48 – info@schaefle.com – Fax (05522) 445484 – geschl. 25. Aug. – 9. Sept und Montag – Dienstag

Rest – *(Mittwoch – Freitag nur Abendessen)* Menü 20/30 € – Karte 17/31 €

♦ Das um 1886 als Wohn- und Landwirtschaftsgebäude erbaute Haus ist heute ein Gasthof mit nettem ländlichem Ambiente und einer schönen Terrasse.

RATTEN – Steiermark – 730 T6 – 1 290 Ew – Höhe 765 m – Wintersport: 1

Wien 135 – Graz 68 – Bruck a.d. Mur 49 – Wiener Neustadt 86 11 **K4**

Stift Vorau★ (Süd-Ost: 21 km)

Gasthof Zur Klause mit Zim

Filzmoos 32 (Nord-Ost: 1 km, Richtung Rettenegg) ✉ 8673 – ✆ (03173) 24 48 – ratten@zurklause.at – Fax (03173) 2448

8 Zim – 30/50 € 60/100 € – ½ P 12 €

Rest – *(geschl. Mittwoch)* Menü 38 € – Karte 16/32 €

♦ Ein im alpenländischen Stil gebautes Gasthaus unter familiärer Leitung, das ein gemütliches Restaurant mit Gaststube beherbergt. Rustikal gestaltete Zimmer.

RAURIS – Salzburg – 730 K7 – 3 110 Ew – Höhe 952 m – Wintersport: 2 200 m 2 7 8 G5

Wien 384 – Salzburg 87 – St. Johann im Pongau 32

Kirchplatz 1, ✉ 5661, ✆ (06544) 2 00 22, info@raurisertal.at

Rauriserhof Rest, Rest,

Marktstr. 6 ✉ 5661 – ✆ (06544) 62 13 – info@rauriserhof.at – Fax (06544) 621390 geschl. 18. Okt. – 20. Dez., 30. März - 8. Mai

75 Zim (inkl. ½ P) – 57/68 € 108/130 € 78/98 € 148/206 €

Rest – (nur Abendessen für Hausgäste)

♦ Das Alpenhotel bietet in warmen Farben freundlich gestaltete Zimmer in neuzeitlichem Landhausstil sowie geräumige Suiten. Großzügiger Freizeitbereich.

Alpina (geheizt) Zim, VISA

Marktstr. 4 ✉ 5661 – ✆ (06544) 65 62 – alpina@salzburg.co.at – Fax (06544) 7348

geschl. 26. Okt. – 15. Dez., April – 9. Mai

48 Zim (inkl. ½ P.) – ☼ 47/65 € 82/118 € ❄ 58/78 € 104/155 €

Rest – (nur Abendessen für Hausgäste) Karte 16/26 €

◆ Das familiengeführte Hotel beherbergt gepflegte, mit hellem Holzmobiliar solide ausgestattete Zimmer, die unterschiedlich im Zuschnitt ausfallen.

Ferienwelt Kristall (geheizt) Zim, Rest, VISA

Marktstr. 2 ✉ 5661 – ✆ (06544) 73 16 – hotel@ferienwelt-kristall.at – Fax (06544) 731641

geschl. 25. März – 3. Mai

65 Zim (inkl. ½ P.) – ☼ 55/72 € 96/118 € ❄ 63/99 € 124/176 €

Rest – (nur Abendessen für Hausgäste)

◆ Ländliches Ambiente in den z. T. mit unbehandeltem hellen Holz oder in rustikaler Eiche ausgestatteten Gästezimmern – einige auch mit separatem Kinderzimmer.

In Rauris-Wörth Süd: 4 km:

Andrelwirt mit Zim

Dorfstr. 19 ✉ 5661 – ✆ (06544) 64 11 – andrelwirt@rauris.net – Fax (06544) 7184

geschl. 20. Okt. – 10. Dez.

10 Zim – 30/45 € 40/60 €

Rest – Karte 21/32 €

◆ Der 500 Jahre alte Gasthof beherbergt gemütliche, auf zwei Ebenen angelegte Stuben, in denen man regionale und internationale Küche serviert.

Gusto VISA AE

Dorfstr. 22 ✉ 5661 – ✆ (06544) 64 04 – gusto@rauris.net – Fax (06544) 64044

Rest – *(nur Abendessen)* (Tischbestellung ratsam) Menü 50 € – Karte 24/44 €

◆ Genießen Sie eine teils regionale, teils internationale Küche in bürgerlicher Atmosphäre – mit sehr freundlichem Service. Netter Terrassenbereich im Sommer.

REICHENAU AN DER RAX – Niederösterreich – 730 T5 – 2 920 Ew – Höhe 485 m – Wintersport: 1 540 m 1 2 – Luftkurort 3 K3

Wien 91 – St. Pölten 81 – Wiener Neustadt 42 – Mürzzuschlag 36

Hauptstr. 63, ✉ 2651, ✆ (02666) 5 28 65, tourismus@reichenau.at

Veranstaltungen

04.07. – 03.08. Festspiele

Höllental★★ (Nord-West: 5 km)

In Reichenau-Hirschwang Nord-West: 2,5 km Richtung Schneeberg:

Seminar-Park-Hotel Hirschwang Zim, VISA

Hirschwang 11 ✉ 2651 – ✆ (02666) 5 81 10 – office@seminarparkhotel.at – Fax (02666) 5811077

geschl. 9. Dez. – 30. Dez.

70 Zim ☕ – 🚹65 € 🚹🚹109 €
Rest – Karte 17/27 €
♦ Hotel in einem 10 000 qm großen Park mit modern und freundlich eingerichteten Gästezimmern, die über eine sehr gute technische Ausstattung verfügen. In neuzeitlichem Stil gehaltenes Restaurant mit Terrasse zum Park hin.

REIFNITZ – Kärnten – siehe Maria Wörth

REIN – Steiermark – 730 R7 – 2 900 Ew – Höhe 500 m 10 J5

Wien 191 – Graz 16 – Leoben 51 – Köflach 33

Gasthof zur Linde mit Zim
Hörgas 1 ✉ 8103 – ✆ (03124) 5 10 69 – gasthof@zurlinde-stiftrein.at – Fax (03124) 51069
geschl. Mitte – Ende Nov. und Mittwoch – Donnerstag
8 Zim ☕ – 🚹35 € 🚹🚹70 €
Rest – Karte 17/37 €
♦ Im Zentrum des kleinen Ortes liegt dieser von der Inhaberfamilie geführte Gasthof – ein unterteiltes gepflegtes Restaurant mit rustikalem Charakter. Solide Zimmer.

REITH BEI KITZBÜHEL – Tirol – siehe Kitzbühel

REITH BEI SEEFELD – Tirol – siehe Seefeld

REITH IM ALPBACHTAL – Tirol – 730 H6 – 2 640 Ew – Höhe 640 m – Wintersport: 2 025 m 1 23 7 E5

Wien 406 – Innsbruck 47 – Wörgl 20 – Schwaz 18
Dorf 41, ✉ 6235, ✆ (05337) 6 26 74, reith@alpbachtal.at

Pirchner Hof (geheizt) Rest, Rest,
Neudorf 42 ✉ 6235 – ✆ (05337) 6 27 49 – info@pirchnerhof.at – Fax (05337) 6274988
geschl. April, Nov. – Mitte. Dez.
76 Zim (inkl. ½ P.) – ☼ 🚹67/73 € 🚹🚹134/148 € ❄ 🚹85/109 € 🚹🚹170/220 €
Rest – Karte 16/35 €
♦ Das Alpenhotel beherbergt gediegene, mit dunklem Holzmobiliar ausgestattete Zimmer – im dazugehörigen Landhaus finden sich z. T. auch Stilmöbel. Der Restaurantbereich ist in Speisesaal und ländliche Stube aufgeteilt.

RETZ – Niederösterreich – 730 T2 – 4 170 Ew – Höhe 264 m 3 K1

Wien 80 – St. Pölten 83 – Stockerau 52 – Krems 59
Hauptplatz 30, ✉ 2070, ✆ (02942) 27 00, tourismus@retz.at
Hauptplatz★
Pulkau (Heilig-Blut-Kirche★) Süd-West: 10 km – Eggenburg (Krahuletz-Museum★, Landschaftsmodell★) Süd-West: 18 km – Schloss Riegersburg★ Nord-West: 21 km

Althof

Althofgasse 14 ✉ 2070 – ✆ (02942) 37 11 – office@althof.at – Fax (02942) 371155

VISA MC AE D

100 Zim – 87 € 138/146 € – ½ P 23 €

Rest – Karte 24/35 €

♦ Der aufwändig renovierte, schöne alte Gutshof überzeugt heute mit geräumigen und technisch sehr gut ausgestatteten, in leicht elegantem Landhausstil eingerichteten Zimmern. Neuzeitliches Restaurant mit hübschem Innenhof und Vinothek.

RETZBACH – Niederösterreich – 730 T2 – 1 040 Ew – Höhe 234 m   3 K1

Wien 81 – Sankt Pölten 130 – Hollabrunn 28

Retzbacher Hof

Bahnstr. 1 ✉ 2074 – ✆ (02942) 20 17 10 – pollak@retzbacherhof.at – Fax (02942) 2017110

gesch. Jan. und Sonntagabend – Mittwochmittag

Rest – Karte 15/29 €

♦ Ein Gasthaus mit ländlichem Salettl und großem Garten mit einer im Sommer sehr reizvollen Terrasse. Die Karte bietet einfache Wirtshausgerichte, aber auch gehobenere Speisen.

REUTHE – Vorarlberg – 730 B6 – 590 Ew – Höhe 650 m   5 A5

Wien 606 – Bregenz 306 – Dornbirn 21 – Lindau 40

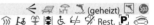

Gesundhotel Bad Reuthe   (geheizt) Rest,

Bad 70 ✉ 6870 – ✆ (05514) 2 26 50 – office@badreuthe.at – Fax (05514) 2265100

130 Zim (inkl. ½ P.) – 82/102 € 144/244 €

Rest – Karte 26/43 €

♦ In einem neueren Anbau dieses Hotels hat man eine großzügige Halle, ganz moderne, angenehm helle Zimmer und einen Kur- und Wellnessbereich mit Mooranwendungen eingerichtet.

REUTTE – Tirol – 730 E6 – 5 720 Ew – Höhe 853 m – Wintersport: 1 900 m 1 9   6 C5

Wien 515 – Innsbruck 90 – Garmisch-Partenkirchen 46 – Kempten 51

Untermarkt 34, ✉ 6600, ✆ (05672) 6 23 36, info@reutte.com

Veranstaltungen

25.07. – 27.07.: Die Zeitreise

Plansee★ (Ost: 6 km)

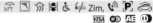

Zum Mohren

Zim,

Untermarkt 26 ✉ 6600 – ✆ (05672) 6 23 45 – info@hotel-mohren.at – Fax (05672) 623456

VISA MC AE D

54 Zim – 67/88 € 104/142 € – ½ P 12 €

Rest – Karte 16/35 €

♦ Der 1765 erstmals erwähnte Gasthof liegt im verkehrsberuhigten Teil des historischen Zentrums. Zimmer mit gutem Platzangebot und ein freundlicher Frühstücksraum. Recht schlichter bürgerlicher Restaurantbereich.

Das Beck garni

Untermarkt 11 ✉ 6600 – ✆ (05672) 6 25 22 – info@hotel-das-beck.at – Fax (05672) 6252235

16 Zim – 42/45 € 68/75 €

◆ Das Hotel ist zentral in der Einkaufszone gelegen und bietet funktionelle und gepflegte Zimmer mit unterschiedlicher Einrichtung. Frühstück serviert man im hauseigenen Café.

RIED IM INNKREIS – Oberösterreich – 730 M4 – 11 410 Ew – Höhe 429 m

Wien 237 – Linz 76 – Gmunden 49 – Passau 52 1 **G3**

Maria Theresia – Haag, Letten 5 ✆ (07732) 39 44

Kobernausserwald – Höhenhart-St.Johann, Straß 1 ✆ (07743) 2 00 66

Veranstaltungen

08.02. – 10.02.: Automesse
29.02. – 02.03.: Sport & Vital
02.10. – 05.10.: Music Austria Eventec
07.11. – 09.11.: Haus & Bau

Der Kaiserhof garni

Friedrich-Thurnerstr. 4 ✉ 4910 – ✆ (07752) 8 24 88 – office@derkaiserhof.at – Fax (07752) 8248828

geschl. 22. Dez. – 7. Jan., 21. – 25. März

33 Zim – 55/65 € 85/100 €

◆ In diesem zentral gelegenen Hotel erwarten Sie ein moderner Hallenbereich sowie neuzeitlich und funktionell ausgestattete Zimmer und ein hübscher Frühstücksraum.

RIED IM OBERINNTAL – Tirol – 730 D7 – 1 220 Ew – Höhe 880 m – Wintersport: 2 300m 1 6 6 **C6**

Wien 529 – Innsbruck 85 – Landeck 16 – Sankt Anton 45

Kirchplatz 48, ✉ 6531, ✆ (05472) 64 21, info@tiroleroberland.at

Linde Zim,

Ried 80 ✉ 6531 – ✆ (05472) 62 70 – info@hotel-linde.at – Fax (05472) 217544

geschl. 6. April – 9. Mai, 26. Okt. – Mitte Dez.

80 Zim (inkl. ½ P.) – 70/80 € 124/140 € 77/100 € 138/174 €
9 Suiten – **Rest** – Karte 18/35 €

◆ Hier erwarten Sie eine großzügige Halle mit Kamin, ein gepflegter zeitgemäßer Wellnessbereich und ein hübscher Garten. Teilweise besonders geschmackvolle Zimmer mit Balkon. A-la-carte-Restaurant im Wintergarten.

RIED IM ZILLERTAL – Tirol – 730 H7 – 1 200 Ew – Höhe 560 m – Wintersport: 7 **E5**

Wien 423 – Innsbruck 50 – Schwaz 22 – Kitzbühel 73

Magdalena (geheizt)

Ried 25a ✉ 6272 – ✆ (05283) 22 43 – magdalena@magdalena.at – Fax (05283) 2034

60 Zim (inkl. ½ P) – 50/60 € 100/120 € 66/99 € 132/198 €
Rest – Karte 16/28 €

◆ Ein gewachsener, solide geführter Familienbetrieb etwas außerhalb des Zentrums mit wohnlichen Zimmern, einem gepflegten Freizeitbereich und einem Garten mit kleinem Teich.

RIEGERSBURG - Steiermark - 730 T7 - 2 570 Ew - Höhe 382 m 11 L5

Wien 162 - Graz 58 - Leibnitz 54 - Fürstenfeld 20

Nr. 4, 8333, (03153) 86 70, tourismus@riegersburg.com

Lage★

Gasthof Fink

Riegersburg 29 8333 - (03153) 82 16 - gasthof@finkwirt.at - Fax (03153) 8216411

geschl. 22. Dez. - 1. März, außer Saison Mittwoch - Donnerstag

Rest - Karte 20/46 €

◆ Der familiengeführte Gasthof bietet einen rustikalen und einen eleganteren Restaurantbereich sowie eine Vinothek mit regionalen Delikatessen und Weinen. Eigene Turmschinkerei.

Rot steht für unsere besonderen Empfehlungen!

RIEZLERN - Vorarlberg - siehe Kleinwalsertal

RITZING - Burgenland - 730 V6 - 900 Ew - Höhe 303 m 4 L3

Wien 89 - Eisenstadt 45 - Wiener Neustadt 44 - Sopron 29

Horvath

Lange Zeile 92 7323 - (02619) 67 22 90 - rest-horvath@netway.at - Fax (02619) 6722920

geschl. 4. - 23. Feb., 18. - 30. Aug. und Montag - Dienstag

Rest - Karte 19/33 €

◆ Im Speisesaal und im Wintergarten dieses Hauses nimmt man an gut eingedeckten Tischen Platz, einfacher ist die bürgerliche Stube. Regionale Küche mit internationalem Einfluss.

RÖTHIS - Vorarlberg - 730 A7 - 2 000 Ew - Höhe 500 m 5 A5

Wien 607 - Bregenz 27 - Feldkirch 12 - Dornbirn 16

Gemeindeamt (1. Stock), Schlößlestr. 31, 6832, (05522) 4 53 25, roehtis@vlbg.at

Rössle Rest, Rest,

Rautenastr. 28 6832 - (05522) 4 43 08 - hotel@roessle.at - Fax (05522) 443088

30 Zim - 52 € 90 €

Rest - *(geschl. Sonntagabend - Montag)* Menü 17 € - Karte 19/24 €

◆ Der im Jahre 1676 als Einkehrhaus erbaute Gasthof im Zentrum befindet sich seit 1876 in Familienbesitz und verfügt über solide möblierte Zimmer. Hübsch im ländlichen Stil eingerichtetes Restaurant.

Torggel

Torkelweg 1 (Richtung Viktorsberg, dann links ab in die Bruchatgasse) 6832 - (05522) 4 40 52 - info@torggel.at - Fax (05522) 440524

geschl. Dienstag

Rest - Menü 38/51 € - Karte 26/48 €

◆ Das Restaurant ist nach einer original erhaltenen Weinpresse von 1674 benannt. Man bietet österreichische Küche und ausgesuchte Weine. Schöner Gastgarten unter Kastanien.

ROHRMOOS – Steiermark – 730 N6 – 1 410 Ew – Höhe 869 m – Wintersport: 1 880 m 12 12 — 9 H5

Wien 291 – Graz 169 – Salzburg 90 – Bischofshofen 50

Schladming, Rohrmoosstr. 234, 8970, (03687) 2 27 77, urlaub@schladming.at

Schladminger Tauern★★ – Hochwurzen★★ (mit) Süd-West: 12 km – Planai★★ (mit) West: 16 km

Schwaigerhof (mit Gästehaus)

Berge, (geheizt) Spa

Schwaigerweg 19 8971
– (03687) 61 42 20 – info@schwaigerhof.at – Fax (03687) 6142252
geschl. 7. – 30. April, 27. Okt. – 5. Dez.

68 Zim (inkl. ½ P.) – 65/110 € 120/200 € 90/150 € 160/300 € – 3 Suiten

Rest – (im Winter nur für Hausgäste) Karte 16/29 €

◆ Ein im alpenländischen Stil gebautes familiengeführtes Hotel am Ortsrand, in dem wohnlich-rustikale Zimmer mit heller Naturholzeinrichtung zur Verfügung stehen.

Schütterhof

Ennstal und Dachstein Massiv, Rest, VISA

Wiesenweg 140
(Nord-Ost: 1,5 km, Richtung Schladming über Rohrmoosstraße) 8971
– (03687) 6 12 05 – hotel@schuetterhof.com – Fax (03687) 61466

54 Zim (inkl. ½ P.) – 75/82 € 130/166 € 93/126 € 166/268 €

Rest – (nur Abendessen für Hausgäste)

◆ Hotel in schöner Hanglage mit neuzeitlichen Zimmern und freundlichem Freizeitbereich mit toller Sicht. Großzügig: die "Large-Zimmer" mit Bio-Einrichtung aus geöltem Vollholz.

Aktivhotel Rohrmooserhof

Berge, (geheizt) Rest,

Schwaigerweg 135 8971
– (03687) 6 14 55 – rohmooserhof@aon.at – Fax (03687) 6145534
geschl. 7. – 30. April, 9. Nov. – 4. Dez.

36 Zim (inkl. ½ P.) – 77/81 € 128/145 € 116/126 € 176/230 € – 6 Suiten

Rest – (nur Abendessen für Hausgäste) Karte 17/25 €

◆ In diesem familiär geleiteten Haus erwarten den Gast wohnlich-solide ausgestattete Zimmer und ein netter heller Saunabereich.

Braunhofer

Bergpanorama, VISA

Teichweg 35 8971 – (03687) 6 15 75 – info@braunhofer.at
– Fax (03687) 6157520
geschl. Mitte Mai – Mitte Juni und Mitte Juni – Okt. Dienstag

Rest – (abends Tischbestellung ratsam) Karte 20/26 €

◆ Ein familiengeführtes Gasthaus in Ortsrandlage. Ein hübscher Kachelofen und die ländliche Einrichtung bestimmen das Ambiente. Terrasse mit Blick auf die Berge.

Landalm

VISA

Bachstr. 120, (Untertal) (Süd-Ost: 2 km) 8971 – (03687) 6 15 73
– info@landauer.cc – Fax (03687) 611666
geschl. 15. – 29. Nov. und Dienstag

Rest – Karte 16/31 €

◆ Aus zwei Bauernhäusern hat man dieses auf zwei Etagen angelegte Restaurant aufgebaut. Die Kombination von altem und neuem Holz schafft ein originelles und warmes Ambiente.

RUDERSDORF - Burgenland - 730 U7 - 2 090 Ew - Höhe 247 m 11 L5

Wien 162 - Eisenstadt 140 - Fürstenfeld 5

Zum alten Weinstock mit Zim Zim, VISA AE

Hauptstr. 13 7571 - (03382) 7 16 21
- gasthof@zumaltenweinstock.at - Fax (03382) 716214
geschl. 23. Dez. - 6. Jan. und Dienstag
10 Zim - 24/29 € 46/54 € - ½ P 18 €
Rest - Karte 17/29 €

◆ Der Gasthof verfügt über eine schlichte, hell eingerichtete Stube und einen Gastgarten unter Bäumen. Die Küche ist frisch, schmackhaft und international-regional. Schöne Gästezimmer in Gartentrakt.

RUSSBACH AM PASS GSCHÜTT - Salzburg - 730 M6 - 810 Ew - Höhe 817 m - Wintersport: 1 618 m 2 31 9 G4

Wien 297 - Salzburg 57 - Berchtesgaden 63 - Bad Ischl 33
Saag 22, 5442, (06242) 5 77, russbach@lammertal.info

Alpenhotel Russbacher Hof garni VISA

Saag 10 5442 - (06242) 2 07 05 - info@russbacherhof.at
- Fax (06242) 2070550
geschl. 7. April - 18. Juli, 29. Sept. - 19. Dez.
14 Zim - 42/52 € 80/110 € 42/55 € 80/116 €

◆ Ein familiär und freundlich geleitetes Hotel, dessen helle Gästezimmer alle über einen Balkon verfügen. Biofrühstück. Für Hausgäste hat man ein kleines Jausenangebot.

Berggasthof zum Hias mit Zim

Saag 51 (West: 1 km, Richtung Abtenau, im Zentrum rechts ab über Bodenberg) 5442 - (06242) 2 20 - info@zumhias.at
- Fax (06242) 36312
geschl. 7. April - 1. Mai, 27. Okt. - 4. Dez.
7 Zim - 33/39 € 56/66 € 43/48 € 74/84 € - ½ P 12 €
Rest - Menü 15/40 € - Karte 17/38 €

◆ In dem familiär geführten Gasthof außerhalb des Ortes erwarten Sie gepflegte Gästezimmer und eine nette Terrasse. Es wird eine Kräuterpfadwanderung mit der Chefin angeboten. Regionale Speisekarte.

RUST AM SEE - Burgenland - 730 W5 - 1 720 Ew - Höhe 123 m 4 M3

Wien 61 - Eisenstadt 14 - Wiener Neustadt 38 - Baden 48
Conradplatz 1, 7071, (02685) 5 02, info@rust.at
Fischerkirche (Fresken★)
Neusiedler See★★ (Ost: 2 km) - Mörbisch am See★ (Süd: 6 km)

Bürgerhaus VISA

Hauptstr. 1 7071 - (02685) 61 62 - office@mooslechners.at
- Fax (02685) 616211
geschl. Feb.
11 Zim - 110/162 € 184/270 €
Rest - (Tischbestellung ratsam) Karte 35/53 €

◆ Einmalig ist das 350 Jahre alte Gästehaus, in dem jedes der Zimmer mit Stil, Liebe und Kreativität eingerichtet ist. Auch schön ist die separate Gästehaus-Suite für 2 Personen. Gemütliches Restaurant mit hübscher Innenhofterrasse.

Seehotel Rest, Rest,
Am Seekanal 2 ✉ 7071 – ✆ (02685) 38 10 – info@seehotelrust.at – Fax (02685) 381419
110 Zim (inkl. ½ P.) – 97/126 € 164/222 € 95/121 € 160/212 € – 5 Suiten
Rest – Karte 20/38 €
♦ Das Hotel am Neusiedlersee bietet neuzeitliche, funktionelle Gästezimmer und einen recht vielfältigen Freizeitbereich mit Beachvolleyball. Gute Tagungsmöglichkeiten. Gediegener Speisesaal.

Sifkovits Rest,
Am Seekanal 8 ✉ 7071 – ✆ (02685) 3 60 – hotel@sifkovits.at – Fax (02685) 36012
geschl. Ende Nov. - Ende März
33 Zim – 55/80 € 75/124 €
Rest – *(geschl. Montag, außer Juli – Aug.)* Karte 18/37 €
♦ Das familiengeführte Haus mit seinen funktionell gestalteten Zimmern liegt nahe dem Neusiedlersee in einem sehr schönen 8 000 qm großen Garten mit Baumbestand. Gepflegtes, solide ausgestattetes Restaurant.

Am Rathausplatz Zim,
Rathausplatz 7 ✉ 7071 – ✆ (02685) 62 02 – am—rathausplatz@rms.at – Fax (02685) 6772
19 Zim – 44/65 € 86/92 €
Rest – *(geschl. Nov. 3 Wochen, Ende Feb. – Anfang März 3 Wochen und Mittwoch, Nov. – März Montag – Mittwoch)* Karte 15/32 €
♦ Im Stadtkern befindet sich dieses Hotel in einem denkmalgeschützen historischen Haus. Die Zimmer sind unterschiedlich und zeitgemäß gestaltet. Restaurant mit ländlichem Charakter und kleine Stube mit Gewölbedecke.

Inamera
Oggauer Str. 29 ✉ 7071 – ✆ (02685) 64 73 – office@inamera.at – Fax (02685) 647318
geschl. Montag – Dienstag, Juli – Aug. nur Montag
Rest – *(Mittwoch – Donnerstag nur Abendessen)* Menü 34/69 € – Karte 29/52 €
♦ Das helle und modern eingerichtete, mit wechselnder Bilderausstellung ausgestattete Restaurant finden Sie am Ortsende von Rust. Regional inspirierte Küche.

Wirtshaus im Hofgassl
Rathausplatz 10 ✉ 7071 – ✆ (02685) 6 07 63 – Fax (02685) 607634
geschl. 7. Jan. – 7. März
Rest – (Tischbestellung ratsam) Menü 30/58 € – Karte 27/44 €
♦ Frisch und sorgfältig wird in diesem Restaurant in einem Gebäude a. d. 16. Jh. gekocht. Zum Haus gehören auch ein schöner Innenhof und ein Kräutergarten.

Rusterhof mit Zim
Rathausplatz 18 ✉ 7071 – ✆ (02685) 6 07 93 – office@mooslechners.at – Fax (02685) 616211
geschl. Nov. – März

4 Zim – 75/90 € 125/150 €
Rest – Karte 18/33 €
◆ Der Drehort der TV-Serie "Der Winzerkönig" ist ein individuelles, gepflegtes und nettes Restaurant mit freundlichem Service, Wirtshauscharakter und traditioneller Küche. Zum Übernachten stehen sehr schöne, originell eingerichtete Suiten zur Verfügung.

SAALBACH-HINTERGLEMM – Salzburg – 730 J6 – 3 020 Ew – Höhe 1 003 m – Wintersport: 2 100 m 14 41 8 F5

Wien 380 – Salzburg 88 – Kitzbühel 75 – Saalfelden 25
Glemmtaler Landesstr. 550, 5753, (06541) 68 00 68, contact@saalbach.com

Veranstaltungen
18.01.: Mountain Attack
02.04. – 06.04.: Musikanten Ski WM

Pinzgauer Spazierweg★★ – Schattberg-Ost★★ (mit) – Zwölferkogel★ (mit)

Im Ortsteil Saalbach

Bauer VISA AE
Oberdorf 232 5753 – (06541) 6 21 30 – office@hotel-bauer.at – Fax (06541) 62135
geschl. Mitte April – Mitte Juni, Mitte Okt. – Anfang Dez.
40 Zim (inkl. ½ P.) – 50/70 € 100/140 € 95/175 € 170/300 €
Rest – Menü 37 € (abends) – Karte 19/39 €
◆ Das Hotel in der Fußgängerzone überzeugt mit schönen, wohnlich gestalteten Gästezimmern und einem ansprechenden Freizeitbereich. Auf Wunsch auch Massage. Elegant-rustikale Restaurantstuben mit sich anschließendem Wintergarten zur Straße hin.

Kendler (geheizt) Rest, VISA AE
Oberdorf 39 5753 – (06541) 6 22 50 – post@kendler.at – Fax (06541) 6335
geschl. Ende März – Ende Nov.
56 Zim (inkl. ½ P.) – 125/260 € 210/386 €
Rest – Menü 51 € (abends) – Karte 23/47 €
◆ Das gewachsene Urlaubshotel verfügt über wohnlich eingerichtete Gästezimmer mit schönen, modernen Bädern sowie ein vielseitiges Wellnessangebot. Am Mittag bietet man eine kleine Karte, abends klassisch-regionale Küche im ländlich-eleganten Kendler's Herzl.

Reiterhof Alpin Resort Rest, VISA AE
Schischulstr. 277 5753 – (06541) 66 82 – info@alpinresort.com – Fax (06541) 668212
geschl. 15. April – 20. Juni, Nov. – 15. Dez.
90 Zim (inkl. ½ P.) – 83/98 € 156/186 € 102/210 € 204/420 €
Rest – (nur für Hausgäste)
◆ Unweit des Dorfplatzes liegt das gewachsene Hotel mit Skischule und nettem Freizeitbereich. Einige Wellnesszimmer mit Infrarotlicht und modernem Bad. Im Sommer all inclusive.

Neuhaus
Zim, Rest, VISA MC

Oberdorf 38 ✉ 5753 – ☎ (06541) 71 51 – saalbach@neuhaus.co.at – Fax (06541) 715174
geschl. 12. April – 22. Mai, Okt. – 1. Dez.
73 Zim (inkl. ½ P.) – ☼ †73/78 € ††130/156 € ❄ †115/181 € ††192/332 €
Rest – Karte 29/42 €
♦ Neben der zentralen Lage sprechen die mit viel hellem Holz angenehm freundlich möblierten Zimmer für dieses Haus. Für Familien stehen Appartements zur Verfügung. Das Restaurant ist in einen Wintergarten und eine kleine Stube unterteilt.

Kohlmais
Schattberg, Zim, VISA MC

Schiliftstr. 469 ✉ 5753 – ☎ (06541) 66 30 – hotel@kohlmais.at – Fax (06541) 663013
geschl. April – 21. Juni, 20. Sept. – 14. Dez.
25 Zim (inkl. ½ P.) – ☼ †61/75 € ††110/138 € ❄ †94/150 € ††170/265 €
Rest – (nur Abendessen für Hausgäste)
♦ Die leicht erhöhte Lage etwas oberhalb des Dorfes und wohnliche Zimmer sprechen für das familiär geleitete Ferienhotel. Bade- und Saunabereich mit schöner Tal-/Bergsicht.

Saalbacher Hof
(geheizt) Zim, VISA MC

Dorfplatz 27 ✉ 5753 – ☎ (06541) 71 11 – hotel@saalbacherhof.at – Fax (06541) 711142
geschl. 6. April – 21. Juni, 4. Okt. – 4. Dez.
88 Zim (inkl. ½ P.) – ☼ †73/94 € ††128/164 € ❄ †114/177 € ††198/324 € – 5 Suiten
Rest – Karte 24/46 €
♦ Gewachsene Ferienadresse in der Fußgängerzone. Die besonders schönen Zimmer im oberen Teil des Hotels sowie Freibad und Liegewiese bieten Berg-/Talblick. Kosmetik und Massage. Das A-la-carte-Restaurant ist ein gemütliches Stüberl.

Post
(geheizt) Zim, VISA MC AE

Dorfplatz 34 ✉ 5753 – ☎ (06541) 62 31 – info@hotelpost-saalbach.at – Fax (06541) 7848
geschl. 15. April – 15. Juni, 15. Sept. – 5. Dez.
45 Zim (inkl. ½ P.) – ☼ †65/95 € ††130/190 € ❄ †98/159 € ††210/330 €
Rest – Karte 19/44 €
♦ Der erweiterte Gasthof a. d. 15. Jh. bietet Wellness mit Kosmetik und Ganzjahresfreibad sowie wohnliche, teilweise besonders komfortable Zimmer. Im Sommer nur all-inclusive. Das Restaurant ist in gemütliche Stuben unterteilt.

Wechselberger mit Zim
VISA MC AE

Oberdorf 178 ✉ 5753 – ☎ (06541) 62 39 – info@wechselberger.at – Fax (06541) 62398
geschl. 15. April - 15. Juni, Okt. – 1. Dez
25 Zim (inkl. ½ P.) – ☼ †50/55 € ††100/110 € ❄ †65/120 € ††120/210 €
Rest – *(geschl. Dienstag)* Menü 19/59 € – Karte 26/46 €
♦ Regionale und mediterrane Küche serviert man Ihnen in diesem von der Inhaberfamilie geführten Haus – gute Weinberatung durch den Patron. Einige der Gästezimmer sind Familienzimmer.

Im Ortsteil Hinterglemm

Theresia Gartenhotel
(geheizt)

Glemmtaler Landstraße 208
(Wiesenegg) ✉ 5754 – ✆ (06541) 7 41 40 – info@hotel-theresia.co.at
– Fax (06541) 7414121
geschl. 9. April – 8. Mai, 28. Okt. – 13. Dez.
47 Zim (inkl. ½ P.) – ☼ 88/198 € 190/280 € ❄ 142/339 € 244/458 € – 10 Suiten
Rest – (nur Abendessen für Hausgäste)

◆ Das familienfreundliche Hotel bietet einen umfassenden Wellnessbereich mit schöner Außenanlage sowie Zimmer von traditionell über klassisch bis zur modernen Design-Suite.

Feriengut Ellmauhof
Reiterkogel und Talschluss, (geheizt) Rest,

Ellmauweg 35 ✉ 5754 – ✆ (06541) 6 43 20
– info-ellmauhof@alpinparadies.at – Fax (06541) 643271
geschl. 20. Okt. – 5. Dez.
40 Zim (inkl. ½ P.) – ☼ 60/67 € 128/154 € ❄ 73/99 € 168/232 €
Rest – Karte 18/26 €

◆ Vielseitige Freizeitangebote wie Kinderhallenbad, Streichelzoo, Reitunterricht und Abenteuerspielplatz machen das malerisch gelegene Hotel besonders für Familien interessant. Hell und freundlich ist der mit viel Holz gestaltete Restaurantbereich.

Sport- und Vitalhotel Ellmau
Reiterkogel, Rest,

Haidweg 357
✉ 5754 – ✆ (06541) 72 26 – info-ellmau@alpinparadies.at
– Fax (06541) 722656
geschl. Mai, Okt. – Nov.
39 Zim (inkl. ½ P.) – ☼ 81/117 € 146/190 € ❄ 105/194 € 182/338 € – 6 Suiten
Rest – Karte 20/51 €

◆ Das Haus etwas oberhalb des Dorfes bietet u. a. einige Feng-Shui-Zimmer und eine Vital Suite mit Lichttherapie und Wasserbett. Großes Freizeitangebot. Im Sommer all-inclusive. Regionstypisch gestaltetes Restaurant.

Salzburg
Zim, Rest,

Reiterkogelweg 182 ✉ 5754 – ✆ (06541) 63 45
– info@hotel-salzburg.at – Fax (06541) 634557
geschl. 13. April – 18. Mai, 12. Okt. – 7. Dez.
29 Zim (inkl. ½ P.) – ☼ 82 € 124/132 € ❄ 130/168 € 180/256 €
Rest *Heurigenstub'n* – (abends Tischbestellung ratsam)
Karte 17/35 €

◆ Ein nettes Hotel unter Leitung der Familie, das über solide, mit hellen Naturholzmöbeln in ländlichem Stil ausgestattete Gästezimmer verfügt. Gemütliche Atmosphäre im rustikalen Restaurant mit Terrasse zur Saalach.

Edelweiß

Zim, Rest,

Dorfstr. 192 ✉ 5754 – ✆ (06541) 63 55 – info@hotel-edelweiss.at – Fax (06541) 635580

geschl. Mai, Okt. – Nov.

40 Zim (inkl. ½ P) – ☼ 62/78 € 107/135 € ❄ 91/164 € 152/280 €

Rest – Karte 24/51 €

◆ Die Gästezimmer dieses im regionstypischen Stil erbauten, engagiert geführten Familienbetriebs sind zeitgemäß eingerichtet und größtenteils recht geräumig. Rustikales Ambiente im A-la-carte-Restaurant mit Kamin und Gartenterrasse.

Zur Dorfschmiede

Dorfstr. 129 ✉ 5754 – ✆ (06541) 74 08 – info@wolf-hotels.at – Fax (06541) 7408309

geschl. 5. April – 10. Mai

48 Zim (inkl. ½ P.) – ☼ 79/102 € 138/154 € ❄ 112/178 € 194/350 € – 5 Suiten

Rest – *(nur Abendessen)* (im Sommer nur für Hausgäste) Karte 23/35 €

◆ Eine gemütliche Halle und freundliche, mit hellen Naturholzmöbeln wohnlich eingerichtete Zimmer sprechen für dieses Haus. Freizeitbereich mit Massageangebot. Im 1. Stock befindet sich das hübsche, rustikale Restaurant.

Zwölfer

Zwölferkogelweg 137 ✉ 5754 – ✆ (06541) 63 17 – info@hotelzwoelfer.at – Fax (06541) 63177

geschl. 5. April – 28. Juni, 20. Sep. – 6. Dez.

28 Zim (im Winter inkl. ½ P.) – ☼ 44/47 € 76/86 € ❄ 92/110 € 164/200 €

Rest – *(geschl. 5. April – 6 Dez.)* Karte 20/31 €

◆ Direkt an der Talstation der Zwölferkogel-Bergbahn liegt dieses Hotel mit neuzeitlich und komfortabel möblierten Zimmern sowie einem netten kleinen Freizeitbereich. Die Lage an der Bergbahn macht das Restaurant für Skifahrer interessant.

Alpenhotel Amalienburg

Zim, Rest,

Kollingweg 147 (West: 2 km) ✉ 5754 – ✆ (06541) 2 00 88 – info@amalienburg.at – Fax (06541) 200884

geschl. 29. März – 24. Mai.

57 Zim (inkl. ½ P.) – ☼ 105/190 € 150/270 € ❄ 109/203 € 150/290 €

Rest – (nur Abendessen für Hausgäste)

◆ Reizvoll im Glemmtal gelegenes Hotel in unmittelbarer Nähe des Hochalmlifts. Die Gästezimmer sind modern eingerichtet, einige als wohnliche Maisonetten angelegt. Restaurant und Terrasse bieten eine schöne Aussicht.

Schachner

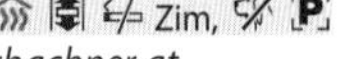

Dorfstr. 163 ✉ 5754 – ✆ (06541) 64 09 – info@hotelschachner.at – Fax (06541) 640995

geschl. Mitte April – Ende Mai, Ende Sept. – Anfang Dez.

24 Zim (inkl. ½ P.) – ☼ 44/64 € 88 € ❄ 64/114 € 128/154 €

Rest – (nur Abendessen für Hausgäste)

◆ Eine sympathische und tadellos gepflegte Ferienadresse direkt am Unterschwarzach-Lift bzw. Skischulsammelplatz. Die Zimmer verfügen größtenteils über einen Balkon.

Oberdanner Rest, VISA
Mühlfeldweg 227 ✉ 5754 – ✆ (06541) 65 86
– oberdanner@hinterglemm.at – Fax (06541) 658669
geschl. 5. April – 22. Mai, 27. Sept. – 8. Dez.
30 Zim (inkl. ½ P.) – ☼ 44/47 € 74/80 € ❄ 68/89 € 116/158 €
Rest – (nur Abendessen für Hausgäste)
◆ Am Ortseingang, nur wenige Schritte vom Bergfried-Lift und nahe dem Hallenbad von Hinterglemm, liegt dieses regionstypische Haus. Alle Gästezimmer mit Balkon.

Das Symbol in Rot weist auf besonders ruhige Häuser hin – hier ist nur der Gesang der Vögel am frühen Morgen zu hören…

SAALFELDEN – **Salzburg** – 730 K6 – **15 100 Ew** – **Höhe 744 m** – **Wintersport: 1 550 m** 3 — 8 **F5**

- Wien 356 – Salzburg 86 – Kitzbühel 50 – Zell am See 14
- Bahnhofstr. 10, ✉ 5760, ✆ (06582) 7 06 60, info@saalfelden-leogang.at
- 18 Urslautal, Schinking 1 ✆ (06584) 20 00
- 18 Salzburg-Brandlhof, Hohlwegen 4 ✆ (06582) 7 48 75
- Saalachtal★

Gut Brandlhof (beheizt) A/C Rest, Rest, Rest, VISA AE
Hohlwegen 4
(Nord: 6 km, an der Straße nach Lofer) ✉ 5760 – ✆ (06582) 78 00
– office@brandlhof.com – Fax (06582) 7800598
200 Zim – 97/130 € 174/240 € – ½ P 25 € – 23 Suiten
Rest – Menü 45 € (abends) – Karte 28/41 €
◆ Seminar- und Wellnessgäste kommen hier gleichermaßen auf ihre Kosten. Im eleganten Landhausstil eingerichtete Zimmer und ein vielfältiges Freizeitangebot. Geschmackvoll gestaltetes Restaurant.

Schörhof Spa VISA
Marzon 10 (Nord: 2 km) ✉ 5760 – ✆ (06582) 7 92 – hotel@schoerhof.at
– Fax (06582) 79245
geschl. 3. – 21. Nov.
46 Zim – ☼ 60/68 € 96/111 € ❄ 75/85 € 125/146 €
– ½ P 13 €
Rest – Karte 16/33 €
◆ Hier ist aus einem ehemaligen Gasthof ein Wellnesshotel mit wohnlichen Zimmern in hellem Holz – auch Familienzimmer – und einem neuzeitlichen Freizeitbereich entstanden. Angenehm helles, in ländlichem Stil gehaltenes Restaurant.

Hindenburg Zim, VISA AE
Bahnhofstr. 6 ✉ 5760 – ✆ (06582) 7 93 – hindenburg@aon.at
– Fax (06582) 79378
70 Zim – ☼ 63/74 € 106/128 € ❄ 78/83 € 136/162 €
– ½ P 18 €
Rest – *(geschl. Sonntag, nur Abendessen)* Karte 15/32 €
◆ Ein tadellos unterhaltener, über 500 Jahre alter Gasthof im Zentrum, der über stilvoll eingerichtete Zimmer mit Holzfußböden verfügt. Mit warmen Farben behaglich gestaltete Gaststuben.

Ritzenhof Rest,

Ritzenseestr. 33 ✉ 5760 – ✆ (06582) 7 38 06 – info@ritzenhof.at – Fax (06582) 7380651

46 Zim (inkl. ½ P.) – ☼ 54/79 € 96/138 € ❄ 59/86 € 106/152 €

Rest – *(geschl. April, Nov.)* Karte 16/26 €

◆ Das Hotel liegt am kleinen Ritzensee und bietet neuzeitlich mit freundlich-hellem Mobiliar ausgestattete Zimmer – kleinere Zimmer mit dunklen Möbeln im Stammhaus. Im Restaurant Orangerie bietet man regionale Küche.

XO VISA

Lofererstr. 15 b, (1. Stock) ✉ 5760 – ✆ (06582) 7 57 17 – office@ixo.at – Fax (06582) 757175

geschl. Sonntag

Rest – *(nur Abendessen)* (Tischbestellung ratsam) Menü 27/49 € – Karte 28/47 €

◆ Restaurant mit geradlinigem, geschmackvoll-modernem Ambiente. Gut sortierte Weinkarte und geschulter Service. In der Bar im EG auch mittags ein kleines Speisenangebot.

Hautemaniere Noël/SCOPE

SALZBURG

Bundesland: Salzburg
Michelin-Karte: **730** L5
Wien 300 – Innsbruck 186 – Bad Reichenhall 20 – München 144

Einwohnerzahl: 148 330 Ew
Höhe: 443 m

8 F4

Salzburg, die stolze Bischofsstadt, verdankt ihren Namen und ihren Reichtum dem Salz, dem weißen Gold, das im nahen Salzkammergut abgebaut wurde. Geprägt wird das Stadtbild noch heute von prächtigen Barockbauten und dem Andenken an den wohl berühmtesten Sohn der Stadt: Wolfgang Amadeus Mozart, der nicht nur aufgrund der berühmten Schokoladenkugeln allgegenwärtig scheint. Zu seinen Ehren werden seit 1920 die Festspiele veranstaltet, die alljährlich im Juni Musikliebhaber aus aller Welt anziehen. Aber nicht nur Kunst und Kultur verleihen der Stadt ihren Reiz. Auch für Feinschmecker haben Salzburg und seine Umgebung viel zu bieten: Die Dichte an guten und sehr guten Adressen ist bemerkenswert, wobei viele der neuen Restaurants in Kontrast zu einem eher schlichten Ambiente eine raffinierte und qualitativ hochwertige Küche anbieten.

PRAKTISCHE HINWEISE

Tourist-Information

Mozartplatz 5 Z, 5020, (0662) 88 98 73 30, tourist@salzburg.info

Autoreisezug

Lastenstraße V

Flughafen

Innsbrucker Bundesstr. 95 (über A 1 V), (0662) 8 58 00
City Air Terminal (Autobusbahnhof), Südtirolerplatz V

Messen

Messezentrum Salzburg, Am Messezentrum 1, 5020, (0662) 2 40 40

30.01. – 02.02.: CASA

14.02. – 17.02.: Bauen u. Wohnen

22.02. – 24.02.: Ferien-Messe Salzburg

08.03. – 09.03.: Salzburger Auto Messe

30.03. – 02.04.: Alles für den Gast

10.05. – 18.05.: Salzburger Dult

29.08. – 31.08.: Tracht & Country

20.11. – 23.11.: BIM

Veranstaltungen

25.01. – 03.02.: Mozartwoche

15.03. – 24.03.: Osterfestspiele

09.05. – 12.05.: Salzburger Festspiele Pfingsten

25.07. – 31.08.: Sommerfestspiele

04.10. – 20.10.: Bachfest

Fußball-Europameisterschaft

10.06., 14.06., 18.06.: Vorrundenspiele

Golfplätze

9 Salzburg-Wals, Schloss Klessheim ✆ (0662) 85 08 51

18 Salzburg-Eugendorf, ✆ (06225) 7 00 00

9 Hof, ✆ (0662) 23 90

18 St. Lorenz, ✆ (06232) 3 83 50

SEHENSWÜRDIGKEITEN

ALTSTADT

Dom★ – Hohensalzburg★★ (Reckturm✳ ★★, Burgmuseum★) – Petersfriedhof★★ – Benediktinerstiftskirche St. Peter★★ – Franziskanerkirche★ **A** – Residenz★★ – Museum der Moderne★ Z – Haus der Natur★★ **M²** – Getreidegasse★ Y – Mirabellgarten★ (monumentale Marmorstiege★★, Salzburger Barockmuseum★ **M³**) V

AUSSICHTSPUNKTE

Mönchsberg ★★ Z, *Hettwer Bastei* ★★ Y

Sacher

Schwarzstr. 5 ✉ 5020 – ✆ (0662) 8 89 77 – salzburg@sacher.com – Fax (0662) 88977551 Y **b**

112 Zim – ✝185/595 € ✝✝220/595 €, ☕ 28 € – 4 Suiten

Rest *Zirbelzimmer* – Menü 53 € – Karte 37/65 €

Rest *Salzachgrill* – Menü 19 € – Karte 26/42 €

♦ Das elegante Grandhotel liegt am Ufer der Salzach und verspricht einen sehr angenehmen Aufenthalt in luxuriösem Ambiente, vervollständigt durch freundliches Personal. Rustikal-geschmackvolles Zirbelzimmer. Salzachgrill mit bezaubernder Terrasse zum Fluss.

Bristol

Zim,

Makartplatz 4 ✉ 5020 – ✆ (0662) 87 35 57 – hotel.bristol@salzburg.co.at – Fax (0662) 8735576

geschl. 3. Feb. – 13. März Y **a**

60 Zim ☕ – ✝150/383 € ✝✝205/450 € – 6 Suiten

Rest – *(geschl. Sonntag, außer Festspielzeit)* Karte 24/56 €

♦ Das traditionelle Stadthotel im Zentrum besticht mit seinen geschmackvollen, individuellen und detailreichen Zimmern und Suiten. Schön gestaltetes Restaurant mit klassischer Küche.

Sheraton

Zim,

Auerspergstr. 4 ✉ 5020 – ✆ (0662) 88 99 90 – sheraton.salzburg@sheraton.com – Fax (0662) 881776 V **s**

162 Zim ☕ – ✝142/507 € ✝✝189/584 € – 8 Suiten

Rest *Mirabell* – Karte 41/53 €

♦ Zwischen dem Kongresszentrum und dem Mirabellengarten liegt das schicke Hotel mit wohnlich-komfortabel ausgestatteten Gästezimmern. Gediegen-elegantes Restaurant mit Terrasse zum Garten und gutem Service.

Altstadt Radisson SAS

Judengasse 15 (Rudolfskai 28) ✉ 5020 – ✆ (0662) 8 48 57 10 – radisson-altstadt@austria-trend.at – Fax (0662) 8485716 Y **s**

62 Zim ☕ – ✝160/345 € ✝✝235/600 € – 13 Suiten

Rest – *(geschl. Sonntag, außer Festspielzeit)* Menü 36/42 € – Karte 25/44 €

♦ Aus der Verbindung mehrerer historischer Häuser entstand dieses hübsche Hotel nahe dem Mozartplatz. Die Zimmer sind mit unterschiedlichen Stilmöbeln schön eingerichtet. Zum Restaurant mit internationaler Speisekarte gehört ein Wintergarten mit Panoramablick.

Goldener Hirsch

Zim,

Getreidegasse 37 ✉ 5020 – ✆ (0662) 8 08 40 – goldener.hirsch@luxurycollection.com – Fax (0662) 843349 Y **e**

69 Zim – ✝151/660 € ✝✝181/660 €, ☕ 28 € – 4 Suiten

Rest – Karte 33/61 €

♦ In dem stilvollen Hotel, das sich in einem Patrizierhaus aus dem Jahre 1407 befindet, kann man je nach Belieben in eleganten oder rustikalen Zimmern wohnen. Das Restaurant bietet internationale Küche, möchte man es regionaler, geht man ins rustikale Herzl.

SALZBURG

Auerspergstr.	V 3	Gstättengasse	X 12	Nußdorfer Str.	X 3
Bürglsteinstr.	X 5	Kaiserschützenstr.	V 20	Rainerstr.	V
Erzabt-Klotz-Str.	X 9	Lindhofstr.	V 22	Schießstrattstr.	V 3
		Mirabellpl.	V 26	Schwatzstr.	V 3
		Nonntaler Hauptstr.	X 29	Späthgasse	X 3

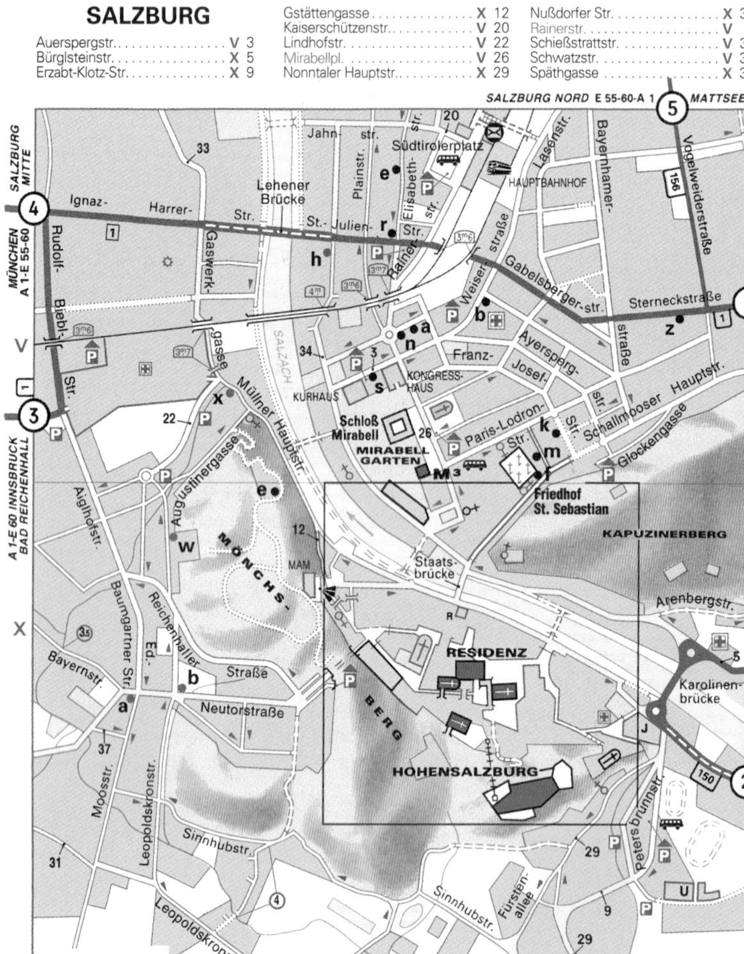

Crowne Plaza-The Pitter

Rainerstr. 6 ✉ *5020*
– ✆ *(0662) 88 97 80* – *crowneplaza.pitter@imlauer.com*
– *Fax (0662) 878893* V **n**

198 Zim ☕ – 🚹 145/285 € 🚹🚹 175/315 €
Rest – *(nur Abendessen)* Menü 19 € – Karte 30/48 €
Rest ***Pitter-Keller*** – Auerspergstr. 23, ✆ (0662) 88 97 87 80 – Karte 16/27 €

◆ Das 1870 erbaute Haus im Herzen Salzburgs verfügt über komfortable und funktionelle Zimmer sowie einen gut ausgestatteten Tagungsbereich. Gediegene Restaurantstube mit elegantem Touch. Im Pitter-Keller gibt es regionale Küche.

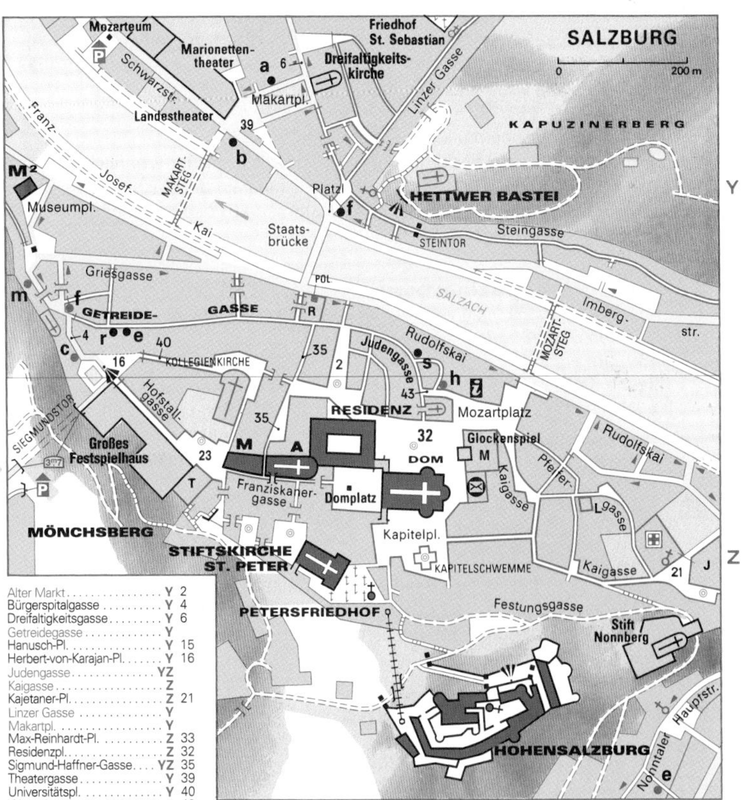

Alter Markt . . . . . . Y 2
Bürgerspitalgasse . . . . . . Y 4
Dreifaltigkeitsgasse . . . . . . Y 6
Getreidegasse . . . . . . Y
Hanusch-Pl. . . . . . . Y 15
Herbert-von-Karajan-Pl. . . . . . Y 16
Judengasse . . . . . . YZ
Kaigasse . . . . . . Z
Kajetaner-Pl. . . . . . . Z 21
Linzer Gasse . . . . . . Y
Makartpl. . . . . . . Y
Max-Reinhardt-Pl. . . . . . . Z 33
Residenzpl. . . . . . . Z 32
Sigmund-Haffner-Gasse . . . . YZ 35
Theatergasse . . . . . . Y 39
Universitätspl. . . . . . . Y 40
Waagpl. . . . . . . Z 43

Schloss Mönchstein

< Salzburg und Umgebung, Rest, VISA AE

Mönchsberg Park 26 ✉ 5020 – ✆ (0662) 8 48 55 50 – salzburg@monchstein.at – Fax (0662) 848559
geschl. Jan. – April X **e**

24 Zim – 192/436 € 240/545 €

Rest – Karte 44/65 €

◆ Das äußerst ansprechende kleine Schloss steht in einem 14 000 qm großen Park oberhalb von Salzburg. Wohnliche und elegante Zimmer, einige mit Blick auf die Stadt. Im Restaurant: zeitgemäße klassische Küche mit mediterranem Einfluss – mittags einfachere Karte.

Castellani Parkhotel

Zim, VISA AE

Alpenstr. 6 (über B 150 X) ✉ 5020 – ✆ (0662) 2 06 00 – info@hotel-castellani.com – Fax (0662) 2060555

151 Zim – 123/196 € 153/236 €

Rest – Karte 24/44 €

◆ Hier hat man Klassisches mit Modernem kombiniert: Geschmackvoll und zeitlos sind die Zimmer in dem unter Denkmalschutz stehenden Haupthaus sowie im Neubau. Restaurant mit hübscher Innenhofterrasse.

Zum Hirschen Biergarten, Zim,

St. Julien Str. 21 ✉ 5020

– ✆ (0662) 88 90 30 – info@zumhirschen.at – Fax (0662) 8890358 V **r**

62 Zim – 83/180 € 110/226 €

Rest – *(geschl. Sonntag)* Menü 24 € – Karte 21/34 €

◆ In Bahnhofsnähe findet man das Hotel, welches über wohnliche Zimmer verfügt, ebenso wie über eine große Sauna auf der Dachterrasse. Die im Wirtshaus verarbeiteten Produkte stammen aus ökologischem Anbau, genau wie ein Teil der Weine.

Mercure Kapuzinerberg Rest, Zim, Rest,

Sterneckstr. 20 ✉ 5020

– ✆ (0662) 8 82 03 10 – h5354@accor.com – Fax (0662) 8820319 V **z**

139 Zim – 95/153 € 115/179 €, 12 € – 4 Suiten

Rest – Karte 25/33 €

◆ Als zentraler Standort empfiehlt sich dieses Hotel, ca. 15 Gehminuten von der Altstadt entfernt. Durch die großzügige Atriumhalle gelangen Sie in funktionelle Zimmer. Restaurant Amadeo mit Terrassengarten.

Stein garni

Giselakai 3 ✉ 5020 – ✆ (0662) 8 74 34 60 – salzburg@hotelstein.at

– Fax (0662) 8743469 Y **f**

55 Zim – 99/155 € 140/185 € – 5 Suiten

◆ Modern hat man die Zimmer in dem 600 Jahre alten Haus direkt an der Staatsbrücke gestaltet. Sechs der Zimmer wurden im Mozartstil eingerichtet. Dachterrasse mit Café und Bar.

Altstadthotel Wolf-Dietrich garni

Wolf-Dietrich-Str. 7 ✉ 5020

– ✆ (0662) 87 12 75 – office@salzburg-hotel.at – Fax (0662) 8712759 V **m**

40 Zim – 71/139 € 114/194 € – 6 Suiten

◆ Das Stadthaus verfügt über gediegene Zimmer und vier aufwändig gestaltete und hübsche Themensuiten. Netter, moderner Badebereich. Frühstück mit Bioprodukten.

NH Salzburg-City Zim,

Franz-Josef-Str. 26 ✉ 5020

– ✆ (0662) 8 82 04 10 – nhsalzburg@nh-hotels.com

– Fax (0662) 874240 V **k**

140 Zim – 90/145 € 105/205 €

Rest – Karte 19/37 €

◆ Unweit vom Mirabellgarten finden Sie in dem besonders auf Geschäftsreisende ausgerichteten Hotel funktionell und sachlich gestaltete Gästezimmer.

arthotel Blaue Gans

Getreidegasse 41 ✉ 5020 – ✆ (0662) 8 42 49 10 – office@blauegans.at

– Fax (0662) 8424919 Y **r**

40 Zim – 109/129 € 145/205 € – 3 Suiten

Rest – *(geschl. Dienstag, außer Festspielzeit)* Karte 27/40 €

◆ Das mit 650 Jahren älteste Gasthaus Salzburgs besitzt moderne, helle und teils mit Designermöbeln ausgestattete Zimmer, ebenso findet man überall zeitgenössische Kunst. Lichtes Restaurant mit schöner Gewölbedecke und netter Terrasse.

Markus Sittikus garni
Markus-Sittikus-Str. 20 ✉ 5020 – ☎ (0662) 8 71 12 10 – hotel@markus-sittikus.at – Fax (0662) 87112158 V **a**
39 Zim – 70/86 € 110/155 €
♦ Im Zentrum liegt das von der Familie geführte, freundliche Stadthotel, das verschieden gestaltete und hübsche Zimmer zur Verfügung stellt.

Lasserhof garni
Lasserstr. 47 ✉ 5020 – ☎ (0662) 87 33 88 – info@lasserhof.com – Fax (0662) 8733886 V **b**
28 Zim – 55/99 € 75/180 €
♦ Dieses gepflegte und solide Hotel verfügt über teils großzügige, immer wohnlich und elegant eingerichtete Gästezimmer.

Haus Arenberg garni
Blumensteinstr. 8 (über Arenbergstr. X) ✉ 5020 – ☎ (0662) 64 00 97 – info@arenberg-salzburg.at – Fax (0662) 6400973
16 Zim – 75/95 € 116/159 €
♦ Gepflegte und modern gestaltete Zimmer, meist mit Balkon und netter Sicht zur Stadt, sowie ein hübscher Garten kennzeichnen das kleine, familiäre Hotel in einer Villengegend.

Altstadthotel Amadeus garni
Linzer Gasse 43 ✉ 5020 – ☎ (0662) 87 14 01 – salzburg@hotelamadeus.at – Fax (0662) 8714017 V **f**
26 Zim – 76/88 € 100/180 €
♦ In dem 500 Jahre alten, freundlich geleiteten Hotel findet man unterschiedlich eingerichtete Zimmer, in denen geschmackvoll mit Farben und Stoffen umgegangen wurde.

Hohenstauffen garni
Elisabethstr. 19 ✉ 5020 – ☎ (0662) 87 76 69 – hohenstauffen@aon.at – Fax (0662) 87219351 V **e**
31 Zim – 72/95 € 99/145 €
♦ Seit 1898 steht das Stadthaus in Elisabethvorstadt, dessen Zimmer individuell und gemütlich eingerichtet wurden, teilweise sind sie auch mit Himmelbetten versehen.

Riedenburg
Neutorstr. 31 ✉ 5020 – ☎ (0662) 83 08 15 – reservierung@riedenburg.at – Fax (0662) 843923
geschl. Sonntag – Montag, außer Festspielzeit X **a**
Rest – (Tischbestellung ratsam) Menü 18 € (mittags)/73 € – Karte 39/66 €
Spez. Hummer im kalten Tomatenfond mit Thaispargel und Arganöl. Wolfsbarsch mit gefüllten Poweraden und Bottarga-Nudeln. Lammrücken mit getrüffelter weißer Bohnencreme.
♦ Hier kocht man eine internationale Küche aus guten Produkten mit regionalen Einflüssen. Serviert wird in den modern-eleganten Gaststuben oder im schönen Gastgarten.

Atelier im Gasthaus zu Schloss Hellbrunn
Fürstenweg 37 (über B 150 X) ✉ 5020 – ☎ (0662) 82 56 08 – office@taste-gassner.com – Fax (0662) 82560842
geschl. 14. Jan. – 20. März und Sonntag – Dienstag, Aug. Montag – Dienstag, Dez. Montag – Dienstag

Rest – *(nur Abendessen)* Menü 38/64 € – Karte 34/51 €
◆ Das hübsche, geradlinig-modern gestaltete Restaurant mit kreativer Küche ist Teil des Renaissance-Lustschlosses. Gasthaus mit einfachem Angebot am Mittag.

XX ✿ **Esszimmer** (Andreas Kaiblinger)
Müllner Hauptstr. 33 ✉ 5020 – ✆ (0662) 87 08 99 – office@esszimmer.com – Fax (0662) 870833
geschl. Anfang Jan. 1 Woche, Sonntag – Montag, außer Dez. und Aug. V **x**
Rest – (Tischbestellung ratsam) Menü 23 € (mittags)/78 € – Karte 46/69 €
Spez. Langostinos mit Paprika, Vanille und Melone. Taube und Maishendl im Kräutercrêpe mit Pfifferlingen. Ziegenkäse mit Erdbeere, dunkler Schokolade, Honig und Rucola.
◆ Ein elegant und modern eingerichtetes Restaurant mit besonderer Note und freundlichem Service. Serviert werden klassisch-kreative Menüs mit den dazu passenden Weinen.

XX **Pan e Vin**
Gstättengasse 1, (1. Etage) ✉ 5020 – ✆ (0662) 84 46 66 – info@panevin.at – Fax (0662) 84466615
geschl. Sonntag, außer Festspielzeit Y **m**
Rest – Menü 67 € – Karte 46/65 €
Rest *Trattoria* – *(geschl. Sonntag – Montag, außer Festspielzeit)* Karte 28/48 €
◆ In dem 600 Jahre alten Haus kann man in zurückhaltender, warmer Atmosphäre italienisch essen und von der guten Weinkarte wählen. Im Untergeschoss des Pan e Vin findet man die Trattoria mit kleiner Showküche.

XX **Culinarium**
St.-Julien-Str. 2, (Eingang Gebirgsjägerplatz) ✉ 5020 – ✆ (0662) 87 88 85 – restaurantculinarium@gmx.at – Fax (0662) 879188
geschl. Mitte Feb. 1 Woche, Anfang Juni 2 Wochen, Okt. 1 Woche und Sonntag, Feiertage, Montagmittag V **h**
Rest – Menü 44/69 € – Karte 33/55 €
◆ Das nett geführte, elegant-gemütliche Restaurant vermittelt Leichtigkeit durch Elemente wie Korbstühle und helle Töne. Offene Küche, in der man Internationales zubereitet.

XX **K+K Restaurant am Waagplatz**
Waagplatz 2, (1. Etage) ✉ 5020 – ✆ (0662) 84 21 56 – kk.restaurant@kuk.at – Fax (0662) 84215633
geschl. 4. Feb. – 3. März Z **h**
Rest – (Tischbestellung ratsam) Menü 49 € – Karte 27/44 €
◆ Teil des bürgerlich-regionalen Restaurants ist das 900 Jahre alte Kellergewölbe, in dem man ein Mittelalterprogramm mit Gauklern, Musikern etc. anbietet.

XX **Trattoria Amici** 
Neutorstr. 28 ✉ 5020 – ✆ (0662) 84 03 32 – Fax (0662) 823360
geschl. Sonn- und Feiertage X **b**
Rest – (Tischbestellung ratsam) Karte 23/41 €
◆ Das typisch italienische Restaurant zeigt sich sehr stimmig in Ambiente und Dekor. Hier findet man sowohl traditionelle Küche sowie freundlichen Service.

Carpe Diem

Getreidegasse 50 ✉ 5020 – ✆ (0662) 84 88 00
– fingerfood@carpediem.com – Fax (0662) 84880088 Y **f**
Rest – Menü 38/85 € – Karte 38/55 €
Rest *Carpe Diem Finest Fingerfood* – Menü 10/45 €
◆ Im 1.OG befindet sich das in warmen Tönen gehaltene Restaurant, in dem man sich internationale Küche schmecken lassen kann. Das Bistro im Erdgeschoss bietet gehobenes Fingerfood in "Cones".

Alt Salzburg

Bürgerspitalgasse 2 ✉ 5020 – ✆ (0662) 84 14 76 – altsalzburg@aon.at
– Fax (0662) 8414764
geschl. 24. Feb. – 3. März, Sonntag – Montagmittag, außer Festspielzeit und Dez. Y **c**
Rest – (abends Tischbestellung ratsam) Menü 48 € – Karte 29/51 €
◆ Nicht nur etwas für Stammgäste ist dieses familiäre Restaurant nahe der Stadtmauer mit seiner gediegenen, elegant-gemütlichen Einrichtung und der überwiegend regionalen Küche.

Magazin

Augustinergasse 13 ✉ 5020 – ✆ (0662) 8 41 58 40 – office@magazin.co.at
– Fax (0662) 8415844
geschl. Sonntag – Montag, außer Festspielzeit X **w**
Rest – (Tischbestellung ratsam) Menü 42/49 € – Karte 41/61 €
Spez. Bouillabaisse mit Atlantikfischen und Sauce Rouille. Asiatisches Schweinsbrüstl mit Jakobsmuscheln und gebackenem Kaviar-Ei. Rinderfilet mit Wasabikruste und geschmortem Minigemüse.
◆ Einzigartig und modern ist das Restaurant mit seiner aparten Mischung aus unverputztem Beton und hochwertiger Einrichtung. Gute Weinauswahl und kreativ-internationale Küche.

In Salzburg-Aigen **Süd-Ost: 6 km über Bürglsteinstraße X:**

Doktorwirt (geheizt) Rest,

Glaser Str. 9 ✉ 5026
– ✆ (0662) 6 22 97 30 – schnoell@doktorwirt.co.at
– Fax (0662) 62297325
geschl. Ende Feb. 2 Wochen, Mitte Okt. – Ende Nov.
41 Zim – 75/98 € 110/165 €
Rest – *(geschl. Sonntagabend – Montag)* Menü 13 € (mittags)/35 € (abends) – Karte 21/39 €
◆ Ein familiärer Gasthof aus dem 12. Jh. mit hübschen Türmchen, gemütlichen Zimmern und gediegener Atmosphäre. Schöner, großzügiger Badebereich. Das Restaurant mit Weinkeller ist auf vier behagliche Stuben verteilt. Freundlicher Service, regionale Küche.

Rosenvilla garni

Höfelgasse 4 ✉ 5020 – ✆ (0662) 62 17 65 – hotel@rosenvilla.com
– Fax (0662) 6252308
14 Zim – 79/168 € 128/199 €
◆ Die charmante Villa mit Feng-Shui-Garten sticht heraus durch ihren zuvorkommenden Service und die eleganten, komfortablen Zimmer. Moderne Bilderausstellung im Haus.

Gasthof Schloss Aigen

Schwarzenbergpromenade 37 ✉ 5026 – ✆ (0662) 62 12 84 – schloss-aigen@elsnet.at – Fax (0662) 6212844
geschl. Dienstag – Donnerstagmittag, außer Festspielzeit
Rest – Menü 39/56 € – Karte 28/47 €
◆ Der am Waldrand gelegene ehemalige Schlossgasthof besticht mit gemütlichem Ambiente und einer schönen Terrasse. Die Spezialität des Hauses sind die Rindfleischgerichte.

In Salzburg-Gneis Süd: 4 km über Nonntaler Hauptstraße Z:

Zum Eigenherr

Josef-von-Eichendorff-Str. 5 ✉ 5020 – ✆ (0662) 83 23 19 – gasthaus.eigenherr@aon.at – Fax (0662) 832319
geschl. 7. – 18. Juli und Montagabend – Dienstag
Rest – Karte 16/38 €
◆ Seit dem 17. Jh. besteht das am Stadtrand gelegene Gasthaus, in dessen neuzeitlichen Restaurantstuben man in netter Atmosphäre speist.

In Salzburg-Gnigl Ost: 3,5 km über Sterneckstraße V:

Pomodoro

Eichstr. 54 ✉ 5023 – ✆ (0662) 64 04 38
geschl. 21. Juli – 21. Aug., über Weihnachten und Montag – Dienstag
Rest – (Tischbestellung ratsam) Karte 25/42 €
◆ Typisch mediterrane Lebensart und die dazu passende frische, italienische Küche finden Sie in dem gemütlichen Restaurant, das mit Fischernetzen rustikal dekoriert wurde.

In Salzburg-Itzling Nord: 1,5 km über Kaiserschützenstraße V:

Gasthof Auerhahn mit Zim

Rest,

Bahnhofstr. 15 ✉ 5020 – ✆ (0662) 45 10 52 – hotel@auerhahn-salzburg.at – Fax (0662) 4510523
geschl. Juni – Juli 2 Wochen und Sonntagabend – Montag, Festspielzeit nur Montag
13 Zim – 45/50 € 75/85 €
Rest – Menü 35/45 € – Karte 21/40 €
◆ In dem Stadthaus am Bahnhof kann man in einem gemütlich-rustikalen Restaurant mit modernem Kaminzimmer internationale und regionale Küche essen. Wohnliche Zimmer stehen zur Übernachtung zur Verfügung.

In Salzburg-Leopoldskron Süd-West: 4 km über Moosstraße X:

Blobergerhof

Zim, Rest,

Hammerauerstr. 4 ✉ 5020 – ✆ (0662) 83 02 27 – office@blobergerhof.at – Fax (0662) 827061
21 Zim – 45/64 € 65/95 €
Rest – *(geschl. 12. – 27. Nov. und Sonntag)* (nur Abendessen für Hausgäste) Menü 17 € – Karte 15/24 €
◆ Der von der Familie geführte Gasthof war ehemals ein kleiner Bauernhof. Heute bietet er wohnliche Zimmer an (manche mit Balkon), teils mit Blick auf den Untersberg. Rustikaler Gastraum mit Holztäfelung und Ofen. Regionale und internationale Küche.

Frauenschuh garni
Gsengerweg 1a ✉ 5020 – ☎ (0662) 83 23 34 – info@frauenschuh.at
– Fax (0662) 83233440
17 Zim – 62/95 € 105/120 €
◆ Nettes, kleines, von der Inhaberfamilie gut geführtes Hotel nahe dem Zentrum. Im Sommer frühstücken Sie auf der Terrasse.

In Salzburg-Liefering **Nord-West: 4 km über Ignaz-Harrer Straße V:**

Brandstätter Rest,
Münchner Bundesstr. 69 ✉ 5020
– ☎ (0662) 43 45 35 – info@hotel-brandstaetter.com
– Fax (0662) 43453590
geschl. 23. – 27. Dez.
35 Zim – 72/140 € 95/155 €
Rest – *(geschl. Sonntag, außer Festspielzeit)* (Tischbestellung ratsam)
Menü 39/69 € – Karte 24/57 €
Spez. Flusskrebserl mit Dillcrème und Häuptlsalat. Kalbssalonbeuschel mit Semmelknödel. Rehrückenmedaillons mit Pilzen und Blaukraut.
◆ Alte Salzburger Bauernmöbel und hübsches Dekor schaffen in dem Gasthof eine charmante Atmosphäre. Die Zimmer liegen zum Teil gartenseitig. Besonders gemütlich sitzt man in der Zirbelstube bei klassischer und traditioneller Küche aus regionalen Produkten.

In Salzburg-Maxglan **Süd-West: 2 km über Neutorstraße X:**

Zur Post garni (mit Gästehäusern)
Maxglaner Hauptstr. 45 ✉ 5020
– ☎ (0662) 8 32 33 90 – info@hotelzurpost.info – Fax (0662) 8323395
geschl. 21. – 26. Dez.
36 Zim – 60/85 € 84/138 €
◆ Ein nettes, gepflegtes Haus, das über wohnliche und freundliche Zimmer verfügt, die gute Technik und moderne Bäder bieten. Neuere Zimmer in einem der Gästehäuser.

Astoria garni
Maxglaner Hauptstr. 7 ✉ 5020 – ☎ (0662) 83 42 77
– hotel.astoria@aon.at – Fax (0662) 83427740
31 Zim – 69/87 € 94/154 €
◆ Eine freundliche, familiär geführte Adresse. Das Haus ist mit zahlreichen Kunstgegenständen und Bildern ausgestattet. Der neuzeitliche Frühstücksraum dient auch als Café.

In Salzburg-Morzg **Süd: 3 km über Nonntaler Hauptstraße Z:**

Zum Buberl Gut
Gneiser Str. 31 ✉ 5020 – ☎ (0662) 82 68 66 – Fax (0662) 8268664
geschl. Feb. 1 Woche, Juli 1 Woche, Okt. 1 Woche und Dienstag
Rest – (Tischbestellung ratsam) Karte 32/49 €
◆ Das komplett sanierte Landgut aus dem 17. Jh. beherbergt das Restaurant mit netter, gemütlicher Atmosphäre, in der regionale Küche mit italienischen Einflüssen serviert wird.

XX **Gwandhaus**
Morzger Str. 31 ✉ 5020 – ✆ (0662) 8 21 02 00
– gwandhaus@gaumenfreunde.com – Fax (0662) 8210204
Rest – Menü 14 € (mittags)/45 € – Karte 30/51 €
◆ Im schmucken Gwandhaus mit Hochzeitsmuseum und Trachtengeschäft speisen Sie in eleganten Restaurantstuben frische regionale Küche und Fischgerichte. Herrlich: die Terrasse.

In Salzburg-Nonntal

XX **Purzelbaum**
Zugallistr. 7 ✉ 5020 – ✆ (0662) 84 88 43 – Fax (0662) 8488433
geschl. Sonntag – Montagmittag, außer Festspielzeit und Dez. Z **e**
Rest – Menü 17 € (mittags)/60 € – Karte 37/52 €
◆ In einem älteren Stadthaus am Zentrumsrand befindet sich das modern gestaltete Restaurant mit saisonaler internationaler Küche – mittags preisgünstige, eher regionale Kost.

In Salzburg-Parsch **Ost: 5 km über Bürgleinstraße X:**

Villa Pace garni – Salzburg und Festung,
Sonnleitenweg 9 ✉ 5020 – ✆ (0662) 64 40 77
– info@villapace.at – Fax (0662) 64407770
geschl. 1. – 28. Feb., 21. – 28. Dez.
12 Zim – 73/109 € 132/178 €
◆ Hoch über Salzburg liegt die freundlich geführte Villa mit schöner Sicht. Individuelle, elegante Zimmer und ein Frühstücksraum mit luxuriösem Touch machen es besonders.

Auf dem Heuberg **Nord-Ost: 3 km über Sterneckstraße V – Höhe 565 m**

Schöne Aussicht
Heuberg 3 ✉ 5023 Salzburg
– ✆ (0662) 64 06 08 – hotel@salzburgpanorama.at – Fax (0662) 6406082
geschl. Jan. – Feb., Nov. 2 Wochen
28 Zim – 59/120 € 75/135 €
Rest – *(geschl. Dienstag – Mittwoch, außer Festspielzeit)* Menü 49 € – Karte 26/46 €
◆ Schön und einsam über den Dächern Salzburgs liegt das etwa 300 Jahre alte familiär geführte Bauernhaus. Zu empfehlen sind die Zimmer mit Balkon und Sicht. Rustikales Restaurant mit Kachelofen und Gartenterrasse mit Blick auf Salzburg und Umgebung.

Auf dem Gaisberg **Ost: 5 km über Sterneckstraße V – Höhe 1 288 m**

Gersberg Alm Rest,
Gersberg 37 ✉ 5020 Salzburg-Gnigl
– ✆ (0662) 64 12 57 – office@gersbergalm.at – Fax (0662) 644278
46 Zim – 95/125 € 137/287 € – 3 Suiten
Rest – (Tischbestellung ratsam) Menü 49 € – Karte 28/43 €
◆ Der erweiterte Gasthof aus dem Jahre 1860 ist sowohl für Tagungen wie auch für Urlauber geeignet. Die Zimmer sind solide und hell möbliert. Das Lokal ist ländlich gestaltet und das Angebot der Saison angepasst.

Beim Flughafen Süd-West: 5 km über Rudolf-Biebl-Straße V:

Airporthotel Zim, Rest,

Dr.-M.-Laireiter-Str. 9 ✉ 5020 Salzburg-Loig

– ✆ (0662) 85 00 20 – airporthotel@aon.at – Fax (0662) 85002044

36 Zim – 90/135 € 125/155 €

Rest – (nur für Hausgäste)

◆ Das aus zwei miteinander verbundenen Landhäusern bestehende Hotel liegt zentral gegenüber dem Flughafen. Die Zimmer sind funktionell und gepflegt. Netter Hallenbadbereich.

Ikarus

Wilhelm-Spazier-Str. 7a (Hangar-7, 1. Etage) ✉ 5020 Salzburg

– ✆ (0662) 21 97 77 – ikarus@at.redbull.com – Fax (0662) 21973786

geschl. 22. Dez. – 3. Jan.

Rest – (Tischbestellung erforderlich) Menü 85/105 € – Karte 55/81 €

◆ Das modern-elegante Restaurant in dem gläsernen Hangar steht für ein ganz besonderes Konzept: Monatlich welchselnde Gastköche präsentieren ganz unterschiedliche Küchenstile.

Nahe der BAB-Ausfahrt Salzburg-Nord Nord: 3 km:

Ibis Nord garni

Carl-Zuckmayr-Str. 1 ✉ 5020 Salzburg-Kasern – ✆ (0662) 21 44

– h3748@accor.com – Fax (0662) 2144555

103 Zim – 60/80 € 84/104 €

◆ Die verkehrsgünstige Lage nahe der Autobahnausfahrt, eine moderne und funktionelle Ausstattung sowie 24-h-Check-in und Snack-Bar sprechen für dieses Kettenhotel.

Beim Stadion Nord-West: 5 km über A 1:

Bulls' Corner

Stadionstr. 4 ✉ 5071 Wals-Siezenheim – ✆ (0662) 43 33 32 45 12

– soccerrbs.bullscorner@rebulls.com – Fax (0662) 4333324483

geschl. 24. Dez. – 6. Jan. und bei Heimspielen

Rest – Menü 10 € (mittags) – Karte 21/43 €

◆ Im Stadion liegt das Restaurant im Stil einer Sportsbar mit Fernsehbildschirmen und nettem Thekenbereich. Angeboten werden internationale und regionale Speisen.

SANKT AEGYD – Niederösterreich – 730 S5 – 2 350 Ew – Höhe 570 m – Wintersport: 1 770 m 4

3 **K3**

Wien 101 – St. Pölten 47 – Baden 78 – Mariazell 31

Klostertal★ (Ost: 38 km)

Zum Blumentritt mit Zim Zim,

Markt 20 ✉ 3193 – ✆ (02768) 22 77 – office@zumblumentritt.at

– Fax (02768) 22771

10 Zim – 35/45 € 70/90 € – ½ P 35 €

Rest – *(geschl. Sonntagabend, Dienstag – Mittwoch)* Menü 32/49 € – Karte 28/41 €

◆ Ein engagiert geführter sympathischer Landgasthof mit gepflegten Räumen im Landhausstil. Geboten wird gute regionale Küche und eine umfassende Weinkarte.

SANKT ANDRÄ – Salzburg – 730 N7 – 740 Ew – Höhe 1 044 m – Wintersport: 9 H5

Wien 285 – Salzburg 127 – Spittal a.d. Drau 64 – Judenburg 81
5580, (06474) 21 47, st-andrae@lungautourismus.at

Gasthof Andlwirt

St. Andrä 21 5572 – (06474) 23 55 – info@andlwirt.at – Fax (06474) 7276
geschl. 7. April – 1. Mai, 3. Nov. – 7. Dez.
27 Zim (inkl. ½ P.) – 38/44 € 76/88 € 42/48 € 83/95 €
Rest – Karte 13/20 €

◆ Tadellos gepflegter Gasthof in der Ortsmitte: Hier erwarten Sie Zimmer in ländlichem Stil, die z. T. über Balkon und Parkettfußboden verfügen. Restaurant mit Nebenzimmer und separater Stube. Auf der Tageskarte empfiehlt man Gerichte aus der Region.

SANKT ANTON AM ARLBERG – Tirol – 730 C7 – 2 530 Ew – Höhe 1 304 m – Wintersport: 2 810 m 10 75 5 B6

Wien 609 – Innsbruck 101 – Imst 46 – Lech am Arlberg 21
Dorfstr. 8, 6580, (05446) 2 26 90, info@stantonamarlberg.com

Veranstaltungen
26.08. – 30.08.: Filmfest

Valluga ★★★ (mit) – Kapall ★★ – Rendl-Kabinenbahn★

Raffl's St. Antoner Hof

Zim, Rest,

Arlbergstr. 69 6580 – (05446) 29 10 – hotel@antonerhof.at – Fax (05446) 3551
geschl. 20. April – 1. Dez.
39 Zim (inkl. ½ P.) – 175/340 € 330/660 € – 12 Suiten
Rest – Karte 33/57 €

◆ Eine gelungene Kombination von Traditionellem und Modernem bestimmt das Ambiente in dem hochwertig eingerichteten Haus. Sehr angenehm ist auch der freundliche Service. Hübsch: die kleine alpenländische A-la-carte-Stube mit internationaler und regionaler Küche.

Schwarzer Adler

Rest,

Dorfst. 35 6580 – (05446) 2 24 40 – hotel@schwarzeradler.com – Fax (05446) 224462
geschl. 20. April – 21. Juni, 5. Okt. – 29. Nov.
70 Zim (inkl. ½ P.) – 70/100 € 140/200 € 100/250 € 200/400 € – 3 Suiten
Rest – *(nur Abendessen)* (im Sommer nur für Hausgäste) Karte 31/47 €

◆ Der am Rand der Fußgängerzone gelegene Gasthof a. d. 16. Jh. ist ein gewachsener Familienbetrieb mit individuellen, recht großzügigen Zimmern. Wellness mit Kosmetikangebot. Hübsche holzvertäfelte Stuben bilden das A-la-carte-Restaurant.

Alte Post

Zim, Rest,

Dorfstr. 11 6580 – (05446) 2 55 30 – st.anton@hotel-alte-post.at – Fax (05446) 255341
geschl. 28. April – 30. Mai, Nov.
62 Zim (inkl. ½ P) – 92/116 € 158/200 € 182/284 € 274/420 €
Rest – *(nur Abendessen)* Karte 26/57 €

◆ Die ehemalige Poststation a. d. 17. Jh. hat sich zu einem regionstypischen Hotel unter familiärer Leitung entwickelt, das über wohnliche Zimmer mit guter Technik verfügt. Gaststuben mit schöner historischer Holztäfelung.

Post Rest, VISA AE

Walter-Schuler-Weg 2 ✉ 6580 – ✆ (05446) 22 13 – info@hotel-post.co.at – Fax (05446) 2343
geschl. 21. April – 22. Juni, 28. Sept. – 30. Nov.
65 Zim (inkl. ½ P.) – ☼ 65/74 € 124/144 € ❄ 99/215 € 176/408 €
Rest – *(geschl. 21. April – 13. Juli, 14. Juli – 27. Sept. Mittwoch)* Karte 29/40 €

♦ Mitten im Zentrum des Ortes liegt dieses Hotel mit seinen wohnlich und funktionell eingerichteten, unterschiedlich geschnittenen Gästezimmern. Gaststuben mit bürgerlichem Ambiente und leicht eleganter Speisesaal.

Lux Alpinae Rest, VISA AE

Arlbergstr. 41 ✉ 6580 – ✆ (05446) 3 01 08 – office@luxalpinae.at – Fax (05446) 30108
geschl. Mai – Nov.
26 Zim (inkl. ½ P.) – ☼ 98/110 € ❄ 189/318 €
Rest – (nur Abendessen für Hausgäste)

♦ Viel Glas, Stahl und Sichtbeton sowie ein supermodernes Design schaffen eine nicht ganz alltägliche Atmosphäre. Eine Kletterwand zieht sich über alle Etagen.

Himmlhof garni

Im Gries 9 ✉ 6580 – ✆ (05446) 23 22 – info@himmlhof.com – Fax (05446) 232214
geschl. 28. April - 11. Juli, 22. Sept. – 28. Nov.
14 Zim – ☼ 84/96 € ❄ 136/228 €
4 Suiten

♦ Mit Engagement leitet die Inhaberfamilie ihr charmantes kleines Hotel. Liebevoll und sehr gemütlich hat man die Gästezimmer und den Frühstücksraum gestaltet.

Europa garni VISA

Dorfstr. 132 ✉ 6580 – ✆ (05446) 34 83 – office@europahotel.at – Fax (05446) 348340
geschl. 27. April – 20. Juni, 28. Sept. – 28. Nov.
13 Zim – ☼ 32/45 € 64/76 € ❄ 100/140 € 136/172 €

♦ Ländlich-moderne Atmosphäre begleitet Sie vom Empfang bis in die hellen, in neuzeitlichem Landhausstil gehaltenen Zimmer mit kleinem Ofen, guter Technik und meist mit Balkon.

Aparthotel Anton Rest, Zim, VISA AE

Kandaharweg 4 ✉ 6580 – ✆ (05446) 24 08 – info@hotelanton.at – Fax (05446) 240819
geschl. Mai – Nov.
14 Zim – 85/120 € 170/240 €
Rest – Karte 19/50 €

♦ Die zentrale Lage an der Galzigbahn sowie funktionelle Zimmer in klarem, modernem Stil – teilweise mit verglasten Bädern – machen dieses kleine Hotel aus. Restaurant mit Bistro-Atmosphäre.

skihotel galzig garni VISA AE
Hannes-Scheider-Weg 5 ✉ 6580 – ✆ (05446) 4 27 70
– info@skihotelgalzig.at – Fax (05446) 4277015
geschl. Mai – Anfang Juli
21 Zim – 140/210 € 150/220 €
◆ Durch und durch modern: von der Holzfassade mit großen Fensterflächen bis zu den hellen, fast schon puristisch eingerichteten Zimmern in geradlinigem Design.

Montjola Rest, P VISA AE
Gastigweg 25 ✉ 6580 – ✆ (05446) 23 02 – info@montjola.com
– Fax (05446) 23029
geschl. Mitte April – Mitte Juni, Ende Sept. – Anfang Dez.
41 Zim (inkl. ½ P.) – ☼ 53/65 € 106/130 € ❄ 95/174 € 154/318 €
Rest – *(geschl. Mitte April – Mitte Dez. und Montag, nur Abendessen)* Karte 28/48 €
◆ Recht ruhig liegt das mit soliden, wohnlichen Zimmern ausgestattete Hotel etwas oberhalb des Ortes. Der Chef bietet für seine Gäste geführte Bergwanderungen. Im Restaurant bietet man u. a. Fondue-Spezialitäten.

Bergschlössl garni VISA
Kandaharweg 13 ✉ 6580 – ✆ (05446) 22 20 – info@bergschloessl.at
– Fax (05446) 2253
geschl. Mai – Mitte Juni
10 Zim – ☼ 64/84 € 128/152 € ❄ 84/141 € 152/249 € – 3 Suiten
◆ Das ca. 100 Jahre alte Haus – einst Kornumschlagstation – ist heute ein kleines Hotel mit schönen, ganz individuellen Zimmern und einem sehr gemütlichen Frühstücksraum.

Arlenburg Zim, Rest, P VISA
Nassereinerstr. 49 ✉ 6580 – ✆ (05446) 31 44 – office@arlenburg.at
– Fax (05446) 314455
23 Zim (inkl. ½ P.) – ☼ 95/115 € 110/150 € ❄ 175/220 € 216/274 € – 13 Suiten
Rest – *(im Sommer Garni, nur Abendessen)* Karte 26/53 €
◆ Ein familiengeführtes neuzeitliches Hotel mit unterschiedlich geschnittenen, funktionell und hochwertig eingerichteten Zimmern/ Appartements im Landhausstil.

Rosa Canina Zim, Rest, P VISA
Untere Nassereinerstr. 39 ✉ 6580 – ✆ (05446) 21 75
– hotel@rosacanina.at – Fax (05446) 21754
geschl. Mai – Juni, Sept. – Nov.
13 Zim (inkl. ½ P.) – ☼ 82/92 € 136/156 € ❄ 123/171 € 172/246 € – 3 Suiten
Rest – (nur Abendessen für Hausgäste)
◆ Dieses sehr gepflegte kleine Landhotel überzeugt mit freundlichen, in ganz hellem Holz modern eingerichteten Zimmern, die z. T. über eine Küchenzeile verfügen.

Sporthotel Rest,

Dorfstr. 48 ✉ 6580 – ✆ (05446) 31 11 – office@sporthotel-st-anton.at – Fax (05446) 311170

geschl. 13. April – 2. Juni, 27. Sept. – 29. Nov.

57 Zim – 49/68 € 94/104 € 110/170 € 220/356 € – ½ P 19 €

Rest – *(geschl. 13. April – 7. Juni)* Karte 26/65 €

◆ Ein von der Inhaberfamilie geleitetes Alpenhotel in der Fußgängerzone mit hellen, funktionell eingerichteten und technisch gut ausgestatteten Gästezimmern. Rustikaler Restaurantbereich – im Winter mit zusätzlicher Steakauswahl.

Montana garni

Dorfstr. 31 ✉ 6580 – ✆ (05446) 32 53 – info@hotelmontana.at – Fax (05446) 32535

geschl. 21. April – 4. Juli, 28. Sept. – 28. Nov.

14 Zim – 60/80 € 80/90 € 150/210 € 170/250 €

◆ Ein familiär geführtes Haus in der Fußgängerzone mit wohnlichen Zimmern im neuzeitlich-alpenländischen Stil, schönem Saunabereich und hellem Frühstücksraum zum Innenhof.

Tyrol Zim, Rest,

Arlbergstr. 77 ✉ 6580 – ✆ (05446) 23 40 – info@tyrolhotel.com – Fax (05446) 2363

geschl. Mai – 15. Juni, 15. Okt. – 1. Dez.

54 Zim (inkl. ½ P.) – 60/90 € 90/120 € 96/191 € 170/360 €

Rest – *(geschl. im Sommer Montag)* Karte 32/62 €

◆ Dieses Bergwanderhotel ist ein gut geführter Familienbetrieb mit hübschem Sauna- und Ruhebereich sowie soliden, teilweise mit kleinem Wohnbereich ausgestatteten Zimmern. Eine gemütliche Atmosphäre herrscht in der Zirbelstube.

Kaminstube am Moos Zim,

Mooserweg 14 ✉ 6580 – ✆ (05446) 26 81 – info@kaminstube.com – Fax (05446) 26815

geschl. Mai – Juni, Sept. – Nov.

26 Zim – 35/40 € 70/80 € 75/87 € 120/164 € – ½ P 28 €

Rest – *(geschl. Mai – Nov.)* Karte 21/40 €

◆ Die Lage oberhalb des Ortes direkt an der Skipiste sowie freundliche, neuzeitlich-wohnlich möblierte Gästezimmer machen dieses Hotel aus. Ländliches Restaurant mit gemütlichem abendlichem Kaminfeuer. Terrasse an der Piste.

Grischuna Zim,

Gastigweg 32 ✉ 6580 – ✆ (05446) 23 04 – hotel@grischuna.at – Fax (05446) 2355

geschl. 16. April – 14. Dez.

21 Zim (inkl. ½ P.) – 77/125 € 120/250 €

Rest – *(nur Abendessen)* Karte 25/43 €

◆ Sehr gepflegt ist dieser in einem ruhigen Wohngebiet gelegene Familienbetrieb. Die Gästezimmer sind wohnlich und funktionell eingerichtet. In der rustikalen Gaststube nehmen Sie an gut eingedeckten Tischen Platz – Aussicht auf das Skigebiet.

Landhaus Strolz garni (mit Gästehaus)

Sonnenwiese 17 ✉ 6580 – ✆ (05446) 23 78 – strolz@arlberg.com – Fax (05446) 23786

geschl. Mai – Juni, 15. Sept – Nov.

12 Zim – ☼ 30/35 € 50/60 € ❄ 72/87 € 120/154 €

◆ Die zwei regionstypischen kleinen Häuser verfügen über helle, solide möblierte und funktionell ausgestattete Zimmer und Appartements sowie nette Frühstücksräume.

Museum

Rudi-Matt-Weg 10 ✉ 6580 – ✆ (05446) 24 75 – museum@st-anton.at – Fax (05446) 272025

geschl. Mai – Mitte Juni, Mitte Sept. – Nov. und Montag sowie Mitte Juni – Mitte Sept. Montag – Dienstag

Rest – *(im Winter nur Abendessen, im Sommer Mittwoch – Freitag nur Abendessen)* Karte 36/55 €

◆ Das Arlberg-Kandahar-Haus von 1912 beherbergt neben dem Ski- und Heimatmuseum mehrere hübsche Stuben, von der komplett vertäfelten Jagdstube bis zur eleganten Bibliothek.

ben.venuto

Hannes-Schneider-Weg 11 , (1. Etage) ✉ 6580 – ✆ (05446) 3 02 03 – info@benvenuto.at – Fax (05446) 302032

geschl. Mai – Nov.

Rest – Menü 41/55 € – Karte 41/56 €

◆ Das Restaurant in der 1. Etage der Ski-WM-Halle besticht durch schlicht-modernes Design: klare Linien, Naturmaterialien und freie Sicht in die Küche und auf die Berge.

Verwallstube Bergpanorama,

Galzig Bergstation, (nur per Seilbahn zu erreichen) ✉ 6580 – ✆ (05446) 2 35 25 01 – fahrner.m@abbag.com – Fax (05446) 2352502

geschl. Mai – 25. Nov.

Rest – *(bis 15.30 Uhr geöffnet, Freitag auch Abendessen)* (Tischbestellung ratsam) Karte 39/57 €

◆ In der Galzig Bergstation in 2 000 m Höhe befindet sich dieses Restaurant mit phantastischem Bergblick. Freitagabends bietet man Live-Musik und ein Candle-Light-Dinner.

Schindler mit Zim Zim,

Alte Arlbergstr. 16 ✉ 6580 – ✆ (05446) 22 07 – info@hotel-schindler.at – Fax (05446) 220722

geschl. Mai – Sept.

9 Zim – 77/144 € 150/198 € – ½ P 25 €

Rest – *(geschl. Okt. – Dez. Sonntag – Dienstag, nur Abendessen)* Karte 25/41 €

◆ Sehr freundlich kümmert man sich in den zwei gemütlichen Restaurantstuben dieses Familienbetriebs um seine Gäste. Geboten werden regionale Speisen. Zum Übernachten stehen individuell und wohnlich ausgestattete Zimmer zur Verfügung.

Frühstück inklusive? Die Tasse steht gleich hinter der Zimmeranzahl.

Im Ortsteil Sankt Jakob **Nord-Ost: 2,5 km Richtung Landeck:**

Zur Pfeffermühle
Zim, Rest, P VISA

Timmlerweg 6 ✉ 6580 – ✆ (05446) 37 40 – office@zurpfeffermuehle.com – Fax (05446) 3741
geschl. 20. April - 27. Juni, 14. Sept. – 28. Nov.
24 Zim (inkl. ½ P) – ☼ 43/59 € 86/118 € ❄ 72/119 € 144/238 €
Rest – *(im Winter nur Abendessen)* Karte 24/42 €

♦ Hinter seiner teils holzverkleideten Fassade beherbergt das gut geführte Alpenhotel mit viel hellem Naturholz und hübschen Stoffen wohnlich eingerichtete Gästezimmer. Im behaglichen, ländlich gestalteten Restaurant ist Mittwoch Fondue-Tag.

Gletscherblick (mit Gästehäusern)
Rest, P

St. Jakober Dorfstr. 35 ✉ 6580 – ✆ (05446) 32 85 – gletscherblick@st-anton.at – Fax (05446) 32608
geschl. 27. April – 28. Juni, 6. Sept. – 28. Nov.
20 Zim (inkl. ½ P) – ☼ 48/55 € 96/110 € ❄ 70/129 € 140/258 €
7 Suiten – **Rest** – (nur Abendessen für Hausgäste)

♦ Sehr gemütlich und ganz im alpenländischen Stil gehalten sind das Hotel, die großzügigen Appartements im Landhaus sowie die geschmackvolle Wohnung im Chalet mit eigener Sauna.

Brunnenhof
P VISA

St. Jakober Dorfstr. 53 ✉ 6580 – ✆ (05446) 22 93 – brunnenhof@arlberg.com – Fax (05446) 22935
geschl. Mai – Dez.
9 Zim (inkl. ½ P.) – 115/135 € 200/270 € – **Rest** – (nur für Hausgäste)

♦ Das einstige Bauernhaus a. d. 17. Jh. ist heute ein familiär geleitetes kleines Hotel in relativ ruhiger Lage etwas abseits des Zentrums. Nett sind die individuellen Zimmer. Eine gemütliche Atmosphäre herrscht in der hübschen holzvertäfelten Bauernstube.

In Sankt Christoph **West: 7 km Richtung Lech – Höhe 1 800 m**

Arlberg Hospiz
Spa Rest, Rest, P VISA AE

St. Christoph 1 ✉ 6580 – ✆ (05446) 2 61 10 – info@arlberghospiz.com – Fax (05446) 3773
geschl. 21. April – Nov.
90 Zim (inkl. ½ P.) – 200/1000 € 400/1300 € – 25 Suiten
Rest *Skiclub Stube* – (Tischbestellung ratsam) Karte 39/68 €

♦ In dem traditionsreichen Hotel vereinen sich alpenländisches Flair und hochwertige Ausstattung. Sehr angenehm ist der engagierte Service im Haus. Großzügiger Spabereich. Rustikal-elegante Skiclub Stube mit klassischem Speisenangebot.

Alpenhotel St. Christoph
Alpenlandschaft, Spa Rest, P VISA

St. Christoph 34 ✉ 6580 – ✆ (05446) 36 66 – alpenhotel@stchristoph.at – Fax (05446) 3618
geschl. 2. Mai – 28. Nov.
36 Zim (inkl. ½ P.) – 150/380 € 200/500 € – 7 Suiten
Rest – Karte 24/47 €

♦ Die leicht erhöhte Lage, geräumige Gästezimmer in neuzeitlichem Stil sowie ein ganz moderner Wellnessbereich machen dieses Hotel aus. Das Restaurant: ein Speisesaal in angenehm hellen Farben und eine rustikale Stube mit Ofen.

Maiensee Rest, VISA AE

St. Christoph 24 ✉ 6580 – ☎ (05446) 21 61 – info@maiensee.com
– Fax (05446) 280456
geschl. 27. April - 28. Nov.
34 Zim (inkl. ½ P.) – 185/235 € 250/418 € – 3 Suiten
Rest – Karte 27/46 €
◆ Direkt am Skilift liegen die zwei miteinander verbundenen regionstypischen Häuser. Neben wohnlichen Zimmern erwartet Sie ein gutes Wellnessangebot. Regionales Speisenangebot im Restaurant.

Hospiz Alm P VISA AE

St. Christoph 16 ✉ 6580 – ☎ (05446) 36 25 – info@hospizalm.at
– Fax (05446) 3625808
geschl. Mai – Nov.
Rest – *(nur Abendessen)* (Tischbestellung ratsam) Karte 46/62 €
◆ Äußerst gemütlich sitzt man in den rustikalen Stuben mit Almhüttencharakter – der herzliche Service unterstreicht die nette Atmosphäre. Einfache Mittagskarte für Skifahrer.

Gute und preiswerte Häuser kennzeichnet das MICHELIN-Männchen, der „Bib": der rote „Bib Gourmand" für die Küche, der blaue „Bib Hotel" bei den Zimmern.

SANKT ANTON IM MONTAFON – Vorarlberg – 730 B7 – 700 Ew – Höhe 650 m

5 **A6**

Wien 581 – Bregenz 58 – Innsbruck 137 – Feldkirch 26

Adler P VISA

Silvrettastr. 21 (B 188) ✉ 6771 – ☎ (05552) 6 71 18
– office@adler-montafon.com – Fax (05552) 6711850
geschl. 4. Nov. – 12. Dez.
45 Zim (inkl. ½ P.) – 74/92 € 122/176 € 90/133 € 152/226 € – 6 Suiten
Rest – Karte 16/43 €
◆ Ein gut geführter Familienbetrieb mit schönem, modernem Spabereich auf ca. 1000 qm. Die Zimmer verteilen sich auf Alt- und Neubau, eingerichtet von rustikal bis neuzeitlich. Klassisches Restaurant und Montafoner Stuben. Im Sommer mit großzügiger Terrasse.

SANKT CHRISTOPH AM ARLBERG – Tirol – siehe Sankt Anton am Arlberg

SANKT FLORIAN BEI LINZ – Oberösterreich – 730 P4 – 5 530 Ew – Höhe 300 m

2 **I3**

Wien 163 – Linz 21 – Steyr 37 – Wels 29
Marktplatz 2, ✉ 4490, ☎ (07224) 56 90, st.florian@oberoesterreich.at
Linz, Tillysburg 28 ☎ (07223) 8 28 73

Veranstaltungen

17.08. – 23.08.: Brucknertage

Stift St. Florian★★ (Altdorfer-Galerie★★★)
Schloss-Museum Hohenbrunn★★ (West: 1,5 km)

Zur Kanne

Marktplatz 7 ✉ 4490 – ✆ (07224) 42 88 – office@gasthof-koppler.at – Fax (07224) 428842
geschl. 5. – 15. Aug., 23. Dez. – 3. Jan.
14 Zim – 52 € 86 €
Rest – *(geschl. Sonntag – Dienstagmittag und Feiertage)* Karte 21/26 €
◆ Ein sehr gut unterhaltener Gasthof aus dem 17. Jh. mit wohnlichen und funktionellen, teils mit Kirschbaummobiliar, teils mit hellem Naturholz eingerichteten Zimmern. Viele kleine Stuben in ländlichem Stil bilden den Restaurantbereich.

SANKT GALLEN – Steiermark – 730 P5 – 1 520 Ew – Höhe 513 m – Wintersport: 900 m 1 10 I4

Wien 186 – Graz 128 – Liezen 39 – Leoben 67
Markt 35, ✉ 8933, ✆ (03632) 77 14, eisenwurzen@xeis.at
Stift Admont★ (Süd-West: 20 km) – Eisenerzer Alpen★ (Süd: 24 km)

Gasthof Hensle (mit Gästehaus) Rest, Zim,

Markt 43, (B 117) ✉ 8933 – ✆ (03632) 71 71 – office@hensle.at – Fax (03632) 717123
geschl. Ende März 2 Wochen, Mitte Sept. 2 Wochen
25 Zim – 35/51 € 70/102 €
Rest – *(geschl. Freitag)* Karte 13/33 €
◆ Solide, wohnliche Gästezimmer in neuzeitlichem Stil stehen in dem familiengeführten Gasthof am Marktplatz zur Verfügung. Mit Fahrrad-Verleih. Das Restaurant: teils bürgerlich mit alter Holzdecke oder Gewölbe.

SANKT GALLENKIRCH – Vorarlberg – 730 B7 – 2 270 Ew – Höhe 900 m – Wintersport: 2 370 m 4 24 5 A6

Wien 660 – Bregenz 72 – Sankt Anton am Arlberg 61 – Feldkirch 41
Silvrettastraße, ✉ 6791, ✆ (05557) 66 00, info@stgallenkirch.at
Valisera-Kabinenbahn★★

Zamangspitze Rest,

Ziggamweg 227 ✉ 6791 – ✆ (05557) 62 38 – info@zamangspitze.at – Fax (05557) 62385
geschl. 6. April – 2. Juni, 16. Nov. – 5. Dez.
44 Zim (inkl. ½ P.) – 67/88 € 134/176 € 83/125 € 166/250 €
Rest – (nur für Hausgäste)
◆ Ruhig liegt das Hotel mit den wohnlichen Zimmern oberhalb des Ortes, schön ist die Aussicht. Zu den Neuerungen des Hauses zählt ein hübscher Sauna- und Ruhebereich.

Alpen Sporthotel Grandau Rest, Rest,

Silvrettastr. 274a (B 188) ✉ 6791 – ✆ (05557) 63 84 – info@grandau.at – Fax (05557) 63847
geschl. 7. April – 12. Mai, 30. Okt. – 10. Dez.
35 Zim (inkl. ½ P) – 70/90 € 140/180 € 90/125 € 180/250 €
4 Suiten – **Rest** – (nur Abendessen für Hausgäste)
◆ In dem familiengeführten Hotel erwarten Sie wohnliche, teils recht geräumige Zimmer in Südlage mit Bergblick und ein neuzeitlicher Freizeitbereich mit Kosmetik. Bar Kuhstall.

Adler Rest,

Silvrettastr. 277 (B 188) ✉ 6791 – ✆ (05557) 6 20 60 – hotel@deradler.at – Fax (05557) 62066
geschl. April – Mitte Juni, Mitte Okt. – Mitte Dez.
43 Zim – 69/89 € 98/134 € 99/128 € 178/226 € – ½ P 20 € – 3 Suiten
Rest *Montafoner- und Jäger Stube* – separat erwähnt
◆ In einem neueren Anbau bietet der Gasthof sehr unterschiedliche, geschmackvoll eingerichtete Zimmer. Schön ist das traditionelle k. u. k. Zimmer mit offenem Kamin.

Montafoner- und Jäger Stube – Hotel Adler

Silvrettastr. 277 (B 188) ✉ 6791
– ✆ (05557) 6 20 60 – hotel@deradler.at – Fax (05557) 62066
geschl. April – Mitte Juni, Mitte Okt. – Mitte Dez.
Rest – *(geschl. Dienstag, Mitte Juni – Mitte Okt. Dienstag – Mittwoch)*
Menü 62/78 € – Karte 25/50 €
◆ Gemütlich-rustikal ist die Atmosphäre in der historischen Montafoner- und Jäger Stube. Im Winter reicht man eine aufwändigere, im Sommer eine einfachere Speisekarte.

SANKT GEORGEN AM LÄNGSEE – Kärnten – 730 P8 – 3 560 Ew – Höhe 593 m

10 I6

Wien 277 – Klagenfurt 25 – St. Veit an der Glan 8 – Völkermarkt 28

Im Ortsteil Dellach West: 5 km über B 82, bei Krottendorf abbiegen:

Moorquell Rest,

Dellacherweg 7 ✉ 9313 – ✆ (04213) 25 90 – hotel@moorquell.at – Fax (04213) 259058
24 Zim (inkl. ½ P.) – 72/93 € 128/170 €
Rest – Karte 19/37 €
◆ Schön liegt das auf Naturwellness ausgerichtete Hotel in einer großzügigen Gartenanlage mit Moorwasser-Badesee und "Park der Balance". Neuzeitliche Zimmer und Ferienwohnungen.

Im Ortsteil Launsdorf Süd-Ost: 6 km über B 82 Richtung Brückl:

Dienstl Gut Zim, Rest,

Wiendorf 1 (West: 4,5 km über die B 82, nach Rain links ab in Richtung Gösseling) ✉ 9314 – ✆ (04213) 21 40 – office@dienstlgut.com – Fax (04213) 21404
geschl. 23. – 27. Dez., 18. – 23. Feb.
24 Zim (inkl. ½ P.) – 83/93 € 176/212 €
Rest – (nur für Hausgäste)
◆ Gutshotel auf einem ca. 52 ha großen Anwesen mit hübschen Zimmern und einer gemütlichen alten Stube. Man bietet auch ein Jugend-Camp und die erste Polo-Schule Österreichs. Ländliches, leicht elegantes Restaurant.

Im Ortsteil Sankt Peter West: 4 km über B 82, bei Krottendorf abbiegen:

Gasthof Liegl mit Zim Rest, P VISA MC AE D
St. Peter bei Taggenbrunn 2 ✉ 9313 – ✆ (04213) 2 12 40
– office@gasthof-liegl.at – Fax (04213) 21244
geschl. Feb. 1 Woche, Okt. 1 Woche
3 Zim – 40/43 € 80/86 €
Rest – *(geschl. Okt. – April Dienstag – Mittwoch)* Karte 29/49 €
◆ In einem kleinen Ortsteil liegt dieser von Familie Liegl engagiert geführte Gasthof. In gepflegtem ländlich-rustikalem Ambiente serviert man Ihnen regionale Speisen.

Im Ortsteil Töplach Nord: 7 km Richtung Friesach, dann rechts:

Seehof Längsee, Zim, P
Töplach 12 ✉ 9313 – ✆ (04213) 22 32 – schratt@hotel-seehof.at
– Fax (04213) 223255
geschl. Nov. – April
27 Zim (inkl. ½ P.) – 58/78 € 114/154 €
Rest – (nur Abendessen für Hausgäste)
◆ Nicht weit vom See liegt das aus einer Pension entstandene Hotel mit zeitgemäßen, freundlichen Gästezimmern und eigener Landwirtschaft.

Dieser Führer lebt von Ihren Anregungen, die uns stets willkommen sind.
Egal ob Sie uns eine besonders angenehme Überraschung
oder eine Enttäuschung mitteilen wollen – schreiben Sie uns!

SANKT GEORGEN AM REITH – Niederösterreich – 730 Q5 – 590 Ew – Höhe 530 m 3 J3

Wien 158 – St. Pölten 101 – Steyr 101 – Amstetten 45

Jagdhof Breitenthal P
Dorf 9 (Ost: 2 km) ✉ 3344 VISA MC AE D
– ✆ (07484) 80 80 – jagdhof@breitenthal.at – Fax (07484) 808045
geschl. 16. – 25. Dez.
20 Zim – 45/55 € 110/120 € – ½ P 15 €
Rest – (nur Abendessen für Hausgäste)
◆ Das a. d. J. 1546 stammende ehemalige Jagdhaus in schöner Alleinlage am Waldrand beherbergt heute überwiegend mit alten Bauernmöbeln wohnlich gestaltete Zimmer.

SANKT GEORGEN IM ATTERGAU – Oberösterreich – 730 M5 – 4 020 Ew – Höhe 540 m – Wintersport: 1 1 G3

Wien 246 – Linz 86 – Salzburg 52 – Gmunden 31
Attergaustr. 31, ✉ 4880, ✆ (07667) 63 86, info@attergau.or.at

Winzer (geheizt) Zim, Rest,
Kogl 66 (Nord-West: 2 km) 4880
– (07667) 63 87 – info@hotel-winzer.at – Fax (07667) 6387111
geschl. Mitte Juni – Mitte Juli
92 Zim (inkl. ½ P.) – 96/110 € 174/228 € – 6 Suiten
Rest – (nur Abendessen für Hausgäste)
◆ Ein familiengeführtes Hotel mit großzügigem Wellnessbereich und Natur-Badeteich. Besonders schön sind die Gästezimmer in der Residenz und im Wellnessschlössl.

SANKT GILGEN – Salzburg – 730 M5 – 3 690 Ew – Höhe 540 m – Wintersport: 1 522 m 1 1 8 G4

Wien 282 – Salzburg 31 – Gmunden 56 – Hallein 36
Mondsee Bundesstr. 1a, 5340, (06227) 23 48, information@wolfgangsee.at
Wolfgangsee★★ – Mondsee★ (Nord: 6 km)

Hollweger
Mondsee Bundesstr. 2 5340 – (06227) 22 26 – office@hollweger.at – Fax (06227) 795652
geschl. 6. – 19. Jan.
53 Zim (inkl. ½ P.) – 99/129 € 174/238 € – 5 Suiten
Rest – Karte 24/38 €
◆ In schöner Lage über dem See befindet sich dieses gepflegte Hotel mit individuellen, wohnlichen Zimmern und lichtdurchflutetem Hallenbad im separaten Glas-Holz-Anbau. Das Restaurant ist teils elegant, teils im ländlichen Stil eingerichtet.

Parkhotel Billroth Wolfgangsee und Berge,
Billrothstr. 2 5340
– (06227) 22 17 – office@billroth.at – Fax (06227) 221825
geschl. 16. Dez. – 21. Jan.
55 Zim – 66/72 € 128/226 € 52/60 € 100/202 € – ½ P 18 €
Rest – *(nur Abendessen)* Karte 20/37 €
◆ Schön liegt das Hotel leicht erhöht über dem See. Man bietet wohnliche Zimmer, einen kleinen Park und einen eigenen Strandbereich. Zum Restaurant gehört eine schöne Terrasse.

Gasthof zur Post Zim, Rest,
Mozartplatz 8 5340 – (06227) 21 57 – office@gasthofzurpost.at – Fax (06227) 2158600
33 Zim – 77/128 € 108/148 €
Rest – *(geschl. Okt. – April Dienstag – Mittwoch)* Karte 18/36 €
◆ Bald 600 Jahre besteht der ehemalige Gutshof, der heute als Gasthof geführt wird. Die neueren Zimmer sind modern. Frühstück wird in der schönen Gaststube serviert. Ländlich-rustikale Atmosphäre, in der regionale Küche angeboten wird.

Schernthaner garni
Schwarzenbrunnerstr. 4 5340 – (06227) 24 02 – office@hotel-schernthaner.at – Fax (06227) 24022
17 Zim – 45/49 € 80/88 €
◆ Wohnliche Zimmer mit Balkon, freundlicher Service und eine nette Sauna sprechen für dieses gepflegte familiär geführte Hotel im Zentrum.

XX **Timbale**

Salzburger Str. 2 ✉ 5340 – ✆ (06227) 75 87 – Fax (06227) 7587
geschl. Sept. – Juli Donnerstag – Freitagmittag
Rest – (Tischbestellung ratsam) Menü 55/65 € – Karte 33/48 €
◆ Ein hell gestaltetes, vom Inhaberehepaar geführtes kleines Restaurant mit intimer Atmosphäre. Die Karte bietet regionale und internationale Speisen.

XX **Tiroler Stub'n** mit Zim

Aberseestr. 9 ✉ 5340 – ✆ (06227) 23 17 – office@haustirol.com
– Fax (06227) 23174
geschl. 20. Okt. - 20. Nov.
11 Zim (inkl. ½ P.) – 🚹54/67 € 🚹🚹108/134 €
Rest – *(geschl. Montag, Dez. – März Montag – Mittwoch)* Karte 20/40 €
◆ Familiärer Gasthof im Zentrum mit ländlichem Ambiente und freundlichem Service durch die Chefin. Das regionale Angebot besteht größtenteils aus Fischgerichten. Gepflegte, wohnliche Gästezimmer.

XX **Enoteca Barbarossa**

Mozartplatz 5 ✉ 5340 – ✆ (06227) 22 45 – Fax (06227) 2245
geschl. Sonntag
Rest – *(nur Abendessen)* (Tischbestellung ratsam) Karte 21/43 €
◆ Eine gemütliche Atmosphäre herrscht in dem ehemaligen Kaufhaus a. d. 17. Jh., das ein italienisches Restaurant beherbergt. Die Speisen werden mündlich angeboten.

X **Wirt am Gries**

Steinklüftstr. 6 ✉ 5340 – ✆ (06227) 23 86 – wirtamgries@aon.at
– Fax (06227) 23863
geschl. 6. Feb. -12. März, Sept. – Juni Dienstag
Rest – Karte 16/36 €
◆ Das von der Inhaberfamilie geführte, nette Restaurant mit rustikalem Charakter bietet seinen Gästen bürgerlich-regionale Kost.

In Sankt Gilgen-Winkl **Nord-Ost: 2 km über B 154 Richtung Mondsee:**

Gasthof Fürberg (mit Gästehaus) ≤ Wolfgangsee und Berge,
Winkl 19 Zim,
(Süd-Ost: 1 km) ✉ 5340 – ✆ (06227) 2 38 50 – gasthof@fuerberg.at
– Fax (06227) 238535
30 Zim – 🚹75/83 € 🚹🚹104/144 € – ½ P 26 €
Rest – Karte 20/34 €
◆ Die ganz besonders schöne Lage direkt am See charakterisiert dieses Hotel. Ländliche Gästezimmer und sehr wohnliche und hübsch gestaltete Komfortzimmer. Gaststube mit bürgerlichem Angebot und Terrasse mit Seeblick.

Gute Küche zu günstigem Preis? Folgen Sie dem „Bib Gourmand"

SANKT JAKOB IM ROSENTAL – Kärnten – 730 O9 – 4 470 Ew – Höhe 450 m 9 I6

▶ Wien 330 – Klagenfurt 35 – Villach 22 – Velden am Wörther See 12
ℹ Gemeindeamt, ✉ 9184, ✆ (04253) 22 95 24, st-jakob-ros@ktn.gde.at

In Sankt Jakob-Mühlbach Nord-West: 3,5 km Richtung Villach:

Rosentaler Hof (geheizt) Zim,
Mühlbach 28 9184 – (04253) 22 41 – office@rosentaler-hof.at – Fax (04253) 22418
geschl. 28. Okt. – 20. Dez., 28. März – 6. Mai
40 Zim (inkl. ½ P.) – 49/75 € 98/150 € 46/66 € 92/132 €
Rest – *(geschl. Dienstag, nur Abendessen)* Karte 20/35 €
♦ Zu den Annehmlichkeiten dieses Hauses zählt ein schöner 10 000 qm großer Park mit Bach. Im Hotel stehen modern oder rustikal eingerichtete Gästezimmer zur Verfügung. Hell und freundlich gestaltetes Restaurant.

SANKT JAKOB IN DEFEREGGEN – Tirol – 730 J8 – 1 010 Ew – Höhe 1 398 m – Wintersport: 2 520 m 1 6 7 F6

Wien 462 – Innsbruck 190 – Lienz 42 – Bruneck 46
Unterrotte 44, 9963, (04873) 6 36 00, stjakob@defereggental.at

Jesacherhof (mit Gästehaus)
Rest,
Ausserrotte 37 (Ost: 3 km) 9963 – (04873) 53 33 – jesacherhof@netway.at – Fax (04873) 533388
geschl. 12. April – Anfang Juni, 26. Okt. – 19 Dez.
74 Zim (inkl. ½ P.) – 98/115 € 196/248 € 119/150 € 238/322 € – 3 Suiten
Rest *Jakobistube* – Karte 20/35 €
♦ Der alpenländische Gasthof mit Balkonfassade liegt direkt am Lift und bietet mit solidem Naturholz wohnlich gestaltete Zimmer. In der Villa: großzügige Maisonetten und Suiten. Die rustikale Jakobistube dient als A-la-carte-Restaurant.

Alpenhof
Rest,
Innerrotte 35 (Ost: 1 km) 9963 – (04873) 53 51 – office@alpenhof-defereggental.at – Fax (04873) 5351500
geschl. 30. Sept. – 21. Dez., 29. März – 14. Juni
82 Zim (inkl. ½ P.) – 59/85 € 118/170 € 80/117 € 160/234 € – 7 Suiten
Rest – (nur Abendessen für Hausgäste)
♦ Am Ortsanfang gelegenes Hotel im Tiroler Stil mit zeitgemäß eingerichteten Zimmern sowie hübschen Suiten – eine davon verfügt über eine eigene Sauna. Stube in Zirbelholz und gepflegter, ländlicher Speisesaal.

Macher's Landhotel
Unterrotte 82 9963 – (04873) 6 36 30 – info@macher.at – Fax (04873) 63636
geschl. 5. April – Mitte Mai, 17. Okt. – Mitte Dez.
20 Zim (inkl. ½ P.) – 59/70 € 96/108 € 80/95 € 130/140 €
Rest – Karte 19/28 €
♦ Fast alle Zimmer dieses Hotels nahe der Kirche liegen nach Süden (mit Balkon) und sind mit viel Holz neuzeitlich und allergikerfreundlich eingerichtet. Bäder mit Tepidarium. Rustikale Pizzeria. Kleine Schnapsbrennerei.

Gasthof Tandlerstuben mit Zim Rest, VISA
Innerrotte 34 (Ost: 2,5 km) ✉ 9963 – ☎ (04873) 63 55
– info@tandler.at – Fax (04873) 63555
geschl. Mitte April – Mitte Mai, Ende Okt. – Ende Nov.
12 Zim (inkl. ½ P.) – ☼ 41/45 € 82/90 € ❄ 43/50 € 86/100 €
Rest – Karte 14/32 €
◆ Das familiengeführte Gasthaus beherbergt bürgerlich-ländliche Stuben sowie einen neuzeitlicheren Restaurantbereich. Die Küche bietet Forellen aus eigener Zucht.

SANKT JAKOB IN HAUS – Tirol – 730 J6 – 640 Ew – Höhe 855 m – Wintersport: 1 500 m 8 7 F5

Wien 354 – Innsbruck 102 – Saalfelden 33 – Kufstein 41
Dorf 2, ✉ 6391, ☎ (05354) 8 81 59, stjakob@pillerseetal.at

Unterlechner Zim, Rest,
Reith 79 ✉ 6391 – ☎ (05354) 8 82 91 – anfrage@unterlechner.com
– Fax (05354) 882914
geschl. April, Nov.
20 Zim (inkl. ½ P.) – ☼ 70/80 € 140/160 € ❄ 70/90 € 140/180 €
Rest – (nur für Hausgäste)
◆ Das kleine Hotel im Tiroler Stil liegt etwas außerhalb des Ortskerns. Besonders gemütlich sind die Zimmer mit schräger Holzdecke im obersten Stock. Selbst gebackener Kuchen!

SANKT JOHANN AM WIMBERG – Oberösterreich – 730 O3 – 1 020 Ew – Höhe 720 m – Wintersport: 850 m 1 2 H2

Wien 211 – Linz 33 – Wels 56 – Freistadt 42
St. Johann am Wimberg 9, ✉ 4172, ☎ (07217) 71 55, gemeinde@stjohannamwimberg.at

Keplingerwirt Biergarten VISA
St. Johann am Wimberg 14 ✉ 4172 – ☎ (07217) 71 05
– keplinger.wirt@aon.at – Fax (07217) 710555
geschl. 7. – 13. Jan., 14. -21. März
17 Zim – 45/55 € 90/100 € – ½ P 40 €
Rest – *(geschl. Sonntagabend – Montag)* Menü 35/49 € – Karte 21/44 €
◆ Seit über 50 Jahren befindet sich der gestandene Gasthof in der Dorfmitte in Familienbesitz. Die Zimmer sind mit Holzböden und hellem Massivholz behaglich eingerichtet. Gaststube mit ländlichem Charakter. Kleine Bilderausstellung.

SANKT JOHANN IM PONGAU – Salzburg – 730 L6 – 10 260 Ew – Höhe 600 m – Wintersport: 1 850 m 2 17 8 G5

Wien 331 – Salzburg 59 – Zell am See 43 – Badgastein 40
Ing.-Ludwig-Pech-Str.1, ✉ 5600, ☎ (06412) 60 36, info@sanktjohann.com

Havannah

Hauptstr. 68 ✉ 5600 – ✆ (06412) 78 83 – havannah@sbg.at
geschl. Montag
Rest – Karte 22/35 €
◆ Ein Büro- und Wohnhaus in der Innenstadt beherbergt das südamerikanisch inspirierte Restaurant – dunkles Holz und Lederpolster bestimmen die Einrichtung.

Cavalli

Hans-Kappacher-Str. 8 ✉ 5600 – ✆ (06412) 2 01 80 – cavalli@aon.at
geschl. Dienstag
Rest – Karte 28/43 €
◆ Ein durch dunkles Holz, dunkles Leder und Reitsport-Dekor geprägtes Restaurant mit Barbereich, in dem man auf Tafeln internationale Küche präsentiert. Kleines Mittagsangebot.

In Sankt Johann-Alpendorf Süd: 5 km – Höhe 800 m

Oberforsthof ← Salzachtal und Hochkönig,

(geheizt) Zim, Rest, VISA AE
Alpendorf 11 ✉ 5600 – ✆ (06412) 61 71 – hotel@oberforsthof.at
– Fax (06412) 7429
83 Zim (inkl. ½ P.) – ☼ †77/103 € ††124/176 € ❄ †138/186 € ††246/342 € – 12 Suiten
Rest – *(geschl. Montag – Dienstag)* Menü 42/68 € – Karte 27/63 €
◆ Das familiengeführte, elegant-rustikale Wellnesshotel verfügt über wohnliche, komfortable Zimmer, die alle mit Balkon versehen sind. U. a. Panoramaschwimmbad mit Außenbereich. Das A-la-carte-Restaurant ist die holzgetäfelte Jägerstube.

Zinnkrügl ← Salzachtal und Hochkönig,
Alpendorf 7 ✉ 5600 Rest, VISA
– ✆ (06412) 61 79 – info@zinnkruegl.at – Fax (06412) 8179
50 Zim (inkl. ½ P.) – ☼ †95/110 € ††160/190 € ❄ †115/150 € ††210/280 € – 15 Suiten
Rest – Karte 31/40 €
◆ Alle Zimmer in dem familiär geführten Ferienhotel sind zum Tal hin gelegen und bestechen mit einer fantastischen Aussicht. Sehr schön, großzügig und hell: der Wellnessbereich. Hübsche, unterschiedlich gestaltete Restaurantstuben.

Dorfhotel Tannenhof ← Salzachtal und Hochkönig,
Alpendorf 3 Rest, Rest, VISA
✉ 5600 – ✆ (06412) 52 31 – info@hotel-tannenhof.at
– Fax (06412) 523161
geschl. 13. April – 10. Mai, 9. Nov. – 1. Dez.
76 Zim (inkl. ½ P.) – ☼ †79/99 € ††138/190 € ❄ †110/164 € ††190/310 € – 12 Suiten
Rest – Karte 20/42 €
◆ Alpenländisch ist das Ambiente im Tannenhof – hier befindet sich auch ein netter "Dorfplatz" als Treffpunkt. Mediterran gibt sich das Alpenschlössl mit schönem Spabereich. Ländliches, leicht elegantes Restaurant mit hübscher Sonnenterrasse.

Sonnhof Salzachtal und Hochkönig, Rest,

Alpendorf 16 5600

– (06412) 72 71 – info@hotel-sonnhof.at – Fax (06412) 727135

geschl. 13. April – 9. Mai, 2. Nov. – 6. Dez.

35 Zim (inkl. ½ P.) – 72/102 € 122/160 € 128/142 € 234/262 € – 3 Suiten

Rest – Karte 24/37 €

◆ Neuzeitliches Ferienhotel unter familiärer Leitung mit meist im eleganten Landhausstil gehaltenen Zimmern und Skischule. Wellness-Juniorsuiten mit Kerzenkamin und Whirlwanne. In rustikale Stuben unterteiltes Restaurant mit sehr schöner Sonnenterrasse direkt an der Piste.

Berghof (mit Gästehaus) Salzachtal und Hochkönig, Rest,

Alpendorf 1

5600 – (06412) 61 81 – info@hotel-berghof.com – Fax (06412) 6515

geschl. 15. April – 1. Mai

70 Zim (inkl. ½ P.) – 51/94 € 122/163 € 73/143 € 165/258 € – 11 Suiten

Rest – Karte 18/37 €

◆ Das älteste Hotel im Ort mit wohnlichen, neuzeitlich-alpenländischen Zimmern und großem Garten. Schöner moderner Freizeitbereich. Im Landhaus: kleinere, sehr rustikale Zimmer. Ländlich gestaltetes, z. T. leicht elegantes Restaurant. Nett: die Bar Hochsitz.

Alpendorf Zim, Rest,

Alpendorf 9 5600 – (06412) 62 59

– info@hotel-alpendorf.at – Fax (06412) 62594

geschl. 6. April – 3. Mai, Nov.

40 Zim (inkl. ½ P.) – 72/77 € 110/152 € 101/117 € 164/218 € – 5 Suiten

Rest – Karte 19/37 €

◆ Ein familiär geführtes Haus mit rustikalem Ambiente. Die Zimmer sind mit soliden Holzmöbeln zeitgemäß ausgestattet. Besonders hübsch sind die Suiten unterm Dach. Restaurant in regionstypischem Stil. Gemütlich: Uko's Hoam-Alm, eine Après-Ski-Bar.

SANKT JOHANN IN TIROL – Tirol – 730 J6 – 7 970 Ew – Höhe 680 m – Wintersport: 1 700 m 3 14 7 E4

Wien 371 – Innsbruck 97 – Kitzbühel 14 – Zell am See 62

Poststr. 2, 6380, (05352) 63 33 50, info@ferienregion.at

GC Lärchenhof, Salzburger Str. 65 (05352) 85 75

Spitalskirche zum hl. Nikolaus in der Weitau★

Brückenwirt Rest,

Kaiserstr. 18 6380 – (05352) 6 25 85 – info@brueckenwirt.co.at

– Fax (05352) 6258514

geschl. Ende März – Mitte Mai, Mitte Okt. – Mitte Dez.

45 Zim (inkl. ½ P.) – 50/70 € 100/200 € 80/119 € 140/240 €

Rest *Ambiente* – (Tischbestellung ratsam) (nur Abendessen) Karte 32/43 €

◆ Ein familiengeführtes Hotel im Zentrum mit eleganter Lobby und ganz individuellen Zimmern – besonders geschmackvoll sind die Deluxe-Zimmer und die Juniorsuiten. Das gediegene Restaurant Ambiente wird ergänzt durch ein gemütlich-rustikales kleines Stüberl.

Gruber garni

Gasteiger Str. 18 ✉ 6380 – ☎ (05352) 6 14 61 – info@hotelgruber.at – Fax (05352) 6146133

geschl. April, Nov.

15 Zim – ☼ 50/60 € 76/90 € ❄ 70/80 € 90/110 €

◆ Das familiär geleitete kleine Hotel liegt an der Kitzbüheler Ache mit schönem Spazierweg. Man bietet wohnliche Gästezimmer und Appartements sowie ein gutes Frühstück.

Crystal

Hornweg 5 ✉ 6380 – ☎ (05352) 6 26 30 – info@hotel-crystal.at – Fax (05352) 6263013

geschl. 1. April – 1. Mai, 18. Okt. – 20. Dez.

40 Zim (inkl. ½ P.) – ☼ 60/68 € 98/122 € ❄ 68/84 € 126/168 €

Rest – (nur für Hausgäste)

◆ Der in einer Seitenstraße unweit der Bergbahn gelegene Familienbetrieb verfügt über mit hellen Naturholzmöbeln solide ausgestattete Gästezimmer. Rustikal gestaltete Restaurantstube.

Grander Schupf

Winkl Schattseite 6 (Süd-Ost: 3,5 km, Richtung Fieberbrunn über B 164, vor der Talstation Eichenhof rechts ab, über Tannweg) ✉ 6380 – ☎ (05352) 6 39 25 – info@eichenhof-lifte.at – Fax (05352) 639257

geschl. April, Anfang Dez. – Ostern Montagabend, Dienstagabend sowie Mai. – Anfang Dez. Montag – Dienstag

Rest – Karte 14/36 €

◆ Urige Hüttenatmosphäre herrscht in dem familiengeführten Berggasthaus in 900 m Höhe. Man verarbeitet Produkte aus eigener Landwirtschaft. Im Winter einfache Mittagskarte.

Unsere „Hoffnungsträger" sind die Restaurants, deren Küche wir für die nächste Ausgabe besonders sorgfältig auf eine höhere Auszeichnung hin überprüfen. Der Name dieser Restaurants ist in „rot" gedruckt und zusätzlich auf der Sterne-Liste am Anfang des Buches zu finden.

SANKT KANZIAN AM KLOPEINERSEE – Kärnten – 730 P9 – 4 300 Ew – Höhe 465 m 10 I6

Wien 299 – Klagenfurt 25 – St. Veit an der Glan 43 – Wolfsberg 38

Klopeiner See – Turnersee, Grabelsdorf 94 ☎ (04239) 38 00

In Sankt Kanzian-Klopein

Amerika-Holzer am See (geheizt) Zim, Rest,

Am See IX

✉ 9122 – ☎ (04239) 22 12 – hotel@amerika-holzer.at – Fax (04239) 2158

geschl. Mitte Okt. – Ende April

65 Zim (inkl. ½ P.) – 92/152 € 146/264 € – 12 Suiten

Rest – *(geschl. Mitte Mai – Anfang Okt., nur Abendessen)* Karte 20/51 €

◆ Eine elegante Halle über mehrere Ebenen empfängt Sie in der aus einer Pension entstandenen Hotelanlage. Sehr gepflegte, wohnlich und funktionell gestaltete Zimmer. Kosmetik. Klassisch-stilvolles Restaurant, schöne Terrasse mit Seesicht und Kastanienbäumen.

In Sankt Kanzian-Seelach

Wellnesshotel Mori (mit Gästehaus) (geheizt) Spa P VISA
Kleinseeweg 20
9122 – (04239) 2 80 00 – office@hotel-mori.at
– Fax (04239) 280061
geschl. Jan. – Mitte März
86 Zim (inkl. ½ P.) – 69/93 € 124/170 €
Rest – Karte 17/38 €
◆ Diese kleine Ferienanlage bietet Appartements, Studios und Komfortzimmer sowie einen großzügigen Wellness- und Freizeitbereich mit eigener Driving Range. Gediegenes Restaurant mit zu den Tennisplätzen hin gelegener Terrasse.

Marko (mit Gästehaus) (geheizt) Rest, P VISA
Seenweg 41 9122 – (04239) 2 26 80
– office@hotel-marko.at – Fax (04239) 226850
geschl. Nov. – März
50 Zim (inkl. ½ P.) – 67/93 € 110/162 €
Rest – Karte 15/29 €
◆ Das tadellos gepflegte und gut geführte Hotel bietet u. a. die 4 Themenzimmer Sonne, Mond, Tango und Doppelleben sowie schöne großzügige Zimmer in der Kunstvilla. Bürgerlich eingerichtetes Restaurant.

Sonne Klopeiner See, Rest, P VISA
Westuferstr. 17 9122 – (04239) 23 37
– sonne@sonne.info – Fax (04239) 233788
geschl. 5. Nov. – 15. März
80 Zim (inkl. ½ P.) – 62/87 € 140/236 €
Rest – *(geschl. 5. Nov. – 30. April)* Karte 16/32 €
◆ In dem aus zwei miteinander verbundenen Häusern bestehenden Hotel am See erwarten Sie ein moderner Hallenbereich und wohnliche Zimmer, meist mit Seeblick. Kosmetikangebot. Restaurant mit sehr schöner Terrasse direkt am Ufer.

Lindenhof (geheizt) P VISA
Seenweg 38 9122 – (04239) 37 26 – office@lindenhof-trinkl.at
– Fax (04239) 372610
geschl. Okt. – 10. April
32 Zim (inkl. ½ P.) – 50/70 € 92/120 €
Rest – (nur für Hausgäste) Karte 16/22 €
◆ Das Hotel mit der gelben Fassade liegt recht ruhig in einer Seitenstraße nahe dem Kleinsee. Es verfügt über solide und funktionell eingerichtete Gästezimmer.

In Sankt Kanzian-Unterburg

Ferienhotel Krainz P VISA AE
Ostuferstr. 27 9122 – (04239) 3 31 10
– office@krainz.at – Fax (04239) 331154
geschl. Okt. – April
52 Zim (inkl. ½ P.) – 49/79 € 98/158 € – 10 Suiten
Rest *St. Georg* – Karte 21/36 €
◆ Eine von der Inhaberfamilie gut geführte Ferienadresse mit gediegenrustikalem Ambiente. Zum Haus gehört ein eigener Strandbereich mit Badesteg. Klassisch gehaltenes Restaurant mit Terrasse zum See.

SANKT KATHREIN AM OFFENEGG – Steiermark – 730 S7 – 1 220 Ew – Höhe 972 m – Wintersport: 1 100 m 4 11 **K4**

Wien 182 – Graz 43 – Leoben 73

Eder

St. Kathrein 3 ✉ 8171 – ☎ (03179) 8 23 50 – eder@almenland.at – Fax (03179) 82355
geschl. März 2 Wochen, 9. – 19. Dez.
23 Zim – 49/58 € 98/114 €
Rest – Karte 12/30 €
◆ Neben zeitgemäßen und solide möblierten Gästezimmern bietet Ihnen dieses am Hang gelegene Hotel einen Freizeitbereich mit Kosmetik und verschiedenen Anwendungen. Gemütlich-ländliches Restaurant mit Wintergartenanbau.

Rot = angenehm. Richten Sie sich nach den Symbolen und in Rot.

SANKT LEONHARD IM LAVANTTAL, BAD – Kärnten – 730 Q8 – 4 820 Ew – Höhe 721 m – Wintersport: 1 818 m 7 10 **J5**

Wien 229 – Klagenfurt 78 – Graz 70

Trippolt Zum Bären

Hauptplatz 7 ✉ 9462 – ☎ (04350) 22 57 – Fax (04350) 2257
Rest – *(geschl. Sept. und Sonntag – Montag, Feiertage, Dienstag – Freitag nur Abendessen)* Menü 67 € – Karte 41/52 €
Rest *Bistro* – *(geschl. Sept. und Samstag – Montag, Feiertage, nur Mittagessen)* Karte 25/45 €
Spez. Gefüllte Tascherl mit zweierlei Schaf-Frischkäse und gedämpftem Apfel-Treviso-Salat. Lammkarree mit Gröstl und Kürbisgemüse. Rehfilet mit Honig-Schalotten und pürierten Erdäpfeln.
◆ Ein netter Familienbetrieb: Vater Josef und Sohn Josef kreieren gemeinsam eine ideenreiche Küche auf klassischer Basis. Freundlicher Service durch die Chefin. Mittags werden im Bistro günstige regionale Speisen angeboten.

In Bad Sankt Leonhard-Kliening Süd-West: 6 km in Richtung Wolfsberg, nach 2 km rechts ab Richtung Klippitztörl:

Moselebauer

(geheizt) Zim, Rest,
Kliening 30
✉ 9462 – ☎ (04350) 23 33 – moselebauer@moselebauer.at – Fax (04350) 233348
82 Zim (inkl. ½ P.) – 83/120 € 136/210 € – 6 Suiten
Rest – Karte 18/39 €
◆ Ein abgelegenes Seminarhotel in einem kleinen Ortsteil mit funktionellen Gästezimmern, Spa und Beauty sowie der "Erlebniswelt" mit Bogenschießen, Quads und Kletterwand. Hell gestalteter Restaurantbereich in ländlichem Stil.

SANKT LEONHARD IM PITZTAL – Tirol – 730 E7 – 1 480 Ew – Höhe 1 370 m 6 **C6**

Wien 524 – Innsbruck 81 – Imst 28 – Sankt Anton 70
in St. Leonhard-Mandarfen, ✉ 6481, ☎ (05414) 8 69 99, info@pitztal.com

In Sankt Leonhard-Mandarfen **Süd: 11,5 km – Höhe 1 680 m**

Wildspitze
Rest, Rest,
Mandarfen 46 ✉ 6481 – ✆ (05413) 8 62 07
– info@verwoehnhotels.at – Fax (05413) 8630360
geschl. Mitte Mai – Ende Juni
54 Zim (inkl. ½ P.) – ☼ 80/100 € 160/190 € ❄ 91/220 €
162/240 € – 20 Suiten
Rest – (nur für Hausgäste)
♦ Das Alpenhotel am Talende überzeugt mit hübschen, wohnlichen Zimmern und Suiten sowie dem auf über 1100 qm angelegten Spabereich "Wildspitz-Alpinarium".

Vier Jahreszeiten
Rest,
Mandarfen 73 ✉ 6481 – ✆ (05413) 8 63 61
– info@hotel-vier-jahreszeiten.at – Fax (05413) 863615
geschl. Mitte Mai – Mitte Juni
67 Zim (inkl. ½ P.) – ☼ 75/86 € 132/158 € ❄ 95/129 €
174/228 €
Rest – (nur für Hausgäste)
♦ In dem familiengeführten Hotel erwarten Sie freundliche Zimmer, darunter auch Allergikerzimmer mit Holzfußboden. Besonders modern und schön: "Elementesuite" nach Feng Shui.

Mittagskogel
Rest,
Mandarfen 86 ✉ 6481 – ✆ (05413) 8 63 86
– info@mittagskogel.at – Fax (05413) 8638633
geschl. Mitte Mai – Anfang Juli
33 Zim (inkl. ½ P.) – ☼ 73/81 € 126/150 € ❄ 92/124 €
164/228 €
Rest – (nur Abendessen) Karte 16/33 €
♦ Hell eingerichtete Zimmer mit gutem Platzangebot und Balkon, einige Familienappartements sowie ein nett gestalteter Badebereich sprechen für dieses Haus.

Rifflsee
Rest,
Mandarfen 52 ✉ 6481 – ✆ (05413) 8 62 96 – rifflsee@pitztal.at
– Fax (05413) 8629620
geschl. Mitte Mai – Anfang Juli
26 Zim (inkl. ½ P.) – ☼ 55/59 € 96/108 € ❄ 69/111 €
118/202 €
Rest – (nur Abendessen für Hausgäste)
♦ Das gepflegte Alpenhotel liegt direkt an der Rifflseebahn. Wohnliche Zimmer und die freundlichen Gastgeber machen es zu einer angenehmen Urlaubsadresse.

In Sankt Leonhard-Neurur **Süd: 5,5 km – Höhe 1 500 m**

Sturpen
Neurur 97 ✉ 6481 – ✆ (05413) 8 72 70 – hotel@sturpen-pitztal.at
– Fax (05413) 872707
geschl. Mai – Juni
24 Zim (inkl. ½ P.) – ☼ 32/36 € 54/62 € ❄ 46/61 € 76/110 €
Rest – (nur Abendessen für Hausgäste)
♦ In dem familiengeführten Hotel am Pitzbach stehen gepflegte, mit solidem Mobiliar in ländlichem Stil eingerichtete Zimmer für Sie bereit.

In Sankt Leonhard-Plangeross Süd: 10 km – Höhe 1 615 m

Gasthof Kirchenwirt

Rest,

Plangeross 10 ✉ 6481 – ✆ (05413) 8 62 15 – hotel@kirchenwirt-pitztal.at – Fax (05413) 862155
geschl. Mai – Juni
24 Zim (inkl. ½ P.) – ☼ 53/76 € 84/130 € ❄ 57/148 € 92/144 €
Rest – (nur Abendessen für Hausgäste)
◆ In nettem regionstypischem Ambiente wohnt man in diesem liebenswerten Haus in gemütlichen, mit Holz ausgestatteten Zimmern. Zwei Gästezimmer verfügen über einen Kachelofen.

Steinkogel

Rest, P VISA

Plangeross 85 ✉ 6481 – ✆ (05413) 8 50 95 – pension@steinkogel.at – Fax (05413) 850955
geschl. Mai
20 Zim (inkl. ½ P.) – 58/69 € 94/115 €
Rest – (nur Abendessen für Hausgäste)
◆ Etwas unterhalb der Talstraße liegt diese familiengeführte kleine Pension, die mit hellem Holz alpenländisch möblierte Zimmer beherbergt.

In Sankt Leonhard-Weisswald Süd: 8,5 km – Höhe 1 560 m

Sport- und Vitalhotel Seppl

(geheizt) Spa P VISA

Weisswald 41 ✉ 6481 – ✆ (05413) 8 62 20 – office@seppl.at – Fax (05413) 86352
geschl. Anfang Mai – Mitte Juni
60 Zim (inkl. ½ P.) – ☼ 73/78 € 160/190 € ❄ 85/120 € 170/260 €
Rest – (nur für Hausgäste)
◆ Ein am Pitzbach gelegenes Alpenhotel mit zeitlos und wohnlich gestalteten Gästezimmern – einige neuzeitlich und leicht elegant im Landhausstil eingerichtet.

SANKT MARTIN BEI LOFER – Salzburg – 730 K6 – 1 160 Ew – Höhe 640 m – Wintersport: 1 8 F4

Wien 336 – Salzburg 44 – Zell am See 35 – Bad Reichenhall 28

Gasthof Bad Hochmoos

P VISA

St. Martin 3 (Wildmoossiedlung, Nord: 1 km)
✉ 5092 – ✆ (06588) 8 22 60 – hochmoos@aon.at – Fax (06588) 822623
geschl. April 2 Wochen, Nov.
59 Zim (inkl. ½ P.) – ☼ 49/67 € 88/110 € ❄ 51/77 € 92/150 €
Rest – Karte 17/35 €
◆ Das mehrfach gewachsene Hotel ist in sechster Generation unter Familienleitung und bietet solide, mit braunem Mobiliar oder hellem Naturholz eingerichtete Zimmer. Unterteilter Restaurantbereich in neuzeitlich-ländlichem Stil.

Der Stern ✿ zeichnet Restaurants mit exzellenter Küche aus.
Er wird an Häuser vergeben, für die man gerne einen Umweg in Kauf nimmt!

SANKT MICHAEL IM LUNGAU – Salzburg – 730 M7 – 3 590 Ew – Höhe 1 075 m – Wintersport: 2 360 m 1 39 9 H5

Wien 297 – Salzburg 108 – Spittal a.d. Drau 45
Raikaplatz 242, 5582, (06477) 89 13, info@stmichael.eu
Lungau, Feldnergasse 165 (06477) 74 48
Radstädter Tauernstr.★ – Schloss Moosham★ (Ost: 6 km)

Eggerwirt (geheizt)
Kaltbachstr. 5 5582 – (06477) 8 22 40
– office@eggerwirt.com – Fax (06477) 822455
geschl. Mitte April – Mitte Mai, Mitte Nov. – Mitte Dez.
75 Zim (inkl. ½ P.) – 116/141 € 232/282 € 118/165 € 236/330 €
Rest – Karte 20/31 €
◆ Das gut geführte Hotel bietet wohnliche Zimmer mit gutem Platzangebot, teils in Südlage und mit Balkon. Großzügiger Wellnessbereich. Ein Naturschwimmteich ergänzt das Freibad. Geräumiger unterteilter Restaurantbereich im alpenländischen Stil.

Am Katschberg Süd: 6 km – Höhe 1 650 m

Falkensteiner Hotel Cristallo (geheizt) Rest,
Katschberghöhe 6
9863 Rennweg – (04734) 3 19 – cristallo@falkensteiner.com
– Fax (04734) 319510
geschl. 5. April – 9. Mai, 3. Nov. – 5. Dez.
130 Zim (inkl. ½ P.) – 73/87 € 116/144 € 86/181 € 142/332 € – 6 Suiten
Rest – (nur für Hausgäste)
◆ Teil der großzügigen Hotelanlage ist der geschmackvoll-moderne Spabereich auf ca. 2000 qm. Familienzimmer und "Falky Land" für Kinder machen das Haus für Familien interessant. In verschiedene regionstypische Stuben unterteiltes Restaurant.

Appart-Hotel Hutter garni
Katschberghöhe 423 5582 St. Michael – (04734) 62 70
– traumurlaub@hutter.at – Fax (04734) 62735
geschl. April – Juni, Okt. – Dez.
23 Zim – 32/38 € 48/58 € 44/73 € 90/150 €
◆ Mit seinen als Appartements angelegten und mit hellem Holz wohnlich eingerichteten Zimmern ist das schön auf einer Anhöhe gelegene Hotel besonders für Familien geeignet.

Sunshine Hotel Sonnalm Zim, Rest,
Katschberghöhe 333
5582 St. Michael – (04734) 49 10 – info@hotel-sonnalm.at
– Fax (04734) 491439
geschl. 7. April - 9. Mai, 26. Okt. – 13. Dez.
51 Zim (inkl. ½ P.) – 50/103 € 86/138 € 75/186 € 134/248 € – 3 Suiten
Rest – (nur für Hausgäste)
◆ Die Lage direkt am Skilift spricht für das Hotel mit der typischen Balkonfassade. Besonders schön ist die Sicht von den Zimmern nach Norden. Suiten mit Sauna und Whirlwanne.

Alpengasthof Bacher ← Bergpanorama,
Katschberg 42 ✉ 5582 St. Michael
– ✆ (04734) 3 18 – gasthof-bacher@sbg.at – Fax (04734) 3184
geschl. 7. April – 14. Juni, Okt. – 1. Dez.
26 Zim (inkl. ½ P.) – ☼ 30/35 € 60/70 € ❄ 48/77 € 80/138 €
Rest – Karte 18/25 €
◆ An einer Skipiste, etwas oberhalb der Katschberghöhe liegt dieses gut unterhaltene Hotel, das mit Naturholzmobiliar ländlich gestaltete Zimmer bietet. Im Restaurant serviert man eine bürgerlich-regionale Küche.

Außerhalb Ost: 2,5 km Richtung Tamsweg:

Stofflerwirt Zim,
Hutterstr. 11 ✉ 5582 St. Michael – ✆ (06477) 82 93 – info@stofflerwirt.at – Fax (06477) 82933
geschl. 1. – 26. April, 24. Okt. – 14. Nov.
28 Zim – ☼ 48/55 € 84/96 € ❄ 50/67 € 86/124 € – ½ P 10 €
Rest – Karte 14/27 €
◆ Ein erweiterter familiengeführter Gasthof, der in einem neueren Anbau über schöne kleine Suiten und Juniorsuiten verfügt. Nett ist der helle Ruhebereich nach Süden hin. Ländliches Ambiente im Restaurant. Sonnenterrasse zur Südseite.

SANKT OSWALD – Niederösterreich – 730 R4 – 1 140 Ew – Höhe 658 m

3 **J2**

Wien 124 – St. Pölten 67 – Krems 59 – Amstetten 42

Landgasthof Fischl (mit Gästehaus) ← (geheizt) Zim, Rest,
St. Oswald 11
✉ 3684 – ✆ (07415) 72 95 – fischl@hoteldesgluecks.at
– Fax (07415) 729535
geschl. 17. – 25. Dez., 4. – 10. Feb., 17. – 23. März, 28. Juli – 3. Aug.
30 Zim – 62 € 108 € – ½ P 15 €
Rest – *(geschl. Dienstag)* (nur für Hausgäste)
◆ Mitten im Dorf liegt der über 300 Jahre alte Landgasthof, der gerne für Tagungen genutzt wird. Die Zimmer sind mit hellem Holz möbliert und funktionell ausgestattet.

SANKT PAUL IM LAVANTTAL – Kärnten – 730 Q8 – 3 680 Ew – Höhe 400 m

10 **J6**

Wien 281 – Klagenfurt 56 – Wolfsberg 19
Stiftsgebäude (Schatzhaus Kärntens★★)

Gasthaus Traube
Hauptstr. 4 ✉ 9470 – ✆ (04357) 20 87 – richard@poppmeier.co.at
– Fax (04357) 3901
geschl. Jan. 3 Wochen, Donnerstag, Sonn- und Feiertage abends
Rest – Karte 15/30 €
◆ Schon viele Generationen befindet sich das Wirtshaus von 1510 in Familienbesitz – ein teils neuzeitlich, teils rustikaler gestaltetes Restaurant mit Gewölbedecke.

SANKT PÖLTEN L – Niederösterreich – 730 S4 – 49 130 Ew – Höhe 267 m – Wintersport: 3 K2

- Wien 63 – Krems 28 – Baden 63 – Melk 29
- Rathausplatz 1, ✉ 3100, ☎ (02742) 35 33 54, tourismus@st-poelten.gv.at
- 18 St. Pölten-Schloss Goldegg, Schloss Goldegg 1 ☎ (02741) 73 60

Veranstaltungen

23.05. – 01.06.: Volksfest
04.07.: Hauptstadtfest

- Institut der Englischen Fräulein★ – Niederösterreichisches Landesmuseum★ **M** Y – Dom Mariä Himmelfahrt★ – Diözesan-Museum★ (Stiftsbibliothek★) – Herrenplatz★ X
- Stift Herzogenburg★ (Nord: 12 km) – Stift Melk★★★ (West: 24 km)

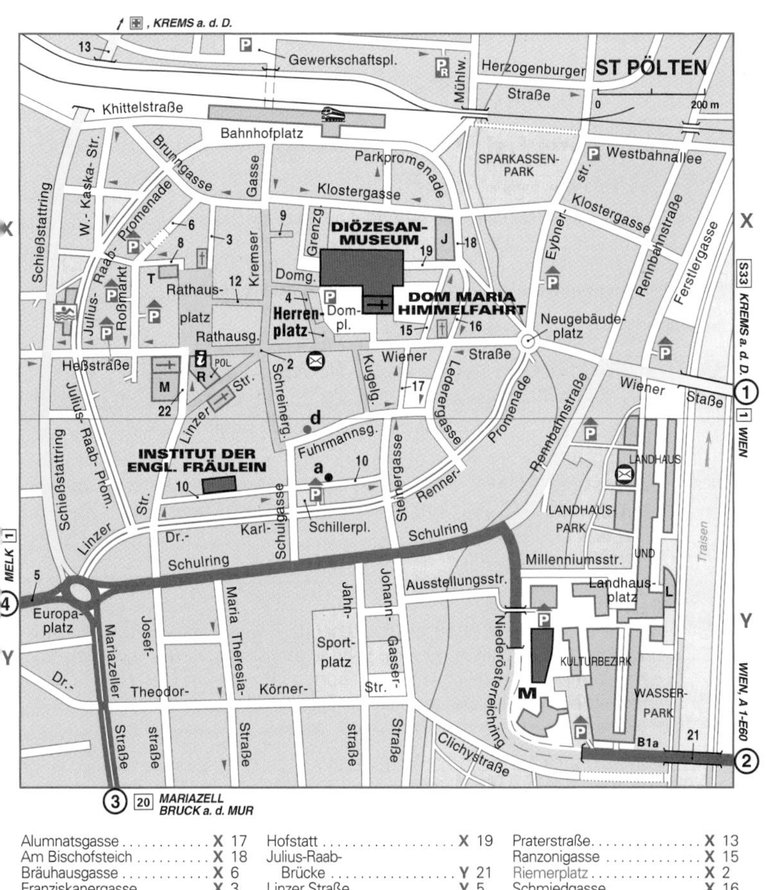

Alumnatsgasse	X 17	Hofstatt	X 19	Praterstraße	X 13
Am Bischofsteich	X 18	Julius-Raab-Brücke	Y 21	Ranzonigasse	X 15
Bräuhausgasse	X 6	Linzer Straße	Y 5	Riemerplatz	X 2
Franziskanergasse	X 3	Marktgasse	X 12	Schmiedgasse	X 16
Heitzlergasse	X 8	Prandtauerstraße	X 22	Schneckgasse	Y 10
Herrengasse	X 4			Stiftsgasse	X 9

Metropol Zim,

Schillerplatz 1 ✉ 3100 – ☎ (02742) 70 70 00 – metropol@austria-trend.at – Fax (02742) 70700133 Y **a**

87 Zim – 123/263 € 143/313 € – 5 Suiten

Rest – (nur für Hausgäste)

◆ In einem modernen Geschäftshaus in der Stadtmitte befindet sich dieses Hotel. Business-Gäste schätzen die neuzeitlich und funktionell eingerichteten Zimmer.

Galerie

Fuhrmanngasse 1 ✉ 3100 – ☎ (02742) 35 13 05 – restaurant@langeneder.at – Fax (02742) 351305

geschl. 11. – 16. Feb., 15. – 25. März, Aug. 3 Wochen und Samstag – Sonntag, Feiertage X **d**

Rest – Menü 24/44 € – Karte 21/48 €

◆ Ein gediegenes Restaurant mit schön eingedeckten Tischen erwartet Sie in dem ehemaligen Fuhrmannshaus a. d. J. 1596. Der Chef gibt am Tisch Tagesempfehlungen.

In Sankt Pölten-Ratzersdorf **Nord-Ost: 4 km über Wiener Straße X:**

Gaststätte Figl

Hauptplatz 4 ✉ 3100 – ☎ (02742) 25 74 02 – gaststaettefigl@aon.at – Fax (02742) 27523

geschl. Jan. 2 Wochen, 11. -27. Aug. und Samstag – Sonntag, Feiertage

Rest – Karte 18/49 €

◆ Familie Reisinger führt dieses gemütliche rustikale Wirtshaus mit überwiegend regionalem Angebot. Nett: die Innenhofterrasse.

SANKT RUPRECHT AN DER RAAB – Steiermark – 730 S7 – 1 880 Ew – Höhe 400 m 11 **K5**

Wien 175 – Graz 37 – Bruck an der Mur 72 – Hartberg 40

Gartenhotel Ochensberger

Untere Hauptstr. 181 Zim,

✉ 8181 – ☎ (03178) 5 13 20 – gartenhotel@ochensberger.at – Fax (03178) 51324

geschl. über Weihnachten

61 Zim (inkl. ½ P.) – 80/101 € 138/180 €

Rest – Karte 13/37 €

◆ Eine aus mehreren Häusern bestehende Hotelanlage mit ganz individuell gestalteten Gästezimmern. Sehr schön ist die Gartenlandschaft, zu der auch ein Naturschwimmteich gehört. Im Restaurant bietet man überwiegend bürgerliche Speisen.

SANKT SEBASTIAN – Steiermark – 730 R5 – 1 180 Ew – Höhe 850 m 3 **J3**

Wien 127 – Graz 122 – Bruck a.d. Mur 66 – Sankt Pölten 73

Lurgbauer mit Zim Zim,

Lurg 1 (Nord: 4,5 km, Richtung St. Pölten über B 20, nach 3 km rechts ab)

✉ 3224 – ☎ (03882) 37 18 – lurgbauer@mariazell.at

5 Zim – 96 € 124 €
Rest – *(geschl. Montag – Dienstag, Okt. – April Montag – Donnerstag)* (Tischbestellung erforderlich) Menü 25 € (mittags)/45 €
♦ Diese nette ländlich-rustikale Adresse ist ein Bauernhof mit eigenen Rindern, Schweinen und Hühnern sowie Hausschlachtung. Idyllisch ist die recht abgeschiedene Lage am Wald. Gemütliche, mit Naturmaterialien eingerichtete Gästezimmer im alten Bauernhaus.

SANKT STEFAN OB STAINZ – Steiermark – 730 R8 – 2 200 Ew – Höhe 404 m

10 **K5**

Wien 213 – Graz 28 – Wolfsberg 54 – Leibnitz 49

Wirtshaus Jagawirt

Zim,

Sommereben 2 (Nord-West: 6 km, Richtung Stainz, dann rechts ab Richtung Greisdorf und Reini) ✉ *8511 –* ✆ *(03143) 81 05 – goach@jagawirt.at – Fax (03143) 81054*
geschl. 2. Jan. – 1. April
15 Zim – 45/50 € 90/100 € – ½ P 21 €
Rest – *(geschl. Mittwoch)* Karte 20/31 €
♦ Schön liegt das alte Wirtshaus mit wohnlich-rustikalen Zimmern und 2 Appartements außerhalb am Wald. Schaf- und Schweinehaltung unterstreicht den ländlichen Charakter. Mit viel Holz und Zierrat behaglich eingerichtete Gaststuben.

Landgasthof Gerngroß mit Zim

Zim, VISA

St. Stefan 9 ✉ *8511 –* ✆ *(03463) 8 11 88 – office@landgasthof-gerngross.at – Fax (03463) 8118815*
geschl. 7. Jan. – 23. Feb. und Sonntagabend – Mittwochmittag
4 Zim – 40 € 60 €
Rest – Menü 33 € – Karte 18/32 €
♦ In dem von Familie Gerngroß geführten Landgasthof bietet man in netten Stuben mit ländlichem Ambiente gute regionale Küche. Zum Übernachten stehen einige solide und gepflegte Gästezimmer bereit.

SANKT VEIT AM VOGAU – Steiermark – 730 S8 – 1 860 Ew – Höhe 600 m

11 **K5**

Wien 232 – Graz 46 – Maribor 24

Thaller

Am Kirchplatz 4 ✉ *8423 –* ✆ *(03453) 25 08 – office@gasthaus-thaller.at – Fax (03453) 2508*
geschl. 17. – 30. März und Dienstag – Mittwoch
Rest – Menü 48/62 € – Karte 14/40 €
♦ Schmackhafte regionale Küche bietet der Gasthof der Familie Thaller in der Ortsmitte. Man sitzt in der getäfelten, mit Bildern dekorierten Gaststube oder im netten Gastgarten.

SANKT VEIT AN DER GLAN – Kärnten – 730 P8 – 12 840 Ew – Höhe 550 m

9 **I6**

Wien 280 – Klagenfurt 21 – Villach 55
Hauptplatz 23, ✉ 9300, ✆ (04212) 5 55 56 68, city@stveit.carinthia.at
Hauptplatz★ – Rathaus★
Burg Hochosterwitz★ (Ost: 5 km) – Schloss Frauenstein★ (Nord-West: 5 km) – Magdalensberg★ (Süd-Ost: 15 km) – Gurk★★ (Nord: 20 km)

La Torre
Grabenstr. 39 ✉ 9300 – ✆ (04212) 3 92 50 – latorre@aon.at – Fax (04212) 39250
geschl. Sonntag – Montagmittag, Sept. – Nov. sowie Jan.- Juni Sonntag – Montag
Rest – Menü 41/58 € – Karte 35/45 €
♦ Ein ehemaliger Wehrturm von 1532 beherbergt heute ein rustikal-elegantes italienisches Restaurant mit dunkler Holzdecke und Kamin. Sehr freundlicher Service durch den Patron.

SANKT VEIT IM DEFEREGGENTAL – Tirol – 730 J8 – 800 Ew – Höhe 1 495 m – Wintersport: 7 F6

Wien 454 – Innsbruck 182 – Lienz 34 – Bruneck 54

An der Straße nach Sankt Jakob West: 4 km, nach Bruggen links:

Gourmethotel Defereggental (mit Gästehaus)
Bruggen 84
✉ 9962 St. Veit im Deferengental – ✆ (04879) 6 64 40 – info@hotel-defereggental.com – Fax (04879) 6644444
geschl. 30. März – 9. Mai, 5. Okt. – 19. Dez.
74 Zim (inkl. ½ P.) – 93/117 € 156/184 € 110/160 € 180/250 € – 18 Suiten
Rest – (nur Abendessen) Karte 26/34 €
♦ Eine private Zufahrt führt Sie zu diesem neuzeitlichen Hotel mit Balkonfassade. Die Suiten, Maisonetten und Doppelzimmer sind freundlich und wohnlich gestaltet. Gratis Skibus. Das Restaurant ist in verschiedene gemütlich-alpenländische Stuben unterteilt.

SANKT VEIT IM PONGAU – Salzburg – 730 L6 – 3 330 Ew – Höhe 763 m – Wintersport: 1 8 G5

Wien 360 – Salzburg 64 – Bischofshofen 16

Sonnhof
Kirchweg 2 ✉ 5621 – ✆ (06415) 43 23 – sonnhof@verwoehnhotel.at – Fax (06414) 731928
geschl. 29. März - 25. Mai, 21. Okt. – 20. Dez.
21 Zim (inkl. ½ P.) – 68/78 € 108/136 € 73/88 € 120/168 €
Rest – *(geschl. Donnerstag, Montag – Samstag nur Abendessen)* (Tischbestellung ratsam) Karte 25/36 €
♦ Das familiär geführte Landhotel bietet mit hellen Naturholzmöbeln und freundlichen Farben wohnlich gestaltete Zimmer mit gutem Platzangebot. In rustikal bis eleganten Restauranträumen wird eine leichte regionale Küche serviert. Terrasse mit schöner Aussicht.

Metzgerwirt (mit Anbau) Zim, Rest,
Markt 5 ✉ 5621 – ✆ (06415) 74 14 – office@metzgerwirt-stveit.com – Fax (06415) 741412
geschl. 7. – 26. April, 16. Nov. – 4. Dez.
36 Zim (inkl. ½ P.) – 66/89 € 98/152 € 69/98 € 108/174 €
Rest – Karte 13/30 €
♦ Ein Gasthof in der Ortsmitte mit einfachen, aber gepflegten Zimmern. In einem nach biologischen Gesichtspunkten gestalteten Anbau sind die Zimmer geräumiger und neuzeitlicher. Gaststube in rustikalem Stil.

SANKT WOLFGANG IM SALZKAMMERGUT – Oberösterreich

– 730 M5 – **2 800 Ew** – **Höhe 539 m** 9 **G4**

Wien 280 – Linz 119 – Salzburg 49 – Gmunden 48

Au 140, ✉ 5360, ✆ (06138) 80 03, info@wolfgangsee.at

Veranstaltungen

19.10.: Int. Lauf rund um den Wolfgangsee

Wolfgangsee★★ – Pfarrkirche★★ (Michael-Pacher-Altar★★★, Schwanthaler-Doppelaltar★)

Salzkammergut★★★ – Schafberg★★ (mit) Nord: 5 km

Im Weissen Rössl

Wolfgangsee und Berge, (geheizt) Rest, VISA AE

Markt 74 ✉ 5360 – ✆ (06138) 2 30 60 – welcome@weissesroessl.at – Fax (06138) 230641

geschl. 24. März – 27. April, 3. Nov. – 20. Nov. (Hotel)

73 Zim – ☼ 110/145 € 150/250 € ❄ 100/145 € 130/250 € – ½ P 25 € – 3 Suiten

Rest *Kaiserterrasse* – *(geschl. 24. März – 1. Mai, 2. – 28. Nov., nur Abendessen)* Karte 34/46 €

Rest *Seerestaurant* – *(geschl. 24. März – 1. Mai, 2. – 28. Nov.)* Karte 25/41 €

♦ Berühmt wurde das Haus durch die gleichnamige Operette von Ralph Benatzky. Schön: die Lage am See sowie sehr individuelle, teils antik möblierte Zimmer. Beauty-Bereich. Kaiserterrasse mit gediegenem Ambiente und klassischer Küche. Angenehm hell: Seerestaurant.

Landhaus zu Appesbach

Wolfgangsee und Berge, Zim, Rest, VISA AE

Au 18

✉ 5360 – ✆ (06138) 22 09 – office@appesbach.com – Fax (06138) 220914

geschl. 7. Jan. – 7. März

27 Zim – ☼ 120/215 € 150/245 € ❄ 100/215 € 130/245 €

Rest – (nur Abendessen für Hausgäste, im Winter Garni)

♦ In malerischer Lage am See befindet sich das einstige Herrenhaus mit gediegen-eleganten Zimmern. Das Prunkstück des Hauses ist die großzügige Windsor-Suite. Bootsverleih.

Seehotel Cortisen

Rest, Rest, VISA AE

Markt 15 ✉ 5360

– ✆ (06138) 2 37 60 – hotel@cortisen.at – Fax (06138) 237644

geschl. 16. März – 26. April, 20. Okt. – 28. Nov.

35 Zim – ☼ 105/145 € 140/195 € ❄ 95/125 € 130/190 € – ½ P 25 €

Rest – (nur für Hausgäste)

♦ Neben der Seelage sprechen auch geschmackvolle Zimmer in angenehmen Farben für das Haus. Schöner Loungebereich am See. Kosmetik-/Massage. Kinder erst ab 12 Jahren willkommen.

Zum Weissen Hirschen

Wolfgangsee und Berge, VISA

Markt 73 ✉ 5360

– ✆ (06138) 22 38 – office@weisserhirsch.at – Fax (06138) 223888

geschl. 7. Jan. – 8. Feb., 3. – 27. Nov.

23 Zim – 70/142 € 108/174 € – ½ P 22 €

Rest – Karte 15/39 €

♦ Das Hotel bietet wohnliche, neuzeitlich eingerichtete Gästezimmer, meist mit Balkon und fast alle mit direktem Seeblick. Dachterrasse mit Whirlwannen und Zugang zum Strandbad. Rustikal gestaltetes Restaurant.

Furian < Zim, Rest, P VISA MC AE
Stern-Allee 196 ✉ 5360 – ☎ (06138) 80 18 – hotel-furian@aon.at – Fax (06138) 801830
geschl. 26. Okt. – 26. Nov.
19 Zim – ☼ 80/90 € 140/180 € ❄ 70/90 € 140/180 € – ½ P 32 €
Rest – *(geschl. 26. März – 2. Mai, nur Abendessen)* (Tischbestellung ratsam) Menü 32 €
◆ Ein Familienbetrieb mit neuzeitlich-gediegenen Zimmern und eleganten Suiten. Eigene Wasserski- und Wakeboard-Schule sowie Boot- und Fahrradverleih. Kleiner Badestrand mit Bar. Teil des Restaurants: ein modern-puristisch gestalteter Raum. Beheizte Terrasse.

Margaretha < Wolfgangsee und Berge, Zim, P VISA MC
Seepromenade 67 ✉ 5360 – ☎ (06138) 23 79 – hotel@wolfgangsee.com – Fax (06138) 237922
geschl. Jan. – April, Nov.
36 Zim – 80/100 € 120/180 € – ½ P 22 €
Rest – Karte 19/35 €
◆ Die wohnlichen Zimmer dieses regionstypischen Hotels sind hell-elegant mit leicht rustikaler Note eingerichtet. Das Strandbad mit Booten ist nur ein paar Schritte entfernt. In ländlichem Stil gehaltenes Restaurant mit schöner Terrasse.

Seevilla garni < P VISA MC AE
Markt 17 ✉ 5360 – ☎ (06138) 2 00 55 – welcome@seevilla.co.at – Fax (06138) 200556
geschl. Feb. – März, Nov.
35 Zim – 95/135 € 140/210 €
◆ Hier wohnt man direkt am See in freundlichen Zimmern, meist mit Seeblick. Garten mit Liegewiese am Wasser. Das Freizeitangebot kann der Gast im Schwesterhotel Scalaria nutzen.

XX **Joseph's** VISA MC AE
Markt 87 ✉ 5360 – ☎ (06138) 2 04 60 – info@dieneuenamsee.at – Fax (06138) 20475
geschl. Jan. – Feb. und Dienstag
Rest – *(nur Abendessen)* (Tischbestellung ratsam) Karte 30/43 €
◆ Sehr freundlich bewirtet man Sie in diesem sympathischen Restaurant im Ortskern mit regionalen wie internationalen Speisen, die auf einer großen Schultafel präsentiert werden.

SAUTENS IM ÖTZTAL – Tirol – 730 E7 – 1 280 Ew – Höhe 810 m 6 C5

Wien 495 – Innsbruck 52 – Imst 17 – Seefeld 36
✉ 6432, ☎ (05252) 65 11, info@sautens.com

Sporthotel Der Ritzlerhof < (geheizt) Rest, P VISA MC
Ritzlerhof 1 ✉ 6432 – ☎ (05252) 6 26 80 – info@ritzlerhof.com – Fax (05252) 626857
geschl. 6. April – 10. Mai, 12. Okt. – 6. Dez.
40 Zim (inkl. ½ P.) – ☼ 60/90 € 96/176 € ❄ 54/112 € 84/224 €
Rest – Karte 17/35 €
◆ Schön liegt das familiengeführte Haus am Waldrand oberhalb des Ortes. Gepflegte, unterschiedlich geschnittene Zimmer und Freizeitangebot mit Volleyball und kleinem Sportplatz. Mit viel hellem Holz neuzeitlich gestaltetes Restaurant.

Gisela Zim, Rest, VISA

Dorfstr. 23 ✉ 6432 – ✆ (05252) 62 15 – info@gisela.at – Fax (05252) 621555 – geschl. 1. Nov. – 20. Dez.

30 Zim (inkl. ½ P) – ☼ 66/79 € 110/136 € ❄ 76/121 € 130/220 € 3 Suiten – **Rest** – (nur Abendessen für Hausgäste)

◆ Dieses gewachsene Haus ist ein tadellos gepflegter Familienbetrieb, in dem Sie ein freundlicher, heller Empfangsbereich sowie solide, wohnlich eingerichtete Zimmer erwarten.

Daniel Berge, VISA

Haderlehnerstr. 20 ✉ 6432 – ✆ (05252) 62 72 – info@hotel-daniel.com – Fax (05252) 62727

geschl. 12. April – 10. Mai, 19. Okt. – 10. Dez.

29 Zim (inkl. ½ P) – ☼ 59/83 € 100/138 € ❄ 60/100 € 102/196 €

Rest – Karte 17/33 €

◆ Etwas oberhalb des Ortes liegt das alpenländische Gasthaus mit seinen wohnlich-ländlichen, z. T. mit Bauernmöbeln ausgestatteten Zimmern. Netter Garten mit Spielplatz.

SCHÄRDING – Oberösterreich – 730 M3 – 5 060 Ew – Höhe 313 m 1 G2

- Wien 261 – Linz 100 – Ried im Innkreis 33 – Passau 18
- Innbruckstr. 29, ✉ 4780, ✆ (07712) 4 30 00, info.schaerding@oberoesterreich.at
- Celtic Golf Course Schärding – Taufkirchen/Pram, Maad 2 ✆ (07719) 8 11 00
- Über den Dächern von Passau – Freinberg 74, ✆ (07713) 84 94
- Stadtplatz (Silberzeile★)

Forstinger garni VISA AE

Unterer Stadtplatz 3 ✉ 4780 – ✆ (07712) 2 30 20 – info@hotelforstinger.at – Fax (07712) 23023

24 Zim – 75/95 € 115/145 €

◆ In dem historischen Stadthaus stehen zeitlos eingerichtete Gästezimmer sowie zwei rustikal-antik gestaltete Räume zur Verfügung. Aufwändiger: die Appartements im Nebenhaus.

Biedermeier Hof Rest, Rest, VISA AE

Passauer Str. 8 ✉ 4780 – ✆ (07712) 3 06 40 – biedermeier-hof@aon.at – Fax (07712) 44648

29 Zim – 44/47 € 72/82 € – ½ P 13 €

Rest – *(nur Abendessen)* Karte 14/21 €

◆ Aus einem alten Gehöft ist dieses gepflegte familiengeführte Hotel mit soliden Gästezimmern geworden. Es werden auch Leihfahrräder angeboten. Eine Holzbalkendecke und Backsteinwände unterstreichen das rustikale Ambiente im Restaurant.

Kupferpfandl VISA AE

Stögergassl 3 ✉ 4780 – ✆ (07712) 20 33 – restaurant@kupferpfandl.at – Fax (07712) 20335

geschl. Mitte Feb. 2 Wochen, Anfang Sept. 2 Wochen und Dienstag sowie Jan. – März auch Sonntagabend

Rest – Menü 35/47 € – Karte 21/39 €

◆ In der Nähe des Stadtplatzes liegt das in freundlich-bürgerlichem Stil eingerichtete Restaurant mit Gewölbedecke und offener Küche. Regionale und internationale Speisen.

SCHALLERBACH, BAD – Oberösterreich – 730 N4 – 3 280 Ew – Höhe 308 m – Wintersport: – Kurort 2 H3

Wien 203 – Linz 42 – Wels 16 – Ried im Innkreis 43

Promenade 2, 4701, (07249) 42 07 10, info@vitalwelt.at

Paradiso (freier Zugang zur Therme) Rest,

Promenade 1
(im EurothermeResort) 4701 – (07249) 44 07 20
– reservierung@eurotherme.at – Fax (07249) 440790
150 Zim (inkl. ½ P.) – 120/145 € 190/240 €
8 Suiten
Rest – (nur Abendessen für Hausgäste)

◆ Die großzügige Hotelanlage etwas außerhalb des kleinen Ortes bietet wohnliche Zimmer mit von Etage zu Etage wechselnder Farbgestaltung sowie direkten Anschluss an die Therme.

Parkhotel Stroissmüller (geheizt)

Badstr. 2 4701 – (07249) 4 87 81
– parkhotel@stroismueller.at – Fax (07249) 487818
geschl. 20. – 25. Dez.
41 Zim – 57/67 € 110/120 € – ½ P 11 €
Rest – Karte 17/29 €

◆ Die zentrale Lage – 500 m von den Thermen entfernt – sowie mit Kirschholzmobiliar solide eingerichtete, neuzeitliche Gästezimmer sprechen für dieses Haus. Gepflegtes Restaurant mit elegantem Touch.

SCHATTWALD – Tirol – 730 D6 – 420 Ew – Höhe 1 100 m – Wintersport: 1 564 m 1 5 B5

Wien 532 – Innsbruck 119 – Reutte 30 – Sonthofen 18

Landhotel Rehbach Schattwalder Gruppe, Rest,

Rehbach 1 (Nord-West: 3 km) 6677
– (05675) 66 94 – info@rehbach.at – Fax (05675) 669415
geschl. Anfang Nov. – Mitte Dez.
16 Zim – 54/64 € 108/128 € – ½ P 8 €
3 Suiten
Rest – *(geschl. Mittwoch)* Karte 13/24 €

◆ Das Gasthaus gefällt mit seiner idyllischen Lage in einem kleinen Weiler, hübschen, wohnlichen Zimmern mit gutem Platzangebot und einem schönen Saunabereich. A-la-carte-Restaurant mit rustikalem Charakter.

Alpengasthof Zur Post Zim,

Schattwald 21 6677 – (05675) 66 01 – info@gz-post.at
– Fax (05675) 66014
geschl. 30. März – 25. April
16 Zim – 33/40 € 66/80 € 33/45 € 66/90 €
Rest – *(geschl. Mittwoch)* Karte 12/32 €

◆ Der 350 Jahre alte Alpengasthof wird freundlich von der Familie geführt und verfügt über tadellos gepflegte, mit soliden Naturholzmöbeln eingerichtete Zimmer. Ländlich dekorierte Gaststuben mit freundlichem Service.

SCHEFFAU AM WILDEN KAISER – Tirol – 730 I6 – 1 210 Ew – Höhe 752 m – Wintersport: 1 800 m 9 84
7 **E5**

Wien 371 – Innsbruck 77 – Kufstein 16 – Kitzbühel 21
Scheffau 202, 6351, (05358) 73 73, tvb@scheffau.net

Kaiser in Tirol
Zim, Rest, VISA AE

Scheffau 145 6351
– (05358) 8 00 00 – welcome@hotel-kaiser-in-tirol.com
– Fax (05358) 8000340
geschl. Ende März – Mitte Mai, Nov. – 23. Dez.
64 Zim (inkl. ½ P.) – 124/154 € 190/258 € – 9 Suiten
Rest – (nur Abendessen für Hausgäste)

◆ Das großzügig angelegte Hotel verfügt über freundliche, funktionelle Zimmer und einen Freizeitbereich mit Kosmetik. Im Sommer überwiegend Wochenpauschalen und All-inclusive.

Sie suchen ein besonderes Hotel für einen sehr angenehmen Aufenthalt? Reservieren Sie in einem roten Haus: … .

SCHIEFLING AM SEE – Kärnten – 730 O9 – 2 270 Ew – Höhe 570 m
9 **I6**

Wien 326 – Klagenfurt 21 – Villach 23 – Velden 6
Pyramidenkogelstr. 150, 9535, (04274) 22 75 22, schiefling@ktn.gde.at

In Schiefling-Goritschach Nord-Ost: 2,5 km über Pyramidenkogelstraße:

Landgasthof Trattnig
VISA AE

Trattnigteichstr. 1 9535 – (04274) 5 00 01
– info@trattnig.at – Fax (04274) 5000145
geschl. März, Nov.
10 Zim – 50/58 € 90/100 € – ½ P 16 €
Rest – Karte 16/29 €

◆ Idyllisch liegt das familiär geführte kleine Hotel an einem Teich. Die Zimmer und Appartements (teilweise mit Wasserbett) – verfügen meist über einen Balkon. Mit viel Holz, Fliesenboden und ländlichem Dekor hübsch gestaltetes Restaurant.

SCHLADMING – Steiermark – 730 N6 – 4 570 Ew – Höhe 750 m – Wintersport: 1 894 m 6 20
9 **H5**

Wien 289 – Graz 167 – Salzburg 88 – Bischofshofen 48
Rohrmoosstr. 234, 8970, (03687) 2 27 77, urlaub@schladming.at
Dachstein Tauern, Oberhaus 59 (03686) 26 30

Veranstaltungen
04.01. – 05.01.: Planai Classic
22.01.: The Night Race
08.07. – 13.07.: Mid Europe

Schladminger Tauern★★ – Planai★★ mit (Süd: 12 km) – Hunerkogel★★★ (Nord-West: 16 km)

Sporthotel Royer (geheizt) Rest,
Europaplatz 583
8970 – (03687) 2 00 – reservierung@royer.at
– Fax (03687) 20094
127 Zim (inkl. ½ P.) – 103/113 € 176/196 € 115/145 €
186/260 €
Rest – Karte 22/34 €
◆ Neben hellen, freundlichen und modernen Zimmern, meist mit Balkon, zählt auch ein gutes Sportangebot mit kleiner Trainingsgolfanlage zu den Vorzügen des Hauses. Das Restaurant teilt sich in das Steirerstüberl und den nur im Winter geöffneten Grill.

Posthotel
Hauptplatz 10 8970 – (03687) 2 25 71
– Info@posthotel-schladming.at – Fax (03687) 225718
42 Zim (inkl. ½ P.) – 61/97 € 118/150 € 82/154 €
158/228 €
Rest – Karte 22/32 €
◆ Das a. d. 17. Jh. stammende Gasthaus im Ortszentrum bietet heute wohnlich und hübsch im Landhausstil eingerichtete Zimmer und einen Saunabereich mit Kosmetik. A-la-carte-Restaurant ist die gemütlich-rustikale Knappenstube mit kleinem Kachelofen.

Mitterhofer (geheizt) Rest, Rest,
Salzburgerstr. 371 8970 – (03687) 2 22 29
– info@mitterhofer.at – Fax (03687) 222298
geschl. 13. April – 5. Mai, 13. Okt. – 29. Nov.
30 Zim (inkl. ½ P.) – 74/80 € 126/152 € 96/118 €
169/227 €
Rest – Karte 15/27 €
◆ Die recht zentrale Lage nicht weit von den Liften sowie funktionell und zeitgemäß ausgestattete Gästezimmer sprechen für dieses gut geführte Hotel. Café mit kleiner Speisekarte.

SCHNEPFAU – Vorarlberg – 730 B6 – 490 Ew – Höhe 734 m – Wintersport: 734 m

5 **A5**

Wien 597 – Bregenz 39 – Dornbirn 29 – Lech am Arlberg 35

Gasthaus Adler
Schnepfau 36 6882 – (05518) 21 04 – adler@moosbrugger.at
– Fax (05518) 21045
geschl. 30. März – 25. April, 2. Nov. – 20. Dez. und Dienstag – Mittwoch
Rest – (Tischbestellung ratsam) Karte 18/33 €
◆ Parkettfußboden, Holztäfelung, Kachelofen und Fotos unterstreichen das bürgerlich-rustikale Ambiente in den Stuben dieses alten Gasthauses.

SCHÖNAU, BAD – Niederösterreich – 730 U6 – 730 Ew – Höhe 490 m – Wintersport: – Kurort

11 **L4**

Wien 95 – St. Pölten 131 – Wiener Neustadt 46
Kurhausstr. 8, 2853, (02646) 82 84, gemeinde@bad-schoenau.gv.at
Golfclub Zöbern, Golfplatz 1 (02642) 84 51

Gesundheitsresort Königsberg (geheizt) Rest,

Am Kurpark 1 ✉ 2853 – ☎ (02646) 82 51
– info@koenigsberg-bad-schoenau.at – Fax (02646) 8251725
221 Zim (inkl. ½ P) – ☼ 87/94 € 162/216 € ❄ 76/102 € 140/234 €
Rest – Menü 48 € – Karte 23/41 €
♦ In dem Hotel oberhalb des Dorfes erwarten Sie eine großzügige Halle, teilweise als Appartements angelegte Zimmer und eine Vielzahl therapeutischer Anwendungen. Teil des gastronomischen Bereichs ist das A-la-carte-Restaurant "Bucklige Welt".

Weber (direkter Zugang zur Kuranstalt) Rest,
Kurhausstr. 16 ✉ 2853 – ☎ (02646) 84 08
– office@hotelweber.at – Fax (02646) 840814
geschl. 28. Jan. – 17. Feb., 20. Juli – 3. Aug.
39 Zim – 50/70 € 100/140 €
Rest – Karte 13/28 €
♦ Der gewachsene Familienbetrieb ist aus einer kleinen Frühstückspension entstanden und verfügt heute über zeitgemäße, solide ausgestattete Zimmer und einen Feng-Shui-Garten. Hell gestaltetes Restaurant mit Wintergarten.

Geier Zim,
Hauptstr. 29 ✉ 2853 – ☎ (02646) 83 83 – hotel.geier@eunet.at
– Fax (02646) 838344
geschl. Feb. 2 Wochen, Nov. 2 Wochen
27 Zim (inkl. ½ P.) – 47/50 € 82/88 €
Rest – *(geschl. Montagmittag)* Karte 12/27 €
♦ In dem von der Inhaberfamilie geführten Haus ganz in der Nähe des Kurzentrums stehen gepflegte und funktionell eingerichtete Gästezimmer bereit. Gaststube mit ländlichem Ambiente.

Triad
Ödhöfen 25 (Nord – West: 1 km) ✉ 2853 – ☎ (02646) 83 17
– triad-machreich@aon.at – Fax (02646) 831733
geschl. 7. – 28. Jan., 21. Juli – 3. Aug. und Montag – Dienstag
Rest – Menü 29/65 € – Karte 21/38 €
♦ Charmant werden Sie in dem gemütlich-rustikalen Restaurant von der Gastgeberin umsorgt – serviert wird gute regionale und internationale Küche. Schöne Terrasse. Driving Range.

SCHÖNBERG IM STUBAITAL – Tirol – 730 G7 – 1 000 Ew – Höhe 1 030 m – Wintersport: 7 D5

Wien 456 – Innsbruck 13 – Hall in Tirol 21 – Seefeld 33
Dorfstr. 10, ✉ 6141, ☎ (0) 5 01 88 15 00, schoenberg@stubai.at

Stubai
Dorfstr. 6 ✉ 6141 – ☎ (05225) 6 25 59 – office@hotel-stubai.at
– Fax (05225) 6295952
geschl. 20. April – 11. Mai, Dez. 2 Wochen
25 Zim – 40/45 € 66/80 € – ½ P 12 €
Rest – *(geschl. Montag – Dienstagmittag)* Karte 13/32 €
♦ In dem Alpenhotel erwarten Sie mit soliden Holzmöbeln in rustikalem Stil eingerichtete, funktionelle Zimmer, die meist über einen Balkon verfügen. Ländlich gestaltetes Restaurant.

Gasthof Handl Zim, Rest,
Handlweg 1 ✉ 6141 – ✆ (05225) 6 25 74
– info@hotel-handl.at – Fax (05225) 625748
geschl. 14. – 30. April, 20. Okt – 10. Dez.
25 Zim – 44/50 € 69/82 € 48/54 € 76/86 €
Rest – Karte 14/32 €
◆ Der historische Gasthof a. d. J. 1882 wurde durch einen modernen Anbau ergänzt, der mit freundlichen, in hellem Holz gehaltenen Zimmern gefällt. Bürgerlich-rustikale Gaststube.

SCHÖNEGG – Oberösterreich – 730 O3 – 560 Ew – Höhe 789 m   2 H2

Wien 222 – Linz 44 – Passau 81 – Freistadt 32
Guglwald 8, ✉ 4191, ✆ (07219) 70 07, rezeption@guglwaldhof.at

Guglwald (geheizt)
Guglwald 8 (West: 4 km Richtung tschechische Grenze) ✉ 4191
– ✆ (07219) 70 07 – rezeption@guglwald.at – Fax (07219) 70075
geschl. Dez. 1 Woche
67 Zim (inkl. ½ P.) – 92/102 € 194/274 € – 5 Suiten
Rest – Karte 17/32 €
◆ In einem kleinen Ort nahe der tschechischen Grenze liegt das Hotel mit schönen, wohnlich gestalteten Zimmern sowie Wellness- und Kosmetikangeboten. Eigener Käutergarten. Rustikal-elegante Stuben, teilweise mit toskanischem Flair. Hübsche Vinothek.

SCHÖRFLING – Oberösterreich – 730 M5 – 3 170 Ew – Höhe 510 m   1 G3

Wien 236 – Linz 76 – Salzburg 61 – Gmunden 22
Hauptstr. 1, ✉ 4861, ✆ (07662) 25 78, info@attersee.at

In Schörfling-Kammer

Langostinos
Bahnhofstr. 4 ✉ 4861 – ✆ (07662) 2 90 50 – office@langostinos.at
– Fax (07662) 29050
geschl. Jan. 2 Wochen, Sept. 1 Woche, Okt. 1 Woche und Mittwoch – Donnerstag
Rest – Menü 42 € – Karte 25/52 €
◆ An einem kleinen Yachthafen liegt das neuzeitliche, leicht maritim dekorierte Gasthaus mit freundlichem Service und sehr nettem Terrassenbereich.

SCHOPPERNAU – Vorarlberg – 730 C7 – 910 Ew – Höhe 860 m – Wintersport: 2 060 m 2 6   5 A5

Wien 590 – Bregenz 46 – Dornbirn 35 – Lech am Arlberg 28
Argenau 376, ✉ 6886, ✆ (05515) 22 88, info@au-schoppernau.at

Wirtshaus zum Gämsle mit Zim
Hinterm Stein 309, (B 200) ✉ 6886 – ✆ (05515) 3 00 62
– hotel@gaemsle.at – Fax (05515) 3006226
geschl. April, Nov.

10 Zim (inkl. ½ P.) – ☼ 60/70 € 112/150 € ❄ 70/90 € 122/176 €
Rest – *(geschl. Montag)* Karte 25/40 €
♦ Das Haus mit der Holzschindel-Fassade beherbergt neben einem gemütlich-rustikalen Gastraum mit Kachelofen und Täfelung auch hübsche, ganz in hellem Holz gehaltene Zimmer.

SCHRÖCKEN – Vorarlberg – 730 C7 – 240 Ew – Höhe 1 260 m – Wintersport: 2 050 m 11

5 **B5**

Wien 580 – Bregenz 56 – Sankt Anton 38 – Dornbirn 45
Heimboden 2, 6888, (05519) 2 67 10, info@schroecken.at

Tannberg

Zim, P

Heimboden 3 (B 200) 6888 – (05519) 2 68 – info@tannberg.at – Fax (05519) 26830
geschl. 15. April – 5.Juli, 13. Okt. – 15. Dez.
22 Zim (inkl. ½ P.) – ☼ 53/57 € 96/104 € ❄ 76/98 € 132/176 €
Rest – *(geschl. im Sommer Mittwoch – Donnerstag)* Karte 19/37 €
♦ Ein gewachsenes familiengeführtes Hotel in einem kleinen Dorf. Die Zimmer sind unterschiedlich in der Größe und mit hellen oder dunklerem Holz möbliert, teils mit Balkon. In rustikale Stuben unterteiltes Restaurant.

SCHRUNS – Vorarlberg – 730 B7 – 3 720 Ew – Höhe 700 m – Wintersport: 2 380 m 3 9

5 **A6**

Wien 588 – Bregenz 65 – Sankt Anton am Arlberg 54 – Feldkirch 33
Haus des Gastes, Silvrettastr. 6, 6780, (05556) 72 16 60, info@schruns-tschagguns.at
Montafon★

Löwen

Spa VISA MC AE

Silvrettastr. 8 6780 – (05556) 71 41 – info@loewen-hotel.com – Fax (05556) 73553
geschl. Mitte April – Mitte Mai, Ende Nov. – Mitte Dez.
83 Zim (inkl. ½ P.) – ☼ 145/155 € 250/270 € ❄ 155/219 € 270/378 € – 4 Suiten
Rest *Edel-Weiß und Montafoner Stube* – separat erwähnt
♦ Sehr wohnliche Räume, geschultes und freundliches Personal sowie ein luxuriöses Spa mit Massage und Kosmetik zeichnen das Hotel aus. Aufwändige Halbpension.

Vitalquelle Gauenstein

Spa Zim, P VISA MC

Außerlitzstr. 80 6780 – (05556) 7 70 49 – hotel@vitalquelle.at – Fax (05556) 77049998
geschl. 2. – 29. Juni
45 Zim (inkl. ½ P.) – ☼ 108/114 € 228/240 € ❄ 118/132 € 258/288 € – 5 Suiten
Rest – *(geschl. Mittwoch, nur Abendessen)* (Tischbestellung erforderlich) Menü 40 € – Karte 27/50 €
♦ Hier erwarten Sie geräumige Zimmer mit geschmackvollem, im gotischen Stil gearbeitetem Altholzmobiliar. Neben Wellness und Beauty bietet das Hotel auch einen Schwimmteich. Restaurant mit rustikalelegantem Ambiente.

Alpenhotel Bitschnau
Rest,

Silvrettastr. 175 ✉ 6780 – ✆ (05556) 7 57 00 – alpenhotel@bitschnau.at – Fax (05556) 757008

geschl. 6. April – Anfang Mai, Ende Nov. – Mitte Dez.

55 Zim (inkl. ½ P.) – ☼ 93/107 € 176/210 € ❄ 107/136 € 208/272 € – 5 Suiten

Rest – Karte 24/35 €

◆ Eine gemütliche Lobby empfängt Sie in dem familiär geführten Hotel. Ganz modern sind der Anbau mit Juniorsuiten im alpinen Stil sowie der Spabereich. Ein Teil der Hotelhalle dient am Abend als A-la-carte-Restaurant – schön ist die Aussicht von hier.

Alpenrose
Rest, VISA

Silvrettastr. 45 ✉ 6780 – ✆ (05556) 7 26 55 – info@spa-alpenrose.at – Fax (05556) 7265577

geschl. 7. April – 7. Mai

50 Zim (inkl. ½ P.) – ☼ 69/137 € 138/202 € ❄ 90/165 € 174/272 € – 3 Suiten

Rest – *(geschl. Dienstag)* Karte 18/51 €

◆ Nett ist die rustikale Atmosphäre in diesem Haus. Die unterschiedlich geschnittenen Zimmer liegen teils nach Süden, meist mit Balkon/Terrasse. U. a. Fitnessraum mit Aussicht. Klassisch-rustikal gestaltetes Restaurant.

Zimba
Rest, VISA

Veltlinerweg 2 ✉ 6780 – ✆ (05556) 7 26 30 – info@hotel-zimba.at – Fax (05556) 7263045

geschl. 6. April – 1. Mai, 19. Okt. – 28. Nov.

71 Zim (inkl. ½ P.) – ☼ 61/65 € 114/130 € ❄ 70/90 € 132/180 €

Rest – Karte 16/30 €

◆ Ein familiengeführtes Hotel mit soliden, zeitgemäßen Gästezimmern. Hübsch ist die freundliche Lobby mit Korbsesseln und großer Fensterfront zum Garten.

Both
Rest, VISA

Auweg 9 ✉ 6780 – ✆ (05556) 7 26 56 – hotel.both@montafon.com – Fax (05556) 726568

33 Zim – ☼ 30/38 € 56/70 € ❄ 42/48 € 84/90 € – ½ P 18 €

Rest – (nur für Hausgäste)

◆ Zwei Familien leiten dieses alpenländische Haus nahe dem Ortszentrum. Gäste wohnen in unterschiedlich möblierten, gepflegten Zimmern, teils mit Balkon.

Auhof

Auweg 14 ✉ 6780 – ✆ (05556) 7 22 69 – auhof@montafon.com – Fax (05556) 722695

geschl. 7. April – 1. Mai, 18. Okt. – 30. Nov.

22 Zim (inkl. ½ P.) – ☼ 41/50 € 82/92 € ❄ 58/70 € 116/132 €

Rest – (nur Abendessen für Hausgäste)

◆ Das in einer Seitenstraße gelegene Hotel unter familiärer Leitung verfügt über solide ausgestattete Zimmer unterschiedlicher Größe sowie 2 Appartements in modernem Design.

Edel-Weiß - Hotel Löwen

Silvrettastr. 8 ✉ 6780 – ✆ (05556) 71 41 – info@loewen-hotel.com – Fax (05556) 73553

geschl. Ende Nov. – Mitte Dez., Mitte April – Mitte Mai und Montag – Dienstag

Rest – *(nur Abendessen)* (Tischbestellung ratsam) Menü 55/84 € – Karte 46/73 €

Spez. Roh marinierter Rehrücken und Steinpilze mit Ingwer-Preiselbeerschaum. Zander mit rotem Mangold und Sommertrüffel im Pergament gegart. Mousse von der Wildrose mit flüssigen Himbeeren und Rosenzuckerl.

♦ Elegantes Ambiente in edlem Weiß sowie kompetenter Service und klassische Küche machen dieses Restaurant zu einer sehr angenehmen Adresse.

Montafoner Stube - Hotel Löwen

Silvrettastr. 8 ✉ 6780 – ✆ (05556) 71 41 – info@loewen-hotel.com – Fax (05556) 73553

geschl. Mitte April – Mitte Mai, Ende Nov. – Mitte Dez.

Rest – Karte 28/51 €

♦ Eine gemütliche Atmosphäre herrscht in der ganz in hellem Holz gehaltenen Montafoner Stube. Geboten wird überwiegend regionale Küche.

Gasthaus zum Kreuz

Kirchplatz 18 ✉ 6780 – ✆ (05556) 7 21 17 – gasthaus.zum.kreuz@montafon.com – Fax (05556) 721174

geschl. Mai, Nov., im Sommer Dienstag

Rest – *(Montag – Samstag nur Abendessen)* (Tischbestellung ratsam) Karte 16/35 €

♦ Mit viel Holz und blanken Tischen, Kamin und regionstypischem Zierrat sind die Gaststuben im Montafoner Stil gehalten. Fondue-Spezialitäten ab 2 Personen.

SCHÜTZEN AM GEBIRGE – Burgenland – 730 V5 – 1 360 Ew – Höhe 124 m 4 L3

Wien 60 – Eisenstadt 8 – Donnerskirchen 7

Taubenkobel (Walter Eselböck) mit Zim Rest,

Hauptstr. 33 ✉ 7081 – ✆ (02684) 22 97 – taubenkobel@relaischateaux.at – Fax (02684) 229718

geschl. Jan. – Mitte Feb.

11 Zim – 144/248 € 180/270 € – 7 Suiten

Rest – *(geschl. Montag – Dienstag, Mittwoch – Freitag nur Abendessen)* (Tischbestellung ratsam) Menü 78/118 €

Spez. Wachtel im Heu. Mozartkugel von der Gänseleber. Brennessel-Chlorophyll mit Fischnockerl.

♦ Stilvolles, individuelles Ensemble mehrerer sanierter Häuser u. a. mit einer Greislerei. Innovative Küche mit lokalen Produkten. Kreativ gestaltete, hübsche Zimmer mit hochwertiger Ausstattung. Schöner Garten mit Teich.

SCHWARZENBERG – Vorarlberg – 730 B6 – 1 670 Ew – Höhe 700 m – Wintersport: 1 467 m 11 5 A5

Wien 640 – Bregenz 24 – Dornbirn 14 – Feldkirch 40
Dorfplatz★ – Bödelesattel ≤★

Hirschen (mit Gästehaus) Rest, VISA
Hof 14 6867 – (05512) 29 44
– info@hirschenschwarzenberg.at – Fax (05512) 294420
geschl. 26. Okt. – 2. Nov.
33 Zim – 101/115 € 145/228 € 92/101 € 132/198 € – ½ P 34 €
Rest – *(geschl. Nov. – Mai Mittwoch – Donnerstagmittag)* Menü 36/55 € – Karte 28/53 €
◆ Hinter seiner Holzfassade gefällt der a. d. J. 1755 stammende Gasthof mit stilvoll-rustikalem Ambiente – das Gästehaus ist mit viel hellem Holz im Landhausstil eingerichtet. Holztäfelung, Kachelofen und Zierrat schaffen im Restaurant ein behagliches Ambiente.

Gasthof Adler VISA
Hof 15 6867 – (05512) 29 66 – adler.schwarzenberg@aon.at
– Fax (05512) 29666
geschl. Jan. 3 Wochen und Montag – Dienstag
Rest – (Tischbestellung ratsam) Menü 40/50 € – Karte 30/46 €
◆ Ein Holzhaus beherbergt das rustikale Restaurant mit gemütlichen Stuben und regionaler Küche. Sehenswert: die Stube mit alten Holztischen. Mit Kastanien bepflanzte Terrasse.

Wie entscheidet man sich zwischen zwei gleichwertigen Adressen? In jeder Kategorie sind die Häuser nochmals geordnet, die besten Adressen stehen an erster Stelle.

SCHWAZ – Tirol – 730 H6 – 12 220 Ew – Höhe 535 m – Wintersport: 2 030 m 5 7 D5

Wien 419 – Innsbruck 28 – Hall in Tirol 21 – Wörgl 33
Franz-Josef-Str. 2, 6130, (05242) 6 32 40, info@silberregion-karwendel.at

Veranstaltungen

05.09. – 20.09.: Klangspuren

Pfarrkirche★ – Franziskanerkirche (Renaissance-Chorgestühl★) – Silberbergwerk★ – Schloss Freundsberg ≤★
Schloss Tratzberg★ (Nord-Ost: 5 km)

Goldener Löwe (mit Gästehaus)
Husslstr. 4 6130 – (05242) 6 23 73 – info@goldenerloewe.at
– Fax (05242) 6237344
geschl. 2. – 14. Nov.
42 Zim – 36/60 € 62/100 € – ½ P 13 €
Rest – *(geschl. Montag)* Karte 15/19 €
◆ Der jahrhundertealte Gasthof ist ein gepflegter und solider Familienbetrieb. Die Zimmer sind unterschiedlich in der Größe und einheitlich mit rustikaler Eiche möbliert. Ländlich gestalteter Restaurantbereich.

SCHWECHAT – Niederösterreich – 730 V4 – 15 290 Ew – Höhe 170 m

4 **L2**

Wien 15 – St. Pölten 85 – Baden 28 – Wiener Neustadt 44

Colony Club Gutenhof – Himberg, (02235) 87 05 50

In Schwechat-Mannswörth Nord-Ost: 3 km:

Hein garni

Mannswörtherstr. 94 ✉ 2320 – (01) 7 07 19 50 – welcome@heinhotel.at – Fax (01) 7071950900

geschl. 23. – 28. Dez.

54 Zim – 83 € 106 €

◆ Ein geradlinig-moderner Stil begleitet Sie vom Empfangsbereich über die funktionell ausgestatteten Gästezimmer bis in den angenehm hellen Frühstücksraum.

Am Flughafen Wien-Schwechat Ost: 6 km:

NH Vienna Airport

Zim,

Hotelstr. 1 (am Flughafen) ✉ 1300 Wien – (01) 70 15 10 – nhviennaairport@nh-hotels.com – Fax (01) 701519571

500 Zim – 130/360 € 130/360 €, 19 €

Rest – Karte 26/56 €

◆ In dem Hotel gegenüber der Ankunftshalle erwarten den Gast eine großzügige, schlicht-elegante Lobby sowie Zimmer in geschmackvollem modernem oder klassischem Stil. Klare Linien kennzeichnen das offen angelegte Restaurant.

SCHWENDAU IM ZILLERTAL – Tirol – 730 H7 – 1 430 Ew – Höhe 680 m

7 **E5**

Wien 436 – Innsbruck 64 – Schwaz 36 – Zell am Ziller 6

Alpenblick

Johann-Sponring-Str. 91 ✉ 6283 – (05282) 36 27 – info@hotel-alpenblick.at – Fax (05282) 3547

geschl. 5. – 30. April, 15. Okt. – 8. Dez.

32 Zim (inkl. ½ P.) – 75/79 € 110/184 € 87/174 € 133/276 €

Rest – Menü 35 € – Karte 25/44 €

◆ Behaglich und wohnlich ist die Atmosphäre in dem Ferienhotel am Ortsrand. Zur Wahl stehen Zimmerkategorien wie Sterngucker, Turmzimmer, Rosen- sowie Kuschelzimmer. Komfortables Restaurant im alpenländischen Stil.

Schrofenblick

Rest,

Burgstall 373 (Süd-West: 2,5 km) ✉ 6290 – (05285) 6 22 76 – info@alpin-hotel.at – Fax (05285) 63437

35 Zim (inkl. ½ P.) – 52/62 € 92/128 € 68/112 € 116/192 €

Rest – Karte 16/38 €

◆ Frische, wohnliche Gästezimmer erwarten Sie in dem etwas außerhalb von Schwendau gelegenen Hotel. Appartements in einem unterirdisch verbundenen Nebengebäude. Teil des rustikalen Restaurants ist die komplett holzverkleidete Zirbelstube.

Sport- und Vitalhotel Stefanie
Johann-Sponring-Str. 90 ✉ 6283 Zim, VISA
– (05282) 36 34 – info@stefanie.at – Fax (05282) 3803
geschl. 12. April – 9. Mai, 25. Okt. – 13. Dez.
35 Zim (inkl. ½ P.) – 80/94 € 140/164 € 87/119 €
154/214 €
Rest – Karte 18/37 €
◆ Das in einer Nebenstraße gelegene Urlaubshotel bietet seinen Gästen wohnliche, z. T. neuzeitlich mit hellem Naturholz möblierte Zimmer und einen freundlichen Freizeitbereich. Rustikal-gediegenes Restaurant.

Neuwirt
Dorf 138 ✉ 6283 – (05285) 6 29 17 – info@ferienhotel-neuwirt.at
– Fax (05285) 6291750
geschl. 20. April – 10. Mai, 26. Okt. – 12. Dez.
33 Zim (inkl. ½ P.) – 53/60 € 90/104 € 66/78 €
118/140 €
Rest – Karte 19/38 €
◆ Ein sehr gepflegtes familiengeführtes Haus, das über mit rustikaler dunkler Eiche oder mit hellem Holz eingerichtete Gästezimmer verfügt. Man bietet Wanderungen/Bergtouren an. Das Restaurant: Wintergarten und bürgerliche Stuben.

Sieghard mit Zim
Zim, VISA
Johann-Sponring-Str. 83 ✉ 6283 – (05282) 33 09
– urlaub@hotel-sieghard.com – Fax (05282) 3732
geschl. 6. April – 9. Mai, 12. Okt. – 8. Dez. und Montag, außer Feiertage
20 Zim (inkl. ½ P.) – 73/88 € 116/146 € 81/115 €
124/192 €
Rest – (Tischbestellung ratsam) Menü 37/50 € – Karte 26/44 €
◆ Im gediegenen Ambiente dieses in der Ortsmitte gelegenen Hauses serviert man Ihnen sowohl regionale als auch klassisch-gehobene Küche. Wohnliche Zimmer in hellem Naturholz.

SCHWERTBERG – Oberösterreich – 730 P4 – 5 170 Ew – Höhe 225 m
2 **I2**

Wien 168 – Linz 27 – Steyr 35 – Freistadt 36

Tinschert
VISA AE
Ing. Schmiedl-Str. 6 ✉ 4311 – (07262) 6 12 76 – info@hotel-tinschert.at
– Fax (07262) 612768
geschl. 1. – 7. Jan., 4. – 17. Aug.
23 Zim – 58 € 92 €
Rest – *(geschl. Samstagabend, Sonn- und Feiertage abends)* Karte 15/28 €
◆ Ein gepflegtes familiengeführtes kleines Hotel in einer Seitenstraße, in dem mit dunklem Holzmobiliar zeitgemäß und funktionell eingerichtete Zimmer bereitstehen. Neuzeitliches, leicht gediegen wirkendes Restaurant mit freundlich gestalteter Gaststube.

SEBERSDORF – Steiermark – 730 T7 – 1 360 Ew – Höhe 298 m 11 **L4**

Wien 136 – Graz 61 – Fürstenfeld 24 – Szombathely 63

Schloss Obermayerhofen
Neustift 1 (West: 1 km) ✉ 8272
– ✆ (03333) 25 03 – schlosshotel@obermayerhofen.at
– Fax (03333) 250350
geschl. 7. Jan. – 28. Feb.
25 Zim – 100/136 € 150/222 €
Rest – *(geschl. Sonntag – Dienstag)* (nur Abendessen für Hausgäste)
Menü 45/68 €
◆ Das schöne Schloss a. d. J. 1130 liegt in einem 12 ha großen, reizvollen Park. Stilvoll wurde der Charme des Anwesens durch Fresken und Antiquitäten bewahrt. Hochzeitskapelle. Rustikal-elegantes Restaurant mit internationaler Karte.

SEE IM PAZNAUNTAL – Tirol – 730 D7 – 1 100 Ew – Höhe 1 050 m – Wintersport: 2 300 m 1 4 — 5 B6

Wien 529 – Innsbruck 85 – Landeck 13 – Sankt Anton 29
Silvrettastr. 178, ✉ 6553, ✆ (05441) 82 96, office@see1.at

Ad Laca (mit Gästehaus Alpenkönigin) Rest,
Au 172 ✉ 6553 – ✆ (05441) 85 80
– info@natur-hotels-see.at – Fax (05441) 858023
geschl. 5. April – 7. Juni
52 Zim (inkl. ½ P.) – 44/60 € 72/104 € 57/88 € 86/176 €
Rest – (nur Abendessen für Hausgäste)
◆ Die soliden, im rustikalen Stil eingerichteten Gästezimmer sowie die Freizeitangebote verteilen sich auf das Hotel Ad Laca sowie das Haus Alpenkönigin. Après-Ski-Bar im UG.

Weisses Lamm
Gries 5 ✉ 6553 – ✆ (05441) 82 90 – hotellamm@aon.at
– Fax (05441) 82905
geschl. Mai – Juni, Okt. – Nov.
35 Zim (inkl. ½ P.) – 42/52 € 82/96 € 45/77 € 114/164 €
Rest – *(nur Abendessen)* Karte 18/33 €
◆ In dem alpenländischen Hotel erwarten Sie neben zeitgemäß ausgestatteten Zimmern eine schöne Saunalandschaft und ein nett angelegter Garten. Gemütlich ist die 200 Jahre alte Zirbenstube.

SEEBODEN – Kärnten – 730 M8 – 6 050 Ew – Höhe 520 m — 9 H6

Wien 341 – Klagenfurt 81 – Villach 46 – Spittal a.d. Drau 5
Hauptplatz 1, ✉ 9871, ✆ (04762) 8 12 10, seeboden.tourist@ktn.gde.at

Landhotel Moerisch (geheizt) Zim, Rest,
Tangern 2
(Nord-Ost: 3 km:) ✉ 9871 – ✆ (04762) 8 13 72 – info@moerisch.at
– Fax (04762) 813728
geschl. 25. März – 25. April, 19. Okt. – 20. Dez.
40 Zim (inkl. ½ P.) – 60/120 € 120/220 €
Rest – *(geschl. Sonntag- Mittwoch, nur Abendessen)* (Tischbestellung ratsam) Menü 35/45 € – Karte 26/38 €
◆ Direkt am Golfplatz liegt dieses nette Landhotel mit geschmackvoll gestalteten, komfortablen Gästezimmern und gutem Freizeitangebot mit Kinderbetreuung. Zu den freundlich gestalteten Restauranträumen gehört eine hübsche Veranda.

Koller's Hotel am See (geheizt)
Seepromenade 2 Rest, VISA AE
9871 – (04762) 8 15 00 – info@kollers.at – Fax (04762) 8150040
geschl. März, Nov.
61 Zim (inkl. ½ P.) – 56/111 € 130/274 € – 3 Suiten
Rest – (nur für Hausgäste) Karte 19/32 €
◆ Herrlich ist die Lage dieses gut geführten Ferienhotels direkt am See. Die Zimmer sind mit italienischen Stilmöbeln wohnlich eingerichtet. Schöner Garten mit Zugang zum See.

SEEFELD – Tirol – 730 F6 – 3 100 Ew – Höhe 1 200 m – Wintersport: 2 100 m 3 27 – Luftkurort 6 C5

Wien 467 – Innsbruck 24 – Garmisch Partenkirchen 35 – Imst 44
Klosterstr. 43, 6100, (050) 88 00, region@seefeld.com
Seefeld-Wildmoos, (0699) 16 06 60 60
Zirlerberg★ – Seefelder Joch★★ mit – Seefelder Sattelstraßen ★★ – Reith★ – Mösern (Friedensglocke des Alpenraums ★★) Süd-West: 3 km

Klosterbräu (geheizt) Rest,
Klosterstr. 30 6100 VISA AE
– (05212) 2 62 10 – info@klosterbraeu.com – Fax (05212) 3885
geschl. Ende März – Anfang Juni, Mitte Okt. – Anfang Dez.
98 Zim – 112/169 € 238/380 € 148/281 € 272/650 € – ½ P 39 € – 15 Suiten
Rest *Ritter-Oswald-Stube* – separat erwähnt
Rest *Bräukeller* – Karte 22/33 €
◆ Sehr persönlich leitet die Familie das ehemalige Klostergebäude a. d. 16. Jh. Die Zimmer sind individuell, geschmackvoll und mit Liebe zum Detail eingerichtet. Gemütliche Atmosphäre und geschulter Service im rustikalen Bräukeller.

Astoria Relax & Spa-Hotel (geheizt)
Rest, VISA AE
Geigenbühel 185 6100 – (05212) 2 27 20
– hotel@astoria-seefeld.com – Fax (05212) 2272100
57 Zim (inkl. ½ P.) – 115/249 € 198/338 € 144/338 € 254/450 €
Rest – *(nur Abendessen)* Karte 30/42 €
◆ Die Einrichtung der individuellen, unterschiedlich geschnittenen Zimmer reicht von gediegen bis luxuriös. Schön ist der Wellnessbereich mit großzügigem Ruheraum. Klassisch gehaltener Speisesaal mit geschmackvollem Dekor.

Dorint Vital Royal Spa (geheizt)
Krinz 32 Rest, VISA AE
6100 – (05212) 4 43 10 – reservierung.seefeld@dorintresorts.com
– Fax (05212) 4431450
126 Zim – 105/245 € 164/384 € – ½ P 35 € – 8 Suiten
Rest *Sonnalm* – *(geschl. Juni -Juli 2 Wochen und 30. März -14. Dez. Sonntag – Montag, nur Abendessen)* (Tischbestellung ratsam)
Menü 48/78 € – Karte 38/49 €
Rest *Zirbenstube* – *(nur Abendessen)* Menü 25 € – Karte 30/34 €
◆ Mit seinem "Vital Royal Spa" auf 3500 qm ist dieses Hotel besonders auf Wellness ausgelegt. Die Zimmer sind mit warmen Tönen wohnlich gestaltet. Sonnalm mit klassisch-zeitgemäßer Küche. Tiroler sowie österreichische und Wiener Schmankerln in der Zirbenstube.

Gartenhotel Tümmlerhof

(geheizt) Rest,

Münchnerstr. 215 6100 – (05212) 25 71 – hotel@tuemmlerhof.at – Fax (05212) 2571104
geschl. 30. März - 8. Mai, 3. Nov. – 21. Dez.
84 Zim (inkl. ½ P.) – 75/125 € 150/250 € 90/204 € 180/408 € – 19 Suiten
Rest – Karte 33/54 €
♦ Ein Hotel, das mit seinen freundlich im Landhausstil eingerichteten Zimmern und einem vielfältigen Freizeitbereich den richtigen Rahmen für einen angenehmen Aufenthalt schafft. Aufmerksamer Service bedient Sie im eleganten Restaurant.

Das Hotel Eden

(geheizt) Rest, Rest,

Münchnerstr. 136
6100 – (05212) 5 04 95 – info@eden-seefeld.at – Fax (05212) 50494
geschl. Nov.
73 Zim (inkl. ½ P.) – 92/144 € 134/228 € 113/229 € 174/328 € – 10 Suiten
Rest – (nur Abendessen für Hausgäste)
♦ In einem großen Park mitten im Ort liegt das gut geführte moderne Hotel. Wohnliche Zimmer in warmen Farben, ausgestattet mit guter Technik. Geschmackvoll: der Spabereich.

Seespitz

(geheizt) Rest,

Innsbruckerstr. 181 6100 – (05212) 22 17 – info@seespitz.at – Fax (05212) 221850
geschl. April, Nov.
61 Zim (inkl. ½ P.) – 109/115 € 160/230 € 118/180 € 196/360 €
Rest – Menü 15 € (mittags)/45 € – Karte 23/44 €
♦ Das Hotel am Wildsee bietet eine hübsche großzügige Halle sowie behagliche, regionstypisch oder modern eingerichtete Gästezimmer und einen neuzeitlichen Freizeitbereich. Im Restaurant: ländliches Ambiente mit elegantem Touch.

Residenz Hochland

Seefeld, Rest,

Wettersteinstr. 184 6100 – (05212) 2 21 10 – info@residenz-hochland.com – Fax (05212) 221115
geschl. April – Mitte Mai, Mitte Okt. – Mitte Dez.
70 Zim (inkl. ½ P.) – 73/192 € 143/240 € 90/299 € 178/374 €
Rest – Karte 21/34 €
♦ Das gewachsene Alpenhotel direkt neben dem Skilift verfügt über wohnliche, teils sehr geräumige Gästezimmer und einen schönen Sauna-bereich. Freundlich gestaltetes Restaurant in ländlichem Stil.

Elite

Zim,

Andreas-Hofer-Str. 39 6100 – (05212) 29 01 – office@elite-seefeld.at – Fax (05212) 21446
geschl. Ende März – Anfang Mai, Nov.
27 Zim – 65/79 € 106/154 € 78/114 € 128/228 € – 3 Suiten
Rest – *(geschl. Anfang Mai – Okt. Montag) (nur für Hausgäste)* Karte 15/30 €
♦ Mit geräumigen, wohnlich eingerichteten Zimmern überzeugt dieses neuzeitliche, im alpenländischen Stil gebaute Hotel. Sehr großzügig ist die Familiensuite. Café-Restaurant mit kleinem Speisenangebot.

Aktivhotel Veronika
Rest,

Riehlweg 161 ✉ 6100
– ✆ (05212) 21 05 – hotel.veronika@seefeld.at – Fax (05212) 3787
geschl. 30. März – 30. April
56 Zim (inkl. ½ P.) – ☼ 77/139 € 140/208 € ❄ 98/190 €
180/320 € – 4 Suiten
Rest – (nur für Hausgäste)
◆ Ein ganz auf Familien eingestelltes Hotel. Schön sind das gemütlich-gediegene Kaminzimmer, die Bar und das moderne Hallenbad. Sehr freundliche Kinderbetreuung im Kiddy's Club.

Sonnenresidenz Alpenpark
(geheizt) Rest,

Speckbacherstr. 182
✉ 6100 – ✆ (05212) 29 51 – alpenpark@kaltschmid.co.at
– Fax (05212) 29515209
geschl. 31. März – 20. Mai, 3. Nov. – 20. Dez.
124 Zim (inkl. ½ P.) – ☼ 74/91 € 142/194 € ❄ 100/146 €
194/308 € – 9 Suiten
Rest – (nur für Hausgäste)
◆ Das Haus steht für ein großes Freizeitangebot mit schönem Badebereich, Sportbar mit Indoor-Golf sowie Squash u. v. a. Wohnliche, meist mit hellem Naturholz möblierte Zimmer.

Seelos
Seefeld, Rest,

Wettersteinstr. 226 ✉ 6100 – ✆ (05212) 23 08 – info@hotel-seelos.at
– Fax (05212) 204541
geschl. 1. April – 15. Juni, 4. Okt. – 6. Dez.
37 Zim (inkl. ½ P.) – ☼ 62/91 € 124/182 € ❄ 75/132 €
150/264 €
Rest – *(im Sommer nur Abendessen)* (nur für Hausgäste) Karte 21/37 €
◆ Sehr schön ist die Lage dieses Alpenhotels mit Panoramablick auf Seefeld. Ein Teil der Zimmer ist etwas eleganter möbliert und nach Süden hin gelegen, mit Balkon.

Die Post
Rest,

Dorfplatz 25 ✉ 6100 – ✆ (05212) 22 01 – post@hotel-post.com
– Fax (05212) 2201500
geschl. April, Nov.
71 Zim (inkl. ½ P.) – ☼ 86/107 € 119/215 € ❄ 101/202 €
139/338 €
Rest – (nur Abendessen für Hausgäste)
◆ Direkt im Zentrum liegt das familiengeführte Hotel mit der gelben Fassade, das mit einer eleganten Halle und wohnlichen, freundlichen Zimmern gefällt. Nette Bar.

Wellnesshotel Schönruh
(geheizt) Rest,

Reitherspitzstr. 356
✉ 6100 – ✆ (05212) 24 47 – schoenruh@kaltschmid.co.at
– Fax (05212) 24477
geschl. 1. April – 9. Mai
99 Zim (inkl. ½ P.) – ☼ 64/134 € 114/204 € ❄ 93/224 €
158/324 € – 10 Suiten
Rest – (nur für Hausgäste)
◆ Ein aus verschiedenen Gebäuden bestehendes Hotel mit hübscher Lobby und großzügigem Badebereich. Besonders schön sind die Royal-Zimmer im Haus Schönruh.

Lärchenhof

Seefeld, Rest,

Geigenbühel 203 ✉ 6100 – ✆ (05212) 23 83 – info@marcati.at – Fax (05212) 238383

geschl. 29. März – 9. Mai, 2. Nov. – 5. Dez.

53 Zim (inkl. ½ P.) – ☼ 72/120 € 104/117 € ❄ 90/165 € 162/362 €

Rest – *(nur Mittagessen)* Karte 21/31 €

◆ Das gewachsene familiengeführte Hotel außerhalb des Zentrums bietet ein wohnliches Ambiente, Spa mit Kosmetik und Massage sowie eine schöne Sicht auf Seefeld. Gediegenes Restaurant.

Alpenhotel Lamm

Dorfplatz 28 ✉ 6100 – ✆ (05212) 24 64 – lamm@alpenhotel.com – Fax (05212) 283434

geschl. April

71 Zim (inkl. ½ P.) – ☼ 105/150 € 180/260 € ❄ 115/175 € 200/310 €

Rest – Karte 22/44 €

◆ Seit 7 Generationen befindet sich das solide geführte Haus im Familienbesitz. Die Zimmer sind neuzeitlich oder rustikal eingerichtet, einige mit Erker. Der modern-rustikale Gewölbekeller mit abendlicher Zittermusik ergänzt das Restaurant.

St. Georg garni

Wasserfallweg 630 ✉ 6100 – ✆ (05212) 31 73 – hotel-stgeorg@seefeld-in-tirol.net – Fax (05212) 31736

geschl. Mai, Nov.

21 Zim – ☼ 37/45 € 74/90 € ❄ 45/64 € 90/128 €

◆ Recht ruhig in einem Wohngebiet liegt das persönlich geführte kleine Hotel mit der regionstypischen Fassade und den im Landhausstil eingerichteten Zimmern.

Central (mit Gästehäusern)

Münchnerstr. 41 ✉ 6100 – ✆ (05212) 32 88 – central@seefeld.at – Fax (05212) 328866

geschl. Anfang April 2 Wochen, Nov.

45 Zim – ☼ 46/71 € 72/122 € ❄ 70/115 € 110/200 € – ½ P 11/15 €

Rest – Karte 20/32 €

◆ Neuzeitliche Gästezimmer – auch Allergikerzimmer mit Holzfußboden – sowie eine hübsche Saunalandschaft sprechen für dieses Hotel. Etwas rustikaler: die Gästehäuser. Bürgerlich gestaltetes Restaurant mit großer Fensterfront.

Zum Gourmet

Zim,

Geigenbühelstr. 158 ✉ 6100 – ✆ (05212) 21 01 – info@zumgourmet.at – Fax (05212) 4382

geschl. 14. – 30 April

30 Zim (inkl. ½ P.) – ☼ 78/137 € 142/182 € ❄ 84/208 € 154/268 €

Rest – *(geschl. Montag – Dienstag)* (nur Abendessen für Hausgäste)

◆ Etwas abseits des Zentrums liegt dieses solide geführte Hotel, das über wohnlich und recht individuell eingerichtete Gästezimmer verfügt. Freundlich gestaltetes Restaurant.

Theresia Zim,

Mösererstr. 198 ✉ 6100 – ✆ (05212) 24 56 – info@theresia-seefeld.com – Fax (05212) 245647
geschl. 25. März – 10. Mai, 4. Okt. – 6. Dez.
27 Zim (inkl. ½ P.) – ☼ †50/73 € ††82/128 € ❄ †73/129 € ††130/240 €
Rest – Karte 17/35 €
♦ Ein familiär geleitetes Hotel mit farblich angenehm gestalteten Gästezimmern, teilweise mit kleinem Wohnbereich, und einer netten, gepflegten Sauna. Italienisch orientierte Küche mit Pizza-/Pasta-Angebot im Restaurant.

Kronenhotel (geheizt) Rest,

Karwendelweg 732 ✉ 6100 – ✆ (05212) 41 06 – info@kronenhotel.com – Fax (05212) 456344
geschl. April, Nov
70 Zim (inkl. ½ P.) – ☼ †50/66 € ††120/154 € ❄ †78/117 € ††142/262 €
Rest – (nur für Hausgäste)
♦ Ein rustikales Ambiente prägt dieses typische Alpenhotel am Ortsende. Die Zimmer sind mit hellem Holz eingerichtet und teils recht großzügig geschnitten.

Haymon Rest,

Kalkkögelweg 264 ✉ 6100 – ✆ (05212) 24 19 – seefeld@haymon.at – Fax (05212) 241993
geschl. 31. März – 3. Mai, 27. Okt. – 6. Dez.
43 Zim (inkl. ½ P.) – ☼ †52/60 € ††90/120 € ❄ †63/89 € ††110/174 €
Rest – (nur Abendessen für Hausgäste)
♦ Das familiengeführte Hotel am Zentrumsrand überzeugt mit wohnlichen, im Tiroler Stil gehaltenen Zimmern der Kategorien Wildmoos, Karwendel oder Kaiser Max – alle mit Balkon.

Solstein Rest,

Hermannstalstr. 558 ✉ 6100 – ✆ (05212) 27 41 – info@hotel-solstein.com – Fax (05212) 27416
geschl. April, Nov.
20 Zim (inkl. ½ P.) – ☼ †50/75 € ††116/136 € ❄ †85/120 € ††170/230 €
Rest – (nur Abendessen für Hausgäste)
♦ In diesem kleinen Hotel erwarten Sie zeitgemäße Zimmer mit gutem Platzangebot und ein schöner, ganz modern gestalteter Saunabereich. Nette Bar. Die im Restaurant verwendeten Fleisch- und Wurstwaren stammen ausschließlich aus der Metzgerei der Familie.

Seefelderhof

Münchnerstr. 146 ✉ 6100 – ✆ (05212) 23 73 – hotel@seefelderhof.com – Fax (05212) 237341
geschl. Ende März – Anfang Mai, Mitte Okt. – Anfang Dez.
50 Zim (inkl. ½ P.) – ☼ †48/97 € ††96/170 € ❄ †65/141 € ††130/264 €
Rest – Karte 22/34 €
♦ Solide ausgestattete Gästezimmer mit unterschiedlichem Platzangebot und ein gepflegter, nett gestalteter Freizeitbereich sprechen für dieses Hotel. Restaurant in regionstypischem Stil.

Christina garni
Reitherspitzstr. 415 ✉ 6100 – ✆ (05212) 25 53 – hotel.christina@aon.at – Fax (05212) 431432
geschl. April – Juni, Nov. – Dez.
14 Zim – ☼ 38/78 € 84/92 € ❄ 52/90 € 104/132 €
♦ Ein sehr familiär geführtes Landhaus mit schönem Garten. Die Zimmer sind hübsch in neuzeitlichem Stil eingerichtet, teils mit kleinem Wohnbereich und Balkon.

Olympia garni
Milserstr. 433 ✉ 6100 – ✆ (05212) 23 34 – info@hotelolympia-seefeld.at – Fax (05212) 44704
geschl. April, Okt. – Nov.
24 Zim – ☼ 35/45 € 64/90 € ❄ 48/57 € 78/108 €
♦ Ein freundlich von der Familie geführtes Hotel, das recht ruhig in einer Nebenstraße liegt und solide, teils hell, teils dunkel möblierte Zimmer bietet.

Schönegg Rest, Rest, P
Speckbacherstr. 174 ✉ 6100 – ✆ (05212) 2 37 50 – info@hotelschoenegg.at – Fax (05212) 2064300
geschl. April – Mai, Nov.
30 Zim (inkl. ½ P.) – ☼ 43/81 € 76/128 € ❄ 65/128 € 112/188 €
Rest – (nur Abendessen für Hausgäste)
♦ Stammgäste schätzen das tadellos unterhaltene Hotel unter familiärer Leitung. Die Zimmer sind mit hellem Holz in ländlichem Stil eingerichtet, z. T. mit kleinem Wohnbereich.

Vergeiner Rest, P
Geigenbühel 692 ✉ 6100 – ✆ (05212) 23 93 – hotel.vergeiner-seefeld@aon.at – Fax (05212) 239334
geschl. 1. April – 9. Mai, 6. Okt. – 19. Dez.
17 Zim (inkl. ½ P.) – ☼ 62/69 € 116/130 € ❄ 90/103 € 172/206 €
Rest – (nur Abendessen für Hausgäste)
♦ Ein sehr gepflegtes kleines Hotel mit wohnlichen Gästezimmern. Das Zentrum sowie ein Skilift befinden sich ganz in der Nähe.

Marthe Rest, P VISA
Krinz 1 ✉ 6100 – ✆ (05212) 25 02 – info@marthe.at – Fax (05212) 250262
geschl. 30. März – 14. Juni, 12. Okt. – 18. Dez.
37 Zim (inkl. ½ P.) – ☼ 46/61 € 84/144 € ❄ 66/90 € 124/185 €
Rest – (nur Abendessen für Hausgäste)
♦ Recht ruhig liegt der Familienbetrieb etwas außerhalb des Ortes. Gepflegter Sauna-/Badebereich; die Zimmer bieten teils Südbalkon. In 1500 m: Reitherjoch-Alm zum Einkehren.

Alpengruss garni
Andreas Hofer Str. 235 ✉ 6100 – ✆ (05212) 26 26 – alpengruss@seefeld-in-tirol.net – Fax (05212) 262620
7 Zim – ☼ 30/55 € 60/80 € ❄ 35/60 € 60/120 €
♦ Die freundliche, familiäre Atmosphäre zeichnet diese Pension aus. Mit Liebe zum Detail wurden die wohnlichen Zimmer eingerichtet. Netter, farblich schöner Frühstücksraum.

Gasthof Batzenhäusl
Klosterstr. 44 ✉ 6100 – ✆ (05212) 22 92
– batzenhaeusel@kaltschmid.co.at – Fax (05212) 22922043
geschl. 26. März – 9. Mai, 20. Okt. – 21. Dez.
29 Zim (inkl. ½ P.) – ☼ 39/75 € 64/100 € ❄ 52/110 € 92/146 €
Rest – Karte 21/37 €
◆ Ein solider Gasthof mit hübscher Balkonfassade, der über recht schlichte, aber gepflegte, mit hellen Naturholzmöbeln regionstypisch eingerichtete Zimmer verfügt. Gemütlich wirkendes Restaurant in bürgerlich-ländlichem Stil. Ab 20 Uhr Tanzlokal.

Egerthof garni
Reitherspitzstr. 294 ✉ 6100 – ✆ (05212) 44 44 – info@egerthof.at
– Fax (05212) 444460
geschl. 27. März – 30. Mai, 4. Okt. – 15. Dez.
26 Zim – ☼ 34/40 € 62/70 € ❄ 51/56 € 88/96 €
◆ Stammgäste schätzen dieses zentrumsnah gelegene Haus mit seinen gepflegten, in rustikaler Eiche möblierten Zimmern. Hell und neuzeitlich gestalteter Saunabereich.

Lindauer garni
Wettersteinstr. 575 ✉ 6100 – ✆ (05212) 20 42 – lindauer@aon.at
– Fax (05212) 20420
geschl. April – Mitte Mai, Mitte Okt. – Mitte Dez.
9 Zim – ☼ 25/45 € 50/90 € ❄ 35/55 € 70/110 €
◆ Sehr familiär wird die von vielen Stammgästen geschätzte kleine Pension geleitet. Schön ist die ruhige Panoramalage. Gemütlich: der mit hellem Holz vertäfelte Frühstücksraum.

Charlotte
Rest, P
Haspingerstr. 475 ✉ 6100 – ✆ (05212) 26 52
– koestinger@hotel-charlotte.com – Fax (05212) 26526
geschl. April – Mitte Mai, Ende Okt. – Mitte Dez.
26 Zim (inkl. ½ P.) – ☼ 57/67 € 100/120 € ❄ 79/99 €
148/188 €
Rest – (nur Abendessen für Hausgäste)
◆ In dem recht ruhig gelegenen Hotel mit Balkonfassade bietet man mit solidem Naturholz eingerichtete Zimmer sowie einige Appartements. Badebereich im Haus gegenüber.

Ritter-Oswald-Stube – Hotel Klosterbräu
Klosterstr. 30 ✉ 6100 – ✆ (05212) 2 62 11 00 – info@klosterbraeu.com
– Fax (05212) 3885
geschl. Ende März – Anfang Juni, Mitte Okt. – Anfang Dez.
Rest – *(nur Abendessen, im Winter Samstag – Sonntag auch Mittagessen)*
Menü 46/62 € – Karte 35/55 €
◆ Gediegenes Ambiente in dem holzverkleideten Restaurant. Erfahrenes Personal serviert mediterran beeinflusste Speisen. Schön ist der Weinkeller unter historischem Kreuzgewölbe.

Südtiroler Stube
Reitherspitzstr. 17 ✉ 6100 – ✆ (05212) 5 04 46
– guido@suedtirolerstuben.com – Fax (05212) 51902
geschl. Ende März – Anfang Mai, Anfang Nov. – Anfang Dez.

Rest – Karte 18/44 €
♦ Viel Holz und Zierrat unterstreichen in den kleinen Stuben des Tiroler Bauernhauses den behaglich-ländlichen Charakter. Regionales Angebot mit Grillspezialitäten.

Kracherle Moos

VISA

Moosweg 758 ✉ 6100 – ✆ (05212) 46 80 – info@kracherlemoos.at – Fax (05212) 468080
geschl. Juni – Juli und Dienstag
Rest – *(Mai und Aug. – Nov. Montag – Freitag nur Abendessen)* (abends Tischbestellung ratsam) Karte 22/43 €
♦ Gemütlich sind die rustikalen Stuben in dem direkt an der Piste gelegenen Bauernhaus. Geboten wird frische regionale Küche – im Winter einfachere Mittagskarte für Skifahrer.

In Reith bei Seefeld Süd-Ost: 3 km Richtung Innsbruck:

Alpenkönig Tirol

(geheizt) Rest, VISA

Gschwandtkopfweg 96 ✉ 6103 – ✆ (05212) 3 32 00 – info@alpenkoenig.at – Fax (05212) 3320700
150 Zim – ☼ 148/208 € 212/272 € ❄ 130/285 € 210/410 € – ½ P 30 € – 25 Suiten
Rest – Menü 48/58 € – Karte 22/40 €
♦ Die große Hotelanlage verfügt über meist sehr geräumige Zimmer mit gepflegter Atmosphäre sowie einen vielseitigen Freizeitbereich mit abwechslungsreichem Programm. Ein aufwändiges Gedeck unterstreicht die elegante Ausstrahlung des Restaurants.

Meilerhof mit Zim

Inntal und Alpen, VISA

Reith 67 (B 177) ✉ 6100 – ✆ (05212) 32 25 – info@meilerhof.at – Fax (05212) 322525
geschl. Nov. 3 Wochen
4 Zim – 50/60 € 80/112 €
Rest – *(geschl. Montag)* Karte 23/47 €
♦ Hier bietet man eine regional geprägte Küche mit internationalem Einfluss – serviert wird im neuzeitlich-ländlichen Restaurant oder auf der Terrasse mit toller Aussicht.

SEEHAM – Salzburg – 730 L5 – 1 680 Ew – Höhe 503 m 1 F3

Wien 299 – Salzburg 21 – Burghausen 35 – Bad Reichenhall 36
Dorf 5, ✉ 5164, ✆ (06217) 54 93, info.seeham@sbg.at

Zum Altwirt

Dorf 1 ✉ 5164 – ✆ (06217) 55 22 – info@altwirt.at – Fax (06217) 612040
25 Zim – 42/56 € 68/96 € – ½ P 10 €
Rest – *(geschl. Feb. und Dienstag)* Menü 10 € – Karte 17/35 €
♦ Im 18. Jh. erbaut wurde der gepflegte Gasthof mit eigener Metzgerei. Die Zimmer sind rustikal und solide mit Eichenmöbeln eingerichtet. Restaurant mit gutbürgerlicher Küche und nettem Heurigen-Garten.

SEEKIRCHEN AM WALLERSEE – Salzburg – 730 L5 – 9 350 Ew – Höhe 512 m 8 G4

Wien 290 – Salzburg 18 – Burghausen 46 – Bad Reichenhall 32
Hauptstr. 3, ✉ 5201, ☎ (06212) 40 35, seekirchen@salzburger-seenland.at

Gasthof zur Post
Hauptstr. 19 ✉ 5201 – ☎ (06212) 22 29 – office@postseekirchen.at – Fax (06212) 7977
28 Zim – 40/45 € 70/80 € – ½ P 12 €
Rest – *(geschl. Sept. – Juni Sonntagabend – Montag)* Karte 14/27 €
◆ Die Zimmer des im Zentrum liegenden Hauses sind teils mit Kirschbaummöbeln, teils mit Naturholz ländlich eingerichtet. Tagungsbereich und nette Terrasse stehen zur Verfügung.

In Seekirchen-Seewalchen Nord-Ost: 1 km:

Schlosswirt Seeburg
Seeburgstr. 8 ✉ 5201 – ☎ (06212) 3 97 12 – schlosswirt.seeburg.marousek@sbg.at – Fax (06212) 39712
geschl. Jan. 2 Wochen, Okt. – Nov. 1 Woche und Montag – Mittwochmittag
Rest – Karte 12/32 €
◆ In dem ehemaligen Schloss unweit des Sees findet man das Restaurant und das Salettl, in denen regional-internationale Küche angeboten wird. Schlosshof mit Bierbrunnen.

SEEWALCHEN AM ATTERSEE – Oberösterreich – 730 M5 – 4 750 Ew – Höhe 495 m 1 G3

Wien 238 – Linz 78 – Salzburg 60 – Vöcklabruck 12

Litzlberger-Keller mit Zim
Moos 8 ✉ 4863 – ☎ (07662) 23 12 – litzlbergerkeller@aon.at – Fax (07662) 231223
geschl. 10. Jan. – 5. Feb. und Dienstag – Mittwoch sowie Juli – Aug. nur Mittwoch
9 Zim – 49/53 € 88/96 €
Rest – Menü 29 € – Karte 19/40 €
◆ Früher Teil der namengebenden Brauerei, heute ein gemütlich-rustikaler Gasthof mit regionaler Küche und einer schönen Terrasse mit Blick auf den See. Bootshaus mit Badesteg.

SEGGAUBERG – Steiermark – 730 S8 – 1 040 Ew – Höhe 350 m 11 K5

Wien 228 – Graz 43 – Maribor 33

Hasenwirt südsteierisches Bergland,
Seggauberg 27 ✉ 8430 – ☎ (03452) 7 45 70 – office@hasenwirt.at – Fax (03452) 7457033
49 Zim – 59/67 € 98/108 € – ½ P 16 €
Rest – Karte 15/28 €
◆ Das familiengeführte Hotel überzeugt mit seiner Lage oberhalb der Weinberge. Alle Zimmer sind nach Süden hin gelegen und bieten eine schöne Aussicht. Restaurant im Landhausstil.

SEKIRN – Kärnten – siehe Maria Wörth

SEMMERING – Niederösterreich – 730 T6 – 610 Ew – Höhe 1 000 m – Wintersport: 1 340 m 1 4 – Heilklimatischer Kurort 11 K4

Wien 92 – St. Pölten 128 – Wiener Neustadt 43 – Mürzzuschlag 15
Passhöhe 248, 2680, (02664) 2 00 25, semmeringtourismus@aon.at
Semmering, Meierei 122 (02664) 81 54
Bahnwanderweg★ (Aussichtswarte am Doppelreiterkogel★★)
Semmeringbahn★ (Nord: 9 km) – Neuberg an der Mürz★ (West: 25 km)

Panhans Hirschenkogel und Sonnewendstein, Zim,
Hochstr. 32b
2680 – (02664) 81 81 – hotel@panhans.at
– Fax (02664) 8181513
113 Zim (inkl. ½ P.) – 106/138 € 158/236 € 117/148 € 174/246 € – 5 Suiten
Rest – Menü 28/39 € – Karte 24/34 €
◆ In dem klassischen Grandhotel aus dem Jahre 1888 erwarten den Gast sehr individuell gestaltete Zimmer von stilvoll-gediegen bis zur Designer-Maisonette. Als Wintergarten angelegtes Restaurant mit eleganter Note.

Panoramahotel Wagner Kalkalpen und Wiener Becken,
Hochstr. 267
2680 – (02664) 2 51 20 – biowelt@panoramahotel-wagner.at
– Fax (02664) 251261
geschl. 25. März – 8. Mai, 20. Okt. – 5. Dez.
24 Zim – 54/75 € 108/150 € – ½ P 18 €
Rest – Karte 25/37 €
◆ Sehr umweltbewusst zeigt sich dieses ganz nach biologischen Richtlinien ausgestattete Haus mit engagierter Gästebetreuung. Bioladen und einige Kosmetikbehandlungen. Auf rein ökologischem Anbau beruhende Speisen werden im Restaurant zubereitet.

SENFTENBERG – Niederösterreich – 730 S3 – 1 980 Ew – Höhe 254 m 3 J2

Wien 86 – Sankt Pölten 45 – Stockerau 60 – Krems an der Donau 9

Weinhaus Nigl mit Zim A/C Zim,
Kirchenberg 1 3541 – (02719) 2 60 95 00
– reservierung@weingutnigl.at – Fax (02719) 2609550
geschl. Jan.
11 Zim – 63/83 € 96/136 €
Rest – *(geschl. Dienstag – Mittwoch)* Menü 36 € – Karte 23/35 €
◆ Unterhalb der Burgruine in einem gotischen Lesehof a. d. 12. Jh. finden Sie dieses Restaurant. Freundlicher Service, regionale Küche und sehr guter Wein aus eigenem Anbau. In den Zimmern wurde Modernes geschmackvoll mit der alten Bausubstanz verbunden.

SERFAUS – Tirol – 730 D7 – 1 100 Ew – Höhe 1 427 m – Wintersport: 2 700 m 10 33 6 C6

Wien 536 – Innsbruck 92 – Sankt Anton am Arlberg 52 – Imst 38
Untere Dorfstr. 13, 6534, (05476) 6 23 90, info@serfaus-fiss-ladis.at

Schalber (geheizt)
Dorfbahnstr. 15 Rest, Rest,
✉ *6534 – ✆ (05476) 67 70 – info@schalber.com – Fax (05476) 677035*
geschl. 7. April – 19. Juni, 10. Nov. – 18. Dez.
84 Zim (inkl. ½ P.) – ☼ 165/175 € 200/300 € ❄ 175/290 €
320/580 € – 22 Suiten
Rest *Jägerstube* – separat erwähnt
◆ Das Hotel mit dem alpenländisch-eleganten Rahmen steht für freundlichen und engagierten Service vom Empfang bis zur Gästebetreuung im schönen großzügigen Wellnessbereich.

Cervosa Rest,
Herrenanger 11 ✉ 6534 – ✆ (05476) 62 11
– info@cervosa.com – Fax (05476) 6736
geschl. 6. April – 15. Juni, 19. Okt. – 7. Dez.
90 Zim (inkl. ½ P.) – ☼ 121/195 € 207/260 € ❄ 182/234 €
286/477 € – 18 Suiten
Rest – (nur Abendessen für Hausgäste)
◆ Ein großzügiger Empfangsbereich mit Flügel und Kaminhalle, wohnlich-elegante Zimmer und Suiten sowie das vielfältige Wellnessangebot machen dieses Hotel aus.

3 Sonnen Zim, Rest,
Untere Dorfstr. 17 ✉ 6534
– ✆ (05476) 62 07 – hotel@dreisonnen.com – Fax (05476) 620755
geschl. Mai, Nov
50 Zim (inkl. ½ P.) – ☼ 109/129 € 198/278 € ❄ 110/259 €
200/578 €
Rest – (nur für Hausgäste)
◆ In diesem sehr netten, persönlich geführten Hotel im Zentrum erwarten Sie wohnliche Gästezimmer mit gutem Platzangebot und ein hübscher Freizeitbereich mit Kosmetik.

Alpenruh Rest, Rest, 
Dorfbahnstr. 10 ✉ 6534 – ✆ (05476) 62 51
– alpenruh@micheluzzihotels.at – Fax (05476) 6531
geschl. 7. April – 7. Juni, 26. Okt. – 12. Dez.
33 Zim (inkl. ½ P.) – ☼ 65/72 € 130/144 € ❄ 80/150 €
160/300 € – 4 Suiten
Rest – (nur Abendessen für Hausgäste)
◆ Dieser Familienbetrieb ist ein sehr gepflegtes Hotel am Ortseingang mit soliden, wohnlich eingerichteten Gästezimmern, die meist über einen Balkon verfügen.

Serfauser Hof Zim,
Dorfbahnstr. 57 ✉ 6534 – ✆ (05476) 63 07 – info@serfauserhof.at
– Fax (05476) 630735
geschl. 7. April – 6. Dez.
19 Zim (inkl. ½ P.) – 145/290 € 200/358 €
Rest – *(nur Abendessen)* Karte 28/42 €
◆ Hübsch hat man das familiär geleitete Haus in der Ortsmitte im gemütlich-rustikalen Stil ausgestattet. Zum Hotel gehört auch ein netter Bade- und Saunabereich. Mit viel Holz behaglich gestaltetes Restaurant.

Alte Schmiede (mit Gästehaus) Rest,
Dorfbahnstr. 64 ✉ 6534
– ✆ (05476) 6 49 20 – info@alte-schmiede-serfaus.at – Fax (05476) 64927
geschl. 15. April – 15. Juni, 15. Okt. – 15. Dez.
35 Zim (inkl. ½ P.) – ☼ 59/67 € 118/134 € ❄ 120/150 € 240/340 € – 19 Suiten
Rest – Karte 15/25 €
◆ Das von der Inhaberfamilie geführte regionstypische Hotel liegt am Zentrumsrand und bietet Ihnen wohnliche Gästezimmer sowie einige geräumige Appartements mit Kochecke. Teil des Restaurants ist das gemütliche Schmiede-Stüberl mit Fondue-Angebot.

Jenny's Schlössl (mit Gästehaus) Rest,
Plojenweg 9 ✉ 6534 – ✆ (05476) 66 54
– jennys@tirol.com – Fax (05476) 665454
geschl. Mitte April – Mitte Mai, Nov.
24 Zim (inkl. ½ P.) – ☼ 67/75 € 114/130 € ❄ 89/130 € 178/260 €
Rest – (nur für Hausgäste)
◆ In Hanglage etwas abseits des Zentrums befindet sich das an ein Schlösschen erinnernde Hotel mit seinen wohnlichen Zimmern; im Gästehaus etwas einfacher. Kosmetik und Massage.

Silvretta Rest, Rest,
Dorfbahnstr. 20 ✉ 6534 – ✆ (05476) 62 56 – info@hotel-silvretta.com
– Fax (05476) 6990
geschl. Anfang April – Mitte Juni, Ende Sept. – Mitte Dez.
36 Zim (inkl. ½ P.) – ☼ 41/50 € 82/100 € ❄ 67/100 € 134/200 €
Rest – (nur Abendessen für Hausgäste)
◆ Zeitgemäß und funktionell eingerichtete Gästezimmer stehen in diesem Hotel in zentraler Lage zur Verfügung. Nett ist die holzgetäfelte Zirbenstube mit Kachelofen.

Castel Rest, VISA
Malbrettweg 13 ✉ 6534 – ✆ (05476) 61 31 – castel@aon.at
– Fax (05476) 61315
geschl. Mai, Nov.
14 Zim (inkl. ½ P.) – ☼ 40/136 € 80/136 € ❄ 63/284 € 126/284 €
Rest – (nur Abendessen für Hausgäste)
◆ Mit ganz hellem Holz hat man die Zimmer und Appartements dieses etwas oberhalb des Ortes gelegenen kleinen Hotels ausgestattet. Schön: der Weinkeller mit Naturfelswänden.

Alpina garni
Dorfbahnstr. 22 ✉ 6534 – ✆ (05476) 62 19 – info@alpina-serfaus.at
– Fax (05476) 62194
geschl. 6. April – 20. Juni, 1. Okt. – 6. Dez.
19 Zim – ☼ 24/33 € 48/66 € ❄ 49/64 € 98/128 €
◆ Das familiengeführte Haus bietet mit hellem Naturholz wohnlich eingerichtete Zimmer und Appartements, einige mit schöner Sicht. Gemütlicher Salon.

Barbara

Rest,

Gänsackerweg 6 ✉ 6534 – ✆ (05476) 62 17 – info@barbara.at – Fax (05476) 6717

geschl. 13. April – 7. Juni, 5. Okt. - 4. Dez.

25 Zim (inkl. ½ P.) – ☼ 50/56 € 94/112 € ❄ 69/102 € 128/204 €

Rest – (nur Abendessen für Hausgäste)

◆ Behagliche, überwiegend mit hellem Holz regionstypisch möblierte Zimmer sowie ein mediterran gestalteter Freizeitbereich erwarten Sie in dem Hotel im Zentrum.

Jägerstube – Hotel Schalber

Dorfbahnstr. 15 ✉ 6534 – ✆ (05476) 67 70 – info@schalber.com – Fax (05476) 677035

geschl. 7. April – 19. Juni, 10. Nov. – 18. Dez. und Mittwoch

Rest – *(nur Abendessen)* (Tischbestellung ratsam) Menü 105 € – Karte 42/52 €

◆ Holztäfelung, Kachelofen und Jagdtrophäen verleihen diesem Restaurant seine gemütliche rustikale Atmosphäre. Kompetenter Service mit guter Weinberatung.

SIBRATSGFÄLL – Vorarlberg – 730 C6 – 430 Ew – Höhe 950 m – Wintersport: 1 100 m 4 — 5 A5

Wien 598 – Bregenz 33 – Dornbirn 30 – Kempten 63

Dorf 18, ✉ 6952, ✆ (05513) 21 21, info@sibra.cnv.at

Gasthof Hirschen

Dorf 31 ✉ 6952 – ✆ (05513) 21 11 – info@derhirschen.at – Fax (05513) 2123

24 Zim – 38/53 € 76/106 €

Rest – Karte 11/29 €

◆ Der alpenländische Gasthof am Zentrumsrand bietet mit soliden Naturholzmöbeln und teils mit Holzboden ausgestattete Zimmer – einige nach Süden gelegen, mit schöner Sicht. Unterteiltes Restaurant mit rustikalem Charakter.

SIERNING – Oberösterreich – 730 O4 – 8 520 Ew – Höhe 369 m — 2 H3

Wien 173 – Linz 34 – Steyr 10 – Wels 37

Kirchenplatz 1, ✉ 4522, ✆ (07259) 22 55 45, claudia.langeder@sierning.ooe.gv.at

Landhotel Forsthof

(geheizt) Zim,

Neustr. 29 ✉ 4522 – ✆ (07259) 2 31 90 – office@forsthof.at – Fax (07259) 231966

50 Zim – 58/68 € 88/98 € – ½ P 20 €

Rest – *(geschl. Sonn- und Feiertage abends)* Karte 16/32 €

◆ Der ehemalige Gutshof aus dem 13. Jh. beherbergt heute ein gut geführtes Seminarhotel mit teils recht großzügigen Zimmern von neuzeitlich bis rustikal in Eiche. Das Restaurant besteht aus mehreren netten ländlichen Stuben, z. T. mit Kachelofen.

SILBERTAL IM MONTAFON – Vorarlberg – 730 B7 – 880 Ew – Höhe 889 m – Wintersport: 1 450 m 4 11 — 5 A6

Wien 593 – Bregenz 70 – Feldkirch 149 – Innsbruck 38

Zentrum 256, ✉ 6780, ✆ (05556) 7 41 12, info@silbertal.at

Bergkristall Zim, Zim,

Zentrum 328 6780 – (05556) 7 41 14
– hotel@bergkristall.com – Fax (05556) 7411431
geschl. nach 15. April – 1. Juni, 15. Okt. – 15. Dez.
22 Zim (inkl. ½ P.) – 89/91 € 152/156 € 100/111 €
174/196 € – 6 Suiten
Rest – *(geschl. im Winter Montag, im Sommer Dienstag)* Karte 24/37 €
♦ Der tipptopp gepflegte Familienbetrieb bietet überwiegend im alpenländischen Stil gehaltene Zimmer, meist mit runden Himmelbetten und teils recht aufwändig gestalteten Bädern.

Hirschen Zim, Zim,

Zentrum 127 6780 – (05556) 7 41 11
– gasthof.hirschen@montafon.com – Fax (05556) 741114
geschl. 7. April – 1. Mai, 19. Okt. – 7. Dez.
22 Zim (inkl. ½ P.) – 78/91 € 130/160 € 86/101 €
146/180 €
Rest – *(geschl. Montag)* Karte 18/30 €
♦ In dem familiengeführten Hotel erwarten Sie wohnliche, mit hellem Naturholzmobiliar regionstypisch eingerichtete Gästezimmer – einige sind besonders geräumig.

SILLIAN – Tirol – 730 J8 – 2 090 Ew – Höhe 1 100 m – Wintersport: 2 407 m 1 5 7 F6

Wien 435 – Innsbruck 144 – Lienz 31 – Cortina d'Ampezzo 48
Gemeindehaus Nr. 86, 9920, (04842) 66 66, info@hochpustertal.com

Dolomiten Residenz Sporthotel Sillian
(geheizt) Rest,

Pustertaler Str. 49d 9920 – (04842) 6 01 10
– info@sporthotel-sillian.at – Fax (04842) 6013
geschl. 6. April – 14. Juni, 8. Nov. – 6. Dez.
106 Zim (inkl. ½ P.) – 106/135 € 170/230 € 117/180 €
204/310 €
Rest – Karte 27/40 €
♦ Zu den Annehmlichkeiten dieses direkt am Skilift gelegenen Hauses zählt ein Wellnessbereich auf 3000 qm mit mehreren Schwimmbecken, Saunen und diversen Kosmetikanwendungen. Restaurant mit gemütlichem rustikalem Ambiente sowie Bauernstube mit Kachelofen.

SÖCHAU – Steiermark – 730 U7 – 1 480 Ew – Höhe 273 m 11 L5

Wien 156 – Graz 57 – Fürstenfeld 10

Oststeirischer Hof (mit Gästehäusern) (geheizt)

Söchau 3 8362 Zim, Rest,
– (03387) 22 32 0 – soechau@maiers.at – Fax (03387) 223232
geschl. 21. – 25. Dez.
58 Zim – 82/87 € 134/144 €
Rest – *(geschl. Sonntagabend)* (nur für Hausgäste)
♦ Vier verschiedene Häuser mit neuzeitlich-funktionellen Zimmern und individuellen Appartements bilden dieses Seminarhotel im Kräuterdorf Söchau. Casanova-Garten mit Pool.

SÖLDEN – Tirol – 730 F8 – 3 070 Ew – Höhe 1 377 m – Wintersport: 3 250 m 5 38 6 C6

Wien 528 – Innsbruck 84 – Imst 50 – Landeck 66

Rettenbach 464, 6450, (05254) 51 00, info@soelden.com

Veranstaltungen

31.08.: Ötztaler Radmarathon

Gaislachkogel ★★

Ventertal★★ (Süd: 5 km) – Gurgler Tal★★ (Süd: 15 km) – Wildes Mannle★★★ (Süd-West: 18 km)

Central

Rest, VISA AE

Auweg 3 6450 – (05254) 2 26 00 – info@central-soelden.at – Fax (05254) 2260511

geschl. Anfang Mai – Mitte Juli

120 Zim (inkl. ½ P.) – 140/193 € 240/364 € 140/224 € 240/426 € – 18 Suiten

Rest Ötztaler Stube – separat erwähnt

◆ Wohnliche Zimmer von modern bis kolonial und der großzügige Wellnessbereich machen das gewachsene Alpenhotel aus. Besonders luxuriös: die Turmsuite Wildspitze auf zwei Etagen.

Castello Falkner

(geheizt) Rest, Rest, VISA

Oberwindaustr. 19 6450 – (05254) 26 00 – info@castello.at – Fax (05254) 260019

geschl. 12. Mai – 21. Juni

48 Zim (inkl. ½ P.) – 79/163 € 158/236 € 92/174 € 184/230 € – 35 Suiten

Rest – Karte 21/34 €

◆ Wie ein kleines Dorf hat man dieses aus mehreren Häusern bestehende Hotel angelegt. Die Zimmer und Suiten sind elegant eingerichtet, einige mit Kachelofen. In rustikale Stuben unterteiltes Restaurant.

Liebe Sonne

Rest, VISA AE

Dorfstr. 58 6450 – (05254) 2 20 30 – liebe.sonne@sonnenhotels.at – Fax (05254) 2423

geschl. Anfang Mai – Ende Juni

60 Zim (inkl. ½ P.) – 65/110 € 130/200 € 80/160 € 150/310 €

Rest – *(nur Abendessen)* Karte 24/33 €

◆ Unweit der Bergbahnen liegt dieses neuzeitliche Hotel. Mit modern-rustikalen Möbeln, Holzfußboden und hübschen Stoffen hat man die Zimmer wohnlich ausgestattet. Eine gemütliche Stube ergänzt den klassisch gestalteten Speisesaal.

Bergland

Rest, Rest, VISA AE

Dorfstrasse 114 6450 – (05254) 2 24 00 – info@bergland-soelden.at – Fax (05254) 2240510

geschl. 4. Mai – 12. Juli

89 Zim (inkl. ½ P.) – 69/92 € 138/210 € 91/149 € 174/322 €

Rest – (Tischbestellung ratsam) Karte 26/46 €

◆ Eine großzügige Halle verbindet die beiden Hotelgebäude "Sölden"- und "Ötztal"-Haus, die mit freundlichen Zimmern in ländlichem Stil gefallen. Angenehm heller Freizeitbereich. Rustikale holzvertäfelte A-la-carte-Stube.

Stefan Zim,
Dorfstr. 50 6450 – (05254) 22 37 – info@hotel-stefan.at – Fax (05254) 223725
geschl. Anfang Mai – Mitte Okt.
35 Zim (inkl. ½ P.) – 86/119 € 172/238 €
Rest – (nur Abendessen für Hausgäste)
♦ Die Gästezimmer dieses nahe den Bergbahnen gelegenen Hotels sind neuzeitlich und sehr gepflegt, verfügen über moderne Bäder und sind z. T. recht geräumig.

Erhart
Windaustr. 24 6450 – (05254) 20 20 – info@hotel-erhart.at – Fax (05254) 20205
geschl. 13. April – 21. Juni
28 Zim (inkl. ½ P.) – 48/73 € 96/146 € 83/143 € 142/246 €
Rest – (nur Abendessen für Hausgäste)
♦ Gut unterhaltene Zimmer, die überwiegend mit hellem Naturholzmobiliar eingerichtet sind, erwarten Sie in dem familiengeführten Alpenhotel. Regionstypische Restaurant-Stube mit Holzfußboden.

Valentin
Dorfstr. 109 6450 – (05254) 22 67 – hotel-valentin@tino.at – Fax (05254) 23708
geschl. Mitte April – Ende Juni, Mitte Sept. – Mitte Okt.
40 Zim (inkl. ½ P.) – 60/80 € 110/140 € 90/140 € 160/240 €
Rest – Karte 20/32 €
♦ Tadellose Pflege, mit dunklem Holz wohnlich-gediegen eingerichtete Zimmer sowie die Lage an der Talstation der Bergbahn sprechen für dieses Hotel. Das Restaurant ist eine in ländlichem Stil gehaltene Stube.

Alpina
Rettenbachstr. 4 6450 – (05254) 5 01 20 – alpina@riml.at – Fax (05254) 501260
geschl. 10. Mai – 13. Juli
54 Zim (inkl. ½ P.) – 66/118 € 116/186 € 84/156 € 152/242 €
Rest – *(geschl. Dienstag)* (nur für Hausgäste)
♦ In einer recht ruhigen Seitenstraße liegt dieses für die Region typische Hotel mit seinen meist im Landhausstil möblierten und freundlich gestalteten Zimmern. Holzvertäfelte Gaststube mit gemütlicher Atmosphäre.

Alphof Rest,
Dorfstr. 202 6450 – (05254) 25 59 – info@alphofsoelden.com – Fax (05254) 210944
geschl. 20. April – 27. Juni, 4. Sept. – 2. Okt.
50 Zim (inkl. ½ P.) – 66/81 € 112/142 € 86/146 € 132/258 € – 3 Suiten
Rest – (nur Abendessen für Hausgäste)
♦ Hinter seiner alpenländischen Balkonfassade beherbergt das familiengeführte Haus am Ortsrand wohnliche Zimmer im Tiroler Stil sowie die Relax Oase mit Panoramapool.

Dominic
Dorfstr. 64 ✉ 6450 – ✆ (05254) 26 46 – info@dominic.at
– Fax (05254) 2975
geschl. Mai- Sept.
22 Zim (inkl. ½ P.) – 🚹99/137 € 🚹🚹134/218 €
Rest – *(nur Abendessen)* Karte 16/39 €
◆ Aus einer Frühstückspension ist dieses neuzeitliche Hotel entstanden. Ein moderner Stil begleitet Sie vom Empfangsbereich bis in die angenehm hell gestalteten Zimmer. Rustikales Restaurant mit schwerer Holzdecke und gepflegter Atmosphäre.

Granat garni
Gemeindestr. 2 ✉ 6450 – ✆ (05254) 20 62 – info@hotel-granat.at
– Fax (05254) 20627
14 Zim ☕ – ☼ 🚹26/48 € 🚹🚹52/96 € ❄ 🚹39/78 € 🚹🚹78/156 €
◆ Zeitgemäße Zimmer mit hellen Naturholzmöbeln stehen in dem kleinen Hotel im Zentrum zur Verfügung. Gratis: die Bade- und Saunalandschaft der Freizeit-Arena.

Hotel am Hof
Auweg 12 ✉ 6450 – ✆ (05254) 22 41 – info@hotel-am-hof.at
– Fax (05254) 2121111
geschl. Mai – Juni
17 Zim (inkl. ½ P.) – ☼ 🚹54/68 € 🚹🚹94/122 € ❄ 🚹85/105 €
🚹🚹148/200 €
Rest – (nur Abendessen für Hausgäste)
◆ Ein netter Familienbetrieb ist dieses kleine Hotel im Tiroler Stil mit ganz rustikal gehaltenen Gästezimmern. Freier Eintritt in Schwimmbad/Sauna der Freizeit-Arena.

XXX **Ötztaler Stube** – Hotel Central
Auweg 3 ✉ 6450 – ✆ (05254) 2 26 00 – info@central-soelden.at
– Fax (05254) 2260511
geschl. Anfang Mai – Mitte Juli
Rest – Menü 44/78 € (abends) – Karte 41/65 €
◆ Gemütlich sitzt man in der ganz mit Zirbelholz vertäfelten Ötztaler Stube. An aufwändig eingedeckten Tischen werden klassische und regionale Speisen serviert.

In Sölden-Hochsölden Nord-West: 6 km Richtung Gletscher:

Schöne Aussicht ← Ötztal und Bergwelt, Rest,
Hochsöldenstr. 3 ✉ 6450
– ✆ (05254) 22 21 – info@schoeneaussicht.at – Fax (05254) 274852
geschl. Mai – Nov.
45 Zim (inkl. ½ P.) – 🚹91/158 € 🚹🚹156/334 €
Rest – (nur für Hausgäste)
◆ Hinter einer zum Teil holzverkleideten Fassade erwartet Sie ein elegant-wohnliches Ambiente. Schön: die ruhige Hanglage an der Piste.

Alpenhotel Enzian ← Ötztal und Bergwelt,
Hochsöldenstr. 7 ✉ 6450
– ✆ (05254) 22 52 – info@hotel-enzian.at – Fax (05254) 2846
geschl. 21. Mai – 28. Juni, 14. Sept. – 28. Nov.

46 Zim (inkl. ½ P.) – ☼ 134/168 € 178/226 € ❄ 153/230 € 206/314 €

Rest – Karte 16/46 €

◆ Die herrliche Panoramalage macht dieses Berghotel aus. Die Zimmer sind unterschiedlich geschnitten und ländlich eingerichtet. Im Winter liegt die Skipiste direkt am Haus. Mit hellem Holz ausgestattetes Restaurant und Terrasse mit beeindruckender Sicht.

In Sölden-Zwieselstein Süd-Ost: 4 km Richtung Timmelsjoch:

Gasthof Zwieselstein mit Zim

Rest, VISA

Kühtrainstr. 14 ✉ 6450 – ✆ (05254) 35 03 – Info@zwieselstein.at – Fax (05254) 350333

10 Zim (inkl. ½ P.) – ☼ 52/56 € 84/92 € ❄ 66/86 € 112/152 €

Rest – *(geschl. 22. Sept. – 20. Okt.)* Karte 22/24 €

◆ Der familiengeführte Gasthof im Tal beherbergt hinter seiner gepflegten Balkonfassade ein holzvertäfeltes Restaurant mit einer alten Stube sowie neuzeitliche Gästezimmer.

In Obergurgl Süd: 14 km Richtung Timmelsjoch – Höhe 1 990 m – Wintersport: 3080 m 2 24

Gurglerstr. 118, ✉ 6456, ✆ (05254) 51 01 00, info@obergurgl.com

Hochfirst

(geheizt) VISA AE

Gurglerstr. 123 ✉ 6456 – ✆ (05256) 6 32 50 – info@hochfirst.com – Fax (05256) 63030

geschl. Mai – Mitte Nov.

90 Zim (inkl. ½ P.) – 114/227 € 214/434 € – 14 Suiten

Rest – (nur für Hausgäste)

◆ Mit einem alpenländisch-wohnlichen Ambiente gefällt dieses komfortable Hotel. Schön: der Wellnessbereich mit großem In-/Outdoorpool und der Saunalandschaft Alpinarium.

Gotthard Zeit

Rest, VISA

Hohe Mutweg 4 ✉ 6456 – ✆ (05256) 62 92 – info@gotthardt-zeit.com – Fax (05256) 6375

geschl. 1. Mai – 25. Juni, 5. Sept. – 20. Nov.

50 Zim (inkl. ½ P.) – ☼ 69/85 € 118/158 € ❄ 97/155 € 170/360 €

Rest – (nur für Hausgäste)

◆ Eine großzügige Lobby empfängt Sie in dem auf einem Plateau gelegenen Alpenhotel. Die Zimmer sind mit hellen Möbeln neuzeitlich-rustikal eingerichtet.

Alpina (mit Gästehaus)

VISA AE

Kressbrunnenstr. 12 ✉ 6456 – ✆ (05256) 60 00 – hotelalpina@hotelalpina.com – Fax (05256) 6234

geschl. 13. April – 15. Nov.

86 Zim (inkl. ½ P.) – 110/233 € 192/466 € – 12 Suiten

Rest – Karte 23/46 €

◆ Etwas oberhalb des Ortes gelegenes Hotel mit zeitlos oder alpenländisch möblierten Zimmern und einem angenehm hell gestalteten Freizeitbereich. Einfacher: das Gästehaus.

Bergwelt Rest,

Kressbrunnenweg 9 ✉ 6456 – ✆ (05256) 62 74
– office@hotelbergwelt.com – Fax (05256) 638372
geschl. 20. April - 17. Nov.
75 Zim (inkl. ½ P.) – 87/224 € 154/378 € – 18 Suiten
Rest – Karte 25/30 €
◆ Teil dieses gewachsenen familiengeführten Hotels ist ein moderner, mit Schindeln verkleideter halbrund angelegter Bau mit hübschen neuzeitlichen Landhauszimmern.

Crystal Zim, Rest,

Gurglerstr. 90 ✉ 6456 – ✆ (05256) 64 54 – info@hotel-crystal.com
– Fax (05256) 636995
geschl. Mai – Nov.
52 Zim (inkl. ½ P.) – 76/155 € 152/310 € – 10 Suiten
Rest *Das kleine Restaurant* – *(nur Abendessen)* (Tischbestellung erforderlich) Karte 34/50 €
◆ Vom Empfang bis in die Gästezimmer hat man dieses Hotel am Ortseingang zeitlos und gediegen gestaltet. 2 Suiten sind als Maisonetten angelegt. Das kleine Restaurant bietet eine kreative, überwiegend internationale Küche.

Josl

Ramolweg 18 ✉ 6456 – ✆ (05256) 62 05 – welcome@josl.at
– Fax (05256) 6460
geschl. 20. April – 28. Juni
43 Zim (inkl. ½ P.) – 58/91 € 108/126 € 86/136 € 180/280 €
Rest – (nur für Hausgäste)
◆ Ein klarer, moderner Stil begleitet durch das gesamte Hotel, vom "Living Room" über die Gästezimmer bis zum Wohlfühlbereich Sky Sphere im 4. Stock. Après-Ski im Josl-Keller.

Olympia Berglandschaft, Zim, Rest,

Kressbrunnenweg 14 ✉ 6456 – ✆ (05256) 62 88 – info@hotel-olympia.at
– Fax (05256) 63927
geschl. 20. April – 21. Juni, 1. Sept. – 21. Nov.
27 Zim (inkl. ½ P.) – 41/44 € 70/82 € 73/112 € 120/198 € – 4 Suiten
Rest – (nur Abendessen für Hausgäste)
◆ Ein gut geführtes Alpenhotel auf einem kleinen Plateau, dessen Zimmer mit hellem Naturholz neuzeitlich und dennoch ländlich, teils leicht elegant eingerichtet sind.

Gasthof Mühle Rest,

Gurglerstr. 87 (Nord: 1 km) ✉ 6456 – ✆ (05256) 67 67
– info@hotel-muehle.com – Fax (05256) 676744
geschl. Mai – 28. Juni, 6. Sept. – 29. Nov.
45 Zim (inkl. ½ P.) – 60 € 110 € 82/153 € 144/324 €
Rest – (nur für Hausgäste)
◆ Ein gewachsener familiärer Gasthof mit soliden Zimmern, zum Tal oder zum Berg/Wald hin gelegen. Für Kinder: Spielraum und Spielplatz. Freizeitbereich mit Massagen/Anwendungen.

Wiesental Zim, VISA

Piccardweg 16 ✉ 6456 – ✆ (05256) 62 63 – info@hotelwiesental.com – Fax (05256) 63583

geschl. Mai – 28. Juni, Okt. – 26. Nov.

26 Zim (inkl. ½ P.) – ☼ 49/53 € 94/102 € ❄ 77/112 € 126/216 €

Rest – Karte 18/29 €

◆ Ein sehr gepflegter Gasthof im Ortszentrum. Es stehen mit hellem Mobiliar solide und wohnlich eingerichtete Zimmer zur Verfügung. Das Restaurant teilt sich in ländlich-rustikale Stuben mit Kachelofen.

Regina Rest, VISA

Kressbrunnenweg 1 ✉ 6456 – ✆ (05256) 62 21 – regina@obergurgl.at – Fax (05256) 63128

geschl. Mai – Juni, Sept. – Mitte Nov.

26 Zim (inkl. ½ P.) – ☼ 61/74 € 86/112 € ❄ 86/142 € 136/248 €

Rest – (nur für Hausgäste)

◆ Hinter der regionstypischen Fassade des Hauses erwarten Sie ein ländlich-rustikal gestalteter Empfangsbereich sowie zeitgemäß und solide ausgestattete Gästezimmer.

Enzian Rest, VISA

Kressbrunnenweg 5 ✉ 6456 – ✆ (05256) 62 35 – enzian@obergurgl.com – Fax (05256) 63405

geschl. Mai – 28. Juni, 7. Sept. – 15. Nov.

27 Zim (inkl. ½ P.) – ☼ 52/57 € 95/114 € ❄ 80/133 € 130/266 € – 4 Suiten

Rest – (nur für Hausgäste)

◆ In dem familiengeführten Hotel oberhalb des Ortes erwarten Sie eine private Atmosphäre sowie gepflegte Gästezimmer mit ländlicher Einrichtung – Suiten teils mit Kachelofen.

Jagd-Haus Panorama garni VISA AE

Hohe Mut Weg 1 ✉ 6456 – ✆ (05256) 62 77 – panorama@obergurgl.com – Fax (05256) 627710

geschl. Anfang Mai – Anfang Nov.

13 Zim – 45/77 € 90/154 €

◆ Das ehemalige Jagdhaus ist heute ein nettes kleines Hotel mit rustikalem Charakter, das sich in unmittelbarer Nähe der Skipiste befindet.

In Hochgurgl **Süd-Ost: 15 km Richtung Timmelsjoch – Höhe 2 150 m – Wintersport: 3080 m 2 24**

Top Hotel Hochgurgl < Ötztal und Bergwelt, Spa Rest, VISA AE

Hochgurgler Str. 8

✉ 6456 – ✆ (05256) 62 65 – tophotel@hochgurgl.com – Fax (05256) 626510

geschl. Anfang Mai – Mitte Nov.

62 Zim (inkl. ½ P.) – 247/417 € 316/656 €

Rest – (Tischbestellung ratsam) Menü 55/65 € – Karte 26/53 €

◆ Schön liegt das Hotel mit dem angenehmen elegant-rustikalen Rahmen an der Skipiste. Zum Angebot zählt u. a. ein moderner Wellnessbereich. Sehr hübsch: die Präsidentensuite. Ganz in Holz gehaltene Restaurantstube mit internationaler und regionaler Küche.

Riml ≤ Ötztal und Bergwelt, Rest, Rest, VISA AE
Hochgurglerstr. 16
6456 – (05256) 62 61 – info@hotel-riml.com – Fax (05256) 6310
geschl. Ende April – Mitte Nov.
99 Zim (inkl. ½ P.) – 96/161 € 180/358 € – 11 Suiten
Rest – (nur Abendessen für Hausgäste)
◆ Wohnliche Zimmer im alpenländischen Stil und ein in hübsch gestalteter Freizeitbereich zeichnen das nahe der Piste gelegene Hotel aus. Mit Indoor-Golfanlage.

Sporthotel Olymp ≤ Bergpanorama, Zim, Rest, VISA AE
Hochgurglerstr. 1
6456 – (05256) 64 91 – office@olymphotel.at – Fax (05256) 638065
geschl. Mitte Mai – Mitte Nov.
75 Zim (inkl. ½ P.) – 118/253 € 176/456 €
Rest *Toni's Almhütte* – (05256) 6 49 17 20 (Tischbestellung erforderlich) Karte 19/38 €
◆ Das typische Alpenhotel verfügt über neuzeitlich wie auch funktionell ausgestattete und sehr gepflegte Gästezimmer im Landhausstil. Das Restaurant ist eine über 400 Jahre alte Almhütte mit derb-rustikalem Charakter.

Angerer Alm ≤ Ötztal und Bergwelt, Rest, Rest, VISA AE
Hochgurgler Str. 3
6456 – (05256) 62 41 – info@hotel-angereralm.at
– Fax (05256) 624124
geschl. 28. April – 15. Nov.
48 Zim (inkl. ½ P.) – 110/185 € 200/350 €
Rest – Karte 20/49 €
◆ Die Lage unterhalb der Skipiste sowie gut unterhaltene, mit hellem oder dunklem Holzmobiliar eingerichtete Zimmer zählen zu den Annehmlichkeiten dieses Hauses. Bürgerlich-rustikales Restaurant mit Wintergarten.

Rot steht für unsere besonderen Empfehlungen!

SÖLL – Tirol – 730 I6 – 3 370 Ew – Höhe 703 m – Wintersport: 1 829 m

9 84 — 7 **E5**

Wien 376 – Innsbruck 71 – Kufstein 14 – Wörgl 13
Dorf 84, 6306, (05333) 52 16, info@soell.at
Hohe Salve ≤★★ (mit)

Alpen Schlössl (mit Gästehaus Agerhof) ≤
Reit 15 (West: 2,5 km) (geheizt) Rest, VISA
6306 – (05333) 64 00 – info@hotel-alpenschloessl.com
– Fax (05333) 6401
geschl. 2. April – 5. Mai, 26. Okt. – 20. Dez.
65 Zim (inkl. ½ P.) – 44/100 € 80/170 € 58/149 € 108/298 €
Rest – *(nur Abendessen)* Karte 15/27 €
◆ Einfach idyllisch liegt dieses aus 3 Häusern bestehende Hotel mit wohnlich-alpenländischem Ambiente. Charmant: die schlichteren, rustikalen Zimmer im 200 Jahre alten Gasthof. Im Agerhof befindet sich die gemütliche A-la-carte-Stube.

Das kleine Hotel Greil Rest, VISA
Pirchmoos 26 6306 – (05333) 52 89
– info@hotelgreil.com – Fax (05333) 5925
geschl. April, Nov.
26 Zim (inkl. ½ P.) – 73/79 € 124/136 € 80/90 € 136/176 € – 4 Suiten
Rest – (nur Abendessen für Hausgäste)
♦ Ein engagiert geführter Familienbetrieb am Ortsrand mit wohnlichen und technisch gut ausgestatteten Zimmern und einem recht aufwändig gestalteten Saunabereich.

Tulpe VISA
Stampfanger 17 6306 – (05333) 52 23 – info@hotel-tulpe.at
– Fax (05333) 5014
geschl. 31. März- 17. Mai, 19. Okt. – 20. Dez.
34 Zim (inkl. ½ P.) – 36/45 € 72/90 € 63/93 € 96/136 €
Rest – (nur Abendessen für Hausgäste)
♦ Helle, moderne Zimmer mit sehr guter Technik und durch Rauchglas abgetrennten Bädern erwarten Sie in dem in unmittelbarer Nähe der Bergbahn gelegenen Haus.

Alpenpanorama VISA
Sonnbichl 18 6306 – (05333) 53 09 – panoramainfo@aon.at
– Fax (05333) 53098
geschl. April
28 Zim (inkl. ½ P.) – 49/61 € 84/104 € 70/91 € 142/160 €
Rest – Karte 16/25 €
♦ Das Hotel liegt am Waldrand etwas oberhalb des Ortes und bietet sehr gepflegte und solide Zimmer, meist mit schöner Sicht. Besonders großzügig sind die Wohlfühlzimmer. Neuzeitlich-ländlich gestaltetes Restaurant. Am Nachmittag Kuchen aus der eigenen Konditorei.

Schindlhaus (Christian Winkler) VISA
Dorf 134 6306 – (05333) 51 61 36 – restaurant.schindlhaus@aon.at
– Fax (05333) 516138
geschl. Montag – Dienstagmittag
Rest – Menü 35/59 € – Karte ca. 25 € (mittags)
Spez. Gefüllte Kerbelknolle mit Ochsenschlepp und Gänseleberauce. Lachsforelle mit Cremespinat und Krensauce. Rosa gebratene Rehhuft mit Mispeln und Serviettenknödel.
♦ Das modern-elegante Restaurant besticht durch die gelungene Kombination von Nussholz und Farbakzenten. Aus der Küche kommt eine kreative Regionalküche.

SPITTAL AN DER DRAU – Kärnten – 730 M8 – 16 050 Ew – Höhe 556 m – Wintersport: 2 142 m 2 10 9 H6

- Wien 341 – Klagenfurt 77 – Villach 41 – Badgastein 44
- Burgplatz 1, 9800, (04762) 5 65 02 20, tourismusbuero@spittal-drau.at
- Schloss Porcia★ (Arkadenhof★, Museum für Volkskultur★★) – Goldeckbahn ★ (mit)
- Gmünd: Stadtbefestigung★★ (Nord: 13 km) – Millstadt am See: Stift★ (Ost: 14 km) – Reißeck-Massiv★★ ab Kolbnitz mit ★ und Eisenbahn (Nord-West: 19 km) – Maltatal★★ (Nord-West: 22 km)

Alte Post

Hauptplatz 13 ✉ *9800 – ✆ (04762) 2 21 70 – hotel.altepost.spittal@aon.at – Fax (04762) 512557*

41 Zim – 58/62 € 99/122 €

Rest – *(geschl. Sonntag)* Karte 19/24 €

◆ Das 700 Jahre alte familiengeführte Haus, früher eine Umspannstation, befindet sich mitten im Zentrum. Die Gästezimmer sind solide ausgestattet und meist recht geräumig. Bürgerliches Restaurant.

Mettnitzer

Neuer Platz 17 ✉ *9800 – ✆ (04762) 3 58 99 – Fax (04762) 35980*
gesch. Juni 2 Wochen, Nov. 2 Wochen und Montag – Dienstag

Rest – Karte 17/39 €

◆ Geschmackvoll hat man die seit 1910 bestehende Weinstube gestaltet. Freundlich serviert man in den drei hübschen vertäfelten Stuben regionale und internationale Gerichte.

In Spittal-Kleinsass Süd-Ost: 6 km über B 100, am Kreisel Zgurn rechts Richtung St. Peter und Oberamlach:

Kleinsasserhof mit Zim

Kleinsass 3 ✉ *9800 – ✆ (04762) 22 92 – walli.josef@kleinsasserhof.at – Fax (04762) 2243*

17 Zim – 54/80 € 96/172 € – ½ P 15 €

Rest – *(geschl. Montag – Mittwoch, Juli – Aug. Montag – Dienstag, wochentags nur Abendessen)* (Tischbestellung ratsam) Karte 18/34 €

◆ Sehr freundlich führt die Familie den mit allerlei Zierrat dekorierten, nicht ganz alltäglichen Gasthof in 720 m Höhe. Einfache bürgerliche Küche aus frischen Produkten. Schlichte, nett und individuell gestaltete Zimmer. Garten mit Naturschwimmteich.

SPITZ AN DER DONAU – Niederösterreich – 730 S3 – 1 770 Ew – Höhe 217 m

3 **J2**

Wien 96 – St. Pölten 42 – Melk 21 – Krems a.d. Donau 20

Mittergasse 3a, ✉ 3620, ✆ (02713) 23 63, info@spitz-wachau.at

Weinberghof garni — Donautal und Spitz,

Am Hinterweg 17 ✉ *3620 – ✆ (02713) 29 39 – hotel@weingut-lagler.at – Fax (02713) 25164*
geschl. Dez. – März

15 Zim – 45/48 € 72/82 €

◆ Schön: Die Lage in den Weinbergen, großzügige, neuzeitliche und wohnliche Zimmer mit hellen Vollholzmöbeln sowie ein Frühstücksraum ganz in Zirbelholz. Weingut mit Heurigem.

Barock-Landhof Burkhardt garni

Kremser Str. 19 ✉ *3620 – ✆ (02713) 23 56 – info@burkhardt.at – Fax (02713) 23564*
geschl. 5. Nov. – März

13 Zim – 46/53 € 72/86 €

◆ In einem großen Garten mit Obstbäumen und Rosen steht der ehemalige Weinlesehof a. d. 18. Jh. Besonders hübsch sind die mit Biedermeiermöbeln bestückten Gemeinschaftsräume.

STAINZ – Steiermark – 730 R8 – 2 350 Ew – Höhe 360 m 10 K5

Wien 217 – Graz 32 – Leibnitz 53 – Köflach 29

Erzherzog-Johann-Str. 3, ✉ 8510, ☎ (03463) 45 18, info@schlicherland.com

Landesmuseum Joanneum (Landwirtschaftliche Sammlung★)

Stainzerhof (mit Gästehaus) VISA AE

Grazer Str. 2 ✉ 8510 – ☎ (03463) 21 15 – hotel@stainzerhof.at – Fax (03463) 211537

30 Zim – 43/84 € 80/114 € – ½ P 18 €

Rest – Karte 14/28 €

◆ In dem a. d. 18. Jh. stammenden familiengeführten Gasthof sowie in einem kleinen Gästehaus stehen solide eingerichtete Zimmer zur Verfügung. Holzmobiliar und Kachelofen geben dem Restaurant seinen rustikalen Charakter. Hübsche innenhofähnliche Terrasse.

Engelweingarten mit Zim ← Steirisches Hügelland, Zim,

Max-Gschiel-Str. 41 (Süd-West: 3,5 km, Richtung Bad Gams, dann rechts ab) ✉ 8510 – ☎ (03463) 23 81 – stainz@engelweingarten.at – Fax (03463) 2381

geschl. Nov. – 24. März, 21. Juli – 4. Aug.

5 Zim – 58 € 73 €

Rest – *(geschl. Sonntag – Montag)* (Tischbestellung ratsam) Karte 15/25 €

◆ Malerisch ist die exponierte Lage dieses sehr netten traditionsreichen Gasthauses. Produkte aus der eigenen Landwirtschaft sind fester Bestandteil der regionalen Küche.

STANS – Tirol – 730 H6 – 1 890 Ew – Höhe 650 m – Wintersport: 750 m 2 7 D5

Wien 422 – Innsbruck 29 – Wörgl 36 – Hall 22

Vogelsang 208 (im Hotel Schwarzbrunn), ✉ 6135, ☎ (05242) 69 09 38 30, tvb.stans1@utanet.at

Schwarzbrunn Rest, VISA AE

Vogelsang 208 ✉ 6135 – ☎ (05242) 69 09 – info@schwarzbrunn.com – Fax (05242) 690974

121 Zim (inkl. ½ P.) – 99/109 € 153/252 € 89/159 € 170/410 € – 7 Suiten

Rest *Landgasthof Marschall* – ☎ (05242) 6 35 81 – Karte 17/36 €

◆ Gewachsenes Alpenhotel mit Zimmern in rustikalem Stil und einem Wellnessbereich auf 1300 qm. Freier Zugang zum öffentlichen Freibad direkt vor dem Haus. All-inclusive-Angebot. Der Landgasthof Marshall ist ein neuzeitlich-ländlich gestaltetes Restaurant.

Brandstetterhof Rest,

Oberdorf 74 ✉ 6135 – ☎ (05242) 6 35 82 – office@brandstetterhof.at – Fax (05242) 66019

geschl. Nov.

20 Zim – 48/52 € 82/90 €

Rest – *(geschl. Mittwoch)* Karte 19/30 €

◆ Das direkt an einem Bach gelegene, fast 400 Jahre alte Bauernhaus beherbergt heute ein kleines Hotel mit wohnlich-ländlichen Zimmern in warmen Farben. Teil des Restaurants ist eine original erhaltene, gemütliche Bauernstube ganz in dunklem Holz.

STEEG – Tirol – 730 C7 – 710 Ew – Höhe 1 124 m 5 B5

Wien 622 – Innsbruck 143 – Bregenz 112 – Reutte 48

Stern Rest, P VISA

Dickenau 14 ✉ 6655 – ✆ (05633) 56 44 – info@gasthof-stern.at – Fax (05633) 56443

geschl. Okt. – 15. Dez, 6. April – 10. Mai

16 Zim – 32/47 € 58/88 €

Rest – *(geschl. Dienstagmittag, Okt. – Mitte Juli Dienstag)* Karte 15/31 €

♦ Dieser gepflegte Gasthof am Lech ist ein sympathischer kleiner Familienbetrieb, dessen Zimmer mit viel Holz behaglich eingerichtet sind. Eine schöne schwere Holzdecke ziert die gemütlich-rustikalen Gaststuben.

Gute Küche zu günstigem Preis? Folgen Sie dem „Bib Gourmand".
– Das freundliche MICHELIN-Männchen heißt „Bib"
und steht für ein besonders gutes Preis-Leistungs-Verhältnis!

STEGERSBACH – Burgenland – 730 U7 – 2 380 Ew – Höhe 262 m 11 L4

Wien 142 – Eisenstadt 120 – Szombathely 41 – Fürstenfeld 19

Thermenstr. 12, ✉ 7551, ✆ (03326) 5 20 52, info@stegersbach.at

GC Golfschaukel, Neudauberg 18 ✆ (03326) 5 50 00

Balance Resort (geheizt) (direkter Zugang zur Therme) Rest, P VISA AE

Panoramaweg 1 ✉ 7551 – ✆ (03326) 5 51 55 – info@balance-resort.at – Fax (03326) 55150

geschl. 20. – 25. Dez.

141 Zim (inkl. ½ P.) – 134/154 € 238/278 € – 5 Suiten

Rest – Menü 21/38 € – Karte 30/34 €

♦ Moderne, lichte Architektur und klare Linien bestimmen hier das Bild. Sehr schön ist der Spa-Bereich auf 2000 qm mit verschiedenen Anwendungen und ärztlicher Betreuung. Restaurant mit großer Terrasse und offener Showküche.

Larimar (Thermal) (Thermal) (direkter Zugang zur Therme) Rest, P VISA AE

Panoramaweg 2 ✉ 7551 – ✆ (03326) 5 51 00 – urlaub@larimarhotel.at – Fax (03326) 55100990

110 Zim (inkl. ½ P.) – 107/137 € 190/250 € – 4 Suiten

Rest – (nur für Hausgäste)

♦ Recht ruhig liegt das Wellnesshotel oberhalb der Therme. Die modernen Biozimmer sind nach den vier Elementen gestaltet. Auch therapeutische Anwendungen werden angeboten.

Landhotel Novosel-Wagner Zim, Rest, P VISA AE

Ägidiplatz 6 ✉ 7551 – ✆ (03326) 5 23 00 – info@hotel-novosel-wagner.at – Fax (03326) 5230020

geschl. 24. Dez. – 5. Jan.

19 Zim – 30/45 € 56/60 € – ½ P 9 €

Rest – *(geschl. Donnerstag, Sonn- und Feiertage, nur Abendessen)* Karte 11/21 €

♦ Die Zimmer dieses gepflegten familiengeführten kleinen Hotels im Zentrum sind recht komfortabel und sehr wohnlich möbliert.

Pirnbacher garni

Neudauerstr. 66 ✉ 7551 – ✆ (03326) 5 20 70 – rezeption@pension-pirnbacher.at – Fax (03326) 5207030

10 Zim – 36 € 64 €

♦ Inmitten verschiedener Golfplätze befindet sich die familiäre Pension mit freundlichem Service, netten Gästezimmern (alle mit Balkon) und einem schönen Garten.

STEINACH AM BRENNER – Tirol – 730 G7 – 3 290 Ew – Höhe 1 050 m – Wintersport: 2 207 m 1 5 7 D6

Wien 469 – Innsbruck 27 – Schwaz 52 – Seefeld 46

Rathaus, ✉ 6150, ✆ (05272) 62 70, tourismus@wipptal.at

Steinacherhof

Bahnhofstr. 168 ✉ 6150 – ✆ (05272) 62 41 – steinacherhof@aon.at – Fax (05272) 624319

geschl. 30. März – 1. Mai, 12. Okt. – 20. Dez.

60 Zim – 54/68 € 86/124 € 56/69 € 88/126 € – ½ P 9 €

Rest – Karte 22/39 €

♦ In dem gegenüber dem Bahnhof gelegenen Hotel erwarten Sie ein gediegener Empfangsbereich und zeitlos eingerichtete Gästezimmer. Teils klassisch, teils rustikal gestaltetes Restaurant.

Gasthof Schützenwirt

Plon 116 ✉ 6150 – ✆ (05272) 63 45 – klotz@schuetzenwirt.com – Fax (05272) 6345

22 Zim – 34/41 € 58/66 € 43/48 € 76/86 € – ½ P 11 €

Rest – Karte 12/27 €

♦ In dem familiär geführten alpenländischen Gasthof oberhalb des Zentrums stehen solide, teilweise in neuzeitlich-rustikalem Stil eingerichtete Zimmer bereit. Bürgerlich-schlichtes Restaurant.

STEINBACH AM ATTERSEE – Oberösterreich – 730 M5 – 910 Ew – Höhe 438 m – Wintersport: 882 m 4 9 G4

Wien 250 – Linz 89 – Salzburg 54 – Gmunden 26

Gemeindeamt 4, ✉ 4853, ✆ (07663) 4 01, info.steinbach@utanet.at

Attersee★

Salzkammergut★★★

In Steinbach-Seefeld Nord: 1 km

Föttinger (mit Gästehaus)

Seefeld 14, (B 152) ✉ 4853 – ✆ (07663) 81 00 – hotel.fœttinger@salzkammergut.at – Fax (07663) 810042

geschl. Jan. 3 Wochen

25 Zim – 44/63 € 92/132 €

Rest – Karte 16/31 €

♦ Ein Garten mit Strand und Blockhaus-Sauna gehört zu diesem Hotel. Zimmer meist mit Seeblick. Im 19. Jh. war Gustav Mahler hier Gast – sein Komponierhäusl ist heute Museum. Restaurant in rustikalem Stil mit Sicht auf den See.

Wien 164 – Linz 44 – Wels 47 – Amstetten 44

Stadtplatz 27, ✉ 4402, ✆ (07252) 53 22 90, info@steyr.info

Veranstaltungen

24.07. – 17.08.: Musikfestival Steyr

Altstadt (Stadtplatz★) Y, Stadtpfarrkirche (Sakramentshäuschen★) Z

Stift Seitenstetten★ Ost: 19 km – Pfarrkirchen: Kirche★West: 20 km

Stadthotel Styria

Stadtplatz 40 ✉ 4400 – ✆ (07252) 5 15 51 – info@styriahotel.at – Fax (07252) 5155151 Z **a**

42 Zim – 84 € 124 €

Rest *Zum Goldenen Ochsen* – *(geschl. Samstagabend – Sonntag)* Karte 13/20 €

Rest *Tabasco* – *(geschl. Montag)* Karte 15/35 €

◆ Aus dem 15. Jh. stammt dieses Haus in der Altstadt. Die mit unterschiedlich eingefärbten Stilmöbeln eingerichteten Gästezimmer sind leicht elegant. Ländlich-rustikal ist das Ambiente im Goldenen Ochsen. Restaurant Tabasco mit Western-Touch.

Landhotel Mader

Zim, VISA AE

Stadtplatz 36 ✉ 4400 – ✆ (07252) 53 35 80 – mader@mader.at – Fax (07252) 533506

geschl. 24. – 26. Dez. Y **c**

60 Zim – 74/88 € 118/140 €

Rest – *(geschl. Sonn- und Feiertage)* Karte 15/34 €

◆ In dem über 500 Jahre alten Stadthaus stehen gepflegte, individuell eingerichtete Zimmer bereit. Hübsche Gewölbedecken zieren einige Bereiche des Hotels. Das Restaurant: gediegen oder ländlich-rustikal, Vinothek mit Backsteingewölbe oder Arkaden-Innenhof.

Parkhotel Styria

Rest, P VISA AE

Eisenstr. 18 (über Z) ✉ 4400 – ✆ (07252) 4 78 31 – parkhotel.styria@liwest.at – Fax (07252) 47831209

45 Zim – 68/85 € 100/128 €

Rest – Karte 17/35 €

◆ Der mit einer alten Villa verbundene Hotelbau beherbergt mit z. T. neuzeitlichen venezianischen Stilmöbeln und moderner Technik ausgestattete Zimmer. Saalartiges Restaurant.

Rahofer

Stadtplatz 9 ✉ 4400 – ✆ (07252) 5 46 06 – cafe-rahofer@liwest.at – Fax (07252) 54606

geschl. Jan. 1 Woche, 15. – 31. Aug. und Sonntag – Montag Y **e**

Rest – Menü 46 € – Karte 25/43 €

◆ Gewölbedecke, Steinfußboden und warme Töne erzeugen in dem Restaurant im Zentrum ein schönes Ambiente. Mediterranes Angebot. Nett: die schattige Innenhofterrasse. Café.

Tabor Turm

Steyr, P VISA

Taborweg 7 ✉ 4400 – ✆ (07252) 7 29 49 – restaurant@taborturm.at – Fax (07252) 72616

geschl. Jan. 3 Wochen, Sept. 2 Wochen und Montag – Mittwochmittag Y **b**

Rest – Menü 45/74 € – Karte 34/44 €

◆ Schön liegt der ehemalige Wachturm erhöht über der Stadt. Eine tolle Panoramasicht bieten sowohl die Restauranträume als auch die Terrasse.

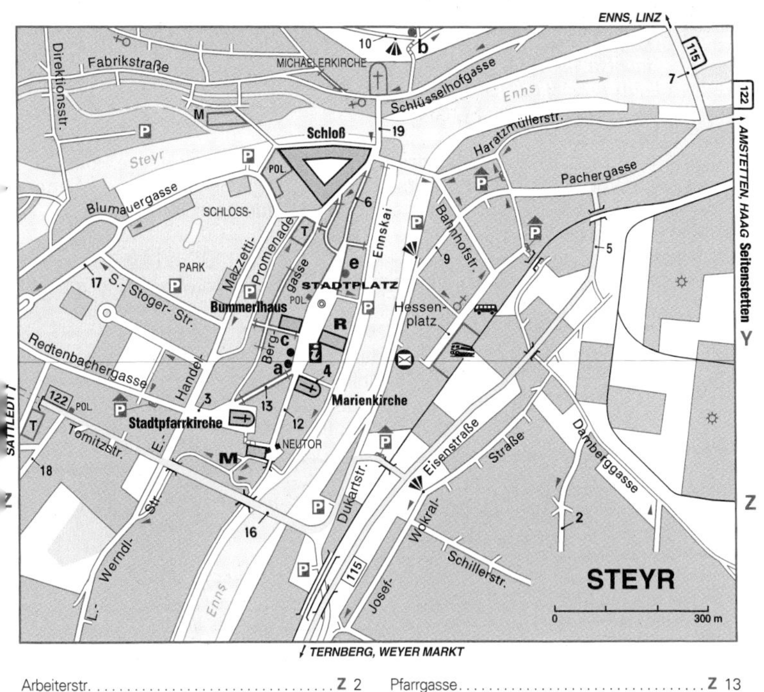

Arbeiterstr.	Z 2	Pfarrgasse	Z 13
Bruckner-Pl.	Z 3	Reder Brücke	Y 7
Dr.-Klotz-Str.	Y 5	Schönauer Brücke	Z 16
Eisengasse	Z 4	Schweizergasse	Y 17
Enge Gasse	Y 6	Stelzhamerstr.	Z 18
Färbergasse	Y 9	Taborweg	Y 10
Grünmarkt	Z 12	Zwischenbrücken	Y 19

An der B 115 **Süd: 3 km über Eisenstraße Z:**

Eckhard

Eisenstr. 94 ✉ 4451 – ✆ (07252) 5 23 26
– eckhard@eisenstrasse.at
– Fax (07252) 48528
34 Zim – 64/74 € 98/118 €
Rest – *(geschl. Sonntag)* Karte 16/38 €
◆ Gerne wird das tadellos unterhaltene familiengeführte Hotel für Seminare genutzt. Die Zimmer sind mit hellen warmen Farben und hübschen Stoffen freundlich eingerichtet. Optisch in 3 Bereiche unterteiltes Restaurant in ländlichem Stil – mittig: ein Kamin.

STOCKERAU – Niederösterreich – 730 U3 – 14 460 Ew – Höhe 174 m

4 **L2**

Wien 30 – St. Pölten 61 – Mödling 49 – Krems 50
Spillern, Wiesener Str. 100 ✆ (02266) 8 12 11
Schloss Schönborn, ✆ (02267) 28 63

City Hotel Zim, Zim,

Hauptstr. 49 ✉ 2000 – ✆ (02266) 62 93 00 – info@cityhotel-stockerau.at – Fax (02266) 629308

93 Zim – 67 € 106 €

Rest – Karte 16/36 €

◆ Tagungsgäste schätzen das an der Ortsdurchfahrt gelegene Hotel mit seinen neuzeitlichen Zimmern und funktionellen Seminarräumen. Netter Saunabereich. Kleine A-la-carte-Stube mit solider Einrichtung.

Drei Königshof Zim,

Hauptstr. 29 ✉ 2000 – ✆ (02266) 62 78 80 – office@dreikoenigshof.at – Fax (02266) 627886

39 Zim – 70/77 € 112/124 €

Rest – *(geschl. Sonntagabend)* Karte 18/36 €

◆ Die zentrale Lage sowie mit Stilmöbeln aus Kirschholz ausgestattete Zimmer sprechen für dieses besonders auf Geschäftsreisende ausgerichtete Hotel. Das Restaurant: teils gemütlich-rustikal, teils modern-elegant.

Gruber's Wirtshaus mit Zim

Donaustr. 26 ✉ 2000 – ✆ (02266) 6 28 20 – grubers.wirtshaus@utanet.at – Fax (02266) 628209

15 Zim – 35/45 € 108/132 €

Rest – *(geschl. 28. Jan. – 3. Feb. und Sonntag- Montag)* (Tischbestellung ratsam) Karte 18/36 €

◆ Das ca. 120 Jahre alte Gasthaus ist ein sehr nettes ländliches Lokal mit freundlichem Service. Für die regionale Küche verarbeitet man überwiegend Produkte hiesiger Landwirte.

STOLZALPE – Steiermark – 730 O7 – 570 Ew – Höhe 1 204 m 9 I5

Wien 260 – Graz 136 – Murau 7 – Sankt Veit an der Glan 79

Alpengasthof Maler Brands Mur Tal,

Stolzalpe 6 (geheizt) Zim, Rest,

(Nord-West: 3,5 km) ✉ 8852 – ✆ (03532) 44 20 – grbrands@murau.at – Fax (03532) 44204

gesch. April, Nov.

8 Zim – 38 € 72 €

Rest – *(geschl. Montag – Dienstag, nur Abendessen)* (Tischbestellung ratsam) Menü 38/49 € – Karte 25/39 €

◆ Abgeschieden und angenehm ruhig liegt der 300 Jahre alte ehemalige Bauernhof hoch in den Bergen. Den Gast erwarten eine herrliche Aussicht und schlichte, gepflegte Zimmer. Im leicht eleganten Restaurant und auf der Terrasse serviert man internationale Küche.

STRADEN – Steiermark – 730 T8 – 1 700 Ew – Höhe 375 m 11 L5

Wien 194 – Graz 74 – Maribor 43 – Leibnitz 38

Castell Puccini garni (geheizt)

Muggendorf 71 (Nord 1,5 km: Richtung Krusdorf) ✉ 8345 – ✆ (03473) 79 02 – office@castell-puccini.at – Fax (03473) 79024

8 Zim – 66 € 112 €

◆ Exklusives kleines Landhotel, in dem sich der Gast wie in der Toskana fühlt. Die Zimmer sind individuell und hochwertig eingerichtet und alle nach einem Komponisten benannt.

Saziani Neumeister 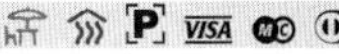
Straden 42 ✉ 8345 – ✆ (03473) 86 51 – saziani@neumeister.cc – Fax (03473) 86514
7 Zim – 100/112 € 160/184 €
Rest *Saziani* – separat erwähnt
Rest *Wirtshaus Saziani* – *(geschl. 7. Jan. – 5. Feb., Juli 1 Woche und Sonntagabend – Dienstag)* Menü 21 € – Karte 20/33 €
◆ In dem an das Weingut angeschlossenen kleinen Hotel "Schlafgut" stehen großzügige, hübsch eingerichtete Gästezimmer und ein schöner Naturbadeteich zur Verfügung. Rustikales Wirtshaus mit schöner Weinlaube.

Saziani – Hotel Saziani Neumeister
Straden 42 ✉ 8345 – ✆ (03473) 86 51 – saziani@neumeister.cc – Fax (03473) 86514
geschl. Mitte Nov. – Mitte März, Juli 1 Woche und Sonntagabend – Dienstag
Rest – (Tischbestellung ratsam) Menü 49/74 € – Karte 36/59 €
Spez. Weizer Berglamm – Schulter in Zweigeltjus geschmort und Rücken mit Kürbiskernen überbacken. Mit Ahornsirup glasierter Rehrücken und Kastaniengnocchi. Gebratener Lungenbraten und geschmortes Backerl vom Almochsen mit Mangold.
◆ Ein ehemaliger Weinkeller beherbergt dieses modern-elegante Restaurant mit Wintergarten. Die Küche ist regional-steirisch und mediterran beeinflusst.

In Hof bei Straden **Süd-Ost: 4,5 km über B 66 Richtung Bad Radkersburg:**

Stöcklwirt mit Zim
Neusetz 44 ✉ 8345 – ✆ (03473) 70 46 – office@stoecklwirt.at – Fax (03473) 7046
geschl. 27. Dez. – Ende Feb. und Montag – Dienstag
4 Zim – 50 € 80 €
Rest – (Tischbestellung ratsam) Menü 23/43 € – Karte 20/32 €
◆ Ein ruhig in den Weinbergen gelegener Gasthof mit hellen, rustikal gestalteten Räumen und regionaler Küche. Mit nettem Bauerngarten und eigener Greißlerei. Hübsch: die modern-ländlich in warmen Farben eingerichteten Gästezimmer.

Krispel mit Zim (Buschenschank) Rest,
Neusetz 29 ✉ 8345 – ✆ (03473) 7 86 20 – wein@krispel.at – Fax (03473) 78624
geschl. Dez. – Feb.
7 Zim – 32/44 € 50/64 €
Rest – *(geschl. 23. Juni – 24. Juli und Montag – Mittwoch, ab 15 Uhr geöffnet)* Karte ca. 10 €
◆ Zum gemütlich-rustikalen Buschenschank gehört auch eine lauschige Weinlaube. Spezialität: Jausen mit Speck vom selbst gezüchteten Wollschwein. Hübsche, wohnliche Gästezimmer.

Gute Küche zu günstigem Preis? Folgen Sie dem „Bib Gourmand"

STRASSEN – Tirol – 730 J8 – 900 Ew – Höhe 1 098 m – Wintersport: 1 5
8 **F6**

Wien 430 – Innsbruck 212 – Lienz 26 – Bruneck 49

Strasserwirt

Strassen 6 9920 – (04846) 63 54 – hotel@strasserwirt.com – Fax (04846) 635455

28 Zim – 57/88 € 94/156 € 58/117 € 96/214 € – ½ P 10 €

Rest – Karte 27/44 €

◆ Mit alten Möbeln hat man den Herrenhauscharakter dieses Gasthofs mit Reitstall bewahrt. Gutes Frühstücksbuffet und Kuchenjause. Schmackhafte regionale Küche und eine gute Weinauswahl erhält man in dem gediegenen Restaurant mit Holztäfelung und Terrakottaboden.

STRENGEN – Tirol – 730 D7 – 1 260 Ew – Höhe 1 000 m
5 **B6**

Wien 563 – Innsbruck 82 – Bludenz 62

Gasthof zur Post
Zim,

Strengen 13 6571 – (05447) 55 19 – haueis.edi@aon.at – Fax (05447) 5318

26 Zim (inkl. ½ P.) – 45/60 € 70/80 € 55/75 € 130/160 €

Rest – Karte 13/28 €

◆ Das familiär geführte kleine Haus in verkehrsgünstiger Lage verfügt über neuzeitlich und funktionell gestaltete Zimmer mit gutem Platzangebot sowie eine nette Lobby mit Bar. Im Restaurant serviert man bürgerliche Küche.

STROBL – Salzburg – 730 M5 – 3 460 Ew – Höhe 542 m – Wintersport: 1 510 m 8
9 **G4**

Wien 275 – Salzburg 43 – Bad Ischl 11 – Gmunden 43

Dorfplatz 17, 5350, (06137) 78 55, office@wolfgangsee.at

Brandauer's Villen

Moosgasse 73 5350 – (06137) 72 05 0 – hotel@brandauers.info – Fax (06137) 720540

geschl. März

30 Zim – 87/181 € 116/214 €

Rest – *(geschl. Montag)* Karte 19/30 €

◆ Die Lage am Wolfgangsee sowie das elegante Ambiente machen die zwei unterirdisch verbundenen Villenbauten aus. Die neuere Villa ist modern gehalten, die ältere ländlicher. Teil des Restaurants mit Terrasse zum See ist eine holzvertäfelte Stube mit Kachelofen.

Wolfgangseehof (mit Gästehäusern)
Zim,

Parkweg 1 5350 – (06137) 6 61 70 – info@wolfgangseehof.at – Fax (06137) 66177

45 Zim – 95 € 138 € 70 € 118 € – ½ P 21/25 €

Rest *Edelweißstube* – Karte 22/35 €

◆ Am Ortsrand liegt das Hotel im Landhausstil mit Blick auf die Berge, es verfügt über wohnliche Zimmer jeweils mit Balkon oder Terrasse. Gutes Tagungs- und Freizeitangebot.

Strobler Hof (geheizt) Zim,

Ischlerstr. 16 ✉ 5350
– ✆ (06137) 73 08 – hotel.stroblerhof@aon.at
– Fax (06137) 522860
geschl. Mitte März – Ende April, Mitte Okt. – Mitte Nov.
25 Zim – 59/69 € 100/120 € – ½ P 20 €
Rest – *(geschl. Montag)* Karte 20/42 €
◆ Im Zentrum gelegener Familienbetrieb mit soliden, ländlich eingerichteten Gästezimmern und schönem Badehaus mit Anwendungen. Restaurant mit regionalen und internationalen Gerichten.

Gasthof Kirchenwirt

Bürglstr. 18 ✉ 5350 – ✆ (06137) 72 07 – info@kirchenwirt.eu
– Fax (06137) 72077
geschl. April, Nov.
22 Zim – 42/52 € 70/90 € – ½ P 11 €
Rest – *(geschl. Mittwoch)* Karte 12/30 €
◆ Familiär geführter Gasthof neben der Kirche mit soliden Zimmern, von denen einige einen schönen Blick auf den See bieten. Hauseigener Badestrand. Einer der drei Restauranträume ist das in ganz hellem Holz gehaltene Jägerstüberl. Terrasse zum Dorfplatz.

In Strobl-Gschwendt **West: 5 km über B 158 Richtung Sankt Gilgen:**

Weidinger Stub'n

Gschwendt 232 ✉ 5342 – ✆ (06137) 71 11 – gerhard.bichler@telering.at
– Fax (06137) 7111
geschl. 14. Jan. – 14. März, 24. Nov. – 5. Dez. und Montag, Sept. – Juni Montag – Dienstag
Rest – (Tischbestellung ratsam) Menü 22 € – Karte 16/35 €
◆ Das kleine Blockhaus beherbergt eine gepflegte, ländlich eingerichtete Stube mit Holztäfelung und recht privater Atmosphäre. Serviert wird frische bürgerliche Küche.

In Strobl-Weißenbach **Süd-Ost: 1,5 km, jenseits der B 158:**

Bergrose Zim,

Weißenbach 162 ✉ 5350 – ✆ (06137) 54 31 – office@bergrose.at
– Fax (06137) 54315
32 Zim – 73/110 € 98/152 €
Rest – Karte 22/37 €
◆ Von der Inhaberfamilie geführtes Hotel in netter ländlicher Umgebung. Die Zimmer sind hell und wohnlich eingerichtet – als Familienzimmer stehen einige Maisonetten bereit. Freundliches, zum Garten hin gelegenes Restaurant mit bürgerlichem Angebot.

STUBEN AM ARLBERG – Vorarlberg – siehe Klösterle

Rot steht für unsere besonderen Empfehlungen!

STUBENBERG AM SEE – Steiermark – 730 T7 – 2 260 Ew – Höhe 451 m
11 K4

Wien 147 – Graz 52 – Leoben 97 – Bruck a.d. Murr 83

Schloss Herberstein★ (Süd: 3 km)

Hotel im Schloss Stubenberg garni

Stubenberg 1 ✉ 8223 – ✆ (03176) 88 64 – hotel@schloss-stubenberg.at – Fax (03176) 20060

geschl. 3. Dez. – Ende März

9 Zim – 75/80 € 110/120 € – 3 Suiten

♦ In dem ca. 700 Jahre alten kleinen Schloss hat man angenehm hell und in neuzeitlichem Stil gehaltene Zimmer eingerichtet. Sehr hübsch: Der Arkaden-Innenhof.

STUMM IM ZILLERTAL – Tirol – 730 H7 – 1 790 Ew – Höhe 550 m – Wintersport:
7 E5

Wien 491 – Innsbruck 52 – Schwaz 24 – Wörgl 39

Pinzger

Dorf 18 ✉ 6272 – ✆ (05283) 22 65 – hotel.info@pinzger.at – Fax (05283) 226517

geschl. Ostern – Mitte Mai, Nov.

57 Zim (inkl. ½ P.) – ☼ 55/68 € 86/112 € ❄ 77/101 € 130/178 €

Rest – Karte 17/38 €

♦ Dieser mitten im Ort gelegene Familienbetrieb bietet wohnliche, teils modern-rustikal möblierte, teils recht großzügige Gästezimmer. Sehr gemütlich sind die ganz mit Naturholz verkleideten Gaststuben.

Landgasthof Linde mit Zim — Rest,

Dorf 2 ✉ 6272 – ✆ (05283) 22 77 – info@landgasthof-linde.at – Fax (05283) 227750

geschl. 16. Juni – 4. Juli, 17. Nov. – 5. Dez.

5 Zim – 55/60 € 88/98 € – ½ P 25 €

Rest – *(geschl. Montag – Dienstag)* Menü 36 € – Karte 19/42 €

♦ Der historische Gasthof beherbergt eine gemütliche Stube ganz in Holz und eine moderne Vinothek im altem Gewölbe. Gute regionale Küche. Schön: die schattige Gartenterrasse.

SULZ – Vorarlberg – 730 A7 – 2 190 Ew – Höhe 485 m
5 A5

Wien 606 – Bregenz 28 – Feldkirch 11 – Dornbirn 17

Altes Gericht

Taverneweg 1 ✉ 6832 – ✆ (05522) 4 31 11 – altes-gericht@aon.at – Fax (05522) 431116

geschl. 11. – 19. Feb, 14. Juli – 14. Aug. und Mittwoch sowie jeden 2. Dienstag

Rest – Menü 65 € – Karte 29/49 €

♦ In seinem ursprünglichen Charakter bewahrt, besticht der Bau a. d. 13. Jh. nun mit dem Charme von 5 ganz in altem Holz gehaltenen Stuben. Sehenswerte historische Malereien.

SULZ IM WIENERWALD – Niederösterreich – siehe Wienerwald

SULZBERG – Vorarlberg – 730 B6 – 1 730 Ew – Höhe 1 015 m – Wintersport: 2 5 A5

Wien 586 – Bregenz 22 – Dornbirn 32 – Lindau 30

Dorf 1, 6934, (05516) 22 13 10, gemeinde@sulzberg.at

Golf Park Bregenzerwald – Riefensberg, Unterlitten 3a (05513) 84 00

Vital Hotel Linde

Bergpanorama, Rest, VISA

Schönenbühl 191 (Süd-West: 3,5 km, Richtung Bregenz) 6934 – (05516) 2 02 50 – linde@bregenzerwaldhotels.at – Fax (05516) 202555

geschl. 1. – 20. Dez., 7. – 17. Jan.

40 Zim (inkl. ½ P.) – 73/96 € 146/164 €

Rest – Karte 22/37 €

♦ Ein recht großzügig angelegtes Hotel mit wohnlichen Gästezimmern – nach Süden hin mit toller Sicht – und einem lichtdurchfluteten Sauna- und Badebereich in modernem Stil. Zur Halle hin offenes Restaurant mit Fensterfront.

Gasthof Ochsen

Bergpanorama, VISA

Dorf 5 6934 – (05516) 21 14 – gasthof@ochsen.at – Fax (05516) 21144

geschl. 10. Nov. – 15. Dez.

14 Zim – 41/51 € 70/90 € – ½ P 17 €

Rest – *(geschl. Montag – Dienstag, nur Abendessen)* Karte 20/35 €

♦ Gepflegte Zimmer mit hellem Holzmobiliar und Dorf- oder Bergsicht sowie ein Saunabereich mit Panorama-Ruheraum sprechen für dieses kleine Alpenhotel. Bürgerlich-rustikales Restaurant mit sehr schöner Aussicht. Am Wochenende: Hausmusik vom Chef.

Gasthof Alpenblick

Bergpanorama, VISA

Dorf 12 6934 – (05516) 22 17 – gasthof@alpenblick.co.at – Fax (05516) 22175

geschl. 1. – 24. Dez und Mittwochabend – Donnerstag

Rest – Karte 19/42 €

♦ Ein netter Gasthof mit gemütlichen Stuben in ländlichem Stil sowie einer beeindruckenden Sicht bis in die Schweiz. Brot und Kuchen werden hier selbst gebacken.

SULZTAL AN DER WEINSTRASSE – Steiermark – 730 S8 – 160 Ew – Höhe 444 m 11 K6

Wien 247 – Graz 62 – Leibnitz 21 – Deutschlandsberg 46

Joseph

Weinberge, Rest, VISA

Sulztal an der Weinstraße 13 8461 – (03453) 45 75 – info@joseph-hotel.com – Fax (03453) 20164

geschl. 16. Dez. – 7. März

8 Zim – 75/135 € 100/180 €

Rest – *(geschl. Sonntag – Mittwoch, nur Abendessen)* Menü 35/45 €

♦ Malerisch in den Weinbergen liegt der einstige Bauernhof, aus dem diese individuelle Adresse in mediterranem Stil entstanden ist. Schöner Garten mit Liegewiese. Große Glasfront und Showküche im modernen Restaurant, in dem regional und mediterran gekocht wird.

TAINACH – Kärnten – 730 P9 – 11 380 Ew – Höhe 450 m 10 **I6**

Wien 300 – Klagenfurt 20 – St. Veit an der Glan 37 – Völkermarkt 10

Sicher

Mühlenweg 2 ✉ 9121 – ✆ (04239) 26 38 – office@sicherrestaurant.at – Fax (04239) 26382

geschl. 30. Dez. – 20. März und Sonntag – Montag, Sept. – Nov. Sonntag – Dienstag

Rest – (abends Tischbestellung ratsam) Menü 75 € – Karte 33/62 €

Spez. Saiblingscarpaccio mit Saiblingskaviar. Tatar vom Bio-Schwein mit pochiertem Ei und Saiblingskaviar. Duett von Huchen und Seeforelle mit Morchel-Erdäpfelragout.

♦ In dem ehemaligen Sägewerk bietet man eine kreative Küche mit Süßwasserfisch, Fleisch, Kräutern und Gemüse aus eigenem Anbau. Spezialität des Hauses ist Saiblingskaviar.

TAMSWEG – Salzburg – 730 N7 – 5 940 Ew – Höhe 1 024 m – Wintersport:

Wien 281 – Salzburg 128 – Bischofshofen 88 – Murau 33 9 **H5**

Kirchengasse 107, ✉ 5580, ✆ (06474) 21 45, tamsweg@lungautourismus.at

Gasthof Gambswirt

Marktplatz 5 ✉ 5580 – ✆ (06474) 23 37 – gambswirt@sbg.at – Fax (06474) 233753

26 Zim – ☼ 42 € 84 € ❄ 44 € 88 € – ½ P 11 €

Rest – Karte 12/28 €

♦ Der 500 Jahre alte familiengeführte Gasthof verfügt über zeitgemäß ausgestattete, mit hellem Naturholz ländlich möblierte Zimmer. Eigene Disco im Haus. Gaststuben in rustikalem Stil.

TANNHEIM – Tirol – 730 D6 – 1 070 Ew – Höhe 1 097 m – Wintersport: 1 820 m 1 6 5 **B5**

Wien 529 – Innsbruck 114 – Kempten 47 – Reutte 25

Oberhöfen 110, ✉ 6675, ✆ (05675) 6 22 00, info@tannheimertal.com

Jungbrunn

(geheizt) Zim, Rest

Oberhöfen 74 ✉ 6675 – ✆ (05675) 62 48 – hotel@jungbrunn.at – Fax (05675) 6544

81 Zim (inkl. ½ P.) – 105/206 € 232/332 € – 11 Suiten

Rest – *(geschl. Dienstag)* Menü 28 € – Karte 29/33 €

Rest *Jungbrunnenstube* – *(geschl. Sonntag, nur Abendessen)* Karte 37/64 €

♦ Ein schönes Ferienhotel, das wohnlich, teils großzügige Zimmer und hübsche Suiten sowie einen ansprechenden und vielfältigen Wellnessbereich bietet. Rustikal-gemütliches Restaurant mit freundlichem Service. Kreative Küche in der Jungbrunnenstube.

Sägerhof

Unterhöfen 35 ✉ 6675 – ✆ (05675) 6 23 90 – hotel@saegerhof.at – Fax (05675) 608859 – geschl. 30. März – 30. April, 26. Okt. – 19. Dez.

60 Zim (inkl. ½ P) – ☼ 77/127 € 129/222 € ❄ 95/150 € 160/276 €

Rest – *(geschl. Donnerstag, Montag – Mittwoch nur Abendessen)* Karte 23/31 €

♦ Das gut unterhaltene Alpenhotel befindet sich mitten im Zentrum. Die gemütlichen Zimmer fallen im Neubau etwas größer und moderner aus. Der Restaurantbereich ist in Stuben und Speisesaal unterteilt – der Gast speist an gut eingedeckten Tischen.

Bogner Hof Zim, Rest,

Bogen 9 6675 – (05675) 62 97 – bogner-hof@netway.at – Fax (05675) 629750
geschl. April – Mitte Mai, Nov. – Mitte Dez.
45 Zim (inkl. ½ P.) – 74/93 € 126/164 € 80/107 € 138/192 €
Rest – Karte 17/36 €
◆ Ruhig gelegenes Hotel mit wohnlichen Gästezimmern und sehr schönem Saunabereich mit Ruhezone. Besonders hübsch: die neueren, z. T. mit Kachelöfen ausgestatteten Zimmer. Geschmackvoll-rustikal gestaltetes Restaurant mit lichtdurchflutetem Wintergarten.

Schwarzer Adler – Sonnenheim

Oberhöfen 49 6675 – (05675) 62 04 – schwarzer-adler@netway.at – Fax (05675) 644426
57 Zim (inkl. ½ P.) – 79/139 € 128/218 € 89/145 € 148/296 € – 5 Suiten
Rest – Karte 19/39 €
◆ Wohnlich-rustikale Zimmer erwarten Sie in diesem Hotel und in dem durch einem unterirdischen Gang verbundenen Gästehaus. Schöner Freizeitbereich mit Kosmetik und Massage. Gemütliche Restaurantstuben in regionstypischem Stil.

Hohenfels das Landhotel Alpenlandschaft, (geheizt) Rest,

Oberhöfen 99 6675 – (05675) 62 86 – info@hohenfels.at – Fax (05675) 5124
geschl. Nov. – Mitte Dez., April
37 Zim – 75/85 € 120/160 € 75/120 € 140/220 € – ½ P 20 € – 6 Suiten
Rest ***Tannheimer Stube*** – *(geschl. Dienstag – Mittwoch, wochentags nur Abendessen)* (Tischbestellung erforderlich) Menü 75/87 € – Karte 48/67 €
Spez. Weißer Tomatenschaum mit gebratenen Jakobsmuscheln. Geschmorte Lammschulter mit Gewürzöl und Parmesanravioli. Topfen-Vanillesoufflé mit Portwein-Kirschen und Joghurteis.
◆ Ein stets freundlicher Service und die persönliche Atmosphäre zeichnen dieses Haus ebenso aus wie die leicht erhöhte Lage und die schönen Zimmer mit Bergblick. Klassische Küche mit regionalen und mediterranen Einflüssen in der gemütlichen Tannheimer Stube.

Vital Hotel zum Ritter

Unterhöfen 19 6675 – (05675) 62 19 – vital@hotel-ritter.at – Fax (05675) 621939
geschl. 30. März – 1. Mai, 2. Nov. – 19. Dez.
65 Zim – 54/101 € 102/152 € 64/132 € 116/214 € – ½ P 19 € – 4 Suiten
Rest – Karte 23/40 €
◆ Das aus einem ursprünglich kleinen Gasthof entstandene Hotel beherbergt z. T. großzügige Zimmer, einige mit Wohnbereich oder begehbarem Schrank. Beautyangebot. Restaurant mit netten rustikalen Stuben.

Moser Hof garni
Berg 54 ✉ 6675 – ✆ (05675) 67 88 – info@moser-hof.at – Fax (05675) 6968
geschl. 6. April – 3. Mai, 2. Nov. – 13. Dez.
14 Zim – ☼ 56/60 € 90/98 € ❄ 60/64 € 98/112 € – 2 Suiten
◆ Ein nettes kleines Hotel unter familiärer Leitung, das Ihnen wohnliche Zimmer im Landhausstil sowie sehr geräumige Ferienwohnungen und Suiten bietet.

Landhaus Sammer garni
Neu-Kienzen 31 (West: 1 km) ✉ 6675 – ✆ (05675) 60 31 – landhaus-sammer@utanet.at – Fax (05675) 5196
geschl. 4. Nov. – 16. Dez., 30. März – 27. April
21 Zim – ☼ 31/33 € 57/86 € ❄ 32/37 € 64/98 €
◆ Das Landhaus mit seinen wohnlichen, meist mit Balkon ausgestatteten Zimmern liegt etwas außerhalb. Zum Haus gehört ein schöner Garten. Netter Saunabereich.

Landhaus Schnöller Zim,
Bogen 28 ✉ 6675 – ✆ (05675) 65 84 – schnoeller.s@netway.at – Fax (05675) 6584122
geschl. April – Mai, 7. Nov. – 15. Dez.
18 Zim (inkl. ½ P.) – ☼ 58 € 110/140 € ❄ 67 € 120/150 €
Rest – (nur Abendessen für Hausgäste)
◆ In dem familiengeführten Hotel erwarten Sie gepflegte, hell und freundlich gestaltete Gästezimmer im Landhausstil sowie der Saunabereich "Vitalcenter" mit Massage.

Gasthof Enzian mit Zim Zim,
Unterhöfen 97 ✉ 6675 – ✆ (05675) 65 27 – info@gasthof-enzian.at – Fax (05675) 6779
geschl. April – 10. Mai, 19. Okt. – 20. Dez.
15 Zim – ☼ 49/52 € 74/97 € ❄ 53/56 € 77/117 € – ½ P 12 €
Rest – *(geschl. Montag, Dienstag – Samstag nur Abendessen)* Karte 18/37 €
◆ Ein Gasthof mit bürgerlich-rustikalem Charakter, der eine regionale Speisekarte und einen netten Terrassenbereich bietet.

TATZMANNSDORF, BAD – Burgenland – 730 U6 – 1 320 Ew – Höhe 346 m – Heilbad

11 **L4**

Wien 123 – Eisenstadt 84 – Neunkirchen 67 – Szombathely 42

Joseph Haydn Platz 3, ✉ 7431, ✆ (03353) 70 15, info@bad.tatzmannsdorf.at

Reiter's Golf und Country Club, Am Golfplatz 2 ✆ (03353) 8 28 20

Reiter's Supreme Hotel (Thermal) Rest, Zim, Rest,
Am Golfplatz 1 ✉ 7431 – ✆ (03353) 8 84 16 07 – info@burgenlandresort.at – Fax (03353) 8841138
geschl. 7. – 19. Dez
177 Zim (inkl. ½ P.) – 114/141 € 198/252 € – 6 Suiten
Rest *Traube* – *(nur Abendessen)* Menü 43/62 € – Karte 34/48 €
◆ Über eine der größten Wellnessanlagen der Region verfügt das Thermenhotel, dessen gediegenes Ambiente man in allen Bereichen wiederfindet. Komfortable Suiten. Das Restaurant Traube ist im klassischen Stil gehalten.

Kur- und Thermenhotel (Thermal) Zim,
Elisabeth-Allee 1 ✉ 7431
– ✆ (03353) 89 40 71 60 – info@kur-undthermenhotel.at
– Fax (03353) 89407199
73 Zim (inkl. ½ P.) – 138/158 € 256/296 € – 3 Suiten
Rest – Karte 24/31 €
♦ Dieses Thermenhotel mit elegantem Rahmen befindet sich in ruhiger Lage und verfügt über einen großen Hallenbereich und zeitgemäß eingerichtete Zimmer.

AVITA (freier Zugang zur Burgenlandtherme) Rest, Rest,
Am Thermenplatz 2 ✉ 7431 – ✆ (03353) 8 99 00 – info@avita.at
– Fax (03353) 899025
86 Zim (inkl. ½ P.) – 89/113 € 178/226 € – 3 Suiten
Rest – (nur Abendessen für Hausgäste)
♦ Direkt mit der Burgenlandtherme verbunden, eignet sich dieses neuzeitliche Hotel mit seinen geschmackvollen Zimmern besonders für Wellnessgäste. Hauseigener Kosmetikbereich.

Reiter's Avance Hotel (Thermal) Rest, Rest,
Am Golfplatz 4 ✉ 7431 – ✆ (03353) 8 84 16 07
– info@burgenlandresort.at – Fax (03353) 8841138
geschl. 7. – 24. Jan
169 Zim (inkl. ½ P.) – 143/160 € 226/260 € – 2 Suiten
Rest – (nur für Hausgäste)
♦ Das All-inclusive-Angebot, der gepflegte Freizeitbereich mit Thermalbad und Sauna, die Kinderbetreuung und die solide eingerichteten Zimmer machen das Hotel aus.

Simon – Das Vitalhotel Rest,
Am Kurpark 3 ✉ 7431
– ✆ (03353) 7 01 70 – info@dasvitalhotel.at – Fax (03353) 701777
geschl. 22. Juni – 7. Juli, 7. – 28. Dez.
46 Zim (inkl. ½ P.) – 60/75 € 120/150 €
Rest – Karte 17/30 €
♦ In dem solide geführten Hotel in der Ortsmitte, nahe dem Kurpark, erwarten Sie eine hübsche Lobby mit Rattansesseln und neuzeitliche, wohnliche Gästezimmer.

Simon Zim, Rest,
Jormannsdorfer Str. 15 ✉ 7431 – ✆ (03353) 7 01 80
– info@hotelsimon.com – Fax (03353) 7018666
geschl. 1. – 13. Jan., 10. – 31. Dez.
35 Zim – 32/38 € 60/72 € – ½ P 10 €
Rest – (nur Abendessen für Hausgäste)
♦ Ein sauberes und gepflegtes Hotel mit funktionell eingerichteten Zimmern in heller Buche und einer Konditorei mit Café. Sie frühstücken im lichten Wintergarten.

TAUPLITZ – **Steiermark** – 730 O6 – **1 010 Ew** – **Höhe 900 m** – **Wintersport: 2 000 m** **18** 9 **H4**

Wien 262 – Graz 140 – Liezen 23 – Bad Aussee 23
Tauplitz 128, ✉ 8982, ✆ (03688) 24 46, info.tauplitz@ausseerland.at

Hechl (geheizt) Rest,
Tauplitz 64 ✉ 8982 – ✆ (03688) 2 26 80 – familiensport@hotel-hechl.at – Fax (03688) 226835
geschl. Anfang April – Mitte Mai, Mitte Okt. – 5. Dez.
30 Zim (inkl. ½ P.) – 56/64 € 96/112 € 68/85 € 120/176 €
Rest – (nur Abendessen) Karte 15/41 €
◆ Dieses gewachsene Hotel ist eine familiäre Adresse mit unterschiedlich eingerichteten Zimmern in überwiegend rustikalem Stil. Besonders großzügig sind die Studios. Bürgerlich-rustikales Restaurant.

In Tauplitz-Tauplitzalm Nord-West: 16 km, über B 145 in Richtung Bad Aussee, ab Bad Mitterndorf über mautpflichtige Tauplitzalm Alpenstraße:

Kirchenwirt Bergpanorama,
Tauplitzalm 26 ✉ 8982 – ✆ (03688) 23 06 – kirchenwirt@tauplitzalm.at – Fax (03688) 230643
geschl. 25. März – Anfang Juni, 15. Okt. – 15. Nov.
34 Zim (inkl. ½ P.) – 59/66 € 108/118 € 79/86 € 148/158 €
Rest – Karte 15/31 €
◆ Ein guter Ausgangspunkt für Wanderer und Skifahrer ist das Haus in 1650 m Höhe, das absolut ruhig in der reizvollen Landschaft liegt. Zeitlos-funktionelle Zimmer.

TECHENDORF – Kärnten – siehe Weissensee

TELFES – Tirol – 730 G7 – 1 370 Ew – Höhe 1 000 m – Wintersport: 2 230 m

1 7 6 **D5**

Wien 460 – Innsbruck 18 – Seefeld 37 – Hall 25
Gemeindehaus, ✉ 6165, ✆ (05225) 6 27 50, telfes@stubai.at
Stubaital★★

Oberhofer Bergpanorama, Rest,
Kapfers 23 ✉ 6165 – ✆ (05225) 6 26 72 – info@hotel-oberhofer.at – Fax (05225) 6361455
25 Zim – 80/110 € 120/172 € 105/184 € 150/228 € – ½ P 22 €
Rest – *(geschl. Anfang Feb. – Ende März) (Tischbestellung erforderlich) (nur Abendessen)* Karte 32/43 €
◆ In diesem Haus bestimmt geradliniges Design das Bild. Man bietet moderne Zimmer, alle mit schöner Aussicht, sowie eine hübsche Gartenanlage mit Teich. Kosmetikbehandlungen. Hell und freundlich gestaltetes Restaurant zur Talseite hin.

Thalerhof Telfes und Bergpanorama,
Kapfers 1 ✉ 6165 – ✆ (05225) 6 26 08 – thalerhof.telfes@aon.at – Fax (05225) 64728
geschl. 1. -15. Mai, 15. Nov. – 15. Dez.
10 Zim – 46/52 € 62/90 €
Rest – (Tischbestellung erforderlich) (nur Abendessen) Menü 42 €
◆ Freundlich leitet die Familie den aus einem alten Bauernhof entstandenen kleinen Gasthof oberhalb des Ortes. Die Zimmer hat man mit hellem Holz wohnlich eingerichtet. Hübsch sind die gemütlich-alpenländischen Restaurantstuben.

TELFS – Tirol – 730 F7 – 12 840 Ew – Höhe 635 m – Wintersport: 1 300 m
6 **C5**

Wien 471 – Innsbruck 28 – Reutte 63 – Seefeld 12
Untermarktstr. 20, 6410, (05262) 6 22 45, info@tirolmitte.at
Stift Stams★★ (Süd-West: 8 km)

Munde

Untermarkt 17 6410 – (05262) 6 24 08 – info@hotel-munde.at
– Fax (05262) 6240862
38 Zim – 47/57 € 76/93 € – ½ P 17 €
Rest – Karte 20/32 €
◆ Direkt im Zentrum liegt dieser 400 Jahre alte Gasthof. Die Zimmer sind mit hellen Naturholzmöbeln ausgestattet, im Anbau besonders geräumig. Restaurant, Bar und Café in neuzeitlichem Stil.

Tirolerhof

Bahnhofstr. 28 6410 – (05262) 6 22 37 – info@der-tirolerhof.at
– Fax (05262) 622379
geschl. 17. – 30. März, 27. Okt. – 3. Nov.
36 Zim – 55/65 € 88/94 € – ½ P 15 €
Rest – *(geschl. Sonntag)* Karte 19/34 €
◆ In diesem soliden und gut geführten Hotel begrüßt Sie zunächst der kleine und nett gestaltete Hallenbereich. Die gepflegten Zimmer sind alle hell möbliert. Freundlicher Service im unterteilten Restaurant in gediegen-bürgerlichem Stil.

Luxuriös oder eher schlicht?
Die Symbole und kennzeichnen den Komfort.

In Telfs-Bairbach Ost: 5,5 km Richtung Seefeld:

Stefan
Inntal,

Bairbach 6a 6410 – (05262) 6 32 60 – restaurant.stefan@aon.at
– Fax (05262) 632604
geschl. 7. – 30. April, 10. Nov. – 10. Dez. und Mittwoch
Rest – Menü 29 € – Karte 17/37 €
◆ Ein ländlich-rustikal eingerichteter Gasthof mit schönem Terrassenbereich und Blick auf das Inntal. In der offenen Küche bereitet man bürgerliche Gerichte.

In Telfs-Buchen Nord-Ost: 8 km Richtung Leutasch:

Interalpen-Hotel Tyrol
Mieminger Kette und Karwendel, (geheizt) Zim, Rest,

Dr.-Hans-Liebherr-Alpenstr. 1
6410 – (05080) 9 30 – reservation@interalpen.com
– Fax (05080) 937190
geschl. 24. März – 8. Juni, 1. – 23. Dez.
286 Zim (inkl. ½ P.) – 165/269 € 330/448 € 177/356 € 354/592 € – 6 Suiten
Rest – Karte 39/54 €
◆ Der Hotelkomplex inmitten des Naturschutzgebiets beeindruckt den Gast mit seiner herrschaftlichen Halle und einem großzügigen Spabereich, der keine Wünsche offen lässt. Das in mehrere Stuben unterteilte Restaurant bietet regional-internationale Küche.

In Mösern Ost: 9 km Richtung Seefeld – Höhe 1 250 m

Inntalerhof Inntal,
Möserer Dorfstr. 2 ✉ 6100
– ✆ (05212) 47 47 – info@inntalerhof.com – Fax (05212) 474747
geschl. 26. Okt. – 13. Dez.
75 Zim (inkl. ½ P.) – ☼ 52/119 € 104/216 € ❄ 79/132 € 165/260 €
Rest – Menü 10 € (mittags)/33 € (abends) – Karte 16/35 €
◆ Am Ortseingang liegt das gewachsene Alpenhotel mit unterschiedlich geschnittenen, solide möblierten Zimmern – meist mit Blick aufs Inntal. Lounge mit Kamin. Kosmetik. Das Restaurant bietet freundlichen Service und eine hübsche Terrasse mit Panoramablick.

Habhof
Brochweg 1 ✉ 6100 – ✆ (05212) 47 11 – hotel@habhof.at
– Fax (05212) 47115
geschl. 25. März – 29. April, 27. Okt. – 6. Dez.
22 Zim (inkl. ½ P.) – ☼ 34/70 € 68/110 € ❄ 52/90 € 92/168 €
Rest – *(geschl. im Sommer Montag)* Menü 35 € – Karte 19/45 €
◆ Das familiengeführte Hotel diente ehemals als Schule und verfügt über gepflegte, mit solidem Mobiliar eingerichtete Gästezimmer. Schöne Aussicht dank der leicht erhöhten Lage. Vertäfelte Restaurantstube mit freundlichem Service und gutem regionalem Angebot.

Frühstück inklusive? Die Tasse ☕ steht gleich hinter der Zimmeranzahl.

THAUR – Tirol – 730 G7 – 3 490 Ew – Höhe 633 m 7 D5

Wien 443 – Innsbruck 8 – Schwaz 25 – Seefeld 32

Gasthof Purner
Dorfplatz 5 ✉ 6065 – ✆ (05223) 4 91 49 – hotel-purner@chello.at
– Fax (05223) 491497
49 Zim ☕ – 68 € 104 € – ½ P 18 €
Rest – Karte 15/44 €
◆ Wohnliche Gästezimmer im Landhausstil mit guter technischer Ausstattung sprechen für dieses von der Familie geführte Hotel. Eine schöne Kreuzgewölbedecke ziert einen der Restauranträume.

THERME-LOIPERSDORF – Steiermark – siehe Loipersdorf und Jennersdorf

THIERSEE – Tirol – 730 I6 – 2 720 Ew – Höhe 790 m – Wintersport: 1 100 m 8 7 E4

Wien 396 – Innsbruck 85 – München 80 – Kufstein 14
Unterer Stadtplatz 8, ✉ 6330, ✆ (05372) 6 22 07, info@kufstein.com

Im Ortsteil Hinterthiersee

Juffing Residenz

Hinterthiersee 79 ✉ 6335 – ✆ (05376) 5 58 50 – residenz@juffing.at – Fax (05376) 5585300

geschl. Mitte Nov. – Mitte Dez.

43 Zim (inkl. ½ P.) – 88 € 150/200 € – 15 Suiten

Rest – (nur Abendessen für Hausgäste)

♦ Mit persönlicher Atmosphäre, geschmackvollen, in warmen Farben eingerichteten Zimmern und einem neuzeitlichen Freizeitbereich überzeugt dieses Hotel hinter der Kirche.

Andrea

Hinterthiersee 105 ✉ 6335 – ✆ (05376) 57 68 – hotel.andrea@aon.at – Fax (05376) 57683

geschl. Nov.

30 Zim (inkl. ½ P.) – 63/95 € 106/170 €

Rest – (nur Abendessen für Hausgäste)

♦ In einer Seitenstraße liegt das familiengeführte Haus in neuzeitlich-alpenländischem Stil. Die überwiegend mit hellen Holzmöbeln eingerichteten Zimmer sind sehr gepflegt.

Sonnhof Kaisertal, Rest, Rest,

Hinterthiersee 16 ✉ 6335 – ✆ (05376) 55 02 – info@hotel-sonnhof.info – Fax (05376) 5902

geschl. 15. – 30. April, 20. Nov. – 15. Dez.

33 Zim (inkl. ½ P.) – 85/115 € 150/210 €

Rest – Karte 20/40 €

♦ Wohnliche, freundlich gestaltete Zimmer sowie ein auf Ayurveda, Yoga, Kräuter und Massage spezialisiertes Beauty- und Wellnessangebot sprechen für dieses Haus. Regionale Küche und ein toller Talblick erwarten Sie im Restaurant.

TIESCHEN – Steiermark – 730 T8 – 1 370 Ew – Höhe 220 m   11 L5

Wien 193 – Graz 81 – Maribor 51

Königsberghof mit Zim Rest,

Tieschen 72 ✉ 8355 – ✆ (03475) 22 15 – info@koenigsberghof.at – Fax (03475) 22154

geschl. 18. – 27. Feb., 7. – 16. Juli

5 Zim – 35 € 60 €

Rest – *(geschl. Dienstag – Mittwoch)* Menü 29/47 € – Karte 18/36 €

♦ Im rustikalen Wirtshaus, im Restaurant-Stüberl oder auf der leicht mediterranen Terrasse bietet man eine kreative Karte und Regionalküche.

TILLMITSCH – Steiermark – 730 S8 – 3 020 Ew – Höhe 276 m   11 K5

Wien 220 – Graz 35 – Maribor 37 – Leibnitz 6

Schmankerlstub'n Temmer 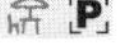

Badstr. 2 ✉ 8430 – ✆ (03452) 8 20 70 – info@schankerlstubn.at – Fax (03452) 82070

geschl. Sonntagabend – Dienstagmittag

Rest – (Tischbestellung ratsam) Karte 15/37 €

♦ Zwei kleine Stuben bilden das Restaurant der Familie Temmer. Die saisonale Küche wird auf einer Tafel oder persönlich vom Chef empfohlen. Netter Gastgarten hinter dem Haus.

TRAISMAUER – Niederösterreich – 730 T3 – 5 620 Ew – Höhe 192 m

Wien 58 – St. Pölten 25 – Krems 17 – Stockerau 50 3 **K2**

Zum Schwan Zim, VISA AE

Wiener Str. 12 ✉ 3133 – ✆ (02783) 62 36 – office@hotel-schwan.at – Fax (02783) 623616

16 Zim – 42/45 € 63/65 €

Rest – *(geschl. Nov. – April)* (nur Abendessen für Hausgäste)

◆ Ganz besonderen Charme haben die ehrwürdigen Gemäuer des in der Altstadt gelegenen über 600 Jahre alten Gebäudes. Wohnliche Gästezimmer und hübscher Innenhof mit Arkadengang.

Zur Weintraube – Nibelungenhof VISA

Wiener Str. 23 ✉ 3133 – ✆ (02783) 63 49 – office@nibelungenhof.at – Fax (02783) 63496 – geschl. 21. Dez. – 8. Jan., Sonntagabend – Montag

Rest – Karte 12/36 €

◆ Gepflegter Gasthof mit ländlichem Charakter. Auf Vorbestellung bereitet der Chef aufwändige Menüs auf Basis konzentrierter, durch "Succomelieren" gewonnener Gemüsesäfte zu.

TRATTENBACH – Niederösterreich – 730 T6 – 620 Ew – Höhe 775 m – Wintersport: 1 256 m 2

11 **K4**

Wien 92 – St. Pölten 127 – Wiener Neustadt 43 – Neunkirchen 24

Dretenpacherhof mit Zim Rest,

Trattenbach 80 ✉ 2881 – ✆ (02641) 82 25 – dretenpacherhof@aon.at – Fax (02641) 822534

6 Zim – 35/42 € 70/80 €

Rest – *(geschl. Dienstagabend – Mittwoch)* Karte 19/24 €

◆ Tadellos sind Führung und Pflege in diesem Landgasthof. Die Gasträume sind ländlich, angenehm hell und freundlich gestaltet. Zimmer mit Kiefernholzmobiliar und Küche.

TRAUNKIRCHEN – Oberösterreich – 730 N5 – 1 770 Ew – Höhe 422 m – Wintersport: 910 m

9 **H4**

Wien 243 – Linz 83 – Salzburg 88 – Gmunden 12

Ortsplatz 1, ✉ 4801, ✆ (07617) 22 34, traunkirchen@traunsee.at

Veranstaltungen 22.05.: Fronleichnamsprozession

Lage★ – Pfarrkirche (Fischerkanzel★)

Das Traunsee Traunsee und Landschaft,

Klosterplatz 4 ✉ 4801 Zim, VISA

– ✆ (07617) 22 16 – traunsee@traunseehotels.at – Fax (07617) 3496

37 Zim – 76/91 € 110/140 € – ½ P 20 €

Rest – (im Winter nur für Hausgäste) Karte 15/42 €

◆ Dieses herrlich direkt am Traunsee gelegene Hotel bietet meist recht geräumige Gästezimmer, viele davon mit Seesicht. Eigene Wasserski- und Tauchschule sowie ein Segelboot. Im Landhausstil eingerichtete Restaurantstuben. Schön ist die Terrasse am See.

Post Zim, Rest, VISA

Ortsplatz 5 ✉ 4801 – ✆ (07617) 2 30 70 – post@traunseehotels.at – Fax (07617) 2809

57 Zim – 68/75 € 106/120 € – ½ P 15 € – **Rest** – Karte 15/32 €

◆ Mitten im Ort, nahe dem See liegt die ehemalige Poststation. Man verfügt über wohnliche, zeitgemäße Zimmer, teils mit Balkon und Blick auf den See. Ländlich-gediegenes Restaurant mit regionaler Küche.

TRAUTENFELS – Steiermark – 730 O6 – 1 020 Ew – Höhe 750 m 9 H4

Wien 254 – Graz 132 – Liezen 15 – Bad Aussee 30
Golf und Landclub Ennstal, Weissenbach-Liezen (03612) 2 48 21
Schloss Trautenfels★★ (Aussichtsturm ←★★)
Pürgg★ Nord-West: 2 km

In Trautenfels-Pürgg Nord: 5 km über B 145 Richtung Bad Aussee: Autos nicht zugelassen

Gasthaus Krenn
Pürgg 11 ✉ 8951 – (03682) 2 22 74 – gasthaus.krenn.puergg@utanet.at – Fax (03682) 222744
geschl. Jan. 2 Wochen und Montag – Dienstag
Rest – (Tischbestellung ratsam) Karte 15/27 €
◆ Sehr gemütlich sitzt man in den charmanten rustikalen Stuben des historischen Schumacherzunfthauses a. d. 14. Jh. Bürgerlich-regionale Karte mit steirischen Gerichten.

TRAUTMANNSDORF – Steiermark – 730 T8 – 880 Ew – Höhe 330 m

Wien 189 – Graz 69 – Maribor 54 – Fürstenfeld 40 11 L5

Steira Wirt VISA
Trautmannsdorf 6 ✉ 8343 – (03159) 41 06 – office@steirawirt.at – Fax (03159) 237640
geschl. 7. Jan. – 5. Feb. und Mittwoch
Rest – Menü 33/43 € – Karte 16/36 €
◆ Hier bietet man Ihnen in gemütlich-rustikalem Ambiente eine verfeinerte Regionalküche. Sehr nett sitzt man in dem mit Weinreben berankten Gastgarten. Hauseigene Metzgerei.

TRAUTMANNSDORF AN DER LEITHA – Niederösterreich – 730 V4 – 2 690 Ew – Höhe 168 m 4 L3

Wien 33 – St. Pölten 100 – Wiener Neustadt 44 – Baden 38
Frühling-Götzendorf, Am Golfplatz (02234) 7 88 78

In Trautmannsdorf-Gallbrunn Nord: 6 km über B 10 Richtung Budapest:

Landgasthof Muhr mit Zim VISA
Hauptstr. 87 ✉ 2463 – (02230) 28 58 – info@muhr.co.at – Fax (02230) 285858
geschl. Feb. 2 Wochen, Aug. 2 Wochen
15 Zim – †49/90 € ††78/126 € – ½ P 20 €
Rest – *(geschl. Montag – Dienstag)* Menü 35 € – Karte 17/39 €
◆ Bürgerliches Ambiente mit passend abgestimmtem Dekor in einem gepflegten, länglich gehaltenen Restaurantbereich. Gut eingedeckte Tische und freundlicher Service.

TREFFEN AM OSSIACHERSEE – Kärnten – 730 N8 – 4 280 Ew – Höhe 545 m – Wintersport: 2 000 m 15 9 H6

Wien 326 – Klagenfurt 41 – Spittal an der Drau 41 – St. Veit an der Glan 47

In Kanzelhöhe Nord-Ost: 13 km über B 98 Richtung Radenthein – Höhe 1 526 m

Sonnenhotel Zaubek Mittelkärnten, Villacher Becken und Seen, Zim, VISA
Kanzelhöhe
Gerlitzen 7 ✉ 9521 – ✆ (04248) 27 13 – zaubek@sonnenhotel.com – Fax (04248) 271361
geschl. April – Mai, Okt. – Nov.
28 Zim (inkl. ½ P.) – ☼ 76/87 € 142/170 € ❄ 82/115 € 146/210 €
Rest – Karte 14/25 €
◆ Die exponierte Lage am Hang und die atemberaubende Sicht machen dieses familienfreundliche Hotel aus. Unterschiedlich geschnittene Zimmer nach Süden. Im Sommer all-inclusive.

TRINS – Tirol – 730 G7 – 1 200 Ew – Höhe 1 214 m 7 D6

Wien 538 – Innsbruck 31 – Schwaz 56 – Seefeld in Tirol 50
Wipptal, Trins 69, ✉ 6152, ✆ (05275) 53 37, info@trins-tirol.at

Zita Zim, Zim,
Trins 132 ✉ 6152 – ✆ (05275) 52 08 – hotel.zita@aon.at
geschl. 15. April – 20. Mai, 15. Okt. – 15. Dez.
20 Zim (inkl. ½ P.) – ☼ 35/42 € 70/84 € ❄ 48/60 € 96/120 €
Rest – *(nur Abendessen)* Karte 15/26 €
◆ Die recht ruhige Lage sowie tadellos gepflegte Zimmer sprechen für dieses nette, von der Familie sehr gut geführte kleine Haus. Restaurant mit rustikal-bürgerlichem Ambiente.

Trinserhof VISA
Trins 106 ✉ 6152 – ✆ (05275) 52 12 – info@trinserhof.com – Fax (05275) 521230
geschl. 20. April – 20. Mai, 10. Okt. – 15. Dez.
22 Zim (inkl. ½ P.) – 39/49 € 78/90 €
Rest – Karte 19/33 €
◆ Der nette Gasthof aus der Jahrhundertwende bietet recht unterschiedlich eingerichtete Zimmer und einen stilvollen Leseraum. Freibad mit schöner Sicht. Gemütliche Restaurantstuben mit Kachelofen bzw. offenem Kamin – Terrasse mit Bergblick.

Hohe Burg Rest, VISA
Trins 107 ✉ 6152 – ✆ (05275) 52 04 – hohe.burg@aon.at – Fax (05275) 5420
geschl. April – Mitte Mai, Ende Okt. – Nov.
22 Zim (inkl. ½ P.) – 48/64 € 84/114 €
Rest – Karte 18/30 €
◆ Das am Ortsausgang gelegene Hotel unter Familienleitung verfügt über meist rustikal eingerichtete sowie einige neuzeitliche Zimmer. "Sumpflöchl" nennt sich die gemütliche Bar. Die Restauranträume sind in alpenländisch-bürgerlichem Stil gehalten.

TSCHAGGUNS – Vorarlberg – 730 B7 – 2 340 Ew – Höhe 700 m – Wintersport: 2 085 m 3 6 5 A6

Wien 587 – Bregenz 64 – Sankt Anton am Arlberg 53 – Feldkirch 32
Latschaustr.1, ✉ 6774, ✆ (05556) 72 16 60, info@schruns-tschagguns.at
Montafon, Zelfenstr. 110 ✆ (05556) 7 70 11

Montafoner Hof (geheizt) P

Kreuzgasse 9 ✉ 6774 – ✆ (05556) 71 00 – info@montafonerhof.com – Fax (05556) 71006
geschl. 6. April – 26. Mai, 26. Okt. – Mitte Dez.
48 Zim (inkl. ½ P.) – ☼ 98/111 € 176/270 € ❄ 109/157 € 198/328 €
Rest *Montafoner Stube* – separat erwähnt
♦ Eine hohe, zum Dach hin offene Lobby mit Kamin und Bar empfängt Sie in dem Familienbetrieb im Zentrum. Wohnliche Zimmer in ländlichem Stil und ein großzügiger Freizeitbereich.

Cresta Rest, P VISA AE

Zelfenstr. 2 ✉ 6774 – ✆ (05556) 7 23 95 – info@cresta-hotel.at – Fax (05556) 723958
geschl. 15. Okt. – 15. Dez.
29 Zim (inkl. ½ P.) – ☼ 59/62 € 106/112 € ❄ 76/79 € 142/148 €
Rest – *(geschl. Dienstag, nur Abendessen)* Karte 20/33 €
♦ Die Zimmer dieses familiengeführten Hauses in der Ortsmitte sind sehr solide und wohnlich mit hellen Holzmöbeln eingerichtet, einige der Doppelzimmer mit Wohnecke. Eine gemütliche kleine Zirbenstube dient als A-la-carte-Restaurant.

Montafoner Stube – Hotel Montafoner Hof P VISA

Kreuzgasse 9 ✉ 6774 – ✆ (05556) 71 00 – info@montafonerhof.com – Fax (05556) 71006
geschl. 6. April – 14. Juni, 26. Okt. – Mitte Dez. und Mittwoch – Donnerstag
Rest – Menü 51/84 € – Karte 37/55 €
♦ Eine gemütliche Atmosphäre herrscht in dieser hübschen holzvertäfelten Stube. Der Service ist aufmerksam, gekocht wird schmackhaft und ambitioniert. Mittags Schmankerlküche.

Gasthof Löwen mit Zim P VISA

Kreuzgasse 4 ✉ 6774 – ✆ (05556) 7 22 47 – info@montafonerhof.com – Fax (05556) 71006
geschl. Mitte Juni – Mitte Juli
5 Zim – ☼ 53/57 € 92/100 € ❄ 48/68 € 82/122 €
Rest – *(geschl. Montag)* Karte 15/33 €
♦ Ein Gebäude a. d. J. 1500 beherbergt die verschiedenen Restaurantstuben mit regionstypischem Charakter. In behaglichem Ambiente serviert man bürgerliche Speisen. Übernachtungsgäste frühstücken im Montafoner Hof – auch der Freizeitbereich dort kann mitbenutzt werden.

TULLN – Niederösterreich – 730 U4 – 13 600 Ew – Höhe 170 m 3 K2

Wien 45 – St. Pölten 43 – Stockerau 18 – Krems 43
Minoritenplatz 2, ✉ 3430, ✆ (02272) 67 56 60, tullner-donauraum@donau.com
Karner★ (Portal★★) – Minoritenkloster★

Sodoma

Bahnhofstr. 48 ✉ 3430 – ✆ (02272) 6 46 16 – Fax (02272) 64616
geschl. Sonntag – Montag
Rest – (Tischbestellung ratsam) Karte 19/43 €
♦ In der gemütlich-ländlichen Gaststube und im neuzeitlicheren Restaurant erwarten Sie freundlicher Service durch die Familie und schmackhafte regionale Küche. Schöne Terrasse.

TULLNERBACH – Niederösterreich – 730 U4 – 2 340 Ew – Höhe 317 m

Wien 26 – St. Pölten 43 – Wiener Neustadt 61 – Baden 46 3 **K2**

Wienerwaldhof (mit Gästehaus)
Strohzogl-Irenental 67 (Nord-West: 5 km) ✉ 3011
– ✆ (02233) 5 31 07 – info@wienerwaldhof.at – Fax (02233) 5310737
geschl. Feb.
80 Zim – 50/75 € 80/108 € – ½ P 11 €
Rest – *(geschl. Montag, Nov. – April Montag – Dienstag)* Karte 13/33 €
♦ Gewachsenes Hotel in einer ehemaligen Jausenstation. Die Zimmer sind mit hellem Naturholz möbliert, im Gästehaus etwas schlichter und in dunkler Eiche. Ländliches Ambiente im mehrfach unterteilten Restaurant.

TULWITZ – Steiermark – 730 S7 – 500 Ew – Höhe 630 m 10 **K4**

Wien 185 – Graz 43 – Bruck an der Mur 42

Gasthof Knoll Pröllhofer
Tulwitzviertel 9 (West: 3,5 km, Richtung Frohnleiten) ✉ 8163
– ✆ (03126) 82 50 – office@proellhofer.at – Fax (03126) 825050
geschl. März 2 Wochen, Sept. 2 Wochen
9 Zim – 31/67 € 72/120 € – ½ P 12 €
Rest – *(geschl. Montag)* Karte 12/31 €
♦ Familiengeführter Gasthof mit modernen, wohnlichen Zimmern – teils als Maisonetten angelegt, eines der Zimmer mit Wasserbett und Whirlpool. Kinderspielplatz hinter dem Haus.

TURNAU – Steiermark – 730 S6 – 1 600 Ew – Höhe 784 m – Wintersport: 1 600 m 4 10 **J4**

Wien 141 – Graz 75 – Bruck an der Mur 26

In Turnau-Pogusch Süd: 3 km Richtung St. Marein im Mürztal:

Wirtshaus Steirereck
Pogusch 21 ✉ 8625 – ✆ (03863) 20 00 – pogusch@steirereck.at
– Fax (03863) 515151
geschl. Jan. 3 Wochen und Montag – Mittwoch
Rest – (Tischbestellung ratsam) Menü 30/38 € – Karte 17/41 €
♦ Mit Engagement leitet Familie Reitbauer diese sympathische Adresse. Für die schmackhaften regionalen Speisen verwendet man teilweise Produkte aus der eigenen Landwirtschaft.

In Turnau-Seewiesen Nord-West: 10 km über B 20 Richtung Mariazell – Höhe 1 000 m

Seeberghof mit Zim
Seewiesen 45, (B 20) ✉ 8636 – ✆ (03863) 81 15 – office@seeberghof.at
– Fax (03863) 8191
geschl. Nov. 3 Wochen
15 Zim – 35/38 € 70/76 € – ½ P 11 €
Rest – *(geschl. Nov. – März Montag – Dienstag)* Karte 15/29 €
♦ Das familiär geleitete Haus ist ein ländlich-rustikal gehaltenes Restaurant, in dem man dem Gast freundlich und aufmerksam regionale Speisen serviert. Zum Übernachten stehen moderne Gästezimmer zur Verfügung.

TURRACHER HÖHE – Kärnten – 730 N8 – **2 030 Ew** – **Höhe 1 763 m** – **Wintersport: 2 200 m** 12 9 **H5**

Wien 286 – Graz 164 – Klagenfurt 61 – Villach 58

Turracher Höhe 218, 8864, (04275) 83 92, info@turracherhoehe.at

Seehotel Jägerwirt (geheizt) Rest, VISA AE

Turracher Höhe 63

8864 – (04275) 8 25 70 – urlaub@seehotel-jaegerwirt.at

– Fax (04275) 8257717

geschl. Mai, Nov.

61 Zim (inkl. ½ P.) – 99/110 € 154/180 € 116/167 € 190/292 €

Rest – Menü 28 €

◆ Das ruhig am See gelegene Hotel mit regionstypischer Balkonfassade ist ein gewachsener Familienbetrieb mit gemütlichen Gästezimmern im Landhausstil.

Schlosshotel Seewirt (geheizt) Zim, Rest, VISA

Turracher Höhe 33 8864

– (04275) 8 23 40 – info@schlosshotel-seewirt.com

– Fax (04275) 8234215

geschl. Mitte April – Anfang Juni, 1. – 19. Juli

40 Zim (inkl. ½ P.) – 60/88 € 120/176 € 73/130 € 146/260 €

Rest – Karte 15/35 €

◆ In diesem Herrenhaus mit Türmchen erwarten Sie unterschiedlich geschnittene Zimmer von modern-gemütlich bis rustikal. Beheizbarer Badeteich. Gediegen-bürgerliche Restauranträume.

Am See Süd: 1 km:

Hochschober (geheizt) Rest, Rest, VISA

Turracher Höhe 5

9565 Turracher Höhe – (04275) 82 13 – holiday@hochschober.at

– Fax (04275) 8368

geschl. 7. April – 28. Mai

100 Zim (inkl. ½ P.) – 144/162 € 276/350 € 147/175 € 294/356 €

Rest – (nur Abendessen für Hausgäste)

◆ Ein sehr angenehmes Ferienhotel mit beeindruckendem Freizeit- und Wellnessangebot. Nicht alltäglich ist der authentische Chinaturm mit Teehaus und fernöstlichen Anwendungen.

TUX – Tirol – 730 H7 – **1 930 Ew** – **Höhe 1 500 m** – **Wintersport: 3 250 m** 17 70 7 **D5**

Wien 451 – Innsbruck 78 – Zell am Ziller 20 – Schwaz 49

Lanersbach 472, 6293, (05287) 85 06, info@tux.at

Tuxertal★★★ – Gefrorene Wand★★★ mit ()

In Hintertux

Neuhintertux VISA AE

Hintertux 783 6294 – (05287) 85 80

– hotel@neu-hintertux.com – Fax (05287) 8580402

geschl. 26. Mai – 16. Juni

64 Zim (inkl. ½ P.) – ☼ †99/112 € ††158/222 € ❄ †117/159 € ††194/318 € – 6 Suiten
Rest – Karte 17/34 €
♦ Die Lage an der Talstation der Gletscherbahn, ein alpenländisch-elegantes Ambiente und ein schöner Wellnessbereich im obersten Stock überzeugen. Geschäfte und Disco im Haus. Rustikaler Restaurantbereich.

Rindererhof Rest, P VISA MC
Hintertux 789 ✉ 6294 – ✆ (05287) 85 58 – hotel@rindererhof.at – Fax (05287) 87502
62 Zim (inkl. ½ P.) – ☼ †72/110 € ††134/186 € ❄ †98/118 € ††176/206 € – 3 Suiten
Rest – Karte 27/40 €
♦ Hinter seiner regionstypischen Balkonfassade beherbergt das an der Gletscherbahn gelegene Hotel Zimmer und Suiten/Juniorsuiten in wohnlich-rustikalem Stil. Das Restaurant: eine gemütliche, holzvertäfelte Stube.

Alpenbad Hohenhaus Rest, Rest, P VISA MC
Hintertux 774 ✉ 6294 – ✆ (05287) 85 01 – info@hohenhaus.at – Fax (05287) 850185
geschl. 4. Mai – 26. Juni
70 Zim (inkl. ½ P.) – ☼ †89/104 € ††150/180 € ❄ †97/131 € ††166/234 €
Rest – (nur Abendessen für Hausgäste)
♦ Die sehr schöne Lage oberhalb des Ortes sowie meist recht geräumige Gästezimmer und eine gemütliche Lobby machen dieses Alpenhotel aus.

In Juns

Höhlenstein (mit Gästehaus) Rest, P VISA MC AE
Juns 586 ✉ 6293 – ✆ (05287) 8 75 23 – info@hoehlenstein.at – Fax (05287) 87523116
geschl. Mitte April – Mitte Mai
30 Zim (inkl. ½ P.) – ☼ †61/78 € ††110/144 € ❄ †78/114 € ††144/208 €
Rest – (nur für Hausgäste)
♦ Das familiengeführte Alpenhotel am Ortsrand verfügt über mit hellen Holzmöbeln ländlich-wohnlich eingerichtete Gästezimmer sowie einige Appartements.

In Lanersbach

Lanersbacher Hof (geheizt) Rest, Rest, P VISA MC
Lanersbach 388 ✉ 6293 – ✆ (05287) 8 72 56 – info@lanersbacherhof.at – Fax (05287) 87453
geschl. 10. April – 21. Juni
37 Zim (inkl. ½ P.) – ☼ †85/131 € ††144/201 € ❄ †107/165 € ††172/252 €
Rest – *(geschl. Montag, Donnerstag, nur Abendessen)* (Tischbestellung erforderlich) Menü 28/53 €
♦ Ein gut geführtes Hotel im regionstypischen Stil, das über behaglich eingerichtete, teilweise recht geräumige Gästezimmer verfügt. Im Restaurant bietet man überwiegend regionale Küche in Menüform.

Sonnleiten

Lanersbach 484 ✉ 6293 – ✆ (05287) 8 72 23 – info@sonnleiten.at – Fax (05287) 872235
geschl. 14. Mai – Juni
22 Zim (inkl. ½ P.) – ☼ 🚹47/62 € 🚹🚹80/124 € ❄ 🚹50/72 € 🚹🚹108/144 €
Rest – (nur Abendessen für Hausgäste)
♦ Die familiengeführte Pension verfügt über wohnliche Gästezimmer, die meist mit hellem, neuzeitlichem Mobiliar eingerichtet sind, einige in Südlage.

Burgschrof'n

Lanersbach 501 ✉ 6293 – ✆ (05287) 8 73 56 – info@burgschrofn.at – Fax (05287) 87701
geschl. Mai – Juni
17 Zim (inkl. ½ P.) – ☼ 🚹53 € 🚹🚹86 € ❄ 🚹66/79 € 🚹🚹112/138 €
Rest – (nur Abendessen für Hausgäste)
♦ Eine kleine alpenländische Pension am Ortsrand mit unterschiedlich geschnittenen, im rustikalen Stil eingerichteten Zimmern, überwiegend mit Balkon.

In Madseit

Alpinhotel Berghaus

Rest,

Madseit 711 ✉ 6293 – ✆ (05287) 8 73 64 – info@hotel-berghaus.at – Fax (05287) 87597
geschl. 12. Mai – 27. Juni
41 Zim (inkl. ½ P.) – ☼ 🚹55/65 € 🚹🚹100/120 € ❄ 🚹77/89 € 🚹🚹144/164 €
Rest – Karte 17/33 €
♦ Der gemütliche modernisierte Traditionsgasthof im schönen Tuxertal ist ein familiengeführtes Hotel mit wohnlichen Gästezimmern. Das Restaurant hat man im regionstypischen Stil eingerichtet.

Zum Sepp mit Zim

Madseit 680 ✉ 6294 – ✆ (05287) 8 77 56 – info@zumsepp.at – Fax (05287) 877568
geschl. 24. Mai – 28. Juni
5 Zim (inkl. ½ P.) – ☼ 🚹41/48 € 🚹🚹82/96 € ❄ 🚹52/58 € 🚹🚹104/116 €
Rest – *(geschl. Mittwoch)* Karte 18/34 €
♦ In dem von der Inhaberfamilie geleiteten Gasthaus erwarten die Besucher ein mit viel Holz behaglich gestaltetes Restaurant. Zum Übernachten stehen gepflegte rustikale Zimmer bereit.

In Vorderlanersbach

Tuxerhof

Vorderlanersbach 80 ✉ 6293 – ✆ (05287) 85 11 – info@tuxerhof.at – Fax (05287) 851150
geschl. 15. April – 21. Juni
50 Zim (inkl. ½ P.) – ☼ 🚹98/164 € 🚹🚹196/218 € ❄ 🚹107/242 € 🚹🚹214/322 €
Rest – (nur Abendessen für Hausgäste)
♦ Hier erwarten Sie freundliche, wohnliche Zimmer, teils mit Kachelofen, sowie ein geschmackvoller, großzügig angelegter Wellnessbereich mit unterschiedlichsten Anwendungen.

Testerhof garni
Vorderlanersbach 286 ✉ 6293 – ✆ (05287) 8 72 97 – info@testerhof.at – Fax (05287) 8729750
geschl. Mai – Juni
25 Zim – 40/41 € 70/80 € 47/50 € 82/102 €
♦ Besonders komfortabel sind die hellen, freundlichen Appartements im Neubau dieses Hotels. Neuzeitlich gestalteter Freizeitbereich mit schönem kleinen Pool.

UDERNS – Tirol – 730 H7 – 1 500 Ew – Höhe 550 m – Wintersport:

7 **E5**

Wien 451 – Innsbruck 49 – Hall in Tirol 40 – Wörgl 35

Der Metzgerwirt
Dorfstr. 6 ✉ 6271 – ✆ (05288) 6 25 59 – info@dermetzgerwirt.at – Fax (05288) 625594
geschl. 7. – 17. Jan. und Montag – Dienstag
Rest – (Tischbestellung ratsam) Menü 32/42 € – Karte 23/45 €
♦ Das freundlich und familiär geleitete alte Wirtshaus beherbergt sehr gemütliche Stuben, in denen man traditionelle Gerichte sowie ambitionierte internationale Küche bietet.

UMHAUSEN – Tirol – 730 E7 – 2 830 Ew – Höhe 900 m – Wintersport: 1 536 m 4

6 **C6**

Wien 506 – Innsbruck 62 – Imst 28 – Sankt Anton 69

In Umhausen-Niederthei Süd-Ost: 5 km in Richtung Ötzi-Dorf – Höhe 1 550 m

Gasthof Tauferberg Zim, Rest,
Niederthai 12 ✉ 6441 – ✆ (05255) 55 09 – info@.tauferberg.com – Fax (05255) 56695
geschl. 6. April – 8. Mai, Nov. – 12. Dez.
25 Zim (inkl. ½ P.) – 41/50 € 74/86 € 46/58 € 84/102 €
Rest – Karte 13/30 €
♦ Hier finden Sie gepflegte Zimmer in alpenländischem Stil, teils mit hellem Naturholzmobiliar, teils mit rustikaler Eiche eingerichtet. Restaurant mit hübscher Holzdecke und Blick in die Küche.

UNKEN – Salzburg – 730 K6 – 1 960 Ew – Höhe 563 m – Wintersport: 1 500 m 4

8 **F4**

Wien 325 – Salzburg 33 – Lofer 8 – Bad Reichenhall 17

Familien Erlebnis Hotel Post
Niederland 28 ✉ 5091 – ✆ (06589) 4 22 60 – info@kinderhotel-zurpost.at – Fax (06589) 422626
geschl. 30. März – 26. April, 4. Nov. – 15. Dez.
50 Zim – 236/396 €
Rest – (nur für Hausgäste)
♦ Auf Familien mit Kindern ist man hier ausgerichtet: Ponys, Streichelzoo, Kino, eine großzügige Außenanlage und wohnliche Familienzimmer /Appartements. All-inclusive-Angebot.

UNTERACH AM ATTERSEE – Oberösterreich – 730 M5 – 1 500 Ew – Höhe 468 m 9 G4

Wien 260 – Linz 100 – Salzburg 45 – Gmunden 46

Hauptstr. 41, 4866, (07665) 83 27, info.unterach@attersee.at

Seegasthof Stadler (mit Gästehaus) Attersee und Bergpanorama,

Stockwinkel 1

(Nord-Ost: 5 km über B 151 Richtung Seewalchen) 4866 – (07665) 83 46 – info@seegasthof-stadler.at – Fax (07665) 834610

geschl. 31. Okt. – Mitte März

45 Zim – 41/52 € 66/98 € – ½ P 11 €

Rest – Karte 19/27 €

♦ Herrlich liegt das für Wassersportler geradezu ideale Ferienhotel am Attersee. Hauseigenes Motorboot, Surfbrett- und Segelbootverleih, direkter Wassereinstieg für Taucher. Rustikales Restaurant mit schöner Terrasse am See.

UNTERPREMSTÄTTEN – Steiermark – 730 S8 – 3 190 Ew – Höhe 360 m 10 K5

Wien 200 – Graz 19 – Maribor 58

Courtyard by Marriott Zim,

Seering 10 (Nord-Ost: 2 km, Nahe der A 9)

8141 – (0316) 8 07 70 – cy.graz@courtyard.com – Fax (0316) 8077666

114 Zim – 87/109 € 87/109 €, 16 €

Rest – Karte 16/32 €

♦ Seine verkehrsgünstige Lage und die funktionelle, neuzeitliche Ausstattung machen dieses Hotel vor allem für Geschäftsleute und Tagungen interessant. Das Restaurant: ein Bistro mit Showküche und großer Fensterfront.

UNTERTAUERN – Salzburg – 730 M7 – 460 Ew – Höhe 1 009 m 9 G5

Wien 318 – Salzburg 82 – Bischofshofen 42 – Liezen 79

Lürzerhof Zim, Rest,

Untertauern 23 5561 – (06455) 2 51 – hotel@luerzerhof.at – Fax (06455) 2514

geschl. 13. April – 1. Juni, 1. Okt. – 1. Dez.

42 Zim (inkl. ½ P.) – 45/57 € 70/81 € 85/132 € 122/201 € – 3 Suiten

Rest – Karte 16/29 €

♦ In diesem gut unterhaltenen Hotel übernachten Sie in wohnlichen Zimmern, teilweise auch mit getrenntem Wohnbereich oder Whirlwanne. Restaurant in alpenländischem Stil – mit Nebenraum.

VELDEN AM WÖRTHERSEE – Kärnten – 730 O9 – 8 550 Ew – Höhe 450 m – Wintersport: 9 I6

Wien 321 – Klagenfurt 26 – Villach 18 – St. Veit an der Glan 43

Villacher Str. 19, 9220, (04274) 21 03, info@velden.at

Wörther See – Köstenberg, Golfweg 41 (04274) 70 45

Wörther See★ – Maria Gail (Flügelaltar★★) West: 13 km – Reifnitz: Pyramidenkogel★ Ost: 18 km

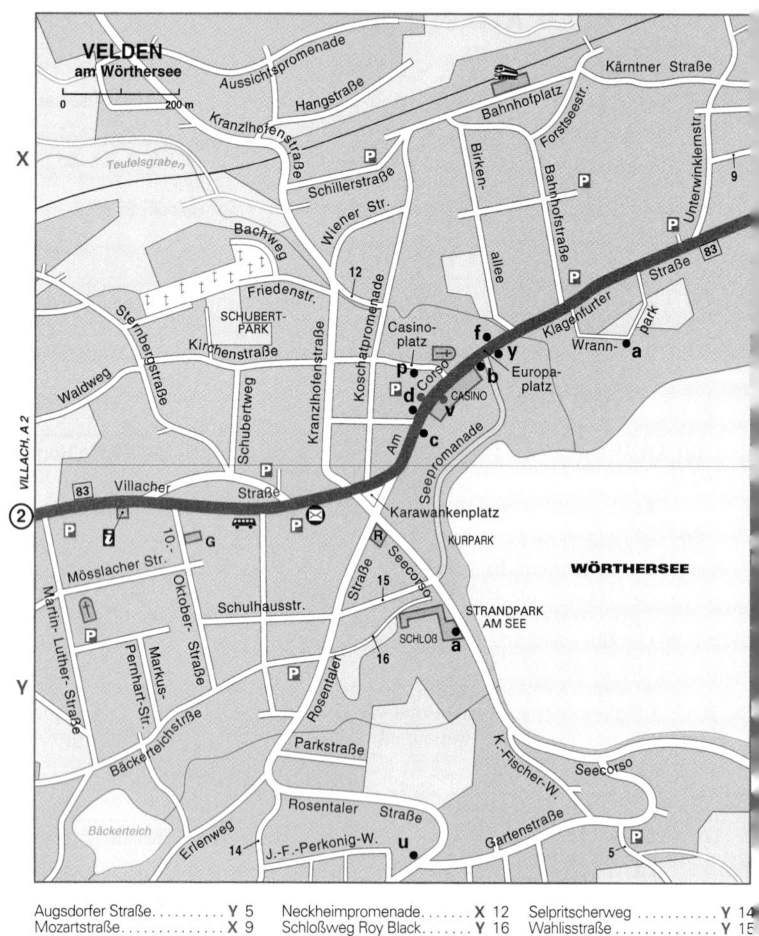

Augsdorfer Straße . . . . **Y** 5	Neckheimpromenade . . . . **X** 12	Selpritscherweg . . . . **Y** 14
Mozartstraße . . . . **X** 9	Schloßweg Roy Black . . . . **Y** 16	Wahlisstraße . . . . **Y** 15

Schloss Velden

Schlosspark 1 (geheizt) Rest,
✉ *9220 – ✆ (04274) 5 20 00*
– info.velden@capellahotels.com
– Fax (04274) 520005368 Y **a**

105 Zim – ☼ 550/850 € 550/850 € ❄ 450/750 € 450/800 €, 29 € – ½ P 75 € – 18 Suiten
Rest *Schlossstern* – separat erwähnt
Rest *Seespitz* – Karte 37/60 €

◆ Das ehemalige Schloss am Wörthersee ist heute ein luxuriöses Hotel, das gelungen Historisches mit Modernem kombiniert. Edel eingerichtete Zimmer mit neuester Technik. Angenehm licht ist das Restaurant Seespitz mit schöner Terrasse direkt am See.

Casinohotel garni
Am Corso 10 ✉ 9220 – ✆ (04274) 5 12 33
– rezeption@casino-hotel.at
– Fax (04274) 51230 X **d**
41 Zim – 115/160 € 178/206 € 82 € 158 €
◆ Das Hotel mit eigenem Bootsanlegesteg befindet sich gegenüber dem Casino. Die Zimmer sind sehr geräumig und modern nach Themen designt – Roulette, Big Apple, Blue Moon...

Seehotel Europa (mit Gästehaus) < Wörthersee, Zim, Rest,
Wrannpark 1 ✉ 9220 – ✆ (04274) 27 70
– seehotel.europa@wrann.at
– Fax (04274) 277088
geschl. Jan. – 25. April, 12. Okt. – Dez. X **a**
85 Zim (inkl. ½ P.) – 95/150 € 178/284 € – 9 Suiten
Rest – Karte 29/53 €
◆ Hotel und Seevilla liegen sehr schön in einem 30 000 qm großen Park am Wörthersee – mit Strand und Bootsverleih. Besonders hübsch sind die Zimmer in der Seevilla. Die Restaurantterrasse bietet See- und Gartenblick.

Seehotel Hubertushof Zim, Rest,
Europaplatz 1 ✉ 9220
– ✆ (04274) 2 67 60 – hotel@hubertus-hof.info
– Fax (04274) 265760
geschl. Ende Okt. - Ende April X **b**
45 Zim – 93/192 € 176/404 € – ½ P 18 €
Rest *Bistro* – Karte 29/44 €
◆ Die zwei nebeneinander stehenden Hotelgebäude beherbergen geschmackvolle Zimmer, z. T. mit Seeblick, sowie einen schönen Spabereich. Sauna direkt am See. Zum Bistro gehört eine mit Weinreben bewachsene Terrasse zur Straße hin.

Werzer's garni < Wörthersee, (geheizt)
Seecorso 64 (Y) ✉ 9220
– ✆ (04274) 38 28 00 – velden@werzers.at
– Fax (04274) 3828040
geschl. Jan. – März
17 Zim – 125/258 € 200/260 € – 3 Suiten
◆ Eine moderne und komfortable kleine Urlaubsadresse mit gutem Freizeitangebot. Die Zimmer bieten meist Seeblick sowie hübsche Bäder mit Whirlwanne und TV. Großer Badesteg.

Villa Bulfon Zim,
Seepromenade 1 ✉ 9220 – ✆ (04274) 26 15
– villabulfon@aon.at – Fax (04274) 263313
geschl. Okt. – Mai X **y**
36 Zim (inkl. ½ P.) – 180/300 € 320/480 € – 5 Suiten
Rest – (nur Abendessen für Hausgäste)
◆ Ein sehenswerter 3,5 ha großer Privatpark mit angeschlossenem eigenem Badestrand verbindet das etwa 500 Jahre alte Herrenhaus mit dem Wörthersee. Restaurant mit eleganter Note. Angenehm sitzt man auf der herrlichen Terrasse im Innenhof.

Seehotel Engstler (geheizt)
Am Corso 21 Zim, Rest,
9220 – (04274) 2 64 40 – info@engstler.com – Fax (04274) 264444
geschl. 13. Okt. – 15. April X **c**
54 Zim – 78/135 € 130/266 € – ½ P 15 € – 3 Suiten
Rest – (nur für Hausgäste)
◆ Von jedem der wohnlichen Gästezimmer dieses Hotels hat man Aussicht auf den Wörthersee. Schön ist auch die Liegewiese am See. Indoor-Tennis und -Golf.

Post Zim, Rest,
Europaplatz 4 9220 – (04274) 21 41 – hotel.post@wrann.at
– Fax (04274) 51120 X **f**
40 Zim – 62/82 € 120/188 € 57/68 € 106/136 € – ½ P 16 €
Rest – Karte 17/44 €
◆ Das familiengeführte Hotel in zentraler Lage verfügt über solide ausgestattete Gästezimmer und besonders komfortable Superior-Zimmer sowie ein eigenes Strandbad. Zum Restaurant gehören das kleine Jägerstüberl, ein Wintergarten und eine schöne Terrasse.

Seeschlössl garni
Klagenfurter Str. 34 (über X) 9220
– (04274) 28 24 – seeschloessl@aon.at – Fax (04274) 282444
geschl. 20. Nov. – 15. März
14 Zim – 85/175 € 130/350 €
◆ In einem weitläufigen Park direkt am Wörthersee steht diese hübsche Villa – ein geschmackvoll eingerichtetes kleines Hotel mit herzlicher Gästebetreuung. Kleines Holzbadehaus.

Goritschnigg garni
Casinoplatz 3 9220 – (04274) 20 35 – info@goritschnigg.com
– Fax (04274) 3452 X **p**
13 Zim – 65/100 € 116/170 €
◆ Die zentrale und doch ruhige Lage sowie schöne, individuelle Gästezimmer sprechen für dieses Haus. Produkte aus der eigenen Metzgerei bereichern das Frühstücksbuffet.

Gästehaus Gudrun garni
Rosentaler Str. 50 9220 – (04274) 25 74
– info@gaestehaus-gudrun.at – Fax (04274) 25745 Y **u**
12 Zim – 43/55 € 86/110 € 43/49 € 86/94 €
◆ Sehr freundlich kümmert man sich in dem kleinen Familienbetrieb um die Gäste. Schön sind die wohnlich-eleganten Zimmer und das gemütliche Kaminzimmer zum hübschen Garten hin.

Schlossstern – Hotel Schloss Velden
Schlosspark 1 9220 – (04274) 5 20 00
– info.velden@capellahotels.com – Fax (04274) 52000759
geschl. 9. – 29. Jan., 10. – 25. März und Montag – Dienstag (außer Juni – Aug.)
Rest – *(nur Abendessen)* Karte 57/80 €
Spez. Gebratene Jakobsmuschelrosette mit Spitzmorcheln im Chablissud. Taubenbrust mit Gemüse und Maxim-Kartoffeln. Topfen-Ingwersoufflé mit gefüllten Schokoladencannelloni.
◆ Der historische Teil des Hotels beherbergt im ersten Stock dieses gediegen-elegante Restaurant mit Blick auf den See. Geboten wird klassische Küche.

XX **Caramé**

Am Corso 10 ✉ 9220 – ✆ (04274) 30 00 – 3000@carame.at – Fax (04274) 51230

gesch. 21. Jan. – 5. Feb., 1. – 14. Nov. und Montag X **d**

Rest – *(nur Abendessen)* Menü 50/79 € – Karte 39/55 €

◆ Gegenüber dem Casino Velden befindet sich der moderne Glasbau in Würfelform. Der Service ist freundlich und kompetent, gekocht wird klassisch mit mediterranem Einfluss.

XX **Casino Restaurant**

Am Corso 17 ✉ 9220 – ✆ (04274) 2 06 45 00 – velden@sweetlife.at – Fax (04274) 2064510 X **v**

Rest – *(nur Abendessen)* Karte 28/52 €

◆ Ganz modern hat man das ins Casino integrierte Restaurant gestaltet. Hier wie auch auf der Terrasse mit Blick auf den Wörthersee reicht man eine internationale Karte.

Luxuriös oder eher schlicht?
Die Symbole X und ⌂ kennzeichnen den Komfort.

In Velden-Auen Ost: 5,5 km über Rosentaler Straße Y und Süduferstraße:

Am Wörthersee Zim,

Quellenweg 97, (Süduferstraße) ✉ 9220 – ✆ (04274) 25 34 – info@flairhotel.de – Fax (04274) 25346

geschl. 22. Okt. – 12. April

28 Zim – 57/110 € 90/180 € – 5 Suiten

Rest – Karte 15/26 €

◆ Ein gepflegtes Ferienhotel am Südufer des Wörthersees mit unterschiedlich eingerichteten Gästezimmern. Am eigenen Badestrand stehen Sonnenliegen und Tretboote zur Verfügung. Eine schöne Sicht auf den See hat man vom Restaurant und der Terrasse.

Gasthof Erlenheim (geheizt) Rest,

Schieflinger Str. 26 ✉ 9220 – ✆ (04274) 24 26 – office@erlenheim.at – Fax (04274) 242612

geschl. Mitte Okt. – Ende Nov.

22 Zim – 39/48 € 88/108 € – ½ P 10 €

Rest – *(geschl. Dez. – April Dienstag – Mittwoch)* Karte 13/31 €

◆ Das kleine Hotel wird von Familie Fritz gut geführt und bietet tipptopp gepflegte, zeitgemäße Zimmer, einige mit Blick zum See. Bürgerliches Restaurant mit Terrasse und Wintergarten.

In Velden-Göriach Nord: 2,5 km über Kranzlhofenstraße X:

X **Landhaus Kutsche**

Göriacherstr. 2 ✉ 9220 – ✆ (04274) 29 46 – office@landhaus-kutsche.at – Fax (04274) 294668

geschl. 7. Jan. – Anfang März und Mittwoch

Rest – *(Montag – Freitag nur Abendessen)* Karte 18/38 €

◆ Ein sympathisches Restaurant mit rustikaler Note – die Decke im Thekenbereich stammt ursprünglich aus einem Osttiroler Bauernhaus. Terrasse mit Aussicht auf die Karawanken.

In Velden-Kranzlhofen Nord: 3 km über Kranzlhofenstraße X :

Gasthof Marko (geheizt) Zim, VISA
Kranzlhofenstr. 70 ✉ 9220 – ✆ (04274) 24 43 – info@marko-velden.at – Fax (04274) 277337
geschl. Nov.
21 Zim – 39/46 € 78/92 € – ½ P 15 €
Rest – *(geschl. Okt. – April Dienstag – Mittwoch)* Karte 15/32 €
◆ Das gepflegte familiengeführte Haus mit Blick auf die Karawanken verfügt über solide möblierte, zeitgemäße Gästezimmer – teils mit Balkon. Ein netter Gastgarten mit altem Baumbestand und schöner Sicht ergänzt das Restaurant.

VIGAUN, BAD – Salzburg – 730 L6 – 1 890 Ew – Höhe 468 m – Wintersport: – Thermalheilbad

8 **G4**

Wien 319 – Salzburg 23 – Bischofshofen 39 – Bad Reichenhall 31
Am Dorfplatz 11, ✉ 5424, ✆ (06245) 8 41 16, info@bad-vigaun.at

Gasthof Langwies Biergarten Zim, VISA
Langwies 22 ✉ 5424 – ✆ (06245) 89 56 – hotel@langwies.at – Fax (06245) 895613
30 Zim – 52/62 € 78/94 € – ½ P 15 €
Rest – *(geschl. 8. – 25. Jan. und Dienstag)* Karte 22/35 €
◆ Das Haus mit familiärer Führung befindet sich etwas außerhalb des Ortes und verfügt über großzügige und wohnliche Zimmer sowie einen Saunabereich mit Zugang zum Garten. Restaurant im regionstypischen Stil mit Biergarten im Innenhof und regionalem Angebot.

Kellerbauer mit Zim VISA
Kellerbauerweg 41 (am Kurzentrum) ✉ 5424 – ✆ (06245) 8 34 74 – kellerbauer@aon.at – Fax (06245) 8347415
geschl. Sonntagabend – Montag
9 Zim – 42 € 70 €
Rest – Menü 25/58 € – Karte 27/47 €
◆ Ein regionstypisches Haus wie aus dem Bilderbuch mit gemütlicher Atmosphäre, freundlichem Service und international-regionaler Küche.

VILLACH – Kärnten – 730 N9 – 57 500 Ew – Höhe 501 m – Wintersport: 2 167 m 8

9 **H6**

Wien 333 – Klagenfurt 39 – Spittal a.d. Drau 41 – Velden 18
Rathausplatz 1, ✉ 9500, ✆ (04242) 2 05 29 00, tourismusinformation.stadt@villach.at

Veranstaltungen

11.07. – 31.08.: Carinthischer Sommer
27.07. – 03.08.: Kirchtagswoche
03.09. – 07.09.: Harley Davidson European Bike Week

Altstadt★ XY – Hauptstadtpfarrkirche St. Jakob (Grabmäler★) – Museum der Stadt Villach★ **M** Y
Villacher Alpenstraße★ – Ossiacher See★ Nord-Ost: 10 km – Burgruine Landskron (Adler-Flugschau★) Nord-Ost: 10 km

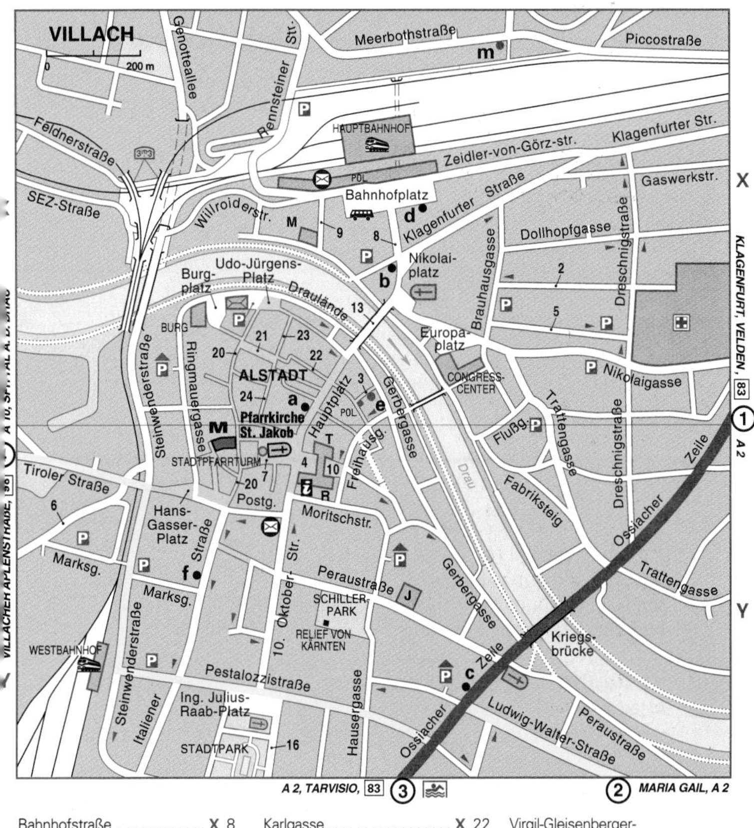

Bahnhofstraße . . . . **X** 8
Bamberger Gasse . . . . **X** 23
Dietrichsteingasse . . . . **X** 3
Franz-von-Tschabuschnig-Straße . . . . **X** 2
Kaiser-Josef-Platz . . . . **X** 21
Karlgasse . . . . **X** 22
Kassinsteig . . . . **X** 9
Kirchenplatz . . . . **Y** 7
Paracelsusgasse . . . . **X** 24
Rathausplatz . . . . **Y** 4
Stadtbrücke . . . . **X** 13
Standesamtsplatz . . . . **Y** 10
Virgil-Gleisenberger-Straße . . . . **X** 5
Völkendorfer Straße . . . . **Y** 6
Widmanngasse . . . . **XY** 20
Wilhelm-Hohenheim-Straße . . . . **Y** 16

Post

Zim, Rest, VISA

Hauptplatz 26 ✉ 9500 – ✆ (04242) 26 10 10 – info@romantik-hotel.com – Fax (04242) 26101420 X **a**

63 Zim – 85/125 € 90/175 € – ½ P 25 € – 5 Suiten

Rest – *(geschl. Sonntag)* Karte 27/44 €

◆ Ein ehemaliges Stadtpalais a. d. 16. Jh. beherbergt individuelle Zimmer, teils im Laura-Ashley-Stil. Freizeitbereich im 3. Stock mit Dachterrasse und Blick über die Stadt. Restaurant mit historischem Kreuzgewölbe. Schön: die begrünte Terrasse im Innenhof.

Mosser garni

VISA

Bahnhofstr. 9 ✉ 9500 – ✆ (04242) 2 41 15 – info@hotelmosser.at – Fax (04242) 24115222 X **b**

50 Zim – 66/90 € 90/145 €

◆ Seit über 250 Jahren – bereits in der 8. Generation – ist dieses Hotel im Besitz der Familie Mosser. Es stehen solide, teilweise sehr geräumige Zimmer zur Verfügung.

Grand Media garni

Ossiacher Zeile 39 ✉ 9500 – ✆ (04242) 2 49 25
– reservation@grandmedia-hotel.eu – Fax (04242) 2492560 Y **c**

93 Zim – 75/135 € 105/155 €

◆ Mit funktionellen, technisch gut ausgestatteten Gästezimmern ist das moderne Hotel am Rande der Innenstadt ganz auf Tagungen und Geschäftsleute ausgelegt.

City garni

Bahnhofplatz 3 ✉ 9500 – ✆ (04242) 2 78 96 – info@hotelcity.at
– Fax (04242) 27896110 X **d**

66 Zim – 70/150 € 100/180 €

◆ Ein gepflegtes Haus gegenüber dem Hauptbahnhof, das auch Geschäftsreisende schätzen. Die Zimmer sind funktionell gestaltet, in den oberen Etagen teils mit schöner Sicht.

Kramer Zim,

Italiener Str. 14, (Zufahrt über Steinwenderstr.) ✉ 9500
– ✆ (04242) 2 49 53 – info@hotelgasthofkramer.at
– Fax (04242) 249533 Y **f**

41 Zim – 47/68 € 84/100 € – ½ P 12 €

Rest – Karte 11/24 €

◆ In diesem gut geführten Gasthof hält man gepflegte, praktisch und solide ausgestattete Zimmer für Sie bereit. Restaurant in ländlichem Stil mit bürgerlicher Karte.

Urbani-Weinstuben

Meerbothstr. 22 ✉ 9500 – ✆ (04242) 2 81 05
– kaspar@restaurant.urbani.at – Fax (04242) 281054
geschl. Anfang Okt.1 Woche und Samstag – Sonntag X **m**

Rest – Karte 20/44 €

◆ Aufmerkam serviert man in den drei unterschiedlich eingerichteten Restaurantstuben moderne wie auch traditionelle Gerichte. Kleine Terrasse vor dem Haus.

Kaufmann & Kaufmann

Dietrichsteingasse 5 ✉ 9500 – ✆ (04242) 2 58 71
– kaufmann@kauf-mann.at – Fax (04242) 258714
geschl. Ende Aug. – Anfang Sept., Montag, Sonn- und Feiertage X **e**

Rest – (Tischbestellung ratsam) Menü 28/34 € – Karte 24/39 €

◆ Das sympathische Lokal in der Innenstadt wird freundlich von Familie Kaufmann geleitet. Die Chefin kocht regionale Speisen mit mediterranem Einfluss. Hübscher Innenhof.

In Villach-Judendorf **3 km über Ossiacher Zeile Y:**

Wirt in Judendorf

Judendorfer Str. 24 ✉ 9504 – ✆ (04242) 5 65 25 – gasthof@wirt-i-page.at
– Fax (04242) 565257
geschl. Jan., Karwoche und Montag

Rest – Karte 20/40 €

◆ Bereits seit über 100 Jahren existiert dieses nette rustikale Kärntner Wirtshaus mit regionaler Küche. Schön sitzt man im Gastgarten unter schattenspendenden Kastanienbäumen.

In Warmbad 4 km über Ossiacher Zeile Y:

Warmbaderhof (Thermal) (Thermal) Rest, Zim, Rest,
Kadischenallee 22 ✉ 9504 – ✆ (04242) 3 00 10
– warmbaderhof@warmbad.at – Fax (04242) 30011309
111 Zim (inkl. ½ P.) – 126/175 € 222/370 € – 12 Suiten
Rest *Das Kleine Restaurant* – Menü 33/69 € – Karte 34/53 €
♦ Das Hotel liegt in einem schönen Park und bietet Zimmer in klassischem Stil sowie einen großzügigen Wellnessbereich. Direkter Zugang zur Therme. Das Kleine Restaurant mit gediegenem Ambiente.

In Drobollach am Faaker See 11 km über Ludwig-Walter Str. Y Richtung Faaker See:

Seeblickstr. 78, ✉ 9580, ✆ (04254) 21 85, tourismusinformation.-drobollach@villach.at

Seehotel Ressmann (mit Gästehaus) Faaker See,
Strandbadstr. 69 ✉ 9580
– ✆ (04254) 22 10 – info@seehotel-ressmann.at – Fax (04254) 221080
geschl. 11. Okt. – 26. April
42 Zim (inkl. ½ P.) – 56/120 € 120/174 €
Rest – Karte 21/32 €
♦ Ein gewachsener Familienbetrieb mit zeitgemäßen Zimmern, meist mit Balkon und Seeblick, sowie einer schönen Liegewiese und Zugang zum See. Eigene Ruderboote. Zum Restaurant gehört eine Terrasse mit Sicht auf See und Berge.

Schönruh
Seeblickstr. 40 ✉ 9580 – ✆ (04254) 21 92 – hotel@schoenruh.net
– Fax (04254) 225393
35 Zim (inkl. ½ P.) – 78/98 € 140/208 €
Rest – Karte 20/31 €
♦ Das Hotel verfügt über unterschiedlich geschnittene Zimmer mit Balkon – teilweise mit Blick auf den See – sowie ein eigenes Strandbad. Man bietet auch Golfpauschalen.

Naturhotel
Strandbadstr. 11 ✉ 9580 – ✆ (04254) 33 12
– naturhotel.faakersee@utanet.at – Fax (04254) 331230
geschl. 26. Okt. – 1. April
10 Zim (inkl. ½ P.) – 67/100 € 120/154 €
Rest – (nur Abendessen für Hausgäste)
♦ Das kleine Nichtraucher-Hotel mit hauseigener Biolandwirtschaft ist schön oberhalb des Sees gelegen. Es erwarten Sie sehr gepflegte Zimmer und Appartements.

In Egg am Faaker See 12 km über Ludwig-Walter Str. Y Richtung Faaker See:

Karnerhof Faaker See und Bergpanorama, (geheizt)
Karnerhofweg 10 ✉ 9580 – ✆ (04254) 21 88 – hotel@karnerhof.com
– Fax (04254) 3650
geschl. 7. Jan. – 15. März, 2. Nov. – 19. Dez.

98 Zim (inkl. ½ P.) – 128/181 € 224/314 € – 3 Suiten
Rest *Götzl Stube* – separat erwähnt
◆ Ein gut geführtes Ferienhotel oberhalb des Sees mit toller Aussicht. Die meisten der wohnlichen und funktionellen Zimmer liegen zum See hin. Vielfältiges Freizeitangebot.

Kleines Hotel Kärnten Faaker See und Bergpanorama, Rest,
Egger Seepromenade 8 ✉ 9580 – (04254) 23 75 – genuss@kleineshotel.at – Fax (04254) 237523
geschl. 15. Okt. – 28. April
16 Zim (inkl. ½ P.) – 111/160 € 196/290 € – 3 Suiten
Rest – (nur für Hausgäste)
◆ Vor allem die ruhige Lage und die tolle Sicht machen dieses persönlich geführte Hotel aus. Neben modernen Zimmern bietet man eine schöne 12 000 qm große Gartenanlage am See.

Harmonie Rest,
Egger Seepromenade 66 ✉ 9580 – (04254) 28 60 – moser@harmonie-hotel.com – Fax (04254) 28604
geschl. Nov. – April
20 Zim – 58/88 € 110/176 € – ½ P 15 €
Rest – *(geschl. Montagabend)* (nur für Hausgäste)
◆ Das Hotel verfügt über geschmackvoll in hellen Farben gehaltene Zimmer und einen hübschen großzügigen Garten zum See hin. Wechselnde Bilderausstellungen zieren das Haus.

Götzl Stube – Hotel Karnerhof Faaker See und Bergpanorama,
Karnerhofweg 10 ✉ 9580 – (04254) 21 88 – hotel@karnerhof.com – Fax (04254) 3650
geschl. Anfang Okt. – Anfang Mai und Montag – Dienstagmittag, Mittwochmittag
Rest – (Tischbestellung ratsam) Menü 42/63 € – Karte 35/49 €
◆ Nach einem hiesigen Maler hat man dieses rustikale Restaurant mit ambitionierter Küche benannt – seine Bilder zieren die Wände. Weinberankte Terrasse mit Berg- und Seesicht.

VIRGEN – Tirol – 730 J7 – 2 130 Ew – Höhe 1 200 m – Wintersport: 1 7 F6

Wien 446 – Innsbruck 164 – Lienz 35 – Matrei in Osttirol 8

Bronte House
Bachweg 4 ✉ 9972 – (04874) 2 00 53 – bronte.house@aon.at – Fax (04874) 2005330
geschl. Mitte Nov. – Mitte Dez
13 Zim – 32/40 € 64/80 € – ½ P 10/12 €
Rest – (nur Abendessen für Hausgäste)
◆ Ein familiär geführtes kleines Haus mit hell und freundlich eingerichteten Gästezimmern und einem großen Garten mit schöner Aussicht.

VITIS – Niederösterreich – 730 R2 – 2 580 Ew – Höhe 558 m 3 J1

Wien 125 – St. Pölten 93 – Zwettl 21 – Gmünd 17

Zum Topf mit Zim
Kaltenbach 26 (Süd: 2 km) ✉ 3902 – ✆ (02841) 83 29 – landgasthof.topf@utanet.at – Fax (02841) 80590
geschl. Feb. 2 Wochen, Juli 2 Wochen
6 Zim – 26 € 48 € – ½ P 10 €
Rest – *(geschl. Montag – Dienstag)* Menü 12/40 € – Karte 16/37 €
♦ Gute Küche bietet das freundlich geführte Restaurant in zwei klassisch eingerichteten Räumen oder auf der wunderschönen Terrasse.

VOITSBERG – Steiermark – 730 O4 – 10 080 Ew – Höhe 395 m 10 J5

Wien 231 – Graz 46

Walter's Restaurant
Hauptplatz 43 ✉ 8570 – ✆ (03142) 2 84 55 – Fax (03142) 28455
geschl. Juli 2 Wochen und Sonntag – Montag
Rest – (nur Abendessen) Menü 33/38 € – Karte 24/41 €
♦ Die Kombination von altem Backsteingewölbe und modernen Elementen bestimmt das Ambiente in diesem Kellerlokal mit Bar – eine Bilderausstellung ziert das Restaurant.

VOLDERS – Tirol – 730 G7 – 4 170 Ew – Höhe 558 m 7 D5

Wien 432 – Innsbruck 15 – Schwaz 15 – Seefeld 37

Landgasthof Jagerwirt
Bundesstr. 15 ✉ 6111 – ✆ (05224) 5 25 91 – knapp@jagerwirt.com – Fax (05224) 5250184
28 Zim – 62 € 88 € – ½ P 15 €
Rest – *(geschl. Karwoche, Ende Okt. 2 Wochen und Montagmittag)* Karte 16/32 €
♦ Gestandener Landgasthof mit funktionellen Zimmern, die ganz mit hellem Naturholz möbliert sind. Kleine Vinothek und Zigarrensalon. Ein Restaurant in ländlich-bürgerlichem Stil mit 300 Jahre alter Zirbenholzstube.

Rossstall-Taverne
Bundesstr. 5 ✉ 6111 – ✆ (05224) 5 52 60 – Fax (05224) 55260
geschl. Ende Juni – Mitte Juli und Sonntag – Montagmittag
Rest – *(Okt. – Mai Montag – Freitag nur Abendessen)* Karte 25/44 €
♦ In dem hell gestrichenen Kellergewölbe einer ehemaligen Pferdeumspannstation serviert man vom Chef persönlich zubereitete regionale und leicht kreative Speisen.

VORCHDORF – Oberösterreich – 730 N4 – 7 270 Ew – Höhe 414 m 2 H3

Wien 27 – Linz 49 – Wels 27 – Vöcklabruck 28

Tanglberg mit Zim
Pettenbacher Str. 3 ✉ 4655 – ✆ (07614) 83 97 – office@tanglberg.at – Fax (07614) 839714
geschl. Sonntagabend – Dienstag
3 Zim – 40 € 70 €
Rest – Menü 75/85 € – Karte 45/60 €
Spez. Trüffel Roger Roucoue. Hecht in Rotweinbutter mit Macis. Filet vom Milchkalb mit Sauce Albufera und Spargel en Papillote.
♦ Hinter einer schlichten Fassade entdecken Sie in charmanter Atmosphäre eine mit Feinsinn zubereitete kreative Küche. Mit im Haus: eine Galerie für zeitgenössische Kunst. Hübsch sind die minimalistisch eingerichteten Gästezimmer.

VORDERLANERSBACH – Tirol – siehe Tux

VORDERSTODER – Oberösterreich – 730 O5 – 770 Ew – Höhe 810 m – Wintersport: 3 9 H4

Wien 224 – Linz 92 – Steyr 62 – Liezen 33

Landhotel Stockerwirt
Vorderstoder 2 4574 – (07564) 8 21 40 – stockerwirt@magnet.at – Fax (07564) 82145
geschl. Ende März – Ende April, Anfang Nov. – Mitte Dez.
15 Zim (inkl. ½ P.) – 55/60 € 88/120 €
Rest – *(geschl. Montagabend – Dienstag)* Karte 15/30 €
◆ Aus dem 17. Jh. stammendes Landhotel mit familiärer Atmosphäre. Viele Familienzimmer, die mit hellem Naturholz möbliert sind, verfügen über einen getrennten Kinderschlafraum. Das Restaurant: gemütliche Gaststuben und ein großer Speisesaal.

WÄNGLE – Tirol – 730 E6 – 920 Ew – Höhe 883 m 6 C5

Wien 503 – Innsbruck 91 – Reutte 2
Oberdorf 4, 6600, (05672) 6 36 01, reutte-waengle-info@netway.at

In Wängle-Hinterbichl über Lechaschau Richtung Wängle, dann der Beschilderung folgen:

Landgasthof Tannenhof Zim, Rest,
Hinterbichl 12 6600 – (05672) 6 38 02 – info@tannenhof.cc – Fax (05672) 71348
geschl. 30. März – 13. April, 26. Okt. – 30. Nov.
25 Zim – 37/40 € 74/80 € – ½ P 12 €
Rest – Karte 15/28 €
◆ Schön und angenehm ruhig liegt dieses Haus in dem kleinen Örtchen. Ein Teil der Gästezimmer ist mit hellem Holz besonders freundlich eingerichtet. Restaurant in bürgerlichem Stil mit netter Terrasse.

WAGRAIN – Salzburg – 730 L6 – 3 130 Ew – Höhe 850 m – Wintersport: 2 014 m 8 36 8 G5

Wien 324 – Salzburg 66 – Bischofshofen 18
Markt 14, 5602, (06413) 84 48, info@wagrain.info

Edelweiss Bergpanorama, Rest,
Weberlandl 65 (Süd-Ost: 3 km, Richtung Flachau, nach 0,5 km rechts ab) 5602 – (06413) 84 47 – hotel@my-edelweiss.at – Fax (06413) 84477
geschl. 14. April – 21. Mai, 29. Sept. – 1. Dez.
35 Zim (inkl. ½ P.) – 64/68 € 114/138 € 79/109 € 140/236 € – 8 Suiten
Rest – (nur Abendessen für Hausgäste)
◆ Hier überzeugen die wunderschöne Lage in 1200 m Höhe (im Winter direkt an der Skipiste) sowie wohnliche, im alpenländischen Stil eingerichtete Zimmer. A-la-carte-Restaurant und Terrasse bieten eine sehr schöne Aussicht.

Alpina Zim, Rest,

Kirchboden 97 ✉ 5602 – ☎ (06413) 83 37 – info@hotelalpina.at – Fax (06413) 833750
geschl. 15. April – 20. Mai, Ende Okt. – Anfang Dez.
30 Zim (inkl. ½ P.) – ☼ 67/88 € 88/144 € ❄ 89/139 € 178/254 €
Rest – (nur Abendessen für Hausgäste)
♦ Wohnliche, technisch gut ausgestattete Gästezimmer und ein neuzeitlicher Freizeitbereich machen das etwas oberhalb des Ortes gelegene Alpenhotel aus. Im Winter dient der Alpinakeller mit Grillgerichten als A-la-carte-Restaurant. Im Sommer: Salzburger Stub'n.

Sporthotel Zim, VISA AE

Hofmark 9 ✉ 5602 – ☎ (06413) 73 33 – info@sporthotel.at – Fax (06413) 7338
geschl. 7. April – 5. Juli
119 Zim (inkl. ½ P.) – ☼ 87/97 € 132/166 € ❄ 99/142 € 150/256 €
Rest – (nur Abendessen für Hausgäste)
♦ Hier erwarten Sie funktionell ausgestattete Zimmer, eine große Halle mit Internetecke und ein Wellnessbereich auf 1 000 qm. Im Sommer bietet man "all inclusive".

Wagrainer Hof VISA

Markt 23 ✉ 5602 – ☎ (06413) 82 04 – info@wagrainerhof.com – Fax (06413) 82047
geschl. 5. April – 1. Mai, Mitte Okt. – Anfang Dez.
43 Zim (inkl. ½ P.) – ☼ 60/78 € 98/134 € ❄ 102/134 € 144/208 €
Rest – (nur Abendessen) Karte 15/34 €
♦ Familiengeführtes Hotel in der Ortsmitte mit sehr gepflegten und sauberen, mit hellen Naturholzmöbeln in neuzeitlichem Stil ausgestatteten Zimmern. Bürgerliche Gaststube.

WAIDHOFEN AN DER THAYA – Niederösterreich – 730 R2 – 5 750 Ew – Höhe 510 m 3 J1

Wien 122 – St. Pölten 93 – Zwettl 30 – Gmünd 27
Hauptplatz 1, ✉ 3830, ☎ (02842) 5 03, info@waidhofen-thaya-stadt.at
Waidhofen, Am Golfplatz 1 ☎ (02842) 5 02

Golfresort Waidhofen Zim, VISA AE

Am Golfplatz 1 (Nord-Ost: 1,5 km)
✉ 3830 – ☎ (02842) 5 02 – tt-hotel@thayatal.at – Fax (02842) 50255
geschl. Jan. – Feb.
40 Zim – 77/97 € 114/154 € – ½ P 25 €
Rest – Menü 49/60 € – Karte 18/33 €
♦ Das Hotel liegt im Grünen, direkt am hauseigenen Golfplatz. Man bietet neuzeitlich und funktionell eingerichtete Gästezimmer, darunter einige Panoramazimmer. Im Restaurant und im Irish Pub bewirtet man nicht nur Golfer.

WAIDHOFEN AN DER YBBS – Niederösterreich – 730 Q5 – 11 670 Ew – Höhe 356 m – Wintersport: 1 111 m ⛷8 ⛷ 2 **I3**

▶ Wien 146 – St. Pölten 89 – Steyr 35 – Amstetten 25
ℹ Oberer Stadtplatz 28, ✉ 3340, ☎(07442) 51 12 55, tourismus@waidhofen.at

Das Schloss an der Eisenstrasse

Am Schlossplatz 1 ✉ 3340 – Zim, VISA AE
– ☎ (07442) 5 05 – info@schlosseisenstrasse.at – Fax (07442) 505505
geschl. 24. Dez. – 7. Jan.
91 Zim – 108/149 € 123/173 € – 8 Suiten
Rest – Karte 22/37 €

◆ Aufwändig restauriertes Schloss a. d. 16. Jh., dessen moderne Einrichtung einen reizvollen Kontrast zum historischen Gebäude bildet. Seminarbereich mit guter Technik. Das Restaurant: angenehm hell und neuzeitlich-schlicht. Schöne Sicht auf Stadt und Fluss.

WAIDRING – Tirol – 730 J6 – 1 780 Ew – Höhe 781 m 7 **F4**

▶ Wien 356 – Innsbruck 107 – Salzburg 54

Tiroler Adler

Rest, Rest, P VISA
Kirchgasse 1 ✉ 6384 – ☎ (05353) 53 11 – info@tiroler-adler.at
– Fax (05353) 531150
geschl. Ende März – Mitte Mai, Anfang Okt. – Anfang Dez.
31 Zim (inkl. ½ P.) – ☼ 54/58 € 88/96 € ❄ 68/92 € 116/164 €
Rest – (nur Abendessen für Hausgäste)

◆ Ein gut gepflegtes, familiär geführtes Haus in zentraler Lage, das über solide ausgestattete Zimmer mit Balkon verfügt. Unterm Dach befinden sich einige einfachere Zimmer.

WALCHSEE – Tirol – 730 I6 – 2 050 Ew – Höhe 668 m – Wintersport: 1 100 m ⛷5 ⛷ 7 **E4**

▶ Wien 371 – Innsbruck 92 – Kufstein 20 – Rosenheim 38
ℹ Dorf 15, Kössen, ✉ 6345, ☎ (0501) 1 00, info@kaiserwinkl.com
⛳ GC Walchsee-Moarhof, Schwaigs 42☎ (05374) 53 78

Golf- und Sport Hotel Moarhof

Schwaigs 42 (Nord-West: 2,5 km) ✉ 6344 P VISA
– ☎ (05374) 53 78 – gcwalchsee@golf.at – Fax (05374) 20065
9 Zim – 64 € 98 € – ½ P 15 € – 4 Suiten
Rest – Karte 15/36 €

◆ Angenehm ruhig liegt das Hotel direkt am hauseigenen Golfplatz und bietet großzügig geschnittene Zimmer mit soliden Naturholzmöbeln im Landhausstil. Freundlich gestaltetes Restaurant.

Schick

Spa Rest, Rest, P VISA
Johannesstr. 1 ✉ 6344 – ☎ (05374) 53 31 – info@hotelschick.com
– Fax (05374) 5331550
geschl. 2. Nov. – 6. Dez., 16. März – 6. April
90 Zim (inkl. ½ P.) – ☼ 70/107 € 140/204 € ❄ 73/112 € 146/224 €
Rest – Karte 20/35 €

◆ Gasthof im alpenländischen Stil im Ortszentrum. Besonders behaglich sind die Zimmer im Anbau. Die Kräuterwickelkur ist die Hausspezialität des Wellnessbereichs. Restaurantstuben mit rustikal-gemütlichem Ambiente.

Am Walchsee Ost: 2 km:

Seehof-Seeresidenz (mit Hotel Panorama) (geheizt) Rest, VISA
Kranzach 20 ✉ 6344 Walchsee – ✆ (05374) 56 61
– panorama@seehof.com – Fax (05374) 5665
geschl. 3. Nov. – 18. Dez.
190 Zim – 95/117 € 148/194 € – ½ P 9 € – 28 Suiten
Rest – Karte 18/31 €
♦ Ein großzügiger Hotelkomplex aus drei sehr komfortablen Häusern mit schöner Thermen- und Saunalandschaft. Luxuriös und äußerst aufwändig gestaltet: die Seeresidenz. Im alpenländischen Stil gehaltenes Restaurant.

WALD IM PINZGAU – Salzburg – 730 I7 – 1 180 Ew – Höhe 885 m – Wintersport: 2 300 m 5 48

7 **E5**

Wien 419 – Salzburg 143 – Kitzbühel 52 – Zell am See 49
Wald Nr. 80, ✉ 5742, ✆ (06565) 82 43, info@wald-koenigsleiten.at

In Wald-Lahn West: 1,5 km:

Schranz Rest, VISA AE
Lahn 18 ✉ 5742 – ✆ (06565) 82 84 – info@gasthofschranz.at
– Fax (06565) 828433
geschl. 20. Okt. – 20. Dez.
35 Zim – ☼ 25/27 € 46/76 € ❄ 31/37 € 58/94 € – ½ P 10 €
Rest – Karte 18/33 €
♦ Recht persönlich führt die Inhaberfamilie dieses Haus. Die in ländlichem Stil gehaltenen Zimmer verfügen alle über einen Balkon. Einige Komfortzimmer. Bürgerliche Gaststuben.

In Königsleiten West: 10 km über Gerlospassstraße – Höhe 1 600 m

Ursprung (mit Gästehaus Panorama) Hohe Tauern und Zillertaler Alpen, VISA
Königsleiten 100
✉ 5742 – ✆ (06564) 82 53 – ursprung@nextra.at – Fax (06564) 82538
geschl. 6. April – 6. Juni, 18. Okt. – 1. Dez.
40 Zim – ☼ 35/40 € 60/80 € ❄ 70/80 € 120/160 €
– ½ P 15 €
Rest – Karte 22/31 €
♦ Ein unverbauter Bergblick zählt zu den Vorzügen dieser beiden alpenländischen Häuser. Die Zimmer sind mit rustikalen Naturholzmöbeln ausgestattet. Gemütliche Gaststuben. Bei schönem Wetter lockt die herrliche Sonnenterrasse.

WALS-SIEZENHEIM – Salzburg – 730 K5 – 11 030 Ew – Höhe 425 m

8 **F4**

Wien 296 – Salzburg 6 – Bad Reichenhall 13 – Bad Ischl 65
Salzburg-Kleßheim, Schloss Kleßheim ✆ (0662) 85 08 51

Grünauer Hof VISA
Grünauer Str. 90, (Grünau) ✉ 5071
– ✆ (0662) 85 04 64 – info@gruenauerhof.at – Fax (0662) 8504648
geschl. 22. – 25. Dez.

50 Zim – 64/75 € 92/120 € – ½ P 20 €
Rest – Karte 12/35 €
◆ Diese Adresse besteht aus drei adretten Häusern in typisch alpenländischem Stil mit rustikalen Zimmern, teils mit Erker. Auch für Tagungen geeignet. Der große Restaurantbereich bietet bürgerliche Küche und einen Kinderspielplatz.

Königgut Rest, Zim, Rest,
Oberfeldstr. 1 (Wals) 5071
– (0662) 85 03 93 – info@koeniggut-salzburg.at – Fax (0662) 85039332
geschl. 17. – 27. Dez.
44 Zim – 60/70 € 100/120 € – ½ P 17 €
Rest – *(geschl. Sonntag)* (nur für Hausgäste)
◆ Wohnlich und funktionell sind die Zimmer des alpenländischen Hotels eingerichtet, das sich besonders für Tagungen eignet. Es gibt einen modernen Freizeitbereich.

Himmelreich garni
Himmelreichstr. 34 5071 – (0662) 85 30 71
– info@hotel-himmelreich.at – Fax (0662) 85307120
geschl. 19. – 29. Dez.
20 Zim – 73/108 € 97/180 € – ½ P 16 €
◆ Die acht elegant-modernen Themenzimmer, benannt nach Planeten, sind besonders schöne Zimmer in diesem Hotel mit wechselnder Bilderaustellung. Naturschwimmteich zum Ausspannen.

Walserwirt Zim, Rest,
Walserstr. 24 (Wals) 5071 – (0662) 85 09 27 – info@walserwirt.com
– Fax (0662) 8509275
geschl. Juli 1 Wochen
25 Zim – 61/95 € 95/165 € – ½ P 19 €
Rest – *(geschl. Sept. – Juli Sonntagabend – Montag)* Karte 18/33 €
◆ Die Zimmer dieses familiengeführten Hotels werden bestimmt von ländlichem Stil. Es stehen Räume für Tagungsgäste und ein ansprechender Freizeitbereich zur Verfügung. Unter anderem bietet man im Restaurant Produkte aus der hauseigenen Metzgerei an.

Gasthof Kamml (mit Gästehaus) Biergarten (geheizt)
Brückenstr. 5 (Siezenheim) 5072
– (0662) 85 02 67 – hotel@kamml.com – Fax (0662) 85026713
49 Zim – 51/65 € 88/110 €
Rest – *(geschl. 22. Dez. – 7. Jan, 5. – 21. Juli, 18. – 27. Okt. sowie Samstag, Sonn- und Feiertage)* Karte 15/30 €
◆ Familiär geführtes Haus mit langer Tradition und gemütlichen Räumen im Landhausstil. Umfangreiches Freizeitangebot; für Radfahrer besonders geeignet. Rustikale Gaststuben im Salzburger Stil mit imposantem Kachelofen.

Gasthof Neuwirt Zim,
Hauptstr. 10 (Wals) 5071 – (0662) 85 00 50 – gasthof@neuwirt.net
– Fax (0662) 854345
15 Zim – 54/58 € 80/110 €
Rest – *(geschl. Mitte – Ende Juli und Samstag – Sonntag)* Karte 12/27 €
◆ Ein recht einfacher typischer Gasthof, der über neuzeitlich-rustikal möblierte Zimmer verfügt, die auch für Allergiker geeignet sind. Ländliche Gaststuben und nettes Heurigenlokal mit Gewölbedecke.

Landgasthof Allerberger
Doktorstr. 1 (Siezenheim) ✉ 5072 – ✆ (0662) 85 02 70 – landgasthof@allerberger.com – Fax (0662) 85040115
geschl. 23. Dez. – 6. Jan.
27 Zim – 50 € 83 €
Rest – *(geschl. Juli 1 Woche, Montag – Dienstag)* Karte 14/36 €
♦ Ursprünglich wurde das Haus im 18. Jh. als Jagdschloss erbaut, nun ist es ein Gasthof mit eigener Brauerei, die Zimmer sind rustikal mit dunklem Holz eingerichtet. Bürgerliche Küche wird in zünftiger Umgebung serviert.

WALTERSDORF, BAD – Steiermark – 730 U7 – 2 030 Ew – Höhe 291 m – Wintersport: – Heilbad

11 **L4**

Wien 137 – Graz 62 – Fürstenfeld 17
Hauptplatz 90, ✉ 8271, ✆ (03333) 31 50, info@badwaltersdorf.com

Safenhof mit Zim
Hauptstr. 78 ✉ 8271 – ✆ (03333) 22 39 – info@safenhof.at – Fax (03333) 223915
geschl. März 2 Wochen und Montag
10 Zim – 37/60 € 64/86 €
Rest – Menü 48 € – Karte 26/41 €
Rest *Dorfheurigen* – ✆ (03333) 22 39 20 *(geschl. Dienstag, wochentags ab 15 Uhr geöffnet)* Karte 14/17 €
♦ Gemütlich ist das in ländlichem Stil gehaltene Restaurant mit Kachelofen und nettem Dekor. Man bietet regionale und internationale Küche. Terrasse an der Safen. Urig: Dorfheuriger im ehemaligen Stall. Hotelbereich mit geschmackvollen Landhauszimmern.

In Bad Waltersdorf-Wagerberg Süd-Ost: 2 km Richtung Heiltherme:

Der Steirerhof (geheizt) (Thermal) A/C Rest, Rest,
Wagerberg 125 ✉ 8271 – ✆ (03333) 3 21 10 – reservierung@dersteirerhof.at – Fax (03333) 3211444
169 Zim (inkl. ½ P.) – 145/165 € 236/278 € 152/175 € 264/370 € – 11 Suiten
Rest – Karte 26/36 €
♦ Auf einem Grundstück von 60 000 qm liegt das Hotel außergewöhnlich schön. Geräumige und wohnliche Zimmer und ein geschmackvoll-moderner Wellnessbereich erwarten den Gast. Großzügiges Restaurant im klassischen Stil.

Thermenhof Paierl (geheizt) (Thermal)
Wagerberg 120
✉ 8271 – ✆ (03333) 28 01 – well-in@thermenhof.at – Fax (03333) 2801400
geschl. 29. Juni – 11. Juli
67 Zim (inkl. ½ P.) – 105/130 € 210/260 € 125/138 € 234/292 €
Rest – (Tischbestellung ratsam) Karte 26/33 €
♦ Hier überzeugen das sehr freundliche Personal, ein großzügig angelegter Wellnessbereich und zeitlos gestaltete Zimmer – einige im japanischen Stil. Vinothek, Zigarren-Lounge. Hell und rustikal-elegant gehaltenes Restaurant.

Panoramahof Ziegler Zim,

Am Sonntagsberg 93 ✉ 8271 – ✆ (03333) 24 80 – hotel@panoramahof.at – Fax (03333) 25714

geschl. 13. – 26. Dez.

30 Zim – 37/51 € 61 € – ½ P 12 €

Rest – *(geschl. Sonntag, nur Abendessen)* Karte 12/20 €

♦ Der Name verspricht nicht zu viel: Die Aussicht auf das Oststeirische Hügelland ist wunderbar. Die Zimmer sind sehr gepflegt und funktionell ausgestattet. Restaurant im Bistrostil.

WARMBAD – Kärnten – siehe Villach

WARTH AM ARLBERG – Vorarlberg – 730 C7 – 210 Ew – Höhe 1 495 m – Wintersport: 2 100 m 14 5 B5

Wien 570 – Bregenz 66 – Sankt Anton 28 – Bludenz 48

Warth 32, Gemeindeamt, ✉ 6767, ✆ (05583) 35 15, tbwarth@warth.at

Sporthotel Steffisalp VISA AE

Warth 36 ✉ 6767 – ✆ (05583) 36 99 – info@steffisalp.at – Fax (05583) 369953

geschl. 6. April – 10. Juli, 28. Sept. – 11. Dez.

56 Zim (inkl. ½ P.) – 89/164 € 178/258 € 155/255 € 180/450 €

Rest – Karte 27/47 €

♦ Durch und durch geradlinig-modern hat man dieses Hotel direkt neben den Skiliften gestaltet. Kosmetikbereich mit hochwertigen Pflegeprodukten. Sie speisen in dem gemütlich-rustikalen traditionellen Gasthaus. Mit SB-Restaurant und Sonnenterrasse.

Walserberg Zim, VISA

Warth 37 ✉ 6767 – ✆ (05583) 35 02 – hotel@walserberg.at – Fax (05583) 350222

geschl. Mai – Juni, Okt. – Nov.

48 Zim (inkl. ½ P.) – 64/71 € 128/152 € 84/124 € 168/288 €

Rest – *(geschl. im Sommer Montag, nur Abendessen)* Karte 17/35 €

♦ Mit modernen Holzmöbeln und hübschen Stoffen hat man die Zimmer wohnlich und funktionell ausgestattet, teilweise mit offenem Bad. Friseur und eigene Bäckerei im Haus. Neuzeitlich und leicht elegant: das Restaurant.

Jägeralpe Bergpanorama, Rest, VISA

Hochkrumbach 5 (Nord-West: 3 km) ✉ 6767 – ✆ (05583) 42 50 – hotel@jaegeralpe.at – Fax (05583) 4243

geschl. Anfang April – Mitte Juni, Mitte Okt. – Anfang Dez.

43 Zim (inkl. ½ P.) – 68/78 € 136/186 € 96/132 € 180/340 €

Rest – Karte 14/50 €

♦ Schön liegt das kinderfreundliche Alpenhotel außerhalb des Ortes an der Skipiste. Die Zimmer sind teils mit bemalten Bauernmöbeln eingerichtet – Romatikzimmer mit Kachelofen. Rustikal ist das Ambiente in den Restaurantstuben. Ganz ungezwungen: die Sennkuchi.

Lechtaler-Hof
Rest,
Warth 55 ✉ 6767 – ✆ (05583) 26 77
– info@lechthalerhof.at – Fax (05583) 26778
geschl. Mai, Okt. – Nov.
20 Zim (inkl. ½ P.) – ☼ 65/90 € 130/180 € ❄ 120/170 €
240/340 €
Rest – *(nur Abendessen)* Karte 21/27 €
◆ Der Berggasthof im Chaletstil beherbergt wohnliche, z. T. geräumige und mit hübschen kleinen Kachelöfen ausgestattete Zimmer. Netter Salon mit Klavier. Alpen Spa mit Kosmetik. Alpenländisch gestaltetes Restaurant mit heller Holztäfelung.

Adler
Hochkrumbach 8 (Nord-West: 4,5 km) ✉ 6767 – ✆ (05583) 42 64
– info@hoteladler.at – Fax (05583) 411266
geschl. 6. April – 1. Juli, 1. Okt. – 5. Dez.
40 Zim – ☼ 42/47 € 70/90 € ❄ 54/75 € 100/158 €
– ½ P 20 €
Rest – (im Winter nur Abendessen für Hausgäste) Karte 17/36 €
◆ Die schöne Lage auf der Passhöhe spricht für dieses familiengeführte Haus. Die Zimmer sind alle in heller Eiche gehalten – in einem Anbau befinden sich einige Appartements. In Stuben unterteiltes Restaurant mit ländlichem Ambiente.

WATTENS – Tirol – 730 G7 – 7 300 Ew – Höhe 567 m – Wintersport: 1 350 m 4

7 D5

Wien 430 – Innsbruck 17 – Schwaz 13 – Seefeld in Tirol 38
Dr.-Felix-Bunzl-Str. 6, ✉ 6112, ✆ (05224) 5 29 04, info@wattensinfo.at

Grander-Restaurant
Dr.-Felix-Bunzl-Str. 6 ✉ 6112 – ✆ (05224) 5 26 26
– info@grander-restaurant.at – Fax (05224) 52628
geschl. Samstagmittag, Sonntag
Rest – (Tischbestellung ratsam) Menü 63/80 € – Karte 37/46 €
◆ Ein Restaurant in modernem Stil mit aufmerksamem Service und gehobener mediterran und klassisch beeinflusster Küche. Mit im Haus: Bar und Vinothek.

Zum Schwan

Swarovskistr. 2 ✉ 6112 – ✆ (05224) 5 21 21 – Fax (05224) 55175
geschl. über Weihnachten 2 Wochen, Samstag, Sonn- und Feiertage
Rest – Menü 32/42 € – Karte 23/41 €
◆ In den auf zwei Etagen angelegten gemütlichen Stuben bietet man eine solide regionale Küche. Am Abend: ein internationales Menü sowie Empfehlungen des Chefs. Nette Terrasse.

Unsere „Hoffnungsträger" sind die Restaurants, deren Küche wir für die nächste Ausgabe besonders sorgfältig auf eine höhere Auszeichnung hin überprüfen. Der Name dieser Restaurants ist in „rot" gedruckt und zusätzlich auf der Sterne-Liste am Anfang des Buches zu finden.

WEER – Tirol – 730 G7 – 1 390 Ew – Höhe 550 m – Wintersport: 1 010 m

Wien 427 – Innsbruck 21 – Schwaz 8 – Hall in Tirol 12 7 **D5**

Weererwirt
(geheizt)

Dorfstr. 5 ✉ 6114 – ☎ (05224) 6 11 40
– info@weererwirt.at – Fax (05224) 611457
geschl. 29. März – 3. Mai, 25. Okt. – 13. Dez.
57 Zim (inkl. ½ P.) – ☼ 39/57 € 78/114 € ❄ 40/78 € 80/156 €
Rest – Karte 16/30 €

◆ Der traditionsreiche Gasthof in der Dorfmitte ist ein kinderfreundlicher Familienbetrieb mit eigener Reithalle und Stallungen. Man kann sogar mit dem eigenen Pferd anreisen! Die Gastronomie verspricht Bodenständigkeit in gemütlichem Rahmen.

WEIDEN AM SEE – Burgenland – 730 W5 – 1 930 Ew – Höhe 124 m

4 **M3**

Wien 55 – Eisenstadt 34 – Wiener Neudorf 67 – Sopron 56
Reiffeisenplatz 5, ✉ 7121, ☎ (02167) 74 27, weiden-tourism@wellcom.at

Zur Blauen Gans (Alain Weissgerber)

Seepark ✉ 7121 – ☎ (02167) 75 10 – restaurant@blaue-gans.at
geschl. Weihnachten – Mitte März und Dienstag – Mittwoch, Juli – Aug. nur Dienstag
Rest – (Tischbestellung ratsam) Menü 54/74 € – Karte 28/50 €
Spez. Gebratene Gänseleber mit Erbsenfond und pochiertem Ei. Zander mit Octopus, Schweinebauch und Lauchnage. Bluttaube mit confiertem Haxerl und Milchpulverhaut.

◆ Gemütlich ist die Atmosphäre in diesem engagiert geleiteten Restaurant mit regional-kreativem Angebot. Bekannt ist der Küchenchef auch durch eine TV-Kochsendung.

WEINZIERL AM WALDE – Niederösterreich – 730 S3 – 1 360 Ew – Höhe 650 m

3 **J2**

Wien 96 – St. Pölten 43 – Krems 19 – Zwettl 40

In Nöhagen Nord: 2 km:

Gasthaus Schwarz

Nöhagen 13 ✉ 3521 – ☎ (02717) 82 09 – office@gasthaus-schwarz.at
– Fax (02717) 82094
geschl. Feb. – März 2 Wochen, Sept. 1 Woche und Montag – Dienstag, Mitte Nov. – April Montag – Donnerstagmittag
Rest – Menü 39 € – Karte 23/35 €

◆ In der gediegen-rustikalen Gaststube oder im lichtdurchfluteten neuzeitlichen Wintergarten bietet man regionale Küche. Besonders gut: die Auswahl an Weißweinen aus der Wachau.

WEISSENKIRCHEN IN DER WACHAU – Niederösterreich – 730 S3 – 1 500 Ew – Höhe 206 m

3 **J2**

Wien 90 – St. Pölten 36 – Krems 14 – Melk 27
Donaulände 262, ✉ 3610, ☎ (02715) 26 00, gaesteinfo@weissenkirchen.at

Renaissancehotel Raffelsberger Hof garni

Weißenkirchen 54 ✉ 3610 – ☎ (02715) 22 01 – office@raffelsbergerhof.at – Fax (02715) 220127 – geschl. Jan. – Ende April

17 Zim – 77/100 € 115/131 €

◆ Das ehemalige Schiffsmeisterhaus a. d. J. 1574 besticht durch seine historischen Gewölbe und Arkaden. Die Zimmer sind recht geräumig und zum Teil mit Antiquitäten bestückt.

Donauhof garni

Rest,

Wachaustr. 298 ✉ 3610 – ☎ (02715) 23 53 – info@hotel-donauhof.at – Fax (02715) 23534 – geschl. 3. Dez. – 15. März

13 Zim – 65 € 104 €

◆ Sehr freundlich leiten Mutter und Tochter gemeinsam das kleine Hotel. Seine individuell eingerichteten Zimmer und das reichhaltige Frühstück in schönem Ambiente überzeugen.

Kirchenwirt

Kremser Str. 17 ✉ 3610 – ☎ (02715) 23 32 – kirchenwirt@weissenkirchen.at – Fax (02715) 2332200

30 Zim – 98/140 € 85/120 € – ½ P 25 €

Rest – *(geschl. Mitte Nov. – Ende März)* Menü 17/30 € – Karte 17/41 €

◆ Über 400 Jahre alt ist dieser familiengeführte Gasthof im Zentrum mit seinen wohnlich-rustikalen Zimmern, einige mit Donaublick. Gewölbezimmer in der Dependance. Das Restaurant teilt sich im mehrere gemütliche kleine Stuben mit Gewölbedecke.

Donauwirt

Wachaustr. 47 ✉ 3610 – ☎ (02715) 22 47 – info@donauwirt.at – Fax (02715) 224747

geschl. Mitte Nov. - Mitte März

12 Zim – 46 € 88/92 € – ½ P 22 €

Rest – *(geschl. Dienstag – Mittwoch)* Karte 20/36 €

◆ Moderner Landgasthof mit angenehm freundlich gestalteten Zimmern in zeitgemäßem Landhausstil und Dielenböden – z. T. mit Dachterrasse und Donaublick. Rustikal-gemütliche Restauranträume mit hübschem Gastgarten.

Holzapfels Prandtauerhof mit Zim

Zim,

Joching 36 ✉ 3610 – ☎ (02715) 23 10 – weingut@holzapfel.at – Fax (02715) 23109

geschl. Anfang Dez. – Anfang März, Sonntagabend – Dienstag

4 Zim – 95 € 145/160 €

Rest – Karte 22/48 €

◆ Gehobener Landhausstil bestimmt den schönen historischen Weinlesehof. Im Restaurant und im traumhaften Arkadenhof serviert man verfeinerte Regionalküche. Weingut, Brennerei. Das Haus verfügt über vier hübsche Appartements.

Florianihof

Wösendorf 74 ✉ 3610 – ☎ (02715) 22 12 – office@florianihof-wachau.at – Fax (02715) 22124

geschl. Feb. 3 Wochen und Mittwoch – Donnerstag

Rest – Menü 35/56 € – Karte 24/49 €

◆ Genießen Sie schmackhafte regionale Küche unter dem schönen Backsteingewölbe des alten Weinlesehofs. Bei schönem Wetter sitzt man nett auf der Terrasse unter Nussbäumen.

Jamek

Joching 45 3610 – (02715) 22 35 – info@weingut-jamek.at – Fax (02715) 223522

geschl. Mitte Dez. – Mitte Jan. und Samstag – Sonntag

Rest – *(Montag – Donnerstag nur Mittagessen)* Menü 18 € – Karte 22/42 €

◆ In dem Haus von 1912 hat man rustikal-elegantes Mobiliar und Dielenboden gelungen mit freundlichen Farben und Stoffen kombiniert. Gutes regionales Angebot. Schöner Garten.

Zum Alten Zechhaus

Bachgasse 83 3610 – (0664) 5 42 44 87 – office@roisl.at – Fax (02266) 61818

geschl. 1. Nov. – 22. März und Freitag

Rest – *(Montag – Donnertag nur Abendessen)* Karte 25/45 €

◆ Der denkmalgeschützte ehemalige Pfarrhof a. d. 13. Jh. ist ein gemütliches, fast intim wirkendes Restaurant unter familiärer Leitung. Sehr nette Gartenwirtschaft.

Heinzle

Weißenkirchen 280 3610 – (02715) 22 31 – restaurant@heinzle.at – Fax (02715) 223119

geschl. Mitte Dez. – Ende Jan. und Montag – Dienstag

Rest – Menü 34 € – Karte 17/35 €

◆ Auf der schönen Terrasse direkt an der Donau und im ländlich-schlicht gestalteten Restaurant serviert man eine regional beeinflusste Fischküche.

Gute und preiswerte Häuser kennzeichnet das MICHELIN-Männchen, der „Bib": der rote „Bib Gourmand" für die Küche, der blaue „Bib Hotel" bei den Zimmern.

WEISSENSEE – **Kärnten** – 730 L8 – **790 Ew** – **Höhe 930 m** – **Wintersport: 1 300 m** 5 — 9 **G6**

Wien 380 – Klagenfurt 102 – Spittal a.d. Drau 45 – Lienz 52

Techendorf 78, 9762, (04713) 2 22 00, info@weissensee.com

Veranstaltungen

23.05. – 24.05.: Angel um die Goldene Forelle

26.07. – 27.07.: Kunsthandwerksmarkt

In Techendorf

Die Forelle (mit Gästehaus)

Techendorf 80 9762 — Zim,

– (04713) 23 56 – info@forellemueller.at – Fax (04713) 23568

geschl. Nov., April

21 Zim (inkl. ½ P.) – 61/90 € 122/180 €

Rest – (nur Abendessen für Hausgäste)

◆ Sehr hübsch und wohnlich sind die Zimmer in diesem familiär geleiteten Haus am See. Der neuzeitliche Saunabereich bietet direkten Zugang zum Garten. Appartements im Gästehaus.

Haus am See Zim, Rest, VISA

Techendorf 73 ✉ 9762 – ✆ (04713) 22 22 – hausamsee@nextra.at – Fax (04713) 22228
geschl. 16. März – 8. Mai, 12. Okt. – 25. Dez.
23 Zim (inkl. ½ P.) – ☼ 76/91 € 128/182 € ❄ 79/86 € 146/172 €
Rest – (nur Abendessen für Hausgäste)
◆ Eine familiengeführte Ferienadresse direkt am Südufer des Weißensees mit freundlicher, behaglicher Einrichtung. Zum Haus gehört auch ein großer Garten am See.

St. Leonhard Rest,

Techendorf 82 ✉ 9762 – ✆ (04713) 2 16 70 – info@hotel-stleonhard.at – Fax (04713) 216722
geschl. 8. März – 15. Mai
17 Zim (inkl. ½ P.) – 68/84 € 136/168 €
Rest – (nur Abendessen für Hausgäste)
◆ Familiäre Atmosphäre herrscht in dem gepflegten kleinen Hotel in Seenähe. Die Zimmer hat man mit hellen Naturholzmöbeln wohnlich eingerichtet. Badehaus mit Saunalandschaft.

Alte Post Seeland Zim, Rest,

Techendorf 13 ✉ 9762 – ✆ (04713) 22 28 – office@seeland.at – Fax (04713) 222840
geschl. 5. März – 10. Mai, 10. Okt. – 25. Dez.
26 Zim (im Winter inkl. ½ P.) – ☼ 48/70 € 96/112 € ❄ 74/90 € 128/140 €
Rest – *(geschl. 10. Mai – 25. Dez.) (nur Abendessen für Hausgäste)*
◆ Die Lage direkt am See mit eigenem Strand und großzügiger Liegewiese sowie solide eingerichtete Zimmer mit Balkon (meist mit Seeblick) sprechen für dieses Haus.

Restaurant Zimmermann VISA

Techendorf 6 ✉ 9762 – ✆ (04713) 22 71 – Fax (04713) 227114
geschl. Nov. und Montag
Rest – Menü 32 € (abends) – Karte 20/34 €
◆ Ein sehr gepflegtes rustikales Restaurant mit freundlichem Service. Nett sind auch das gemütliche Nichtraucher-Stüberl und die überdachte Terrasse vor dem Haus.

In Gatschach West: 1 km ab Techendorf:

Gasthof Weissensee Zim, Rest,

Gatschach 3 ✉ 9762 – ✆ (04713) 22 14 – fam.koch@gasthofweissensee.at – Fax (04713) 2170
geschl. April, Nov.
31 Zim (inkl. ½ P.) – 50/63 € 100/116 €
Rest – *(geschl. Mittwoch, nur Abendessen)* Karte 21/34 €
◆ Ein Bauernhaus von 1618 ist dieser nette, traditionsreiche Gasthof mit hauseigenem Badestrand und soliden, gepflegten Zimmern. Gemütlich sitzt man in den Restaurantstuben.

In Neusach Ost: 1,5 km ab Techendorf:

Seehotel Enzian garni
Neusach 32 ✉ 9762 – ✆ (04713) 22 21 – enzian@cieslar.at – Fax (04713) 2221430
geschl. 10. März – 1. Mai, 12. Okt. – 15. Dez.
22 Zim – 42/92 € 74/204 €
◆ Wohnliche Gästezimmer, ein netter Frühstücksraum und ein wunderschönes, direkt am See gelegenes Saunahäuschen mit toller Aussicht sprechen für dieses gut geführte Hotel.

Fergius
Neusach 18 ✉ 9762 – ✆ (04713) 22 19 – fergius@hotelweissensee.at – Fax (04713) 2305
geschl. 30. Okt. – 22. Dez.
36 Zim (inkl. ½ P.) – 80/160 € 118/276 € – 2 Suiten
Rest – (nur für Hausgäste)
◆ Eine gemütliche Lobby mit Bar und wohnliche Zimmer mit neuzeitlicher Technik – fast alle mit Balkon und Blick zum See – erwarten Sie in diesem Ferienhotel.

Ronacherfels
See, Zim,
Neusach 40 ✉ 9762 – ✆ (04713) 21 72 – info@ronachacherfels.at – Fax (04713) 217224
geschl. 7. März – 9. Mai, 4. Okt. – 26. Dez.
9 Zim (inkl. ½ P.) – 74/94 € 108/190 €
Rest – *(geschl. Montag, Dienstagabend)* (Tischbestellung erforderlich) Karte 20/37 €
◆ Das wohnlich gestaltete kleine Hotel besticht durch seine verkehrsfreie Lage direkt am See sowie die herzliche Gästebetreuung. Anfahrt mit dem Auto nur für Übernachtungsgäste. Im hübschen Seepavillon bietet man regionale und internationale Küche.

Gralhof (mit Gästehaus)
Rest,
Neusach 7 ✉ 9762 – ✆ (04713) 22 13 – gralhof@aon.at – Fax (04713) 221375
geschl. April, Nov. – 25. Dez.
15 Zim (inkl. ½ P.) – ☼ 45/70 € 70/120 € ❄ 79/93 € 114/146 €
Rest – (nur Abendessen für Hausgäste, im Sommer garni)
◆ Nach wie vor betreibt man auf diesem über 500 Jahre alten Anwesen eine Landwirtschaft, deren Bioprodukte den Hausgästen zugute kommen. Am Seestrand: Saunahaus mit Ausblick.

In Kreuzberg Nord-West: 4 km ab Techendorf Richtung Greifenburg:

Familienhotel Kreuzwirt
(geheizt) Rest,
Kreuzberg 2 ✉ 9762 – ✆ (04713) 22 06 – info@hotelkreuzwirt.at – Fax (04713) 220650
geschl. 26. März – 30. April, 20. Okt. – 15. Dez.
42 Zim (inkl. ½ P.) – 60/88 € 130/176 €
Rest – Karte 18/30 €
◆ Ganz auf Familien ist dieses gewachsene Alpenhotel ausgelegt. Zum Angebot gehören ein Kinderhallenbad, Spielzimmer mit Betreuung sowie ein großer Spielplatz. Restaurant mit ländlich-rustikalem Ambiente.

WEISSKIRCHEN IN STEIERMARK – Steiermark – 730 Q7 – 1 340 Ew – Höhe 681 m 10 **J5**

Wien 202 – Graz 80 – Knittelfeld 12 – Judenburg 7

k.u.k. Wirtshaus Taverne

Judenburgerstr. 13 ✉ 8741 – ✆ (03577) 8 22 55 – taverne.breznik@ainet.at – Fax (03577) 8225555
geschl. März 2 Wochen, Okt. 2 Wochen und Dienstag, Juni – Mitte Sept. nur Dienstagmittag
Rest – Karte 18/37 €
♦ Dieses seit mehreren Generationen in Familienbesitz befindliche Haus a. d. J. 1612 empfängt Sie in seinen rustikalen Stuben mit einem Hauch k. u. k. Nostalgie.

WEISTRACH – Niederösterreich – 730 P4 – 2 200 Ew – Höhe 352 m 2 **I3**

Wien 157 – St. Pölten 100 – Steyr 15 – Amstetten 29

Landgasthof Kirchmayr

Weistrach 9 ✉ 3351 – ✆ (07477) 4 23 80 – rest@kirchmayr.net – Fax (07477) 4238024
geschl. Jan. 3 Wochen sowie Montag – Dienstag, Sonn- und Feiertage abends
Rest – Karte 14/35 €
♦ Die Ursprünge des Hauses reichen bis ins 12. Jh. zurück, seit dem beginnenden 19. Jh. wird es von der Familie Kirchmayr als bodenständiger Gasthof geführt.

Wir bemühen uns bei unseren Preisangaben um größtmögliche Genauigkeit. Aber alles ändert sich! Lassen Sie sich daher bei Ihrer Reservierung den derzeit gültigen Preis mitteilen.

WEIZ – Steiermark – 730 S7 – 8 950 Ew – Höhe 477 m 11 **K4**

Wien 168 – Graz 29 – Bruck a.d. Mur 63 – Fürstenfeld 48
Hauptplatz 18, ✉ 8160, ✆ (03172) 2 31 96 60, office@tourismus.com

Gasthof Allmer

Biergarten

Wegscheide 7 (Ost: 1,5 km, Richtung Birkfeld, dann rechts ab) ✉ 8160 – ✆ (03172) 22 58 – office@gasthof-allmer.at – Fax (03172) 225822
27 Zim – 42 € 70 €
Rest – *(geschl. Dienstag)* Karte 11/27 €
♦ Der am Ortsrand gelegene Gasthof mit seinem freundlichen, hellen Äußeren hält saubere und gepflegte, zeitgemäß möblierte Zimmer bereit. Gaststuben in ländlicher Aufmachung, mit Wintergarten.

Altes Rathaus

Klammstr. 4 ✉ 8160 – ✆ (03172) 4 66 60 – office@gastro-weiz.com – Fax (03172) 443815
geschl. Sonntag, Feiertage abends
Rest – Menü 26 € – Karte 15/33 €
♦ Das ehemalige Rathaus bietet einen historischen Rahmen für dieses Restaurant mit Gewölbekeller. Internationale Küche aus saisonalen Produkten. Terrasse zur Fußgängerzone.

WELS – Oberösterreich – 730 O4 – 56 480 Ew – Höhe 317 m 2 **H3**

- Wien 195 – Linz 34 – Steyr 47 – Gmunden 37
- Kaiser-Josef-Platz 22, ✉ 4600, ✆ (07242) 4 34 95, office@tourism-wels.at
- GC Wels-Weißkirchen, Golfplatzstr. 2 ✆ (07243) 5 60 38
- Kremstal-Kematen a.d.K., Schachen 20 ✆ (07228) 7 64 40

Veranstaltungen

23.01. – 25.01.: PRObau u. PROsicherheit
07.03. – 09.03.: Energiesparmesse
04.04. – 06.04.: Volksfest, Blühendes Österreich u. Biker
25.05. – 31.05.: Richard Wagner Festival
03.09. – 07.09.: Agraria & Herbstmesse
14.11. – 16.11.: Gesund Leben

- Altstadt (Stadtplatz★) AB
- Schmiding: Zoologischer Garten★ Nord-West: 7 km – Lambach: Stift★ Süd-West: 16 km – Stadl-Paura: Wallfahrtskirche★ Süd-West: 18 km

WELS

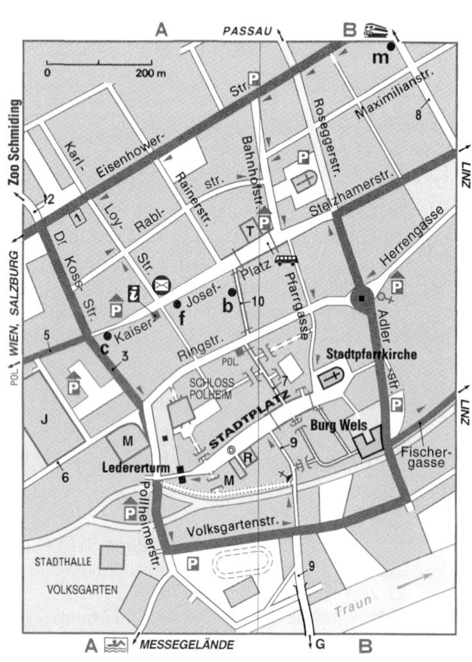

 **Alexandra** garni

Dr.-Schauer-Str. 23 ✉ 4600 – ✆ (07242) 4 72 14 – office@hotelalexandra.at – Fax (07242) 4721455
geschl. 22. Dez. – 6. Jan B **m**
22 Zim – 🛉92 € 🛉🛉124 €

◆ Ein gemeinsamer Hallenbereich verbindet diese schmucke Stadtvilla mit dem von der selben Familie geleiteten Bayrischen Hof. Wohnliche, in warmen Farben gehaltene Zimmer.

Hauser Rest,

Bäckergasse 7 ✉ 4600 – ✆ (07242) 4 54 09 – office@hotelhauser.com – Fax (07242) 4540945 A **b**

42 Zim – 81/101 € 108/128 €

Rest – (nur Abendessen für Hausgäste)

◆ Modern und geschmackvoll zeigt sich die Einrichtung dieses ehemaligen Bürgerhauses. Bei gutem Wetter serviert man das Frühstück auf der Terrasse über den Dächern von Wels.

Ploberger garni

Kaiser-Josef-Platz 21 ✉ 4600 – ✆ (07242) 6 29 41 – reservierung@hotel-ploberger.at – Fax (07242) 62941110 A **f**

82 Zim – 73/97 € 99/126 €

◆ Zentral und doch relativ ruhig liegt dieses Haus. Die Zimmer in der Bel Etage überzeugen mit extra großem Arbeitsbereich und schönem Marmorbad.

Bayrischer Hof Zim,

Dr. Schauer-Str. 21 ✉ 4600 – ✆ (07242) 4 72 14 – office@bayrischerhof.at – Fax (07242) 4721455
geschl. 22. Dez. – 6. Jan. B **m**

48 Zim – 58 € 86 €

Rest – *(geschl. Samstag – Sonnntag, Feiertage)* Karte 21/28 €

◆ Eine hübsche weiß-blaue Fassade ziert dieses in Bahnhofsnähe gelegene, mit dem Hotel Alexandra verbundene Haus. Man bietet unterschiedlich möblierte Gästezimmer. Restaurant mit bürgerlich-rustikalem Ambiente.

Maxlhaid

Maxlheid 9 (über Stelzhamer Str. B: 4 km) ✉ 4600 – ✆ (07242) 4 67 16 – maxlhaid@liwest.at – Fax (07242) 61632
geschl. 23. Dez. – 7. Jan.

30 Zim – 53 € 80 €

Rest – *(geschl. Samstag – Sonntag, Feiertage)* Karte 17/35 €

◆ Ein Gasthof mit Geschichte: Von 1835 bis 1855 diente er als Station der Pferdeeisenbahn. Heute beherbergt man Gäste in unterschiedlichen Zimmern. Pferdeeisenbahnmuseum. Nett gestaltete Räumlichkeiten mit Gewölbedecke dienen als Restaurant.

Gösserbräu Biergarten Rest, Zim,

Kaiser-Josef-Platz 27 ✉ 4600 – ✆ (07242) 6 04 60 – office@goesserbraeu.at – Fax (07242) 56312 A **c**

21 Zim – 55/65 € 85/95 €

Rest – Karte 15/29 €

◆ Stilvolle Möbel, Parkettböden und edle Stoffe tragen zur Individualität und Wohnlichkeit dieser Welser Traditionsadresse bei, die bereits im 16. Jh. namentlich erwähnt wurde. Rustikal-gemütliches Ambiente im Restaurant, draußen der herrliche Gastgarten.

Wirt am Berg

*Salzburger Str. 227 (Süd-West: 5 km über Eisenhower Straße **A**) ✉ 4600 – ✆ (07242) 4 50 59 – office@wirtamberg.at – Fax (07242) 450599*
geschl. 24. Dez. – 7. Jan., 16. – 25. März, 28. Juli – 11. Aug., 19. – 27. Okt. und Sonntag – Montag

Rest – (Tischbestellung ratsam) Menü 44/60 € – Karte 29/49 €
◆ Seit 1881 wird das schöne Anwesen a. d. J. 1630 von der Familie geführt. Stilvolles Ambiente, freundlicher Service und gutes Essen gehen hier Hand in Hand. Innenhofterrasse.

WENNS – Tirol – 730 E7 – 2 020 Ew – Höhe 982 m – Wintersport: 2 450 m 1 7 6 C6

Wien 507 – Innsbruck 63 – Imst 11 – Landeck 27
Unterdorf 18, 6473, (05414) 8 69 99, info@pitztal.com

Alpen
Zim,
Oberdorf 711 6473 – (05414) 86 11 10 – info@hotel-alpen.at – Fax (05414) 861114
geschl. 15. April – 1. Juni, 28. Okt. – 1. Dez.
18 Zim (inkl. ½ P.) – 60/105 € 80/140 € 65/128 € 90/170 €
Rest – (nur Abendessen für Hausgäste)
◆ Von der regionstypischen Holzbalkonfassade bis in die Gästezimmer zeigt das am Ortsrand gelegene kleine Hotel seinen rustikalen Charakter.

WERFEN – Salzburg – 730 L6 – 3 090 Ew – Höhe 600 m 8 G4

Wien 343 – Salzburg 47 – Bischofshofen 8 – Hallein 32
Markt 24, 5450, (06468) 53 88, info@werfen.at

Erzherzog Eugen garni
Markt 38 5450 – (06468) 5 21 00 – obauer-krieger@sbg.at – Fax (06468) 75523
11 Zim – 50/88 € 80/95 €
◆ Der nette Familienbetrieb ist ein idealer Ausgangspunkt für die Besichtigung der Burg Werfen und der Eisriesenwelt. Zimmer mit individuell angefertigten, hellen Holzmöbeln.

Karl & Rudolf Obauer mit Zim
Rest,
Markt 46 5450 – (06468) 5 21 20 – ok@obauer.com – Fax (06468) 521212
geschl. 16. Juni – 10. Juli
12 Zim – 80/155 € 125/225 €
Rest – *(geschl. Montag – Dienstag, außer Saison)* (Tischbestellung erforderlich) Menü 35 € (mittags)/95 € – Karte 47/86 €
Spez. Geräucherte Kalbsleber mit Speck, Zwetschkenchutney und Safranapfel. Steinbutt mit Safran-Kalbshax'lsaft und Solofino-Spargel. Lamm mit Rosmarinpolenta und Rettich.
◆ Das elegante Restaurant überzeugt mit der regional geprägten Küche der Gebrüder Obauer. Schön ist die Terrasse hinter dem Haus. Wohnlich und modern eingerichtete Gästezimmer mit Balkon.

In Werfen-Imlau Süd: 1,5 km Richtung Bischofshofen:

Landgasthof Reitsamerhof (mit Gästehäusern)
Reitsam 22 5450 – (06468) 53 79 – office@reitsamerhof.at – Fax (06468) 53794
geschl. nach Ostern 2 Wochen, Mitte Nov. 3 Wochen

25 Zim – 31/39 € 54/68 € – ½ P 11 €
Rest – *(geschl. Montag – Dienstag)* Karte 12/30 €
♦ Das für die Region typische Haus unter Leitung der Familie liegt verkehrsgünstig nahe der A 10 und bietet wohnlich und solide eingerichtete Zimmer. Das Restaurant wird im Sommer um schöne Terrassenplätze im Grünen ergänzt.

WERFENWENG – Salzburg – 730 L6 – 770 Ew – Höhe 950 m – Wintersport: 1 836 m 1 9 — 8 G4

Wien 346 – Salzburg 50 – Bischofshofen 12 – Hallein 35
Skimuseum, Weng 138, 5453, (06466) 42 00, tourismusverband@werfenweng.org
Höhlen Eisriesenwelt★★ Nord-West: 20 km

Elisabeth

Zim,

Weng 41 5453 – (06466) 4 00 – werfenweng@hotelelisabeth.at – Fax (06466) 4004
geschl. Nov.
34 Zim (inkl. ½ P.) – 68/74 € 116/128 € 77/109 € 148/218 € – 3 Suiten
Rest – (nur Abendessen für Hausgäste)
♦ Das Hotel beherbergt einen großzügigen Hallenbereich und teils recht geräumige Zimmer im neuzeitlichen Landhausstil – einige mit toller Sicht. Kosmetik-Angebot.

WESTENDORF – Tirol – 730 I6 – 3 460 Ew – Höhe 800 m – Wintersport: 1 865 m 12 76 — 7 E5

Wien 380 – Innsbruck 76 – Wörgl 15 – Kitzbühel 17
Schulgasse 2, 6363, (05334) 62 30, westendorf@kitzbuehel-alpen.com

Vital Landhotel Schermer

(geheizt) Rest, VISA

Dorfstr. 106 6363 – (05334) 62 68 – welcome@vitalhotelschermer.at – Fax (05334) 626866
geschl. 1. – 30. – April, 11. Nov. – 11. Dez.
67 Zim (inkl. ½ P.) – 97/109 € 164/188 € 108/142 € 186/254 € – 19 Suiten
Rest – Karte 13/38 €
♦ Wohnliche Gästezimmer in neuzeitlichem Stil sowie ein freundlich gestalteter, moderner Wellnessbereich machen diesen Familienbetrieb in der Ortsmitte aus. Die Restaurantstuben sind teilweise rustikal gehalten.

Glockenstuhl

Rest,

Dorfstr. 27 6363 – (05334) 61 75 – westendorf@glockenstuhl.at – Fax (05334) 2472
geschl. 30. März – 22. Mai, 19. Okt. – Mitte Dez.
20 Zim (inkl. ½ P.) – 66/76 € 112/118 € 85/113 € 150/196 € – 4 Suiten
Rest – *(geschl. Mitte Mai – Mitte Okt. Dienstag, nur Abendessen)* Karte 15/37 €
♦ Das regionstypische Haus am Ortsrand bietet hübsche, zeitgemäß ausgestattete Gästezimmer mit Balkon sowie einen netten Bade-/Saunabereich und Massage. Charmantes, ganz mit Holz verkleidetes Restaurant mit freundlichem Service.

Residenz 4-Jahreszeiten garni
Holzham 93 (Süd-West: 1 km) ✉ 6363
– ✆ (05334) 3 00 31 – info@4-jahres-zeiten.at – Fax (05334) 3003131
geschl. April – Juni, Okt. – Dez.
16 Zim – ☼ 28 € 87 € ❄ 55/65 € 153/173 €
◆ Recht ruhig liegt das Hotel in einem kleinen Weiler. Es stehen gepflegte, mit modernen Holzmöbeln eingerichtete Zimmer zur Verfügung.

Bichlingerhof Rest,
Bichling 105 (Nord-Ost: 1 km) ✉ 6363 – ✆ (05334) 63 26
– hotel@bichlingerhof.at – Fax (05334) 6383
geschl. April, Nov.
21 Zim – ☼ 34 € 68 € ❄ 57/61 € 104/112 € – ½ P 7 €
Rest – Karte 13/31 €
◆ In dem etwas außerhalb gelegenen, familiär geleiteten Ferienhotel erwarten Sie hell möblierte, zeitgemäße Gästezimmer, alle mit Balkon. Restaurant mit gemütlicher Zirbenstube und Kachelofen.

Gasthof Aschenwald
Bahnhofstr. 19 (Nord-Ost: 1,5 km, an der B 170) ✉ 6363
– ✆ (05334) 22 74 – gasthof@aschenwald.at – Fax (05334) 22744
geschl. April – 1. Juni, 18. Okt. – 1. Dez.
22 Zim (inkl. ½ P.) – ☼ 44 € 88 € ❄ 49/54 € 88/108 €
Rest – Karte 18/29 €
◆ Ein familiengeführter Gasthof mit sehr gepflegten und soliden Zimmern, die mit hellem Naturholz oder dunkler Eiche ausgestattet sind. Bürgerlich-rustikale Restaurantstuben.

Bestecke ✕ und Sterne ✿ sollten nicht verwechselt werden!
Die Bestecke stehen für eine Komfortkategorie, die Sterne zeichnen Häuser mit besonders guter Küche aus - in jeder dieser Kategorien.

WEYREGG AM ATTERSEE – Oberösterreich – 730 M5 – 1 500 Ew – Höhe 482 m – Wintersport: 790 m 3 1 G3

Wien 241 – Linz 81 – Salzburg 65 – Gmunden 27
Weyregger Str. 69, ✉ 4852, ✆ (07664) 22 36, info.weyregg@attersee.at
GC Weyregg am Attersee, Wachtbergstr. 30 ✆ (07664) 2 07 12

✕ **Wirtshaus Häupl am Berg** < Attersee,
Wachtbergstr. 30 ✉ 4852 – ✆ (07664) 2 07 27
– info@haeupl-am-berg.at
geschl. Sept. – Juni Montag – Dienstag
Rest – Karte 16/39 €
◆ Das Restaurant mit bürgerlich-regionalem Angebot befindet sich direkt am Golfplatz mit herrlicher Sicht über den Attersee. Im Haus befindet sich auch eine kleine Vinothek.

In Weyregg-Alexenau **Süd: 2,5 km Richtung Bad Ischl:**

Gasthof zur Bramosen

Rest,

Alexenau 8 ✉ 4852 – ✆ (07664) 22 91
– ecker@hotel-bramosen.at – Fax (07664) 229144
geschl. Jan. – Feb.
34 Zim – 53/63 € 92/122 € – ½ P 25 €
Rest – Karte 18/35 €

♦ Nicht weit vom Attersee gelegenes Hotel mit soliden Zimmern und einem eigenen Strandbereich mit Liegewiese. In einem kleinen Haus nebenan hat man Appartements eingerichtet. Restaurant und Terrasse bieten eine schöne Sicht auf den See.

Wien: Stephandom

WIEN

L **Bundesland:** Wien
Michelin-Karte: 730 UV4
▶ München 439 – Praha 296
– Salzburg 304 – Graz 199

Einwohnerzahl: 1 550 130 Ew
Höhe: 156 m

4 L2

Die ehemalige Kaiserstadt Wien ist eine der bedeutendsten Kunstmetropolen Europas. Sammlungen von Weltrang und einzigartige Baudenkmäler spannen den Bogen von der Vergangenheit in die Gegenwart. Vieles erinnert an die glanzvollen Epochen unter den Habsburgern, manches an berühmte Musiker, die hier bedeutende Kapitel der Musikgeschichte schrieben. Und noch immer schwingt der Walzer seinen Taktstock über dem geschäftigen Treiben rund um den Stephansdom. Wien ist als Regierungssitz Stadt der Ministerien und Verwaltungen und seit 1979 auch einer der ständigen Sitze der Vereinten Nationen. Für viele Einheimische und Besucher ist Wien aber vor allem die Stadt der Kaffeehäuser, Beisln und Heurigen, in denen die traditionelle Gastlichkeit weiterhin hochgehalten wird.

PRAKTISCHE HINWEISE

Tourist-Information

Albertinaplatz JR, ✉ 1010, ✆ (01) 2 45 55, info@wien.info

Flughafen

✈ Wien-Schwechat (über A 4 CZ), ✆ (01) 7 00 70

Messen

Wiener Messe, Messeplatz 1, ✉ 1021, ✆ (01) 1 72 72 00

17.01. – 20.01.: Ferien-Messe u. Vienna Autoshow

05.02. – 07.02.: ITnT

21.02. – 24.02.: Bauen & Energie

08.03. – 16.03.: Wohnen & Interieur

12.04. – 15.04.: Vinova u. Alles für den Gast

24.04. – 27.04.: VIENNAFAIR u. Austropharm

27.05. – 29.05.: Real Vienna

07.10. – 10.10.: VIENNA-TEC

16.10. – 18.10.: GLORIA

23.10. – 26.10.: Modellbau-Messe

20.11. – 23.11.: Vienna Boat Show

Veranstaltungen

01.01.: Neujahrskonzert der Wiener Philharmoniker

31.01.: Opernball

30.03. – 04.05.: Wiener Frühlingsfestival

09.05. – 15.06.: Wiener Festwochen

17.10. – 29.10.: Viennale (Internationales Filmfestival)

15.11. – 24.12.: Christkindlmarkt

Fußball-Europameisterschaft

08.06., 12.06., 16.06.: Vorrundenspiele

20.06., 22.06.: Viertelfinale

26.06.: Halbfinale

29.06.: Finale

Golfplätze

18 GC Wien, Freudenau 65a ✆ (01) 7 28 95 64 CY

9 C & C Golfclub am Wienerberg, Gutheil-Schoder-Gasse 9 ✆ (01) 6 61 23 70 00 BZ

18 Club Danube Golf Wien, Weingartenallee 22 ✆ (01) 2 56 82 82

HAUPTSEHENSWÜRDIGKEITEN

DIE HOFBURG

Gebäude und Plätze: Michaelertrakt★ – Josefsplatz★ – Heldenplatz★

Museen und Sammlungen: Kaiserappartements★ – Sisi-Museum★ – Hofsilber- und Tafelkammer★ – Schatzkammer★★★ – Spanische Hofreitschule★★ – Österreichische Nationalbibliothek★ – Albertina: Graphische Sammlung★★ – Ephesos-Museum★★ – Sammlung alter Musikinstrumente★★ – Hofjagd- und Rüstkammer★★ – Museum für Völkerkunde★ JR

SCHLOSS SCHÖNBRUNN

Schlossbesichtigung★★ – Wagenburg★ (Imperialwagen★★) – Schlosspark★★ (Tiergarten★, Palmenhaus★) – Gloriette★★ AZ

GEBÄUDE UND DENKMÄLER

Stephansdom★★★ – Jesuitenkirche★ KR – Kapuzinergruft★★ – Peterskirche★ JR – Oberes Belvedere★★ (Sammlungen des 19. und 20. Jh.★★) FV – Unteres Belvedere★ (Barokmuseum★★, Museum mittelalterlicher Kunst★) FU – Karlskirche★★ CY – Burgtheater★ HR – Maria am Gestade★ JP

JUGENDSTIL UND SECESSION

Postsparkasse★ LR – Wagner-Pavillons★ – Secessionsgebäude★★ (Beethovenfries★★) JS – Otto-Wagner-Wohnhäuser an der Linken Wienzeile★ FU – Kirche am Steinhof★★ AY

PLÄTZE, PARKS UND STRASSEN

Graben (Pestsäule★★) – Neuer Markt (Donnerbrunnen★★) JR – Schwarzenbergplatz★ KS – Volksgarten★ HR – Prater★ (Riesenrad★★) GU – Rundfahrt über den Ring★

MUSIKALISCHES WIEN

Staatsoper★★ JS – Haus der Musik★★ KS – Pasqualatihaus (Beethoven)★ HP – Figarohaus (Mozart)★ KR – Schubert-Gedenkstätte★ **M**[5] FT – Haydn-Gedenkstätte★ **M**[10] EV – Johann-Strauß-Gedenkstätte★ LP

MUSEEN, GALERIEN, SAMMLUNGEN

Kunsthistorisches Museum★★★ – Museumsquartier★★ (Leopold Museum★) HS – Akademie der bildenden Künste: Gemäldegalerie★★ JS – MAK (Österreichisches Museum für angewandte Kunst)★★ LR – Historisches Museum der Stadt Wien★ KS - Naturhistorisches Museum★ HR – Jüdisches Museum★ – Uhrenmuseum★ **M**[17] JR – Heeresgeschichtliches Museum★ **M**[23] GV – Schatzkammer des Deutschen Ordens★ – Dom- und Diözesanmuseum★ **M**[19] KR – Technisches Museum★ **M**[2] AZ – Kaiserliches Hofmobiliendepot★ **M**[11] EU – Liechtensteinmuseum★★ **M**[27] FT

STRASSENVERZEICHNIS WIEN

Straße	Planquadrat	Nr.
Adalbert-Stifter-Str.	CX	3
Albertinapl.	JS	
Alserbachstr.	EFT	4
Alser Str.	EU	
Altes Landgut	CZ	
Altmannsdorfer Str.	AZ	6
Amundsenstr.	AY	
Am Heumarkt	KLS	
Am Hof	JR	
Annagasse	JKS	
Arsenalstr.	FGV	
Aspernbrücke	LPR	
Atzgerdorfer Pl.	AZ	
Auerspergstr.	HR	
Augartenbrücke	JP	
Babenbergerstr.	HJS	
Bäckerstr.	KR	9
Ballhauspl.	HJR	
Bankgasse	HJR	
Bauernmarkt	KR	10
Beatrixgasse	LS	
Beethovenpl.	KS	
Berggasse	HP	
Biberstr.	LR	
Billrothstr.	ET	12
Blumauergasse	LP	
Börsegasse	JP	
Börselpl.	JP	
Bognergasse	JR	13
Bräunerstr.	JR	15
Breitenfurter Str.	AZ	16
Breitenleer Str.	CX	
Breite Gasse	HRS	
Brigittenauer Lände	FT	
Brünner Str.	CX	
Burggasse	HRS, EU	
Burgring	HR	
Cobenzlgasse	AX	
Concordiapl.	JP	
Dampfschiffstr.	LPR	
Döblinger Hauptstr.	BXY	21
Dominikanerbastei	KR	22
Donaufelder Str.	CX	
Donaustadtstr.	CXY	24
Dornbacher Str.	AY	
Dorotheergasse	JR	25
Dresdner Str.	CXY	
Dr-Ignaz-Seipel-Pl.	KR	27
Dr-Karl-Lueger-Ring	HPR	
Dr-Karl-Renner-Ring	HR	
Eichenstr.	EV	
Eipeldauerstr.	CX	
Engerthstr.	GT	
Erdberger Lände	CYZ, GU	28
Erdbergstr.	CY	30
Erzherzog-Karl-Str.	CY	31
Europapl.	EU	
Exelbergstr.	AXY	
Falkestr.	KLR	33
Favoritenstr.	FV	34
Felderstr.	HR	
Fleischmarkt	KR	
Flötzersteig	AY	
Floridsdorfer Brücke	CX	36
Flurschützstr.	EV	
Franz-Josefs-Kai	KLPR	
Freyung	JR	
Friedrichstr.	JS	38
Friedrich-Schmidt-Pl.	HR	
Gablenzgasse	AY	
Garnisongasse	HP	
Georg-Coch-Pl.	LR	40
Gersthofer Str.	AY	
Getreidemarkt	HJS	42
Glockengasse	LP	
Graben	JR	
Gregor-Mendel-Str.	ET	43
Grenzackerstr.	CZ	45
Griechengasse	KR	46
Grinzinger Allee	BX	48
Grinzinger Str.	BX	49
Grünbergstr.	AZ, FGV	
Gudrunstr.	BCZ	
Gumpendorfer Str.	HS	
Gutenberggasse	HS	51
Hadikgasse	AYZ	
Hafenzufahrtstr.	CY	
Haidgasse	KP	
Handelskai	CXY	
Hasenauerstr.	ET	54
Hauptallee	CY	
Hauptstr.	AX	
Heiligenkreuzer Hof	KR	55
Heiligenstädter Lände	FT	57
Heiligenstädter Str.	FT	58
Heinestr.	FGT	
Heinrichsgasse	JP	
Hermesstr.	AZ	
Hernalser Hauptstr.	AY	
Herrengasse	JR	
Hetzendorfer Str.	AZ	
Hietzinger Kai	AZ	60
Himmelpfortgasse	KR	61
Hintere Zollamtsstr.	LR	
Hirschstettner Str.	CX	63
Hoche Warte	BX	64
Hörlgasse	HJP	
Hohenstr.	AX	
Hoher Markt	KR	
Hollandstr.	KP	
Hütteldorfer Str.	ABY	
Invalidenstr.	LR	
Jägerstr.	FT	
Johannesgasse	KRS	
Josefspl.	JR	
Josefstädter Str.	EU	
Judengasse	KR	66
Judenpl.	JR	67
Kärntner Ring	JKS	
Kärtner Str.	JRS	
Kahlenberger Str.	BX	
Karlspl.	JS	
Kohlmarkt	JR	70
Krottenbachstr.	ABX	
Kulmgasse	AY	23
Kundmanngasse	GU	71
Laaer-Berg-Str.	CZ	
Lainzer Str.	AZ	
Landesgerichtsstr.	HPR	
Landstr. Gürtel	FGV	
Landstr. Hauptstr.	LR, GUV	72
Lange Gasse	EU	73
Lassallestr.	CY, GT	74
Laxenburger Str.	CZ, FV	
Leopoldauer Str.	CX	
Leopoldsgasse	KP	
Lerchenfelder Str.	EU	
Lichtenfelsgasse	HR	
Lichtensteg	KR	78
Liechtensteinstr.	HP	
Linke Bahngasse	LS	
Linke Wienzeile	BYZ, EV	
Linzer Str.	AY	
Löwelstr.	HR	79
Löwengasse	GU	
Lothringerstr.	KS	
Lugeck	KR	
Marc-Aurel-Str.	KPR	81
Margaretengürtel	EFV	
Margaretenstr.	BCYZ	82
Mariahilfer Str.	HS, EU	
Maria-Theresien-Pl.	HRS	
Maria-Theresien-Str.	HJP	
Marienbrücke	KP	
Maurer Hauptpl.	AZ	
Maurer-Lange-Gasse	AZ	83
Meidlinger Hauptstr.	BZ	84
Michaelerpl.	JR	
Millöckergasse	JS	29
Minoritenpl.	JR	
Mölkerbastei	HP	85
Museumspl.	HS	
Museumstr.	HR	
Naglergasse	JR	
Neubaugasse	EU	86
Neubaugürtel	EU	
Neuer Markt	JR	87
Neustiftgasse	HR	88
Neuwaldegger Str.	AY	89
Nibelungengasse	HJS	
Nordbahnstr.	CY	
Nordbrücke	CX	
Nußdorfer Str.	ET	
Obere Augartenstr.	FT	
Obere Donaustr.	KP	
Operngasse	JS	
Opernring	JS	
Oppolzergasse	HR	90
Parkring	KLR	
Philharmonikerstr.	JS	91
Plankengasse	JR	92
Postgasse	KR	
Prager Str.	CX	
Praterbrücke	CY	
Praterstr.	LP, FGU	
Prinz-Eugen-Str.	CY, FUV	93
Raffineriestr.	CY	
Rathauspl.	HR	
Rautenweg	CX	
Raxstr.	BZ	94
Rechte Bahngasse	LS	
Reichsbrücke	CY	
Reisnerstr.	LS	
Renngasse	JPR	95
Rennweg	CYZ	
Rooseveltpl.	HP	
Roßauer Brücke	JP	
Rotensterngasse	LP	
Rotenturmstr.	KR	
Rudolfspl.	JKP	
Rudolf-Sallinger-Pl.	LS	
Salvatorgasse	JPR	96
Salztorbrücke	KP	
Salztorgasse	KP	
Schauflergasse	JR	97
Schlachthausgasse	CY	98
Schlickpl.	JP	
Schönbrunner Str.	ABZ, EV	99
Schönlaterngasse	KR	100
Schottengasse	HP	102
Schottenring	JP	
Schreyvogelgasse	HR	103
Schubertring	KS	
Schüttelstr.	CY, GU	
Schulhof	JR	105
Schwarzenbergpl.	KS	
Schwarzspanierstr.	HP	
Schwedenbrücke	KPR	
Schwertgasse	JP	106
Seilerstätte	KRS	
Seitzergasse	JR	107
Seyringer Str.	CX	
Siebenbrunnengasse	EFV	
Siebensterngasse	HS	
Siemensstr.	CX	
Sieveringer Str.	AX	
Simmeringer Hauptstr.	CZ	
Singerstr.	KR	
Sonnenfelsgasse	KR	108
Sonnwendgasse	FV	
Speisinger Str.	AZ	109
Spiegelgasse	JR	
Spitalgasse	EU	111
Spittelauer Lände	FT	112
Spittelberggasse	HS	114
Stephanspl.	KR	115
Stock-im-Eisen-Pl.	JR	116
Stromstr.	FT	
Stubenbastei	KR	
Stubenring	LR	
Südosttangente	CY	
Taborstr.	KLP	
Tegetthoffstr.	JR	117
Tiefer Graben	JPR	120
Traisengasse	FGT	
Triester Str.	BZ, FV	
Tuchlauben	JR	123
Türkenstr.	HJP	
Ungargasse	LS	
Universitätsstr.	HP	
Untere Donaustr.	LP	
Uraniastr.	LR	124
Veitingergasse	AZ	126
Vordere Zollamtsstr.	LR	
Währinger Gürtel	ETU	
Währinger Str.	HP, ET	
Wagramer Str.	CXY	
Wallnerstr.	JR	
Wattgasse	AY	
Webgasse	EV	68
Weihburggasse	KR	
Weiskirchnerstr.	LR	130
Weißgerberlände	GU	129
Wiedner Gürtel	FV	131
Wiedner Hauptstr.	JS, FV	132
Wienerbergstr.	BZ	134
Wipplingerstr.	JPR	
Wollzeile	KR	
Zieglergasse	EU	135
Zirkusgasse	LP	

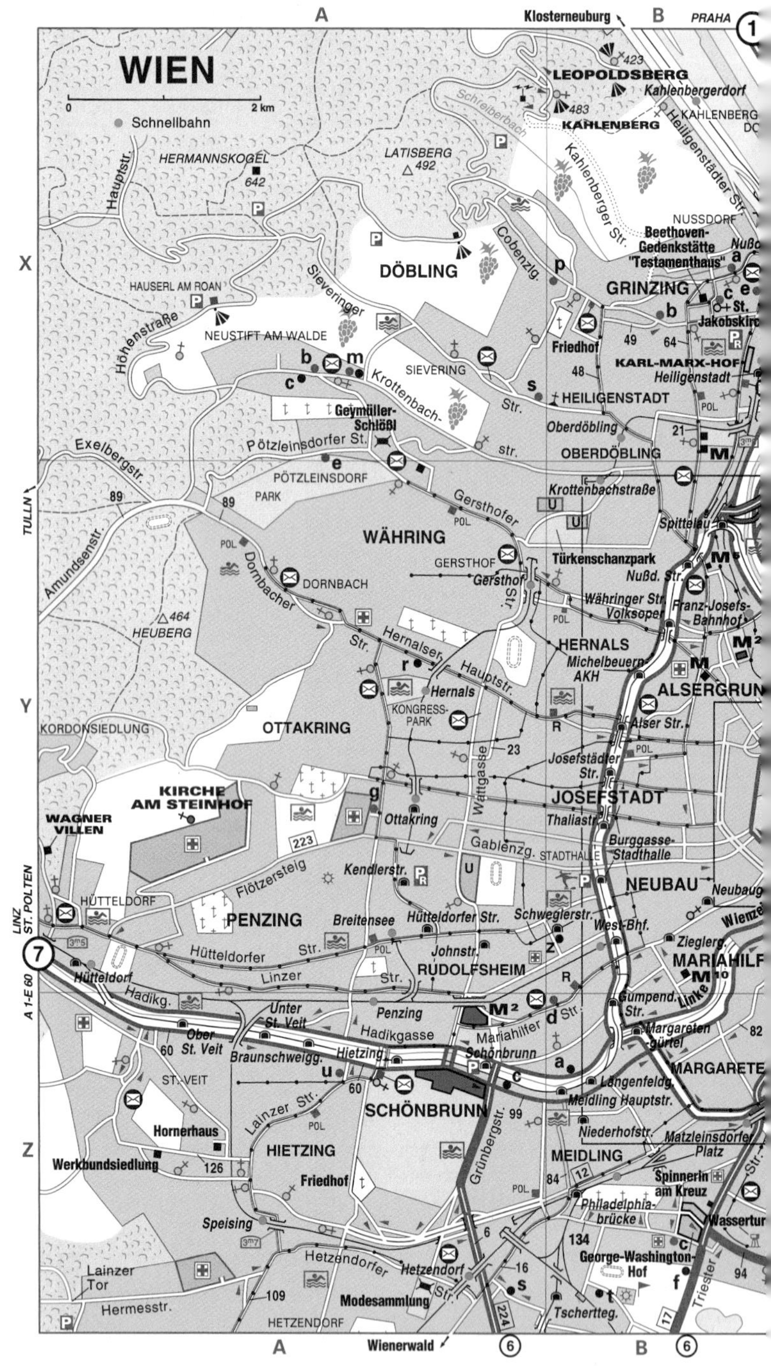
WIEN
0
2 km
Schnellbahn
Klosterneuburg
PRAHA
LEOPOLDSBERG
Kahlenbergerdorf
KAHLENBERG
HERMANNSKOGEL
642
LATISBERG
492
DÖBLING
GRINZING
NUSSDORF
Beethoven-Gedenkstätte "Testamenthaus"
HAUSERL AM ROAN
NEUSTIFT AM WALDE
SIEVERING
HEILIGENSTADT
KARL-MARX-HOF
Heiligenstadt
Geymüller-Schlößl
OBERDÖBLING
Oberdöbling
Pötzleinsdorfer St.
PÖTZLEINSDORF
PARK
Exelbergstr.
TULLN
WÄHRING
Krottenbachstraße
Spittelau
Türkenschanzpark
GERSTHOF
Gersthof
DORNBACH
Währinger Str. Volksoper
Franz-Josefs-Bahnhof
HEUBERG
464
HERNALS
Michelbeuern-AKH
ALSERGRUND
Hernals
KONGRESS-PARK
KORDONSIEDLUNG
OTTAKRING
Alser Str.
Josefstädter Str.
JOSEFSTADT
Thaliastr.
KIRCHE AM STEINHOF
WAGNER VILLEN
Ottakring
Gablenzg.
STADTHALLE
Burggasse-Stadthalle
Kendlerstr.
NEUBAU
Neubaug.
LINZ ST. PÖLTEN
HÜTTELDORF
PENZING
Breitensee
Hütteldorfer Str.
Schweglerstr.
West-Bhf.
Zieglerg.
MARIAHILF
RUDOLFSHEIM
Johnstr.
Hütteldorf
Hadikg.
Penzing
Gumpend. Str.
Ober St. Veit
Unter St. Veit
Hadikgasse
Margaretengürtel
MARGARETEN
Braunschweigg.
Hietzing
Schönbrunn
Längenfeldg.
ST.-VEIT
SCHÖNBRUNN
Meidling Hauptstr.
Niederhofstr.
Matzleinsdorfer Platz
Hornerhaus
Werkbundsiedlung
HIETZING
MEIDLING
Friedhof
Spinnerin am Kreuz
Speising
Philadelphiabrücke
Wasserturm
George-Washington-Hof
Lainzer Tor
Hetzendorfer Str.
Hetzendorf
Hermesstr.
Modesammlung
HETZENDORF
Tscherttteg.
Wienerwald
A
B
X
Y
Z
1
6
7
A 1-E 60

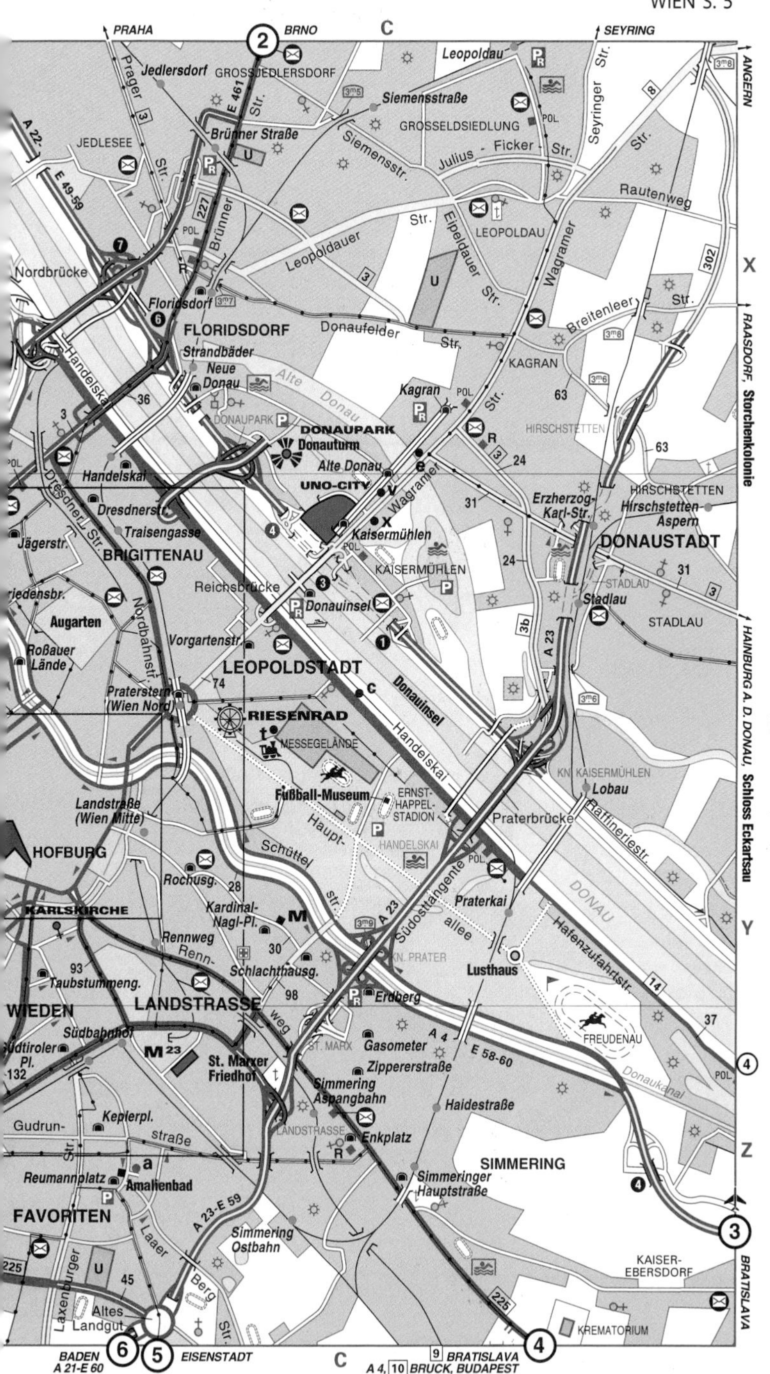
PRAHA
BRNO
SEYRING
ANGERN
RAASDORF, Storchenkolonie
HAINBURG A. D. DONAU, Schloss Eckartsau
BRATISLAVA
BADEN A 21-E 60
EISENSTADT
9 BRATISLAVA
A 4, 10 BRUCK, BUDAPEST
Jedlersdorf
GROSSJEDLERSDORF
Leopoldau
Siemensstraße
GROSSELDSIEDLUNG
Brünner Straße
JEDLESEE
Julius - Ficker Str.
Seyringer Str.
Rautenweg
LEOPOLDAU
Leopoldauer Str.
Eipeldauer Str.
Wagramer Str.
Nordbrücke
Floridsdorf
FLORIDSDORF
Donaufelder Str.
Breitenleer Str.
KAGRAN
Strandbäder
Neue Donau
Alte Donau
DONAUPARK
Donauturm
Kagran
HIRSCHSTETTEN
UNO-CITY
Kaisermühlen
Erzherzog-Karl-Str.
Hirschstetten-Aspern
DONAUSTADT
Handelskai
Dresdnerstr.
Traisengasse
Jägerstr.
BRIGITTENAU
KAISERMÜHLEN
STADLAU
Stadlau
Reichsbrücke
Donauinsel
Augarten
Roßauer Lände
Vorgartenstr.
LEOPOLDSTADT
Praterstern (Wien Nord)
RIESENRAD
MESSEGELÄNDE
Fußball-Museum
ERNST-HAPPEL-STADION
KN KAISERMÜHLEN
Lobau
Praterbrücke
Raffineriestr.
Landstraße (Wien Mitte)
HOFBURG
HANDELSKAI
DONAU
Schüttelstr.
Haupt-allee
Südosttangente
Rochusg.
Kardinal-Nagl-Pl.
KARLSKIRCHE
Praterkai
Rennweg
Hafenzufahrtstr.
Lusthaus
Schlachthausg.
KN. PRATER
Taubstummeng.
WIEDEN
LANDSTRASSE
Erdberg
Südbahnhof
FREUDENAU
Südtiroler Pl.
St. Marxer Friedhof
ST. MARX
Gasometer
Zippererstraße
Donaukanal
Simmering Aspangbahn
Haidestraße
Keplerpl.
Gudrunstraße
LANDSTRASSE
Enkplatz
SIMMERING
Reumannplatz
Amalienbad
Simmeringer Hauptstraße
FAVORITEN
Simmering Ostbahn
KAISER-EBERSDORF
Laxenburger Str.
Laaer Berg Str.
Altes Landgut
KREMATORIUM

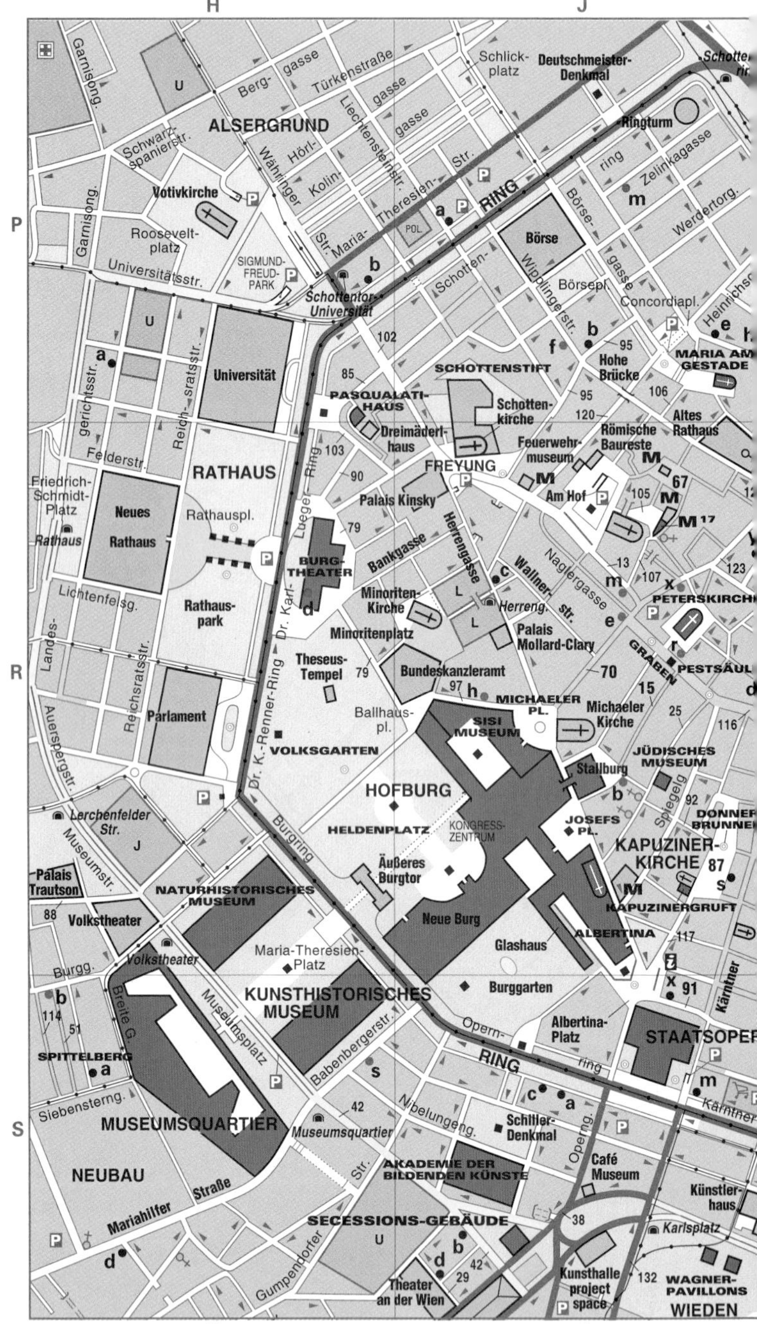
H
J
P
R
S
ALSERGRUND
Votivkirche
Roosevelt-platz
SIGMUND-FREUD-PARK
Schottentor-Universität
Universität
RATHAUS
Neues Rathaus
Rathauspl.
Rathaus-park
Parlament
BURG-THEATER
PASQUALATI-HAUS
Dreimäderlhaus
SCHOTTENSTIFT
Schotten-kirche
FREYUNG
Palais Kinsky
Börse
Ringturm
Deutschmeister-Denkmal
Schlick-platz
Hohe Brücke
MARIA AM GESTADE
Altes Rathaus
Römische Baureste
Feuerwehr-museum
Am Hof
Minoriten-Kirche
Minoritenplatz
Theseus-Tempel
Bundeskanzleramt
Palais Mollard-Clary
MICHAELER PL.
Michaeler Kirche
SISI MUSEUM
VOLKSGARTEN
HOFBURG
HELDENPLATZ
KONGRESS-ZENTRUM
Äußeres Burgtor
Neue Burg
Stallburg
JOSEFS PL.
JÜDISCHES MUSEUM
KAPUZINER-KIRCHE
KAPUZINERGRUFT
ALBERTINA
Glashaus
Burggarten
Albertina-Platz
STAATSOPER
PETERSKIRCHE
GRABEN
PESTSÄULE
DONNERBRUNNEN
Palais Trautson
Volkstheater
NATURHISTORISCHES MUSEUM
Maria-Theresien-Platz
KUNSTHISTORISCHES MUSEUM
MUSEUMSQUARTIER
SPITTELBERG
NEUBAU
Mariahilfer Straße
AKADEMIE DER BILDENDEN KÜNSTE
SECESSIONS-GEBÄUDE
Theater an der Wien
Schiller-Denkmal
Café Museum
Künstlerhaus
Karlsplatz
Kunsthalle project space
WAGNER-PAVILLONS
WIEDEN
RING
Dr. K.-Renner-Ring
Dr. Karl-Lueger-Ring
Burgring
Opernring
Schottenring
Universitätsstr.
Währinger Str.
Herrengasse
Bankgasse
Wallnerstr.
Naglergasse
Wipplingerstr.
Börsepl.
Concordiapl.
Lerchenfelder Str.
Museumstr.
Museumsplatz
Babenbergerstr.
Nibelungeng.
Operng.
Gumpendorfer Str.
Siebensterng.
Breite G.
Burgg.
Landesgerichtsstr.
Reichsratsstr.
Felderstr.
Lichtenfelsg.
Auerspergstr.
Friedrich-Schmidt-Platz
Garnisong.
Schwarzspanierstr.
Berggasse
Türkenstraße
Liechtensteinstr.
Hörlgasse
Kolingasse
Maria-Theresien-Str.
Schottengasse
Zelinkagasse
Werdertorg.
Börsegasse
Heinrichsgasse
Spiegelg.
Kärntner Str.
Ballhauspl.
Rathaus
Herreng.
Volkstheater
Museumsquartier

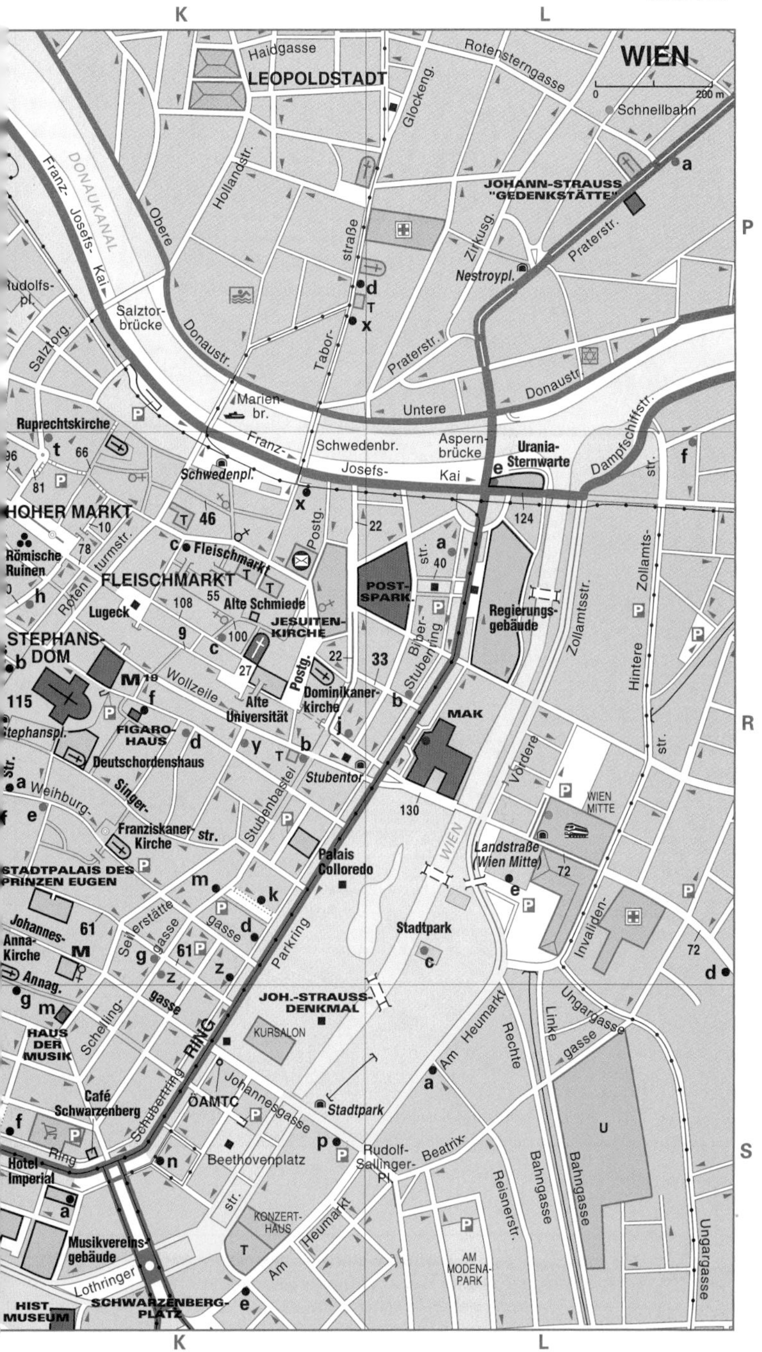
WIEN
LEOPOLDSTADT
Haidgasse
Rotensterngasse
Glockeng.
Schnellbahn
Hollandstr.
JOHANN-STRAUSS "GEDENKSTÄTTE"
Praterstr.
Zirkusg.
Nestroypl.
Obere
DONAUKANAL
Franz-Josefs-Kai
Taborstraße
Rudolfspl.
Salztorbrücke
Donaustr.
Salztorg.
Marienbr.
Untere
Donaustr.
Dampfschiffstr.
Ruprechtskirche
Schwedenbr.
Aspernbrücke
Urania-Sternwarte
Schwedenpl.
HOHER MARKT
Postg.
Römische Ruinen
Rotenturmstr.
Fleischmarkt
FLEISCHMARKT
POSTSPARK.
Regierungsgebäude
Zollamtsstr.
Hintere Zollamtsstr.
Lugeck
Alte Schmiede
JESUITENKIRCHE
STEPHANSDOM
Wollzeile
Alte Universität
Dominikanerkirche
Biberstr.
Stubenring
MAK
Stephanspl.
FIGARO-HAUS
Deutschordenshaus
Stubentor
Weihburg-
Singerstr.
Stubenbastei
Vordere
WIEN MITTE
Franziskanerkirche
Palais Colloredo
WIEN
Landstraße (Wien Mitte)
STADTPALAIS DES PRINZEN EUGEN
Seilerstätte
Parkring
Stadtpark
Johannes-gasse
Anna-Kirche
Annag.
Invalidenstr.
JOH.-STRAUSS-DENKMAL
KURSALON
Schellinggasse
HAUS DER MUSIK
RING
Am Heumarkt
Rechte
Linke
Ungargasse
Bahngasse
Café Schwarzenberg
Schubertring
ÖAMTC
Johannesgasse
Stadtpark
Rudolf-Sallinger-Pl.
Beatrixg.
Hotel Imperial
Beethovenplatz
Reisnerstr.
Lothringerstr.
KONZERTHAUS
Musikvereinsgebäude
AM MODENA-PARK
HIST MUSEUM
SCHWARZENBERG-PLATZ
K
L
P
R
S
0
200 m

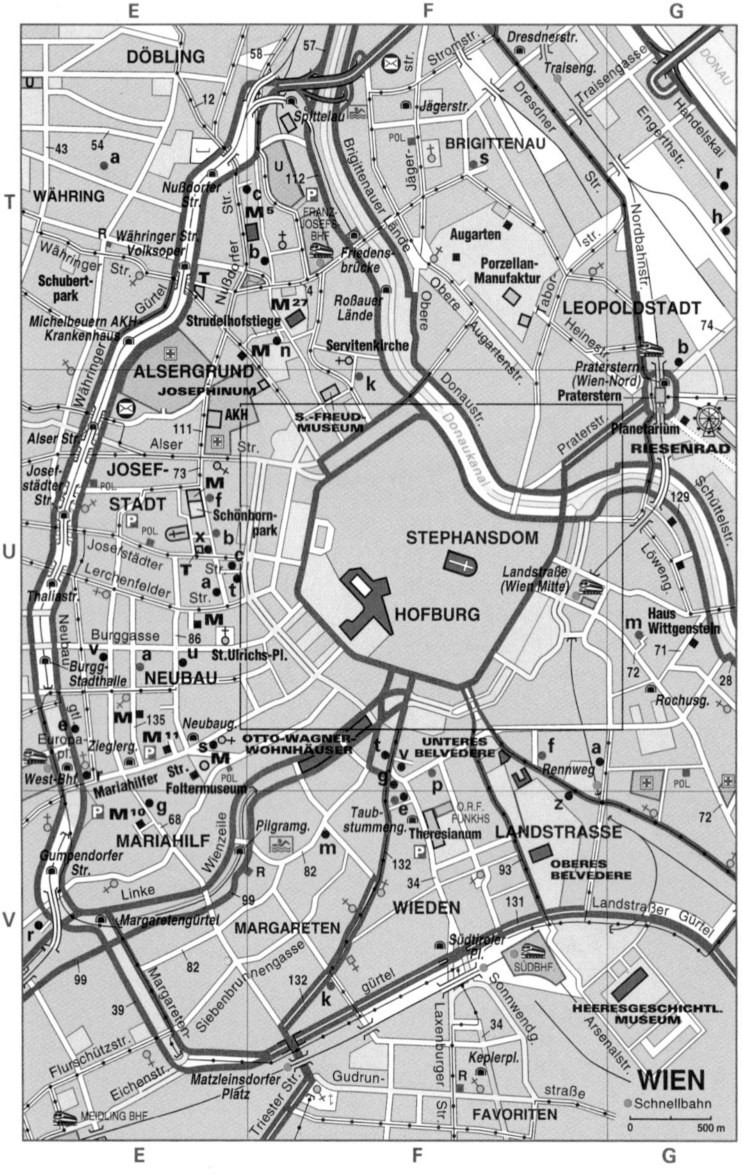

E F G

DÖBLING
WÄHRING
Nußdorfer Str.
Spittelau
Brigittenauer Lände
Jägerstr.
Stromstr.
Dresdnerstr.
Traiseng.
Traisengasse
Dresdner Str.
BRIGITTENAU
Engerthstr.
Handelskai
DONAU
FRANZ-JOSEFS-BHF
Friedensbrücke
Augarten
Porzellan-Manufaktur
Währinger Str. Volksoper
Währinger Str.
Schubertpark
Gürtel
Nußdorfer Str.
Strudelhofstiege
Roßauer Lände
Obere Augartenstr.
Taborstr.
Nordbahnstr.
LEOPOLDSTADT
Heinestr.
Michelbeuern AKH-Krankenhaus
ALSERGRUND
JOSEPHINUM
Servitenkirche
Donaustr.
Donaukanal
Praterstern (Wien-Nord)
Praterstern
Planetarium
RIESENRAD
AKH
S.-FREUD-MUSEUM
Alser Str.
Alser Str.
Josefstädter Str.
JOSEF-STADT
Schönbornpark
Praterstr.
Schüttelstr.
Löweng.
STEPHANSDOM
Josefstädter Str.
Lerchenfelder Str.
Thaliastr.
Landstraße (Wien Mitte)
HOFBURG
Haus Wittgenstein
Burggasse
Neubau
Burgg.-Stadthalle
St.Ulrichs-Pl.
NEUBAU
Rochusg.
Neubaug.
Europa-pl.
Zieglerg.
West-Bhf.
OTTO-WAGNER-WOHNHÄUSER
UNTERES BELVEDERE
Rennweg
Mariahilfer Str.
Foltermuseum
MARIAHILF
Wienzeile
Pilgramg.
Taubstummeng.
O.R.F. FUNKHS
Theresianum
LANDSTRASSE
OBERES BELVEDERE
Gumpendorfer Str.
Linke
Margaretengürtel
MARGARETEN
WIEDEN
Landstraßer Gürtel
Südtiroler Pl.
SÜDBHF.
Siebenbrunnengasse
Margareten-
gürtel
Sonnwendg.
Laxenburger Str.
HEERESGESCHICHTL. MUSEUM
Arsenalstr.
Flurschützstr.
Eichenstr.
Matzleinsdorfer Platz
Triester Str.
Gudrun-straße
Keplerpl.
FAVORITEN
MEIDLING BHF
WIEN
Schnellbahn
0 500 m

E F G

Wie entscheidet man sich zwischen zwei gleichwertigen Adressen?
In jeder Kategorie sind die Häuser nochmals geordnet,
die besten Adressen stehen an erster Stelle.

Alphabetische Liste der Hotels und Restaurants

A — Seite

B — Seite

C — Seite

D — Seite

E — Seite

F — Seite

G — Seite

H — Seite

I — Seite

J — Seite

K — Seite

Restaurants, die sonntags geöffnet sind

Stadt Zentrum Stadtbezirke 1 – 9

Imperial
Zim, Rest,

Kärntner Ring 16 ✉ 1015 **U** *Karlsplatz – ✆ (01) 50 11 00*
– hotel.imperial@luxurycollection.com – Fax (01) 50110410 KS **a**
138 Zim – †355/1080 € ††355/1080 €, ☕ 37 € – 31 Suiten
Rest *Imperial* – *(nur Abendessen)* (Tischbestellung ratsam) Karte 46/77 €
Rest *Café Imperial* – Karte 32/54 €
♦ Das noble Grandhotel von 1873 besticht durch seinen eindrucksvollen historischen Rahmen, perfekten Service und hochwertigste Ausstattung. Luxus pur bieten die Suiten. Stilvoll-gediegen ist das Restaurant. Café Imperial mit dem Flair eines Wiener Kaffeehauses.

Palais Coburg
Zim,

Coburgbastei 4 ✉ 1010 **U** *Stubentor*
– ✆ (01) 51 81 80 – hotel.residenz@palais-coburg.com
– Fax (01) 51818100 KR **m**
35 Suiten ☕ – †490/2140 € ††490/2140 €
Rest *Restaurant Coburg* – separat erwähnt
Rest *WeinBistro* – ✆ (01) 51 81 88 70 – Karte 27/45 €
♦ Eleganz und Großzügigkeit begleiten den Gast hier auf Schritt und Tritt. Hinter der beeindruckenden Fassade des 1840 errichteten Palais verbirgt sich ein edles Interieur. WeinBistro: angenehm lichter, begrünter Pavillon und Weinbar.

Grand Hotel
Zim,

Kärntner Ring 9 ✉ 1010 **U** *Karlsplatz*
– ✆ (01) 51 58 00 – sales@grandhotelwien.com
– Fax (01) 5151312 KS **f**
205 Zim – †340/440 € ††390/490 €, ☕ 30 € – 11 Suiten
Rest *Le Ciel* – ✆ (01) 5 15 80 91 00 *(geschl. Sonntag)* Menü 36 € (mittags)/60 € – Karte 47/71 €
Rest *Unkai* – ✆ (01) 5 15 80 91 10 *(geschl. Montagmittag)* Menü 38/99 € – Karte 18/74 €
Rest *Grand Café* – ✆ (01) 5 15 80 91 20 – Menü 26 € – Karte 26/46 €
♦ Eine repräsentative Halle empfängt Sie in dem schönen Grandhotel mit historischem Flair. Klassisch-elegantes Ambiente zieht sich durch das gesamte Haus. Le Ciel ist ein vornehmes Restaurant im 7. Stock mit hübscher Terrasse. Japanische Küche im Unkai.

Sacher
Zim, Rest,

Philharmonikerstr. 4 ✉ 1010 **U** *Karlsplatz*
– ✆ (01) 51 45 60 – wien@sacher.com
– Fax (01) 51456810 JS **x**
152 Zim – †385/650 € ††385/650 €, ☕ 30 € – 7 Suiten
Rest *Anna Sacher* – *(geschl. Juli – August und Montag)* Menü 62/94 € – Karte 38/77 €
Rest *Rote Bar* – Karte 33/72 €
♦ Das luxuriöse Traditionshaus von 1876 ist eine äußerst stilvolle Adresse mit erstklassigem Service und schönem Freizeitbereich. Suiten mit Terrasse und Blick über Wien. Anna Sacher: klassisch-elegant. Edle Rote Bar in rotem Samt, mit traditioneller Küche.

Bristol

*Kärntner Ring 1 ✉ 1015 **U** Karlsplatz – ✆ (01) 51 51 60 – hotel.bristol@luxurycollection.com – Fax (01) 51516550* JS **m**

140 Zim – 235/550 € 235/630 €, ☕ 33 € – 10 Suiten

Rest *Korso* – separat erwähnt

Rest *Sirk* – *(geschl. Juli – Aug. 4 Wochen)* Karte 32/70 €

◆ Ein durch und durch stilvolles Hotel mit professionellem Service. Prunkvoll und sehr luxuriös ist die "Prince of Wales"-Suite mit eigenem Fitness- und Saunabereich. Im Restaurant Sirk gibt eine große Fensterfront den Blick auf die Staatsoper frei.

Le Méridien

*Opernring 13 ✉ 1010 **U** Karlsplatz – ✆ (01) 58 89 00 – info.vienna@lemeridien.com – Fax (01) 588909090* JS **c**

294 Zim – 175/285 € 175/285 €, ☕ 28 € – 17 Suiten

Rest *Shambala* – Karte 34/52 €

◆ Hinter seiner klassischen Fassade überrascht dieses Hotel mit geschmackvollem, geradlinig-modernem Design. Die Zimmer sind technisch auf dem neuesten Stand. Der klare Stil des Hotels setzt sich auch im Restaurant Shambala fort.

InterContinental

*Johannesgasse 28 ✉ 1037 **U** Stadtpark – ✆ (01) 71 12 20 – vienna@ihg.com – Fax (01) 7134489* KS **p**

453 Zim – 189/499 € 189/499 €, ☕ 27 € – 61 Suiten

Rest – Karte 30/41 €

◆ Der großzügige Rahmen und zeitgemäße, auf Businessgäste zugeschnittene Zimmer mit guter Technik kennzeichnen das Hotel. Die oberste Etage bietet eine tolle Aussicht auf Wien. Leicht mediterran gestaltetes Restaurant mit Showküche und Wintergarten.

Marriott

*Parkring 12a ✉ 1010 **U** Stadtpark – ✆ (01) 51 51 80 – vienna.marriott.info@marriotthotels.com – Fax (01) 515186510* KR **d**

313 Zim – 249/300 € 249/300 €, ☕ 24 € – 5 Suiten

Rest – Karte 26/56 €

◆ Von der im Atriumstil angelegten Lobby des Hauses gelangen Sie in die wohnlichen, in warmen Tönen gehaltenen Gästezimmer, einige mit Blick auf den Stadtpark. Das Garten-Café ist in die Hotelhalle integriert. Geboten wird internationale Küche.

Hilton Vienna Plaza

*Schottenring 11 ✉ 1010 **U** Schottentor-Universität – ✆ (01) 31 39 00 – info.vienna-plaza@hilton.com – Fax (01) 3139022009* JP **a**

218 Zim – 139/359 € 139/359 €, ☕ 26 € – 10 Suiten

Rest – Karte 31/46 €

◆ Dieses Hotel in der Innenstadt überzeugt mit großzügigen und technisch gut ausgestatteten Zimmern sowie luxuriösen Designer-Suiten. Restaurant mit modernem Ambiente.

Radisson SAS Palais

Zim,

Parkring 16 ✉ *1010* **U** *Stadtpark*
– ✆ *(01) 51 51 70 – sales.vienna@radissonsas.com*
– *Fax (01) 5122216* KR **z**

247 Zim – 260 € 260 €, 25 € – 10 Suiten

Rest ***Le siècle*** – ✆ (01) 5 15 17 34 40 *(geschl. 16. Juli – 19. Aug. sowie Sonn- und Feiertage)* Karte 45/65 €

Rest ***Palais Café*** – ✆ (01) 5 15 17 34 70 – Karte 26/44 €

♦ Das Hotel gegenüber dem Stadtpark besteht aus zwei miteinander verbundenen Palaisbauten a. d. 19. Jh. Mit stilvoller Einrichtung wird man dem historischen Rahmen gerecht. Le siècle: klassisches Restaurant mit Blick auf den Park. Palais Café im Wintergarten.

Hilton Vienna

Zim, Rest,

Am Stadtpark 3 ✉ *1030* **U** *Landstraße*
– ✆ *(01) 71 70 00 – reservation.vienna@hilton.com*
– *Fax (01) 7130691* LR **e**

579 Zim – 139/279 € 139/279 €, 26 € – 41 Suiten

Rest – Karte 29/48 €

♦ Ein großes Tagungshotel in zentraler Lage mit Atriumhalle und modern eingerichteten Gästezimmern. Von den oberen Etagen hat man eine tolle Aussicht. Restaurant in neuzeitlichem Stil.

Hotel de France

Zim,

Schottenring 3 ✉ *1010* **U** *Schottentor-Universität*
– ✆ *(01) 31 36 80 – defrance@austria-hotels.at*
– *Fax (01) 3195969* HP **b**

194 Zim – 170/275 € 200/305 €, 25 €

Rest – Karte 19/49 €

♦ Das klassisch-elegante Stadthotel verfügt über komfortable Zimmer, die modern oder traditionell gestaltet sind. Im obersten Stockwerk befinden sich großzügige Maisonetten. No. 3 nennt sich das brasserieartige Restaurant.

Ambassador

Kärntner Str. 22 ✉ *1010* **U** *Stephansdom* – ✆ *(01) 96 16 10*
– *office@ambassador.at – Fax (01) 5132999* JR **s**

86 Zim – 240/439 € 304/550 €, 25 €

Rest ***Mörwald im Ambassador*** – separat erwähnt

♦ Eine gelungene Kombination aus Tradition und Moderne bieten die stilvollen, technisch gut ausgestatteten Zimmer. Die Themenzimmer sind berühmten Persönlichkeiten gewidmet.

Renaissance Penta

Zim,

Ungargasse 60 ✉ *1030* **U** *Rochusgasse*
– ✆ *(01) 71 17 50 – renaissance.penta.vienna@renaissancehotels.com*
– *Fax (01) 711758143* FU **a**

339 Zim – 139/360 € 139/360 €, 21 €

Rest – Karte 16/35 €

♦ Der historische Rahmen macht die einstige k. u. k. Militärreitschule aus. Ein hohes, von Säulen getragenes Kreuzgewölbe ziert den schönen Hallenbereich. Funktionelle Zimmer. Restaurant mit elegantem Ambiente.

Do & Co Hotel Vienna Zim,
Stephansplatz 12 (6. Stock) ✉ *1010* VISA
U *Stephansplatz – ✆ (01) 2 41 88 – hotel@doco.com*
– Fax (01) 24188444 JR **d**
43 Zim – 🚹215/450 € 🚹🚹215/450 €, ☕ 25 €
Rest – Karte 32/52 €
◆ Das Hotel direkt am Stephansdom ist durch und durch in topmodernem Design gehalten. Äußerst geschmackvoll sind die edel ausgestatteten Zimmer. Euroasiatisches bereitet man in der Showküche des in der 7. Etage gelegenen Restaurants. Terrasse mit Domblick.

Radisson SAS Style Hotel Zim, Rest,
Herrengasse 12 ✉ *1010* VISA AE
U *Herrengasse – ✆ (01) 22 78 00 – info.style@radissonsas.com*
– Fax (01) 2278077 JR **c**
78 Zim – 🚹260/300 € 🚹🚹260/315 €, ☕ 23 € – 6 Suiten
Rest *Sapori* – *(geschl. Aug. und Sonntag, Feiertage, Juli Samstagmittag, Sonntag)* Menü 35 € (mittags)/60 € – Karte 39/48 €
◆ Eine moderne, hochwertige Ausstattung in geradlinigem Stil begleitet Sie von der als Rundbau angelegten Halle bis in die eleganten Zimmer des einstigen Bankgebäudes. Im ehemaligen Tresorraum im UG hat man das Sapori eingerichtet. Italienische Küche.

Das Triest Zim, VISA AE
Wiedner Hauptstr. 12 ✉ *1040* **U** *Karlsplatz – ✆ (01) 58 91 80*
– office@dastriest.at – Fax (01) 5891818 FU **t**
72 Zim ☕ – 🚹210 € 🚹🚹270 € – 3 Suiten
Rest – *(geschl. 3. – 17. Aug. und Samstagmittag, Sonntag)* Menü 40 € – Karte 30/53 €
◆ Die von Sir Terence Conran designten Zimmer sind in klaren Linien gehalten und mit guter Technik ausgestattet – funktionell und dennoch wohnlich. Restaurant mit modernem Ambiente und italienischer Küche.

NH Belvedere garni VISA AE
Rennweg 12a ✉ *1030* **U** *Karlsplatz – ✆ (01) 2 06 11*
– nhbelvedere@nh-hotels.com – Fax (01) 2061115 FV **z**
114 Zim – 🚹90/155 € 🚹🚹90/155 €, ☕ 15 €
◆ Ein modernes Hotel, entstanden im klassizistischen Gebäude der ehemaligen Bundesdruckerei. Überzeugende Zimmer, teils mit Blick auf den Botanischen Garten, Bistro mit Snacks.

Hilton Vienna-Danube (geheizt)
Handelskai 269 Zim, Rest, P VISA AE
✉ *1020 – ✆ (01) 7 27 77 – info.vienna-danube@hilton.com*
– Fax (01) 7277782200 CY **c**
367 Zim – 🚹135/260 € 🚹🚹135/260 €, ☕ 22 €
Rest – Karte 27/43 €
◆ Hotel in einem ehemaligen Speichergebäude an der Donau mit recht großzügigen, technisch gut ausgestatteten Zimmern. Tagungsbereich z. T. im 8. Stock mit Blick über die Stadt. Vom Restaurant aus genießen Sie die Aussicht auf den Fluss.

The Levante Parliament Zim,

Auerspergstr. 9 1080 **U** *Rathaus*

– (01) 22 82 80 – parliament@thelevante.com – Fax (01) 2282828 HR **t**

70 Zim – 130/220 € 155/286 €

Rest – *(geschl. Sonntag)* Karte 26/45 €

◆ Hinter einer Steinfassade verbirgt sich das durch und durch geradlinig-modern designte Hotel – Glaskunst setzt interessante Akzente. Zimmer mit neuester Technik. In dem puristisch gestalteten Restaurant offeriert man eine internationale Küche.

Kaiserhof garni

Frankenberggasse 10 1040 **U** *Karlsplatz – (01) 5 05 17 01*

– wien@hotel-kaiserhof.at – Fax (01) 505887588 FU **v**

74 Zim – 130/180 € 165/260 € – 3 Suiten

◆ Freundlich und aufmerksam kümmert man sich in diesem sehr schön eingerichteten Haus von 1896 um seine Gäste – zwei Etagen sind besonders modern. Snackkarte im Barbereich.

Fleming's Hotel Wien-Westbahnhof

Neubaugürtel 26 Rest,

1070 **U** *Wien Westbahnhof – (01) 22 73 70*

– wien@flemings-hotels.com – Fax (01) 227379999 EU **e**

146 Zim – 125/175 € 145/211 € – 4 Suiten

Rest – Karte 20/36 €

◆ Die zentrumsnahe Lage und klarer, moderner Stil vom Empfangsbereich bis in die hochwertig eingerichteten Zimmer zeichnen das Hotel aus. Restaurant mit Brasserie-Atmosphäre.

Hollmann Beletage

Köllnerhofgasse 6 1010 **U** *Stephansplatz – (01) 9 61 19 60*

– hotel@hollmann-beletage.at – Fax (01) 961196033 KR **c**

16 Zim – 140/180 € 140/180 €

Rest – *(geschl. Sonntag, Feiertag)* Menü 12 € *(mittags)*/49 € – Karte 26/43 €

◆ Eine interessante Adresse ist dieses individuelle kleine Hotel. Hinter der klassischen Stadthausfassade überrascht ganz modernes, geradliniges Design. Das Restaurant Hollmann Salon befindet sich im "Heiligenkreuzerhof" gegenüber dem Hotel.

K+K Hotel Maria Theresia garni

Kirchberggasse 6 1070 **U** *Volkstheater*

– (01) 5 21 23 – kk.maria.theresia@kuk.at – Fax (01) 5212370 HS **a**

123 Zim – 185/210 € 250/275 €

◆ Im Künstlerviertel Spittelberg gelegenes Hotel. Besonders schön: die Zimmer mit Blick auf Wien. In der großzügigen Halle befindet sich eine Bar mit kleiner Speisekarte.

Kaiserin Elisabeth garni

Weihburggasse 3 1010 **U** *Stephansplatz – (01) 51 52 60*

– info@kaiserinelisabeth.at – Fax (01) 515267 KR **a**

63 Zim – 126/180 € 216/230 €

◆ Mozart und Wagner waren Gäste in diesem Hotel nahe dem Stephansdom, das seit 1809 als Herberge dient. Elegantes, dunkles Massivholzmobiliar im Stil der Jahrhundertwende!

Mercure Grandhotel Biedermeier garni

Landstraßer Hauptstr. 28 (Am Sünnhof)
✉ 1030 **U** Landstraße – ✆ (01) 71 67 10 – h5357@accor.com
– Fax (01) 71671503 LR **d**

201 Zim – 156/205 € 184/233 €, ☕ 15 € – 12 Suiten

◆ In einem Stadthaus mit schöner Ladenpassage ist dieses Hotel angesiedelt. Geschmackvoll sind die Zimmer mit Kirschbaummöbeln im Biedermeierstil eingerichtet.

König von Ungarn

AC Zim, VISA AE

Schulerstr. 10 ✉ *1010* **U** *Stephansplatz – ✆ (01) 51 58 40 – hotel@kvu.at*
– Fax (01) 515848 KR **f**

33 Zim ☕ – 145/165 € 208 €

Rest – *(nur Abendessen)* Karte 24/36 €

◆ Hinter dem Stephansdom liegt das mit viel Stil und warmen Farbtönen klassisch eingerichtete Haus aus dem 16. Jh. Besichtigen Sie den sehenswerten Innenhof! Das Restaurant befindet sich in dem Haus, in dem Mozart einmal lebte.

Das Tyrol garni

Mariahilfer Str. 15 ✉ *1060* **U** *Museumsquartier – ✆ (01) 5 87 54 15*
– reception@das-tyrol.at – Fax (01) 58754159 HS **d**

30 Zim ☕ – 109/209 € 149/259 €

◆ Das sorgsam restaurierte Eckhaus beherbergt mit zeitgemäßen Möbeln geschmackvoll ausgestattete Zimmer. Bilder moderner österreichischer Künstler finden sich im ganzen Haus.

Altstadt Vienna garni

Kirchengasse 41 ✉ *1070* **U** *Volkstheater – ✆ (01) 5 26 33 99*
– hotel@altstadt.at – Fax (01) 5234901 EU **u**

42 Zim ☕ – 109/149 € 129/189 € – 8 Suiten

◆ Jedes Zimmer des Patrizierhauses hat sein eigenes Gesicht. Die Räume haben hohe Decken, Parkett und sind mit ausgesuchten Kunstobjekten bestückt.

Sofitel

AC Zim,

Am Heumarkt 35 ✉ *1030* **U** *Stadtpark – ✆ (01) 71 61 60*
– h1276@accor.com – Fax (01) 71616844 KS **e**

211 Zim – 116/297 € 141/297 €, ☕ 19 €

Rest – *(geschl. Samstagmittag, Sonntagmittag, Feiertage mittags)*
Karte 23/48 €

◆ Jugendstilelemente und Klimt-Reproduktionen geben den Räumen mit den zeitlosen Naturholzmöbeln und moderner Technik eine freundliche Atmosphäre. Schön: die Pullmannbar. Im Restaurant serviert man dem Gast internationale und Wiener Gerichte.

Rathauspark garni

Rathausstr. 17 ✉ *1010* **U** *Rathaus – ✆ (01) 40 41 20*
– rathauspark@austria-trend.at – Fax (01) 40412761 HP **a**

117 Zim – 200/300 € 240/350 €, ☕ 15 €

◆ Ein schöner stuckverzierter Eingangsbereich empfängt Sie in dem schmucken Haus a. d. J. 1880. Die meist hohen Räume sind modern-elegant eingerichtet. Original erhaltener Lift.

Falkensteiner Am Schottenfeld garni
Schottenfeldgasse 74 ✉ 1070
U *Burggasse Stadthalle – ✆ (01) 5 26 51 81*
– schottenfeld@falkensteiner.com
– Fax (01) 5265181160 EU **v**
95 Zim – 133/169 € 169/219 €
◆ Vom recht großen Empfangsbereich bis in die angenehm hell möblierten, funktionell ausgestatteten Zimmer ist das in eine Häuserreihe integrierte Hotel ganz modern gestaltet.

K+K Palais Hotel garni
Rudolfsplatz 11 ✉ 1010 **U** *Schwedenplatz – ✆ (01) 5 33 13 53*
– kk.palais.hotel@kuk.at – Fax (01) 533135370 JP **h**
66 Zim – 180 € 240 €
◆ Funktionelle und dennoch wohnliche Zimmer sowie ein Frühstücksraum in warmen Farben bietet dieses historische Stadtpalais. Stephansdom und U-Bahn sind ganz in der Nähe.

Rathaus garni
Lange Gasse 13 ✉ 1080 **U** *Rathaus – ✆ (01) 4 00 11 22*
– office@hotel-rathaus-wien.at – Fax (01) 400112288
geschl. 22. – 26. Dez EU **a**
40 Zim – 118/138 € 148/198 €, 13 €
◆ Äußerst geschmackvoll und modern wurde das originelle Stadthotel von 1890 gestaltet. Jedes Zimmer wurde einem österreichischen Winzer gewidmet, nach dem Motto "Wein&Design".

Strudlhof garni
Pasteurgasse 1 ✉ 1090 **U** *Währinger Str.-Volksoper*
– ✆ (01) 3 19 25 22 – hotel@strudlhof.at
– Fax (01) 3192522800 FT **n**
84 Zim – 142/149 € 189/209 €
◆ In diesem Hotel stehen technisch gut ausgestattete Gästezimmer zur Verfügung. Einen stilvollen Rahmen zum Tagen finden Sie im rückwärtig gelegenen Palais.

Am Opernring garni
Opernring 11 ✉ 1010 **U** *Karlsplatz – ✆ (01) 5 87 55 18*
– hotel@opernring.at – Fax (01) 587551829 JS **a**
35 Zim – 140/200 € 155/240 €
◆ Vis-à-vis der Staatsoper liegt dieses Hotel mit der schönen Jugendstilfassade. Geräumige Zimmer vereinen Wohnlichkeit mit der Funktionalität moderner Hotellerie.

Mercure Secession garni
Getreidemarkt 5 ✉ 1060 **U** *Museumsquartier*
– ✆ (01) 5 88 38 – h3532@accor.com – Fax (01) 58838212 JS **b**
70 Zim – 99/165 € 122/206 €
◆ Dank seiner zentralen Lage ist dieses Haus ein guter Ausgangspunkt für die Erkundung der Stadt. Sie werden in wohnlichen und bequemen Zimmern untergebracht. Auch Appartements.

Starlight Suiten Salzgries garni 
Salzgries 12 ✉ 1010 **U** *Schwedenplatz*
– ✆ (01) 5 35 92 22 – reservation@starlighthotels.com
– Fax (01) 535922211 JP **e**
49 Suiten – 153/183 € 183/211 €
◆ Gutes Platzangebot und Funktionalität machen die modern ausgestatteten Suiten des zentral gelegenen Hotels aus. Kleines Zimmerfrühstück inkl., Frühstücksbuffet gegen Aufpreis.

Starlight Suiten Heumarkt garni
Am Heumarkt 15 ✉ 1030 **U** *Stadtpark*
– ✆ (01) 7 10 78 08 – reservation@starlighthotels.com
– Fax (01) 710780811 LS **a**
50 Suiten – 153/183 € 183/211 €
◆ Nicht nur für Geschäftsreisende: gut geführte Adresse nahe dem Stadtpark mit neuzeitlichen, geräumigen Suiten. Kleines Zimmerfrühstück inkl., Frühstücksbuffet gegen Aufpreis.

Starlight Suiten Renngasse garni
Renngasse 13 ✉ 1010 **U** *Schottenring*
– ✆ (01) 53 39 98 90 – reservation@starlighthotels.com
– Fax (01) 533998911 JP **b**
50 Suiten – 153/183 € 183/211 €
◆ Das Hotel im Zentrum verfügt über komfortable Suiten – einheitlich möbliert und mit frischen Farben gestaltet. Kleines Zimmerfrühstück inkl., Frühstücksbuffet gegen Aufpreis.

Cordial Theaterhotel garni
Josefstädter Str. 22 ✉ 1080 **U**
Josefstädterstr. – ✆ (01) 4 05 36 48 – chwien@cordial.at
– Fax (01) 4051406 EU **x**
54 Zim – 196 € 220 € – 4 Suiten
◆ Direkt neben dem Theater in der Josefstadt finden Sie in diesem restaurierten Jugendstilhaus ein praktisches, sehr gepflegtes Quartier. Kleines Café-Restaurant für Hungrige.

Am Parkring Wien, Zim, Rest,
Parkring 12 ✉ 1010 **U** *Stubentor*
– ✆ (01) 51 48 00 – parkring@schick-hotels.com – Fax (01) 5148040 KR **k**
58 Zim – 109/168 € 129/247 € – 8 Suiten
Rest – *(Juli – Aug. nur Abendessen)* Karte 27/47 €
◆ Gegenüber dem Stadtpark, in den obersten Stockwerken des Gartenbauhochhauses finden Sie moderne Räume mit toller Aussicht. Fragen Sie nach Zimmern mit Balkon! Vom Hotelrestaurant Himmelsstube schaut man auf die Skyline der Stadt.

Am Stephansplatz garni
Stephansplatz 9 ✉ 1010 **U** *Stephansplatz*
– ✆ (01) 53 40 50 – office@hotelamstephansplatz.at
– Fax (01) 53405710 KR **b**
56 Zim – 130/265 € 195/310 €
◆ Ein moderner, klarer Stil zieht sich wie ein roter Faden durch das gesamte Haus. Die Gästezimmer sind funktionell ausgestattet, z. T. mit Blick auf den Stephansdom.

IN HOC SIGNO VINCES
RAMOS PINTO
Est.1880

Der MICHELIN-Führer

Eine Kollektion zum Genießen!

Belgique & Luxembourg
Deutschland
España & Portugal
France
Great Britain & Ireland
Italia
Nederland
Österreich
Portugal
Suisse-Schweiz-Svizzera
Main Cities of Europe

Und auch:

Las Vegas
London
Los Angeles
New York City
Paris
San Francisco
Tokyo

Arkadenhof garni
Viriotgasse 5 ✉ *1090* **U** *Nußdorferstr. – ✆ (01) 3 10 08 37*
– office@arkadenhof.com – Fax (01) 3107686 EFT **c**
45 Zim – 105/126 € 145/165 €
◆ Solide und wohnlich in der Ausstattung, bietet Ihnen diese Adresse ein gepflegtes und zeitgemäßes Zuhause auf Zeit. Zentrale Lage nahe dem Franz-Josefs-Bahnhof.

Lassalle garni
Engerthstr. 173 ✉ *1020* **U** *Vorgartenstr. – ✆ (01) 21 31 50*
– lassalle@austria-trend.at – Fax (01) 21315100 GT **r**
140 Zim – 75/250 € 99/300 €, 13 € – 4 Suiten
◆ Das in einer Seitenstraße nahe der Innenstadt gelegene Haus überzeugt durch modern und funktionell ausgestattete Gästezimmer und eine Business-Etage.

Hotel Messe garni
Messestr. 2 ✉ *1020* **U** *Praterstern – ✆ (01) 72 72 70*
– messe@austria-trend.at – Fax (01) 72727100 CY **t**
243 Zim – 125/162 € 170/246 €
◆ In der Nähe von Prater und Messe hält dieser moderne verglaste Bau zweckmäßige Zimmer für Sie bereit. Schön ist die Aussicht aus den Businesszimmern in den oberen Stockwerken.

Erzherzog Rainer A/C Rest, Zim,
Wiedner Hauptstr. 27 ✉ *1040* **U** *Taubstummengasse – ✆ (01) 5 01 11*
– rainer@schick-hotels.com – Fax (01) 50111350 FU **g**
84 Zim – 99/151 € 123/203 €
Rest – Karte 22/35 €
◆ Wiener Institution mit gemütlich-klassischen Zimmern, teils mit Jugendstil-Möbeln: In diesem Haus wohnten schon Marika Rökk, Rudolf Schock und Marie Curie. In der rustikalen "Wiener Wirtschaft" bietet man Wiener Küche mit Schwerpunkt auf Gulaschgerichten.

Holiday Inn Vienna City A/C Zim,
Margaretenstr. 53 ✉ *1050*
U *Kettenbrückengasse – ✆ (01) 5 88 50 – vienna.city@holiday-inn.at*
– Fax (01) 58850899 FV **m**
101 Zim – 215/230 € 230/245 €
Rest – Karte 19/32 €
◆ Das Stadthotel in Margareten bietet Übernachtungsgästen zwei Zimmerkategorien: modern mit hellem Naturholz eingerichtet oder elegant und etwas geräumiger ausgelegt. Modernes Restaurant mit Spiegel-Optik. Hübsch: die Terrasse hinter dem Haus.

Stefanie A/C Zim, Rest,
Taborstr. 12 ✉ *1020* **U** *Schwedenplatz – ✆ (01) 21 15 00*
– stefanie@schick-hotels.com – Fax (01) 21150160 KLP **d**
122 Zim – 109/157 € 153/224 €
Rest – Karte 21/41 €
◆ Genießen Sie Wiener Atmosphäre in einem Haus mit Charme: Möbel im klassischen Wiener Stil verleihen dem Hotel nostalgisches Flair. Eine Gartenterrasse mit schattenspendenden Bäumen ergänzt das Restaurant.

Amadeus garni

Wildpretmarkt 5 ✉ 1010 **U** *Stephansplatz – (01) 5 33 87 38 – office@hotel-amadeus.at – Fax (01) 533873838*
geschl. 21. – 28. Dez. JR **y**

30 Zim – 90/170 € 160/178 €

◆ Weiße Schleiflack-Stilmöbel, die dekorativ mit roten Teppichböden und Sitzpolstern kontrastieren, prägen die sympathische, familiäre Adresse im Künstlerviertel Wildpretmarkt.

Anatol garni

Webgasse 26 ✉ 1060 **U** *Zieglergasse – (01) 59 99 60 – anatol@austria-trend.at – Fax (01) 5999655* EV **g**

62 Zim – 169 € 199 €, 15 €

◆ Vom Empfangsbereich bis in die technisch gut ausgestatteten Zimmer überzeugt das Hotel mit Funktionalität und schlicht-moderner Einrichtung in angenehmen Farben.

Capricorno garni

Schwedenplatz 3 ✉ 1010 **U** *Schwedenplatz – (01) 53 33 10 40 – capricorno@schick-hotels.com – Fax (01) 53376714* KR **x**

46 Zim – 146 € 194 €

◆ Wiener Atmosphäre und Jugendstil-Elemente begegnen Ihnen im ganzen Haus! Auch die teils mit Stilmöbeln bestückten Zimmer beeindrucken durch ihr geschmackvolles Innenleben.

Kummer Zim,

Mariahilfer Str. 71a ✉ 1060 **U** *Neubaugasse – (01) 5 88 95 – kummer@austria-hotels.at – Fax (01) 5878133* EU **s**

95 Zim – 120/235 € 155/275 €

Rest – Karte 19/37 €

◆ Inmitten eines der lebendigsten Geschäftsviertel von Wien warten hinter der klassizistischen Fassade aus der Jahrhundertwende geräumige Zimmer mit klassischen Stilmöbeln. Genießen Sie eine Ruhepause im charmanten Restaurant.

Johann Strauss garni

Favoritenstr. 12 ✉ 1040 **U** *Taubstummengasse – (01) 5 05 76 24 – info@hotel-johann-strauss.at – Fax (01) 5057628* FV **e**

53 Zim – 110/160 € 145/180 €

◆ Der "ungekrönte König des Walzers" gab diesem Haus aus der Jugendstilzeit seinen Namen. Hinter der schönen historischen Fassade erwarten den Gast komfortable Zimmer.

Suitehotel Wien Messe garni

Radingerstr. 2 ✉ 1020 **U** *Vorgartenstr. – (01) 24 58 80 – h3720@accor.com – Fax (01) 24588188* GT **h**

158 Zim – 97/99 € 97/99 €, 12 €

◆ Ein neuartiges Konzept: Sie bewohnen 30 qm große, modern und farbenfroh eingerichtete Zimmer, die mit Trennwänden in Wohn- und Schlafbereich unterteilt werden können.

Mercure Josefshof garni
*Josefsgasse 4 ✉ 1080 **U** Rathaus*
– ✆ (01) 4 04 19 – office@josefshof.com – Fax (01) 40419150 EU **c**
119 Zim – 119/185 € 119/209 €, ☕ 14 €
◆ Hinter seiner gelben Fassade beherbergt das Hotel wohnliche Zimmer, teils mit Parkettfußboden. Im Sommer wird das Frühstück auf der Innenhof-Terrasse serviert.

Albatros garni
*Liechtensteinstr. 89 ✉ 1090 **U** Volksoper – ✆ (01) 3 17 35 08*
– albatros@austria-trend.at – Fax (01) 317350885 FT **b**
70 Zim ☕ – 130/250 € 150/300 €
◆ Die Zimmer dieses Hotels sind in ihrer funktionellen Art ganz auf den Businessgast ausgelegt. Frühstücksraum sowie ein separater Aufenthaltsraum befinden sich im 1. Stock.

Beethoven garni
*Millöckergasse 6 ✉ 1060 **U** Karlsplatz – ✆ (01) 58 74 48 20*
– info@beethoven.bestwestern.at – Fax (01) 5874442 JS **d**
36 Zim ☕ – 90/150 € 120/240 €
◆ In einer Seitenstraße unweit des Naschmarktes gelegenes Hotel mit wohnlich eingerichteten Zimmern. Im Sommer wird das Frühstück auch im kleinen Innenhof serviert.

Römischer Kaiser garni
*Annagasse 16 ✉ 1010 **U** Stephansplatz – ✆ (01) 51 27 75 10*
– info@rkhotel.bestwestern.at – Fax (01) 512775113 KS **g**
24 Zim ☕ – 120/240 € 130/290 €
◆ Wiener Charme verbreiten die schöne Halle mit hoher Decke sowie die technisch gut ausgestatteten Zimmer und Bäder im Versace-Design.

Am Schubertring garni
*Schubertring 11 ✉ 1010 **U** Karlsplatz – ✆ (01) 71 70 20*
– hotel.amschubertring@chello.at – Fax (01) 7139966 KS **n**
39 Zim ☕ – 99/135 € 128/218 € – 3 Suiten
◆ Die Lage nahe Konzerthaus, Akademietheater und Staatsoper spricht für dieses Hotel. Die Zimmer sind individuell eingerichtet, einige mit Blick über die Dächer der Stadt.

City-Central garni
*Taborstr. 8 ✉ 1020 **U** Schwedenplatz – ✆ (01) 21 10 50*
– city.central@schick-hotels.com – Fax (01) 21105140 KP **x**
58 Zim ☕ – 102/150 € 143/210 €
◆ Hinter der stilvollen Fassade des traditionsreichen Hauses verbergen sich Räume mit modernem Komfort, die dennoch die typische Wiener Atmosphäre nicht vermissen lassen.

InterCityHotel Zim, Rest,
*Mariahilferstr. 122 ✉ 1070 **U** West – Bahnhof – ✆ (01) 52 58 50*
– reception@wien.intercityhotel.at – Fax (01) 52585111 EU **r**
179 Zim ☕ – 70/149 € 99/249 € – **Rest** – Karte 20/35 €
◆ Zweckmäßiges Quartier am Westbahnhof: Mit dem Zimmerausweis in der Tasche sind Sie mobil, denn die Nutzung des öffentlichen Nahverkehrs ist im Zimmerpreis inbegriffen!

Ibis Messe Zim,

*Lassallestr. 7a ✉ 1020 **U** Praterstern – ✆ (01) 21 77 00 – h2736@accor.com – Fax (01) 21770555* GT **b**

166 Zim – †66 € ††81 €, ☕ 9 € – **Rest** – Karte 16/25 €

◆ Neuzeitliche und funktionelle Zimmer mit hellen Möbeln warten in der Nähe des Praters. Auf moderne Technik muss man ebensowenig verzichten wie auf große Schreibtische.

XXXX ✿✿ **Steirereck** (Heinz Reitbauer Jun.)

*Am Heumarkt 2 (Stadtpark) ✉ 1030 **U** Stadtpark – ✆ (01) 7 13 31 68 – wien@steirereck.at – Fax (01) 71331682*

geschl. Samstag – Sonntag, Feiertage LR **c**

Rest – (Tischbestellung ratsam) Menü 49 € (mittags)/98 € – Karte 47/85 €

Spez. Steinpilze mit Meeresfrüchtesalat und marinierter Gänseleber. Pogusch Lamm aus eigener Landwirtschaft. Reh mit Wald- und Wiesenaromaten.

◆ Das elegante Restaurant im Stadtpark bietet eine kreative Küche aus überwiegend regionalen Produkten. Typische Mehlspeisen in der angeschlossenen Milch- und Käsebar Meierei.

XXXX **Korso** – Hotel Bristol

*Kärntner Ring 1 ✉ 1015 **U** Karlsplatz – ✆ (01) 51 51 65 46 – Fax (01) 51516575*

geschl. Aug. und Samstagmittag JS **m**

Rest – Menü 48 € (mittags)/86 € – Karte 62/86 €

◆ Hier genießen Sie in klassischem Ambiente das ebenso klassische Speisenangebot. Eine beleuchtete Onyx-Wand ziert das Restaurant.

XXXX ✿ **Restaurant Coburg** – Hotel Palais Coburg

*Coburgbastei 4 ✉ 1010 **U** Stubentor – ✆ (01) 51 81 88 00 – restaurant@palais-coburg.com – Fax (01) 51818818*

geschl. Sonntag – Montag KR **m**

Rest – *(nur Abendessen)* Menü 78/108 € – Karte 46/75 €

Spez. Kalbskutteln mit roten Rüben und Kaviar. Zanderfilet im Räucherpilzfond mit Gnocchetti. Lammrücken mit Senfjus und Spitzkraut.

◆ Sehr angenehm sitzt man in diesem eleganten Restaurant. Christian Petz' klassische Küche wird ergänzt durch eine beachtliche Weinauswahl mit ca. 5000 Positionen.

XXX **Mörwald im Ambassador**

*Kärntner Str. 22, (1. Stock) ✉ 1010 **U** Stephansplatz – ✆ (01) 96 16 11 61 – ambassador@moerwald.at – Fax (01) 96161160* JR **s**

Rest – (Tischbestellung ratsam) Menü 39 € (mittags)/125 € – Karte 52/74 €

◆ Das Restaurant mit französischer Küche ist angeschlossen an eine schöne Atriumbar. Vom Wintergarten blickt man auf den Neuen Markt – im Sommer bei offener Glasfront.

XXX **Niky's Kuchlmasterei** mit Zim Zim, Zim, Zim,

Obere Weissgerberstr. 6 ✉ 1030 – ✆ (01) 7 12 90 00 – office@kuchlmasterei.at – Fax (01) 712900016

geschl. Sonn- und Feiertage, außer Dez. LR **f**

7 Suiten – †250 € ††250 €, ☕ 13 €

Rest – Menü 29 € (mittags)/52 € – Karte 35/58 €

◆ Reichlich Dekor und viele Originale bestimmen das Bild in diesen nicht ganz alltäglichen Restaurantstuben. Schöne Terrasse und riesiger Weinkeller. Individuelle, exklusive Suiten.

Julius Meinl am Graben

Graben 19 (1. Stock) ✉ 1010 **U** *Stephansplatz – ✆ (01) 5 32 33 34 60 00 – restaurant@meinlamgraben.at – Fax (01) 53233341290*
geschl. Sonn- und Feiertage JR **e**
Rest – (Tischbestellung erforderlich) Menü 34 € (mittags)/89 € (abends) – Karte 48/70 €
♦ In einem traditionsreichen Feinkostgeschäft liegt dieses gut besuchte Restaurant mit klassischer Küche. Von den Fensterplätzen aus blickt man auf den Graben und die Pestsäule.

Grotta Azzurra

Babenbergerstr. 5 ✉ 1010 **U** *Museumsquartier – ✆ (01) 5 86 10 44 – office@grotta-azzurra.at – Fax (01) 586104415* HS **s**
Rest – Menü 70 € – Karte 32/49 €
♦ Österreichs ältestes italienisches Restaurant ist diese seit den 50er Jahren bestehende Adresse. Details wie hohe Decken, schöne Leuchter und Bilder bestimmen die Atmosphäre.

Steirer Stub'n

Wiedner Hauptstr. 111 ✉ 1050 – ✆ (01) 5 44 43 49 – steirerstuben@chello.at – Fax (01) 5440888
geschl. Sonn- und Feiertage, Juli – Aug. Samstag – Sonntag FV **k**
Rest – (Tischbestellung ratsam) Menü 25 € – Karte 33/43 €
♦ Eine Wiener Institution: In den geschmackvoll eingerichteten, rustikalen Gasträumen bietet man regionale und internationale Gerichte.

Selina

Laudongasse 13 ✉ 1080 **U** *Rathaus – ✆ (01) 4 05 64 04 – Fax (01) 4080459* EU **f**
Rest – Menü 49/68 € – Karte 21/43 €
♦ In modern-elegantem Ambiente mit südländischem Touch serviert man neben gehobener internationaler Küche auch mediterran-orientalische Speisen.

Novelli

Bräunerstr. 11 ✉ 1010 **U** *Herrengasse – ✆ (01) 5 13 42 00 – novelli@haslauer.at – Fax (01) 51342001*
geschl. Sonntag JR **b**
Rest – (Tischbestellung ratsam) Menü 26 € (mittags) – Karte 33/54 €
♦ Hier erwarten Sie italienische Küche und freundlicher Service. Kräftige warme Farben geben diesem neuzeitlichen Restaurant eine mediterrane Note.

Vestibül

Dr. Karl-Lueger-Ring 2 (Burgtheater) ✉ 1010 **U** *Herrengasse – ✆ (01) 5 32 49 99 – restaurant@vestibuel.at – Fax (01) 532499910*
geschl. Samstagmittag, Sonn- und Feiertage sowie Juli – Aug. auch Samstagabend HR **d**
Rest – Menü 39 € – Karte 29/49 €
♦ Im Seitenflügel des Burgtheaters befindet sich heute ein stilvoll mit Marmor und Stuck gestaltetes Restaurant. Man verwöhnt Sie mit guten regionalen und mediterranen Speisen.

Walter Bauer

Sonnenfelsgasse 17 ✉ 1010 **U** *Stubentor – ✆ (01) 5 12 98 71*
– restaurant.walter.bauer@aon.at – Fax (01) 5129871
geschl. Karwoche, 21. Juli – 15. Aug., Samstag – Montagmittag KR **c**
Rest – (Tischbestellung ratsam) Menü 49/69 € – Karte 45/65 €
Spez. Steinbutt an der Gräte gebraten. Entrecôte mit Kräuterbutter und hausgemachten Pommes Frites. Crème brûlée mal drei.
◆ Etwas versteckt liegt das Altstadthaus a. d. 14. Jh. in einer kleinen Gasse. Unter einem schönen Kreuzgewölbe genießen Sie eine moderne Küche.

Zum weißen Rauchfangkehrer

Weihburggasse 4 ✉ 1010 **U** *Stephansplatz – ✆ (01) 5 12 34 71*
– rauchfangkehrer@utanet.at – Fax (01) 512347128
geschl. Mitte Juli – Mitte Aug. und Sonntag – Montag KR **e**
Rest – *(nur Abendessen)* (Tischbestellung ratsam) Karte 45/77 €
◆ Eine angenehme Atmosphäre herrscht in dem traditionsreichen Gasthaus. Sehr freundlich umsorgt man Sie in gemütlichen, hübsch dekorierten Stuben mit Wiener Küche.

Fabios

Tuchlauben 6 ✉ 1010 **U** *Stephansplatz – ✆ (01) 5 32 22 22*
– fabios@fabios.at – Fax (01) 5322225
geschl. Sonntag JR **x**
Rest – (Tischbestellung erforderlich) Karte 46/63 €
◆ Sehr lebendig und recht kosmopolitisch geht es in diesem modern designten Restaurant am Ende der Fußgängerzone zu. Geboten wird ambitionierte mediterrane Küche.

Indochine 21

Stubenring 18 ✉ 1010 **U** *Stubentor – ✆ (01) 5 13 76 60*
– restaurant@indochine.at – Fax (01) 513766016 LR **b**
Rest – Menü 27/90 € – Karte 38/67 €
◆ In bester Stadtlage lässt diese Trendadresse ein Stück koloniales Indochina wieder aufleben. Serviert wird Fusion-cooking auf hohem Niveau: asiatisch mit französischem Akzent.

Zum Schwarzen Kameel

Bognergasse 5 ✉ 1010 **U** *Herrengasse – ✆ (01) 5 33 81 25*
– info@kameel.at – Fax (01) 533812523
geschl. Sonn- und Feiertage JR **m**
Rest – (Tischbestellung erforderlich) Menü 29 € (mittags)/64 € – Karte 34/59 €
◆ Nahe dem Stephansdom befindet sich das hübsche, im Jugendstil gehaltene Restaurant mit dem Charme eines Wiener Kaffeehauses. Mit eigenem Feinkostgeschäft.

RieGi

Schauflergasse 6 ✉ 1010 **U** *Herrengasse – ✆ (01) 5 32 91 26*
– world@barbaro.at – Fax (01) 532912620
geschl. Anfang Jan. 1 Woche, Ende Juli - Mitte Aug. und Sonntag – Montag, Feiertage JR **h**
Rest – Menü 45/78 € – Karte 47/59 €
Spez. Jakobsmuschelravioli im Tomatensud mit Pesto. Warme Pastete vom Perlhuhn mit Gänseleber und Spargelgemüse. Geschmorte Lammschulter mit jungen Artischocken.
◆ In dem modern-eleganten Restaurant unweit der Hofburg überzeugt internationale Küche mit mediterranem Einfluss. Interessant ist die aufwändig beleuchtete Decke, der Himmel.

SKY Restaurant

Kärntner Str. 19, (im Kaufhaus Steffl, 7. Etage) ✉ 1010
U *Stephansplatz – ✆ (01) 5 13 17 12 – office@skybox.at*
– Fax (01) 513171220
geschl. Sonntag KR **f**
Rest – *(nur Abendessen)* Karte 31/50 €
◆ Beste Lage: Im 7. Stock eines Kaufhauses mitten in der Fußgängerzone befindet sich dieses neuzeitliche, aber dennoch klassische Restaurant mit dunklem Parkettfußboden.

da moritz

Schellinggasse 6 ✉ 1010 **U** *Stubentor – ✆ (01) 5 12 44 44*
– tisch@damoritz.at – Fax (01) 5135644
geschl. Sonntag KR **g**
Rest – Menü 15 € (mittags)/55 € – Karte 33/40 €
◆ Eine trendige Adresse ist das auf zwei Etagen angelegte Restaurant in einem schönen Eckhaus. Das Speisenangebot ist mediterran ausgelegt.

Mezzo

Esteplatz 6 ✉ 1030 **U** *Landstr. – ✆ (01) 7 15 51 48 – mezzo@mezzo.cc*
– Fax (01) 7155148
geschl. 24. Dez. – 7. Jan. und Samstag – Sonntag, Feiertage GU **m**
Rest – Menü 27/59 € – Karte 27/42 €
◆ Puristisch-modern präsentiert sich das in warmen Tönen gehaltene Restaurant in einem Stadthaus am Zentrumsrand. Internationale Karte mit mediterranem und regionalem Einfluss.

Salut

Wildpretmarkt 3 ✉ 1010 **U** *Stephansplatz – ✆ (01) 5 33 13 22*
– salut.gastronomie.gmbh@chello.at – Fax (01) 5082865
geschl. Jan. 2 Wochen, Aug. 3 Wochen und Sonntag, Feiertage JR **y**
Rest – Karte 33/56 €
◆ In der Stadtmitte, nahe dem Stephansplatz gelegener Familienbetrieb, dessen Küche und Weinkarte auf Frankreich ausgerichtet sind.

Gußhaus

Gußhausstr. 23 ✉ 1040 **U** *Taubstummengasse*
– ✆ (01) 5 04 47 50 – gusshaus@kainz-wexberg.at
– Fax (01) 5059464
geschl. Samstagabend, Sonn- und Feiertage FU **p**
Rest – Karte 26/42 €
◆ Stillleben zieren die in warmen Tönen gestrichenen Wände dieses Restaurants im Bistrostil, das seinen Namen einer im Nebenhaus befindlichen k. u. k. Erzgießerei verdankt.

Plachutta

Wollzeile 38 ✉ 1010 **U** *Stubentor – ✆ (01) 5 12 15 77*
– wollzeile@plachutta.at – Fax (01) 512157720 KR **b**
Rest – (Tischbestellung ratsam) Karte 27/43 €
◆ Familie Plachutta fühlt sich seit Jahren der großen Wiener Rindfleischtradition verpflichtet und serviert dieses gekocht in allen Variationen in der grüngetäfelten Gaststube.

Cantinetta Antinori

Jasomirgottstr. 3 ✉ 1010 **U** *Stephansplatz – ✆ (01) 5 33 77 22 – reservations@cantinetta-antinori.at – Fax (01) 533772211* KR **s**

Rest – (Tischbestellung ratsam) Karte 38/49 €

◆ Genießen Sie die klassische toskanische Küche inmitten von stilvollem Bistro-Ambiente und typischem Dekor. Große Auswahl bester Antinori-Weine, auch glasweise!

Fadinger

Wipplingerstr. 29 ✉ 1010 **U** *Schottentor-Universität – ✆ (01) 5 33 43 41 – restaurant@fadinger.at – Fax (01) 5324451*

geschl. 11. – 17. August sowie Samstagmittag, Sonn- und Feiertage JP **f**

Rest – (Tischbestellung ratsam) Menü 20 € (mittags)/55 € (abends) – Karte 26/50 €

◆ Eine sympathische Adresse ist das Restaurant nahe der Börse mit seiner lebendig-quirligen Atmosphäre. Die schmackhafte Küche ist international und regional. Gute Weinauswahl.

Bordeaux Bar à vin

Servitengasse 2 ✉ 1090 **U** *Roßauer Lände – ✆ (01) 3 15 63 63 – office@bordeauxbar.at – Fax (01) 315636363*

geschl. Sonn- und Feiertage FU **k**

Rest – Menü 35 € – Karte 25/47 €

◆ Ein nettes Ambiente erwartet Sie in dem modernen, in angenehm warmen Farben gehaltenen Restaurant mit großer Bar. Man bietet eine kleine Auswahl an internationalen Gerichten.

Cantino

Seilerstätte 30 (im Haus der Musik) ✉ 1010 **U** *Stephansplatz – ✆ (01) 5 12 54 46 – restaurant@cantino.at – Fax (01) 512555028*

geschl. 12. Juli – 24. Aug. und Samstagmittag, Sonntagabend KS **m**

Rest – Menü 37/45 € – Karte 26/39 €

◆ Schlicht-modern gehaltenes Restaurant ganz oben im Haus der Musik – Panoramafenster bieten freie Sicht über Wien. Internationale Küche mit großer Tapas-Auswahl.

Österreicher im MAK

Stubenring 5, (im Museum MAK) ✉ 1010 Wien **U** *Stubentor – ✆ (01) 7 14 01 21 – office@oesterreicherimmak.at – Fax (01) 7101021* LR

Rest – Karte 20/37 €

◆ In dem historischen Gebäude des Museums für Angewandte Kunst serviert man in geradlinig-modernem Ambiente regionale Speisen. Mit schönem Gastgarten.

Schnattl

Lange Gasse 40 ✉ 1080 **U** *Rathaus – ✆ (01) 4 05 34 00 – Fax (01) 4053400*

geschl. nach Ostern 2 Wochen, Ende Aug. 2 Wochen und Samstag, Sonntag, Feiertage EU **b**

Rest – Menü 35/50 € – Karte 31/47 €

◆ Das gepflegte kleine Restaurant mit seinem schlichten, aber nicht ungemütlichen Ambiente ist am Rande der Innenstadt platziert. Nett sitzt es sich auf der Innenhofterrasse.

Weibels Wirtshaus

Kumpfgasse 2 ✉ 1010 **U** *Stubentor – ✆ (01) 5 12 39 86*
– Fax (01) 5123986 KR **d**
Rest – (Tischbestellung ratsam) Menü 30/36 € – Karte 22/40 €
◆ Sehr gemütlich sitzt man in diesem typischen Beisel in der Innenstadt. Hier wie auch im netten Außenbereich bewirtet man Sie freundlich mit Wiener Küche.

Weibel 3

Riemergasse 1 ✉ 1010 **U** *Stubentor – ✆ (01) 5 13 31 10*
– Fax (01) 5133110
geschl. Sonntag – Montag, Feiertage KR **y**
Rest – *(nur Abendessen)* (Tischbestellung ratsam) Menü 48 € – Karte 32/45 €
◆ In dem kleinen Restaurant mit Beisel-Atmosphäre sitzt man recht eng, aber gemütlich. Speisekarte mit überwiegend spanischem Angebot und gute Weinauswahl.

Artner

Floragasse 6 ✉ 1040 **U** *Taubstummengasse – ✆ (01) 5 03 50 33*
– restaurant@artner.co.at – Fax (01) 5035034
geschl. Samstagmittag, Sonn- und Feiertage mittags FV **e**
Rest – Menü 30/50 € – Karte 25/45 €
◆ Ein in klarem, modernem Stil gehaltenes Restaurant, in dem man seinen Gästen zeitgemäße Regionalküche mit internationalen Einflüssen bietet. Preiswertes Mittagsmenü.

Tempel

Praterstr. 56 ✉ 1020 **U** *Nestroyplatz – ✆ (01) 2 14 01 79*
– restaurant.tempel@utanet.at – Fax (01) 2140179
geschl. 22. Dez. – 7. Jan., Aug. 2 Wochen und Samstagmittag, Sonntag – Montag LP **a**
Rest – Menü 15 € (mittags)/39 € – Karte 23/32 €
◆ In dem kleinen bistroartigen Restaurant in einem Innenhof bietet man international beeinflusste regionale Küche und täglich wechselnde preiswerte Mittagsmenüs. Nette Terrasse.

Urania

Uraniastr. 1 ✉ 1010 **U** *Landstr. – ✆ (01) 7 13 30 66*
– office@barurania.com – Fax (01) 7157297 LR **e**
Rest – *(Montag – Freitag nur Abendessen)* (Tischbestellung ratsam) Karte 28/35 €
◆ Trendrestaurant im Gebäude einer Sternwarte. Hinter einer verglasten Fassade erwartet Sie ein puristisches Interieur in dezenten Farben. Im Sommer Dachterrasse mit Donaublick.

Pan e Wien

Salesianergasse 25 ✉ 1030 **U** *Stadtpark – ✆ (01) 7 10 38 70*
– office@panewien.at
geschl. Samstagmittag, Sonn- und Feiertage FU **f**
Rest – Karte 28/41 €
◆ In einem Wohngebiet gelegenes Restaurant mit typischem Bistro-Ambiente – hohe Räume mit blanken Tischen und Weinregalen. Große Piemonteser Weinkarte. Netter Schanigarten.

Harry's Time

Dr. Karl Lueger Platz 5 ✉ 1010 **U** *Stubentor – ✆ (01) 5 12 45 56 – office@harrys-time.at – Fax (01) 512455610*
geschl. Samstagmittag, Sonn- und Feiertage KR **j**
Rest – (Tischbestellung ratsam) Karte 28/47 €
◆ In klarem, modernem Design präsentiert sich dieses familiengeführte Restaurant mit internationaler und regionaler Küche. Spezialität: Ente. Terrasse zur Seitenstraße.

Wrenkh

Bauernmarkt 10 ✉ 1010 **U** *Stephansplatz – ✆ (01) 5 33 15 26 – bauernmarkt@wrenkh.at – Fax (01) 5350840*
geschl. Sonn- und Feiertage KR **h**
Rest – Karte 21/29 €
◆ Das in der Innenstadt gelegene Restaurant ist angenehm schlicht im modernen Bistrostil gehalten. Auf den Tisch kommen überwiegend vegetarische Gerichte.

Livingstone

Zelinkagasse 4 ✉ 1010 **U** *Schottenring – ✆ (01) 5 33 33 93 12 – office@livingstone.at – Fax (01) 53333935* JP **m**
Rest – *(nur Abendessen)* Karte 29/45 €
◆ In einem ehemaligen Tuchlager im jüdischen Viertel von Wien befindet sich das Restaurant im Kolonialstil. Sehr gemütlich: die Bar Planter's Club.

Zu ebener Erde und erster Stock

Burggasse 13 ✉ 1070 **U** *Volkstheater – ✆ (01) 5 23 62 54*
geschl. 1. – 7. Jan., 13. Juli – 4. Aug. und Samstagmittag, Montag, Sonn- und Feiertage HS **b**
Rest – (Tischbestellung ratsam) Menü 32/45 € – Karte 24/36 €
◆ Ein Stück Alt-Wien vermittelt dieses Biedermeierrestaurant am Spittelberg. Im Erdgeschoss gibt's einfache Küche, im Obergeschoss österreichische Küche mit mediterranem Touch.

Yohm

Petersplatz 3 ✉ 1010 **U** *Stephansplatz – ✆ (01) 5 33 29 00 – restaurant@yohm.at – Fax (01) 533290016 –* **Rest** *– Karte 30/51 €* JR **r**
◆ Restaurant in einem modernen Gebäude direkt an der Peterskirche. Große Fenster und Wände in kräftigen Farben schaffen ein helles, freundliches Ambiente. Asiatische Küche.

Huth

Schellinggasse 5/3 ✉ 1010 **U** *Stubentor – ✆ (01) 5 13 56 44 – info@zum-huth.at – Fax (01) 5135644 –* **Rest** – Karte 19/35 € KR **z**
◆ Eine modern designte, recht lebendige Gastwirtschaft. Im Keller: der Livingroom mit Ziegelgewölbe und Club-Atmosphäre. Man bietet Wiener Küche sowie Internationales.

Gaumenspiel

Zieglergasse 54 ✉ 1070 **U** *Zieglergasse – ✆ (01) 5 26 11 08 – essen@gaumenspiel.at – Fax (01) 526110830*
geschl. Samstagmittag, Sonntag – Montagmittag EU **a**
Rest – (Tischbestellung ratsam) Menü 32/39 € – Karte 31/43 €
◆ Recht schlicht gehaltenes Bistro mit freundlich-versiertem Service. Holzfußboden und ein warmer Rotton unterstreichen die nette Atmosphäre. Mittags kleinere, einfachere Karte.

Le Salzgries
Marc-Aurel-Str. 6 ✉ 1010 **U** *Schwedenplatz – ✆ (01) 5 33 40 30 – restaurant@le-salzgries.at – Fax (01) 5334020*
geschl. 1. – 14. Jan., 26. Juli – 18. Aug. und Sonn- und Feiertage KR **t**
Rest – Karte 37/68 €
◆ Eine nette moderne Brasserie in einem typischen Wiener Stadthaus mit zeitgemäß zubereiteter klassisch-französischer Küche und freundlichem Service. Kleiner Schanigarten.

Stadtbezirke 10 – 15

Holiday Inn Vienna-South Zim,
Hertha-Firnberg-Str. 5 ✉ 1100 – ✆ (01) 6 05 30 – hivienna@whgeu.com – Fax (01) 60530580 BZ **f**
174 Zim – 115/210 € 115/230 €, ☕ 22 € – 4 Suiten
Rest – Karte 22/42 €
◆ Das Hotel liegt am Stadtrand in einem Business-Park mit Shopping-Center – ein modernes Haus, dessen funktionelle Einrichtung die Gäste schätzen. Schwerpunkt im Restaurant Brasserie California ist das große kalt-warme Buffet.

Renaissance Wien Zim,
Linke Wienzeile/Ullmannstr. 71 ✉ 1150 **U** *Meidling Hauptstr. – ✆ (01) 89 10 20 – rhi.viehw@renaissancehotels.com – Fax (01) 89102300* BZ **a**
309 Zim – 115/295 € 115/330 €, ☕ 22 €
Rest – Karte 26/40 €
◆ Die Zimmer dieses Hauses sind mit hellem Holzmobiliar funktionell ausgestattet – geräumiger sind die Executive-Zimmer. Hallenbad im 7. Stock mit Panoramablick über die Stadt. Elegant wirkt das Restaurant.

Landhaus Tschipan garni
Friedhofstr. 12 (über Laaer-Berg-Str. CZ) ✉ 1100 – ✆ (01) 6 89 40 11 – office@tschipan.at – Fax (01) 689401135
29 Zim ☕ – 75/85 € 105/125 €
◆ Ein netter und gut geführter Familienbetrieb am Stadtrand! In den gepflegt und wohnlich wirkenden Zimmern mit italienischen Stilmöbeln fühlt man sich als Gast gut aufgehoben.

Courtyard by Marriott Zim,
Schönbrunner Schlossstr. 38 ✉ 1120 **U** *Schönbrunn – ✆ (01) 8 10 17 17 – info@courtyard-vienna.at – Fax (01) 8101717177* AZ **c**
118 Zim – 110/180 € 110/180 €, ☕ 14 €
Rest – *(nur Abendessen)* Karte 19/32 €
◆ Beim Schloss Schönbrunn liegt dieses neuzeitliche Stadthaus mit modernen, funktionellen Zimmern. Die Konferenzräume sind mit neuester Technik ausgestattetet.

Gartenhotel Altmannsdorf (mit Gästehaus) Zim,
Hoffingergasse 26 ✉ 1120 **U** *Schöpfwerk – ✆ (01) 8 01 23 – office@gartenhotel.com – Fax (01) 8012351*
geschl. über Weihnachten AZ **s**

190 Zim – 100/150 € 129/180 €
Rest – Menü 25 € – Karte 20/41 €
◆ Vor allem Tagungsgäste schätzen die funktionellen Zimmer des Hotels am Stadtrand. Modernes Gästehaus mit Seminarraum und Cafeteria. Sehr schön: die Zimmer mit Parkblick. In einem ehemaligen Gewächshaus liegt das Restaurant in ansprechendem Wintergarten-Stil.

Bosei

Zim, VISA MC AE D

Gutheil-Schoder-Gasse 7b ✉ 1100 – ✆ (01) 66 10 60 – bosei@austria-trend.at – Fax (01) 6610699 BZ **t**
195 Zim – 120 € 150 €
Rest – Karte 22/32 €
◆ Am Rande eines Sport- und Erholungsparks (u. a. mit Golf- und Tennisplatz) liegt das moderne Hotel. Die funktionellen Zimmer bieten ein recht gutes Platzangebot. Das Restaurant besticht durch die große Fensterfront mit Blick auf den Golfplatz.

Stadthalle garni

VISA MC

*Hackengasse 20 ✉ 1150 **U** Schweglerstr. – ✆ (01) 9 82 42 72 – office@hotelstadthalle.at – Fax (01) 982723256* BY **z**
44 Zim – 79/105 € 105/135 €
◆ Nahe dem Westbahnhof gelegenes Hotel mit neuzeitlichem und freundlichem Ambiente. Ein schön begrünter Innenhof dient als Frühstücksterrasse.

Reither garni

VISA MC AE D

*Graumanngasse 16 ✉ 1150 **U** Lengenfeldgasse – ✆ (01) 8 93 68 41 – hotel.reither@aon.at – Fax (01) 8936835*
geschl. 22.- 27. Dez. EV **r**
50 Zim – 95/125 € 126/165 €
◆ Die Zimmer dieses Familienbetriebs sind gut unterhalten, zeitgemäß und praktisch eingerichtet und verfügen teilweise über Balkon oder Terrasse.

XX das Turm

Wien, VISA MC AE D

Wienerbergstr. 7, (22. Etage) (im Business Park Wienerberg) ✉ 1100 – ✆ (01) 6 07 65 00 – office@dasturm.at – Fax (01) 607650080
geschl. Samstag – Sonntag BZ **c**
Rest – Menü 22 € (mittags)/74 € – Karte 47/57 €
◆ Eine phantastische Aussicht auf die Stadt genießt man vom 22. Stock dieses modernen Hochhauses. In dem rund angelegten Restaurant wird kreative Küche serviert.

XX Vikerl's Lokal

Würffelgasse 4 ✉ 1150 – ✆ (01) 8 94 34 30 – office@vikerls.at – Fax (01) 8943430
geschl. Anfang Jan. 1 Woche, Karwoche, Aug. 2 Wochen und Samstagmittag, Sonntagabend – Montag sowie Juni – Aug. Samstagmittag, Sonntag – Montag BZ **d**
Rest – (Tischbestellung ratsam) Menü 36/45 € – Karte 21/40 €
◆ Am Rande der Innenstadt liegt das in nette rustikale Stuben unterteilte Restaurant mit guter regionaler Küche und freundlichem Service unter der Leitung der Chefin.

XX **Plachutta Hietzing**

Auhofstr. 1 ✉ 1130 **U** *Hietzing – ✆ (01) 87 77 08 70*
– hietzing@plachutta.at – Fax (01) 877708722
geschl. Mitte Juli – Mitte Aug. AZ **u**
Rest – (Tischbestellung ratsam) Karte 29/46 €
◆ Viele Rindfleischgerichte bietet man in dem Haus mit der Jugendstilfassade: Kavalierspitz, Hüferscherzel und andere Spezialitäten speisen Sie in gehobenem Wirtshausambiente.

X **Meixner's Gastwirtschaft**

Buchengasse 64 (Ecke Herndlgasse) ✉ 1100
U *Reumannplatz – ✆ (01) 6 04 27 10 – k.meixner@aon.at*
– Fax (01) 6063400 CZ **a**
Rest – Karte 20/39 €
◆ Gemütlich eingerichtete Traditions-Gastwirtschaft, in der Sie die Chefin mit einer unverfälschten Regionalküche bekocht. Netter Schanigarten hinterm Haus.

Stadtbezirke 16 – 19

Schild garni

Neustift am Walde 97 ✉ 1190 – ✆ (01) 44 04 04 40
– office@hotel-schild.at – Fax (01) 4404000 AX **c**
29 Zim – 88/160 € 150/190 €
◆ Ein recht modernes Hotel mit wohnlichen, funktionellen Zimmern unterschiedlicher Größe, die mit italienischen Möbeln ausgestattet sind. Im Sommer Frühstück im Garten.

Landhaus Fuhrgassl-Huber garni

Rathstr. 24 ✉ 1190
– ✆ (01) 4 40 30 33 – landhaus@fuhrgassl-huber.at
– Fax (01) 4402714 AX **m**
38 Zim – 85 € 135/138 €
◆ Wohnlich sind die im Landhausstil eingerichteten Zimmer dieses schön gelegenen Familienbetriebs. Im Sommer frühstücken Sie im hübschen Innenhof – Buffet mit guter Auswahl.

Jäger garni

Hernalser Hauptstr. 187 ✉ 1170 – ✆ (01) 48 66 62 00
– hoteljaeger@aon.at – Fax (01) 48666208 AY **r**
17 Zim – 85/120 € 120/170 €
◆ Das engagiert geführte Haus mit hübschem Vorgarten befindet sich seit Jahrzehnten in Familienbesitz. Wohnlich sind die mit hübschen Tapeten und Stoffen ausstaffierten Zimmer.

XX **Plachutta**

Heiligenstädter Str. 179 ✉ 1190 – ✆ (01) 3 70 41 25
– nussdorf@plachutta.at – Fax (01) 370412520 BX **e**
Rest – Karte 24/44 €
◆ In diesem freundlichen Lokal wird Rindfleischkultur gepflegt: In Kupferkesseln serviert man kraftvolle Suppen mit Schulterscherzel, Hüferschwänzel und anderen Gustostückerln.

XX **Eckel**

Sieveringer Str. 46 ✉ 1190 – ✆ (01) 3 20 32 18 – restaurant.eckel@aon.at – Fax (01) 3206660
geschl. 23. Dez. – 21. Jan., 10. – 25. Aug. und Sonntag – Montag AX **s**
Rest – Karte 27/48 €
◆ Das Landhaus beherbergt nette, teilweise holzgetäfelte Stuben, in denen man eine überwiegend traditionelle Küche serviert. Schöne Terrasse.

X **Steirerstöckl**

Pötzleinsdorfer Str. 127 ✉ 1180 – ✆ (01) 4 40 49 43 – steirerstoeckl@jagawirt.at – Fax (01) 4406449
geschl. Montag – Dienstag AX **e**
Rest – (abends Tischbestellung ratsam) Karte 19/35 €
◆ Ein gemütlicher Gasthof am Waldrand mit ländlich-rustikalem Flair. Die verschiedenen Gaststuben sind mit viel Holz gestaltet – freundlicher Service und nette Gartenterrasse.

X **Das Cottage**

Cottagegasse 6 ✉ 1180 – ✆ (01) 4 79 03 76 – office@das-cottage.com – Fax (01) 4790382 ET **a**
Rest – Karte 20/40 €
◆ Hier bietet man eine zeitgemäße Wiener Küche mit internationalem Einfluss, die man auch in dem sehr angenehmen, hübschen Schanigarten unter großen Kastanienbäumen serviert.

Stadtbezirke 21 – 22

NH Danube City Zim,

Wagramer Str. 21 ✉ 1220 **U** *Alte Donau – ✆ (01) 26 02 00 – nhdanubecity@nh-hotels.com – Fax (01) 2602020* CY **v**
252 Zim – 99/252 € 99/252 €, 19 € – 3 Suiten
Rest – Menü 28 € (mittags Buffet) – Karte 27/48 €
◆ Das Hotel nahe der UNO-City ist mit technisch modernen, funktionellen Gästezimmern und Konferenzräumen sowie einem Businesscenter besonders auf Geschäftsreisende ausgelegt. Das Restaurant ist neuzeitlich gestaltet und schließt sich offen an die Halle an.

Park Inn garni

Wagramer Str. 16 ✉ 1220 **U** *Kaisermühlen – ✆ (01) 26 04 00 – reservation.vienna@rezidorparkinn.com – Fax (01) 26040699* CY **x**
135 Zim – 153/166 € 183/195 €
◆ Das Hotel bietet sehr geräumige, geschmackvoll-ländlich mit Weichholzmöblen eingerichtete Zimmer, die funktionell und dennoch wohnlich sind.

Strandhotel Alte Donau garni

Wagramer Str. 51 ✉ 1220 **U** *Alte Donau – ✆ (01) 2 04 40 40 – welcome@strandhotel-alte-donau.at – Fax (01) 204404040* CX **e**
19 Zim – 65/88 € 92/115 €
◆ In der Dependance eines älteren Gasthauses befinden sich sehr gepflegte, neuzeitliche und technisch gut ausgestattete Zimmer. Lage beim Erholungsgebiet Alte Donau.

Mraz & Sohn

Wallensteinstr. 59 ✉ 1200 **U** *Friedensbrücke – ✆ (01) 3 30 45 94 – Fax (01) 3501536*
geschl. 24. Dez. – 6. Jan., 11. – 31. Aug. und Samstag – Sonntag, Feiertage FT **s**
Rest – (Tischbestellung ratsam) Menü 38/89 € – Karte 47/57 €
Spez. Gänseleber mit Kirschen und Frenchtoast. Ox mit Knoblauchschnecken. Rösthaselnuss-Mousse.
◆ Engagiert leitet Familie Mraz dieses hübsche, individuell gestaltete Restaurant. Die kreative Küche wird ergänzt durch eine interessante Weinauswahl.

Heurige – überwiegend Selbstbedienung vom Buffet, Preise nach Gewicht

Schübel-Auer

Kahlenberger Str. 22 (Döbling) ✉ 1190 – ✆ (01) 3 70 22 22 – daniela.somloi@schuebel-auer.at – Fax (01) 3702222
geschl. 22. Dez. – Jan., 16. – 24. April und Sonntag – Montag BX **a**
Rest – *(ab 16 Uhr geöffnet)* Menü 18 € (Buffet)
◆ Der ehemalige Auerhof wurde 1642 als Winzerhaus mit Mühle und Mühlgang erbaut. 1972 hat man das Gebäude umsichtig renoviert und liebevoll ausgestattet. Innenhofterrasse.

Feuerwehr-Wagner

Grinzingerstr. 53 (Heiligenstadt) ✉ 1190 – ✆ (01) 3 20 24 42 – heuriger@feuerwehrwagner.at – Fax (01) 3209141 BX **b**
Rest – *(ab 16 Uhr geöffnet)* Karte ca. 15 € (Buffet)
◆ Vor allem Stammgäste schätzen diesen typischen Heurigen – mit dunklem Holz und blanken Tischen gemütlich-rustikal gestaltet. Sehr nett: der terrassenförmig angelegte Garten.

Mayer am Pfarrplatz

Pfarrplatz 2 (Heiligenstadt) ✉ 1190 – ✆ (01) 3 70 12 87 – mayer@pfarrplatz.at – Fax (01) 3704714
geschl. 20. Dez. – 15. Jan. BX **c**
Rest – *(Montag – Samstag ab 16 Uhr geöffnet)* Karte ca. 19 € (Buffet)
◆ Eine Heurigen-Adresse wie sie im Buche steht: rustikales Inventar, Schrammelmusik und eine schöne Innenhof-Terrasse. Eine Besonderheit: 1817 wohnte Beethoven hier im Haus!

Fuhrgassl Huber

Neustift am Walde 68 ✉ 1190 – ✆ (01) 4 40 14 05 – weingut@fuhrgassl-huber.at – Fax (01) 4402730 AX **b**
Rest – *(ab 14 Uhr geöffnet)* Menü 13 €
◆ Die Stuben laden ein, edle Tropfen zu probieren. Sehenswert sind vor allem das Stadl mit Kamin und Galerie sowie der herrliche Innenhof. Mit Schrammelmusik.

Wolff

Rathstr. 44 (Neustift) ✉ 1190 – ✆ (01) 4 40 23 35 – wolff@wienerheuriger.at – Fax (01) 4401403 AX **m**
Rest – Karte 10/20 €
◆ In urigem Ambiente bieten das Weingut und der nebenan gelegene Buschenschank ein Buffet und eine kleine Karte. Nett ist der mit Glas überdachte Arkadenhof.

Altes Preßhaus

Cobenzlgasse 15 (Grinzing) ✉ 1190 – ✆ (01) 3 20 02 03 – office@altes-presshaus.com – Fax (01) 320020323
geschl. Jan. – März BX **p**
Rest – Karte 20/37 €
◆ Das Haus gilt als der älteste Heurige in Grinzing! Bei typischer Heurigenmusik sitzt man in gemütlicher Atmosphäre. Eine Besonderheit ist die historische Weinpresse im Keller.

Wien-Flughafen – siehe Schwechat

WIENER NEUSTADT – Niederösterreich – 730 U5 – 37 630 Ew – Höhe 265 m

4 **L3**

Wien 47 – St. Pölten 91 – Baden 29 – Sopron 43
Hauptplatz 3, ✉ 2700, ✆ (02622) 37 33 11, buerger-tourist@wiener-neustadt.at
Föhrenwald, Kleinwolkersdorf 217 ✆ (02622) 2 91 71
Neuklosterkirche (Grabplatte★) – Dom (Brauttor★)
Burg Forchtenstein★ Süd-Ost: 25 km

Corvinus

Zim, Zim, VISA AE

Bahngasse 29 ✉ 2700 – ✆ (02622) 2 41 34 – hotel@hotel-corvinus.at – Fax (02622) 24139
68 Zim – 75/79 € 116/120 €
Rest – Karte 21/43 €
◆ Kubische Formen außen und funktionelle zeitgemäße Zimmereinrichtungen prägen dieses auch für Seminarveranstaltungen geeignete Hotel. Hübsch eingedeckte Tische erwarten Sie im Restaurant.

Gastwirtschaft Brod

VISA AE

Bahngasse 1 ✉ 2700 – ✆ (02622) 2 81 07 – office@gastwirtschaftbrod.at – Fax (02622) 28107
geschl. 14. – 27. Juli, 27. – 30. Dez. sowie Sonn- und Feiertage – Montag
Rest – (Tischbestellung ratsam) Menü 35/56 € – Karte 23/44 €
◆ Ein nettes, bewusst schlicht gehaltenes Restaurant in einem der ältesten Häuser der Stadt. Gäste schätzen den freundlichen Service und die produktbezogene regionale Küche.

WIENERWALD – Niederösterreich – 730 U4 – 2 410 Ew – Höhe 400 m

3 **K2**

Wien 17 – St. Pölten 63 – Baden 12
Perchtoldsdorf (Pfarrkirche zum Hl. Augustinus★)

In Sulz im Wienerwald

Postschänke zu Sulz

P VISA

Hauptstr. 51 ✉ 2392 – ✆ (02238) 81 35 – Fax (02238) 71988
geschl. 21. Jan. – 19. Feb. und Montag – Dienstag
Rest – *(Okt. – April Mittwoch – Freitag nur Abendessen)* Karte 21/39 €
◆ An gut eingedeckten Tischen werden in den vier urig-rustikalen Stuben des altösterreichischen Gasthauses regionale, böhmische und Wiener Gerichte angeboten.

X **Stockerwirt**

Hauptstr. 36 (Süd: 1,5 km) ✉ 2392 – ✆ (02238) 82 59 – landgasthaus@stockerwirt.com – Fax (02238) 82594
geschl. Montag – Dienstag
Rest – *(Okt. – April Mittwoch – Freitag nur Abendessen)* Karte 16/38 €
◆ Eine nette Adresse ist dieses Gasthaus mit regional-internationaler Küche. Die schöne Terrasse liegt zum Garten mit Teich und alten Apfel- und Nussbäumen.

Wir bemühen uns bei unseren Preisangaben um größtmögliche Genauigkeit. Aber alles ändert sich! Lassen Sie sich daher bei Ihrer Reservierung den derzeit gültigen Preis mitteilen.

WILDERMIEMING – Tirol – siehe Mieming

WILDSCHÖNAU – Tirol – 730 I6 – 4 020 Ew – Höhe 828 m – Wintersport: 1 903 m 2 36 7 E5

Wien 401 – Innsbruck 73 – Wörgl 15 – Kitzbühel 36
Oberau 337, ✉ 6311, ✆ (05339) 8 25 50, info@wildschoenau.com

In Wildschönau-Auffach

Platzl (geheizt) Zim,

Auffach 177 ✉ 6313 – ✆ (05339) 89 28 – hotel@platzl.at – Fax (05339) 892828
geschl. April, Nov.
50 Zim – ☼ 38/40 € 64/70 € ❄ 42/60 € 70/100 € – ½ P 10 €
Rest – Karte 16/33 €
◆ Das gut unterhaltene familiengeführte Hotel im Ortszentrum verfügt über funktionelle, mit soliden Naturholzmöbeln ausgestattete Gästezimmer. Bürgerlich präsentiert sich das Restaurant.

Gasthof Weissbacher

Auffach 4 ✉ 6313 – ✆ (05339) 89 34 – gh.weissbacher@aon.at – Fax (05339) 2673
geschl. 30. März – 18. Mai,19. Okt. – 13. Dez.
27 Zim – ☼ 34/38 € 60/66 € ❄ 47/54 € 78/92 €
Rest – *(geschl. Mitte Mai – Mitte Okt. Mittwoch)* Karte 16/30 €
◆ In diesem über 100 Jahre alten Gasthof finden Sie freundlichen Service und Zimmer, die mit rustikaler Eiche oder hellem Naturholz eingerichtet sind. Gemütliche Restaurantstuben z. T. mit Zirbenholzvertäfelung.

In Wildschönau-Mühltal

X **Thalmühle** 

Mühltal 7 ✉ 6311 – ✆ (05339) 89 19 – thalmuehle@utanet.at
geschl. Nov. 2 Wochen und im Sommer Sonn- und Feiertage sowie im Winter Dienstag
Rest – (abends Tischbestellung ratsam) Karte 15/24 €
◆ Genießen Sie in der urigen Atmosphäre der 250 Jahre alten ehemaligen Mühle die Spezialität des Hauses: Brez'n Supp'n – freundlicher Service durch den Chef.

In Wildschönau-Niederau

Wastlhof (mit Gästehaus)
Wildschönauer Str. 206 ✉ 6314
– ✆ (05339) 82 47 – info@hotelwastlhof.at – Fax (05339) 82477
geschl. 1. April – 10. Mai, 21. Okt. – 20. Dez.
50 Zim (inkl. ½ P.) – ☼ 57/64 € 104/142 € ❄ 64/78 € 118/186 € – 3 Suiten
Rest – Karte 14/34 €
♦ Das Alpenhotel bietet einen Freizeitbereich mit Kosmetik und eine hauseigene Reitschule. Besonders wohnlich: die leicht eleganten, in warmen Farben gehaltenen neueren Zimmer. Bürgerlich-gediegene Restaurantstuben.

In Wildschönau-Oberau

Silberberger
Rest,
Roggenboden 216 ✉ 6311 – ✆ (05339) 84 07 – hotel@silberberger.at – Fax (05339) 840788
geschl. 29. März – 1. Mai, 1. Nov. – 20. Dez.
51 Zim (inkl. ½ P.) – ☼ 59/63 € 96/100 € ❄ 69/84 € 110/140 € – 3 Suiten
Rest – (nur Abendessen für Hausgäste)
♦ Am Skigebiet Roggenboden liegt dieses familiengeführte Hotel, das gemütliche, unterschiedlich möblierte Zimmer und geräumige Suiten bietet.

Apparthotel Talhof
Zim,
Roggenboden 190 ✉ 6311 – ✆ (05339) 84 65 – info@talhof.at – Fax (05339) 846522
geschl. 28. Okt. – 15. Dez., 15. April – 15. Mai
15 Zim – ☼ 46/65 € 92/110 € ❄ 64/82 € 110/141 €
Rest – *(geschl. Dienstag)* Karte 15/33 €
♦ Die im Landhausstil gehaltenen Zimmer verfügen immer über eine kleine Küche und getrennte, z. T. sehr großzügige Wohn- und Schlafbereiche – viele auch mit Kachelofen. Im Restaurant speisen Sie in gepflegter Atmosphäre.

Landhaus Marchfeld garni
Roggenboden 167 ✉ 6311 – ✆ (05339) 24 03 – rainer@silberberger.at – Fax (05339) 240360
geschl. 15. April – 1. Mai, 18. Okt. – 22. Dez.
9 Zim – ☼ 40/42 € 66/76 € ❄ 42/48 € 76/84 €
♦ Eine herzliche, familiäre Atmosphäre macht den etwas außerhalb am Hang gelegenen kleinen Familienbetrieb aus. Die Zimmer sind mit soliden hellen Naturholzmöbeln eingerichtet.

Tirolerhof
Oberau 275 ✉ 6311 – ✆ (05339) 8 11 80 – info@hoteltirolerhof.at – Fax (05339) 811833
geschl. 7. – 30. April, 3. Nov. – 20. Dez.
59 Zim (inkl. ½ P.) – ☼ 59/64 € 100/110 € ❄ 63/79 € 108/140 €
Rest – *(geschl. Mai. - Anfang Nov. Dienstag)* Karte 14/28 €
♦ Eine gepflegte Adresse im Zentrum: Direkt neben dem Anfängerskilift finden Sie hier gut unterhaltene Zimmer in rustikal-gediegenem Stil. Das A-la-carte-Restaurant ist in einem ländlichen Stüberl untergebracht.

Kellerwirt mit Zim — Zim, VISA

Oberau 72 ✉ 6311 – ✆ (05339) 81 16 – info@kellerwirt.com
– Fax (05339) 2413
geschl. 10. Apr. – 10. Mai, 15. Nov. – 10. Dez.
28 Zim – ☼ 45/55 € 70/88 € ❄ 50/58 € 70/90 € –
½ P 15 €
Rest – *(geschl. Mittwoch)* Karte 20/35 €
◆ Der Gasthof a. d. 13. Jh. teilt sich in urige kleine Stuben – mit Kreuzgewölbe, bemalter Holzkassettendecke oder mit alter Holztäfelung. Die Küche: regional bis international.

Wie entscheidet man sich zwischen zwei gleichwertigen Adressen?
In jeder Kategorie sind die Häuser nochmals geordnet,
die besten Adressen stehen an erster Stelle.

WILHELMSBURG – Niederösterreich – 730 S4 – 6 660 Ew – Höhe 320 m

3 **K3**

Wien 70 – St. Pölten 13 – Krems 50 – Melk 35
Stift Lilienfeld★ Süd: 11 km

Landgasthof Reinberger — Rest, VISA AE

Kreisbacher Str. 11 ✉ 3150
– ✆ (02746) 23 64 – reinberger@synops.at – Fax (02746) 236435
geschl. 27. Dez. – 13. Jan.
14 Zim – 42/50 € 72/80 €
Rest – *(geschl. Sonntagabend – Montag)* Karte 14/30 €
◆ Eine traditionsreiche Adresse ist dieses familiär geleitete historische Gasthaus. Das kleine Hotel bietet u. a. einige besonders wohnliche und freundliche Komfortzimmer. Gepflegtes Restaurant im ländlichen Stil.

WINDISCHGARSTEN – Oberösterreich – 730 P5 – 2 350 Ew – Höhe 600 m – Wintersport: – Lufkurort

9 **I4**

Wien 258 – Linz 90 – Steyr 59 – Liezen 27
Hauptstr. 28, ✉ 4580, ✆ (07562) 52 66, info@pyhrn-priel.net
Spital am Pyhrn (Stiftskirche★) Süd: 10 km

Dilly's Wellness-Hotel — (geheizt) Rest, VISA

Pyhrnstr. 14 ✉ 4580
– ✆ (07562) 5 26 40 – wellness@dilly.at – Fax (07562) 5264500
80 Zim (inkl. ½ P.) – 96/124 € 192/216 €
Rest – (nur für Hausgäste)
◆ Eine Spielhalle für Kinder über zwei Etagen und die Zimmerausstattung z. T. mit Himmelbetten sind bei diesem Familienhotel besonders hervorzuheben.

WINZENDORF-MUTHMANNSDORF – Niederösterreich – 730 U5 – 1 720 Ew – Höhe 320 m

4 **L3**

Wien 57 – St. Pölten 93 – Wiener Neustadt 10 – Baden 31

Schmutzer

Hauptstr. 12, (Winzendorf) ✉ 2722 – ☎ (02638) 2 22 37 – gasthaus-schmutzer@aon.at – Fax (02638) 222374
geschl. 4. Feb. – 3. März, 18. Aug. – 2. Sept. und Montag
Rest – Menü 33/67 € – Karte 19/51 €
Rest *Der Kleine Schmutzer* – Karte 15/23 €
◆ Ländlich-eleganter familiengeführter Gasthof mit sehr gut eingedeckten Tischen und freundlichem Service. Gute Auswahl an österreichischen Weinen. Gastgarten mit Kastanienbaum. Rustikal-schlicht, aber dennoch gemütlich zeigt sich der Kleine Schmutzer.

Puchegger-Wirt mit Zim

Bahnhofplatz 86, (Winzendorf) ✉ 2722 – ☎ (02638) 2 22 24 – info@puchegger.at – Fax (02638) 22224105
7 Zim – 35 € 56 €
Rest – *(geschl. Sonntagabend – Dienstag)* Menü 30 € – Karte 20/36 €
◆ Viele Stammgäste schätzen diesen familiengeführten Landgasthof, der neben einem ländlich-gemütlichen Restaurant mit Bauernmöbeln eingerichtete Gästezimmer bietet.

WÖRGL – Tirol – 730 I6 – 10 890 Ew – Höhe 513 m – Wintersport: 850 m 2

7 **E5**

Wien 387 – Innsbruck 59 – Kitzbühel 15 – Kufstein 31
Rattenberg★ Süd-West: 15 km – Kramsach: Freilichtmuseum Tiroler Bauernhöfe★ Süd-West: 17 km

Gasthof Weisses Lamm

Innsbrucker Str. 7 (B 171) ✉ 6300 – ☎ (05332) 7 22 01 – gh-lamm@woergl.at – Fax (05332) 722014
geschl. Nov. – 10. Dez.
33 Zim – 40 € 70 €
Rest – *(geschl. Samstag – Sonntag)* Karte 12/28 €
◆ Dieser über 250 Jahre alte Gasthof unter Familienleitung beherbergt solide und zeitgemäße mit Naturholzmöbeln ausgestattete Zimmer. Gemütliches Ambiente in den Gaststuben.

WOLFSBERG – Kärnten – 730 Q8 – 25 310 Ew – Höhe 490 m – Wintersport: 2 100 m 28

10 **J5**

Wien 263 – Klagenfurt 58 – Graz 77 – Köflach 49
Getreideplatz 3, ✉ 9400, ☎ (04352) 33 30, tourismusbuero@wolfsberg.at
Wolfsberg- St. Michael, Hattendorf 25 ☎ (04352) 6 16 88
Schloss (Stucksaal★)
Autobahnbrücke des Lavanttales★ (Nord: 14 km)

Hecher Zim, Rest,

Wiener Str. 6 ✉ 9400 – ☎ (04352) 29 46 – hotel@hecher.at – Fax (04352) 294645
38 Zim – 48 € 75 €
Rest – (nur Abendessen) Karte 14/25 €
◆ Mitten im Zentrum gelegenes Hotel mit durchweg sehr gepflegten und wohnlichen Zimmern. Man bietet auch ein Café mit Kuchen aus der hauseigenen Konditorei.

In Wolfsberg-St. Margarethen **Nord-West: 2 km über BAB-Ausfahrt Wolfsberg Nord:**

Gasthof Stoff

Zim, Rest,

St. Margarethen 14 ✉ 9412
– ✆ (04352) 22 97 – ghstoff@gmx.at – Fax (04352) 229750

48 Zim – 39/45 € 70/74 €

Rest – Karte 14/20 €

◆ Ein gewachsener familiengeführter Gasthof in einem kleinen Ortsteil, der über recht unterschiedliche Zimmer von schlicht bis zeitgemäß verfügt. Nett und zwanglos ist die Atmosphäre im bürgerlich-ländlichen Restaurant.

In Wolfsberg-St. Stefan **Süd: 2 km über BAB-Ausfahrt Wolfsberg Süd:**

Alter Schacht mit Zim

Hauptstr. 24 ✉ 9431 – ✆ (04352) 31 21 – office@alterschacht.at
– Fax (04352) 312111
geschl. Feb. 2 Wochen, Juli 1 Woche, Sept. 1 Woche und Sonntagabend – Montag

10 Zim – 41 € 72 €

Rest – Menü 30 € – Karte 14/39 €

◆ In dem familiär geleiteten Gasthof mit gediegen-rustikalem Charakter serviert man Ihnen freundlich regionale Speisen. Gute Weinauswahl. Zum Übernachten stehen einige gepflegte Zimmer bereit.

Rot steht für unsere besonderen Empfehlungen!

WOLKERSDORF – Niederösterreich – 730 V3 – 6 200 Ew – Höhe 178 m

4 **L2**

Wien 27 – St. Pölten 85 – Mödling 45 – Stockerau 30

Klaus im Weinviertel

Zim, Rest,

Julius-Bittner-Platz 4 ✉ 2120
– ✆ (02245) 2 22 40 – info@hotel-klaus.at – Fax (02245) 4286
geschl. 22. – 28. Dez.

70 Zim – 50/60 € 75/80 €

Rest – *(nur Abendessen)* Karte 16/40 €

◆ Gewachsener Gasthof in der Ortsmitte mit unterschiedlich ausgestatteten Zimmern. Dank des direkten Schnellbahnanschlusses auch für Wien-Besucher interessant. Neuzeitlich gestaltetes Restaurant mit Wintergarten.

In Wolkersdorf-Kronberg **Nord: 4 km über B 7 Richtung Mistelbach:**

Kronberghof

Am Russbach 3 ✉ 2123 – ✆ (02245) 43 04 – info@kronberghof.at
– Fax (02245) 43044

15 Zim – 46/54 € 74/86 €

Rest – *(geschl. Montag – Dienstag)* Karte 16/26 €

◆ Eine ehemalige Hofmühle war der Ursprung dieses Anwesens, das wegen der eigenen Reithalle und der Pferdeeinstellmöglichkeiten vor allem für Reiter interessant ist. Gemütliche und rustikale Atmosphäre zeichnet das Restaurant aus.

In Wolkersdorf-Riedenthal Nord: 3 km über B 7 Richtung Mistelbach:

XX **Buchingers Zur Alten Schule**

Wolkersdorfer Str. 6 ✉ 2120 – ✆ (02245) 8 25 00
– manfred@buchingers.at – Fax (02245) 83702
geschl. Feb. – Mitte März, Aug. und Montag – Mittwoch
Rest – Karte 21/35 €
♦ Die ehem. Dorfschule beheimatet heute ein Restaurant mit zum Teil holzvertäfelten Wänden. Im Sommer stehen zusätzlich reizvolle Terrassenplätze zur Verfügung.

ZAMS – **Tirol** – 730 D7 – **3 390 Ew** – **Höhe 780 m** – **Wintersport: 2 212 m** 1 7 5 **B6**

Wien 514 – Innsbruck 70 – Imst 32 – Sankt Anton 15

X **Post-Gasthof Gemse**

Hauptplatz 1 ✉ 6511 – ✆ (05442) 6 24 78 – haueis@aon.at
– Fax (05442) 68276
geschl. Nov. und Mittwoch
Rest – Karte 18/24 €
♦ Seit 1726 ist der Gasthof in der Ortsmitte im Besitz der Familie Haueis. Gemütlich sitzt man in der traditionell gestalteten Gaststube. Bilder von Künstlern zieren das Haus.

ZAUCHENSEE – **Salzburg** – **siehe Altenmarkt im Pongau**

ZEISELMAUER – **Niederösterreich** – 730 U4 – **1 970 Ew** – **Höhe 175 m** 4 **L2**

Wien 28 – St. Pölten 53 – Krems 49 – Stockerau 24

X **Zum lustigen Bauern**

Kirchenplatz 1 ✉ 3424 – ✆ (02242) 7 04 24
– zum.lustigen.bauern@aon.at
geschl. 4. – 10. Feb. und Mittwoch
Rest – Karte 14/33 €
♦ Der auf römischen Grundmauern erbaute Gasthof bietet eine aparte Mischung aus historischem und modernem Charme. Bedient von freundlichem Personal speist man hier regional.

ZELL AM SEE – **Salzburg** – 730 K7 – **9 640 Ew** – **Höhe 757 m** – **Wintersport: 1 969 m** 6 22 8 **F5**

Wien 369 – Salzburg 98 – Kitzbühel 55 – Bad Reichenhall 62

Brucker Bundesstr. 1a, ✉ 5700, ✆ (06542) 77 00, welcome@europasportregion.info

36 Zell am See-Kaprun, Golfstr. 25 ✆ (06542) 56 16 10

Schmittenhöhe★★ (mit) Y – Pinzgauer Spazierweg★★

Saalachtal★ Nord: 15 km

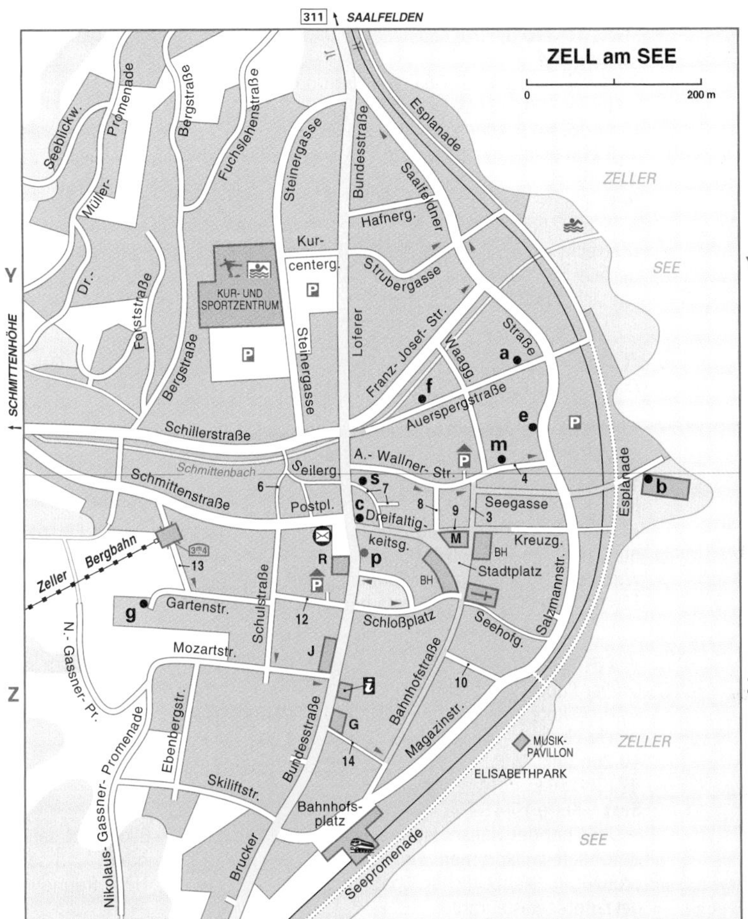

Salzburgerhof (geheizt)
Auerspergstr. 11 Rest, VISA AE
✉ 5700 – ✆ (06542) 7 65 – 5sterne@salzburgerhof.at – Fax (06542) 76566
geschl. Nov. Y **a**
63 Zim (inkl. ½ P.) – ☼ 140/195 € 250/360 € ❄ 170/240 € 300/440 € – 15 Suiten
Rest – (Tischbestellung ratsam) Menü 65 € – Karte 28/55 €
◆ Wohnlich elegante Zimmer, luxuriöse Suiten und ein großzügiger Wellnessbereich mit allerlei Anwendungen erwarten Sie in dem vornehmen Hotel. Badeteich im hübschen Garten. Aufmerksamer Service serviert Ihnen internationale und regionale Speisen.

Grand Hotel (mit Gästehaus) Rest, Rest, Rest,

Esplanade 4

✉ 5700 – ✆ (06542) 7 88 – info@grandhotel-zellamsee.at – Fax (06542) 788305

geschl. 5. – 25. April, 12. Okt. – 22. Nov. YZ **b**

110 Zim (inkl. ½ P.) – ☼ 98/128 € 166/226 € ❄ 115/190 € 200/350 € – 11 Suiten

Rest – Karte 21/42 €

◆ Schön liegt das im klassischen Stil gebaute Haus direkt am See. Die recht unterschiedlich geschnittenen Zimmer bieten z. T. eine wunderbare Sicht. Etwas einfacheres Gästehaus. Rustikal-gemütlich präsentieren sich die Restaurantstuben.

Tirolerhof Rest,

Auerspergstr. 5 ✉ 5700 – ✆ (06542) 77 20 – welcome@tirolerhof.co.at – Fax (06542) 77270

geschl. 29. März – 17. Mai, 12. Okt. – 13. Dez. Y **f**

86 Zim (inkl. ½ P.) – ☼ 94/133 € 160/180 € ❄ 129/219 € 210/294 €

Rest – Karte 22/38 €

◆ Sehr gut geführtes und tadellos gepflegtes Haus. Sucht man Entspannung, bleiben im großzügig angelegten Wellnessbereich Aquarena keine Wünsche offen. Elegantes Ambiente, stimmiges Dekor und freundlicher Service sprechen für das Restaurant.

Badhaus

Loferer Bundesstr. 77 (über Y) ✉ 5700 – ✆ (06542) 7 28 62 – hotel@hotel-badhaus.at – Fax (06542) 7286244

geschl. 6. April – 10. Mai, 1. Okt. – 13. Nov.

40 Zim (inkl. ½ P.) – ☼ 66/90 € 116/164 € ❄ 80/143 € 130/256 €

Rest – Karte 16/41 €

◆ Der Chef des Hauses ist begeisterter Motorradfahrer – Biker sind daher besonders willkommen. Ein Teil der Zimmer ist ganz modern und sehr großzügig. Neuzeitlicher Spabereich. Mit viel hellem Holz freundlich gestaltetes Restaurant.

Zum Hirschen Zim,

Dreifaltigkeitsgasse 1 ✉ 5700 – ✆ (06542) 7 74 – hotel@zum-hirschen.at – Fax (06542) 47166

geschl. 25. März – 16. April, 20. Okt. – 1. Dez. Z **c**

45 Zim (inkl. ½ P.) – ☼ 72/82 € 124/164 € ❄ 92/127 € 164/234 €

Rest – Menü 19/35 € – Karte 19/44 €

◆ Behagliche Wärme strahlen die mit viel Holz eingerichteten Zimmer dieses Gasthofes im Ortszentrum aus. Ein kleiner Freizeitbereich steht zur Verfügung. Das Restaurant glänzt durch stilvolle Atmosphäre mit ländlichem Charme.

Zum Metzgerwirt (geheizt)

Sebastian-Hörl-Str. 11 ✉ 5700 – ✆ (06542) 7 25 20 – info@romantik-hotel.at – Fax (06542) 7252034

geschl. April, Nov. Y **e**

39 Zim (inkl. ½ P.) – ☼ 🚹73/115 € 🚹🚹126/196 € ❄ 🚹98/178 € 🚹🚹156/316 € – 3 Suiten
Rest – *(geschl. März Montagmittag, Okt. Montagmittag)* Karte 17/43 €
◆ Der im Kern über 500 Jahre alte familiengeführte Gasthof mit mehreren Anbauten bietet solide eingerichtete Zimmer. Lage nahe dem See. Gewölbe und dunkles Holz prägen das Ambiente des Restaurants.

Heitzmann
Zim, Rest, P, VISA, AE

Weißgerbergasse 1 ✉ 5700 – ☎ (06542) 7 21 52 – office@zellamsee-hotel.at – Fax (06542) 7215233
geschl. 5. April – 17. Mai, 27. Sept. – 20. Dez. Z **s**
26 Zim (inkl. ½ P.) – ☼ 🚹77/93 € 🚹🚹132/162 € ❄ 🚹91/160 € 🚹🚹155/270 €
Rest – (nur Abendessen für Hausgäste)
◆ Mitten im Zentrum liegt das von der Familie geleitete Alpenhotel, dessen Gästezimmer wohnlich eingerichtet und z. T. recht verspielt dekoriert sind.

Sporthotel Alpin
Rest, P, VISA, AE

Gartenstr. 11 ✉ 5700 – ☎ (06542) 7 69 – welcome@sporthotelalpin.com – Fax (06542) 76971
geschl. Ende März – Mitte Mai, Mitte Okt. – Mitte Dez. Z **g**
40 Zim (inkl. ½ P.) – ☼ 🚹125/148 € 🚹🚹231/255 € ❄ 🚹138/209 € 🚹🚹235/379 €
Rest – (nur für Hausgäste)
◆ Für Skifans ideale Lage an der Skipiste und der Talstation der Zeller Bergbahn. Recht einheitlich geschnittene Zimmer mit solider Ausstattung. Restaurant im Stil der für die Region typischen traditionellen Gaststuben.

Der Waldhof
(geheizt) Rest, P, VISA

Schmittenstr. 47 (über Y) ✉ 5700 – ☎ (06542) 7 75 – waldhof@sbg.at – Fax (06542) 77528
geschl. Anfang Okt. – Anfang Dez.
79 Zim (inkl. ½ P.) – ☼ 🚹94/106 € 🚹🚹166/190 € ❄ 🚹119/180 € 🚹🚹188/310 €
Rest – (nur für Hausgäste)
◆ Ein gestandenes Hotel im alpenländischen Stil etwas außerhalb des Zentrums. Sehr komfortabel: die Juniorsuiten im modernen Gästehaus gegenüber. Im Sommer all inclusive.

Landgasthof Stadt Wien
(geheizt) Spa, Zim, P

Schmittenstr. 41 (über Y) ✉ 5700 – ☎ (06542) 7 62 – hotel@hotel-stadtwien.at – Fax (06542) 76251
geschl. 6. April – 1. Mai, Nov. – 1. Dez.
57 Zim (inkl. ½ P.) – ☼ 🚹66/116 € 🚹🚹126/231 € ❄ 🚹94/151 € 🚹🚹158/302 €
Rest – (nur für Hausgäste)
◆ Eine angenehm unkomplizierte und lockere Atmosphäre sowie wohnlich-funktionelle Zimmer verschiedener Kategorien sprechen für den Familienbetrieb etwas außerhalb des Zentrums.

St. Georg Rest,

Schillerstr. 32 (über Y) ✉ 5700 – ✆ (06542) 7 68 – st.georg@zell-am-see.at – Fax (06542) 768300
geschl. Mitte April – Mitte Mai, Mitte Okt. – Ende Nov.
38 Zim (inkl. ½ P.) – ☼ 56/79 € 112/157 € ❄ 84/143 € 168/286 €
Rest – *(nur Abendessen)* Karte 24/36 €
◆ Für die Region typisches Hotel mit unterschiedlich geschnittenen, funktionell eingerichteten Zimmern. Die Zeller Bergbahn liegt praktisch vor der Haustür.

Grüner Baum (mit Gästehaus)

Seegasse 1 ✉ 5700 – ✆ (06542) 77 10 – hotel@gruener-baum.at – Fax (06542) 47188 Y **m**
53 Zim (inkl. ½ P.) – ☼ 54/59 € 94/112 € ❄ 62/80 € 102/144 €
Rest – Karte 15/32 €
◆ Mitten im Zentrum, in der Fußgängerzone angesiedeltes Hotel mit drei Teilhäusern. Gepflegte Zimmer mit teils hellem, teils dunklem Mobiliar. Restaurant im gemütlichen Wirtshausstil.

Gasthof Steinerwirt mit Zim Zim, Zim,

Dreifaltigkeitsgasse 2 ✉ 5700 – ✆ (06542) 7 25 02 – office@steinerwirt.com – Fax (06542) 7250247
geschl. Juni Z **p**
28 Zim (inkl. ½ P.) – ☼ 45/65 € 90/130 € ❄ 55/78 € 110/156 €
Rest – Karte 14/35 €
◆ Historischer Gasthof a. d. J. 1493 im Zentrum: Das Ambiente der unterteilten Stuben reicht von urig-gemütlich bis rustikal-bürgerlich. Hübscher Gastgarten mit Kastanienbäumen. Moderne Gästezimmer.

In Zell-Prielau **Nord: 2 km über Loferer Bundesstraße Y, dann Richtung Thumersbach:**

Schloss Prielau Zim,

Hofmannsthalstr. 12 ✉ 5700 – ✆ (06542) 72 91 10 – info@schloss-prielau.at – Fax (06542) 7291111
geschl. Nov.
10 Zim – 110/130 € 220/260 € – ½ P 25 €
Rest *Mayer's* – separat erwähnt
Rest *Schlossküche* – *(geschl. Dienstag, nur Mittagessen)* Karte 19/40 €
◆ Ein Privatpark mit Wildgehege gehört zu diesem schönen Anwesen, das durch persönliche Gästebetreuung und sehr hübsche, behagliche Zimmer mit antiken Möbelstücken überzeugt. Gemütlich ist die Schlossküche mit internationalen Gerichten und Brotzeiten bis 18 Uhr.

Mayer's – Hotel Schloss Prielau

Hofmannsthalstr. 12 ✉ 5700 – ✆ (06542) 72 91 10 – info@schloss-prielau.at – Fax (06542) 729111
geschl. Nov.
Rest – *(geschl. Dienstag, Montag – Freitag nur Abendessen)* (Tischbestellung ratsam) Menü 68/98 €
Spez. Variation von der Gänseleber. Gebratenes Zanderfilet mit Kalbsschwanztapioka und Meerrettichschaum. Zweierlei vom Kalb mit Petersilienpüree und Trüffelschaum.
◆ Dieses Restaurant bietet in eleganter Atmosphäre eine modern interpretierte klassische Küche. Freundlicher und kompetenter Service.

In Zell-Schüttdorf Süd: 1,5 km über Brucker Bundesstraße Z:

Sporthotel Alpenblick (geheizt) Zim, Rest,

Alte Landesstr. 6
✉ 5700 – ✆ (06542) 54 33 – hotel@alpenblick.at – Fax (06542) 54331
geschl. April
100 Zim (inkl. ½ P.) – ☼ 65/77 € 130/202 € ❄ 113/152 € 150/218 € – 8 Suiten
Rest – Karte 20/45 €
♦ Das komfortable Ferienhotel mit über 500 Jahre altem Stammhaus bietet wohnliche, überwiegend großzügig geschnittene Zimmer und einen neuzeitlichen Wellnessbereich auf 1100 qm. Die kleine Turmstube dient als A-la-carte-Restaurant.

Mavida

Kirchenweg 11 ✉ 5700 – ✆ (06542) 54 10 – info@mavida.at – Fax (06542) 56760
47 Zim – ☼ 115/125 € 210/250 € ❄ 135/185 € 250/370 € – ½ P 25 €
Rest – Karte 32/46 €
♦ Vom Empfang bis in die technisch sehr gut ausgestatteten Zimmer bestimmen heimische Naturmaterialien und modernes Design das Bild. Schön: der aufwändig gestaltete Spabereich. Geradliniger Stil und warme Töne im Restaurant. Mit begehbarem gläsernem Weinschrank.

amiamo – Familotel Zim, Rest,

Am Schüttgut 20 ✉ 5700 – ✆ (06542) 5 53 55 – hotel@amiamo.at – Fax (06542) 5535534
geschl. 5. April – 24. Mai, Nov. – 15. Dez.
40 Zim (inkl. ½ P.) – ☼ 57/79 € 126/178 € ❄ 82/120 € 194/262 €
Rest – (nur für Hausgäste)
♦ Das von der Porsche AG erbaute Haus liegt reizvoll direkt an der Piste und ist ganz auf Familien ausgelegt. Betreuung und eigener Speisesaal für Kinder. All-inclusive-Angebot.

In Zell-Thumersbach Nord-Ost: 4 km über Loferer Bundesstraße Y:

XX **Landhotel Erlhof** mit Zim

Erlhofweg 11 ✉ 5700 – ✆ (06542) 56 63 70 – erlhof@aon.at – Fax (06542) 5663763
geschl. Nov.
14 Zim – 57/70 € 100/140 € – ½ P 25 €
Rest – *(geschl. Mittwoch)* Menü 48 € – Karte 26/49 €
♦ Auf fast 1000 Jahre Geschichte kann das Gut in schöner Lage mit Blick auf See und Gebirge zurückschauen. In netten kleinen Stuben wird regional-klassische Küche serviert. Zum Übernachten stehen den Gästen im Landhausstil eingerichtete Zimmer zur Verfügung.

ZELL AM ZILLER – Tirol – 730 H7 – 1 890 Ew – Höhe 580 m – Wintersport: 2 505 m 5 45 7 E5

Wien 434 – Innsbruck 61 – Schwaz 32 – Wörgl 47
Dorfplatz 3a, ✉ 6280, ✆ (05282) 22 81, info@zell.at
Veranstaltungen 30.04. – 04.05.: Gauderfest
Kirche★
Gerlos-Alpenstraße★ – Zillertal★★

Theresa SPA-Wellness Hotel (geheizt)

Bahnhofstr. 15 Rest,

6280 – (05282) 2 28 60 – info@theresa.at – Fax (05282) 4235

geschl. Mitte April – Mitte Mai, Mitte Nov. – Mitte Dez.

60 Zim (inkl. ½ P.) – 146/224 € 237/299 € 164/242 € 272/429 € – 8 Suiten

Rest – (nur Abendessen für Hausgäste)

◆ Gewachsener Alpengasthof mit weit gefächertem Zimmerangebot von rustikal bis klassisch-gediegen. Schön: der großzügig angelegte Wellnessbereich.

Bräu

Dorfplatz 1 6280 – (05282) 2 31 30 – info@hotel-braue.com – Fax (05282) 231317

geschl. 25. März – Anfang Mai, Nov.

40 Zim (inkl. ½ P.) – 51/80 € 112/160 € 62/107 € 124/214 €

Rest – Karte 14/40 €

◆ Ein über 500 Jahre alter Gasthof im Zentrum mit hauseigener Brauerei. Die Zimmer unterscheiden sich in Einrichtung und Größe, z. T. im historischen Stil gehalten. Das Restaurant: drei gemütlich-rustikale Stuben mit Kachelofen.

Englhof

Zellbergeben 17 6280 – (05282) 31 34 – info@englhof.at – Fax (05282) 3135

geschl. 13. April – 1. Mai, 12. Okt. – 20. Dez.

30 Zim (inkl. ½ P.) – 49/60 € 92/104 € 61/72 € 116/128 €

Rest – *(nur Abendessen für Hausgäste)* Karte 18/36 €

◆ Individuell eingerichtete Zimmer, teils mit Möbeln aus rustikaler Eiche, teils mit hellem Naturholz, bietet das solide, familiengeführte Haus. Restaurant mit hübschem Dekor im ländlichen Stil.

Dieser Führer lebt von Ihren Anregungen, die uns stets willkommen sind. Egal ob Sie uns eine besonders angenehme Überraschung oder eine Enttäuschung mitteilen wollen – schreiben Sie uns!

ZELTWEG – Steiermark – 730 Q7 – 7 840 Ew – Höhe 650 m 10 J5

Wien 198 – Graz 76 – Leoben 38 – Judenburg 10

Hubertus-Hof

Bahnhofstr. 81 8740 – (03577) 2 23 15 – empfang@hotelhubertushof.at – Fax (03577) 2231531

geschl. 22. – 25. Dez.

21 Zim – 49/59 € 96/116 € – ½ P 12 €

Rest – *(geschl. Juli – August Sonn-und Feietage abends)* Menü 27 € – Karte 14/36 €

◆ Das Hotel befindet sich gegenüber dem Bahnhof und verfügt über gepflegte, funktionell eingerichtete Gästezimmer mit Schallschutzfenstern. Zum Restaurant gehört ein netter Gastgarten mit Kastanien.

Im Schloss Farrach West: 2,5 km:

Schlosstaverne
Schlossweg 13 ✉ 8740 Zeltweg – ✆ (03577) 2 52 57 – schloss-taverne@aon.at – Fax (03577) 2525724
geschl. 1. – 7. Jan., Juli 1 Woche und Montag
Rest – (Tischbestellung ratsam) Menü 23/45 € – Karte 23/41 €
♦ Dieses Schloss a. d. J. 1670 mit seiner schönen Mosaikfassade bietet einen stilvollen Rahmen, z. T. mit historischem Kreuzgewölbe. Freundlich leitet die Chefin den Service.

ZIRL – Tirol – 730 F7 – 6 120 Ew – Höhe 620 m – Wintersport: 6 D5

Wien 457 – Innsbruck 13 – Seefeld 13 – Imst 47
Dorfplatz 3, ✉ 6170, ✆ (05238) 5 22 35, innsbruck-west@netway.at

Tyrolis
Meilstr. 36 ✉ 6170 – ✆ (05238) 5 15 54 – hotel@tyrolis.com – Fax (05238) 51552
27 Zim – 48/69 € 79/158 €
Rest – *(geschl. Montag)* Karte 19/36 €
♦ Von der Fassade über den schönen Empfangsbereich bis in die hochwertig eingerichteten Zimmer ist dieses Haus ganz im Tiroler Stil gehalten. Holztäfelung und eine aufwändig gearbeitete Holzdecke bestimmen im Restaurant das Bild. Bürgerliche Küche.

Sie suchen ein besonderes Hotel für einen sehr angenehmen Aufenthalt?
Reservieren Sie in einem roten Haus: ... .

ZISTERSDORF – Niederösterreich – 730 W3 – 5 640 Ew – Höhe 200 m 4 L1

Wien 61 – St. Pölten 119 – Stockerau 64 – Bratislava 74
Niedersulz (Weinviertler Museumsdorf★) Süd-West: 10 km

Zum grünen Baum
Landstr. 1 ✉ 2225 – ✆ (02532) 8 15 55 – gasthaus@gmx.at
geschl. Samstag, Sonntagabends
Rest – Karte 12/32 €
♦ Einfaches, schnörkelloses, aber dennoch gepflegtes Dekor machen den Reiz dieses Dorfwirtshauses aus. Bei schönem Wetter bewirtet man Sie auch auf der hübschen Terrasse.

ZÖBLEN – Tirol – 730 D6 – 250 Ew – Höhe 1 100 m – Wintersport: 1 500 m 3 5 B5

Wien 530 – Innsbruck 117 – Reutte 28 – Sonthofen 20

Wildanger garni
Zöbeln 55 ✉ 6677 – ✆ (05675) 66 85 – info@wildanger.com – Fax (05675) 668577
23 Zim – 47/63 € 70/82 €
♦ Die Zimmer in diesem Haus sind mit hellem Naturholz wohnlich eingerichtet. Der rustikale Frühstücksraum mit netter Sicht dient am Tag als Café. Kleine Gerichte für Hausgäste.

ZÜRS AM ARLBERG – Vorarlberg – siehe Lech am Arlberg

ZWETTL – Niederösterreich – 730 R3 – 11 630 Ew – Höhe 520 m 3 J2

Wien 124 – St. Pölten 73 – Krems 50 – Gmünd 27

Hauptplatz 4, ✉ 3910, ✆ (02822) 50 31 29, touristinfo.zwettl@wvnet.at

Weitra, Hausschachen 313 ✆ (02856) 20 58

Stift Zwettl★ Ost: 3 km – Burg Rapottenstein★ Süd-West: 15 km

In Zwettl-Friedersbach Süd-Ost: 8 km über B 38 Richtung Krems:

Schweighofer Zim,
Friedersbach 53 ✉ 3533 VISA AE
– ✆ (02822) 77 51 10 – rezeption@hotel-schweighofer.at
– Fax (02822) 7751154
geschl. 13. – 18. Feb.
45 Zim – 53/64 € 90/116 € – ½ P 13 €
Rest – *(geschl. Jan. – März Sonntagabend – Montag)* Karte 16/35 €
♦ Aus einer kleinen Pferdestation mit Postamt ist in mehr als 100 Jahren dieser Landgasthof gewachsen. Es erwarten Sie ein großzügiger Hallenbereich und unterschiedliche Zimmer. Die urig-gemütliche Zirbelstube ist das Herzstück des Restaurants.

In Zwettl-Geschwendt Süd-West: 3,5 km über B 36 Richtung Ottenschlag, nach 2 km rechts:

Schwarz-Alm VISA
Almweg 1 ✉ 3910 – ✆ (02822) 5 31 73 – info@schwarzalm.at
– Fax (02822) 5317311
38 Zim – 72 € 120/128 € – ½ P 16 €
Rest – Karte 14/32 €
♦ Von einer Almhütte entwickelte sich dieses Anwesen im Grünen zum Seminarhotel, das nach Feng-Shui-Grundsätzen funktionell und wohnlich zugleich eingerichtet ist. In mehrere verschiedene Bereiche unterteiltes Restaurant, z. T. mit schönem Ausblick auf die Landschaft.

In Zwettl-Schloss Rosenau Süd-West: 8 km Richtung Weitra, nach 3 km links:

Schlosshotel Rosenau
Schloss Rosenau 1 ✉ 3924 VISA AE
– ✆ (02822) 58 22 10 – schloss.rosenau@wvnet.at – Fax (02822) 582218
geschl. 7. – 31. Jan.
17 Zim – 78/98 € 140/184 € – ½ P 25 € – 3 Suiten
Rest – Karte 23/42 €
♦ Das Renaissanceschloss a. d. J. 1593 besticht mit sehr individuellen, geschmackvollen Zimmern, schönen Veranstaltungsräumen und der reizvollen Lage. Freimaurermuseum im Haus. Im Restaurant: historische Gewölbedecken und angenehm schlichtes Dekor.

→ *Die besten Restaurants entdecken ?*
→ *Das nächst gelegene Hotel finden ?*
→ *Ein Haus auf den Karten suchen ?*
→ *Unsere Symbole verstehen…*

Folgen Sie dem roten Bib !

Der Rat des **Koch-Bib** zu unseren Restaurantempfehlungen.

Die Informationen und kleinen Tips des augenzwinkernden **cleveren Bib** um sich unterwegs zurechtzufinden.

Der Rat des **Pagen-Bib** zu unseren Hotelempfehlungen.

Ferientermine 2008
(Angegeben ist jeweils der erste und letzte Tag der Ferien)

Vacances scolaires
(Premier et dernier jour de vacances)

School holidays
(Dates of holidays)

Vacanze scolastiche
(primo ed ultimo giorno di vacanza)

	Winter	Semester	Ostern	Pfingsten	Sommer
Burgenland	24.12. - 06.01.	11.02 - 16.02.	15.03. - 25.03.	10.05. - 13.05.	28.06. - 30.08.
Kärnten	24.12. - 06.01.	18.02. - 23.02.	15.03. - 25.03.	10.05. - 13.05.	05.07. - 06.09.
Niederösterreich	24.12. - 06.01.	11.02. - 16.02.	15.03. - 25.03.	10.05. - 13.05.	28.06. - 30.08.
Oberösterreich	24.12. - 06.01.	18.02. - 23.02.	15.03. - 25.03.	10.05. - 13.05.	05.07. - 06.09.
Salzburg	24.12. - 06.01.	18.02. - 23.02.	15.03. - 25.03.	10.05. - 13.05.	05.07. - 06.09.
Steiermark	24.12. - 06.01.	18.02. - 23.02.	15.03. - 25.03.	10.05. - 13.05.	05.07. - 06.09.
Tirol	24.12. - 06.01.	18.02. - 23.02.	15.03. - 25.03.	10.05. - 13.05.	05.07. - 06.09.
Vorarlberg	24.12. - 06.01.	11.02. - 16.02.	15.03. - 25.03.	10.05. - 13.05.	05.07. - 06.09.
Wien	24.12. - 06.01.	11.02. - 16.02.	15.03. - 25.03.	10.05. - 13.05.	28.06. - 30.08.

Gesetzliche Feiertage 2008

01.01.	Neujahr	**15.08.**	Mariä Himmelfahrt
06.01.	Heilige Drei Könige	**26.10.**	Nationalfeiertag
24.03.	Ostermontag	**01.11.**	Allerheiligen
01.05.	Tag der Arbeit	**08.12.**	Mariä Empfängnis
01.05.	Christi Himmelfahrt	**25.12.**	1. Weihnachtsfeiertag (Christtag)
12.05.	Pfingstmontag	**26.12.**	2. Weihnachtsfeiertag (Stephanitag)
22.05.	Fronleichnam		

Entfernungen

EINIGE ERKLÄRUNGEN

In jedem Ortstext finden Sie Entfernungen zur Bundeshauptstadt, zur Landeshauptstadt sowie zu den nächstgrößeren Städten in der Umgebung. Die Kilometerangaben der Tabelle ergänzen somit die Angaben des Ortstextes. Da die Entfernung von einer Stadt zu einer anderen nicht immer unter beiden Städten zugleich aufgeführt ist, sehen Sie bitte unter beiden entsprechenden Ortstexten nach. Eine weitere Hilfe sind auch die am Rande der Stadtpläne erwähnten Kilometerangaben. Die Entfernungen gelten ab Stadtmitte unter Berücksichtigung der günstigsten (nicht immer kürzesten) Strecke.

Distances

QUELQUES PRÉCISIONS

Au texte de chaque localité vous trouverez la distance de la capitale, de la capitale du « Land » et des villes environnantes. Les distances intervilles du tableau les complètent. La distance d'une localité à une autre n'est pas toujours répétée en sens inverse : voyez au texte de l'une ou l'autre. Utilisez aussi les distances portées en bordure des plans. Les distances sont comptées à partir du centre-ville et par la route la plus pratique, c'est-à-dire celle qui offre les meilleures conditions de roulage, mais qui n'est pas nécessairement la plus courte.

Distances

COMMENTARY

The text on each town includes its distances to the capital, to the "land" capital and to its neighbours. The distances in the table complete those given under individual town headings for calculating total distances. To avoid excessive repetition some distances have only been quoted once, you may, therefore, have to look under both town headings. Note also that some distances appear in the margins of the town plans. Distances are calculated from centres and along the best roads from a motoring point of view - not necessarily the shortest.

Distanze

QUALCHE CHIARIMENTO

Nel testo di ciascuna località troverete la distanza dalla capitale, dalla capitale del « land » e dalle città circostanti. Le distanze tra le città della tabella le completano. La distanza da una località ad un'altra non è sempre ripetuta in senso inverso : vedete al testo dell'una o dell'altra. Utilizzate anche le distanze riportate a margine delle piante. Le distanze sono calcolate a partire dal centro delle città e seguendo la strada più pratica, ossia quella che offre le migliori condizioni di viaggio, ma che non è necessariamente la più breve.

Entfernungen zwischen den größeren Städten
Distances entre principales villes
Distances between major towns
Distanze tra le principali città

	Bad Gastein	Bad Ischl	Baden	Bischofshofen	Eisenstadt	Feldkirch	Fürstenfeld	Gmunden	Graz	Innsbruck	Judenburg	Kitzbühel	Klagenfurt	Krems an der Donau	Kufstein	Leibnitz	Leoben	Lienz	Liezen	Linz	Reutte	Ried im Innkreis	Salzburg	Schärding	Seefeld in Tirol	Spittal an der Drau	St. Anton am Arlberg	St. Pölten	Steyr	Villach	Wels	Wien	Wiener Neustadt	Wolfsberg	Zell am See
Bad Ischl	120																																		
Baden	351	269																																	
Bischofshofen	46	79	309																																
Eisenstadt	354	287	35	313																															
Feldkirch	351	403	631	377	677																														
Fürstenfeld	322	256	133	281	135	647																													
Gmunden	176	34	236	132	282	411	284																												
Graz	258	191	170	217	172	583	60	220																											
Innsbruck	197	250	478	224	523	155	494	259	430																										
Judenburg	209	143	181	168	183	534	152	171	87	382																									
Kitzbühel	98	146	374	123	420	254	393	155	329	101	315																								
Klagenfurt	119	224	282	177	284	471	197	299	152	321	103	237																							
Krems an der Donau	370	244	93	326	138	605	242	212	280	452	289	351	384																						
Kufstein	194	176	404	150	450	229	421	185	356	77	342	37	317	379																					
Leibnitz	293	226	199	252	201	618	89	255	43	465	122	363	155	308	391																				
Leoben	223	157	135	182	137	548	132	185	67	395	52	294	147	244	321	104																			
Lienz	61	214	414	167	416	328	329	246	284	177	235	93	144	440	129	302	285																		
Liezen	140	73	213	99	215	465	184	110	119	312	106	210	158	250	238	157	84	221																	
Linz	236	111	188	192	233	472	290	78	225	319	211	217	263	162	245	262	190	309	112																
Reutte	288	289	517	263	563	152	534	298	469	93	456	192	409	492	167	506	434	266	351	358															
Ried im Innkreis	198	78	242	154	287	406	305	51	241	274	227	179	279	216	200	278	205	271	128	82	332														
Salzburg	95	56	300	50	346	336	348	81	284	183	270	79	217	275	109	321	248	209	138	141	223	104													
Schärding	219	157	273	175	318	396	336	125	271	264	258	196	310	247	190	309	236	288	159	113	322	42	124												
Seefeld in Tirol	219	271	500	246	545	142	516	280	452	24	438	122	340	474	98	489	417	196	333	340	80	298	208	286											
Spittal an der Drau	47	153	344	105	346	400	259	227	214	249	165	165	74	421	244	231	215	73	158	287	338	249	146	270	268										
St. Anton am Arlberg	293	346	574	320	620	68	591	355	526	98	512	197	414	549	172	563	491	271	408	415	94	373	282	360	85	343									
St. Pölten	336	210	67	292	112	571	216	177	254	418	263	317	358	36	344	283	218	409	212	129	458	185	238	213	440	387	515								
Steyr	230	105	167	186	212	466	257	72	192	313	179	211	231	141	239	230	157	302	80	51	353	107	133	136	334	239	409	107							
Villach	82	188	310	140	312	435	225	262	179	284	131	200	40	419	279	197	181	108	193	322	373	284	181	305	303	38	378	393	276						
Wels	207	82	202	163	247	443	261	49	196	290	182	189	235	176	216	233	161	281	84	42	330	52	110	81	312	258	386	142	47	294					
Wien	381	275	41	340	60	636	164	242	201	483	211	381	306	77	409	231	165	445	244	194	523	250	303	278	505	375	579	73	173	341	207				
Wiener Neustadt	327	261	32	286	30	652	110	284	147	499	156	398	251	141	425	176	111	390	189	236	539	292	345	320	521	320	595	115	215	287	249	61			
Wolfsberg	180	225	239	237	241	532	128	253	83	381	54	297	61	348	376	101	99	205	153	258	470	277	278	305	401	135	475	321	227	101	231	268	215		
Zell am See	49	125	354	49	357	307	325	157	261	154	247	55	221	351	91	298	226	92	142	217	246	179	84	198	176	150	251	317	212	185	189	377	330	283	
Zwettl	331	206	139	287	184	566	288	173	326	414	335	313	430	50	339	355	290	404	208	100	453	181	234	209	435	382	510	83	125	422	138	123	187	393	315

Leoben – Wien: 165 km

Karte der Wintersportorte

- ● Wintersportorte
- Seilbahn
- Autotransport per Bahn
- 11-5 Ggf. Wintersperre. (Bsp.: Nov.-Mai)

Cartes des stations de sports d'hiver

- ● Stations de sports d'hiver
- Téléphérique
- Transport des autos par voie ferrrée
- 11-5 Fermeture possible en période d'enneigement *(ex : Nov.-Mai)*

Map of winter sports stations

- ● Winter sports resort
- Cablecar
- Transportation of vehicles by rail
- 11-5 Approximate period when roads are snowbound and possibly closed. (Ex: Nov.-May)

Carte delle stazioni di sport invernali

- ● Stazione di sport invernali
- Funivia
- Trasporto auto su treno
- 11-5 Chiusura possibile in periodo d'innevamento. (Esempio : Nov.-Maggio)

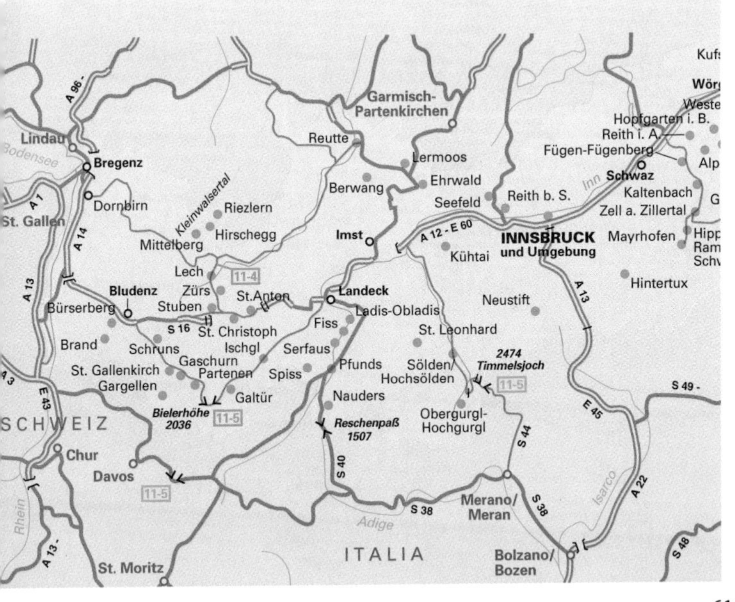

E 49
E 53
Vltava
E 56
Regen
Ceské Budejovice
A 3-
E 55
E 56
A 92
Freistadt
Passau
DONAU
Isar
Landshut
Schärding
A 7
DEUTSCHLAND
Inn
Eferding
LINZ
A 8
A 1 -
A 94
E 552
Braunau
Ried
i. Innkreis
E 56
Wels
Steyr
A 9
Vöcklabruck
Salzach
Gmunden
Enns
A 1
Grünau
im Almtal
Bad Ischl
SALZBURG
E 52 - 60
E 45 - 52
Hallein
Liezen
Tauplitz
A 93
Scheffau a. W. K.
Rußbach
Gosau
Bad Mitterndorf
Ellmau
Lofer
A 10
Going a. W. K.
Leogang
Pichl-Mandling
Annaberg
Ramsau a. D.
Kufstein
St. Johann i. T.
Saalfelden
Aich-Assach
Maria Alm
Filzmoos
E 651
Söll
Oberndorf
Haus im Ennstal
Wörgl
Mühlbach
a. H.
Bischofs-
hofen
Reith b. K.
Schladming
Kitzbühel
Westendorf
Rohrmoos
Brixen
im Thale
Kirchberg
in T.
Saalbach-
Hinterglemm
Dienten a. H.
Altenmarkt-Zauchensee
arten i. B.
Wildschönau
St. Johann i. P.
Flachau
Obertauern
Zell am See
Alpbach
Wagrain
Dorfgastein
Neukirchen
a. G.
A 10
Tamsweg
Mittersill
Kaprun
Rauris
Großarl
nbach
lertal
Gerlos
Wald im Pinzgau
Bad Hofgastein
Mur
St. Michael
im Lungau
Krimml
Großglockner-
Hochalpenstraße
2505
11-4
Bad Gastein
fen
Hippach,
Ramsau,
Schwendau
ertux
Heiligenblut
Turracher Höhe
Flattach
St. Jakob
in Defereggen
Bad
Kleinkirchheim
Feldkirchen
i. Karnten
Lienz
Spittal
a. d. Drau
Drau
Treffen
S 49 -
A 10
Ossiach
a. S.
E 66
Hermago
Villach
12-4
Gail
S 51
Plöckenpaß
1360
Sonnalpe
Naßfeld
201
A 2
Jesenice
Cortina
d'Ampezzo
S 528
ITALIA
A 23
- E 55
S 48
S 51
Tagliamento
Piave

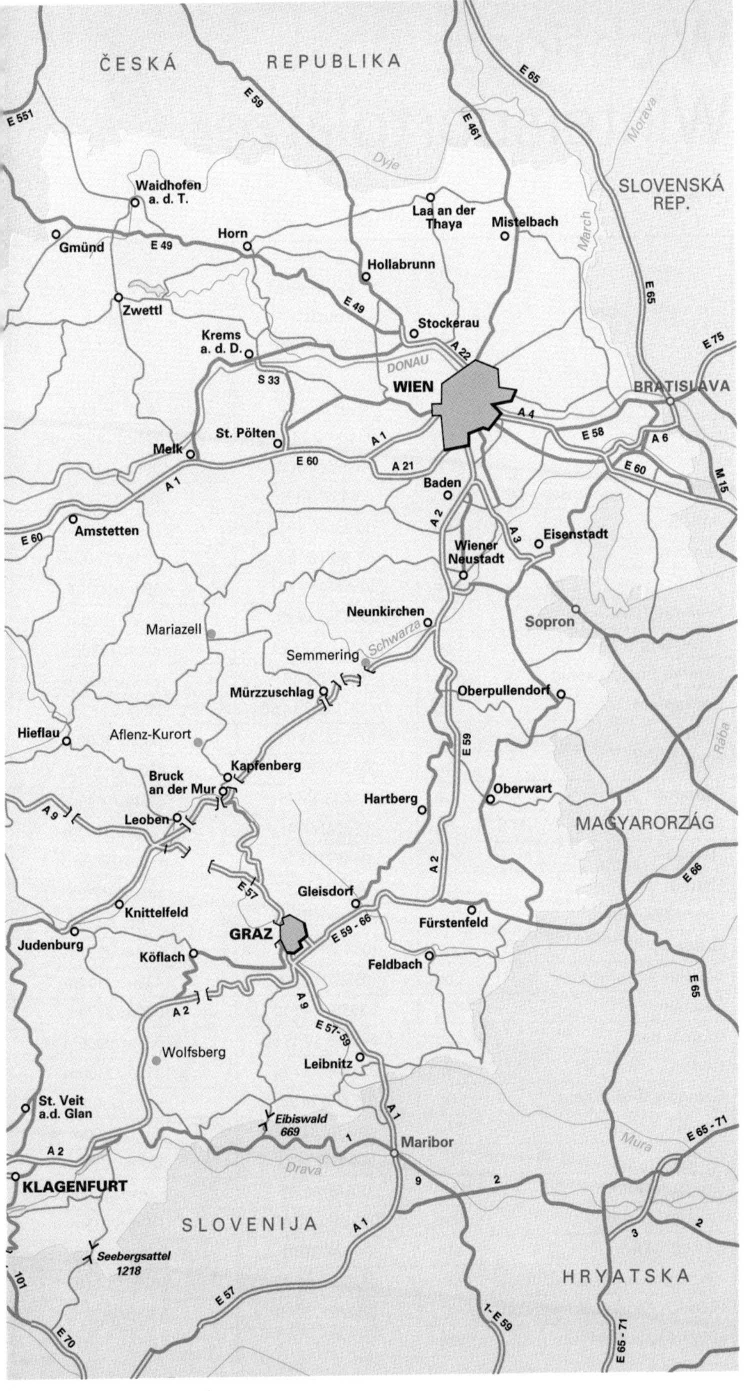

ČESKÁ REPUBLIKA
SLOVENSKÁ REP.
MAGYARORZÁG
SLOVENIJA
HRYATSKA
WIEN
GRAZ
BRATISLAVA
KLAGENFURT
Waidhofen a. d. T.
Gmünd
Horn
Zwettl
Krems a. d. D.
Laa an der Thaya
Mistelbach
Hollabrunn
Stockerau
DONAU
Melk
St. Pölten
Amstetten
Baden
Eisenstadt
Wiener Neustadt
Neunkirchen
Sopron
Mariazell
Semmering
Schwarza
Mürzzuschlag
Oberpullendorf
Hieflau
Aflenz-Kurort
Kapfenberg
Bruck an der Mur
Leoben
Hartberg
Oberwart
Gleisdorf
Knittelfeld
Judenburg
Fürstenfeld
Köflach
Feldbach
Wolfsberg
Leibnitz
St. Veit a.d. Glan
Eibiswald 669
Maribor
Drava
Mura
Seebergsattel 1218
Dyje
Morava
March
Rába

Wichtigste Wintersportplätze

Ort	Bundesland	Telefon (Tourist-Information)	Höhe
Aflenz-Kurort	Stm	(03861) 37 00	765m/1810m
Aich-Assach	Stm	(03686) 2 23 40	694m/2015m
Alpbach	Tir	(05336) 60 00	1000m/2100m
Altenmarkt-Zauchensee	Sbg	(06452) 56 11	856m/2130m
Annaberg	Sbg	(06243) 40 40 57	777m/1618m
Berwang	Tir	(05674) 82 68	1336m/1740m
Brand	Vbg	(05559) 55 50	1050m/2000m
Brixen im Thale	Tir	(05334) 84 33	800m/1829m
Bürserberg	Vbg	(05552) 6 33 17	900m/1850m
Dienten am Hochkönig	Sbg	(06461) 2 63	1071m/1826m
Dorfgastein	Sbg	(06432) 3 39 34 60	835m/2033m
Ehrwald	Tir	(05673) 23 95	1000m/3000m
Ellmau	Tir	(05358) 23 01	820m/1550m
Filzmoos	Sbg	(06453) 82 35	1054m/1645m
Fiss	Tir	(05476) 64 41	1436m/2700m
Flachau	Sbg	(06457) 22 14	925m/1980m
Flattach	Ktn	(04785) 6 15	699m/3120m
Fügen-Fügenberg	Tir	(05288) 6 22 62	550m/2400m
Galtür	Tir	(05443) 85 21	1584m/2297m
Gargellen	Vbg	(05557) 63 03	1430m/2300m
Gaschurn	Vbg	(05558) 8 20 10	1000m/2370m
Gastein, Bad	Sbg	(06432) 3 39 35 60	1083m/2686m
Gerlos	Tir	(05284) 5 24 40	1250m/2300m
Going am Wilden Kaiser	Tir	(05358) 24 38	800m/1500m
Gosau	Ooe	(06136) 82 95	756m/1800m
Großarl	Sbg	(06414) 2 81	920m/2033m
Grünau im Almtal	Ooe	(07616) 82 68	527m/1600m
Haus im Ennstal	Stm	(03686) 2 23 40	740m/2015m
Heiligenblut	Ktn	(04824) 20 01	1301m/2912m
Hermagor (Sonnalpe Naßfeld)	Ktn	(04282) 2 04 30	600m/2000m
Hippach, Ramsau, Schwendau	Tir	(05282) 25 93	600m/1830m
Hirschegg (s. Kleinwalsertal)	Vbg		

Principales stations de sports d'hiver
Main winter sport stations
Principali stazioni di sport invernali

Seilbahn	Lift	Abfahrt	Loipen	Eisbahn	Rodelbahn	Pferdeschlitten	Ort
0	8	20	10	X	X	X	Aflenz-Kurort
2	13	35	40	X		X	Aich-Assach
1	18	45	22	X	X	X	Alpbach
3	20	150	150	X	X	X	Altenmarkt-Zauchensee
2	31	65	25		X	X	Annaberg
	12	40	27	X	X	X	Berwang
	13	50	16		X	X	Brand
9	84	250	44	X	X	X	Brixen im Thale
	13	50	15		X		Bürserberg
1	17	80	7		X		Dienten am Hochkönig
4	16	80	20		X	X	Dorfgastein
1	10	45	60	X		X	Ehrwald
10	104	285	80	X	X	X	Ellmau
1	11	32	35		X	X	Filzmoos
9	31	160	55	X	X	X	Fiss
9	44	220	150	X	X	X	Flachau
2	9	49	28	X	X		Flattach
3	16	48	30	X	X	X	Fügen-Fügenberg
	10	40	45	X	X	X	Galtür
1	7	33					Gargellen
4	24	110	30	X	X	X	Gaschurn
7	20	150	31	X	X	X	Gastein, Bad
3	41	115	25	X	X	X	Gerlos
1	25	52	35	X	X	X	Going am Wilden Kaiser
2	35	80	50			X	Gosau
4	17	80	17	X	X	X	Groβarl
1	13	40	20	X	X		Grünau im Almtal
2	13	35	40	X		X	Haus im Ennstal
3	11	55	53	X	X	X	Heiligenblut
5	25	101	100	X	X	X	Hermagor (Sonnalpe Naβfeld)
1	13	20	21	X	X		Hippach, Ramsau, Schwendau
							Hirschegg (s. Kleinwalsertal)

Ort	Bundesland	Telefon (Tourist-Information)	Höhe
Hofgastein, Bad	Sbg	(06432) 33 93	870m/2300m
Hopfgarten im Brixental	Tir	(05335) 23 22	620m/1825m
Innsbruck und Umgebung	Tir	(0512) 59 85 00	575m/2256m
Ischgl	Tir	(05444) 5 26 60	1377m/2872m
Kaltenbach	Tir	(05283) 22 18	558m/2300m
Kaprun	Sbg	(06547) 7 70	800m/3029m
Kirchberg in Tirol	Tir	(05357) 23 09	860m/1995m
Kitzbühel	Tir	(05356) 7 77	800m/2000m
Kleinkirchheim, Bad	Ktn	(04240) 82 12	1100m/2055m
Kleinwalsertal (Hirschegg, Mittelberg, Riezlern)	Vbg	(05517) 5 11 40	1100m/2080m
Krimml	Sbg	(06564) 7 23 90	1076m/2040m
Kühtai	Tir	(05239) 52 22	2020m/2520m
Kufstein	Tir	(05372) 6 22 07	503m/1900m
Ladis-Obladis	Tir	(05472) 66 01	1200m/2540m
Lech und Zürs	Vbg	(05583) 2 16 10	1450m/2444m
Leogang	Sbg	(06583) 82 34	800m/1914m
Lermoos	Tir	(05673) 2 40 11 00	1004m/2250m
Lienz	Tir	(04852) 6 52 65	673m/2290m
Lofer	Sbg	(06588) 8 32 10	640m/1747m
Maria Alm	Sbg	(06584) 78 16	800m/2000m
Mariazell	Stm	(03882) 23 66	864m/1635m
Mayrhofen	Tir	(05285) 67 60	680m/2250m
Mittelberg (s. Kleinwalsertal)	Vbg		
Mitterndorf, Bad	Stm	(03623) 24 44	812m/1965m
Mittersill	Sbg	(06562) 42 92	790m/1894m
Mühlbach am Hochkönig	Sbg	(06467) 72 35	854m/1826m
Nauders	Tir	(05473) 8 72 20	1394m/2750m
Neukirchen am Grossvenediger	Sbg	(06565) 65 50 74	856m/2150m
Neustift	Tir	(05226) 22 28	1000m/3250m
Obergurgl-Hochgurgl	Tir	(05256) 64 66	1990m/3080m
Oberndorf	Tir	(05352) 6 29 27	700m/1466m
Obertauern	Sbg	(06456) 72 52	1750m/2335m
Ossiach am See	Ktn	(04243) 4 97	510m/1911m
Partenen	Vbg	(05558) 8 31 50	1050m/2370m
Pfunds-Spiss	Tir	(05474) 52 29	970m/2850m
Pichl-Mandling	Stm	(06454) 73 80	841m/2000m
Ramsau (s. Hippach)	Tir		
Ramsau am Dachstein	Stm	(03687) 8 18 33	1100m/2700m
Rauris	Sbg	(06544) 2 00 22	952m/2200m
Reith bei Kitzbühel	Tir	(05356) 7 77 35	800m/2000m

Seilbahn	Lift	Abfahrt	Loipen	Eisbahn	Rodelbahn	Pferdeschlitten	Ort
5	16	150	21	X	X		Hofgastein, Bad
9	84	250	11	X	X	X	Hopfgarten im Brixental
3	7	25	12	X	X	X	Innsbruck und Umgebung
5	36	200	48	X	X	X	Ischgl
2	16	86	41	X		X	Kaltenbach
6	22	55	18	X	X		Kaprun
5	55	158	45	X	X	X	Kirchberg in Tirol
5	55	164	120	X	X	X	Kitzbühel
4	22	90	16	X	X	X	Kleinkirchheim, Bad
2	34	120	42	X	X	X	Kleinwalsertal (Hirschegg, Mittelberg, Riezlern)
4	61	155	40	X	X	X	Krimml
9	85	250	30	X	X	X	Kühtai
	11	40	30	X	X	X	Kufstein
9	33	160	111	X	X		Ladis-Obladis
5	28	110	23	X	X	X	Lech und Zürs
11	45	200	38		X	X	Leogang
1	8	30	103	X	X	X	Lermoos
1	16	41	110	X	X		Lienz
2	12	46	34	X	X		Lofer
3	31	150	33		X	X	Maria Alm
1	4	11	88	X	X	X	Mariazell
7	39	148	20	X	X	X	Mayrhofen
							Mittelberg (s. Kleinwalsertal)
	21	25	75	X	X	X	Mitterndorf, Bad
	15	25	44	X	X	X	Mittersill
1	22	80	12	X	X	X	Mühlbach am Hochkönig
3	27	111	80	X	X	X	Nauders
2	12	35	35	X	X	X	Neukirchen am Grossvenediger
4	24	67	40	X	X	X	Neustift
2	21	110	12	X			Obergurgl-Hochgurgl
2	15	60	25		X	X	Oberndorf
1	27	100	18		X	X	Obertauern
1	18	37	180	X	X		Ossiach am See
4	24	110	30	X	X	X	Partenen
3	25	110	115	X	X	X	Pfunds-Spiss
1	18	36	20	X	X	X	Pichl-Mandling
							Ramsau (s. Hippach)
1	17	30	155		X	X	Ramsau am Dachstein
2	8	30	42			X	Rauris
5	59	159	40	X	X	X	Reith bei Kitzbühel

Ort	Bundesland	Telefon (Tourist-Information)	Höhe
Reith bei Seefeld	Tir	(05212) 31 14	1130m/2100m
Reith im Alpbachtal	Tir	(05337) 6 26 74	640m/2025m
Reutte	Tir	(05672) 6 23 36	851m/1900m
Riezlern (s. Kleinwalsertal)	Vbg		
Rohrmoos	Stm	(03687) 2 27 77	869m/1850m
Rußbach	Sbg	(06242) 5 77	817m/1618m
Saalbach-Hinterglemm	Sbg	(06541) 6 80 00	1003m/2100m
Saalfelden	Sbg	(06582) 7 06 60	744m/1550m
Sankt Anton/Sankt Christoph	Tir	(05446) 2 26 90	1304m/2810m
Sankt Christoph (s. Sankt Anton)	Tir		
Sankt Gallenkirch	Vbg	(05557) 6 60 00	900m/2370m
Sankt Jakob in Defereggen	Tir	(04873) 6 36 00	1398m/2520m
Sankt Johann im Pongau	Sbg	(06412) 60 36	600m/1850m
Sankt Johann in Tirol	Tir	(05352) 63 33 50	680m/1700m
Sankt Leonhard	Tir	(05413) 8 50 50	1370m/3440m
Sankt Michael im Lungau	Sbg	(06477) 89 13	1075m/2360m
Scheffau am Wilden Kaiser	Tir	(05358) 73 73	752m/1800m
Schladming	Stm	(03687) 2 27 77	750m/1894m
Schruns	Vbg	(05556) 72 16 60	700m/2380m
Schwendau (s. Hippach)	Tir		
Seefeld	Tir	(05212) 23 13	1200m/2100m
Semmering	Noe	(02664) 2 00 25	1000m/1340m
Serfaus	Tir	(05476) 6 23 90	1427m/2700m
Sölden/Hochsölden	Tir	(05254) 51 00	1377m/3250m
Söll	Tir	(05333) 52 16	703m/1829m
Sonnalpe Nassfeld (s. Hermagor)	Ktn		
Spittal an der Drau	Ktn	(04762) 5 65 02 20	556m/2142m
Stuben	Vbg	(05582) 3 99	1409m/2800m
Tauplitz	Stm	(03688) 2 44 60	900m/2000m
Treffen	Ktn	(04248) 23 36	545m/2000m
Turracher Höhe	Ktn/Stm	(04275) 83 92	1763m/2200m
Tux, Hintertux	Tir	(05287) 85 06	1500m/3250m
Wagrain	Sbg	(06413) 84 48	850m/2014m
Wald im Pinzgau	Sbg	(06565) 8 24 30	885m/2300m
Westendorf	Tir	(05334) 62 30	800m/1865m
Wildschönau	Tir	(05339) 82 55	828m/1903m
Wolfsberg	Ktn	(04352) 33 40	490m/2100m
Zell am See	Sbg	(06542) 7 70	757m/1969m
Zell im Zillertal	Tir	(05282) 22 81	580m/2408m
Zürs (s. Lech)	Vbg		

Seilbahn	Lift	Abfahrt	Loipen	Eisbahn	Rodelbahn	Pferdeschlitten	Ort
2	15	21	240	X	X		Reith bei Seefeld
1	23	45	15	X	X	X	Reith im Alpbachtal
1	8	19	180	X	X	X	Reutte
							Riezlern (s. Kleinwalsertal)
12	12	70	60	X	X	X	Rohrmoos
2	31	65	5		X	X	Rußbach
11	44	200	11	X	X	X	Saalbach-Hinterglemm
	3	3	80	X	X	X	Saalfelden
11	74	260	22	X	X	X	Sankt Anton/Sankt Christoph
							Sankt Christoph (s. Sankt Anton)
4	24	110	30		X	X	Sankt Gallenkirch
1	8	34	75	X	X	X	Sankt Jakob in Defereggen
2	17	70	10	X	X	X	Sankt Johann im Pongau
3	14	60	70	X	X	X	Sankt Johann in Tirol
3	9	50	20	X	X	X	Sankt Leonhard
1	24	105	39	X	X	X	Sankt Michael im Lungau
9	84	250	70	X	X		Scheffau am Wilden Kaiser
4	20	53	20	X	X	X	Schladming
3	9	47	14	X	X	X	Schruns
							Schwendau (s. Hippach)
3	20	37	250	X	X	X	Seefeld
1	4	14	18	X	X	X	Semmering
9	33	160	20	X	X	X	Serfaus
5	38	170	16	X	X	X	Sölden/Hochsölden
9	84	250	150	X	X	X	Söll
							Sonnalpe Nassfeld (s. Hermagor)
2	10	27	80	X	X	X	Spittal an der Drau
4	35	185	3	X	X	X	Stuben
	19	40	80			X	Tauplitz
	15	16	23	X	X	X	Treffen
	11	30	25	X	X	X	Turracher Höhe
17	70	321	20	X	X		Tux, Hintertux
8	36	150	45	X	X	X	Wagrain
4	51	155	23	X	X	X	Wald im Pinzgau
8	40	250	30	X	X	X	Westendorf
3	36	42	30	X	X	X	Wildschönau
	28	86	62	X	X		Wolfsberg
6	22	75	38	X	X	X	Zell am See
3	37	115	20	X	X	X	Zell im Zillertal
							Zürs (s. Lech)

Telefon-Vorwahlnummern international

Wichtig : bei Auslandsgesprächen darf die Null (0) der Ortsnetzkennzahl nicht gewählt werden (außer bei Gesprächen nach Italien).

Indicatifs téléphoniques internationaux

Important : pour les communications internationales, le zéro (0) initial de l'indicatif interurbain n'est pas à composer (excepté pour les appels vers l'Italie).

von \ nach	A	B	CH	CZ	D	DK	E	FIN	F	GB	GR
A Österreich		0032	0041	00420	0049	0045	0034	00358	0033	0044	0030
B Belgien	0043		0041	00420	0049	0045	0034	00358	0033	0044	0030
CH Schweiz	0043	0032		00420	0049	0045	0034	00358	0033	0044	0030
CZ Tschechische Rep.	0043	0032	0041		0049	0045	0034	00358	0033	0044	0030
D Deutschland	0043	0032	0041	00420		0045	0034	00358	0033	0044	0030
DK Dänemark	0043	0032	0041	00420	0049		0034	00358	0033	0044	0030
E Spanien	0043	0032	0041	00420	0049	0045		00358	0033	0044	0030
FIN Finnland	0043	0032	0041	00420	0049	0045	0034		0033	0044	0030
F Frankreich	0043	0032	99041	00420	0049	0045	0034	00358		0044	0030
GB Großbritannien	0043	0032	0041	00420	0049	0045	0034	00358	0033		0030
GR Griechenland	0043	0032	0041	00420	0049	0045	0034	00358	0033	0044	
H Ungarn	0043	0032	0041	00420	0049	0045	0034	00358	0033	0044	0030
I Italien	0043	0032	0041	00420	0049	0045	0034	00358	0033	0044	0030
IRL Irland	0043	0032	0041	00420	0049	0045	0034	00358	0033	0044	0030
J Japan	00143	00132	00141	001420	00149	00145	00134	001358	00133	00144	00130
L Luxemburg	0043	0032	0041	00420	0049	0045	0034	00358	0033	0044	0030
N Norwegen	0043	0032	0041	00420	0049	0045	0034	00358	0033	0044	0030
NL Niederlande	0043	0032	0041	00420	0049	0045	0034	0358	0033	0044	0030
PL Polen	0043	0032	0041	00420	0049	0045	0034	00358	0033	0044	0030
P Portugal	0043	0032	0041	00420	0049	0045	0034	00358	0033	0044	0030
RUS Russ. Föderation	81043	81032	81041	810420	81049	81045	*	810358	81033	81044	*
S Schweden	00943	00932	00941	009420	00949	00945	00934	009358	00933	00944	00930
USA	01143	01132	01141	011420	01149	01145	01134	01358	01133	01144	01130

* Automatische Vorwahl nicht möglich

* Pas de sélection automatique

International Dialling Codes

Note: When making an international call, do not dial the first (0) of the city codes (except for calls to Italy).

Indicativi Telefonici Internazionali

Importante: per le comunicazioni internazionali, non bisogna comporre lo zero (0) initiale del prefisso interurbano (esclude le chimate per l'Italia)

H	I	IRL	J	L	N	NL	PL	P	RUS	S	USA	
0036	0039	00353	0081	00352	0047	0031	0048	00351	007	0046	001	**A Österreich**
0036	0039	00353	0081	00352	0047	0031	0048	00351	007	0046	001	**B Belgien**
0036	0039	00353	0081	00352	0047	0031	0048	00351	007	0046	001	**CH Schweiz**
0036	0039	00353	0081	00352	0047	0031	0048	00351	007	0046	001	**CZ Tschechische Rep.**
0036	0039	00353	0081	00352	0047	0031	0048	00351	007	0046	001	**D Deutschland**
0036	0039	00353	0081	00352	0047	0031	0048	00351	007	0046	001	**DK Dänemark**
0036	0039	00353	0081	00352	0047	0031	0048	00351	007	0046	001	**E Spanien**
0036	0039	00353	0081	00352	0047	0031	0048	00351	007	0046	001	**FIN Finnland**
0036	0039	00353	0081	00352	0047	0031	0048	00351	007	0046	001	**F Frankreich**
0036	0039	00353	0081	00352	0047	0031	0048	00351	007	0046	001	**GB Großbritannien**
0036	0039	00353	0081	00352	0047	0031	0048	00351	007	0046	001	**GR Griechenland**
	0039	00353	0081	00352	0047	0031	0048	00351	007	0046	001	**H Ungarn**
0036		00353	0081	00352	0047	0031	0048	00351	*	0046	001	**I Italien**
0036	0039		0081	00352	0047	0031	0048	00351	007	0046	001	**IRL Irland**
00136	00139	001353		001352	00147	00131	00148	001351	*	00146	0011	**J Japan**
0036	0039	00353	0081		0047	0031	0048	00351	007	0046	001	**L Luxemburg**
0036	0039	00353	0081	011352		0031	0048	00351	007	0046	001	**N Norwegen**
0036	0039	00353	0081	00352	0047		0048	00351	007	0046	001	**NL Niederlande**
0036	0039	00353	0081	00352	0047	0031		00351	007	0046	001	**PL Polen**
0036	0039	00353	0081	00352	0047	0031	0048		007	0046	001	**P Portugal**
81036	*	*	*	*	*	81031	81048	*		*	*	**RUS Russ. Föderation**
00936	00939	009353	0981	009352	00947	00931	00948	009351	0097		0091	**S Schweden**
01136	01139	011353	01181	011352	01147	01131	01148	011351	*	01146	–	**USA**

* Direct dialing not possible

* Selezione automatica impossibile

Ort mit mindestens

einem Hotel oder Restaurant • Linz
einem angenehmen Hotel oder Restaurant
einem Hotel mit
einem sehr ruhigen und abgelegenen Hotel
einem Restaurant mit

Localité offrant au moins

une ressource hôtelière • Linz
un hôtel ou restaurant agréable
bonnes nuits à petits prix
un hôtel très tranquille, isolé
une bonne table à

Place with at least

a hotel or restaurant • Linz
a pleasant hotel or restaurant
good accommodation at moderate prices
a quiet, secluded hotel
a restaurant with

La località possiede come minimo

una risorsa alberghiera • Linz
albergo o ristorante ameno
buona sistemazione a prezzi contenuti
un albergo molto tranquillo, isolato
un'ottima tavola con

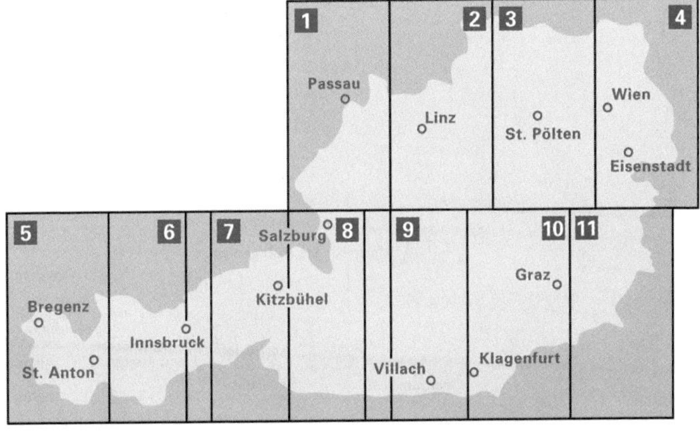

F
G
1
1
Vltava
A 3
E 56
A 92
E 53
A 3
DONAU
Passau
2
DEUTSCHLAND
Schärding
Inn
A 8
E 56-552
Gurten
Ried Im Innkreis
Inn
3
Alz
Hochburg-Ach
Feldkirchen bei Mattighofen
Salzach
Franking
Lenzing
Ager
Schörfling
Seewalchen
Mattsee
Seeham
Köstendorf
St. Georgen
i. Attergau
Attersee
Obertrum a. S.
Neumarkt a. W.
Weyregg
7
8
F
Seekirchen a. Wallersee
G
Nussdorf
Anthering
Mondsee
Eugendorf
Steinbach

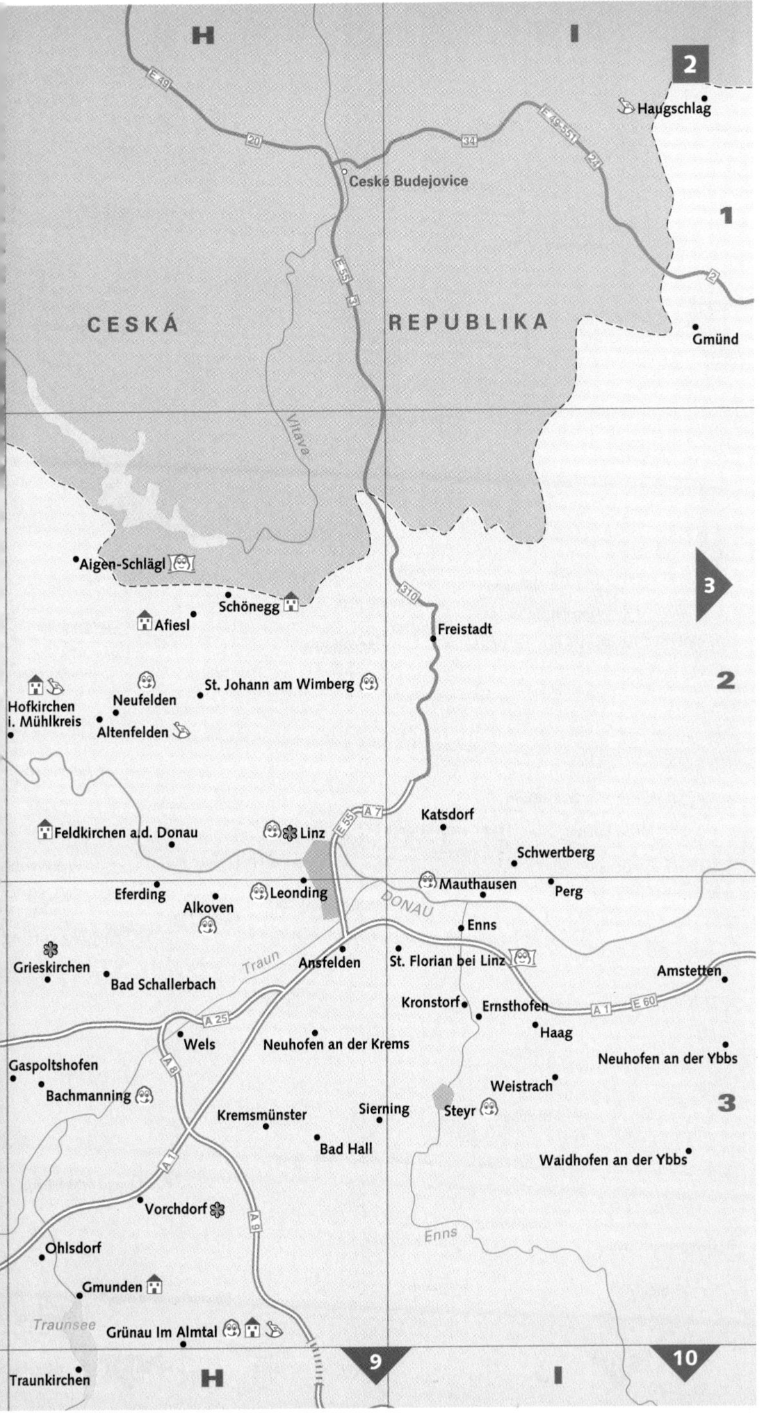

H
I
2
Haugschlag
E 49
20
34
E 49-551
24
Ceské Budejovice
1
2
E 55
3
CESKÁ
REPUBLIKA
Gmünd
Vltava
Aigen-Schlägl
3
310
Schönegg
Afiesl
Freistadt
St. Johann am Wimberg
2
Hofkirchen
i. Mühlkreis
Neufelden
Altenfelden
A 7
Katsdorf
E 55
Feldkirchen a.d. Donau
Linz
Schwertberg
Mauthausen
Perg
Eferding
Alkoven
Leonding
DONAU
Enns
Grieskirchen
Traun
Ansfelden
St. Florian bei Linz
Amstetten
Bad Schallerbach
Kronstorf
Ernsthofen
A 25
A 1
E 60
Haag
Wels
Neuhofen an der Krems
Neuhofen an der Ybbs
Gaspoltshofen
A 8
Weistrach
Bachmanning
Kremsmünster
Sierning
Steyr
3
Bad Hall
Waidhofen an der Ybbs
A 1
Vorchdorf
A 9
Enns
Ohlsdorf
Gmunden
Traunsee
Grünau Im Almtal
9
10
Traunkirchen
H
I

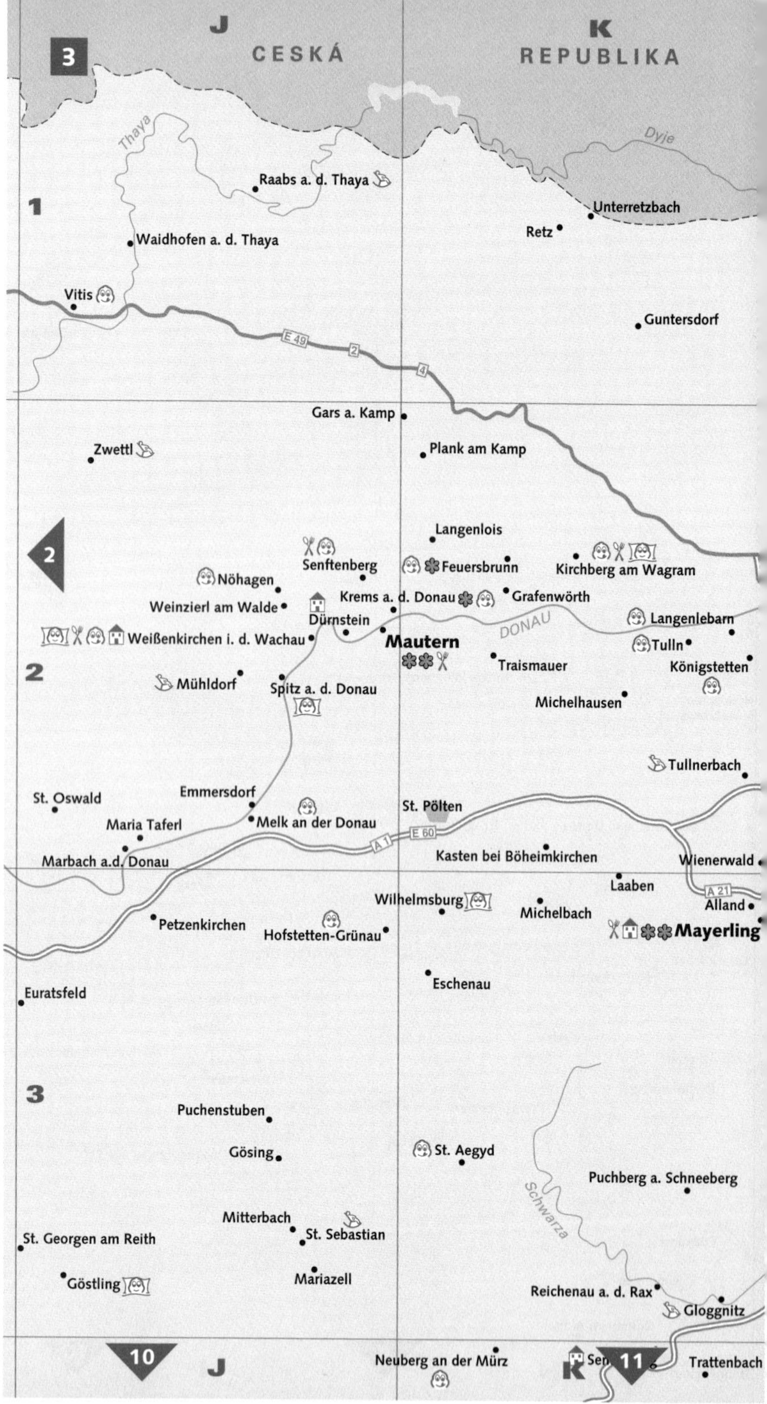
3
J
CESKÁ
K
REPUBLIKA
Thaya
Dyje
1
Raabs a. d. Thaya
Unterretzbach
Retz
Waidhofen a. d. Thaya
Vitis
Guntersdorf
E 49
2
4
Gars a. Kamp
Zwettl
Plank am Kamp
2
Langenlois
Senftenberg
Feuersbrunn
Kirchberg am Wagram
Nöhagen
Krems a. d. Donau
Grafenwörth
Weinzierl am Walde
Dürnstein
DONAU
Langenlebarn
Weißenkirchen i. d. Wachau
Mautern
Tulln
Traismauer
Königstetten
2
Mühldorf
Spitz a. d. Donau
Michelhausen
Tullnerbach
St. Oswald
Emmersdorf
St. Pölten
Maria Taferl
Melk an der Donau
E 60
A 1
Marbach a.d. Donau
Kasten bei Böheimkirchen
Wienerwald
Laaben
A 21
Wilhelmsburg
Alland
Michelbach
Petzenkirchen
Hofstetten-Grünau
Mayerling
Eschenau
Euratsfeld
3
Puchenstuben
Gösing
St. Aegyd
Puchberg a. Schneeberg
Schwarza
Mitterbach
St. Sebastian
St. Georgen am Reith
Mariazell
Göstling
Reichenau a. d. Rax
Gloggnitz
10
J
Neuberg an der Mürz
K
11
Trattenbach

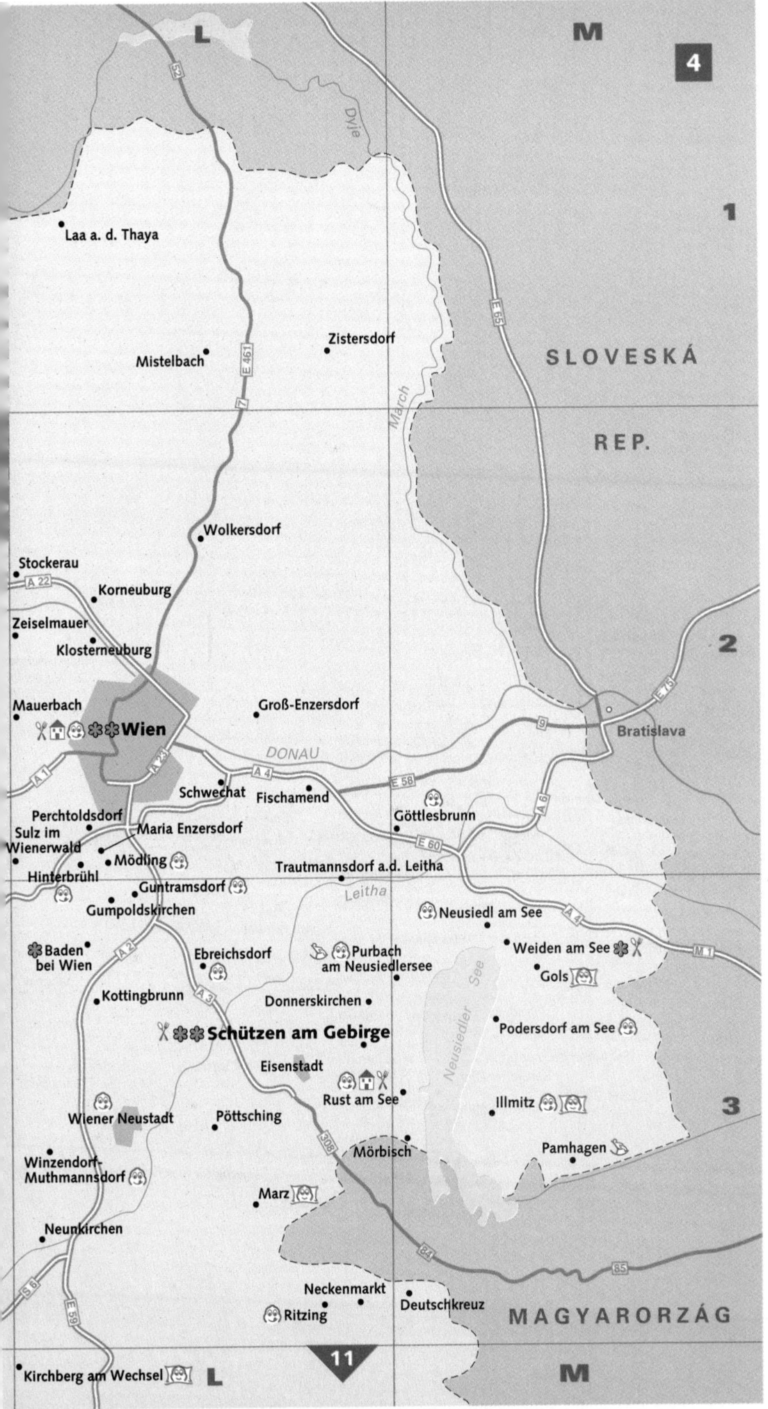

L
M
4
1
2
3
Laa a. d. Thaya
Zistersdorf
Mistelbach
SLOVESKÁ
REP.
Wolkersdorf
Stockerau
Korneuburg
Zeiselmauer
Klosterneuburg
Mauerbach
Groß-Enzersdorf
Wien
Bratislava
DONAU
Schwechat
Fischamend
Göttlesbrunn
Perchtoldsdorf
Maria Enzersdorf
Sulz im Wienerwald
Mödling
Hinterbrühl
Trautmannsdorf a.d. Leitha
Guntramsdorf
Leitha
Gumpoldskirchen
Neusiedl am See
Baden bei Wien
Ebreichsdorf
Purbach am Neusiedlersee
Weiden am See
Gols
Kottingbrunn
Donnerskirchen
Podersdorf am See
Schützen am Gebirge
Neusiedler See
Eisenstadt
Rust am See
Illmitz
Wiener Neustadt
Pöttsching
Mörbisch
Pamhagen
Winzendorf-Muthmannsdorf
Marz
Neunkirchen
Neckenmarkt
Deutschkreuz
Ritzing
MAGYARORZÁG
11
Kirchberg am Wechsel
L
M
Dyje
March

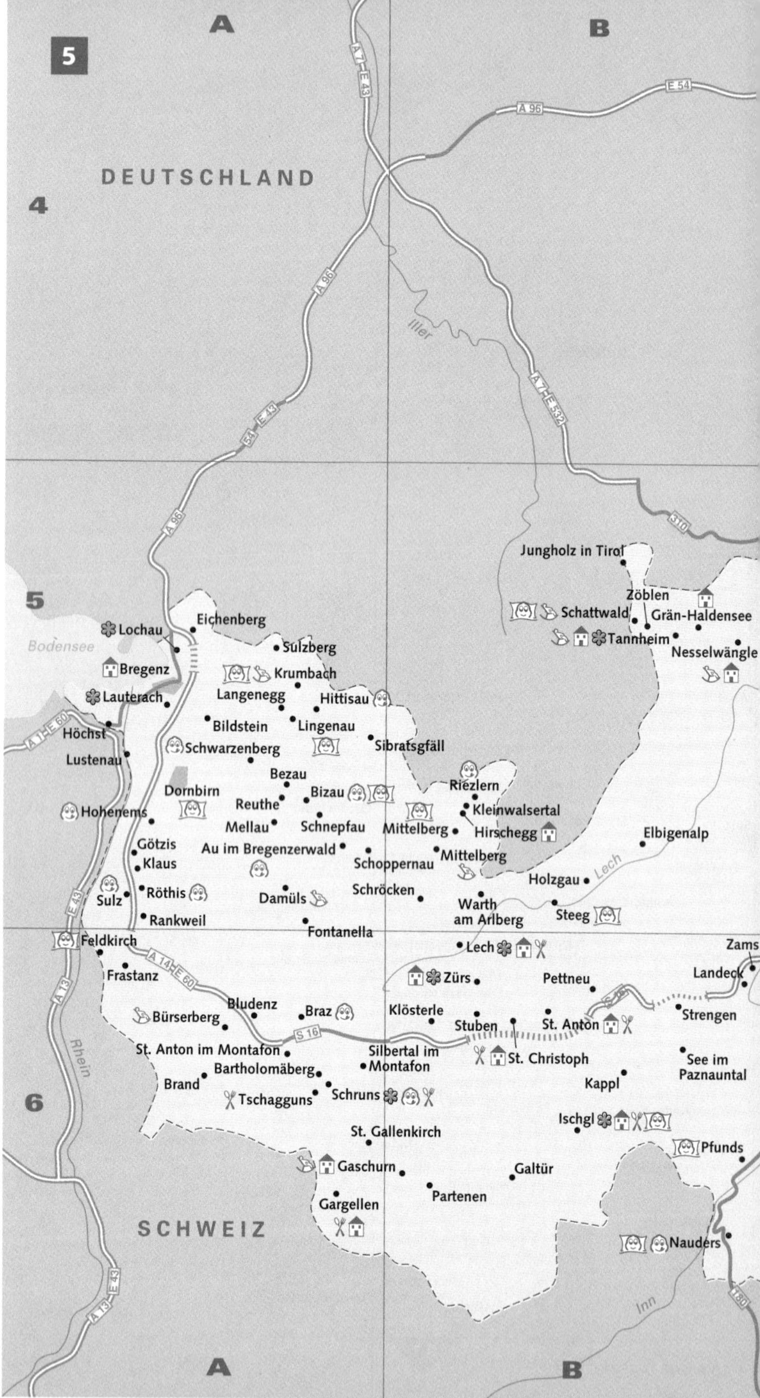
5
A
B
DEUTSCHLAND
4
5
6
SCHWEIZ
Bodensee
Iller
Lech
Rhein
Inn
Lochau
Eichenberg
Bregenz
Sulzberg
Krumbach
Lauterach
Langenegg
Hittisau
Höchst
Bildstein
Lingenau
Lustenau
Schwarzenberg
Sibratsgfäll
Bezau
Dornbirn
Bizau
Riezlern
Reuthe
Hohenems
Kleinwalsertal
Mellau
Schnepfau
Mittelberg
Hirschegg
Götzis
Au im Bregenzerwald
Schoppernau
Klaus
Mittelberg
Sulz
Röthis
Damüls
Schröcken
Holzgau
Warth am Arlberg
Steeg
Rankweil
Fontanella
Feldkirch
Lech
Zams
Frastanz
Zürs
Pettneu
Landeck
Bludenz
Braz
Klösterle
Strengen
Bürserberg
Stuben
St. Anton
St. Anton im Montafon
Silbertal im Montafon
St. Christoph
See im Paznauntal
Brand
Bartholomäberg
Kappl
Tschagguns
Schruns
Ischgl
St. Gallenkirch
Pfunds
Gaschurn
Galtür
Partenen
Gargellen
Nauders
Jungholz in Tirol
Zöblen
Schattwald
Grän-Haldensee
Tannheim
Nesselwängle
Elbigenalp
A 7
E 43
E 54
A 96
A 7
E 532
310
54
A 1
E 60
E 43
A 13
A 14
S 16
180

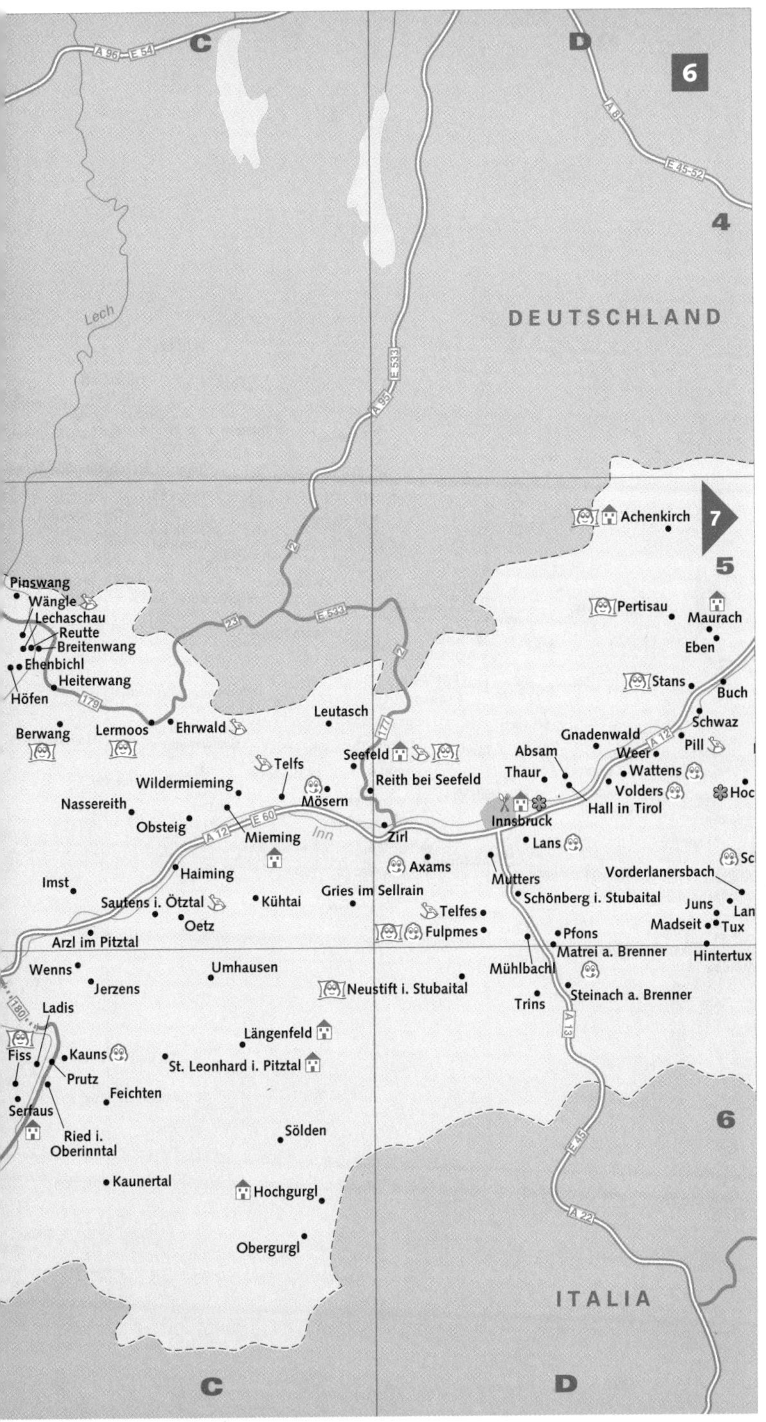

6
C
D
A 96
E 54
A 8
E 45-52
4
DEUTSCHLAND
Lech
A 95
E 533
7
5
2
23
Achenkirch
Pinswang
Wängle
Lechaschau
Reutte
Breitenwang
Ehenbichl
Heiterwang
Höfen
179
Pertisau
Maurach
Eben
Stans
Buch
Schwaz
Pill
Berwang
Lermoos
Ehrwald
Leutasch
Gnadenwald
Absam
Weer
Wattens
Volders
Thaur
Hall in Tirol
Innsbruck
Seefeld
Reith bei Seefeld
Telfs
Mösern
Wildermieming
Nassereith
Obsteig
Mieming
A 12
E 60
Inn
Zirl
Lans
Axams
Mutters
Vorderlanersbach
Schönberg i. Stubaital
Juns
Madseit
Tux
Hintertux
Imst
Haiming
Gries im Sellrain
Telfes
Fulpmes
Sautens i. Ötztal
Kühtai
Oetz
Arzl im Pitztal
Pfons
Matrei a. Brenner
Mühlbachl
Wenns
Umhausen
Jerzens
Neustift i. Stubaital
Steinach a. Brenner
Trins
A 13
180
Ladis
Fiss
Kauns
Prutz
Längenfeld
St. Leonhard i. Pitztal
Feichten
Serfaus
Ried i. Oberinntal
Sölden
Kaunertal
Hochgurgl
Obergurgl
E 45
A 22
6
ITALIA
C
D

7
D
E
F
4
5
6
DEUTSCHLAND
ITALIA
Inn
Salzach
A 8
E 45-52
E 52-60
A 12
E 45-60
A 13
E 45
A 22
S 49
E 66
178
161
Erl
Kössen
Walchsee
Ebbs
Erpfendorf in Tirol
Waidring
Going a. Wilden Kaiser
Thiersee
Kufstein
St. Jakob i. Haus
Ellmau
St. Johann i. T.
Scheffau a. Wilden Kaiser
Mariastein
Söll
Oberndorf i. T.
Achenkirch
Bad Häring
Reith b. Kitzbühel
Wörgl
Brixen i. Thale
Kitzbühel
Kramsach
Hopfgarten
Kirchberg
Aurach
Westendorf
Pertisau
Maurach
Brixlegg
Eben
Reith i. Alpbachtal
Alpbach
Wildschönau
Jochberg
Stans
Buch
Fügenberg
Fügen
Schwaz
Uderns
Bramberg am Wildkogel
Mittersill
Neukirchen am Großvenediger
Hollersbach
Gnadenwald
Pill
Stumm
Absam
Weer
Ried
Thaur
Wattens
Aschau
Königsleiten
Wald im Pinzgau
Volders
Hochfügen
Zell am Ziller
Gerlos
Krimml
Hall in Tirol
Innsbruck
Hainzenberg
Lans
Hippach
Ramsau
Schwendau
Mutters
Vorderlanersbach
Mayrhofen
Schönberg i. Stubaital
Finkenberg
Juns
Lanersbach
Madseit
Tux
Pfons
Matrei a. Brenner
Hintertux
Mühlbachl
Virgen
Steinach a. Brenner
Trins
St. Veit im Defereggental
St. Jakob in Defereggen
Innervillgraten
Sillian
6

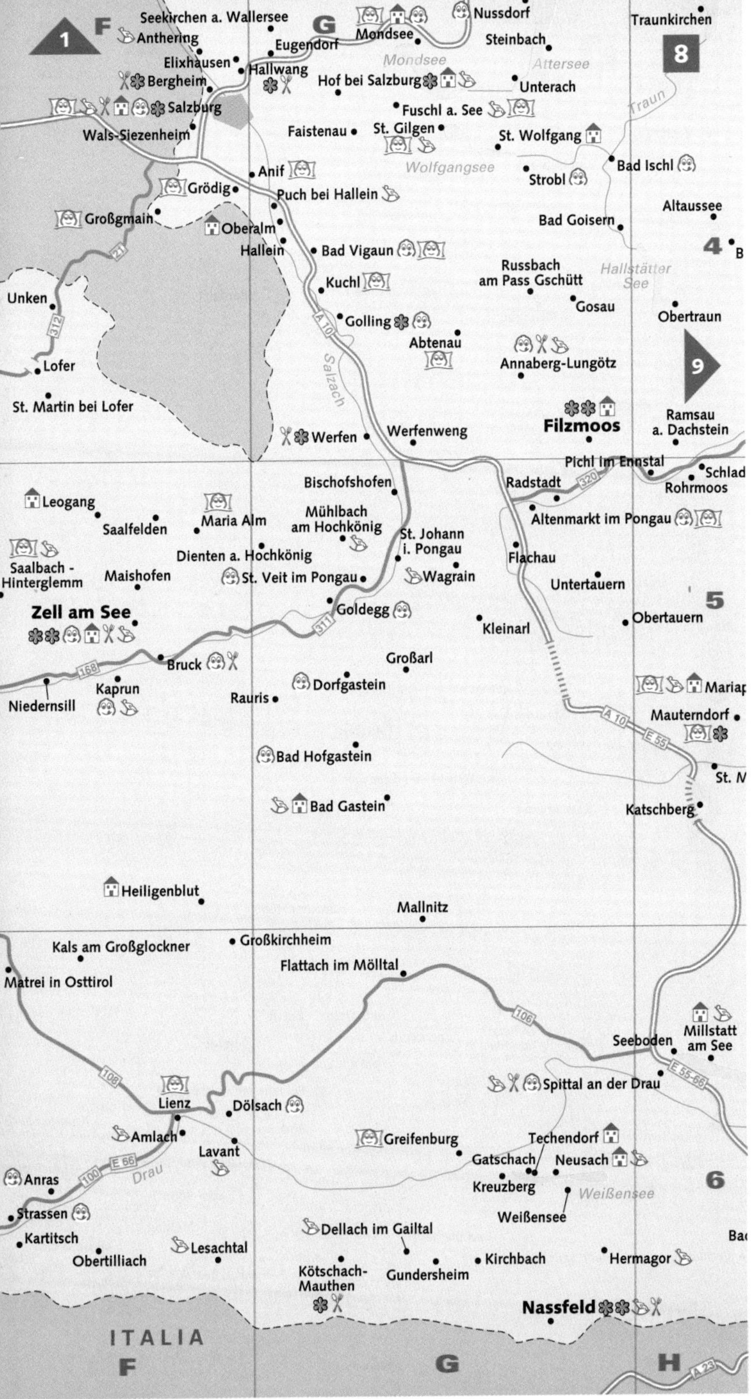
1
F
G
H
8
4
9
5
6
Seekirchen a. Wallersee
Anthering
Elixhausen
Bergheim
Salzburg
Wals-Siezenheim
Eugendorf
Hallwang
Mondsee
Nussdorf
Steinbach
Traunkirchen
Attersee
Unterach
Hof bei Salzburg
Fuschl a. See
Traun
Faistenau
St. Gilgen
St. Wolfgang
Wolfgangsee
Bad Ischl
Anif
Grödig
Strobl
Puch bei Hallein
Großgmain
Oberalm
Hallein
Bad Vigaun
Altaussee
Bad Goisern
Russbach am Pass Gschütt
Hallstätter See
Kuchl
Unken
Gosau
Obertraun
Golling
Abtenau
Annaberg-Lungötz
Lofer
Salzach
St. Martin bei Lofer
Ramsau a. Dachstein
Filzmoos
Werfen
Werfenweng
Pichl im Ennstal
Schlad
Rohrmoos
Radstadt
Bischofshofen
Leogang
Saalfelden
Maria Alm
Mühlbach am Hochkönig
St. Johann i. Pongau
Altenmarkt im Pongau
Dienten a. Hochkönig
Flachau
Saalbach - Hinterglemm
Maishofen
St. Veit im Pongau
Wagrain
Untertauern
Zell am See
Goldegg
Kleinarl
Obertauern
Bruck
Großarl
Niedernsill
Kaprun
Dorfgastein
Rauris
Mariap
Mauterndorf
Bad Hofgastein
St. M
Bad Gastein
Katschberg
Heiligenblut
Mallnitz
Kals am Großglockner
Großkirchheim
Flattach im Mölltal
Matrei in Osttirol
Millstatt am See
Seeboden
Spittal an der Drau
Lienz
Dölsach
Amlach
Lavant
Greifenburg
Techendorf
Gatschach
Neusach
Kreuzberg
Weißensee
Anras
Drau
Strassen
Dellach im Gailtal
Kartitsch
Lesachtal
Obertilliach
Kötschach-Mauthen
Gundersheim
Kirchbach
Hermagor
Bad
Nassfeld
ITALIA
A 10
A 23
E 55
E 55-66
E 66
21
312
311
168
320
106
108
100

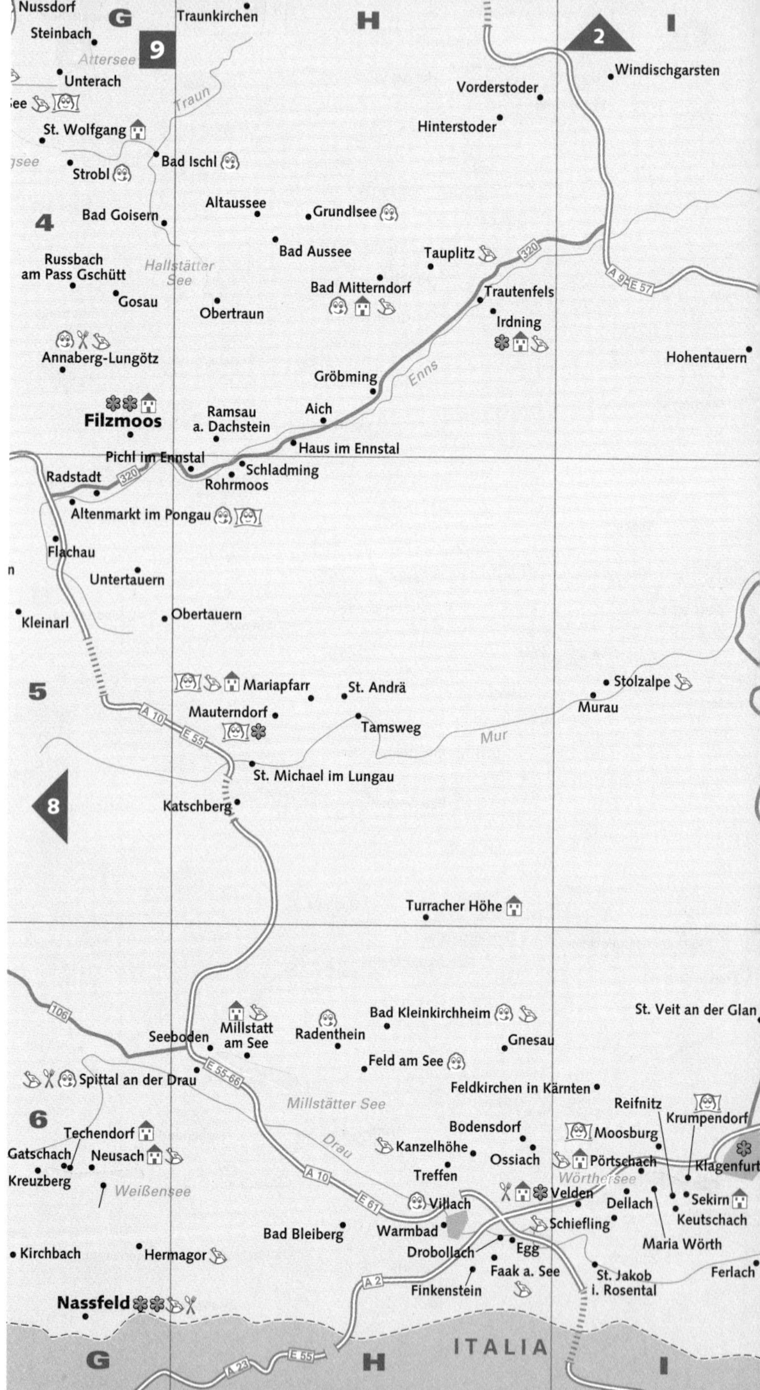

G
H
I
9
2
4
5
6
8
Nussdorf
Steinbach
Attersee
Unterach
St. Wolfgang
Strobl
Traunkirchen
Traun
Bad Ischl
Bad Goisern
Altaussee
Grundlsee
Bad Aussee
Russbach am Pass Gschütt
Hallstätter See
Gosau
Obertraun
Bad Mitterndorf
Tauplitz
320
A 9 E 57
Trautenfels
Irdning
Vorderstoder
Hinterstoder
Windischgarsten
Hohentauern
Annaberg-Lungötz
Filzmoos
Ramsau a. Dachstein
Aich
Gröbming
Enns
Haus im Ennstal
Pichl im Ennstal
Radstadt
Schladming
Rohrmoos
Altenmarkt im Pongau
Flachau
Untertauern
Kleinarl
Obertauern
Mariapfarr
St. Andrä
Mauterndorf
Tamsweg
Stolzalpe
Murau
Mur
A 10
E 55
St. Michael im Lungau
Katschberg
Turracher Höhe
106
Seeboden
Millstatt am See
Radenthein
Bad Kleinkirchheim
Gnesau
St. Veit an der Glan
Feld am See
Spittal an der Drau
E 55-66
Millstätter See
Feldkirchen in Kärnten
Reifnitz
Krumpendorf
Techendorf
Bodensdorf
Moosburg
Gatschach
Neusach
Kanzelhöhe
Ossiach
Pörtschach
Klagenfurt
Kreuzberg
Drau
Treffen
Wörthersee
Weißensee
A 10
Velden
Dellach
Sekirn
Villach
E 61
Keutschach
Bad Bleiberg
Warmbad
Schiefling
Maria Wörth
Kirchbach
Hermagor
Drobollach
Egg
St. Jakob i. Rosental
Ferlach
A 2
Faak a. See
Finkenstein
Nassfeld
ITALIA
E 55
A 23

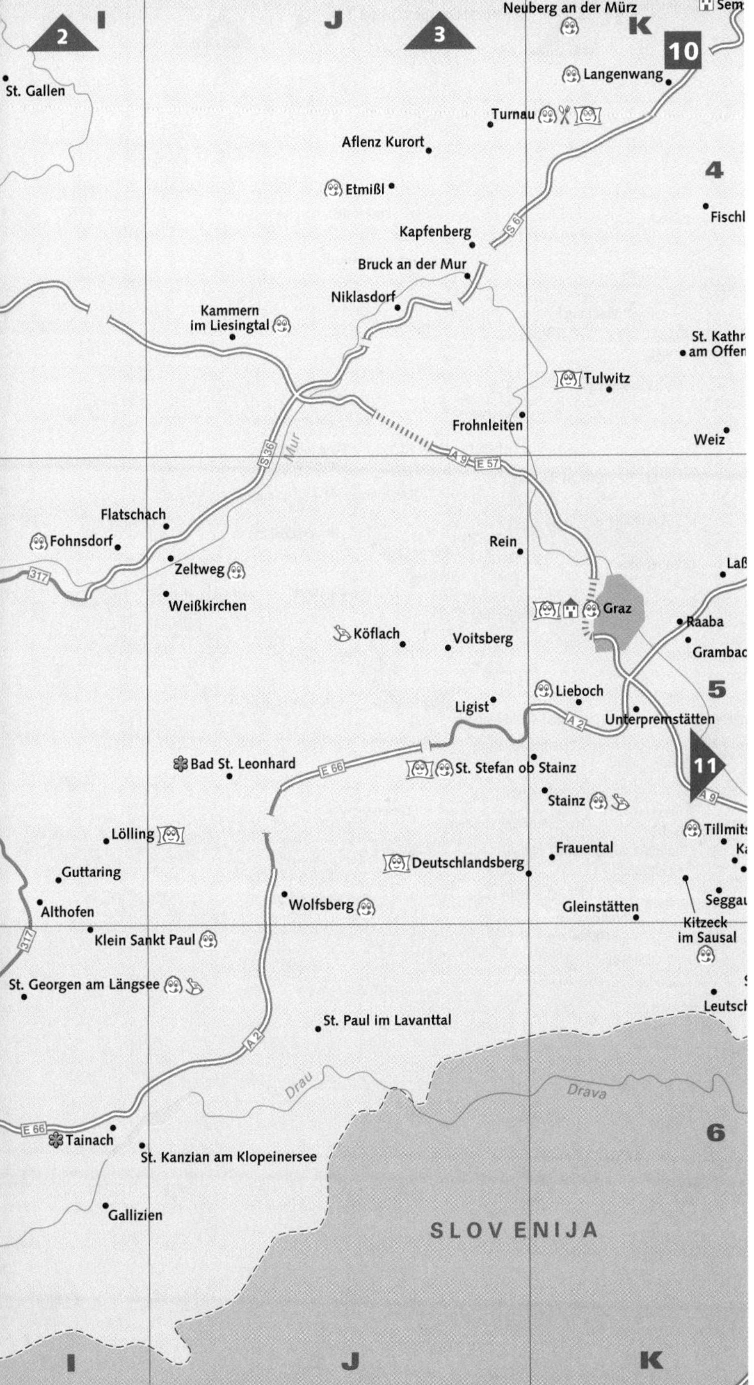

I
J
K
2
3
10
Neuberg an der Mürz
Sem
Langenwang
St. Gallen
Turnau
Aflenz Kurort
Etmißl
4
Fischl
Kapfenberg
S 6
Bruck an der Mur
Niklasdorf
Kammern
im Liesingtal
St. Kathr
am Offen
Tulwitz
Frohnleiten
Weiz
S 36
Mur
A 9
E 57
Flatschach
Fohnsdorf
Rein
Zeltweg
317
Laß
Weißkirchen
Graz
Raaba
Köflach
Voitsberg
Grambac
5
Lieboch
Ligist
A 2
Unterpremstätten
Bad St. Leonhard
E 66
St. Stefan ob Stainz
11
A 9
Stainz
Lölling
Tillmits
Frauental
Deutschlandsberg
Guttaring
Wolfsberg
Gleinstätten
Seggau
Althofen
Kitzeck
im Sausal
Klein Sankt Paul
317
St. Georgen am Längsee
Leutsch
St. Paul im Lavanttal
A 2
Drau
Drava
E 66
6
Tainach
St. Kanzian am Klopeinersee
Gallizien
SLOVENIJA
I
J
K

Semmering
Trattenbach
Kirchberg am Wechsel
K
L
M
11
3
4
Lutzmannsburg
Bad Schönau
A 2
Ratten
4
Fischbach
Pinkafeld
Bad Tatzmannsdorf
Birkfeld
Pöllauberg
St. Kathrein
am Offenegg
Hartberg
Stubenberg
Ollersdorf im Burgenland
Sebersdorf
Stegersbach
Weiz
Bad Waltersdorf
Burgauberg-
Neudauberg
St. Ruprecht an der Raab
Bad Blumau
Kukmirn
Gleisdorf
E 59-66
Heiligenbrunn
Rudersdorf
Fürstenfeld
Laßnitzhöhe
Söchau
Loipersdorf
Heiligenkreuz
Raaba
Riegersburg
Grambach
Jennersdorf
Feldbach
5
Kapfenstein
Minihof-Liebau
stätten
Bad Gleichenberg
10
Trautmannsdorf
Bairisch Kölldorf
MAGYARORZÁG
A 9
Straden
Tieschen
Hof bei Straden
Tillmitsch
Kaindorf an der Sulm
Klöch
Leibnitz
St. Veit am Vogau
Seggauberg
Bad Radkersburg
Ehrenhausen
Kitzeck
im Sausal
Berghausen
Mur
Mura
Gamlitz
Sulztal a. d. Weinstr.
Leutschach
E 59
Maribor
6
Drava
A 1
E 57
HRVATSKA
K
L
M